What is Psychology?

Custom Version for FIT

3rd Edition

Ellen Pastorino | Susann Doyle-Portillo

CENGAGE
Learning·

Australia • Brazil • Japan • Korea • Mexico • Singapore • Spain • United Kingdom • United States

What is Psychology?

What is Psychology?, 3rd Edition
Ellen E. Pastorino | Susann M. Doyle-Portillo

© 2012 Cengage Learning. All rights reserved.

Senior Project Development Manager:
Linda deStefano

Market Development Manager:
Heather Kramer

Senior Production/Manufacturing Manager:
Donna M. Brown

Production Editorial Manager:
Kim Fry

Sr. Rights Acquisition Account Manager:
Todd Osborne

For product information and technology assistance, contact us at
Cengage Learning Customer & Sales Support, 1-800-354-9706

For permission to use material from this text or product,
submit all requests online at **cengage.com/permissions**
Further permissions questions can be emailed to
permissionrequest@cengage.com

This book contains select works from existing Cengage Learning resources and was produced by Cengage Learning Custom Solutions for collegiate use. As such, those adopting and/or contributing to this work are responsible for editorial content accuracy, continuity and completeness.

Compilation © 2012 Cengage Learning

ISBN-13: 978-1-285-56181-3

ISBN-10: 1-285-56181-3

Cengage Learning
5191 Natorp Boulevard
Mason, Ohio 45040
USA
Cengage Learning is a leading provider of customized learning solutions with office locations around the globe, including Singapore, the United Kingdom, Australia, Mexico, Brazil, and Japan. Locate your local office at:
international.cengage.com/region.

Cengage Learning products are represented in Canada by Nelson Education, Ltd.
For your lifelong learning solutions, visit **www.cengage.com/custom.**
Visit our corporate website at **www.cengage.com.**

Printed in the United States of America

STUDENTS: Accessing Your Aplia Course Through CengageBrain

CENGAGEbrain.com

CREATING YOUR APLIA ACCOUNT ON CENGAGEBRAIN BY VISITING:
login.cengagebrain.com

What is login.cengagebrain.com? Imagine that you are using Aplia along with another online study tool from Cengage Learning. Rather than having separate logins and passwords for both applications, Cengage offers a single access point through login.cengagebrain.com.

When you visit login.cengagebrain.com, you will see the following:

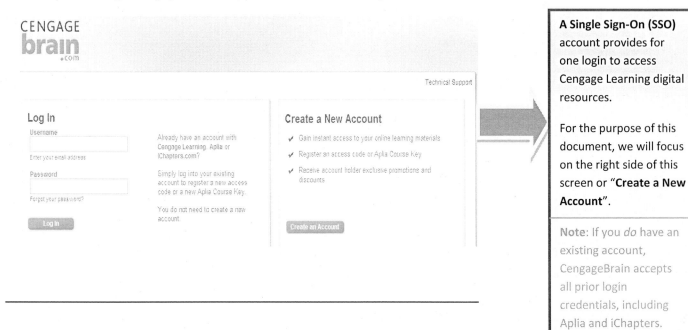

A Single Sign-On (SSO) account provides for one login to access Cengage Learning digital resources.

For the purpose of this document, we will focus on the right side of this screen or "**Create a New Account**".

Note: If you *do* have an existing account, CengageBrain accepts all prior login credentials, including Aplia and iChapters.

Step 1 | Begin by Creating an Account

1. Click the "Create an Account" button
2. The following page will load. Enter in the Aplia Course Key

YOUR COURSE KEY IS PROVIDED BY YOUR INSTRUCTOR TO ACCESS APLIA.

Instructors often provide the Aplia Course Key on their **syllabus**, or the course web site. If you need help locating the **Aplia Course Key**, ask your instructor.

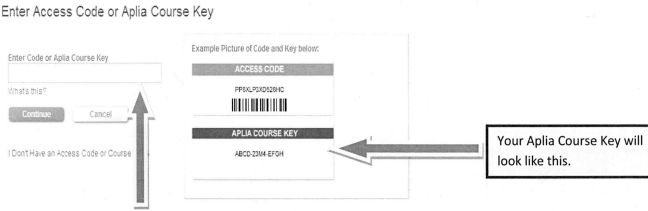

Your Aplia Course Key will look like this.

Step 2 | Confirm Your Course Information

The graphic below serves as an illustration for what you will see. Please confirm the displayed screen represents your enrolled course.

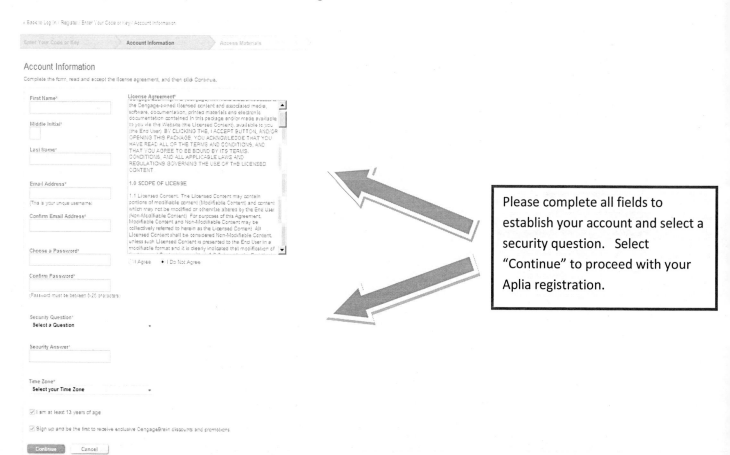

« Back to Log In / Register / Confirm Course

Enter Your Code or Key   Account Information   Access Materials

Confirm Course Information

Please confirm that this is the Aplia course for which you want to register

School:	Aplia university
Instructor:	Support Team
Course Name:	Principles of Economics Spring 2010
Start Date:	April 19, 2010
End Date:	July 26, 2010
Not the right course?	edit course key

Continue

> Confirm that the course information shown matches the course you are enrolled in. If yes, click the "**Continue**" button. If not, click on the "edit course key" link to re-enter the correct Course Key.

Step 3 | Complete Registration Form

As a new user, you must complete all fields in the registration form and click "Continue"

« Back to Log In / Register / Enter Your Code or Key / Account Information

Enter Your Code or Key   Account Information   Access Materials

Account Information

Complete the form, read and accept the license agreement, and then click Continue.

First Name*

Middle Initial*

Last Name*

Email Address*

(This is your unique username)

Confirm Email Address*

Choose a Password*

Confirm Password*

(Password must be between 6-20 characters)

Security Question*
Select a Question

Security Answer*

Time Zone*
Select your Time Zone

☑ I am at least 13 years of age

☑ Sign up and be the first to receive exclusive CengageBrain discounts and promotions

Continue   Cancel

License Agreement*

the Cengage-owned licensed content and associated media, software, documentation, printed materials and electronic documentation contained in this package and/or made available to you via this Website (the Licensed Content), available to you (the End User) BY CLICKING THE, I ACCEPT BUTTON, AND/OR OPENING THIS PACKAGE, YOU ACKNOWLEDGE THAT YOU HAVE READ ALL OF THE TERMS AND CONDITIONS, AND THAT YOU AGREE TO BE BOUND BY ITS TERMS, CONDITIONS, AND ALL APPLICABLE LAWS AND REGULATIONS GOVERNING THE USE OF THE LICENSED CONTENT

1.0 SCOPE OF LICENSE

1.1 Licensed Content. The Licensed Content may contain portions of modifiable content (Modifiable Content) and content which may not be modified or otherwise altered by the End User (Non-Modifiable Content). For purposes of this Agreement, Modifiable Content and Non-Modifiable Content may be collectively referred to herein as the Licensed Content. All Licensed Content shall be considered Non-Modifiable Content, unless such Licensed Content is presented to the End User in a modifiable format and it is clearly indicated that modification of

○ I Agree   ● I Do Not Agree

> Please complete all fields to establish your account and select a security question. Select "Continue" to proceed with your Aplia registration.

Step 4 | My Home Dashboard Review

You have arrived at your "**My Home**" page. Here you can verify your e-Mail address with CengageBrain and pay for your course **(See Step 5).** Note that any prior (and future) Cengage Learning purchases will appear on this page. Additionally, the page provides support resources and a transaction history of your Cengage purchases – digital products, textbooks or rentals.

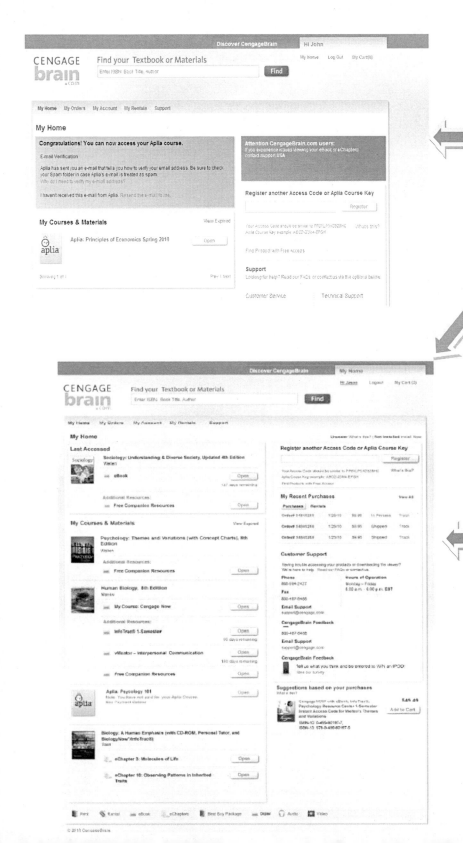

IMPORTANT: CengageBrain requires you to verify your e-mail address. Please go to your e-mail and check for a message from CengageBrain.com with the Subject "**Aplia Verification E-Mail**". If you don't see the message, check your SPAM folder.

Click the link to verify your e-mail. **Once verified, you will be prompted to log back in again with your e-mail and password from Step 3 above. Once you do, you will be brought back to your "My Home" Dashboard as shown below.**

Here is a complete view of the Dashboard showing all Cengage Learning resources instantly available in one spot. Also note transaction history and support options in the right hand field.

Step 5 | Completing Payment For Your Aplia Course

NOTE: YOUR APLIA PAYMENT CODES ARE BOUND WITHIN THIS BOOK. THERE ARE <u>NO</u> <u>ADDITIONAL CHARGES TO ACCESS APLIA</u>. SIMPLY COMPLETE THE PAYMENT PROCESS BY CLICKING ON THE "SEE PAYMENT OPTIONS LINK" CIRCLED IN GREEN.

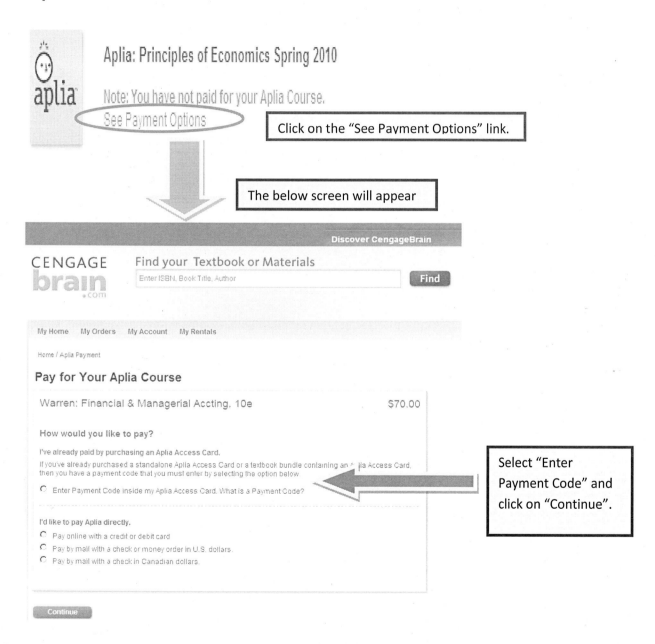

My Courses & Materials

Aplia: Principles of Economics Spring 2010

Note: You have not paid for your Aplia Course.

See Payment Options

Click on the "See Payment Options" link.

The below screen will appear

Discover CengageBrain

CENGAGE brain .com

Find your Textbook or Materials

Enter ISBN, Book Title, Author   [Find]

My Home   My Orders   My Account   My Rentals

Home / Aplia Payment

Pay for Your Aplia Course

Warren: Financial & Managerial Accting, 10e $70.00

How would you like to pay?

I've already paid by purchasing an Aplia Access Card.

If you've already purchased a standalone Aplia Access Card or a textbook bundle containing an Aplia Access Card, then you have a payment code that you must enter by selecting the option below.

○ Enter Payment Code inside my Aplia Access Card. What is a Payment Code?

I'd like to pay Aplia directly.

○ Pay online with a credit or debit card
○ Pay by mail with a check or money order in U.S. dollars.
○ Pay by mail with a check in Canadian dollars.

Select "Enter Payment Code" and click on "Continue".

[Continue]

Step 5 | Completing Payment For Your Aplia Course (cont.)

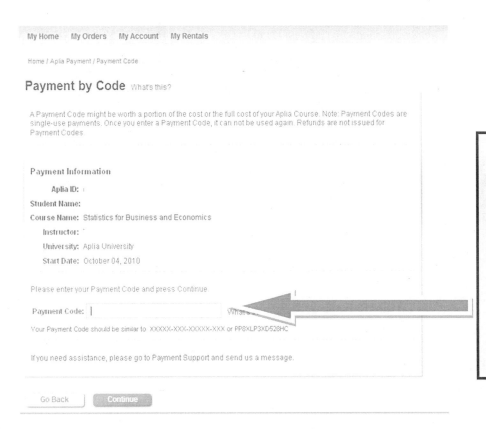

My Home   My Orders   My Account   My Rentals

Home / Aplia Payment / Payment Code

Payment by Code What's this?

A Payment Code might be worth a portion of the cost or the full cost of your Aplia Course. Note: Payment Codes are single-use payments. Once you enter a Payment Code, it can not be used again. Refunds are not issued for Payment Codes.

Payment Information

Aplia ID:

Student Name:

Course Name: Statistics for Business and Economics

Instructor:

University: Aplia University

Start Date: October 04, 2010

Please enter your Payment Code and press Continue.

Payment Code: [   ]   What's

Your Payment Code should be similar to XXXXX-XXX-XXXXX-XXX or PP8XLP3XD528HC

If you need assistance, please go to Payment Support and send us a message.

Go Back   Continue

Enter the payment code that is **bound within your book.** Your payment code will look like the one shown below.

Payment Code
BQQFF-FNB-JPCPQ-PXH

NOTE: Your payment code *is not* the same as your Course Key provided by your Instructor.

My Home   My Orders   My Account   My Rentals

Payment Confirmation

Please print this page for your records.

Your Payment Code has been accepted as payment for your Aplia course.

Order Summary

Student name:

Aplia ID:

Course: Statistics for Business and Economics

Instructor:

School: Aplia University

Course start date: 10/04/10

Course end date: 12/26/10

Grace period ends: 10/25/10

Payment code used: ZTRKF-FNB-JPGNP-PCB

Date and time of payment: 10/19/10, 08:21 AM

Please note that your Payment Code has now been used and will no longer work for any subsequent Aplia course.

Refund Policy

There are no refunds for Payment Codes. For more information, please read Aplia's Terms

If you have questions about your payment, please contact Aplia Supp

Continue

This is a **Payment Confirmation** screen. Feel free to print the screen by clicking on the link that says "print" in blue at the top of the page.

- - - - - - - - - - - - - - - - - - -

Click "Continue" to return to your My Home Dashboard and click on the "OPEN" button next to your Aplia course.

Step 6 | Accessing Your Course

Once click on the "Open" button, you will be directed to your Aplia course as shown below.

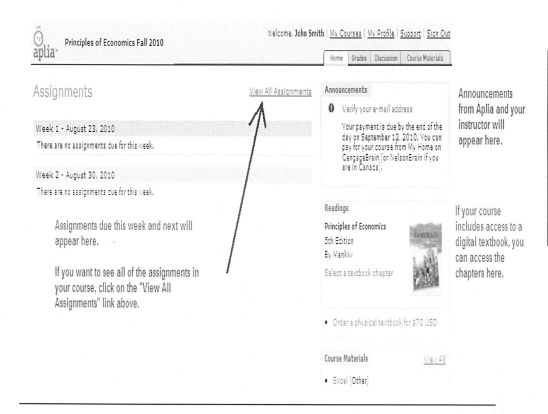

Congratulations!

You have successfully accessed your Aplia course! This page is your Aplia Home Page. Make note of Assignments, Instructor Announcements, access your eBook, etc.

Step 7 | Re-Entering Your Course After Logging Out

Now that you have created an account at login.cengagebrain.com, you can gain immediate access to your "My Home" page, simply by logging in at login.cengagebrain.com. Fill in your username and password to go directly to your "My Home" page and access your course!

Still Need Help?

Problems with your CengageBrain account?

- Check the FAQs in the Support area of your CengageBrain home.

  OR

- Write to **cengagebrain.support@cengage.com**

  OR

- Call 866-994-2427 Monday through Friday from 8 AM to 6 PM EST

Problems with your Aplia course?

- Click on the Support link in your Aplia course

  OR

- Write to **support@aplia.com**

  OR

- Start a chat with a Support representative Monday through Friday from 8 AM to 5 PM PST.

For my siblings—Karen, Lisa, Nanci, and Rick. Thank you for your encouragement, advice, friendship, and support over the years. You are all a part of who I am and I love you.

Ellen Pastorino

For my husband, Eulalio Ortiz Portillo. Knowing you has made me a better person. Eres mi vida, mi amor.

Susann Doyle-Portillo

ABOUT THE AUTHORS

ELLEN E. PASTORINO

Ellen E. Pastorino (Ph.D., Florida State University, 1990) is a developmental psychologist who established her teaching career at Gainesville State College in Georgia. As a tenured professor she created and developed the college's Teaching and Learning Center, working with faculty to promote student learning. For the past 13 years she has been teaching at Valencia Community College in Orlando, Florida. Here, too, she has worked with faculty in designing learning-centered classroom practices. Ellen has won numerous teaching awards including the University of Georgia, Board of Regents Distinguished Professor, the NISOD Excellence in Teaching Award, and Valencia's Teaching and Learning Excellence Award. Ellen has published articles in *The Journal of Adolescent Research* and *Adolescence,* and actively participates in many regional and national teaching conferences. However, her main passion has always been to get students excited about the field of psychology. Ellen is a member of the Association for Psychological Science (APS) and currently serves as the Psychology Department Coordinator at Valencia's Osceola Campus. Ellen has authored test banks, instructor manuals, and student study guides. While working as a consultant for IBM Corporation she developed numerous educational materials for teachers and students. Her current interests include assessment, inclusion, service learning, and reaching underprepared students. Ellen strives to balance her professional responsibilities with her love of physical fitness and family life.

SUSANN M. DOYLE-PORTILLO

A professor of psychology at Gainesville State College for the past 16 years, **Dr. Susann M. Doyle–Portillo** earned her Ph.D. in Social Cognition in 1994 from the University of Oklahoma. Prior to her doctoral program, Susann earned bachelors degrees in engineering and psychology. This exposure to both the hard sciences and the social sciences helped to ground her firmly in the experimental tradition of psychology. She has published articles in *Social Cognition* and *Contemporary Social Psychology,* but the main focus of her career has and will always be teaching. During her tenure at Gainesville State College, Susann has earned a reputation as an excellent, but challenging instructor. Her annual teaching evaluations regularly rank her performance as being "superior" and "excellent" and she has three times been listed in *Who's Who Among America's Teachers.* Susann is also actively engaged in student learning outside of the classroom. One of her major goals is to help students learn by getting them involved in conducting original research, and she was named the 2010 Gainesville State College Best Practices Award winner for her work in this area. In addition to her teaching duties, Susann has pursued professional development opportunities in the area of learning outcome assessment and currently serves as the coordinator of General Education Assessment at Gainesville State College.

BRIEF CONTENTS

CONTENTS

CHAPTER 2

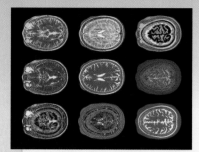

How Does Biology Influence Our Behavior? 40

CHAPTER 3

CHAPTER 4

CONSCIOUSNESS: WIDE AWAKE, IN A DAZE, OR DREAMING? 132

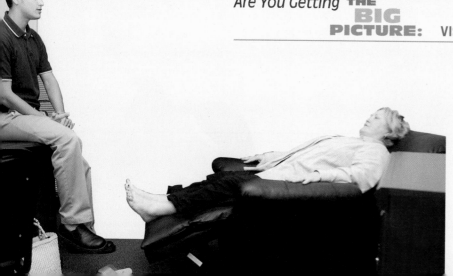

HOW DO WE LEARN? 174

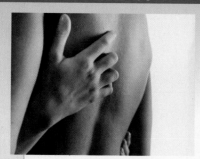

CHAPTER 10

How Do Gender and Sexuality Affect Our Behavior? 402

THE BIG PICTURE: **HOW DO WE DEVELOP A GENDER AND SEXUAL IDENTITY? 403**

SOCIAL PSYCHOLOGY: HOW DO WE UNDERSTAND AND INTERACT WITH OTHERS? 446

THE BIG PICTURE: HOW DO WE NAVIGATE OUR SOCIAL WORLD? 447

CHAPTER 12

HEALTH, STRESS, AND COPING: HOW CAN YOU CREATE A HEALTHY LIFE? 496

THE BIG PICTURE: WHAT CAN PSYCHOLOGY TELL US ABOUT HEALTH? 497

WHAT IS PERSONALITY AND HOW DO WE MEASURE IT? 534

THE BIG PICTURE: HOW CAN WE UNDERSTAND PERSONALITY? 535

PREFACE
TO THE INSTRUCTOR

Together, we have over 35 years of experience teaching introductory psychology. We each teach 3–6 sections of Introductory or General Psychology each semester—it is our bread and butter so to speak. So, it's a good thing that intro psych is also our favorite course. Contrary to what many may think of professors teaching the same course over and over, it never grows old for us. Teaching intro allows us to touch on many different aspects of our fascinating field and to work with diverse students from all walks of life such that no two classes are ever alike.

The uniqueness of each class is just one of the challenges that keep us excited about teaching this course. There are others. General psychology classes are often full of students who are just beginning their academic careers—some are fresh from high school—others are returning, non-traditional students who've been out of the classroom for several years. They come to us with the desire to learn about psychology, but often they face serious obstacles. Some are overworked in their personal lives. Some have lingering academic deficiencies. And most expect learning to be easier than we know it to be. As such, a big part of our mission is to help students overcome these obstacles and obtain success.

Getting students to read their textbook in preparation for lectures and exams is one of the biggest problems we face as instructors. Like many instructors, our experience has been that few students read assigned chapters prior to lecture, and some even fail to read the chapters by the time they take exams. For years, we have tried various methods of motivating students to read—pop quizzes, reading quizzes, test questions from material in the book but not covered in lecture, and so on. None of these methods seemed to have much of an impact on students.

Students' free time is, of course, in short supply. And when they do have free time, reading a textbook doesn't always seem like an attractive option. Students often find their texts difficult to read, boring, and full of content that is far removed from the concerns of their daily lives. One of us overheard students speaking before class the second week of the semester. One student asked those sitting around him if they had read the reading assignment—most replied they had not. He then said, "I read it, but man I have no idea what they were saying in that chapter!" If we want students to read their books, we will have to give them books that they will *want* to read, and that means giving them a book that they can understand and one that *they* find relevant enough to be worth the time it takes to read. That is why we've written this text. Our goal was to write an "untextbook" textbook—a book with a clean, non-distracting format that students would find interesting to read, easy to read, and memorable.

UNLOCKING CURIOSITY IN STUDENTS BY MAKING PSYCHOLOGY INTERESTING

One of the best ways to motivate students to read is to capture their curiosity from the very beginning. Each chapter opens with The Big Picture, a real-life story of a person whose experience illustrates the concept of the chapter. For example, Chapter 2, *How Does Biology Influence Our Behavior?* opens with the story of Jean-Dominique Bauby, a man who became a prisoner in his own body after a stroke damaged his brainstem. Despite the fact that the stroke left him almost completely paralyzed and able only to blink his left eye, Bauby still managed to write a book. Students will find this inspirational story intriguing and hard to forget. And after reading of Bauby, their curiosity will drive them to want to know more about the content of Chapter 2, the brain and how it influences our behavior.

Another wonderful feature of the Big Picture stories is that the majority of them come from popular books that students can read to further explore the lives of these intriguing people. Professors interested in adding an interdisciplinary element to their course could also assign these books as supplementary texts.

MAKING PSYCHOLOGY RELEVANT FOR ALL PEOPLE

There is little doubt that students learn best when they become personally invested in the material that they are reading and studying. However, for this to occur, students must actually find the material to be applicable to their lives. Given that today's college students are a diverse group of people, writing a text that is relevant to today's student means writing a text that embraces their diversity. Due to the essential role of diversity in modern psychology, in the third edition, we have fully integrated all diversity topics into the body of the text. Throughout the text, we have used examples of real people, who reflect the diversity seen in our classrooms. Where applicable, we have cited and highlighted research that reflects many aspects of diversity, including gender differences, racial diversity, cultural diversity, and age and socioeconomic differences (see the Diversity Theme Index found on the inside back cover). The art program for the text was carefully chosen to reflect the diversity of our social world. Even the subjects of the Big Picture stories used throughout the text were selected in part because they celebrate people from many walks of life. In all, we have increased our coverage of diversity in the third edition, referencing people from some 135 countries and/or cultural groups.

Countries and Cultural Groups Referenced in *What Is Psychology?*

Afghanistan
Africa/African
African Americans
Alaska Natives
Algeria
Americans
American Navajos
Arabs
Arab Americans
Argentina
Asia/Asians
Asian Americans
Asian Indian Americans
Australia
Austria
Bashi people of Africa
Belgium
Black
Brazil/Brazilians
British
Bulgaria
Canada
Central America/Central
    Americans
China
Chinese
Chinese Americans
Collectivistic cultures
    (worldwide)

Collectivistic cultures (U.S.)
Croatia
Cuba
Cuban Americans
Cyprus
Czech Republic
Dani
Denmark/Danish
East Africans
East Asians
Egypt/Egyptians
El Salvador
English
Estonia
Europe/Europeans
European Americans
European Union
Finland
France/French
Gabonese
Galapagos Islands
Georgian (U.S.)
Germany
Great Britain
Greece
Greenland
Hindus
Hispanic
Hispanic Americans

Hong Kong
Hungary
Iceland
India
Individualistic cultures
    (worldwide)
Individualistic state cultures
    (U.S.)
Indonesia
Iran
Iraq
Ireland
Israel/Israeli
Islamic/Muslim
Italy
Jamaica
Japan/Japanese
Japanese Americans
Jewish
Jordan
Kiriwina
Korea/Korean
Korean Americans
Latino
Latino Americans
Latvia
Lithuania
Malaysia
Mauritania

Mayan	Pacific Islander	Sweden
Mexico	Philippines	Switzerland/ Swiss
Mexican Americans	Poland	Taiwan/Taiwanese
Morocco	Portugal	Thailand
Multiracial	Puerto Rico	Turkey
Multiracial Americans	Quebecois	Ukraine
Namibia	Romania	United Arab Emirates
Nubian	Russia/Russian	United Kingdom
Native Americans	Scotland	United States
Native Hawaiian	Setswana	Viennese
Netherlands	Seventh Day Adventists	Vietnam
New Yorkers	Singapore	Vietnamese Americans
New Zealand	Slovakia	Wales
Non-Western countries	South Africa	Western countries (cultures,
North American	South America/South	nations, societies)
North Ireland	American	Western Europe
North Korea	Southeast Asian	White/Caucasian
Norway	South Korea	
Oceania	Spain/Spanish	

MAKING PSYCHOLOGY ACCESSIBLE WITHOUT DUMBING IT DOWN

Motivating students to read the text is, of course, a primary concern of instructors. But reading the text does no good if the student does not understand what he or she has read. The student comment we mentioned previously is very telling. He read the assignment, but he did not understand it. We doubt this did much to encourage him to read his next reading assignment! A major goal of this text is to bring psychology to the student by making it understandable and to do so without sacrificing content. We believe that it is not necessary to condescend to students to get them to understand. Rather, you just have to explain difficult concepts thoroughly and clearly.

Engaging Narrative Writing Style

Throughout the text, we have adopted an engaging narrative writing style that will not intimidate students. Difficult concepts (e.g., neural transmission, classical conditioning) are given extended description and many examples are used to illustrate and clarify points. The language we use in the text strongly reflects the way we speak to our students during class. We attempted to use our prose to tell students the *story* of psychology, as opposed to a mere litany of theories and research findings. We believe we have succeeded. Throughout the process of writing this text, many faculty reviewers and students have consistently praised our writing style for its clarity and accessibility. One reviewer commented that it was obvious that this text was written by authors who have spent much time in the classroom in front of students.

ENHANCING MOTIVATION AND LEARNING BY MAKING PSYCHOLOGY PRACTICAL

A key point in getting students to read a text and retain what they've read is making the material applicable to their lives. When information is associated with the self, it becomes more easily retrieved from memory. So, when students can see how psychology relates to their personal lives, they are much more likely to find it interesting and a lot less likely to forget it. Throughout the text, we have made a concerted effort to use practical, everyday examples to illustrate the concepts of psychology.

What's Happening in Your Brain?

The *What's Happening in Your Brain?* feature emphasizes the personal relevance of psychology by showing students what likely happens in their brains when they engage in certain mental processes and behavior. For example, in Chapter 8, *Motivation and Emotion: What Guides Our Behavior?*, a brain scan showing the effects of alcohol abuse on the adolescent brain is provided. *What's Happening in Your Brain?* also fosters the Big Picture of psychology by tying the chapter content back to the biological psychology discussed in Chapter 2.

Technology and Behavior

New to the third edition is a *Technology and Behavior* feature in each chapter that shows students the psychological relevance of the modern technologies they use on a daily basis. For example, in Chapter 6, *How Does Memory Function?*, we examine the effects that laptops and cell phones in the classroom have on learning and memory. In Chapter 2, *How Does Biology Influence Our Behavior?*, we address the debate on whether or not cell phone use is linked to increased brain tumors. This feature is sure to resonate with today's technologically savvy students.

Integrated Applications

Another way in which students can see how psychology relates to their personal lives is through integrated applications. Throughout the text, we give numerous examples of how psychology is related to everyday life. For example, in Chapter 5, *How Do We Learn?*, we discuss how habituation can be used in physical therapies that treat people suffering from chronic vertigo or motion sickness. In Chapter 7, *Cognition, Language, and Intelligence: How Do We Think?*, we give examples of how creativity can be used to solve everyday problems, such as using a cell phone as a homing device to find a lost purse or backpack.

Try This Demonstration

Each chapter also includes at least one *Try This Demonstration*, in which students are asked to engage in a simple demonstration of a chapter topic. For example, in Chapter 3, *How Do We Sense and Perceive the World?*, we show students how to prove to themselves that the moon illusion is just an illusion caused by perceptual processes by having them look at the moon from an unusual vantage point. In Chapter 11, *Social Psychology: How Do We Understand and Interact With Others?*, students explore their own attributional biases when making judgments about celebrities.

Applying Psychology

In the end-of-chapter material, we have also included *Use It or Lose It* questions. These short-answer questions ask students to apply their knowledge to solving a problem—again emphasizing the usefulness of psychology. For instance, in Chapter 4, *Consciousness: Wide Awake, In a Daze, or Dreaming?*, we include the following applied exercise:

> Keep a dream log for a week. Using the different theories on dreaming, interpret what your dreams mean. Which of these interpretations seems the most plausible, and why?

ENHANCING LEARNING BY MAKING PSYCHOLOGY THOUGHT-PROVOKING

Another way to enhance learning is to get students to read in an active fashion. All too often students read in a very passive, in-one-ear-and-out-the-other mode. Students must be enticed to actually *think* while they are reading. To further enhance active engagement in the material, we have embedded thought-provoking questions in the text material. These questions appear in blue and are designed to spur students to engage in goal-directed reading. For example, in Chapter 11, *Social Psychology: How Do We Understand and Interact With Others?*, we pose the question, "Do we want someone who is similar to us, or are we looking for someone who is different to complement our personality?" immediately before we discuss how attitudes affect romantic attraction. By reading in a goal-directed fashion, students are more likely to engage in elaborative rehearsal of the material and will better retain what they've read.

Let's Review

Critical thinking involves analyzing and evaluating information and applying it to other situations. The ability to think critically is an essential learning outcome of both a good psychology course and an undergraduate education. To help foster critical thinking in students, *Let's Review* sections at the end of each major section offer students an opportunity to test their knowledge of the preceding section. The questions are arranged according to difficulty with easier questions coming before more difficult ones. Easy questions require students to use lower level critical thinking skills such as identification and recall of concepts and facts. More difficult questions require students to comprehend and apply psychological concepts or require analysis, synthesis, and discrimination of psychological information. The *Let's Review* feature will help students begin to distinguish superficial learning of material from deeper levels of understanding—an important skill for academic success.

MAKING LEARNING MORE PERMANENT BY GIVING STUDENTS THE BIG PICTURE OF PSYCHOLOGY

As instructors, one of our greatest frustrations has been that many students seem to learn merely for the moment. They come to class, do their assignments, take their exams, and then immediately forget the material they were just tested on. What a waste of energy! One of our goals was to write a text that would help prevent this common problem.

Linking Concepts Together

As we wrote each of the chapters, we were very conscious of the *story* we were telling students. Our purpose was to get students to see the *big picture* of psychology as opposed to seeing the material as a mere collection of ideas and data. Within each chapter, we made a concerted effort to link the concepts together into an integrated whole by frequently making reference to concepts covered earlier in the chapter, by asking questions that touch on more than one concept, by using examples that unify the material, and by threading the Big Picture stories that open each chapter throughout the chapter.

Cross-Chapter References

Likewise, we encourage readers to see that the different areas of psychology are not mutually exclusive or independent by making many cross-chapter references to relevant material. For example, in Chapter 5, *How Do We Learn?*, we relate habituation to natural selection, which is discussed in Chapter 2. These references will encourage students to see that material from other chapters can enrich their understanding of the chapter at hand and motivate them to reread previous sections that need refreshing.

The Big Picture Review Tables

Each chapter includes a *Big Picture Review* table that summarizes a body of content from the chapter. For example, in Chapter 12, *Health, Stress, and Coping: How Can You Create a Healthy Life?*, techniques that reduce stress are summarized. The *Big Picture Review* aids student retention by presenting information in a concise fashion for easy review while reading and studying.

Learning Challenge

New to the third edition is a 15-question *Learning Challenge* quiz at the end of each chapter. Just as in the *Let's Review,* the *Learning Challenge* quiz contains questions at three different levels of mastery. One-point questions require students to use lower level critical thinking skills such as identification and recall of concepts and facts. Two-point questions require students to comprehend and apply psychological concepts. Three-point questions are at the highest level of critical thinking and require analysis, synthesis, and discrimination of psychological information. After taking the quiz, students can calculate their overall level of mastery using a scoring key. Students not achieving the advanced level are then directed to restudy the chapter's content and try again to reach this highest level of mastery.

Critical Thinking for Integration

To help students further develop a *big picture* of psychology, we include *Critical Thinking for Integration* questions at the end of the chapter—a feature that was consistently praised by our many reviewers. These short-answer questions require that the student apply concepts from more than one chapter in solving a problem. Instructors could also assign these questions as written assignments to keep students current on material from chapters covered earlier in the course. For instance, in Chapter 4, *Consciousness: Wide Awake, in a Daze, or Dreaming?,* we include the following question, integrating material from Chapter 4 with information about the brain from Chapter 2:

> Using Chapter 2 as a guide, draw a model of the brain and graphically represent where in the brain various psychoactive drugs have their effects. Also represent on this visual schema the neurotransmitters that affect these areas of the brain.

Are You Getting the Big Picture? Visual Summaries

An *Are You Getting the Big Picture?* visual summary of the chapter is also included in the end-of-chapter material to allow students to truly *see* the *big picture* of the chapter. This feature provides a visual summary of all the major concepts and theories of the chapter depicted in a graphical format. This tool will be especially helpful to students who prefer to learn through visual means.

NEW FEATURES IN THE THIRD EDITION—NEW WAYS TO UNLOCK STUDENT CURIOSITY!

The feedback we received on the second edition of this text from students and instructors alike reaffirmed our original mission to write a book that motivates students to read by capturing their interest and unlocking their curiosity. As a result, our mission in this third edition is to continue to show students that psychology is not only interesting, but also practical and relevant for everyone. We also continue to encourage students to develop a mental *Big Picture* of psychology as they read to facilitate long-term learning and retention of the material. To help us accomplish this ongoing mission, we've added some new features and improvements to the third edition:

- *Big Picture Review* tables have been streamlined in the third edition to only include review material.
- To make psychology as inclusive as possible, we've further integrated diversity throughout the text including the research cited, examples and cases cited, and the art program. In all, 135 different ethnic and cultural groups are mentioned in the text. In addition, based on reviewer feedback and our own commitment to writing an even more inclusive text, the *Spotlight on Diversity* features from the second edition have been completely integrated into the text in the third edition so that students are not tempted to either ignore this mate-

rial or see it as an add-on. We have not reduced diversity coverage; it has just been integrated to streamline the text, simplify reading, and help ensure student exposure to this essential content. The Diversity Theme Index on the book's inside back cover highlights the diversity coverage by chapter.

- Because today's students are accustomed to using technology in many aspects of their daily lives, we have included a new *Technology and Behavior* feature in the third edition. This feature examines both the psychological pros and cons of having these new technologies in our lives. For example, in Chapter 11, *Social Psychology: How Do We Understand and Interact with Others?*, we examine the use of social networking sites to produce "flash mobs," or impromptu gatherings of people in public settings. Flashmobs can be powerful political and artistic statements, but they can also get out of hand and lead to rioting. Social psychology helps understand why this happens.

- To help students develop better insight into their own learning processes, we added a 15-question *Learning Challenge* quiz at the end of each chapter. The *Learning Challenge* replaces the Concept Check found in the second edition. Whereas the Concept Check asked students to master material at a factual level, the *Learning Challenge* quiz contains questions at three different levels of mastery. One-point questions require students to use lower level critical thinking skills such as identification and recall of concepts and facts. Two-point questions require students to comprehend and apply psychological concepts. Three-point questions are at the highest level of critical thinking and require analysis, synthesis, and discrimination of psychological information. After taking the quiz, students can calculate their overall level of mastery using a scoring key. Students not achieving the advanced level are then directed to restudy chapter content and try again to reach this highest level of mastery. A major benefit of the *Learning Challenge* is that it makes salient for students the difference between being familiar with concepts and actually knowing the material. This understanding will help students further their own metacognitive skills.

- To further streamline the text, in the third edition we have integrated the *Are You Getting the Big Picture* feature (which recapped the opening Big Picture case study and chapter content at the end of the chapter) into the Visual Summary at the end of the chapter. By uniting these features, students have just one place to go for a concise Big Picture review of the chapter.

- To keep abreast of the ever-changing face of research and give students the best possible understanding of psychology, we've added over 925 new references to the third edition. Take a look at some of the topics that have been added to each of the chapters in this edition:

CHAPTER 1

What Is Psychology?

- New Big Picture story on Michael Oher opens the chapter
- Titchener's and Washburn's contribution to structuralism emphasized
- Gestalt psychology covered in history section
- New section on birth of positive psychology
- New key terms added and defined: positive psychology, neuroscience, stimulus, response, experimental group, control group, placebo effect, and double-blind study
- Updated information on undergraduate degrees in psychology and work settings of psychologists
- More detailed information on minority contributions to psychology including Clark's and Clark's doll experiments and Inez Prosser's research
- Updated information on women and minorities in the field of psychology
- A new *What's Happening in Your Brain?* study detailing the effect of playing violent video games on the brain
- A new *Technology and Behavior* feature covering psychological research and the Internet

CHAPTER 2

How Does Biology Influence Our Behavior?

- New discussion of epigenetics for a cutting edge look at the nature vs. nurture debate
- New debate on the number of neurons and glial cells in the brain
- Updated information on neurotransmitters and their relationship to mental health issues
- A *Technology and Behavior* feature examining the link between cell phone use and brain tumors
- Diffusion tensor imaging and transcranial magnetic stimulation added to the list of technologies used in studying the brain

CHAPTER 3

How Do We Sense and Perceive Our World?

- New information on visual perception in the cortex and the fusiform face area of the temporal lobe
- New information on hearing loss and memory
- New *Technology and Behavior* feature on ipods, earbuds, and hearing loss
- Updated information on lock and key theory of olfaction
- Updated information on pheromones and the olfactory epithelium
- New information on artists and binocular depth cues
- New discussion of Western vs. Asian perceptual styles

CHAPTER 4

Consciousness: Wide Awake, in a Daze, or Dreaming?

- New *Big Picture* stories of Charlie Parker and Andre Agassi open the chapter
- New *Technology and Behavior* feature discusses sleep texting
- New discussion of fatal familial insomnia
- The fear-extinction purpose of dreaming
- Tryptophan's relationship to serotonin and facilitating sleep
- Enhanced description of the nature of crack cocaine
- New discussion of caffeine intoxication and popularity of energy drinks loaded with caffeine
- Updated information on drug use by age, gender, and ethnicity

CHAPTER 5

How Do We Learn?

- New *Big Picture* story on Michael Gates Gill, author of *How Starbuck's Saved My Life*, opens the chapter
- New *Technology and Behavior* feature discussing if Leap Pads, PlayStations, and Xboxes are the Skinner boxes of the 21st century
- New *Try This Demonstration* on orienting reflexes
- Updated information on European bans on corporal punishment

CHAPTER 6

How Does Memory Function?

- New *Try This Demonstration* on implicit memory
- New *Technology and Behavior* feature on laptops and cell phones in classrooms and their effect on learning and memory
- Ebbinghaus' forgetting curves
- New *Try This Demonstration* on autobiographical memory
- Enhanced explication of elaborative rehearsal

- Updated information on biological evidence for separate episodic and semantic memory systems
- Updated information on the difference between episodic and autobiographical memory
- Updated information on the consistency of flashbulb memories
- New section on storing memory at the synapse
- Updated information on the hippocampus and procedural memory

CHAPTER 11

Social Psychology: How Do We Understand and Interact With Others?

- New *Big Picture* story on Rose Mahoney's cultural odyssey of rowing a boat down the Nile River opens the chapter
- New information on aversive racism
- New *Technology and Behavior* feature on social networking flash mobbing
- New information on culture and helping behavior
- New section on social facilitation and social loafing

CHAPTER 12

Health, Stress, and Coping: How Can You Create a Healthy Life?

- New *Technology and Behavior* feature on technology's health effects
- The potential positive effect of stressful life experiences for *some* people, referred to as *post-traumatic growth* or *benefit-finding*
- Coverage on the Type C personality
- New section includes detailed information on physical activity, eating healthy, and getting enough sleep
- New section details research on the five factors that contribute to happiness and well-being

CHAPTER 13

What Is Personality, and How Do We Measure It?

- New *Technology and Behavior* feature on personality and online game play
- More explanation on each of the five factors of personality
- Emergence of positive psychology as a rebirth of the humanistic perspective

CHAPTER 14

What Are Psychological Disorders, and How Can We Understand Them?

- New *Big Picture* stories including Howie Mandel, Nathaniel Ayers, and JK Rowling open the chapter
- A new *Technology and Behavior* feature explores Internet addiction
- Dissociative fugue disorder coverage
- Enhanced coverage on symptoms of schizophrenia
- Updated information on suicide
- Dissociative and somatoform disorder sections now follow anxiety disorders as they are believed to be similar in nature

CHAPTER 15

What Therapies Are Used to Treat Psychological Problems?

- Counterconditioning and Mary Cover Jones' contribution to behavior therapy
- Eye Movement Desensitization Reprocessing (EMDR) therapy
- New *Technology and Behavior* feature details the nature of cybertherapy
- Coverage of 12-step program format under group therapy
- Discussion of valproate's popularity over lithium in treating bipolar disorder

AVAILABLE SUPPLEMENTS

Instructor Resources

Instructor's Resource Manual

ISBN: 978-1-111-34871-7

Written by Diane Cook, Gainesville State College, and Thomas Hancock, University of Central Oklahoma, this manual contains learning objectives, lecture outlines, ideas for instruction, suggested answers to the end-of-chapter Critical Thinking questions, and annotated lists of supplemental readings, videos, and websites. An extensive "ideas for instruction" section for each major chapter section includes lecture topics, activities, student projects, journal prompts, and handouts. Also included—discussion, teaching, and technology tips suggested by the text's authors.

Test Bank
ISBN: 978-1-111-34873-1
Written by Kelly Bouas Henry of Missouri Western State College, this is a printed selection of more than 200 multiple-choice questions, 15 true/false questions, and 10 short answer questions for each chapter, plus *Making Connections* items that ask students to answer questions based on material learned in earlier chapters. All questions are keyed to the book's learning objectives.

New Design! PowerLecture™ With JoinIn™ and ExamView®
ISBN: 978-1-111-34874-8
A fast and easy way to build customized, media-rich lectures, **PowerLecture™** provides a collection of newly-designed, book-specific Microsoft® PowerPoint® lecture slides—reflecting instructional design principles that define how we best process information. Slides strategically combine text (including talking point examples not cited in the text), visuals, and one-click links to narrated animations to engage students and optimize their learning. You'll also find **JoinIn™ Student Response System** content on slides (for use with "clickers"), allowing you to ask questions and see students' responses, and **ExamView™** computerized testing, featuring printed Test Bank items in electronic format.

Wadsworth Psychology Video Library
Available upon adoption are a variety of videos to spark student interest and illuminate the relevance of psychology, including news segments, clips from Hollywood films, introductions to eminent researchers and their work, Candid Camera-like segments depicting people in socially challenging situations, and more.

New! Introductory Psychology Video—Video Provided by BBC Motion Gallery
ISBN: 978-1-111-35260-8

ABC® News on DVD, Introductory Psychology
Vol. 1 ISBN: 978-0-495-50306-4
Vol. 2 ISBN: 978-0-495-59637-0
Vol. 3 ISBN: 978-0-495-60490-7

Research in Action
Vol. I ISBN: 978-0-495-59520-5
Vol. II ISBN: 978-0-495-59813-8

Psych in Film
ISBN: 978-0-618-27530-4

Revealing Psychology
ISBN: 978-0-547-01453-1

Wadsworth Guest Lecture Series
ISBN: 978-0-547-00401-3

Online Resources

Contact your Cengage Learning representative for assistance with packaging any of the resources below with student texts.

Aplia™ for *What Is Psychology?*, Third Edition   aplia
www.aplia.com
Aplia™ is an online interactive learning solution that improves comprehension and outcomes by increasing student effort and engagement. Aplia provides automatically graded assignments with detailed, immediate explanations on every question. Aplia presents a vari-

ety of question types to reinforce student reading and require them to demonstrate their understanding of the material in multiple ways. Short engagement activities—such as experiments, videos, and surveys—provide experiential learning opportunities while illustrating concepts, piquing students' interest, and motivating them to learn more. As students complete assignments, grades flow directly into your Aplia gradebook.

For a demo, visit **www.aplia.com.**

Psychology CourseMate

Printed Access Card: 1-111-67734-4
Instant Access Code: 1-111-67733-6
Cengage Learning's **Psychology CourseMate** includes interactive teaching and learning tools including an integrated eBook, quizzes, flashcards, videos, learning modules, and more to support the printed textbook. It also features *Engagement Tracker,* a first-of-its-kind tool that monitors student engagement in the course.

CengageNOW™ for *What Is Psychology?* Third Edition
CENGAGENOW™
Printed Access Card: 1-111-67780-8
Instant Access Code: 1-111-67779-4
CengageNOW™ is an easy-to-use online resource that helps students study in less time to get the grade they want—NOW. Featuring **CengageNOW™ Personalized Study** (a diagnostic tool containing text-specific resources), the program helps students learn more in less time by focusing their attention on what they don't know. Students can also link to the **Psychology Resource Center.** Automatic grading saves you time.

Psychology Resource Center
Printed Access Card: 0-495-59712-0
Instant Access Code: 0-495-59713-9
The **Psychology Resource Center** offers 24/7 access to hundreds of videos, learning modules, simulations, and more to help students better understand psychology and study for exams. Access is available separately or through **CengageNOW.**

WebTutor™ on Blackboard® or WebCT®
Jumpstart your course with customizable, text-specific content for use within your course management system, including media assets, quizzes, web links, and more.

Student Supplements

Study Guide
ISBN: 978-1-111-34881-6
Written by Susann Doyle-Portillo and Ellen Pastorino, this guide presents learning objectives, key points, fill-in chapter review items, and self-check questions (true/false, multiple-choice, and short-answer).

Supplementary Books
There are several other supplementary books that offer help to students.

Challenging Your Preconceptions: Thinking Critically About Psychology, Second Edition
ISBN: 0-534-26739-4
This paperbound book, written by Randolph Smith, helps students strengthen their critical thinking skills. Psychological issues such as hypnosis and repressed memory, statistical seduction, the validity of pop psychology, and other topics arc used to illustrate the principles of critical thinking.

Writing Papers in Psychology: A Student Guide
ISBN: 0-495-50956-6
The eighth edition of *Writing Papers in Psychology,* by Ralph L. Rosnow and Mimi Rosnow, is a valuable "how-to" manual for writing term papers and research reports. This new edi-

tion has been updated to reflect the latest APA guidelines. The book covers each task with examples, hints, and two complete writing samples. Citation ethics, how to locate information, and new research technologies are also covered.

Writing With Style: APA Style Made Easy
ISBN: 0-8400-3167-X

This accessible and invaluable workbook-style reference guide will help students smoothly make the transition from writing for composition classes to writing for psychology classes. In her fifth edition of *Writing With Style,* author Lenore T. Szuchman succinctly provides the basics of style presented by the fifth edition of the APA's *Publication Manual.* This unique workbook format offers both a quick reference to APA style and interactive exercises that give students a chance to practice what they've learned.

Challenging Your Preconceptions: Thinking Critically About Psychology
ISBN: 0-534-26739-4

This supplement supports the development of critical thinking skills necessary to success in the introductory psychology course. The chapter sequence mirrors the organization of the typical introductory psychology course. In the first chapter, the author identifies seven characteristics of critical thinkers, and in the following chapters he dissects a challenging issue in the discipline and models critical thinking for the reader. Each chapter concludes with an analysis of the process, exercises for the student, and extensive references. This useful volume supports the full semester of the course.

Critical Thinking in Psychology: Separating Sense from Nonsense
ISBN: 0-534-63459-1

Do your students have the tools to distinguish between the true science of human thought and behavior from pop psychology? The second edition of John Ruscio's book provides a tangible and compelling framework for making that distinction. Because we are inundated with "scientific" claims, the author does not merely differentiate science and pseudoscience, but goes further to teach the fundamentals of scientific reasoning on which students can base their evaluation of information.

Cross-Cultural Perspectives in Psychology
ISBN: 0-534-54653-6

How well do the concepts of psychology apply to various cultures? What can we learn about human behavior from cultures different from our own? These questions lie behind a collection of original articles written by William F. Price and Rich Crapo. The fourth edition of *Cross-Cultural Perspectives in Psychology* contains articles on North American ethnic groups as well as cultures from around the world.

Introduction to Positive Psychology
ISBN: 0-534-64453-8

This brief paperback presents in-depth coverage of the relatively new area of positive psychology. Topically organized, it looks at how positive psychology relates to stresses and health within such traditional research areas as developmental, clinical, personality, motivational, social, and behavioral psychology.

ACKNOWLEDGMENTS

Writing a college textbook has been an exhausting yet rewarding experience. We are ordinary community college professors who teach four to six classes every semester, so we are often writing in whatever free time we have—weekends, nights, and holidays. We do not live in a "publish or perish" environment. Instead we are valued for our contributions to student learning and service to our institutions. Yet, we have grown so much as educators and psychologists in tackling this project. This would not have been possible without the support of many people who deserve our acknowledgement.

We would like to thank Dean Melissa Pedone at Valencia Community College and Chuck Karcher at Gainesville State College for their administrative support. We would like to thank Jaime Perkins at Cengage Learning for being the best publisher in the world! We would also like to thank Kristin Makarewycz and Christy Frame from Cengage Learning for being great editors and managers of this project. Your assistance and criticism has been invaluable. We also owe great debts of gratitude to Liz Rhoden, Kim Russell, Vernon Boes, Roman Barnes, Lauren Keyes, Paige Leeds, Phil Hovanessian and the rest of the team at Cengage Learning for all that you do. We also gratefully acknowledge Nicole Lee Petel at Lachina Publishing Services for skillfully guiding the book through the various stages of production.

We also would like to thank the following reviewers for their insightful comments and expert guidance in developing this text:

Belinda Blevins-Knabe, *University of Arkansas at Little Rock*; Pamela Costa, *Tacoma Community College*; Michael G. Dudley, *Southern Illinois University Edwardsville*; Mominka Fileva, *Davenport University*; Deborah Garfin, *Georgia State University*; John H. Hummel, *Valdosta State University*; Cameron R. John, *Utah Valley University*; Franz Klutschkowski, *North Central Texas College*; Kenneth Koenigshofer, Ph.D., *University of Maryland*; Debra J Matchinksy, *North Hennepin Community College*; Laura N. May, *University of South Carolina Aiken*; David Monetti, *Valdosta State University*; Cindy Nordstrom, *Southern Illinois University Edwardsville*; Ann Phillips, *University of Michigan*; Jason S. Spiegelman, *Community College of Baltimore County*; Mary Stelma, *Lansing Community College*; Karla West, *Boise State University*; Kevin M. P. Woller, *Rogers State University*.

We are grateful to the reviewers from the second edition:

Angela Allen, *Roanoke College*; Cheryl Anagnopoulos, *Black Hills State University*; Jo Ann Armstrong, *Patrick Henry Community College*; Linda Bastone, *Purchase College, SUNY*; Guin "Buck" Christmas, *North Florida Community College*; Claudia Cochran, *El Paso Community College*; Donna Dahlgren, *Indiana University Southeast*; Susan Edwards, *Mott Community College*; Christopher France, *Cleveland State University*; Eugenio Galindro, *El Paso Community College*; Mark Garrison, *Kentucky State University*; Julie Gurner, *Community College of Pennsylvania*; Verneda Hamm Baugh, *Kean University*; Joseph Hardy, *Harrisburg Area Community College*; Milton Hatcher, *Arkansas State University*; Holly Haynes, *Georgia Gwinnett College*; Debra Hollister, *Valencia Community College*; Tonya Honeycutt, *Johnson County Community College*; Matthew Krug, *Wisconsin Lutheran College*; Sandra Lancaster, *Grand Rapids Community College*; Christopher LeGrow, *Marshall University*; Sonya Lott-Harrison, *Community College of Philadelphia*; Debra Matchinsky, *North Hennepin Community College*; Robert Matchock, *Penn State Altoona*; Clark McKinney, *Southwest Tennessee Community College*; Martha Mendez-Baldwin, *Manhattan College*; Todd Nelson, *California State University, Stanislaus*; Henry Pines, *Canisius College*; Jim Previte, *Victor Valley College*; Amira Rezec, *Saddleback College*; Ronda Rhoden, *El Paso Community College*; Nicole Roberts, *University of Wisconsin*; Edna Ross, *University of Louisville*; Patricia Sawyer, *Middlesex Community College*; Nancy Simpson, *Trident Technical College*; Katrina Smith, *Southern Catholic College*; Mark Stewart, *American River College*; Anita Tam, *Harrisburg Area Community College*; Joycelyn Williams, *Kingwood College, North Harris*; *Montgomery Community College District*; Anthony Zainea, *Grand Rapids Community College*.

We would also like to thank the reviewers from the first edition:

Mark Agars, *CSU San Bernardino*; Yuki Aida, *Austin Community College*; Rahan Ali, *Penn State University*; Margaret Armitage, *Howard Community College*; JoAnn Armstrong, *Patrick Henry Community College*; Ted Barker, *Okaloosa-Walton College*; Linda Bastone, *Purchase College, SUNY*; Saundra Boyd, *Houston Community College System*; Norma Caltagirone, *Hillsborough Community College—Ybor Campus*; Herb Coleman, *Austin Community College*; Perry Collins, *Wayland Baptist University*; Mary Coplen, *Hutchinson Community College*; Donna Dahlgren, *Indiana University Southeast*; Stephen Donohue, *Grand Canyon*

University; Michael Durnam, *Adams State College;* Ray Eilenstine, *Southeastern Community College;* Thomas Estrella, *Lourdes College;* Michael Firmin, *Cedarville University;* Rita Flattley, *Pima Community College;* Jana Flowers, *Richland College;* Nancy Foster, *Mississippi State University;* Karen Freiberg, *University of Maryland, Baltimore County;* Robert Gehring, *University of Southern Indiana;* Stan Gilbert, *Community College of Philadelphia;* Kendra Gilds, *Lane Community College;* Frank Hager, *Allegany College of Maryland;* Kaira Hayes, *Fort Hays State University;* Debra Hollister, *Valencia Community College;* Jaye Johnston, *Kingwood College;* Bradley Karlin, *Texas A&M University;* Irina Khramtsova, *Arkansas State University;* Shirin Khosropour, *Austin Community College;* Matthew Krug, *Wisconsin Lutheran College;* Ernest Marquez, *Elgin Community College;* Anne McCrea, *Sinclair Community College;* Martha Mendez-Baldwin, *Manhattan College;* Glenn Meyer, *Trinity College;* Leslie Minor-Evans, *Central Oregon Community College;* Karen Mor, *Cuyamaca College;* Dean Murakami, *American River College;* Debbie Podwika, *Kankakee Community College;* Jeff Reber, *State University of West Georgia;* Tanya Renner, *Kapiolani Community College;* Edna Ross, *University of Louisville;* Patricia Sawyer, *Middlesex Community-Tech College;* Jeff Schaler, *Johns Hopkins University;* Jean Selders, *Arapahoe Community College;* Kimberley Smirles, *Emmanuel College;* Mark Stewart, *American River College;* Greg Turek, *Fort Hays State University;* Denise Valenti-Hein, *University of Wisconsin, Oshkosh.*

We would also like to thank our friends and colleagues at Gainesville State College and Valencia Community College for their support and latitude over the past decade. We would especially like to thank the thousands of students we have worked with over the years. In your own way, each of you has helped us to become better teachers and better people. Our hope is that this book will touch many other students and foster an interest in and passion for psychology.

Finally, we would like to thank our families. Susann would like to thank her husband, Eulalio Ortiz Portillo, for being a man who will, unasked, bring his wife a hot tea while she is writing. Your love and support make my life possible. Ellen would like to thank Christian, Andrew, and Scott for tolerating the "Do Not Disturb" sign while she was writing, even when they were hungry. Ellen also would like to thank her WonderBoy husband, Dave, for his technical assistance, his tireless rereading of material, and his patience and support. Love is indeed something that you do.

WHAT IS PSYCHOLOGY?

THE BIG PICTURE

What Do Psychologists Study?

Welcome to the world of **psychology**, the scientific study of behavior and mental processes. But what exactly does that include? Behavior includes actions, feelings, and biological states. Mental processes include problem solving, intelligence, and memory, to name just a few. Psychology is a science because psychologists conduct research in accord with the **scientific method**. They analyze the behavior of humans as well as other species.

For centuries people have been trying to understand the mind and behavior. Psychology is probably one of the few disciplines in which students come to the first class believing they already know much about the topic. We see psychologists and psychiatrists on talk shows and reality television (Dr. Phil, Dr. Drew) and listen to them on the radio. We frequently see them depicted on television (*Lie to Me, Law & Order: SVU, Criminal Minds, Bones*) and in the movies (*Shutter Island; Running With Scissors; I, Robot; Prime*). Many of these portrayals are quite entertaining, but they do not always represent psychology accurately. As a result, the public image of the discipline tends to be distorted.

The purpose of this textbook is to help you develop a deeper understanding of psychology. In this chapter, we explain what psychologists do, how they think, and where they work. It is a general overview, or "big picture," of the field of psychology, an introduction to the more specific areas of psychology discussed in subsequent chapters.

Each chapter begins with a "Big Picture" section to help you integrate the chapter material into the broader field of psychology. This big picture incorporates accounts of real people and events. We hope that by reading these real-life stories, you will find psychological topics easier to understand and will be better able to apply psychological principles and concepts to your own life. To begin, consider the following story.

One afternoon Tony Henderson left Hurt Village, a gang-infested housing project in West Memphis, and drove east to Briarcrest Christian School to enroll his son, Steven. He also had with him Steven's friend, Michael, who had been crashing on the floor at his house for some time and who he feared would drop out of school, hit the streets selling drugs, and end up dead or in jail.

Steven was a model student and talented basketball player who had no difficulty being accepted. However, Michael was a different story. Michael had no dad, and his mother was in rehab. He had spent time in several foster homes and at other times had no known address. He had been enrolled in eleven different schools in nine years,

CHAPTER OUTLINE

- What Is Psychology?
- How Did Psychology Become a Science? The Origins of Psychology
- What Is Psychology Like Today?
- How Is Psychological Research Conducted? Hypotheses and Methods
- What Are the Ethical Rules of Psychological Research?

© Whisson/Jordan/Corbis

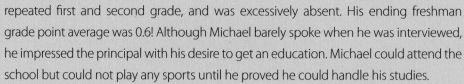

The story of Michael Oher and his adoptive family, the Tuohys, powerfully illustrates how people can change their circumstances and behavior to better themselves, despite overwhelming odds.

psychology the scientific study of behavior and mental processes

scientific method a systematic process used by psychologists for testing hypotheses about behavior

repeated first and second grade, and was excessively absent. His ending freshman grade point average was 0.6! Although Michael barely spoke when he was interviewed, he impressed the principal with his desire to get an education. Michael could attend the school but could not play any sports until he proved he could handle his studies.

As a new student Michael was hard to miss. He was one of the few African American students at this predominately White private school. He was 6'5" tall and weighed close to 350 pounds. Everyone knew who Michael was even though he rarely spoke. His teachers tried to engage him, but he didn't speak in class, never had his books, and was soon failing his classes. Then things started to change. First, his biology teacher gave him an oral instead of a written test and realized that Michael was learning! He had a fantastic memory and could understand many concepts if he could see them or have them explained in visual detail.

For a year and a half several families at the school gave Michael a place to sleep, including the Tuohys. Sean Tuohy knew what it was like to be a poor kid in a private school and to use sports to pay for an education. His college education was courtesy of a basketball scholarship at the University of Mississippi. Now a self-made success, Sean owned a chain of fast-food restaurants and dedicated his time and money to help the "poor jocks" at his kids' school. It started with a lunch account, but when his wife, Leigh Anne, got involved, Michael soon became a member of their family. "When I moved in with Leigh Anne and Sean, I felt loved," said Michael, "like part of a family. In the other houses I didn't feel like part of the family. I didn't feel like they wanted me there" (Lewis, 2009, p.150).

Leigh Anne took him shopping for clothes, provided food, tuition, and medical care, and gave him his own room—a first for Michael. She required that he visit his mother. She educated Michael on the details of upper-middle-class American life from restaurant dining to the meaning of such words as *foyer*. She treated Michael as she did her two other children, providing material goods, spiritual and emotional guidance, and love.

By the spring of his sophomore year, Michael was earning Ds in his classes while spending five hours a day after school with private tutors. He was playing basketball and soon afterward throwing the discus for the track team. It wasn't until his junior year that Michael started to play football. Despite his size, here too Michael had problems. He seemed confused and passive and didn't want to hit anyone. But his size got him noticed by a national college football scout. He attended elite football camps in the summer and received additional training from his coaches. He became a pre-season High School All-American football pick. Division I college coaches showed up in droves, and Michael became one of the most sought after offensive linemen in the nation. Sean was mystified: "I was under the impression Michael sucked at football," he said. "I was trying to get him a basketball scholarship" (Lewis, 2009, p. 98).

The changes in Michael's environment brought changes in Michael. He smiled and laughed more often. He became more talkative and sure of himself. With the help of a personal tutor, his grades significantly improved. By his senior year, he was making all As and Bs and was named to the Honor Roll. His football playing improved too, and his team clinched the Tennessee state championship. Michael Oher was soon named Tennessee's high school football Player of the Year. He was the first in his biological family to graduate from high school, and he received a full athletic scholarship to the University of Mississippi. Here too he continued to thrive with the help of his support system—the Tuohys, his tutor, his coaches and friends. In 2009, he graduated from Ole Miss with a degree in criminal justice. That summer, he became the first round draft pick for the NFL Baltimore Ravens, signing a 5-year, $13.8 million contract.

Michael Oher's story, originally published by Michael Lewis in the book *The Blindside: Evolution of a Game* before being made into a motion picture, reflects the effects of poverty, racism, drug abuse, and child neglect but also highlights human resiliency, motivation, kindness, love, and optimism. Michael's story includes both the best and the worst of human behavior—all of which is of interest to psychologists. His story richly illustrates the depth and breadth of the field of psychology.

In this chapter, we introduce you to psychology: what it is and what it is not, how it became a science, and what the field is like today. We also describe the goals of psychological research and how psychologists study behavior. As you read this chapter and those that follow, keep Michael Oher's story in mind. Consider how psychologists might study his behavior and that of those around him. By doing this, you will have started to think like a psychologist. This perspective will help you integrate the different areas of psychology into a whole and keep the big picture of psychology in your mind.

WHAT IS PSYCHOLOGY?

LEARNING OBJECTIVES

What Should You Know?
- Identify common misconceptions about the field of psychology.
- Define psychology.

When you think about Michael Oher's story, you might suppose that psychologists would be most interested in studying how he coped: how he dealt with his mother's drug use, how he adapted to being virtually homeless, what his fears were in transferring to new schools and new environments, and how he managed the stress of school, football, and being adopted by a family of a different racial and economic background. Many people assume that psychologists only study people who are in crisis or who have mental health problems. This belief is just one of many common misconceptions about the field of psychology. Let's look at some others.

Correcting Common Misconceptions About the Field of Psychology

You are probably reading this book because you have enrolled in a general psychology course. Your expectations of what you will learn have been influenced by your general impressions of psychology. Much of the psychological information presented in the media focuses on practitioners, therapy, and helping others, and you may have the impression that psychology is all about how you feel and how you can feel better. Although a large proportion of psychologists counsel or otherwise treat clients, most of these professionals hold a doctorate degree in psychology, which required that they study scientific methodology and complete a considerable amount of research.

APA Style:

Author, A. A., Author, B. B., & Author, C. C. (Year). Title of article:

Subtitle of article. *Title of Periodical or Journal, Vol #,* pages.

Example:

Snibbe, A. C. (2003). Cultural psychology: Studying the exotic other.

APS Observer, 16, 30–32.

FIGURE 1.1

● **Reference Citations in Psychology**

The References section at the end of this book lists the complete source for each citation. Here is the APA style format for psychological references. The citation for this particular reference would appear in the text as (Snibbe, 2003).

TABLE 1.1

● **How Much Do You Know About Behavior?**

Indicate whether you believe each statement is true (T) or false (F).

1. We are either left brain or right brain thinkers. T F

2. Genes only work during prenatal development. T F

3. No new neurons develop after infancy. T F

4. Brain injury in children is always worse than brain injury in adults. T F

5. Stress is caused by bad things that happen to you. T F

6. During sleep, the brain rests. T F

7. There are female and male brains. T F

8. Males are better at math than females. T F

9. We only have five senses. T F

10. Legal drugs don't hurt the brain but illegal ones do. T F

11. Our memory works like a video recorder. T F

12. Schizophrenia means you have multiple personalities. T F

theory an explanation of why and how a behavior occurs

Psychology is rooted in scientific research. The information in this book is research based. Every idea put forward in the field is subject to scientific study. You will notice that many statements in this text are followed by names and years in parentheses—for example, (Pastorino, 2011). These text citations refer to the scientific studies on which the stated conclusions are based, with the researcher name(s) and date of the study. All the research citations (● FIGURE 1.1) can be found in the References section at the end of this book.

A psychologist's explanation of a particular behavior is generally presented as a theory. A **theory** is an explanation of why and how a behavior occurs. It does not explain a particular behavior for all people, but it does provide general guidelines that summarize facts and help us organize research on a particular subject.

We all, at times, fancy ourselves as psychologists. We interact with people all the time, we observe others' behaviors, and we have our own personal experiences. Therefore, we might naturally think that we already know a lot about psychology. People often behave the way we think they will behave, so psychology seems as though it is just common sense. However, we often overlook the examples of behavior that don't confirm our expectations or support our preexisting beliefs. Psychologists systematically test their ideas about behavior using the prescribed methods and procedures we will describe later in this chapter.

Take a look at ● TABLE 1.1 and answer the questions about behavior. All the statements are false. Yet, many students hold these misconceptions or myths about behavior. Psychological findings do not always confirm our everyday observations about behavior. By objectively measuring and testing our ideas and observations about behavior, we can determine which ideas are more likely to stand up to scientific scrutiny. Behavior is much more complex than the simple statements in Table 1.1 suggest.

Although some psychologists specialize in mental illness, many others work in academic settings, in the business world, in education, or in government agencies. Psychology is an extremely diverse field, and new specialties are appearing each year. Psychologists are interested in numerous topics, including learning, memory, aging, development, gender, motivation, emotion, sports, criminal behavior, and many other subjects. We cannot cover every area of psychology in this textbook, but we will give you an overview of the main areas of psychological research.

Psychology Will Teach You About Critical Thinking

If you asked 10 of your friends how to tell when pasta has been adequately cooked, you probably would not get the same answer from each person. Some may focus on how tender the pasta is; others may rely on how well the pasta sticks to the wall; still others may just follow the package directions. Similarly, psychologists do not necessarily agree on why people behave as they do.

Human beings are extremely complex. Many variables influence why a particular person in a particular place behaves in a specific way on a certain occasion. One psychologist may focus on possible external reasons for behavior, such as the influence of others or the environment in which people live. That psychologist's explanations will differ from those of a psychologist who focuses on internal reasons for behavior, such as people's physical health, their degree of motivation, or how they feel about themselves.

Because behavior is so complex, psychological theories generally don't definitively explain the behavior of all people. To think like a psychologist, you must think critically to analyze and evaluate information. You must be able to distinguish true psychological information from *pseudoscience*. Pseudoscientific findings sound persuasive, but they are not necessarily based on scientific procedures. Their conclusions may go far beyond the scope of their actual data. For example, have you ever heard that people use only 10% of their brain? Many college students believe this false statement despite evidence that shows it is not true (Higbee & Clay, 1998). To think like a psychologist, you must be skeptical rather than accepting about explanations of behavior.

Critical thinking involves analyzing and evaluating information and applying it to other situations. Critical thinking makes you an intelligent consumer of information, and you will be encouraged to practice this skill throughout the book as you read the chapter material and test your mastery of the material in the Let's Review sections at the end of each main topic and in the questions at the end of each chapter.

Because we all engage in behavior, much of the information in this text will apply to your life. Like Michael Oher, we all dream, remember, like or dislike others, are motivated, have high or low self-esteem, behave aggressively, help others, learn, perceive, and use our senses. Consequently, we recommend that you apply the material in this text to your own behavior as much as possible. This connection will increase your interest in the text, and you will study more effectively.

Let's REVIEW

REVIEW In this section we defined psychology and identified several misconceptions about the field. For a quick check of your understanding, try answering the following questions at increasing levels of difficulty.

1. Which of the following statements is *true*?

   a. Psychology is just common sense.
   b. Psychologists only study abnormal behavior.
   c. Psychologists know why people behave the way that they do.
   d. Psychologists test ideas about behavior according to the scientific method.

2. Which of the following topics would a psychologist most likely study?

   a. weather patterns in Africa
   b. memory changes in adults
   c. causes of the Vietnam War
   d. all of the above

3. Which of the following statements is *not* a pseudoscientific claim?

   a. Transplant organs carry personality traits that are always transferred from donors to receivers.
   b. Walking on hot coals without burning one's feet requires paranormal abilities.
   c. You can make a blood clot in your brain disappear by humming and praying.
   d. Several studies show a relationship between academic achievement and self-esteem.

ANSWERS 1. d; 2. b; 3. d

LEARNING OBJECTIVE

What Should You Know?
- Describe the early schools of psychology and identify the major figures that influenced its development.

HOW DID PSYCHOLOGY BECOME A SCIENCE? THE ORIGINS OF PSYCHOLOGY

How did psychology become a science? Psychology has been described as having "a long past but only a short history" (Ebbinghaus, 1910, p. 9). Although psychology did not formally become a science until the 1870s, people have always been interested in explaining behavior. The roots of psychology can be traced to philosophy and medicine in ancient Egypt, Greece, India, and Rome. Philosophers debated whether the mind, or the thinking part of a human, could be studied scientifically; they discussed the nature of the mind and where it was located. Because of the mind's association with the body, much of what we consider psychology today was then part of the field of medicine. Hippocrates (460–377 BCE), the father of medicine, believed that personality was in part a reflection of the mix of chemicals in the body, and abnormal behavior was typically treated with medical procedures. The ancient Indian texts of knowledge, *The Vedas* (2000–600 BCE), describe *chakras* or energy processing centers within the body that govern physical, mental, emotional, and spiritual health.

Continued debate in these disciplines throughout the Renaissance (1400–1500) and post-Renaissance (1500–1600) periods influenced early psychologists' attempts to formulate a science of the mind. Although these issues were not considered "psychological" at the time, doctors and philosophers debated many of the same issues that concern modern psychologists.

Early Approaches: Structuralism, Functionalism, and Psychoanalysis

When did psychology become a separate field of study? Traditionally, psychology's birth is linked with the first psychology laboratory, which was established by Wilhelm Wundt in 1879 at the University of Leipzig, in Germany. As you will see, some of the people who brought psychology into the scientific arena were trained as physicians; others were more philosophical in nature. Communication was much slower in those days, and psychology developed in different ways in different countries. However, these differences produced a psychology that was broad and complex, with many avenues of exploration.

Wilhelm Wundt (1832–1920) wanted to know what psychological processes enable us to experience the external world. His approach today is referred to as structuralism.

© Bettmann/Corbis

Wilhelm Wundt, Edward Titchener, and Structuralism

For Wilhelm Wundt (1832–1920), the goal of psychology was to study conscious processes of the mind and the body. He wanted to know what thought processes enabled us to experience the external world. In particular, Wundt attempted to detail the *structure* of our mental experiences. Like a chemist who questions what elements combine to create different substances, Wundt questioned what elements, when combined, would explain mental processes. Wundt's view that mental experiences were created by different elements is referred to as **structuralism**, a term coined not by Wundt but by his student Edward Titchener.

To identify the structure of thought, Titchener used a process known as **introspection**, a self-observation technique. Trained observers were presented with an event and asked to describe their mental processes. The observations were repeated many times. From these introspections, Titchener identified three basic elements of all conscious experiences: sensations, images, and feelings. For example, try this demonstration.

structuralism an early psychological perspective concerned with identifying the basic elements of experience

introspection observing one's own thoughts, feelings, or sensations

TRY THIS DEMONSTRATION

Apply the technique of introspection to determine what this object is.

Look at the accompanying photo of an object. If you were asked to describe the object, what would you say? How do you know that the object is a potato? Does the object fit your visual image or memory of a potato? That is, does it look like a potato? If the object were in front of you right now, how else might you conclude it is a potato? Does it smell like a potato, taste like a potato, and feel like a potato? Using your senses, you deduce that the object before you is a potato.

© David Young-Wolff/PhotoEdit

Wundt's and Titchener's research went beyond introspection and structuralism to encompass a very broad view of psychology. They conducted detailed studies on color vision, visual illusions, attention, and feelings. They also influenced the field of psychology through their students, many of whom went on to establish psychology departments and laboratories in the United States. For example, Titchener's first graduate student, Margaret Washburn, became the first woman to earn a doctorate in psychology. Washburn did not share Titchener's emphasis on structuralism and instead investigated the connection between motor movement and the mind and conducted extensive research on animal behavior. Other psychologists also reacted against the very limited view of the mind that structuralism presented as it did not adequately explain how we actively organize or *perceive* our sensations. Such disagreement gave rise to another early school of psychology called **Gestalt psychology**. The word *Gestalt* is German for "whole form." Gestalt psychology, founded by Max Wertheimer in the early 1900s, emphasized how our minds organize sensory stimuli to produce the perception of a whole form (such as perceiving a group of stars in the night sky as the Big Dipper). Researchers discovered a number of principles of perception that are detailed further in Chapter 3.

History of American Psychology, U. of Akron, Akron, Ohio

The first woman to be awarded a doctorate in psychology was Margaret Washburn (1871–1939).

William James and Functionalism

William James (1842–1910), a U.S. professor of psychology, was responsible for introducing experimental psychology to U.S. college students. He had visited Wundt's laboratory but did not share Wundt's focus on breaking down mental events to their smallest elements. Rather, James proposed a focus on the wholeness of an event and the impact of the environment on behavior. He emphasized *how* a mental process operates as opposed to the structure of a mental process. He came to believe that consciousness and thought evolved through the process of natural selection, to help the organism adapt to its environment (Nielsen & Day, 1999). *Evolution* and *natural selection* were ideas that were then quite new. Evolution refers to the development of a species—the process by which, through a series of changes over time, humans have acquired behaviors and characteristics that distinguish them from other species. For James, the question was not what elements contribute to one's experience but rather what *function* does the event serve for the person or animal. How does a particular behavior help an organism adapt to its environment and thereby increase its chances of surviving and reproducing? James's perspective on psychology became known as **functionalism**.

Functionalism's focus on the adaptive value of behavior was influenced by Charles Darwin's theory of evolution. Darwin's theory speculated that certain behaviors or traits that enhance survival are naturally selected. For example, Darwin had collected several different types of birds in the Galapagos Islands. The birds were all about the same size but had different beaks (see photo). Through research with other scientists in London, Darwin discovered that the birds were all finches and that each species was uniquely related to a specific island. Darwin thought that the different species had been formed from a small number of common ancestors. The differences in their beaks could be attributed to adapting to different food supplies on each island. According to James, if human behavior is naturally selected like Darwin's finches' beaks, it is important for psychologists to understand the function or survival value of a behavior.

Functionalism was less rigid and not as bound to laboratory methods and experimentation as was Wundt's structuralism. However, just as Wundt did not restrict himself to structuralism, functionalism was not the whole of James's work in the young field of psychology. James suggested applications of psychology to teaching and created the field of *educational psychology*. For example, James's book, *Talks to Teachers* (1899), described how psychological knowledge about creating associations and making connections could be used to help students learn—techniques that continue to inform school practices today. Another contribution to psychology by James was in the area of emotions. The James-Lange theory of emotion, formulated by James and a Danish physiologist, Carl Lange, at about the same time, describes how physical sensations give rise to emotions (more on this in Chapter 8). In addition, James published books on religious experiences and philosophy. James's open-mindedness also influenced psychology when he became intrigued by the unorthodox ideas of a Viennese physician named Sigmund Freud.

William James (1842–1910) introduced experimental psychology to U.S. college students and is associated with functionalism.

© Mary Evans Picture Library/Alamy

Darwin's finches illustrated the interaction between genes and adaptation to the environment. The different species originated from common ancestors (genes), yet variations in their beaks arose as they adapted to different food supplies on each island.

Sigmund Freud and Psychoanalytic Theory

Sigmund Freud is probably the best known historical figure in psychology. Did Freud have such a huge influence on the beginnings of psychology, or is his contribution overrated? Historians and psychologists continue to debate this

Sigmund Freud's (1856–1939) focus on the unconscious was unique and led to his formulation of psychoanalytic theory.

Gestalt psychology an early psychological approach that emphasized how our minds organize sensory stimuli to produce the perception of a whole form

functionalism an early psychological perspective concerned with how behavior helps people adapt to their environment

LUXURY REBORN

www.belvedere-vodka.com

Can you identify the Freudian symbols in this advertisement?

psychoanalytic theory Sigmund Freud's view that emphasizes the influence of unconscious desires and conflicts on behavior

behaviorism a psychological perspective that emphasizes the study of observable responses and behavior

stimulus any object or event that is perceived by our senses

response an organism's reaction to a stimulus

Ivan Pavlov's studies illustrated that behavior is influenced by stimuli in one's environment.

issue, but there is no doubt that Freud's ideas about behavior were radical for that time. Freud's ideas permeate Western culture in music, media, advertising, art, and humor—a testament to his influence and importance.

Freud (1856–1939) studied medicine, focusing on neurology and disorders of the nervous system. He began seeing people with all kinds of "nervous" disorders, such as an intense fear of horses or heights or the sudden paralysis of an arm. Freud became interested in the use of hypnosis and what was then referred to as "the talking cure" to treat these nervous disorders, yet neither worked as effectively as he had hoped. He began asking patients to express any and every thought that occurred to them, no matter how trivial or unpleasant. Freud theorized that encouraging patients to say whatever came to mind allowed them to recall forgotten memories that seemed to underlie their problems. This process, known today as *free association*, is one element of *psychoanalysis*, a therapy that Freud developed.

From these experiences, Freud came to believe that the *unconscious* plays a crucial role in human behavior. For Freud, the unconscious was that part of the mind that includes impulses, behaviors, and desires that we are unaware of but that influence our behavior. Until this time, much of psychology had focused on conscious mental processes. Freud's focus on the unconscious was unique and led to his formulation of **psychoanalytic theory**. According to this theory, humans are similar to animals in that they possess basic sexual and aggressive instincts that motivate behavior. However, unlike animals, humans can reason and think, especially as they mature. In childhood we learn to use these conscious reasoning abilities to deal with and to suppress our basic sexual and aggressive desires so that we can be viewed approvingly by others. For Freud, the conflict between the conscious reasoning part of the mind and the unconscious instinctual one was key to understanding human behavior. Although controversial, Freud's theory dominated European psychology. However, in the early 1900s in the United States, Freud's ideas were overshadowed by another approach to understanding behavior called *behaviorism*.

Behaviorism: A True Science of Psychology

While Freudian psychology was going strong in Europe in the 1920s, in the United States functionalism was slowly being replaced by a school of thought referred to as **behaviorism**. A growing number of psychologists believed that in order for psychology to be taken seriously as a "true" science, it must focus on observable behavior and not on the mind. You can't see the mind or what a person thinks; you can only see what a person does. Behaviorists believed that only overt, observable behaviors could truly be measured consistently from person to person. One of the most vocal proponents of this school of thought was John B. Watson (1878–1958).

John B. Watson's Behaviorism and Ivan Pavlov's Experiments

Watson was influenced by Russian physiologist Ivan Pavlov's studies of digestion in dogs. While measuring and analyzing the first process of digestion (salivation), Pavlov noticed that his dogs started to salivate before he gave them meat powder. When the experiments first started, the salivation had occurred only *after* the dogs were given the meat powder. To further study this curious change in response, Pavlov performed experiments to train the dogs to salivate to other nonfood stimuli. (You will learn more about Pavlov's classic experiments in Chapter 5.)

Pavlov's experiments were important to Watson as examples of how behavior is the product of *stimuli* and *responses*. A **stimulus** is any object or event that is perceived by our senses. A **response** is an organism's reaction to a stimulus. To further his point, Watson and his associate, Rosalie Rayner, performed an experiment on a 9-month-old infant named Albert. Watson first presented Albert with the stimulus of a white rat. Albert played with the white rat and showed no fear of it (response). Knowing that infants do fear loud noises, Watson paired the two stimuli, first presenting the rat to Albert and then presenting a loud gong sound behind Albert's head.

Little Albert reacted to the loud noise with the startle, or fear, response. Over and over again, Watson repeated the procedure of pairing the two stimuli—presenting the rat followed by the loud gong. Then, when Watson presented the rat to Albert with no gong, the infant responded with the startle response. Watson had conditioned Little Albert to fear a white rat, a rat that Albert had played with earlier without fear. This demonstrated for Watson that observable stimuli and responses should be the domain of psychology. Unfortunately for Watson, a personal scandal resulted in his dismissal as the chair of the psychology department at Johns Hopkins University, and he later became a psychological consultant to an advertising firm (Buckley, 1989). Thus, we probably could consider Watson the first *consumer* psychologist. Think about how advertisers today associate certain stimuli with products to get consumers to purchase them. For example, young, beautiful people, laughing and having a great time, may be associated with a particular brand of beer.

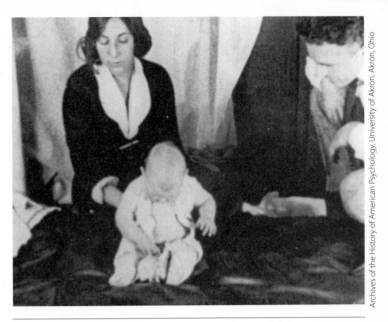

Archives of the History of American Psychology, University of Akron, Akron, Ohio

John B. Watson and Rosalie Rayner showed how stimuli and responses could be studied in their experiment on baby Albert.

B. F. Skinner and Behavioral Consequences

Although Watson was no longer within mainstream psychology, behaviorism remained strong in the United States, partially due to the work of B. F. Skinner (1904–1990). Skinner, like Watson, believed that psychology should focus on observable behavior. But Skinner added a dimension to Watson's framework: *consequences*. Skinner believed that psychologists should look not only at the stimuli in the environment that cause a particular response but also at what happens to a person or animal after the response—what Skinner called the consequences of a behavior. To illustrate consequences, let's look at Little Albert's behavior from Skinner's perspective. Once Albert was afraid of the rat, how would he act when he saw the rat? If Albert moved away from the rat, his behavior effectively reduced his fear. Feeling less fear or anxiety is a good (positive) consequence, or outcome. Whenever Albert saw the rat again, he probably moved away even faster. Skinner asserted that positive consequences, such as the reduction of Albert's anxiety, would lead him to engage in the same behavior again. Negative consequences, or outcomes that are not desirable, would lessen Albert's desire to engage in the behavior again. We know these processes as *reinforcement* and *punishment*, topics that are explored further in Chapter 5.

© Michael Newman/PhotoEdit

By associating their products with beautiful, smiling people, advertisers are hoping consumers will purchase their brands.

Beyond Behaviorism: Humanism, Cognitive Psychology, and the Birth of Positive Psychology

Behaviorism was a dominant force in American psychology until the 1960s. By that time, it became evident that this one theory could not study all behaviors. Behaviors such as feelings and thoughts could not easily be reduced to stimuli and responses. This criticism, combined with the social climate of the times, opened the door for other views on behavior and a willingness to explore topics previously ignored.

© Bettmann/Corbis

B. F. Skinner's (1904–1990) behaviorism emphasized the influence of consequences on behavior.

The Humanists

Discontent with behaviorism and the social upheaval of the 1960s led to a growing interest in an approach toward treatment called **humanism**. Many psychologists did not accept the behaviorists' view that humans were governed by stimuli and responses, with no will of their own to change their behavior. In the 1960s, societal values were rapidly changing, and the civil rights movement and the Vietnam War sparked widespread civil disobedience. Many young Americans were endorsing women's rights, free love, and free will. Psychology was changing too, and humanists emphasized that everyone possesses inner resources for personal growth and development. The goal of humanistic therapy, therefore, would be to help individuals use these inner resources to make healthier choices and thus lead better lives. Humanism stressed the free will of individuals to choose their own patterns of behavior. Two well-known humanists are Abraham Maslow and Carl Rogers. You will read more about their ideas and theories in Chapters 8 and 13.

Cognitive Psychology and the Birth of Positive Psychology

While humanism was changing how psychologists were treating clients, changes were also occurring in research psychology. Researchers were becoming disenchanted with the limits of testing stimuli, responses, and consequences in the laboratory, and there was renewed interest in the study of conscious mental processes, which had originated with Wilhelm Wundt. Research expanded to subjects such as memory, problem solving, and decision making. However, unlike the earlier functionalism and structuralism, this new study of mental processes was based not on introspection but on more objective experimental methods. Acknowledging that mental processes are not directly observable to the eye, scientists believed that reasonable inferences about mental processes could be made from performance data. For example, in studying memory processes in children, a researcher can ask children what strategies or techniques they use to remember a list of items. If children using a particular strategy (Strategy A) remember more compared to children using a different strategy (Strategy B), then one can infer that there must be something about Strategy A that facilitates memory. This conclusion is reasonable even though we can't directly see the children use

Gaye Gerard/Getty Images

humanism a psychological perspective that emphasizes the personal growth and potential of humans

Martin Seligman (second from right), shown here with the Dalai Lama (left), adopted the term *positive psychology* in 1998 to emphasize research focused on describing those factors that contribute to happiness, positive emotions, and well-being.

the techniques. Such reasoning led to much experimental research on mental processes, or *cognition*. By the 1980s the study of cognitive processes, **cognitive psychology**, was a part of mainstream psychology.

Focusing on *how* we think, particularly whether our thoughts are pessimistic or optimistic in nature, soon led to a growing emphasis on human strengths and on how humans attain happiness, called **positive psychology**. Led by Martin Seligman (Seligman & Csikszentmihalyi, 2000) and Ed Diener, positive psychology has produced an explosion of research over the past 10 years describing the factors that contribute to happiness, positive emotions, and well-being (Ruark, 2009; Wallis, 2005). By scientifically studying positive aspects of human behavior, the goal of positive psychology is to enable individuals, families, and communities to thrive.

Let's
REVIEW
In this section we discussed the early theories of psychology. For a quick check of your understanding, try answering the following questions at increasing levels of difficulty.

1. Which historical approach emphasized the importance of unconscious drives and instincts on behavior?

   a. psychoanalytic   c. structuralism

   b. functionalism   d. cognitive

2. Javier wants to know how aggression helps a person adapt to the environment. Which historical approach is Javier emphasizing?

   a. structuralism   c. functionalism

   b. psychoanalysis   d. humanism

3. Which of the following people would be *least* likely to emphasize the influence of stimuli and responses on behavior?

   a. John Watson   c. Rosalie Rayner

   b. Carl Rogers   d. B. F. Skinner

ANSWERS: 1. a; 2. c; 3. b

cognitive psychology the study of mental processes such as reasoning and problem solving

positive psychology the study of factors that contribute to happiness, positive emotions, and well-being

LEARNING OBJECTIVES

What Should You Know?
- Distinguish among the seven modern perspectives of psychology and understand the nature of the eclectic approach.
- Describe the training of a psychologist and compare and contrast the different specialty areas of the profession.

WHAT IS PSYCHOLOGY LIKE TODAY?

How do psychologists explain behavior today? Given the historical sketch of psychology we have just provided, it is probably no surprise to learn that modern psychology is a very broad profession. In the past, not everyone agreed on how to explain behavior, just as many debate the causes of behavior today. Many modern perspectives are an extension of the historical schools of thought. Here we discuss seven orientations or perspectives on behavior (● FIGURE 1.2): *biological, evolutionary, cognitive, psychodynamic, behavioral, sociocultural,* and *humanistic*. A person's training and personal views on behavior influence the perspective or perspectives a modern psychologist adopts.

Explaining Behavior: Modern Perspectives and the Eclectic Approach

Psychologists who adopt a **biological** or **physiological perspective** look for a physical cause for a particular behavior. In this perspective, genetic, biochemical, and nervous system (brain functioning) relationships to behavior and mental processes are examined. This perspective

biological/physiological perspective focuses on physical causes of behavior

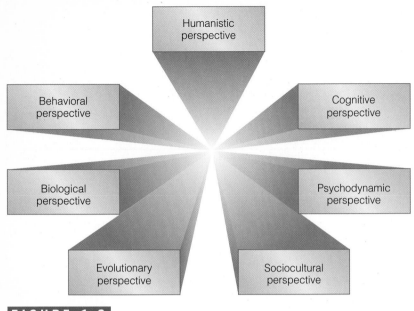

FIGURE 1.2

● **Psychological Perspectives** Just as a photograph or a piece of art can be examined from many different angles, so too can mental processes and behavior. We call these angles perspectives. Each offers a somewhat different picture of why people behave as they do. Taken as a whole, these perspectives underscore the complex nature of behavior.

neuroscience science that investigates the relationships between the nervous system and behavior/mental processes

evolutionary perspective focuses on how evolution and natural selection influence behavior

cognitive perspective focuses on how mental processes influence behavior

psychodynamic perspective focuses on internal unconscious mental processes, motives, and desires that may explain behavior

behavioral perspective focuses on external, environmental influences on behavior

sociocultural perspective focuses on societal and cultural factors that may influence behavior

humanistic perspective focuses on how an individual's view of himself or herself and the world influence behavior

is also a branch of science referred to as **neuroscience**. (We discuss the physical processes of genes and the nervous system in Chapter 2.) For example, a biological explanation of aggression may focus on specific brain areas that are activated when we perceive a threat in our environment, as illustrated in ● WHAT'S HAPPENING IN YOUR BRAIN?

Very closely aligned to the biological perspective is the **evolutionary perspective**. This approach is similar to the biological approach in that the cause of behavior is biological. However, this is where the similarity ends. The evolutionary perspective proposes that natural selection is the process at work. Behaviors that increase your chances of surviving are favored or selected over behaviors that decrease your chances of surviving. Remember James's functionalism? One could say that James was an early evolutionary psychologist. Similarly, this approach analyzes whether a particular behavior increases a person's ability to adapt to the environment, thus increasing the chances of surviving, reproducing, and passing one's genes on to future generations (Buss, 2009).

This approach often creates controversy because it seems to ignore environmental influences on behavior. An example will help illustrate this controversy. Both men and women can be jealous, yet psychological research has found that the type of jealousy exhibited by men and women is different. Men tend to be more jealous of sexual infidelity—that is, if their mate has sex with another person. In contrast, women report more jealousy over emotional infidelity—that is, if their mate establishes a close attachment to another person (Buss, Larsen, Westen, & Semmelroth, 1992; Buunk, Angleitner, Oubaid, & Buss, 1996; Levy & Kelly, 2010). Many argue that this difference stems from how boys and girls have been raised, an environmental influence. However, some psychologists have argued that this difference in jealousy stems from evolutionary forces. Heterosexual men need to know that their offspring are in fact theirs, which is why sexual infidelity would be so upsetting to them. For heterosexual women, help in child rearing requires a continued attachment with their mate. Consequently, emotional infidelity is more distressing to women. Keep in mind that not all psychologists support this particular explanation of gender differences in jealousy (DeSteno & Salovey, 1996; Harris, 2003; Levy & Kelly, 2010). It is one perspective among several for looking at and explaining this behavior.

The **cognitive perspective** explains behavior with an emphasis on thoughts and interpretations based on memory, expectations, beliefs, problem solving, or decision making. A cognitive view focuses on how people process information and on how that process may influence behavior. We saw from the opening case study that Michael's memory for school information was influenced by how the material was presented to him. How he *processed* the information influenced his learning. You will learn more about these cognitive processes in Chapters 6 and 7, when we discuss such topics as memory, problem solving, thinking, decision making, intelligence, and language.

The **psychodynamic perspective** is a collective term that refers to those assumptions about behavior originally conceived by Freud, which have been modified by his followers. The psychodynamic view focuses on internal, often unconscious mental processes, motives, and desires or childhood conflicts to explain behavior. For example, in 2009 at the Fort Hood military base in Texas, Nidal Malik Hasan entered the Soldier Readiness Center where he worked and shot at soldiers and civilians, killing 13 people and wounding 30 others before he was incapacitated by civilian police officers. The psychodynamic view might suggest that Nidal had some frustrated desires or unresolved childhood conflicts that erupted into hostility and anger that he unleashed on the soldiers. These conflicts and frustrated desires also

WHAT'S HAPPENING IN YOUR BRAIN?

Comstock Images/Getty Images

A biological perspective focuses on physical explanations of behavior. For example, in one study (Radiological Society of North America, 2006) investigating the impact of violent video game exposure on brain functioning, teenagers played either a violent video game or a nonviolent video game for 30 minutes. During the teens' game-play, researchers measured brain functioning using functional magnetic resonance imaging (fMRI) that shows what part(s) of the brain are active during the task. Brain regions that are active show up as brightly colored areas on the image. As you can see, the two groups showed marked differences in brain activation. Compared to the group that played the nonviolent game, the group that played the violent video game demonstrated less activity in the prefrontal area of the brain, which is associated with focus, concentration, and self-control, and more activity in the amygdala, which is involved in emotional arousal.

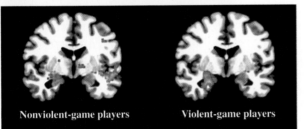

Wang, Y., M.D., Kalnin, A. J., M.D., Mosier, K. M., D.M.D, Ph.D., Dunn, D.W., M.D., and Kronenberger, W.G., Ph.D. (2006). Violent video games leave teenagers emotionally aroused. *Radiological Society of North America*, Nov. 29, 2006.

Nonviolent-game players   **Violent-game players**

---

may explain why Nidal was not able to control his hostile feelings—feelings that everyone has from time to time but that most people do not act upon.

The **behavioral perspective** focuses on external causes of behavior. It looks at how stimuli in our environment or the rewards and punishments we receive or both of these influence our behavior and mental processes. This approach suggests that behavior is learned and is influenced by other people and events. For example, if a student studies and then aces an exam, that reward may encourage her to study again the next time. If she only gets an average score, merely passing the test may not be rewarding enough to encourage the student to study for future exams. This perspective stems, as you might guess, from Watson's and Skinner's behaviorist views (more on this in Chapter 5).

The **sociocultural perspective** adopts a wider view of the impact of the environment on behavior. It suggests that your society or culture influences your actions. Michael Oher's change from a culture of poverty and neglect to one of support and means influenced his school performance and demeanor. The sociocultural perspective would attribute these changes to aspects of society such as changes in family structure, socioeconomic status, and connectedness among people in communities. Sociocultural views will be evident throughout this textbook when differences due to culture, income level, or gender are highlighted.

The **humanistic perspective** explains behavior as stemming from your choices and free will. These choices are influenced by

The psychodynamic view would examine unconscious motives to explain Nidal Malik Hasan's behavior at Fort Hood in 2009.

Paul J. Richards/AFP/Getty Images

your self-concept (how you think of yourself) and by your self-esteem (how you feel about yourself). This view of the self and feelings toward the self direct you to choose certain behaviors over others. For example, if you see yourself as a low achiever in school as Michael initially did, you may be less likely to take challenging courses or to apply yourself in the courses that you do take. Humanistic views of behavior are explored in Chapters 8, 13, and 15.

Most psychologists do not rigidly adhere to just one of these perspectives but are likely to take what is referred to as an **eclectic approach** when explaining behavior. This eclectic approach integrates or combines several perspectives to provide a more complete, yet complex picture of behavior. ● THE BIG PICTURE REVIEW illustrates these approaches and shows how a combined approach gives a more expansive understanding of behavior than any single approach could.

Training to Be a Psychologist

What type of education and training do I need to become a psychologist? The majority of psychologists hold a doctorate in psychology—usually a PhD (Doctor of Philosophy)

eclectic approach integrates and combines several perspectives when explaining behavior

basic research scientific study about the specifics of a behavior without concern for its application

applied research scientific study to solve a problem

THE BIG PICTURE *review*

Looking at Anxiety From Modern Perspectives

PSYCHOLOGISTS CAN EXAMINE BEHAVIOR FROM MANY DIFFERENT PERSPECTIVES

Biological	Anxiety is related to chemicals in the body or to genetics (heredity).
Evolutionary	Anxiety is an adaptive response that prepares one to respond to potential threats in the environment. This response helps humans survive because it warns them of danger and thereby helps them avoid situations or people that may harm them. However, in modern times, these threats tend to be ongoing: traffic jams, crowding, and the hectic pace of consumerism.
Cognitive	Focuses on how anxious people think differently from nonanxious people. Anxious people may engage in more pessimistic thinking or worry that everything will go wrong.
Psychodynamic	Anxiety is the product of unresolved feelings of hostility, guilt, anger, or sexual attraction experienced in childhood.
Behavioral	Anxiety is a learned behavior much like Albert's fear of the white rat. It is a response that is associated with a specific stimulus or a response that has been rewarded.
Sociocultural	Anxiety is a product of a person's culture. In the United States more women than men report being anxious and fearful, and this gender difference results from different socialization experiences. Men in the United States are raised to believe that they must not be afraid, so they are less likely to acknowledge or report anxiety. Women do not experience this pressure to hide their fears, so they are more likely to tell others and to seek treatment.
Humanistic	Anxiety is rooted in people's dissatisfaction with their real self (how they perceive themselves) as compared to their ideal self (how they want to be).
Eclectic	Anxiety stems from various sources depending on the individual. One person may be prone to anxiety because many people in his family are anxious and he has learned to be anxious from several experiences. Another person may be anxious because she is dissatisfied with herself and believes that everything always goes wrong in her life.

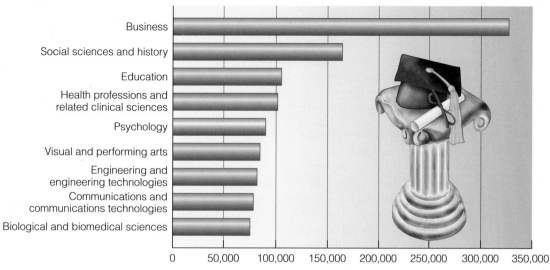

Number of bachelor's degrees awarded

FIGURE 1.3

● **Undergraduate Degrees in Psychology** Psychology is a popular undergraduate degree. It ranked fifth following business, social sciences and history, education, and health professions in number of degrees awarded in 2006–2007. *Source: Data from U.S. Department of Education, National Center for Education Statistics, 2009.*

or a PsyD (Doctor of Psychology). A PhD program focuses more on research whereas the PsyD focuses more on clinical training. To obtain either doctorate, psychologists must first complete a bachelor's and a master's degree. The road to a doctoral degree is long, usually 4 to 7 years after the undergraduate degree. Most doctoral programs require extensive study of research methods and statistics, and most require that students do some form of research.

What if I'm interested in doing research? There are two general types of psychological research: basic research and applied research. **Basic research** focuses on uncovering the specifics about a behavior. An example of basic research is the work of a number of teams to pinpoint the chemicals in the brain that are involved in memory. **Applied research** seeks to solve a problem (possibly using the findings of basic research). Determining how to reduce aggression or prejudice is an example of applied research. Another example is testing which of two therapy techniques works better in treating people who are depressed.

What if I don't get a PhD or PsyD? Those who study psychology to the point of a bachelor's or master's degree aren't excluded from the profession. A bachelor's degree in psychology may qualify you to assist psychologists in mental health centers or rehabilitation and correctional programs or to serve as a research assistant. Without additional academic training, the opportunities for advancement in the profession are limited (Appleby, 1997), but 20% of students who graduate with a bachelor's degree in psychology do find work in social services or public relations. The skills an undergraduate psychology major acquires are valued by employers in business, industry, and government (American Psychological Association [APA], 2000a). As you can see in ● FIGURE 1.3, psychology is a popular degree among undergraduate students.

A master's degree typically requires 2 to 3 years of graduate work. Master's-level psychologists may administer tests, conduct research, or counsel patients under the supervision of a doctoral-level psychologist. In a few states, they may be able to practice independently. They may teach in high schools or community colleges, work in corporate human resources departments, or work as school psychologists.

A large percentage of psychologists affiliated with colleges and universities teach and do research. Psychologists also work in school systems, hospitals, business, government, and other human services settings (APA Center for Workforce Studies, 2007; ● FIGURE 1.4). Psychologists perform many functions in many different roles. Their job descriptions may include conducting research, counseling clients, and teaching college courses.

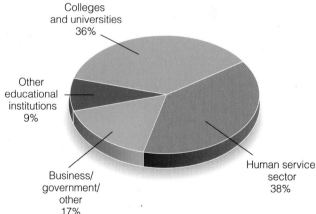

Colleges and universities
36%

Other educational institutions
9%

Business/ government/ other
17%

Human service sector
38%

FIGURE 1.4

● **Work Settings of Psychologists** A large percentage of psychologists affiliated with colleges and universities teach and do research. Psychologists also work in school systems, business, and government, or are employed in health-related or other human services settings. *Source: 2007 Doctorate Employment Survey. APA Center for Workforce Studies.*

Known as the father of African American psychology, Francis Sumner (1895–1954) in 1920 became the first African American to receive a doctorate from a U.S. university.

The findings of Kenneth and Mamie Clark's doll experiments on the self-esteem of Black children were noted in the landmark 1954 case *Brown v. Board of Education of Topeka*, in which the Supreme Court ruled segregation of public schools unconstitutional.

A related profession is *psychiatry*. A psychiatrist holds a medical degree (MD) and then specializes in mental health. A psychiatrist's graduate work includes a medical internship and residency, followed by training in treatment of mental health disorders. As medical practitioners, psychiatrists have extensive training in the use of therapeutic drugs, and they may dispense or prescribe medication and order medical procedures such as brain scans.

Specialty Areas in Psychology

What are the different types of psychologists? In addition to the various approaches or perspectives psychologists take, they also study different aspects of behavior, which correspond to specialty areas of psychology. A number of these specialty areas are depicted in ● TABLE 1.2, but keep in mind that there are many more. This diversity stems from the complexity of behavior and the interrelatedness of different areas. What a developmental psychologist studies, for example, is connected to and may have an impact on the work of social, clinical, and educational psychologists. In each of these areas, some psychologists perform basic research, others conduct applied research, and some do both.

Gender, Ethnicity, and the Field of Psychology

Our review of psychology's past and present has shown the evolution of a professional field from one based on philosophy and medicine to one that has increasingly expanded and become more diverse in scope. Such a change can also be seen in the representation of women and minorities in the field of psychology.

In the early development of psychology, women and minorities were not allowed in many instances to receive graduate degrees despite completing all the requirements for a doctorate. Despite these constraints and many other societal hurdles, several women and minority individuals contributed significantly to the field. As previously mentioned, Margaret Washburn (1871–1939) became the first woman to be awarded a doctorate in psychology in 1894 (Furumoto, 1989). Mary Calkins (1863–1930) became the first female president of the American Psychological Association in 1905. She studied at Harvard University with William James and performed several studies on the nature of memory. Christine Ladd-Franklin (1847–1930) studied color vision in the early 1900s. Karen Horney (1885–1952) focused on environmental and cultural factors that influence personality development (see Chapter 13).

Few degrees were awarded to minority students in the early 1900s. Gilbert Haven Jones (1883–1966) was the first African American to earn a doctorate in psychology—in Germany in 1909. Francis Sumner (1895–1954) was the first African American to receive a doctorate in psychology from a university in the United States (in 1920) and is known as the father of African American psychology for his many contributions to the education of Black people. His research focused on equality between Blacks and Whites, refuting the idea that African Americans were inferior. He helped establish an independent psychology department at Howard University, a historically Black college. Two of his students, Kenneth and Mamie Clark, performed research on the self-perceptions of Black children. The Clarks' doll experiments (K. B. Clark, 1950; K. B. Clark & Clark, 1950) found that Black children often preferred to play with White dolls over Black dolls and attributed positive descriptors such as *good* and *pretty* to the color white and negative descriptors such as *bad* and *ugly* to the color black. The Clarks' findings were noted in the landmark 1954 case *Brown v. Board of Education of Topeka*, in which the Supreme Court ruled segregation of public schools unconstitutional.

Inez Prosser was the first African American woman to be awarded a doctorate in psychology, in 1933. Her doctoral dissertation (Prosser, 1933) studied the self-perceptions

TABLE 1.2

● **Specialty Areas in Psychology**

	TOPICS OF INTEREST
Experimental psychology	Conducts basic research on sensation, perception, learning, motivation, and emotion.
Developmental psychology	Researches how we develop physically, cognitively, socially, and emotionally over the life span.
Biopsychology	Researches the biological processes that underlie behavior, including genetic, biochemical, and nervous system functioning.
Personality psychology	Researches how people differ in their individual traits, how people develop personality, whether personality traits can be changed, and how these qualities can be measured.
Social psychology	Researches how our beliefs, feelings, and behaviors are influenced by others, whether in the classroom, on an elevator, on the beach, on a jury, or at a football game.
Cognitive psychology	Studies mental processes such as decision making, problem solving, language, and memory.
Industrial/organizational (I/O) psychology	Examines the relationship between people and their work environments. May study applied issues such as increasing job satisfaction or decreasing employee absenteeism, or focus on understanding the dynamics of workplace behavior, such as leadership styles or gender differences in management styles.
Human factors psychology	Researches human capabilities as they apply to the design, operation, and maintenance of machines, systems, and environments to achieve optimal performance. For example, designing the most effective configuration of control knobs in airplane cockpits for pilots.
Forensic psychology	Works with mental health issues within the context of the legal system. May study a certain type of criminal behavior such as rape or murder, or may be asked to determine a person's competence to stand trial.
Cross-cultural psychology	Investigates cultural similarities and differences in psychological traits and behaviors.
Health psychology	Researches ways to promote health and prevent illness. May be concerned with issues such as diet and nutrition, exercise, and lifestyle choices that influence health.
Educational psychology	Researches how people learn and how variables in an educational environment influence learning. May develop materials and strategies to enhance learning.
Clinical psychology	Researches, assesses, and treats children, adolescents, and adults who are experiencing difficulty in functioning or who have a serious mental health disorder such as schizophrenia.
Counseling psychology	Researches, assesses, and treats children, adolescents, and adults who are experiencing adjustment difficulties.
School psychology	Assesses students' psychoeducational abilities (academic achievement, intelligence, cognitive processing) and shares test results with teachers and parents to help them make decisions regarding the best educational placement for students.
Sports psychology	Investigates the mental and emotional aspects of physical performance.
Community psychology	Seeks to understand and enhance the quality of life for individuals, communities, and society. Focuses on early intervention in and prevention of individual and community problems.
Positive psychology	Seeks to discover and promote those factors that contribute to happiness, positive emotions, and well-being.
Environmental psychology	Examines the relationship between environments and human behavior. Focuses on designing, managing, protecting, and/or restoring environments to enhance behavior. Also studies environmental attitudes, perceptions, and values to promote environmentally appropriate behavior.

of Black children. She compared the self-esteem of Black children attending a segregated school to that of Black children attending an integrated school. She found that the Black children at the segregated school fared better. The Black children from the integrated school were more likely to feel inferior and report less satisfactory social relations (Benjamin, Henry, & McMahon, 2005). Given the probable prejudicial attitudes of the White people at the integrated school, it is not surprising that the Black children from the integrated school did not have positive experiences.

Have times changed for women and minorities in psychology? Women have indeed made great progress in the field of psychology. From 1920 to 1974, 23% of doctorates in psychology went to women (APA, 2000b), and from 1960 to 1999, the greatest percentage increase in science and engineering doctorates earned by women was in psychology (National Science Foundation [NSF], 2006). Currently, far more women than men earn psychology degrees. In 2007, nearly 80% of master's degrees and 73% of doctorate degrees in psychology were awarded to women (U.S. Department of Education, 2009). Educational gains have in some ways been followed by progress in the careers of women in psychology. In 2003, 47% of the full-time psychology faculty at degree-granting institutions were women (U.S. Department of Education, 2005). However, female psychology faculty members are less likely than males to be promoted to the rank of full professor. In a faculty salaries survey conducted by the American Psychological Association (APA) in 2006–2007, women represented only 29% of full professors and 35% of tenured faculty members in U.S. psychology graduate departments (APA Center for Psychology Workforce Analysis and Research, 2007a). Although psychology has become more fully open to both men and women at the educational level, inequities at the professional level still exist.

Likewise, although the numbers of racial and ethnic minorities in psychology have increased, progress has been slow. Although approximately 33% of the U.S. population are minorities (U.S. Census Bureau, 2006), only 20% of newly enrolled full-time students in graduate schools in psychology were minorities in 2006–2007 (APA Center for Psychology Workforce Analysis and Research, 2007b). Between 1976 and 1993, close to 8% of all doctorates in psychology were awarded to minorities (APA, 1997). By 2007 that number had increased to almost 25% (U.S. Department of Education, 2009). This means that 3 out of 4 psychology doctorates are granted to Whites, regardless of gender. Despite increases in advanced degrees awarded to minorities, they are still underrepresented as faculty in colleges. In 2006–2007, minorities represented less than 9% of full professors and 10% of tenured faculty members in psychology graduate departments (APA Center for Psychology Workforce Analysis and Research, 2007b). The APA has established several programs to attract more minorities to the field of psychology to address this lack of minority representation.

Let's
REVIEW
In this section, we discussed modern psychological perspectives, described the training that is necessary to be a psychologist, and surveyed a number of the specialty areas of psychology. For a quick check of your understanding, try answering the following questions at increasing levels of difficulty.

1. Which modern psychological perspective emphasizes the importance of thought processes for understanding behavior?

   a. behavioral
   b. humanistic

   c. sociocultural
   d. cognitive

2. A psychologist who studies individual differences in shyness is probably from which specialty area?

   a. cognitive
   b. social

   c. developmental
   d. personality

3. Dr. Martinez is conducting a study on the nature of emotion. What type of research is Dr. Martinez doing?

   a. applied
   b. basic

   c. consumer
   d. preventative

ANSWERS 1. d; 2. d; 3. b

HOW IS PSYCHOLOGICAL RESEARCH CONDUCTED? HYPOTHESES AND METHODS

Though psychologists in various specialty areas study and emphasize different aspects of behavior, they all share similar goals. The main goals of psychology and psychological research are:

- To describe behavior
- To predict behavior
- To explain behavior
- To control or change behavior

Description involves observing events and describing them. Typically, description is used to understand how events are related to one another. For example, you may notice that your health club tends to get more crowded in the months of January, February, and March. This observation describes an event.

If you observe that two events occur together rather reliably or with a general frequency or regularity, you can make *predictions* about or anticipate what events may occur. From your observations, you may predict that the health club will be more crowded in January. You may arrive earlier for a parking spot or to get a place in the spinning class.

Although it may be known that two events regularly occur together, that doesn't tell us what caused a particular behavior to occur. Winter months do not cause health clubs to become crowded. These two events are related, but one event does not cause the other. Therefore, an additional goal of psychology is to *explain* or understand the causes of behavior. As stated previously, psychologists usually put forth explanations of behavior in the form of theories. A theory is an explanation of why and how a particular behavior occurs. We introduced seven types of explanations, or perspectives, earlier in the chapter. For example, how do we explain higher health club attendance in the winter months? Is it a behavior that is influenced by the environment? Perhaps health clubs are more crowded because the weather makes outdoor exercise more difficult. Is it a behavior that is influenced by our biology? As these ideas are tested, more and more causes and predictors of behavior are discovered. Some of these explanations or theories will be modified, some will be discarded, and new ones will be developed.

The purpose behind explaining and understanding the causes of behavior is the final goal of psychology, *controlling* or *changing* behavior. It relates to the goal of explanation because one needs to understand what is causing a behavior in order to change or modify it. For example, let's say that the weather is a factor in health club attendance. Health clubs could offer outdoor fitness activities beginning in mid-March to prevent declining enrollment. Many psychologists go into the field in the hope of improving society. They may want to improve child care, create healthier work environments, or reduce discrimination in society. Such sentiments reflect the goal of control and underscore the potential impact of good research. ● FIGURE 1.5 summarizes the goals of psychology.

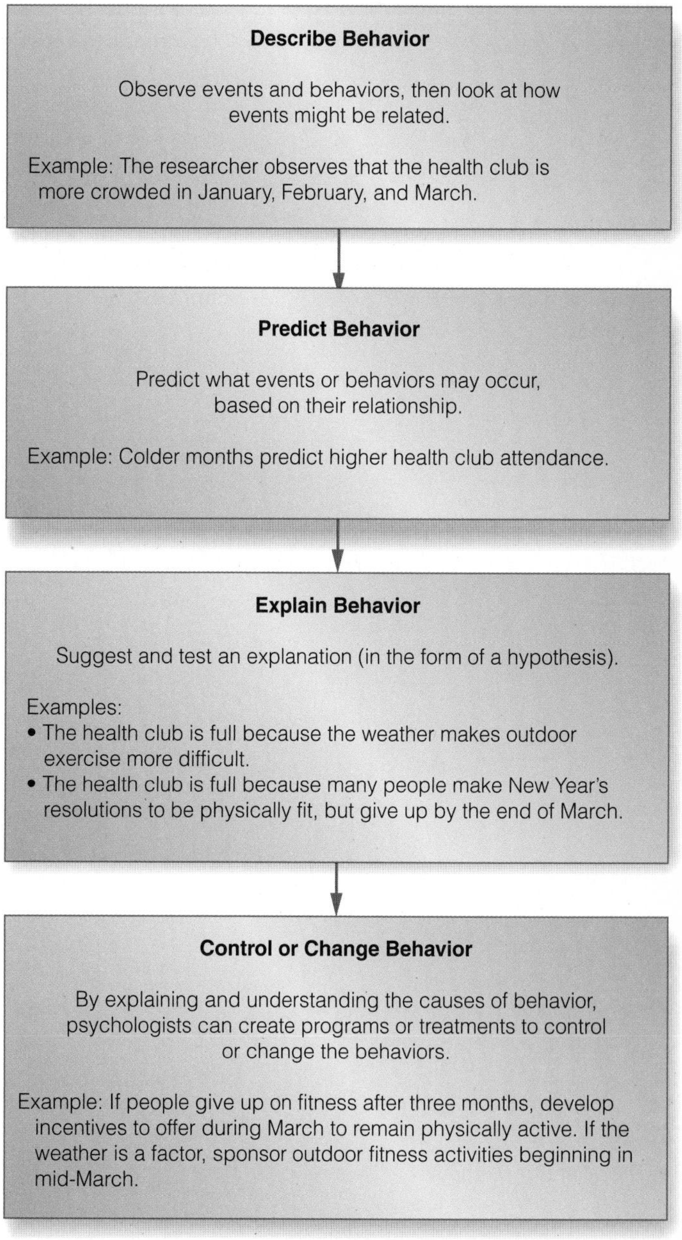

LEARNING OBJECTIVES

What Should You Know?

- Identify the four goals of psychological research.
- Outline the steps of the scientific method and distinguish between predictive and causal hypotheses.
- Describe the advantages and disadvantages of observational, correlational, and experimental research methods and the types of conclusions that can be drawn from each method.

FIGURE 1.5

● **Goals of Psychology**

Psychologists attempt to describe, predict, explain, and ultimately control or change behavior.

Describe Behavior

Observe events and behaviors, then look at how events might be related.

Example: The researcher observes that the health club is more crowded in January, February, and March.

Predict Behavior

Predict what events or behaviors may occur, based on their relationship.

Example: Colder months predict higher health club attendance.

Explain Behavior

Suggest and test an explanation (in the form of a hypothesis).

Examples:
- The health club is full because the weather makes outdoor exercise more difficult.
- The health club is full because many people make New Year's resolutions to be physically fit, but give up by the end of March.

Control or Change Behavior

By explaining and understanding the causes of behavior, psychologists can create programs or treatments to control or change the behaviors.

Example: If people give up on fitness after three months, develop incentives to offer during March to remain physically active. If the weather is a factor, sponsor outdoor fitness activities beginning in mid-March.

The Scientific Method

The purpose of psychological research is to test ideas about behavior. As previously stated, researchers use the scientific method when testing ideas about behavior. The scientific method is a set of rules for gathering and analyzing information that enables you to test an idea or hypothesis. All scientists adhere to these same steps even though they may use different techniques within each step. The decisions the scientist makes at each step of the scientific method will ultimately affect the types of conclusions that can be made about behavior.

How can the scientific method be used to meet the goals of psychology? Let's say that you have an interest in understanding beer drinking among college students. You want to make some predictions (a goal of psychology) about beer drinking. You use the scientific method to test this idea, as outlined in ● FIGURE 1.6.

1. *Define and describe the issue to be studied.* You might hypothesize that college students who buy pitchers of beer tend to drink more than college students who purchase bottles of beer (a **prediction**). You study previous research in scientific journals on alcohol consumption.
2. *Form a testable hypothesis.* Students who buy pitchers of beer tend to drink more than students who buy beer in bottles. This **hypothesis** must be phrased in a way that can be objectively measured—that is, in such a way that another person can test the same hypothesis to verify or *replicate* your results.
3. *Choose an appropriate research strategy.* This step involves many decisions. You will need to choose a group of people to observe (college students) and a research method that allows you to measure objectively how much beer students who buy pitchers drink versus how much beer students who buy bottles drink. You must also decide where your study will be conducted. Will it be in the environment where the behavior naturally occurs (such as the local college bar) or will it be in a laboratory (a more controlled setting)? You must decide who you will use as *participants*. Will you use animals or humans? If using humans, how will they be selected? If using animals, what species will you use?

prediction an expected outcome of how variables will relate

hypothesis an educated guess

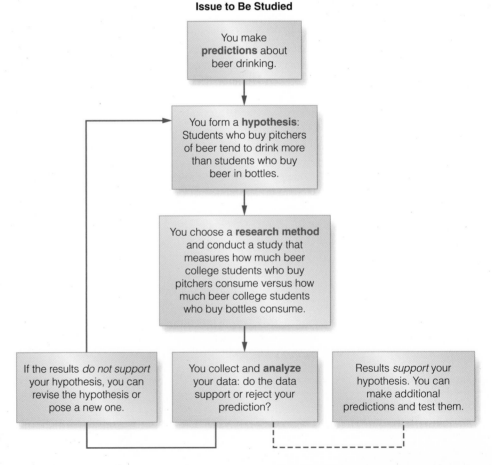

Issue to Be Studied

You make **predictions** about beer drinking.

You form a **hypothesis**: Students who buy pitchers of beer tend to drink more than students who buy beer in bottles.

You choose a **research method** and conduct a study that measures how much beer college students who buy pitchers consume versus how much beer college students who buy bottles consume.

If the results *do not support* your hypothesis, you can revise the hypothesis or pose a new one.

You collect and **analyze** your data: do the data support or reject your prediction?

Results *support* your hypothesis. You can make additional predictions and test them.

FIGURE 1.6

● **The Scientific Method** The scientific method enables researchers to test ideas about behavior.

4. *Conduct the study to test your hypothesis.* Run the study and collect the data based on the decisions in steps 1–3.

5. *Analyze the data to support or reject your hypothesis.* Analysis of data is usually conducted using statistics. If the result does not support your hypothesis, you can revise it or pose a new one. If the result does support your hypothesis, you can make additional predictions and test them. Geller, Russ, and Altomari (1986) actually included this prediction in a larger study on beer drinking among college students and found support for the hypothesis that buying pitchers was associated with consuming larger amounts of beer.

No matter which goal of psychology you are addressing, the process is the same. The goal merely influences the decisions that you make when testing an idea through the scientific method. If your goal is description or prediction, your hypothesis will state what you expect to observe or what relationships you expect to find. Your research strategy will then be designed to measure observations or relationships, and your analysis of the data will employ statistics that enable you to support or refute your hypothesis. It is in this way that the scientific method allows us to test the ideas of psychology.

Asking Questions: Hypotheses

What types of questions do psychologists ask when doing research? As you have seen, one of the first steps of the scientific method is to formulate a question or hypothesis about behavior. These hypotheses generally fall into one of two categories: *predictive hypotheses* and *causal hypotheses.*

Predictive Hypotheses

A **predictive hypothesis** makes a specific set of predictions about the relationships among variables. It is used to address two goals of psychology: description and prediction. The previous example on beer drinking among college students illustrated a predictive hypothesis: The study predicted that students who buy pitchers of beer tend to drink more than students who buy beer in bottles. Predictive hypotheses are made when the researcher measures the variables of interest but does not manipulate or control the variables in the study. Because the researcher does not control the variables, conclusions of research studies that test predictive hypotheses are limited. The conclusions can only state what was observed, or what variables appear to be related to one another. They cannot be used to draw cause-and-effect conclusions; in other words, buying pitchers of beer doesn't *cause* a person to drink more beer. To determine the cause, you must form and test a causal hypothesis.

Causal Hypotheses

A **causal hypothesis** specifically states how one variable will influence another variable. Causal hypotheses can be tested only when the researcher is able to control or manipulate the main variables in a study. The researcher sets up different conditions in a study and then observes whether there is a change in behavior because of the different conditions. For example, suppose a researcher has developed a new strategy to teach children how to read. The researcher hypothesizes that this program will cause greater gains in reading than the standard method for teaching reading. This is a causal hypothesis. Some students are assigned to the new reading program, and others are assigned to the standard program. The researcher then measures the children's gains in reading at the end of the year to see if there is a difference. As you will soon see, causal hypotheses can only be tested by means of an experiment. To test a causal hypothesis, a researcher must be able to conclude how one variable affects or causes a change in another variable.

Research Methods

Once you have stated a hypothesis, the next step in the research process is to decide on a research strategy and a way of selecting participants. The type of hypothesis you make (predictive or causal) typically determines which research methods you can employ. You are more likely to use some research methods to test predictive hypotheses and other methods to test causal hypotheses.

predictive hypothesis an educated guess about the relationships among variables

causal hypothesis an educated guess about how one variable will influence another variable

A school playground could be an environment for naturally observing children's behaviors.

What research methods are used to test predictive hypotheses? Several types of research methods are used to test predictive hypotheses: *naturalistic observations, case studies, surveys,* and *correlational research.* All these methods are used when the researcher cannot control or manipulate the main variables in the study. Each method has its advantages and disadvantages.

Naturalistic Observations

Naturalistic observations are research studies that are conducted in the environment in which the behavior typically occurs. For example, Belsky, Woodworth, and Crnic (1996) wanted to investigate whether the quality of family interaction identifies which families have more difficulty managing their firstborn sons at 2 years of age. The researchers measured family interaction by observing the parents and their toddlers on two occasions around dinnertime—an environment that naturally produces child management issues. The researcher in a naturalistic study is a recorder or observer of behavior who then describes or makes predictions about behavior based on what he or she has observed. Because the researcher does not control events in a naturalistic study, it is not possible to pinpoint the causes of behavior. Therefore, naturalistic studies are predominantly used to achieve the goals of description and prediction. The observations of Belsky et al. (1996) suggest that the child's temperament, the parents' personalities, and the quality of the parents' marriage were just 3 out of 9 measurements that predicted which families might have difficulty controlling their toddlers.

Suppose you want to observe and describe childhood aggression. Would this lend itself to naturalistic observation? Where might you conduct such a study? A naturalistic environment for observing childhood aggression may be a school playground. However, not all behavior lends itself to naturalistic observation. For example, if you want to study helping behavior in an emergency situation, it would be very difficult to conduct a naturalistic study. Where would you make your observations? You could go to disaster scenes, but these observations would be taking place *after* the emergency had occurred. Even if you decided on a place, you could be waiting there a very long time before an emergency actually occurred!

While naturalistic observation does allow a researcher to paint a picture of behavior as it normally occurs, researchers need to consider the influence of *reactivity.* Consider the example of studying childhood aggression by observing students on a school playground. What might happen if you were to simply enter the playground, sit down, and start writing about what you saw? The children might behave differently because of your presence or because of their awareness that they are being observed or both; as a result, your observations of aggression might not be reliable or true. Consequently, when conducting a naturalistic observation, researchers attempt to minimize reactivity. In this way, they can be sure that they are observing the true behavior of their participants.

Case Studies

A **case study** is an in-depth observation of one participant. The participant may be a person, an animal, or even a setting such as a business or a school. Every chapter of this book opens with a brief case study. As with naturalistic observation, in case studies researchers do not control any variables but merely record or relate their observations. Case studies provide in-depth information on rare and unusual conditions that we might not otherwise be able to study. For example, much of what we know about dissociative identity disorder, formerly called multiple personality disorder, comes from case studies that have been turned into books and films such as *Sybil, When Rabbit Howls,* and *The Three Faces of Eve.* However, the main disadvantage of the case study method is its limited applicability to other situations.

naturalistic observation observing behavior in the environment in which the behavior typically occurs

case study an in-depth observation of one person

© Ariel Skelley/Corbis

It is very difficult to take one case, especially a rare case, and say that it applies to everyone. In other words, case studies lack **generalizability**; because of this, the conclusions that are drawn from case studies are limited to the topic being studied.

Surveys

Many times psychologists want to study a whole group of people but in less depth. A **survey** can accomplish this task by asking a large group of people about their attitudes, beliefs, behaviors, or any combination of these. A large group of people can quickly respond to questions or statements in their homes, online, over the phone, or out in public. Have you ever filled out a questionnaire, participated in a phone interview, or completed a survey at the mall? You were probably asked many questions such as your age, income level, gender, race, and what products you buy or how you feel about a particular issue or candidate. Your responses are then sorted by these attributes to see whether, for instance, men are more likely than women to buy a particular product or vote for a certain candidate.

What are surveys used for? Survey data are used to make predictions and test predictive hypotheses. Knowing which people are more likely to buy a product enables a company to market its product more effectively and perhaps devise new strategies to target individuals who are not buying its products. Similarly, knowing which behaviors are related to a higher frequency of illness enables a psychologist to predict who is more at risk for physical or mental illness. However, *who* you ask to complete a survey and *how* you ask them are critical elements in distinguishing good survey research from biased research.

How do you select the people who will take your survey? In a perfect world, researchers would include every person they are interested in studying. This is termed the **population of interest**. For a developmental psychologist who specializes in infant development, all infants would be the population of interest. It is impossible to test everyone, so researchers select a portion, or subset, of the population of interest called a **sample**. Because the sample will be used to make inferences or judgments about the entire population, the sample should reflect the whole population as much as possible; that is, it should be a *representative sample*. Random sampling of participants ensures a representative sample. In a *random sample*, every member of the population has an equal chance of being selected to participate in the study; thus, *sampling bias* is not introduced into the research.

Take a look around at your classmates in your general psychology course. Would this group qualify as a random sample of your college? Probably not. All the students in the college did not have the same chance to choose the course. Registration is typically staggered such that students with more credits get to register earlier than students with fewer credits. So your class is not a random sample. Would the group qualify as a representative sample of college students? Probably not. As a group, this class may not represent the college student population in terms of age, race, income level, major, geographic region, and other characteristics.

The more representative the sample is, the more the results will generalize to the population of interest. But random sampling is not always possible. Consequently, psychological research often uses *samples of convenience*, or groups of people who are easily accessible to the researcher. The students in your psychology course are a sample of convenience. In fact, much psychological research relies on using college students as the sample of convenience! In the United States only 29% of those over the age of 25 have college degrees, so these samples probably do not represent all types of people and groups (U.S. Census Bureau, 2008).

A second critical element of the survey method is the wording of the questions. A respondent has to be able to understand the question and interpret it in the way the researcher intended. For example, suppose you were asked to complete a survey at your college that included this question: How would you rate the services provided to you by the college over the last semester? And the answer choices were Very Good, Good, Adequate, and Not Good. The question is assuming that (1) you know what services the college provides, (2) you have used them, and (3) all respondents evaluate the word *good* in the same way. Notice too that only one of the answer choices reflects less than average performance by the college; this imbalance in the answers could skew or create bias in the results. For these reasons, it's important to make questions clear and precise to obtain accurate estimates of people's feelings, beliefs, and behavior. Differences in survey question wording have been found in part

generalizability how well a researcher's findings apply to other individuals and situations

survey a research method that asks a large group of people about their attitudes, beliefs, and/or behaviors

population of interest the entire universe of animals or people that could be studied

sample the portion of the population of interest that is selected for a study

to influence rape estimates (Fisher, 2009) and estimates on adolescent sexual behaviors (Santelli, Lindberg, Abma, McNeeley, & Resnick, 2000), to name just two.

In summary, surveys are advantageous in that they allow psychologists to ask lots of questions of a large sample of people. Accurate information can be gathered in a relatively short time. Yet, the survey wording, the representativeness of the sample, and whether people choose to answer the questions honestly can bias the results.

Correlational Studies

Correlational studies test the relationship, or **correlation**, between two or more variables: television watching and violent behavior, the presence of malls in a community and employment rates, or depression and gender, for example. Again, in correlational studies the researcher does not control variables but rather measures them to see if any reliable relationship exists between them. For example, if we were to measure your weight (one variable), what other variable might show a relationship to your weight? Your height? Your calorie consumption? Your gender? Your age? Your life expectancy? If you were to measure all these variables, you might find that all of them vary in relation to weight. These relationships are correlations.

The strength of a correlation is measured in terms of a *correlation coefficient*, which is a statistic that tells us the strength of the relationship between two factors. Correlation coefficients range from −1.00 to +1.00. The closer the correlation coefficient is to −1.00 or +1.00, the stronger the correlation, or the more related the two variables are. The closer the correlation coefficient is to 0, the weaker the correlation—that is, one variable does not reliably predict the other variable. For example, in a study on the quality of parent–infant relationships and the degree of later problem behavior in their children, Rothbaum, Schneider-Rosen, Pott, & Beatty (1995) found a −.50 correlation between the mother's quality of attachment to the infant and later problem behavior in the child. The correlation between the father's quality of attachment to the infant and later problem behavior was −.15. The higher correlation found with mothers suggests that the quality of the mother–child relationship is a better predictor of subsequent problem behavior than is the quality of the father–child relationship. Generally, the stronger the correlation between two variables, the more accurate our predictions, but perfect (−1.00 or +1.00) correlations rarely happen in psychology. Human behavior is too complex for such perfect relationships to occur.

What do the positive and negative signs in front of the correlation mean? The sign before the correlation coefficient tells us how the variables relate to one another (● FIGURE 1.7). A **positive correlation** means that as one variable increases, the second variable also tends to increase, or as one variable decreases, the other variable tends to decrease. In both cases, the variables are changing in the same direction. An example of a positive correlation is marijuana use and lung cancer. As marijuana use increases, so does the likelihood of developing lung cancer (Caplan & Brigham, 1990; "Marijuana as Medicine," 1997). Another example of a positive correlation is similarity in attitudes and attraction. The more similar two people are in attitudes, the more likely they are to be attracted to one another (Byrne, 1969; Fig. 1.7).

correlation the relationship between two or more variables

positive correlation a relationship in which increases in one variable correspond to increases in a second variable

FIGURE 1.7

● **Correlation** Correlation, a research method used for prediction, shows how two variables are related.

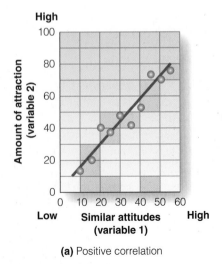

(a) Positive correlation

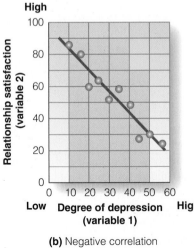

(b) Negative correlation

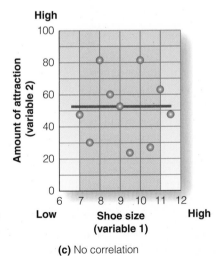

(c) No correlation

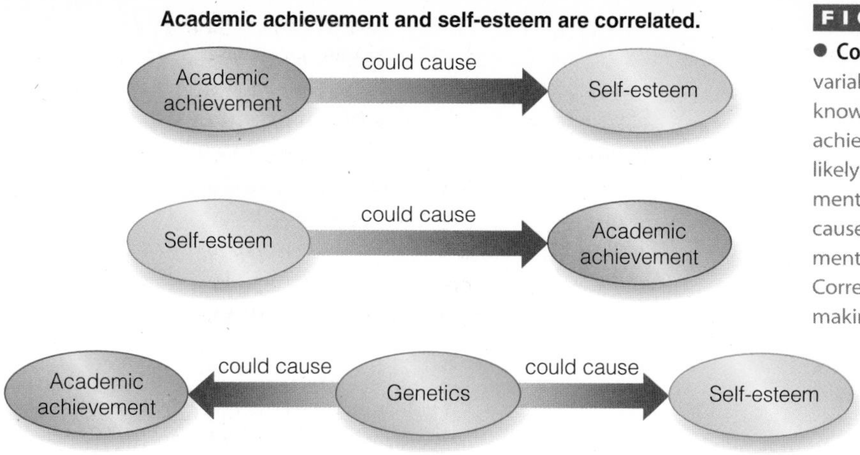

Academic achievement and self-esteem are correlated.

FIGURE 1.8

● **Correlation Does Not Mean Causation** When two variables are correlated or related, it does not mean that we know why they are related. It could be that high academic achievement causes high self-esteem. However, it is equally likely that high self-esteem causes high academic achievement. It is also possible that a third variable, such as genetics, causes both high self-esteem and high academic achievement, resulting in a relationship between the two variables. Correlation can only be used for making predictions, not for making cause-and-effect statements.

In a **negative correlation**, as one variable increases the other variable tends to decrease in what is referred to as an *inverse* relationship. Notice that the variables are changing in *opposite* directions. An example of a negative correlation is exercise and anxiety. The more people exercise, the less anxiety they tend to experience (Morgan, 1987). Or consider the negative correlation between relationship satisfaction and depression. As relationship satisfaction increases, feelings of depression decrease (Beach, Sandeen, & O'Leary, 1990; Fig, 1.7).

Correlational studies enable researchers to make predictions about behavior, but they do *not* allow us to make cause-and-effect conclusions (● FIGURE 1.8). For example, there is a positive correlation between academic achievement and self-esteem. Students who have high academic achievement also tend to have high self-esteem. Similarly, students who have low academic achievement tend to have low self-esteem. High academic achievement may cause an increase in self-esteem. However, it is just as likely that having high self-esteem causes one to do better academically. There may be a third variable, such as the parents' educational level or genetics, which actually causes the relationship between academic achievement and self-esteem. A correlational study does not tell us which of these explanations is correct. The only research method that permits us to draw cause-and-effect conclusions is the experiment.

Experiments

What research method is used to test causal hypotheses? Although several types of research methods are used to test predictive hypotheses, only one research method can test a causal hypothesis: the **experiment**. We will discuss several features of the experiment, including its advantages and disadvantages.

Necessary Conditions for an Experiment Two main features characterize an experiment. First, the variables in the study are controlled or manipulated. Second, participants are randomly assigned to the conditions of the study. When these two conditions have been met, causal conclusions *may* be drawn. Let's first turn our attention to the issue of experimenter control.

The point of the experiment is to manipulate one variable and see what effect this manipulation has on another variable (● FIGURE 1.9). These variables are termed the *independent* and *dependent variables*, respectively. The **independent variable** is the variable that the experimenter manipulates; it is the cause in the experiment. The **dependent variable** measures any result of manipulating the independent variable; it is the effect in the experiment.

The typical experiment divides participants into two types of groups: *experimental groups* and *control groups*. The **experimental groups** are those participants who receive the manipulation that is being tested. The **control groups** do not receive the manipulation that is being tested; they serve as a baseline comparison for the experimental group. Both groups are then measured on the dependent variable to see if there is a difference *between* the groups. In some experiments the control group receives a *placebo* or inactive substance such as a sugar pill

negative correlation a relationship in which increases in one variable correspond to decreases in a second variable

experiment a research method that is used to test causal hypotheses

independent variable the variable in an experiment that is manipulated

dependent variable the variable in an experiment that measures any effect of the manipulation

experimental group the group of participants that receive the manipulation that is being tested

control group the group of participants that do not receive the manipulation that is being tested

Elements of an Experiment

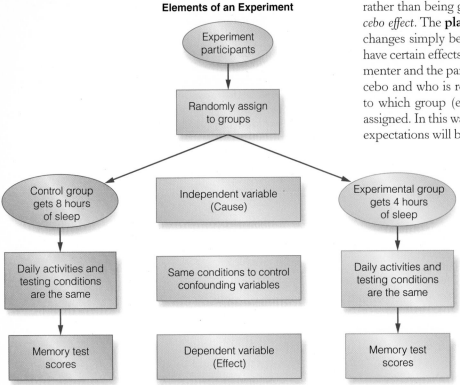

● **Elements of an Experiment** The two main ingredients of an experiment are (1) variables that are controlled or manipulated and (2) participants that are randomly assigned to the conditions of the study. When these two conditions have been met, causal conclusions may be drawn.

placebo effect a measurable change in participants' behavior due to the expectation or belief that a treatment will have certain effects

double-blind study an experiment in which both the experimenter and the study participants do not know to which group (experimental or control) participants have been assigned

confounding variable any factor other than the independent variable that affects the dependent measure

rather than being given nothing. This is to control for the *placebo effect*. The **placebo effect** occurs when participants show changes simply because they believe or expect a treatment to have certain effects. In **double-blind studies**, both the experimenter and the participants are not told who is receiving a placebo and who is receiving the actual treatment; they are *blind* to which group (experimental or control) a person has been assigned. In this way neither the participant's or experimenter's expectations will bias the results.

Suppose, for example, that we want to study the effects of sleep deprivation. Specifically, we hypothesize that sleep deprivation causes deficits in memory. This is a causal hypothesis that can be tested with an experiment. We decide to manipulate the amount of sleep participants receive to see if it has any effect on memory. In this example, the amount of sleep is our independent variable. Some participants will be allowed to sleep 8 hours per night for the week of our study (control group). Others will be allowed to sleep only 4 hours each night (experimental group). The experimenter has set, or controlled, the amount of sleep (the independent variable) at two levels: 8 hours and 4 hours. Each day of our study we measure the participants' memory (the dependent variable) by having them complete several memory tasks. At the end of the study, we compare the memory scores of those participants who received 8 hours of sleep (control group) with those who received only 4 hours of sleep (experimental group).

To be sure that it is the amount of sleep affecting memory and not something else, we need to be sure that we have controlled any variable (other than the independent variable) that may influence this relationship. These potentially problematic variables are called **confounding variables**. What confounding variables might we need to control? Maybe age influences one's memory or how one handles sleep deprivation. If either of these is true, we would want to control the age of our participants. We also would want to make sure that participants had not used any substances known to affect memory or the sleep cycle prior to their participation in the experiment. Consequently, we would control for this variable too.

Both groups must be treated the same except for the amount of sleep they receive, so the researcher sets the conditions of the experiment to be the same for both groups. For example, every participant should complete the memory tasks at the same time of day, and every participant should complete the same memory tasks. The criteria for scoring the memory tasks must be the same as well. The instructions for completing the tasks must be the same. The lighting, temperature, and other physical features of the room in which the participants sleep and complete the memory tasks should be the same for all participants. Our purpose is to design a study in which we manipulate the independent variable to see its effect on the dependent variable. If we control any potentially confounding variables that influence this relationship and find a difference in the dependent variable between our groups, that difference is most likely due to the independent variable, and we have established a cause-and-effect relationship.

What if the experimenter does not control a confounding variable? We now have more than one variable that could be responsible for the change in the dependent variable: the independent variable and the confounding variable. When this occurs, the researcher is left with an alternative explanation for the results. The change in the dependent variable could have been caused by the independent variable, but it also could have been caused by the confounding variable. Consequently, causal conclusions are limited.

Let's not forget the second condition necessary for an experiment—how participants are assigned to the conditions of the independent variable. Just as we do not want any differences in the nature of our conditions other than the amount of sleep, we must be sure that there are no differences in the composition of our groups of participants. Psychologists eliminate this problem through **random assignment** of participants to the conditions of the study. In our example on sleep and memory, assigning all the males in the sample to the 4-hour sleep condition and all the females to the 8-hour sleep condition would create a confounding variable. Gender differences might have an effect on memory scores. It may be that gender (the confounding variable) rather than sleep deprivation (the independent variable) is the cause of a difference in memory. To eliminate the influence of such confounding variables, experimenters randomly assign participants to conditions. Each participant has an equal chance of being placed in either condition. Male participants are just as likely to be assigned to the 4-hour condition as they are to the 8-hour condition, and the same is true for female participants. In this way, any participant variable that has the potential to influence the research results is just as likely to affect one group as it is the other. Without random assignment, confounding variables could affect the dependent variable. This is typically what occurs in *quasi-experiments*.

A **quasi-experiment** is in some ways like an experiment. The researcher manipulates the independent variable and sets the other conditions to be the same for both groups. However, the second requirement for an experiment—randomly assigning participants to conditions—has not been met. Quasi-experiments use existing groups of people who differ on some variable. For example, suppose you want to see if smoking cigarettes during pregnancy causes lower-birth-weight babies. For ethical reasons, you cannot assign some pregnant women to smoke and prevent others from smoking. Instead, for your smoking condition, you must select pregnant women who already smoke. These women may differ on other variables when compared to pregnant women who do not smoke. For example, their eating habits may differ. As a result, a confounding variable (the diet of the mothers) rather than smoking could cause a difference in the dependent variable (the birth weight of the offspring). Because quasi-experiments do not meet the conditions necessary for a "true" experiment, causal conclusions based on these designs should be made cautiously (Shadish, Cook, & Campbell, 2002; West, 2009).

Advantages and Disadvantages of Using Experiments

Experiments have several advantages. First, it is only through experimentation that we can approach two of the goals of psychology: explaining and changing behavior. An experiment is the only research method that enables us to determine cause-and-effect relationships. This advantage makes interpreting research results less ambiguous. In an experiment we attempt to eliminate any confounding variables through experimenter control and random assignment of participants to groups. These techniques enable us to draw clearer conclusions from research results.

If experiments are so great, why don't we just use them all the time? First, experiments do not address the first two goals of psychology: describing and predicting behavior. These are often the first steps in understanding behavior, and naturalistic observation, surveys, and correlational studies are quite useful for doing this. Second, in an attempt to control confounding variables, experiments conducted in laboratory settings may create an artificial atmosphere. It is then difficult to know if the same result would occur in a more natural setting. This may be another reason to conduct naturalistic observations or correlational studies. Third, sometimes employing the experimental method is simply

random assignment participants have an equal chance of being placed in any condition of the study

quasi-experiment a research study that is not a true experiment because participants are not randomly assigned to the different conditions

By studying behavior in a lab environment, researchers are better able to control the variables in an experiment.

not possible for ethical or practical reasons. As we mentioned in the case of quasi-experimental designs, we cannot force people to be randomly assigned to a condition that would harm them (such as smoking) or that does not pertain to them (such as having high blood pressure). Psychologists must follow certain ethical guidelines and practices when conducting research. We turn our attention to this topic next.

Let's REVIEW

In this section we detailed the goals of psychology, identified the steps of the scientific method, and described methods of research. For a quick check of your understanding, try answering the following questions at increasing levels of difficulty.

1. The more hours that students work, the less successful they are academically. This is an example of what type of correlation?

   a. zero
   b. positive

   c. perfect
   d. negative

2. In an experiment on attitudes, participants are given either positive or negative information about a speaker and then asked to evaluate the effectiveness of the speaker. In this experiment, which is the independent variable?

   a. the effectiveness of the speaker
   b. the type of information the participant is given
   c. attitude change
   d. the speaker

3. When we know that two events regularly occur together, which goal of psychology can be met?

   a. predicting behavior
   b. changing behavior

   c. understanding behavior
   d. explaining behavior

ANSWERS 1. d; 2. b; 3. a

LEARNING OBJECTIVE

What Should You Know?
• Describe the main ethical principles that guide psychologists as they conduct research.

WHAT ARE THE ETHICAL RULES OF PSYCHOLOGICAL RESEARCH?

Generally, psychologists affiliated with universities and colleges cannot conduct research unless their research proposal has passed review by an **Institutional Review Board (IRB)**. The function of the IRB is to ensure that the research study being proposed conforms to a set of ethical standards or guidelines. This section details who sets these standards and what the main responsibilities are for psychologists who conduct research.

Ethical Guidelines for Participants

Who sets the ethical guidelines for psychological research? The American Psychological Association (APA), one of the main professional organizations for psychologists, has taken the lead in establishing ethical guidelines, or professional behaviors that psychologists must follow. These guidelines, the "Ethical Principles of Psychologists and Code of Conduct" (APA, 2002), address a variety of issues, including general professional responsibility, clinical practice, psychological testing, and research. Here we look at the guidelines psychologists must follow when conducting research with humans and animals. The ethical duties of psychologists who treat clients are discussed in Chapter 15.

What is the Golden Rule for conducting research on human participants? One of the main concerns of the IRB is to ensure that the proposed research has met the ethical

Institutional Review Board (IRB)
a committee that reviews research proposals to ensure that ethical standards have been met

guideline of respect and concern for the dignity and welfare of the people who participate (APA, 2002). Researchers must protect participants from any potential harm, risk, or danger as a result of their participation in a psychological study. If such effects occur, the researcher has the responsibility to remove or correct these effects. In the experiment that Watson and Rayner conducted on 9-month-old Albert discussed earlier in the chapter, the fear that Albert developed toward white rats was never removed. Today the procedure for this experiment would be considered unethical. Watson caused harm to Albert and did not remove his fear at the end of the experiment.

A fundamental principle of ethical practice in research is **informed consent**. Researchers inform potential participants of any risks during the informed consent process, wherein the researcher establishes a clear and fair agreement with research participants prior to their participation in the research study (APA, 2002). This agreement clarifies the obligations and responsibilities of the participants and the researchers and includes the following information:

- The general purpose of the research study, including the experimental nature of any treatment
- Services that will or will not be available to the control group
- The method by which participants will be assigned to treatment and control groups
- Any aspect of the research that may influence a person's willingness to participate in the research
- Compensation for or monetary costs of participating
- Any risks or side effects that may be experienced as a result of participation in the study

Prospective participants are also informed that they may withdraw from participation in the study at any time, and they are informed of any available treatment alternatives. In addition, the researcher agrees to maintain **confidentiality**. Personal information about participants obtained by the researcher during the course of the investigation cannot be shared with others unless explicitly agreed to in advance by the participant or as required by law or court order. See the ● TECHNOLOGY AND BEHAVIOR box for concerns regarding online research.

Can you trick participants in an experiment? It is not always possible to fully inform participants of the details of the research, as it may change their behavior. For this reason, psychologists sometimes use *deception* in their research. For example, suppose we wanted to research student cheating. If we tell participants we are studying cheating behavior, it will likely influence their behavior. If we tell participants we are investigating student–teacher behavior, we can measure student cheating more objectively. However, the use of deception must be justified by the potential value of the research results. Moreover, deception can be used only when alternative procedures that do not use deception are unavailable.

If participants have been deceived in any way during the course of a study, the researcher is obligated to *debrief* participants after the experiment ends. **Debriefing** consists of full disclosure by the researcher to inform participants of the true purpose of the research. Any misconceptions that the participant may hold about the nature of the research must be removed at this time. For example, suppose you volunteer to participate in a psychological experiment on attitudes toward your school. You arrive at the psychology lab at the appropriate time and are asked to wait in a room for a moment with two other participants. While in the waiting room, the other participants start talking to you. One is very pleasant and kind, but the other is rude, negative, and overbearing. The researcher then arrives and escorts you to another room in which you complete a self-esteem questionnaire. After completing the questionnaire, you are then told that the true purpose of the study was to investigate your reaction to the people in the waiting room. The researcher is exploring how positive and negative behaviors influence another person's self-esteem. The two people in the waiting room were not really participants but *confederates*, individuals who pose as participants but who are really working for the researcher. In such an experiment, you were not physically or psychologically harmed, so the deception and subsequent debriefing were ethical. This ethical standard was not always met in the past. Consider the following research study.

In the 1960s Stanley Milgram (1963) set out to determine if the average person could be induced to hurt others in response to orders from an authority figure. (You will read more about Milgram's research in Chapter 11.) Participants were deceived into believing that they

informed consent research participants agree to participate after being told about aspects of the study

confidentiality researchers do not reveal which data were collected from which participant

debriefing after an experiment, participants are fully informed of the nature of the study

TECHNOLOGY and BEHAVIOR

ONLINE PSYCHOLOGY LABS

Over 2 million hits occur when you type "online psychology lab" into any search engine. Many of these results will direct you to research laboratories at well-known universities across the United States where you can participate in online experiments and surveys—performing tasks or answering questionnaires from the convenience of your own home. What are the advantages and disadvantages of online research, and are the results from such research believable? The answer is perhaps.

Numerous online psychology labs now exist where people can participate in psychological research from the convenience of their own home.

Image Source/PhotoLibrary

In many ways online psychological research is subject to the same methodological concerns as traditional research. How you design your study, give directions, and ask questions can be interpreted differently by your participants, and thereby influence your results. Participants may not give honest answers, or they may answer questions to make themselves look better or to support or disprove what they believe to be the researcher's hypothesis. However, using the Internet for psychological research presents additional challenges in the areas of sampling and ethics.

On the plus side, researchers conducting online research have the distinct advantage of soliciting a larger and more diverse sample at a fraction of the cost, with improved efficiency and data storage (Gosling & Johnson, 2010). Thousands of participants from all over the world may be gathered over the Internet as opposed to a few hundred that can be collected on-site. However, recall that the people you get to participate in your study are very important to the conclusions of your study. Internet research does not ensure a representative sample. Some people do not have access to a computer or may not know how to use the Internet. Web surveys often produce a lower response rate than traditional formats (Fan & Yan, 2010), and people who complete online research may be different in some way from people who are less willing to complete online research. This produces a confounding variable that presents an alternative explanation for one's results. Moreover, researchers may not be able to ensure that participants are who they say they are. People can more easily falsify their identity on the Internet than they can in person, calling into question the "true" characteristics of the sample that is generated.

In addition to sampling concerns, online research presents unique ethical challenges (Eynon, Schroeder, & Fry, 2009). Psychologists have a duty to maintain confidentiality and privacy of participants' data and personal information. Researchers may or may not consider security as part of their data collection plan or may not have the necessary training to implement electronic security. In such cases, researchers may need to consult technical experts to ensure the security of online information. Even with the best security, databases may still be compromised. Universities and professional organizations will need to develop ethical practices to address these issues.

Although Stanley Milgram debriefed his participants, he still caused them psychological harm. Such a study violates current ethical standards of psychological research.

Obedience © 1965, Stanley Milgram

were participating in a research study on learning rather than on obedience. Participants were told that they would be playing the role of a "teacher" in the experiment. Participants were introduced to a "learner" who was then led to a separate room. The teacher's job was to administer electric shocks to the learner every time the learner made a mistake in an effort to help the learner better learn a list of words. In reality, the participant was not actually shocking the learner. The learner's responses were prerecorded on a tape, but the participants did not know this and believed they were, indeed, shocking the learner.

Despite the fact that participants believed the learner to be ill or worse, most of them continued to follow the experimenter's orders. A full 65% of the participants shocked the learner all the way up to the highest shock level. During the procedure, Milgram's participants exhibited emotional distress. Although Milgram debriefed his participants after the study, he still violated the ethical principle of psychological harm. He was criticized for exposing participants to the trauma of the procedure itself and for not leaving the participants in at least as good a condition as they were prior to the experiment (Baumrind, 1964). Because of these ethical problems, a study such as this would not be approved today.

We should also note that for years the primary focus in research was on White males. Women and minorities were not only discouraged from becoming professionals in psychology but also were largely ignored or neglected when studying psychological issues. Many minority and female as well as male psychologists have contributed to the field of psychology by addressing these shortcomings and designing research that looks specifically at the behaviors of minorities and women.

Ethical Guidelines for Animal Research

Animal studies have advanced our understanding of many psychological issues, including the importance of prenatal nutrition, our treatment of brain injuries, and our understanding of mental disorders (Domjan & Purdy, 1995). Psychologists must meet certain standards and follow ethical guidelines when conducting research with animals. Psychological research using animal subjects must also be approved by an IRB. Less than 10% of all psychological studies involve animal subjects, and these consist mainly of rodents and birds (APA, 1984). Animals must be treated humanely and in accord with all federal, state, and local laws and regulations. Researchers are responsible for the daily comfort, housing, cleaning, feeding, and health of animal subjects. Discomfort, illness, and pain must be kept at a minimum, and such procedures can only be used if alternative procedures are not available. Moreover, harmful or painful procedures used on animals must be justified in terms of the knowledge that is expected to be gained from the study. Researchers must also promote the psychological well-being of some animals that are used in research, most notably primates (APA, 2002).

In the chapters that follow, we will detail more specifically psychological research in the main specialty areas of psychology. For example, in the next chapter, we start with the biological processes that underlie all behavior. Each chapter will prepare you for mastering the concepts of the next chapter, and we frequently remind you of concepts presented in earlier chapters to help you connect the information. A visual summary entitled *Are You Getting the Big Picture?* concludes each chapter. It will help you remember the topics and concepts that have been introduced and further your understanding of how these concepts relate to one another.

Let's REVIEW

As a quick check of your understanding of ethical considerations in research, try answering the following questions at increasing levels of difficulty.

1. What is the rule for deceiving participants in a psychological study?

    a. Deception is never allowed in psychological research. It is against the law and you go to jail if you use it.

    b. Deception is allowed only when using animals as subjects; human beings are too intelligent for deception.

    c. Deception is allowed when alternative procedures are unavailable and participants are debriefed at the end of the study.

    d. Deception can be done under any circumstances because psychological research never harms participants.

2. Which of the following is *not* an ethical guideline psychologists must follow when conducting research?

    a. paying participants for their participation   c. freedom from harm

    b. informed consent   d. confidentiality

3. Dr. Kwan is performing case study research. She should be most concerned with which of the following ethical principles?

    a. deception   c. debriefing

    b. physical harm   d. confidentiality

ANSWERS 1. c; 2. a; 3. d

STUDYING the CHAPTER

KEY TERMS

psychology (3)
scientific method (3)
theory (6)
structuralism (8)

introspection (8)
Gestalt psychology (8)
functionalism (9)
psychoanalytic theory (10)

behaviorism (10)
stimulus (10)
response (10)
humanism (12)

cognitive psychology (13)
positive psychology (13)
biological/physiological
   perspective (13)

neuroscience (14)
evolutionary perspective (14)
cognitive perspective (14)
psychodynamic
   perspective (14)
behavioral perspective (15)
sociocultural perspective (15)
humanistic perspective (15)
eclectic approach (16)
basic research (17)

applied research (17)
prediction (22)
hypothesis (22)
predictive hypothesis (23)
causal hypothesis (23)
naturalistic observation (24)
case study (24)
generalizability (25)
survey (25)
population of interest (25)

sample (25)
correlation (26)
positive correlation (26)
negative correlation (27)
experiment (27)
independent variable (27)
dependent variable (27)
experimental group (27)
control group (27)
placebo effect (28)

double-blind study (28)
confounding variable (28)
random assignment (29)
quasi-experiment (29)
Institutional Review
   Board (IRB) (30)
informed consent (31)
confidentiality (31)
debriefing (31)

LEARNING CHALLENGE

Now that you have studied the chapter, assess your comprehension of the material by answering the following questions. Then use the key at the end to determine if your understanding is at the basic, intermediate, or advanced level. For a more comprehensive assessment of your learning, please see your student study guide and your Psychology CourseMate (www.cengagebrain.com).

1. Which of the following topics would a psychologist have the least interest in?

a. learning
b. sexuality
c. weather patterns
d. color perception

2. Which of the following is the most likely educational attainment of the majority of psychologists?

a. doctorate degree
b. master's degree
c. bachelor's degree
d. associate's degree

3. Dr. Vaz conducted an experiment in which she randomly assigned her participants to one of two conditions. In the first condition, the participants were shown visual images of common objects and then one hour later asked to recall as many of the objects as they could remember. In the second condition, the participants heard the names of the same objects and then one hour later were asked to recall as many of the objects as they could. Dr. Vaz then compared the number of items recalled for these two groups of participants. In this experiment, which of the following is the independent variable?

a. the number of items recalled
b. whether the participants saw or heard the objects
c. the sex of the participants
d. the room in which the participants took the exam

4. Given the information in the preceding question, which of the following would be considered a confounding variable?

a. the objects
b. random assignment of participants
c. any visual or hearing deficits the participants may have
d. the recall of the participants

5. Which of these modern perspectives most emphasizes external causes of behavior?

a. biological
b. behavioral
c. psychodynamic
d. evolutionary

6. Which of the following professionals is most likely to prescribe medication for a mental health disorder?

a. a clinical psychologist
b. a psychiatrist
c. a biopsychologist
d. an experimental psychologist

7. Theories are used for which goal of psychology?

a. describe
b. observe
c. predict
d. explain

8. Correlational studies test which type of hypotheses?

a. predictive
b. causal
c. both predictive and causal
d. neither predictive nor causal

9. As an educational psychologist, you might use naturalistic observations of college students in a test-taking environment to get at which of psychology's goals?

a. change behavior
b. predict behavior
c. explain behavior
d. describe behavior

10. Psychology is the scientific study of _____.

a. behavior only
b. mental processes only
c. behavior and mental processes
d. the brain and the body

11. Many modern psychologists follow the _____ approach to psychology, in that they do not adhere strictly to one psychological perspective.

a. eclectic
b. pragmatic
c. functional
d. common sense

12. Dr. Wernike performs basic research in the areas of sensation, perception, and learning. Dr. Wernike is what type of psychologist?

a. health
b. experimental
c. developmental
d. social

13. Psychologists test ideas about behavior by following a set of rules called the _____.

a. eclectic approach
b. survey method
c. hypothesis testing
d. scientific method

14. Dr. Pi wants to test the hypothesis that smoking marijuana impairs one's ability to remember information. What type of research method will Dr. Pi most likely have to use to test this hypothesis?

a. a true experiment
b. a case study
c. a quasi-experiment
d. a survey

15. The longer the commute for a student to a college campus, the less likely he or she is to complete a degree. This is an example of a _____.

a. negative correlation
b. positive correlation
c. zero correlation
d. perfect correlation

Scoring Key

Below are the answers and the associated point values for each of the Learning Challenge questions. Circle the associated points for each question that you answered correctly. To obtain your Learning Challenge Score, add up the points you circled and write the total in the blank below.

1. C, 1 pt   **6.** B, 2 pts   **11.** A, 1 pt
2. A, 1 pt   **7.** D, 3 pts   **12.** B, 2 pts
3. B, 2 pts   **8.** A, 3 pts   **13.** D, 1 pt
4. C, 3 pts   **9.** D, 2 pts   **14.** C, 3 pts
5. B, 3 pts   **10.** C, 1 pt   **15.** A, 2 pts

Learning Challenge Score _____

(27–30) Congratulations! You scored at the advanced level. You are well on your way to mastering the material. Take the next step by answering the questions in your Student Study Guide or your Psychology CourseMate (www.cengagebrain.com).

(21–26) You are almost there! You scored at the intermediate level. Review the material you missed before moving on to answer the questions in your Student Study Guide or your Psychology CourseMate (www.cengagebrain.com).

(20 and below) You are on your way, but you're not there yet! You scored at the beginner level. It appears that you need to carefully review the chapter to improve your mastery of the material.

USE IT OR LOSE IT: APPLYING PSYCHOLOGY

1. Suppose Wilhelm Wundt, William James, and Sigmund Freud had the opportunity to sit down and discuss the causes of behavior. What might this conversation sound like? On what issues might they agree? On what issues might they disagree?

2. Explain depression from each of the modern perspectives and using the eclectic approach. Use The Big Picture Review as a guide if you need help.

3. Design a research study to test the idea that listening to rock music while studying facilitates learning. What type of hypothesis would you make? Could this idea be tested by naturalistic observation? How could you set up a cor-relational study to test this idea? Could an experiment be designed to address this issue? What types of conclusions could you reach from these different research methods? What ethical considerations would you follow when conducting this study?

4. Explain how you can apply the scientific method to decide on a college major or a career choice. Could this method also be used as part of your decision-making process when purchasing a large item such as a car or a house? Explain how it could be used for these major purchases.

CHAPTER STUDY RESOURCES

Student Study Guide

To help organize your learning, work through Chapter 1 of the *What Is Psychology? Student Study Guide*. The study guide includes learning objectives, a chapter summary, fill-in review, key terms, a practice test, and activities.

CengageNOW

Go to **www.cengage.com/login** to link to CengageNOW, your online study tool. First take the Pre-Test for this chapter to get your personalized study plan, which will identify topics you need to review and direct you to online resources. Then take the Post-Test to determine what concepts you have mastered and what you still need work on.

CourseMate

Access an interactive eBook, chapter-specific interactive learning tools, including flashcards, quizzes, videos, and more in your Psychology CourseMate, available at **CengageBrain.com**.

Aplia

Aplia™ is an online interactive learning solution that helps you improve comprehension—and your grade—by integrating a variety of tools such as video, tutorials, practice tests, and interactive eBook. Founded by a professor to enhance his own courses, Aplia provides automatically graded assignments with detailed, immediate explanations on every question, and innovative teaching materials. More than 1,000,000 students like you have used Aplia at over 1,800 institutions. Aplia should be purchased only when assigned by your instructor as part of your course.

WHAT IS PSYCHOLOGY?

Chapter 1 has given you an overview of the field of **psychology** and how psychologists do research. We hope that as you read this chapter, you were able to see how Michael Oher's story highlights many behaviors psychologists study such as motivation, racism, the effects of poverty, and love.

© Whisson/Jordan/Corbis

WHAT *IS* PSYCHOLOGY?

- To think like a psychologist, you must be skeptical about explanations of behavior, rather than accepting of them. Psychology is *not* simply giving advice, *not* just "common sense," and *not* limited to studying mental illness.

- Psychologists study all types of behaviors, from helping behavior to how people manage stress to love, aggression, and so on using the **scientific method**.

HOW DID PSYCHOLOGY BECOME A SCIENCE?

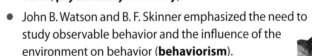

- Psychology became a distinct field of scientific study when Wilhelm Wundt established the first psychology laboratory, in Germany, in 1879. Wundt and Titchener studied the elements that explained mental processes (**structuralism**).

- William James's focus was on how particular behaviors helped people adapt to their environment (**functionalism**).

© Bettmann/Corbis

Wilhelm Wundt

- Sigmund Freud, one of the most famous people to influence psychology, believed the key to understanding behavior was uncovering unconscious motivations (**psychoanalytic theory**).

- John B. Watson and B. F. Skinner emphasized the need to study observable behavior and the influence of the environment on behavior (**behaviorism**).

- In contrast to the environmental focus of behaviorism, Carl Rogers and Abraham Maslow emphasized free will and personal growth in determining behavior (**humanism**).

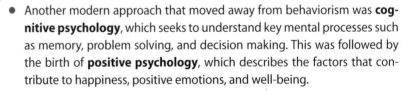

Sigmund Freud

© Topham/The Image Works

- Another modern approach that moved away from behaviorism was **cognitive psychology**, which seeks to understand key mental processes such as memory, problem solving, and decision making. This was followed by the birth of **positive psychology**, which describes the factors that contribute to happiness, positive emotions, and well-being.

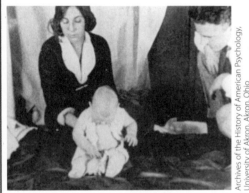

Archives of the History of American Psychology, University of Akron, Akron, Ohio

Rosalie Rayner and John B. Watson

WHAT ARE THE FOUR GOALS OF PSYCHOLOGICAL RESEARCH?

- To describe behavior
- To predict behavior
- To explain behavior
- To control or change behavior

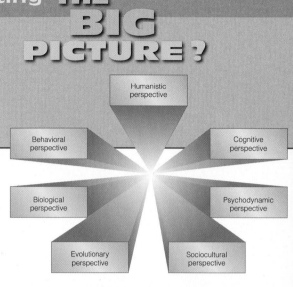

WHAT IS PSYCHOLOGY LIKE TODAY?

- Other major forces in psychology today include:
  - **biological** psychology, which examines the physiological contributions to behavior
  - **evolutionary** psychology, which looks at how behaviors may be genetically programmed to help us adapt better for survival
  - **sociocultural** psychology, which researches behaviors across ethnic groups and nations
- Psychologists today embrace an **eclectic** approach to studying and understanding behavior.
- Psychologists typically have a doctorate in psychology, which usually involves 5–7 years of postgraduate study and research beyond the undergraduate degree.
- There are numerous specialty areas of psychology, including:
  - developmental psychology (which studies child and adult development)
  - social psychology (which examines ways in which we are influenced by others)
  - industrial/organizational psychology (which looks at behavior in the workplace)
  - experimental psychology (which performs basic research on sensation, perception, and learning)
  - health psychology (which focuses on ways to promote health and prevent illness)
  - clinical or counseling psychology (administering therapy to assist individuals with mental health problems)

- Of those pursuing graduate work in psychology, women now outnumber men although they still lag behind men as a percentage of full professors and tenured faculty at U.S. psychology graduate departments.
- There has been an increase in the number of racial and ethnic minority students majoring in psychology, but their numbers are still smaller than their percentage in the general population.

HOW IS PSYCHOLOGICAL RESEARCH CONDUCTED?

- Psychologists form **predictive** and **causal hypotheses**, and then conduct research using the **scientific method**.
- Predictive hypotheses are tested by **naturalistic observation**, **case studies**, **surveys**, and **correlational studies**.
- Causal hypotheses are tested by **experiments** in which variables are controlled and care is taken to test a random sample of a **population of interest**. The **experimental group** is compared to the **control group** on the **dependent variable** to see if the **independent variable** had an effect.
- To ensure humane conduct of experiments, the American Psychological Association has established a strict set of ethical guidelines that must be followed when researchers study animals and humans.

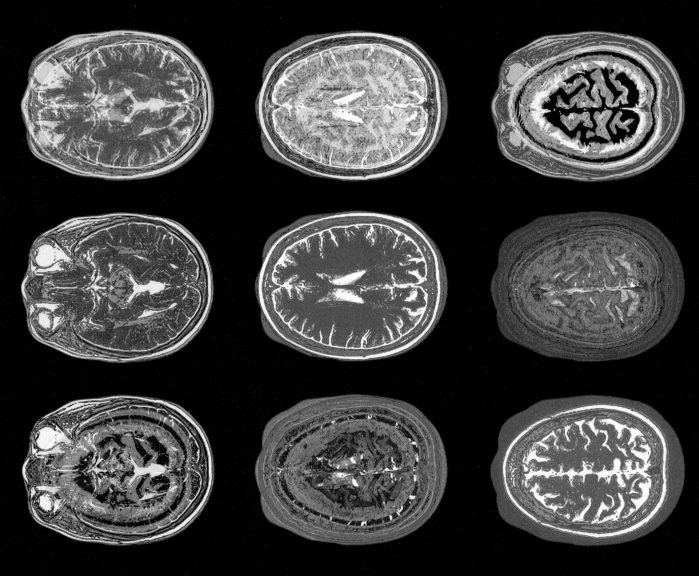

HOW DOES BIOLOGY INFLUENCE OUR BEHAVIOR?

THE BIG PICTURE

What Would We Be Without a Healthy Brain?

When did you last stop to wonder how your brain works? For most of us, the answer to that question is probably never! Most of us lead our lives without giving our brain much thought. Every day we go about our business, taking for granted our ability to move, speak, feel, and breathe. We seldom, if ever, stop to think about the amazing internal systems that allow us to accomplish these tasks. Sometimes the best way to gain an appreciation for things we take for granted is to see what life would be like without them. In the following case study, we see what life was like for Jean-Dominique Bauby when he suddenly lost much of his brain function. After reading his story, you will probably have more respect for your own brain and the abilities it gives you.

When Jean-Dominique Bauby began his day on December 8, 1995, his life was the essence of success. At age 43 he was editor-in-chief of the French fashion magazine *Elle*, the father of two loving children, a world traveler—a man who seemed to have everything. But all of this was about to change. That afternoon, as Bauby was driving, he suddenly began to experience unusual neurological problems. As he drove along, Bauby began to feel as if he were moving in slow motion. His vision began to blur and double, and familiar landmarks along the road seemed only vaguely recognizable. Realizing that he was in trouble, Bauby pulled off the road and attempted to get out of the car, only to find that he was unable to walk. He collapsed and was rushed to a nearby hospital where he lapsed into a coma that lasted nearly three weeks.

As you may have guessed, Bauby experienced a stroke on that December afternoon. Blood flow to the brainstem was disrupted, leaving Bauby with what physicians call "locked-in syndrome." Those with locked-in syndrome remain conscious but are almost completely unable to move or speak. They are essentially trapped or "locked" inside their bodies. When Bauby awoke from his coma, he was aware of his surroundings but unable to move any part of his body except for his left eyelid. He was also completely mute and half deaf, and because he was unable to blink his right eye, it had to be sewn shut to protect his cornea. Bauby lived the remaining 15 months of his life in this locked-in state, unable to move or speak but very aware of his surroundings and quite able to think and feel.

If Bauby's story ended here, it would certainly be a sad tale, but there was more to his life than this tragedy. There was also the remarkable triumph of an intelligent and

CHAPTER OUTLINE

- How Does the Brain Communicate?

- How Do Neurotransmitters, the Brain's Chemical Messengers, Work?

- Is the Nervous System a Single System?

- How Is the Brain Organized?

- How Do We Study the Brain?

- How Does the Endocrine System Influence Our Behavior?

- What Makes Us Who We Are—Our Biology or the Environment?

Don Farrall/Getty Images

Jean-Dominique Bauby blinked more than 200,000 times to write *The Diving Bell and the Butterfly* after having a stroke and ending up in a locked-in state. In 2007, the book was made into a motion picture that was nominated for and won many awards, including prizes at the Cannes Film Festival.

resourceful man. Bauby gradually learned to communicate with others by doing the only thing he could—blinking his left eye. Using an ingenious system, an assistant would read off the letters of the alphabet one at a time. When the assistant read the appropriate letter, Bauby would blink and the assistant would gradually compile the words and phrases that Bauby spelled out. Although it was painstaking, this system allowed Bauby to communicate with those who were patient enough to go through the process. Through blinking, Bauby was able to free himself to a small but meaningful degree from the prison of locked-in syndrome.

Not only did Bauby communicate with his family and friends, he also dictated a best-selling book that was later made into a major motion picture in 2007. It is estimated that Bauby had to blink his eye more than 200,000 times to dictate the manuscript (MacIntyre, 1998). *The Diving Bell and the Butterfly* (Bauby, 1997), published in France just days after his death on March 9, 1997, recounts Bauby's struggle to cope with the infirmities he suffered as a result of his devastating stroke, as well as his musings on the life he lost that December day. It also serves as a testament to the awesome complexity and power of the human brain. We take for granted that our brain and nervous system will function properly and allow us to do just as we wish. Bauby himself wrote of how unaware he had been of the functioning of his brainstem until it failed him and he was locked forever inside his body.

In this chapter we explore many aspects of the biological processes that underlie our behavior. You will begin to recognize the amazing intricacy and precision with which the systems within our bodies influence even our simplest behaviors. Keep the story of Jean-Dominique Bauby in mind as you read this chapter. Be aware that right now, as you read this page, everything you are doing—reading, learning, holding the book, blinking, breathing, and so on—originates in your wonderfully complex nervous system. By the end of the chapter, you'll have a better understanding of how your nervous system makes all these behaviors possible.

How Does the Brain Communicate?

As the case of Jean-Dominique Bauby makes painfully apparent, we rely on our bodies to do everything for us. We do not question that our brain will somehow store the information we just learned in psychology class and that on exam day it will retrieve that information. We take for granted that we will be able to walk, to talk, to play baseball, and to maintain a constant body temperature and a steady heart rate. But how are such everyday miracles accomplished? How does your brain know when you need to eat or sleep? How does your brain tell the muscles of your arm to contract so you can throw a baseball? In short, how does the brain communicate?

The brain communicates with itself and the rest of the body over networks of specialized information-carrying cells called **neurons**. Neurons use a sophisticated communication system to conduct the signals that allow us to control our bodies. For example, when you touch a hot stove, neurons in your fingertips send information up your arm to your spinal column. In response to this possible threat, signals are sent back out from the spine to the muscles of your arm. The result is a quick, reflexive jerking of your arm away from the hot stove (● FIGURE 2.1).

Using newly developed techniques, some researchers now estimate that the average adult male brain weighs about 1.5 kg (about 100 g more than the average female brain) and contains roughly 86 billion neurons, far less than the often cited estimate of 100 billion neurons. In addition to the neurons, the brain contains approximately the same number of **glial cells** (Azevedo et al., 2009). Glial cells have been traditionally thought to outnumber neurons (by about 10 to 1) and merely provide support functions for them, such as providing nutrients and removing wastes. However, both of these assumptions have recently been called into doubt. Some researchers now believe that glial cells do not outnumber neurons in the brain (Azevedo et al., 2009), and rather than merely supporting neurons, the glial cells can directly regulate the signals that neurons send to one another (Araque, 2008; Huang & Bergles, 2004; Overstreet, 2005; Volterra & Steinhauser, 2004). Although researchers continue to investigate the role of glial cells in information processing in the brain, we already have abundant evidence of the important support functions of glial cells.

For starters, glial cells help maintain the chemical environment of the neuron, and they help repair neural damage after injuries. However, one of their most important functions is forming **myelin**. Myelin is a whitish, fatty, waxy substance that coats many neurons. This protective coating insulates and speeds up neural signals. Much like rubber or plastic insulation on an electrical cord, myelin helps the signal get where it is going quickly. Myelinated neurons can conduct signals much faster than unmyelinated neurons. To appreciate what myelin does for neural communication, let's look at what happens when myelin is lost due to illness.

Multiple sclerosis (MS) is a disease that attacks and destroys the myelin insulation on neurons and also damages the neurons themselves (Herz, Zipp, & Siffrin, 2009). People with MS have difficulty controlling the actions of their body and have sensory problems, including numbness and vision loss. When myelin breaks down, neural signals are greatly slowed down or halted altogether. Initially, movement becomes

neurons cells in the nervous system that transmit information

glial cells brain cells that provide support functions for the neurons and may play a role in regulating neural signaling

myelin fatty, waxy substance that insulates portions of some neurons in the nervous system

FIGURE 2.1

The Neurons Involved in a Reflex
When you touch a hot stove, neurons in your fingertips send information up your arm to your spinal column. In response to this possible threat, signals are sent out from the spine to the muscles of your arm. The result is a quick, reflexive jerking of your arm away from the hot stove.

3 In the spinal cord, information travels from **sensory neurons** to **motor neurons**.

4 Motor (efferent) neurons send information from your spinal cord to your arm muscles, signaling them to contract, jerking your hand away.

Spinal cord (cross section)

2 Sensory (afferent) neurons send information from your (hot) fingertips up your arm and to your spinal cord.

1 You touch the hot stove; the heat registers in your skin's sensory receptors.

Courtesy of William L. Breneman

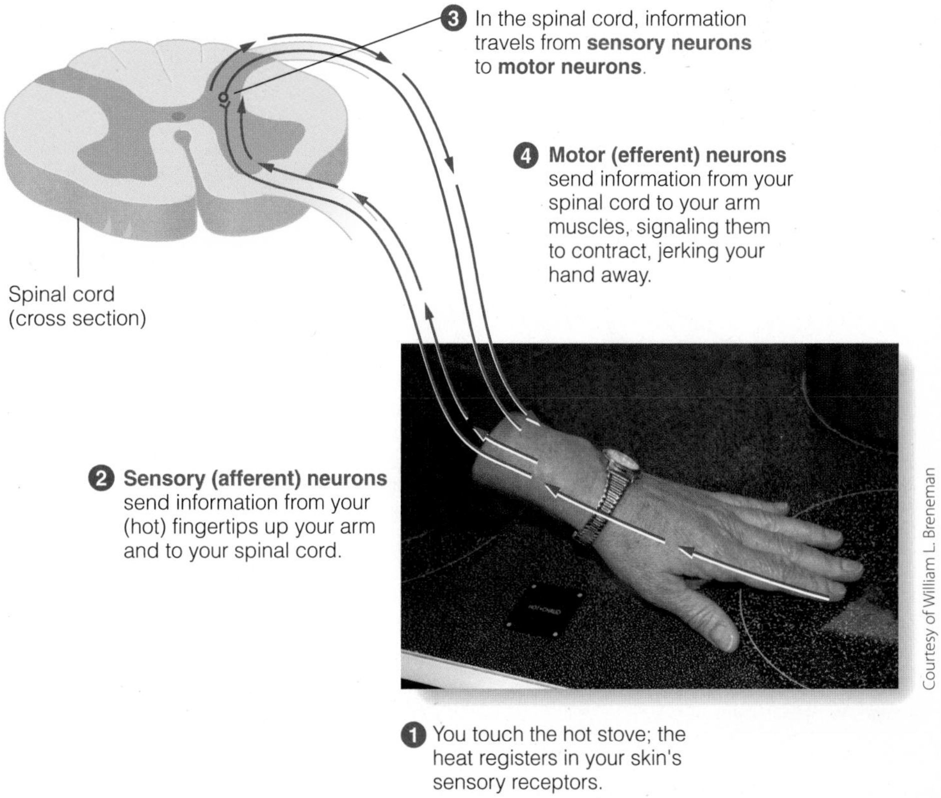

Television talk show host Montel Williams has multiple sclerosis, a disease that results in destruction of myelin. As the myelin is destroyed, patients may suffer from a variety of neurological symptoms including difficulty moving and sensory loss.

difficult; as the disease progresses, voluntary movement of some muscles may become impossible. Sensory systems such as vision may also fail because incoming signals from the eye do not reach the vision processing parts of the brain. Life often becomes very challenging for people with MS as the "orders" sent to and from the brain are delayed or lost along the way.

Without myelin our nervous system cannot function properly—our neurons cannot efficiently carry information from one point to another. As psychologists, we are particularly interested in understanding how *healthy* neurons send signals throughout the nervous system. Before we can examine how neurons transmit signals, we must first examine the anatomy of neural cells and how they connect with one another in the nervous system.

What Does a Neuron Look Like?

Like any cell in the body, the neuron has a **cell body** that contains a nucleus (● FIGURE 2.2). The cell body is somewhat similar in shape to a fried egg with the nucleus being the yolk. Like the nucleus of any cell, the nucleus of the neuron contains **DNA (deoxyribonucleic acid)**, the chemical that contains the genetic blueprint that directs the development of the neuron. Growing out of the cell body are branchlike structures called **dendrites** (from the Greek word for tree branch). The dendrites receive incoming signals from other neurons.

Growing out of the other end of the cell body is a long tail-like structure called an **axon**, which carries signals away from the cell body. When a neuron is insulated with myelin, it is the axon that is covered, or *myelinated*. As you can see in Figure 2.2, myelin does not continuously cover the entire length of a neuron's axon. Rather, the myelin covers segments of the axon with a *myelin sheath*. Axons vary in length from a few hundred micrometers to many centimeters, depending on where in the nervous system they are located. Axons in the brain are typically very short (1 millimeter or less) whereas other axons in the body, such as

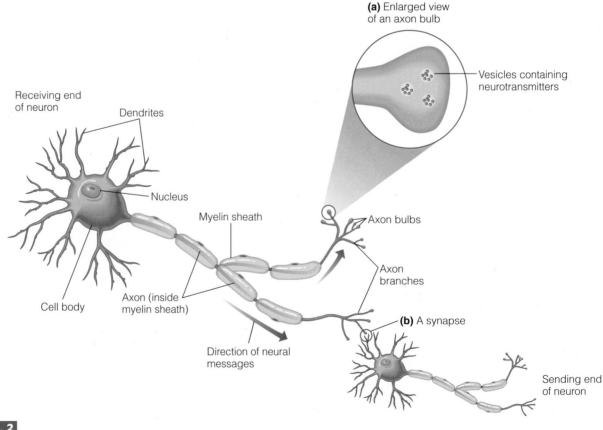

FIGURE 2.2

● **A Typical Neuron** The arrows indicate the flow of information from the dendrites on the cell body of the neuron to the axon bulbs at the end of the neuron. Neurons may have many dendrites and axon branches, and some neurons are insulated with myelin, which helps speed up neural signals in the neuron. *From Gaudin and Jones,* Human Anatomy and Physiology, *Fig 11.3a, p. 263. Reprinted by permission of the author.*

FIGURE 2.3

● **Detail of a Synapse** A synapse is formed when the axon bulb of one neuron comes in proximity to the receptors on the dendrites of the postsynaptic neuron.

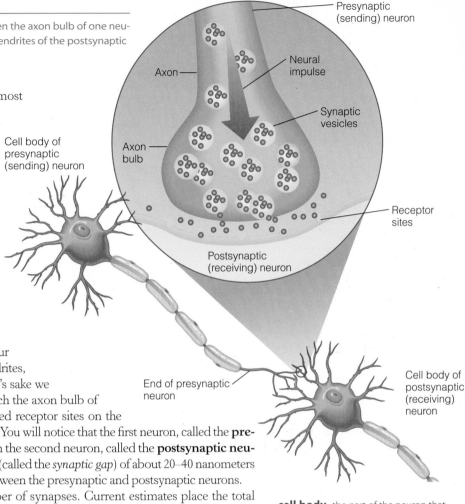

those that extend down the legs, can be almost in length (Purves et al., 1997).

The end of the axon splits into separate branches (Figure 2.2). At the end of each branch is an axon bulb, which houses small storage pouches or *synaptic vesicles*. These vesicles contain **neurotransmitters**, the chemical messengers that carry signals across the synapse. A **synapse** is the junction between two neurons where the axon bulb of one neuron comes into proximity with specialized *receptor sites* on the dendrites of another neuron.

The neural structure of the brain is extremely complex, and synapses can occur at several places along a neuron (e.g., dendrites, axon, or cell body). However, for simplicity's sake we will discuss only the type of synapse in which the axon bulb of the first neuron is in proximity to specialized receptor sites on the dendrites of a second neuron (● FIGURE 2.3). You will notice that the first neuron, called the **presynaptic neuron**, does not physically touch the second neuron, called the **postsynaptic neuron**. At a synapse, there is a measurable gap (called the *synaptic gap*) of about 20–40 nanometers (a nanometer is one billionth of a meter) between the presynaptic and postsynaptic neurons.

Humans have an extremely large number of synapses. Current estimates place the total number of synapses in the trillions (Morrow, Roffman, Wolf, & Coyle, 2008; Pakkenberg et al., 2003). Think about this for a moment. **How is it possible for humans to have trillions of synapses but only billions of neurons?** It's possible because the neurons of the brain do not synapse in a *one-to-one* fashion. Rather, each neuron can synapse with up to 10,000 other neurons (F. Bloom, Nelson, & Lazerson, 2001). Look again at the neurons in Figure 2.2. Synapses can occur at any place along any of the dendrites of these neurons. (Are you getting a feel for the complexity of the brain?) Keep in mind as you read the rest of this chapter that although we will describe simple one-to-one connections between neurons, this is merely for ease of discussion. The reality of the brain is much more complex: 86 billion neurons and trillions of neural connections.

This vast network of neurons and synapses gives our nervous system the ability to generate and send the messages that are necessary to govern our bodies. Let's take a closer look at how these signals are generated within the neuron and how the signals jump across the synapse as they travel through the nervous system.

How Do Neurons Send Signals?

Neural signals underlie much of the action in our bodies—breathing, moving, using our senses, and so on. Because Jean-Dominique Bauby was still able to send neural signals from his brain to the muscles of his eyelid, he was able to communicate with others. To understand how these neural signals are generated within a neuron, we must first understand the chemical environment of the neuron. Understanding brain chemistry is important because the brain uses *electrochemical* energy that is produced by charged particles called **ions** to send neural signals. Brain tissue is made up largely of densely packed neurons and glial cells. Brain tissue is surrounded by a constant bath of body fluid that contains many different ions. Some of the ions that play a particularly important role in neural signaling are sodium (Na^+), potassium (K^+), chloride (Cl^-), and negatively charged protein molecules called *anions*.

cell body the part of the neuron that contains the nucleus and DNA

DNA the chemical found in the nuclei of cells that contains the genetic blueprint that guides development in the organism

dendrites branchlike structures on the cell body of the neuron that receive incoming signals from other neurons in the nervous system

axon the long tail-like structure that comes out of the cell body of the neuron and carries action potentials that convey information from the cell body to the synapse

neurotransmitters chemical messengers that carry neural signals across the synapse

synapse the connection formed between two neurons when the axon bulb of one neuron comes into proximity with the dendrite of another neuron

presynaptic neuron the neuron that is sending the signal at a synapse in the nervous system

postsynaptic neuron the neuron that is receiving the signal at a synapse in the nervous system

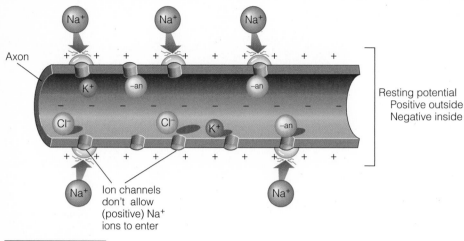

Axon

Resting potential
Positive outside
Negative inside

Ion channels
don't allow
(positive) Na⁺
ions to enter

● **Resting Potential**   When a neuron is at rest, the ion channels do not allow large sodium ions
(Na⁺) to enter the cell. As a result of the high concentration of Na⁺, the predominant charge on the
outside of the neuron is positive. The predominant charge inside the neuron is negative because of
the high concentration of negatively charged protein molecules called anions (−an) found there.
This difference in charge between the inside and the outside of the cell is called the resting potential.

When a neuron is at rest, meaning
it is not actively conducting a signal,
there is an imbalance in the types of
ions found inside and outside the cell
walls of the neuron. This imbalance
exists because openings in the axon,
called *ion channels*, only allow some
ions to pass into and out of the neuron.
Small ions such as K⁺ can pass through
the ion channels, but larger ions such
as Na⁺ cannot. Because Na⁺ cannot
enter the axon, high concentrations
of K⁺ and negative anions are found
inside the neuron and a high concentration of Na⁺ is found *outside* the neuron
(● FIGURE 2.4). Having a high concentration of negative anions on the *inside*
of the cell and a high concentration of
Na⁺ ions on the *outside* of the neuron
is crucial to the neuron's ability to send
neural signals.

Resting Potential

Figure 2.4 shows that this imbalance of ions causes an imbalance of electrical charges inside
and outside of the neuron. Because the charge outside the cell differs from the charge inside
the cell, the cell is said to be *polarized*. Look again at Figure 2.4. What type of charge dominates the inside of the neuron? What charge dominates the outside of the cell? The inside of
the cell is more negatively charged than the outside because there are a lot of positive sodium
ions (Na⁺) on the outside and a lot of negative anions on the inside of the cell. This polariza-
tion of the cell is called a potential difference, and the potential difference of a neuron at *rest*
is called the **resting potential**. In mammals, the resting potential is about −70 millivolts (a
millivolt, mv, is 1/1000 of a volt). This means that when resting, the inside of the neuron is
about 70 mv more *negative* than the outside of the neuron. Even though the resting potential
is a small potential difference, it is an important driving force in creating neural signals.

The Action Potential and the Threshold of Excitation

When a neuron receives input from other neurons, these incoming signals enter at the dendrites and travel across the cell body to the axon. These signals can make the inside of the cell
more positive or more negative. If the incoming signals make the inside of the neuron more
positive, the inside of the neuron may become positive enough to reach the neuron's **threshold of excitation** (about −55 mv in mammals). When the threshold of excitation is reached,
the ion channels along the axon suddenly open and allow Na⁺ ions to enter the cell. As Na⁺
ions flood into the cell, the inside of the neuron becomes rapidly more and more positive,
which causes the neuron to fire. These "firings" or neural impulses within the neuron are
called **action potentials** (● FIGURE 2.5a).

All neural impulses are equally strong. If a neuron reaches threshold and fires an action
potential, the neural signal will reach the synapse. A neuron firing an action potential is like
firing a gun. You either shoot or you don't, and once the shot is fired, it's not going to stop
in midair. Because all action potentials are equally strong and because, once fired, they will
reach the synapse, action potentials are said to fire in an **all-or-none fashion**.

The Refractory Period

As the action potential travels down the axon, the inside of the axon becomes more and
more positive as Na⁺ floods into the neuron. Consequently, the potential difference inside
the cell reverses, becoming more positive. At the same time, the outside of the cell becomes

ions charged particles that play an
important role in the firing of action
potentials in the nervous system

resting potential potential difference
that exists in the neuron when it is resting
(approximately −70 mv in mammals)

threshold of excitation potential
difference at which a neuron will fire an
action potential (−55 mv in mammals)

action potential neural impulse fired
by a neuron when it reaches −55 mv

all-or-none fashion all action
potentials are equal in strength; once a
neuron begins to fire an action potential,
it fires all the way down the axon

more negative because much of the available Na$^+$ enters the neuron through the ion channels. This change in the charges inside and outside the neuron will eventually reverse the flow of Na$^+$. As the outside of the cell becomes more negative than the inside, sodium will no longer be allowed into the cell. Furthermore, positive potassium ions (K$^+$) will be pumped out of the cell until the resting potential (-70 mv) is restored ($\bullet$ FIGURE 2.5b). This resetting of the resting potential is analogous to cocking a gun after it has been fired; it enables the neuron to fire future action potentials. After a neuron fires an action potential, it enters a brief **refractory period** while the resting potential is being restored. During this time, it cannot fire another action potential. Because of the refractory period, there is a limit to how fast neurons can fire. Nonetheless, our neurons are easily able to fire hundreds of action potentials per second—which is all the speed we need to function.

So far, we've looked at how a neural signal travels down the axon, but what happens when the action potential hits the axon bulb at the end of the axon? How does the signal get across the synapse?

How Do Signals Jump the Synapse?

When the action potential reaches the axon bulb of the presynaptic (sending) neuron, it causes the vesicles in the axon bulb to open and dump the neurotransmitters they contain into the synapse. The neurotransmitter molecules float in the fluid-filled synapse ($\bullet$ FIGURE 2.6). Some of them will quickly drift across the synapse and come into contact with the tulip-shaped receptor sites lined up on the dendrites of the postsynaptic (receiving) neuron.

Each type of neurotransmitter has a specific molecular shape, and each type of receptor site has a specific configuration. Only certain types of neurotransmitters open specific receptor sites. Just as you must have the correct key to open a lock, a particular receptor site will only be activated by a specific neurotransmitter. When a neurotransmitter finds the correct receptor site on the postsynaptic neuron, it *binds* with the receptor site and causes a change in the electrical potential inside the postsynaptic neuron (Figure 2.6).

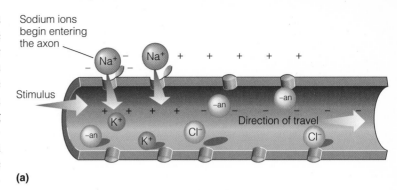

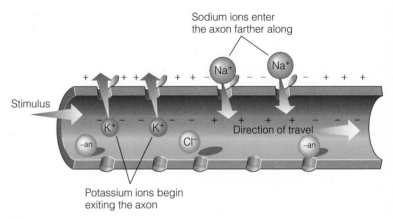

Sodium ions begin entering the axon

Stimulus

Direction of travel

(a)

Sodium ions enter the axon farther along

Stimulus

Direction of travel

Potassium ions begin exiting the axon

(b)

FIGURE 2.5

$\bullet$ **Action Potential**   The action potential shown here (a) occurs all the way down the axon and is how we send neural signals in our nervous system. As the action potential travels down the axon (b), the sodium channels close and potassium (K$^+$) channels open, allowing potassium to leave the cell. As the K$^+$ leaves the cell, the inside of the cell becomes more negative. Potassium will continue to leave the cell until the neuron has returned to its resting potential. *Source: Modified from Starr & Taggart (1989).*

refractory period   brief period after a neuron has fired an action potential in which the neuron is inhibited and unlikely to fire another action potential

Just as one must cock a gun again after firing, neurons must return to their resting potential before they can send more action potentials. The brief period of time it takes for the neuron to return to its resting potential is known as the refractory period.

Just as we must use the correct key to open a lock, a neuron can only be stimulated when the correct neurotransmitter binds with its receptor sites.

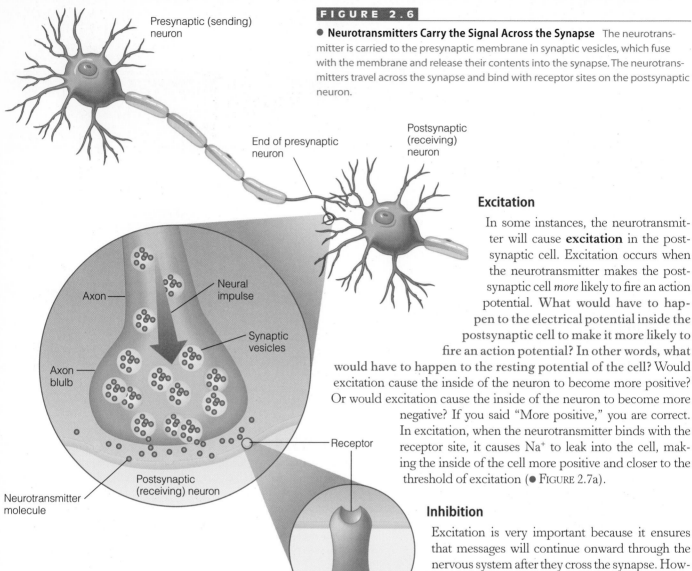

FIGURE 2.6

● **Neurotransmitters Carry the Signal Across the Synapse** The neurotransmitter is carried to the presynaptic membrane in synaptic vesicles, which fuse with the membrane and release their contents into the synapse. The neurotransmitters travel across the synapse and bind with receptor sites on the postsynaptic neuron.

Labels: Presynaptic (sending) neuron; End of presynaptic neuron; Postsynaptic (receiving) neuron; Axon; Neural impulse; Synaptic vesicles; Axon blulb; Postsynaptic (receiving) neuron; Neurotransmitter molecule; Receptor

Excitation

In some instances, the neurotransmitter will cause **excitation** in the postsynaptic cell. Excitation occurs when the neurotransmitter makes the postsynaptic cell *more* likely to fire an action potential. What would have to happen to the electrical potential inside the postsynaptic cell to make it more likely to fire an action potential? In other words, what would have to happen to the resting potential of the cell? Would excitation cause the inside of the neuron to become more positive? Or would excitation cause the inside of the neuron to become more negative? If you said "More positive," you are correct. In excitation, when the neurotransmitter binds with the receptor site, it causes Na⁺ to leak into the cell, making the inside of the cell more positive and closer to the threshold of excitation (● FIGURE 2.7a).

Inhibition

Excitation is very important because it ensures that messages will continue onward through the nervous system after they cross the synapse. However, sometimes we need to stop the message from continuing onward (for example, to relax a tensed muscle). This process is called **inhibition**. Inhibition occurs when the neurotransmitter makes the postsynaptic cell *less* likely to fire an action potential. As you may have guessed, inhibition causes the inside of the postsynaptic cell to become more negative. Generally, inhibitory neurotransmitters cause chloride (Cl^-) to *enter* the postsynaptic neuron or potassium (K^+) to *leave* the postsynaptic neuron. The net effect is to make the postsynaptic cell less likely to fire by making the inside of the cell more negative (● FIGURE 2.7b).

Recall how we began our discussion of action potentials with the incoming signals at the dendrites of a cell. Inhibition and excitation at the synapse are where those signals originate. Inhibition at the synapse produces negative (−) signals that inhibit the postsynaptic cell's ability to fire an action potential. Excitation produces positive (+) signals that facilitate the postsynaptic cell's ability to fire an action potential.

How Do Excitation and Inhibition Interact?

Because of the complexity of the brain, a single postsynaptic cell can simultaneously receive excitatory (+) and inhibitory (−) signals from a great number of presynaptic neurons. So, how does the postsynaptic cell know whether or not to fire an action potential and send the signal down the line? All the incoming signals converge on the axon, which acts like an adding machine, summing up the excitatory (+) and inhibitory (−) signals. Only when the sum

excitation when a neurotransmitter binds with the postsynaptic cell and makes it more likely to fire an action potential

inhibition when a neurotransmitter binds with the postsynaptic cell and makes it less likely to fire an action potential

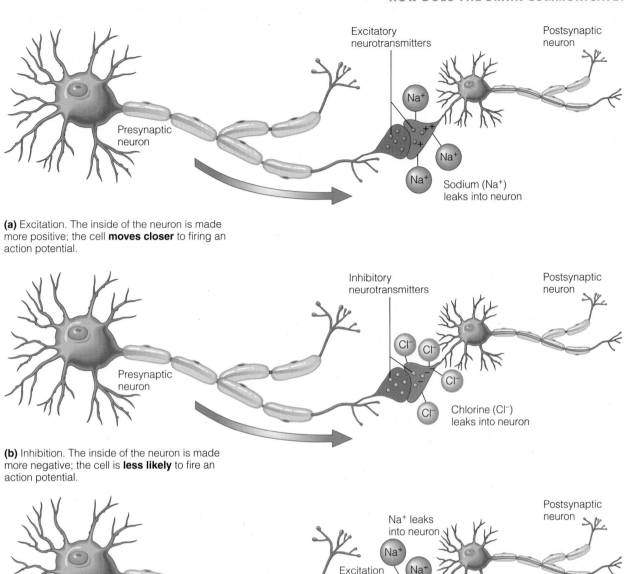

(a) Excitation. The inside of the neuron is made more positive; the cell **moves closer** to firing an action potential.

(b) Inhibition. The inside of the neuron is made more negative; the cell is **less likely** to fire an action potential.

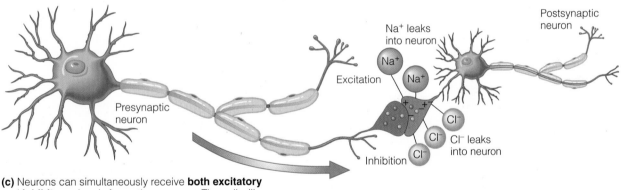

(c) Neurons can simultaneously receive **both excitatory** and **inhibitory** signals from other neurons. The cell will fire an action potential only if it reaches threshold.

FIGURE 2.7

● **Excitation and Inhibition in the Synapse** Excitatory neurotransmitters cause sodium (Na^+) to enter the postsynaptic cell (a), making it more positive on the inside and bringing it closer to firing an action potential. Inhibitory neurotransmitters cause chloride (Cl^-) to enter (or potassium, K^+, to leave) (b), making the cell more negative on the inside and moving it farther away from firing an action potential. A neuron can simultaneously receive both excitatory and inhibitory signals from other neurons (c), but it will fire an action potential only if it reaches threshold at −55 mv. *From Gaudin and Jones,* Human Anatomy and Physiology, *Fig. 11.3a, p. 263. Reprinted by permission of the author.*

of the signals moves the resting potential at the axon to threshold (−55 mv) will the neuron fire an action potential. If the threshold is not reached, the signal simply does not go any farther at this time. The axon will continue to sum up the incoming signals until the threshold mark is reached and only then will the neuron fire an action potential (● FIGURE 2.7c).

The function of excitation in the nervous system is pretty clear. Excitation starts actions in the nervous system. But why do we need inhibition in the nervous system? Simply put, inhibition is required to slow down and shut off certain processes in the nervous system. Many processes in the body require both excitation and inhibition. For example, bending your arm to touch your shoulder requires contraction (excitation) of the bicep muscles and relaxation (inhibition) of the tricep muscles on the backside of the arm.

Cleaning Up the Synapse: Reuptake

When neurotransmitters cross the synapse to bind with postsynaptic receptor sites, not all of these floating neurotransmitters will find available receptors to bind with. **What happens to the unused neurotransmitters left in the synapse?** Unused neurotransmitters are recycled and returned to the vesicles of the presynaptic neuron by a process called **reuptake**. Reuptake accomplishes two goals. First, it resupplies the vesicles with neurotransmitters so that the next signal sent by the presynaptic neuron can also jump the synapse. Second, reuptake clears the synapse of the unused neurotransmitters, thereby ensuring that just the right amount of excitation or inhibition occurs in the postsynaptic neuron.

When neurotransmitters bind with receptor sites, they cause either excitation or inhibition. Afterward, the molecules either dislodge from the receptor site or are broken down by specialized chemicals called *enzymes*. These used neurotransmitters, or the pieces of them, are then taken up by the presynaptic neuron and recycled. If reuptake did not occur, once the receptor sites were cleared out, other unattached neurotransmitters in the synapse would bind with the sites, causing further excitation or inhibition. This duplication of signals could cause confusion or dysfunction in the nervous system. Therefore, reuptake is essential to healthy functioning of our brain and nervous system.

Later in this chapter, you will see that some beneficial drugs act on the body by altering this process of reuptake. In fact, most drugs have their effect in the body at the synapse. We look more closely at how drugs act at the synapse in Chapter 4. For now, let's turn our attention to the types of neurotransmitters and their basic influence on behavior.

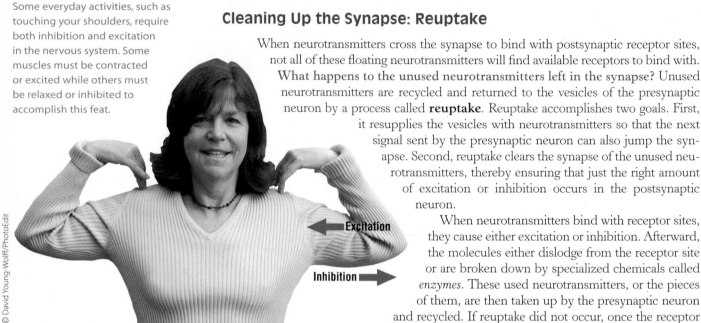

Some everyday activities, such as touching your shoulders, require both inhibition and excitation in the nervous system. Some muscles must be contracted or excited while others must be relaxed or inhibited to accomplish this feat.

© David Young-Wolff/PhotoEdit

reuptake process by which unused neurotransmitters are recycled back into the vesicles

Let's
REVIEW In this section, we described the structure and function of the neurons in the nervous system. For a quick check of your understanding, try answering the following questions at increasing levels of difficulty.

1. Which of the following chemicals enters the axon of the neuron as it begins to fire an action potential?

    a. potassium (K^+)
    b. sodium (Na^+)

    c. chloride (Cl^-)
    d. dopamine

2. Inside the neuron, excitation is to _____ as inhibition is to _____.

    a. increasing positivity; decreasing negativity
    b. increasing negativity; decreasing positivity

    c. increasing positivity; increasing negativity
    d. decreasing positivity; decreasing negativity

3. Suki takes a drug that causes potassium ions to leave her neurons. This drug is likely to produce what type of effect on her neurons?

    a. increased firing
    b. excitation

    c. inhibition
    d. both excitation and inhibition

ANSWERS 1. b; 2. c; 3. c

HOW DO NEUROTRANSMITTERS, THE BRAIN'S CHEMICAL MESSENGERS, WORK?

Well over 100 different chemical compounds have been identified as neurotransmitters (Morrow, Roffman, Wolf, & Coyle, 2008), and researchers continue to investigate more substances that may affect neural signaling. For example, some forms of the sex hormone *estrogen* that regulate certain aspects of reproduction in the body have recently been shown to also behave like neurotransmitters in the brain (Balthazart & Ball, 2006). A complete review of all known neurotransmitters is well beyond the scope of this text, but we will look at the ones that most influence our moods and behavior.

The First Neurotransmitter: Acetylcholine

Acetylcholine (ACh) was the first neurotransmitter discovered. Like many neurotransmitters, ACh is found at both excitatory and inhibitory synapses. In the early part of the 20th century, ACh was found to inhibit the action of the heart and to excite skeletal muscles. Today, ACh is thought to play a role in our awareness or consciousness and to have a role in memory (E. Perry, Walker, Grace, & Perry, 1999). This hypothesized role in memory originated in the discovery that during the course of their disease, people with Alzheimer's have loss of functioning in neurons that release ACh into their synapses (Martorana et al., 2009). Because Alzheimer's disease is associated with extreme dysfunction of memory and loss of ACh action in the brain, it appears that ACh may help the brain store or process memory or do both. Subsequent animal research continues to support and clarify ACh's role in memory. For example, mice with genetically low ACh action in the brain have been shown to have specific deficits in motor skill learning and object recognition memory (de Castro et al., 2009).

Because memory problems are associated with low ACh activity in the brain, drugs that are used to treat Alzheimer's disease often work to increase ACh functioning in the brain and temporarily improve memory function (Colombres, Sagal, & Inestrosa, 2004). However, these drugs do not stop the progression of this fatal disease. Before moving on, try this demonstration on therapeutic drugs.

TRY THIS DEMONSTRATION

Do an online search using the keywords "Aricept" and "prescribing information" to find the information that doctors use to determine whether to prescribe a drug. Aricept is used to treat the symptoms of Alzheimer's disease. How does Aricept affect the synapses of the brain? Does it affect acetylcholine? What warnings and contraindications are there for Aricept? You can also find prescribing information for other drugs in this manner. For example, try searching for Cymbalta, Strattera, Paxil, or Haldol.

Parkinson's Disease and Schizophrenia: Dopamine

Dopamine is primarily inhibitory in the brain, but like most neurotransmitters it is also known to be excitatory. Dopamine appears to influence several processes, including movement, learning, and attention. Dopamine may also play an important role in motivation by making some activities such as sex and eating very pleasurable or rewarding for us. The reward produced by dopamine may even play a role in the development of certain types of substance abuse (Nestler & Carlezon, 2006; H. D. Schmidt & Pierce, 2006). We discuss substance abuse more fully in Chapter 4.

Parkinson's disease is associated with the loss of neurons in an area of the brain richest in dopamine. Drugs used to treat Parkinsonian symptoms work to indirectly increase the amount of dopamine in the brain. Care must be used in administering such drugs, though, because too much dopamine in the brain produces some very troubling symptoms—in particular, symptoms similar to those of schizophrenia.

acetylcholine (ACh) neurotransmitter related to muscle movement and perhaps consciousness, learning, and memory

dopamine neurotransmitter that plays a role in movement, learning, and attention

Actor Michael J. Fox has Parkinson's disease, a degenerative disease that results in decreased dopamine action in the brain, which causes tremors and other neurological symptoms. Former boxer Mohammed Ali likely has Parkinsonianism, a related condition resulting from repeated brain injury.

Schizophrenia is a serious psychiatric disorder (see Chapter 14). People with schizophrenia are unable to think clearly and are often troubled by hallucinations and delusions. Drugs used to treat schizophrenia block the action of dopamine at the synapse. Regulating brain chemistry is not simple. As you might imagine, prolonged use of dopamine-blocking drugs can cause Parkinsonian-like side effects. Think about it. Too little dopamine and one has Parkinsonian symptoms; too much dopamine and the result is schizophrenic symptoms. It appears that healthy functioning requires just the right amount of dopamine in the brain.

Playing a Part in Depression: Serotonin and Norepinephrine

Serotonin is thought to play a role in many different behaviors, including sleep, arousal, mood, eating, and pain perception. It is primarily an inhibitory neurotransmitter and has received a great deal of media attention during the last 20 years. Since the discovery of serotonin in the 1940s, an understanding of its function has become increasingly important to the understanding of human behavior and mental disorders.

A lack of serotonin in the brain has been linked to several mental and behavioral disorders. Drugs that increase the action of serotonin at the synapse by preventing its reuptake are called *selective serotonin reuptake inhibitors* (SSRIs). Prozac and other SSRIs have been used to successfully treat depression, eating disorders, compulsive behavior, and pain. However, not all drugs that act on serotonin are therapeutic. The illegal drug MDMA, or Ecstasy, may actually reduce serotonin action in the brain (Xie et al., 2006). This loss of serotonin action may account for reports of depression following Ecstasy highs in some users. We will discuss MDMA and other drugs more in Chapter 4.

By inhibiting the reuptake of serotonin, Zoloft increases the amount of serotonin activity in the synapse, which may reduce depressive symptoms in some patients and allow them to once again enjoy the pleasurable moments of their lives.

Norepinephrine (NOR) is also primarily inhibitory. It is thought to play a role in regulating sleep, arousal, and mood. Some drugs that alleviate depression have an effect on NOR as well as on serotonin. For example, the antidepressant Cymbalta alleviates depression by selectively inhibiting the reuptake of both serotonin and norepinephrine. NOR may also play a role in regulating brain development during childhood (Sanders, Happe, Bylund, & Murrin, 2005) and recovery of functioning after brain injury (Bueno-Nava et al., 2008).

Inhibiting and Exciting the Brain: GABA and Glutamate

Gamma amino butyric acid (GABA) is thought to regulate arousal or our general level of energy and alertness. It is estimated that one third of all synapses and most inhibitory synapses in the brain use GABA as their neurotransmitter. Therefore, it appears that GABA plays an essential role in normal brain function. Loss of GABA in the brain can produce seizures, because without GABA's inhibitory effects, arousal levels become too high. Some anticonvulsant drugs work by lessening the effects of enzymes that destroy GABA molecules (Rowlett, Cook, Duke, & Platt, 2005). GABA may also play a role in mediating anxiety. Rats injected with drugs that increase GABA action in certain parts of the brain demonstrate less anxiety-related behaviors (e.g., Degroot, 2004), and drugs that increase GABA action in the brain are often used to calm and sedate humans. These drugs include tranquilizers (such as Valium) and alcohol. We will discuss treatment of anxiety again in Chapter 15.

Whereas GABA is the chief inhibitory neurotransmitter, **glutamate** is the chief excitatory neurotransmitter in the brain. More than 50% of all synapses in the brain use glutamate as a neurotransmitter, and without it many brain processes would not take place. Ironically, glutamate can also be a deadly force in the brain. When diseases, such as Alzheimer's disease, affect glutamate-bearing neurons, glutamate molecules may be released in abnormally large quantities. Large amounts of extracellular glutamate can cause brain cell death as the neurons literally become excited to death when the glutamate causes them to fire a frenzy of action potentials (Bossy-Wetzel, Schwarzenbacher, & Lipton, 2004). It appears that in the brain too much excitation is a very bad thing.

On the other hand, not having enough glutamate action in the brain is also associated with problems. For example, low activity in a certain type of glutamate receptor, called the NMDA receptor, is associated with some of the symptoms of schizophrenia (Coyle, Tsai, & Goff, 2003).

Pain in the Brain: Endorphins and Substance P

Have you ever heard the term *endorphin*? If you have, what was the context? Many people's first exposure to endorphins is in the context of exercise or physical injuries. **Endorphins** are neurotransmitters that are chemically very similar to the class of narcotic drugs called *opiates* (such as opium, heroin, morphine, and codeine). Endorphins are released in the central nervous system during times of stress, such as physical exertion or physical injury, to protect us from pain. Endorphins work by blocking the action of another neurotransmitter, *substance P*, which carries pain messages in the central nervous system. When endorphins are released, we feel less pain and a mild sense of euphoria. This is the "runner's high" that long-distance runners often report experiencing. Some evidence even suggests that substance P may play a role in carrying signals of "emotional pain," and drugs that reduce substance P activity in the brain are currently being investigated as potential antidepressants (Rakofsky, Holtzheimer, & Nemeroff, 2009). In addition to their role as painkillers, endorphins may play a role in regulating eating behavior and cardiovascular functioning.

In summary, communication in the nervous system is complex. Action potentials release neurotransmitters that carry the signal across the synapse to other neurons. In turn, these receiving neurons are either excited or inhibited. Our next step is to take a look at how this neural signaling fits into the structure of the nervous system. Before moving on, take a moment to look at ● THE BIG PICTURE REVIEW for a recap of the types of neurotransmitters and their functions.

Stockbyte/Getty Images

Exercise can lead to the release of endorphins, producing feelings of pleasure and well-being that are sometimes called a "runner's high."

serotonin neurotransmitter that plays a role in many different behaviors, including sleep, arousal, mood, eating, and pain perception

norepinephrine (NOR) neurotransmitter that plays a role in regulating sleep, arousal, and mood

gamma amino butyric acid (GABA) the body's chief inhibitory neurotransmitter, which plays a role in regulating arousal

glutamate the chief excitatory neurotransmitter in the brain, found at more than 50% of the synapses in the brain

endorphins neurotransmitters that act as a natural painkiller

THE BIG PICTURE review

Some Neurotransmitters, Their Functions, and Related Diseases and Clinical Conditions

NEUROTRANSMITTER	FUNCTIONS	RELATED DISEASES AND CLINICAL CONDITIONS
Acetylcholine	Excites skeletal muscles; inhibits heart action; memory	Alzheimer's disease
Dopamine	Movement; learning; attention; motivation and reward	Parkinson's disease; schizophrenia; substance abuse
Serotonin	Sleep; arousal; mood; eating; pain perception	Depression; obsessive compulsive disorder; some eating disorders; chronic pain
Norepinephrine	Sleep; arousal; mood	Depression
GABA	Chief inhibitor; regulates arousal	Some anxiety disorders; some seizure disorders
Glutamate	Chief excitatory neurotransmitter; many diverse functions	Neural death following head injuries and disease; schizophrenia
Endorphins	Suppression of pain; eating; cardiovascular functioning	Some indication of link to mood
Substance P	Carries pain signals	Linked to depression

Let's REVIEW

In this section, we described some of the major neurotransmitters and the roles they may play in our functioning. For a quick check of your understanding, try answering the following questions at increasing levels of difficulty.

1. Depression is associated with low levels of which neurotransmitter?

a. dopamine

b. serotonin

c. glutamate

d. acetylcholine (ACh)

2. _____ is thought to be the most important neurotransmitter in the brain because it is the _____ neurotransmitter.

a. Glutamate; most common

b. GABA; most common

c. Glutamate; strongest

d. GABA; rarest

3. Sasha has been drinking an herbal tea that she believes boosts her body's ability to manufacture acetylcholine. Why do you suppose Sasha is so interested in drinking this tea?

a. She is trying to improve her memory.

b. She is trying to treat her depression.

c. She is hoping it will help her have more energy.

d. She is hoping it will help her sleep better.

ANSWERS 1. b; 2. a; 3. a

IS THE NERVOUS SYSTEM A SINGLE SYSTEM?

Our **nervous system** is the vast, interconnected network of all the neurons in our body. Every single facet of our body's functioning and our behavior is monitored and influenced by the nervous system. The nervous system is arranged in a series of interconnected subsystems, each with its own specialized tasks. Because the brain acts as the command center of our nervous system, the brain, along with the spinal cord, is traditionally viewed as a separate subdivision of the nervous system called the **central nervous system (CNS)**. All other components of the nervous system are referred to collectively as the **peripheral nervous system (PNS)** (● FIGURE 2.8). We discuss the CNS in detail later in this chapter when we examine the brain. First, however, let's take a look at the parts of the PNS.

Messages From the Body: The Peripheral Nervous System

The functions of the PNS are twofold. First, the PNS must ensure that the CNS is informed about what is happening inside and outside our body. To this end, the PNS is equipped with **sensory (afferent) neurons** that convey information to the CNS from the outside world, such as sights and sounds, as well as information from our internal world, such as aches and pains. Second, the PNS acts out the directives of the CNS. The PNS is equipped with **motor (efferent) neurons** that carry signals from the CNS to our muscles. For example, when you see a juicy apple, the sensory neurons of your eye send this information upward to the part of the brain that processes visual information. Here the brain recognizes the apple, and you decide to eat the apple. The brain then sends signals downward to the motor neurons of your hand and arm, which, in turn, direct you to reach out and grasp the apple with your hand (● FIGURE 2.9). In this fashion, the sensory pathways send sensory information *to* the spinal cord and brain, and the motor pathways carry "orders" *away* from the brain and spinal cord to the rest of the body.

Traditionally, psychologists and physiologists have further subdivided the neurons of the PNS into two subsystems: the *somatic nervous system* and the *autonomic nervous system* (Purves et al., 1997).

LEARNING
OBJECTIVE

What Should You Know?
● Describe the major parts of the nervous system and what types of information they process.

nervous system an electrochemical system of communication within the body that uses cells called neurons to convey information

central nervous system (CNS) the brain and the spinal cord

peripheral nervous system (PNS) all of the nervous system except the brain and spinal cord

sensory (afferent) neurons neurons that transmit information from the sense organs to the central nervous system

motor (efferent) neurons neurons that transmit commands from the brain to the muscles of the body

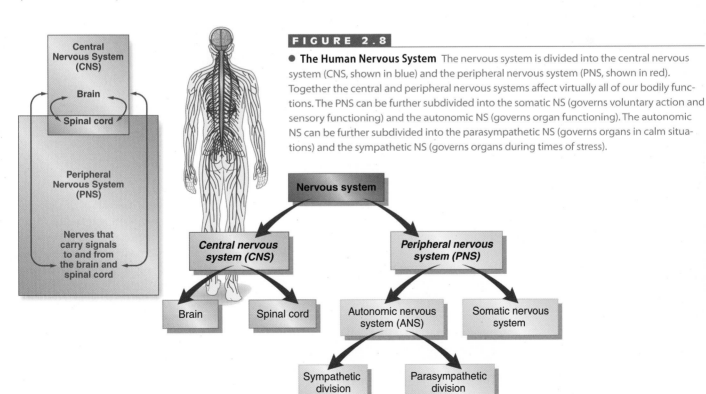

FIGURE 2.8

● **The Human Nervous System** The nervous system is divided into the central nervous system (CNS, shown in blue) and the peripheral nervous system (PNS, shown in red). Together the central and peripheral nervous systems affect virtually all of our bodily functions. The PNS can be further subdivided into the somatic NS (governs voluntary action and sensory functioning) and the autonomic NS (governs organ functioning). The autonomic NS can be further subdivided into the parasympathetic NS (governs organs in calm situations) and the sympathetic NS (governs organs during times of stress).

FIGURE 2.9

● **Sensory and Motor Pathways**

Reaching for an apple involves both afferent sensory pathways (shown in red), efferent motor pathways (shown in blue), and interneuron pathways (shown in green).

Interneurons process information within the brain

Sensory pathways carry visual information **to** the brain

Visual sensory information travels to the eye

Motor pathways carry information **away** from the brain

Courtesy of William L. Breneman

Reaching Out: The Somatic Nervous System

The **somatic nervous system** includes those neurons that control the skeletal muscles of the body (*soma* is Greek for "body") and is therefore largely concerned with voluntary actions. Reaching for an apple is an example of a voluntary action that involves the somatic division of the PNS. The CNS made the decision to reach for the apple, and then this "order" was sent downward, across the motor neurons of the somatic nervous system that control the muscles of the arm. The arm muscles then react to the orders from the CNS, and you reach for the apple. The functioning of the somatic nervous system enables us to control our bodies in a deliberate and flexible manner.

Although controlling body movements is important, it is equally advantageous to have some processes in the body frequently controlled automatically and involuntarily. **What processes in your body do you have little conscious control over?** Did you think of heart rate, digestive function, and breathing? These are some of the processes that are controlled by the autonomic division of the PNS.

Looking Inside: Organ Function and the Autonomic Nervous System

The neurons of the **autonomic nervous system** control the smooth muscles of the internal organs, the muscles of the heart, and the glands. By automatically regulating organ functions, the autonomic nervous system frees up our conscious resources and enables us to respond quickly and efficiently to the demands placed on us by the environment. Imagine how hard life would be if you had to remember to breathe, tell your heart to beat, and remind your liver to do its job! You would have little energy and attention left for thinking and learning, let alone responding quickly to threatening situations. Thankfully, we have the autonomic nervous system—composed of the *sympathetic* and *parasympathetic* divisions—to regulate our organ functions, and it is equipped with separate divisions to help us survive in an ever-changing and sometimes dangerous world.

The Sympathetic Nervous System

In threatening situations, we must react—fast—to save ourselves. To help us react quickly, the **sympathetic** division of the autonomic nervous system takes over primary regulation of our

somatic nervous system branch of the peripheral nervous system that governs sensory and voluntary motor action in the body

autonomic nervous system branch of the peripheral nervous system that primarily governs involuntary organ functioning and actions in the body

sympathetic nervous system branch of the autonomic nervous system most active during times of danger or stress

TABLE 2.1

● **Functions of the Sympathetic and Parasympathetic Systems**

The sympathetic and parasympathetic divisions of the autonomic nervous system have different effects on the organs of the body.

© Science Photo Library/Alamy

Wave RF/PhotoLibrary

SYMPATHETIC		PARASYMPATHETIC
Dilates pupils, inhibits tears	**Eyes**	Contracts pupil, stimulates tears
Inhibits salivation (dry mouth)	**Salivary glands**	Activates salivation
Dilates bronchi, increases respiration	**Lungs**	Constricts bronchi, calms respiration
Accelerates heart rate	**Heart**	Slows heart rate
Goose bumps; activates sweat glands	**Skin, sweat glands**	No goose bumps; inhibits sweat glands
Inhibits activity	**Stomach, intestines, pancreas, gallbladder**	Stimulates activity
Stimulates glucose release	**Liver**	Slows glucose release
Releases adrenalin	**Adrenal gland**	Stops releasing adrenalin
Contracts blood vessels	**Blood vessels of internal organs**	Dilates blood vessels
Relaxes bladder; inhibits elimination	**Bladder, bowels**	Constricts bladder; stimulates elimination
Promotes ejaculation and vaginal contractions	**Genitals**	Stimulates genitals

organ functions during times of stress. The sympathetic nervous system evolved to protect us from danger. When it is activated, heart rate increases, breathing becomes more rapid, blood pressure increases, digestion slows, muscle tissue becomes engorged with blood, the pupils dilate, and the hair on the back of the neck stands up (as in a cat confronted by a strange dog). All these changes help to prepare us (and the cat) to defend our body from threat. For this reason, the actions of the sympathetic nervous system are often referred to as the *fight or flight* response (see ● TABLE 2.1). The increased cardiovascular activity quickly pumps oxygenated blood away from internal organs and to the muscles of the arms and legs so that the animal or person can swiftly attack, defend itself, or run away. Because the sympathetic nervous system plays an important role in our response to stress, it also plays an important role in our health. We explore this connection in Chapter 12.

The Parasympathetic Nervous System

Once the danger has passed, the **parasympathetic** division of the autonomic nervous system takes control of our organ function, and heart rate, respiration, blood pressure, and pupil dilation return to normal (see Table 2.1). In general, the parasympathetic nervous system operates when we are calm and relaxed. As you read this page, it is very likely (unless you find psychology terrifying) that your parasympathetic nervous system is primarily responsible for regulating the functions of your internal organs. When the parasympathetic nervous system is active, heart rate, blood pressure, and respiration are kept at normal levels. Under parasympathetic control, blood is circulated to the digestive tract and other internal organs so that they can function properly, and your pupils are not overly dilated. Your body is calm, and everything is running smoothly.

parasympathetic nervous system
branch of the autonomic nervous system most active during times of normal functioning

Let's REVIEW

Let's REVIEW In this section, we described the structure of the nervous system, including the central and peripheral nervous systems. For a quick check of your understanding, try answering the following questions at increasing levels of difficulty.

1. Which branch of the autonomic nervous system is most active when we are relaxed?

   a. parasympathetic   c. endocrine

   b. sympathetic   d. spinal

2. The sensory neurons are to the _____ nervous system as brain cells are to the _____ nervous system.

   a. central; peripheral   c. autonomic; somatic

   b. peripheral; central   d. somatic; autonomic

3. An increased risk of heart disease would most likely correlate with overuse of which of the following branches of the nervous system?

   a. somatic nervous system   c. sympathetic nervous system

   b. autonomic nervous system   d. parasympathetic nervous system

ANSWERS 1. a; 2. b; 3. c

What Should You Know?

● Be able to locate the hindbrain, midbrain, and forebrain, list their parts, and explain what they do.

hindbrain primitive part of the brain that comprises the medulla, pons, and cerebellum

medulla part of the hindbrain that controls basic, life-sustaining functions such as respiration, heart rate, and blood pressure

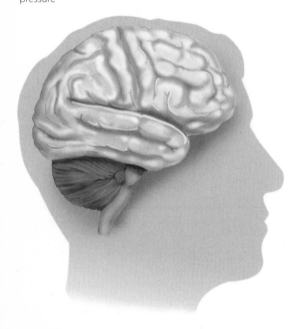

HOW IS THE BRAIN ORGANIZED?

Brain tissue is composed largely of neurons and glial cells. These cells form the brain structures that control our physiological and psychological functioning. The brain is organized into systems of structures that control specific functions, such as emotion, memory, movement, and so on. We'll begin our discussion with the *hindbrain*, where some of our most basic bodily functions are controlled. Next, we'll examine the *midbrain*, before concluding with a discussion of the *forebrain*, where some of our most humanlike and sophisticated abilities are controlled.

The Hindbrain

The **hindbrain** sits directly above the spinal cord and is named for its position at the bottom of the brain (● FIGURE 2.10). The hindbrain is the most "primitive" part of the brain, involved in the most basic life-sustaining functions, such as respiration and heartbeat. The term *brainstem* refers to a series of brain structures that are essential for life. The hindbrain makes up a good portion of the brainstem.

   The hindbrain consists of three structures: the *medulla*, the *pons*, and the *cerebellum*. The most crucial parts of the hindbrain are the medulla and the pons. The **medulla** sits at the top of the spinal column at the point where the spinal cord enters the base of the skull (● FIGURE 2.11). The medulla regulates heartbeat and respiration, and even minor damage to the medulla can result in death from heart or respiratory failure (e.g., Hershman, Halberthal, Goldsher, Golz, & Bar-Joseph, 2009). It also plays a role in sneezing, coughing, vomiting, swallowing, and digestion.

FIGURE 2.10

● **The Human Hindbrain, Midbrain, and Forebrain** The human hindbrain (shown in blue) governs basic and life-sustaining functions. The midbrain (shown in red) connects the lower structures of the hindbrain with the higher structures of the forebrain. The forebrain (shown in gold) governs complex processes such as cognition, sensory processing, and the planning and execution of behaviors.

FIGURE 2.11

● **The Brain and Its Structures** This figure shows the cortex and the subcortical structures of the brain.

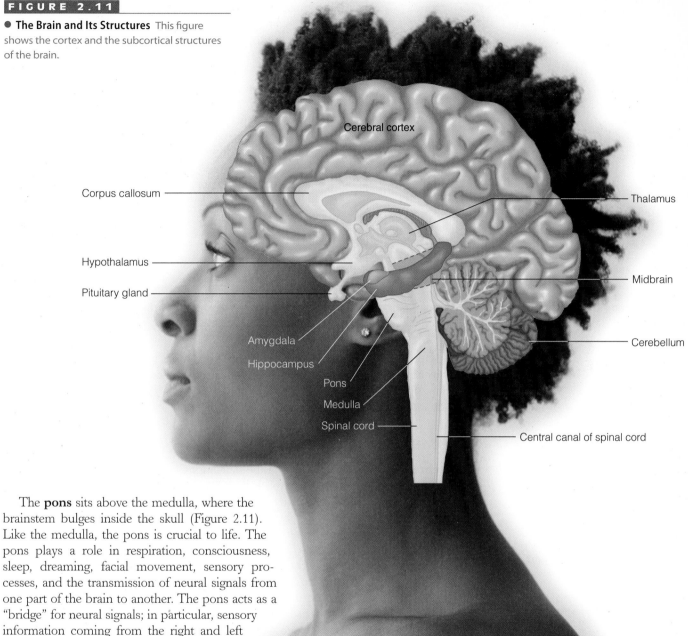

Cerebral cortex

Corpus callosum

Thalamus

Hypothalamus

Midbrain

Pituitary gland

Amygdala

Hippocampus

Pons

Medulla

Spinal cord

Cerebellum

Central canal of spinal cord

The **pons** sits above the medulla, where the brainstem bulges inside the skull (Figure 2.11). Like the medulla, the pons is crucial to life. The pons plays a role in respiration, consciousness, sleep, dreaming, facial movement, sensory processes, and the transmission of neural signals from one part of the brain to another. The pons acts as a "bridge" for neural signals; in particular, sensory information coming from the right and left sides of the body crosses through the pons before moving on to other parts of the brain. If the pons becomes damaged, the "bridge" is out, and serious impairments result. The pons was probably damaged when Jean-Dominique Bauby had his stroke. Cases of locked-in syndrome like Bauby's are most often associated with damage in the ventral (facing the throat) regions of the pons (Luxenberg, Goldenberg, Frank, Loch Macdonald, & Rosengart, 2009; Gallo & Fontanarosa, 1989; Virgile, 1984).

The final part of the hindbrain is the **cerebellum**. The cerebellum is the large, deeply grooved structure at the base of the brain (Figure 2.11). Although not as crucial to survival as the pons and medulla, the cerebellum is necessary for balance, muscle tone, and motor skills (Seidler et al., 2002). It also plays a critical role in the learning of motor skills (Hikosaka, Nakamura, Sakai, & Nakamura, 2002) and the execution of certain behaviors (B. R. Walker, Diefenbach, & Parikh, 2007). A recent study found that relative to nonplayers, basketball players had structural differences in their cerebellums, suggesting that their extensive practice of the sport may have changed their cerebellar structure (Park et al., 2009). Furthermore, damage to the cerebellum leads to loss of balance and coordination. Alcohol impairs the

pons hindbrain structure that plays a role in respiration, consciousness, sleep, dreaming, facial movement, sensory processes, and the transmission of neural signals from one part of the brain to another

cerebellum hindbrain structure that plays a role in balance, muscle tone, and coordination of motor movements

4x5 Coll-Francisco Cruz/PhotoLibrary

Without the cerebellum we would not be able to accomplish tasks such as learning to ride a bicycle.

midbrain brain structure that connects the hindbrain with the forebrain

reticular formation part of the midbrain that regulates arousal and plays an important role in attention, sleep, and consciousness

forebrain brain structures including the limbic system, thalamus, hypothalamus, and cortex that govern higher-order mental processes

● **The Cerebral Hemispheres** The cerebrum is divided into right and left hemispheres. The outside covering of the hemispheres, the cortex, is where the higher-order processing in the brain takes place.

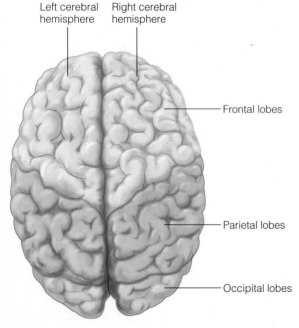

Left cerebral hemisphere   Right cerebral hemisphere

— Frontal lobes

— Parietal lobes

— Occipital lobes

© JLP/Jose Luis Pelaez/zefa/Corbis

functioning of the cerebellum (as well as the functioning of some important forebrain structures), producing the familiar symptoms of staggering, clumsiness, and slowed reaction time. Police officers assess these behaviors when they give motorists a field sobriety test of balance, coordination, and reaction time.

Recently, the traditional view that the cerebellum is involved only in motor functioning has been challenged. There is growing evidence that the cerebellum may also affect cognitive functioning. New studies indicate that damage to the cerebellum can be related to deficits in language, attention, and memory (Baillieux et al., 2009).

The Midbrain

The **midbrain** structures connect the hindbrain with the more sophisticated forebrain. For psychologists, one of the most interesting midbrain structures is the **reticular formation**. The reticular formation, located near the pons, is a network of neurons that extends from the hindbrain region into the midbrain. One function of the reticular formation is to regulate arousal levels (Kinomura, Larsson, Gulyas, & Roland, 1996); as such, the reticular formation plays an important role in attention, sleep, and consciousness (Hudson, 2009; Izac, 2006). The reticular formation functions as a type of "on switch" for the high-level thinking centers of the forebrain. Additionally, the reticular formation appears to play a role in regulating cardiovascular activity, respiratory functioning, and body movement.

The Forebrain

The **forebrain** resides in the top part of the skull and regulates complex mental processes such as thinking and emotional control. It is the largest region of the brain and includes several subsystems that regulate many emotional, motivational, and cognitive processes. Without such a well-developed forebrain, we humans would not have the mental abilities we do: problem solving, thinking, remembering, using language, and so on. Bauby's stroke spared his forebrain, and his "mind" was left intact—recall that he was able to think, feel, and remember. He was even able to write a memoir in his head!

The forebrain contains several groups of structures that function as subsystems. The structures of the **limbic system** and other forebrain structures govern sensory, emotional, and motivational processes. Finally, the wrinkled and folded external surface of the brain, the **cerebral cortex**, governs high-level processes such as cognition and language. In ● FIGURE 2.12 you can see that the forebrain is divided into the right and left **cerebral hemispheres**. For the most part, forebrain structures are duplicated in the right and left hemispheres.

The Limbic System

Do you ever wonder why humans experience emotions? What is the value of feeling angry, afraid, or happy? One possible answer is that emotion helps us survive in a dangerous world. Fear may warn us of danger, and anger may help us fight to protect ourselves. Pleasurable feelings such as happiness and love can bind people together and foster cooperation. In this way, emotion functions as an early warning system, and to some extent it is a motivating force for our behavior. The series of brain structures collectively called the *limbic system* regulates some of our basic emotional reactions. Two limbic structures are located deep in the central region of the brain, above the hindbrain and beneath the cerebral cortex: the *amygdala* and the *hippocampus* (● FIGURE 2.13).

The **amygdala** is an almond-shaped structure located almost directly behind our temples. The amygdala governs the emotions of fear and aggression (Sah, Faber, Lopez De Armentia, & Power, 2003). More specifically, the amygdala may play a role in our memory for frightening events (Ou, Yeh, & Gean, 2009) as well as the way we perceive and respond to emotion-evoking stimuli (Adolphs, 2002; Isenberg et al., 1999). For example, surgical lesions were made in a woman's amygdalae in an attempt to lessen her epileptic seizures. As a result, she lost the ability to perceive the emotional tone of others' voices. She could no longer recognize angry and frightened vocal intonations although she could hear and comprehend spoken words (S. K. Scott, Young, Calder, & Hellawell, 1997). Other studies have found that participants with amygdala damage have a difficult time making accurate judgments about others' mood states by looking at their facial expressions. This is especially true when participants are making judgments about other people's level of fear and anger (Adolphs, Tranel, & Damasio, 1998; R. Graham, Devinsky, & LaBar, 2007).

Recently, researchers have shown that individuals with *autism* or *Asperger's syndrome*, psychological disorders characterized by severe deficits in social behavior, experience abnormal patterns of amygdala activation when perceiving fear in other people's faces (Ashwin, Baron-Cohen, Wheelwright, O'Riordan, & Bullmore, 2007). Studies like these suggest that the amygdala may play an essential role in helping us size up social situations and, in turn, regulating our emotional reactions to these situations.

The **hippocampus** is the other structure of the limbic system that we will describe. Like the amygdalae, hippocampal regions are found in both hemispheres of the brain. The hippocampus is a long, curved structure shaped somewhat like a sea horse (Figure 2.11). The word *hippocampus* comes from the Greek *hippokampos*, which means "sea horse." The hippocampus appears to play a crucial role in the processes of learning and memory.

Much of what we know about the function of the hippocampus is from case studies of people who have suffered damage to the hippocampus. The most famous case of such damage was a young man named H.M. who had severe, uncontrollable epilepsy that did not respond to medication. In a last-ditch effort to reduce the severity of H.M.'s seizures, doctors decided to take the drastic measure of destroying the parts of H.M.'s brain that were producing the seizures, including the hippocampus (Scoville & Milner, 1957). The surgery did reduce H.M.'s seizures, but it also produced some devastating and unexpected side effects. After the surgery, it became apparent that H.M. was suffering from *anterograde amnesia*, the inability to store *new* memories. H.M. could hold information in consciousness the way we briefly hold a phone number in mind while we dial, and his memory for events that occurred prior to the surgery remained intact. But H.M. was unable to form new memories for concepts and events. He would forget conversations seconds after they occurred. He was unable to learn new facts. Oddly, though, H.M. could store new motor skills (for example, he could learn new dance steps), but later he would have no recollection of having ever executed the new skill. H.M.'s misfortune provided scientists an early and unprecedented opportunity to study the role that the hippocampus plays in forming memories.

Many subsequent case studies and controlled animal experiments have supported the hypothesis that the hippocampus is important to learning and memory. For example, researchers used brain-imaging techniques to compare the hippocampi of London taxi drivers to those of London bus drivers. They found that certain areas of the hippocampus were enlarged in the taxi drivers but not in the bus drivers. Furthermore, the number of years a participant had been driving a taxi was positively correlated with the size of certain hippocampal areas. These data suggest that portions of the hippocampus enlarged as the taxi drivers memorized

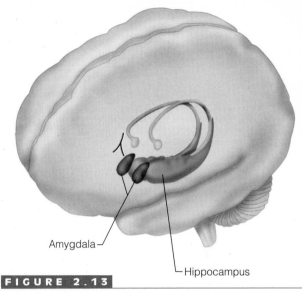

Amygdala

Hippocampus

FIGURE 2.13

● **The Limbic System** Limbic system structures including the amygdala and hippocampus process specific aspects of emotion and memory.

© Jose Luis Pelaez, Inc./Corbis

The amygdala plays a role in emotions such as fear and aggression.

limbic system system of structures including the amygdala and hippocampus that govern certain aspects of emotion, motivation, and memory

cerebral cortex thin, wrinkled outer covering of the brain in which high-level processes such as thinking, planning, language, interpretation of sensory data, and coordination of sensory and motor information take place

cerebral hemispheres right and left sides of the brain that to some degree govern different functions in the body

amygdala part of the limbic system that plays a role in our emotions of fear and aggression

hippocampus part of the brain that plays a role in the transfer of information from short- to long-term memory

complicated maps of the entire city (see ● WHAT'S HAPPENING IN YOUR BRAIN?). For bus drivers, who only had to memorize a small number of bus routes, length of time driving a bus did not correlate with the size of their hippocampi (Maguire, Woollett, & Spiers, 2006).

Recently, researchers compared the hippocampi of medical doctors, who also have to learn vast amounts of information, to people of similar intelligence who were not doctors. They found no difference in the size of the hippocampus between these two groups. It appears that having a larger hippocampus is only associated with performing tasks that specifically involve spatial memory (Woollett, Glensman, & Maguire, 2008).

Keep in mind, however, that this research is merely correlational in nature. For example, from this research alone, it is impossible to tell whether the differences seen in the taxi drivers' hippocampi were directly caused by memorizing the maps or by some other activity. For example, perhaps taxi drivers spend more time talking to passengers than bus drivers do, and this interaction influenced their hippocampal development. This is just one of many possibilities that need further investigation.

A similar debate concerns the relationship between the amount of stress we experience and hippocampal size. Studies have shown that prolonged exposure to certain hormones released during times of stress can damage hippocampal tissue (Sapolsky, 2000a; Tata & Anderson, 2009) and that people who have suffered from prolonged stress (such as combat or childhood abuse) have smaller hippocampi (Sapolsky, 2002). At first glance, the conclusion looked simple—stress shrinks the hippocampus. However, it may not be that simple. Some studies suggest that having a smaller hippocampus to begin with may predispose one to developing posttraumatic stress. For example, combat veterans who suffered from *posttraumatic stress disorder* (*PTSD*) had smaller hippocampi—but so did their identical twin brothers who never faced combat (Gilbertson et al., 2002). Additionally, people with PTSD

WHAT'S HAPPENING IN YOUR BRAIN?

HIPPOCAMPAL SIZE AND MEMORY

These regions of the hippocampus (shown in yellow) were found to be larger in London taxi drivers than the same hippocampal regions of London bus drivers. Furthermore, the size of these regions was positively correlated with the amount of time a cab driver had been driving. These data suggest that these hippocampal regions may increase as a cab driver uses his or her brain to memorize complicated street maps.

Source: Maguire, Woollett, & Spiers (2006).

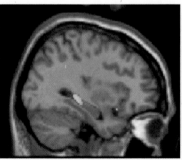

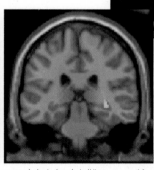

© Peter Turnley/Corbis

London taxi drivers and bus drivers: A structural MRI and neuropsychological analysis. (*Hippocampus*, 16 (12), pp. 1091–1101. Magure, E. A., Woollett, K., & Spiers, H. J. © 2006. Reprinted with permission of Wiley-Liss, Inc., a subsidiary of John Wiley & Sons, Inc.

were found to have smaller hippocampi regardless of whether their PTSD resulted from years of trauma or a single episode of trauma in adulthood. Perhaps having a smaller hippocampus is associated with the tendency to store unusually intense memories of traumatic events (Bonne et al., 2008). Subsequent studies are needed to isolate exactly how stress affects the structure of the hippocampus and how the hippocampus affects our reaction to stress.

The Thalamus and Hypothalamus

Outside the limbic system are two more important forebrain structures, the *thalamus* and the *hypothalamus*. Their names are similar, but the thalamus and the hypothalamus have considerably different functions in the forebrain. The **thalamus** plays a role in the attention we pay to things that stimulate our senses (G. A. Michael, Boucart, Degreef, & Goefroy, 2001) and functions as a relay station for information coming from our senses to the brain (see Chapter 3). Most of the input from our senses first travels to the thalamus before being sent on to the appropriate part of the cortex for further processing.

The thalamus also plays a role in brain functioning during sleep, particularly during *rapid eye movement*, or REM, sleep where much of our dreaming occurs. During REM sleep, the thalamus seems to help keep particular areas of the brain's cortex activated (Miyauchi, Misaki, Kan, Fukunaga, & Koike, 2009; Murillo-Rodriguez, Arias-Carrión, Sanguino-Rodriguez, González-Arias, & Haro, 2009). We will discuss the process of sleep more fully in Chapter 4.

Nestled below the thalamus is the **hypothalamus** (the prefix *hypo* means "below"). The hypothalamus maintains **homeostasis** in the body, a state of internal equilibrium across a variety of bodily systems. In maintaining homeostasis, the hypothalamus is responsible for monitoring and regulating body temperature, thirst, hunger, sleep, autonomic nervous system functioning, and some sexual and reproductive functions, and can change hormone levels in the bloodstream. To maintain homeostasis, the hypothalamus must ultimately motivate us to engage in certain behaviors. For example, when our body needs fuel, the hypothalamus motivates us with hunger. When we need sleep, the hypothalamus makes us sleepy, and we are motivated to go to bed. No other part of the nervous system plays a more central role in physiological motivation. Without the hypothalamus, we would not know when to engage in the behaviors that keep our bodily systems in balance.

The Cortex

The most noticeable structure on the external surface of the brain is the cerebral cortex, or simply the cortex. The cortex is the thin (approximately 2 mm thick), wrinkled layer of tissue that covers the outside of the cerebral hemispheres (● FIGURE 2.14). The cortex is arguably the most sophisticated part of the brain and is responsible for the highest levels of processing—cognition and such mental processes as planning, decision making, perception, and language. It is no coincidence that the human cortex is the most developed of all known creatures and that we humans also have the most highly developed cognitive skills of all known species. Compare the photographs in Figure 2.14. Notice that the human cortex is very folded and convoluted, whereas the cat's brain is much less so. The folds allow for more cortical surface

thalamus part of the forebrain that functions as a sensory relay station in the brain

hypothalamus part of the forebrain that plays a role in maintaining homeostasis in the body involving sleep, body temperature, sexual functions, thirst, and hunger; also the point where the nervous system intersects with the endocrine system

homeostasis an internal state of equilibrium in the body

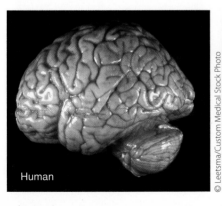
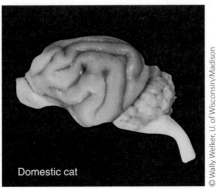

Human

© Leetsma/Custom Medical Stock Photo

Domestic cat

© Wally Welker, U. of Wisconsin/Madison

FIGURE 2.14

● **Cortex of a Human Brain and a Cat Brain** Note how much more convoluted or folded the human brain is compared to the cat brain. Many of the higher-order processes that humans engage in, such as language and thinking, are processed in the cortex.

area within the confines of the skull cavity. A cat has proportionately less cortical area than a human does, and this reduction in cortex translates into fewer cognitive abilities for the cat.

Lateralization and the Lobes of the Cortex

The human cortex is divided into four distinct physical regions called *lobes*. These are the **frontal lobe**, the **parietal lobe**, the **occipital lobe**, and the **temporal lobe** (● FIGURE 2.15a). The lobes of the cortex are structurally symmetrical in both hemispheres of the brain, meaning that the brain has both right and left frontal lobes, right and left temporal lobes, and so on. However, the functions of the right and left lobes are often somewhat different.

So, why isn't the brain a seamless whole? Functions are *lateralized*, or found in only one hemisphere of the brain, for two reasons. One reason is that the lobes of the brain tend to be wired in a *contralateral* fashion, with the right side of the brain governing the left side of the body and the left side of the brain governing the right side of the body. Although contralateral wiring is the norm in the brain, some neural pathways carry information to and from the body to the same hemisphere of the brain.

The Left and Right Hemispheres

Another reason for lateralization is that the right and left hemispheres process somewhat different types of information (Stephan et al., 2003). For example, most people process language largely in the left hemisphere. Although some people have major language centers in the right hemisphere, and some have major language centers in both hemispheres, for the average person language is located in the left hemisphere. As a result, when people suffer major damage to the left hemisphere (as from a stroke), their ability to use language often suffers. Two examples illustrate this *hemispheric specialization* of language.

When people suffer severe damage to **Broca's area** in the left frontal lobe (● FIGURE 2.15b), they are unable to produce understandable speech, a type of condition known as **aphasia** (Geschwind, 1975; Geschwind & Levitsky, 1968). When damage is confined to **Wernicke's area** in the left temporal lobe, the resulting aphasia makes the person unable to understand spoken language. People with damage to this area may also have difficulty pro-

---

frontal lobe cortical area directly behind the forehead that plays a role in thinking, planning, decision making, language, and motor movement

parietal lobe cortical areas on the top sides of the brain that play a role in touch and certain cognitive processes

occipital lobe cortical area at the back of the brain that plays a role in visual processing

temporal lobe cortical areas directly below our ears that play a role in auditory processing and language

Broca's area a region in the left frontal lobe that plays a role in the production of speech

aphasia an impairment of language, most often resulting from brain damage, in which the person may have difficulty producing speech, understanding speech, or both

Wernicke's area a region in the left temporal lobe that plays a role in the comprehension of speech

---

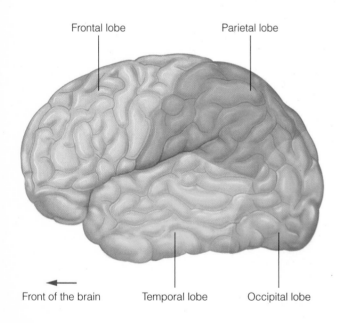

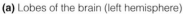

(a) Lobes of the brain (left hemisphere)

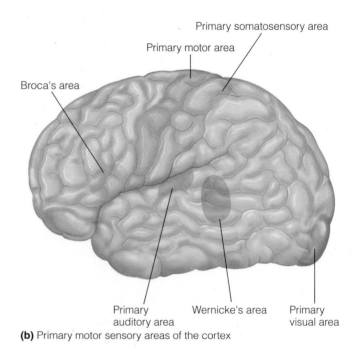

(b) Primary motor sensory areas of the cortex

FIGURE 2.15

● **The Human Brain**   (a) The lobes of the brain. (b) The language centers of the brain are found in the left hemisphere. Wernicke's area in the left temporal lobe allows us to comprehend speech. Broca's area in the left frontal lobe allows us to produce speech. *From Gaudin and Jones,* Human Anatomy and Physiology, *Fig. 12.2, p. 294. Reprinted by permission of the author.*

ducing understandable speech due to their inability to comprehend and monitor their own speech. However, when the damage is confined to the right side of the brain, patients usually remain able to understand and produce speech, but they have some difficulty processing certain types of spatial information (such as judging the distance between two objects). Differences in the linguistic and spatial processing of the left and right hemispheres once led scientists to broadly conclude that the hemispheres of the brain processed very different categories of information: they surmised that the left hemisphere processed verbal information and the right hemisphere processed spatial information.

However, the brain may not divide its functions as neatly as once thought. In fact, the right hemisphere does seem to process certain aspects of language, including such subtleties as the sound of speech, visual details of printed words, unusual uses of words (e.g., calling a man a "cat"), and novel metaphors (Beeman & Chiarello, 1998; Mashal & Faust, 2008). Newer research also indicates that both hemispheres process different aspects of spatial information (Amorapanth, Widick, & Chatterjee, 2009; Chabris & Kosslyn, 1998). To sum up, we are coming to understand that the hemispheres perform complementary functions. Both sides of the brain work together to enable us to fully understand language and visual perception.

The Corpus Callosum

Whether the hemispheres process different information or merely different aspects of the same information, they must have some means of coordinating the information they process. The **corpus callosum** is a dense band of neurons that sits just below the cortex along the midline of the brain (Banich & Heller, 1998; Figure 2.11). This band physically connects the right and left cortical areas and ensures that each hemisphere "knows" what the other hemisphere is doing. The corpus callosum passes information back and forth between the right and left hemispheres, allowing us to integrate these somewhat independent functions. Does this mean that communication between the hemispheres reduces lateralization in the brain?

Sex Differences in the Corpus Callosum and Brain Lateralization

Some studies of gender differences in the brain have suggested that certain areas of the corpus callosum may be larger in women than in men. In particular, the back part of the corpus callosum, an area called the *splenum*, appears to be slightly larger in females than it is in males. However, this size difference is controversial because it is most likely to be found by researchers who adjust their data for the fact that males tend to have larger brains (Driesen & Raz, 1995). In fact, some have suggested that this size difference may have less to do with gender and more to do with brain size itself. In other words, men with small brains may also have large corpora callosa. If this is true, larger corpora callosa may be found in people with smaller brains, regardless of gender (Leonard, 1997).

A clearer picture is seen in another brain structure that allows for communication across the hemispheres. The *anterior commissure* tends to be larger in females, and this size difference is found even when researchers do not correct their data to account for the smaller brain size of females. Similarly, the *massa intermedia*, a structure that connects the two sides of the thalamus, also seems to be larger in women (Allen & Gorski, 1991). It appears that women may have somewhat more connections between the left and right hemispheres of the brain, but what does this imply about behavior? One possibility is that because women have more connections between hemispheres, the functioning of the female brain is less lateralized, or more integrated (Reite et al., 1995). This interpretation is supported by the fact that at least during the performance of spatial and verbal tasks, the pattern of electrical activity in male brains tends to be more confined to one hemisphere than it is in female brains (Koles, Lind, & Flor-Henry, 2009). Nonetheless, others argue that the overall research does not support the idea of anatomical and functional differences in the language centers of male and female brains (see Wallentin, 2009). Or, that increased communication between hemispheres may even increase lateralization in the brain (Kimura, 2000). Although a clear picture of sex differences in the corpus callosum and brain lateralization has not yet emerged, psychologists do have a much clearer understanding of what happens to the brain when the corpus callosum fails to do its job.

corpus callosum a thick band of neurons that connects the right and left hemispheres of the brain

The Split Brain

split brain a brain with its corpus callosum severed; sometimes done to control the effects of epilepsy in patients who do not respond to other therapies

FIGURE 2.16

● **A Typical Split-Brain Study** In a typical split-brain experiment, an image is flashed to a split-brain person's right or left visual field, and she is asked to identify the object in the image. When the image is flashed to the person's right visual field, she is able to name it, but when it is flashed to her left visual field, she is unable to name it because the information cannot travel to the language centers in the left hemisphere.

Physicians have at times willfully disrupted communication between the hemispheres by destroying the corpus callosum in the human brain. Such a drastic measure is taken in cases in which people have severe, uncontrollable epilepsy. In severe epilepsy, abnormal electrical activity can build up in one hemisphere and spread across the corpus callosum to engulf the opposite hemisphere. This short-circuiting of both hemispheres produces a severe, life-threatening seizure called a *grand mal seizure*. If drugs cannot control the seizures, surgery may be performed to cut the corpus callosum and thereby contain the short-circuiting to one hemisphere only. The patient still has seizures, but they are not as severe. Patients who have had this surgery are referred to as having a **split brain** because the hemispheres are no longer connected by neural pathways. Split-brain patients provide scientists with an opportunity to study the lateralization of the brain.

Working with split-brain patients, researchers can study the functioning of each hemisphere independent of the other. For example, split-brain research helped scientists conclude that the left hemisphere enables us to produce speech (● FIGURE 2.16). Researcher Michael Gazzaniga (1967) briefly flashed pictures of familiar objects to the right and left visual fields of split-brain patients and asked them to identify the objects (Figure 2.16). When an object is briefly presented to our right peripheral field of vision, the resulting visual information is sent directly to the left hemisphere of the brain. Because Broca's area is in the left hemisphere for most people, Gazzaniga found that the average split-brain patient could verbally identify the object. But what about an object presented to the patient's left peripheral field of vision? When an object is briefly shown on our far left side, the resulting visual information is sent directly to the right hemisphere of the brain. In a normal brain, the information travels from the right hemisphere across the corpus callosum to the language centers in the left hemisphere. However, in a split-brain patient this transfer cannot happen. Without the corpus callosum, Gazzaniga's split-brain patients could not transmit the knowledge of what they were seeing to the language centers in their left hemisphere. The right brain knew what the objects were, but it could not inform the "speaking" left brain. Predictably, the split-brain patients were unable to name the objects they saw in their left visual fields. Interestingly, in this situation split-brain patients would be able to point to the objects in a drawing—provided they used their left hand (which is controlled by the right brain). Split-brain research has helped us to begin sorting out the relative contributions that the right and left hemispheres make to everyday cognitive processes.

Within the different lobes of the brain there is also specialization. Let's take a look.

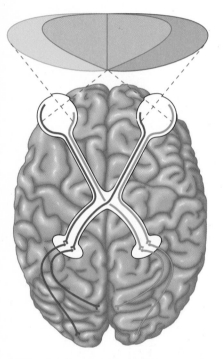

(a) Visual pathways in the brain

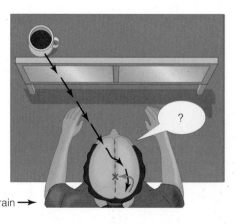

Normal brain

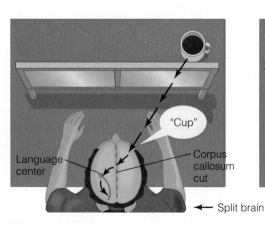

←— Split brain —→

(b) Split brain

The Specialization of Function in the Lobes of the Cortex

About 25% of the total surface area of the cortex is dedicated to motor and sensory functions such as vision, hearing, movement, and tactile sensation. Specific motor-sensory areas can be found in all the lobes of the brain (frontal, parietal, occipital, and temporal). The remaining 75% of the cortical area is devoted to higher-order processes that involve the integration of information, such as thinking, planning, decision making, and language. Collectively, this 75% is referred to as the **association cortex** because these areas involve the processing and integration of information from the motor-sensory areas of the cortex.

We do not yet completely understand the functions of specific areas of the association cortex. Often, damage to the association areas produces general changes and deficits in behavior. However, stimulation of specific areas of the association cortex does not usually lead to specific, predictable physical reactions. It is thought that the association cortex plays a role in general cognition, such as planning and decision making. Where applicable, we will discuss the known functions of the association areas for the specific lobes of the brain.

The Frontal Lobe

The frontal lobe is the area of the cortex that lies closest to the forehead (Figure 2.15a). Much of the frontal lobe is association cortex, including Broca's area, which is involved in the production of speech. The frontal lobe association areas play a role in cognitive processes such as attention, problem solving, judgment, the planning and executing of behavior, and certain aspects of personality. These cognitive functions are illustrated in a famous 1848 case study of a railway worker named Phineas Gage. Gage suffered severe trauma to his *prefrontal cortex* (the association area at the very front part of the frontal lobe) when a metal rod was shot through his head in an explosion. Although he survived his injuries, they resulted in some dramatic personality changes. Whereas Gage had been a calm, responsible man prior to his injuries, he became impulsive, emotionally volatile, and irresponsible afterward. Because the prefrontal cortex is important for the regulation of emotion (R. J. Davidson, Putman, & Larson, 2000), the damage to Gage's brain robbed him of his ability to control his emotions and make good judgments (Damasio, Grabowski, Frank, Galaburda, & Damasio, 1994).

At the back of the frontal lobe (behind the prefrontal cortex) lies the **motor cortex**, a narrow band of cortex that allows us to execute motor movements. The motor cortex on the right side of the brain affects movement on the left side of the body, and vice versa. Additionally, specific points along the motor cortex correspond to particular points on the body. ● FIGURE 2.17a is a rendering of a *homunculus*, a humorous mapping of body parts onto their appropriate motor cortical points. If stimulation were applied to these points along the motor cortex, the result would be movement of the corresponding body part. During brain surgery, surgeons may apply electrical stimulation to the brain before making incisions in the cortical tissue; the patient's subsequent movements or other responses indicate where the surgical instruments are located along the motor cortex (and other areas). Without such precautionary measures, a physician could accidentally cause paralysis with a misplaced cut along the motor cortex.

The Parietal Lobe

Parts of the parietal lobe play a role in sensation. A thin strip of the parietal lobe affects our sense of touch, pressure, and pain. This strip, called the **somatosensory cortex**, lies directly behind the motor cortex, along the leading edge of the parietal lobe (Figure 2.15b). The somatosensory cortex is wired much like the motor cortex, and specific points along the somatosensory cortex correspond to particular points on the body (● FIGURE 2.17b). Damage to the somatosensory cortex often results in numbness of the corresponding body part.

The Occipital Lobe

The occipital lobe of the brain is located at the very back of the skull, above the cerebellum (Figure 2.15a). Much of the occipital lobe is dedicated to processing visual information. The **visual cortex** of the occipital lobe is composed of layers of tissue that contain long axonal fibers. An action potential is stimulated in specialized cells of the visual cortex when our eyes

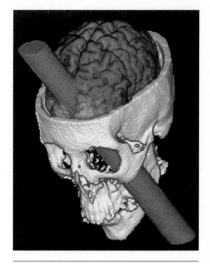

Phineas Gage was a responsible, mild-mannered worker on a railway construction crew until a rod like this one was shot through his head in a freak accident. Gage survived, but he was never the same. The damage to Gage's prefrontal cortex coincided with dramatic changes in his personality. The once calm Gage became emotionally volatile and difficult. As a result, he was unable to perform his former job with the railroad.

Reprinted with permission from Damasio, H., Grabowski, T., Frank, R., Galaburda, A. M., & Damasio, A. R. (1994). The return of Phineas Gage: The skull of a famous patient yields clues about the brain. *Science, 264*, 1102-1105. © 1994, AAAS.

association cortex areas of the cortex involved in the association or integration of information from the motor-sensory areas of the cortex

motor cortex a strip of cortex at the back of the frontal lobe that governs the execution of motor movement in the body

somatosensory cortex a strip of cortex at the front of the parietal lobe that governs our sense of touch

visual cortex a region of cortex found at the back of the occipital lobe that processes visual information in the brain

FIGURE 2.17

● **Motor and Sensory Homunculi** Homunculi are humorous depictions of the localization of function on the cortex. *From Penfield and Rasmussen, The Cerebral Cortex of Man (1950). Reprinted by permission of Gale, a division of Thomson Learning: www.thomsonrights.com. Fax 800-730-2215.*

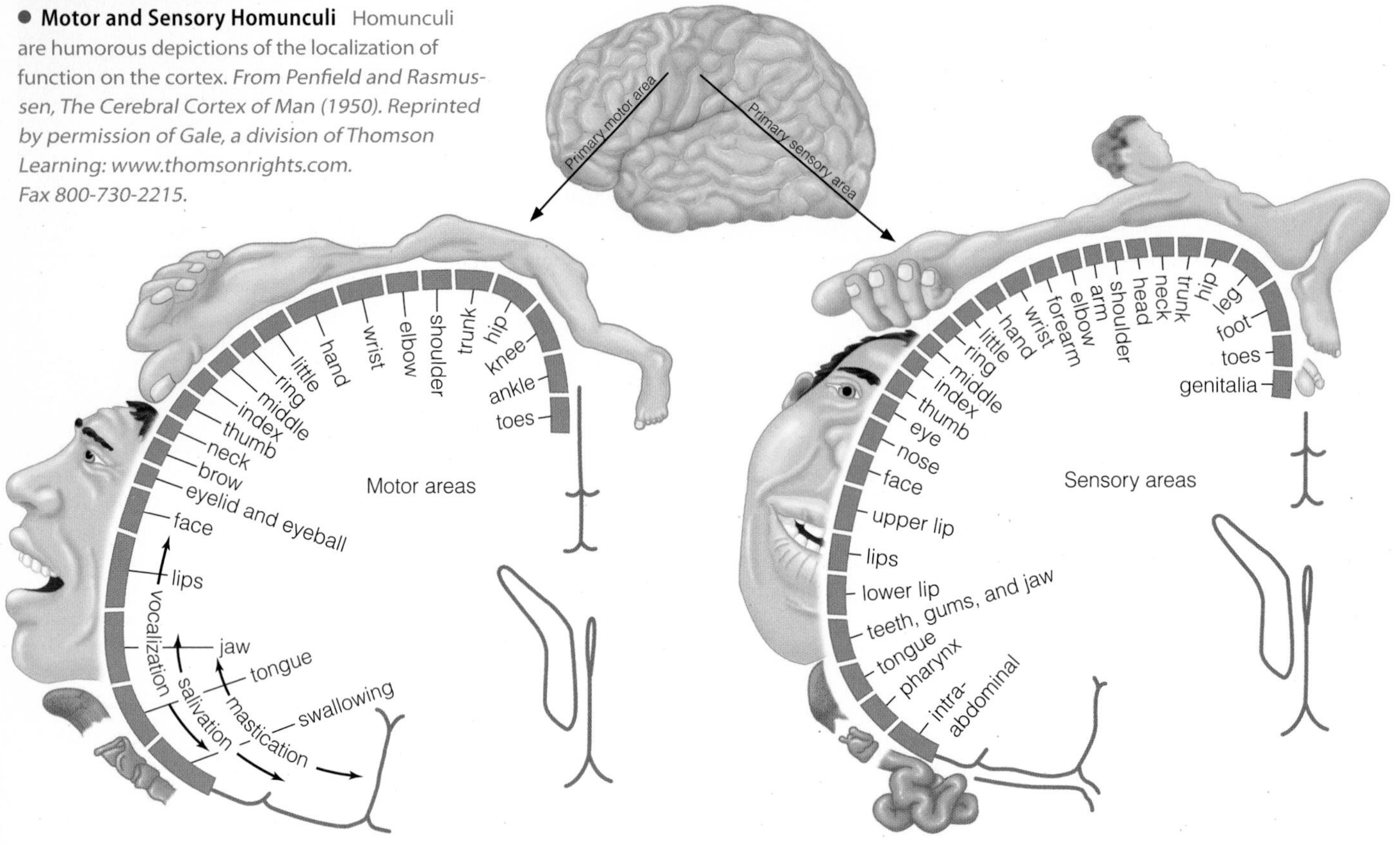

(a) The motor homunculus

(b) The sensory homunculus

see specific types of visual stimuli in the outside world. For instance, some cells begin to fire only when we see lines, and other cells fire only when we see circular shapes. Like a computer, our brain integrates all the incoming neural impulses from these specialized cells in the visual cortex to enable us to perceive what we are viewing. Without the operation of the visual cortex, our brain could not make sense of what our eyes see. Damage to the visual cortex can result in partial or complete blindness. In cases of visual cortex damage, blindness may occur even though the eyes are functioning properly. This would be like taking a photograph but not developing the film correctly. The camera (the eye) does its job, but we fail to develop the picture (the function of the cortex).

The Temporal Lobe

The temporal lobe is in front of the occipital lobe and just below the parietal and frontal lobes—roughly behind our ears inside the skull. Not surprisingly, one of the major functions of the temporal lobe is the processing of auditory information or hearing. The temporal lobe areas devoted to hearing are the **auditory cortex**, located on the upper edge of the temporal lobe (Figure 2.15b). In addition to the auditory cortex, the left temporal lobe of most people contains Wernicke's area. As we've already seen, Wernicke's area is responsible for the comprehension of speech. People who have suffered major damage to Wernicke's area often cannot understand the meaning of spoken words. They hear the words, but they can't make sense of them.

auditory cortex a region of cortex found in the temporal lobe that governs our processing of auditory information in the brain

Now that you have learned about the structure and function of the brain, we hope that you are suitably impressed. We have merely begun to explore the function of our nervous system in this chapter, and scientists are far from completely understanding this amazing system. As research continues, scientists learn more about how our physiology influences our thoughts and behaviors. Luckily researchers have a great deal of modern technology to help them learn about the brain.

Let's
REVIEW
In this section, we dealt with the structure and function of the hindbrain, midbrain, and forebrain. The hindbrain is primarily involved in life-sustaining functions, and the midbrain connects the hindbrain with the sophisticated structures of the forebrain. The function of the cortex and lateralization of the cortex were also described. For a quick check of your understanding, try answering the following questions at increasing levels of difficulty.

1. The occipital lobe is where much of our _____ processing occurs.

   a. auditory
   b. emotional
   c. motor memory
   d. visual

2. Which of the following brain structures is arguably *most* essential to life?

   a. frontal lobe
   b. amygdala
   c. medulla
   d. hippocampus

3. Billy suffered a stroke on the left side of his brain. Most of his left frontal lobe was destroyed. What symptoms would you *most* expect to see in Billy as a result of this damage?

   a. paralysis on the right side of his body and an inability to speak
   b. paralysis on the right side of his body and an inability to understand speech
   c. paralysis of his left leg, partial deafness, and stuttering
   d. paralysis on the left side of his body and an inability to understand speech

ANSWERS 1. d; 2. c; 3. a

HOW DO WE STUDY THE BRAIN?

LEARNING OBJECTIVE

What Should You Know?
- Describe brain-imaging techniques and other ways we can study the brain, and explain their advantages and limitations.

Psychologists have many methods for studying the brain. Some of these procedures are invasive (they require surgery); others are noninvasive. Some procedures allow researchers to examine only the structure of the brain, whereas others indicate which areas of the brain are most active at a given moment. Because these techniques can be used on living brain tissue, they can give researchers important information about the specific behavioral functions that are governed by particular areas of the brain. Medically, these techniques are also used in cases like Jean-Dominique Bauby's to diagnosis neurological problems associated with injuries and disease. We summarize some of the most useful technologies available for helping us to better understand the inner workings of the brain—*CAT scans, MRIs, DTIs, PET scans, SPECT scans, fMRIs, angiograms, EEGs, ERPs, brain lesions, brain stimulation, TMS,* and *single cell recordings*—in ● TABLE 2.2.

The technologies described in Table 2.2 have helped psychologists to better understand how the brain works to regulate and control our mental processes and behavior. Through the use of these technologies, we have learned that the human nervous system is an extremely impressive and important network. However, the nervous system is not the only communication system within the body. We turn now to the other major communication network, the endocrine system.

TABLE 2.2

● **Common Techniques for Studying the Brain and Examples of Their Use**

TECHNIQUE FOR STUDYING THE BRAIN	DESCRIPTION	WHAT INFORMATION DOES IT YIELD?	WHEN WOULD THIS TECHNIQUE BE USED?
Computerized Axial Tomography (CAT Scan)	Multiple X-ray beams are passed through the brain from different angles. As they pass through the brain, the X-rays are slowed down by the brain tissue. The computer then analyzes the speed at which the X-rays exit the head and uses this information to build a picture of the brain and its structures.	A computer-generated picture of the brain and its structures is given. No information on brain function is provided.	To diagnose tumors, strokes, certain diseases, and structural abnormalities in the brain.
Magnetic Resonance Imaging (MRI)	A magnetic field is used to excite the atoms in the body, and the energy emitted by these atoms is used to construct a computer-generated picture of the brain.	A highly detailed, structural picture of the brain is given. No information on brain function is provided.	To diagnose tumors, strokes, certain diseases, and structural abnormalities in the brain. Structures as small as 1–2 mm can be identified (Raichle, 1994).
Diffusion Tensor Imaging (DTI)	MRI technology is used to measure the diffusion of water in certain brain tissue.	An extremely detailed, structural picture of specific neural tracts in the brain's white matter is generated.	Researchers can study specific neural networks in the brain's white matter. Doctors can examine specific neural problems in patients (e.g., in cases of Alzheimer's disease; Stebbins & Murphy, 2009).
Positron Emission Tomography (PET Scan)	Radioactive glucose (the brain's fuel source) is injected into the bloodstream. The computer measures which areas of the brain are most active and consuming the most glucose.	PET scans can indicate which parts of the brain are most active at a given moment. Structural information is very limited.	To diagnose areas of the brain that have ceased functioning due to disease or injury; to help researchers correlate brain activity with behavior.
Single Photon Emission Computerized Tomography (SPECT Scan)	Radioactive isotopes are injected into the bloodstream and absorbed by different parts of the body.	SPECT scans can indicate blood flow and organ activity in the body. Structural information is very limited.	Usage is similar to PET scans.
Functional MRI (fMRI)	Uses MRI technology to track which neurons in the brain are most active at a given moment by examining the energy released by hemoglobin molecules in the bloodstream.	fMRIs yield a highly detailed picture of brain structures and can also indicate which brain areas are most active at any particular moment.	Used in a fashion similar to PET/SPECT scans, fMRIs also help researchers to correlate brain function with behavior.
Angiograms	An X-ray is taken of the brain after a special dye has been injected into the bloodstream.	A picture of the blood-flow patterns in the brain is given. The only structures seen on an angiogram are the blood vessels.	Useful for diagnosing blood-flow problems such as the blood clots or arterial plaques commonly found in stroke victims.

● **Common Techniques for Studying the Brain and Examples of Their Use,** *continued*

TECHNIQUE FOR STUDYING THE BRAIN	DESCRIPTION	WHAT INFORMATION DOES IT YIELD?	WHEN WOULD THIS TECHNIQUE BE USED?
Electroencephalography (EEG)	An EEG measures changes in electrical voltage at points along the scalp.	A gross picture of brain activity is given. No structural information is provided.	Assesses gross patterns of brain activation in brain-injured patients; can be used to measure normal participants' brain activity during certain processes such as sleep or mental tasks.
Evoked Response Potentials (ERPs)	In ERPs, successive EEGs are averaged to remove the electrical interference and background noise found in traditional EEG tests.	A gross picture of brain activity is given. No structural information is provided.	Usage is similar to EEG.
Brain Lesions	Specific parts of the brain are intentionally destroyed.	By creating lesions in specific areas of the brain, researchers can see what effect these lesions have on behavior.	Used to help determine the function of specific brain structures; may also be used therapeutically to destroy malfunctioning parts of the brain. (Pfann, Penn, Shannon, & Corcos, 1998).
Brain Stimulation	Small electrodes are inserted into the brain, and specific parts of the brain are intentionally stimulated with mild electrical currents.	By stimulating specific areas of the brain, researchers can see what effect this stimulation has on behavior.	Used to help determine the function of specific brain structures; also used in new therapies to treat conditions such as depression by stimulating brain function in specific areas of the brain.
Transcranial Magnetic Stimulation (TMS)	A targeted magnetic field is applied to specific locations on the outside of the head to stimulate underlying neurons to fire action potentials.	TMS provides a noninvasive and relatively pain-free method of stimulating the brain so that researchers can see what effect this stimulation has on behavior.	TMS can be used to determine the function of specific cortical regions, allowing doctors and researchers to "map" the brain (e.g., Picht, Mularski, Kuehn, Vajkoczy, Kombos, & Suess, 2009).
Single Cell Recordings	Electrodes are implanted in specific neurons to record their rate of neural firing.	By recording which neurons begin to fire during certain activities, researchers can learn about the function of specific neurons.	Useful in basic research—for example, in determining how the brain responds to certain sensory input.

Let's
REVIEW
In this section, we outlined some brain-imaging technologies. For a quick check of your understanding, try answering the following questions at increasing levels of difficulty.

1. Which of the following techniques measures electrical activity in the brain?

   a. EEG
   b. PET

   c. fMRI
   d. angiogram

2. Which of the following techniques would researchers probably be most reluctant to use on a human research participant?

   a. lesions
   b. TMS

   c. fMRI
   d. CAT scan

3. Which of the following techniques can show the brain's structures in the greatest amount of detail?

   a. MRI
   b. angiogram

   c. EEG
   d. DTI

ANSWERS 1. a; 2. a; 3. d

LEARNING
OBJECTIVE

What Should You Know?

● Explain how the endocrine system works and list the endocrine glands.

HOW DOES THE ENDOCRINE SYSTEM INFLUENCE OUR BEHAVIOR?

We have seen that because of its electrochemical nature, the nervous system is especially good at quickly conveying information within the body. It is the speed of the nervous system that enables us to react quickly to changes in our environment. Messages are sent, decisions are made, and actions are taken—all accomplished with the speed of firing action potentials. At times, however, we require communication within the body that is slower and produces more long-lasting effects. In these circumstances, the *endocrine system* is called into action.

The endocrine system is a chemical system of communication that relies on the action of specialized organs called **endocrine glands** that are located throughout the body (● FIGURE 2.18). When stimulated, endocrine glands release chemicals called **hormones** into the bloodstream. These hormones circulate through the bloodstream until they reach other organs in the body. Our internal organs are equipped with special receptor sites to accept these hormones.

The endocrine system is considerably slower than the nervous system in relaying messages because it relies on blood circulating through the veins and arteries of the cardiovascular system to transport hormones throughout the body. The effects of hormones in the bloodstream, however, tend to last longer than the stimulation caused by action potentials at the synapse. Some of the bodily processes that are heavily influenced by hormonal activity include sexual activity, eating, sleeping, general physiological arousal, and growth.

Communication between the nervous and endocrine systems takes place through the hypothalamus and its connection with the **pituitary gland**. The pituitary gland, situated in the vicinity of the limbic system under the hypothalamus (Figure 2.18), is responsible for regulating hormone release in all the other endocrine glands. When the endocrine system is called into action, the hypothalamus sends a signal to the pituitary gland. The pituitary gland then releases hormones that travel through the bloodstream to the other endocrine glands, stimulating them to release the hormones they produce into the bloodstream. These hormones circulate to their target organs, where they bring about specific changes in the functioning of these organs.

Our bodies are equipped with a great number of endocrine glands throughout the body (Figure 2.18). Probably the best known endocrine glands are the *ovaries* and *testes*, which are

endocrine glands organs of the endocrine system that produce hormones and release them into the bloodstream

hormones chemical messengers of the endocrine system

pituitary gland master gland of the endocrine system that controls the action of all other glands in the body necessary for sexuality and reproduction. Ovaries are the female sex glands, located in the abdominal cavity. Ovaries are directly responsible for the production of female eggs (ova) and the release of female sex hormones, or **estrogens**. Testes are the male sex glands, located in the testicles. Testes produce male sex cells (sperm) and male hormones, or **androgens**. Despite being typically associated with either male or female sexuality, estrogens and androgens are found in both men and women and affect multiple systems in the body (such as hair and muscle growth, metabolism, and so on; see Chapter 10).

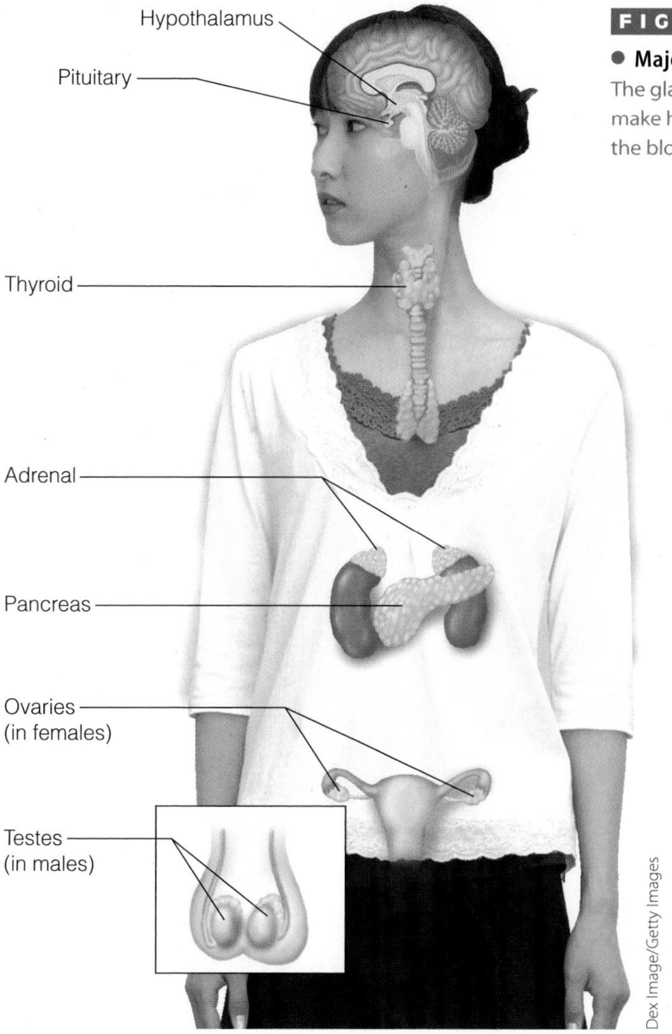

The *adrenal glands* sit just above the kidneys in both males and females and are important for regulating arousal and sexual behavior, among many things. The inside of the adrenal gland, the **adrenal medulla**, is particularly important in sympathetic nervous system reactions. When the sympathetic nervous system becomes active during times of stress, the adrenal medulla releases norepinephrine and epinephrine (also known as

Dex Image/Getty Images

FIGURE 2.18

● **Major Endocrine Glands of the Body**
The glands of the endocrine system make hormones and release them into the bloodstream.

Hypothalamus
Pituitary
Thyroid
Adrenal
Pancreas
Ovaries (in females)
Testes (in males)

adrenalin) into the bloodstream. When norepinephrine and epinephrine are released in the body outside the central nervous system, they function as hormones. The sudden flooding of the bloodstream with these hormones causes increased heart rate, blood pressure, and respiration.

The external part of the adrenal glands, the **adrenal cortex**, plays many roles in the endocrine system. Among other things, the adrenal cortex produces *adrenal androgens*, which are male sex hormones found in both males and females. These androgens control many aspects of our sexual characteristics and basic physiological functioning.

The *thyroid gland*, located in the throat, governs important aspects of metabolism. Dysfunction of the thyroid can lead to serious physical symptoms. *Hyperthyroidism*, or an overactive thyroid, is associated with increased metabolism, weight loss, bulging eyes, weakness, high blood pressure, and cardiac problems. *Hypothyroidism*, or an underactive thyroid, is related to lowered metabolism, weight gain, sluggishness, thin brittle hair, menstrual abnormalities in females, and depression. The symptoms of hypothyroidism often mimic those of depressive psychological disorders. Prior to treatment for depression, a routine thyroid check should be done to avoid misdiagnosis.

The nervous and endocrine systems are nothing short of amazing in their intricate structure and function. The importance of these systems to everyday life is especially apparent in cases like Bauby's where damage has rendered part of the communication system useless. How did we develop such complex systems in the first place? Certainly the human nervous

estrogens a class of female sex hormones that regulate many aspects of sexuality and are found in both males and females

androgens a class of male hormones found in both males and females

adrenal medulla center part of the adrenal gland that plays a crucial role in the functioning of the sympathetic nervous system

adrenal cortex outside part of the adrenal gland that plays a role in the manufacture and release of androgens and therefore influences sexual characteristics

and endocrine systems are far advanced when compared to those of other species. Why are we so complex, and what accounts for the traits humans possess? These questions lead us into the areas of genetics and evolution.

Let's REVIEW

In this section, we described the endocrine system and its relationship to the nervous system. For a quick check of your understanding, try answering the following questions at increasing levels of difficulty.

1. An overactive thyroid gland is also known as _____.

  a. hypothyroidism   c. pituitary disorder
  b. hyperthyroidism   d. dwarfism

2. A malfunction in which of the following endocrine glands would be *most* disruptive to the overall functioning of the endocrine system?

  a. thymus   c. pituitary
  b. ovaries   d. adrenal

3. Juanita was just frightened by a snake. Which of the following endocrine glands most likely played the biggest role in her response to danger?

  a. thymus   c. adrenal cortex
  b. thyroid   d. adrenal medulla

ANSWERS 1. b; 2. c; 3. d

LEARNING OBJECTIVES

What Should You Know?

- Give an overview of the nature versus nurture debate, and describe genetic and environmental factors in human development.
- Give an overview of the theory of evolution, and explain how the human nervous system may have developed through natural selection.

WHAT MAKES US WHO WE ARE—OUR BIOLOGY OR THE ENVIRONMENT?

One question that has plagued humankind for centuries is how we become the people we become. Each person is a unique collection of physical characteristics, personality traits, and abilities. What makes us different from one another? For example, Jean-Dominique Bauby was, among other things, a gifted author, a courageous man, and, unfortunately, a man who was susceptible to a stroke. Why? Did Bauby become the man he was because of the environment he grew up in? Were Bauby's traits, abilities, and weaknesses predestined by the genes he inherited from his parents? To answer these questions, we look next at the contributions our genes and our environment make to our development.

Nature Versus Nurture and Interactionism

Explaining how and why we develop as we do is the central issue in the age-old **nature–nurture debate**. Those on the *nature* side of this debate claim that intelligence, kindness, athletic ability, and other characteristics are largely determined by one's **genes**. Genes are the strands of deoxyribonucleic acid (DNA) that are found in the nuclei of all living cells. DNA directs the development of proteins within the cells of the body. By instructing a cell to make specific kinds of protein molecules, the genes direct the development of the different organs and systems of the body.

Those on the *nurture* side view behavior as being molded by environmental influences such as the way your parents treat you, the educational opportunities you have, and even the technologies to which you are exposed (see the ● TECHNOLOGY AND BEHAVIOR box, p. 75). From the nurture point of view, our traits and other characteristics are acquired totally by experience. What do you think? Are you a product of the genes you inherited? Or are you a product of your environment?

nature–nurture debate the degree to which biology (nature) or the environment (nurture) contributes to one's development

genes strands of DNA found in the nuclei of all living cells

interactionism perspective that our genes and environmental influences work together to determine our characteristics

TECHNOLOGY and BEHAVIOR

DO CELL PHONES CAUSE BRAIN TUMORS?

The modern cell phone was invented at Motorola in 1973, but it wasn't until the 1990s that cell phones became small enough and cheap enough to appeal to the public (Federal Communications Commission [FCC], 2004). Today, cell phones are used in most countries and have even replaced traditional home phone service for many people. Think about it—how many people do you know who do *not* have a cell phone?

Cell phones have made our lives easier by enabling us to stay in touch with family and friends. They allow us to work more efficiently and give us easy access to coworkers and clients. Cell phones have also made our lives safer by giving us easier access to emergency help and the ability to monitor the whereabouts of our children.

Yet, as with many new products, there have been questions about the safety of cell phones. Cell phones emit certain levels of nonionizing radiation in the form of radio frequency energy. Nonionizing radiation such as radio frequency energy is thought to be safer than ionizing radiation (e.g., X-rays), but it does cause a heating effect in affected areas. In fact, microwave ovens work by focusing radio frequency energy on the water and fat molecules within foods. So, when we hold a cell phone to our head, how do the emitted radio frequencies affect our nearby brain?

The research on the safety of cell phones has yielded a mixed and somewhat confusing pattern of results (Kan, Simonsen, Lyon, & Kestle, 2008). Because cell phones have only been in widespread use since the mid-1990s, and the effects of radiation exposure on the brain often take decades to develop, we are just now starting to see the results of long-term studies (Hardell & Carlberg, 2009). Some of these studies suggest that long-term cell phone use may be related to an increased risk of developing certain brain tumors.

Swedish researcher Lennart Hardell and his colleagues (the Hardell-group) have been studying the health of cell phone users for over a decade. In one study, they found that 10 or more years of cell phone use was associated with an increased incidence of two types of brain tumors, acoustic neuromas (a rare tumor of the auditory nerve) and gliomas (tumors of the brain's glial cells) (Hardell, Carlberg, Söderqvist, Mild, & Morgan, 2007). In a follow-up study, the Hardell-group found more evidence suggesting that long-term cell phone use is associated with increased risk of astrocytoma brain tumors (the most common type of glioma) on the same side of the head as the cell phone is used. In this study, the risk was highest for participants who had begun using cell phones prior to age 20, followed by those using cell phones for more than 10 years (Hardell & Carlberg, 2009).

Does this research prove that cell phones cause brain tumors? The jury is still out. The available research on cell phone use and brain tumors in humans has relied on participants' retrospective recall of their cell phone usage and has all been correlational in nature. For ethical reasons, researchers will not purposely assign participants to heavy cell phone use conditions when it is hypothesized that these conditions could be harmful. At best, the available research suggests a correlation between cell phones and brain tumors, which doesn't necessarily mean that cell phones cause brain tumors. Nonetheless, it is hard to ignore the increased risk that the Hardell-group has shown for both young and long-term cell phone users. Until researchers have a clear answer to this question, you may wish to be extra careful by using hands-free cell phone technology. So far, no one has found evidence that cell phone radiation is harmful unless the phone is pressed to one's head.

Some researchers have found that long-term cell phone use of 10 years or more is associated with an increased risk of certain brain tumors. Although we have not yet determined that cell phones cause brain tumors, you may choose to take the precaution of using your speaker phone feature or headset to avoid holding the phone close to your head for prolonged periods.

Teo Lannie/PhotoAlto Agency/PhotoLibrary

© Reuters/Corbis

Scientists like Dr. Robert Waterson have been working to map the entire genetic makeup of human beings in the Human Genome Project. One of the most surprising results of the project was the discovery that humans have only around 30,000 genes. It had been previously thought that we had almost 100,000 genes.

Most current psychologists would answer both. Today, the dominant perspective on the nature–nurture debate is **interactionism**. Most psychologists now believe that genetic influences interact with environmental influences to produce our traits and behavior. For example, Bauby's amazing creativity was probably due in part to the genes he received from his parents and in part to the environments he encountered at home, in school, at work, and elsewhere.

Interactionism has become extremely important with the recent discovery that environmental factors can change the way genes function in our bodies without altering the DNA sequence of the gene, a phenomenon referred to as **epigenetics**. For example, environmental factors can change which genes become active or inactive in the body. This switching on and off of genes can ultimately change the way the body develops and functions. For instance, inactivation of gene p53, a tumor suppressor gene, in humans results in an increased risk of cancer (Machado-Silva, Perrier, & Bourdon, 2010). If an environmental factor alters the functioning of our genes (e.g., by switching some on or off), this change in gene expression can, in some cases, be passed down to future generations. For example, one study found that Swedish men's mortality was correlated with whether or not their paternal grandfathers experienced famine during critical points in their childhoods. The researchers also found that women's mortality was related to their paternal grandmother's childhood experience of famine (Pembrey et al., 2006). Although exactly which genes were involved in these cases is still unknown, studies like this one suggest that a combination of environment and genetics may not only affect an individual but also have a lasting effect on future generations.

The discovery of epigenetics arose out of researchers' continuing efforts to understand the complex interplay of nature and nurture influences on specific traits. We will discuss the nurture influences on development more fully in Chapters 5, 7, and 9 when we discuss learning, intelligence, and development. For now, let's focus our attention on the more biological genetic, or nature, side of this debate.

Genetic Blueprint for Traits

Development is not chaotic; rather, it usually happens in a predictable and orderly way. Much of this order stems from the fact that all living organisms develop according to a "blueprint" or plan contained in the genes that an organism inherits from its parents. **How many genes make up the blueprint for human development?**

To answer this question, the U.S. government began a mammoth project, the *Human Genome Project*, in which scientists sought to map out the human *genome*—in other words, the entire set of DNA found in the human body. Mapping of the millions of chemical bases that make up the genome began in 1990 and was completed by 2003. To date, one of the most surprising findings of the project was that the total number of genes in the human genome is about 30,000. Originally, scientists had predicted that they would find approximately 100,000 genes. The fact that a mere 30,000 genes direct the development of something as complex as us humans was a surprise (U.S. Department of Energy, 2007).

As a species, we are human because the 30,000 genes of the human genome direct our bodies to develop as human bodies. As individuals, we have unique characteristics because we inherited a particular mix of genes for specific traits from our parents. At conception, we get half our genes from our mother and the other half from our father. From this combination of genes, we develop our characteristics. The genetic code that we inherit for a particular trait is called the **genotype**. But recall that the genotypes we inherit only partly determine the traits we actually acquire. The environment plays a role as well. The actual

epigenetics the principle that environmental factors can alter the expression of genes in our bodies without altering the DNA sequence of the gene

genotype inherited genetic pattern for a given trait

trait or characteristic we develop is referred to as the **phenotype**. The phenotype is a product of the genotype an organism inherits and the environment in which it lives. For example, Siamese cats have a characteristic look because all Siamese cats share some common genes that are particular to the breed. However, the climate a Siamese cat is raised in affects the color of its coat. Siamese cats raised in hot climates tend to be light, whereas Siamese cats reared in cold climates develop darker fur (W. Gallagher, 1994). Inherited genotypes direct the cat to develop as a Siamese, but environmental influences produce further variations in the phenotypes that result. The same principle holds true for humans. The exact shade of your hair, the level of your intelligence, the speed with which you run—all are phenotypes, which are the expression of inherited genotypes and environmental influences.

Genetically speaking, the human species has done quite well. We are the most highly developed species on earth. Our cortex is more developed than those of other species, and as a result we have many well-developed abilities that are lacking in other species. We use spoken language to communicate, we have well-developed self-concepts, we can imagine the future, and we are adept problem solvers, to name a few of our high-level abilities. We can thank our genes for these wonderful advances that separate us from the rest of the animal kingdom, but why are we humans genetically different from other animals? Why do different species exist? Many scientists believe the answer to this question is found in the process of *evolution*.

BIZARRO

GOLLY DARN, BUDDY BOB! WHAT'S A GIANT-SCREEN T.V. DOING OUT HERE IN THE SWAMP?!

WHO CARES?! FINDERS KEEPERS!

EVOLUTION WINS AGAIN

© BIZARRO © DAN PIRARO. KING FEATURES SYNDICATE.

The Evolution of Species: Natural Selection

In 1859 Charles Darwin published *On the Origin of Species by Means of Natural Selection* (Darwin, 1859). In this text, Darwin outlined what has become the basis for modern theories of evolution, the process of **natural selection**. Natural selection is a simple but powerful process that can change, kill, or create a species over time. The central principle of natural selection is that for characteristics to be retained in a species, genes for these traits must be passed on to offspring. If an organism does not reproduce, its genes die with it. If a specific trait is *maladaptive* and tends to prevent an organism from surviving and procreating, then the genes for this trait are not as likely to be passed on to offspring. Over time, these maladaptive genes should die out in the species. In contrast, *adaptive* genes, which give rise to traits that help an organism reproduce, will be passed on to future generations. Over time, through *natural selection*, these adaptive genes will become more widespread in the species (see also Chapter 1).

The effects of evolution can be seen in the human nervous system. As we've mentioned, human brains differ from nonhuman brains in some important ways. The most notable differences are seen when comparing the human cortex to the cortices found in other species. The human cortex is more highly evolved (see Figure 2.14, p. 63). Genes that supported such a highly evolved cortex were presumably selected in our species over millions of years of natural selection and evolution. Can you see how some of our cortical functions could have contributed to our ancestors' reproductive success? For example, how could the capacity for language have aided our ancestors? Could being able to communicate danger to others have helped many of our ancient ancestors survive, reproduce, and safeguard their offspring? There is little doubt that having a large cortex and all the associated perks such as language, problem-solving skills, memory, and planning skills helped our species survive and flourish. We hope the knowledge about our amazing nervous system that you have learned here will help you realize just how kind evolution has been to us.

phenotype actual characteristic that results from the interaction of the genotype and environmental influences

natural selection cornerstone of Darwin's theory of evolution, which states that genes for traits that allow an organism to be reproductively successful will be selected or retained in a species and genes for traits that hinder reproductive success will not be selected and therefore will die out in a species

Let's REVIEW

In this section, we described several aspects of the genetic bases for traits and behavior. For a quick check of your understanding, try answering the following questions at increasing levels of difficulty.

1. Genes are made up of _____.

    a. DNA   c. phenotypes

    b. ACh   d. GABA

2. A phenotype for a particular trait, such as hair color, is the product of the organism's _____.

    a. genotype   c. environment

    b. DNA   d. genotype and environment

3. Dr. Jasper is a scientist who believes that environmental influences can affect the way that our genes are expressed during development. In his studies, he is examining how maternal environment can affect fur coloring in subsequent generations of rats. Dr. Jasper is *least* likely to agree that our traits are the result of_____.

    a. epigenetics   c. nature forces

    b. interactionism   d. a and b

ANSWERS 1. a; 2. d; 3. c

STUDYING the CHAPTER

KEY TERMS

neurons (43)
glial cells (43)
myelin (43)
cell body (44)
DNA (44)
dendrites (44)
axon (44)
neurotransmitters (45)
synapse (45)
presynaptic neuron (45)
postsynaptic neuron (45)
ions (45)
resting potential (46)
threshold of excitation (46)
action potential (46)
all-or-none fashion (46)
refractory period (47)
excitation (48)
inhibition (48)
reuptake (50)
acetylcholine (ACh) (51)
dopamine (51)

serotonin (52)
norepinephrine (NOR) (53)
gamma amino butyric acid
   (GABA) (53)
glutamate (53)
endorphins (53)
nervous system (55)
central nervous system
   (CNS) (55)
peripheral nervous system
   (PNS) (55)
sensory (afferent)
   neurons (55)
motor (efferent) neurons (55)
somatic nervous system (56)
autonomic nervous
   system (56)
sympathetic nervous
   system (56)
parasympathetic nervous
   system (57)
hindbrain (58)

medulla (58)
pons (59)
cerebellum (59)
midbrain (60)
reticular formation (60)
forebrain (60)
limbic system (60)
cerebral cortex (60)
cerebral hemispheres (60)
amygdala (61)
hippocampus (61)
thalamus (63)
hypothalamus (63)
homeostasis (63)
frontal lobe (64)
parietal lobes (64)
occipital lobe (64)
temporal lobes (64)
Broca's area (64)
aphasia (64)
Wernicke's area (64)
corpus callosum (65)

split brain (66)
association cortex (67)
motor cortex (67)
somatosensory cortex (67)
visual cortex (67)
auditory cortex (68)
endocrine glands (72)
hormones (72)
pituitary gland (72)
estrogens (73)
androgens (73)
adrenal medulla (73)
adrenal cortex (73)
nature–nurture debate (74)
genes (74)
interactionism (76)
epigenetics (76)
genotype (76)
phenotype (77)
natural selection (77)

LEARNING CHALLENGE

Now that you have studied the chapter, assess your comprehension of the material by answering the following questions. Then use the key at the end to determine if your understanding is at the basic, intermediate, or advanced level. For a more comprehensive assessment of your learning, please see your your student study guide and your Psychology CourseMate (www.cengagebrain.com).

1. The part of the neuron that receives incoming signals is the _____.

a. axon
b. dendrites
c. cell body
d. vesicles

2. Homeostasis is an internal equilibrium controlled by the _____ of the brain.

a. medulla
b. thalamus
c. hippocampus
d. hypothalamus

3. _____ is to danger as _____ is to calm.

a. Somatic; autonomic
b. Parasympathetic; sympathetic
c. Central; peripheral
d. Sympathetic; parasympathetic

4. The principle of epigenetics is most compatible with _____.

a. nature
b. nurture
c. interactionism
d. endocrinology

5. Hugh had a stroke in the right occipital lobe of his brain. Which of the following symptoms is most likely to occur due to this damage?

a. inability to hear sounds from the left side of his body
b. inability to feel the left side of his body
c. inability to see things on the left side of his body
d. paralysis on the left side of his body

6. Letha injured her head in a car accident. As a result of her injuries, she can no longer understand others' speech, and she often says things that make little sense. Where is the most likely site of Letha's brain injury?

a. left frontal lobe
b. right frontal lobe
c. left temporal lobe
d. right temporal lobe

7. The _____ is important for regulating arousal in the brain.

a. thalamus
b. reticular formation
c. medulla
d. hypothalamus

8. Which of the following neurotransmitters is most analogous to the brakes on a car?

a. GABA
b. glutamate
c. acetylcholine (ACh)
d. serotonin

9. Tad takes a drug that stimulates his adrenal medulla. What symptoms is this drug likely to cause in Tad?

a. panic
b. sleepiness
c. sexual arousal
d. abdominal pain

10. In a split-brain surgery, doctors cut the _____ of the brain to reduce seizures.

a. reticular formation
b. hippocampus
c. corpus callosum
d. amygdala

11. The _____ is to fast as the _____ is to slow.

a. central nervous system; endocrine system
b. endocrine system; central nervous system
c. autonomic nervous system; central nervous system
d. central nervous system; peripheral nervous system

12. Kim was born with a deformity in his brain that causes him to lack the ability to balance his body and inhibits his ability to learn new motor skills. The most likely site of Kim's deformity is his _____.

a. parietal lobe
b. medulla
c. thalamus
d. cerebellum

13. During brain surgery, Dr. Li stimulates the brain of her patient by touching an electrode to the surface of the cortex. When Dr. Li applies the stimulation, the patient does not have any noticeable reaction. Where is Dr. Li most likely stimulating the brain?

a. motor cortex
b. somatosensory cortex
c. association cortex
d. visual cortex

14. Which brain structure is most closely associated with amnesia?

    a. thalamus

    b. hypothalamus

    c. hippocampus

    d. corpus callosum

15. Which of the following is part of the limbic system?

    a. hypothalamus

    b. cerebellum

    c. amygdala

    d. thalamus

Scoring Key

Below are the answers and the associated point values for each of the Learning Challenge questions. Circle the associated points for each question that you answered correctly. To obtain your Learning Challenge Score, add up the points you circled and write the total in the blank.

1. B, 1 pt   **6.** C, 3 pts   **11.** A, 2 pts

2. D, 1 pt   **7.** B, 1 pt   **12.** D, 3 pts

3. D, 2 pts   **8.** A, 2 pts   **13.** C, 3 pts

4. C, 2 pts   **9.** A, 3 pts   **14.** C, 2 pts

5. C, 3 pts   **10.** C, 1 pt   **15.** C, 1 pt

Learning Challenge Score _____

(27–30) Congratulations! You scored at the advanced level. You are well on your way to mastering the material. Take the next step by answering the questions in your Student Study Guide or your Psychology CourseMate (www.cengagebrain.com).

(21–26) You are almost there! You scored at the intermediate level. Review the material you missed before moving on to answer the questions in your Student Study Guide or your Psychology CourseMate (www.cengagebrain.com).

(20 and below) You are on your way, but you're not there yet! You scored at the beginner level. It appears that you need to carefully review the chapter to improve your mastery of the material.

USE IT OR LOSE IT: APPLYING PSYCHOLOGY

1. Jean-Dominique Bauby was still able to think, feel, and remember the events of his life after a stroke left him in a permanent state of locked-in syndrome. Now that you know something about the brain, can you explain why he retained these abilities?

2. If a person were injected with a drug that blocked the action of acetylcholine in the brain, what would you expect to happen?

3. What human traits do you believe to be adaptive at this point in our evolutionary history? If we assume that natural selection is still occurring, in a million years what would you expect humans to be like?

4. Your best friend is interested in what you are learning in your psychology class. He asks you to explain how the endocrine system differs from the nervous system. What would you tell him?

5. Your best friend's grandmother has just suffered a stroke. This stroke has left her with an inability to speak, but she can still understand what others say to her. She also has paralysis on the right side of her body. Your friend wants to know what part of her grandmother's brain was likely damaged by the stroke. Based on your understanding of the brain, what would you tell your friend?

CRITICAL THINKING FOR INTEGRATION

1. Design an *experiment* to test the hypothesis that the amygdala plays a role in the processing of emotional memories.

2. You want to test the hypothesis that low levels of serotonin are related to obesity in humans. Which type(s) of research design(s) would you *not* want to use? Why?

3. Discuss the ethical considerations involved in using invasive techniques for studying the brains of animals.

4. What questions would a developmental psychologist be *most* interested in asking about the nervous system?

CHAPTER STUDY RESOURCES

Student Study Guide

To help organize your learning, work through Chapter 2 of the *What Is Psychology? Student Study Guide*. The study guide includes learning objectives, a chapter summary, fill-in review, key terms, a practice test, and activities.

CengageNOW

Go to **www.cengage.com/login** to link to CengageNOW, your online study tool. First take the Pre-Test for this chapter to get your personalized study plan, which will identify topics you need to review and direct you to online resources. Then take the Post-Test to determine what concepts you have mastered and what you still need work on.

CourseMate

Access an interactive eBook, chapter-specific interactive learning tools, including flashcards, quizzes, videos, and more in your Psychology CourseMate, available at **CengageBrain.com**.

Aplia

Aplia™ is an online interactive learning solution that helps you improve comprehension—and your grade—by integrating a variety of tools such as video, tutorials, practice tests, and interactive eBook. Founded by a professor to enhance his own courses, Aplia provides automatically graded assignments with detailed, immediate explanations on every question, and innovative teaching materials. More than 1,000,000 students like you have used Aplia at over 1,800 institutions. Aplia should be purchased only when assigned by your instructor as part of your course.

Together, the nervous system and endocrine system influence *every* action of your body—every movement, every biological process, and every thought. The tragic case of Jean-Dominique Bauby illustrates just how important a healthy brain is to our ability to carry out our daily activities. In the few moments it took the stroke to destroy crucial parts of his brainstem, Jean-Dominique lost nearly all his ability to engage in voluntary behaviors. Now that you have a greater understanding of how your nervous system and endocrine system work, we hope you have a greater appreciation for what these systems do *for* you.

HOW DOES BIOLOGY INFLUENCE OUR BEHAVIOR?

HOW DOES THE BRAIN COMMUNICATE?

- **Neurons** use electrochemical energy to generate **action potentials** that travel to the end of the neuron and cause the release of **neurotransmitters**.

- Action potentials or neural signals are fired when a neuron is depolarized enough to reach its **threshold of excitation** (−55 mv).

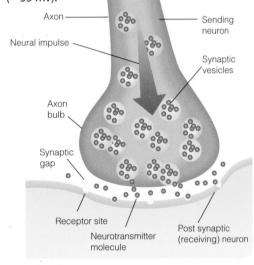

Axon

Neural impulse

Sending neuron

Synaptic vesicles

Axon bulb

Synaptic gap

Receptor site

Neurotransmitter molecule

Post synaptic (receiving) neuron

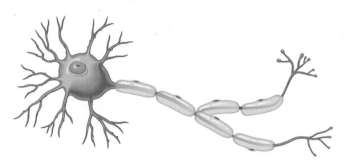

- Neurotransmitters are chemical compounds that carry signals across neurons. Some of the key neurotransmitters are **acetylcholine**, **dopamine, serotonin**, **norepinephrine**, **GABA**, and **glutamate**.

- Neurotransmitters play significant roles in regulating behavior and mood.

IS THE NERVOUS SYSTEM A SINGLE SYSTEM?

The **nervous system** is organized into a hierarchy of systems:

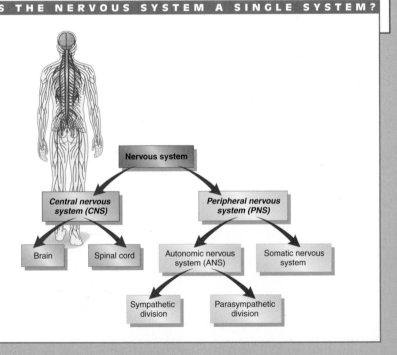

Nervous system

Central nervous system (CNS)

Peripheral nervous system (PNS)

Brain

Spinal cord

Autonomic nervous system (ANS)

Somatic nervous system

Sympathetic division

Parasympathetic division

HOW IS THE BRAIN ORGANIZED AND HOW DO WE STUDY THE BRAIN?

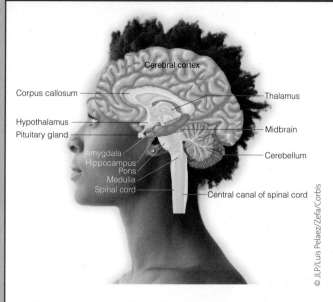

Cerebral cortex
Corpus callosum
Hypothalamus
Pituitary gland
Amygdala
Hippocampus
Pons
Medulla
Spinal cord
Thalamus
Midbrain
Cerebellum
Central canal of spinal cord

© JLP/Luis Pelaez/Zefa/Corbis

- The brain is divided into three key regions: the **hindbrain**, the **midbrain**, and the **forebrain**. The forebrain regulates higher order processes such as thinking and emotional control.

- The brain regulates motor activity, sensation and perception, emotions, our ability to learn and remember, and all the other elements of human behavior.

- The **cerebral cortex** is a thin layer of wrinkled tissue that covers the outside of the brain and is most responsible for the cognition, decision making, and language capabilities that are unique to humans.

- The brain is divided into right and left hemispheres. The left hemisphere generally governs the right side of the body, whereas the right hemisphere governs the left side of the body.

- To assist in studying the brain and its functioning, technology such as CAT scans, MRIs, fMRIs, PET scans, and SPECT scans are all important tools.

© Lester Lefkowitz/Corbis

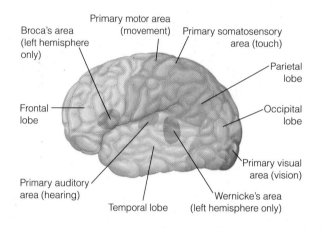

Broca's area (left hemisphere only)
Primary motor area (movement)
Primary somatosensory area (touch)
Parietal lobe
Frontal lobe
Occipital lobe
Primary visual area (vision)
Primary auditory area (hearing)
Wernicke's area (left hemisphere only)
Temporal lobe

HOW DOES THE ENDOCRINE SYSTEM INFLUENCE OUR BEHAVIOR?

The endocrine system contains **glands** that release chemical messengers—**hormones**—into the bloodstream. Compared to the nervous system, the endocrine system is slower and more long-lasting in its effects.

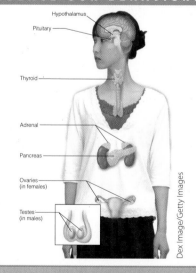

Hypothalamus
Pituitary
Thyroid
Adrenal
Pancreas
Ovaries (in females)
Testes (in males)

Dex Image/Getty Images

WHAT MAKES US WHO WE ARE—OUR BIOLOGY OR THE ENVIRONMENT?

The **phenotype** or actual trait = Inherited genes or the **genotype** (nature) + Environmental influences (nurture)

Natural selection → genotypes that aid reproductive success remain in the gene pool

© Reuters/Corbis

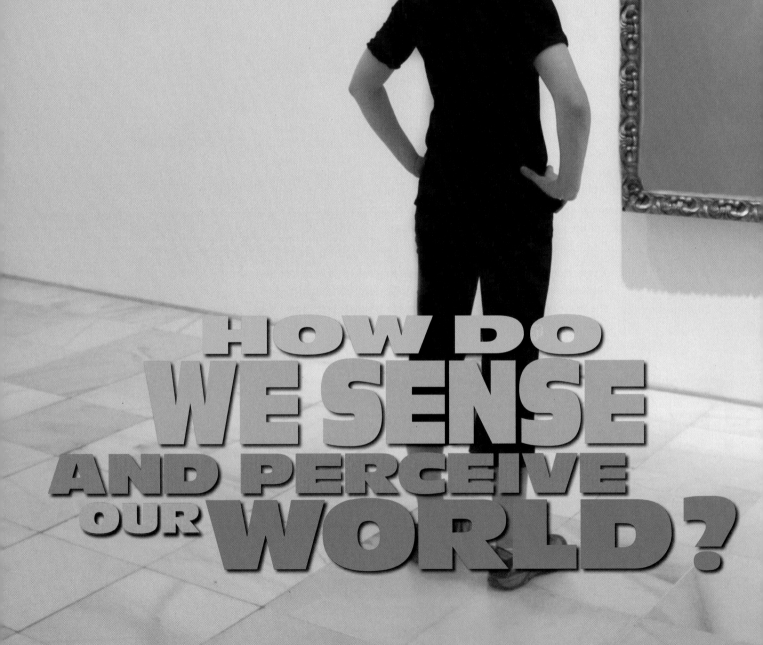

HOW DO WE SENSE AND PERCEIVE OUR WORLD?

THE BIG PICTURE

How Do We Take It All In?

At this moment, you are reading this textbook in an attempt to learn more about human behavior—and to do well in your psychology class. Take a moment to think about what is actually taking place as you read this page. How do you get the visual information printed on this page into your brain where it can be stored for future use?

To read this page, you must first focus your conscious awareness or **attention** on the page and be able to *see* the images printed on it. Seeing is an example of what psychologists call **sensation**. In sensation, sense organs of the body, such as the eyes, convert environmental energy, such as the light that is bouncing off the book page, into *action potentials* that the brain can then process. Sensation—in this case, seeing— is the first step to getting information into our minds. If you did not have sense organs such as your eyes, ears, tongue, nose, and nerve endings, you would not be able to accomplish **transduction**, or the conversion of environmental stimuli into a form that your nervous system can process. Without sensation, you would not be able to learn.

After sensation, the next step is **perception**. You must understand what the images printed on the page mean. Perception occurs when you interpret the meaning of the information gathered through your senses. In this case, reading this page requires that you use your prior knowledge of the English language to help you perceive the meaning of the printed letters and words. Likewise, when you listen to a lecture, sensation occurs as your ears do their job of transducing sound into neural impulses. Then perception occurs as you use your knowledge of spoken language to interpret the information your ears have sent your brain.

What you already know about the world often helps you interpret your current experience. As you look around your room right now, what do you see, hear, smell, taste, and feel? To answer these questions, you must use your senses to take in information from your environment. Then you must use what you know about the world to help you perceive what you see, hear, smell, taste, and feel. However, because perception depends in part on the experiences and knowledge we have, people do not always perceive things the same way. For instance, two people looking at the same cloud may each think that the cloud looks like a different animal.

CHAPTER OUTLINE

- Measuring Sensation and Perception: How Sensitive Are Our Senses?

- How Do We See the World?

- How Do We Hear the World?

- What Other Senses Do We Have?

- Perception: How Do We Make Sense of It All?

- How Accurate Are Our Perceptions?

Grant Faint/Getty Images

(continued)

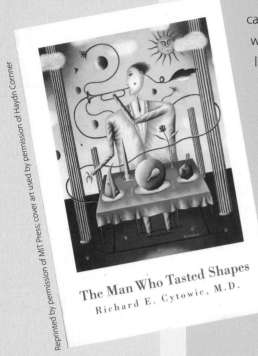

The Man Who Tasted Shapes
Richard E. Cytowic, M.D.

Reprinted by permission of MIT Press; cover art used by permission of Haydn Cornner

Dr. Richard Cytowic wrote *The Man Who Tasted Shapes* about his friend Michael Watson's unusual case of synesthesia.

attention conscious awareness; can be focused on events that are taking place in the environment or inside our minds

sensation the process through which our sense organs transduce environmental energies such as light and sound into neural impulses

transduction the process through which our sense organs convert environmental energies into neural impulses

perception the process through which we interpret sensory information

Individual differences exist in *how* you sense things as well. Some people cannot see well without glasses. Some people have very acute hearing abilities, whereas others cannot discriminate well between different sounds—and some, like Michael Watson, have very unusual sensory and perceptual abilities indeed.

All his life, Michael had experienced sensations and perceptions differently than other people did. When Michael (an amateur gourmet cook) tasted foods, he also *felt* the sensation of certain geometric shapes on his body. For example, when tasting a chicken dish, he might have the sensation of feeling rounded shapes pressed against his body, especially on his face and hands. Consequently, when developing new recipes, Michael's goal might be to produce a dish that would taste *pointed* rather than *rounded*—as opposed to a dish that would be salty or spicy.

Michael's unique shape tasting is an interesting case of a very rare condition called *synesthesia*. Synesthesia, which affects only about 10 out of every 1 million people, is characterized by cross-linkages among the senses (Cytowic, 1999; J. Ward, 2003). When a person with synesthesia senses a stimulus with one sense, he or she experiences sensations in another sense. In general, the cross-linkage seems to be one-way. For example, hearing a sound may evoke the sight of a color, but the sight of a color does not evoke the hearing of a sound.

In Michael's case, taste invoked sensations of touch. Sometimes Michael felt the shapes over his entire body. Other times, such as when tasting sweets, he only felt the shapes in his hands. He felt most shapes in his face, hands, and shoulders. Because of his unique abilities, Michael attracted the attention of his good friend, neurologist Dr. Richard Cytowic. Richard studied Michael for many years in an attempt to better understand his friend's unique abilities and the way in which the brain influences sensation and perception—a journey he chronicled in a fascinating book entitled *The Man Who Tasted Shapes* (Cytowic, 1999).

As you might have guessed, Richard found that people like Michael do not process sensory information in the typical way. But how does the average person's brain process sensory information? Answering these questions will be the focus of this chapter. As you read through the chapter, keep Michael Watson's story in the back of your mind. What must it be like to actually taste shapes?

MEASURING SENSATION AND PERCEPTION: HOW SENSITIVE ARE OUR SENSES?

Psychologists who study sensation and perception are most interested in understanding how we process sensory stimuli such as sights, sounds, and smells. For instance, what occurs when you look at an apple? How does your mind interpret the color of the light bouncing off the surface of the apple? Why do some apples appear to be greenish-red and others appear to be deep ruby red? What makes the different notes of a musical piece sound different? What physical properties of a food make it taste sweet or bitter? Questions like these are the focus of the branch of psychology called **psychophysics**.

Absolute Thresholds

One of the fundamental questions psychophysicists have sought to answer concerns the limits of human sensory capabilities. How faint a light can humans see? How soft a tone can we hear? At what concentration can you first taste sugar dissolved in a glass of water? How intense a pressure must be placed on the arm for you to feel it?

Psychophysicists have conducted many experiments to answer these questions. These experiments typically involve presenting stimuli of gradually increasing or decreasing intensity (along with some trials in which the stimulus is not presented at all). Participants are asked to report whether they can detect the presence of the stimulus. In this way psychophysicists establish an *absolute threshold*. **Absolute threshold** is defined as the minimum intensity of a stimulus that can be detected 50% of the time. This 50% mark is used because the level of the stimulus required for it to *just* be perceived varies from trial to trial and from person to person during an experiment.

One reason for variations in participants' reports of absolute threshold is changes in the individual's *response bias*, or tendency to report detecting the presence of the stimulus whether or not the stimulus is actually present. Because it can be very difficult to tell whether we can actually sense stimuli when they are presented at very low levels, sometimes we tend to guess. Have you ever thought you heard the phone ring while you were in the shower, only to find that you were mistaken? Many of us have had this frustrating experience. Why does this occur? A simple explanation is that we are listening intently for the phone to ring. Because we *expect* the ring to be very faint over the sound of the shower, we convince ourselves that we hear a sound that simply isn't present.

The same thing sometimes occurs during laboratory experiments that examine absolute threshold. If you are listening intently to hear a very faint sound over a pair of headphones, you may think you hear a stimulus when it isn't actually there. On another day, you may not make this same mistake. Your absolute threshold may appear to move around a bit. ● TABLE 3.1 lists the approximate established absolute thresholds for the five senses, described in familiar descriptive terms.

LEARNING OBJECTIVE

What Should You Know?
- Explain the concepts of absolute threshold, just noticeable difference (jnd), and signal detection used in measuring sensation and perception.

TABLE 3.1

SENSE		ABSOLUTE THRESHOLD
Vision		A candle seen from 30 miles away on a clear, dark night.
Hearing		A ticking watch that is 20 feet away in an otherwise quiet room.
Smell		One drop of perfume diffused in a three-room apartment.
Taste		One teaspoon of sugar dissolved in 2 gallons of water.
Touch		The wing of a bumblebee falling on one's cheek from a distance of 1 centimeter.

Paul Bricknell/Getty Images

© Peter Baxter/ Shutterstock

Image Source/ Getty Images

Ken Karp/PhotoLibrary

Andre Skonieczny/ PhotoLibrary

psychophysics the study of how the mind interprets the physical properties of stimuli

absolute threshold the minimum intensity of a stimulus at which participants can identify its presence 50% of the time

This girl can feel this insect only when its weight exceeds her absolute threshold for touch.

Keiji Iwai/PhotoLibrary

FIGURE 3.1

● **Possible Judgments in Detecting the Presence of a Stimulus** Imagine that you are expecting an important phone call, but you need to take a shower. While you're in the shower, listening for the phone, these are the possible situations that might arise and the judgments you might make in these situations. Signal detection theory uses the proportion of hits and false alarms that a subject makes to separate response bias from actual ability to detect the presence of the stimulus.

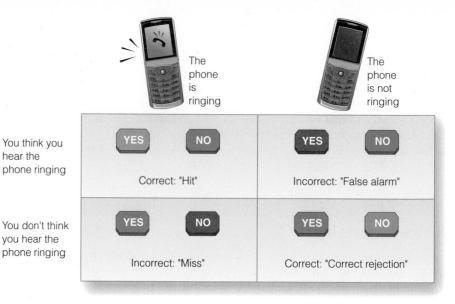

The phone is ringing

The phone is not ringing

You think you hear the phone ringing

| YES | NO | | YES | NO |

Correct: "Hit"

Incorrect: "False alarm"

You don't think you hear the phone ringing

| YES | NO | | YES | NO |

Incorrect: "Miss"

Correct: "Correct rejection"

signal detection a method of analyzing the relative proportions of hits and false alarms to eliminate the effects of response bias in a participant's detection of a stimulus

Air traffic control displays must be designed to maximize controllers' hits and correct rejections while minimizing their misses and false alarms.

Signal Detection Theory

Some theorists propose that to get a true measure of the participants' sensory abilities researchers must go a step further by separating out the influence of response bias. **Signal detection** is a method of analyzing the proportion of correct judgments (*hits*) and errors (*false alarms*) that a participant makes in trying to detect a stimulus or signal. By applying statistical measures to these proportions, researchers can eliminate the effects of response bias and thereby get a truer measure of the participant's ability to actually detect the presence of the signal or stimulus (Parasuraman, Masalonis, & Hancock, 2000). ● FIGURE 3.1 illustrates the types of judgments you could make in a signal detection situation (such as hearing the phone ring while you're in the shower) and the signal detection terminology for each possible response: hit, false alarm, miss, and correct rejection.

Signal detection has great significance in the real world. For instance, air traffic controllers monitor computer screens for unauthorized air traffic entering their airspace. In experiments on air traffic control, researchers can monitor participants' hit and false alarm rates for detecting intruding aircraft on a mock radar screen. Studies like these help researchers design radar screens and computer displays that will allow air traffic controllers to maximize their *hits* while minimizing their *false alarms*.

Signal detection is obviously useful in improving job performance, but does it also apply to other real-world situations? Researchers now believe that signal detection can be applied to more complex situations in which people have to judge whether they have seen a person's face before, as in eyewitness testimony (Macmillian & Creelman, 1991; Podd, 1990). In this application a hit would mean correctly identifying a face you had seen before. A false alarm would be incorrectly identifying a face as one you had seen before when in fact you had not seen it before.

By applying signal detection to eyewitness testimony in controlled laboratory experiments, researchers study whether the average witness can reliably and accurately identify faces seen before. As we will see in this chapter and again in Chapter 6, many studies have shown that eyewitness testimony is often inaccurate. This, of course, has implications for our legal system as well as for psychologists studying sensation and perception.

© Matthew McVay/Getty Images

Just Noticeable Difference

In addition to establishing absolute thresholds for the senses, psychophysicists have tried to establish the minimum *change* in the intensity of a stimulus that can be detected 50% of the time. This barely noticeable change in the stimulus is referred to as the *difference threshold* or the **just noticeable difference (jnd)**. In the early 1800s, psychophysicist Max Weber discovered something very interesting about the jnd. Because sensation is subjective, the amount of change in the stimulus that is necessary to produce a jnd depends on the intensity at which the stimulus is *first* presented. For example, if you are holding a 10-pound weight, it will take more added weight for you to notice a change than it would if you started out holding a 5-pound weight. After many experiments, Weber determined that he could express the relationship between the stimulus's original intensity and the amount of change in the stimulus that is required to produce a jnd by means of the equation now known as **Weber's law** ($\Delta I/I = k$). Weber's law states that when the change in a given stimulus (ΔI) required to produce a jnd is divided by the initial intensity of the stimulus (I), the result is a constant number (k). However, this constant varies for each of the five senses; that is, the k, or constant, for vision is different from the k constants for hearing, taste, smell, and touch.

John Eder/Getty Images

There is no good scientific evidence to suggest that moviegoers can be coerced into buying refreshments through subliminal persuasion.

If we know the k value for a particular stimulus, we can use Weber's law to predict the change in the stimulus that would be needed to produce a jnd in the average participant. For example, for taste, $k = 1/5$. So, if you begin with 5 teaspoons of salt in a pot of soup, you would have to add one teaspoon of salt to produce a jnd. However, the same amount of stimulus change (ΔI) does not always produce a jnd. If your soup originally contains 10 teaspoons of salt, you will need an additional 2 teaspoons of salt to produce a jnd. Weber's law clearly demonstrates the subjectivity of sensation and perception. One additional teaspoon of salt in a very salty pot of soup is not noticeable, but that same teaspoon of salt added to a less salty pot of soup is noticeable.

Research on absolute and difference thresholds deals with our ability to *consciously* perceive sensory stimuli—to be *aware* that we are perceiving the stimuli. But what happens when sensory stimuli are presented at intensities too weak to be consciously perceived? If we are not consciously aware of sensory stimuli, can they still affect our behavior?

Processing Without Awareness: Subliminal Stimulation of the Senses

In psychological terms, when sensory stimuli are presented at intensities that are too weak to reach absolute threshold, the stimuli are said to be **subliminal**. Subliminal perception became a topic of many debates in the late 1950s when a man named James Vicary attempted to use subliminal persuasion to convince moviegoers at a public theater to buy more popcorn and soda. Vicary flashed messages such as "Eat popcorn" and "Drink Coca-Cola" between the frames of a movie at a speed so fast that moviegoers did not have time to consciously perceive the messages. Because the messages were flashed so briefly, the moviegoers never consciously saw anything other than the movie.

Vicary reported that as a result of his "experiment," concession sales rose 18%. As it turns out, James Vicary admitted in 1962 that he had not conducted a true experiment. The data that he collected were so few that they could not be used for scientific purposes (Epley, Savitsky, & Kachelski, 1999; Pratkanis, 1992). After Vicary's attempts at subliminal persuasion, researchers began to carefully examine the effects of subliminal persuasion both in the real world and in the laboratory. To date, most studies have failed to yield convincing evidence for the effectiveness of subliminal persuasion (see Pratkanis, Epley, Savitsky, & Kachelski, 2007).

just noticeable difference (jnd) the minimum change in intensity of a stimulus that participants can detect 50% of the time

Weber's law a psychophysical formula used to predict the jnd for a given stimulus: $\Delta I/I = k$, where ΔI is the change in the stimulus required to produce a jnd, I is the original intensity of the stimulus, and k is a constant that varies for each of the five senses

subliminal when the intensity of a stimulus is below the participant's absolute threshold and the participant is not consciously aware of the stimulus

Furthermore, when these studies do show that subliminal perception can affect behavior, the effects are nowhere near as impressive as Vicary's claims. For example, in one study, researchers were able to show that being subliminally exposed to the brand name *Lipton Ice* affected participants' choice of an iced tea drink—*but only if they were already thirsty*. It did not influence those participants who were not already motivated to drink (Karremans, Stroebe, & Claus, 2006). At present, the Federal Communications Commission has a ban on subliminal ads on TV and radio, but there is little reason to be afraid that subliminal messages will take away our free will and give advertisers the power to directly control our behavior.

Now that we have a basic understanding of how psychologists measure the limits of our sensory abilities, we will examine how our bodies accomplish the process of sensation.

Let's REVIEW

In this section, we have given you a quick overview of some important aspects of measuring sensation and perception—absolute threshold, signal detection theory, just noticeable difference, and subliminal stimulation of the senses. For a quick check of your understanding, try answering the following questions at increasing levels of difficulty.

1. In signal detection theory, correctly identifying the presence of a stimulus is called a _____.

   a. hit   c. correct rejection
   b. false alarm   d. miss

2. According to Weber's law, adding one more teaspoon of sugar to a glass of tea would be most noticeable when _____.

   a. the tea initially had no sugar in it
   b. the tea initially had 2 teaspoons of sugar in it
   c. the tea initially had 3 teaspoons of sugar in it
   d. the tea initially had 5 teaspoons of sugar in it

3. Jerry wants to sweeten his iced tea. He adds one teaspoon of sugar, but the tea does not taste sweet to him. When Jerry adds one more teaspoon of sugar to his tea, he finds that the tea now tastes sweet—but just barely. Two teaspoons of sugar seem to correspond to Jerry's _____.

   a. just noticeable difference   c. signal detection threshold
   b. absolute threshold   d. stimulus threshold

ANSWERS 1. a; 2. a; 3. b

LEARNING OBJECTIVES
What Should You Know?

● Describe the physical properties of light—wavelength, amplitude, and the visible spectrum—and how they relate to human vision.

● Describe the anatomy of the eye and the layers of the retina and how they function.

● Explain how we adapt to light and dark, how we see color, and how the brain processes what we see.

HOW DO WE SEE THE WORLD?

Our eyes are at the front of our skulls, so you might assume that vision is a direct transfer from object to eye to brain. Vision is more complicated than that, however, and researchers have studied vision more than the other senses. To understand vision, we'll look at the properties of light that apply to vision, the anatomy of the eye, the layers of the retina, and how we process visual information in the brain.

How Vision Works: Light Waves and Energy

When we see an object, what we really see are the light waves that are reflected off the surface of the object. Thus a blue shirt will appear blue because blue is the only color of light that is reflected by the shirt. The shirt absorbs all other colors of light.

Measuring Light: Wavelength and Amplitude

● FIGURE 3.2 depicts the *electromagnetic spectrum*, which includes visible light. Electromagnetic energies, including light, result from disturbances in the electrical and magnetic fields

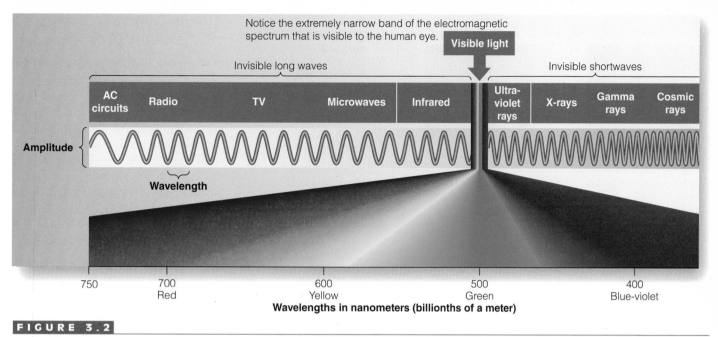

● **The Visible Spectrum of Light** *From Psychology, 3/e by Don H. Hockenbury and Sandra E. Hockenbury. © 2003 by Worth Publishers. Used with permission.*

that exist in the universe. Like all electromagnetic energies, light waves are characterized by their **wavelength** and **amplitude**. The wavelength of light is the distance between the peaks of consecutive waves. The amplitude of the light wave is the height of each wave peak. These distances are typically measured in nanometers (nm).

The human eye cannot sense all electromagnetic energy. In fact, the **visible spectrum** for humans is only a very narrow band of the electromagnetic spectrum that spans from about 360 nm to 750 nm (Figure 3.2). Other species can sense electromagnetic wavelengths that are beyond the human visible spectrum. Some snakes sense infrared rays, allowing them to sense other animals' body heat (Sinclair, 1985). Some fish, reptiles, birds, insects, rodents, and other vertebrates are able to sense ultraviolet (UV) light (Boulcott & Braithewaite, 2005). Some animals, such as spiders and rats, use their ability to sense UV light during hunting (Bhaskara, Brijesh, Ahmed, & Borges, 2009) or in tracking other animals (Pickerell, 2003). If you are hiking through the woods, keep in mind that certain animals may be able to see you before you see them!

Properties of Light: Hue, Brightness, and Saturation

Although our eyes cannot sense much of the electromagnetic spectrum, we are capable of seeing millions of different combinations of color, richness, and brightness of light (M. H. Bornstein & Marks, 1982; Linhares, Pinto, & Nascimento, 2008). The wavelength of the light wave corresponds to the color or **hue** of the light we see. Shorter wavelengths correspond to cool colors such as blues and purples; longer wavelengths correspond to warmer colors such as yellows and reds (Figure 3.2). The amplitude of the light wave corresponds to its **brightness**. The higher the amplitude of the light wave, the brighter the color we perceive. One other characteristic of light, **saturation**, corresponds to the purity of the light. Light that consists of a single wavelength will produce the most saturated, or richest, color. Light that is a mixture of wavelengths produces less saturated colors. For example, pure blue light is high in saturation, but a mixture of blue and white light produces a less saturated blue light. ● FIGURE 3.3 illustrates the differences in brightness and saturation for a particular hue of blue.

For vision to occur, our eyes must be able to convert the electromagnetic waves of the visible spectrum into action potentials that our brains can process. In the next section, we will look at the anatomy of the eye to get a feel for how this conversion occurs.

wavelength a physical property of some energies that corresponds to the distance between the wave peaks

amplitude a physical property of some energies that corresponds to the height of the wave peaks

visible spectrum the spectrum of light that humans can see

hue the color of a light

brightness the intensity of light; it corresponds to the amplitude of the light waves

saturation the purity of light; pure light or saturated light consists of a single wavelength

a. Hue
Pure Saturated Blue

The hue (blue) corresponds to the wavelength on the visible spectrum. This blue is highly saturated—the purest blue.

b. Brightness
Brighter Intensity of the Same Blue

The higher the amplitude of the lightwave, the brighter the hue (blue) appears.

c. Saturation
Less Saturated Blue

Light that is from more than one wavelength—here, blue light mixed with white light—is less saturated than the pure blue in (a).

FIGURE 3.3

● **Brightness and Saturation for a Hue of Blue**

The Anatomy of the Outer Eye

The process of vision begins with the parts of the eye we can readily see: the clear cornea that covers the iris (the colored part of your eye) and the pupil (the opening in the iris). From there, light is eventually focused on the retina at the back of your eye. The white part, the sclera, is a supporting structure that doesn't play a part in the processing of visual information.

The Cornea, Pupil, Iris, and Lens

When light enters the eye, the first structure it passes through is the cornea (● FIGURE 3.4). The *cornea* is the clear, slightly bulged-out outer surface of the eye. It protects the eye and begins the focusing process. The light that is reflected from an object in the environment must eventually be focused on the rear surface of the eye if we are to see the object clearly. As light waves pass through the material of the cornea, they slow down and bend—just as they do when they pass through a camera lens. This bending of the light waves plays an essential role in focusing images on the back of your eye. A damaged cornea can make it impossible for a person to see clearly.

Directly behind the cornea is the **pupil**. This black opening in the center of your eye is not really a structure. Rather, it is an opening, or aperture, through which light passes into the center of the eye. Light cannot pass through the white part of the eye, or the *sclera*. Therefore, it must pass through the cornea and pupil to enter the eye. The *iris*, the colored part of the eye surrounding the pupil, is constructed of rings of muscles that control the size of the pupil. In dimly lit conditions, the iris relaxes to dilate the pupil, allowing the maximum amount of light into the eye. In brightly lit conditions, the iris constricts to close the pupil, thus reducing the amount of light entering the eye so as not to overwhelm the light-sensitive cells in the eye. Although the pupil constricts rapidly in bright conditions, it is not always fast enough for us to avoid some discomfort. Anyone who has ever had someone turn on the bedroom light at night can attest to this!

Directly behind the iris and the pupil is the **lens** of the eye. The lens is a clear structure that is attached to the eye with strong *ciliary muscles*. The lens of the eye is rather like the lens of a camera—its job is to bring the light waves entering the eye into sharp focus on the back of the eye. A camera adjusts by moving the lens in and out (by turning it) until the image is in focus. Our eyes focus light not by moving the lens in and out, but by changing the thickness of the lens itself. Unlike the rigid glass of a camera lens, the lens of the eye is somewhat soft and flex-

pupil the hole in the iris through which light enters the eye

lens the part of the eye that lies behind the pupil and focuses light rays on the retina

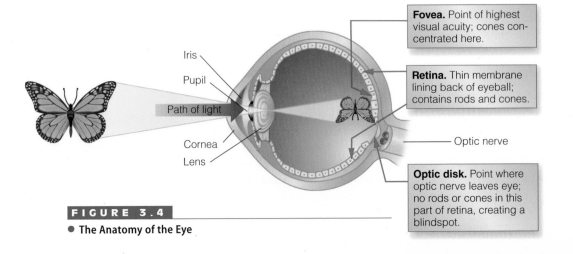

Iris
Pupil
Path of light
Cornea
Lens

Fovea. Point of highest visual acuity; cones concentrated here.

Retina. Thin membrane lining back of eyeball; contains rods and cones.

Optic nerve

Optic disk. Point where optic nerve leaves eye; no rods or cones in this part of retina, creating a blindspot.

FIGURE 3.4

● **The Anatomy of the Eye**

ible. The shape of the eye's lens can adjust, or undergo **accommodation**, so that the image passing through it is focused properly. When we look at an object that is far away (more than 20 feet), the ciliary muscles stretch and flatten the lens. This way light waves passing through the lens bend very little and the image appears in focus on the back of the eye. When we look at an object that is close at hand, the ciliary muscles contract and push on the lens to make it thicker. In this state, light waves bend so as to focus the nearby image on the back of the eye.

The Retina: Light Energy To Neural Messages

Once the light waves have been focused on the back of the eye, transduction of light waves into neural impulses occurs in the **retina**, the surface that lines the inside of the back of the eyeball. In the retina, specialized cells called **rods** and **cones** transduce light into action potentials. Without these cells, vision would not be possible. Before we look at how transduction occurs, it will be helpful if we describe the anatomy of the retina and the pathways through which visual information is processed there.

The Anatomy of the Retina

The diagram in ● FIGURE 3.5 shows a cross section of the layers in the human retina. The *ganglion cells* are on the surface of the retina, followed by successive layers of *amacrine*, *bipolar*, and *horizontal cells*, and finally the light-sensitive rods and cones. Look closely at Figure 3.5 and you will see that the light entering the eye must filter through all the layers of the retina before finally striking the rods and cones.

Incoming light passes unimpeded through the transparent layers of the retina to reach the rods and cones, which transduce the light energy into neural impulses. These signals travel back out to the ganglion cells on the surface of the retina. Along the way, the horizontal, bipolar, and amacrine cells funnel and consolidate the neural information from the rods and cones so that we can see a unified, coherent image. The signals that reach the ganglion cells in the top layer of the retina are to some degree summaries of the visual information from the rods and cones.

The Optic Nerve and the Blindspot

Once the neural impulses reach the ganglion cells, they exit the retina and travel to the brain via the **optic nerve**, which is composed of the axons of the ganglion cells (see Figures 3.4 and 3.5). The optic nerve actually exits the retina on the *surface* of the retina; there are no light-sensitive rods or cones at the point where the optic nerve leaves the retina. With no rods or cones at this spot, each of our eyes has a **blindspot**, which is a point in our visual field where we cannot see.

Luckily, however, our blindspots do not pose much of a problem. For one thing, the blindspot is at the side of our visual field, where we normally do not bring objects into focus in the first place (see Figure 3.4). If the blindspot were located at the *fovea* (the point directly behind the pupil), it is possible that we would be much more aware of it. Another reason is that we have two eyes. Whatever part of the world we miss seeing because of the blindspot in our left eye we see with our right eye, and vice versa.

Now that we have a picture of how the retina is constructed, let's turn our attention to a more careful look at how the rods and cones allow us to see.

The Rods and Cones

The rods and cones that line the inside layer of the retina play different roles in the process of vision. The rods, which are long and skinny, are sensitive to all colors of light, but they do not transmit information about color to the brain (see Figure 3.5). You can think of the rods as being black-and-white receptors. If you had only rods in your retina, you'd see everything in black and white. We see the world in color because of the cone cells in the retina. The cones, which are shorter and fatter than the rods, are responsible for transmitting information about color to the brain.

Relative to rods, the cones of the eye require a higher intensity of light to become activated. Because of this, we do not have good color vision in dimly lit situations—especially at night

Ray Hendley/Indexstock

Vision problems can strike at any age. Nearsightedness, or not seeing distant objects well, is common at all ages. Another condition, presbyopia, is more common after middle age. Presbyopia occurs when, as we age, the lens of the eye becomes more rigid and the eye is less able to accommodate to close objects. Because of presbyopia, many middle-aged and older adults need reading glasses or bifocals.

accommodation the process through which the lens is stretched or squeezed to focus light on the retina

retina the structure at the back of the eye that contains cells that transduce light into neural signals

rods the light-sensitive cells of the retina that pick up any type of light energy and convert it to neural signals

cones the cells of the retina that are sensitive to specific colors of light and send information to the brain concerning the colors we are seeing

optic nerve the structure that conveys visual information away from the retina to the brain

blindspot the point where the optic nerve leaves the retina and where there are no rods or cones

The back of the retina, which lines the back interior surface of the eye

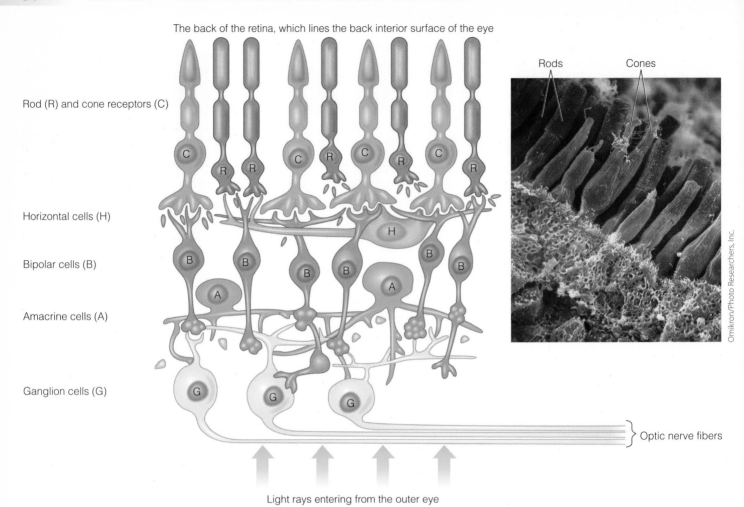

Rod (R) and cone receptors (C)

Rods   Cones

Horizontal cells (H)

Bipolar cells (B)

Amacrine cells (A)

Ganglion cells (G)

Optic nerve fibers

Light rays entering from the outer eye

Omikron/Photo Researchers, Inc.

FIGURE 3.5

● **A Cross Section of the Retina** Above is a schematic of the retina with the rods shown in purple and the cones in pink. To the right is an electron micrograph of the retina showing the rods and cones. *From "Organization of the Primate Retina," by J. E. Dowling and B. B. Boycott, in* Proceedings of the Royal Society of London, 16, *Series B, 80–111. Copyright © 1966 by the Royal Society.*

(Manning & Brainard, 2009). Think about driving at night. When light levels are not very intense, it may be possible to see objects in the distance, but impossible to discern their color.

In each eye you have about 100 million rods but only about 5 million cones (Matlin & Foley, 1997). Having so many rods and so few cones in the retina indicates that perceiving shape and form takes precedence over perception of color. If you think about it for a minute, this arrangement makes sense. Which information would you need first: to see the shape of a car speeding toward you in the dark, or to see the color of the car? Your first concern would be seeing the car to avoid a collision.

In addition to being differentially sensitive to light energy, the rods and cones of the eye are not distributed evenly across the surface of the retina. The highest concentration of cones is at the fovea, with fewer and fewer cones toward the peripheral edges of the retina. The density of rods follows the opposite pattern, with the highest concentration at the peripheral edges of the retina and fewer and fewer rods as you move toward the fovea (see ● FIGURE 3.6). This arrange-

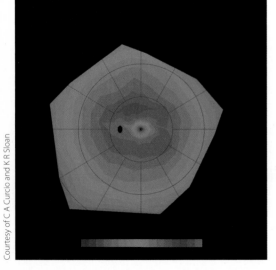

Courtesy of C A Curcio and K R Sloan

FIGURE 3.6

● **The Ratio of Rods to Cones in the Retina** This figure shows the ratio of rods to cones in the human retina. The darker, cooler colors signify a decreasing rod to cone ratio. Notice that at the fovea (the dark blue center of the retina) we find only cones. This high concentration of cones at the fovea gives us our best color vision for objects that are viewed head-on.

TRY THIS DEMONSTRATION

Where's Your Best Color Vision? Close your eyes and have a friend hand you a colored crayon without telling you what color it is. Sit upright in a chair with the crayon in your hand, extend your arm directly out to the side so that your arm forms a 90-degree angle with the side of your body (● FIGURE 3.7). Fix your eyes directly in front of you and open your eyes. In this position, the crayon should be outside your range of vision.

Now slowly move your extended arm forward in an arc toward the front of your head. Don't move your eyes. Keep them fixed directly ahead. As you move your arm slowly forward, keep noticing whether or not you can see the crayon. When you can just see the crayon, stop moving your arm. Now, can you tell what color the crayon is? Don't cheat and move your eyes!

At this point, you should be able to see the crayon, but you should not be able to tell what color it is. This is because you are seeing the crayon on the edges of your retina, where you have only rods. The rods are good at picking up the image of the crayon, but they can't tell your brain the color of the crayon. Now, slowly move your arm forward again, until you can just perceive the crayon's color. You have now moved your arm forward enough that light from the crayon is striking some of your cones (closer to the center of your eye). At this point, your perception of the color should be washed out, because you are still seeing the crayon with mostly rods.

FIGURE 3.7

● **Color Vision and Position in the Visual Field** When you hold a crayon to the side, you cannot perceive its color because there are no cones on the peripheral edges of the retina. When you hold a crayon directly in front of your eyes, the high density of color-sensitive cones at the fovea gives you the best color perception.

As you continue to move the crayon slowly forward, be aware of how the color seems to deepen and intensify. The closer to the front of your face you move the crayon, the more cones you are using, and the better your color vision becomes. When the crayon is directly in front of your eyes, its color appears most vivid. You are now seeing the crayon primarily with your cones because it is directly in front of your fovea.

ment means that our best color vision is for objects placed directly in front of us, whereas our color vision for objects seen out of the corners of our eyes is very poor. To demonstrate this for yourself, try this simple demonstration. You'll need a set of crayons, a chair, and the help of a friend.

Turning Light Energy Into Neural Messages

The rods and cones of the eye are able to transduce light into neural impulses because they contain light-sensitive **photopigments**, chemicals that are activated by light energy. When a rod is not receiving light input, its photopigment molecules are stable. However, when light strikes the rod, this incoming light energy splits the photopigments apart (Yau & Hardie, 2009). As the photopigments break up, they set off a complex chain of chemical reactions that change the rate at which the neurons of the visual system fire action potentials. The brain uses the pattern of these action potentials to interpret what we are seeing.

Adapting To Light and Darkness

Have you ever had to wait at the back of a dark theater for your eyes to adjust before you could find your seat? This type of adaptation is referred to as **dark adaptation**. It also takes our eyes a while to adapt to

photopigments light-sensitive chemicals that create electrical changes when they come into contact with light

dark adaptation the process through which our eyes adjust to dark conditions after having been exposed to bright light

Because cones require more light energy than rods, it can be difficult to discriminate among colors at night. Even though you can clearly make out the shapes of the oncoming cars, you may not be able to discern their color.

Eddie Hironaka/Getty Images

sudden increases in light brightness, or undergo **light adaptation**. Adaptation to both light and dark is important because the lighting conditions of our environment can vary widely. A sunny day is at least 10^9 times brighter than a moonless night (Rieke & Rudd, 2009).

Dark and light adaptation are accomplished, in part, by changes in pupil size. Unfortunately, the amount of dilation and constriction that our pupils can accomplish is limited, and they alone cannot fully account for the adaptations we experience. Another mechanism of adaptation is found in the photopigments themselves. If you were to enter a completely darkened room, no light would enter your eyes and no photopigments would break down. After remaining in these darkened conditions for a period of time, the photopigment levels in your eyes would build up. This is what occurs when we sleep at night. With a large store of photopigments, your eyes are very sensitive to light. If someone were to suddenly turn on the lights in the bedroom, you would experience a bright flash of light and perhaps even pain as a large number of photopigments break down all at once. It would take about one minute for your eyes to adjust to the light (Hood & Finkelstein, 1986).

The process of dark adaptation is the opposite of what occurs during light adaptation. Under normal daytime lighting conditions, we constantly use our photopigments to see our surroundings. So, at any given moment during the day, a certain percentage of our photopigments are broken down. If you suddenly enter a darkened theater after being in bright daylight, you will not have enough photopigments to be able to see well. It will take more than 30 minutes for your photopigment levels to fully build up, giving you complete dark adaptation (Hood & Finkelstein, 1986). This is why you may have to stand, popcorn in hand, at the back of the darkened theater for several minutes before you can find your seat.

How We See Color

Like the rods, the cones of the retina also contain photopigments. However, there is an important distinction between the photopigments in the rods and cones. All rods contain the same photopigment. In contrast, there are three different types of cones, each containing a slightly different photopigment. **Why do we need three types of cones in our eyes?** The answer seems to be that three different cones are necessary for color vision.

The Colors of Light

You may have learned in elementary school about three primary colors (red, yellow, and blue) from which all other colors can be made. But did you know that these primary colors refer to reflected colors (such as in paint or crayons) and not colors of light? When you mix paints together, what your eyes are actually seeing is the light that is reflected from the surface of the paint. Because your eyes are sensitive to *light energy*, your perception of color is due to the color of the light that enters your eye. When you see a surface that's painted blue, it appears blue because blue is the only color of light that is reflected by that surface. All other colors of light are being absorbed by the blue paint.

Mixing colored light is different from mixing reflected colors of paints, crayons, or dyes. When colors of light are combined, you see the direct mix of light and not the light that's being reflected from a surface. Therefore, the primary colors of light are different from those of paints, and thus the combinations formed by mixing primary colors of light are different from the combinations of similarly colored paints.

light adaptation the process through which our eyes adjust to bright light after having been exposed to darkness

When you step out of the darkness into bright light, you may experience a flash of pain as the built-up photopigment in your eyes reacts all at once to the bright light.

Jack Wild/Getty Images

The primary colors of light are *red, green,* and *blue.* All other colors of light can be made from these three colors. If you mix all the primary colors of light together, you get white light. In contrast, if you mixed red, blue, and yellow paint together, you would get black paint (● FIGURE 3.8). When we describe color vision and combinations of colors, remember to think in terms of *light,* and not in terms of paint.

The Trichromatic Theory of Color Vision

By now, perhaps some of you have made the connection between the three primary colors of light and the three different types of cones in our retinas. Could it be that each type of cone detects the presence of a different primary color of light? This is the central assumption of the **trichromatic theory of color vision**.

The exact origin of the trichromatic theory of color vision is not really known (W. A. H. Rushton, 1975; G. S. Wasserman, 1978). Most psychologists credit Hermann von Helmholtz (1821–1894) with proposing this theory in the mid-1800s. According to the trichromatic theory, we have three different types of cones in our eyes, each of which contains a slightly different photopigment that makes the cell particularly sensitive to a certain wavelength of light.

One type of cone is particularly sensitive to long wavelengths of light (red), another is very sensitive to medium wavelengths of light (green), and the third is most sensitive to short wavelengths of light (blue). Notice that these colors correspond to the primary colors of light. These differentially sensitive cones give our brain a means of knowing what color of light we are seeing at any particular moment (B. R. Conway, 2009; G. Wald, 1964).

For example, if the brain receives input that the red cones are very active and the green and blue are not very active, the brain knows you are seeing the color red. This same logic can be applied to seeing the colors green and blue, but how does it apply to seeing nonprimary colors? All colors of light are some combination of red, green, and blue light (see Figure 3.8). So, the brain processes the proportions of red, green, and blue cones that are firing intensely to know what color you are seeing.

Color Blindness

Does trichromatic color vision mean that all people have red, green, and blue cones? Curiously, research in the last decade or so suggests that some people with normal color vision may have more than three types of cones. The presence of additional types of cones may cause some people to perceive colors differently from others (Nathans, Merbs, Sung, Weitz, & Wang, 1992; Neitz, Neitz, & Jacobs, 1993). There is also abundant evidence that some people have fewer than three types of cones. **Color blindness**, or the inability to see one or more colors, is often the result of missing cones in the retina. A particularly common type of color blindness is red–green color blindness, a genetic disorder that occurs in approximately 1 out of 20 males in the United States (Neitz, Neitz, & Kainz, 1996) who are born missing either red or green cones.

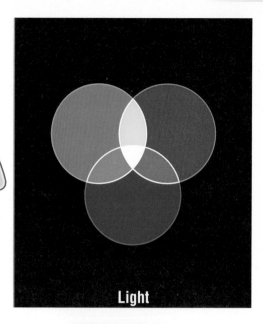

Paint   Light

FIGURE 3.8

● **Primary Colors of Paint and Light**
Mixing paint is not the same as combining colors of light.

trichromatic theory of color vision the idea that color vision is made possible by the presence of three different types of cones in the retina that react, respectively, to either red, green, or blue light

color blindness a condition in which a person cannot perceive one or more colors because of a lack of specific cones in the retina

If you were missing all of your cones, this piece of art would be perceived in grayscale instead of color.

The red–green color-blind person has only blue and red cones *or* blue and green cones in his retina. The lack of red (or green) cones results in an inability to discriminate between red and green. At a stoplight, a red–green color-blind person must look at the position of the red and green lights, because the lights appear to be the same color.

Curiously, being color-blind may not always be a bad thing. In one study, researchers found that monkeys with only two types of cones in their retina were better at detecting a camouflaged stimulus than were trichromatic monkeys. Perhaps color blindness has not been selected out of primates because it can be advantageous—for example, for seeing hidden food or predators (Saito et al., 2005).

Although trichromatic theory explains certain aspects of color vision, it does not explain all aspects of vision. Trichromatic theory cannot explain *negative afterimages*. To understand what an afterimage is, you'll need ● FIGURE 3.9 in your textbook and a blank sheet of white paper.

TRY THIS DEMONSTRATION

A Negative Afterimage. Set the blank paper aside. Stare at the black dot in the center of Figure 3.9 without blinking or moving your eyes. Continue staring for 60 to 90 seconds. Then quickly move your gaze to the blank sheet of white paper. What do you see? You should see the image of a green shamrock with a yellow border on the blank sheet of white paper. The shamrock is a negative afterimage. Notice that the colors you see in the afterimage are different from the colors in the original.

Why would you see different colors in your afterimage? The trichromatic theory of color vision cannot explain this phenomenon. One theory that does so is the opponent-process theory of color vision.

FIGURE 3.9

● **Negative Afterimages**
See text for instructions.

The Opponent-Process Theory of Color Vision

In contrast to the trichromatic theory of color vision, which proposes cones that detect single colors of light, the **opponent-process theory** proposes a different type of color-sensitive cell in the visual system, a cell that is sensitive to two colors of light. There are thought to be three types of opponent-process cells in our visual system: red/green, yellow/blue, and black/white. The key to opponent-process theory is that these cells can detect the presence of only one color at a time. The colors *oppose* one another so that the opponent-process cell cannot detect the presence of both colors at the same time. For example, a red/green cell can detect either red or green light at any one time. If you shine a red light in the eye, the red/green cells tell our brain that we are seeing red. If you shine a green light in the eye, the red/green cells tell our brain that we are seeing green. But these red/green cells cannot detect red and green at the same time. Opponent-process theory is consistent with the finding that if we simultaneously shine red and green lights into your eye, you will likely see a neutral shade that is neither red nor green (Hurvich & Jameson, 1957/2000).

Opponent-process theory can explain the phenomenon of negative afterimages. Recall the demonstration you tried with Figure 3.9. After staring at the red and blue shamrock, you saw the green and yellow afterimage. Opponent-process theory proposes that as you stared at the red and blue shamrock, you were using the red and blue portions of the opponent-process cells. After a period of 60–90 seconds of continuous staring, you expended these cells' capacity to fire action potentials. In a sense, you temporarily "wore out" the red and blue portions of these cells. Then you looked at a blank sheet of white paper. Under normal conditions, the white light would excite *all* of the opponent-process cells. Recall that white light contains all colors of light. But, given the exhausted state of your opponent-process cells, only parts of them were capable of firing action potentials. In this example, the green and yellow parts of the cells were ready to fire. The light reflected off the white paper could excite only the yellow and green parts of the cells, so you saw a green and yellow shamrock.

opponent-process theory proposes that we have dual-action cells beyond the level of the retina that signal the brain when we see one of a pair of colors

Trichromatic Theory or Opponent-Process Theory?

We've seen that trichromatic theory and opponent-process theory each explain certain aspects of color vision. So, which theory is correct? Both theories seem to have merit. It is generally believed that these two theories describe processes that operate at different places in the visual system (Hubel, 1995).

Trichromatic theory does a good job of explaining color vision at the level of the rods and cones. The available evidence does indeed suggest that the photopigments in the cones of the retina are differentially sensitive to particular colors of light (Abramov & Gordon, 1994; W. A. H. Rushton, 1958, 1975).

Opponent-process theory best explains the processing of color vision beyond the level of the rods and cones. When we described opponent-process theory, we talked about opponent-process cells, but we didn't indicate where these cells are in the visual system. It turns out that some cells in the retina other than cones function as opponent-process cells, responding to pairs of colors (Gouras, 1991). Evidence suggests that some ganglion cells (see Figure 3.5, p. 94) operate as opponent-process cells (B. R. Conway, 2009; DeValois & DeValois, 1975). When a ganglion cell receives input from the cones, it will detect only the presence of one of its two designated colors. For example, a ganglion cell designated as a red/green cell will detect signals that indicate the presence of red *or* green light. In true opponent-process fashion, the red/green ganglion cell cannot detect the presence of red and green light at the same time.

Opponent-process theory may also explain the action of the other layers of the retina—the amacrine, horizontal, and bipolar cells. In fact, opponent processing may even occur after information leaves the retina and travels to the visual cortex (see B. R. Conway & Livingstone, 2005). In the next section, we will trace the path that visual information takes as it leaves the retina and enters the brain.

The Visual Pathways of the Brain

Once the rods and cones of the retina transduce light into action potentials, this information begins its journey into the brain. Recall from Chapter 2 that the ultimate destination of visual information in the brain is the visual cortex of the occipital lobe (see p. 64). As visual information travels from the individual rods and cones of the retina to the visual cortex of the brain, it is continually processed and combined to ultimately give us a coherent perception of what we see in the environment.

As we have already discussed, the process of combining the input from the millions of rods and cones begins while the information is still in the retina. The bipolar, horizontal, and amacrine cells (see Figure 3.5, p. 94) gather the information from the rods and cones and funnel it to the ganglion cells. The ganglion cells join together to form the optic nerve, which carries visual information into the brain.

The Optic Chiasm and Our Cross-Wired Brain

Information traveling along the optic nerve is processed *contralaterally* in the brain. Just as movement in the body is controlled by the opposite side of the brain, visual information from the right side of the body travels to the left hemisphere, and information from the left side travels to the right hemisphere. The point at which the optic nerve from the left eye and the optic nerve from the right eye cross over is called the **optic chiasm**. From the optic chiasm, most visual information travels to a part of the thalamus called the **lateral geniculate nucleus (LGN)**. The LGN is thought to act as a filter for visual information coming from the retina, and some opponent-processing of color may occur in the LGN (see B. R. Conway & Livingstone, 2005).

After leaving the LGN, visual information travels directly to the visual cortex, where specialized cells interpret the input (see ● Figure 3.10). Many of these cortical cells function as **feature detectors** that fire only when they receive input that indicates we are looking at a particular shape, color, angle, or other visual feature. We have feature detectors for many different specific features of visual stimuli (B. R. Conway, 2003; Hubel, 1995;

optic chiasm the point in the brain where the optic nerve from the left eye crosses over the optic nerve from the right eye

lateral geniculate nucleus (LGN) the part of the thalamus that processes visual information en route to the cortex

feature detectors specialized cells in the visual cortex that fire only when they receive input that indicates we are looking at a particular shape, color, angle, or other visual feature

---

FIGURE 3.10

● **The Visual Pathways in the Brain**
You can see that visual information from your right side travels to the visual cortex on the left side of the brain and information from your left side travels to the visual cortex on the right side.

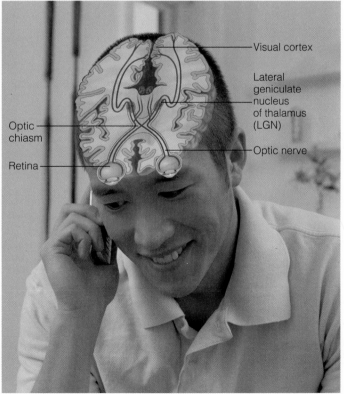

Visual cortex

Lateral geniculate nucleus of thalamus (LGN)

Optic chiasm

Optic nerve

Retina

Hulbert, 2003; Seiffert, Somers, Dale, & Tootell, 2003; Xiao, Wang, & Felleman, 2003). The visual cortex and other parts of the brain gather information from our various feature detectors and combine it to help give us a coherent picture of whatever it is we are seeing (S. Jackson & Blake, 2010; Lumer, Friston, & Rees, 1998; S. O. Murray, Olshausen, & Woods, 2003).

Yet, the world is a complex place full of rich visual detail. Is it possible that all of our visual perception of the world results from feature detectors that respond to simple geometric shapes? Maybe not. In fact, evidence is mounting to suggest that other areas of the brain may be organized to further process certain complex stimuli. For example, we have a region in the temporal lobe called the *fusiform face area*, which enlarges and specializes during childhood to selectively process the faces we see (Peelen, Glaser, Vuilleumier, & Eliez, 2009). Likewise, other areas have been shown to selectively process body parts (Cross, Mackie, Wolford, & de C. Hamilton, 2009) and pictures of indoor and outdoor scenes (Kanwisher, 2003).

Do Men and Women See the World Differently?

Recent evidence suggests that when it comes to processing visual information, men and women see things differently. Females tend to be better at discriminating one object from another (Overman, Bachevalier, Schuhmann, & Ryan, 1996), naming colors (M. H. Bornstein, 1985), and accurately identifying facial expressions (Vassallo, Cooper, & Douglas, 2009). Females also tend to show a preference for using many colors and seem to prefer warm colors to cool ones. Males tend to be better at processing moving objects and the spatial aspects of objects (G. M. Alexander, 2003).

Researcher Gerianne Alexander (2003) has argued that these gender differences in visual processing are neurological and that they have evolved to facilitate the performance of traditional male–female roles in society. In many societies, males have historically hunted for food, whereas women have gathered crops and nurtured their children. By being able to discriminate among objects and colors well, females are well suited to gathering food. For example, good color vision allows you to see a ripe fig among the green leaves of a tree. On the other hand, male ability to process movement and spatial information may have helped them perform hunting duties. We'll have more to say about gender roles and gender differences in Chapter 10. For now, let's turn our attention to our other senses.

Let's
REVIEW
In this section, we discussed vision, including the physical properties of light, the anatomy of the eye and the retina, how we adapt to light and dark, how we see color, and the role of the brain in vision. For a quick check of your understanding, try answering the following questions at increasing levels of difficulty.

1. We are able to see color because of the presence of _____ cells in our retinas.

   a. rod

   b. cone

   c. amacrine

   d. bipolar

2. Which theory best accounts for the presence of negative afterimages in vision?

   a. the opponent-process theory

   b. the trichromatic theory

   c. the rod-and-cone theory

   d. the theory of red–green color blindness

3. You have just returned to a darkened theater after a trip to the concession stand. Now you have a problem—you can't find your seat in the dark. Knowing what you do about vision, which of the following would *most likely* help you to find your seat?

   a. Stare straight ahead at the seats.

   b. Search for your seat out of the corner of your eye.

   c. Go back out into the bright light and allow your eyes to deplete their photopigments.

   d. Cross your eyes and search for your seat.

ANSWERS 1. b; 2. a; 3. b

HOW DO WE HEAR THE WORLD?

Like vision, hearing is one of our most important senses; much of what we learn in life depends on these two senses. Additionally, hearing plays an important role in our ability to communicate with others. To understand hearing, we will describe the physical properties of sound waves, the anatomy of the ear, and how our brain processes sound.

How Hearing Works: Vibrating Sound Waves

As was the case with vision, hearing requires that environmental energy be transduced into neural impulses. In the case of vision, the energy is electromagnetic. In hearing, the environmental energy takes a different form. Sounds, such as a human voice, produce waves of compressed air that our ears convert to neural impulses. You can feel these waves by holding your fingertips directly in front of your mouth while speaking. It may be hard to believe, but sound waves are a physical force that can even break glass!

Like light waves, sound waves have their own psychophysical properties. A sound wave has both peaks and valleys (● FIGURE 3.11a). A **cycle** includes the peak of the wave and the valley that immediately follows it. Counting the number of cycles in a given time frame allows us to determine the **frequency** of a sound wave. Traditionally, the frequency of sound waves is measured in hertz (Hz), or the number of cycles completed per second. A sound wave with a frequency of 1000 Hz would complete 1,000 cycles per second.

The frequency of a sound wave corresponds to the **pitch** of the sound we perceive. The higher the frequency of the sound wave, the higher the pitch we perceive when hearing it. The average young adult can perceive sounds that range from a low of 20 Hz to a high of 20000 Hz (Gelfand, 1981). We lose some of this range as we age, particularly our ability to hear high pitches. Those of us who live and work in noisy environments may be even more likely to suffer hearing loss as we age (see the ● TECHNOLOGY AND BEHAVIOR box on iPods, earbuds, and hearing loss, p. 102). For instance, people who live in North American urban areas experience greater age-related hearing loss than do people who live in quiet rural areas of Africa (W. I. Bennett, 1990). Most of the everyday sounds we hear fall well below the 20000-Hz level. But, if we begin to have difficulty hearing sounds at 1800 Hz and below, our ability to comprehend speech may suffer (Welford, 1987). Researcher Teresa Cervera and colleagues (2009) found that hearing loss in 55–65-year-old participants was a good predictor of problems in processing speech as well as certain memory problems. Specifically, those with hearing loss were likely to have greater trouble on tasks that required *working memory* or the ability to hold information in our conscious mind while processing it.

cycle a physical characteristic of energy defined as a wave peak and the valley that immediately follows it

frequency a physical characteristic of energy defined as the number of cycles that occur in a given unit of time

pitch the psychophysical property of sound that corresponds to the frequency of a sound wave

(a) Frequency determines pitch

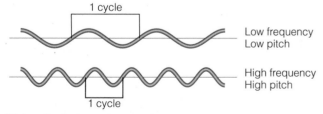

1 cycle

Low frequency
Low pitch

High frequency
High pitch

1 cycle

(b) Amplitude determines loudness

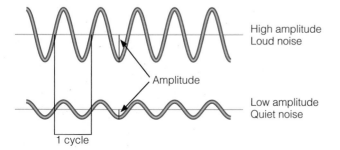

High amplitude
Loud noise

Amplitude

Low amplitude
Quiet noise

1 cycle

FIGURE 3.11

● **The Amplitude and Frequency of Sound Waves**
The frequency, or number of cycles per second, determines the sound's pitch. The higher the wave's frequency, the higher the sound's pitch will be (**a**). The height, or amplitude, of a sound wave determines its loudness. Higher amplitudes correspond to louder sounds (**b**).

TECHNOLOGY and BEHAVIOR

IPODS, EARBUDS, AND HEARING LOSS

Do you own an iPod, Zune, or other personal listening device (PLD)? Do you listen to these devices while using earbuds (small speakers that fit into the ear canal) or headphones? If so, you are not alone. According to some researchers, college students probably spend more time listening to PLDs than does any other age group (Danhauer, Johnson, Byrd, & DeGood, 2009). There is little doubt that PLDs have made our lives much more entertaining and enjoyable. Many of us enjoy listening to music while exercising, studying, taking a long flight, and so on. Modern PLDs, such as the iPod, provide us with the unprecedented convenience of being able to carry thousands of our favorite songs with us wherever we go. We have even seen hoodies with iPod earbuds sewn directly into the garment so that the wearer could be unobtrusively plugged in all day long!

Caterina Bernardi/Getty Images

PLDs are a great way to enjoy music and other media, but don't forget to follow the 60–60 rule.

Sounds great, right? But, as with most things, moderation may be an important consideration. Increased levels of noise have long been a consideration in the industrialized world. In fact, roughly 10% of Americans between the ages of 20 and 69 have suffered some level of permanent damage to their hearing as a result of overexposure to noise (Griest, Folmer, & Hal Martin, 2007). This damage results from noise in the workplace, environmental noise, and perhaps even from leisure activities, such as listening to PLDs at too high a level. Some PLDs are capable of outputting sounds at more than 130 dB (Danhauer et al., 2009). To put this number in context, a circular saw puts out roughly 99 dB (National Institute for Occupational Safety and Health, 2010). Given that we might be tempted to listen for literally hours to a PLD full of great songs, this sound exposure may be equivalent to listening to power tools, unprotected, for several hours a day. Furthermore, researchers have discovered that when listening to a PLD with earbud-style headphones in noisy background conditions, people tend to play the device at a higher level (89 dB) than do listeners who use in-ear earphones that sit directly in the ear canal (78 dB). This tendency occurs because earbuds do not

block out background noise, forcing the wearer to turn up the volume to hear well. In quiet background environments, earbud wearers and in-ear wearers listen at comparable levels (Fligor & Ives, 2006, cited in Danhauer et al., 2009).

Initially, researchers suggested limiting PLD use to what is called the 60–60 rule: no more than 60 minutes per day of listening to your PLD at 60% of its maximum volume (Fligor & Cox, 2004). However, based on further research, some now suggest a more lenient guideline: no more than 4.6 hours per day of listening at 70% of maximum volume (Portnuff and Fligor, 2006, cited in Danhauer et al., 2009).

So, do people (including college students) follow either of these guidelines? Well, the good news is that several studies have suggested that many people are more cautious when listening to PLDs than perhaps we would expect, given the media concern over potential hearing loss (see Danhauer et al., 2009 for a review). The bad news is that a minority of people out there are possibly endangering their hearing by not following these guidelines.

Jeffrey Danhauer and colleagues (2009) surveyed 609 American college students and found that although the majority of students were within the guidelines of the 60–60 rule, approximately 25% were not. There were also some who were outside the more conservative guidelines for listening at 70% full volume. Approximately 12% of the participants said that they listened at 70% or more of full volume for 3+ hours a day. So, even by the most conservative estimates, Danhauer and colleagues found that approximately 10% of college students may be endangering their hearing with their PLD use.

To minimize your risk, you might invest in some in-the-ear headphones to block background noise better than earbuds, use your PLD software to limit the maximum volume of your PLD to 60–70% of maximum, and limit your exposure. This is one case where less is better.

Like light waves, sound waves differ in amplitude (see Figure 3.11b). The amplitude of a sound wave corresponds to the **loudness** of the sound we hear as well as the amount of pressure the compressed waves of air exert on the eardrum. The higher the amplitude, the more pressure is exerted on the eardrum, and the louder the sound is. Loudness is usually measured in **decibels (dB)**. ● TABLE 3.2 shows the decibel levels for some common sounds. Note that the sensory threshold for sound in humans is defined as 0 decibels.

Let's turn our discussion to the ear itself and how it allows us to transduce sound waves into neural impulses. As we did with the eye, we will begin by taking a closer look at the anatomy of the ear.

The Anatomy and Function of the Ear

The structures of the ear are well designed to accomplish the task of hearing. As we examine these structures, we will divide the ear into three sections: the *outer ear*, *middle ear*, and *inner ear* (● FIGURE 3.12).

The Outer Ear

The very outside of the outer ear is called the *pinna*. It includes the part of the body normally referred to as the ear and earlobe. The pinna acts as a funnel to gather sound waves. After being gathered by the pinna, sound waves are channeled through the *auditory canal* where sounds are amplified and then strike the membrane at the end of the auditory canal, the *eardrum*.

The Middle Ear

The eardrum, or *tympanic membrane*, is a very thin membrane that vibrates as the incoming sound waves strike it, much as the head of a drum vibrates when a drumstick strikes it. The three bones, or *ossicles*, of the middle ear that are directly behind the eardrum are the *hammer* (or malleus), *anvil* (or incus), and *stirrup* (or stapes). These very small bones that rest against one another transmit vibrations from the eardrum to the inner ear. The middle ear connects to the inner ear at the point where the stirrup rests against the *oval window* (see Figure 3.12). The oval window is found on the outer end of the **cochlea**, one of the major components of the inner ear. The cochlea is a coiled, fluid-filled tube about 1.4 inches long that resembles a snail (Matlin & Foley, 1997). The curled nature of this structure may help to focus incoming sound waves as they are transduced into neural impulses within the cochlea (Manoussaki, Chadwick, Ketten, Arruda, Dimitriadis, & O'Malley, 2008).

The Inner Ear

If you were to uncoil the cochlea, you would see that it resembles a flexible tube that is closed off at the end. The inside of the tube is partitioned into three ducts, or canals, each filled with fluid. These are the *vestibular canal*, the *cochlear duct*, and the *tympanic canal* (● FIGURE 3.13). In our quest to

---

TABLE 3.2

● **The Decibel Levels of Some Common Sounds**

DECIBELS	EXAMPLE
Little or No Chance of Damage	
0	The softest detectable sound
20	A soft whisper
30	A quiet library
40	A quiet neighborhood
50	A refrigerator running
60	The average conversation
Prolonged Exposure Can Cause Damage	
70	A noisy restaurant
80	A loud radio
90	A lawn mower
100	Heavy traffic
120	A very loud thunder clap
Sounds of These Intensities Can Quickly Cause Damage	
140	A jet airplane taking off
160	Extremely loud rock music
180	The launch of a spacecraft

---

loudness the psychophysical property of sound that corresponds to the amplitude of a sound wave

decibels (dB) the unit of measure used to determine the loudness of a sound

cochlea the curled, fluid-filled tube that contains the basilar membrane in the inner ear

FIGURE 3.12

● **The Anatomy of the Ear**

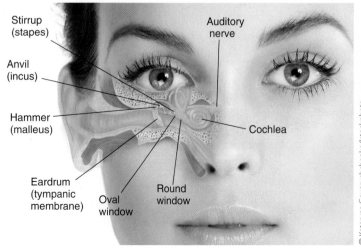

Stirrup (stapes)
Anvil (incus)
Hammer (malleus)
Eardrum (tympanic membrane)
Oval window
Round window
Auditory nerve
Cochlea

FIGURE 3.13
● **Enlarged Detail of the Inner Ear**

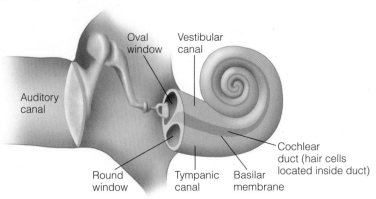

basilar membrane the structure in the cochlear duct that contains the hair cells, which transduce sound waves into action potentials

hair cells neurons that grow out of the basilar membrane and transduce sound waves into action potentials

auditory nerve the nerve that carries information from the inner ear to the brain

place theory proposes that our brain decodes pitch by noticing which region of the basilar membrane is most active

understand how hearing occurs, we are most concerned with the cochlear duct because that is where transduction occurs. The floor of the cochlear duct is lined with the **basilar membrane**. Growing out of the basilar membrane are specialized **hair cells** that transduce sound wave energy into neural impulses.

Recall our discussion about the transmission of sound waves through the outer and middle ears, and then look once again at Figures 3.12 and 3.13. Incoming sound waves cause the ossicles to vibrate. This vibration is transferred to the cochlea because the stirrup rests against the oval window. The vibration of the stirrup against the oval window sets up a wave action inside the fluid-filled vestibular canal. As this wave travels through the vestibular canal, the cochlear duct begins to ripple. Inside the cochlear duct, the traveling wave ripples across the hair cells, causing them to begin sending neural impulses.

The Auditory Pathways of the Brain

Once the hair cells transduce sound into neural impulses, these impulses must be sent to the brain for further processing. Attached to the end of the cochlea is the **auditory nerve** (Figure 3.12). The bundled neurons of the auditory nerve gather the information from the hair cells to relay it to the brain. ● FIGURE 3.14 shows the path that auditory information takes from the ears to the brain. Notice that auditory information from each ear reaches both sides of the brain.

The auditory cortex (see Chapter 2, p. 64) has the capacity to decode the meanings of the sounds we hear (see ● WHAT'S HAPPENING IN YOUR BRAIN). Our next task is to examine how the brain perceives, or makes sense of, the auditory information it receives from the ears.

FIGURE 3.14
● **The Auditory Pathways in the Brain**

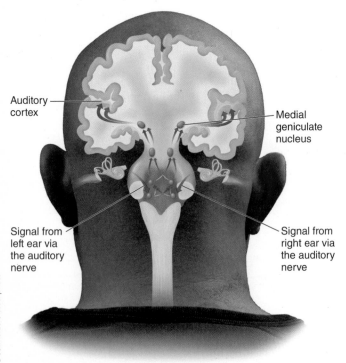

Place Theory of Pitch Perception

Several theories have been proposed to explain how we perceive pitch. Hermann von Helmholtz, who is credited with the trichromatic theory of color vision, also studied pitch perception. Helmholtz contributed to our understanding of sound perception with his **place theory** of pitch perception (Helmholtz, 1863/1930), which proposes that sounds of different frequencies excite different hair cells at particular points along the basilar membrane. According to place theory, the brain receives information on pitch from the location, or *place*, on the basilar membrane that is being most excited by incoming sound waves. Evidence suggests that place theory may indeed explain some of our ability to perceive pitch.

WHAT'S HAPPENING IN YOUR BRAIN?

PROCESSING MUSIC IN THE BRAIN

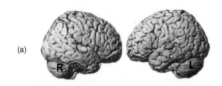
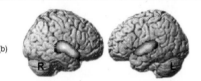

(a)

R   L

(b)

R   L

L. Ruytjens, A. T. M. Willemsen, P. Van Dijk, H. P. Wit, & F. W. J. Albers (2006). Functional imaging of the central auditory system using PET. *Acta Oto-Laryngologica*, 2006; 126: pgs. 1236-1244. © 2006 Taylor & Francis.

Radius Images/PhotoLibrary

Researchers have long used brain imaging scans like PET scans to observe neural processing during sensory stimulation. One area where this technology has been particularly useful is in studying how the brain processes auditory information. By exposing participants to certain auditory stimuli while they are in a PET scan machine, researchers can map the neural activity of hearing. In panel (a), you can see how the brain responds to noise. Unsurprisingly, hearing noise results in a great deal of activity in the primary auditory cortex of the brain. On the other hand, what happens when the participants are exposed to more complex sounds, such as music? Would sensing and perceiving music result in more widespread activation in the brain than noise would? As it turns out, it does. Hearing music not only results in brain activation of the primary auditory cortex, it also results in activity in the surrounding secondary auditory areas (panel b) suggesting that auditory processing occurs in multiple cortical steps (Ruytjens, Willemsen, Van Dijk, Wit, & Albers, 2006).

In the early 1960s, Georg von Békésy conducted some important studies using pure tones, made up of single sound waves, which revealed that different pitches caused the most vibration at different points along the basilar membrane. Low-frequency sounds activate the far end of the basilar membrane the most. High-frequency sounds cause the most activation at the front part of the basilar membrane, near the oval window. This makes sense in light of what we know about hearing loss resulting from damage. As we age, many of us lose some of our hearing as a result of wear and tear on the hair cells of the basilar membrane. It stands to reason that hair cells at the front of the basilar membrane are more vulnerable to damage because they experience the most intense vibrations coming in from the outside world. If we lose our front hair cells first and place theory has merit, this would explain why age-related hearing loss first affects our ability to hear higher pitches.

Although Békésy's research on place theory does describe some of our ability to perceive pitch, it did not take into account that most of the sounds we hear are complex, made up of many separate pure tones. When place theory is put to the test using complex sounds rather than pure tones, it does not fare as well as it does in explaining perception of pure tones (Matlin & Foley, 1997). What other explanations have been offered for our ability to perceive pitch?

Frequency Theory of Pitch Perception

Frequency theory proposes that our brain receives information about pitch directly from the frequency at which the hair cells are firing (Rutherford, 1886; Wever, 1949/1970). An incoming sound wave will cause the hair cells to fire action potentials at a frequency that is equal to the frequency of the sound wave. For example, a sound wave at 500 Hz would cause

frequency theory proposes that our brain decodes pitch directly from the frequency at which the hair cells of the basilar membrane are firing

the hair cells to fire 500 action potentials per second; a sound wave at 750 Hz would produce 750 action potentials per second.

Frequency theory is a very simple concept, but it has a severe limitation. Hair cells can fire only at a maximum rate of 1,000 action potentials per second (1000 Hz), yet we can hear sounds in the range of 20–20000 Hz. Frequency theory obviously falls short in explaining perception of pitches over 1000 Hz.

Volley Theory of Pitch Perception

Volley theory is an updated version of frequency theory that seeks to explain perception of sounds over 1000 Hz (Wever, 1949/1970). According to volley theory, "teams" of hair cells work together to give us the perception of sounds over 1000 Hz. For example, let's say you hear a tone of 3000 Hz. No single hair cell can fire at 3000 Hz, but three hair cells, each firing at 1000 Hz, can work together to tell your brain that you are hearing a 3000-Hz tone. Three cells firing in turn at their maximum rate can send the signal as a group at 3000 Hz. Hair cells that work together can thus accomplish what single hair cells cannot.

Duplicity Theory: An Integration

Volley theory seems adequate to explain pitch perception, but we still have to deal with place theory, which also seems to explain some aspects of our perception. Recall that Georg von Békésy (1960) did find that different pitches excite different parts of the basilar membrane. Volley theory cannot explain why this would be the case. So, what is going on in our ears? Is it the place or the frequency of the excited hair cells that tell us what pitch we are hearing? It may well be that it is *both*.

Today it is widely believed that we perceive pitch through a combination of volley theory and place theory. This combination of perceptual processes is called **duplicity theory**. Researchers strongly suspect that frequency and place information work together to give us pitch perception, but we don't yet understand exactly how these two mechanisms work together. Before moving on, take a moment to look at ● THE BIG PICTURE REVIEW for a recap of the theories of pitch perception.

volley theory proposes that our brain decodes pitch by noticing the frequency at which *groups* of hair cells on the basilar membrane are firing

duplicity theory proposes that a combination of volley and place theory explains how our brain decodes pitch

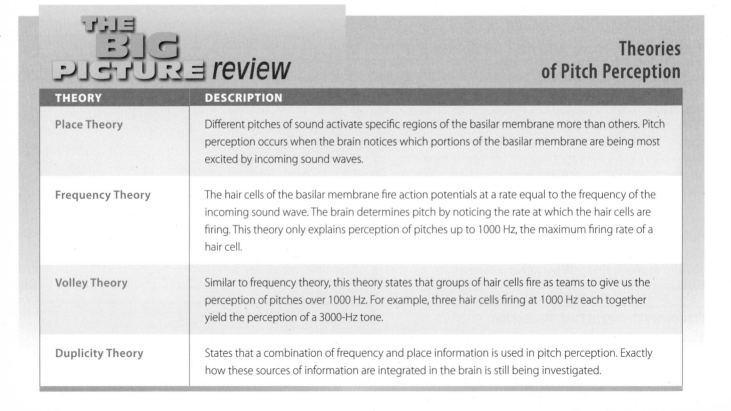

THE BIG PICTURE *review*

Theories of Pitch Perception

THEORY	DESCRIPTION
Place Theory	Different pitches of sound activate specific regions of the basilar membrane more than others. Pitch perception occurs when the brain notices which portions of the basilar membrane are being most excited by incoming sound waves.
Frequency Theory	The hair cells of the basilar membrane fire action potentials at a rate equal to the frequency of the incoming sound wave. The brain determines pitch by noticing the rate at which the hair cells are firing. This theory only explains perception of pitches up to 1000 Hz, the maximum firing rate of a hair cell.
Volley Theory	Similar to frequency theory, this theory states that groups of hair cells fire as teams to give us the perception of pitches over 1000 Hz. For example, three hair cells firing at 1000 Hz each together yield the perception of a 3000-Hz tone.
Duplicity Theory	States that a combination of frequency and place information is used in pitch perception. Exactly how these sources of information are integrated in the brain is still being investigated.

Let's
REVIEW
In this section, we looked at the process of hearing: the psychophysics of sound, the anatomy of the ear, the brain's role in hearing, and theories of pitch perception. For a quick check of your understanding, try answering the following questions at increasing levels of difficulty.

1. _____ theory proposes that pitch is perceived when the brain locates the region of the basilar membrane that is firing the most action potentials.

a. Frequency

b. Basilar

c. Place

d. Volley

2. Volume is to _____ as pitch is to _____.

a. amplitude; frequency

b. wavelength; frequency

c. peak height; amplitude

d. frequency; amplitude

3. Frequently violating the 60–60 rule when listening to your PLD would be most likely to result in _____.

a. total deafness

b. deafness for low pitches

c. deafness for medium pitches

d. deafness for high pitches

ANSWERS 1. c; 2. a; 3. d

LEARNING
OBJECTIVE
What Should You Know?

● Explain the processes involved in taste, smell, touch, and the body senses.

WHAT OTHER SENSES DO WE HAVE?

Although we learn a great deal about the world through our senses of vision and hearing, our ability to function also rests on our ability to taste, smell, touch, and sense our bodies. For Michael Watson, whose story opened this chapter, the sensory pathways for some of these senses were interconnected. For Michael, taste resulted in touch, making his synesthesia one of the rarest forms known. Most of us can't even imagine what Michael experiences while eating a sandwich! However, we can examine what happens when we nonsynesthetes experience the sensations of *taste*, *smell*, and *touch*, as well as what we call the *body senses*.

Taste: Information From the Tongue

Most of us will never experience taste as a tactile sensation, the way Michael Watson does. However, for us the senses of taste and smell are interconnected. These two senses are called chemical senses, because they require that certain chemicals come into direct contact with our sense organs. Vision and hearing don't require such direct contact; you can perceive visual and auditory stimuli at a distance. But for taste, or **gustation**, to occur, certain chemicals in foods and other substances must be dissolved in our saliva and come into direct contact with the sense organ commonly known as the tongue. For smell, chemicals in the nearby air—from food or other substances—must come into contact with cells in the nasal cavity.

Properties of Taste: The Four—or Five—Tastes

It is widely believed that humans are sensitive to at least four different types of tastes: bitter, sweet, salty, and sour (Bartoshuk & Beauchamp, 1994). It makes good sense that our tongues are designed to detect these tastes, because they are associated with certain types of foods that have implications for our survival (T. R. Scott & Plata-Salaman, 1991). Sweet flavors are associated with organic molecules that contain hydrogen, carbon, and oxygen. Sugars are organic molecules, so our ability to taste sugars may ensure that we take in enough to fuel our bodies. Salty flavors are associated with foods that release ions, or charged particles. As we saw in Chapter 2, ions such as sodium are crucial for normal functioning of the nervous system. Our ability to taste salts ensures that we take in enough of these critical ions. Sour

gustation the sense of taste

tastes are generally associated with acidic substances, and bitter flavors are often found in substances that contain nitrogen. Our ability to sense sour and bitter tastes may help us to regulate the level of acidity (pH) in our bodies. Bitter tastes are often associated with toxic substances. Therefore, tasting bitterness may steer us away from certain poisons.

In addition to these four basic tastes, some researchers have proposed that humans may be sensitive to a fifth taste called *umami*, or glutamate (Rolls, 2000). Umami is a meaty, brothy flavor that is more common in Asian foods than it is in Western cuisine (MSG, or monosodium glutamate, is a common ingredient in Asian dishes). So, Westerners are not likely to be as familiar with umami's flavor as they are with the other basic tastes. Nonetheless, preliminary studies indicate that the ability to taste umami exists (Damak et al., 2003; Hodson & Linden, 2006). So, how does the tongue detect the presence of these four (or five) basic flavors?

The Anatomy and Function of the Tongue

When you look at your tongue in the mirror, you normally see a bunch of little bumps lining its surface. We'll guess that you were taught to refer to these visible bumps as taste buds. This is incorrect—the bumps you see are the **papillae** of the tongue. Your **taste buds** actually reside in the pits between the papillae (● FIGURE 3.15). Your taste buds are what transduce the chemicals in the foods you eat into the neural impulses that convey taste information to your brain. Most people have between 2,000 and 5,000 taste buds on their tongue (I. J. Miller & Bartoshuk, 1991). Unlike some types of sensory cells, taste buds can regenerate. This is important because we damage our taste buds on a regular basis. Have you ever eaten a very hot slice of pizza and as a result lost some of your sense of taste for a few days? You probably killed many of your taste buds with that molten mozzarella, and you had to wait for them to grow back!

We also lose some of our taste buds permanently with age. This may contribute to the diminished sense of taste that is often seen in older adults (Nordin, Razani, Markison, & Murphy, 2003). It might appear that one way to maintain an elderly person's appetite is a diet that includes many richly flavored foods. However, studies have shown that this strategy may not always work (Essed, van Staveren, Kok, & de Graaf, 2007).

papillae bumps on the tongue that many people mistake for taste buds

taste buds the sense organs for taste that are found between the papillae on the tongue

FIGURE 3.15

● **Papilla and Taste Buds** Taste buds are the sensory receptors for taste. Contrary to popular belief, the bumps on our tongues are not taste buds—they are papillae. Our taste buds are located next to the papillae on the tongue.

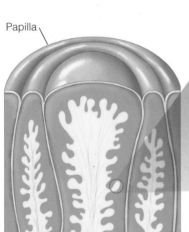
Papilla

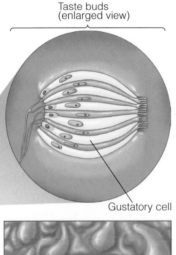
Taste buds (enlarged view)

Gustatory cell

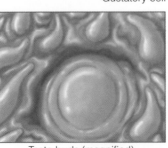
Taste buds (magnified)

If you burn your taste buds with a slice of hot pizza, you will experience temporary loss of taste sensation until the taste buds grow back.

AP Photo/Dima Gavrysh

Many researchers believe that, like the cones of the eye, different taste buds seem to be maximally sensitive to one of the four basic flavors (Shallenberger, 1993). Thus taste perception on the tongue appears to work very much like color perception in the retina. If the brain is informed that the "sweet taste buds" are very active, we taste a sweet flavor. If the "sour taste buds" are most active, we taste something sour. If all flavors are some combination of sweet, salty, sour, bitter, and perhaps umami, the presence of four or five types of taste buds is sufficient to explain our taste perception (Chandrashekar, Hoon, Ryba, & Zuker, 2006). **But, is taste perception solely dependent on these four or five flavors?** New research suggests that taste perception can be modified by certain compounds that have no flavor of their own, yet they are able to enhance the flavors of sweet, salty, and umami. Use of these flavor-enhancing compounds, called *Kokumi taste*, is much more common in Japanese cooking than it is in Western cuisine. And, at this time, we do not understand how Kokumi taste works (Ohsu et al., 2010).

Loss of taste buds may reduce our ability to taste as we grow older. A bland diet may only make this problem worse.

A good deal of our ability to taste certain flavors also depends on where on the tongue the substance is placed. The different types of taste buds are concentrated in certain locations. Over the years, there has been significant disagreement as to exactly where these areas of sensitivity can be found on the tongue. There is more agreement on the sweet and sour tastes. Sweet tastes are best detected at the front of the tongue, and sour tastes are best detected on the sides (Shallenberger, 1993). Salty tastes are thought to be detected best near the front of the tongue (Shallenberger, 1993).

You may be surprised to learn that the center of the tongue lacks taste buds. You won't taste flavors that are placed directly in the center of your tongue. In a sense, this region of the tongue is like the blindspot in the eye—no taste sensation can occur here (Matlin & Foley, 1997). Despite this taste blindspot, we still manage to taste the foods we eat because chewing distributes food across the tongue.

Of course, only after your brain has done its part can you become consciously aware of the flavor of your food. Next, we will look at the taste pathways in the brain.

Taste Pathways in the Brain

Each taste bud is connected to a neuron that receives input from the taste bud. These neurons join together to form three nerves. One nerve gathers input from the front of the tongue, another from the back of the tongue, and a third from the throat. These nerves travel to the medulla and the pons of the brainstem before conveying the taste information to the thalamus (see Figure 2.11, p. 59). Like most sensory information, taste information travels from the thalamus to the "thinking" part of the brain, the cortex. Most of the taste information ends up in the somatosensory cortex of the parietal lobe, but some of the information is diverted to the limbic system before reaching the cortex (see Figure 2.15b, p. 64).

Michael Watson's special sense of taste is linked to abnormal processing in the left limbic and left cortical areas of his brain. In Watson's case, his synesthesia seemed to coincide with a *reduction* in the activity of his left cortical areas and an *increase* in processing in his subcortical left limbic regions. In essence, when he "tasted shapes," the "thinking" part of his brain shut down on the left side.

Given that Michael Watson's sense of taste is so unusual, it is likely that his food preferences were affected by his synesthesia. However, even for people with a normal sense of taste, food preferences can be a very individual thing. The food choices we make may be a product of our genetics, learning, and even our culture.

Taste Preferences: Would You Eat That?

How would you like to have a bowl of soup made with fresh iguana meat and vegetables? Sound good? It may surprise you, but to many it would! The spouse of one of the authors is from El Salvador, where iguana meat is considered a treat enjoyed mostly by the wealthy. In

© Catherine Karnow/Corbis

© Bios/Peter Arnold, Inc.

To some, this meal would be appetizing; to others, it would be disgusting. Our cultural background heavily influences the foods we like.

Whether you like certain foods may depend on your genetic ability to taste certain flavors or your cultural background or both.

the United States, iguana is strangely absent from most restaurant menus. Around the world, taste preferences for food are as varied as the cultures in which they are found.

It seems likely that several factors account for the diet of a particular culture. The availability of food sources dictates what a particular people *can* eat. Central Americans eat iguana meat today partly because their ancestors once ate the wild iguanas that roamed there. Every culture must take advantage of the food sources at its disposal, and hunger can make foods taste better, especially when those foods provide needed nutrients (Mobini, Chambers, & Yeomans, 2007). Ecological and practical concerns also affect food choices. The use of camel blood as a food in East Africa makes sense because camels do not reproduce very quickly. If East Africans slaughtered their camels for meat, they might quickly deplete their stock. Bleeding the camels and consuming the blood utilizes the animals as a more sustainable food source (E. A. Stephens, 2000).

Religious values and traditions also shape cultural food preferences. Many of the world's religions influence the diet of their followers. For example, Jews and Muslims will not eat pork, Hindus do not eat beef, and Seventh Day Adventists frown upon the use of chili pepper and black pepper (Grivetti, 2000).

As with these cultural food preferences, many of our individual food preferences develop through learning—some of it very early in life. Research shows that the foods a mother eats can affect the flavor of her breast milk, and exposure to these flavors during breastfeeding can affect her child's later taste preferences (Mennella & Beauchamp, 1991). It has also been shown that being exposed to a variety of flavors in infancy tends to make infants more open to new and novel foods (Gerrish & Mennella, 2001).

Although the influence of learning on food preferences is strong, evidence also suggests that biological factors can affect our sense of taste. Prior to menopause, women's ability to taste fluctuates with hormonal levels, and after menopause it declines (Prutkin et al., 2000). There are also some genetic variations in the ability to taste. Some people, called *supertasters*, have taste buds that allow them to strongly taste a bitter compound called 6-n-propylthiouracil (PROP). In contrast, *nontasters* perceive very little or no bitterness from PROP (Bartoshuk, 2000). Nontasters have been shown to eat a wider variety of foods than supertasters do (Azar, 1998; Pasquet, Obeerti, Ati, & Hladik, 2002). Compared to nontasters, female PROP tasters tend to eat more fat and less fruit in their diets (Yackinous & Guinard, 2002). Supertasters may avoid some foods that are rich in cancer-fighting compounds but also have bitter flavors (such as brussels sprouts).

Our sense of taste is not influenced solely by our taste buds, however. Our sense of taste is also heavily dependent on our sense of smell (G. M. Shepard, 2006). If you've ever tried to taste food when you've had a bad cold, you know that your sense of smell makes a significant contribution to taste and that clogged nasal passages tend to make food taste bland.

Smell: Aromas, Odors, and a Warning System

Olfaction, our sense of smell, has adaptive value. Smells can alert us to danger. The ability to smell smoke enables us to detect a fire long before we see flames. The rotten smell of spoiled food warns us not to eat it. Without such odoriferous warnings, we could easily find ourselves in harm's way. Despite the usefulness of olfaction, compared to other animals, humans do not have a very good sense of smell. Dogs, for example, are much better at detecting odors. Some have argued that as humans evolved trichromatic color vision, we lost some of our ability to smell. With the ability to see ripe fruits and blushing mates, we didn't need to rely on a keen sense of smell. So, smell diminished as color perception increased (Kleiner, 2004).

Interestingly, recent research links further declines in olfaction with an increased risk of developing Alzheimer's disease (Fusari & Molina, 2009) and cognitive impairments (Swan & Carmelli, 2002), and with already having Alzheimer's disease (Motomura & Tomota, 2006). Although it's too soon to know the exact implications of these findings, they underscore the need for researchers to further understand olfaction. **So, just how does olfaction work?**

Like our sense of taste, our sense of smell is a chemical sense that relies on our ability to detect the presence of certain chemicals in the air we breathe. Odors come from chemicals that are *volatile* and evaporate easily. When a volatile chemical evaporates, its molecules become diffused in the air. When we inhale these molecules into our nose, we may experience smelling the substance. Our sense of smell is quite sensitive. Recall from our earlier discussion of sensory thresholds that we can detect the presence of a single drop of perfume in a three-room apartment (see Table 3.1). When it comes to discriminating between odors, we can detect roughly 500,000 different scents (Cain, 1988), and we can identify by name about 10,000 different smells (Lancet et al., 1993).

The inability to smell also limits the ability to taste.

Olfactory Pathways: The Limits of Our Knowledge

Researchers have not been able to determine precisely how our sense of smell works. Of the senses we have described to this point, smell is by far the least understood. What we do know is that we are able to smell because of a special piece of skin that lines the top of the nasal cavity (● FIGURE 3.16). This special piece of skin, the **olfactory epithelium**, probably contains only a few hundred different types of odor receptors (Lancet et al., 1993). When we breathe in odor-laden air, the odor molecules reach the receptors in the olfactory epithelium and stimulate these cells. This stimulation accomplishes the transduction of odor into smell, but just how our brain understands what we smell is not well understood at this time (Matlin & Foley, 1997). One theory, **lock-and-key theory**, proposes that olfactory receptors are excited by odor molecules in much the same way that neurotransmitters excite receptor sites on the postsynaptic neuron (Amoore, 1970, see Chapter 2). According to lock-and-key theory, specific odor molecules have the power to "unlock" or excite certain olfactory receptors in the olfactory epithelium.

Despite the logic of lock-and-key theory, there is reason to doubt that this theory really explains how we perceive smells. Current research suggests that the idea that one odor (the key) excites one receptor (the lock), leading to the perception of a specific smell, may be too simplistic a model to capture the complexity of human olfaction (Triller et al., 2008). Clearly, we have more to learn about smell.

Yet, we do know that once the cells of the epithelium have transduced odor into neural impulses, these signals travel across the *olfactory nerve* to the *olfactory bulb* of the brain. The olfactory bulb is located just below the bottom edge of the frontal lobe of the brain (see Figure 3.16). The olfactory bulb processes incoming information before sending it on to other parts of the brain. Some olfactory information goes directly to the primary smell cortex, in the temporal lobes of the brain.

Other olfactory information is sent to both the cortex and the limbic system. Recall from Chapter 2 that the limbic system regulates emotional and motivational activity. The limbic system (see Figure 2.13, p. 61) seems to be heavily involved in the processing of olfactory information. This may explain the strong emotional reactions we often have to certain smells. For example, one of the authors has a strong emotional reaction to smelling grease and gasoline odors. These smells always remind her of her deceased father, who was an airplane

olfaction the sense of smell

olfactory epithelium a special piece of skin at the top of the nasal cavity that contains the olfactory receptors

lock-and-key theory proposes that olfactory receptors are excited by odor molecules in a fashion that is similar to how neurotransmitters excite receptor sites

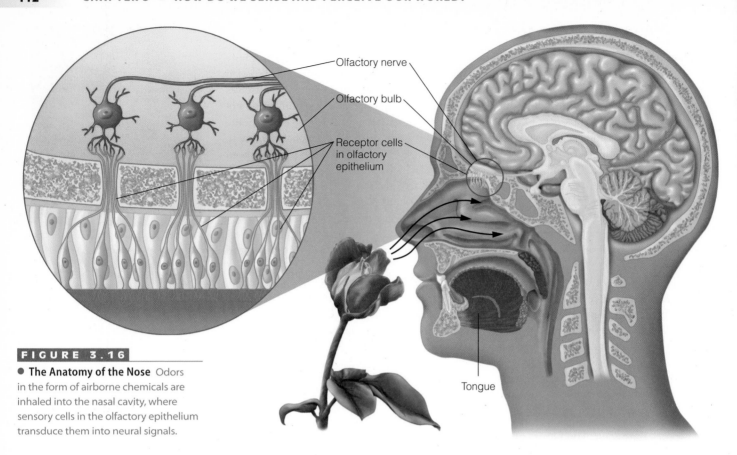

Olfactory nerve

Olfactory bulb

Receptor cells in olfactory epithelium

Tongue

FIGURE 3.16

● **The Anatomy of the Nose** Odors in the form of airborne chemicals are inhaled into the nasal cavity, where sensory cells in the olfactory epithelium transduce them into neural signals.

pheromones airborne chemicals that are released from glands and detected by the vomeronasal organs in some animals and perhaps humans

Many mammals use pheromones to communicate with each other. This cat is passing pheromone-laden air over vomeronasal organs in the roof of its mouth.

mechanic, and causes her to miss him. Are there particular smells that bring back emotionally charged memories for you?

Pheromones

Some researchers believe that humans have yet another sense somewhat related to smell. This sense, the *vomeronasal*, is well documented in animals (Doty, 2001). Many animals communicate with each other via airborne chemicals called **pheromones**. Pheromones are produced by glands in the animal's body and dispersed into the air, where other animals then inhale them. Such animals are equipped with vomeronasal organs that can detect the presence of inhaled pheromones. Perhaps you have seen a cat inhale deeply through its open mouth—a process called *flehmen*. The cat is passing pheromone-laden air over special organs, called Jacobson's organs, in the roof of its mouth. These organs can detect the presence of pheromones. The presence of such an organ in humans has been the subject of controversy. Some researchers have found evidence that some people have vomeronasal organs in their nasal cavities (Rapiejko, Zielnik-Jurkiewicz, Wojdas, Ratajczak, & Jurkiewicz, 2008). Yet, others claim that even if present, vomeronasal organs do not function in adults, and detection of pheromones may actually occur elsewhere in the olfactory epithelium (Wang, Nudelman, & Storm, 2007).

The evidence does suggest that pheromones affect certain aspects of human sexual behavior (Tirindelli, Dibattista, Pifferi, & Menini, 2009). For example, when a woman is exposed to pheromones in the underarm secretions of another woman, her menstrual cycle tends to synchronize with the other woman's cycle (Larkin, 1998; K. N. Stern & McClintock, 1998). When women are exposed to a pheromone that is released from men's hair follicles, they tend to increase their social interactions with males (E. Miller, 1999). Other pheromones found in men's sweat tend to improve a woman's mood state (Monti-Bloch, Diaz-Sanchez, Jennings-White, & Berliner, 1998). Current evidence, however, does not support the idea that pheromone-laden perfumes can make one wildly attractive to the other sex. It's more likely the case that the vomeronasal sense is just one of the senses involved in sexuality.

Touch: The Skin Sense

The sense of touch was the other half of Michael Watson's synesthesia. When he tasted a food, he felt geometric shapes pressed against certain parts of his body. For most of us, our senses of touch and taste are not intertwined the way they are for Michael Watson. For us, touch has little to do with the flavor of a food. So, what role does touch play in our lives? Touch is associated with many of life's pleasurable experiences. Feeling a friendly pat on the back can certainly enhance our social interactions. Sexual activity depends heavily on our ability to feel touch. But our ability to sense with our skin also affects our survival. Through our skin we feel touch, temperature, and pain. The importance of touch is clearly seen in cases of people who are born without the ability to feel pain, or who lose that ability as a result of disease or injury. For such people, repeated, unnoticed injuries can be a serious problem and may lead to fatal infection (e.g., Melzack & Wall, 1988; Sternbach, 1963).

Our keen sense of touch originates in our skin. Our skin is composed of several layers that contain touch receptors. The inner layer, the **dermis**, contains most of the touch receptors (● FIGURE 3.17). Our skin's outer layer is the **epidermis**, which consists of several layers of dead skin cells. The epidermis also contains touch receptors, especially in areas of the skin that do not have hair, such as the fingertips.

We have different types of receptors for touch, temperature, and pain (Figure 3.17). We know more about the function of the touch receptors than about the pain and temperature receptors. Pressure on the skin pushes against the axons of the touch receptors. This causes a change in the axonal membrane's permeability to positive ions, allowing them to enter the cell (Loewenstein, 1960; Hu, Chiang, Koch, & Lewin, 2010). As you recall from Chapter 2, as positive ions enter the cell, an action potential becomes more likely to fire. If the touch is intense enough to allow the receptors to reach threshold, neural impulses will be fired. These impulses travel to the spinal cord, and then to the brain. In the brain, the signals enter the thalamus and then go on to the somatosensory cortex of the parietal lobe. Some signals, particularly those indicating the presence of threatening stimuli, go to the limbic system as well as the somatosensory cortex (Coren, Ward, & Enns, 1999). Once the signals reach the somatosensory cortex, our brain interprets the sensation and directs us to take the appropriate action.

dermis the inner layer of the skin that contains most of the touch receptors

epidermis the outer layer of the skin that contains some touch receptors

The Body Senses: Experiencing the Physical Body in the Environment

So far, we have covered what are referred to as the five senses: vision, hearing, taste, smell, and touch. Do we possess other senses? The answer is yes, but we're not talking about a sixth sense, clairvoyance, or ESP. We are referring to the body senses, the senses that help us experience our physical bodies in the environment: *kinesthesis* and the *vestibular sense*.

FIGURE 3.17

● **Anatomy of the Skin and Its Receptors** Different types of skin receptors pick up different types of stimulation.

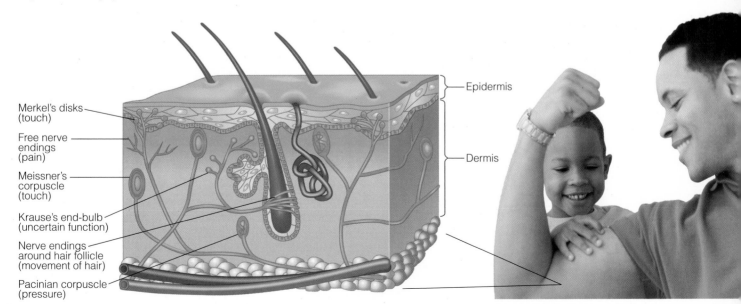

Merkel's disks (touch)
Free nerve endings (pain)
Meissner's corpuscle (touch)
Krause's end-bulb (uncertain function)
Nerve endings around hair follicle (movement of hair)
Pacinian corpuscle (pressure)

Epidermis
Dermis

© Jose Luis Pelaez Inc/Blend Images/Corbis

Our vestibular sense keeps us balanced, and the kinesthetic sense allows this skateboarder to perform intricate moves without falling.

Kinesthesis

Kinesthesis refers to our ability to sense the position of our body parts in space and in relation to one another. As you walk, you are aware of where your arms, legs, and head are in relation to the ground. Kinesthetic sense is important to athletes, especially to gymnasts and high divers. It allows them to know where their bodies are as they execute their routines and dives. Our kinesthetic sense uses information from the muscles, tendons, skin, and joints to keep us oriented at all times. The information from these sources is processed in the somatosensory cortex and the cerebellum of the brain (see Chapter 2 for a review of the cerebellum's role in balance and motor skills).

kinesthesis the ability to sense the position of our body parts in relation to one another and in relation to space

vestibular sense the sense of balance

FIGURE 3.18

● **The Vestibular Organs** The vestibular system helps us balance our body by monitoring the position and acceleration of our head as we move. To accomplish this, a gel-like fluid in the semicircular canals, saccule, and utricle presses against hair cells much like those found in the cochlea of the inner ear. When the hair cells of the vestibular system are moved, they signal the brain with information about the orientation of our head in three-dimensional space. *Based on S. Iurato (1967). Submicroscopic Structure of the Inner Ear. Pergamon Press.*

The Vestibular Sense

Another important body sense is our sense of balance, or **vestibular sense**. The vestibular system uses input from the semicircular canals and the vestibular sacs of the inner ear to keep us balanced (● FIGURE 3.18). These structures are filled with a fluid gel that surrounds hair cells much like those in the cochlea. When your head moves in any direction, the gel inside these structures moves in the opposite direction. The movement of the gel bends the hair cells and stimulates them to send neural impulses to the brain, which then uses these signals to determine the orientation of your head. Our vestibular system allows us to do such everyday tasks as walking, driving a car, and bending over to pick up a pencil from the floor. Without our vestibular sense, we would simply topple over.

On the other hand, rapid movements of your head, such as those you experience on spinning carnival rides, can overstimulate the vestibular system. Such movements can cause a violent wave action in the fluid gel of the vestibular system. When the gel crashes against the sensory cells, the result can be dizziness and nausea. People vary with respect to the degree of vestibular stimulation that they can comfortably tolerate. For example, some people are prone to motion sickness while simply riding in cars, whereas others can ride the most extreme amusement park rides with no ill effects.

You now have a working knowledge of how our sensory organs transduce environmental energies into neural impulses. Our next topic is perception, or how we make sense of all of this sensory information.

Nick Laham/Getty Images

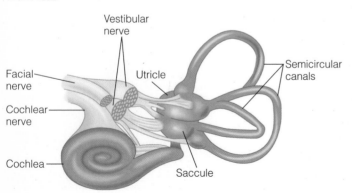

Vestibular nerve

Facial nerve

Utricle

Cochlear nerve

Semicircular canals

Cochlea

Saccule

Let's
REVIEW
In this section, we explained the chemical senses, taste and smell; touch; and the body senses, kinesthesis and the vestibular sense. For a quick check of your understanding, try answering the following questions at increasing levels of difficulty.

1. Which of the following is *not* thought to be a taste for which your tongue has receptors?

    a. salty   c. hot
    b. sour   d. bitter

2. Which of the following senses is most closely related to your sense of hearing?

    a. taste   c. smell
    b. touch   d. vestibular sense

3. Manuel has a horrible head cold. Which of his senses is *least likely* to be affected by the cold?

    a. taste   c. smell
    b. touch   d. vestibular sense

ANSWERS 1. c; 2. d; 3. b

LEARNING OBJECTIVES

What Should You Know?
- Describe top-down and bottom-up perceptual processing and explain the differences between them.
- Give an overview of perceptual constancy theories and how we perceive depth.

PERCEPTION: HOW DO WE MAKE SENSE OF IT ALL?

At the beginning of this chapter, we defined perception as *the interpretation of sensory information*. That's it in a nutshell. When you look at your friend's face, light bounces off his or her face. This light strikes your retina and the rods and cones transduce the light into neural impulses. Sensation is complete. But now your brain must interpret the meaning of the neural impulses so you will recognize your friend's face. The fact that you believe that you are seeing your friend's face and not, say, a dog or a cat, is the result of perceptual processes in your brain.

Likewise, for Michael Watson, once his tongue had transduced the flavor of the chicken dish, his brain interpreted, or perceived, that taste to be "pointed." Certainly most of us could have tasted the same chicken dish and had a different perception. We might have said that the dish was salty or spicy, but we wouldn't have perceived it as "pointy." Psychologists do have some understanding of how perception occurs for most of us, even if they don't completely understand Michael Watson's taste-related perceptions. In the coming sections, we will examine some of the theories psychologists have about the ways we perceive.

Using What We Know: Top-Down Perceptual Processing

Top-down perceptual processing occurs when we use previously gained knowledge to help us interpret a stimulus. For instance, let's go back to the example of perceiving your friend's face. When you see a face that you recognize as a friend's, what leads you to this recognition? Your memory helps you understand the "meaning" of the face you see. You know that faces usually contain two eyes, a nose, a mouth, and so on. Furthermore, you know how your friend's particular eyes, nose, and other features look. This stored knowledge allows you to quickly perceive the face of a friend. Given the usefulness of top-down perceptual processing, it's not surprising that we begin using our knowledge to help us perceive the world within the first year of life (Gliga, Volein, & Csibra, 2010).

Top-down perceptual processing can also fill in parts of the stimulus that are missing from our actual sensation of it. For example, look at ● FIGURE 3.19. You cannot see the left leg or the feet of this man, but you probably assume that they are there. Your knowledge of the human body tells you that the odds are slim that he is actually missing the leg and feet you cannot see. Consequently, in perceiving this picture, you implicitly assume that the "missing" leg and feet do, in fact, exist. This effect is so strong that later when you recall this picture, you might even remember having seen his leg and his feet—complete with tennis shoes on them!

© Novastock/Index Stock Imagery, Inc.

Errors in top-down perceptual processing can lead to faulty eyewitness testimony. Even though this suspect's face can't be seen, an eyewitness may make automatic judgments about this person's appearance based on his or her expectations of what a criminal is like.

PM Images/Getty Images

● **Top-Down Perceptual Processing** When you perceive the image in this photograph, your knowledge of the human body leads you to have certain expectations about the person in the picture. Because of top-down perceptual processing, you do not perceive that the man is missing his leg or his feet.

Unfortunately, this "filling-in" of missing details can sometimes lead to mistakes in perception. This can be a real problem in eyewitness accounts of crimes. One study showed that 75% of a sample of falsely convicted people were mistakenly identified as the criminal by an eyewitness (Wells & Olson, 2003). **So, why are eyewitnesses so frequently inaccurate?**

Sometimes your expectations about the world can *bias* your perception. Recent evidence even suggests that your perception of color is affected by your expectations. You see a banana as yellow, in part because you expect it to be yellow (Hansen, Olkkonen, Walter, & Gegenfurtner, 2006). So, imagine how perception can be distorted in social situations, given all the notions we each have about how people tend to behave in the world. For example, let's say that you are having lunch at a sidewalk café. Suddenly, your lunch is disrupted by a commotion at the bank across the street. You look up just in time to see someone run out of the bank. The person is dressed head-to-toe in black, wearing a black ski mask, and carrying a gun. The person is about 5'10" and about 150 lbs., but you have only a few-second glimpse before the figure pushes through the crowd and runs down the street. As you read this description, did you have a mental picture of this scene? If so, what assumptions did you automatically make? Did you assume that the bank robber was male? If you are like most people, you probably did. Furthermore, if you actually witnessed this event, you are likely to have told the police to look for a 5'10" male when, in reality, the robber could have been a female. After all, you never saw the robber's face.

Building a Perception "From Scratch": Bottom-Up Perceptual Processing

So, what do we do when we have very little or no stored knowledge to help us perceive a stimulus? We use a different perceptual process, one that does not rely on stored knowledge or expectations of the stimulus. In **bottom-up perceptual processing**, we use the properties of the stimulus itself to build our perception of that stimulus.

top-down perceptual processing perception that is guided by prior knowledge or expectations

bottom-up perceptual processing perception that is not guided by prior knowledge or expectations

TRY THIS DEMONSTRATION

● **Top-Down Versus Bottom-Up Processing** What is this picture? With no expectations to guide your perception, you are forced to rely mainly on bottom-up processes. Because the picture is ambiguous, bottom-up processes do not lead to a quick recognition of the stimulus. Now turn to Figure 3.21 (p. 118), which will enable you to engage your top-down perceptual processes. After looking at Figure 3.21, you should be able to quickly recognize the figure in this picture because you now have expectations to guide your perception.

Look at ● FIGURE 3.20. What do you see? With few clues about what this stimulus is, you cannot easily use your knowledge to help you perceive it. The stimulus is too ambiguous. Without top-down processing, you are forced to use bottom-up processes to perceive the stimulus. You build your perception of the picture by piecing together your perceptions of the many different components that make up this stimulus. You perceive the lines, curves, dots, shaded areas, and shapes. You then try to fit these components together to figure out what the drawing means. Most people find it very difficult to figure out what Figure 3.20 is using only bottom-up perceptual processes!

If you are ready to give up and try top-down perceptual processing, look at ● FIGURE 3.21 (p. 118). Now turn back to Figure 3.20. You will likely find that you can now readily perceive the image in Figure 3.20. You now have knowledge of what to look for, so perception becomes much easier. Your knowledge of what the picture is guides the way you piece together the components of the stimulus. When you switch to top-down processing, the picture becomes almost obvious.

In the course of a typical day, we probably use both top-down and bottom-up perceptual processes continually. We use bottom-up processes to piece together perceptions of ambiguous stimuli and top-down processes to tell us what we can expect to perceive in certain situations. Perception can be complicated in a three-dimensional world that is full of shapes and forms. To make perception even more complicated, our bodies do not remain stationary during perception. We move. The objects we perceive sometimes move. As a result, the information our senses receive from our world is highly variable. Our perceptual processes must be able to deal with these dynamic conditions. So, how do we organize and make sense of our perceptions?

Understanding What We Perceive: Interpreting Size, Shape, and Brightness

When you see a tiny person, how do you know that he or she is actually far away? How do we develop an understanding of what the sensory data mean? One of the problems encountered in interpreting sensory data is that of *perceptual constancy*. When you look at a visual stimulus, the image it projects on your retina is highly influenced by the perspective from which you view the object. Yet your perception of the object is not as dependent on perspective as your sensation is. For example, if you view a friend from a distance of 3 feet, an image of a certain size is projected onto your retina. If you move away and view the same friend from a distance of 6 feet, a smaller image of your friend is projected on your retina. Your *sensation* has changed (due to the smaller image projected on the retina), but you will not perceive that your friend has shrunk. If the image projected on your retina shrinks, why don't you perceive that your friend is also shrinking? Your brain appears to step in to correct your perception, to give you a *constant* perception of the objects that you see in the world. There is evidence that our brains correct not only for *size constancy*, but also for *shape constancy*, *brightness constancy*, and *color constancy* (● FIGURE 3.22).

Depth Perception: Sensing Our 3-D World With 2-D Eyes

Another perceptual challenge is *depth perception*. The world we view is three-dimensional, but the image it projects onto our retina is two-dimensional, like a photograph. Somehow,

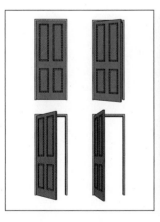   

(a)　　　　　　　　　(b)　　　　　　　　　(c)　　　　　　　　　(d)

Matthias Clamer/Getty Images

FIGURE 3.22

● **Perceptual Constancies**

(a) The shape of the image this door projects onto the retina changes dramatically as the orientation of the door changes. Yet we still perceive that the door is rectangular because of shape constancy.

(b) Even though the size of the image this person projects onto the retina shrinks as he walks away, because of size constancy we do not perceive that he is shrinking.

(c) The coal may reflect more light in the sun than the paper does in the shade, yet we still perceive that the paper is brighter than the coal because of brightness constancy.

(d) Even though this apple is in the shade, we still perceive it as being red because of color constancy.

FIGURE 3.21

● **Solution to the Problem in Figure 3.20** After looking at this picture, can you easily find the cow in Figure 3.20?

our brains must be able to determine depth from the information our eyes receive from the outside world. What makes this possible?

Binocular Depth Perception

One way that we perceive depth is through binocular depth cues. The term *binocular* means "two-eyed." **Binocular depth cues** rely on information from both eyes—specifically, information based on **retinal disparity**. Retinal disparity refers to the fact that each of our eyes sees a slightly different view of the world, because our eyes are set a few centimeters apart.

TRY THIS DEMONSTRATION

To check this disparity, try this demonstration. Look across the room and carefully note how your view changes as you close first your right eye and then your left. Notice that the view changes most for objects that are close to you, and less for objects that are distant. In short, the amount of retinal disparity we experience is a function of the distance from which we view an object (● FIGURE 3.23). Our brain uses the amount of retinal disparity we experience to calculate how far the object is from us, enabling us to perceive depth in the world.

Monocular Depth Cues

Binocular disparity is an important depth cue, but it is not the only way we perceive depth. If it were, we would be in serious trouble if we lost the use of one of our eyes. We also would not be able to perceive depth in paintings or photographs. Luckily, we have another means of depth perception that requires the use of only one eye: **monocular depth cues**.

Many of you may have learned about monocular depth cues when you began drawing and painting as a child. Because a canvas has no depth, all parts of the painting are the same distance from the viewer's eyes, and retinal disparity does not help us perceive depth. Interestingly, seeing the world without binocular depth cues may help some artists to draw and paint better. An analysis of the famous Dutch painter Rembrandt's self-portraits suggests

binocular depth cues depth cues that utilize information from both eyes

retinal disparity a binocular depth cue that uses the difference in the images projected on the right and left retinas to inform the brain about the distance of a stimulus

monocular depth cues depth cues that require information from only one eye

Gestalt approach a psychological school of thought originating in Germany that proposed that the whole of a perception must be understood rather than trying to deconstruct perception into its parts

figure-ground a Gestalt principle of perception that states that when we perceive a stimulus, we visually pull the *figure* part of the stimulus forward while visually pushing backward the background, or *ground*, part of the stimulus

closure a Gestalt principle of perception that states that when we look at a stimulus, we have a tendency to see it as a closed shape, rather than lines

© David Young-Wolff/PhotoEdit

FIGURE 3.23

● **Binocular Depth Cues** The brain uses retinal disparity, or the degree to which the images projected on the right and left retinas differ from each other, to calculate how far away an object is. The farther away the object, the smaller the degree of retinal disparity.

that he had a misalignment of his eyes that would have dramatically impaired his binocular depth cues. Being forced to perceive the world with only monocular depth cues may have enhanced his ability to render realistic images on a two-dimensional canvas (Dingfelder, 2010). ● TABLE 3.3 describes some of the most useful monocular depth cues that allow artists to paint realistic scenes and also help us perceive depth in the world.

Perceptual constancy and depth perception are both important components of our perceptual processing. But how do we perceive the cylindrical shape of a soda can or the rectangular shape of a shoe box? To understand this level of perceptual processing, we will examine theories of form perception.

Perceiving Form: The Gestalt Approach

One influential approach to understanding form perception is the **Gestalt approach** (see Chapter 1). According to the Gestalt approach, the whole of a perception is greater than the sum of its parts. In fact, the word *Gestalt* is German for "whole form." According to the Gestaltists, when you look at your friend's face, the resulting perception is not merely a sum of the angles, curves, shapes, and lines that make up the face; rather, you perceive the stimulus *as a whole*. In this case, you perceive a face because your mind has implicitly grouped all of the stimuli that make up that face into a coherent whole.

One of the major contributions of Gestalt theory is a series of perceptual laws that attempt to explain how our minds automatically organize perceptual stimuli together to produce the perception of a whole form (Wertheimer, 1923). One of the most important Gestalt concepts of perceptual organization is **figure-ground**. When you look at your world, you see a multitude of objects or figures that seem to stand away from the background. For instance, imagine you are in psychology class and your professor is standing at the whiteboard. You perceive that your professor is in front of the board, and the board is seen as the background. As you look at her, you visually pull her form, or *figure*, to the foreground and push the image of the whiteboard to the background, or *ground*.

● FIGURE 3.24 shows figure-ground in action. You should have different perceptions of this picture, depending on what you visually pull forward as the figure and what you push back to the ground. What do you see when you look at it?

Another Gestalt principle is **closure**. When we perceive a stimulus such as the one in ● FIGURE 3.25, we tend to mentally fill in, or *close*, the object. The stimulus is not a complete triangle, but nearly everyone will perceive it as complete. According to the principle of closure, we have a preference for viewing solid shapes as opposed to lines.

The Gestalt principles of **proximity** and **similarity** help explain how we group objects together. These rules state that we group together stimuli that are close to each other, or proximal, and also stimuli that are similar. What do you see *first* when you look at the pictures in ● FIGURE 3.26? Do you see 60 different objects in each of these pictures? In Figure

TABLE 3.3
● **Monocular Depth Cues**

MONOCULAR DEPTH CUE	DESCRIPTION	EXAMPLE
Interposition	More distant objects are partially hidden by closer objects.	© Robert Estall/Corbis
Height on the horizon	More distant objects are placed higher on the horizon than closer objects.	© Richard T. Nowitz/ Corbis
Relative size	More distant objects are seen as smaller than closer objects of the same size.	© W. Cody/Corbis
Texture gradient	More distant objects have less texture or detail than closer objects.	© Corbis
Aerial perspective	More distant objects are hazier and blurrier than closer objects.	© Sylvain Grandadam/ Getty Images
Linear perspective	Converging lines indicate distance or depth.	© Sylvain Grandadam/ Getty Images
Motion parallax	More distant objects appear to move more slowly than closer objects as we pass by them.	© Steven Lam/Getty Images

proximity a Gestalt principle of perception that states that we tend to group close objects together during perception

similarity a Gestalt principle of perception that states that we tend to group like objects together during perception

© Octavio Ocampo

FIGURE 3.24

● **Figure-Ground** What do you see when you look at this picture? Depending on how you use the perceptual rule of figure-ground, you will see different things in this work by Octavio Ocampo. Do you see bunnies? A cat? Men's faces?

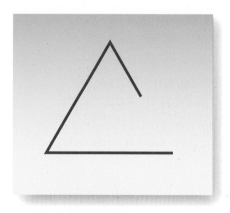

FIGURE 3.25

● **Closure** According to the Gestaltists, we tend to mentally fill in, or close, solid forms during perception.

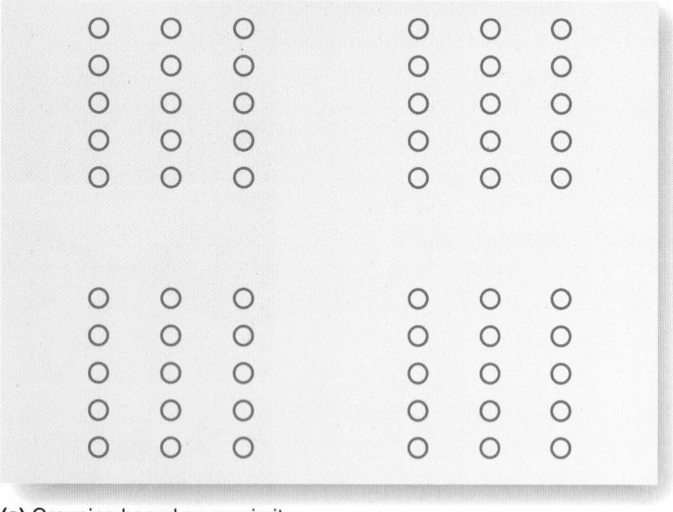

(a) Grouping based on proximity

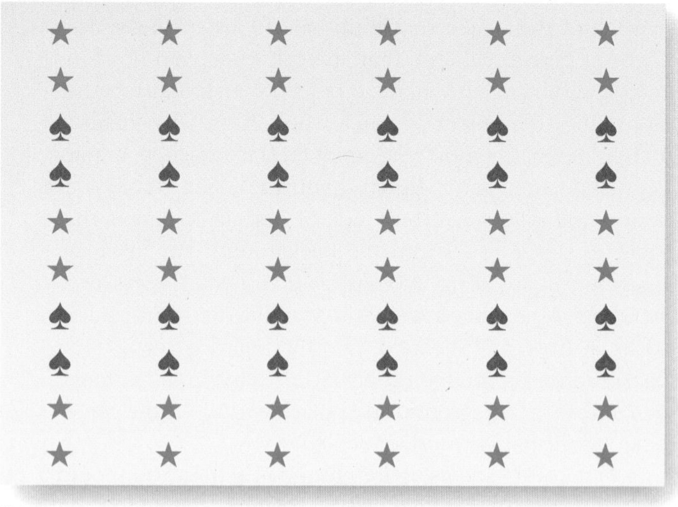

(b) Grouping based on similarity

FIGURE 3.26

● **The Gestalt Rules of Similarity and Proximity**

good continuation a Gestalt principle of perception that states that we have a preference for perceiving stimuli that seem to follow one another as being part of a continuing pattern

3.26a, because of proximity, you probably perceive a group of four squares. In Figure 3.26b, because of similarity, you probably perceive alternating pairs of rows of clubs and diamonds. As you read this page, you are continually using proximity to discriminate between the words that make up the sentences. Without proximity, you would see a mass of letters, but you would not know where one word ends and another begins.

The final Gestalt principle that we will look at is **good continuation**. The principle of good continuation states that we prefer to perceive stimuli that seem to follow one another

© Corbis

(a)   **(b)**

FIGURE 3.27

● **Two Instances of Good Continuation** Good continuation ensures that we perceive continuous patterns in the world. This perceptual principle is vital to the survival of the animal in (**b**).

as being part of a continuing pattern. For example, look at ● FIGURE 3.27a. How would you describe this stimulus? Many describe it as looking like the top of a castle wall. When we look at this stimulus, we tend to see the overall pattern as opposed to seeing myriad dashes on a piece of paper. Camouflage works on the principle of good continuation. Can you see the hidden animal in Figure 3.27b? This animal's very survival depends on its predator's use of good continuation!

Perceiving Form: Feature Detection Theory

Feature detection theory states that we have cells in our visual cortex that fire only in response to certain stimuli. Researchers studied this theory in animals, using electrodes to measure the activity of single neurons in the visual cortex. With an electrode in place, the researchers presented the animal with a certain visual stimulus, such as a bar of light, then checked to see whether the neuron fired. Through a process of elimination, the researchers determined what particular stimulus was needed to cause the specific neuron to fire (Hubel & Weisel, 1965).

Using this approach, researchers found that some cells of the cortex respond to particular combinations of lightness and darkness, lines of differing thickness, location, and orientation (Hubel & Wiesel, 1979). The neurons that fire only when certain visual stimuli are presented may work as feature detectors. Presumably, the human brain also has feature detectors, and by noticing which of our feature-detecting neurons are firing, our brain determines the form of the stimulus we are viewing. The square in ● FIGURE 3.28 is made up of two horizontal lines of identical length and two vertical lines of identical length. If each of these four lines is detected by a different set of feature-detecting neurons, two detectors for vertical lines and two detectors for horizontal lines, then our brain can deduce that we are looking at a rectangle.

Feature detection research holds much promise, but it is difficult to conduct (Hubel, 1990). Each neuron of the visual system has to be tested to determine what feature it detects. Mapping the entire visual system of feature detectors is likely to take a long time.

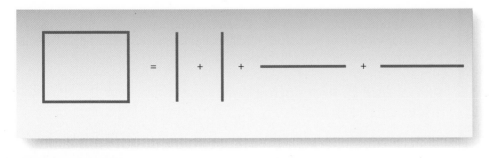

feature detection theory a theory of perception that proposes the existence of feature detectors or cortical cells that only fire when we see certain visual stimuli such as shapes, colors of light, or movements

---

FIGURE 3.28

● **An Example of Feature Detection** Feature-detecting neurons fire for each of these four lines.

Let's REVIEW

In this section, we described perception and perceptual organization, including top-down and bottom-up perception; ways that our brain corrects our perception to give us perceptual constancy; how our brain uses monocular and binocular depth cues to perceive depth; and two theories of form perception. For a quick check of your understanding, try answering the following questions at increasing levels of difficulty.

1. Which of the following is a binocular depth cue?

   a. motion parallax

   b. interposition

   c. retinal disparity

   d. textural gradient

2. Cultural influences would be *most likely* to affect which of the following perceptual processes?

   a. bottom-up perceptual processing

   b. top-down perceptual processing

   c. Gestalt perceptual processing

   d. feature detection processing

3. A brain tumor in your occipital lobe might result in distorted visual perception. This result is *most* consistent with which theory of perception?

   a. feature detection theory

   b. Gestalt theory of perceptual organization

   c. top-down perceptual processing theory

   d. bottom-up perceptual processing theory

ANSWERS 1. c; 2. b; 3. a

Because of top-down processing, it would take a long time to accurately perceive this laptop computer in the road. We simply don't expect to see laptop computers in the middle of the highway; therefore, our perception is slowed down.

ThinkStock/Getty Images

HOW ACCURATE ARE OUR PERCEPTIONS?

One of our students once had a frightening experience in which he misinterpreted a visual stimulus. He was driving in the mountains of northern Georgia when he passed a bear on a distant hillside. The bear was standing on its hind legs, towering over the 20-foot-tall pine trees that surrounded it. But the student knew that this was very unlikely, so he turned his car around and went back for another look. On closer inspection of the scene, he saw that all of the pine trees on the mountainside were newly planted saplings, about 3 feet high. The bear that towered over them was only an average-sized Georgia black bear! Our student was able to go back and correct his perception, but this is not always the case. We may never discover that we have misperceived a situation. Why do we sometimes misperceive our world?

Errors Due to Top-Down Processing: Seeing What We Expect to See

Why do you think the student misperceived the size of the black bear? The key to his misperception of the bear was in his misperception of the size of the pine trees. When driving through the mountains, most Georgians do not expect to see hillsides of baby trees. It's more typical to see mountainsides covered with mature pine trees that can be well over 20 feet tall. Because this is the normal expectation, the student used top-down processing and simply took for granted that the trees were a mature height. It wasn't until he saw the pine trees up close that he realized that his top-down processing had failed him. Because he misperceived the trees, he also misperceived the height of the bear.

Errors Due to Perceptual Constancy: Tricks of the Brain

Errors that are caused by top-down processing relate to the knowledge and the expectations we have of our world. Misperceptions occur for other reasons, too. Sometimes we misperceive things when our brain's attempts to give us perceptual constancy go awry.

The Moon Illusion

Have you ever noticed how the moon appears to be much larger as it rises over the horizon than when it is directly overhead? Many people think it is because the earth is closer to the moon when it is at the horizon but this is not true. The answer lies in our brain's attempt to correct for what it thinks is a mistake in perception. The moon projects the same size image on our retina when it is on the horizon as it does when it is directly overhead. But when the moon is on the horizon, our brain is tricked into thinking that the moon is actually farther away than it is when it's overhead. When we view the moon on the horizon, many interposition cues, such as trees and buildings that stand between the moon and us, indicate distance to our brain. But when we view the moon directly overhead, there are no interposition cues to indicate distance. Consequently, our brain thinks the moon is farther away when it is on the horizon, even though the image it projects on the retina is the same size as the one projected by the "closer" moon directly overhead. The logic involved is this: if the moon is farther away on the horizon, but it still projects the same size image on the retina as the moon overhead, then the moon on the horizon must be bigger than the moon overhead. The brain tries to *fix* the inconsistency by inflating our perception of the size of the moon on the horizon (Kaufman & Rock, 1989).

The moon illusion occurs because our brain distorts our perception.

© Jeremy Woodhouse/Masterfile

TRY THIS DEMONSTRATION

Undoing the Moon Illusion Just in case you need convincing, try this demonstration. You can stop your brain from trying to maintain consistency. Next time a full moon is rising, allow yourself to experience the illusion that the moon on the horizon is huge. Then turn so that you are facing away from the moon on the horizon. Bend over and spread your legs so that you can view the moon upside down between your legs. When you view the moon this way, it will look as small as it does when you view it overhead. When your head is upside down, your brain doesn't use its normal processes to correct for perceptual inconsistency, so the illusion disappears. When you stand up, turn around, and view the moon on the horizon from a normal position, it will again look larger.

The Ponzo Illusion

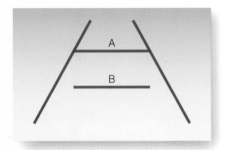

FIGURE 3.29

● **The Ponzo Illusion** Line segments A and B are both the same length, but we perceive that A is longer than B.

The Ponzo Illusion

This same logic underlies the *Ponzo illusion*. Lines of equal length that lie across converging lines appear to be unequal in length (● FIGURE 3.29). In the Ponzo illusion, linear perspective and height on the horizon cues tell the brain that the top line is farther away than the bottom one. Yet, both lines project the same size image on the retina. In an attempt to maintain size constancy, the brain inflates our perception of the top line's length, thus causing the illusion that the top line looks longer than the bottom line. This illusion occurs even though we do not consciously perceive that the line on top is farther away (Gillam, 1980).

The Müeller-Lyer Illusion

Size constancy probably also plays a role in the *Müeller-Lyer illusion* (● FIGURE 3.30; Weidner & Fink, 2007). In this illusion, our perception of the length of the vertical line segments changes, depending on the direction of the arrows at either end of the line. When the arrows extend away, the line looks longer.

Although researchers are not quite sure why the Müeller-Lyer illusion occurs, it is thought that the arrows serve as depth cues, much as we might find in the concave and convex angles of a building. If you look at Figure 3.30c, you can see that this type of corner produces a surface that is closer to the viewer than the recessed corner in Figure 3.30d. These depth cues may set off a process of compensation for size consistency that is very similar to those found in the moon illusion and the Ponzo illusion.

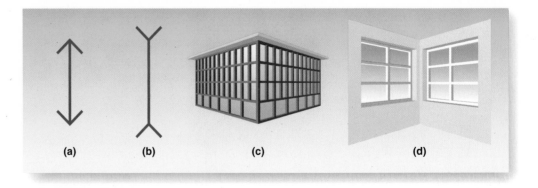

(a)　　(b)　　(c)　　(d)

FIGURE 3.30

● **The Müeller-Lyer Illusion** In the Müeller-Lyer illusion, the line in (**a**) is perceived as being shorter than the line in (**b**), even though they are of equal length. The Müeller-Lyer illusion is often seen in rectangular, "carpentered" buildings. The vertical line in the outside corner (**c**) looks shorter than the vertical line in the inside corner (**d**)—yet they are the same length. Architects use the Müeller-Lyer illusion to create certain perceptions of their buildings.

Cultural Factors in Perception

As we've discussed, your beliefs and expectations of the world can influence your top-down perceptual processing. Given that culture and environment influence many of our beliefs and expectations (remember our student and the Georgia bear?), it isn't surprising that cultural differences in perception have been demonstrated. For example, when viewing scenes, Westerners tend to focus on the details of objects (such as the people and objects), suggesting an analytic style of perception. In contrast, East Asians tend to spend more time focusing on the contextual relationships (such as how the people and objects are related to one another) in the scene, suggesting a more holistic style of perception (Goh & Park, 2009).

The Müeller-Lyer illusion provides another example of the influence of culture on perception. People who live in "carpentered" environments, where many of the buildings are wood-framed rectangular structures, have much experience with the architectural angles that produce the Müeller-Lyer illusion. Is it possible that these people also experience the Müeller-Lyer illusion to a greater degree than those who've lived their lives in "noncarpentered" worlds (where rectangular structures are rare)? This seems to be the case. The Bashi people of Africa traditionally live in round dwellings. When compared to Europeans, the Bashi are often found to be less susceptible to the Müeller-Lyer illusion (Bonte, 1962). A similar effect has been found among American Navajos. When traditional Navajos who live in round homes called *hogans* were compared to Navajos who grew up in rectangular buildings, they were found to be less likely to experience the Müeller-Lyer illusion (D. M. Pedersen & Wheeler, 1983). These studies suggest that our perceptions are influenced by elements in our culture that prepare us to see the world in a particular manner.

People who grow up in noncarpentered environments, where structures tend to be like this round hogan, are less likely to experience the Müeller-Lyer illusion.

Rob Crandall/The Image Works

Let's REVIEW

In this section, we dealt with errors in perception and several common perceptual illusions. For a quick check of your understanding, try answering the following questions at increasing levels of difficulty.

1. In the _____ illusion, parallel lines appear to converge as they recede into the distance.

   a. Ponzo
   b. Müeller-Lyer
   c. moon
   d. all of the above

2. The Ponzo illusion most likely occurs due to which perceptual process?

   a. monocular depth cues
   b. binocular depth cues
   c. top-down processing
   d. subliminal perception

3. A friend asks you to explain how culture affects perception. From what you have learned in this chapter, you should tell him that culture can affect _____.

   a. top-down perception
   b. bottom-up perception
   c. feature detection -down and bottom-up perception
   d. none of the above

ANSWERS 1. a; 2. a; 3. a

STUDYING the CHAPTER

KEY TERMS

attention (85)
sensation (85)
transduction (85)
perception (85)
psychophysics (87)
absolute threshold (87)
signal detection (88)
just noticeable difference (jnd) (89)
Weber's law (89)
subliminal (89)
wavelength (91)
amplitude (91)
visible spectrum (91)
hue (91)
brightness (91)
saturation (91)
pupil (92)
lens (92)

accommodation (93)
retina (93)
rods (93)
cones (93)
optic nerve (93)
blindspot (93)
photopigments (95)
dark adaptation (95)
light adaptation (96)
trichromatic theory of color vision (97)
color blindness (97)
opponent-process theory (98)
optic chiasm (99)
lateral geniculate nucleus (LGN) (99)
feature detectors (99)
cycle (101)
frequency (101)

pitch (101)
loudness (103)
decibels (dB) (103)
cochlea (103)
basilar membrane (104)
hair cells (104)
auditory nerve (104)
place theory (104)
frequency theory (105)
volley theory (106)
duplicity theory (106)
gustation (107)
papillae (108)
taste buds (108)
olfaction (111)
olfactory epithelium (111)
lock-and-key theory (111)
pheromones (112)
dermis (113)

epidermis (113)
kinesthesis (114)
vestibular sense (114)
top-down perceptual processing (115)
bottom-up perceptual processing (116)
binocular depth cues (118)
retinal disparity (118)
monocular depth cues (118)
Gestalt approach (119)
figure-ground (119)
closure (119)
proximity (119)
similarity (119)
good continuation (120)
feature detection theory (121)

TEST YOURSELF!

Now that you have studied the chapter, assess your comprehension of the material by answering the following questions. Then use the key at the end to determine if your understanding is at the basic, intermediate, or advanced level. For a more comprehensive assessment of your learning, please see your student study guide and your Psychology CourseMate (www.cengagebrain.com).

1. _____ is the focusing of your awareness on stimuli inside your mind or in the outside world.

   a. Perception
   b. Sensation
   c. Attention
   d. Transduction

2. Sensation is the _____ of environmental energy into neural impulses.

   a. transduction
   b. perception
   c. signal detection
   d. sublimation

3. In signal detection theory, being correct is to _____ as being wrong is to _____.

   a. false alarm; hit
   b. hit; false alarm
   c. false alarm; correct rejection
   d. correct rejection; hit

4. Taste is most closely associated with which other sense?

   a. vision
   b. hearing
   c. smell
   d. touch

5. Typical color blindness is best explained by the _____ theory.

   a. opponent process
   b. duplicity
   c. trichromatic
   d. place

6. Being blindfolded for an hour would be most likely to *reduce* the time it would take you to undergo _____.

   a. top-down perceptual processing
   b. light adaptation
   c. dark adaptation
   d. retinal disparity

7. The theory that best explains olfaction is the _____ theory.

   a. opponent process
   b. place
   c. duplicity
   d. lock-and-key

8. Sally is sewing, and she drops her needle on the highly patterned rug in her sewing room. After searching for 5 minutes, Sally is unable to find the lost needle. Which of the following best describes why Sally is having trouble finding the needle?

   a. perceptual constancy
   b. proximity
   c. similarity
   d. good continuation

9. Wilbur has a bad ear and sinus infection. Which of Wilbur's senses would be *least* likely to be affected?

   a. hearing
   b. vestibular sense
   c. kinesthetic sense
   d. olfaction

10. _____ are cells in the visual cortex that fire only when certain stimuli are seen.

   a. Epithelial cells
   b. Feature detectors
   c. Papillae
   d. Hair cells

11. The vomeronasal sense is most closely associated with which other sense?

   a. vision
   b. taste
   c. olfaction
   d. vestibular sense

12. Tasting which of the following flavors would most likely cause more than one type of taste bud to begin firing neural signals?

   a. the fishy flavor of sushi
   b. the saltiness of pretzels
   c. the bitterness of cranberries
   d. the brothy flavor of a soup

13. Gilda is deaf. Gilda's deafness is possibly the result of damage to her _____.

   a. hair cells
   b. cochlea
   c. basilar membrane
   d. all of the above

14. Which of the following theories of sensation and perception is *most* analogous to a choir singing a three-part harmony?

   a. place theory
   b. volley theory
   c. opponent process theory
   d. the Gestalt approach

15. The outermost layer of our skin is the _____.

    a. epidermis
    b. dermis
    c. basilar membrane
    d. papillae

Scoring Key

Below are the answers and the associated point values for each of the Learning Challenge questions. Circle the associated points for each question that you answered correctly. To obtain your Learning Challenge Score, add up the points you circled and write the total in the blank.

1. C, 1 pt	**6.** C, 3 pts	**11.** C, 2 pts
2. A, 1 pt	**7.** D, 1 pt	**12.** A, 3 pts
3. B, 2 pts	**8.** D, 3 pts	**13.** D, 3 pts
4. C, 2 pts	**9.** C, 3 pts	**14.** B, 2 pts
5. C, 2 pts	**10.** B, 1 pt	**15.** A, 1 pt

Learning Challenge Score _____

(27–30) Congratulations! You scored at the advanced level. You are well on your way to mastering the material. Take the next step by answering the questions in your Student Study Guide or your Psychology CourseMate (www.cengagebrain.com).

(21–26) You are almost there! You scored at the intermediate level. Review the material you missed before moving on to answer the questions in your Student Study Guide or your Psychology CourseMate (www.cengagebrain.com).

(20 and below) You are on your way, but you're not there yet! You scored at the beginner level. It appears that you need to carefully review the chapter to improve your mastery of the material.

USE IT OR LOSE IT: APPLYING PSYCHOLOGY

1. Your younger sister listens to music at a very loud level on her iPod nearly every day. What would you tell her to convince her to turn down the volume?

2. Because you are studying sensation in psychology, your uncle asks you to explain why he cannot distinguish red objects from green objects. What would you tell him?

3. Assume you work on the staff of a nursing home. Most of your clients are people in their 80s and 90s. How can you use your knowledge of sensation and perception to do your job better? In other words, what changes can you expect to see in your clients' sensory and perceptual abilities, and how can you accommodate those changes?

4. You have been charged with determining the additional amount of sugar one would have to add to a cup of coffee that already contained 2 teaspoons of sugar to produce a jnd. How would you go about determining this?

5. Find a picture of Vincent Van Gogh's painting *Starry Night*. What monocular depth cues are used in this painting? Provide specific examples of your choices.

6. Can you identify specific examples of how your cultural background has affected your perception?

CRITICAL THINKING FOR INTEGRATION

1. Explain how top-down perceptual processing may affect the testimony of a person who has witnessed an armed robbery.

2. If Ali has a brain tumor in his occipital lobe, how might this affect his sensory and perceptual processes?

3. How might strongly held beliefs, such as racial prejudices, affect perception?

4. Design a research study to test the hypothesis that males and females have different food preferences.

CHAPTER STUDY RESOURCES

Student Study Guide

To help organize your learning, work through Chapter 3 of the *What Is Psychology? Student Study Guide*. The study guide includes learning objectives, a chapter summary, fill-in review, key terms, a practice test, and activities.

CengageNOW

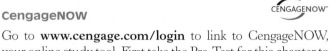

Go to **www.cengage.com/login** to link to CengageNOW, your online study tool. First take the Pre-Test for this chapter to get your personalized study plan, which will identify topics you need to review and direct you to online resources. Then take the Post-Test to determine what concepts you have mastered and what you still need work on.

CourseMate

Access an interactive eBook, chapter-specific interactive learning tools, including flashcards, quizzes, videos, and more in your Psychology CourseMate, available at **CengageBrain.com**.

Aplia

aplia

Aplia™ is an online interactive learning solution that helps you improve comprehension—and your grade—by integrating a variety of tools such as video, tutorials, practice tests, and interactive eBook. Founded by a professor to enhance his own courses, Aplia provides automatically graded assignments with detailed, immediate explanations on every question, and innovative teaching materials. More than 1,000,000 students like you have used Aplia at over 1,800 institutions. Aplia should be purchased only when assigned by your instructor as part of your course.

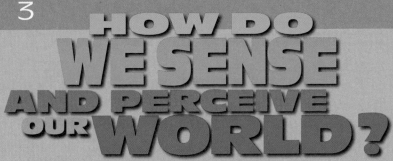

HOW DO WE SENSE AND PERCEIVE OUR WORLD?

Michael Watson's synesthesia gave us a memorable glimpse of atypical sensory processing. In large measure, our sense of reality is determined by how we sense and perceive the world around us. **Sensation** is the means by which information from the outside world enters our mind. Then **perception** occurs as we interpret and make sense of this information. Without these processes, we would be cut off from the outside world.

MEASURING SENSATION AND PERCEPTION: HOW SENSITIVE ARE OUR SENSES?

- **Psychophysics** is the branch of psychology that studies how we process sensory stimuli.
- Psychophysicists conduct experiments to determine the **absolute threshold** and **just noticeable difference** of each of the five senses.
- **Weber's law** is the relationship between the original intensity of a stimulus and the amount of change that is required to produce a jnd.
- When sensory stimuli are too weak in intensity to reach absolute threshold, the stimuli are said to be **subliminal**.

HOW DO WE SEE THE WORLD?

- Light is electromagnetic energy, measured primarily by **wavelength** and **amplitude**.

  Wavelength = **Hue**; Amplitude = **Brightness**
- The **visible spectrum** of light is the narrow band we are able to see. Some animals are able to see a much broader spectrum.

Notice the extremely narrow band of the electromagnetic spectrum that is visible to the human eye.

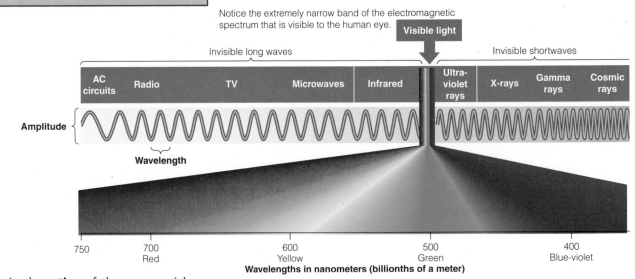

Visible light

Invisible long waves | Invisible shortwaves

| AC circuits | Radio | TV | Microwaves | Infrared | Ultra-violet rays | X-rays | Gamma rays | Cosmic rays |

Amplitude

Wavelength

750 Red   700   600 Yellow   500 Green   400 Blue-violet

Wavelengths in nanometers (billionths of a meter)

- In the **retina** of the eye, specialized cells known as **rods** and **cones** convert light into neural impulses, which eventually travel to the brain via the **optic nerve**.
- The **trichromatic theory of color vision** and the **opponent-process theory** are both used to explain how we process color.
- **Color blindness** is the inability to see certain colors and is often the result of missing cones in the retina.

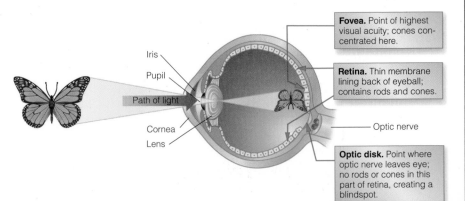

Iris

Pupil

Path of light

Cornea

Lens

Fovea. Point of highest visual acuity; cones concentrated here.

Retina. Thin membrane lining back of eyeball; contains rods and cones.

Optic nerve

Optic disk. Point where optic nerve leaves eye; no rods or cones in this part of retina, creating a blindspot.

Are You Getting THE BIG PICTURE?

HOW DO WE HEAR THE WORLD?

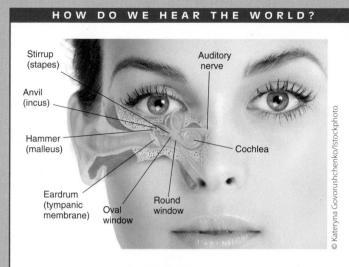

Stirrup (stapes)
Auditory nerve
Anvil (incus)
Hammer (malleus)
Cochlea
Eardrum (tympanic membrane)
Oval window
Round window

© Kateryna Govorushchenko/Istockphoto

- Sounds are produced by waves of compressed air. **Frequency = Pitch**; Amplitude = **Loudness**
- The eardrum, or tympanic membrane, is a very thin membrane in the middle ear that vibrates to incoming sounds. It begins transmitting those sounds through small bones to the **hair cells** in the fluid-filled **cochlea**, where neural impulses are generated.
- The **auditory nerve** carries sounds we hear into the brain.

WHAT OTHER SENSES DO WE HAVE?

- Humans are sensitive to at least four types of taste: bitter, sweet, salty, and sour.
- The **taste buds**, which reside in the pits between the **papillae** on your tongue, transduce the chemicals in the food you eat into neural impulses.
- The sense of smell operates by converting odors captured by a special piece of skin that lines the top of the nasal cavity to neural impulses that travel via the olfactory nerve to the olfactory bulb in the brain.
- Many animals (and perhaps humans) have a vomeronasal system that allows them to communicate with other animals via airborne chemicals known as **pheromones**.
- The sense of touch originates in the skin, with the inner layer—the **dermis**—containing most of the touch receptors.
- **Kinesthesis** refers to our ability to sense the position of our body parts in space and in relation to one another.
- The **vestibular sense** monitors the position of our head in space and helps us to stay balanced.

© Catherine Karnow/Corbis

PERCEPTION: HOW DO WE MAKE SENSE OF IT ALL AND HOW ACCURATE ARE OUR PERCEPTIONS?

© Octavio Ocampo

- **Top-down perceptual processing** refers to using previously gained knowledge to interpret a sensory stimulus.
- **Bottom-up perceptual processing** refers to using properties of the stimulus itself to form our perception of a stimulus.
- Perceptual constancies, depth cues, and **feature detection** are among the mental shortcuts we automatically employ to assist in perceiving stimuli.
- Perceptual errors can occur for a variety of reasons. They are often due to misapplied expectations that lead us to think we have seen or heard things we have not.

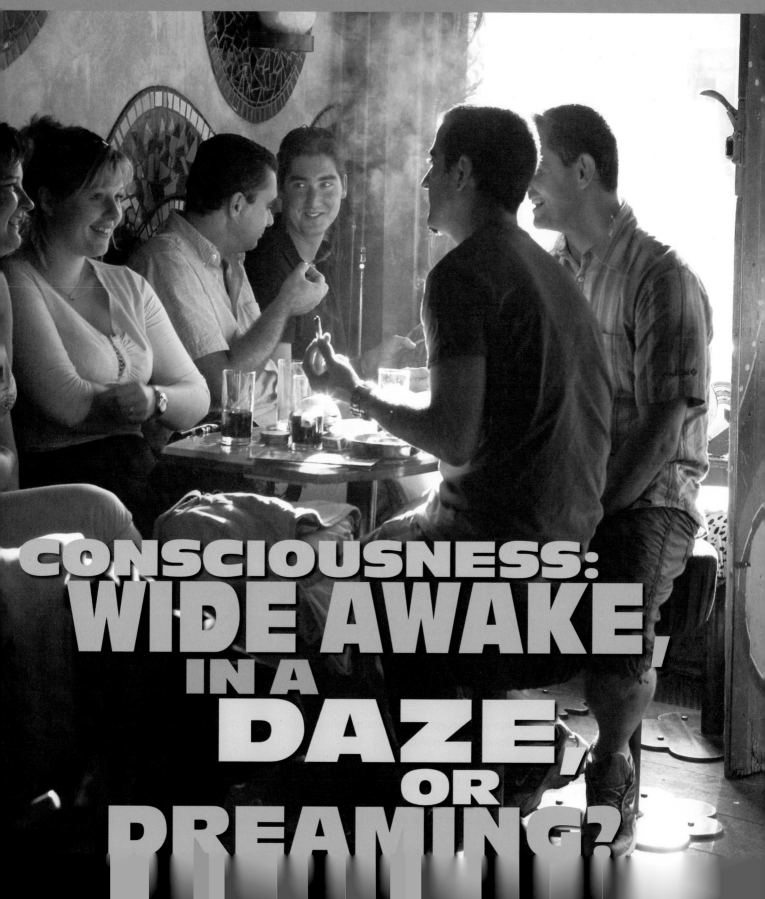

CHAPTER 4

CONSCIOUSNESS: WIDE AWAKE, IN A DAZE, OR DREAMING?

THE BIG PICTURE

What Is Consciousness?

In previous chapters we examined psychologists' interests in the more biological domains of behavior—sensation, perception, the nervous system, and the hormonal system. For the most part these chapters focused on conscious behavior. **Consciousness**, in psychological terms, includes the feelings, thoughts, and aroused states of which we are aware. This chapter examines the levels, or gradations, of consciousness itself—when you are *not* fully awake, alert, aware, or perhaps of sound mind. For example, psychologists have done quite a bit of research in three areas: sleep, hypnosis, and the effects of various psychoactive drugs.

Today, conferences on consciousness draw everyone from quantum physicists to philosophers, and there is ample debate about what is unique about human consciousness. Yet changes in consciousness occur because of changes in the body and brain. In this chapter, you will see how brain functions and chemistry discussed in Chapters 2 and 3 actually operate and affect our awareness. Consider the following stories:

Charlie "Bird" Parker is one of the most well-known figures of jazz music. His mother bought him a saxophone when Charlie entered high school, and Charlie taught himself how to play it. He practiced for hours and hours, and listened to jam sessions at jazz clubs. He quit school at the age of 15 to become a professional musician, playing with several well-known local big bands in Kansas City, Kansas. At the same time, he got married and began using drugs, most notably alcohol and heroin. Parker was especially gifted on the sax—playing incredibly fast and with unparalleled phrasing and rhythm. Sadly, his drug use caused him to miss many performances over his career and resulted in several failed marriages and several stints in rehab. Eventually, Charlie landed in Bellevue Psychiatric Hospital in 1954. He was diagnosed with acute and chronic alcoholism and narcotic addiction. His then common-law wife indicated that Charlie had suicidal tendencies when he was drinking. After a brief discharge, Charlie readmitted himself to the hospital because he was back to drinking and feared for his own safety. After drying out, Charlie tried to put his life back together. He lived in Greenwich Village, appearing occasionally at a club called the Open Door. Unfortunately, he died suddenly at the age of 34 in the New York City apartment of a friend.

After 20 years in professional tennis, eight-time Grand Slam champion Andre Agassi retired from tennis following the 2006 U.S. Open. His connection with tennis began

Ticket/Photolibrary

Michael Ochs Archives/Getty Images

A great jazz saxophonist, Charlie Parker battled alcohol and narcotic addiction throughout his short life.

Ethan Miller/Getty Images

very early in life—at the age of 3. As detailed in Agassi's memoir, *Open: An Autobiography* (2009), his overbearing father valued tennis over education, and Andre was forced to practice for hours each day on the backyard tennis court his father had built at their modest Las Vegas home. At 13, Andre was sent to a Florida tennis camp that felt more like a prison. He dropped out of school in the ninth grade and turned professional at 16.

After stumbling in three Grand Slam finals, Agassi won his first major championship at Wimbledon in 1992 at the age of 22. Three years later, Agassi reached the World No. 1 ranking. However, Andre's career was soon in disarray. A recurring wrist injury made playing tennis (let alone winning) difficult, and Andre became depressed and unmotivated and started using crystal methamphetamine. The drug made him feel energetic and invincible, able to go days without sleep—but it did not help his tennis game. By late 1997, Agassi had dropped to No. 141 in the rankings and failed an ATP (Association of Tennis Professionals) drug test at a tournament. "My name, my career, everything is now on the line, at a craps table where no one wins. Whatever I've achieved, whatever I've worked for, might soon mean nothing" (p. 255).

After quitting crystal meth and pulling out of that slump, Agassi went on to win five Grand Slam tournaments and reclaim the World No. 1 ranking, becoming the oldest men's player ever to do so at the age of 32. Since retirement, he has been heavily involved in charity work through his Andre Agassi Charitable Foundation and Andre Agassi College Preparatory Academy, a charter school for underprivileged children.

You may not feel that these stories have any relevance to you, let alone to psychology—but they do. Separated by 50 years, Charlie's and Andre's lives are remarkably similar. Both men were extremely talented in their professions, and both fell into the abyss of drug use. Although one ends in tragedy and the other in triumph, both illustrate that drug addiction has no boundaries. It does not discriminate by social class, age, gender, or ethnicity. It is also one of the primary ways in which we alter our consciousness—the focus of this chapter. We alter consciousness when we sleep, daydream, meditate, or drink alcohol or caffeine. We may also witness altered states in the lives of those we love. By closely examining these states, we may better understand our behavior and the behavior of those around us. We will start with the altered state we all experience—sleep.

consciousness feelings, thoughts, and aroused states of which we are aware

WHAT HAPPENS WHEN WE SLEEP? REST, DREAMING, AND CIRCADIAN RHYTHM

Many of us never question what goes on in our bodies and minds as we sleep. But sleep offers plenty of behaviors for psychologists to explore. First, we will look at *why* we sleep, or the benefits of sleep. Then we will discuss what occurs in our brains and bodies as we sleep. We will explore the purpose of dreams and whether dreams have meaning. We will conclude by describing different types of sleep disorders. We caution you that just reading about sleep can make you drowsy!

Functions of Sleep: Why Do We Sleep, and What If We Don't?

What would happen if you tried to stay awake? William C. Dement, a pioneer in sleep research, actually tried this experiment himself. As we will see, Dement's lack of sleep made him a danger to himself and others, but he was not in danger of dying from lack of sleep. Eventually he fell asleep. In the same way that you cannot hold your breath until you die, you cannot deprive yourself of all sleep. Sleep always wins. We drift into repeated *microsleeps* (Goleman, 1982). A **microsleep** is a brief (3- to 15-second) episode of sleep that occurs in the midst of a wakeful activity. We are typically unaware of its occurrence unless we are behind the wheel of a car or another similar environment. In such circumstances, microsleeps could cause a disaster. Yet microsleeps appear to help us survive by preventing total sleep deprivation. There is a rare inherited genetic disorder called *fatal familial insomnia* in which protein buildup in the thalamus of the brain causes increasing insomnia, hallucinations, weight loss, dementia, and then death (Dauvilliers et al., 2004; Krasnianski et al., 2008). However, for most people, sleep deprivation eventually results in falling asleep.

Sleep ensures our continued physical and mental health in several ways.

© Tom Carter/PhotoEdit

It is estimated that more than 24,000 deaths occur annually in accidents caused directly or in part by drowsy drivers.

- *Sleep restores your body tissues and facilitates body growth.* Sleep allows your immune system, nervous system, and organs time to replenish lost reserves and energy and to repair any cellular damage. This prepares the body for action the next day and ensures the continued health of the body. Sleep also activates growth hormone, which facilitates physical growth during infancy, childhood, and the teen years (Gais et al., 2006; Szentirmai et al., 2007). Lack of adequate sleep can also affect energy levels, often making us feel drowsy and fatigued (K. Murphy & Delanty, 2007; Oginska & Pokorski, 2006).
- *Sleep increases immunity to disease.* During sleep, the production of immune cells that fight off infection increases. Therefore, your immune system is stronger when you receive the appropriate amount of sleep (Beardsley, 1996; Born et al., 1997; Lange et al., 2006; Motivala & Irwin, 2007). When you deprive your body of sleep, your natural immune responses are reduced (Irwin et al., 2003; K. Murphy & Delanty, 2007). This is in part why you are encouraged to sleep and rest when you are ill. This effect on immunity occurs after as few as two days of total sleep deprivation or even several days of partial sleep deprivation (Heiser et al., 2000; Irwin et al., 1996; Ozturk et al., 1999; N. L. Rogers et al., 2001). For college students, this may mean you are more susceptible to colds and flu at midterm and final exam time. You are more likely to sleep less at these times, thereby decreasing your immune system's ability to combat illnesses. Fortunately, after a night or several nights of recovery sleep, your natural immune functions return to normal (Irwin et al., 1996; Ozturk et al., 1999). Sleeping truly is good medicine.

microsleep brief episode of sleep that occurs in the midst of a wakeful activity

- *Sleep keeps your mind alert.* When people do not get enough sleep, they are more likely to be inattentive and easily distracted (Jennings, Monk, & van der Molen, 2003; Kahol et al., 2008; Kendall et al., 2006; Koslowsky & Babkoff, 1992; Murphy & Delanty, 2007). Sleep makes your body more sensitive to norepinephrine—the neurotransmitter that keeps you alert during the day—as we discussed in Chapter 2 (Steriade & McCarley, 1990).

- *Sleep helps learning and memory.* When you sleep, emotional experiences as well as information that you have reviewed or rehearsed are more likely to be remembered (Fogel, Smith, & Cote, 2007; Gais, Lucas, & Born, 2006; Karni et al., 1994; Payne et al., 2008; Racsmany, Conway, & Demeter, 2010; Rasch & Born, 2008; Stickgold & Walker, 2007; M. P. Walker, 2009; M. P. Walker & Stickgold, 2004). **Does this mean that you can learn while you sleep?** No. Chapter 6 offers an in-depth look at memory processing, but a brief discussion here will help you understand the connection between sleep and memory.

In order to get information into your memory, you must *encode* it, or do something to remember the information. This may mean repeating the information over and over again. Other encoding methods include visualizing the information or associating it with a personal experience. When information is thoroughly encoded, it can be more easily transferred to long-term memory so that we can retrieve it later.

So, back to the question of learning while you're sleeping. Information that you process during sleep must be well encoded while you're awake in order for memory to benefit from sleep. Sleep allows you to better store what material was actually processed (that is, encoded well enough) during studying. Information that you can't readily retrieve in the morning probably wasn't encoded well enough, and you will need to study it again. You can see the advantage of a good night's sleep before an exam.

Sleep's connection to memory processing may also explain why problem solving seems to improve after a night's sleep (Ellenbogen et al., 2007). You may think about a problem repeatedly during the day, frustrated by your inability to find a solution. The next day you awaken with a solution in mind. This suggests that pertinent details about the problem are processed during sleep. The phrase "sleep on it" really does have merit.

- *Sleep enhances your mood.* Sleep activates many chemicals that influence your emotions and mood. Consequently, if you are deprived of sleep, you are more likely to be irritable, cranky, and unhappy, in addition to being tired (Boivin et al., 1997; Durmer & Dinges, 2005; Murphy & Delanty, 2007). This effect is even more pronounced in children, adolescents, and young adults, perhaps because as we get older we get better at regulating our emotions such that they may be less affected by lack of sleep (O'Brien, 2009; Ready, Marquez, & Akerstedt, 2009).

Research also suggests that sleep may have evolved as a necessary behavior for humans (Hirshkowitz, Moore, & Minhoto, 1997; Webb, 1983). When humans lived in caves, it was dangerous for them to go out at night to hunt for food because they had very little night vision and were relatively small compared to other species. If they did go outside at night, they were likely to be the food for larger predators. Consequently, humans who stayed inside the cave at night were more likely to survive and produce offspring. Over time, these offspring may have adapted to the pattern of nighttime sleeping and daytime hunting and gathering.

As you can see, sleep is a necessity, not a luxury. Sleep offers many benefits to our functioning and ensures that we will be healthy, alert, and happy.

How Much Sleep Do We Need?

Is there an optimal number of hours of sleep (6, 8, or 10) that each of us requires? Unfortunately, there is no definitive answer. People show differences in the amount of sleep they need. Some people brag about how little sleep they need. Yet research shows that although the amount of sleep we need depends on several factors, many of us are not getting enough. Here are some sleep factors and facts:

- *Age.* Who sleeps more, the young or the old? The older we get, the less sleep we need (● Figure 4.1). Babies require a lot of sleep, between 16 and 18 hours a day. Preschoolers

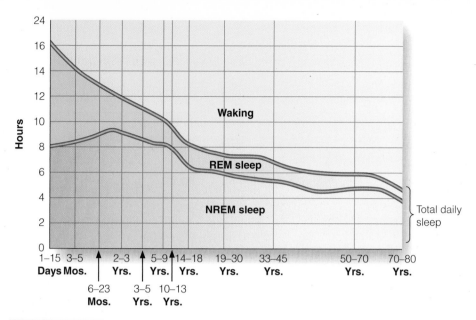

FIGURE 4.1

● **Age Differences in Sleep Needs** Newborns sleep an average of 16 hours a day. Preschoolers require less sleep, about 10 to 12 hours. Most teenagers and adults require 8 hours. *From "Ontogenetic Development of Human Sleep-Dream Cycle," by H. P. Roffwarg, J. N. Muzino, and W. C. Dement,* Science, *1966, 152:604–609. Copyright 1966 by the AAAS. Reprinted by permission.*

require less sleep, about 10 to 12 hours a day, typically including a midday nap. Teenagers and young adults need less sleep than children, but they still require 8 to 10 hours of sleep a night. However, just 1 in 5 teenagers gets an optimal 9 hours of sleep on school nights (National Sleep Foundation, 2006). People between the ages of 25 and 34 are more likely to report insufficient rest or sleep than are people over the age of 65 (McKnight-Eily et al., 2009). On average, college students sleep 6.1 hours—2 hours less than they need—each night (Maas, 1998). Adults, on average, sleep 6.7 hours a night on weekdays (National Sleep Foundation, 2009). According to sleep experts, most adults and teenagers require at least 8 hours of sleep a night.

● *Lifestyle (Environment).* Our lifestyle habits and our environment also influence the amount of sleep that we need or get. If you were raised in a home in which everyone was up early on the weekends to do chores, you adapted to a different sleep schedule than someone who slept until 10 a.m. or noon on weekends. In one study of college students, good sleepers were more likely to have regular bedtime and rise time schedules than poorer sleepers (Carney et al., 2006). Keep in mind too that stressors and responsibilities change as we get older. Job responsibilities, parenting, or living on one's own also brings about changes in our sleep schedule. Recall how Andre Agassi's drug use altered his sleep and the poor performance on the tennis court that ensued.

● *Genetics.* Genes may also play a role in the amount of sleep that each of us requires. For example, studies that measured the sleep patterns of identical twins compared to fraternal twins found more similar sleep needs and sleep behaviors among identical twins (de Castro, 2002; Webb & Campbell, 1983). Additional research also suggests that genes may influence our propensity to be either "night owls" or "early birds." Some people may be genetically predisposed to get up early in the morning and go to bed earlier, whereas others may prefer getting up later and going to bed later (J. P. Guthrie, Ash, & Bendapudi, 1995; Mongrain et al., 2004; Tankova, Adan, & Buela-Casal, 1994). To assess your propensity toward morningness or eveningness, complete the brief scale in ● Table 4.1.

TRY THIS DEMONSTRATION

Read each question in Table 4.1 carefully. Select the most appropriate answer and note the corresponding value next to it.

TABLE 4.1

● Morningness–Eveningness Scale

QUESTION	ANSWER	VALUE
If you were entirely free to plan your evening and had no commitments the next day, at what time would you choose to go to bed?	8 P.M.–9 P.M.	5
	9 P.M.–10:15 P.M.	4
	10:15 P.M.–12:30 A.M.	3
	12:30 A.M.–1:45 A.M.	2
	1:45 A.M.–3 A.M.	1
You have to do 2 hours of physically hard work. If you were entirely free to plan your day, in which of the following periods would you choose to do the work?	8 A.M.–10 A.M.	4
	11 A.M.–1 P.M.	3
	3 P.M.–5 P.M.	2
	7 P.M.–9 P.M.	1
For some reason you have gone to bed several hours later than normal, but there is no need to get up at a particular time the next morning. Which of the following is most likely to occur?	Will wake up at the usual time and not fall asleep again	4
	Will wake up at the usual time and doze thereafter	3
	Will wake up at the usual time but will fall asleep again	2
	Will not wake up until later than usual	1
You have a 2-hour test to take that you know will be mentally exhausting. If you were entirely free to choose, in which of the following periods would you choose to take the test?	8 A.M.–10 A.M.	4
	11 A.M.–1 P.M.	3
	3 P.M.–5 P.M.	2
	7 P.M.–9 P.M.	1
If you had no commitments the next day and were entirely free to plan your own day, what time would you get up?	5 A.M.–6:30 A.M.	5
	6:30 A.M.–7:45 A.M.	4
	7:45 A.M.–9:45 A.M.	3
	9:45 A.M.–11 A.M.	2
	11 A.M.–12 P.M.	1
A friend has asked you to join him twice a week for a workout in the gym. The best time for him is between 10 P.M. and 11 P.M. Bearing nothing else in mind other than how you normally feel in the evening, how do you think you would perform?	Very well	1
	Reasonably well	2
	Poorly	3
	Very poorly	4
One hears about "morning" and "evening" types of people. Which of these types do you consider yourself to be?	Definitely a morning type	6
	More a morning than an evening type	4
	More an evening than a morning type	2
	Definitely an evening type	0

Now add the scores together to get your total. Compare your total score with the table to the right to get an idea of your *chronotype*.

Adapted from "A Self Assessment Questionnaire to Determine Morningness–Eveningness in Human Circadian Rhythms," by J. A. Horne and O. Ostberg, International Journal of Chronobiology, 4 (1976): 97–110.

MORNINGNESS–EVENINGNESS SCALE	
Definitely morning type	32–28
Moderately morning type	27–23
Neither type	22–16
Moderately evening type	15–11
Definitely evening type	10–6

Circadian Rhythm and the Biological Clock

Our cycle of sleep is also greatly influenced by our biological clocks. For example, if you were put in a cave and had no cues as to time—no watches, light, or clocks—your body would exhibit a natural rhythm of sleeping and waking that closely resembles a 25-hour cycle. This phenomenon is referred to as a **circadian rhythm**. This circadian rhythm is programmed by a group of brain cells in the hypothalamus called the **suprachiasmatic nucleus (SCN)** (Zee & Manthena, 2007). The SCN works very much like an internal clock—signaling other brain areas when to be aroused (awake) to start the day and when to shut down (sleep) for the day.

How does the SCN know when it is time to be awake or asleep? The SCN is very responsive to light changes and takes its cues from your eyes. When your eyes transmit light information to the SCN, they are in essence telling it whether it is light or dark outside (● FIGURE 4.2). The light information helps the SCN direct the release of **melatonin**, the hormone that facilitates sleep. Melatonin regulates your circadian rhythm and helps you get to sleep. As darkness increases, so does the production of melatonin in your body (J. Arendt, 2006; Brzezinski, 1997). It is known as the "Dracula hormone" because it comes out at night.

We stated that the SCN functions on a 25-hour cycle. But our days are 24 hours long. Each day we ask our SCN to reset the clock by one hour. It does this automatically and without much consequence to our functioning. Yet when we try to reset the clock by several or more hours, we disrupt our body's natural circadian rhythm. We lose the benefits of sleep we discussed previously.

A significant amount of research now suggests that a developmental change in our intrinsic sleep–wake cycle occurs during puberty (Carskadon, Acebo, & Jenni, 2004; Crowley, Acebo, & Carskadon, 2007; Jenni, Achermann, Carskadon, 2005; Munch et al., 2005; D. J. Taylor et al., 2005). Changes in melatonin secretion and light sensitivity alter the timing of our cycle. We are more likely to want to stay up later in the evening and sleep longer in the morning. Although teenagers' social calendars often strengthen this tendency, the fact that part of this change is developmental in nature does have serious implications for high school starting times and adolescent academic performance.

circadian rhythm changes in bodily processes that occur repeatedly on approximately a 24- to 25-hour cycle

suprachiasmatic nucleus (SCN) a group of brain cells located in the hypothalamus that signal other brain areas when to be aroused and when to shut down

melatonin hormone in the body that facilitates sleep

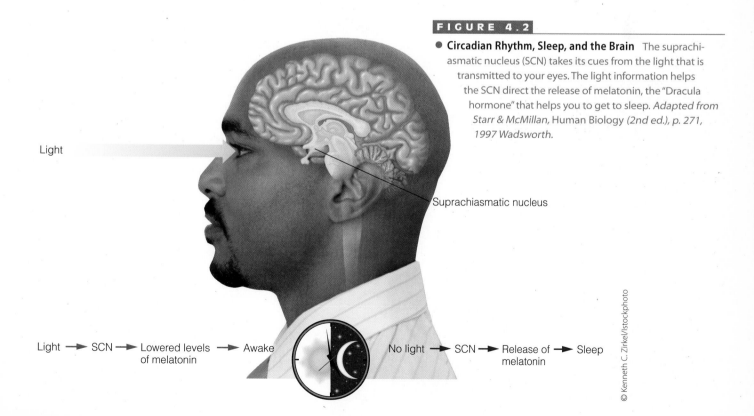

FIGURE 4.2

● **Circadian Rhythm, Sleep, and the Brain** The suprachiasmatic nucleus (SCN) takes its cues from the light that is transmitted to your eyes. The light information helps the SCN direct the release of melatonin, the "Dracula hormone" that helps you to get to sleep. *Adapted from Starr & McMillan,* Human Biology *(2nd ed.), p. 271, 1997 Wadsworth.*

Light

Suprachiasmatic nucleus

Light → SCN → Lowered levels of melatonin → Awake

No light → SCN → Release of melatonin → Sleep

© Kenneth C. Zirkel/Istockphoto

Paula Bronstein/Getty Images

Sleeping on the plane may help to reduce jet lag when traveling to other time zones.

"Weekend Lag" and Jet Lag

Many of us disrupt our circadian rhythm on a weekly basis. We attempt to maintain a routine sleep schedule on weekdays, going to bed around the same time every night so that we can get up in the morning for work or school. Then the weekend comes, and what do we do? Many of us stay up *later* and "sleep in" on the weekends, forcing our SCN to reset its cycle. Then Sunday night arrives. We may have the best intentions—getting to bed at a decent hour so that we'll get enough sleep to meet the demands of our Monday schedules. But instead, we toss and turn, look at the clock, and wonder when we are going to fall asleep. When Monday morning comes, we feel tired. We may hit the snooze button several times, oversleep, or take a long shower to help us wake up. Why? Because we just asked our internal clock to reset itself by three, four, or more hours! Disrupting our circadian rhythm to this extent makes us irritable, tired, less attentive, and moody.

How does a time change affect our circadian rhythm? This rhythm must be reset to adapt to the one-hour time change that takes place in the fall and spring in most parts of the United States and in many other countries. It must also be reset when we travel to different time zones, and we may experience *jet lag* as we adjust. On average, for each hour of time change, it takes one day to reset our circadian rhythm. However, you can minimize the effects of jet lag when you travel to other time zones. Some people start adapting their sleep schedule to the destination time zone before they depart. Others adapt to the new time zone as soon as they arrive. For instance, one of the authors took a 14-hour flight from Los Angeles to Auckland, New Zealand, arriving at 8:00 a.m. New Zealand time. Although she was tired, she went to the hotel, ate breakfast, and toured the city. She went to bed a little earlier than her usual bedtime and awoke the next day feeling refreshed and energized. Her jet lag symptoms were minimal.

Shift work may interfere with normal sleep patterns, affecting job performance.

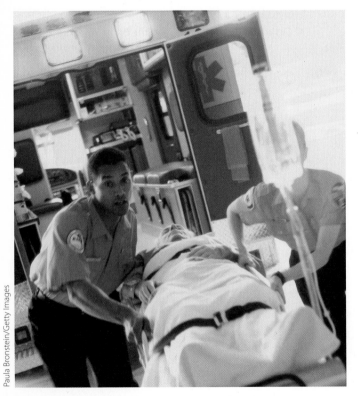

Paula Bronstein/Getty Images

Working the Night Shift

Our body's circadian rhythm also has implications for roughly the 15% of full-time workers in the United States who do shift work. In many professions (police work, firefighting, airline flight crew, medical care, and the military), people may be assigned to work 8-, 12-, or even 24-hour shifts, at varying times on different days. When you work Sunday and Monday nights, but Tuesday through Thursday mornings, it is more difficult for your body to reset its circadian rhythm. This disruption can impair your thinking and your health. Shift workers in general report more sleep disturbances, more hormonal irregularities (for women), more accidents, injuries, and illnesses, and decreased cognitive performance (Barger et al., 2009; Berger & Hobbs, 2006; Haus & Smolensky, 2006; Kahol et al., 2008; Rouch et al., 2005). If late night or early morning shifts are regular, then your body can adapt to the new rhythm. However, if the shift hours are constantly changing, your circadian rhythm is disrupted, and your sleep benefits diminish. Hence, you may be less alert, more easily distracted, and more prone to mental errors.

Stages of Sleep: What Research Tells Us

Not only do our bodies show a rhythm in relation to sleeping and waking, there is also a biological rhythm to the way we sleep. Using electroencephalogram (EEG) technology, sleep researchers have identified five stages of sleep. Recall from Chapter 2 that EEGs examine the electrical activity of relatively large areas of the brain. This technique works by using electrodes placed on the scalp and body that measure changes in brain activity and the related physical responses of the body. These changes, called brain waves, are then plotted on graph paper or a computer screen. The patterns the brain waves create give researchers an image of our brain activity when we are awake and when we are asleep. Brain waves vary in terms of the height of the wave (amplitude) and the number of waves per second (frequency). Brain-wave patterns are usually categorized as *alpha*, *beta*, *delta*, or *theta* waves. See the ● WHAT'S HAPPENING IN YOUR BRAIN? feature.

WHAT'S HAPPENING IN YOUR BRAIN?

BRAIN ACTIVITY DURING WAKEFULNESS AND THE VARIOUS STAGES OF SLEEP

Electroencephalogram technology records brain-wave activity during wakefulness and the various stages of sleep. When awake yet relaxed, the brain emits alpha waves. Brain activity during non-REM sleep progressively slows from theta waves (stage I) to delta waves (stage IV). REM sleep is characterized by rapid and fast brain waves. The brain scan images also differentiate slow-wave sleep, REM sleep, and wakefulness. Notice how your brain looks as though it is awake while you are in REM sleep! The brain scans labeled "awake" and "REM sleep" look very similar whereas the portion labeled "slow-wave sleep" looks quite different.

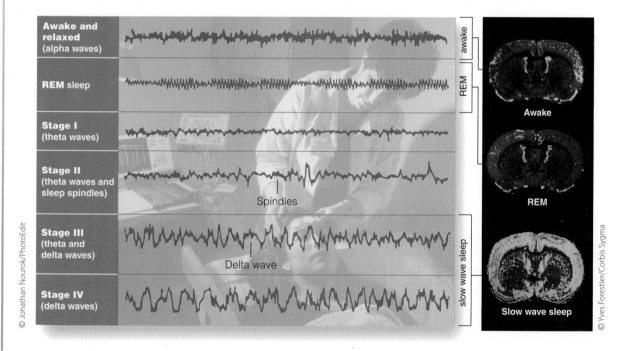

© Jonathan Nourok/PhotoEdit

© Yves Forestier/Corbis Sygma

When we are awake and alert, our brain (as measured by an EEG) emits *beta* waves. Beta brain waves are rapid, with a high number of cycles per second. This indicates frequent impulses of electrical activity in the brain. When we are awake but relaxed, our brain emits *alpha* waves. Alpha waves are somewhat slower and less frequent than beta waves. As we sleep, our brain-wave patterns change in a predictable sequence.

If you watch someone sleep, you will notice that at times the person's eyes move under the eyelids, showing rapid eye movement (REM). At other times during sleep, such eye movement is absent. From such observations, researchers have identified two distinct sleep patterns: **non-REM sleep** and **REM sleep**. When your eyes do not move during sleep, it is

non-REM sleep relaxing state of sleep in which the individual's eyes do not move

REM sleep active state of sleep in which the individual's eyes move

referred to as non-rapid-eye-movement, or non-REM, sleep. The state in which our eyes do move is called rapid-eye-movement, or REM, sleep. As we will see, during these two states of sleep our bodies and brains are experiencing very different activities. Non-REM sleep is a progressively relaxed state. In contrast, REM sleep is very active. During a night of sleep, our bodies and brains move back and forth between states of relaxation and activity until we wake up in the morning (Armitage, 1995; Dement & Kleitman, 1957). Our nights begin in non-REM sleep.

The Stages of Non-REM Sleep

When we fall asleep at night, our bodies and brains progress through a series of non-REM sleep stages:

- *Stage I sleep* is a light sleep and is characterized by *theta* waves. Notice in the What's Happening in Your Brain? feature that theta waves are slower and less frequent than beta or alpha waves. During this stage, your breathing and heart rates slow down. You may experience sensations such as falling or floating. You can easily awaken from stage I sleep, which typically lasts from 1 to 7 minutes.
- *Stage II sleep* is characterized by *sleep spindles* and lasts approximately 20 minutes. Sleep spindles (see What's Happening in Your Brain?) are a pattern of slower theta waves sporadically disrupted by bursts of electrical activity. During stage II sleep, breathing, muscle tension, heart rate, and body temperature continue to decrease. You are clearly asleep and not easily awakened. Recent findings suggest that stage II sleep spindles help us process both simple and complex motor skills that we have learned (Fogel & Smith, 2006; Fogel et al., 2007; Kuriyama, Stickgold, & Walker, 2004; Tucker & Fishbein, 2009).
- *Stages III and IV sleep* are referred to as *slow-wave sleep*. In stage III sleep you begin showing *delta* brain-wave patterns. Delta waves are large, slow brain waves. When a consistent pattern of delta waves emerges, you have entered stage IV sleep. Stage IV sleep is referred to as deep sleep. The body is extremely relaxed. Heart rate, respiration, body temperature, and blood flow to the brain are reduced. Growth hormone is secreted. It is believed that during this deep sleep, body maintenance and restoration occur (Porkka-Heiskanen et al., 1997). For example, your proportion of deep sleep increases after a day of increased physical activity (Horne & Staff, 1983). It is difficult to awaken people from deep sleep. When they are awakened, they may be disoriented or confused. Your first hour of sleep is predominately slow-wave sleep. Slow-wave sleep then progressively gets shorter the longer you sleep.

REM Sleep: Dream On

After approximately 30–40 minutes of slow-wave sleep, your brain and body start to speed up again. You cycle back through stage II of non-REM sleep and then enter REM (rapid-eye-movement) sleep. REM sleep is a very active stage. Your breathing rate increases, and your heart beats irregularly. Blood flow increases to the genital area and may cause erections in males (Somers et al., 1993). However, your muscle tone significantly decreases, leaving the muscles extremely relaxed and essentially paralyzed. The What's Happening in Your Brain? feature shows that your REM brain-wave patterns are similar to your brain-wave patterns when you are awake. As you can see in the brain scan images, when you enter REM sleep your brain looks as though it is awake while you sleep! The brain scans labeled "awake" and "REM sleep" look almost exactly alike. You can see that the portion labeled "slow-wave sleep" looks quite different.

REM sleep is intimately connected to dreaming. Although you can dream in some form in all sleep stages, dreams during REM sleep are more easily recalled. More than 80% of people awakened from REM sleep report dreaming (Hirshkowitz et al., 1997). The body paralysis that occurs during REM prevents you from acting out your dreams. However, in rare instances, people do not experience the paralysis that normally accompanies REM sleep. This condition, which mainly affects older men, is referred to as **REM behavior disorder**. People with REM behavior disorder may thrash about while in REM sleep, sometimes causing harm to themselves or others (Gugger & Wagner, 2007; Plazzi et al., 1997).

REM behavior disorder a condition in which normal muscle paralysis does not occur, leading to violent movements during REM sleep

Why do we have REM sleep? The purpose for REM sleep is constantly being questioned. Some studies indicate a connection between REM sleep and memory processing. People who are deprived of REM sleep and dreaming are less likely to recall complex information learned earlier in the day than are people who were not deprived of REM sleep (Chollar, 1989; Karni et al., 1994). REM-deprived people also report having difficulty concentrating when they awaken. These findings have led researchers to speculate that REM sleep—and perhaps dreaming—facilitates the storage of memories as well as mental strategies that are useful to us (Diekelmann & Born, 2010; Rauchs et al., 2004). At the same time, REM appears to help us process recent emotional experiences (Walker & van der Helm, 2009) and to "discard" information that is trivial or less important to us (F. Crick & Mitchison, 1995; C. Smith, 1995). Other research shows no relationship between time spent in REM sleep and memory problems (J. M. Siegel, 2001). The exact connection between REM sleep and memory continues to be investigated (B. Carey, 2007).

Another curiosity of REM sleep is referred to as **REM rebound**. When people lose REM sleep because of medications, drugs, or sleep deprivation, they make up for it on subsequent nights by spending more time dreaming (Dement, 1960). Before we look at theories and research on dreaming, let's review what happens during a typical night of sleep.

A Typical Night's Sleep

A typical night of sleep consists of cycling through non-REM stages and REM sleep (● Figure 4.3). We progress through stages I, II, III, and IV of non-REM sleep. We revisit stages III and II of non-REM sleep. We then enter REM sleep. After a brief period in REM sleep, we begin the cycle again, starting with the non-REM stages. The pattern repeats throughout the night. One complete cycle of non-REM and REM sleep takes about 90 minutes. But

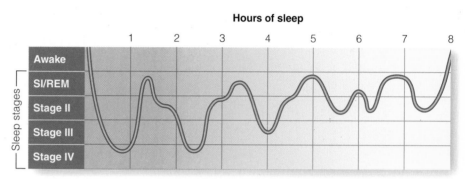

notice from Figure 4.3 that as the night progresses we spend less time in slow-wave sleep and more time in REM sleep. This means that the body-restoring function of slow-wave sleep takes place early on, during the first few cycles of sleep. After these early cycles with longer non-REM sleep, we spend longer in REM sleep as the night progresses. If you are not getting enough sleep, you will miss out on the longest period of REM sleep. On average, we spend around 20% of our total sleep time each night in REM sleep. If you sleep 8 hours a night, you spend roughly 90 minutes of that time in REM sleep. That means each night you spend approximately 90 minutes having REM dreams. These dreams occur at intervals during the night. Why do we dream, and do our dreams have meaning? Let's find out.

FIGURE 4.3

● **A Typical Night of Sleep** As the night progresses, we spend less time in slow-wave sleep (stages III and IV) and more time in REM sleep.

Dreaming: The Night's Work

Do you remember your dreams? Although not everyone reports remembering their dreams when they awaken, everyone, regardless of culture, progresses through dream states during sleep. Dreams do show some similarities in content from one culture to another. For example, dream themes that focus on basic needs or fears (sex, aggression, and death) seem to be universal. Other content seems to be specific to its presence in a culture. For instance, today's Alaskan natives may have dreams that include snowmobiles, but their ancestors of 100 years ago obviously did not. People dream about what they know, which is influenced by the culture in which they live (Price & Crapo, 2002).

Sigmund Freud's Interpretation of Dreams

Psychologists, along with other scientists and philosophers, have had a longstanding interest in the purpose and reason for dreaming. One of the most controversial and best-known theories of dreaming is Sigmund Freud's. In his *Interpretation of Dreams* (1900/1980), Freud

REM rebound loss of REM sleep is recouped by spending more time in REM on subsequent nights

called dreams "the royal road to the unconscious." According to Freud, dreams allow us to express fears and sexual and aggressive desires without the censorship of our conscious thought processes. Having straightforward dreams about these "unacceptable" desires would cause us anxiety. Instead, we dream in symbols that represent our unconscious desires. For Freud, dreams contained both **manifest content** and **latent content**. The manifest content of a dream is what you recall when you awaken. The latent, or hidden, content of the dream is the symbolic interpretation. For example, a young girl may dream of coming home from school one day to find the house deserted. She runs from room to room, looking for her parents or some sign that they will be returning soon (manifest content). Such a dream among children may signify the anxiety of being left alone, deserted, uncared for, or unprotected (latent content).

Dreams as Coping, Evolutionary Defense, or Just Biology at Work

Many psychologists and psychiatrists have challenged Freud's excessive emphasis on sex and aggression. Some have proposed alternative explanations for why we dream. For example, the *continuity hypothesis* suggests that dreaming is a way of coping with daily problems and issues. We dream about everyday experiences and current concerns in an effort to resolve these issues (Cartwright, 1993; Pesant & Zadra, 2006; Schredl, 2009; Schredl & Erlacher, 2008). In this view, dreams are not as symbolic as Freud suggested. *Memory theory* suggests that dreams are a way to consolidate information and to get rid of trivial details in our memories (Eiser, 2005; Porte & Hobson, 1996). From this viewpoint, dreams represent a function of memory.

The **threat simulation theory (TST)** suggests an evolutionary function of dreams. TST proposes that dreaming is essentially an ancient biological defense mechanism that allows us to experience potentially threatening situations so that we can rehearse our responses to these events. Although studies do show that childhood trauma or recurrent dreams are associated with a greater number of threatening dream events, not all of our dreams involve themes of survival (Valli & Revonsuo, 2009; Valli et al., 2005; Zadra, Desjardins, & Marcotte, 2006). More recently, researchers Levin and Nielsen (2009) have proposed a fear-extinction purpose of dreaming—allowing us to experience fearful situations over and over again so that we are less likely when awake to automatically respond to such stimuli with fear.

A biologically based theory is the **activation-synthesis theory** (Hobson & McCarley, 1977), which suggests that dreaming is just a consequence of the highly aroused brain during REM sleep, when the brain shows activation of millions of random neural impulses. The cortex of the brain attempts to create meaning out of these neural impulses by synthesizing them into familiar images or stories based on our stored memories. These images and stories may reflect our past, our emotions, our personal perspectives, and information accessed during waking (Hobson, Pace-Schott, & Stickgold, 2000), but they have no hidden "Freudian" meaning. However, because we are the ones who integrated these images into a plot, the story line may provide us with insights about ourselves (McCarley, 1998).

So, What Do Dreams Mean?

Have you ever been chased in a dream? Have you ever had the experience of flying in a dream? Have you ever had a recurring dream? Have your dreams ever made you feel anxious, worried, or fearful? You are not alone. Others' dreams share these themes and emotions (Merritt et al., 1994; Van de Castle, 1994). Why do many of us experience thematically similar dreams if dreams represent our personal issues and concerns? What about age as a factor in dreaming? Infants spend significantly more time in REM sleep, and therefore more time dreaming, than do older people. What psychological issues would infants be resolving through their dreams?

All mammals experience REM sleep. But do they dream? Watching your pet dog or cat run or cry out during sleep would lead you to believe that they do dream. Do cats and dogs have unconscious psychological issues to resolve as well? Obviously, our understanding of the purpose and meaning of dreaming is incomplete. Dreaming and dreams offer plenty of research opportunities.

Dreams aside, sleep research indicates that not everyone always gets a good night's sleep. Some of us exhibit sleep disturbances, our next topic of discussion.

manifest content according to Freudian theory, what the dreamer recalls on awakening

latent content according to Freudian theory, the symbolic meaning of a dream

threat simulation theory (TST) suggests that dreaming is an ancient biological defense mechanism that allows us to repeatedly simulate potentially threatening situations so that we can rehearse our responses to these events

activation-synthesis theory suggests that dreams do not have symbolic meaning, but are the by-product of the brain's random firing of neural impulses during REM sleep

Sleep Disorders: Tossing and Turning—and More

Not everyone goes to sleep in the predictable pattern of stages described previously. Some people have a **sleep disorder**, or a disturbance in the normal pattern of sleep. It is estimated that 95% of American adults experience a sleep disorder at some point in their lives (Dement & Vaughan, 1999). Sleep disorders also affect approximately 25% to 40% of children and adolescents (Meltzer & Mindell, 2006). Sleep disorders include *insomnia*, *narcolepsy*, *sleep apnea*, *sleepwalking*, *night terrors*, and *enuresis*.

Insomnia: There Is Help!

Insomnia, the most commonly reported sleep disorder, is the inability to get to sleep or stay asleep or both. Occasional insomnia is quite common, with as many as 50% of adults reporting insomnia at some time in their lives (Nowell et al., 1998). Insomnia is associated with a multitude of factors including stress, coping with the loss of a loved one, a change in sleep schedule, obesity, chronic pain, anxiety, depression, or drug abuse as the opening case study illustrated (T. Roth, Krystal, & Lieberman, 2007).

Insomnia can be treated medically using antianxiety or sedative medications such as Xanax or Ambien, or by taking over-the-counter medications such as Sominex and Nytol that contain antihistamines and pain relievers to induce sleepiness. However, long-term use of these drugs (discussed later in this chapter) may lead to dependence and serious side effects, including memory loss, fatigue, and increased sleepiness. Chronic insomnia is best treated with a combination of taking medication for a limited time, cognitive-behavioral therapy (which focuses on changing thoughts and behaviors that interfere with restful sleep—discussed more in Chapter 15), and following several sleep guidelines that have evolved from our study of how we sleep (Bootzin & Rider, 1997; Morin et al., 2009; Riemann & Perlis, 2009; T. Roth et al., 2007):

- Establish a regular sleep–wake cycle to work your body's circadian rhythm. Go to bed at the same time every evening and wake up at the same time every morning. Even if you have difficulty falling asleep at night, continue to get up at the same time each morning.
- Avoid long naps during waking hours. Naps can disrupt your circadian rhythm. **But, what about children who take daily naps, and adults who "power nap" or use siestas?** Children's naps and siestas typically occur at the same time every day and thereby work with, rather than against, the circadian rhythm. Power naps are short periods of rest (15–20 minutes) that are relaxing and that can reenergize the body and mind, and because they are short, generally do not interfere with our sleep cycles (Milner & Cote, 2009).
- Don't use your bed for anything other than sleeping. For example, people with insomnia should not eat, study, work, or watch television in bed. The bed should be associated only with sleeping.
- If you can't get to sleep after 15 minutes, get up and do something that you think will make you tired enough to get to sleep, such as reading (but not in your bed). Then try again to fall asleep.
- Avoid sleeping pills, alcohol, cigarettes, and caffeine. These are all drugs that interfere with your natural sleep cycle and disrupt REM sleep. Foods such as fruits, vegetables, beans, and whole grains, which provide carbohydrates, produce a rise in blood insulin that helps the amino acid *tryptophan* make serotonin, a neurotransmitter that facilitates sleep (see Chapter 2) (Silber & Schmitt, 2010). A glass of milk also provides a dose of tryptophan, which may be helpful.
- Exercise during the day can promote good sleep. But avoid physical workouts within an hour of bedtime. Your body should be relaxed prior to sleeping.

Narcolepsy

Narcolepsy, a rare sleep disorder that affects approximately 140,000 to 250,000 Americans, occurs when a person falls asleep during alert times of the day (Zeman et al., 2004). This is not the same as a microsleep, though. The person with narcolepsy experiences brief periods of REM sleep that may be accompanied by muscle paralysis, a condition called *cataplexy*.

sleep disorder a disturbance in the normal pattern of sleeping

insomnia a sleep disorder in which a person cannot get to sleep or stay asleep or both

narcolepsy a rare sleep disorder in which an individual falls asleep during alert activities during the day

Cataplexy occurs in about 70% of people with narcolepsy (American Psychiatric Association, 2000a). People with narcolepsy may fall down or otherwise injure themselves during these episodes. If you have ever seen what are called fainting dogs or fainting goats, you have seen (at least in animals) the nature of narcolepsy. Narcolepsy is thought to stem from a loss of neurons in the hypothalamus of the brain. These neurons are responsible for producing a chemical called *hypocretin* that helps to control the sleep–wake cycle (J. M. Siegel & Boehmer, 2006; Nishino, 2007; Zeitzer, Nishino, & Mignot, 2006). Those with the condition typically take the drug *modafinil* to improve wakefulness (Becker et al., 2004; Gallopin et al., 2004; T. Roth, Schwartz et al., 2007) and *sodium oxybate*, the only FDA-approved medication for cataplexy (Thorpy, 2007).

Sleep Apnea and SIDS

Sleep apnea is a disorder in which a person stops breathing while sleeping. In an attempt to get air, people with sleep apnea often emit loud snores or snorts that may awaken them or their partners. This pattern may occur hundreds of times during the night. People afflicted may feel sluggish, tired, irritable, or unable to concentrate the next day because of the nighttime sleep disruption (Naegele et al., 1995). Obesity, being overweight, and the use of alcohol or sedatives increase one's chances of developing sleep apnea (Ball, 1997; Resta et al., 2001). Once diagnosed, sleep apnea may be treated in various ways. If obesity is a factor, a weight-loss program is the first treatment. In addition, a nasal mask (called a Continuous Positive Airway Pressure, or CPAP, device) that blows air into the nose to facilitate continuous breathing can be worn at night. Wearing mouth retainers can help in some cases. In severe cases, removing the tonsils or surgery to alter the position of the jaw can be performed (Saskin, 1997). Considerable evidence suggests a genetic basis for sleep apnea (Chiang, 2006; Polotsky & O'Donnell, 2007). Estimates of sleep apnea in the general population range from 3 to 28% (Chiang, 2006).

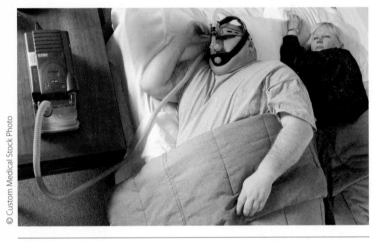

A Continuous Positive Airway Pressure, or CPAP, device blows air into the nose to facilitate continuous breathing for people who have sleep apnea.

Sleep apnea has also been suggested as one cause for *sudden infant death syndrome (SIDS)*, or "crib death," when apparently healthy babies die while they are sleeping. They stop breathing for reasons that are not yet understood. SIDS affects babies whose average age is 4 months. African American and American Indian babies are at greater risk than White or Hispanic babies, and the risk is higher for males than for females (Lipsitt, 2003). Lower birth weight combined with bed-sharing with an adult and maternal smoking also puts babies at higher risk for SIDS (McGarvey et al., 2006; Ostfeld et al., 2006). The practice of laying babies on their stomachs to sleep puts them more at risk for SIDS (Hirshfeld, 1995); as a result, the American Academy of Pediatrics recommends that newborns be put on their sides or on their backs to sleep. Parents and caretakers are also advised to remove large stuffed animals or heavy coverings such as blankets or pillows from cribs. This ensures that the infant's mouth and nose are not obstructed.

Sleepwalking: Wake Me Up!

Sleepwalking, or somnambulism, occurs during non-REM slow-wave sleep. People with this disorder get up and walk around during deep sleep, sometimes performing actions that make them appear to be awake. They may cook, eat, open doors, or engage in minimal conversation. **Should you awaken someone who is sleepwalking?** Yes, if you can. Because sleepwalkers are asleep, they may injure themselves or others. Wake them up or guide them back to bed. They may be initially disoriented or confused, but you will not do harm by awakening them. **Are sleepwalkers acting out their dreams?** Remember that most dreams occur during REM sleep, which is accompanied by body paralysis (unless one has REM behavior disorder). Walking and moving during REM sleep would not be possible. It is estimated that between 1% and 15% of the general population sleepwalk. It is more common in children than in adults (National Sleep Foundation, 2004).

sleep apnea a sleep disorder in which a person stops breathing during sleep

sleepwalking a sleep disorder in which a person is mobile and may perform actions during stage IV sleep

© Custom Medical Stock Photo

TECHNOLOGY and BEHAVIOR

R U SLEEP-TEXTING?

An increasing number of people report on blogs, message boards, and Facebook pages that they are "sleep-texting"— sending text messages to friends while they are asleep. Is this possible? No one really knows. People have been shown to perform a variety of activities while asleep such as sleepwalking, sleep talking, and sleep eating—behaviors that are performed routinely and automatically in daily life. Yet, sending a text message is a more complex behavior than eating, talking, or walking. It requires a person to select several options on a cell phone and type the message. According to a Nielsen report on media trends (2009), the average number of texts by young teens has gone up 566% in just 2 years. It is possible, therefore, that young people who routinely send text messages may automate this behavior so that it can be performed without much thought during sleep. Yet, many sleep researchers believe that the message would not be coherent or understandable if generated during sleep. However, there are several alternative explanations for sleep-texting. It could be that the person simply does not remember sending the text. Often, we may briefly awaken during the night and go to the bathroom or answer the phone and not recall the incident in the morning. Similarly, a person may wake up in the middle of the night, text someone, go back to sleep, and not remember doing so, because the act didn't last long enough to enter memory. It also is possible that a person regrets what he or she sent in the text and uses "sleep-texting" as a rationale or excuse for the behavior.

Although no studies have been published in the United States on sleep-texting, research has documented the disruptive effect of night texting on a person's sleep cycle (Van den Bulck, 2003, 2007). Many young people often sleep with their cell phones right next to them. This vigilance to a "possible" incoming message as well as the vibration or sound that occurs when a message is received interrupt the natural sleep cycle and make deep sleep less likely. As a result, the person may be more tired and less focused the next day. For this reason, it is recommended that people turn off their cell phones prior to sleeping.

© Bill Aron/PhotoEdit

Night Terrors and Enuresis

Night terrors also occur during non-REM slow-wave sleep. Although night terrors can occur anytime in one's life, they are more commonly reported in children between the ages of 4 and 12 and in older adults with various neurological and cognitive disorders such as Parkinson's disease and elderly dementia (Abad & Guilleminault, 2004). During night terrors, children awaken in an apparent state of fear. Their heart rates and breathing are rapid, and they may scream loudly and sit up in bed, wide-eyed with terror. People rarely recall the incident in the morning (Hartmann, 1981). An attack may last 5 to 20 minutes. In the United States, an estimated 1–6% of children experience night terror episodes. For adults, estimates are less than 1% (American Psychiatric Association, 2000a).

Why night terrors occur is still a mystery, although the disorder does tend to run in families (Guilleminault et al., 2003). Keep in mind that people who are having night terrors do not know what is occurring. Simply reassure the person that everything is all right and to go back to sleep. Night terrors are different from *nightmares*. **Nightmares** are brief scary dreams that typically occur during REM sleep and are often recalled in vivid detail in the morning.

Enuresis is bedwetting, but it does not refer to the occasional nighttime bedwetting that is common among young children. Enuresis is diagnosed when a child who is at least 5 years old wets his or her bed or pajamas at least twice a week over a 3-month period (American Psychiatric Association, 2000a). It is estimated that 15–20% of 5-year-olds are diagnosed with enuresis, but by adolescence the prevalence decreases to about 1%. Enuresis is more common in males and tends to run in families. Approximately 75% of children with enuresis have biological relatives who had the disorder (Ondersma & Walker, 1998). Such a high percentage suggests that enuresis may be inherited. However, the behavior may also occur during times of stress, such as when a new sibling is born or familial conflict is high, and may accompany night terrors.

Enuresis occurs during slow-wave sleep when the child is extremely relaxed. The child is unaware that he or she is wetting the bed, and he or she is not engaging in this behavior to purposely or subconsciously frustrate and annoy his parents. Parents frequently ask, "Then why doesn't he wet the bed when he spends the night at other people's houses?" The answer is that when children aren't at home, they do not sleep as deeply—and therefore are not as relaxed—so the bedwetting does not occur. Scolding or punishing a child seldom has any effect on the bedwetting. In fact, scolding can potentially damage the child's self-esteem and the parent–child relationship. Several treatment methods are available, and most children outgrow the behavior (A. K. Berry, 2006).

Gender and Ethnic Differences in Sleep

Sleep research has also investigated the degree to which gender and ethnicity influence sleep. Several studies have found that men report needing less sleep than women to function at their best and that women are more likely than men to sleep 8 hours or more. Women are more likely than men to report insufficient rest or sleep (McKnight-Eily et al., 2009), daytime sleepiness, and needing 30 minutes or more to fall asleep (National Sleep Foundation, 2005; Oginska & Pokorski, 2006). One research study (Adan & Natale, 2002) has also indicated potential gender differences in the circadian rhythm of males and females. In the area of sleep disorders, two consistent gender differences have emerged. Insomnia tends to be more frequent in women (Morlock, Tan, & Mitchell, 2006; R. E. Roberts, Roberts, & Chan, 2006; Voderholzer et al., 2003; B. Zhang & Wing, 2006), and snoring and sleep apnea are more common in men (Jordan & McEvoy, 2003).

Only a limited number of studies have compared sleep variables across ethnic groups. Those that have suggest that African Americans sleep worse than European Americans. They report poorer sleep quality, more variation in sleep time, and taking longer to fall asleep (Durrence & Lichstein, 2006; McKnight-Eily et al., 2009; Nunes et al., 2008). However, African Americans are also more likely to live in urban areas, a variable that is associated with poorer sleep quality (Hale & Do, 2007). Asian Americans were most likely of any ethnic group to say they get a good night's sleep (National Sleep Foundation [NSF], 2010). African American, American Indian, and Hispanic adults are also at higher risk for sleep apnea, although these

night terrors very frightening non-REM sleep episodes

nightmare a brief, scary REM dream that is often remembered

enuresis a condition in which a person over the age of 5 shows an inability to control urination during sleep

observed ethnic differences are mainly explained by a higher rate of obesity among these groups (Fiorentino et al., 2006; NSF, 2010; Villaneuva et al., 2005).

In summary, sleep is as necessary to our survival as food and shelter. Sleep refuels our bodies and minds, preparing us for the challenges of the next day. When we skip sleep, change our sleep cycle, or experience disturbances in our sleep, we may feel irritable, less alert, and tired the next day.

Let's REVIEW

In this section, we described why we sleep, what influences the amount of sleep we need, and the stages we progress through on a typical night. We outlined several theories of dreaming and described some common sleep disorders. For a quick check of your understanding, try answering the following questions at increasing levels of difficulty.

1. Maria falls asleep during alert daytime activities. Maria would most likely be diagnosed with which sleep disorder?

   a. narcolepsy   c. sleep apnea

   b. insomnia   d. enuresis

2. Ronnie has a dream that he is being chased by a golden goose. He is told that this reflects his anxiety about impregnating women. This analysis represents the _____ of his dream.

   a. manifest content   c. activation synthesis

   b. latent content   d. mental reprogramming

3. Which of the following is *not* characteristic of REM sleep?

   a. rapid eye movements   c. shortening periods as the night progresses

   b. paralysis of body musculature   d. increased heart rate

ANSWERS 1. a; 2. b; 3. c

LEARNING OBJECTIVES

What Should You Know?

- Detail the experience of hypnosis and explain several theories about how hypnosis occurs.
- Distinguish between what hypnosis can and cannot do for you.

HYPNOSIS: REAL OR IMAGINED?

What is hypnosis? Can anyone be hypnotized? Is hypnosis fake? Are all psychologists hypnotists? Can a hypnotist make you do something outrageous, such as squawk like a chicken or get naked in a room full of people? Students often ask these questions about hypnosis. This section will describe the experience of hypnosis, explain several ideas about how hypnosis occurs, and delineate what hypnosis can and cannot do for you.

The Hypnosis Experience

Not all psychologists are hypnotists, and not all hypnotists are psychologists. **Hypnosis** is a method used by researchers and psychologists (and hypnotists) to create a state of heightened suggestibility in others. Typically, if you are undergoing hypnosis, you are asked to focus on an object, an image, or the hypnotist's voice. For several minutes, you are told that you are getting sleepy and becoming more relaxed (Druckman & Bjork, 1994). You don't fall asleep—though EEG brain-wave patterns of hypnotized people show an increase in alpha waves—and this isn't followed by the non-REM pattern of sleep stages discussed earlier (Graffin, Ray, & Lundy, 1995). After inducing you into this relaxed hypnotic state, the hypnotist makes suggestions about what you are seeing, feeling, or perceiving. For example, one suggestion might be to lift your left arm over your head. A more complex suggestion might be that your eyelids feel as though they are glued shut and you cannot open them. Although accounts vary widely, many hypnotized people report that they feel as though they are floating or that their bodies are sinking. Under hypnosis, they remain in control of their bodies and are aware of their surroundings (Kirsch & Lynn, 1995).

hypnosis a state of heightened suggestibility

Hypnotic Susceptibility

Hypnotic susceptibility is the ability to become hypnotized. Some people have a low degree of susceptibility—they cannot easily be hypnotized. Others have a high susceptibility, meaning that they can easily be hypnotized. One well-known standard test for measuring the degree to which people respond to hypnotic suggestions is the *Stanford Hypnotic Susceptibility Scale*. The scale assesses your suggestibility to certain tasks while in a state of hypnosis with a trained hypnotist. The tasks range from pulling apart your interlocked fingers to hallucinating the presence of a buzzing fly.

Contrary to what you may see on television or in the movies, research using such measures has found that not everyone can be hypnotized. The critical factor appears to be whether you want to be hypnotized, rather than the skill of the hypnotist (Kirsch & Lynn, 1995). About 10% of adults are extremely difficult to hypnotize (Hilgard, 1982).

Can you be hypnotized against your will? No, you cannot be hypnotized against your will. People who are easily hypnotized tend to be better able to focus their attention (Crawford, Brown, & Moon, 1993; Egner, Jamieson, & Gruzelier, 2005; Raz, 2005), have vivid imaginations (Silva & Kirsch, 1992; Spanos, Burnley, & Cross, 1993), and have positive expectations about hypnosis (Bates, 1994). Neuroimaging studies even document differences in brain activation between people who are highly hypnotizable and those who are low in hypnotic susceptibility (Naish, 2010; Nash, 2005; Raz, Fan, & Posner, 2006). In Western cultures, children between the ages of 8 and 12 are more susceptible to hypnosis than adults (Bates, 1994). In some non-Western cultures, this childhood susceptibility does not diminish in adulthood. It may be that achieving a trance state is more valued or widely accepted in these cultures (C. Ward, 1994). Hypnotic suggestibility does not appear to be related to such factors as intelligence, gender, sociability, or gullibility (Kirsch & Lynn, 1995), although in one study (Page & Green, 2007), female undergraduates did score higher than males on the Harvard Group Scale of Hypnotic Susceptibility.

Explaining Hypnosis: Is It an Altered State?

Currently, there are two theories explaining hypnosis: *dissociation theory* and the *response set theory*. Ernest Hilgard's (1977, 1992) **dissociation theory** suggests that hypnosis is truly an altered state of consciousness: a person feels, perceives, and behaves differently than in a conscious state. To dissociate means to split or break apart. Hilgard maintains that under hypnosis, your consciousness divides into two states. One level of your consciousness voluntarily agrees to behave according to the suggestions of the hypnotist. However, at the same time, a *hidden observer* state exists. This hidden observer is aware of all that is happening.

We all engage in dissociation at times. Have you ever driven to a familiar location and realized when you arrived that you couldn't consciously remember driving there? Have you ever dissociated in a class—paying attention to the lesson while at the same time doodling or mentally organizing the rest of your day? If you have experienced any of these behaviors, then you are familiar with the concept of dissociation. Hilgard believes that hypnosis works in much the same way, allowing the person to attend to the hypnotist's suggestions while still being aware of what is happening through the hidden observer.

In a classic demonstration, Hilgard hypnotized participants and suggested that they would feel no pain. The participants were then instructed to submerge their arms in ice-cold water. When Hilgard asked them whether they felt pain, the participants replied "No." However, when they were asked to press a key with their other hand if they felt pain, the participants did so. On one level, they agreed with the hypnotist that

dissociation theory Hilgard's proposal that hypnosis involves two simultaneous states: a hypnotic state and a hidden observer

Not everyone can be hypnotized. You have to want to be hypnotized and believe it will work for you.

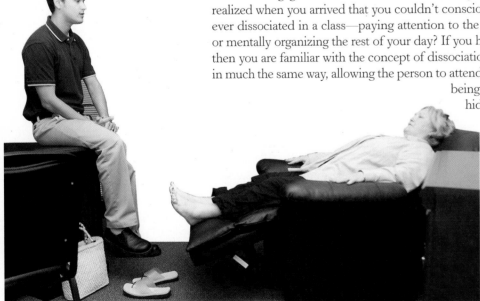

© AP Photo/News Tribune/Stephen Brooks

there was no pain, while at the same time a part of them indicated that there was pain (Hilgard, Morgan, & MacDonald, 1975).

Another view, the **response set theory of hypnosis** (Kirsch, 2000; Kirsch & Lynn, 1997; Lynn, 1997), asserts that hypnosis is *not* an altered state of consciousness. Rather, hypnosis is merely a willingness to respond appropriately to suggestions. Several studies do support that people's response expectancies influence their responsiveness to hypnosis (Benham et al., 2006; Milling, Reardon, & Carosella, 2006). Highly hypnotizable people enter hypnosis with the intention of behaving as a "hypnotized person" and hold the expectation that they will succeed in following the hypnotist's suggestions. Their intentions and expectations trigger their positive response to being hypnotized. Nonhypnotized participants show behaviors similar to those of hypnotized people, such as behaving in strange ways or acting like a young child, simply because they are willing to do what the hypnotist asks them to do (Dasgupta et al.,1995; Kirsch, 1994).

The debate over whether hypnosis is truly an altered state continues (Holroyd, 2003; Rainville & Price, 2003). Unfortunately, hypnosis has acquired the reputation for doing some things that it cannot. Let's look at these myths and realities of hypnosis.

What Hypnosis Can and Cannot Do

Can hypnosis cure your smoking addiction? Can hypnosis help you recover lost memories from your childhood? A certain mystique surrounds hypnosis, leading some to believe that it is similar to a magic spell that can cure all ills and bestow special powers. Psychological research has investigated these issues in an attempt to separate fact from fiction. To date, research reveals the following:

- *Relieving Pain.* One of the best documented uses for hypnosis is pain relief (Clay, 1996; Wiechman Askay & Patterson, 2007). Under hypnosis, clients relax, which reduces pain, or distract themselves from the pain by focusing on more pleasant and pain-free scenarios, or do both. Hypnosis has been used to minimize pain in childbirth, to block pain during medical or dental treatments, and to relieve chronic pain from arthritis and from migraine headaches (Chaves, 1994; Liossi, White, & Hatira, 2006; Nolan et al.,1995; Pinnell & Covino, 2000; VandeVusse et al., 2007). This pain relief is more pronounced for people who have a high susceptibility to hypnosis (Bates, 1994). Effective pain relief also can be achieved by nonhypnotic treatments such as deep relaxation training or distraction techniques (Chaves, 1989; D. R. Patterson et al., 2006). Hypnosis does not reduce the sensation of pain. The pain is still there, but hypnosis changes a person's subjective experience of pain (Rainville et al., 1997).

- *Curing Addictions.* Posthypnotic suggestions have proven less successful for treating addictions or self-control behaviors, even in people with a high susceptibility to hypnosis (Bowers & LeBaron, 1986). Although hypnosis has been used as a treatment to stop smoking, nail biting, overeating, gambling, alcoholism, and other addictions, it has proven no more successful than other treatments at controlling these behaviors (Bates, 1994; J. P. Green & Lynn, 2000). Self-control behaviors such as smoking and alcoholism are some of the most difficult behaviors to change, as Charlie Parker's story illustrates (Rabkin et al., 1984).

- *Enhancing or Recovering Memory.* One of the most controversial applications of hypnosis has been in the area of memory enhancement. Research in this area has focused on two key issues: age regression and recovered memories.

Can hypnosis help a person relive earlier childhood experiences? This is referred to as *age regression.* Numerous studies on age regression demonstrate that under hypnosis, adults act the way they *expect* children to behave (Spanos, 1996). They may write, sing, or behave like a child, but it is more like an adult playing the role of a child. Their behavior is not different from that of nonhypnotized people who are asked to behave like a child (Nash, 1987).

Can hypnosis help a person recall repressed events or information, such as from a crime scene or from one's childhood? This is referred to as *recovered memories.* Being in a

response set theory of hypnosis
asserts that hypnosis is *not* an altered state of consciousness, but a cognitive set to respond appropriately to suggestions. The intent to behave as a "hypnotized person" and the expectation that one will succeed in following the hypnotist's suggestion becomes a response set that triggers the hypnotic response automatically.

Hypnosis is no more effective than other treatment approaches at curing addictions.

relaxed state may facilitate recall under certain circumstances. However, research reveals that hypnotized people may also recall untrue events. For this reason, information gathered under hypnosis is not permissible in a court of law in the United States, Australia, or Great Britain. People are more suggestible under hypnosis, and consequently their memories are more likely influenced by the suggestions, tone, hints, questions, and remarks of the hypnotist. They may recall just as many events that did not occur as events that did, and they may also be more prone to distort information (Scoboria, Mazzoni, & Kirsch, 2006; Scoboria et al., 2002). For these reasons, the use of hypnosis in the area of memory enhancement should be viewed with skepticism (H. B. Gibson, 1995; McConkey, 1995; C. Perry, 1997).

● *Enhancing Physical Performance.* Hypnosis does not create superhuman capacities. However, being in a relaxed state such as hypnosis can enhance physical performance. The person can more readily visualize optimal performance and reduce self-doubt or nerves. This enhancement can also be achieved through other techniques, such as deep muscle relaxation and guided imagery (Druckman & Bjork, 1994).

● *Decreasing Anxiety and Enhancing Psychotherapy.* Hypnosis has proven useful in decreasing fears and anxieties for people with a high susceptibility to hypnosis (Saadat et al., 2006). Clinicians sometimes use hypnosis in therapy to help their clients solve problems or cope with bodily symptoms such as headaches or stomach pains that appear to be related to psychological stress. Hypnosis has been helpful in reducing pain and tension. Again, it is most effective for clients who have a high susceptibility to hypnosis (Kirsch, Montgomery, & Sapirstein, 1995).

To summarize, hypnosis does not endow us with superhuman strength, allow us to reexperience childhood events, cure addictions, or improve the accuracy of our memories. However, hypnosis may be of some benefit in decreasing pain, promoting relaxation, and perhaps enhancing therapy for *some* people. These benefits are not universal. The person must want to be hypnotized and have positive beliefs about hypnosis.

Let's REVIEW

In this section, we detailed the experience of hypnosis, explored two theories about how hypnosis occurs, and discussed what hypnosis can and cannot do for you. For a quick check of your understanding, try answering the following questions at increasing levels of difficulty.

1. Research on hypnosis suggests that it is *least* helpful for which of the following?

   a. pain relief   c. quitting smoking

   b. reduction of anxiety   d. childbirth

2. Which of the following statements about hypnosis is *false*?

   a. Everyone can be hypnotized.

   b. Hypnosis is real; people are not just faking it.

   c. Memories recalled under hypnosis are not always accurate.

   d. Not all psychologists agree as to whether hypnosis is an altered state of consciousness.

3. Cecilia has been hypnotized and told that she will not feel pain in her right hand. Her right hand is then immersed in freezing cold water. According to the dissociation theory of hypnosis, what part of Cecilia will report feeling pain?

   a. the secret hypnotist   c. the conscious self

   b. the posthypnotic suggester   d. the hidden observer

ANSWERS 1. c; 2. a; 3. d

WHAT ARE THE EFFECTS OF PSYCHOACTIVE DRUGS?

Psychoactive drugs are substances that influence the brain and thereby a person's behavior, as illustrated in the opening stories of Charlie Parker and Andre Agassi. Over the past 25 years, millions of teenagers and children in the United States have routinely been educated about the effects of drugs. The most popular of these programs, Drug Abuse Resistance Education, or DARE, began in 1983. Yet despite widespread education programs, many misperceptions about drugs still exist. For example, name the three most widely used psychoactive drugs in American society. The three drugs most commonly used by Americans over the age of 12 are alcohol, nicotine, and caffeine (see ● FIGURE 4.4)—substances that are all legal for adults to use (Substance Abuse and Mental Health Services Administration [SAMHSA], 2009). We tend to overlook the abuse of these drugs and focus on illegal substances such as cocaine and marijuana.

In 2008, 47% of people in the United States age 12 or older admitted to having tried an illegal substance at some time in their lives (SAMHSA, 2009a). Exposure to alcohol and illegal drugs prior to the age of 15 increases one's risk of developing adult substance dependence, herpes infection, early pregnancy, and crime (Odgers, Caspi, Nagin, et al., 2008). Illicit drug use is highest among young adults between the ages of 18 and 25 and higher in males than in females (SAMHSA, 2009a). Substance use in the United States also varies considerably by ethnic group (● FIGURE 4.5; SAMHSA, 2009a). Multiracial, African American, and American Indian/Alaska Native groups have the highest rates of current illegal drug use, and Asians have the lowest. This section addresses the most frequently used drugs and their effects, and describes how these drugs work and how they cause damage.

Drug Tolerance, Dependence, and Substance Abuse

In order to understand the effects of psychoactive drugs, it is important to establish the scientific meaning of two specific drug terms: *tolerance* and *substance dependence*. Defining these terms will help you understand the effects of different psychoactive drugs.

Tolerance has to do with the amount of a drug required to produce its effect. After repeated use of a drug, it is usually the case that more and more of it is needed to achieve its initial effect (American Psychiatric Association, 2000a). For example, when someone first drinks alcohol, he or she may have one beer or one glass of wine and get a buzz from it. However, after drinking alcohol frequently, this person will require more beers or glasses of wine to achieve the same high. This person has increased his or her tolerance for alcohol.

psychoactive drugs substances that influence the brain and thereby the behavior of individuals

tolerance a condition in which after repeated use, more of a drug is needed to achieve the same effect

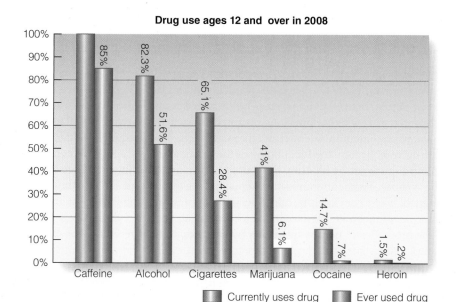

Drug use ages 12 and over in 2008

- Caffeine: 100% / 85%
- Alcohol: 82.3% / 51.6%
- Cigarettes: 65.1% / 28.4%
- Marijuana: 41% / 6.1%
- Cocaine: 14.7% / .7%
- Heroin: 1.5% / .2%

■ Currently uses drug   ■ Ever used drug

FIGURE 4.4

● **Drug Use in the United States**
Caffeine, alcohol, and nicotine (the active ingredient in tobacco) are the three most commonly used psychoactive drugs in the United States. *Source: SAMHSA, Office of Applied Studies, National Survey on Drug Use and Health, 2008.*

FIGURE 4.5

● **Ethnicity and Illicit Drug Use** Substance use in the United States varies considerably by ethnic group. Multiracial, African American, and American Indian/Alaska Native groups have the highest rates of illegal substance abuse; Asians have the lowest incidence. *Source: SAMHSA, Office of Applied Studies, Results from the 2008 National Survey on Drug Use and Health: National Findings, 2009.*

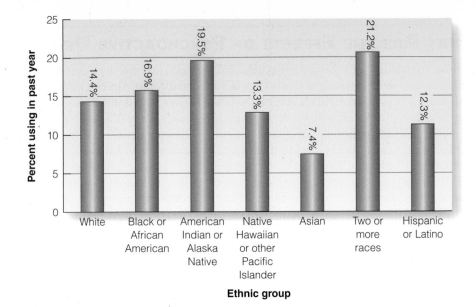

However, as tolerance develops, the difference between a safe dose and a potentially harmful dose, called the *margin of safety*, narrows. Some drugs (like barbiturates) have a very narrow, or small, margin of safety; that is, their too-high, toxic dose differs only slightly from their too-low, ineffectual dose. In order to obtain the same level of intoxication, a user who has developed tolerance may raise his or her dose to a level that may result in coma or death—the too-high, toxic dose.

Related to tolerance is **substance dependence**, which occurs when someone is either physically or psychologically reliant on a drug's effects. Charlie Parker's 20-year use of alcohol and heroin exemplifies this dependence. Typically, dependence is operating when the person stops using the drug and experiences **withdrawal symptoms**. Withdrawal symptoms may include physical symptoms such as vomiting, shaking, sweating, physical pain, hallucinations, or headaches. People may also experience behavioral withdrawal symptoms when they are deprived of responses or rituals, such as injecting a drug or lighting a cigarette, that help them cope with negative emotions (Baker et al., 2006; S. Siegel, 2005). Not all drugs produce the same withdrawal symptoms. In many cases, people continue to use a drug just to ward off the unpleasantness of the physical withdrawal effects or emotional distress. Psychologists typically use the term **substance abuse** to indicate that someone has lost control over his or her drug use.

How Drugs Work: Biology, Expectations, and Culture

Psychoactive drugs alter your state of functioning by interfering with the normal workings of the nervous system. How do psychoactive drugs affect brain functioning? Some drugs slow down normal brain activity whereas others speed it up. Typically, drugs achieve these effects by interfering with or mimicking neurotransmitters in the brain. Recall from Chapter 2 how neurotransmitters are released into the synapse. Neurotransmitters influence the activity of the nervous system, the functioning of the brain, and thus a person's behavior. Some psychoactive drugs act by blocking the reuptake of neurotransmitters as they are removed from the synapse. The neurotransmitters remain in the synapse longer, affecting functioning in a variety of ways. For example, the popular antidepressant drug Prozac inhibits the reuptake of the neurotransmitter serotonin, thereby affecting one's mood and sleep. Other drugs mimic the properties of neurotransmitters by attaching to their receptor sites (Stahl, 1996). For example, drugs such as morphine and codeine relieve pain by mimicking the effects of the neurotransmitter endorphin.

Do psychological factors such as the environment and expectations influence a drug's effect? Yes, they do. Exposure to stress or trauma increases a person's vulner-

substance dependence a condition in which a person needs a drug in order to maintain normal functioning

withdrawal symptoms physical or behavioral effects that occur after a person stops using a drug

substance abuse loss of control over one's drug use

ability to drug dependence (Goeders, 2004; Rohrbach et al., 2009). Environmental stimuli such as where a drug is taken or whether drug paraphernalia are present become associated with drug taking and later trigger the craving for the drug sensation (Crombag & Robinson, 2004; S. Siegel, 2005). Playing at jazz clubs where alcohol was in abundance could have likely been a trigger for Charlie Parker's alcoholism. If you expect a drug to alter your behavior in a particular way, you are more likely to change your behavior to fit your expectations. For example, in several studies people who believed that they had consumed alcohol behaved as if they had been drinking alcohol (Leigh, 1989). Whether or not they had actually consumed it, their behavior was influenced by their expectations about the effects of alcohol. They reported strong sexual fantasies or drove more recklessly when they thought they had been drinking alcohol (Abrams & Wilson, 1983; McMillen, Smith, & Wells-Parker, 1989). Several studies have shown that people who believe that alcohol will help them handle stress better are more likely to develop drinking-related problems (M. L. Cooper et al., 1992; Schuckit, 1998).

One's culture also influences drug use. For example, rates of alcohol abuse are very low in China, where traditional beliefs scorn alcohol use or behaving as if one is under the influence of alcohol. People in China are not only less likely to drink alcohol, they are also less likely to advertise the fact that they have been drinking. In contrast, Korean men have a high rate of alcohol abuse, and Korean Americans have higher rates of alcohol use than other Asian subgroups (SAMHSA, 2006). Their culture encourages drinking in social situations (Helzer & Canino, 1992).

How might North American attitudes toward alcohol influence your expectations about drinking alcohol and its effect? Drinking beer while you watch sports events such as football, baseball, and hockey is an accepted custom. Advertisers capitalize on this cultural "value" by depicting sports fans having a great time drinking beer at a game. Therefore, when you attend a football, baseball, or hockey game—or watch it on television—you may feel compelled to have a beer. You may be more likely to cheer, yell, and blow off steam because you believe that you are expected to behave this way. Culture and expectations, therefore, can influence the use and actual effects of drugs.

The variety of psychoactive drugs in use today can be classified into four main groups: *depressants, opiates, stimulants,* and *hallucinogens.* ● THE BIG PICTURE REVIEW provides a summary comparing the effects of these drugs. We'll begin with depressants.

Is the behavior of these fans due to alcohol or to their cultural expectations of alcohol?

Alcohol and Other Depressants

Depressant drugs interfere with brain functioning by inhibiting or slowing normal neural functioning. In low doses, depressants often cause a feeling of well-being, or a "nice buzz." Anxiety is reduced when the nervous system slows down. This may be why many people mistakenly believe that alcohol is an "upper." In high dosages, depressants can cause blackouts, coma, or death. The deaths of Anna Nicole Smith, Heath Ledger, and Michael Jackson were attributed in part to overdoses of depressants. Depressants are usually grouped into *alcohol, barbiturates,* and *sedatives.*

Health Effects of Alcohol

After cancer and heart disease, alcoholism is the third leading health problem in the United States today (Centers for Disease Control and Prevention [CDC], 2004a). It is estimated that excessive alcohol consumption costs Americans more than $185 billion per year because of its negative effects on health and the ability to work (Harwood, 2000). Hundreds of thousands of lives are lost each year as a result of alcohol-related crimes and accidents (Rivers, 1994). Despite these statistics, alcohol remains one of the most popular drugs worldwide (Alvarez, Delrio, & Prado, 1995).

depressants drugs that inhibit or slow down normal neural functioning

THE BIG PICTURE *review*

Psychoactive Drugs and Their Effects

The four groups of substances most often leading to substance dependence are (1) depressants, (2) opiates, (3) stimulants, and (4) hallucinogens.

SUBSTANCE	TRADE NAMES STREET NAMES	MEDICAL USES	ROUTE OF ADMINISTRATION	MAIN EFFECTS
Depressants				
Alcohol	Beer, wine, liquor	Antidote for methanol poisoning, antiseptic	Oral, topical	Relaxation; lowered inhibitions; impaired reflexes, motor coordination, and memory
Barbiturates	Nembutal, Seconal, Phenobarbital; **Barbs**	Anesthetic, anticonvulsant, sedative, relief of high blood pressure	Injected, oral	Anxiety relief, euphoria, severe withdrawal symptoms
Benzodiazepines	Librium, Rohypnol, Valium, Xanax, **roofies, tranks**	Antianxiety, sedative, sleeping disorders	Injected, oral	Anxiety relief, irritability, confusion, depression, sleep problems
Opiates				
Codeine	Tylenol with codeine, Fiorinal with Codeine	Pain relief, antitussive	Injected, oral	Euphoria, constipation, loss of appetite
Heroin	**Horse, smack**	None	Injected, smoked, sniffed	Euphoria, pain control, constipation, loss of appetite
Methadone	Amidone, Methadose	Pain relief, treatment for opiate dependence	Injected, oral	Relief from withdrawal symptoms, constipation, loss of appetite
Morphine	Roxanol	Pain relief	Injected, oral, smoked	Euphoria, pain control
Opium	Laudanum; **Dover's Powder**	Pain relief, antidiarrheal	Oral, smoked	Euphoria, pain control
Stimulants				
Caffeine	Coffee, tea, soda, chocolate, energy drink	Treatment for migraine headaches	Oral	Alertness, insomnia, loss of appetite, high blood pressure
Nicotine	Nicorette gum, Nicotrol; **cigars, cigarettes, snuff**	Treatment for nicotine dependence	Smoked, sniffed, oral, transdermal	Alertness, calmness, loss of appetite
Cocaine	**coke, crack, rocks, snow, blow**	Local anesthetic; vasoconstrictor in Europe	Injected, smoked, sniffed	Increased energy, excitation, insomnia, loss of appetite, mood swings, delusions, paranoia, heart problems

Psychoactive Drugs and Their Effects (*continued*)

SUBSTANCE	TRADE NAMES STREET NAMES	MEDICAL USES	ROUTE OF ADMINISTRATION	MAIN EFFECTS
Amphetamine	Dexedrine; **Black beauties; crosses**	ADHD, obesity, narcolepsy	Injected, oral, smoked, sniffed	Increased alertness and energy, insomnia, loss of appetite, delusions, paranoia
Methamphetamine	**Crank, crystal, ice, meth**	ADHD, short-term aid to weight loss	Injected, oral, smoked, sniffed	Mood elevation, alertness, insomnia, loss of appetite, anxiety, paranoia
MDMA	**Adam, Ecstasy, XTC**	None	Oral	Increased insight and emotion, muscle tension, sleep problems, anxiety, paranoia
Hallucinogens				
Marijuana	**Grass, herb, pot, reefer, weed, sinsemilla**	Glaucoma, nausea from chemotherapy	Oral, smoked	Relaxation, altered perceptions, sleep problems, paranoia, amotivation
Phencyclidine	PCP; **Angel dust, hog**	Anesthetic (veterinary)	Injected, oral, smoked	Euphoria, unpredictable moods, hostility
LSD	**Acid, microdot**	None	Oral	Altered perceptions, distortion of senses, panic reactions, flashback effects

Alcohol affects the neurotransmitter GABA, which is related to anxiety levels. In low dosages, alcohol may make one feel more sociable and relaxed. Alcohol also depresses the functioning of the cerebral cortex. So, in addition to feeling calm and relaxed, we are more likely to shed our inhibitions in regard to our thoughts and behaviors (Koob & Bloom, 1988; Stahl, 1996). When we drink alcohol, we are more willing to be silly or aggressive, share our emotions, or engage in behaviors that we would think twice about if we were sober.

Alcohol also inhibits the functioning of the brain stem, impairing motor functioning and coordination. Reaction time and reflexes are slowed. When your tolerance is exceeded, your speech becomes slurred and your judgment is impaired. It is also harder for your brain to sustain attention, process information, and form new memories (Givens, 1995; Tsai, Gastfriend, & Coyle, 1995; Sayette, Reichle, & Schooler, 2009). Alcohol may cause *memory blackouts*—after a heavy night of drinking, you may not remember the events of the night before. Alcohol also reduces the time spent in REM sleep, which as we have discussed plays a pivotal role in memory processing. Alcohol may make you drowsy, and you may even pass out, but the type of sleep you are getting in this state is not the type of sleep you need. Chronic alcoholism can lead to *Korsakoff's syndrome*, a memory disorder caused by a deficiency of vitamin B (thiamine). A person who is an alcoholic often substitutes alcohol for more nutritious foods, which results in numerous vitamin deficiencies. Unfortunately, these memory deficits tend to be irreversible.

Because drinking alcohol results in reduced inhibitions, people are more likely to engage in sexual activity (A. Cooper, 2002; K. C. Davis et al., 2009; Patrick & Maggs, 2009). But alcohol impairs sexual performance. It makes it more difficult for a male to get and maintain an erection. The ability to achieve orgasm is also hampered by the effects of alcohol. We may think and feel that we are better lovers when under the influence of alcohol, but in reality we are not.

Alcohol's effect on motor coordination can be seen in a police sobriety test.

Women who drink alcohol heavily during pregnancy put their unborn child at risk for **fetal alcohol syndrome (FAS)**. Ingested alcohol does cross the placenta. Children born with FAS tend to have low birth weight; exhibit limb, head, and facial deformities; and suffer brain abnormalities that retard intellectual functioning and cause difficulties in learning, memory, problem solving, and attention (Ikonomidou et al., 2000; Kumada et al., 2007; N. K. Young, 1997). Because of the negative effects of alcohol on prenatal development, even moderate drinking during pregnancy is not recommended.

Does everyone experience the same effects from alcohol? No. The degree to which each of us experiences these effects depends on several factors. For example, alcohol has either more or less effect depending on your tolerance level: the higher your tolerance, the more alcohol you can consume before feeling its effects. Another factor is the rate of consumption. The faster you drink, the faster the alcohol is absorbed into the blood, increasing the alcohol's effect. Gender influences alcohol's effect as well. Metabolic and weight differences between males and females make it easier for male bodies to tolerate higher levels of alcohol (York & Welte, 1994). ● TABLE 4.2 details the typical effects of certain blood alcohol concentrations.

Alcohol and Genetics

Research suggests a possible genetic factor in alcohol's effect (Stacey, Clarke, & Schumann, 2009). Studies of twins show that if one identical twin is an alcoholic, the other twin has

TABLE 4.2

● **Typical Effects of Blood Alcohol Concentrations (BAC)** Alcohol intoxication varies greatly among individuals. Some people become intoxicated at lower blood alcohol concentration levels.

BAC	TYPICAL EFFECTS
.02–.03	Slight euphoria and loss of shyness; light-headedness. Depressant effects of alcohol are not yet apparent.
.04–.06	Feelings of well-being, relaxation, and lowered inhibitions; minor impairment of reasoning and memory; lowered alertness
.07–.09	Feelings of well-being; slight impairment of balance, speech, vision, reaction time, and hearing; reduced judgment and self-control; impaired reasoning and memory
.10–.125	Significant impairment of motor coordination; loss of judgment; slowed thinking; slurred speech; impairment of balance, vision, reaction time, and hearing
.13–.15	Gross motor impairment and lack of physical control; blurred vision and major loss of balance; severely impaired judgment. Feelings of well-being are reduced.
.16–.20	Anxiety, restlessness, sadness; nausea and vomiting; feeling dazed and confused; blackouts
.25	Severely impaired physical and mental abilities; increased risk of injury by falls or accidents
.30	Stupor; little comprehension of whereabouts; loss of consciousness
.35	Possible coma
.40+	Onset of coma; possible death due to respiratory arrest

fetal alcohol syndrome (FAS) a birth condition resulting from the mother's chronic use of alcohol during pregnancy that is characterized by facial and limb deformities and intellectual impairment

almost a 40% chance of developing a drinking problem. Rates for fraternal twins are much lower (Prescott et al., 1994). Research on sons of alcoholic fathers also suggests a possible genetic predisposition to alcohol dependence. The sons are likely to have an overall higher tolerance for alcohol, requiring more alcohol before feeling its effects, and are therefore at greater risk for abusing alcohol (Schuckit & Smith, 1997). More recently, researchers have located specific strands of genes that regulate the function of GABA. These genes vary across families with multiple members who have alcohol problems and may contribute to a person's vulnerability to alcoholism (Edenberg & Foroud, 2006; Krystal et al., 2006; Soyka et al., 2008).

Cultural studies also support a possible genetic link. For instance, in some ethnic groups such as Japanese and Chinese, drinking alcohol can cause facial flushing. This sudden reddening of the face is a genetic trait that rarely occurs in Europeans. The physical and social discomfort of facial flushing tends to reduce the rate of alcohol consumption and alcoholism in these groups. People in ethnic groups that do not experience facial flushing are more likely to become alcoholics (Helzer & Canino, 1992).

Alcohol and Ethnicity in the United States

Patterns of drinking also vary across ethnic groups in the United States. National surveys and studies of adult community samples have generally found the highest drinking levels among European Americans, multiracial Americans, and American Indians, followed by Latino/ Hispanic Americans. The lowest drinking levels are for African Americans and Americans of Asian Indian descent (Herd, 1990, 1994; SAMHSA, 2009a). These findings are consistent with drinking patterns among college and secondary school students as well (Skager, Frifth, & Maddahian, 1989; Welte & Barnes, 1987; SAMHSA, 2009a). European American, American Indian, and Latino/Hispanic American college students tend to binge drink in higher numbers than do African American and Asian American students (SAMHSA, 2009a). Gender differences in drinking among most ethnic minorities parallel those found in the majority culture: males typically consume more alcohol and do so more often than females (Mooney et al., 1987; SAMHSA, 2009a; Welte & Barnes, 1987).

Can we assume that ethnicity is the cause of these differences in alcohol use? The answer is no. These findings are correlational, not causal (a person's ethnicity doesn't *cause* his or her rate of alcohol consumption), and causal conclusions cannot be drawn from correlational data (Chapter 1) because factors other than ethnicity may be operating. Thus, these findings should be interpreted with caution. Each ethnic group is highly diverse. Hispanic Americans include groups whose ancestors originated from such diverse regions as Central America, Puerto Rico, Cuba, Spain, Mexico, and South America. Asian Americans include groups originating from China, Japan, Korea, and Vietnam. Drinking levels and frequency within each subgroup may differ. For example, Cuban Americans consistently report more use of alcohol than other Hispanic groups (SAMHSA, 2006). Reported alcohol use among Japanese Americans and Korean Americans over the age of 12 is higher than for Chinese Americans and Vietnamese Americans (SAMHSA, 2006). Moreover, attitudes toward alcohol may vary considerably within these subcultures, influencing the level of drinking. Broad-based national surveys fail to consider such diversity when compiling data on alcohol consumption (J. Jung, 2001).

Alcohol use also varies across social classes. This factor is not typically controlled for when studying rates of alcohol use among different ethnic groups (J. Jung, 2001). For example, African American men from lower socioeconomic levels report more drinking problems than do European American men from lower socioeconomic levels. The reverse appears to apply at higher socioeconomic levels—European American males report more drinking problems than African American males do (M. C. Jones, Webb, Hsiao, & Hannan, 1995). Consequently, one cannot tell whether the differences in alcohol use are due to socioeconomic level or ethnicity.

Many other factors also may play a role in ethnic differences in alcohol use, including education level, urban–rural differences, and the impact of having minority status in a majority culture. Environmental factors such as learning also play a role. Children of alcoholics have an increased risk of developing alcoholism that cannot be attributed solely to genetics. As adults, they are more likely to cope with personal or work-related stress by imitating the behavior of

Alcohol has devastating effects on families.

their alcoholic parent (Blane, 1988; Rivers, 1994). Clearly, the effects of alcohol and whether or not one becomes an abuser of alcohol depend on the interaction among genetic, cultural, individual, and environmental factors.

Social Costs of Alcohol Use

Alcohol dependence is devastating to individuals, families, and society in general. According to the National Highway Traffic Safety Administration (NHTSA), almost 32% of all traffic deaths in the United States are alcohol-related (NHTSA, 2008). Alcohol-impaired driving is highest for people between the ages of 21 and 24 and more common for males than for females (CDC, 2002; Chou et al., 2006). More than half of rapists report that they drank alcohol before committing their crime. In college campus surveys, alcohol plays a role in the majority of sexual assaults and rapes. More than half of spousal abuse incidents involve alcohol (J. Adler & Rosenberg, 1994; Camper, 1990; Seto & Barbaree, 1995). Millions of children who live with alcoholic parents are also seriously affected. High levels of conflict—as well as physical, emotional, and sexual abuse—are likely in these households (Mathew et al., 1993). Alcohol abuse also has economic costs. Alcohol abuse is associated with excessive absenteeism, lost productivity at work, and higher rates of on-the-job injury. Recall that Charlie Parker often missed many performances and experienced several divorces due in part to his alcohol use. These costs also tend to be significantly higher for heavy drinkers (C. A. Fisher et al., 2000; Gorsky, Schwartz, & Dennis, 1988; S. Jones, Casswell, & Zhang, 1995). Alcohol-related car accidents cost about $51 billion each year in the United States (Blincoe et al., 2002). Alcohol, contrary to the beer commercials, is indeed dangerous to our health and our society.

Barbiturates and Sedatives

Barbiturates, commonly called "downers," are a category of depressants that are typically prescribed to reduce anxiety or to induce sleep. Well-known barbiturate drugs include Nembutal and Seconal. Sedatives or tranquilizers are also prescribed to reduce anxiety. They include a class of drugs called the *benzodiazepines*, including Valium and Xanax. Both types of depressants have effects similar to alcohol. In small dosages, they slow the nervous system, promoting relaxation. In high dosages, though, they severely impair motor functioning, memory, and judgment. Like alcohol, these drugs influence the functioning of the neurotransmitter GABA (Barbee, 1993). When these drugs are taken in combination with alcohol, they are potentially lethal because they can cause suppression of those brain areas that control breathing and heart rate, which can lead to unconsciousness, coma, or death.

You may have heard of the tranquilizer called Rohypnol ("roofies"), commonly known and used as a *date rape drug*. It is placed in a woman's drink at a party or club without her knowledge or consent, and the combined effect of alcohol and Rohypnol renders her unconscious. In this state she is then sexually assaulted or raped. In the morning, because of the drugs' effects on memory, she may not recall the event (Navarro, 1995).

When used as prescribed, barbiturates and sedatives can be helpful in the short-term treatment of anxiety disorders and sleeping problems such as insomnia. However, over the long term, there is a risk of dependence. Long-term use of barbiturates actually alters sleep patterns, lessening time spent in REM sleep (Kales & Kales, 1973). Severe emotional depression also may set in, increasing the risk of suicide. Long-term use of tranquilizers leads to memory loss and actually heightens anxiety. When the effect of the drug has worn off, the body goes into "overdrive" to overcome its depressing effects (McKim, 1997). Withdrawal from these drugs can be brutal and includes convulsions, hallucinations, and intense anxiety.

Opiates (Narcotics): Morphine, Codeine, Opium, and Heroin

The **opiates**, or narcotics, are drugs that are used to treat pain by mimicking pain-inhibiting neurotransmitters in the body such as endorphins. Opiates include morphine, codeine, opium, and heroin, although heroin and opium are not considered or prescribed as a medicine. While depressing some brain areas, these drugs create excitation in other brain areas. In addition to blocking pain, they produce a feeling of pleasure that is almost like floating on a cloud or being in a dreamlike state (Bozarth & Wise, 1984). The opiates are extremely addictive, causing dependence within a few weeks. When you take opiates, your brain recognizes an abundance of pain inhibitors in the body and decreases its own production of endorphins. So when the effect of the opiate wears off, you feel your earlier pain *and* the absence of pleasure, and you will want another, larger dose (Hughes et al., 1975; Zadina et al., 1997). It is for this reason that narcotic administration is so closely monitored by health professionals.

Physical withdrawal symptoms related to opiate use include hot and cold flashes, cramps, sweating, and shaking. These symptoms typically last anywhere from 4 to 7 days, but they are not life-threatening. What *is* life-threatening is the risk of overdose. Street concentrations of narcotic drugs such as heroin and opium can vary widely. In addition, a person's sensitivity to opiates—either self-administered or medically given to prevent withdrawal symptoms—may fluctuate on a daily basis (Gallerani et al., 2001). The user never knows, therefore, if the concentration of drug he or she is taking will exceed the body's ability to handle it. There is an added risk of contracting HIV/AIDS and hepatitis C from using contaminated needles because opiates are often injected into a vein.

Currently, many heroin addicts are treated with the chemical *methadone* or buprenorphine. Each reduces the unpleasantness of the withdrawal symptoms yet does not produce the intense high of heroin. They are both equally effective in treating heroin dependence (Fiellin, Friedland, & Gourevitch, 2006; Payte, 1997; Vigezzi et al., 2006).

Stimulants: Legal and Otherwise

The **stimulants** include drugs that interfere with brain functioning by speeding up normal brain activity. Five stimulant substances we will review are *caffeine, nicotine, cocaine, amphetamines,* and *MDMA* (Ecstasy).

Caffeine: Java Jitters

Do you consider caffeine a drug? Because many of us wake up each morning reaching for that cup of coffee or that can of Monster or Red Bull to get us going, we may not even consider caffeine a mind-altering drug. Yet, caffeine is a psychoactive drug because of its effects on the brain. It is perhaps the most frequently used psychoactive drug in the world. Caffeine is an active ingredient in coffee, tea, sodas, some energy drinks, chocolate, migraine headache medications, and some diet pills. It stimulates the brain by blocking neurotransmitters (primarily adenosine) that slow down our nervous system and cause sleep (Julien, 1995). In small doses, caffeine gives us a boost, keeping us more alert and helping us focus. It helps problem solving and decreases reaction time (Warburton, 1995). However, in large doses, caffeine can "wire" you, causing insomnia, upset stomach, racing heartbeat, nervousness, and irritability. There are increasing reports of "caffeine intoxication" resulting from the use

IMPictures/FilmMagic/Getty Images

© John G. Mabanglo/epa/Corbis

The combined effects of pain medications and depressant drugs were a major factor in the accidental deaths of Heath Ledger and Michael Jackson.

opiates painkilling drugs that depress some brain areas and excite others

stimulants drugs that speed up normal brain functioning

The caffeine content of energy drinks varies, with some containing the equivalent of 14 cans of Coca-Cola, which can result in "caffeine intoxication"—nervousness, anxiety, restlessness, insomnia, upset stomach, tremors, rapid heartbeat, and in rare cases, death.

© Richard Levine/Alamy

of energy drinks as well as the mixing of energy drinks high in caffeine with alcohol, increasing alcohol-related injuries such as falls and car accidents (Reissig, Strain, & Griffiths, 2009).

Regular caffeine use can lead to dependence. If you suddenly stop drinking coffee or kick your cola habit, you will likely experience headaches, irritability, tiredness, and flu-like symptoms (Schuh & Griffiths, 1997). These withdrawal symptoms, even if they aren't severe, can last a week. Excessive caffeine use increases the risk of high blood pressure and encourages the development of fibroid cysts in women's breasts. Pregnant women in particular should reduce caffeine intake because high amounts of caffeine are associated with an increased risk of miscarriage and have been linked with birth defects (Infante-Rivard et al., 1993). As you can see, caffeine is a potent psychoactive drug. An even more potent stimulant is nicotine.

Nicotine: A Really Bad Habit

Nicotine is an addictive substance that makes it difficult for young people to quit smoking once they have started.

© Penny Tweddie/Getty Images

Nicotine, the active ingredient in tobacco and the source of a smoker's craving for cigarettes, is a powerful stimulant. Tobacco use is the most preventable cause of death in the United States. More than 440,000 deaths result each year from tobacco use, at an annual price tag of more than $193 billion in health-related economic costs (CDC, 2008c). Tobacco use has been linked to lung cancer, throat cancer, emphysema, and heart disease (Noah & Robinson, 1997). Women who smoke during pregnancy reduce the flow of oxygen to the fetus. Their babies tend to be irritable, have respiratory problems, and have lower birth weight (Rosenblith, 1992).

Most adult smokers started smoking before the age of 18, and every day more people under the age of 18 become regular smokers (● FIG-URE 4.6) (Johnston et al., 2009a). Although the percentage of people in the United States who smoke has decreased considerably over the last 50 years, 23.1% of adult men and 18.3% of adult women continue to smoke regularly (CDC, 2009a). The percentages are significantly higher for adults ages 21–29 years (37%) (SAMHSA, 2009a). American Indians have the highest rates of tobacco use, and African American and Southeast Asian men have high rates of smoking. Asian American and Hispanic women have the lowest rates (CDC, 2006; SAMHSA, 2009a).

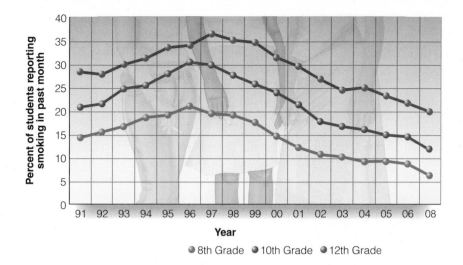

8th Grade ● 10th Grade ● 12th Grade

Why is nicotine so addictive? Much of nicotine's allure comes from its effect on the brain. Nicotine affects several neurotransmitters. It influences acetylcholine and glutamate such that in low doses, nicotine improves attention and memory (McGehee et al., 1995). Nicotine also elevates dopamine levels, leading to feelings of pleasure and reward (Pidoplichko et al., 1997). In high doses, nicotine causes vomiting, diarrhea, sweating, and dizziness. Yet users quickly develop a tolerance to nicotine.

The U.S. Food and Drug Administration officially named nicotine an addictive substance in 1997 because users can become dependent, often in just a few days. Withdrawal from chronic nicotine use rivals withdrawal from other abused drugs such as cocaine, morphine, and alcohol (Epping-Jordan et al., 1998). Withdrawal symptoms, lasting anywhere from 2 to 6 weeks, include headaches, irritability, stomach upset, difficulty sleeping, and an intense craving for the drug. This helps explain why it is so hard for people to stop smoking. Although 3 out of every 4 smokers have tried to quit, only 2 out of 10 succeed. High relapse rates occur. On average, it takes smokers four to five attempts at quitting before they succeed (Jarvik, 1995). This indeed illustrates the power of dependence.

Cocaine and Crack

In 2009, Adam Goldstein, known as DJ AM, was found dead in his New York City apartment due to the combined effects of cocaine and sedatives. Quiet Riot singer Kevin DuBrow, 52, was found dead in his Las Vegas home due to an accidental cocaine overdose. Supermodel Kate Moss's battle with cocaine addiction also has played itself out in the media. Cocaine and its derivative, crack, are powerful and dangerous stimulant drugs. Snorted, smoked, or injected, cocaine is quickly absorbed into the body and thus reaches the brain rapidly. Crack is powdered cocaine mixed with water and other additives that is then boiled until a solid mass forms. It is broken into rocks and smoked with a long glass tube called a crack pipe. Inhaling the smoke delivers large quantities of the drug to the lungs and produces an intense and immediate high.

What does cocaine do to the brain? Cocaine, in all its forms, blocks a protein called the dopamine transporter (DAT), which helps the reuptake of dopamine into the neuron (Chapter 2). Because reuptake is blocked, free dopamine in the brain increases. Cocaine also affects norepinephrine and serotonin transporter proteins in a similar way, but its action on the dopamine system is generally thought to be the most important (Hummel & Unterwald, 2002; Nestler, 2006; J. M. Williams & Galli, 2006). The buildup of dopamine produces an instant surge of arousal, a feeling of pleasure and optimism. Appetite decreases, but heart rate, blood pressure, and alertness increase. Used in low doses, the effect of cocaine is short-lived—lasting roughly 10 to 30 minutes. However, users typically repeat doses, making its effect last longer. When the effect of the cocaine wears off, the person "crashes," showing decreased energy and depressed mood. This low creates an intense craving for the drug that sets up a cycle of continued use and dependence (Gawin, 1991). High doses of cocaine

Rob Loud/Getty Images

© PACHA/Corbis

People pay a high price for using stimulant drugs. Adam Goldstein, "DJ AM," died from an overdose of cocaine and sedatives. Supermodel Kate Moss was dropped from several ad campaigns after photos of her allegedly snorting cocaine were revealed by the media.

(relative to one's tolerance) can cause paranoia, sleeplessness, delusions, seizures, strokes, and potentially cardiac arrest (Lacayo, 1995). Users who are dependent on cocaine may lose interest in their usual friends and activities, lose weight, and have chronic sore throats and difficulty sleeping; there may also be a noticeable change in their finances.

Health effects of repeated use of cocaine also include chronic nosebleeds, damage to nasal cartilage (from snorting), and respiratory and heart problems. Miscarriages are common for pregnant women who use cocaine. If the pregnancy continues, the infant is more likely to be born premature and, as a newborn, must be weaned from the effects of the drug. However, the long-term impact of prenatal exposure to cocaine continues to be in question. Earlier research indicated that by school age, children with prenatal exposure to cocaine were more likely to be hyperactive and to show delayed language learning and disorganized thinking (Konkol et al., 1994; B. M. Lester, Corwin et al., 1991; Mayes et al.,1996). However, more recent research suggests that the home environment may play a stronger role in a child's development than prenatal cocaine exposure (R. E. Arendt et al., 2004; Hurt et al., 2005; Kilbride, Castor, & Fuger, 2006). For example, Hurt and colleagues (2005) have followed a group of 135 urban schoolchildren, 62 with prenatal exposure to cocaine and 73 without. Now in the fourth grade, children from both groups have shown similar poor school performance. In both groups, children with successful school performance were more likely to have come from better home environments regardless of prenatal cocaine exposure.

Amphetamines

Amphetamines, called "uppers" or "speed," have effects similar to those of cocaine. However, the high produced by these drugs is less intense but generally lasts longer (a few hours). At one time amphetamines such as Dexedrine, Methedrine, and Benzedrine were widely prescribed for weight loss and depression. So many people became dependent on them that their use is now limited to treating people with narcolepsy and children who are diagnosed with attention deficit hyperactivity disorder (ADHD). They may be abused in these situations as well, and other medications are available for these conditions.

Currently, the most abused form of amphetamine is *methamphetamine*, commonly called crystal meth, crystal, ice, chalk, or crank. This is the drug that Andre Agassi used. Methamphetamine use is the fastest-growing drug problem in much of the United States. According to the 2008 National Survey on Drug Use and Health (NSDUH), 5% of the U.S. population age 12 or over has used methamphetamine at least once (SAMHSA, 2009a). Approximately 4.1% of college students and 8.3% of young adults between the ages of 19 and 28 have tried methamphetamine (National Institute on Drug Abuse [NIDA] & University of Michigan, 2006).

How is methamphetamine made? Methamphetamine is easily "cooked" in labs with a variety of easily available ingredients. Pseudoephedrine, the main chemical ingredient in methamphetamine, is a key component of cold remedies such as Sudafed. The pseudoephedrine is combined with other chemicals readily available in gasoline, rubbing alcohol, pool cleaning supplies, or drain cleaners to produce methamphetamine. Methamphetamine can be injected, snorted, smoked, or ingested orally. To reduce the number of meth labs in the country, the Combat Methamphetamine Epidemic Act of 2005, passed in 2006, placed national restrictions on the sales of pseudoephedrine. It is no longer available on open shelves; purchasers must sign a sales log, must show identification, and can buy no more than 3.6 grams a day and 9 grams a month (Government Printing Office, 2006).

Methamphetamine, like cocaine, affects dopamine, serotonin, and norepinephrine levels in the brain (Volkow et al., 2001). As we saw in Andre's behavior, the result is enhanced mood and pleasure, energy, alertness, and reduced appetite. Heart rate and blood pressure also increase. Like cocaine, methamphetamine leads to a crash to low energy levels, paranoia, and depressed mood when the effects of the drug have subsided. However, methamphetamine remains present in the brain longer than cocaine. It not only blocks the reuptake of dopamine but also increases the release of dopamine, leading to a more toxic effect on the central nervous system (NIDA, 2006b). Continued use results in insomnia, paranoia, agitation, confusion, violent behavior, memory loss, and dependence. Methamphetamine use can also cause strokes, cardiovascular problems, and extreme anorexia. An overdose can cause coma and death. Users who inject the drug and share needles are also at risk for acquiring HIV/AIDS and hepatitis C (Bezchlibnyk-Butler & Jeffries, 1998).

MDMA (Ecstasy)

MDMA, called "Ecstasy," "Adam," or "XTC," is a drug chemically similar to amphetamine. In its "pure" form, Ecstasy is called MDMA, but street Ecstasy typically contains other drugs such as amphetamine, ketamine, caffeine, and ephedrine (Walters, Foy, & Castro, 2003). After becoming a street drug in the 1980s, MDMA's use dramatically increased as a "club drug" in the 1990s and early 2000s, particularly among college students and young adults. In 2008, 5.2% of people over the age of 12 reported using Ecstasy at some point in their lives (SAMHSA, 2009a). It is also being used at relatively high levels by high school students in the United States with 4.3% of twelfth graders having tried the drug (Johnston et al., 2009). In the United States, use is also spreading beyond predominantly European American youth to African American and Hispanic populations (Boeri, Sterk, & Elifson, 2004; Maxwell & Spence, 2003), and Ecstasy has become a popular drug among urban gay males (NIDA, 2006a).

How does Ecstasy affect a person? Taken orally, usually in a tablet or a capsule, Ecstasy enhances mood and energy levels and heightens users' sensations. Users report increased self-confidence, increased feelings of love and warmth toward others, emotional openness, and lack of inhibition (Fry & Miller, 2002). The effect begins very fast, within half an hour of consumption, and lasts approximately 3 to 6 hours. Negative effects of Ecstasy use are insomnia, teeth clenching, nausea, increases in heart rate and blood pressure, fatigue, and blurred vision. Most of these negative effects subside within 24 hours. Paranoia, depression, drug craving, overheating, cardiac problems, kidney failure, seizures, strokes, loss of touch with reality, or any combination of these effects may also occur (Bezchlibnyk-Butler & Jeffries, 1998).

Although MDMA increases the activity of several neurotransmitters in the brain, it is the serotonin pathway that has received the most attention. Ecstasy binds to the serotonin transport protein such that the availability of free serotonin increases (Britt & McCance-Katz, 2005; Colado, O'Shea, & Green, 2004). Ecstasy is a relatively "young" drug. The long-term effects of its use on the human brain are not yet fully understood (R. L. Cowan, 2007). However, disrupted sleep patterns and subtle, persistent deficits in memory have been documented (Kuypers, Wingen, & Ramaekers, 2008; McCann et al., 2009; Randall et al., 2009). It also is unclear whether Ecstasy has properties of the hallucinogens. Users regularly report hallucinations, but it is impossible to know whether they have really been using pure MDMA or have bought low doses of LSD instead. More about LSD will be revealed as we now turn our attention to the hallucinogens.

Hallucinogens: Distorting Reality

Hallucinogens are drugs that interfere with brain functioning by simultaneously exciting and inhibiting the nervous system. These contrasting effects often cause distortions in perception, or *hallucinations*. Hallucinogenic substances include *marijuana*, *PCP*, and *LSD*.

Marijuana

Marijuana—also called pot, reefer, or weed—is a mild hallucinogen. It rarely, if ever, leads to overdoses that cause death (Zimmer & Morgan, 1997). Thirteen states currently allow for its medicinal use. It has been prescribed for medical conditions such as glaucoma, chronic

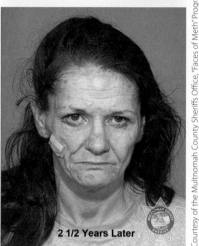

Methamphetamine abuse can radically alter one's physical appearance as it causes skin lesions and tooth decay.

hallucinogens drugs that simultaneously excite and inhibit normal neural activity, thereby causing distortions in perception

Uriel Sinai/Getty Images

Although controversy continues over the medicinal uses of marijuana, smoking pot increases one's chances of respiratory problems and lung damage.

pain, and nausea from cancer chemotherapy and has been found moderately effective in clinical trials for muscle spasms and multiple sclerosis (Croxford, 2003; Grinspoon & Bakalar, 1995; Iverson, 2003; T. W. Klein & Newton, 2007). It is also the most widely used illegal substance in the United States, with 41% of people over the age of 12 reporting having tried the drug. Past-year usage is highest among 16- to 25-year-olds, and males report higher usage than females. American Indians report the highest use and Asian Americans the lowest (SAMHSA, 2007, 2009).

The effects of marijuana depend on the expectations and current mood of the user (R. T. Jones, 1971; Moreira & Lutz, 2008). If you expect to become mellow under the influence of pot, you are more likely to act mellow when you're high. Similarly, if you are depressed before smoking pot, the drug is more likely to intensify this mood. Of course, marijuana's effect will also depend on your tolerance level and the amount of the drug consumed.

The active ingredient in marijuana is **THC (tetrahydrocannabinol)**. THC is absorbed by the lungs and produces a high that lasts for several hours. THC binds to the neurotransmitter called anandamide that influences learning, short-term memory, motor coordination, emotions, and appetite—behaviors that are all affected when people are high on marijuana (Matsuda et al., 1990). In low doses, THC makes users feel good and experience vivid sensations. THC also slows reaction time and impairs judgment and peripheral vision. For this reason, marijuana users are just as dangerous driving a car or operating machinery as users of other drugs. Marijuana use also interferes with memory, disrupting both the formation of memories and the recall of information (Nestor et al., 2008; H. G. Pope & Yurgelun-Todd, 1996; Ranganathan & D'Souza, 2006). Its stimulation of appetite and increased sensitivity to taste may result in an attack of the "munchies." In high doses, THC may produce hallucinations, delusions, paranoia, and distortions in time and body image (Hanson & Venturelli, 1998; Morrison, Zois, McKeown et al., 2009). Long-term marijuana use can lead to dependence. Many people report mild withdrawal symptoms when marijuana use is stopped including irritability, sleeplessness, decreased appetite, anxiety, and drug cravings (Cooper & Haney, 2008; de Fonseca et al., 1997; Grinspoon et al., 1997; R. S. Stephens, Roffman, & Simpson, 1994; Vandrey et al., 2008; Wickelgren, 1997).

Studies on long-term users of marijuana have shown long-lasting cognitive effects including impaired attention, learning, and motor coordination (H. G. Pope & Yurgelun-Todd, 1996; Volkow et al., 1996). However, permanent structural changes in the brain have not been identified with chronic use (Quickfall & Crockford, 2006). Marijuana also has serious long-term health effects. Because it is typically smoked, users may experience respiratory problems such as bronchitis and lung damage (Tashkin, 2005). A few marijuana cigarettes (or joints) contain more carcinogenic substances than a half pack of cigarettes (Ferrell, 1996).

PCP

In the 1950s, Parke, Davis and Company developed PCP (phencyclidine) as an anesthetic for surgery. However, following surgery, patients showed worrisome side effects including hallucinations, delirium, and disorientation. Consequently, it was removed from the market (for humans) in 1965 and sold to veterinarians for use in animal surgery. Its use as a street drug spread significantly until 1978, when it was taken off the market completely—even for animals (Rudgley, 1998). Today, PCP is manufactured illegally and sold on the street by such names as "angel dust" and "rocket fuel." "Sherm," "killer joints," or "KJs" are names that refer to PCP poured over cigarettes or marijuana joints. PCP can be eaten, snorted, smoked,

THC (tetrahydrocannabinol) the active ingredient in marijuana that affects learning, short-term memory, coordination, emotion, and appetite

or injected. Although the use of PCP has declined steadily since 1979, in 2008, 2.7% of people over the age of 12 reported having tried PCP, with males again outnumbering females (SAMHSA, 2009a).

PCP has hallucinogenic properties as well as stimulant and depressant effects. These unpredictable effects often lead to distress, mood swings, and confusion. PCP inhibits the neurotransmitter glutamate, which is involved in the perception of pain, responses to the environment, and memory. In low doses, PCP produces a sudden increase in blood pressure, pulse rate, and breathing. Flushing, profuse sweating, and numbness of the limbs may also occur. Out-of-body experiences and the sensation of walking on a spongy surface are also reported. In higher doses, PCP causes a drop in blood pressure, pulse rate, and respiration. This may be accompanied by nausea, vomiting, blurred vision, drooling, loss of balance, and dizziness. Hallucinations, confusion, paranoia, and garbled speech also result. Users may become severely disoriented or suicidal and may therefore be a danger to themselves or others. Seizures, coma, or death may also occur (Rudgley, 1998).

Using PCP can lead to dependence. Users often crave the feelings of strength, power, and invulnerability and the escape from real life that PCP brings. Long-term use of PCP is associated with memory loss and difficulty in speaking and thinking, and may lead to permanent changes in fine motor abilities (NIDA, 2001).

LSD

LSD (lysergic acid diethylamide), more commonly referred to as acid, is the most potent perception-altering drug known. In 2008, 9.4% of people over the age of 12 reported having tried LSD at some time in their lives; males were more likely to have tried the drug than were females (SAMHSA, 2009a). LSD's effects typically begin 30 to 90 minutes after ingestion and can last anywhere from 6 to 12 hours.

How does LSD affect a person? Users of LSD may experience increased blood pressure and heart rate, dizziness, loss of appetite, and nausea, but the drug's main effects appear to be emotional and sensory. Even at very low doses, LSD causes bizarre hallucinations, distortions in time and body image, and intense emotions that together are often referred to as "tripping." Emotions may shift rapidly from fear to happiness, and the user may seem to experience several emotions at once. Colors, smells, sounds, and other sensory stimuli seem highly intensified and may even blend in what is known as *synesthesia*, in which a person seems to hear or feel colors and see sounds (NIDA, 2001). Recall from Chapter 3 the story of Michael Watson, who had synesthesia and tasted shapes. These effects are due to LSD's resemblance to the neurotransmitter serotonin (Aghajanian, 1994). LSD stimulates serotonin receptors, influencing perceptions, emotions, and sleep. However, whether one's "trip" is pleasant or unpleasant is unpredictable and depends on the user's expectations and mood. On good trips, users experience enjoyable sensations, but bad trips produce terrifying thoughts and feelings, including fears of insanity, death, or losing control. Although withdrawal symptoms from LSD have not been documented, users quickly develop tolerance (N. S. Miller & Gold, 1994; NIDA, 2001).

Two long-term effects of LSD in some users are *persistent psychosis* and *hallucinogen persisting perception disorder (HPPD)*, more commonly referred to as "flashbacks." Persistent psychosis is a long-lasting psychotic-like state after the trip has ended. It may include dramatic mood swings, visual disturbances, and hallucinations. These effects may last for years and can affect people who have no history or other symptoms of a psychological disorder. HPPD, or flashbacks, is a reexperiencing of the sensations originally produced by the LSD hours, weeks, or even years after its initial use. It typically consists of visual disturbances such as seeing bright or colored flashes and trails attached to moving objects. HPPD often persists even years after people have stopped using the drug (NIDA, 2001). Knowledge on the causes and treatment for persistent psychosis and HPPD are very limited; further studies are needed (J. H. Halpern & Pope, 2003). Additional lasting side effects of LSD use may include short-term memory loss, paranoia, nightmares, and panic attacks (Gold, 1994).

Despite the different effects of the drugs discussed, they all have one thing in common: they alter our state of consciousness—in sometimes unpredictable, and occasionally tragic, ways. Although much is still unknown about many of these drugs, it is clear from the opening stories and the research that has been cited that the long-term negative effects outweigh the short-term high and feelings of well-being that they produce. By understanding these effects, you may well avoid or prevent their abuse in the future.

Let's REVIEW

In this section, we detailed the nature of psychoactive drugs—from caffeine to heroin—including how they work and their effects. As a quick check of your understanding, try answering the following questions at increasing levels of difficulty.

1. Which category of drugs has its main effects by slowing down normal neural processing?

   a. stimulants   c. depressants

   b. hallucinogens   d. amphetamines

2. Rolanda takes a drug that raises her blood pressure and heart rate, makes her feel euphoric and excited, and suppresses her appetite. Rolanda in all likelihood has *not* taken _____.

   a. cocaine   c. methamphetamine

   b. alcohol   d. crack

3. The designer drug Ecstasy, or MDMA, produces effects similar to what two categories of drugs?

   a. stimulants and depressants   c. stimulants and hallucinogens

   b. hallucinogens and depressants   d. opiates and depressants

ANSWERS 1. c; 2. b; 3. c

STUDYING the CHAPTER

KEY TERMS

consciousness (133)
microsleep (135)
circadian rhythm (139)
suprachiasmatic nucleus (SCN) (139)
melatonin (139)
non-REM sleep (141)
REM sleep (141)
REM behavior disorder (142)
REM rebound (143)
manifest content (144)

latent content (144)
threat simulation theory (TST) (144)
activation-synthesis theory (144)
sleep disorder (145)
insomnia (145)
narcolepsy (145)
sleep apnea (146)
sleepwalking (146)
night terrors (148)

nightmare (148)
enuresis (148)
hypnosis (149)
dissociation theory (150)
response set theory of hypnosis (151)
psychoactive drugs (153)
tolerance (153)
substance dependence (154)
withdrawal symptoms (154)

substance abuse (154)
depressants (155)
fetal alcohol syndrome (FAS) (158)
opiates (161)
stimulants (161)
hallucinogens (165)
THC (tetrahydrocannabinol) (166)

LEARNING CHALLENGE

Now that you have studied the chapter, assess your comprehension of the material by answering the following questions. Then use the key at the end to determine if your understanding is at the basic, intermediate, or advanced level. For a more comprehensive assessment of your learning, please see your student study guide and your Psychology CourseMate (www.cengagebrain.com).

1. Hap is at a workshop and falls asleep. He is relaxed and his brain-wave pattern would show long waves—but not delta waves—interrupted by short bursts of electrical activity. Hap is in what stage of sleep?

a. stage I
b. stage II
c. stage IV
d. REM

2. Which of the following statements about sleep is *false*?

a. Sleep patterns change with age.
b. Everyone needs at least 8 hours of sleep a night.
c. Some people are night owls whereas others are early birds.
d. Circadian rhythms influence the sleep cycle.

3. At a nightclub one weekend, someone slipped a drug into Aoki's drink that made her "pass out" and have no recall of the events of the evening. What type of drug was most likely put in Aoki's drink?

a. stimulant
b. hallucinogen
c. sedative
d. opiate

4. Which of the following drugs is *least* likely to lead to physical withdrawal symptoms?

a. marijuana
b. heroin
c. alcohol
d. nicotine

5. Which of the following categories of drugs produces the most intense withdrawal effects once the person stops using the drug?

a. hallucinogens
b. barbiturates
c. stimulants
d. a and c

6. Deep sleep occurs during _____ sleep.

a. stage I
b. stage II
c. stage III
d. stage IV

7. Which neurotransmitter does nicotine *not* affect?

a. acetylcholine
b. dopamine
c. serotonin
d. glutamate

8. After repeated use, drug users develop _____ and may become reliant on a drug.

a. tolerance
b. withdrawal
c. a margin of safety
d. flashbacks

9. Under hypnosis, a person shows increased _____ brain waves.

a. delta
b. REM
c. beta
d. alpha

10. Dr. Surrell believes that dreams do not have symbolic meaning but are merely the by-product of electrical signals being fired in the brain. Dr. Surrell is endorsing which dream theory?

a. Freudian theory
b. continuity
c. activation synthesis
d. threat simulation

11. Benita often wakes up in the morning feeling very tired, despite sleeping 9–10 hours. Her husband has noticed that she often emits loud snores and seems to have erratic breathing while she is sleeping. Benita most likely has which sleep disorder?

a. insomnia
b. sleep apnea
c. narcolepsy
d. enuresis

12. People who are easily hypnotized tend to have which of the following traits?

a. positive expectations about hypnosis
b. higher intelligence
c. higher sociability
d. all of the above

13. Which of the following drugs is most likely to be prescribed to reduce pain?

a. stimulant
b. depressant
c. hallucinogen
d. opiate

14. Why is melatonin referred to as the "Dracula hormone"?

    a. because it decreases during the day

    b. because it increases at night

    c. both a and b

    d. neither a nor b

15. Which of the following is *not* a documented use of hypnosis?

    a. decreasing anxiety

    b. relieving pain

    c. recovering memories

    d. enhancing therapy

Scoring Key

Below are the answers and the associated point values for each of the Learning Challenge questions. Circle the associated points for each question that you answered correctly. To obtain your Learning Challenge Score, add up the points you circled and write the total in the blank.

1. B, 2 pts	**6.** D, 1 pt	**11.** B, 2 pts
2. B, 1 pt	**7.** C, 3 pts	**12.** A, 3 pts
3. C, 2 pts	**8.** A, 1 pt	**13.** D, 1 pt
4. A, 3 pts	**9.** D, 1 pt	**14.** C, 3 pts
5. B, 3 pts	**10.** C, 2 pts	**15.** C, 2 pts

Learning Challenge Score _____

(27–30) Congratulations! You scored at the advanced level. You are well on your way to mastering the material. Take the next step by answering the questions in your Student Study Guide or your Psychology CourseMate (www.cengagebrain.com).

(21–26) You are almost there! You scored at the intermediate level. Review the material you missed before moving on to answer the questions in your Student Study Guide or your Psychology CourseMate (www.cengagebrain.com).

(20 and below) You are on your way, but you're not there yet! You scored at the beginner level. It appears that you need to carefully review the chapter to improve your mastery of the material.

USE IT OR LOSE IT: APPLYING PSYCHOLOGY

1. How would you rate your hypnotic susceptibility? Under what circumstances would you consider using hypnosis as a therapy or treatment, and why?

2. Using the theories on hypnosis as a guide, explain how stage hypnotists alter the behavior of their audience volunteers.

3. How prevalent is drug use at your campus? Design a survey to assess this issue at your school. Administer the survey to student volunteers, and tabulate the results. What conclusions can be drawn from your results? What factors may have influenced your results?

4. Given the numerous factors, such as age and lifestyle, that influence the amount of sleep a person needs, detail how each of these factors influences the amount of sleep you get. How can you improve the quality of your sleep? What benefits might this change bring you?

5. Keep a dream log for a week. Using the different theories on dreaming, interpret what your dreams mean. Which of these interpretations seems the most plausible, and why?

CRITICAL THINKING FOR INTEGRATION

1. Using the information from Chapter 1 on research methods, design a study that will confirm that sleep changes as we age.

2. Using Chapter 2 as a guide, draw a model of the brain and graphically represent where in the brain four psychoactive drugs have their effects. Also represent on this visual schematic the neurotransmitters that affect these areas of the brain.

3. Explain differences in hypnotic suggestibility as a result of variations in sensation, expectations, and perceptual errors. Use the information from Chapter 3 as a guide in formulating your answer.

CHAPTER STUDY RESOURCES

Student Study Guide

To help organize your learning, work through Chapter 4 of the *What Is Psychology? Student Study Guide*. The study guide includes learning objectives, a chapter summary, fill-in review, key terms, a practice test, and activities.

CengageNOW

CENGAGENOW™

Go to **www.cengage.com/login** to link to CengageNOW, your online study tool. First take the Pre-Test for this chapter to get your personalized study plan, which will identify topics you need to review and direct you to online resources. Then take the Post-Test to determine what concepts you have mastered and what you still need work on.

CourseMate

Access an interactive eBook, chapter-specific interactive learning tools, including flashcards, quizzes, videos, and more in your Psychology CourseMate, available at **CengageBrain.com**.

Aplia

aplia

Aplia™ is an online interactive learning solution that helps you improve comprehension—and your grade—by integrating a variety of tools such as video, tutorials, practice tests, and interactive eBook. Founded by a professor to enhance his own courses, Aplia provides automatically graded assignments with detailed, immediate explanations on every question, and innovative teaching materials. More than 1,000,000 students like you have used Aplia at over 1,800 institutions. Aplia should be purchased only when assigned by your instructor as part of your course.

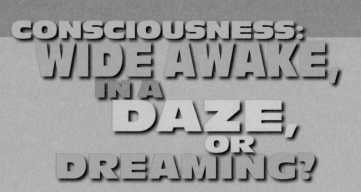

CONSCIOUSNESS: WIDE AWAKE, IN A DAZE, OR DREAMING?

Consciousness includes the feelings, thoughts, and aroused states in which we are aware. Altered states of consciousness occur when we sleep, daydream, meditate, are hypnotized, or take any psychoactive drug. We have seen how these seemingly simple states can powerfully influence behavior and the lives of people such as Charlie Parker and Andre Agassi.

WHAT HAPPENS WHEN WE SLEEP?

- When teenagers and adults get at least 8 hours of sleep, the benefits include restored body tissues, body growth, immunity to disease, an alert mind, processing of memories, and enhanced mood.

- The **circadian rhythm** is a natural rhythm of sleep and waking programmed by a group of brain cells in the hypothalamus called the **suprachiasmatic nucleus**.

- A typical night of sleep involves cycling through two states of sleep: **non-REM sleep**, which progressively relaxes the person; and **REM (rapid-eye-movement) sleep**, which is very active.

- Freud believed that dreams allow us to express fears and desires without conscious censorship. Most psychologists and psychiatrists dispute Freud's emphasis on sex and aggression in interpreting dreams.

- **Threat simulation theory (TST)** proposes that dreaming is an evolved defense mechanism that allows us to rehearse our responses to threatening situations.

- **Activation-synthesis theory** suggests that dreaming is just a consequence of the highly aroused brain during REM sleep.

- **Insomnia** is the inability to get to sleep or to stay asleep. It is the most common **sleep disorder.**

- Other sleep disorders include **sleep apnea**, in which a person stops breathing while asleep, and a rarer condition called **narcolepsy**, in which a person falls asleep during alert times of the day.

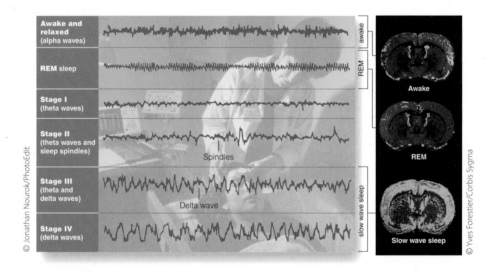

Awake and relaxed (alpha waves) — awake

REM sleep — REM

Stage I (theta waves)

Stage II (theta waves and sleep spindles) — Spindles

Stage III (theta and delta waves) — Delta wave — slow wave sleep

Stage IV (delta waves)

© Jonathan Nourok/PhotoEdit

Awake

REM

Slow wave sleep

© Yves Forestier/Corbis Sygma

HYPNOSIS: REAL OR IMAGINED?

- **Hypnosis** is a technique used to create a state of heightened suggestibility. Hypnosis usually involves being asked to mentally focus on an object, image, or the hypnotist's voice, thus inducing a highly relaxed state.

- Hypnotic susceptibility varies greatly and does not seem to be related to intelligence, gender, or sociability. People who are easily hypnotized tend to be better able to focus their attention, have vivid imaginations, and have positive expectations about hypnosis.

- Hypnosis has been shown to be effective for some people in providing pain relief and decreasing anxiety. It has not been shown to be as effective in curing addictions or recovering accurate memories.

© AP Photo/News Tribune/Stephen Brooks

WHAT ARE THE EFFECTS OF PSYCHOACTIVE DRUGS?

- **Psychoactive drugs** are substances that influence the brain and therefore the behavior of a person.

- Drug **tolerance** refers to the amount of a drug required to produce its effects. After repeated use of a drug, more of it is usually needed to achieve its initial effect.

- **Substance dependence** refers to a person's need of a drug in order to function emotionally or physically.

- **Depressants** such as alcohol, sedatives, and barbiturate drugs interfere with brain functions by inhibiting or slowing normal neural function.

- **Opiates** such as morphine, codeine, and opium are used to treat pain by mimicking the effects of naturally occurring pain-reducing neurotransmitters such as endorphins.

- **Stimulants** are drugs such as caffeine, nicotine, cocaine, and amphetamines that interfere with brain functioning by speeding up normal brain activity.

© Blend Images/Alamy

- **Hallucinogens**, including marijuana and LSD, are drugs that interfere with brain functioning by simultaneously exciting and inhibiting normal neural activity. These contrasting effects often cause disruptions in perception or hallucinations.

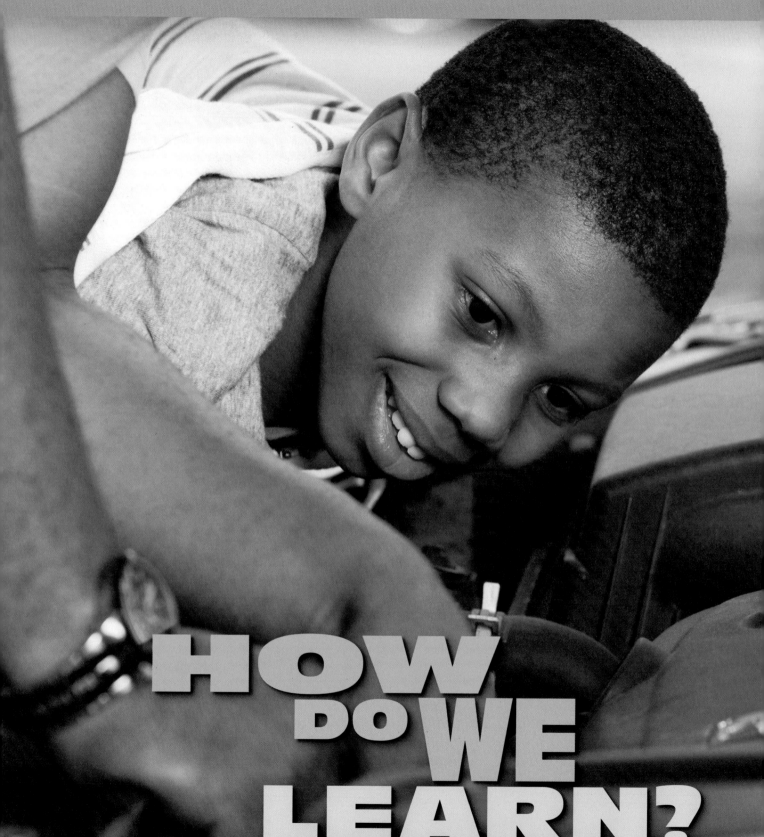

CHAPTER 5

HOW DO WE LEARN?

THE BIG PICTURE

From Socialite to Pauper: Learning to Live Again

As you learned in Chapter 2, *nature* influences our traits and behavior through our genes, but environmental influences or *nurture* can also affect our development in very significant ways. One of the ways that our environment nurtures us is through *learning*. Learning is a crucial part of life. It is through learning that we acquire many of the skills we need to survive in our world.

Michael Gates Gill was a man who had it all. A son of privilege, Michael had grown up with opportunities that many of us only dream of having. Educated at Yale, Michael had rubbed shoulders with the rich and famous—people like Ernest Hemingway and the Queen of England. After college, a friend set Michael up with a job at a prestigious advertising firm, where for the next 25 years he worked tirelessly to build a successful and profitable career. Before long, Michael had landed the accounts of some of the biggest companies in the world, including Ford, Burger King, and IBM. This hard work brought many rewards, and life was good. Not only did Michael rise quickly through the ranks in his firm, he married, had four children, bought an expensive house in the suburbs of New York, traveled, and earned a six-figure income. What more could a person want?

Michael was soon to learn the answer to that question. One morning, after 25 years of service to his firm, Michael was asked to breakfast by his boss and summarily fired. She told him that it was purely a matter of finances. They could hire a younger person to do his job for less money. After 25 years of loyalty, Michael was now viewed as unnecessary overhead.

Over the next 10 years, Michael saw his life deteriorate considerably. Shortly after being fired, he began an affair with Susan, a woman at his gym. The affair offered some comfort but also resulted in a fifth child and the death of his marriage. Michael found himself with a new son for whom he could not provide. Soon, Susan lost interest in having an older boyfriend with few assets, and the relationship waned. Michael was now all alone, and the worst was yet to come. The final blow came when Michael was diagnosed with a rare brain tumor that affected his hearing and required delicate brain surgery—bad news for a man without health insurance.

At 63, Michael was broke, on the verge of homelessness, and ill. And then, a chance meeting opened a door through which Michael would find the greatest happiness of his life. It all started with a cup of coffee. Michael stopped in for coffee at a Starbucks on a day when the company was having a hiring fair. As he was drinking his coffee

CHAPTER OUTLINE

- How Does Learning Help Us?

- Classical Conditioning: Can We Learn Through Association?

- Operant Conditioning: What Do We Learn From the Consequences of Our Actions?

- Observational Learning or Modeling: Can We Learn by Watching Others?

© Colin Hawkins/cultura/Corbis

and reading the paper, he heard someone to his side speak these life-changing words: *"Would you like a job?"* Looking up, he realized that the woman had been speaking to him. Although she had been half-joking in her question, Michael was indeed interested, especially when he learned that Starbucks offered full benefits to all its employees. Michael quickly made it his mission to convince this woman, Crystal, to hire him.

This was a tough sell, however. Mike (he now dropped the formal name of his past life) and Crystal could not have been more different. Mike was a fallen son of the white, privileged upper class. Crystal was the African American daughter of a drug addict who had overcome poverty and hardship with hard work and determination. She was successful and rightfully proud of her achievements. But her pride and past struggles had not hardened her. She believed in giving others a chance to succeed as well—even down-on-their-luck socialites. She hired Mike.

Mike quickly found himself working in a neighborhood he never would have ventured into in his previous life and with people he would never have associated with in the past. He also found himself doing work that he would never have dreamed of doing—cleaning restrooms, taking out trash, running a cash register. One real surprise for Mike was that some of these jobs, which many consider to be unskilled labor, actually were very challenging tasks. Things like taking complicated drink orders and running a computerized cash register were terrifying to Mike, despite all his previous Madison Avenue successes. Yet, Mike knew that he had to succeed. This job was his only chance of being able to afford health insurance and to care for both himself and his young son. What he didn't know at first was that this job was also the means by which he would regain his self-worth, cast aside his prejudices, and finally learn the meaning of happiness.

Mike committed himself entirely to learning how to be a good Starbucks employee. Under Crystal's supervision, the Starbucks philosophy that all people have equal value and all jobs must be done well and with respect became Mike's own point of view. Mike learned to take pride in a job well done and to see good work as its own reward, even when that work was scrubbing a bathroom floor. He came to value all the diverse people he worked with and served. People from all walks of life—the homeless man, the executive, the young parents, the college students, the would-be musicians, the underprivileged minority members, the people just trying to survive in New York City— all became valuable and worthy of respect to Michael Gates Gill. And, perhaps most surprising of all, Mike became respectable to Michael Gates Gill as well. He became a man proud of the work he did. He became a man who respected others and felt their love and respect in return.

After a year of working under Crystal's supervision, Mike was confident enough to transfer to another Starbucks location, where he continues his career in coffee. He also wrote about his transformation in an inspiring book entitled *How Starbucks Saved My Life: A Son of Privilege Learns to Live Like Everyone Else* (Gill, 2008).

For Michael Gates Gill, working at Starbucks was a life-changing experience through which he learned to be truly happy.

© Bill Aron/PhotoEdit

Early in life, Michael Gates Gill had to learn to live among the rich and powerful—a task he adapted to very successfully. Late in life, Mike had to learn to live among the less privileged—a task he struggled with, but ultimately mastered. Like Mike, we are all affected by our experiences. Every day, we learn from the people and events in our lives. Sometimes these lessons are painful, but many times they are also happy for it is through learning that we grow as human beings. In this chapter, we will examine some of the ways in which our experiences influence our behavior as we explore the different types of learning.

Before you continue reading, take a moment to consider this question: What have been the most important learning experiences of your life? Keep these events in mind as you read. Seeing the personal relevance of learning will help you retain this information for your next exam.

HOW DOES LEARNING HELP US?

When you hear the term *learning*, it probably brings to mind studying textbooks and lecture notes in preparation for exams. This isn't surprising because you are, after all, a college student. Much of your life now is spent in the pursuit of this particular type of learning. Although it is true that a lot of learning does occur in school, an extraordinary amount of learning occurs outside the classroom.

Think about it—what have you learned outside school? Here are just a very few of the possibilities. You learned to walk, to speak your native tongue, to have social skills, to have a sense of right and wrong, and possibly to play baseball. Now how did you learn these things? Perhaps you learned by watching others, by listening to others, by reading, or by doing. Learning occurs through a variety of means and in a variety of situations. For psychologists, learning must be defined in terms broad enough to encompass all these types of experiences. That is, **learning** *is a relatively permanent change in behavior or the potential for behavior that results from experience.* Many different types of experiences lead to learning. And, when learning occurs, we are changed. At times learning results in actual behavior change—for example, losing money in a vending machine may make you less likely to put in more money. At other times, learning only gives us additional knowledge but doesn't impact our behavior—for example, watching skiing on TV may give you some knowledge of how to ski, but if you never actually go skiing, this knowledge will not show up in your behavior.

Whether learning impacts our behavior or just increases our knowledge, learning may not remain with us forever. Learning that is routinely exercised tends to stay with us longer than learning that we do not use. For example, knowing how to play childhood games may dwindle as we no longer play these games. But, knowing how to drive a car may stay with us for all of our adulthood. Like many things in life, learning is often a case of use it or lose it.

Carlos Davila/Getty Images

Learning is a relatively permanent change in behavior or the potential for behavior that occurs as a result of experience. This girl is engaged in learning.

In this chapter, we will examine four types of experience that lead to learning—*habituation*, *classical conditioning*, *operant conditioning*, and *observational learning*. As you read about these different types of learning, keep in mind that it is through learning that we gain the knowledge and skills necessary to survive in the world. For example, Michael Gates Gill used his ability to learn to help him adapt to having his world turned upside down by unemployment, illness, and rejection. Likewise, you also use learning to navigate the changes and challenges in your world. We'll begin our quest to understand how we learn by looking at one of the simplest types of learning there is—*habituation*.

Orienting and Habituation: Learning to Ignore

Suppose you are sitting in class, listening to your psychology professor and taking notes. All of a sudden there is a loud banging noise directly outside your classroom. What would your very *first* reaction to the unexpected noise be? If you are like most people, you would immediately stop listening to the lecture and turn your head in the direction of the noise. This very normal response is called an **orienting reflex** (Pavlov, 1927/1960). Orienting reflexes occur when we stop what we are doing to orient our sense organs in the direction of unexpected stimuli.

In our example, the stimulus was auditory, but this doesn't have to be the case. If you were standing in line at the cafeteria and someone poked you in the back, you would most likely turn to see what the person wanted. If you were having dinner in a restaurant and someone began to take pictures using a flash camera, you would likely look in the direction of the flashes of light. In short, we exhibit the orienting reflex to any type of novel stimulus.

TRY THIS DEMONSTRATION

Your course syllabus probably contains some warning about coming to class on time. Here's one reason why—notice what happens to you and your classmates the next time a student comes in late to class. Does everyone automatically look toward the door as the student comes through it? This is also an orienting reflex—one that distracts from your ability to learn the course material.

© Arclight/Alamy

learning a relatively permanent change in behavior or behavior potential as a result of experience

orienting reflex the tendency of a person or animal to orient its senses toward unexpected stimuli

After people live in this house for a while, habituation will ensure that they barely even notice the sounds of the jets like this one as they take off and land.

Why do you think we exhibit orienting reflexes? What is the benefit of automatically paying attention to novel stimuli? If you said "self-protection," you would be correct. Orienting reflexes allow us to quickly gather information about stimuli that could potentially be threatening. For instance, that banging noise in the hallway could be a student dropping her books, or it could be a fight. In the case of a fight, you may want to take steps to ensure that the fight doesn't affect you in a negative way. By orienting your senses toward the event, you can quickly assess what, if any, action is needed to protect yourself.

The benefit of having orienting reflexes is limited, though. Suppose that after looking up at the sound of the banging, you see that it is only a worker hammering as he installs a new bulletin board in the hallway. You would likely return your attention to the psychology lecture. If the banging noise continues, your tendency to look up at the noise in the hall would steadily decrease. In other words, your orienting reflex would diminish over time. This decrease in responding to a stimulus that occurs as the stimulus is repeated over and over is called **habituation**.

Despite its name, habituation does not refer to forming a habit. Instead, habituation ensures that we do not waste our energy and mental resources by responding to irrelevant stimuli. In our previous example, after you have established that the noise in the hallway is not threatening, there is no reason to keep looking up. If you did keep exhibiting the orienting reflex, you would needlessly miss part of your psychology lecture as well as waste energy that could be spent more usefully.

Almost all creatures, including those with very simple nervous systems, seem to have the capacity for habituation (J. D. Harris, 1943). This universality of habituation implies that habituation is the simplest type of learning seen in living things (M. Davis & Egger, 1992). Habituation can be seen in newborn infants (Lavoie & Desrochers, 2002; S. A. Rose, 1980) and even in fetuses (Van Heteren, Boekkooi, Jongsma, & Nijhuis, 2000). Recent studies have suggested that the cerebellum, which is part of the more primitive hindbrain (see Chapter 2), plays a role in certain instances of habituation (Frings et al., 2006). These findings seem to indicate the primitive nature of habituation. Furthermore, because almost all species seem to habituate, it is likely that habituation evolved through *natural selection*. Recall from Chapter 2 that as a result of natural selection, characteristics that promote reproductive success will be retained in a species. It is likely that habituation allowed our ancestors to deal more adaptively with their environment because it allowed them to ignore useless repetitive information.

Habituation allows us to tune out unnecessary stimuli so that we can concentrate on the task at hand.

habituation the tendency of a person or animal to ignore repeated stimuli

Habituation as an Adaptive Asset

To get a better feel for the adaptive value of habituation, imagine what life would be like if you could *not* habituate. Without habituation, you would reflexively respond to every sight, sound, touch, and smell you encountered every time you encountered it. You would not be able to ignore these stimuli. Think of how this would limit your ability to function. Every time the worker hammered the bulletin board in the hall, your attention would move away from the lecture and toward the hall. You certainly would not learn much psychology under these circumstances! With habituation, you get the best of both worlds. You can respond to new, novel stimuli that may pose a danger, and you can also ignore stimuli that have been checked out and deemed to be harmless. Habituation gives you flexibility in that you don't have to continue to respond to a stimulus. But once you have habituated to a stimulus, will you ignore the stimulus forever?

Dishabituation

Another aspect of this flexibility is that you can also stop habituating when the circumstances warrant it. **Dishabituation** occurs when a person or animal begins to respond more intensely to a stimulus to which it had previously habituated. Let's return to our example of the worker in the hallway. Although you find the hammering distracting at first, you soon habituate to the sound. Then after several minutes of ignoring the steady hammering, you hear a new sound. The worker has turned on a radio at a rather high volume. Will you ignore this sound, too? No, you likely will not. Because the quality of the stimulus has changed dramatically, you will dishabituate. You will again find yourself orienting toward the hallway. This new sound is too dissimilar to the hammering, and you have to check it out. Once you recognize that it is the worker's radio (and that it poses no threat), you will likely habituate to this new sound as well as to the hammering.

A change in the quality of the stimulus is not the only thing that can cause dishabituation. So can the passage of time. For instance, if the worker took an hour-long lunch break and then went back to hammering, you might briefly dishabituate to the hammering. This would not last long, however—after just a few bangs of the hammer, you would reenter habituation and return your attention to the lecture. As you can see, adaptive functioning is a balance of responding—habituating and dishabituating at the appropriate time. In addition to helping us function on a daily basis, sometimes habituation principles can be applied to help people who suffer from certain physical problems.

Practical Applications of Habituation

One practical application of habituation is the use of habituation training for people who suffer from chronic motion sickness that may include nausea and intense dizziness, or *vertigo*. Motion sickness can be caused when the brain receives conflicting information from the visual and vestibular systems that you learned about in Chapter 3. These conflicts can be set off by certain movements or exposure to certain stimuli that give the illusion of movement, such as computer displays. For people who suffer from chronic motion sickness, simple tasks like working at a computer may be impossible. Physical therapists often use habituation techniques to help people overcome chronic motion sickness. By repeatedly exposing clients to the stimulation that produces motion sickness, the therapist can gradually train these clients to habituate, or stop responding, to some of the visual and vestibular signals that would normally cause them to feel sick (Yardley & Kirby, 2006). Similar techniques have been used to train figure skaters (Tanguy, Quarck, Etard, Gauthier, & Denise, 2008), pilots, and astronauts to do their jobs without experiencing motion sickness (e.g., Bagshaw, 1985).

Habituation is quite important to everyday life, but it is still a very simple type of learning. Habituation does not explain the bulk of the learning that we engage in during our lifetime, such as learning to play tennis or ride a bike. Nor does habituation explain how we come to associate certain emotions and physiological reactions with certain stimuli, such as learning to fear snakes or feeling happy when we smell Grandma's perfume. For explanations of these more complex events, we will have to turn our attention to more sophisticated and complex types of learning.

dishabituation to begin re-responding to a stimulus to which one had been habituated

Let's REVIEW

In this section, we have given you an overview of learning and a discussion of the simplest type of learning, habituation, and the related concepts of orienting reflexes and dishabituation. For a quick check of your understanding, try answering the following questions at increasing levels of difficulty.

1. Psychologists define learning as _____ .

    a. a change in behavior as a result of experience

    b. a change in the potential for behavior as a result of experience

    c. a relatively permanent change in behavior or the potential for behavior as a result of experience

    d. adding to your knowledge by going to school

2. Which of the following would likely have the capacity for habituation?

    a. a 3-month-old human baby   c. an adult dog

    b. an adult monkey   d. all of the above

3. Habituation describes how one learns to _____.

    a. ski   c. function well despite having vertigo

    b. study with the TV on   d. b and c

ANSWERS 1. c; 2. d; 3. d

CLASSICAL CONDITIONING: CAN WE LEARN THROUGH ASSOCIATION?

The discovery of classical conditioning was something of an accident. In Russia around the turn of the 20th century, a physiologist named Ivan Pavlov (1849–1936) was doing research on the digestive processes of dogs (for which he would eventually win a Nobel Prize). Pavlov was investigating the role that salivation plays in digestion. He had surgically implanted devices in the cheeks of dogs so that he could measure how much saliva they produced. His experimental method was to place the dog in a harness, present the dog with some food, and then measure the amount of saliva the dog produced (see ● FIGURE 5.1).

While conducting these studies, Pavlov noticed that sometimes the dogs began to salivate *before* the food was presented to them. Sometimes the mere sight of the food dish or the sound of the approaching experimenter was enough to produce salivation. So what was going on here? Why would a dog start to salivate when it heard footsteps or saw an empty food bowl? Pavlov reasoned that the dog had learned to *associate* certain cues or stimuli with the presentation of food. To the dog, the approach of footsteps had come to mean that food was soon going to appear. Consequently, the dog had become *conditioned*, or taught, to respond to the footsteps the same way that it responded to the food—by salivating. Unwittingly, Pavlov had discovered a learning process, one that became extremely influential in psychology.

Pavlov began to investigate the learning process itself. He systematically paired different stimuli with food to see which could be conditioned to produce the reflexive

LEARNING OBJECTIVES

What Should You Know?

● Describe Pavlov's paradigm of classical conditioning.

● Define classical conditioning and discuss the factors that affect it.

● Explain how classical conditioning occurs in humans.

● Describe the process through which classically conditioned responses are removed.

FIGURE 5.1

● **Pavlov's Original Experiment** The dog was held in the harness and food was placed before it. The presence of the food (unconditioned stimulus, or US) caused the dog to salivate (unconditioned response, or UR). After a while, cues in the laboratory situation (lights, sounds, or sights) became conditioned stimuli (CS) that also caused the dog to salivate (conditioned response, or CR).

TABLE 5.1
● **Some Examples of US–UR Pairs**

UNCONDITIONED STIMULUS (US)	UNCONDITIONED RESPONSE (UR)	
A puff of air to the eye	Eye blink	
Ingestion of a toxin	Nausea	
Being stuck with a pin	Flinching away from pin	
Sour food placed on the tongue	Salivation	
A light shone in the eye	Pupil contraction	
A blow to the knee	Knee-jerk reflex	

Michael L. Abramson/Time Life Pictures/Getty Images

© David Young-Wolff/PhotoEdit

Jose Luis Pelaez/Getty Images

MedioImages/Photodisc/Getty Images

Altrendo images/Getty Images

Michael Donne/Photo Researchers, Inc.

unconditioned stimulus (US)
a stimulus that naturally elicits a response in a person or animal

unconditioned response (UR)
the response that is elicited by an unconditioned stimulus

neutral stimulus (NS) a stimulus that does not naturally elicit an unconditioned response in a person or animal

conditioned stimulus (CS)
a stimulus that elicits a conditioned response in a person or animal

conditioned response (CR)
the response elicited by a conditioned stimulus in a person or animal

response of salivation. In one of these investigations, Pavlov sounded a buzzer just before he gave the dog some food. He repeated these trials several times while measuring the amount of saliva the dog produced. After repeated pairing of the buzzer and the food, the dog soon began to salivate on hearing the buzzer—even on trials in which *the food was not presented after the buzzer sounded!* The dog had become conditioned to associate the buzzer with the presentation of food. As a result, the buzzer had taken on the same power as food to cause the dog to salivate.

The Elements of Classical Conditioning

This process of learning that Pavlov discovered is commonly referred to as *classical conditioning,* or *Pavlovian conditioning.* We will define it in a minute, but first let's look at the process that produces a conditioned response.

1. *The Unconditioned Stimulus and Response.* In order to classically condition a person or animal, you must begin with a stimulus that naturally and reliably causes some response in the person or animal. Because this stimulus naturally causes the reflexive response, it is referred to as an **unconditioned stimulus (US)**, and the response it evokes is called an **unconditioned response (UR)**. The term *unconditioned* refers to the fact that the association between the stimulus and the response is unlearned. In Pavlov's case, the food was the US and salivation was the UR. You do not need to teach a dog to salivate when food is presented. Instead, salivation occurs naturally when a dog sees food. ● TABLE 5.1 gives some more examples of US–UR pairs that could be used in classical conditioning.

2. *The Neutral Stimulus.* The next step is the selection of a **neutral stimulus (NS)** that does *not* naturally elicit the UR. In Pavlov's case, the NS used was a buzzer. Prior to training or conditioning, a dog would not be likely to salivate when it heard a buzzer. Therefore the buzzer is said to be *neutral.* It has no power to naturally cause the UR.

3. *Pairing the Neutral and Unconditioned Stimuli.* The third step is to systematically pair the neutral stimulus with the unconditioned stimulus. Pavlov accomplished this by repeatedly sounding the buzzer (NS) just prior to presenting the dog with the food (US). Through this repeated association of the US and the NS, the NS eventually loses its neutrality. In Pavlov's case, the dog began to salivate when the buzzer was presented without the food. At this point, classical conditioning had occurred because the buzzer was no longer neutral. The buzzer had become a **conditioned stimulus (CS)** that had the power to produce the **conditioned response (CR)** of salivation (● FIGURE 5.2).

We would define **classical conditioning** as *learning that occurs when a neutral stimulus is paired with an unconditioned stimulus that reliably causes an unconditioned response, and because of this association, the neutral stimulus loses its neutrality and takes on the same power as the unconditioned stimulus to cause the response.* This definition may seem a bit complex, but classical conditioning is actually a fairly simple process. It merely involves learning to associate two stimuli, the unconditioned stimulus and the neutral stimulus. Through this association, the NS becomes a CS (see ● The Big Picture Review, p. 184). In the next section, we will examine some of the factors that affect the strength of the association.

Factors Affecting Classical Conditioning

Exactly what is being learned in classical conditioning? Up to this point, we have sort of skirted around this issue. We said that the person or animal learns to associate the

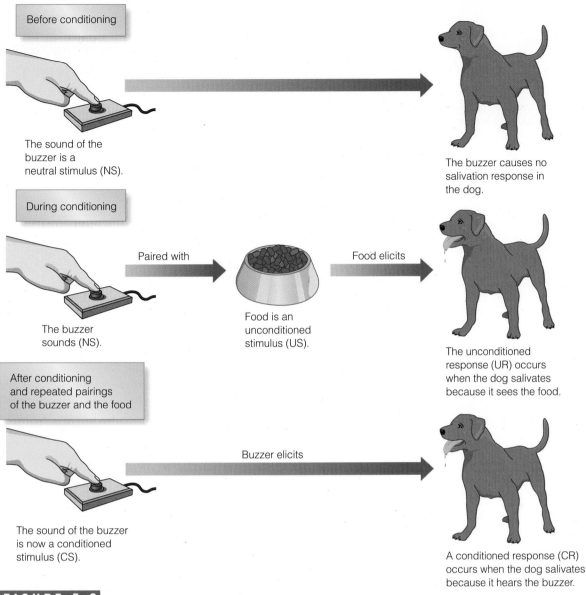

Before conditioning

The sound of the buzzer is a neutral stimulus (NS).

The buzzer causes no salivation response in the dog.

During conditioning

The buzzer sounds (NS).

Paired with

Food is an unconditioned stimulus (US).

Food elicits

The unconditioned response (UR) occurs when the dog salivates because it sees the food.

After conditioning and repeated pairings of the buzzer and the food

The sound of the buzzer is now a conditioned stimulus (CS).

Buzzer elicits

A conditioned response (CR) occurs when the dog salivates because it hears the buzzer.

FIGURE 5.2

● **Pavlov's Classical Conditioning Paradigm** Before conditioning, the neutral stimulus has no power to cause the response. After repeated pairings of the neutral stimulus with an unconditioned stimulus, which naturally elicits an unconditioned response, the neutral stimulus becomes a conditioned stimulus with the power to elicit the response—now called the conditioned response.

NS/CS with the US. This is true, but what is the nature of this association? Why do these two particular stimuli become associated? Why did Pavlov's dog associate the buzzer with the food instead of associating other stimuli from the situation with the food? Why didn't the dog begin to salivate when it heard the laboratory door open, or when the laboratory lights turned on? Why did it wait for the buzzer? To answer these questions, psychological researchers have experimentally examined different facets of the relationship between NS/CS and the US.

Relationship in Time: Contiguity

One variable that emerged from this research as an important factor in classical conditioning is contiguity. **Contiguity** refers to the degree to which the NS/CS and US occur close together in time. Generally speaking, for classical conditioning to occur, the NS/CS and the

classical conditioning learning that occurs when a neutral stimulus is repeatedly paired with an unconditioned stimulus; because of this pairing, the neutral stimulus becomes a conditioned stimulus with the same power as the unconditioned stimulus to elicit the response in the person or animal

contiguity the degree to which two stimuli follow one another in time

The Components of Classical Conditioning

ABBREVIATION	TERM	DEFINITION
US	Unconditioned stimulus	A stimulus that naturally and reliably evokes a response in the person or animal
UR	Unconditioned response	The response that is naturally and reliably elicited by the unconditioned stimulus
NS	Neutral stimulus	A stimulus that does not initially elicit the unconditioned response in the person or animal
CS	Conditioned stimulus	A stimulus that was once neutral, but through association with the unconditioned stimulus, now has the power to elicit the response in the animal or person
CR	Conditioned response	After conditioning has occurred, the response that is elicited in the person or animal by the conditioned stimulus

Forward (delayed) conditioning: CS comes first, but continues until US starts. Conditioning occurs readily.

Forward (trace) conditioning: CS comes first, ends before start of US. Conditioning occurs readily, but response is somewhat weak.

Forward trace conditioning with longer delay: Conditioning is weaker.

Simultaneous conditioning: In most cases, conditioning is weak or hard to demonstrate.

Backward conditioning: After a few repetitions, CS becomes inhibitory—that is, a signal for a time of *absence* of the US, and conditioning is weak.

FIGURE 5.3

● **Possible Placements of the CS and the US in Classical Conditioning**
Relative positions of the CS and US are shown for five different versions of classical conditioning: forward delayed, forward trace, forward trace with longer delay, simultaneous, and backward conditioning.

contingency the degree to which the presentation of one stimulus is contingent on the presentation of the other

US must be separated by only a short period of time (Bangasser, Waxler, Santollo, & Shors, 2006; E. A. Wasserman & Miller, 1997). If the interval between the presentation of the NS/CS and the US is too long, the two stimuli will not be associated and conditioning will not occur. If Pavlov had sounded the buzzer and then 3 hours later given the dog some food, imagine what would have happened. It is very unlikely that the dog would have been conditioned to salivate when it heard the buzzer.

Classic studies have shown that in most cases, if the US lags behind the NS/CS for more than a few seconds, conditioning will not be as strong as it could have been (Church & Black, 1958; Noble & Harding, 1963; M. C. Smith, Coleman, & Gormezano, 1969). However, the exact length of the optimal interval of time between presentation of the NS/CS and the US varies depending on what response is being conditioned (see J. Jones, 1962).

Another aspect of contiguity is the relative placement of the NS/CS and the US in time—in other words, whether the NS/CS precedes the US or follows it. Imagine if Pavlov had first given the dog the food and *then* sounded the buzzer. In that case the dog would not have been as likely to associate the food with the buzzer. ● FIGURE 5.3 shows the five major ways to place the NS/CS and the US in classical conditioning. Of these placements, *delayed conditioning* produces the strongest conditioning, and *backward conditioning* produces the weakest conditioning (S. B. Klein, 1987).

Consistency and Reliability: Contingency

Although contiguity is necessary for conditioning, it alone does not guarantee that conditioning will occur. Conditioning also requires **contingency**, which refers to the degree to which the NS/CS reliably signals that the US is going to be presented. If the NS/CS does not reliably predict the onset of the US, then strong conditioning will not occur (Bolles, 1972; Rescorla, 1967; for review, see D. S. Wheeler & Miller, 2008). For example, if Pavlov had sometimes fed the dog after sounding the buzzer and sometimes fed the dog without sounding the buzzer, conditioning would have been weakened. This inconsistency would not send the dog a clear message that the buzzer meant food was coming. Therefore, the dog would be less likely to salivate on hearing the buzzer. Given that both contiguity and contingency are necessary for strong classical conditioning, the best way to ensure strong conditioning is to consistently present only one NS/CS immediately before presenting the US.

The process of classical conditioning seems a bit complex, doesn't it? It also seems as if it could occur only in a laboratory (where USs and NSs could be systematically paired)—but this is untrue. Classical conditioning occurs frequently in everyday life. In fact, each of us has probably felt the effects of classical conditioning many times. For example, we have been classically conditioned to have certain emotional reactions in our lives. You may feel happy when you smell a perfume that reminds you of your mother. You may feel fear when you see a snake. For a view of what happens inside your brain during classical conditioning, take a look at ● WHAT'S HAPPENING IN YOUR BRAIN?.

As we look at classical conditioning in the real world, keep in mind the general definition of classical conditioning, and try to generate your own examples of real-world classical conditioning. ● TABLE 5.2 gives some helpful tips for identifying classical conditioning situations and understanding the different components they involve.

Real-World Classical Conditioning: What Responses Can Be Classically Conditioned in Humans?

As you will recall, the starting point for classical conditioning is a preexisting US–UR relationship. Because of the nature of most US–UR relationships (see Table 5.1), the types of responses that can be classically conditioned usually fall into two categories: *emotional responses* and *physiological responses*.

TABLE 5.2

● **Tips for Identifying and Analyzing Classical Conditioning Situations**

1. Classical conditioning begins with a US–UR relationship. Because of this requirement, most classical conditioning situations involve the conditioning of *emotional or physiological responses*, such as fear, nausea, happiness, anger, sweating, or salivation.

2. In a classical conditioning situation, *the UR and the CR are the same response*. The only difference is which stimulus elicits this response. For example, in Pavlov's experiment, salivation was the UR when it was caused by the food, but it also was the CR when it was caused by the buzzer.

3. In a classical conditioning situation, *the NS is the same stimulus as the CS*. The only difference is whether or not the stimulus has the power to elicit the response. In Pavlov's experiment, the buzzer began as a neutral stimulus with no power to cause salivation. But after conditioning, it became a CS with the power to cause salivation.

4. In a classical conditioning situation, *the NS/CS is not the same stimulus as the US*. For conditioning to occur, the CS must begin as a neutral stimulus. Because the US is never neutral (it always has the power to cause the response), the CS and the US have to be different stimuli.

WHAT'S HAPPENING IN YOUR BRAIN?

CLASSICAL CONDITIONING IN THE BRAIN

When you receive a puff of air to the eye, you cannot help blinking. Anyone who's had a glaucoma test during an eye exam can attest to this. Because eye blinks are easily elicited, they can also be easily conditioned. In this fMRI, you are looking at the bottom of the brain. The grooved structure to the left of the image is the bottom of the cerebellum. This participant has been classically conditioned to blink when a tone is heard. This was accomplished by presenting a tone (NS/CS) followed by a puff of air to the eye (US) to elicit an eye blink (UR/CR). Activity in the cerebellum was shown to increase (in the region shown in yellow) as the participant came to expect the puff of air after hearing the tone.

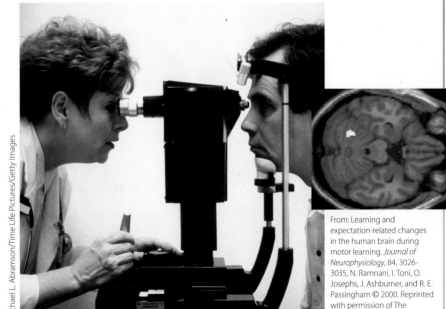

Michael L. Abramson/Time Life Pictures/Getty Images

From: Learning and expectation-related changes in the human brain during motor learning. *Journal of Neurophysiology*, 84, 3026-3035, N. Ramnani, I. Toni, O. Josephs, J. Ashburner, and R. E. Passingham © 2000. Reprinted with permission of The American Physiological Society.

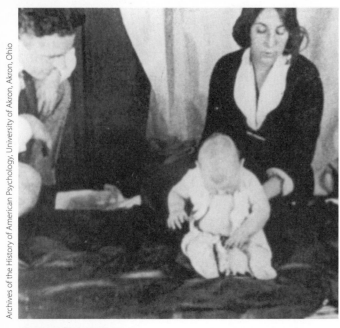

FIGURE 5.4

● **The Little Albert Experiment**
Watson and his assistant, Rosalie Rayner, classically conditioned Albert to fear a white lab rat.

stimulus generalization responding in a like fashion to similar stimuli

Many phobias are classically conditioned responses. A fear-producing encounter with a stimulus can result in the stimulus—a needle—becoming a CS that elicits fear.

Classical Conditioning of Emotional Responses

The classical conditioning of emotional responses was clearly demonstrated in a famous—now infamous—set of experiments conducted by John B. Watson and his student Rosalie Rayner in the early 1900s (Watson & Rayner, 1920). Watson set out to show that classical conditioning could be used to condition fear responses in a child. Because Watson used a 9-month-old boy named Albert, the experiments are now commonly referred to as the "Little Albert" experiments.

In the Little Albert experiments, Watson classically conditioned Albert to fear a white rat. To do this, Watson first gave Albert a white lab rat and allowed him to play with it. In the beginning, the rat was an NS for Albert because it did not cause him to be afraid. A few minutes after giving Albert the rat, Watson made a very loud noise by striking a piece of metal with a hammer. As with most 9-month-olds, a loud noise such as this was a US for Albert that reliably produced the UR of frightening Albert and making him cry. Over and over, Watson repeated this sequence of presenting the rat (NS), then making the noise (US), with the result that Albert would become afraid and cry (UR) (● FIGURE 5.4).

Can you see the parallels here between what Watson and Rayner were doing to Albert and what Pavlov did with his dogs? In the same way that Pavlov conditioned his dogs to salivate at the sound of the buzzer, Watson conditioned Albert to fear a white rat by associating the rat with a frightening noise. After several trials of pairing the noise and the rat, all Watson had to do to get Albert to cry was to show him the rat. Because the rat had been paired with the noise, the rat lost its neutrality and became a CS that was able to evoke the CR of fear.

Emotional reactions such as fear are also classically conditioned outside the laboratory. For example, one of us once had a professor who had an intense fear of bees because earlier in his life, several bees had stung him after he accidentally disturbed a beehive. In this case of classical conditioning, the multiple bee stings were a US that elicited the UR of fear. The bees were initially an NS, but because they were paired with the bee stings, they became a CS that could produce the CR of fear. From that day onward, all the professor had to do was to see a bee to feel intense fear. Classically conditioned emotional responses, such as fear, may provide a protective function for us. Fearing bees may have made the professor more cautious around bees and prevented him from having another, very painful encounter with bees.

In fact, the professor's fear of bees may have protected him from other insects as well. After developing his fear of bees, he soon found that not only was he afraid of bees, he was also afraid of wasps, yellow jackets, and any other flying insect that could sting. In psychological terms, his fear had undergone **stimulus generalization**, which occurs when stimuli that are similar to the CS have the same power to elicit the CR even though they have never been paired with the US. The professor had never been stung by a wasp, yet he feared them because they are similar to bees.

Stimulus generalization also occurred in the Little Albert experiments. After being conditioned to fear the rat, Albert also exhibited fear when presented with a dog, a rabbit, a fur coat, and a fake white Santa Claus beard. His fear of white rats had generalized to several *furry* things (Watson & Rayner, 1920). This may leave you wondering what happened to Little Albert. Unfortunately, Albert's mother withdrew him from the program and moved away before Watson and colleagues could remove the fear they had conditioned in Albert.

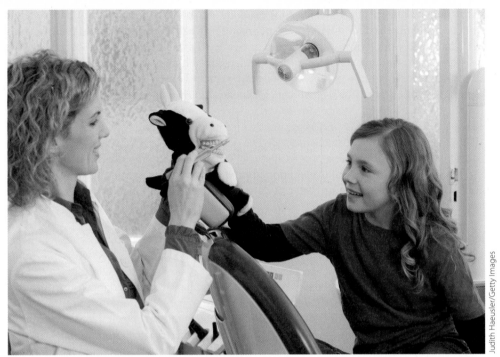

Judith Haeusler/Getty Images

FIGURE 5.5

● **Counterconditioning** Dentists often use counterconditioning to reduce the fear that children feel during dental exams. By associating a trip to the dentist with nonthreatening things, such as stuffed animals and cartoon characters, children become conditioned to feel more positive emotions and less fear at the dentist's office.

A few years after the end of the Little Albert experiments, one of Watson's students, Mary Cover Jones, developed a technique for removing conditioned fears (Klein, 1987). Jones's technique involved gradually moving the fear-producing stimulus closer and closer to the participant while the participant was engaged in some task that made him or her have a positive emotional response, such as reading. By pairing the feared stimulus with positive emotion, Jones reduced the participant's phobia (● FIGURE 5.5). This type of technique is called **counterconditioning** because the participant is slowly classically conditioned to have a positive rather than a negative reaction to the stimulus. Today, *systematic desensitization* is a modern technique for treating phobias that is based on Jones's procedure (Wolpe, 1958; Choy, Fyer, & Lipsitz, 2007). We will explain systematic desensitization in more detail in Chapter 15 when we discuss psychotherapy.

Unfortunately, Albert was unable to benefit from any therapeutic intervention. Having possibly left Albert in a state of fearing furry things violates one of the most important ethical rules of psychology: that researchers should not do lasting

counterconditioning using classical conditioning to remove an undesired conditioned response in a person or animal

For those who handle poisonous and nonpoisonous animals, being able to generalize and discriminate among them is an extremely important ability. Successful, experienced snake handlers, such as Jeff Corwin, treat poisonous snakes with more caution than they treat nonpoisonous ones.

Kevin Winter/Getty Images

harm to their participants. To be fair to Watson and Rayner, it is unknown if Albert suffered from a lasting phobia after leaving the experiment, or whether any conditioned fear generalized in the real world. However, the mere possibility that Albert may have been scarred by his experience warrants serious ethical consideration. Phobias can be debilitating and are some of the most common psychological disorders in the United States. In one study of more than 18,000 Americans, 19.9% of African Americans, 12.7% of Hispanics, 11.5% of European Americans, and 6.6% of Asians were found to have suffered from the symptoms of a phobia although they may not have been diagnosed with a phobic disorder (A. Y. Zhang & Snowden, 1999). In addition, a more recent study of 8,205 people 65 and older found that 6.05% of them had actually had a diagnosable phobia at some point in their lifetime (K. L. Chou, 2009).

However, not all classically conditioned responses will generalize. The opposite process, **stimulus discrimination**, often occurs. In stimulus discrimination, the CR occurs in response to a particular CS, but it does *not* occur in response to other stimuli that are similar to the CS. For instance, a woman who works in the reptile house at the zoo is probably not afraid of most snakes, but if she found herself face-to-face with a poisonous king cobra, she would likely feel afraid. In other words, she has learned to discriminate between poisonous and nonpoisonous snakes. For her, this discrimination is very useful. It allows her to do her job without constant fear, but it also allows her to protect herself in truly dangerous situations.

Although conditioned fear may serve to protect us from harm by motivating us to avoid certain dangers, positive emotions can also be classically conditioned. For example, Michael Gates Gill has positive emotional reactions to Starbucks. Cues associated with Starbucks may act as CSs for Mike because they were associated with other stimuli that brought about positive emotional feelings in him. Consider a hypothetical example: smelling Starbucks coffee (NS/CS) makes Mike feel happy (UR/CR) because he has associated this scent with the respect and friendship the Starbucks employees gave him (US). Many of our reactions are the result of real-world classical conditioning. Given this, can classical conditioning be used to intentionally control our reactions to certain stimuli? In other words, is classical conditioning useful in everyday life?

Many advertisers use classical conditioning to get consumers to respond positively to their products. For example, television ads often use images of beautiful people, adorable animals, and beautiful scenery to sell products (Pleyers, Corneille, Luminet, & Yzerbyt, 2007). The hope here is that the positive emotions (UR) elicited by these images (US) will become CRs that are elicited by the product (NS/CS). If you feel warm and fuzzy about the product, you may be more likely to buy it.

Evidence suggests that this application of classical conditioning does indeed work. In fact, classically conditioned positive emotions can have a greater impact on consumers' attitudes about a product than does actual knowledge about the product. This is especially true when exposure to the product has been limited (Greenvale, Jeen-Su, & Mukesh, 1998). For example, even if you are not a beer drinker, you may feel happy when you see a store display for a particular brand of beer because you associate this brand with a cute, funny animal from the beer commercials on TV. With little firsthand knowledge of the product (you don't drink beer), this positive emotion might be just enough to get you to buy this brand for your next party. No wonder companies spend so much money developing ads that will make us feel good.

stimulus discrimination responding only to particular stimuli

---

By making them laugh, the Geico Gecko may classically condition consumers to feel good about Geico Insurance. This positive emotion, in turn, may influence their future decisions about car insurance.

© Tony Freeman/PhotoEdit

Classical Conditioning of Physiological Responses: The Special Case of Taste Aversion

Emotions are not the only things that can be classically conditioned. Pavlov's original demonstrations of classical conditioning show a physiological response, salivation. But what other kinds of physiological responses can be classically conditioned? Table 5.1 (p. 182) gives a list of some of the US–UR relationships that could form the basis of classical conditioning. Of these, one of the most important and common is the classical conditioning of nausea.

Have you ever eaten a food that you liked and soon after become sick to your stomach with the flu, food poisoning, motion sickness, or some other ailment? Then, after recovering from your sickness, did you find the sight, smell, or even the idea of that food nauseating? If you answered yes to both of these questions, you have experienced what psychologists call classically conditioned **taste aversion**, also known as the *Garcia effect* in tribute to psychologist John Garcia, who did much of the classic work on this type of learning.

One of the authors can vividly remember going through this type of conditioning as a child. After she ate a big dessert of peppermint ice cream, she came down with a severe case of tonsillitis that was accompanied by nausea and vomiting. After she recovered from the tonsillitis, it was *years* before she could even think about peppermint ice cream without feeling queasy. The same author regularly holds an informal contest in her classes to see who has had the longest-running taste aversion. The current record stands at more than 20 years!

It seems that taste aversion is something that we learn with particular ease (Garcia & Koelling, 1966). Taste aversion is unique in two ways. First, it often occurs with only one pairing of the NS/CS and the US. Unlike most cases of classical conditioning, in taste aversion a single pairing of the food (NS/CS) and the virus (US) is usually sufficient to cause strong conditioning. The second difference is that in taste aversion, the interval between the NS/CS and the US can be very long. Intervals as long as 24 hours can result in conditioning (Garcia, Ervin, & Koelling, 1966; Logue, 1979). Because taste aversion is an exception to some of the rules of conditioning, some psychologists believe that our genes biologically predispose or prepare us to learn taste aversion easily (M. E. P. Seligman, 1970; Yamamoto, 2008).

By learning taste aversion easily, we are better able to avoid certain poisonous plants and substances. Once something has made us sick, we want no part of it in the future. No doubt the ability to learn taste aversion quickly and consequently avoid poisonous substances has survival value. Therefore, through natural selection, genes that enabled our ancestors to learn taste aversion quickly would have been retained because animals with those genes— human and nonhuman—would have lived whereas those with a sluggish response to taste aversion would likely die. Taste aversion is widely seen in many species of animals (Garcia, 1992).

In one famous study, Garcia and colleagues showed that taste aversion can be used to help control the pesky nature of some animals (Gustavson & Garcia, 1974). In the western United States, coyotes often sneak into sheep pastures and kill sheep rather than hunt for food in the wild. Decades ago, frustrated sheep ranchers would be very tempted to either shoot the coyotes on sight or poison them. Garcia suggested a more humane and ecologically sound alternative—using taste aversion to condition the coyotes to dislike sheep as a food source. As part of the study, a few sheep were slaughtered and their carcasses were treated with a chemical that causes nausea in coyotes. The tainted carcasses were then left out for the coyotes to eat. Because coyotes can't pass up a free meal, they ate the sheep and got very sick to their stomachs. After they recovered, they wanted nothing to do with sheep because of conditioned taste aversion, giving today's ranchers a nonviolent solution to the coyote problem.

taste aversion classical conditioning that occurs when a person or animal pairs the experience of nausea with a certain food and becomes conditioned to feel ill at the sight, smell, or idea of the food

Coyotes like these were classically conditioned to have taste aversion for sheep meat. This conditioning provided a nonviolent, ecologically sound way for ranchers and coyotes to coexist in harmony.

Charles Volkland/PhotoLibrary

TRY THIS
DEMONSTRATION

You can use taste aversion to help yourself eat more healthily. Think of a food that you frequently overindulge in, but wish you wouldn't (e.g., pizza, candy). Several times a day, imagine a delicious serving of this food. While thinking of this food, also think of something disgusting such as a bunch of worms squirming on your chosen food. If you repeat this procedure for several weeks, you may find yourself less motivated to indulge in this food. In a different approach, psychologists have classically conditioned children to like healthful vegetables by pairing new vegetable flavors (NS/CS) with the flavor of sugar (US) to produce liking (UR/CR) (Havermans & Jansen, 2007).

© Martyn F. Chilmaid/Photo Researchers, Inc.

Hangovers are nature's way of discouraging future intoxication. If you experience a hangover after getting drunk, alcohol may become a conditioned stimulus for nausea. This classically conditioned taste aversion may help ensure that you do not drink to excess again in the future.

Aversion can also be used to treat alcoholism. The idea behind this **aversion therapy** is to condition a taste aversion to alcohol (S. Ross & Peselow, 2009). The client takes the drug Antabuse. If he or she then drinks alcohol, the result is intense nausea and headache, which often leads to conditioned taste aversion. Aversion therapy has been shown to be modestly helpful in motivating people with alcoholism to remain abstinent (J. W. Smith, Frawley, & Polissar, 1997). However, it does not represent a "cure" for alcoholism. In one study, only 20% of the people with alcoholism who were tested remained abstinent for 1 year after being treated with aversion therapy alone (Landabaso et al., 1999). So although aversion therapy may be a useful part of a comprehensive treatment program, it should not be the only treatment used for alcoholism (Finn, 2003; R. R. Hunt, 2002).

The failure of aversion therapy to reliably produce long-term avoidance of alcohol indicates that although taste aversion is often an enduring type of learning, it doesn't necessarily last forever. What do you think causes the conditioned aversion to disappear? Or, more generally, what brings about the end of any classically conditioned response?

Extinction of Classically Conditioned Responses

Let's assume that you had the misfortune of developing a classically conditioned taste aversion to your favorite food because you ate this food just before you became ill with the flu. Furthermore, let's assume that you wanted to be able to eat your favorite food again without feeling sick to your stomach. How would you go about ridding yourself of your acquired taste aversion? One way would be to force yourself to eat the food over and over again. At first, you would feel nauseated because of the conditioning, but if you continued to eat the food, your conditioned nausea would eventually decrease, or undergo **extinction**.

In classical conditioning, extinction can be brought about by presenting the CS to the participant without also presenting the US. In our example, extinction would begin when you ate your favorite food (CS) and you did not have the flu (US). When the CS is presented alone, it no longer predicts the onset of the US, and the CR decreases. Years later, the author finally got over her taste aversion to peppermint ice cream after she took a job in a restaurant that sold a great deal of it. After scooping many scoops of peppermint ice cream, she found that the sight and smell of it no longer made her feel sick. It wasn't long before she was even able to eat peppermint ice cream without a problem.

Recently, some have argued that habituation may also play a role in extinction (McSweeney & Swindell, 2002). According to this argument, repeated exposure to the CS causes one to habituate to it. As long as you ignore the stimulus, it is less likely to elicit a response from you, and extinction ensues. But what if you have trouble ignoring the CS? One recent study

aversion therapy a type of therapy that uses classical conditioning to condition people to avoid certain stimuli

extinction the removal of a conditioned response

found that characteristically anxious children exhibited more fear while habituating to a loud sound than nonanxious children did. The anxious children also showed slower extinction of their fear of the sound, suggesting that personality factors may affect both habituation and extinction (Liberman, Lipp, Spence, & March, 2006).

Pavlov's experiments with dogs also included extinction trials with the dogs. ● FIGURE 5.6 shows the **acquisition**, or learning, curve for the CR and the extinction curve for the CR in Pavlov's experiment. As you can see from this figure, the CR of salivation to the buzzer was acquired over several trials in which the CS and the US were paired. In the extinction trials, the buzzer was sounded but no food was presented, and there was a fairly steady decrease in the CR. In other words, the dog became less and less likely to salivate when it heard the buzzer. **Does this mean that once a response has been extinguished, it is gone forever?**

The extinction curve in Figure 5.6 does not show a completely continuous pattern of decrease in the CR. Sometimes, after a response has been extinguished, there will be a temporary increase in the CR. This phenomenon, called **spontaneous recovery**, can occur at any point during extinction (e.g., Troisi, 2003) and may be especially likely when a response is extinguished immediately after it is originally learned (Huff, Hernandez, Blanding, & LaBar, 2009). Let's go back to our example of taste aversion for peppermint ice cream. Today, although your author does not have an active, ongoing taste aversion for peppermint ice cream, every now and again when she thinks of peppermint ice cream, she will feel a bit sick. Thankfully, her spontaneous recovery doesn't last long. She soon reenters extinction, and she can think of peppermint ice cream and even eat it without a trace of nausea.

What do you suppose would happen if she happened to eat some peppermint ice cream on a hot day and suffered from a *small* amount of heat-induced nausea? Do you think her taste aversion to peppermint ice cream would return? It is likely that it would. In fact, responses that are extinguished are usually reacquired more easily than they were in the first place. Extinction does *not* mean that we forget that there once was a connection between the CS and the US; it simply means that the CR is less likely to occur when the CS is presented.

So far, we have seen that learning can occur through habituation and classical conditioning. Habituation explains how we learn to ignore familiar stimuli, and classical conditioning explains how we come to have certain emotional and physiological responses to stimuli. Both of these types of learning occur frequently and are important to our ability to function, but together they do not explain all behaviors. For example, neither habituation nor classical conditioning can explain how we learn to drive a car or how a child learns to clean his room every day. To understand how we acquire these types of behavior, we will have to explore other types of learning.

acquisition the process of learning a conditioned response or behavior

spontaneous recovery during extinction, the tendency for a conditioned response to reappear and strengthen over a brief period before reextinguishing

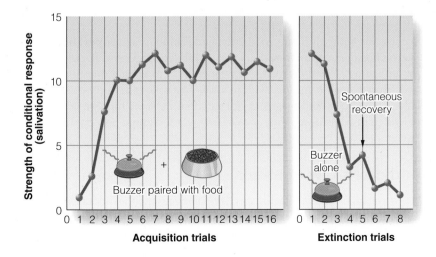

FIGURE 5.6

● **The Phases of Classical Conditioning** These plots show the number of conditioning trials on the *x* axis and the strength of the conditioned response on the *y* axis. During acquisition, the response increases in strength as a function of the number of times the CS and US have been paired together. During extinction, the CS is presented without the US, which leads to a decrease in the strength of the CR. Note that during extinction, sometimes there is a temporary, sharp increase in the strength of the CR despite the fact that the CS has not been recently presented with the US. This is called spontaneous recovery.

Let's REVIEW

In this section, we have given you a brief overview of some of the important issues in classical conditioning. For a quick check of your understanding, try answering the following questions at increasing levels of difficulty.

1. In Pavlov's original studies with the dog, the food was the_____.

a. US

b. UR

c. CS

d. CR

2. In classical conditioning, which of the following is most closely related to the NS?

a. US

b. CS

c. UR

d. CR

3. Janna, a real-estate agent, desperately wants to sell a home. She tells the owner to place a pan of vanilla extract in the oven and heat it just before the prospective buyers arrive to look at the house. Janna knows that the smell of vanilla in the house will increase the chance that the buyers will like the house because they have been classically conditioned to respond favorably to the smell of vanilla. In this example, what is the CR?

a. the pleasant emotions evoked by the smell of vanilla

b. the smell of vanilla

c. the memory of Grandma baking cookies at Christmas

d. the house

ANSWERS 1. a; 2. b; 3. a

operant conditioning a type of learning in which the person or animal learns through the consequences of its behavior

LEARNING OBJECTIVES

What Should You Know?

- Explain how classical conditioning and operant conditioning differ.
- Explain the law of effect and the experiments that led to its discovery.
- Describe the contributions that B. F. Skinner made to the study of operant conditioning.
- Describe the phases of operant conditioning.
- Describe the factors that affect the process of operant conditioning.
- Describe generalization, discrimination, and shaping as they relate to operant conditioning.
- Describe the decisions that must be made when applying operant conditioning in the real world.

law of effect a principle discovered by E. L. Thorndike that states that random behaviors that lead to positive consequences will be strengthened and random behaviors that lead to negative consequences will be weakened

OPERANT CONDITIONING: WHAT DO WE LEARN FROM THE CONSEQUENCES OF OUR ACTIONS?

Suppose you are sitting in your psychology class, listening to a lecture, when your professor asks the class a question. For some reason, you raise your hand to answer the question even though you have never made a comment in this class before. The professor calls on you, and you give the correct answer. In response to your answer, the professor smiles broadly and praises you for giving such an accurate and insightful answer.

How do you think this scenario would affect you? As a result of the professor's reaction, would you be more or less likely to raise your hand in the future when she asked a question? If you are like most people, this type of praise would indeed encourage you to raise your hand in the future. But what would happen if instead of praising you, she frowned and said that your answer was one of the stupidest she had ever heard? How would this reaction affect your behavior? Obviously, after such a cruel response, many of us would be very unlikely to answer any more questions in that professor's class.

Both of these examples illustrate another type of learning, called **operant conditioning**. *In operant conditioning, we learn from the consequences of our behavior.* In our example, being praised for answering a question makes one more likely to answer questions in the future; being called "stupid" makes one less likely to answer future questions. We will see that operant conditioning is a powerful means of learning that explains how we learn many of the important lessons in our lives. But first, we will begin by looking at how operant conditioning was discovered.

E. L. Thorndike's Law of Effect

At about the same time that Ivan Pavlov was developing his theories about learning in Russia, American psychologist E. L. Thorndike (1874–1949) was busy conducting experiments on operant conditioning in New York. Thorndike was working with cats in specially constructed *puzzle boxes.* A puzzle box is a box with a lid or door that locks into place so that an animal can be locked inside. Once inside the box, the animal must activate some type of unlatching device to win its release. The device that unlatches the lid may be a rope pull, a pedal that needs to be pushed, or a switch that needs to be flipped. ● FIGURE 5.7 shows a typical puzzle box with a foot-pedal release.

In his research, E. L. Thorndike (1898) locked a hungry cat in one of these puzzle boxes and placed some food outside the box. Then he recorded how long it took the cat to figure out how to get out of the box. Once the cat activated the device and got out of the box, Thorndike would take the cat and place it back in the puzzle box. Over and over, Thorndike repeated this procedure of imprisoning the cat and measuring the time it took the cat to win its release.

Thorndike observed in these studies that when the cat was first placed in the puzzle box, it thrashed around randomly until, by accident, it tripped the mechanism and got out of the box. However, after several more trials, the cat's behavior became less random, and the time it took to get out of the box declined. This decrease in the amount of time it took the cat to get out of the box indicated to Thorndike that *learning* was taking place: The cat was learning to associate its behavior with the consequences that its behavior brought about.

Based on what he observed in his puzzle box studies, Thorndike developed a principle of learning that he called the **law of effect**. *The law of effect states that in a given situation, behaviors that lead to positive, satisfying consequences will be strengthened, such that the next time the situation occurs, the behavior is more likely to be repeated. In addition, the law of effect states that in a given situation, behaviors that lead to negative, discomforting consequences will be weakened, such that the next time the situation occurs, the behavior will be less likely repeated* (Thorndike, 1905).

Reinforcement

Let's examine the law of effect in terms of a hungry cat in a puzzle box. When the cat is first trapped in the box, it will likely perform many random behaviors. For instance, it may claw, hiss, bite at the bars, roll over on its back, or meow. But none of these behaviors will open the box. The cat's early responses to being stuck in the box are random or "trial-and-error." After some time, let's say that the cat happens to step on the foot pedal that opens the puzzle box and is able to get out to where the food is waiting. This particular random behavior has led to a consequence that is far more rewarding than any of the other random behaviors the cat has tried. The law of effect states that this particular response is strengthened, or *reinforced*, because it was instrumental in evoking a reward. This process of **reinforcement** means that the rewarded behavior will become more likely in the future. The next time the cat is locked in the box, it will be more likely to step on the pedal than to try the other behaviors that did not lead to release on prior trials. Over many trials, the law of effect results in the cat's becoming more and more likely to step on the pedal and less and less likely to use other behaviors that were not reinforced in the past. The behaviors that were not rewarded—and therefore not reinforced—are likely to die out (see ● FIGURE 5.8).

Positive and Negative Reinforcement

The two types of reinforcement are *positive reinforcement* and *negative reinforcement* (see ● FIGURE 5.9). In **positive reinforcement**, the behavior leads to the *addition* of something pleasant to the person or animal's environment. For instance, Thorndike positively reinforced the cat for stepping on the pedal by giving the cat food when it got out of the puzzle box.

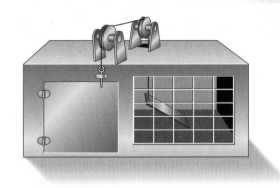

FIGURE 5.7

● **Puzzle Box** This is an example of a puzzle box like those used by Thorndike. To get out of the box, the cat would have to pull the string or step on the pedal.

reinforcement the strengthening of a response that occurs when the response is rewarded

positive reinforcement strengthening a behavior by adding something pleasant to the environment of the person or animal

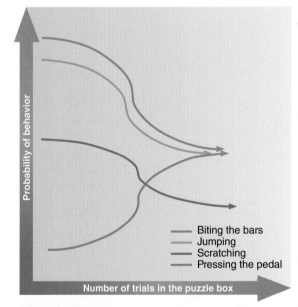

FIGURE 5.8

● **Reinforcement of a Successful Response in a Puzzle Box Experiment** The law of effect predicts that behaviors that lead to positive consequences will be strengthened whereas behaviors that fail to do so will weaken and be eliminated. Over the trials of Thorndike's study, the cats became successively less likely to engage in nonproductive behaviors—biting at the bars and jumping up and down—and more likely to engage in pressing the pedal.

FIGURE 5.9

● **The Four Types of Consequences of Behavior** Reinforcement increases the likelihood of a behavior; punishment decreases it.

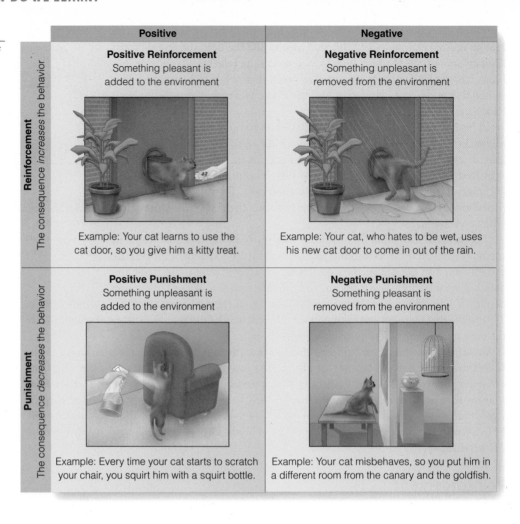

	Positive	Negative
Reinforcement *The consequence increases the behavior*	**Positive Reinforcement** Something pleasant is added to the environment Example: Your cat learns to use the cat door, so you give him a kitty treat.	**Negative Reinforcement** Something unpleasant is removed from the environment Example: Your cat, who hates to be wet, uses his new cat door to come in out of the rain.
Punishment *The consequence decreases the behavior*	**Positive Punishment** Something unpleasant is added to the environment Example: Every time your cat starts to scratch your chair, you squirt him with a squirt bottle.	**Negative Punishment** Something pleasant is removed from the environment Example: Your cat misbehaves, so you put him in a different room from the canary and the goldfish.

In **negative reinforcement**, the behavior is rewarded by the *removal* of something unpleasant from the person or animal's environment. In Thorndike's case, the cat was negatively reinforced for stepping on the pedal because this behavior led to the removal of its imprisonment in the puzzle box. We are, of course, assuming that the hungry cat did *not* enjoy being trapped in the box.

The difference between *punishment* and negative reinforcement is a point that gives many students great trouble because they tend to think that negative reinforcement is a type of punishment. This is not the case. The "negative" in negative reinforcement refers to the fact that negative reinforcement *removes* something from the person's or animal's environment; it does not refer to a negative or unpleasant consequence of the behavior. When you see the term *reinforcement*, keep in mind that reinforcement leads to an *increase* in behavior. **Punishment**, on the other hand, is an unpleasant consequence that leads to a *decrease* in behavior. (We'll discuss punishment in more detail in a moment.)

A Japanese View of Reinforcement

The United States, like many Western cultures, is an *individualistic* society; people are judged on their individual accomplishments in life. To be successful in America, you must show that you have accomplished something of value—a prestigious job, an ability or talent that few others have, and so on. In Japan (and several other Asian cultures), accomplishments of the individual are not valued nearly as much as accomplishments of the *group*. For this reason, Japan is referred to as a *collectivistic* culture. To be successful in Japan, you must show that you have helped the group succeed. For example, a successful employee helps his company achieve prestige and financial gain; his success is not measured by how much he, as an individual, attains.

negative reinforcement strengthening a behavior by removing something unpleasant from the environment of the person or animal

punishment the weakening of a response that occurs when a behavior leads to an unpleasant consequence

Given that psychologists are influenced by the cultures in which they live, it is understandable that our U.S. view of what is reinforcing and punishing reflects a bias toward individualistic rewards and punishments. So how might a Japanese psychologist view the concept of reinforcement in a collectivistic culture?

Researcher Yutaka Haruki has developed a theory of *human reinforcement* that describes additional consequences that are reinforcing. Haruki's reinforcements go beyond the Western notions of positive and negative reinforcement (Ogawa & Haruki, 2002; Haruki, 2000; Haruki, Shigehisa, Nedate, Wajima, & Ogawa, 1984), and his theory does not apply to nonhuman reinforcement because it reflects the values found in a collectivistic human society. According to Haruki's human reinforcement theory, there are four types of consequences that reinforce human behavior:

External reinforcement (oshitsuke): You are rewarded by someone else with either positive or negative reinforcement. For example, a parent gives a child a new toy for earning a good grade on an exam.

Self-reinforcement (makase): You reward yourself—with either positive or negative reinforcement—for your own behavior. For example, you buy yourself a new CD or allow yourself to skip a day at the gym for doing well on an exam.

Internal reinforcement (uketome): You reward someone else for your own behavior. For example, you shake your professor's hand after earning an A in the professor's course.

Alien reinforcement (mitome): You reward yourself when someone else engages in a desired behavior. For example, you may be proud when your child scores a soccer goal. If your child accepts that you are proud of this behavior, the child is also rewarded.

The Japanese view of conditioning emphasizes the role that the opinions and actions of others play in reinforcing a person's behavior. This is what one would expect to see in a collectivistic culture, in which one's behavior is judged not on an individual basis, but rather on how that behavior affects the group. Numerous studies done by Yutaka Haruki and colleagues (for a review, see Haruki, 2000) have indicated that Japanese children can be conditioned by these types of reinforcement. Interestingly, Haruki and Shigehisa (cited in Triandis, 1994, p. 35) found that although Americans can be conditioned by both external and alien reinforcement, Americans learn best through external reinforcement. It appears that culture can influence what we find reinforcing.

Punishment

As you can see from Figure 5.9, punishment also comes in two varieties. **Positive punishment** occurs when a behavior results in the *addition* of something *unpleasant* to the person's or animal's environment. For example, a puzzle box could be rigged to electrify the floor of the cage every time the cat stepped on the pedal. The cat would then be positively punished every time it stepped on the pedal because the resulting shock would add pain to the cat's environment.

In **negative punishment**, the behavior leads to the *removal* of something *pleasant* from the person's or animal's environment. A puzzle box could be rigged so that when the cat presses the pedal, a drape falls over the cage, and the cat can no longer see outside the cage. If the cat enjoys seeing outside the cage, then stepping on the pedal would lead to negative punishment because it leads to the loss of a pleasant privilege for the cat. The effect of punishment is to decrease a behavior, regardless of whether the punishment is positive or negative.

How Do Classical and Operant Conditioning Differ?

You may be wondering how operant conditioning differs from classical conditioning. In the real world, classical and operant conditioning often occur simultaneously (Bitterman, 2006). So, it is very important that you learn to distinguish between these two types of learning. One way operant conditioning differs from classical conditioning is that in classical conditioning, the person or animal plays a rather passive role. A US naturally evokes a UR, and learning occurs because a CS is paired with the US. The person or animal doesn't have to actively do anything; it merely responds reflexively to the stimuli, just as Pavlov's dogs naturally salivated

positive punishment weakening a behavior by adding something unpleasant to the person's or animal's environment

negative punishment weakening a behavior by removing something pleasant from the person's or animal's environment

when food was presented. In operant conditioning, however, the person or animal plays a more active role. The person or animal has to *first* engage in some nonreflexive behavior before learning can occur. In our example, the student had to first answer a question in class before any operant conditioning could occur (see p. 192). There is no US that will reliably cause a student to answer a question in class. The student must decide to answer on her own.

Another difference between classical and operant conditioning is that in classical conditioning, there is one clear response that is required of the person or animal. For example, in Pavlov's experiments the food would cause only salivation in the dog. Therefore, the only response that could be conditioned in this case would be salivation. In operant conditioning, the person or animal may engage in any number of responses. For instance, while sitting in class, a student could answer the professor's question, not answer it, sleep, read a book, and so on. Any of these responses *could* be operantly conditioned to become stronger, but only if it evokes positive consequences from the environment.

A final difference is in the types of responses conditioned through these two processes. As you will recall, emotional and physiological responses tend to be classically conditioned. In operant conditioning, the responses that are conditioned tend to be more complex behaviors as opposed to simple emotional or physiological reactions. Operant conditioning can explain things as complex as how a student learns to freely answer questions in class or how a child learns to speak politely in public. Classical conditioning cannot account for these types of learning because there is no US that will evoke these types of responses, and without a preexisting US–UR relationship, there can be no classical conditioning.

As you study this material and prepare for your exams, keep in mind the important ways that classical and operant conditioning differ from each other. Keeping the points that distinguish these two types of learning foremost in your thoughts as you study and take exams can only help you succeed!

B. F. Skinner and Operant Responses

One psychologist who was concerned with clearly distinguishing operant conditioning from classical conditioning was B. F. Skinner (1904–1990). Although E. L. Thorndike is generally credited with beginning the experimental study of operant conditioning, Skinner is more commonly associated with this type of learning. Skinner began to formally study operant conditioning in the late 1920s when he was a graduate student at Harvard University. During his long career—from the 1920s to the 1990s—Skinner made many significant contributions to our understanding of operant conditioning (Schultz & Schultz, 2000). Perhaps some of Skinner's most obvious contributions were to introduce new terminology and technology to the study of this type of learning.

Skinner actually introduced the term *operant* to the study of this type of conditioning. When E. L. Thorndike first wrote the law of effect, he referred to learning from the consequences of behavior as *instrumental conditioning* because behavior was "instrumental" in obtaining certain consequences. Yet, Skinner felt that the term *operant* better distinguished this type of learning from classical conditioning than the term *instrumental* did. Skinner wanted to emphasize the fact that in classical conditioning, the person or animal does not actively choose to operate on the environment to produce some consequence; rather, the response is forced from the animal.

In contrast, Skinner wanted to emphasize that in operant conditioning, the animal makes a choice to respond to its environment in a certain way. Therefore, Skinner chose to refer to instrumental behavior as **operant behavior**—behavior that *operates* on the environment to produce some consequence (Skinner, 1938). Today, most psychologists take their lead from B. F. Skinner, using the term *operant conditioning*.

Another of Skinner's contributions to the study of operant conditioning was the method he developed for studying animal behavior. Skinner felt that Thorndike's use of puzzle boxes required too much time for each trial. It took the animal a long time to figure out how to open the box and receive its reward, which limited the number of trials that could be run in a given experiment and caused problems for researchers because the animal might get tired before it had completed enough trials to be conditioned. To solve this problem,

operant behavior behavior that operates on the environment to cause some sort of consequence to occur

Skinner constructed an apparatus that allowed him to study the operant conditioning of a simpler response. This device, now called a **Skinner box**, is a chamber large enough to house a small animal, typically a rat (● FIGURE 5.10). Inside the chamber is a lever or bar that the rat can press down. When the animal depresses the lever or bar, it receives reinforcement in the form of a pellet of food from an automatic feeding device attached to the chamber. Skinner boxes are also built for pigeons; the pigeon receives a reward by pecking at a disk on the side of the box.

To study operant behavior, Skinner would place a hungry rat in the Skinner box and wait for the rat to accidentally press the bar. Once the rat pressed the bar, a pellet would drop into the chamber to reinforce this operant behavior. The rat was free to press the bar as often as it wanted and whenever it wanted. By recording the number of bar presses and when they occurred, Skinner could get a good picture of the acquisition of the operant behavior. Using the Skinner box, researchers have been able to learn a great deal about the different aspects of operant conditioning. This advance in the methodology and apparatus for studying animal learning is one of B. F. Skinner's major contributions to psychology. Skinner box technology has also been adapted for use in developing educational toys. For a look at some of these modern "Skinner boxes," see ● TECHNOLOGY AND BEHAVIOR.

Acquisition and Extinction

Two areas that Skinner explored were acquisition and extinction. You may recall from our discussion of classical conditioning that acquisition refers to the conditioning of a response and extinction refers to the loss of a conditioned response. As in classical conditioning, it is possible to plot acquisition and extinction curves for operantly conditioned behaviors. The rat learns that pressing the bar leads to obtaining food, and its tendency to press the bar increases. However, the rat can eat the pellets only so fast. Therefore, the number of times the rat will press the bar in a given time frame is limited by the speed at which it eats (● FIGURE 5.11).

Extinction also occurs in operant conditioning, but it is caused by circumstances that differ from those that cause extinction in classical conditioning. In classical conditioning, extinction occurs because the CS is presented without the US. In operant conditioning, extinction occurs because the behavior is no longer reinforced (see Figure 5.11). Many of us hold jobs, and going to work is an example of an operantly conditioned response. We

Photo Researchers, Inc. (both)

FIGURE 5.10

● **Skinner Box** In these operant chambers the animals can be reinforced with food for pressing the bar or pecking the disk. Skinner boxes like these allow researchers to efficiently gather data on operant conditioning.

FIGURE 5.11

● **Acquisition and Extinction in Operant Conditioning** Just as we saw in classical conditioning, operant responses can also undergo acquisition, extinction, and reacquisition.

Skinner box a device created by B. F. Skinner to study operant behavior in a compressed time frame; in a Skinner box, an animal is automatically rewarded or punished for engaging in certain behaviors

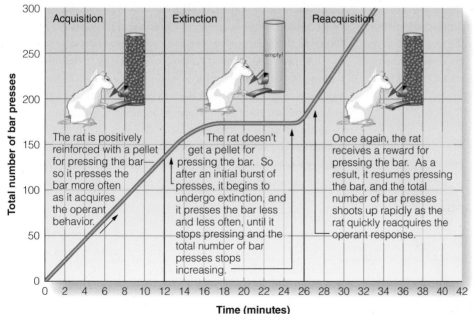

The Phases of Operant Conditioning

Acquisition — The rat is positively reinforced with a pellet for pressing the bar—so it presses the bar more often as it acquires the operant behavior.

Extinction — The rat doesn't get a pellet for pressing the bar. So after an initial burst of presses, it begins to undergo extinction, and it presses the bar less and less often, until it stops pressing and the total number of bar presses stops increasing.

empty!

Reacquisition — Once again, the rat receives a reward for pressing the bar. As a result, it resumes pressing the bar, and the total number of bar presses shoots up rapidly as the rat quickly reacquires the operant response.

Total number of bar presses

Time (minutes)

TECHNOLOGY and BEHAVIOR

ARE LEAP PADS, PLAYSTATIONS, AND XBOXES THE SKINNER BOXES OF THE 21ST CENTURY?

In 1958, B. F. Skinner wrote an article, entitled *Teaching Machines,* in which he argued that psychologists and educators should apply their understanding of operant conditioning to develop devices that would allow children to learn at their own pace (Skinner, 1958). In Skinner's view, these teaching machines would present the learner with a question or task to answer or complete. If the learner's answer was correct, the machine would allow her to advance to the next question, thereby reinforcing the learner for getting the correct answer. If the learner's answer was incorrect, she would not be allowed to advance until she provided the right answer, thus withholding reinforcement for the incorrect response.

Before advanced computer technology became part of everyday life, such teaching machines were elaborate and cumbersome to construct. The personal computer changed all this. Today, we have abundant examples of these "teaching machines," although we rarely refer to them as such. They are now known as *Leap Pads, Nintendo DS, Xbox, Wii, PlayStation,* and so on. Some of these products were developed with the specific goal of being educational, teaching machines. Others were not. We'll see, however, that regardless of their intended use, these devices can condition users in both positive and negative ways.

In playing electronic games, players are rewarded for their behavior in various ways. A child selecting a correct answer on a Leap Pad hears a reward tone and is congratulated. A gamer scores points for shooting the bad guy, gets to see the next level after successful play, receives feedback on his exercise form from a Wii console, and so on. Players can also be punished. If you make a bad decision, your character might be killed or you may lose points or resources. You may hear a disappointed failure tone if you spell a word incorrectly, and so on.

Many of us do not realize that while we are playing electronic and video games, we are being conditioned by these high-tech devices.

A large amount of research has documented the negative impact these games have on behavior, especially games that have violent or sexual content or both. For example, in young children, playing violent video games is associated with poorer attention, and spending more time gaming in general is associated with increased aggression and poorer competence at school (Hastings et al., 2009). For college students, playing video games in which women are portrayed as sex objects resulted in increased tendencies to treat women inappropriately (Yao, Mahood, & Linz, 2010). In addition, young men randomly assigned to play the video game *Grand Theft Auto III* were found to exhibit more uncooperative behavior and more permissive attitudes about alcohol and drugs than did a control group that played a low-violence game (S. S. Brady & Matthews, 2006).

Is the news all bad? Or, can these modern-day Skinner boxes also condition us in positive ways? Research does suggest that these technologies can be beneficial. In a preliminary study, kindergarteners who used a Leap Pad experienced an increase in reading enjoyment, reading proficiency, and reading engagement (Munson, 2006). Another study showed that older people using Nintendo DS to play "brain training" games that exercise cognitive function were more engaged in the games and enjoyed them more than doing the same sorts of exercises in a paper and pencil format (Nacke, Nacke, & Lindley, 2009). Given that numerous studies suggest that exercising cognitive function in adulthood may help us keep our cognitive abilities longer (Valenzuela & Sachdev, 2009), having engaging devices like the Nintendo DS to encourage such exercise is a good thing.

It appears that gaming *content* holds the key to determining whether or not these technologies produce beneficial learning. For example, games that depict prosocial themes (such as helping others) have been shown to increase actual prosocial behavior in gamers (Greitemeyer & Osswald, 2010). Playing fast-action games tends to increase our speed in performing subsequent perceptual tasks, but if you want to increase your perceptual accuracy you should play puzzle games (Nelson & Strachan, 2009).

Like most things, it appears that these electronic games can be both beneficial and harmful. To minimize the possibility of negative outcomes, play games with nonviolent themes and place reasonable limits on gaming time.

Bruce Laurance/Getty Images

go to work because we expect to be reinforced for this behavior on payday. What would it take to extinguish your going-to-work behavior? The answer is simple, isn't it? All it would take is the removal of your reinforcement. If your boss stopped paying you, you would likely stop going to work. In operant conditioning, withholding the reinforcement that maintains the behavior causes the extinction of that behavior.

Like acquisition, extinction does not typically happen in one trial. Even if your boss failed to pay you on payday, you might very well return to work for a few days. In fact, you might even experience a temporary **extinction burst**, during which you worked *harder* in an attempt to obtain reward immediately after your boss withholds your pay (e.g., Galensky, Miltenberger, Stricker, & Garlinghouse, 2001). At the very least, you probably would not entirely abandon work until it became very clear that reinforcement would no longer be forthcoming. Extinction tends to occur over a number of trials. Each time the person or animal emits the operant response without being reinforced, its tendency to repeat the response diminishes (see Figure 5.11).

Because extinction removes responses, it has many practical applications. One way to stop someone from engaging in an annoying behavior is to extinguish it by removing the reinforcement for that behavior. Take the example of a parent and child shopping together in a department store. The child sees a toy that he wants, but his parent refuses to buy it. At this refusal, the child begins to whine and cry, but instead of punishing the child for this behavior, the parent ignores the child. By not reinforcing the whining and crying, the parent begins to extinguish this annoying behavior. Once the child learns that crying and whining do not lead to reward, the child will stop using this behavioral strategy to get what he wants.

The trick to using extinction to reduce unwanted behaviors is figuring out what is actually reinforcing the behavior, removing that reinforcement, and then making sure that no other reinforcement of the unwanted behavior is occurring (G. Martin & Pear, 1983). If Dad ignores the child's tantrums when he takes the child shopping but Mom gives in and buys the child toys, then the behavior will not be completely extinguished.

Shaping New Behaviors

Before a behavior can be operantly conditioned, the person or animal must first engage in the behavior spontaneously. Before Thorndike's cat learned to quickly receive its reward by stepping on the foot-release in the puzzle box, it first had to accidentally or spontaneously step on the pedal and open the box. Learning occurs only *after* the behavior has been emitted and the person or animal has been either punished or rewarded. **Given this, how can operant conditioning explain the development of** *novel* **behaviors?** For example, how could an animal trainer use operant conditioning to teach a dog to do a trick that involves walking on its hind legs?

Animal trainers use an operant conditioning technique called **shaping**, in which a novel behavior is slowly conditioned by reinforcing *successive approximations* of the final desired behavior. In the case of training the dog, the trainer will reinforce *any* spontaneous behavior that is in the direction of the final desired behavior. The trainer may start by rewarding the dog for looking at him. Once the dog learns to pay attention, it may expand on this behavior by sitting up. This will also lead to a treat. Then the dog must sit up to get the treat. Once the dog learns to sit up, it may go a bit further and rear up a bit on its hind legs. This will also earn the dog a treat. Now that the dog can rear up, it must do so to get a treat. After rearing up for a time, the dog may spontaneously go up all the way onto its hind legs. The trainer responds with more treats. Soon the dog will progress to standing on its hind legs, and the trainer will reciprocate with more treats every time the dog stands up on its hind legs. The final step comes when the dog spontaneously takes its first steps after being conditioned to stand on its hind legs. At this point, all the trainer has to do is reward the dog for walking on its hind legs.

Noel Hendrickson/Masterfile

By ignoring this child's tantrum, the parent is placing the child on an extinction schedule. If the parent does not reward the child for this behavior, the behavior should be less likely to occur in the future. Keep in mind, however, that extinction bursts may cause temporary increases in the behavior along the way.

extinction burst a temporary increase in a behavioral response that occurs immediately after extinction has begun

shaping using operant conditioning to build a new behavior in a person or animal by rewarding successive approximations of the desired response

Animal trainers such as the Dog Whisperer, Cesar Milan, sometimes use shaping to get animals to perform new behaviors.

Nelson Barnard/Getty Images

Shaping has many useful purposes in the real world. A parent could use shaping to help a child become more successful in school. At first the parent could reward the child for any study-related behavior, such as doing reading assignments or homework. Then the parent could progress to rewarding the child for earning good grades on individual assignments, followed by a reward only for good grades on individual exams. Then the parent could reward the child for making good grades in individual courses. Finally, the parent could reward the child only for making good grades in *all* courses. By slowly rewarding closer and closer approximations of the final desired behavior, the parent can shape a behavior in the child that would, perhaps, have never occurred on its own.

Schedules of Reinforcement

Acquisition and extinction of operant behavior seem simple enough, but numerous Skinner box studies have taught us that many factors can affect the rate at which responses are acquired or extinguished. One extremely important factor is the **schedule of reinforcement**—the timing and the consistency of the reinforcement.

Continuous Schedules of Reinforcement

Conceptually, the simplest type of reinforcement schedule is **continuous reinforcement**, in which each and every instance of the desired behavior is rewarded. In a Skinner box study, every time the rat presses the bar, a pellet of food is delivered to the rat. In real life, many simple behaviors are reinforced on a continuous schedule. One example is when we reach for objects. The act of reaching is reinforced when we actually grasp the object we were trying to get. Except in unusual circumstances, such as reaching for an object on a shelf that is too high, reaching is rewarded every time we reach (Skinner, 1953). Unfortunately, continuous schedules of reinforcement are often not very helpful when using operant conditioning to modify behavior.

There are two main reasons that continuous reinforcement is often not very helpful. The first drawback is a practical one. Let's say that you were going to use continuous reinforcement to change a child's behavior. You want your child to be polite when speaking to others, so you decide to use a continuous schedule and reinforce your child with praise *every time* she is polite. Would this be feasible? We doubt it. A continuous schedule of reinforcement would mean that you would have to be around your child every time she was polite, and you would have to praise or otherwise reward her for this politeness. This just isn't practical or possible.

The second problem is that continuously reinforced behaviors are vulnerable to extinction. What happens when your children are not in your presence, and you are not there to continually reinforce their good behavior? As we have already seen, when reinforcement is withheld, behavior often starts to extinguish. The problem with using continuous schedules of reinforcement is that they lead to behaviors that extinguish very quickly once the reinforcement ceases (Nevin & Grace, 2005).

Why would this be true? When a behavior has been continuously reinforced, there is a very clear *contingency* between the behavior and the reward. The person or animal learns that the behavior should *always* lead to a reward. When the reinforcement stops, a clear signal is sent that the contingency no longer holds true, and extinction occurs relatively rapidly. If the behavior is reinforced only *some* of the time, the child or animal is less likely to see the lack of reinforcement as a sign that the contingency is no longer operating. Schedules of reinforcement that reinforce a behavior only some of the time are called **partial reinforcement schedules**. *Ratio schedules* of partial reinforcement are based on the number of responses, whereas *interval schedules* are based on the timing of the responses.

schedule of reinforcement the frequency and timing of the reinforcements that a person or animal receives

continuous reinforcement a schedule of reinforcement in which the person or animal is rewarded for every instance of the desired response

partial reinforcement schedule a schedule of reinforcement in which the person or animal is rewarded for only some instances of the desired response

fixed ratio schedule a schedule of reinforcement in which the person or animal is rewarded for every xth instance of the desired response

variable ratio schedule a schedule of reinforcement in which the person or animal is rewarded on average for every xth instance of the desired response

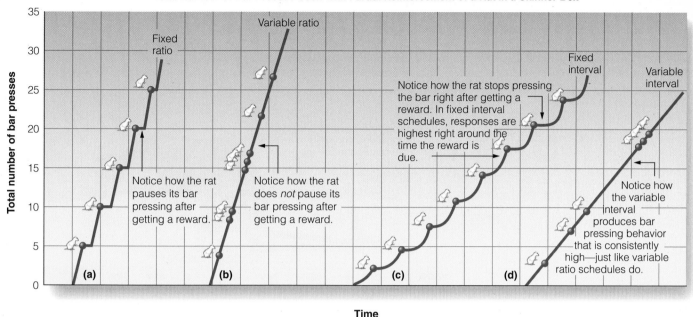

Total Number of Bar Presses Seen with Partial Reinforcement of a Rat in a Skinner Box

● = Reward given for the bar press

FIGURE 5.12

● **Partial Reinforcement of a Rat in a Skinner Box** This graph plots the rates of response for different schedules of reinforcement and the points at which the rat is reinforced. Notice how the rat's bar-pressing behavior changes before and after it receives a pellet on the different schedules of reinforcement. Which schedule would you use if you were going to use positive reinforcement to train your dog?

Ratio Schedules of Reinforcement

In a **fixed ratio schedule**, a set number of responses must be emitted before a reward is given. For example, suppose every third response is rewarded. A rat in a Skinner box would have to press the bar three times to get a food pellet. In the real world, some people are paid on fixed ratio schedules. A person who works in a manufacturing plant and is paid a bonus for every 100 parts assembled is being reinforced on a fixed ratio, as are agricultural workers who are paid per bushel of fruit picked, garment workers who are paid per piece sewn, and so on.

Besides producing slower extinction than continuous reinforcement, fixed ratio schedules also lead to fairly high response rates (● FIGURE 5.12a). High rates of responding are especially likely if it takes many responses to get a reward (Collier, Hirsch, & Hamlin, 1972; C. E. Stephens, Pear, Wray, & Jackson, 1975). If your goal is to produce many instances of the behavior, such as many filled boxes of raspberries, in a short time frame, a fixed ratio schedule may just do the trick.

The second type of ratio schedule is the **variable ratio schedule**, in which the exact number of responses that are required to receive a reward varies around some average. For example, the rat may have to press the bar two times to receive the first reward, one time to receive the second reward, and then six times to receive the third reward.

Variable ratio schedules of reinforcement yield high rates of response (Figure 5.12b) and even slower rates of extinction than fixed ratio schedules. A real-world example of variable ratio reinforcement is slot machines, which pay off on a variable ratio schedule of reinforcement. You never know how many pulls of the handle it will take to lead to the reward of a payoff. Consequently, people will play slot machines for long periods of time, even when

Slot machines pay off on a variable ratio schedule of reinforcement. Because it is hard to predict when the next reward is due, people playing the machine are likely to show high rates of responding and very slow rates of extinction. This translates into big profits for the casinos!

FIGURE 5.13

● **Fixed Interval (FI) Schedule of Reinforcement** This is an example of an FI 10-minute schedule of reinforcement for a rat in a Skinner box. The blue dots indicate when the rat pressed the bar, and the red dots indicate when the rat was rewarded for its bar-pressing behavior. On an FI of 10 minutes, the rat will receive a maximum of one reinforcement during any one 10-minute interval. Over time, the rat learns to press the bar only when a reward is due—right around the 10-minute interval mark. Yes, rats do have some sense of time!

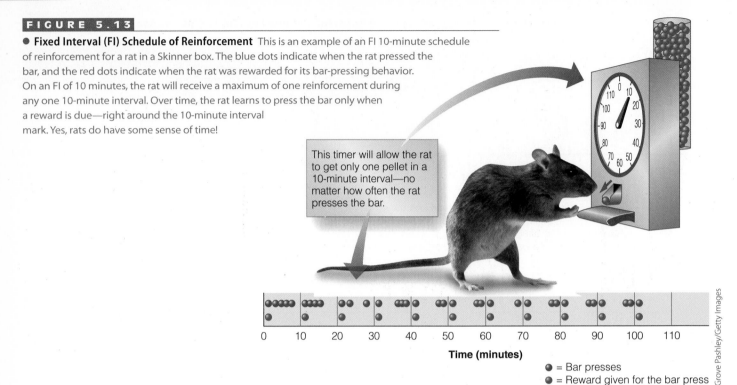

This timer will allow the rat to get only one pellet in a 10-minute interval—no matter how often the rat presses the bar.

Time (minutes)

● = Bar presses
● = Reward given for the bar press

Grove Pashley/Getty Images

they haven't hit the jackpot. One of us once knew a person who claimed to have lost $2,000 in slot machines during a weekend in Las Vegas. That type of resistance to extinction keeps many a casino owner very happy.

Interval Schedules of Reinforcement

Ratio schedules of reinforcement are based on the number of responses emitted by the person or animal. In interval schedules of reinforcement, the person or animal is rewarded only once per some interval of time. In a **fixed interval schedule**, the person or animal is rewarded for the first instance of the desired response, after which a set interval of time must pass before any other instances of the response will be rewarded. For example, if a rat in a Skinner box is reinforced on a fixed interval of 10 minutes, it will be rewarded for its first bar press, but not again until after 10 minutes have passed—no matter how many more times it presses the bar. Then the first bar press after the 10-minute mark has passed will be rewarded (● Figure 5.13).

The typical pattern of responding with a fixed interval schedule is to see most of the responding right around the time at which the reward is due. Then once the person or animal has received its reward for an interval, it usually stops responding for most of the remainder of the interval. One example of a fixed interval schedule is a yearly performance review at work. If an employee knows that she is going to be evaluated every January, she might be tempted to work her hardest in December. Immediately after being reviewed, the employee may be tempted to reduce her performance because she knows that she will not be reviewed again for another year. But as the end of the interval approaches and the next performance evaluation looms near, we can expect to see another increase in the employee's performance. This characteristic pause after reinforcement on a fixed interval schedule has been seen in rats (Innis, 1979) as well as humans (Shimoff, Catania, & Matthews, 1981; see Figure 5.12c).

One way to avoid this pause in the behavior immediately after reinforcement is to make the interval *variable*. Similar to what we saw in the variable ratio schedule, in a **variable interval schedule**, the length of the interval varies. What if our employee from the previous example did not know when to expect her next evaluation? What if she could be evaluated during any month of the year? Under these circumstances, her only choice would be to always perform well—assuming, of course, that she wanted to do well on her evaluation. As you can see from Figure 5.12d, variable interval schedules produce steady rates of responding in rats. Another

fixed interval schedule a schedule of reinforcement in which the person or animal is rewarded for the first desired response in an *x*th interval of time

variable interval schedule a schedule of reinforcement in which the person or animal is rewarded for the first desired response in an average *x*th interval of time

benefit of variable interval schedules is that they produce behaviors that are more resistant to extinction than those produced with fixed interval schedules.

In summary, when it comes to the effects that these different schedules have on operant conditioning:

1. Continuous reinforcement leads to high rates of responding but the quickest extinction.
2. Ratio schedules lead to higher rates of responding than do interval schedules.
3. Variable schedules lead to behaviors that are the most resistant to extinction.

Discrimination and Generalization

Just as classically conditioned responses undergo discrimination and generalization, so do operantly conditioned responses. By learning to discriminate and generalize appropriately, we learn to maximize the number of reinforcements and limit the number of punishments we receive in life.

Discrimination

In operant conditioning, discrimination occurs when the person or animal learns to distinguish among similar stimulus situations and to offer a particular response only in those specific situations in which reinforcement will be forthcoming. Discrimination occurs regularly in our lives. For instance, when students learn that they will be rewarded for sitting quietly and attentively during a teacher's lecture, the reward may be the teacher's favor or being able to hear the lecture and learn from it. In this situation, sitting quietly is the "right" thing to do in that it will lead to reinforcement. But will being quiet always elicit reinforcement in the classroom? Of course not. When the teacher asks a student a question, remaining quiet and refusing to speak will not lead to reinforcement. In fact, silence could even lead to punishment if the teacher becomes frustrated with the student. Therefore, the student must learn to *discriminate* between situations in which remaining silent will and will not lead to reinforcement. As you can see, not only does the ability to discriminate lead us to reward, it can also keep us out of trouble.

Generalization

Equally important is our ability to generalize our operant responses. Generalization occurs when the same operant behavior is emitted in response to different but similar stimuli. Let's say that you study very hard for your next psychology exam. You do your reading on time. You attend all lectures and take good notes. You study your psychology materials for at least 30 minutes each day, and you begin to study for the exam several days in advance. As a result of these good study habits, you earn an A on the exam. Receiving this A is a big reinforcement for your study habits. Given the success of your study methods in psychology, do you think that you might try these methods in your other courses? If so, your study behavior will generalize to your other courses. In this example, generalization is a good thing because it leads to greater success in all your courses.

In the previous examples, discrimination and generalization led to positive outcomes. Unfortunately, this is not always the case. One example of the negative aspects of discrimination and generalization is found in prejudice and discrimination against certain groups of people. In prejudice, one's negative feelings about a few members of a group generalize to most or all members of that group. Similarly, one learns to treat members of some groups in a kind manner and to treat all or most members of a disliked group in an unkind manner, thus discriminating against them. Here what we commonly refer to as discrimination in the social sense is also an example of what psychologists refer to as discrimination in learning. We will explore the downside of discrimination and generalization in Chapter 11 when we look at social psychology and the development of prejudices such as racism and gender bias.

Decisions That Must Be Made When Using Operant Conditioning

If used correctly, operant conditioning can be very effective in modifying behavior in both people and animals. However, the use of operant conditioning as a parental tool provides a

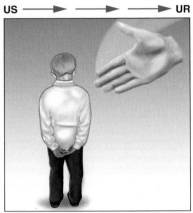

FIGURE 5.14

● **Classical Conditioning of Fear During a Spanking** Even though a parent may only intend to use operant conditioning when spanking a child, it is possible that the child may also experience classical conditioning. Because the parent is delivering the punishment, the parent can become a conditioned stimulus that elicits fear in the child.

nice backdrop for discussing some of the choices one must make before implementing an operant conditioning program of behavior modification with any person or animal.

One of the first decisions that has to be made when using operant conditioning to change behavior is which type of consequence to use. Recall from Figure 5.9 (p. 194) that there are two basic types of consequences that follow behavior—reinforcement and punishment. When designing an operant conditioning program of behavior modification, one must first decide whether to punish or reinforce the behavior. Sometimes this choice will be a very clear one, but often it will not be.

Punishment or Reinforcement?

At times, a parent will have a choice either to *reinforce* a child's *good* behavior or to *punish* the child's *bad* behavior. For example, suppose your child is not studying. You can punish the child for *not* studying, or you can reward the child *for* studying. Which of these methods do you think will be more successful and safer (that is, causes fewer negative reactions)? If you guessed that reinforcement is the safer, more effective route, you guessed correctly. In fact, one of the most effective ways of controlling children's behavior is to show them how you want them to respond and then reward them for behaving that way (Kochanska, 1997; Zahn-Waxler & Robinson, 1995). **So what makes punishment riskier and less effective?**

● *Punishment doesn't teach the correct behavior in a given situation.* Think about it for a moment. Let's say you hear your daughter getting frustrated with the family dog and cussing at the dog. As a result, you immediately yell at her. What have you taught her? You have taught her not to use whatever cuss word she uttered at the dog. What you have *not* taught her, however, is how she *should have responded* in this situation. The next time she is frustrated with the dog, she will not know how to express her frustration appropriately. Because punishment does not teach the correct response, any use of punishment should include a discussion of appropriate behavior and reinforcement of that behavior (G. Martin & Pear, 1983).

● *Harsh punishment, especially physical punishment, teaches aggressive behavior.* Harsh punishment provides an aggressive model for the child. When a parent physically punishes a child, the parent is teaching the child two things: first, that the child's behavior has had aversive consequences; and second, that being aggressive is a powerful means of controlling other people's behavior. In later sections of this chapter, we will see that children often imitate the behavior of others (Bandura, 1977). Therefore, while harsh punishment may stop an unwanted behavior, it may also teach the child to be aggressive. The next time the child feels frustrated or upset with another person, he or she may try using aggression to express those feelings. This is rarely the goal most parents have in mind.

● *Harsh punishment is often ineffective at producing behavior change* (Gershoff, 2002). When punished, children often stop engaging in the undesired behavior, but only for as long as their parents are around. When the parents are out of sight—and the threat of immediate punishment is gone—the undesired behavior returns. Because the goal is usually to ensure that the child behaves even when the parents are not around, punishment is not always effective.

● *Harsh punishment often leads to negative emotional reactions* (Gershoff, 2002; Skinner, 1953). These negative reactions include anger, fear, and anxiety. If a child experiences fear and anxiety when a parent punishes him, he may come to fear the parent. Just as Little Albert came to associate the white rat with loud, frightening noises, a child can come to associate a parent with pain and humiliation. Through classical conditioning, the parent can become a conditioned stimulus that evokes negative emotions in the child, and this conditioned fear can lead the child to want to avoid the parent (● FIGURE 5.14).

Harsh punishment, in particular, is less effective than reinforcement. **If you do choose to use punishment on your children, how can you ensure its effectiveness?** Before we begin, let us first state that *physical* punishment or spanking should be avoided. Years of research have shown us that children who experience physical punishment are more likely to be aggressive and experience lower levels of mental health than children who are not hit (Gershoff, 2002). Similarly, parents who use physical punishment have been shown to be

TABLE 5.3

● Austria, Bulgaria, Croatia, Cyprus, Denmark, Finland, Germany, Greece, Hungary, Iceland, Latvia, Netherlands, Norway, Portugal, Romania, Spain, Sweden, and Ukraine have all banned physical punishment of children (Council of Europe, 2008). This doesn't mean that these governments advocate not disciplining children. There are many effective alternatives to physical punishment that can be used to discipline children.

NONPHYSICAL PUNISHMENTS	EXAMPLE
Timeout: The child is sent to sit in a quiet place.	Devon, 5 years old, is sent to sit in the laundry room for 5 minutes after hitting his sister. There are no toys, friends, or other reinforcements present.
Restitution: The child has to give up something.	Sabina broke her sister's toy on purpose. Now Sabina has to give one of her own toys to her sister.
Fines: The child has to pay a fine.	Every time a family member uses inappropriate language, he or she has to put 50 cents in the "swear jar."
Loss of privileges: The child loses a privilege.	Giorgio lost his cell phone privileges for 2 weeks for breaking curfew and talking back to his parents.

NONPUNISHMENT METHOD	EXAMPLE
Empathy training: Teach the child to empathize with others. If the child hurts another, she is encouraged to imagine what that person might have felt as a result of being hurt. The ability to empathize reduces the motivation to hurt others.	Suzy intentionally breaks Jimmy's toy. To teach her empathy, Suzy's mother asks her to think about how she felt when Bobby broke her toy last week. Then Suzy is asked to think about whether Jimmy might be feeling the same way now that Suzy broke his toy. This should make Suzy feel bad about having hurt Jimmy.
Differential reinforcement of incompatible responses (DRI): The child is rewarded for engaging in a desirable behavior that cannot be emitted at the same time as the undesirable behavior.	Marya's parents reward her for being quiet in church as opposed to punishing her for being loud in church.

more hostile and to have higher levels of conflict in their marriages (Kanoy, Ulku-Steiner, Cox, & Burchinal, 2003).

There are a number of alternatives to physical punishment, many of which are listed in ● TABLE 5.3. If used properly, these techniques will most likely prove effective. Here are a few tips for making punishments like the ones in Table 5.3 more effective in general:

1. Tell the child what the appropriate behavior is, and then reinforce it.
2. Minimize situations that tempt the child to engage in bad behavior.
3. Use a punishment that really is punishing. If the child does not find the punishment aversive, it will fail to decrease the behavior.
4. Punishment must occur immediately after the bad behavior occurs.
5. Punishment must occur each and every time that the bad behavior occurs. Otherwise, the bad behavior is partially reinforced when the child escapes the punishment.
6. Remain calm while you are punishing a child. This will help ensure that you do not abuse the child.

As you can see, punishment, especially physical punishment, is riddled with possible dangers. These potential dangers have motivated the Council of Europe to launch a campaign to end corporal punishment of children in Europe. As of 2008, 18 of the 47 member states of the Council of Europe had legislatively banned corporal punishment and 7 more had committed to instituting bans in the near future (Council of Europe, 2008). When you have a choice, it is much safer and often more effective to use reinforcement of good behavior to control behavior. However, there are things to consider if you want to be sure your program of reinforcement has the desired effect on the behavior you are trying to change.

Choosing a Reinforcer That Is Reinforcing

It may seem like a trivial issue, but the first consideration in developing a program of reinforcement is to choose a reinforcer that is actually reinforcing for the person you are trying to condition. If the reinforcer is not something the person likes or values, it will not work. For example, if your significant other cleans the whole house, and you reward him by cooking a meal that he does *not* like, then he will not be more likely to clean the house again. Your attempt at operant conditioning will have failed.

On the surface, it may seem that choosing reinforcers that are reinforcing is a simple issue, but there are situations in which this task is not so simple, such as when you are trying to modify the behavior of people who are challenged by mental illnesses. One of the authors once tried to reinforce a man with mental illness by giving him some new clothes. To her dismay, he promptly traded these clothes to a fellow patient for a single pack of cigarettes! Obviously, cigarettes were more reinforcing for him than clothes. The author made this mistake because she was thinking about what would reinforce her—not what would be reinforcing for him. As a result, her program of reinforcement was not very effective. When choosing a reinforcer, you must break out of your own way of thinking to consider what the other person is likely to find reinforcing.

Primary and Secondary Reinforcers

Reinforcers can be categorized as either **primary** or **secondary reinforcers**. A primary reinforcer is one that is directly reinforcing. Examples of primary reinforcers are food, water, a warm bed, and sexual pleasure. These reinforcers are primary because they are pleasurable in and of themselves. If you are hungry, then food will reinforce you by removing your hunger.

In contrast, secondary reinforcers are rewarding only because they lead to primary reinforcers. A wonderful example of a secondary reinforcer in Western society is money. By itself, a dollar bill is not reinforcing. What makes a dollar reinforcing is what you can buy with it—food, water, shelter, and other primary reinforcers. When you get right down to it, you don't go to work for money per se. You go to work to ensure that you will be able to purchase an adequate supply of primary reinforcers.

One method of secondary reinforcement is to use a *token economy* (see Chapter 15 also). A **token economy** reinforces desired behavior with a token of some sort (e.g., a poker chip or a gold star) that can later be cashed in for primary reinforcers (see G. Martin, England, Kaprowy, Kilgour, & Pilek, 1968). Token economies are often used to control the behavior of groups of people such as schoolchildren (Salend, 2001), children receiving treatment for intellectual disabilities and autism (Matson & Boisjoli, 2009), or prisoners. Token economies can also be used in the context of a family (Kazdin, 1977).

To set up a token economy, the first step is to draw up a list of desired and undesired behaviors that you will try to control. The next step is to decide how many tokens to give (or take away) for each of the behaviors, and develop some sort of recordkeeping system to keep track of each participant's tokens. One recordkeeping approach is to draw a chart like the one shown in ● FIGURE 5.15 and hang it on the wall in a prominent place.

There are two main advantages to using token economies. One is that a token economy is effective when trying to simultaneously modify a number of behaviors in a group of people. For example, a token economy can be used with an entire class, which is easier than trying to develop an individual operant conditioning program for each student.

The second major advantage is that token economies allow for immediate reinforcement with a token, even when it is not practical to immediately present the primary reinforcer. For example, it's disruptive for a teacher to stop the class to give a child a toy as a reinforcer. However, the teacher can immediately hand the child a token that can be used at week's end to purchase a toy. The use of tokens helps to bridge the gap between the behavior and the eventual primary reinforcement of the behavior.

A potential problem with token economies is that the behavior is often reinforced continuously. As we saw in previous sections, continuous reinforcement can lead to behavior that is vulnerable to extinction. It is possible that a token economy may lessen a person's desire to engage in a behavior when the behavior is not likely to lead to a token or some other reward. This potential problem may be outweighed, however, by the usefulness of the token economy in controlling the immediate behavior of the people in the program. For instance, in a prison you may be more worried about controlling the immediate, day-to-day behavior of the prison population. Facilitating the future motivation of the inmates to behave in a particular way once they are out of the token economy is likely to be of less concern.

primary reinforcer a reinforcer that is reinforcing in and of itself

secondary reinforcer a reinforcer that is reinforcing only because it leads to a primary reinforcer

token economy a system of operant conditioning in which participants are reinforced with tokens that can later be cashed in for primary reinforcers

Mrs. Duncan's Class

FIGURE 5.15

● **A Sample Point System From a Token Economy**

Participants	Paying attention in class, +5 tokens	On time for class, +3 tokens	Homework completely done, +7 tokens	B or better on daily quiz, +10 tokens	Talking in class, −5 tokens	Fighting, −10 tokens	Calling people names −10 tokens
Jose							
Mary							
Luis							
Billy							
Omar							
Eddie							
Terrika							

Token values
25 tokens = 1 sticker, eraser, or pencil
50 tokens = 1 small toy
75 tokens = 1 medium-size toy
100 tokens = 1 coupon for free pizza
125 tokens = 1 DVD

The Role of Cognition in Learning

So far in this chapter, we have discussed three major types of learning—habituation, classical conditioning, and operant conditioning—which have some important things in common. One common feature is that all these types of learning require that the person or animal *do something* before learning can occur. In habituation, the person or animal must emit an orienting reflex. In classical conditioning, the person or animal must have an unconditioned response. In operant conditioning, the person or animal must first engage in some random behavior that is either reinforced or punished.

Another common feature of these learning theories is that they do not emphasize the role that mental or cognitive processes play in learning. Researchers such as Ivan Pavlov, John B. Watson, E. L. Thorndike, and B. F. Skinner did not discuss thoughts and feelings and how these may affect the learning process. B. F. Skinner, in particular, argued that psychology should not seek to study the cognitive aspects of behavior because he believed that these things could not be studied scientifically and objectively. Skinner did not deny that humans and animals had thoughts and feelings; he simply held that they could not be studied adequately. Therefore, Skinner subscribed to a type of psychology called *behaviorism* (see Chapter 1), which states that the *only* aspect of living things that can and should be studied scientifically is behavior. Thus, Skinner tried to explain behavior without discussing cognitive or mental processes (Skinner, 1953).

Because strict behaviorism totally ignores the influence of cognitive processes, it does not explain some of the learning we see in the real world, or in the lab. In the early 1900s, some researchers, including Wolfgang Köhler, became aware that cognitive processes must play a role in learning. Köhler observed that chimpanzees did not always attempt to solve problems in a trial-and-error fashion as predicted by the law of effect. Rather, they often seemed to study a problem for a long time as if formulating a mental plan—before attempting to solve it. In one experiment, Köhler placed a banana just out of reach on the outside of a chimpanzee's cage, and he placed a stick inside the cage. The law of effect would predict that the chimpanzee would try many random behaviors—like shaking the bars and jumping up and down—before picking up the stick and using it to reach the banana. But this is not what Köhler observed. Instead, the chimpanzee studied the situation and then appeared to suddenly come up with the solution. After this flash of **insight** into how to solve its dilemma, the chimpanzee picked up the stick and used it to scoot the banana to a point where it could be reached (Köhler, 1925).

insight a new way of looking at a problem that leads to a sudden understanding of how to solve it

© Penny Tweedie/Alamy

Wolfgang Köhler found that chimpanzees, like this one, can acquire insight into how to solve problems by watching and studying situations before acting. This type of problem solving suggests that cognitive processes can play an important role in learning.

Köhler's work shows that learning can be a purely cognitive task. The chimpanzee did not have to wait for the consequences of its behavior to rule out behavioral strategies that would not accomplish the goal of obtaining the banana. Rather, the chimpanzee appeared to reason its way to a solution *before* acting.

In the 1930s, Edward Tolman found additional support for the idea that cognition plays a role in learning. Tolman discovered that rats would learn to run through a maze even when they were not rewarded for doing so (Tolman & Honzik, 1930). In Tolman's experiment, one group of rats was allowed to wander through the maze, and they were rewarded with food if they found their way to the end of the maze. Another group of rats was also allowed to explore the maze, but they were not rewarded even if they found their way to the end. As you might expect, after 10 days of training in the maze, the group that was rewarded could run through the maze more quickly than the unrewarded group could. On the 11th day, Tolman began to give rats in *both* groups a reward at the end of the maze. After just a few rewarded trials, the previously unrewarded rats could run through the maze just as fast as the rats that had been rewarded all along. This rapid learning in the previously unrewarded rats indicates that these rats had been learning even when they were not being rewarded.

Tolman's findings cannot be explained by operant conditioning alone because learning occurred *without* reinforcement. Tolman interpreted his results as being evidence that the rats had engaged in **latent learning**, or learning that cannot be directly observed through behavior. He proposed that while the unrewarded rats were wandering through the maze, they were developing a **cognitive map**, or mental representation of the maze in their heads. Once the reward was presented, they used this map to help them get to the reward more quickly.

Although Tolman's experiments pointed to cognitive processes at work during learning, many psychologists ignored the impact of cognition on learning because of behaviorism's dominance in psychology at the time. It was not until the 1960s that learning researchers really began to look at the role of cognition in learning and behavior.

Let's REVIEW

In this section, we have given you a quick overview of some of the important issues in operant conditioning, including the law of effect, the factors that affect operant conditioning, the differences between operant conditioning and classical conditioning, and B. F. Skinner's contributions to operant conditioning. For a quick check of your understanding, try answering the following questions at increasing levels of difficulty.

1. Which of the following schedules of reinforcement is associated with the quickest extinction rates?

   a. fixed ratio   c. variable ratio

   b. variable interval   d. continuous

2. In operant conditioning, which two things are being associated?

   a. a CS and a US   c. a behavior and a consequence

   b. an NS and a CR   d. an environmental situation and a consequence

3. Which of the following is an example of negative reinforcement?

   a. receiving an allowance for doing your chores

   b. taking a drug to avoid painful withdrawal symptoms

   c. taking away your child's TV because she is making poor grades in school

   d. receiving a fine for speeding on the highway

latent learning learning that cannot be directly observed in a person's or animal's behavior

cognitive map a mental representation of the environment

ANSWERS 1. d; 2. c; 3. b

OBSERVATIONAL LEARNING OR MODELING: CAN WE LEARN BY WATCHING OTHERS?

As we saw in the previous discussion, learning can occur without reinforcement, but even Tolman's unrewarded rats had at least engaged in the behavior of moving through the maze. Does all learning require that we actually engage in the behavior? As it turns out, we can learn by simply observing the behaviors of others. In this type of learning, called **observational learning**, we *observe* others and imitate, or *model*, their behavior. For that reason, observational learning is sometimes referred to as *modeling*. Our opening story of Michael Gates Gill provides a good example of observational learning in action. Crystal was a very important mentor and role model for Mike in his new life. Many times, he witnessed Crystal treating all people, even difficult people, with respect and value. Mike learned to model this attitude of respect. Mike also learned to model Crystal's work ethic. Whether she was cleaning a bathroom floor or making a cappuccino, she did everything to the best of her ability—a trait that Mike adopted as well.

As you read the following sections, keep in mind that observational learning departs from the behaviorism that Skinner so forcefully advocated on two major points. First, it acknowledges that learning can occur without an overt change in behavior; second, it takes into account the role of cognition in the learning process.

Albert Bandura and the Bobo Doll Experiments

In the 1960s, psychologist Albert Bandura (b. 1925) conducted several experiments on observational learning, now considered classic psychological experiments, that contributed to his development of *social learning theory*. Collectively, these experiments are referred to as the *Bobo doll experiments* because the experimental procedure utilized a blow-up plastic "Bobo" doll, a popular children's toy.

In the Bobo doll experiments, children watched films in which a woman beat up the Bobo doll. She hit him with a mallet, sat on him, threw him in the air, and so on (Bandura, Ross, & Ross, 1961). After the children viewed the films, Bandura and his colleagues placed them in a room alone with the Bobo doll and observed their behavior without their knowledge. If the children imitated the characteristic behaviors of the model, then Bandura knew that learning had occurred (● FIGURE 5.16).

In one of the Bobo doll experiments (Bandura, 1965), three groups of children watched three different films. In the *reward* film condition, the model was rewarded after beating up on Bobo. In the *punishment* film condition, she was punished after beating up on Bobo. In the *no consequences* film condition, nothing happened to the model after she beat up on Bobo.

observational learning learning through observation and imitation of others' behavior

FIGURE 5.16

● **Bandura's Bobo Doll Experiments**
These photos, taken from the Bobo doll experiments, clearly show the children (panel B) modeling what they saw the model (panel A) doing to Bobo.

©Albert Bandura

After viewing one of these films, the children were observed with Bobo, and their aggressive behaviors were recorded. As you might expect, the children who had seen the model rewarded for beating up Bobo were most likely to beat up on him themselves. However, an unexpected finding of the study was that the children who had seen the *no consequences* film were equally likely to beat up on Bobo. This means that seeing someone merely get away with aggressive behavior is just as likely to lead to modeling as seeing aggression rewarded. The only thing that deterred the children's aggression toward Bobo was having seen the film in which the model was punished for treating Bobo badly. Only these children were more hesitant to beat up on Bobo when they were left alone with him in the observation room.

By leaving the children alone with Bobo and recording their aggressive behavior, Bandura was able to assess how willing the children were to beat up on Bobo as a function of the consequences they expected would follow such aggression. But what about what they learned about how to be aggressive toward Bobo? Is it possible that some of the children who did *not* beat up Bobo had still learned *how* to beat up Bobo? To test the children's level of *learning*, Bandura (1965) asked the children to show him exactly what they had seen in the films. Here, the children were free to model the behavior without fear of any type of punishment. Under these conditions, Bandura found that there were no significant differences across the three groups. All of the groups exhibited equal levels of learning when it came to knowing how the model had beat up Bobo.

The Bobo doll experiments show us two things. First, you don't have to engage in a behavior or experience reinforcement for learning to occur. Second, just as Tolman discovered with his rats in the mazes, learning can be latent. The children who viewed the *punishment* film had learned how to beat up Bobo, but they were reluctant to beat him up because they feared there would be negative consequences for them if they did. We hope that the Bobo doll experiments make you think about the potential impact that violent movies, video games, and television may have on the children who view them because some very recent research seems to underscore the notion that kids do not merely watch TV—rather, they learn from TV.

Researchers Donna Mumme and Anne Fernald (2003) have found that children as young as 12 months pay attention to how a televised model reacts to certain stimuli, and they model their own reaction to the stimulus after the model's reaction. In this study, 12-month-old infants watched a televised actress interacting with certain toys. The actress responded either positively, neutrally, or negatively to certain toys. Later, the infants were allowed to play with the same toys. The results showed that the infants were most likely to react favorably to the toys that the actress had either been neutral about or liked. Conversely, the infants were less likely to want to play with the toys to which the actress had reacted negatively. It seems that the infants disliked these toys simply because they had seen the actress reacting negatively toward them. Thus, the observational learning that occurs when watching TV may have the power to influence the attitudes that even very young children hold about the objects in their world.

Think about the impact that this process may have on learning stereotypes and prejudices. If a child is subjected to models (in real life or on TV) who react negatively to specific groups of people, could this lead to modeling in which the child comes to react negatively to certain types of people simply because he or she has seen this reaction in others? It seems likely that it could, and perhaps at a very young age. Later in this text, we will explore the causes of aggression and prejudice in our discussions of social psychology in Chapter 11. But for now, let's take a closer look at this process of observational learning and the variables that affect it.

Observational Learning and Cognition

The role of cognition in observational learning can be clearly seen when you examine the conditions that are necessary for modeling to occur. According to Bandura (1986), modeling is a four-step process.

1. *Attention.* The observer must first pay attention to the model's behavior before he or she can model it. Research shows that children tend to model their behavior after people who are warm, nurturant, or powerful (Bandura, 1977)—especially when they can directly interact with these models (Nielsen, Simcock, & Jenkins, 2008). For example, a child may pay attention to the behavior of loving parents, a nurturant teacher, or a popular and seemingly powerful classmate. As we have already seen, another type of model that is particu-

larly good at grabbing our attention is televised models (Bandura, Grusec, & Menlove, 1966). As a result, it is quite common to see children on the playground modeling the behavior of their favorite TV cartoon character. As we age and mature, however, we tend to seek out models that seem similar to us in some way (Bandura, 1986). For example, we may model our behavior after people of the same sex, ethnicity, or occupation.

2. *Retention in memory.* The observer must retain a cognitive representation or memory of the model's behavior. For children on the playground to model the behavior of TV characters, they must have memories of what they have previously seen on TV.

3. *Reproduction of the behavior.* The observer must have a mental representation of the behavior stored in memory that can be retrieved and used to reproduce the behavior. Of course, the person must have the physical abilities to actually reproduce the behavior if modeling is to occur. For instance, a child may remember seeing a cartoon superhero flying. Although the child may be able to model an approximation of this behavior, he will not be able to model the behavior precisely.

4. *Motivation.* After retrieving the memory of the behavior and figuring out how to produce the behavior, the observer must be motivated to actually execute the behavior. As we saw in the Bobo doll experiments, the observer may sometimes not *want* to execute the behavior. This is especially true if the observer believes that execution of the behavior may lead to punishment.

Bandura's work on observational learning brings an additional element to the study of learning in that it addresses the role of cognition in the learning process. In the next two chapters, we will consider cognitive processes more carefully, looking at how memory works in Chapter 6 and at the cognitive processes involved in solving problems and making decisions and judgments in Chapter 7.

What do we learn from watching TV and playing video games?

Franco Vogt/PhotoLibrary

Let's REVIEW

In this section, we have given you a brief overview of some important aspects of observational learning, including Bandura's Bobo doll experiments, the steps involved in modeling, and the role that cognition plays in observational learning. For a quick check of your understanding, try answering the following questions at increasing levels of difficulty.

1. The first step in observational learning is _____.

    a. retaining the behavior in memory

    b. being motivated to execute the behavior

    c. paying attention to the behavior

    d. reproducing the behavior

2. Observational learning differs from operant conditioning in that _____.

    a. in observational learning, the person is less aware that learning is taking place

    b. in operant conditioning, the person is less aware that learning is taking place

    c. in observational learning, the person does not have to engage in the response

    d. in operant conditioning, the person does not have to engage in the response

3. Ty watches a violent TV show, but he has never been seen to model any of the behaviors he has seen on the show. Which of the following statements is true regarding Ty's learning?

    a. Ty has not learned anything from watching the show.

    b. Ty has definitely learned something from watching the show.

    c. Ty may have learned something from watching the show.

    d. At some point in time, Ty's behavior will definitely change as a result of watching the show.

ANSWERS 1. c; 2. c; 3. c.

STUDYING the CHAPTER

KEY TERMS

learning (177)
orienting reflex (178)
habituation (179)
dishabituation (180)
unconditioned stimulus (US) (182)
unconditioned response (UR) (182)
neutral stimulus (NS) (182)
conditioned stimulus (CS) (182)
conditioned response (CR) (182)
classical conditioning (182)

contiguity (183)
contingency (184)
stimulus generalization (186)
counterconditioning (187)
stimulus discrimination (188)
taste aversion (189)
aversion therapy (190)
extinction (190)
acquisition (191)
spontaneous recovery (191)
operant conditioning (192)
law of effect (193)
reinforcement (193)
positive reinforcement (193)

negative reinforcement (194)
punishment (194)
positive punishment (195)
negative punishment (195)
operant behavior (196)
Skinner box (197)
extinction burst (199)
shaping (199)
schedule of reinforcement (200)
continuous reinforcement (200)
partial reinforcement schedule (200)

fixed ratio schedule (201)
variable ratio schedule (201)
fixed interval schedule (202)
variable interval schedule (202)
primary reinforcer (206)
secondary reinforcer (206)
token economy (206)
insight (207)
latent learning (208)
cognitive map (208)
observational learning (209)

LEARNING CHALLENGE

Now that you have studied the chapter, assess your comprehension of the material by answering the following questions. Then use the key at the end to determine if your understanding is at the basic, intermediate, or advanced level. For a more comprehensive assessment of your learning, please see your student study guide and your Psychology CourseMate (www.cengagebrain.com).

1. Learning to re-respond to a stimulus that you have previously learned to ignore is also known as _____.

a. habituation
b. dishabituation
c. orienting reflex
d. classical conditioning

2. Wilbur has a crush on his first-grade teacher. Every time he smells her perfume, he feels happy. Wilbur's happiness is likely the result of which type of learning?

a. habituation
b. classical conditioning
c. operant conditioning
d. observational learning

3. If Pavlov had only sometimes given the dog food after buzzing the buzzer, this would have most clearly disrupted the _____ of the CS and the US.

a. timing
b. contiguity
c. contingency
d. extinction

4. In _____ we remove an undesired conditioned response using classical conditioning.

a. extinction
b. counterconditioning
c. operant conditioning
d. extinction bursts

5. As taste aversion undergoes extinction, _____ might occur.

a. punishment
b. shaping
c. spontaneous recovery
d. insight

6. Learning is to _____ as _____ is to forgetting.

a. acquisition; extinction
b. extinction; extinction burst
c. shaping; insight
d. insight; shaping

7. Which of the following would lead to an increase in behavior?

a. positive reinforcement
b. negative reinforcement
c. shaping
d. all of the above

8. Avoiding public speaking because it makes you nervous is an example of _____.

a. habituation
b. classical conditioning
c. operant conditioning
d. observational learning

9. Sadie the dog scratches faster and louder on the back door when her owner fails to let her out for her walk. This increased scratching behavior is an example of _____.

a. extinction burst
b. stimulus generalization
c. stimulus discrimination
d. latent learning

10. You are a manager who wants to implement an operant conditioning program to reward employees for coming to work on time. Which of the following approaches will likely be most effective in getting employees to come on time, even after the program has ended?

a. continuous reinforcement
b. fixed interval reinforcement
c. fixed ratio reinforcement
d. variable ratio reinforcement

11. _____ is reinforcing successive approximations of a final desired behavior.

a. Shaping
b. Insight learning
c. Observational learning
d. Cognitive mapping

12. A _____ is particularly useful for conditioning the behavior of a group of people.

a. variable interval schedule
b. Skinner box
c. primary reinforcer
d. token economy

13. Latent learning is most closely associated with which of the following concepts?

a. habituation
b. classical conditioning
c. operant conditioning
d. observational learning

14. Which of the following are secondary reinforcers?

a. trophies
b. candy
c. water
d. a warm blanket

15. _____ conducted the experiments on observational learning in which children were shown a model behaving aggressively toward a blow-up toy clown.

a. Ivan Pavlov
b. B. F. Skinner
c. Albert Bandura
d. E. L. Thorndike

Scoring Key

Below are the answers and the associated point values for each of the Learning Challenge questions. Circle the associated points for each question that you answered correctly. To obtain your Learning Challenge Score, add up the points you circled and write the total in the blank.

1. B, 1 pt	**6.** A, 2 pts	**11.** A, 1 pt
2. B, 3 pts	**7.** D, 2 pts	**12.** D, 1 pt
3. C, 2 pts	**8.** C, 3 pts	**13.** D, 2 pts
4. B, 1 pt	**9.** A, 3 pts	**14.** A, 3 pts
5. C, 2 pts	**10.** D, 3 pts	**15.** C, 1 pt

Learning Challenge Score _____

(27–30) Congratulations! You scored at the advanced level. You are well on your way to mastering the material. Take the next step by answering the questions in your Student Study Guide or your Psychology CourseMate (www.cengagebrain.com).

(21–26) You are almost there! You scored at the intermediate level. Review the material you missed before moving on to answer the questions in your Student Study Guide or your Psychology CourseMate (www.cengagebrain.com).

(20 and below) You are on your way, but you're not there yet! You scored at the beginner level. It appears that you need to carefully review the chapter to improve your mastery of the material.

USE IT OR LOSE IT: APPLYING PSYCHOLOGY

1. Identify a situation in which you were classically conditioned. Then identify the NS/CS, US, and UR/CR.

2. Think about two different environments that you frequently experience (e.g., school, work, hanging with your friends). What behaviors are likely to be rewarded in these environments? What behaviors are likely to be punished? Are some behaviors rewarded in one environment but punished in the other? How will these rewards and punishments affect your future behavior? Explain.

3. How do the types of learning in this chapter apply to parents and their children? In other words, how do parents use these types of learning in their roles as parents?

4. If you were an employer who wanted to maximize employee productivity, which schedule of reinforcement would you use when creating a timetable for performance reviews of your employees? Defend your choice.

CRITICAL THINKING FOR INTEGRATION

1. Design an experiment to test the hypothesis that continuous reinforcement leads to behaviors that are more easily extinguished than behaviors that are built with partial reinforcement. Describe your design in detail.

2. What role might the four types of learning play in drug addiction?

3. What role might the four types of learning play in a therapy program for people addicted to drugs?

4. What role does culture play in the four types of learning?

CHAPTER STUDY RESOURCES

Student Study Guide

To help organize your learning, work through Chapter 5 of the *What Is Psychology? Student Study Guide*. The study guide includes learning objectives, a chapter summary, fill-in review, key terms, a practice test, and activities.

CengageNOW

Go to **www.cengage.com/login** to link to CengageNOW, your online study tool. First take the Pre-Test for this chapter to get your personalized study plan, which will identify topics you need to review and direct you to online resources. Then take the Post-Test to determine what concepts you have mastered and what you still need work on.

CourseMate

Access an interactive eBook, chapter-specific interactive learning tools, including flashcards, quizzes, videos, and more in your Psychology CourseMate, available at **CengageBrain.com**.

Aplia   aplia

Aplia™ is an online interactive learning solution that helps you improve comprehension—and your grade—by integrating a variety of tools such as video, tutorials, practice tests, and interactive eBook. Founded by a professor to enhance his own courses, Aplia provides automatically graded assignments with detailed, immediate explanations on every question, and innovative teaching materials. More than 1,000,000 students like you have used Aplia at over 1,800 institutions. Aplia should be purchased only when assigned by your instructor as part of your course.

HOW DO WE LEARN?

In this chapter, we looked at four different types of learning: **habituation**, **classical conditioning**, **operant conditioning**, and **observational learning**. These learning theories explain much of the behavior seen in Michael Gates Gill, the man profiled at the beginning of the chapter. Like us, Mike habituated to life's annoyances, such as the buzzing in his ear. He was classically conditioned to have particular emotional reactions to people and things. He was operantly conditioned by the rewards and punishments he encountered, and he ultimately learned how to embrace his new life by modeling his behavior after his mentor, coworkers, and other important models.

© Arclight/Alamy

HOW DOES LEARNING HELP US?

- **Learning** is a relatively permanent change in behavior or the potential for behavior that results from experience.
- **Orienting reflexes** allow us to respond to unexpected stimuli.
- **Habituation** allows us to stop responding to stimuli that are repeated over and over.
- **Dishabituation** allows us to re-respond to a stimulus that was previously habituated.

CLASSICAL CONDITIONING: CAN WE LEARN THROUGH ASSOCIATION?

- Ivan Pavlov discovered classical conditioning while studying salivation in dogs.
- **Classical conditioning** occurs when a **neutral stimulus** is paired with an **unconditioned stimulus** that reliably causes an **unconditioned response**, and because of this association, the neutral stimulus loses its neutrality and becomes a **conditioned stimulus** that elicits the **conditioned response**.
- Classical conditioning is most effective when the NS/CS and US are separated by only a brief period of time (**contiguity**), and the NS/CS must reliably predict the US (**contingency**).
- The Little Albert experiments of John Watson and Rosalie Rayner studied how emotional responses could be classically conditioned in humans.
- **Stimulus generalization** occurs when we respond to similar stimuli with the same conditioned response.
- **Stimulus discrimination** occurs when the conditioned response is only elicited by a particular CS.
- **Taste aversion** occurs when a particular food is associated with some other ailment or condition that causes nausea and the food becomes a conditioned stimulus for nausea.
- The elimination of a conditioned response is known as **extinction**.

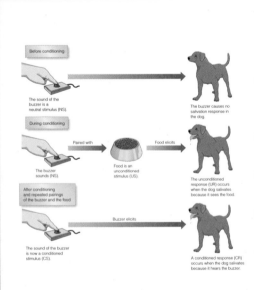

Before conditioning

The sound of the buzzer is a neutral stimulus (NS).

The buzzer causes no salivation response in the dog.

During conditioning

The buzzer sounds (NS).

Paired with

Food is an unconditioned stimulus (US).

Food elicits

The unconditioned response (UR) occurs when the dog salivates because it sees the food.

After conditioning and repeated pairings of the buzzer and the food

The sound of the buzzer is now a conditioned stimulus (CS).

Buzzer elicits

A conditioned response (CR) occurs when the dog salivates because it hears the buzzer.

OPERANT CONDITIONING: WHAT DO WE LEARN FROM THE CONSEQUENCES OF OUR ACTIONS?

- In **operant conditioning**, we learn from the consequences of our actions.

- E. L. Thorndike developed the **law of effect**, which emphasized the negative and positive consequences of behavior.

- The Four Consequences of Behavior:

The Four Types of Consequences of Behavior		
	Add to Environment	**Remove from Environment**
Increase Behavior	+ Reinforcement	- Reinforcement
Decrease Behavior	+ Punishment	- Punishment

© Masterfile

- B. F. Skinner, a strong proponent of *behaviorism*, coined the term *operant conditioning* to refer to how certain behavior operates on the environment to produce some consequence. The **Skinner box** is a chamber used to study animal learning.

- Five schedules of **reinforcement**—**continuous, fixed ratio, variable ratio, fixed interval**, and **variable interval**—describe the timing and number of responses required to receive reinforcement.

- In **shaping**, a novel behavior is slowly conditioned by reinforcing successive approximations of the final desired behavior.

- **Primary reinforcers** are reinforcing in themselves. **Secondary reinforcers** are rewarding because they lead to primary reinforcers.

- A **token economy** reinforces desired behavior with a token of some sort that can later be cashed in for primary reinforcers.

OBSERVATIONAL LEARNING OR MODELING: CAN WE LEARN BY WATCHING OTHERS?

- **Observational learning** is learning that occurs by observing others and modeling their behavior.

- Albert Bandura's Bobo doll experiments showed that you do not have to engage in a behavior or experience for learning to occur and that learning can be **latent**.

- In contrast to behaviorists such as Skinner, observational learning theorists emphasize the role that cognitive processes (attention and retention in memory), reproduction of the behavior, and motivation play in learning.

Bruce Laurance/Getty Images

Franco Vogt/PhotoLibrary

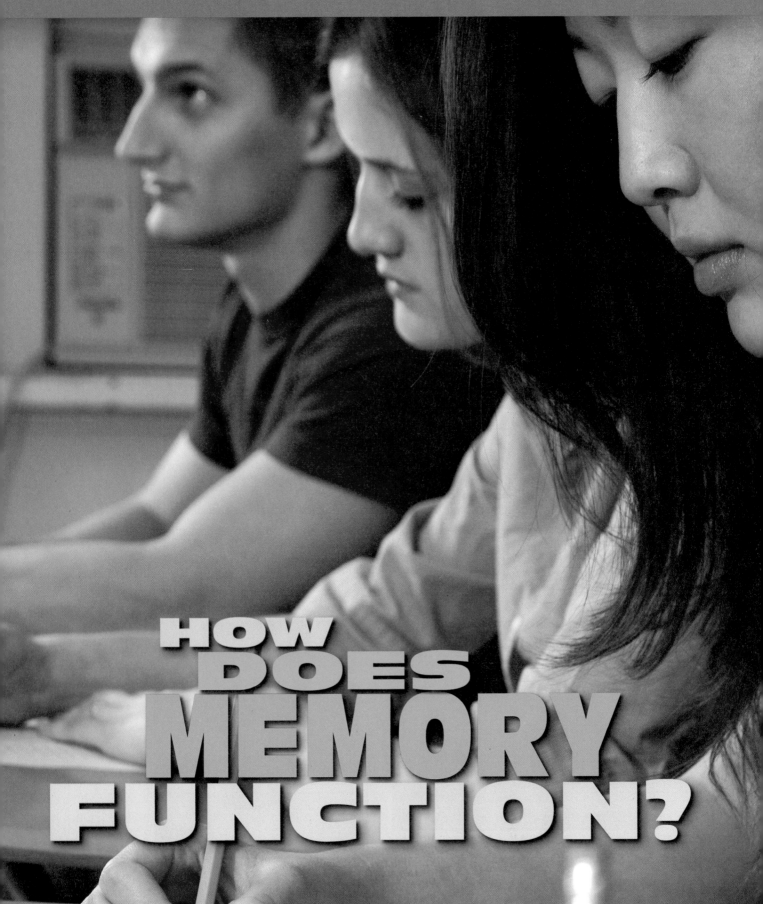

CHAPTER 6

HOW DOES MEMORY FUNCTION?

THE BIG PICTURE

The Real Rain Man: Does Extraordinary Memory Come at a Price?

Using our memory, we can remember things that have happened in the past: our first date, the antics of childhood friends, the name of our second-grade teacher, lessons we have learned, and so on. It is our ability to remember that gives us our sense of self. Our memory connects us to the past and all the people, places, and experiences we have encountered in our lifetime. For most of us, memory works well, but it is not perfect. As students, you know that committing information to memory takes effort, and even with significant effort, forgetting can still occur. Wouldn't it be nice if you could read your psychology textbook once and remember everything? Before you answer, read the story of a remarkable man, Kim Peek, the real life "Rain Man" portrayed by Dustin Hoffman in the Oscar-winning movie of that name.

Kim, who passed away in December 2009 from a heart attack, was different from the moment of his birth. His head was 30% larger than normal. He did not respond normally to stimulation. His eyes moved independently of one another, and he had a large blister-like growth across the back of his head that doctors could not identify.

At age 3, the growth on Kim's head suddenly began to relocate, growing into the back of his skull, and exploding the right half of his cerebellum into many separate pieces. Later it was discovered that Kim had no corpus callosum and that the two hemispheres of his brain were fused into one large mass (see Chapter 2). Despite these brain abnormalities, Kim excelled at certain aspects of memory. At age 6, Kim was memorizing parts of encyclopedias, and his ability to memorize information continued to become more impressive as he aged. By adulthood, he exhibited extraordinary mental abilities in more than a dozen topic areas. Kim spent most of his time voraciously reading—phone books, maps, history books, album covers—all with near total recall. In fact, he could simultaneously read two passages at the same time—one with his left eye and one with his right eye! If you told Kim your date of birth, he could *immediately* tell you the day of the week you were born on and the year and date when you could retire at age 65. If you told him your hometown, he could tell you your zip code, telephone prefix, and most likely the history of your town. He could also hum almost any piece of music on demand and do mental mathematics at an astounding level.

© Frederick Bass/fstop/Corbis

219

Yet, Kim's genius did not extend to all types of mental functioning. He had extreme difficulty learning motor skills, most likely because of his damaged cerebellum. He could not brush his teeth or dress without assistance. By age 14, Kim completed his high school requirements at home, but he couldn't attend public school because of his extreme hyperactivity. Kim's mind constantly jumped from idea to idea, and he could not concentrate on one task at a time. He was quite poor at tasks that involve analytical reasoning or conceptual thought. For example, he could memorize a history book, but had difficulty discussing the meaning of "democracy." Kim's score on traditional intelligence tests was approximately 74, in the range that indicates mental retardation. On tests that only measure knowledge, he scored around 175—*way* above average.

For unknown reasons, Kim's damaged brain seemed to give him the amazing ability to process massive amounts of information. The price for this ability seemed to be that Kim's mind was constantly besieged by its own mental connections. His mind wandered along a meandering sequence of related facts, exhausting Kim's cognitive resources and leaving him with little capacity for higher-order thought processes (e.g., reasoning and problem solving).

So, think about it once again. Which would you value more—the ability to memorize every word of this textbook, or the ability to understand and apply the knowledge it contains? We would certainly choose the latter. While it's true that most of us have to put much more effort into our memory than Kim did, if you understand how your own memory works, you can minimize your effort and maximize your effectiveness (think test scores!). So, let's take a look at how normal memory works, starting with the basic functions of memory.

Kim Peek was the remarkable man who inspired the character of the Rain Man in the Oscar-winning movie of the same name.

DOES MEMORY FUNCTION LIKE A COMPUTER?

Kim Peek's father affectionately referred to Kim as the "Kimputer" because of his amazing memory skills. Many psychologists also use a computer analogy to help them understand the mind. The *information-processing approach* in cognitive psychology assumes that the mind functions like a very sophisticated computer. A computer accepts input—the information you type into it—stores and processes the information, and allows you to go back and retrieve the same information. In essence, this is also what your mind does with information. As you read this chapter, you are inputting, or **encoding**, information into your memory in the form of **memory traces**, which are stored bits of information in memory. Your mind will process this information and put it into memory **storage**, and then on test day or some other day when the information is needed, you will use **retrieval** processes to recall and output the information from memory as you answer questions on an exam.

The parallels between computers and the mind are hard to miss. After all, we built computers to mimic the mind's processing of information. We even speak of computers in human terms. We speak of computer *memory*, computer *languages*, and computers *talking* to other computers via modems and networks. Scientists have developed software programs that allow computers to solve complex problems, such as making medical and psychological diagnoses (Patel & Ramoni, 1997; Vetterlein, Mandl, & Adlassnig, 2010), using what scientists call *artificial intelligence*. We humans built computers to take over some of our everyday processing of information, but does this mean that computers really function the same way as our minds do? No—even the fastest computers in the world cannot outthink the human mind.

One of the greatest differences between computers and the human mind is the human capacity for consciousness, or awareness of one's own thoughts and the external world. When we focus our attention on something, we bring the stimulus into our consciousness and become consciously aware of it. If we turn our attention inward, we become conscious of our own thoughts. If we focus our attention outward, we become conscious of the outside world (see Chapter 4). Computers do not have this ability because computers lack consciousness. Whether or not programmers will ever be able to develop a computer that has consciousness is a topic of interesting debate among scientists (Buttazzo, 2008). At least for now, consciousness seems to be solely for the living.

Explicit and Implicit Memory

Psychologists define the *conscious* use of memory as **explicit memory** (Bush & Geer, 2001; Graf & Schacter, 1985). We use explicit memory when we consciously search our memory for a previously stored bit of information. For example, try to answer the following question: "What part of the brain's cortex processes visual information?" To answer, you must consciously search your memory for the information you learned in Chapter 2. We hope your search led you to the correct answer, the occipital lobe! While you were trying to answer this question, you were fully aware that you were searching your memory for the answer. In this respect, you were utilizing your memory explicitly. **But do we always know what's going on inside our own memory?**

Not always—sometimes we access and retrieve memories without having consciously tried to do so. For example, have you ever heard a song on the radio that caused you to spontaneously recall an old memory—perhaps a memory of a childhood friend you associate with the song or the exact place where you first heard the song? Or have you ever had some old memory pop into your head for no obvious reason? Most of us have had these experiences, in which previously stored memories were pulled into consciousness without our having consciously searched for them. These examples illustrate the phenomenon of **implicit memory**, which is the *unconscious* use of memory (Graf & Schacter, 1985; Reder, Park, & Kieffaber, 2009). For example, when we brush our teeth, tie our shoes, or make our bed, we usually do so without much conscious awareness of our body movements.

encoding the act of inputting information into memory

memory traces the stored code that represents a piece of information that has been encoded into memory

storage the place where information is retained in memory

retrieval the process of accessing information in memory and pulling it into consciousness

explicit memory the conscious use of memory

implicit memory the unconscious use of memory

Implicit Memory and Word-Stem Completions

Numerous studies on implicit memory have shown that even when we are not consciously aware of it, our memory is still at work (for a review, see Richardson-Klavehn & Bjork, 1988). You can see this for yourself by trying the following demonstration.

TRY THIS DEMONSTRATION

Try this demonstration on yourself by answering the following questions:

1. How much do you weigh? _____
2. On a scale of 1 to 10 (1 = very unhappy; 10 = very happy), rate how happy you are with your appearance. _____
3. On a scale of 1 to 10 (1 = very unhappy; 10 = very happy), rate how happy you are with your current major. _____

Next, complete the following word-stems with whatever word *first* comes to mind.

For example: EXA_____ could be EXA*m* or EXA*mple* or EXA*ct*, and so on.

1. PRE_____
2. DIE_____
3. THI_____
4. MUS_____
5. SKI_____
6. OBE_____
7. CAL_____
8. SLE_____

Now take a look at the words you completed on the word-stem completion part of the questionnaire. Were most of your words somehow related to physical appearance (e.g., pretty, diet, thin, muscle, skinny, obese, calorie, slender, and so on)? Or, were most of your words not appearance-related (e.g., present, died, think, music, skillet, obey, calm, slept, and so on)? Given the conditions in this demonstration, many people would complete the word-stems with appearance-related words.

This demonstration is a modified version of a procedure used by researchers in Australia (Tiggeman, Hargreaves, Polivy, & McFarlane, 2004). They found that exposing participants to media images of thin models or asking participants to think about their own appearance influenced participants to generate more appearance-related words on a word-stem completion task. It appears that seeing images of an ideal body or thinking about one's own appearance activates or *primes* concepts stored in memory, which are related to appearance. Later, when the participants were asked to do the word-stem completions, they may have not been consciously aware that these appearance-related concepts were activated. Yet, they were activated, and they influenced the participants' choice of words to complete the word-stems. Were you aware that your answers to the first two questions were influencing your choices on the word-stem completion task? If not, don't feel bad; it was just your implicit memory helping you out.

We have seen in this section that the function of memory involves three distinct processes: encoding, storage, and retrieval. We also saw that memory can be used in both a conscious, explicit fashion and an unconscious, implicit fashion. With this basic understanding of what memory does, we will move on to look at psychological theories of the structure and process of memory.

Let's REVIEW

In this section, we discussed the functions of memory and described the difference between implicit and explicit use of memory. For a quick check of your understanding, try answering the following questions at increasing levels of difficulty.

1. Recalling information from memory is known as_____.

   a. encoding
   b. storage
   c. retrieval
   d. forgetting

2. _____ is to conscious as _____ is to unconscious.

   a. Implicit memory; explicit memory
   b. Explicit memory; implicit memory
   c. Encoding; retrieval
   d. Retrieval; encoding

3. Which of the following *best* illustrates the use of implicit memory?

   a. knowing the correct answer on a multiple-choice test
   b. trying to remember where you left your car keys
   c. forgetting where you left your car keys
   d. on a hunch, you guess the right answer on a multiple-choice test

ANSWERS 1. c; 2. b; 3. d

THE TRADITIONAL THREE STAGES MODEL OF MEMORY: ARE WE SERIAL PROCESSORS?

Traditionally, memory has been explained as having three distinct stages of storage, called the **three stages model** of memory (R. C. Atkinson & Shiffrin, 1968). When information enters memory, its first stop is **sensory memory**. In sensory memory, information that comes in from our eyes, ears, and other senses is briefly stored in a sensory form, most often a sound or a visual image. If we pay attention to the information in our sensory memory, the information is sent on to the second stage, **short-term memory (STM)**, for further processing. Short-term memory functions as a temporary holding tank for a limited amount of information. We can hold information in short-term memory for only a few seconds before we must act either to send it further on in the memory system or to keep it in short-term memory by refreshing it. If we decide to further process the information in short-term memory, we can move the information from temporary storage to the permanent storage system of **long-term memory (LTM)** (● FIGURE 6.1).

Sensory Memory: Where It All Begins

All the information that enters our memory from the outside world must first pass through our senses. The information we receive from our sense organs lasts for a very brief time after the sensory stimulation has ended. This holding of sensory information after the sensory stimulus ends is sensory memory. Perhaps you have noticed your sensory memory at work. Have you ever heard a fire engine's siren and then found that you could still hear the sound

three stages model an early model of memory proposing that information is stored in three sequential stages: sensory, short-term, and long-term memory.

sensory memory a system of memory that very briefly stores sensory impressions so that we can extract relevant information from them for further processing

LEARNING OBJECTIVES

What Should You Know?
- Describe the three stages model of memory.
- Describe the function and characteristics of sensory, short-term, and long-term memory.
- Describe the newer conception of working memory and how it relates to the three stages model's concept of short-term memory.

short-term memory (STM) a system of memory that is limited in both capacity and duration; in the three stages model of memory, short-term memory is seen as the intermediate stage between sensory memory and long-term memory

long-term memory (LTM) a system of memory that works to store memories for a long time, perhaps even permanently

FIGURE 6.1

● **The Traditional Three Stages Model of Memory** The traditional three stages model of memory proposes that in forming new memories, information passes sequentially from sensory memory to short-term memory to long-term memory.

```
Information → Sensory memory → Short-term memory ⇄ Long-term memory
```

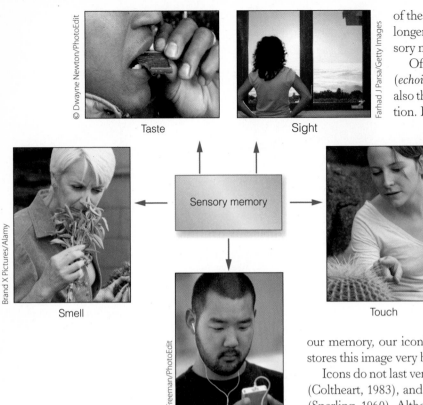

Taste

Sight

Smell

Sensory memory

Touch

Hearing

FIGURE 6.2

● **Sensory Memory** Psychologists believe that we have sensory memory for each of our senses. In sensory memory, we store a brief sensory impression of the object we are sensing.

of the siren in your head for a short time after you could no longer actually hear the siren? If so, you caught your sensory memory at work.

Of all our senses, sight (*iconic memory*) and hearing (*echoic memory*), the two most studied by psychologists, are also the primary means through which we acquire information. But they are not the only useful senses. We also learn through our senses of taste, smell, and touch (*haptic memory*). Psychologists assume that we have sensory memories for each of the senses (see ● FIGURE 6.2).

Visual Sensory Memory: Iconic Memory

Iconic memory is the sensory memory for visual stimuli. As we saw in Chapter 3, when you look at something, your eyes take in this information and *transduce* it into neural impulses. These sensory impulses are then sent to the brain for further processing. To get information on what we have seen into our memory, our iconic memory takes a "snapshot" of our sensation and stores this image very briefly. This stored image is referred to as an *icon*.

Icons do not last very long. As soon as we see an object, an icon is formed (Coltheart, 1983), and it lasts for only about half a second before it decays (Sperling, 1960). Although icons do not last long, they last long enough for our minds to extract information about what we have seen and send it on to short-term memory. If the icon remained in our minds for a longer time, it is likely that it would overlap with icons for new visual stimuli, creating a confusing effect similar to that of superimposed photographs.

When you watch a movie, you experience this phenomenon of overlapping icons, but in this case the overlap leads to the illusion of movement. A movie is made up of frames, still shots all strung together, yet we perceive movement on the screen. **How can we perceive movement when all we are seeing is a series of still pictures?** The answer lies in the speed with which the frames of the movie are changed on the screen. The frames are projected on the screen at a speed faster than one frame per half second, so the icon we make of an individual frame is still in our head when our eyes see the next frame. The icon we make for the second frame will be superimposed on the icon for the first frame, and we will perceive movement on the screen. To destroy the illusion of movement on the screen, all you would have to do is slow down the film. If you've ever watched old silent films, such as Charlie Chaplin films, you've probably noticed this effect. Silent films were shot and projected at slower speeds, with fewer frames per second. The result is less overlap of icons in the viewer's sensory memory, and so the movement in the film looks jerky and halting. Our icons remain in effect long enough to allow us to perceive movement in movies, but not so long as to cause problems in our everyday perception of the world. We need to retain the icon only long enough for us to pay attention to it and transfer it to short-term memory. A similar process occurs when we hear something.

Auditory Sensory Memory: Echoic Memory

Auditory sensory memory is called **echoic memory**. When you hear something, your echoic memory makes an auditory image or recording of that sound and stores it briefly. This recording is called an *echo*. Echoes have a much longer duration than visual icons. Echoes last up to 2 seconds after your ears stop hearing the sound (Klatzky, 1980; Triesman, 1964). Holding information you've just heard in echoic memory for 2 seconds gives you more time to process the information, which reduces the chance that you might miss something you hear. This is especially important for auditory information because once auditory information is lost, it is generally more difficult to retrieve than visual information.

iconic memory sensory memory for visual information

echoic memory sensory memory for auditory information

For example, if your professor writes some important information on the board concerning an upcoming exam and you are not paying attention, all you have to do is look at the board again. If, instead, your professor gives the class the information verbally, and you do not hear the announcement the first time, you will be out of luck unless you can get someone to repeat the message for you. This is not as sure a bet as simply looking at the board again.

Because auditory information is easily lost, echoic memory plays a crucial role in our processing of information. The echo you store of your professor's voice gives you a full 2 seconds after the message ends to process the information before it is lost. Perhaps you have reaped the benefits of echoic memory in the past. Have you ever asked someone to repeat herself, only to realize that you did, in fact, know what she had said? If so, you knew what she had said because your echoic memory gave you a second shot at processing her message. Think of how much you might have missed if it weren't for your echoic memory.

Transferring Information From Sensory to Short-Term Memory

As we have seen, the function of sensory memory is to hold sensory information long enough for us to process it and send it on to short-term memory for further processing. How do we transfer information from sensory memory to short-term memory? **Does all sensory information reach short-term memory? Or do we lose some sensory information before it reaches short-term memory?**

We receive an enormous amount of information every day through our senses. Some of this information is important and needs to be processed more thoroughly in memory, but much of it does not need to be remembered or processed further. For example, as you hold this book, do you need to be aware of the feel of the pages as you turn them? Tomorrow, will you have to recall and describe the ink color of these words, the exact texture of these pages, and the sounds the pages make as you turn them? What is important is the message of the text; the rest is inconsequential. Because we receive so much useless sensory information each day, our memory system has mechanisms for getting rid of unneeded sensory information.

According to the three stages model, the transfer point between sensory memory and short-term memory provides one opportunity to eliminate unneeded information. For information to be transferred from sensory memory to short-term memory, we must first pay attention to the sensory information. We pay attention to something by focusing our consciousness on that stimulus. As you read a phone number in a phone book, you pay attention to the number and bring it into your consciousness. As you do this, you ensure that the sensory information held in the icon of the number will be transferred from iconic memory into short-term memory (see ● FIGURES 6.3a and 6.3b). If you are distracted or unmotivated, you may gaze at the page without paying attention to the number. In that case, the sensory information in the icon will be lost because icons decay after a half second. As you can see, if you don't pay attention to what you are reading, you are wasting your time.

Attention is a necessary step in getting information into memory, but there is more to it than that. Once information makes it to your short-term memory, you have to take active steps to keep this information in memory.

As you carry on a conversation, your echoic memory briefly stores a "recording" of the sounds you hear. This recording, called an echo, may help you avoid missing part of the conversation. If you didn't quite catch what your friend has just said, you have up to 2 seconds in which to reprocess the information still contained within the echo before this information is lost.

Short-Term Memory: Where Memories Are Made (and Lost)

The three stages view of memory conceptualizes short-term memory as a temporary holding tank for information that has been transferred in from sensory memory. In sensory memory, information is encoded in its natural sensory form. Short-term memory uses a **dual coding system** in which memories can be stored either visually or acoustically (Paivio, 1982).

dual coding system a system of memory that encodes information in more than one type of code or format

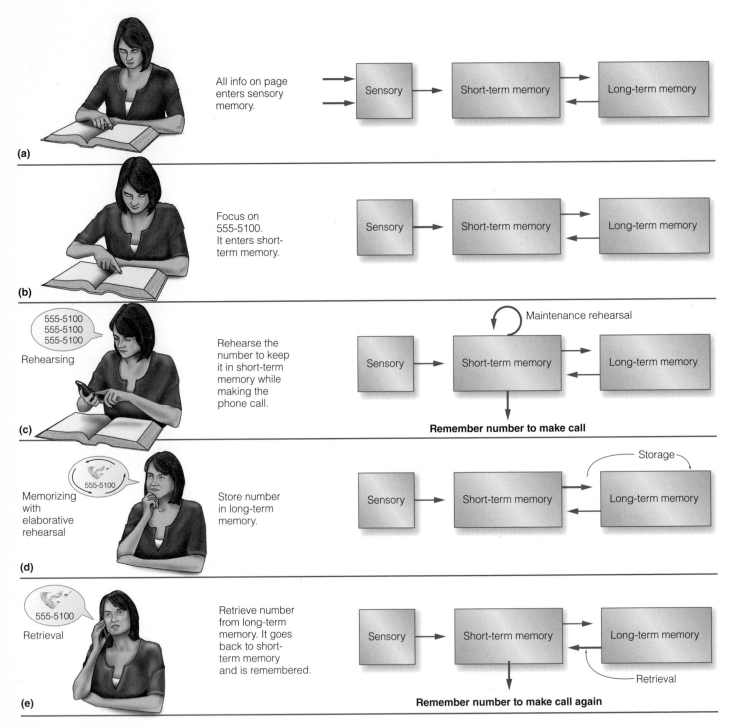

FIGURE 6.3

● **The Three Stages Model of Memory** (a) As Juanita looks up the phone number, the information enters into her visual sensory memory. (b) As she focuses her attention on the phone number, the information now moves to her short-term memory. (c) To keep the number in mind while she goes to the phone and dials the pizza shop, Juanita uses maintenance rehearsal, repeating the number over and over to herself. (d) As Juanita continues to think about the number, she engages in elaborative rehearsal by associating the number with the idea of pizza in her mind; as a result, the number is now stored in her long-term memory. (e) Later, Juanita retrieves the number from long-term memory when once again she wants to order a pizza.

Most verbal information appears to be encoded in short-term memory in an *acoustic* form. In other words, the information we store in short-term memory is primarily about the *sound* of the words that we are storing. This appears to be true even when the information we are storing comes from our visual sensory memory. So, even if you initially read the material, you are still more likely to encode the information in an acoustic form (R. Conrad, 1964; Paivio, 1971).

When we see or hear a word, we draw out the sounds of the word from our sensory memory and temporarily store this information in our short-term memory. Try this example. Think about what you did yesterday. Can you "hear" your own voice describing the events in your mind? Most of us can. In this example, you are using the stored acoustic aspects of your memory as you recall yesterday's events. This type of acoustic information is what is most often stored in short-term memory.

We often store acoustic information in short-term memory, but we are also able to store visual information in short-term memory. When we are presented with information that is nonverbal, we may store it in a visual form in short-term memory. For example, if you see a picture of a house, you might store the memory of the house in the form of a visual image. The fact that information can be stored in short-term memory in either acoustic or visual form gives us flexibility as we process information. Thus, you may recall the directions to a place of business in the next town visually or auditorily.

Although short-term memory serves us well, it is another point in the system where information can be lost. Because short-term memory is designed for temporary memory storage, both its capacity and its duration are limited. You can hold only a small amount of information in STM, and only for a short time. If you've ever tried to hold a phone number in your head while you make it to the phone, then you know just how limited short-term memory is and how susceptible it is to forgetting.

The Capacity of Short-Term Memory: Seven (Plus or Minus Two)

In 1956, psychologist George Miller published a landmark paper on what he called the *magic number 7* or the capacity of short-term memory (Miller, 1956) In this research, Miller had participants try to remember as many items from a list as they could. Using this type of approach, Miller found that the average person could hold about 7 ± 2 items in short-term memory. This 7 ± 2 capacity applies to such items as numbers, words, and other small bits of information. Recently, researchers studying the brain have suggested that the rather small capacity of our short-term memory might be due to the manner in which neurons in the hippocampus code and store information (Migliore, Novara, & Tegolo, 2008).

Nonetheless, our 7 ± 2 capacity easily allows us to hold a phone number, a short grocery list, or the name of a person we just met in our short-term memory. But what if we need to hold more information in our short-term memory? **Can we fit more than seven items in this memory store?** Maybe. One technique for extending the amount of information we can hold in short-term memory is called **chunking** (Simon, 1974). Chunking involves grouping information together into meaningful units, or *chunks*. For example, many of the important numbers in our culture—social security numbers, phone numbers, license plates, credit card numbers, and so on—are usually separated by dashes or spaces to facilitate our remembering them.

However, there is also a limit to how much information can be chunked. The number of chunks that we can store in short-term memory decreases as the chunks get larger. In other words, you can hold more 3-digit numbers in short-term memory than you can 8-digit numbers (Simon, 1974). Think of short-term memory as a bookshelf. You can fit only so many books on the shelf at one time. If the books are skinny, you can fit as many as 9. If the books are fat, you will be able to fit only 4 or 5. If you add more books to an already full shelf, some books will be pushed off. Like the bookshelf in our metaphor, the capacity of short-term memory is similarly limited. The magic number 7 holds, but only for relatively small chunks of information.

The Duration of Short-Term Memory: It's Yours for 30 Seconds

Duration is the second major limitation on short-term memory. Once information passes into short-term memory, it can only be kept there for around 30 seconds without some type of rehearsal or refreshing of the material (J. A. Brown, 1958; L. R. Peterson & Peterson, 1959).

In a typical experiment to determine the duration of short-term memory, participants hear a three-letter combination or nonsense syllable (such as HYL) and are asked to remember it. Immediately after, the participants are asked to start counting backward by threes from some starting number (for example, starting with 505: 502, 499, 496, . . .). Counting backward prevents the participants from studying or rehearsing the syllable they heard. To measure how well

chunking a means of using one's limited short-term memory resources more efficiently by combining small bits of information to form larger bits of information, or chunks

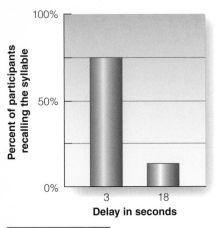

FIGURE 6.4

● **Short-Term Memory Duration**
As you can see, the duration of short-term memory is very limited. Without rehearsal, information stored in short-term memory will be lost in a matter of seconds. L. R. Peterson and Peterson (1959) found that participants could remember most of a list of words 3 seconds after hearing it, but few of the words were recalled after 18 seconds.

maintenance rehearsal repeating information over and over again to keep it in short-term memory for an extended period of time

elaborative rehearsal forming associations or links between information one is trying to learn and information already stored in long-term memory so as to facilitate the transfer of this new information into long-term memory

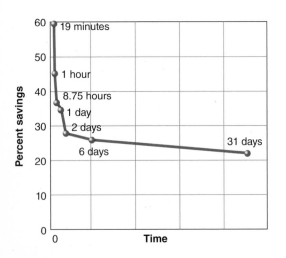

participants retain the syllable in short-term memory, the researchers stop the counting at specific intervals and ask participants to recall the syllable. ● FIGURE 6.4 shows the data from one such study. As you can see, for these participants retention dropped off rapidly. After only 18 seconds, many were unable to recall the syllable (L. R. Peterson & Peterson, 1959).

What if you have to keep some information in short-term memory for more than 30 seconds? Suppose you look up a phone number and have to remember it while you take a 2-minute walk to the phone. If you can't write the phone number down, you need to find a way to keep it in your short-term memory for longer than 30 seconds. Off the top of your head, what do you think you would do in this situation? One simple solution would be to repeat the phone number over and over out loud as you walk to the phone. This repetition of the material in short-term memory, called **maintenance rehearsal**, is useful for extending the duration of short-term memory (Nairne, 2002; see Figure 6.3c, p. 226). When you repeat the information over and over again, you resupply it to short-term memory before it can decay, thus extending its retention for another 30 seconds or so before you must repeat the number to yourself again.

How We Transfer Information From Short-Term to Long-Term Memory

Maintenance rehearsal may be useful for keeping information in short-term memory (see Figure 6.3c), but what if you want to move information from short-term memory into permanent, long-term memory storage? Unfortunately, you will likely have to do more than merely repeat the information if you want to store it permanently in long-term memory. Maintenance rehearsal accomplishes only a *weak* transfer of information into long-term memory (Glenberg, Smith, & Green, 1977; Lockhart & Craik, 1990). And, memories encoded using maintenance rehearsal are easily forgotten with time (see ● FIGURE 6.5). You may have learned this lesson the hard way if repetition is your primary means of studying material for exams. If you simply repeat information over and over in your head, or repeatedly read over the information in your text and notes, your studying will not accomplish strong transfer of information into long-term memory, and you may find yourself in trouble on test day.

Elaborative Rehearsal

Repetition of information is merely maintenance rehearsal. As we just saw, the main function of maintenance rehearsal is to keep information in short-term memory—and information in short-term memory is only temporary. To really get information into your long-term memory, you use another technique, called **elaborative rehearsal** (Craik & Lockhart, 1972; see Figure 6.3d, p. 226). Elaborative rehearsal involves forming *associations*, or mental connections, between the information in short-term memory that you want to store and information you already have stored in your permanent long-term memory. To memorize a phone number forever, it helps to associate the number with other information that you have stored in LTM. For example, advertisers often use jingles to get customers to recall a business's phone number. Associating the phone number with the melody serves to elaborate it in memory. Elaborative rehearsal also explains why many of us can easily recall the words to a song as we are singing it, but have a very difficult time reciting the lyrics without the aid of singing.

FIGURE 6.5

● **Retention After Maintenance Rehearsal** Psychologist Hermann Ebbinghaus learned lists of nonsense syllables (e.g., NOH) using maintenance rehearsal and then calculated how much of this learning was retained over various periods of time—a factor he called savings in learning. A savings score of 100% would mean that no learning was lost with time. As you can see, memory for the syllables dropped off very quickly over time. After only 2 days, nearly 75% of the learning was lost. These data clearly indicate that maintenance rehearsal is a relatively poor means of storing information in long-term memory. If you want to really retain what you have learned, you should use elaborative rehearsal. (Based on data from Ebbinghaus, 1885/1913).

Another powerful means of elaborative rehearsal is to connect new material to one's self (Gutchess, Kensinger, Yoon, & Schacter, 2007). We have been encouraging you to generate personally relevant examples of the material you are learning in this text so that you can reap the benefits of elaborative rehearsal as you read this text. Every time you generate an example from your own life that demonstrates a psychological principle, you are engaging in elaborative rehearsal and increasing the chances of retrieving the material later (see Figure 6.3e, p. 226).

Levels of Processing

This notion that the more thoroughly or deeply you process information, the more strongly you transfer it to long-term memory is referred to as the **levels-of-processing model** of memory (Craik & Lockhart, 1972). When Fergus Craik and Robert Lockhart (1972) first proposed the levels-of-processing approach, it was assumed that the *only* way to get information into long-term memory was to use elaborative rehearsal. Subsequent research has shown that this isn't necessarily the case. Although maintenance rehearsal is a shallow form of processing that doesn't involve much elaboration of the material, it does allow for some transfer of information into long-term memory (Lockhart & Craik, 1990). For example, you may eventually remember your checking account number if you have to write it, and thus repeat it, frequently enough. However, the type of transfer to long-term memory that occurs with maintenance rehearsal doesn't really help students pass an exam in which they actually have to understand what they are talking or writing about. In one study, it was found that if you increase the amount of maintenance rehearsal by 9 times (900%), you increase your recall of the information by only 1.5% (Glenberg et al., 1977). Elaborative rehearsal, in contrast, involves a very deep level of processing. To elaborate material, you must access information stored in long-term memory and associate it with the information you are trying to learn. This requires much more effort and thought than merely repeating the information over and over. The good news is that this effort pays off in terms of better memory for the information. Elaborative rehearsal is clearly your best bet if you want to successfully master material, whether it be in a course or in life.

levels-of-processing model
a model that predicts that information that is processed deeply and elaboratively will be best retained in and recalled from long-term memory

As an example, let's say that you attend a multicultural fair at your school in which students bring foods from their native cultures for everyone to try (one of the author's schools regularly holds such an event). You sample a West African dish called a *puff-puff*, a type of slightly sweet, fried bread that is often eaten with kidney bean stew. Finding the puff-puff delicious, you decide to commit it to memory so that you can later find some means of obtaining more—trust us, they're that good!

Puff-puffs are a West African fried bread traditionally eaten with kidney bean stew.

If you want to commit information about the puff-puff to long-term memory, you must associate it with what you already know. You might think about how a puff-puff looks very much like an American doughnut hole. You may note that the puff-puff contains nutmeg, which reminds you of drinking eggnog with nutmeg during the winter. You might associate the puff-puff with similar fried breads in other cultures, such as Native American fry bread or beignets from New Orleans. Or you might associate puff-puffs with your friend Denis from West Africa.

Susann Doyle-Portillo

Do you see what we're doing here? We are finding ways to *associate* and *link* the puff-puff to concepts that you already have stored in long-term memory, such as doughnuts, nutmeg, and a friend. This is what elaborative rehearsal is all about. You go beyond simply repeating information to actually *thinking* about the information, and in doing so, you process the information deeply enough to efficiently transfer it to long-term memory. When you use elaborative rehearsal as you learn, you will retain the information in the permanent storage system of long-term memory in a way that maximizes the chances that you will be able to retrieve it when you need it, such as on test day or when searching online for West African recipes.

Does Short-Term Memory Really Exist?

Recall that the three stages model proposes short-term memory as a separate, intermediate stage of memory that is limited in capacity and duration (see Figure 6.1, p. 223). As you learned in Chapter 1, any scientific theory must be backed up by the results of scientific experiments before we place much stock in it. As you will shortly see, not all of the available research supports the three stages model, particularly in its conception of short-term memory. Let's take a look at the evidence that supports and that calls into doubt the three stages model.

The Serial-Position Curve: Primacy and Recency

In a serial-position experiment, participants listen to a list of around 20 words slowly read aloud by the experimenter. Immediately following the last word, the participants are asked to engage in *free recall* of the words—that is, to recall the words in any order that they can. The tendency for participants to recall each word correctly is plotted against the position of the word in the original list. ● FIGURE 6.6 shows a typical serial-position curve. You will notice in Figure 6.6 that not all of the words in the list have an equal chance of being recalled. Rather, words at the beginning and the end of the list are recalled better than words in the middle of the list.

The overall shape of the serial-position curve fits well with the three stages view of memory. In fact, the three stages model predicts that you will obtain a curve like that shown in Figure 6.6. The tendency for words at the beginning of the list to be better recalled, called the **primacy effect**, can be explained in terms of long-term memory. As participants listen to the list of words, they spend considerable time rehearsing the words at the beginning of the list in their short-term memory. While they are doing this, they have no short-term memory capacity left to rehearse the words in the middle of the list. Therefore, words in the middle of the list are lost from short-term memory, but the words at the beginning of the list are moved to long-term memory and thus are remembered well at recall.

The words at the end of the list are also well remembered, in what is called the **recency effect**. The recency effect is thought to occur because participants still have these words in short-term memory at the time they are asked to recall the list. Therefore, all the participants

primacy effect the tendency for people to recall words from the beginning of a list better than words that appeared in the middle of the list

recency effect the tendency for people to recall words from the end of a list better than words that appeared in the middle of the list

● **Serial-Position Curve** In a serial-position experiment (Murdoch, 1962), participants are asked to remember a list of words that are read aloud to them. In such experiments, words at the beginning of the list (primacy effect) and words at the end of the list (recency effect) are remembered best.

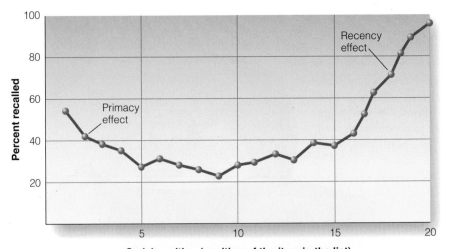

Serial position (position of the item in the list)

have to do is dump these words from their short-term memory before going on to retrieve the other words (from the beginning of the list) from long-term memory. In the serial-position experiment, participants should be able to recall the last two or three words they heard (Glanzer & Cunitz, 1966). The recency effect does not extend to the full 7 ± 2 capacity of short-term memory because some of the capacity of short-term memory is taken up in rehearsing the words from the start of the list and in continuing to hear new words.

Interestingly, memory for recent events is one of the aspects of memory that is most affected by normal aging (Wingfield & Kahana, 2002). As we get older, our short-term memory tends to suffer more than our distant long-term memories. One of the authors, who is only 48, sometimes shops with a mental grocery list and often leaves the grocery store without buying everything she needs. This type of forgetting almost never occurred in her 20s. However, not all short-term memory suffers as we age. In one study, participants of different ages were shown a series of three pictures in rapid succession. Seconds later, they were shown a test picture and asked to determine if the test picture was one of the pictures they had just seen. In this case, younger and older participants showed serial-position curves that were strikingly similar. The older participants did *not* have poorer recency memory than the younger participants (Sekuler, McLaughlin, Kahana, Wingfield, & Yotsumoto, 2006). It appears that aging negatively affects recency memory for verbal information much more than for visual information. Perhaps the author should *visualize* what she needs to buy at the store instead of naming the items—maybe she'd avoid so many return trips!

Although numerous serial-position experiments like these support the three stages model of memory, some scientists still express doubts about the model, especially its conception of short-term memory. One lingering question is whether short-term memory is one single storage system. Anecdotal evidence from case studies suggests that short-term memory may not be a single storage system. One case concerns a man named K.F., who suffered damage to his left parietal and occipital lobes in a motorcycle accident. After the accident, K.F. had no impairment of long-term memory, but he did experience problems with short-term memory. K.F.'s memory span was greatly reduced, and he had a very small recency effect during serial-position experiments (Shallice & Warrington, 1970). These findings indicate that K.F. had lost some of his short-term memory functioning, but further research produced findings that are inconsistent with the three stages view of short-term memory. K.F. was found to have noticeable problems with his short-term memory for orally presented letters and digits, but fewer problems with visually presented stimuli (Warrington & Shallice, 1972). K.F. also had no short-term memory problems for sounds that were not words, such as sirens and car horns (Shallice & Warrington, 1974). These findings suggest that K.F.'s short-term memory was not a single storage system. If it had been, he would have had problems with *all* types of short-term memory.

The case study of K.F. does not prove that short-term memory consists of multiple storage systems. As you learned in Chapter 1, cases studies are of limited value in helping us understand how the average person functions. It is possible that K.F.'s brain and mind functioned differently from other people's even before his accident. However, the case of K.F. raises some interesting concerns about the three stages view of short-term memory.

Another potential problem with the three stages model has to do with how we process information in memory. The three stages model proposes that the only route by which information can reach long-term memory is through short-term memory. There is some doubt as to whether this is true (Logie, 1999). If information must pass from sensory memory into short-term memory without having made contact with long-term memory, then long-term memory is activated only *after* information is processed in short-term memory. The problem is that this is not always the case. If you are given a list of seven words to remember, you will likely use maintenance rehearsal (repeating the words over and over to yourself) to keep these words in short-term memory. To do so, however, you will have to know how to pronounce the words, which you can only know by accessing your knowledge (from long-term memory) of how to pronounce the words. You must access and retrieve information in long-term memory *before* you have processed the information into long-term memory (Logie, 1999).

These questions about whether or not short-term memory is a single storage system and whether or not short-term memory is wholly separate from long-term memory have cast doubt on the traditional three stages model of memory and led to the development of alternative views of memory. One of the most influential alternatives to the three stages model is the *working memory* view of memory (Baddeley, 1986; Baddeley & Hitch, 1974).

The Working Memory View: Parallel Memory

Today, many researchers reject the notion that information passes sequentially through the three stages of memory and instead propose a new type of memory called **working memory** (see Baddeley, 2002). The working memory model views the memory stages in more of a *parallel* fashion as opposed to a *serial* fashion. In other words, the working memory model assumes that we process different aspects of memory at the same time rather than in a series of stages as predicted by the three stages model.

In this view, working memory and short-term memory are parts contained within long-term memory (● FIGURE 6.7). Working memory moves information into and out of long-term memory, whereas short-term memory operates as the part of working memory that briefly stores the information we are using at any particular time.

Suppose a bee stings you. Your haptic sensory memory registers the pain of the sting, and your visual sensory memory captures the sight of the bee. These sensory impressions are then sent to working memory, where they are combined into an integrated memory representation of being stung by the bee (c.f., Y. Kessler & Meiran, 2006). At the same time, your working memory may activate a long-term memory of what you learned in first-aid class about allergic reactions to bee stings. Working memory pulls this information on allergic reactions into short-term memory, and you now consciously think about the signs of an allergic reaction as you check to see if you are having one. You conclude that you are not having an allergic reaction. So you cease to think about the possibility of an allergic reaction, and working memory transfers the new knowledge that you are not allergic to bee stings to long-term memory.

As you can see, in this view of memory, information does not flow sequentially from sensory to short-term to long-term memory. Rather, working memory plays several roles. The short-term memory part of working memory acts as a storage system for information that is currently being used. At the same time, other parts of working memory act to retrieve information, process new information, and send new and revised information on to long-term memory. The order in which the different memory stages are activated can vary depending on the circumstances.

One advantage of the working memory model is that it can explain why we sometimes seem to access long-term memory before we process information in short-term memory. Take, for instance, the phenomenon of *top-down perceptual processing* that you learned about in Chapter 3. Top-down perceptual processing occurs when we use stored knowledge (from long-term memory) to interpret sensory information. As you read the words on this page, you must access information that you have stored in long-term memory about the English language so that you can pronounce and read these words. As the words on the page enter your

working memory a multifaceted component of long-term memory that contains short-term memory, a central executive, a phonological loop, and a visuospatial sketch pad; the function of working memory is to access, move, and process information that we are currently using

FIGURE 6.7

● **The Working Memory View of Memory** In the working memory view of memory, the stages of memory work more in a parallel fashion than in a sequential fashion. In this view, short-term memory and working memory are parts of memory that are contained within long-term memory. Working memory moves information into and out of both short-term and long-term memory as necessary.

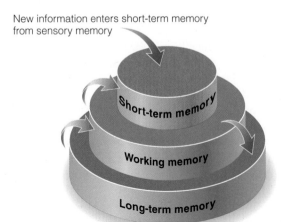

New information enters short-term memory from sensory memory

Short-term memory

Working memory

Long-term memory

• Working memory retrieves information from long-term memory to help process information in short-term memory; for example, the meaning of words stored in short-term memory may be accessed from long-term memory.

• Working memory also retrieves stored information when you need it—for an exam, your address, directions to your aunt's house—and sends it to short-term memory.

• Working memory also moves information from short-term memory into long-term memory for storage; for example, when you are studying, working memory will move the information you want to remember into long-term memory.

short-term memory, you know what they mean and how they are pronounced. The working memory view of memory can explain this, but the three stages model cannot. Because the working memory view is more of a parallel processing model, it allows for the possibility that you can access long-term memory as you are reading the words on the page. In this model, you can go to your long-term memories to help you process perceptual information in a top-down fashion (Logie, 1996).

Another advantage of the working memory view of memory is that it can explain some of the memory data found in people like K.F. who experience brain damage. As you will recall, the three stages model of memory didn't fit K.F.'s case because he had problems with some, but not all, aspects of short-term memory. The selective nature of K.F.'s short-term memory problems argued against the three stages model of a single short-term memory store (Shallice & Warrington, 1974; Warrington & Shallice, 1972). In the working memory model, such selective problems can occur because working memory is not viewed as a single entity (Baddeley, 2002).

The Central Executive

One of the more prominent theories of a multicomponent working memory proposes that working memory contains a **central executive** component and two subordinate systems: the **phonological loop**, which processes auditory information (e.g., the buzzing of a bee), and the **visuospatial sketch pad**, which processes visual and spatial information (e.g., the sight of a bumblebee) (Baddeley, 2002; Baddeley, 1992; Baddeley & Hitch, 1974). These systems are called *subordinate systems* because they fall under the control of the central executive (● FIGURE 6.8).

The central executive functions as an attention-controlling mechanism within working memory. The central executive must coordinate the actions of the subordinate systems and integrate information that comes in from these systems (e.g., directing you to pay attention to how close a bee gets to your arm). This makes the central executive component especially important when we are engaged in tasks that require attention and the coordination of visual and auditory information, such as when playing a video game (Baddeley, 1992). Recently, some researchers have proposed that faulty executive functioning—or an inability to direct one's attention while using working memory—may be one of the underlying mechanisms in attention deficit hyperactivity disorder (ADHD) in children (Sonuga-Barke, Dalen, & Remington, 2003). Similarly, Kim Peek's inability to keep his mind from jumping from idea to idea suggests some impairment of executive functioning.

Interestingly, there is also evidence to suggest that one of the results of Alzheimer's disease, which is characterized by progressive memory loss, is a loss of central executive functioning (Crowell, Luis, Vanderploeg, Schinka, & Mullan, 2002). This loss of central executive functioning can be seen when Alzheimer's patients are asked to do visual and auditory tasks at the same time. Because their central executive is not functioning properly, Alzheimer's patients have trouble coordinating and integrating information from visual and auditory sources, and they experience more problems than a healthy person does on the simultaneous tasks. However, when Alzheimer's patients are tested on a single task that is scaled to their ability, they do not perform more poorly than control participants (Logie, Della Sala, Wynn, & Baddeley, 2000). This pattern of results supports

central executive in the working memory model, the attention-controlling component of working memory

phonological loop in the working memory model, the part of working memory that processes the phonological, or sound, qualities of information

visuospatial sketch pad in the working memory model, the part of working memory that processes the visual and spatial aspects of information

FIGURE 6.8

● **Baddeley's Central Executive Model of Working Memory** In Baddeley's model of working memory, the central executive integrates visual information from the visuospatial sketch pad and auditory information from the phonological loop. The integration of information that the central executive provides is crucial when we are engaged in activities that require us to use both visual and auditory information—as in deciding how to react when you both see and hear nearby bumblebees.

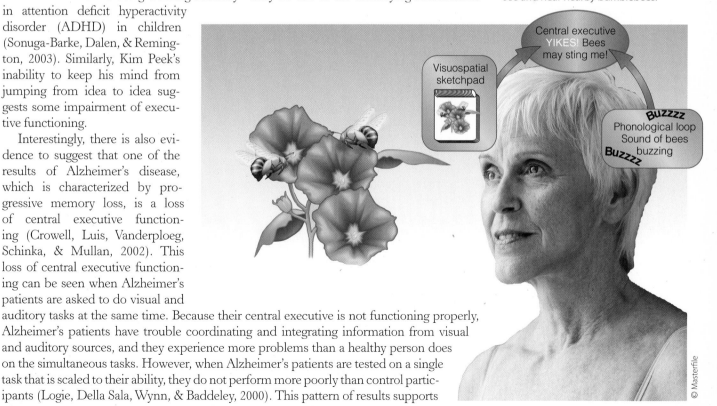

© Masterfile

TABLE 6.1

● **Differences Between the Traditional Three Stages Model of Memory and the Working Memory Model**

THREE STAGES MODEL	WORKING MEMORY MODEL
Memory consists of three separate stages: sensory memory, STM, and LTM.	Memory consists of several interacting components: sensory memory, working memory, and LTM.
STM is a single component of memory that is separate from LTM.	Working memory is a multicomponent part of LTM that includes STM, the central executive, the phonological loop, and the visuospatial sketch pad.
Memory operates in a serial fashion.	Memory operates in a parallel fashion.
The three stages model cannot easily explain some cognitive processes such as top-down perceptual processing.	Because the working memory model is a parallel model of memory, it can better account for processes such as top-down perceptual processing

the notion that the structure of working memory has multiple components, with at least one component that integrates information.

The central executive model of working memory also fits well with K.F.'s memory problems. As you will recall, K.F. had substantial problems holding most auditory information in short-term memory. The pattern of K.F.'s problems seems consistent with the idea of a central executive and its two subordinate systems, the phonological loop and the visuospatial sketch pad. If we assume that K.F.'s brain damage affected the phonological loop part of his working memory but not the visuospatial sketch pad, we would expect him to have trouble processing auditory information but not to have trouble processing visual information. This is exactly what we see in the case of K.F.!

The working memory view offers a more complex model than the traditional three stages model (see ● TABLE 6.1), one that explains more of what researchers observe about memory. This does not mean, however, that psychologists have a complete understanding of how memory works. There is disagreement even among working memory theorists as to exactly what role working memory plays in the memory system (for example, see Buehner, Mangels, Krumm, & Ziegler, 2005). Theorists also disagree as to whether working memory is separate from long-term memory. Not all researchers are convinced that working memory is composed of multiple components, and those who are convinced of its multiplicity do not agree on the number of components. Even Alan Baddeley, the original author of the working memory model, freely acknowledged that our understanding of working memory is still actively developing (Repovs & Baddeley, 2006). Still, relative to the three stages model, the working memory model represents a better explanation of memory (see Table 6.1).

Let's REVIEW

In this section, we described the three stages model of memory and its limitations. We also introduced the newer idea of working memory that deals with some of the limits of the three stages model. For a quick check of your understanding, try answering the following questions at increasing levels of difficulty.

1. Which view of memory holds that information must pass through the memory storage systems in a serial fashion?

   a. the three stages model
   b. the working memory view of memory
   c. the parallel processing view of memory
   d. all of the above

2. When you are listening to music, which component of working memory are you *least* likely to be using?

   a. the phonological loop
   b. the central executive
   c. the visuospatial sketch pad
   d. short-term memory

3. Which of the following is the *best* example of elaborative rehearsal?

   a. reading and outlining a chapter in your text
   b. outlining the material from your text and your lecture notes
   c. using flashcards of key concepts in the chapter
   d. repeatedly reading over your lecture notes

ANSWERS 1. a; 2. c; 3. b

LONG-TERM MEMORY: HOW DO WE STORE INFORMATION FOR THE LONG HAUL?

According to both of the two memory models we've explored—the three stages model and the working memory model—long-term memory is our largest and most permanent memory storage system (Figures 6.3, p. 226, and 6.7, p. 232). Long-term memory is where we store information that we wish to keep for a long period of time. Information there remains unconscious until we activate it and call it into working memory or short-term memory. Let's begin by getting a better feel for the nature of long-term memory.

LEARNING OBJECTIVES

What Should You Know?
- Explain how information is organized in long-term memory.
- Describe the different types of long-term memory and their characteristics.

The Capacity of Long-Term Memory

For all practical purposes, long-term memory seems to have a limitless capacity. To date, psychologists have not found any reason to believe that long-term memory has a limited capacity, as short-term memory and working memory do. We can safely say that you are unlikely to ever run out of room in your long-term memory. It may sometimes feel as though your brain is full, but you still have the capacity to store more information in long-term memory. What you are feeling is more likely to be related to problems in focusing your attention or a lack of available capacity in short-term or working memory. If you can pay enough attention to move the information through sensory memory to short-term/working memory, and then rehearse the material enough to get it to long-term memory, you will find that you have ample storage space for the information.

Encoding in Long-Term Memory

Information is encoded in long-term memory in several forms. As in the other parts of memory storage, information in long-term memory may be stored in both acoustic and visual forms (Paivio, 1986). However, we more often encode long-term memories semantically, in terms of the meaning of the information. **Semantic encoding** stores the gist, or general meaning, of the stimulus rather than storing all of the sensory details (J. R. Anderson, 1974; Gernsbacher, 1985; Wanner, 1968).

Semantic encoding offers some distinct advantages over acoustic and visual encoding in long-term memory even though it sacrifices a lot of the details. For example, if you read a description of a West African puff-puff in a cookbook, you could store information about the sound of the word *puff-puff* or the visual image of a puff-puff in your long-term memory, but this wouldn't really help you make a puff-puff. In fact, you could memorize an exact picture of a puff-puff and still not know what it is. On the other hand, if you stored semantic information about the puff-puff—that it is a West African food consisting of a fried ball of dough made of flour, eggs, sugar, nutmeg, shortening, milk, and baking powder—you would potentially have enough understanding of a puff-puff to actually make one. A picture couldn't give you that.

Similarly, as you read this page, you do not need to store a visual image of the page or an acoustic recording of your voice reading these words. You need to store the gist of the information contained on the page and how the information relates to what you have already stored in long-term memory. You accomplish this by encoding the information—in a semantic code—and connecting this new information with the other information you have already stored in long-term memory.

Kablonk/PhotoLibrary

Although you may sometimes feel as if your long-term memory is "full," you always have the capacity to store information—provided that you are not too tired, distracted, or unmotivated to rehearse and elaborate the material you wish to learn.

Organization in Long-Term Memory

One aspect of encoding information in long-term memory is how we organize it. What would life be like if you did not organize the contents of your long-term memory? Think

semantic encoding encoding memory traces in terms of the meaning of the information being stored

of your long-term memory as a library. Imagine going to the library to look for a specific book, only to find that the librarians had been tossing the books up on the shelf, in no particular order, for the last 10 years. How would you find the book you need? You would have to start on the first shelf of the first bookcase and search book by book until you found the book that you were seeking. This could take considerable time, and you could also make a mistake and overlook the book you were searching for.

The same thing would occur if your long-term memory had no organization. Every time you tried to retrieve a memory or a bit of knowledge, you might have to search through everything in your memory. To make matters worse, you have much more information in your long-term memory than there are books in a library (Landauer, 1986).

In some ways, Peek's story illustrates how important organization is to memory functioning. Kim spent most of his time reading and studying phone books, encyclopedias, maps, and so on. In fact, he spent his life creating a well-organized database of obscure information in his long-term memory. As a result, he could retrieve the zip code of a complete stranger's hometown from his memory at a moment's notice.

Over the years, psychologists have proposed various means by which we organize our knowledge categorically (for a review, see J. R. Anderson, 2000). One of these strategies involves the use of a generalized knowledge structure called a **schema** (Bartlett, 1932; Rumelhart, 1980). We have *schemata* (plural of *schema*) for people, places, concepts, events, groups of people, and just about everything else that we know.

Schemata can be thought of as filing systems we use for knowledge about particular concepts. Schemata contain general information on the characteristics of the concept's category, its function, and so on. For each of these general characteristics, the schema has slots for information specific to the concept. For example, let's look at a portion of a hypothetical schema for a puff-puff. On the left are the names of the slots in the schema found for *breads*. On the right are the specific bits of information that would be placed in these slots for the puff-puff.

Slots	*Puff-Puff*
Is a:	bread
Contains:	flour, sugar, shortening, nutmeg, eggs, etc.
Method of preparation:	fried
Uses:	energy source; eaten with kidney bean stew
Appearance:	small, doughnut-hole sized
Origin:	West Africa

These slots can also have default values that are used when information is missing from our perception. For instance, if you did not read that the puff-puff is fried, you might assume that because a puff-puff is bread, it must be baked. One of the default values for the slot "method of preparation" may be "baked." We probably rely on these default values in schemata when we engage in *top-down perceptual processing* (Chapter 3).

Obviously, breads are not the only objects for which we have schemata. In fact, we have schemata for many different types of information. In addition to schemata for objects, we have schemata for abstract concepts such as love, hate, and psychology. We also have schemata to categorize our social world. We use *person schemata* for specific people, such as best friend, mother, or brother; *stereotypes* for groups of people, such as Blacks, Whites, or Latinos; and *scripts* for events, such as going to the doctor, eating at a fancy restaurant, or going on a date. In Chapter 11, we will take a closer look at how schemata affect our behavior in social situations. However, for right now, take a look at ● FIGURE 6.9 and see what types of assumptions you make based on your own schemata.

Types of Long-Term Memory

Most research on memory has concerned itself with a type of explicit memory called **declarative memory**. Declarative memory is memory for

schema an organized, generalized knowledge structure in long-term memory

declarative memory a type of long-term memory that encompasses memories that are easily verbalized, including episodic and semantic memories

FIGURE 6.9

● **Schematic Assumptions** Schematic assumptions help us fill in missing details in our perceptions and memories. As you look at this picture, what assumptions do you make about this person? These assumptions are likely to result from your stereotypes for categories of people, such as men, people of color, or young people. Think about your assumptions. What do they say about you and the schemata you have stored in your long-term memory?

Hitoshi Nishimura/Getty Images

knowledge that can be easily verbalized: names, dates, events, concepts, and so on. Declarative memory can be divided into two subtypes: **semantic memory**, which is memory for concepts, and **episodic memory**, which is memory for the events in one's life.

Kim Peek was a master at adding to his semantic memory. We may not be able to memorize encyclopedias as he did, but we are still able to store enormous amounts of semantic memories. In fact, as you read and study this chapter, you will add to the schemata you have stored in long-term memory for the concepts in the chapter. For example, you may think of semantic and episodic memories from your own life and tie your growing knowledge of psychology to the well-formed schemata you have for the world. By building and strengthening these schemata, you are helping to build a knowledge base for psychology that will later enable you to apply this information to problems that require some understanding of psychology, including the exam on test day.

As you read this chapter, you are also adding to your episodic memory (Tulving, 1972; M. A. Wheeler, Stuss, & Tulving, 1997). Episodic memory contains your memories of what has recently happened in your life (Conway, 2001). You store memories of your conversations with others, events you have attended, and your activities in your episodic memory. Episodic memories are associated with a unique sense of personal awareness (Wheeler et al., 1997). Later, when you remember reading this chapter, you will experience a sense of *self-knowing* as you recall this episodic memory. You'll think, *I* was there. *I* remember reading that chapter.

Because our lives are a series of events, our episodic memories are constantly updated. We don't seem to retain the actual details of events in memory for very long (Conway, 2001). For example, you probably don't recall what you wore to class three weeks ago. Instead, episodic memories are quickly integrated into **autobiographical memory,** our more general memory of our own personal history (Burt, Kemp, & Conway, 2008; Conway, 2001). Autobiographical memories are less detailed than episodic memories. For example, you may remember the highlights of high school, but not recall every day you spent there. Even if some of the details are missing, autobiographical memory gives us cherished memories of childhood, our first date, or days spent with friends.

Take a moment now to recall some of your own autobiographical memories. Is it easy to recall the events of your life, or is it a struggle? Interestingly, researchers have found that how easily you recall autobiographical memories may be a function of your gender (Colley, Ball, Kirby, Harvey, & Vingelen, 2002; Niedzwienska, 2003). Why would gender be related to recall of autobiographical memories? Let's take a look.

semantic memory long-term, declarative memory for conceptual information

episodic memory long-term, declarative memory for the events in our lives

autobiographical memory memory for our past that gives us a sense of personal history

Autobiographical memory gives us our past—such as these childhood memories.

Michael Dunning/Getty Images

Gender and Autobiographical Memory

To illustrate one of the characteristic features of autobiographical memory, try this demonstration. You will need paper, pencil, and a timer.

TRY THIS DEMONSTRATION

Get out a sheet of paper and write down as many memories of your past as you can in the next four minutes. After you are finished, look over your list and put a star by all of the memories that involve emotions—for example, memories of times where you felt happy, sad, excited, and so on. Now count the number of starred and unstarred memories. Which do you have more of—emotional or nonemotional memories? For many of us, autobiographical memories tend to be fairly emotional.

It is this emotional quality of autobiographical memories that seems to explain why women sometimes have better recall of autobiographical memories than men. In fact, women *only* outscore men when recalling memories of emotion-laden events. When it comes to recalling nonemotional events from the past, men and women perform equally (P. J. Davis, 1999). But, why would this be?

From the time we are children, our parents talk with us about the past, encouraging us to recall the events of our lives. When conversing with us, however, parents tend to treat boys and girls differently. Research suggests that parents tend to discuss past events, especially emotional social events, more frequently and in greater detail with their daughters (Buckner & Fivush, 2002). These childhood conversations may serve to make females more likely than males to elaborate emotional autobiographical memories more in long-term memory. As you learned earlier in this chapter, greater elaboration at encoding leads to greater ease of retrieval later on.

The idea that women are more elaborative in their autobiographical memory has been supported by other studies as well. In one study, researchers asked older men and women (ages 68–79) to recall and tell their life histories during an interview. The researchers then analyzed the amount of specific detail in the participants' stories. They found that the women's recollections were significantly more detailed and specific than the men's. This suggests that older women may place more value on remembering the past than older men do (Pillemer, Wink, DiDonato, & Sanborn, 2003). Perhaps women place more value on detailed memories of the past because of the social functions of autobiographical memory. After all, it is through autobiographical memory that we share ourselves and our past with others.

In fact, researchers have found that for women (but not men), having vivid, more detailed autobiographical memories is positively correlated with having higher degrees of *empathy* or an ability to feel what others are feeling (Pohl, Bender, & Lachmann, 2005). This suggests that having a detailed, elaborated memory of our own past may also be related to our ability to have insight into other people, which may in turn help us connect with them on an emotional level (J. A. Robinson & Swanson, 1990).

These studies suggest, in part, that just as for semantic memory, elaboration enhances episodic memory. Does this mean that our episodic and semantic memories are stored in the same fashion?

Episodic and Semantic Memory: Two Systems or One?

Currently in psychology, there is some debate over whether episodic memories are stored in the same manner as semantic memories. Although the findings are controversial, a number of studies suggest that episodic and semantic memory may indeed be separate memory systems (K. S. Graham, Simons, Pratt, Patterson, & Hodges, 2000; M. A. Wheeler et al., 1997). Some of the most persuasive research on this issue comes from studies utilizing the PET and fMRI scanning technologies that you learned about in Chapter 2. These scans allow researchers to see which parts of the brain are most active while the participant is engaged in certain activities. By scanning participants' brains while they perform semantic and episodic

Research suggests that relative to males, females are better at recalling emotionally charged autobiographical memories. Later in life, this female may recall this happy graduation day better than her male classmates do.

Realistic Reflections/Getty Images

memory tasks, researchers can get a feel for which parts of the brain are involved in these two types of memory.

The results of such brain scanning studies suggest that executing episodic and semantic memory tasks results in activation in some common areas of the brain, such as the prefrontal cortex, but also in some unique patterns of activation (Cabeza & Nyberg, 2000; B. Levine et al., 2004; Nyberg et al., 2003). At present, all we can say is that the available data *suggest* that episodic and semantic memory are separate memory systems, but more research is needed to further assess the validity of this suggestion.

Regardless of whether or not semantic and episodic memory are part of the same memory system, they share the characteristic of being easily verbalized. This is not true of all of our knowledge. **Procedural memory**, our memory for skills, is not readily declarative in nature. To illustrate the difference between declarative and procedural memories, take a moment to try the following demonstration.

TRY THIS DEMONSTRATION

First, think of a skill that you know very well, such as walking, riding a bike, or driving a car. Then attempt to tell someone else how to execute that skill without showing how to do it. You can use only words to describe the skill. Now, choose something about which you have declarative memory—the directions to your favorite electronics store or the plot of your favorite movie—and try to communicate that using only words.

Which task did you find to be more difficult? We bet that you found the first task to be much harder than the second! The first task asked you to verbalize a procedural memory, whereas the second asked you to verbalize a semantic memory. Procedural memories are not easily verbalized, and we've demonstrated just how hard it can be to find words to describe even everyday skills.

Another defining characteristic of procedural memory is that it is often *implicit* memory (N. J. Cohen, 1984; Squire, Knowlton, & Musen, 1993). Recall that implicit memory is memory that is used unconsciously. We remember without being aware that we are remembering. For the most part, the skills we execute every day are done in an unconscious, implicit fashion. As you walk to your classes, are you consciously aware of what you need to do to get your body to walk? When you take notes in class, are you aware of what you need to do to get your hand to write? Of course not. We walk, write, drive a car, and so on without thinking about it. The fact that procedural memories are implicit may also help explain why we have a difficult time verbalizing them. How can you verbalize your execution of a behavior when you are not aware of how you do it? You can't.

A final aspect of procedural memory that separates it from declarative memory is its longevity. Procedural memories tend to last for a long time in long-term memory. You've probably heard the saying "It's like riding a bike. You never forget how to do it." There is a great deal of truth in this folk wisdom—once we have mastered a skill, it does stay with us for a long time. For example, one of the authors recently purchased a bike. She hadn't ridden one in almost 10 years, but when she tried it, it was as if she had ridden just yesterday. Declarative memory, on the other hand, does not enjoy the same longevity as procedural memory. If you put aside your studies of psychology and never thought about it, how much psychology do you think you would be able to recall 10 years from now?

As you can see, procedural memory seems to differ substantially from declarative memory. The degree of disparity between these two types of memory brings up the question of whether they are separate memory systems. Strong evidence to support the notion that procedural memory is a separate memory system comes from studies done with people suffering from *amnesia*.

Amnesia: What Forgetting Can Teach Us About Memory

Amnesia is a condition in which a person cannot recall certain declarative memories. Amnesia can be classified as retrograde or anterograde (● FIGURE 6.10). **Retrograde amnesia**

procedural memory long-term memory for skills and behaviors

retrograde amnesia a type of amnesia in which one is unable to retrieve previously stored memories from long-term memory

Retrograde:
A person with retrograde amnesia cannot remember what they have done in the past.

Anterograde:
A person with anterograde amnesia cannot form new memories even though they experience new events.

© Chris Hendrickson/Masterfile

FIGURE 6.10

● **Amnesia Affects a Person's Memory in Dramatic Ways**

is an inability to recall previously stored declarative memories; **anterograde amnesia** is an inability to encode new declarative memories in long-term memory. In short, retrograde amnesia is amnesia for one's past, and anterograde amnesia is amnesia for one's present and future.

There are several causes of amnesia, but of most interest to us here is amnesia that is caused by brain injury or illness. In particular, studies of brain-injured people with anterograde amnesia have taught us much about the distinction between declarative and procedural memory. One of the most famous cases of anterograde amnesia involved H.M. (Corkin, 1968), who suffered from severe epilepsy that was centered in the vicinity of his hippocampal regions in the temporal lobe (Chapter 2) and did not respond to medication. In an effort to curb H.M.'s seizures, doctors removed the hippocampal regions in both hemispheres of his brain (Squire, 1992). The surgery was successful, in that H.M.'s seizures were drastically reduced. However, in another sense, the operation was a serious failure. After H.M. recovered from the surgery, it became apparent that he could no longer store new declarative memories. He could not remember seeing his doctor seconds after the doctor left the room. He was also unable to read an entire magazine article. By the time he got to the end of a long paragraph, he would have forgotten what he'd just read. It was clear that H.M. had severe anterograde amnesia, a condition he lived with for the next 55 years until his death in 2008 at age 82 (B. Carey, 2008).

Interestingly, however, H.M. did not completely lose his ability to store new long-term memories. After the surgery, he could still store procedural memories. For instance, H.M. could learn to do certain perceptual-motor tasks, such as tracing a stimulus while looking at its image in a mirror. Furthermore, he was seen to improve on these tasks with time (Milner, 1962). Results similar to those found in H.M. have also been found in other people with amnesia (e.g., Cermak, Lewis, Butters, & Goodglass, 1973). The fact that H.M. and other people with amnesia can still learn new skills indicates that procedural memory is not stored in long-term memory in the same way as declarative memory.

Most of us will never face amnesia to the degree that H.M. did. However, amnesia may be more common than you think. All of us experience some degree of *infantile amnesia*, in which we cannot recall events that occurred before age 3. Recall that episodic memory is an explicit, verbally based memory system. In infancy, we do not have the verbal skills or underlying brain development to support episodic memory (L. J. Carver & Bauer, 2001).

Brain damage is another common cause of amnesia. In the United States, some 50,000 to 300,000 athletes can be expected to experience a concussion during a given sports season. Many of these injured athletes will have at least mild, temporary amnesia (M. W. Collins et al., 2003). If you add to these numbers the people who will suffer from other forms of brain injury—from car accidents, illnesses, drug overdoses, and falls—you can see how amnesia may be more common than you might think. This is why it is important to always follow safety procedures, such as wearing a helmet while bicycling.

Even without brain injury or amnesia, you may still encounter mild problems with your memory from time to time. Normal, everyday forgetting can be an annoyance. In the next sections, we will discuss how we retrieve information from long-term memory and theories of why we sometimes forget the information we have encoded in our memory.

anterograde amnesia a type of amnesia in which one is unable to store new memories in long-term memory

Let's
REVIEW In this section, we described the characteristics, types, and organization of long-term memory. For a quick check of your understanding, try answering the following questions at increasing levels of difficulty.

1. Memories for concepts and knowledge are part of _____ memory.

   a. semantic   c. episodic

   b. procedural   d. sensory

2. Which of the following belong to the category, schema?

   a. stereotypes   c. scripts

   b. person schemata   d. all of the above

3. Which of the following is the *best* example of semantic encoding in long-term memory?

   a. remembering how to play the tune to your favorite song on a guitar

   b. remembering the name of the artist who sings your favorite song

   c. hearing the tune to your favorite song in your head

   d. seeing the face of the artist who sings your favorite song in your head

ANSWERS 1. a; 2. d; 3. b

How Do We Remember and Why Do We Forget?

We store memories so that we can later retrieve them. *Retrieval* is the act of moving information from long-term memory back into working memory or consciousness. Retrieval occurs when we send a *probe* or *cue* into long-term memory in search of *memory traces* or encoded memories that we have stored there. A probe or cue can be many things—a test question, the sight of a playground, the sound of a roller coaster, or the smell of popcorn. For example, if you see an old friend on the street, the sight of her face may act as a cue that allows you to retrieve her name from your long-term memory. If you had not seen your friend on the street, her name would not have spontaneously popped into your consciousness. Rather, it would have remained tucked away in your long-term memory. Seeing her face was the cue that prompted your recall of her name. Similarly, on exams, your professor's test questions act as probes that prompt you to search your long-term memory for the answers.

Think for a moment about the types of exams you have had in the past—for example, multiple-choice, essay, fill-in-the-blank, and true/false. Which of these is your *least* favorite type of exam question? If you are like the typical college student, you probably dislike the dreaded essay test the most. Why are essay exams so much harder than multiple-choice exams? The answer lies in the type of retrieval task we engage in when we take these types of exams.

Recognition and Recall

An essay question is an example of a **recall** task. In a recall task, the probe is relatively weak and does not contain a great deal of information to go on as you search your memory for the answer. You can't guess your way through an essay test. You must really know the information to answer the question. If you have not elaborated the material in long-term memory, you will likely find it difficult to recall.

A multiple-choice question, on the other hand, is an example of a **recognition** task. In recognition, the probe is stronger and contains much more information than does a recall

LEARNING
OBJECTIVES

What Should You Know?
- Explain retrieval processes in memory.
- Describe and give examples of the various theories of forgetting in long-term memory.

recall a type of retrieval process in which the probe or cue does not contain much information

recognition a type of retrieval process in which the probe or cue contains a great deal of information, including the item being sought

Eric Audras/PhotoLibrary

Many things can function as memory probes—test questions, sights, sounds, smells, and so on. These probes have the power to retrieve memories and bring them to consciousness. For example, smelling your grandmother's perfume may bring a host of pleasant memories to mind.

cue. Several researchers have proposed theories to explain why recognition is typically easier than recall (e.g., Gillund & Shiffrin, 1984; Tulving, 1983). One theory proposes that recognition is easier because of the overlap between the content of the probe and the content of the memory trace (Tulving, 1983). Think about it for a minute: In a multiple-choice question, the answer is actually part of the probe.

One word of caution: As you study for exams, keep in mind that recognition tasks are easier than recall tasks. If you quiz yourself using multiple-choice questions (such as those provided in this book), keep in mind that you are testing yourself in the easiest possible way because the probe itself provides much of the answer. Just because you can pass a multiple-choice test on the material doesn't mean that you could pass a recall test on the material. If you really want to test your knowledge, you would do better to test yourself using some form of recall test instead, with short answer or fill-in-the-blank questions. This strategy will help ensure your success and long-term retention of the material.

Unfortunately, no method of study is foolproof. Despite your best efforts at studying, there will always be times when retrieval is difficult. We've all known times when the probes and cues we sent into long-term memory were not successful in retrieving the desired information. For a memory to actually be retrieved from long-term memory, two conditions must be met: the memory must be both *available* and *accessible*. A memory is available when it has been encoded in long-term memory and the memory trace is still present in long-term memory. Obviously, if you never encoded the memory in long-term memory, you won't be able to retrieve it later. The memory must be available if retrieval is to occur.

Have you had the frustrating experience of being unable to remember something that you *know* you know, but you just can't seem to recall it? Psychologists refer to this as the *tip-of-the-tongue (TOT)* phenomenon. You know the information is in your mind, on the tip of your tongue, so to speak, but you can't retrieve it. The TOT phenomenon shows us that availability is not enough by itself to ensure retrieval. Accessibility of the memory trace is also important. If the probe cannot reach the memory trace in long-term memory, the memory will not be retrieved, even if it is available. As we will see in the next section, there are a variety of circumstances in which the probe fails to retrieve an available, but inaccessible, memory.

When Retrieval Fails: Forgetting

What student hasn't asked herself this question: "I studied that material, so why did I forget it on the test?" Forgetting occurs when we cannot, for some reason, retrieve information from long-term memory. One theory of forgetting, **decay theory**, maintains that once a memory trace is stored in long-term memory, it must be routinely activated to keep it there (Ebbinghaus, 1885/1913). If we store a memory and then fail to recall it periodically, the memory trace weakens and decays. If the decay is not stopped by recalling the memory, the memory trace will be lost forever from long-term memory.

Although decay theory seems to make sense, there are some good reasons to doubt that memory traces decay from disuse. One is that memories seem to last for very long periods of time, even when we do not routinely access these memories. For example, in one study, participants' recognition of English–Spanish vocabulary words was tested anywhere from 1 to 50 years after they had studied Spanish. The results showed that recognition memory for these vocabulary words declined little over the years (Bahrick, 1984).

Another reason to doubt decay theory comes from the methodology used in the experiments that have been done to support it. These experiments usually involve having participants learn a list of words or syllables and then testing the participants on their recall of the items at various intervals of time (e.g., J. G. Jenkins & Dallenbach, 1924). These experiments usually show that memory for the items drops off as time passes, suggesting that memory

decay theory a theory of forgetting that proposes that memory traces that are not routinely activated in long-term memory will degrade

traces do decay with time. However, interpreting the results of such experiments is tricky. The participants' tendency to forget the material could have been due to decay, or it could have been due to another process called *interference*.

Interference occurs in both working memory and long-term memory when other information blocks the retrieval of a memory trace. In interference, the memory trace is still available, but it is inaccessible. **Proactive interference** occurs when older information inhibits our ability to retrieve other, newer information from memory. For example, one of the authors spells her first name in an unusual way that often causes proactive interference in others. Her name is pronounced *Suzanne*, but it is spelled *Susann*. Because of its spelling, people often pronounce her name as *Susan* when they first see it in print. Then, no matter how many times she corrects them, they seem to always want to call her *Susan*. This example is one of proactive interference because the *older* pronunciation of her name inhibits the *newer* pronunciation in people's memory. It's also the reason she started going by *Sue* early in childhood!

We can also experience **retroactive interference**, in which *newer* information inhibits the retrieval of *older* information in memory. Suppose you move to a new home and work very hard to memorize your new address and phone number. Chances are you will soon find it hard to recall your old address and phone number. This is an example of retroactive interference, when the newer phone number and address interfere with your ability to retrieve the old phone number and address from long-term memory.

Unfortunately, our susceptibility to both proactive (Emery, Hale, & Myerson, 2008) and retroactive interference (Ebert & Anderson, 2009; Hedden & Park, 2003) tends to increase as we age. One explanation for why interference increases with age is that our central executive function tends to decline with advancing age. As the central executive becomes less efficient, it is also less able to suppress interfering memory traces (Hedden & Yoon, 2006).

Interference theory does seem to describe one way in which we forget information, but there is reason to suspect that interference may not occur as often in the real world as it does in laboratory experiments (Slameka, 1966). **Cue-dependent forgetting** may be a better explanation of forgetting in the real world. Cue-dependent forgetting (Tulving, 1974) asserts that the amount of information we can retrieve from long-term memory is a function of the type of cue or probe we use. If the memory cues we use are not the right ones, we may experience forgetting. For example, assume you have the following words to memorize:

Bread	*Sally*
Soda	*Pearl*
Bologna	*Laura*
Pear	*Mary*
Potato chips	*Candy*

and later you are asked to recall all of the foods on the list. You are likely to recall *Bread*, *Soda*, *Bologna*, *Pear*, and *Potato chips*, but what about *Candy*? You are likely to forget about *Candy* because you encoded *Candy* as a name and not as a food. If the cue used at recall is stated "Recall all of the names you learned," you will surely recall the word *Candy*. Your forgetting was cue-dependent.

The cue-dependent forgetting theory is part of the *encoding specificity principle* that was developed by Endel Tulving (S. Wiseman & Tulving, 1976). According to this principle, we encode aspects of the context in which we learn information, later using these contextual aspects as cues to help us retrieve the information from long-term memory. If the encoding specificity principle is correct, then we should have better memory when we retrieve information in the same setting that we learned it. **Does this mean that taking a test in the same room in which you had lectures improves your retrieval?** Yes! If you take an exam in the room in which you heard lectures on the material, you should be able to retrieve somewhat more information than if you take the test in another room. In one distinctive study, researchers asked divers to learn a list of words while they were either on shore or 20 feet under the water (Godden & Baddeley, 1975). Later, researchers tested the divers' recall for the words in either the context in which they studied the words or the context in which they did not study the words. Consistent with the encoding specificity principle, the researchers found that when the divers recalled the words in the same context in which they had learned the

proactive interference a type of forgetting that occurs when older memory traces inhibit the retrieval of newer memory traces

retroactive interference a type of forgetting that occurs when newer memory traces inhibit the retrieval of older memory traces

cue-dependent forgetting a type of forgetting that occurs when one cannot recall information in a context other than the context in which it was encoded

FIGURE 6.11

● **The Encoding Specificity Principle**
Studies show that we best remember information when we retrieve it in the same context in which it was learned. Godden & Baddeley (1975) found that divers who learned a list of words while underwater also recalled more of the words while submerged than they did on the dock. Studies like this one suggest that a change in context may be one reason we sometimes forget.

Nicole Duplaix/Getty Images

words, their recall was better (● FIGURE 6.11).

Encoding specificity has also been shown to hold true for mood states and states of consciousness. People can recall information they learned while drinking alcohol better when they have been drinking (Eich, Weingartner, Stillman, & Gillin, 1975). Information learned while smoking marijuana is better recalled while smoking marijuana (E. S. Parker, Birnbaum, & Noble, 1976). And information learned while in a bad mood is better recalled in a negative mood state than when one is happy (Teasdale & Russell, 1983). These findings do not mean that it is better to learn while in these states. For example, alcohol can reduce one's ability to encode information in the first place (E. S. Parker et al., 1976).

The final theory of forgetting we will discuss is Sigmund Freud's (1915, 1943) proposal that the emotional aspects of a memory can affect our ability to retrieve that memory. According to Freud, when we experience emotionally threatening events, we push or *repress* these memories into an inaccessible part of our mind called the *unconscious* (Chapter 1). This **repression** results in amnesia for this information.

Repression of memories has become a very controversial subject in the past 25 years because of its relationship to cases of childhood sexual abuse. Some people have claimed that they suddenly "remembered" abuse that had occurred many years before. After many years have passed, there is often no corroborating evidence to support such claims. Furthermore, some experiments indicate that the details of memories for past events can be incorrect, and that this may be especially true for children (Brainerd & Reyna, 2002; Howe, 2000). In one study, researchers found that preschool children could not distinguish memories for fictitious events from memories for real events after 10 weeks of thinking about the events. More alarming was the fact that the children were able to give detailed accounts of the fictitious events, and they seemed to really believe that the fictitious events had happened (Ceci, 1995).

The frequent lack of corroborating evidence for recovered memories, along with experimental evidence that questions the accuracy of memory, has led some to charge that these are in fact *false memories*. The debate is further fueled by the lack of experimental data to support the notion that repression can occur. To test the theory of repression, researchers would have to traumatize participants and then see whether they repressed their memories of the trauma. Obviously, this type of study cannot be done for ethical reasons. So, for now, psychologists cannot say for sure whether or not repression is one of the reasons we forget. The debate over whether memories of abuse that are "de-repressed" by therapeutic suggestion are true memories is one aspect of a larger issue concerning memory—that of just how accurate our memory generally is. Before moving on, take a moment to look at ● THE BIG PICTURE REVIEW for a recap of the theories of forgetting.

repression a type of forgetting proposed by Sigmund Freud in which memories for events, desires, or impulses that we find threatening are pushed into an inaccessible part of the mind called the unconscious

THE **BIG PICTURE** *review*

Theories
of Forgetting

THEORY	DEFINITION	EXAMPLE
Decay	Memory traces that are not routinely activated erode and disappear over time.	You haven't thought of your best friend from kindergarten in 15 years. When you meet your friend, you cannot recall his or her name.
Proactive interference	Older memory traces inhibit the retrieval of newer memory traces.	You can't seem to remember your friend's new, married name, but you can recall her maiden name.
Retroactive interference	Newer memory traces inhibit the retrieval of older memory traces.	You can't recall your old cell phone number, but you can recall your new cell phone number.
Cue-dependent forgetting	Memories are not as easily retrieved when the retrieval cues do not match the cues that were present during encoding.	You run into a classmate at the grocery store, and you can't recall her name. But you do recall her name when you see her at school.
Repression	Threatening memories are pushed into the inaccessible unconscious part of the mind.	You are in a horrible car accident in which other people are seriously injured. Although you are uninjured, you later cannot recall details of the accident.

Let's REVIEW

In this section, we discussed how information is retrieved from long-term memory and presented some theories of why we sometimes forget information that we have stored in long-term memory. For a quick check of your understanding, try answering the following questions at increasing levels of difficulty.

1. Essay exam questions are an example of _____.

   a. recall

   b. recognition

   c. implicit retrieval

   d. retrieval based on encoding specificity

2. Decay is most related to _____ whereas interference is most related to _____.

   a. availability; accessibility

   b. accessibility; availability

   c. encoding; accessibility

   d. encoding; availability

3. Mary and Karl have worked together for 3 years. Mary is at home, trying to remember Karl's new cell phone number, but the only phone number that comes to mind is their work number. Mary is experiencing which memory phenomenon?

   a. encoding specificity

   b. memory trace decay

   c. proactive interference

   d. retroactive interference

ANSWERS 1. a; 2. a; 3. c

IS MEMORY ACCURATE?

Can you remember what you were doing when you heard that

- O. J. Simpson was suspected of murder?
- the Federal Building in Oklahoma City had been bombed?
- Princess Diana died in a car crash?

LEARNING OBJECTIVE

What Should You Know?

- Describe the accuracy of memory and its implications for eyewitness memory.

- terrorists had attacked the World Trade Center on September 11, 2001?
- Hurricane Katrina had caused massive damage to New Orleans?
- a gunman had gone on a murderous rampage at Virginia Tech?

Can you recall the details of what you were doing when you heard of any of these events? If you can, then you have what psychologists call a **flashbulb memory**—an unusually detailed memory for an emotionally charged event (R. Brown & Kulik, 1977). Often people claim that they can recall the exact details: where they were, what they were doing, what they were wearing, what the weather was like at the moment when they heard of emotional events like these.

For example, one of your authors recalls watching the news coverage of the September 11 attacks in Georgia on a big screen TV in the library of her school. She also recalls that September 11, 2001, was a sunny day in Georgia. But was it? She also remembers seeing the bright blue sky in the news footage from New York. Is it possible that her memory that it was also a bright and sunny day in Georgia is biased by her memory of the television footage of the World Trade Center? Maybe. We will see that frequently, memory is not as accurate as it seems.

TRY THIS DEMONSTRATION

Do you remember where you were on September 11, 2001, at the time of the attacks on the World Trade Center? Like your author, do you recall watching the live TV coverage as the tragedy was taking place? If so, answer this question: How long after the plane hit the first tower did it take for both towers to fall? Researchers interviewed 690 people 7 weeks after the attack and asked them this question. On average, the participants reported that it took 62 minutes for the towers to collapse—when in reality it took almost 2 hours. On the day of the attack, do you remember watching news coverage of the first plane hitting the towers? If so, you are not alone—despite the fact that this video footage did not air until the next day (Perina, 2002). So how did you do on this task? How accurate (or inaccurate) is your memory of that day?

flashbulb memory an unusually detailed and seemingly accurate memory for an emotionally charged event

Do you remember what you were doing when you heard about the September 11 attacks?

© Steve McCurry/Magnum Photos

Some researchers now suspect that stress hormones that act on the amygdala (Chapter 2) may be responsible for certain aspects of flashbulb memories. A current theory is that when you experience an emotional event, such as watching a horrific terrorist attack, your body releases stress hormones that direct your brain's amygdala to initiate storage of a long-term memory of that event. However, these stress hormones also seem to block the formation of accurate memories for what was happening immediately before the emotional event. Therefore, you may end up with a memory for the emotional event that may not be entirely accurate because you have something of a "gap" in your memory (Bower, 2003).

Although flashbulb memories may contain inaccuracies, the details of these memories tend to remain consistent over time. One study found that participants retained approximately 75% of their initial flashbulb memories of how they learned about the September 11 attacks one year after the event. Interestingly, this was true of both young and older participants (S. R. Davidson, Cook, & Glisky, 2006). Perhaps the consistency of flashbulb memories contributes to our belief that the details are true and accurate—even if they are not.

Memory Is Not Like a Video Camera

Does it surprise you to know that memory is often inaccurate? When we store memories of the everyday events in our lives, we do not store memory traces for every detail. Memory does not work like a video camera! It's more of a construction project. We store the gist of the information in long-term memory with the help of schemata, but we do not store all of the exact details of the event. This means that when we retrieve a memory from long-term memory, we do not simply recall all of the details of the event and then use them to *reconstruct* the event. Memory is more than just **reconstructive**, or based on actual events. It is also *constructive*.

Memory is **constructive** in that we use the knowledge and expectations that we have stored in our schemata to help us fill in the missing details in our stored memories. It is very possible that you filled in the gaps in your memory of September 11, 2001. Likewise, the author may associate September 11, 2001, with the bright blue New York sky shown in photos like the one on page 246. She may be using this information as she *constructs* her memory of that fateful day. Yet these filled-in details feel very much as if they are true. Without some corroborating evidence, we cannot say for sure what the sky was like in Georgia on September 11, 2001.

Most of the time, it makes little difference whether or not we recall such details accurately. In reality, it does not matter what the weather was like in Georgia on September 11, 2001. But sometimes the details of our recollections can be extremely important, even a matter of life and death.

Eyewitness Memory

The available research on eyewitness memory shows that we can make serious errors without knowing it. What kinds of situations make such errors in eyewitness memory more likely?

Psychologist Elizabeth Loftus has spent a good part of her career showing that eyewitness memory can be manipulated by the expectations we hold about the world. For example, in one experiment (Loftus & Palmer, 1974), Loftus showed participants a film of a car accident. After viewing the film, the participants were randomly divided into several groups and questioned about their memory of the film. In one group, the participants were asked, "About how fast were the cars going when they *smashed into* each other?" In another group, the participants were asked, "About how fast were the cars going when they *hit* each other?" In the control group, the participants were not asked to estimate the speed of the cars. The results showed that the verb used in the question affected participants' estimates of the speed of the cars. Participants in the "smashed into" group estimated the speed of the cars, on average, at 41 mph; the average estimate for participants in the "hit" group was 34 mph; and the control group estimated the speed to be 32 mph. It seems that the words *smashed* and *hit* activated different expectations that were used to fill in the missing details in the participants' memories of the film, and the result was that they remembered the film differently. Imagine how a lawyer's choice of words might influence a witness's memory on the witness stand.

Even more dramatic is the fact that our memories can be permanently altered by things that happen *after* we encode the memories. In another study (Loftus & Zanni, 1975), Loftus showed participants a film of a car crash and then asked them a series of questions about the accident. The participants in one group were asked, "Did you see *a* broken headlight?" In a second group, the participants were asked, "Did you see *the* broken headlight?" Although there had been no broken headlight in the film, some of the participants reported that they had seen one. Of those who were asked about *a* broken headlight, only 7% reported that they had seen a broken headlight in the film. On the other hand, of the participants who were asked about *the* broken headlight, 17% said they had seen it. By subtly suggesting to them that there *had* been a broken headlight, Loftus caused the participants to remember seeing something that they had not seen. She created a false memory in her participants.

These false memories do not seem to be motivated by a participant's desire to please the researcher. In another study Loftus offered participants $25 if they could accurately recall an event. Even with this motivation to be accurate, the participants could not prevent their memories from being distorted by the misleading information they heard *after* viewing the incident (Loftus, 1979).

Although it is clear that eyewitness memory is susceptible to errors, there is some disagreement as to why these errors occur. According to Elizabeth Loftus (2000), we accept subsequent misinformation as being correct, and this information becomes part of our memory for the original event. Others propose that eyewitness memory becomes faulty when we make errors in identifying the source of information we have stored in long-term memory

reconstructive memory memory that is based on the retrieval of memory traces that contain the actual details of the events that we have experienced

constructive memory memory that utilizes knowledge and expectations to fill in the missing details in retrieved memory traces

(M. K. Johnson, Hashtroudi, & Lindsay, 1993). According to this view, when we retrieve a memory for a particular event from long-term memory, we also retrieve information from other sources relevant to the event. For instance, we might retrieve information from times when we discussed the event with others, from comments others made about the event, from things we read about the event in a magazine, and so on. Because there is considerable overlap between our memory for the original event and our memories of information related to the event, it is easy for us to get confused about the source of these bits of information. We might misattribute the source of a particular detail to our memory of the original event, when we actually encoded it in another situation.

Regardless of which interpretation is correct, after we witness the original event, the more information we are faced with, the more likely it is that our memory will become faulty. The same problems that plague eyewitness memory also affect our memory for the everyday events in our lives. It may be unsettling to you to realize that your memory can be faulty. But don't despair—we don't always make mistakes, and many times when we do, they are not of great consequence.

Let's REVIEW

In this section, we discussed the accuracy of memories we retrieve from long-term memory—in particular, eyewitness accounts of events. For a quick check of your understanding, try answering the following questions at increasing levels of difficulty.

1. _____ occurs when we fill in the missing details of our stored memories.

   a. Constructive memory
   b. Reconstructive memory
   c. Procedural memory
   d. Encoding specificity

2. _____ is to accurate as _____ is to inaccurate.

   a. Reconstructive; constructive
   b. Constructive; reconstructive
   c. Constructive; video
   d. Video; reconstructive

3. Martha is 55 years old. One of her childhood memories is of hearing about the assassination of President Kennedy in her elementary school classroom. She recalls that she was wearing a red dress and had a math test that day. According to the research on flashbulb memories, it's likely that Martha's memory of this day has been influenced by which of the following memory processes?

   a. constructive memory
   b. reconstructive memory
   c. retrograde amnesia
   d. both a and b

ANSWERS 1. a; 2. a; 3. d

LEARNING OBJECTIVE

What Should You Know?
• Discuss what is known about the biology of memory.

HOW IS MEMORY STORED IN THE BRAIN?

So far, we have confined our discussion of memory to understanding the manner in which information is processed in the mind. Using a computer analogy for the mind, we have been looking at the *software* and *data* of our memory systems. But, what role does our *hardware*, the brain, play in memory? How are memories stored in the brain?

Storing Memory at the Synapse

Recall from Chapter 2 that neurons in the brain connect with one another at *synapses* (see Figure 2.3, p. 45). When the presynaptic cell releases neurotransmitters, they travel across the synapse and bind with the receptor sites on the postsynaptic cell. Here, they stimulate the postsynaptic cell and change its rate of firing action potentials. Psychologist Daniel Hebb

(1948) first proposed that memories are stored in the brain as a result of changes in the structure and function of specific synapses. According to Hebb, when we process new information and new memory traces are encoded, specific neurons in the brain fire and release neurotransmitters into their synapses. When a synapse is activated, protein molecules in the neurons are changed, which reconfigures the synapse and makes it better able to convey neural signals to the postsynaptic side. With repeated exposure to the information and repeated activation of specific neural pathways in the brain, the synapses along the way become facilitated and strengthened. This change, called **long-term potentiation**, can last for months and is thought to be one mechanism through which the brain stores new memories.

Long-term potentiation can help explain how memories are stored at the level of the neuron and synapse. Currently, researchers are examining the exact biological mechanisms that change the structure of synapses and produce long-term potentiation (e.g., Sacktor, 2010). Next, we'll take a look at what is known about the role that brain structures play in memory.

Brain Structures Involved in Memory

Much of what we know about the role that specific brain structures play in memory comes from studies of people with amnesia. People with amnesia often experience severe memory problems that can be traced to damage or disease in particular parts of the brain. Recall the case of H.M., discussed earlier in this chapter. H.M.'s hippocampal regions were removed in an attempt to control his epilepsy. As a result of the surgery, H.M. could no longer undergo **memory consolidation** (the stabilization and long-term storage of memory traces in the brain) for his declarative memories (● FIGURE 6.12). Other amnesic cases, too, have supported the notion that the hippocampus plays a significant role in the storage and consolidation of declarative memories (Parkin & Leng, 1993).

Scientists also use brain-imaging technology, discussed in Chapter 2, to study the function of the brain during memory tasks (e.g., see Finn, 2004). These studies indicate that the hippocampus plays an important role in the declarative memory function of people without amnesia. For instance, PET scans show that blood flow in the normal brain is higher in the right hippocampal region during declarative memory tasks, but not during procedural memory tasks (Schacter, Alpert, Savage, Rauch, & Alpert, 1996; Squire et al., 1992).

Research on both animals (Iso, Simoda, & Matsuyama, 2006) and humans (Woollett, Glensman, & Maguire, 2008) suggests that the degree to which we use certain types of memory may have implications for the structure of our brain, particularly in the area of the hippocampus. Do you recall the study of London taxi drivers from Chapter 2? That study used MRI technology to show that London cab drivers have specific hippocampal regions that are larger than those found in London bus drivers. London's street system is old and complicated, and taxi drivers must memorize the entire city, not just a single bus route, in order to be licensed. Is it possible that these drivers experienced greater hippocampal development because they relied on their memory so much in doing their job? No one can say for sure at this time, but consistent with this notion, the researchers did find that the taxi drivers who had been driving the longest tended to have the biggest hippocampal regions (Maguire, Woollett, & Spiers, 2006).

Because the hippocampus appears to play an important role in the formation of new memories, researchers are currently investigating whether drugs that stimulate neural growth and function in the hippocampus may also provide useful treatments for people experiencing memory-robbing diseases such as Alzheimer's disease (e.g., Frielingsdorf, Simpson, Thal, & Pizzo, 2007).

Like the hippocampus, the frontal lobe seems to play a significant role in the processing of declarative memory. Evoked response potential (ERP) recordings have revealed that the left frontal lobe is very active during the processing of verbal information. This makes sense because one of the language centers of the brain, Broca's area (Chapter 2), is in the left frontal lobe (J. R. Anderson, 2000). Similarly, PET scans of the brain in action have revealed that the amount of left frontal lobe activation seems to be related to the degree to which the participant is processing the material. Left frontal lobe activity is especially likely to occur when participants are *deeply* processing the material. In fact, the more activation there is in the participants' left frontal lobe, the better they tend to recall the information (Kapur et al., 1994). Findings like these seem to suggest that the levels-of-processing approach to memory may

long-term potentiation as neurons are repeatedly stimulated, it becomes easier for them to fire action potentials

memory consolidation the stabilization and long-term storage of memory traces in the brain

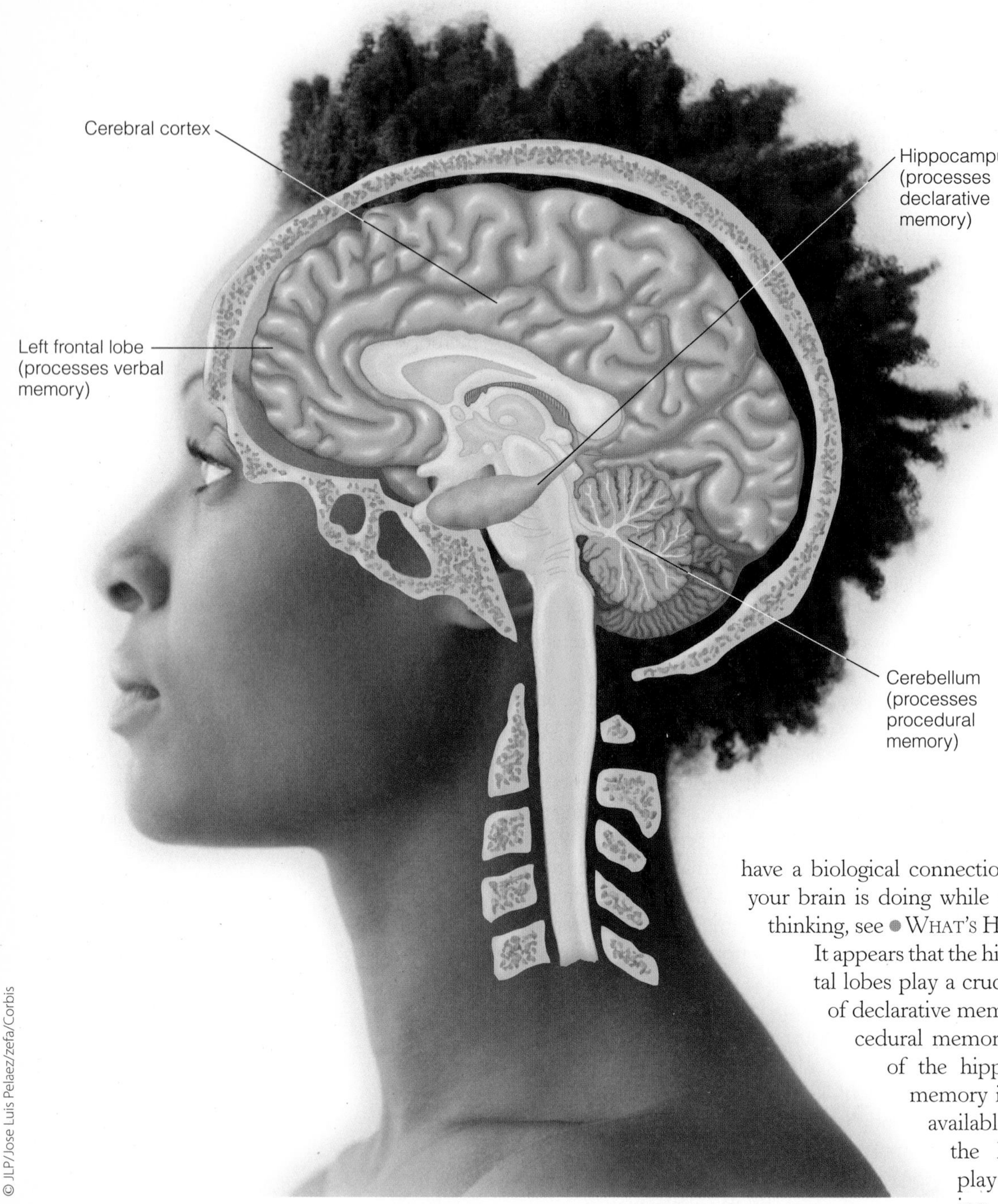

Cerebral cortex

Hippocampus (processes declarative memory)

Left frontal lobe (processes verbal memory)

Cerebellum (processes procedural memory)

FIGURE 6.12

● **Brain Structures That Are Important to Memory** The hippocampus processes declarative memories, the left frontal lobe processes verbal memories, and the cerebellum processes procedural memories.

have a biological connection. For a picture of what your brain is doing while you are engaged in such thinking, see ● WHAT'S HAPPENING IN YOUR BRAIN? It appears that the hippocampus and the frontal lobes play a crucial role in the processing of declarative memory, but what about procedural memory? At this time, the role of the hippocampus in procedural memory is less clear. Much of the available research suggests that the hippocampus does not play a central role in processing procedural memories. Declarative memory is usually explicit, but procedural memory is typically executed in an implicit, nonconscious manner. Therefore, we may gain some insight into how the brain processes procedural memory by examining the brain function that underlies implicit memory. To examine brain function during implicit memory processing, researchers took PET scans of participants while they completed implicit and explicit memory tasks. As expected, the explicit memory task was associated with increased blood flow in the hippocampal regions of the brain. However, when the participants used their implicit memory, all of the blood flow changes that occurred were *outside* the hippocampal regions of the brain (Schacter et al., 1996). This suggests that the hippocampus is not involved when memory is processed implicitly, or when we process procedural memories.

WHAT'S HAPPENING IN YOUR BRAIN?

This PET scan shows that regions of the left frontal lobe, shown in red, are very active during thinking (lower right). When listening, the brain shows high activity in the temporal lobe (upper left). When speaking, high activity is seen in the left frontal lobe along the motor cortex and in Broca's area (lower left).

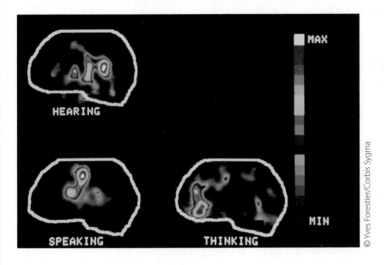

© Yves Forestier/Corbis Sygma

© Ron Chapple Stock/Alamy

Other brain-imaging studies have shown that procedural memory is linked to brain structures outside the hippocampus. For instance, motor skill memory seems to rely, in part, on the cerebellum (Sanes, Dimitrov, & Hallett, 1990; ● Figure 6.12). This explains why people like H.M. are able to acquire new skills, simply because procedural memories do not rely on the function of the hippocampus. This also explains why Kim Peek, who had severe cerebellum damage, could memorize large volumes of information but had difficulty learning new skills. This damage meant that Kim had to relearn basic skills on a daily basis, such as brushing his teeth. On the other hand, Kim excelled at the odd task of reading mirror images of words. Perceptual skills like these seem to rely on certain parts of the cortex and do not require the cerebellum (Poldrack, Desmond, Glover, & Gabrieli, 1996).

Yet, some very recent studies have suggested that the hippocampus may play some role in processing procedural memories after all. For example, fMRI brain scans revealed activation in the left hippocampus as participants learned new skills by repeatedly performing the skill (Gheysen, Van Opstal, Roggeman, Van Waelvelde, & Fias, 2010). Activity in the hippocampus has also been shown to coincide with the overnight memory consolidation of newly learned motor skills (Albouy et al., 2008). Studies like these suggest that we still have more to learn about the role of the hippocampus (and other brain structures) in memory.

Let's
REVIEW   In this section, we discussed the biological underpinnings of memory. Research indicates that the synapses, frontal lobes, hippocampus, and cerebellum all play roles in memory processing. For a quick check of your understanding, try answering the following questions at increasing levels of difficulty.

1. _____ occurs when neurons fire more easily after repeated stimulation.
   a. Long-term potentiation
   b. Proactive interference
   c. Retroactive interference
   d. Forgetting

2. Which of these brain structures is least likely to play a role in storing new memories?
   a. cerebellum
   b. medulla
   c. hippocampus
   d. frontal lobe

3. Jose was in a car accident, and he damaged his cerebellum. Which of the following tasks would be most difficult for Jose after his accident?
   a. learning to play the piano
   b. learning psychology
   c. recalling his childhood
   d. remembering what he had for breakfast

ANSWERS 1. a; 2. b; 3. a

HOW CAN YOU IMPROVE YOUR MEMORY?

Much of one's academic performance relies on the ability to remember information, and unlike Kim Peek, most of us cannot store entire books in our long-term memory. Don't despair, though. Now that you have learned a bit about how your memory works, you can apply this knowledge to your own life and improve your memory. As you have seen in this chapter, memory involves three processes: encoding, storage, and retrieval. To be a successful student, you have to study in a way that works with these processes, not against them. We'll outline some strategies that will help maximize your memory.

Pay Attention

Attention is the first step in getting information into memory. If you are distracted while studying, you won't be able to devote your full attention to the information you are trying to learn, and your ability to recall the information later may be affected (Iidaka, Anderson, Kapur, Cabeza, & Craik, 2000). Therefore, you should study when and where you can focus your full attention on your studies. Try studying in a quiet, distraction-free environment. Turn off the music and the TV, and focus on what you are doing. Don't try studying while lying on your bed because the next thing you know, you'll be asleep. Sitting upright at a desk in a quiet room is the best setting. Luckily, most college libraries offer just such a place. Try using the library if you can't find peace and quiet at home or in your dorm room.

Don't forget that paying attention is also important in the classroom. If you are distracted in class, information may not be encoded into short-term memory—making later study useless. For a closer look at how some modern technologies *may* distract us during class, see the ● TECHNOLOGY AND BEHAVIOR box on cell phones and laptops in the classroom.

Do Not Cram for Exams

Cramming is one of the worst ways to study for an exam. Unfortunately, many students procrastinate and then try to make up for it by pulling an all-nighter right before the exam. If this

TECHNOLOGY and BEHAVIOR

CELL PHONES AND LAPTOPS IN THE CLASSROOM—USEFUL OR DISTRACTING?

Have you ever sent text messages in class? Used a laptop? Played a game on your cell phone? Today, students have unprecedented access to technology in the classroom and beyond. For some of us, our cell phone or laptop is vital to everyday life. We use these technologies to remain connected, store important information, find our way from here to there, and so on. But, do these technologies help us learn? Or, do they present distractions that impede our use of memory?

How many times have you been in class when another student's cell phone began to ring? Has this ever happened during an exam? Aside from being annoying, research suggests that a ringing cell phone can impair memory. In a classroom setting, Christian End and colleagues randomly assigned some students to watch a video during which the researchers called a classmate's phone twice, letting it ring for 5 seconds each time. In the control condition, students watched the video uninterrupted. Later, all students were given a multiple-choice test on the content of the video. The results showed that relative to the control group, students in the cell phone condition performed more poorly on the exam. They were also more likely to have incomplete class notes on the video content (End, Worthman, Mathews, & Wetterau, 2010). These results indicate that ringing cell phones affect students' attention and later memory for course content. It appears that muting your cell phone is more than just a matter of politeness. Your academic success may depend on it.

Like cell phones, laptops are becoming increasingly popular in classrooms. On the surface, laptops seem to provide wonderful advantages to students. You can use them to take notes, download online lecture slides, or perhaps even connect to the Internet to look up material related to the lecture. Sounds good, but what do students actually do with their laptops in class?

Using technologies like cell phones and laptops in class will only aid your memory if you use them appropriately. If you allow these technologies to distract you from the lecture, your memory will likely suffer. Remember that you can't learn well if you don't pay attention!

To answer this question, researchers Tomas Lindroth and Magnus Bergquist (2010) studied college students over a period of years to examine their actual use of laptops in class. The researchers discovered that as a technology, laptops can be both useful and harmful to learning. It all depends on how students use them. Five main points emerged from their research:

- Using a laptop forces a student to take more responsibility for his own learning. With all the distractions that laptops present (e.g., YouTube, instant messaging, Facebook, etc.), students have to choose whether to stay on task (i.e., the lecture content) or not. When laptops are used to take notes, look up topics relevant to the lecture, or discuss lecture material, they can help students learn. When used off-topic, they are more likely to do harm.
- Students need to learn how to use technologies appropriately. For example, they should know the limitations of Wikipedia, Facebook, and the like as information services.
- Laptops are mobile. If used correctly, they can help learning by allowing the student to have her notes, online sources of information, and communication software always at hand.
- Laptops compete with lecturers and can easily distract students, hurting learning. For example, when students begin instant messaging or emailing each other during the lecture about things that are not relevant to the lecture, the distraction prevents students from encoding lecture content. Likewise, when students watch the content on the screens of other students' laptops (e.g., YouTube videos), learning falters. To minimize these distractions, Lindroth and Bergquist suggest that professors try to integrate laptop use into the lecture. Others go further to argue that unless they are integrated, laptops should be banned in class (Fried, 2008).
- The physical attributes of laptops—whirring fans and blinking lights—are distracting and may impede learning.

These studies underscore the importance of attention in allowing us to successfully encode memories. It is likely that anything that distracts us from the material will also cause our memory to suffer. Yet, the news is not all bad. The problem is not these technologies, but rather how we choose to use them. If used responsibly, cell phones and laptops can be beneficial to learning and memory.

Vicki Kerr/Getty Images

is the way that you approach your studies, you are begging for failure. Even if you manage to pull it off, and you actually pass the exam, the information you stored in long-term memory is likely to become inaccessible shortly after the exam. In short, you waste your time when you cram.

Studies have shown that **massed practice**—when you try to learn a great deal of information in one study session—results in poor recall of the information. Recall suffers because massed practice results in fatigue, which leads to a lack of attention, and the shortened time frame also does not give you time to adequately rehearse information. Without adequate attention and elaborative rehearsal, information will not be efficiently stored in long-term memory.

A better way to study is to use **distributed practice**, distributing your study time across multiple days (with gaps in between during which you don't study) rather than bunching it up on one day (or night). The beauty of distributed practice is that you don't necessarily have to study *longer*, you just need to space out the time you spend studying. For example, in one study (Krug, Davis, & Glover, 1990), participants who repeatedly read a passage over a series of sittings recalled more of the passage than those who repeatedly read the passage multiple times in a single sitting. Furthermore, taking longer breaks in between study sessions may help you retain the information longer (Cepeda et al., 2009). So, it's not necessarily how long you study, but rather the timing of your study that matters.

Use Elaborative Rehearsal

As we saw in the *levels-of-processing model* of memory (p. 229), how you rehearse material affects how well you will be able to retrieve that material. Maintenance rehearsal does not aid retention and retrieval of information in long-term memory as well as elaborative rehearsal does. If you study by reading the material over and over, you use maintenance rehearsal, which is only meant to keep information in short-term memory.

To study efficiently, you must process the information at a deeper level, finding ways to elaborate on the *meaning* of the material in your memory. This means you must form connections or associations among the bits of information you are trying to learn and the information you already know. Outlining is one way to do this. Take all of the material you are trying to learn, and organize it into an outline. When you create an outline, you must elaborate the material because you have to think about the relationships among concepts. It also helps to come up with your own original examples of the concepts you are learning—a technique we've encouraged you to use throughout this text. By generating examples, you once again elaborate the material. If the examples are from your own life, this is even better because they tie the material to your *self*, and we remember information that relates to the self better than information that does not (Gutchess et al., 2007).

Use Overlearning

Overlearning is a technique in which you learn the material until you feel that you have mastered it, and then you *continue* to study it some more. By doing this, you help ensure that you will be able to retrieve it at a later date because every time you activate information in long-term memory, you help to make it more available for retrieval. Overlearning can also make you feel more confident as you sit down to take an exam. Knowing that you really know the material, as opposed to "sort of" knowing it, can lessen the anxiety that you feel during an exam, which in turn can improve your performance.

Mnemonics Make Your Memory Mighty

If you find it difficult to elaborate the material, you might try using **mnemonic devices**, memory tricks that help you recall information. There are many different types of mnemonics. Here are a few that you might try.

massed practice cramming or attempting to learn large amounts of information in a single session of study

distributed practice spreading one's study time across a series of study sessions

overlearning improving memory for material that is already known by continuing to rehearse it

mnemonic device a cognitive procedure or mental trick that is designed to improve one's memory

Acronyms

To create an acronym, you take the first letter of each word you want to remember and use these first letters to form a word. For example, *USA* stands for *United States of America*. *ESR* could stand for the three memory processes of *encoding*, *storage*, and *retrieval*. Acronyms can also be useful in many practical situations. For example, nurses use the acronym *SPICES* to remember to evaluate *Sleep, Problems with eating and feeding, Incontinence, Confusion, Evidence of falls, and Skin breakdown* in determining the level of decline in nursing home residents (Montgomery, Mitty, & Flores, 2008).

Acrostics

Using an acrostic, you create a rhyme or saying in which each word starts with the first letter of each of the to-be-remembered words. For example, *Ellen steals rabbits* could be an acrostic to help you remember the three memory processes of *encoding*, *storage*, and *retrieval*.

Pegword System

Using a pegword system, you associate each to-be-remembered word or concept with an easily remembered pegword. For example, a classic pegword system uses the old counting rhyme—"one is a bun, two is a shoe, three is a tree, four is a door"—as the basis for the pegs. Each to-be-remembered item is tied in memory to one of these phrases. If you wanted to remember *decay, interference, repression*, and *change in context* as forms of forgetting, you would associate each of these concepts with one of the pegs. You might think of *decaying buns, interfering shoes, repressed trees*, and *changing the context by opening the door*. Then by recalling the well-remembered rhyme, you will be cueing your memory for the to-be-remembered concepts.

Method of Loci

Using the method of loci, you connect each to-be-remembered item to the visual image of a point along a path you are very familiar with. You might, for instance, use the visual image of the route you take to walk (or drive) to school. You would mentally place a bizarre visual image of each to-be-remembered item at a specific point along this route. To recall the items, you would visualize yourself taking this route and encountering the concepts along the way. For example, to remember the types of forgetting, you might visualize a heap of *decaying* trash next to your front door; a TV with *interference* on the screen along the road you take to get to school; an image of a very *repressed*, uptight person sitting huddled by the door to your building at school; and an image of a clown that is out of *context* because it is in the middle of the hallway of your classroom building at school.

The SQ3R Method

SQ3R is an acronym mnemonic for Survey, Question, Read, Recite, and Review. Using this method when studying a chapter, you first *survey* the whole chapter, noting the section headings. As you survey them, you formulate *questions* based on these headings. Then, as you *read* the chapter, you search for answers to your questions. After you read the chapter, you reread the material and *recite*, or summarize, the meaning of each section. Finally, you *review* what you have learned from reading and reciting the material. The SQ3R seems to foster memory because it encourages elaboration and integration of the material. Give it a try when you read the next chapter.

Let's REVIEW

In this section, we discussed some techniques for improving your memory. For a quick check of your understanding, try answering the following questions at increasing levels of difficulty.

1. Which of the following is not a mnemonic device?

   a. encoding specificity   c. pegword

   b. acrostic   d. method of loci

2. Sally studies psychology for 12 hours on Saturday. Billy studies psychology for 1 hour each day for 12 days. All other factors being equal, who is likely to do better on the upcoming psychology exam?

   a. Sally

   b. Billy

   c. Both Sally and Billy have an equal chance of doing well on the exam.

   d. We don't have enough information to predict who will do better.

3. Which of the following study techniques would likely foster the *most* elaboration of the material one is trying to remember?

   a. an acronym

   b. re-reading the material 3 times

   c. generating personal examples of the material

   d. all of the above would foster equal amounts of elaboration

ANSWERS 1. a; 2. b; 3. c

STUDYING the CHAPTER

KEY TERMS

encoding (221)
memory traces (221)
storage (221)
retrieval (221)
explicit memory (221)
implicit memory (221)
three stages model (223)
sensory memory (223)
short-term memory (STM) (223)
long-term memory (LTM) (223)
iconic memory (224)
echoic memory (224)

dual coding system (225)
chunking (227)
maintenance rehearsal (228)
elaborative rehearsal (228)
levels-of-processing model (229)
primacy effect (230)
recency effect (230)
working memory (232)
central executive (233)
phonological loop (233)
visuospatial sketch pad (233)
semantic encoding (235)
schema (236)

declarative memory (236)
semantic memory (237)
episodic memory (237)
autobiographical memory (237)
procedural memory (239)
retrograde amnesia (239)
anterograde amnesia (240)
recall (241)
recognition (241)
decay theory (242)
proactive interference (243)
retroactive interference (243)

cue-dependent forgetting (243)
repression (244)
flashbulb memory (246)
reconstructive memory (247)
constructive memory (247)
long-term potentiation (249)
memory consolidation (249)
massed practice (254)
distributed practice (254)
overlearning (254)
mnemonic device (254)

TEST YOURSELF!

Now that you have studied the chapter, assess your comprehension of the material by answering the following questions. Then use the key at the end to determine if your understanding is at the basic, intermediate, or advanced level. For a more comprehensive assessment of your learning, please see your student study guide and your Psychology CourseMate (www.cengagebrain.com).

1. Stored memories are referred to as _____.

   a. trace codes
   b. memory traces
   c. elaborations
   d. semantics

2. Psychologists believe that we have sensory memories for which of the following senses?

   a. sight
   b. hearing
   c. touch
   d. all of the above

3. Which of the following memories is more closely related to our ability to execute skills such as brushing our teeth?

   a. explicit
   b. implicit
   c. iconic
   d. echoic

4. The fact that elaborative rehearsal leads to better memory than maintenance rehearsal is best accounted for by which of these theories?

   a. three stages model
   b. levels-of-processing model
   c. implicit memory model
   d. working memory model

5. Which of the following types of memory is *least* likely to be accurate in its detail?

   a. constructive memories
   b. reconstructive memories
   c. sensory memories
   d. short-term memories

6. If an advertiser wants viewers to forget that its product is more expensive than the competition's product, where should the advertiser place this information in a 60-second television commercial?

   a. 5 seconds into the commercial
   b. 27 seconds into the commercial
   c. 39 seconds into the commercial
   d. 55 seconds into the commercial

7. A _____ is a generalized knowledge structure in long-term memory.

   a. trace
   b. code
   c. schema
   d. phonological loop

8. As you read this sentence, which part of it would likely be processed by the visuospatial sketch pad?

   a. the meanings of the words
   b. how the words are pronounced
   c. the font (typeface) in which the words are printed
   d. all of the above

9. Most long-term memory traces use a _____ coding scheme.

   a. visual
   b. auditory
   c. haptic
   d. semantic

10. Kashia did not recognize her friend from school when she ran into him at the movies Friday night. Yet, she did recognize him when she saw him in class on Monday morning. Kashia's failure to recognize her friend Friday night is best explained by_____.

   a. a lack of availability in memory
   b. proactive interference
   c. retroactive interference
   d. cue-dependent forgetting

11. Which of the following is a false statement?

   a. Flashbulb memories are episodic memories.
   b. Flashbulb memories last longer than regular long-term memories.
   c. The details of flashbulb memories are much more accurate than those of regular long-term memories.
   d. Flashbulb memories often contain inaccuracies.

12. Belinda immigrated to the United States from her native Brazil 7 years ago. After speaking English for several years, she now finds that she can no longer recall the Portuguese words for some common items. Yet, when reading Portuguese, she never has trouble understanding these words. Belinda's experience is best explained by _____.

   a. a lack of availability in memory
   b. cue-dependent forgetting
   c. proactive interference
   d. retroactive interference

13. Deschaun was at home when a tornado leveled the house. Luckily, he was uninjured, but the house was a total loss. Now, 6 months later, when Deschaun tries to remember the night of the tornado, he draws a blank. Deschaun's forgetting is best explained by _____.

a. decay
b. proactive interference
c. repression
d. cue-dependent forgetting

14. _____ is to short-term memory as _____ is to long-term memory.

a. Dual coding; semantic coding
b. Semantic coding; dual coding
c. Verbal coding; visual coding
d. Visual coding; verbal coding

15. _____ is spacing your study time over a period of days.

a. Distributed practice
b. Massed practice
c. Elaborative rehearsal
d. Maintenance rehearsal

Scoring Key

Below are the answers and the associated point values for each of the Learning Challenge questions. Circle the associated points for each question that you answered correctly. To obtain your Learning Challenge Score, add up the points you circled and write the total in the blank.

1. B, 1 pt	**6.** B, 3 pts	**11.** C, 2 pts
2. D, 1 pt	**7.** C, 1 pt	**12.** D, 3 pts
3. B, 2 pts	**8.** C, 3 pts	**13.** C, 3 pts
4. B, 2 pts	**9.** D, 1 pt	**14.** A, 2 pts
5. A, 2 pts	**10.** D, 3 pts	**15.** A, 1 pt

Learning Challenge Score _____

(27–30) Congratulations! You scored at the advanced level. You are well on your way to mastering the material. Take the next step by answering the questions in your Student Study Guide or your Psychology CourseMate (www.cengagebrain.com).

(21–26) You are almost there! You scored at the intermediate level. Review the material you missed before moving on to answer the questions in your Student Study Guide or your Psychology CourseMate (www.cengagebrain.com).

(20 and below) You are on your way, but you're not there yet! You scored at the beginner level. It appears that you need to carefully review the chapter to improve your mastery of the material.

USE IT OR LOSE IT: APPLYING PSYCHOLOGY

1. If you were going to design a computer that "thinks" like a human does, what would you have your computer do?

2. Your best friend tells you about a very detailed memory she has for her first day of kindergarten 16 years ago. She claims to recall all of the details of that special day—everything from what she had for breakfast to the color and design of the dress she wore. After telling you of her memory, your friend asks you how it is possible that she can remember that day in such detail. Given what you know about memory, what would you say to your friend about her childhood memory?

3. Assume that you are a psychologist who is called to testify in court. The defense attorney asks you to describe for the jury how humans store memories for everyday events. What would your testimony be about the accuracy of memory?

4. Your grandmother thinks she is having some problems with her memory. However, her doctor has assured her that her forgetting is normal and that she does *not* have Alzheimer's disease. How would you explain to her why she sometimes forgets things that she meant to buy at the store and the names of old friends that she hasn't seen in years?

CRITICAL THINKING FOR INTEGRATION

1. Explain the evolutionary value of implicit memory.

2. How does getting a good night's sleep relate to memory?

3. What types of questions would a developmental psychologist ask about memory?

4. Use what you have learned about learning in Chapter 5 *and* what you have learned about memory in this chapter to design a plan to make yourself a more motivated, successful student.

CHAPTER STUDY RESOURCES

Student Study Guide

To help organize your learning, work through Chapter 6 of the *What Is Psychology? Student Study Guide.* The study guide includes learning objectives, a chapter summary, fill-in review, key terms, a practice test, and activities.

CengageNOW

Go to **www.cengage.com/login** to link to CengageNOW, your online study tool. First take the Pre-Test for this chapter to get your personalized study plan, which will identify topics you need to review and direct you to online resources. Then take the Post-Test to determine what concepts you have mastered and what you still need work on.

CourseMate

Access an interactive eBook, chapter-specific interactive learning tools, including flashcards, quizzes, videos, and more in your Psychology CourseMate, available at **CengageBrain.com**.

Aplia   aplia

Aplia™ is an online interactive learning solution that helps you improve comprehension—and your grade—by integrating a variety of tools such as video, tutorials, practice tests, and interactive eBook. Founded by a professor to enhance his own courses, Aplia provides automatically graded assignments with detailed, immediate explanations on every question, and innovative teaching materials. More than 1,000,000 students like you have used Aplia at over 1,800 institutions. Aplia should be purchased only when assigned by your instructor as part of your course.

HOW DOES MEMORY FUNCTION?

For Kim Peek, brain damage to his cerebellum and other structures left him with both astounding abilities and dramatic impairments of memory. He could memorize entire encyclopedias and phone books, and yet every day he had to relearn how to brush his teeth. The human brain **encodes**, stores, and processes information, and allows us to use memory both **explicitly** (consciously) and **implicitly** (unconsciously). Kim Peek's story both awes us with the power of memory and saddens us with the realization of how difficult life can be when memory fails us.

THE TRADITIONAL THREE STAGES MODEL OF MEMORY: ARE WE SERIAL PROCESSORS?

Many researchers today reject the rigid **three stages model** of memory and suggest a different type of memory, called **working memory**, that is important in moving information in and out of **long-term memory**.

Information → Sensory memory → Short-term memory → Long-term memory

New information enters short-term memory from sensory memory

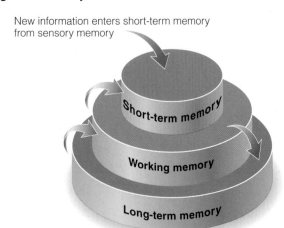

Short-term memory

Working memory

Long-term memory

• Working memory retrieves information from long-term memory to help process information in short-term memory; for example, the meaning of words stored in short-term memory may be accessed from long-term memory.

• Working memory also retrieves stored information when you need it—for an exam, your address, directions to your aunt's house—and sends it to short-term memory.

• Working memory also moves information from short-term memory into long-term memory for storage; for example, when you are studying, working memory will move the information you want to remember into long-term memory.

LONG-TERM MEMORY: HOW DO WE STORE INFORMATION FOR THE LONG HAUL?

Long-term memory is organized into **schemata**, which allow us to quickly and efficiently use our memory. In a sense, schemata are like a filing system for the library of knowledge we have stored in our long-term memory.

PhotoSpin, Inc/Alamy

HOW IS INFORMATION STORED IN LONG-TERM MEMORY?

Declarative memory   **Procedural memory**

Semantic memory
+
Episodic memory

Are You Getting THE BIG PICTURE?

HOW DO WE REMEMBER AND WHY DO WE FORGET?

Despite our best efforts to retain information, sometimes forgetting occurs. Forgetting may be due to **decay** of memory traces, **interference**, **cue-dependent forgetting**, or perhaps even **repression**.

- **Flashbulb memories** are unusually detailed memories for emotionally charged events—memories that are quite powerful but not always accurate.
- In general, we are prone to many memory errors. In cases of eyewitness testimony, these errors can have serious consequences.

IS MEMORY ACCURATE?

HOW IS MEMORY STORED IN THE BRAIN?

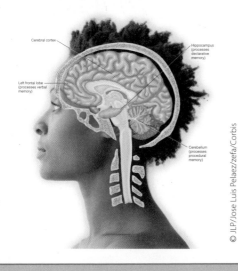

Cerebral cortex

Hippocampus (processes declarative memory)

Left frontal lobe (processes verbal memory)

Cerebellum (processes procedural memory)

- Information is stored at the synapse via **long-term potentiation**.
- Brain-imaging research shows that people who use their memory a great deal may have structural differences in their hippocampal regions. The hippocampus and frontal lobe seem to play significant roles in processing **declarative memory**.
- Studies suggest that **procedural memory** is linked to the cerebellum.

HOW CAN YOU IMPROVE YOUR MEMORY?

- Pay attention to what you are trying to remember; avoid distractions.
- Do not cram for exams.
- Use **elaborative rehearsal** to reinforce retention of information.
- Use **overlearning**.
- **Mnemonics** make your memory mighty.
- The SQ3R method encourages a process of Survey, Question, Read, Recite, Review.
- Use technologies, such as laptops and cell phones, appropriately while in class!

CHAPTER 7

COGNITION, LANGUAGE, AND INTELLIGENCE: HOW DO WE THINK?

Juan Silva/Getty Images

THE BIG PICTURE | What Would Life Be Without Language?

What if you had no words to describe or represent the objects in your world? What if you didn't even know that you had a name? Or what names are? Without language what would your thoughts and memories be like? Because language touches so many aspects of our lives, it is virtually impossible for us to truly understand what life would be like if we knew *no* language at all. Even those with deafness or those who don't speak the dominant language in their culture still have ways of symbolizing the world. Very few people make it to adulthood without developing some form of verbal or gestural language. This is the story of one man who did—a man known as Ildefonso.

Ildefonso was born in a rural area of Oaxaca in southern Mexico. When Ildefonso's parents realized that he had been born completely deaf, they labeled him a "dummy" and refused to send him to school. By the time he was about 5, Ildefonso was working in the sugarcane fields and tending farm animals. When work was not available, Ildefonso would beg for money and food. When Ildefonso was 10, his parents sent him to live with his grandfather in Mexico City, but there, too, he was deprived of any formal education. Without education or exposure to people who knew sign language, Ildefonso grew up without learning a language. He had *no* understanding of any spoken or signed language. He knew no Spanish, English, American Sign Language, or Mexican Sign Language. In fact, Ildefonso did not even know that language existed or that he had a name!

Without words with which to communicate, Ildefonso used spontaneous pantomiming to communicate his thoughts and desires. Using improvised gestures allowed Ildefonso to communicate with others in a crude fashion. And, after Ildefonso immigrated to the United States, he managed to make a living as a field hand. But, his lack of language isolated him from others and prevented him from understanding much of his world.

At age 27, Ildefonso met Susan Schaller, a teacher at a Los Angeles deaf education program. At first, Susan had little success in working with Ildefonso. Susan began teaching sign language, or signing, to Ildefonso, but she found it impossible to teach him sign language using conventional methods of instruction. She would sign a word and then point to the thing it represented in the real world. For example, she would sign the word *tree* and then point to a tree in the yard. Ildefonso would mimic her actions. He would sign the word *tree* and point to the tree, but he did not understand what she meant. He did not understand that things had *labels*. Even though Susan tried to stop Ildefonso from mimicking her gestures, no amount of signing and pointing to objects

263

Susan Schaller's book *A Man Without Words* chronicles the time she spent teaching Ildefonso, who was unable to hear or speak, his first language.

Early access to sign language allows many deaf children to acquire sign language as hearing children acquire a first spoken language. Ildefonso's lack of access prevented him from learning to sign as a child. In fact, Ildefonso did not know that language existed when he met Susan Schaller.

cognition the way in which we use and store information in memory

seemed to reach him. He continued mimicking Susan's signs without understanding the significance of his own actions.

Then Susan had an inspiration. Instead of repeatedly signing a word and pointing to its referent, she acted out a skit of a teacher teaching a student to sign words. In this skit, she played both the role of the teacher and the role of the student. She would pantomime a teacher signing the word *cat*, and then she would write the word *cat* on the board and pantomime stroking the fur of an imaginary cat. Then she would play the role of the student, who sat and watched what the teacher was doing, studied the sign for the word, and then appeared to understand the significance of the word and its sign. The genius of this approach was that it freed Ildefonso to merely sit back and watch. During the skit, Susan completely ignored Ildefonso, so there was no need for him to concentrate on mimicking her actions. All he had to do was watch and try to understand the meaning of the skit. When Ildefonso was free to merely watch, with no pressure to mimic the signs he was seeing, he finally began to understand the message Susan was trying to convey. He finally understood that things, such as a cat, had labels and that these labels could be written words or gestured signs. He finally understood the concept of language.

Once Ildefonso recognized the existence of language in the world, he realized how much he had been deprived of as a child. His first reaction was one of sorrow, and he wept openly at the knowledge of all that he did *not* know. Then he got down to the business of learning his first language, American Sign Language (ASL), at age 27!

Eventually, Ildefonso learned enough ASL to function adequately in the deaf world. With his newfound abilities, Ildefonso got a good job as a landscape artist and continued to study ASL while mentoring other languageless people, including his own brother who had also been born deaf. In short, Ildefonso became an engaged and productive citizen of the world.

The story of Ildefonso is a glimpse into a world that most of us can barely imagine. Ildefonso's lack of language touched nearly every aspect of his life, particularly his thinking. People with language—most of us—tend to think in terms of words. For us, much of our knowledge is stored in a verbal form, but for Ildefonso that was impossible. His knowledge of the world had to be stored in some other form, most likely in pictures. This no doubt affected the way that he thought and solved problems, and even the way that he viewed himself—Ildefonso wasn't aware that he had a name until he learned language. Despite his lack of language, Ildefonso was obviously an intelligent man, even though he would have scored low on many commonly used intelligence tests because they are verbally based.

By considering the case of Ildefonso, we see the interconnectedness of thought, language, and intelligence. This interdependence is also true for the vast majority of us who use language every day. Language is related to just about every aspect of the way in which we store and use information, or what psychologists refer to as **cognition.** In this chapter, we will explore many aspects of cognition, including *thinking, language,* and *intelligence.* As you read this chapter, reflect on your own use of language and try to imagine what life must be like for those who've been deprived of language because of prejudice against people who are deaf or a lack of exposure to appropriate deaf education.

THINKING: HOW DO WE REPRESENT OUR WORLD?

We engage in some sort of thinking every waking moment. We think about others, we think hard on exams, and we think about what we'll have for dinner. But most of us would have difficulty defining what it is that we actually *do* when we think. As we saw in Chapters 3 and 6, we are continually taking in information from the outside world, some of which we process and store in long-term memory. The information we store in long-term memory about the world and how it works constitutes our **knowledge** base. Psychologists define **thinking** as the use of knowledge to accomplish some sort of goal: to perceive and understand our world, to communicate with others, and to solve the problems we encounter in our lives (R. E. Mayer, 1983). Every time you retrieve some bit of knowledge from long-term memory to help answer a test question or remember the name of an old friend, you are *thinking*.

Thinking involves the use of all types of knowledge. In our long-term memory, we store our knowledge as **mental representations**—bits of memory that represent objects, events, people, and so on, that are not actually present now. For instance, most of us can close our eyes and think about what our best friend looks like even though she isn't present. To do this, we call on the mental representations we have stored of our knowledge of what our friend looks like. Similarly, we can recall the name of our best friend, the smell of her perfume, and the color of her hair by recalling the various mental representations of her that we have stored in our knowledge base.

In general, thinking involves the use of two broad classes of mental representations: those based on *sensory* aspects of the object, such as its visual appearance, smell, taste, and so forth; and those based on the *meaning* of the object, such as its name, definition, and properties. We will now turn our attention to a discussion of the best-studied forms of these mental representations: *visual images* and *concepts*.

Visual Images: How Good Is the Mental Picture?

With no words to work with, Ildefonso probably encoded much of his knowledge of the world as visual images. Prior to learning his first language, Ildefonso's knowledge must have been primarily a conglomeration of pictures. Unlike Ildefonso, most of us have the ability to store information in a verbal form, but this does not mean that visual images are not important means of storing knowledge of the world. The ability to "see" a friend's face in our mind or to visualize a map of our hometown in our head can be very useful in everyday life. Over the years, psychologists have studied visual images by examining how people perform on certain tasks in which they must mentally manipulate visual images.

One task that is used to study visual images is *mental rotation*. In a mental rotation task, participants are asked to rotate, or turn, an image in their head (Macramalla & Bridgeman, 2009). For example, in one classic study, participants were shown a series of letters that were oriented at different angles. In addition to being rotated, some of the letters were normal (right-reading), whereas others were reversed in mirror-image format (● FIGURE 7.1). After viewing the letter, the participant had to determine whether the letter was normal or reversed. The results of the experiment showed that as the letter was rotated farther from an upright position, it took the participant more time to judge whether the letter was normal or reversed (L. A. Cooper & Shepard, 1973). These results indicate that the task required participants to mentally rotate a visual image of the letter from its rotated position back to an upright position before they made a judgment. The farther rotated the stimulus letter was, the farther they had to rotate their visual image, and the longer it took them.

The results of this and numerous other mental rotation experiments (see R. N. Shepard, 1978, for a review) suggest that visual images may have all the spatial properties of the real stimulus. In other words, the visual image we store is essentially a *copy* of the stimulus we see in the world. Another line of evidence for this match between mental image and external reality comes from *image-scanning* studies that examine how we mentally scan images in our head (Denis & Borst, 2006; Kosslyn, Ball, & Reiser, 1978/2004).

knowledge information stored in our long-term memory about the world and how it works

thinking the use of knowledge to accomplish some sort of goal

mental representation memory traces that represent objects, events, people, and so on, that are not present at the time

Normal		Mirror-image	
R 0°	Я 300°	Я 0°	Я 300°
Я 60°	Я 240°	Я 60°	Я 240°
Я 120°	R 180°	Я 120°	R 180°

FIGURE 7.1

● **A Mental Rotation Task** In this task, participants were asked to determine whether the letter was right-reading or reversed. The greater the rotation, the longer it took. *Source: M. W. Eysenck and M. T. Keene, Cognitive Psychology, 4th ed., p. 258. Psychological Press.*

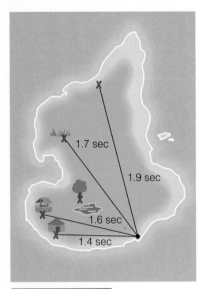

● **An Image-Scanning Task** In this task, participants were asked to imagine a black dot moving across the map to the points indicated by the Xs. The average amount of time to do this task was proportionate to the distance between the starting point and the ending point on the map. *Source: © Stephen Kosslyn, 1983.*

In a typical image-scanning experiment, like the one pioneered by Stephen Kosslyn and colleagues (Kosslyn et al., 1978/2004), participants are asked to memorize a map of a fictitious island with several objects depicted on it (see ● FIGURE 7.2). After the participants have memorized the map, they are then asked to mentally scan the path that a black dot would take as it travels from one point on the map to another. Because the points exist at various distances from one another, researchers can correlate the time it takes the participants to mentally scan the image with the distance between the points on the actual map. If the participants' visual images of the map are copies of the actual map, then the time it takes to scan longer distances should be longer than the time it takes to scan shorter distances on the map. This is exactly what Stephen Kosslyn found (see Figure 7.2). The time it took to scan distances increased proportionately with the increase in the actual distances on the map. For a look at how the brain responds during image scanning, take a look at ● WHAT'S HAPPENING IN YOUR BRAIN?.

The Limits of the Mental Picture

As convincing as the mental rotation and image-scanning experiments are in supporting the argument that visual images have spatial properties that mimic those of the actual stimulus, the question remains: Do we actually store photographic images of the things that we see? As it turns out, there are reasons to suspect that we generally do not. Several studies indicate that mental rotation does not always correlate with the physical properties of the stimulus (Boden, 1988; Hinton, 1979), and there is also evidence to suggest that we cannot always manipulate our visual images in the same manner that we could manipulate the actual object (Chambers & Reisberg, 1985).

For example, participants in one study were shown an ambiguous figure, like that shown in ● FIGURE 7.3, and asked to form a visual image of it in their heads. Because this figure can be interpreted as a duck or a rabbit, some of the participants interpreted the image in their heads as a duck and others as a rabbit. While the participants were holding the image of the ambiguous figure in their heads, they were asked to reinterpret it as something else—to see it as a duck if they had originally seen it as a rabbit, or vice versa. Astonishingly, none

WHAT'S HAPPENING IN YOUR BRAIN?

BRAIN ACTIVITY DURING IMAGE-SCANNING TECHNIQUES

During a typical image-scanning experiment, participants are first asked to memorize a map. Then they are asked to mentally scan the image of the map as they hold it in memory. Researchers have used PET scans to scan participants' brains while they are engaged in image-scanning tasks (Mellet et al., 2002). During scanning, participants showed increased activity in the right medial temporal lobe, near the hippocampus. This result makes sense in that the hippocampus has been shown to play a role in spatial memory (remember the London taxi drivers from Chapter 2, p. 62?).

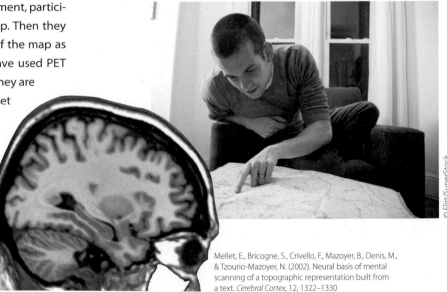

Mellet, E., Bricogne, S., Crivello, F., Mazoyer, B., Denis, M., & Tzourio-Mazoyer, N. (2002). Neural basis of mental scanning of a topographic representation built from a text. *Cerebral Cortex, 12,* 1322–1330

© Flirt/SuperStock

of them could do so. They could see the image in their heads only as being what they had originally interpreted it to be. However, the participants were able to draw a picture of the figure, and once they had drawn it, they could interpret the figure as being either a duck or a rabbit (Chambers & Reisberg, 1985). If the visual image in their heads had all the same properties as the actual stimulus, then why were the participants unable to reinterpret their visual image? Apparently, although the visual images we have in our heads do retain some characteristics of the actual stimulus, they are also influenced by the verbal interpretation we place on them (Chambers & Reisberg, 1992).

TRY THIS DEMONSTRATION

How good is the map in your mind? Let's look at your ability to answer questions about a visual stimulus that you have seen many times, a map of North America. Answer these questions:

Which is farther east: Reno, Nevada, or San Diego, California?

Which is farther north: Montreal, Canada, or Seattle, Washington?

Which is farther west: the Atlantic or the Pacific entrance to the Panama Canal?

The answers may seem obvious, but researchers have found that most people answer them incorrectly (A. Stevens & Coupe, 1978). The correct answers are San Diego, Seattle, and the Atlantic entrance. Are you surprised? Take a look at ● FIGURE 7.4, which shows that these are the correct answers.

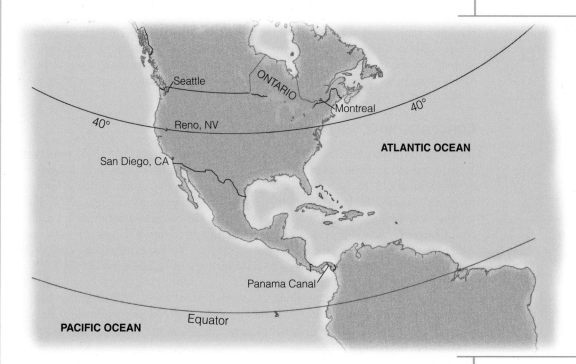

FIGURE 7.3

● **An Ambiguous Figure** What do you see when you *first* look at this picture?

FIGURE 7.4

● **A Map of North and Central America** Most people answer many questions about this map incorrectly even though they have seen it many times before. It is highly unlikely that we have an exact visual image of this map stored in our long-term memory.

Why so many of us answer these questions incorrectly has to do with how we have organized our knowledge about the geography of the world, in what are called **cognitive maps**. We introduced cognitive maps in Chapter 5 in our discussion of the role cognition plays in learning—remember Edward Tolman's work with rats learning the path through a maze (p. 208)? In this case, our cognitive maps are mental representations for geographical information. It appears that we do not store an exact visual image of a map of the world in our

cognitive map a mental representation of the environment

cognitive map. Rather, we store an approximate visual image of the map as well as some general knowledge about the geography of the area. Furthermore, when we try to visualize maps in our heads, we tend to think of geographical locations in terms of larger units (A. Stevens & Coupe, 1978), and we use this knowledge to help us deduce the needed geographical information (B. Tversky, 1981). In response to the first question, for example, we know that San Diego is in California, and we know that California is west of Nevada. Therefore, when we recall our cognitive map of the United States, we assume that Reno, Nevada, must be east of San Diego, and we visualize a map in which this is true. In fact, it is not true, as you can see in Figure 7.4.

So, where does all this research leave us with respect to visual images? Isn't it a bit contradictory? Some studies suggest that visual images are precise mental copies of the actual stimuli, but other studies show that visual images may deviate significantly from the actual stimuli. According to Stephen Kosslyn (1994), our mental representation of visual stimuli relies on *both* visual images and verbal knowledge. In other words, we use both types of mental representations—sensory (pictures) and meaning (words)—to fully represent visual stimuli. The pictures represent parts of the stimulus, and the words describe the stimulus and tell us how the pieces of the picture fit together. For example, when you look at a flower, you might store, among other things, a visual image of the shape of a petal, the stem, and the center, along with verbal instructions that the petals are placed around the center and the stem descends from the bottom of the flower. In Kosslyn's view, we do not store a carbon copy of the flower. Instead, we use this mixture of verbal and pictorial pieces to *construct* our visual image of the flower. This should ring some bells in your head. As we learned in Chapter 6, memory is *constructive*, and unfortunately, the constructive nature of memory does sometimes lead to inaccuracies. So, don't feel bad if you thought Reno was east of San Diego!

It appears that language plays an important role in our representation of knowledge even when we are dealing with visual information. It would be interesting to know how Ildefonso stored visual images without the use of any verbal instructions. We will never know how Ildefonso's mind was able to cope with this lack of language. Psychologists have not had much opportunity to study people like Ildefonso, but we have had the chance to study those of us who do use language as part of our mental representation of the world. Later in this chapter, we will take a closer look at how we use language to represent the *meaning* of our world.

Concepts: How We Organize What We Know

As we saw in Chapter 6, we have a tendency to organize our knowledge in long-term memory. We store mental representations for related objects together in the same mental category. For example, we would store our knowledge of cats, dogs, and elephants together in the category for *animals*, and apple, oranges, and grapes together in the category for *fruits*. This tendency to organize information based on similarity shows the *conceptual* nature of human cognition. **Concepts**, the mental categories that contain related bits of knowledge, are organized around the *meaning* of the information they represent. For instance, *animal* is a concept. In our mind we know what it means to be an animal. Animals are living beings, but we also distinguish animals from humans, and so on.

At times, when we store conceptual information of an object, we encode the characteristics and features of the object in a *semantic* form. For example, you may encode knowledge about the features of a car (e.g., has tires, drives, made of metal, and so on) in long-term memory (A. M. Collins & Quillian, 1969). Recent research suggests that we may also store the *perceptual* experiences we have of objects in long-term memory. For example, when we see a car, our eyes send this visual information to our brain and a specific pattern of neural activity in the visual cortex results. We then capture and store information on this pattern of neural activity and later can use this information to recreate the visual perception of the car in our mind. Likewise, we would store our perceptual experience of the smell of the car, the sound of its engine, and so on (Barsalou, 2008; Marques, 2010).

Later, we use this semantic and perceptual information to perceive, think about, and deal with our world. Conceptually organizing our knowledge helps us use that knowledge more

concept mental category that contains related bits of knowledge

efficiently. Concepts can be viewed as a type of mental shorthand that both organizes and saves space in our cognitive system. Let's look at an example of a well-known concept: oranges. Close your eyes and picture an orange in your mind's eye. Can you see it clearly? Can you describe it in detail? Most of us can do this easily for something as familiar as an orange. Now look carefully at your mental orange. Is this concept that you have stored in your mind an *actual* orange that you have seen? In other words, is this orange number 123,675 that you saw one Sunday morning at the local market? Not likely. Instead, your concept of an orange is an abstraction, or a general idea, of what an orange is. You don't have to store mental representations for each and every orange you have seen. Rather, you only need to store a generalized concept of what an orange is and what it looks like. This ability is a great cognitive space-saver when you think about all the oranges you'll see in your lifetime.

Organizing Concepts Into Categories

Another benefit of mental concepts is that we can organize them into hierarchical categories (Markman & Ross, 2003). Psychologists have found that we tend to organize our knowledge into three levels of categorization (Rosch, Mervis, Gray, Johnson, & Boyes-Braem, 2004). The highest, most general level is called the **superordinate category**. The superordinate level contains concepts that are broad and general in their description. For example, fruit would be considered a superordinate category. The intermediate level of categorization is the **basic level category**. The basic level seems to be the level that we use most often to think about our world. For example, when we write out a shopping list, we probably list basic level concepts, such as oranges rather than fruit.

The third level in the hierarchy is the **subordinate category**. Concepts at the subordinate level are less general and more specific than those at the basic level. When speaking of oranges, the subordinate category would contain items like Valencia oranges, navel oranges, and blood oranges. Although the subordinate level is the most specific, it is not the first level that springs to mind when we think about our world. You would be much more likely to place the basic level concept—oranges—on your shopping list than you would be to place Valencia oranges. Interestingly, the basic level is also the first level of knowledge young children acquire (P. C. Quinn & Tanaka, 2007; Rosch et al., 2004).

The basic level category *apples* falls under the superordinate category *fruit*. The label *Granny Smith* is a subordinate category of the basic level concept *apples*.

Formal and Natural Categories

So, how do we acquire concepts in the first place? Simply put, we acquire concepts from an early age as we observe and learn from our world. We acquire **formal concepts** as we learn the rigid rules that define certain categories of things. For example, for an animal to be considered a member of the category *female*, it must possess certain attributes or characteristics. All females are genetically designed to produce either offspring or eggs. If an animal does not have this attribute, it cannot be a female.

The lines that define formal categories are very clear-cut. Unfortunately, life is not always so neat and tidy as to provide us with formal rules for everything, and much of our knowledge of the world does not fit cleanly into only one category. For example, do you consider a tomato a fruit or a vegetable? How do you categorize cucumbers? Many people consider tomatoes and cucumbers to be vegetables, whereas others—including botanists—categorize them as fruits. Why the confusion? Perhaps because we associate fruits with sweetness, we tend not to classify cucumbers and tomatoes as fruit even though they do contain seeds, which is a defining attribute of fruit. Most of us are aware of the rules for membership as a female, but not aware of the botanical definition of a fruit. We have organized our fruit and vegetable concepts in a less distinct and orderly fashion based on our own experiences with them.

superordinate category the highest, most general level of a concept

basic level category the intermediate level of categorization that seems to be the level that we use most to think about our world

subordinate category the lowest level of categorization, which contains concepts that are less general and more specific than those at the basic level

formal concept concept that is based on learned, rigid rules that define certain categories of things

Concepts that develop naturally as we live our lives and experience the world are referred to as **natural concepts**. We do not learn formal rules for these concepts; rather, we intuit and create the rules as we learn about our world. As such, the boundaries defining natural concept categories are often blurry, or "fuzzy" (Rosch, 1973a; Rosch et al., 2004). Our example of the tomato is a good illustration of this conceptualizing. You can classify the tomato as a vegetable, a fruit, or both, depending on your experience. How do you see it? Because natural concepts are a by-product of our day-to-day experience, they develop in a relatively effortless and *natural* manner as we live our lives.

When categorizing information in the real world, we tend to do well with the fuzzy boundaries of natural concepts, but we are not perfect. The difficulty involved in deciding which concepts to include in and which to exclude from a category varies considerably. Sometimes it's an easy task, and other times it's not.

TRY THIS DEMONSTRATION

Take a look at ● FIGURE 7.5 below, and answer the questions as quickly as you can. Which of the questions are you able to answer quickly? Which ones take longer? Why do you think some of them are easier than others?

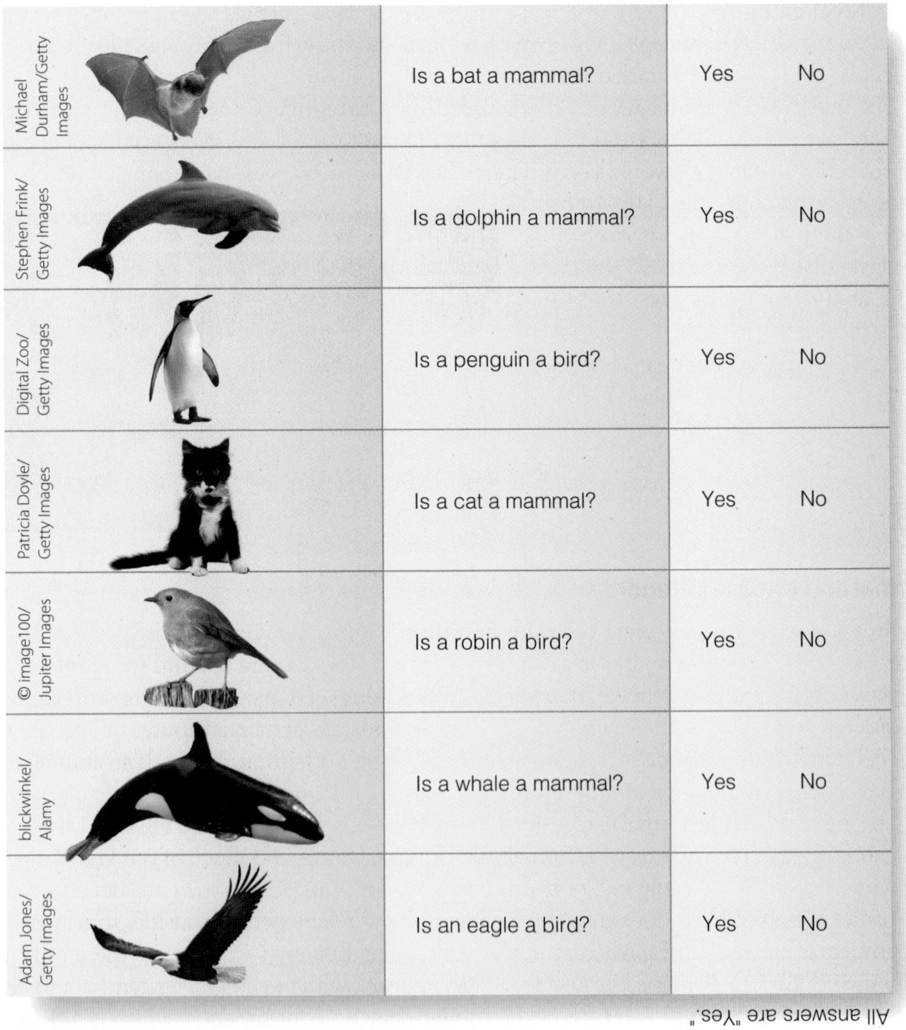

Michael Durham/Getty Images	Is a bat a mammal?	Yes	No
Stephen Frink/Getty Images	Is a dolphin a mammal?	Yes	No
Digital Zoo/Getty Images	Is a penguin a bird?	Yes	No
Patricia Doyle/Getty Images	Is a cat a mammal?	Yes	No
© image100/Jupiter Images	Is a robin a bird?	Yes	No
blickwinkel/Alamy	Is a whale a mammal?	Yes	No
Adam Jones/Getty Images	Is an eagle a bird?	Yes	No

All answers are "Yes."

FIGURE 7.5

● **Natural Concept Categories**

natural concept concept that develops naturally as we live our lives and experience the world

Most people find it easier to decide that a robin is a bird than that a penguin is a bird. But why? One possibility is that a robin is a more typical example of the category *bird* than a penguin is. According to some researchers, we form what are called **prototypes** for natural concept categories, much like the mental image of the orange we examined on page 269. A prototype is our concept of the most typical member of the category—in essence, a summary of all the members of the category. When we judge whether or not something belongs in a natural concept category, we compare it to the prototype of the category (Minda & Smith, 2002). The more similar the object is to the prototype, the faster we judge it to be a member of the concept category.

However, other researchers argue that instead of using abstracted prototypes, we judge category membership by comparing an item to the memories that we have stored for actual examples or **exemplars** of that concept category (Nosofsky & Zaki, 2002; Rehder & Hoffman, 2005; Voorspoels, Vanpaemel, & Storms, 2008). In this view, you would determine that the robin in your backyard is a bird by comparing this robin to the memories or exemplars of the actual birds you have seen during your lifetime. Unless you live where penguins are common, you are likely to have many more songbird exemplars than penguin exemplars available in your memory. Because robins resemble the songbird exemplars that quickly come to mind more closely than penguins do, you are quicker to decide that a robin belongs in the category of birds.

The debate over whether we use prototypes or exemplars to judge category membership is ongoing. Some argue that we may even use both (Ashby & Maddox, 2005; G. Storms, DeBoeck, & Ruts, 2001). Regardless of how we go about making category judgments, these judgments are crucial to our ability to think about our world. In the next section, we will see just what we can accomplish with all our thinking. But first, take a moment to test your knowledge of this last section on the following quiz.

prototype our concept of the most typical member of the category

exemplar a mental representation of an actual instance of a member of a category

Let's
REVIEW
In this section, we discussed thinking and how we represent information in memory. We discussed not only the format of stored knowledge but also its organizational structure. For a quick check of your understanding, try answering the following questions at increasing levels of difficulty.

1. _____ is/are bits of stored knowledge.

   a. Thinking   c. Schemas

   b. Mental representations   d. Prototypes

2. Which of the following would be a superordinate concept for the category *hammers*?

   a. ball-peen hammers   c. tools

   b. saws   d. screwdrivers

3. In an experiment, Dr. Kelly asks participants to name the first example of a "vehicle" that comes to mind. Based on what you know about concepts, which of the following vehicles would the average participant be *most* likely to name?

   a. a tractor   c. an airplane

   b. a train   d. a car

ANSWERS 1. b; 2. c; 3. d

PROBLEM SOLVING: WHERE DOES OUR THINKING GET US?

Imagine that you get into your car one morning, only to find that it won't start. It's 7:30 and you have an 8:00 class. Today of all days, you don't need this hassle because you have a final exam in your psychology class. You have a problem! As you can see from this example, we never know when a problem will arise. What would you do in this situation? Call a friend for a ride?

LEARNING OBJECTIVES

What Should You Know?

- Describe the different types of problems we face and the ways in which we may try to solve them.
- Describe common obstacles to problem solving.

TABLE 7.1

● **The Steps to Problem Solving**

PROBLEM-SOLVING STEP	EXAMPLE
Identify the problem.	The car won't start, and I have a final exam.
Represent the problem.	If I miss this exam without permission, I'll fail the course.
Plan a solution.	I will call a taxi.
Execute the plan.	Call the taxi.
Evaluate the plan.	The taxi will get me to school, but I will be late. Maybe I should also have called my professor.
Evaluate the solution.	I did make it to school, and I took the exam. My professor was a bit angry that I didn't call to say I'd be late, but I did pass the exam. I handled this situation adequately, but next time I'll call my professor.

Source: J. R. Hayes, 1989.

well-structured problem problem for which there is a clear pathway to the solution

algorithm a method of solving a particular problem that always leads to the correct solution

heuristic a shortcut or rule of thumb that may or may not lead to a correct solution to the problem

Walk to school? Call your professor and arrange to take a makeup final? Or fix your own car? In general, when we solve problems, we go through a series of six stages (J. R. Hayes, 1989), outlined in ● TABLE 7.1.

Although the prospect of missing a final exam is frightening, there are a variety of obvious solutions to this problem. This is not the case for all problems, however. If it were, we would have ended hunger, war, and pollution long ago. Why do some problems seem to have obvious possible solutions whereas others do not? The answer lies in the type of problem we are facing.

Well-Structured Problems: The Answer Is Out There

Well-structured problems are problems for which there is a clear pathway to the solution. For example, what if your best friend asks you to bake him a cake for his birthday? Even if you don't know how to bake a cake, you know that you can find a recipe and follow the instructions to produce the desired result. Baking may be new to you, but you can get the information you need to accomplish your goal.

We face well-structured problems every day. Programming your DVR, balancing your checkbook, and finding the cheapest hotel at your vacation destination are all examples of well-structured problems. When we solve well-structured problems, we tend to go about it in one of two ways. We use either an *algorithm* or a *heuristic* to achieve a solution.

Deciding how much paint to buy for a home improvement project is an example of a task that can be most accurately solved using an algorithm.

Algorithms and Heuristics: The Long and Short of Problem Solving

An **algorithm** is a method of solving a particular problem that always leads to the correct solution; a **heuristic** is a shortcut or rule of thumb that may or may not lead to a correct solution. Imagine that you're going to paint your bedroom, but you don't know how much paint to buy. The algorithmic solution to this problem is to measure the height and width of all your walls, calculate the area, and look up how many gallons of paint are required to cover this area. This algorithm will lead to the correct answer, and as a result, you will buy just the right amount of paint. However, this strategy also takes considerable time. You must measure the walls, find the formula for paint coverage, and calculate the required figures. If you are in a hurry or impatient, this strategy may not be your first choice.

So how can you solve your problem more quickly? You could use a heuristic, such as simply guessing how much paint you will need to do the job. Guessing is quick, but you do run the risk of not buying the right amount of paint. You might have to go back to the store for more paint, or you might have a lot of paint left over. *Guessing* and repeated guessing, or *trial and error*, are two very common heuristics.

As you look at this example, you may think that it seems foolish to guess at the amount of paint to buy when a clear algorithm exists for this problem. Why would

Black/Getty Images

anyone approach a problem in this seemingly haphazard fashion? There are several reasons one would choose a heuristic over an algorithm. First, heuristics can save time. Heuristics are mental shortcuts that can quickly lead us to solutions. You might guess correctly that you need 2 gallons of paint to cover your room, especially if you have experience painting rooms. In this case, measuring the room would be an unnecessary waste of time. Second, we do not always know the correct algorithm for the problem we are facing. What if you lack the mathematical knowledge to calculate the surface area of your bedroom walls? Even though there is a formula for calculating the surface area and paint coverage, if you don't know what it is, you cannot implement the algorithm, and you would have to use a heuristic.

Ill-Structured Problems: The Answer May Be Out There

Ill-structured problems are problems for which there is no known algorithm. For example, do you know an algorithm for bringing about world peace? Unfortunately, neither do we. In the case of an ill-structured problem, we have no choice but to use a heuristic, but this restriction does not mean that there is no chance the problem will be solved. Try solving this ill-structured problem, which is like the one used by researcher James Adams (1976).

Aside from an unwillingness to use socially undesirable methods of solving problems, we may not even *think* of certain possible solutions. This situation is often the case with ill-structured problems. We get stuck in particular ways of trying to solve problems, and we lack

ill-structured problem a problem for which an algorithm is not known

TRY THIS
DEMONSTRATION

Assume that you are one of six people in a room. In the center of the room is a pipe that is embedded in the concrete floor (● FIGURE 7.6). The pipe extends 4 inches above the surface of the floor. In the pipe is a Ping-Pong ball. The Ping-Pong ball has a diameter of 1.5 inches, and the inside diameter of the pipe is 2.1 inches. Among the six people in the room, you have the following items: a file, 100 feet of clothesline, a hammer, a chisel, a box of corn-flakes, a wire coat hanger, a monkey wrench, and a lightbulb. Your task is to remove the Ping-Pong ball from the pipe *without* damaging the pipe, the floor, or the ball.

With no clear algorithm for this problem, how would you proceed? Most people would probably use some form of the trial-and-error heuristic to get the ball out. You might try to hit the pipe with the hammer in hopes of vibrating the ball upward. You might try using the wire from the coat hanger to lift the ball out. Or you might try sucking the ball out of the pipe with your mouth because Ping-Pong balls are so light. But these techniques are unlikely to achieve the desired result. Many of us would be stumped by this problem, especially if we are from a Western culture. That's a hint! Why would your culture make a difference in this case? One interesting thing about culture is that it influences the approach we take to solving problems. In the United States, we have learned to approach problems like this one with tools, so our first instinct is to make or use some sort of tool to mechanically remove the ball from the pipe. Our culture also dictates what is and is not appropriate public behavior. There is a way to get the ball out of the pipe, but to do it, you have to break one of our Western cultural taboos. Have you guessed the solution yet? ***Have one of the people in the room pee into the pipe.*** The ball will float to the surface on the urine. By now, you're probably saying, "Yuck! I don't want to get the ball out of the pipe that badly!" Your disgust for this solution is part of the point. In many Western cultures, urinating in public is considered to be socially unacceptable behavior. Therefore, many Westerners would not attempt to solve this problem in this fashion. However, in a culture in which public urination is not so taboo, people would have no qualms about using this effective strategy.

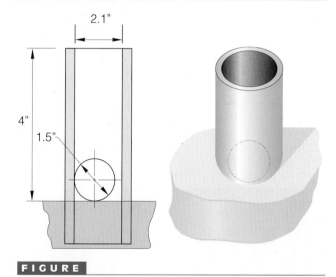

FIGURE

● **An Ill-Structured Problem** How would you get the ball out of the pipe?

the **insight** required to find a true solution. Insight occurs when we find a new way of looking at the problem that leads to a sudden understanding of how to solve it (Dominowski & Dallob, 1995; Qiu et al., 2010). Because of its perceived suddenness, insight is often referred to as the "Aha!" experience. Insight often feels as if a "lightbulb" has turned on, illuminating the answer for us. Yet, research indicates that insight isn't such a sudden process. Insight often occurs only after we have thought about the problem for a while (C. A. Kaplan & Simon, 1990). Truly understanding a problem and how to solve it often occurs only as the result of much thought and gradual acquisition of knowledge about the problem (Hamel & Elshout, 2000).

Creativity: Overcoming Obstacles to Problem Solving

We do not need to tell you that some problems in life are more difficult to face than others are. At times, all of us may encounter problems that challenge even our best problem-solving skills. For example, Susan Schaller's early attempts to teach language to Ildefonso failed. To solve the difficult problem of getting Ildefonso to grasp the concept of language, Schaller had to use what we commonly refer to as *creativity*. To reach Ildefonso, Schaller came up with the unconventional idea of ignoring him while she pantomimed a scene of a teacher teaching language to an imaginary student. She had to abandon the typical approaches to teaching sign language that had worked for her in the past in favor of this novel, creative approach.

For more than 50 years, psychologists have been trying to define exactly what creativity is and what abilities or traits creative people possess (Mumford, 2003). To date, the major agreement among researchers has been that **creativity** involves the ability to combine mental elements in new and useful ways (e.g., Sternberg, 1999; O. Vartanian, Martindale, & Kwiatkowski, 2003). Creativity may mean finding a novel solution to a problem, as Schaller did, or coming up with a unique approach to creating some new product—a piece of music, a painting, or a scientific theory that is widely recognized by society as being creative (Gelade, 2002).

Certainly all of us can think of people we consider creative. But what makes one person more creative than another? Are there special traits or abilities that creative people possess? Over the years, psychologists have proposed several variables that may underlie creativity, but the one that has received the most attention is a skill called *divergent thinking* (O. Vartanian et al., 2003). Divergent thinking is the ability to generate many ideas quickly in response to a single prompt (Eysenck, 1995). For example, a divergent thinker can quickly come up with many different ways to tie a scarf or many different uses for an ink pen.

Divergent thinking aids creativity because it allows you to come up with many different ideas about how to solve a problem. As we will see, when you can think quickly to generate many different ideas, you are less likely to be blocked by some of the common obstacles to problem solving, including *functional fixedness* and *mental sets*.

insight a new way of looking at a problem that leads to a sudden understanding of how to solve it

creativity the ability to combine mental elements in new and useful ways

functional fixedness being able to see objects only in their familiar roles

Creativity requires us to think divergently. In creating this piece of art, the artist has found a new use for these common items.

© Accretion by Beverly Rayner

Functional Fixedness

When we attempt to solve problems, we often rely on well-used strategies. We look at the tools that we have at our disposal, and we evaluate them in terms of their common, everyday uses. We think of a hammer as a tool for pounding and a box as an object for holding other objects. We often cannot conceive of using these tools in new, novel ways. This limitation of being able to see objects only in their familiar roles is called **functional fixedness**. Functional fixedness can prevent us from solving problems that otherwise could be solved. But as the following story illustrates, sometimes we must break out of functional fixedness and find creative ways to solve our problems.

One of your authors has a bad habit of leaving things, such as her purse, in places where they don't belong. One day, she could not find her purse anywhere, and she needed to get to class. After searching for a bit, she called her cell phone, which was in the purse, and used her ringing phone to direct her to its location under a pile of books and papers. Using a cell phone as a homing beacon of sorts requires one to break out of functional fixedness to realize that a phone can be used for purposes other than its typical uses.

Mental Sets

Another obstacle to problem solving is a **mental set**. A mental set is a tendency to habitually use the methods of problem solving that have worked for you in the past. Mental sets become an obstacle when we persist in trying solutions that may have worked in the past but are *not* working in the current situation.

TRY THIS
DEMONSTRATION

Will you be a victim of mental sets? Try solving this riddle from Gayle Dow and Richard Mayer (2004): *One morning a woman's earring fell into a cup that was filled with coffee, yet her earring did not get wet. How could this be?* (See ● Figure 7.7, p. 276, for the answer.)

If you find yourself having little success in solving a problem, stop working on the problem for a while and let it *incubate*. **Incubation**, or a period of not thinking about the problem, sometimes helps us solve a problem (Sio & Ormerod, 2009). When we incubate, the unproductive strategies recede from memory, and we are better able to attack the problem from a fresh, more productive perspective when we return to it. If we are locked in a mental set, incubation may be just what is needed to solve the problem.

As we've seen in this section, problem solving is a matter of generating possible solutions and then selecting from them the solution that will ultimately solve the problem. If your car broke down tomorrow, how would you decide which course of action to take? Would you call in absent to school? Call a mechanic? Call a taxi? Walk to school? Go back to bed and forget it? Many times, choosing the *best* solution from among all the possibilities is the real task. In our next section, we will look a bit closer at the cognitive processes that we engage in when we reason, make decisions, and make judgments.

Let's
REVIEW
In this section, we discussed the process of problem solving, including the types of problems we might face, the manner in which we tend to solve such problems, and common obstacles to problem solving. For a quick check of your understanding, try answering the following questions at increasing levels of difficulty.

1. A(n) _____ problem has a clear path to its solution.
   a. ill-structured
   b. well-structured
   c. insight
   d. divergent-thinking

2. Incubation is most closely related to which of the following concepts?
   a. well-structured problems
   b. insight
   c. prototypes
   d. exemplars

3. Sue used a chair with wheels to carry a load of books to her car. She piled the books in the seat of the chair and pushed it to her car. Trina, on the other hand, carried her books by hand, even though she also had a chair with wheels in her office. Trina was most likely suffering the effects of _____.
   a. functional fixedness
   b. an ill-structured problem
   c. insight
   d. mental sets

ANSWERS 1. b; 2. b; 3. a

mental set the tendency to habitually use methods of problem solving that have worked for you in the past

incubation a period of not thinking about a problem that helps one solve the problem

© Susann Doyle-Portillo

FIGURE 7.7

- **Solution to the Earring in the Coffee Cup Problem** The earring doesn't get wet because the cup is full of dry coffee grounds, not liquid coffee! Did you get caught in the mental set of thinking that a *cup of coffee* implies a cup of liquid coffee? Don't feel bad if you did; many of us would make the same mistake.

reasoning drawing conclusions about the world based on certain assumptions

deductive reasoning reasoning from the general to the specific

inductive reasoning reasoning from the specific to the general

decision making making a choice from among a series of alternatives

judgment the act of estimating the probability of an event

availability heuristic a heuristic in which we use the ease with which we can recall instances of an event to help us estimate the frequency of the event

representativeness heuristic a heuristic in which we rely on the degree to which something is representative of a category, rather than the base rate, to help us judge whether or not it belongs in the category

ARE WE ALWAYS LOGICAL WHEN REASONING, MAKING DECISIONS, OR MAKING JUDGMENTS?

Reasoning, decision making, and judgments are cognitive processes that use some of the same strategies as problem solving. We engage in *reasoning* when we draw conclusions based on certain assumptions about the world. For example, you might reason that your friend Jamal is a nice person because he has many friends. *Decision making* is choosing among several options, as in our example of what you might do if your car breaks down. *Judgments* are a type of problem solving in which we estimate the likelihood of some event—for example, judging the chance of rain today. In making judgments, we often use two particular heuristics that we'll discuss.

Deductive and Inductive Reasoning

We engage in **reasoning** when we draw conclusions that are based on certain assumptions about the world. For example, you might reason that your friend Rick has money because he drives a nice car. Or, based on your experiences, you might reason that studying leads to better grades. Psychologists who study reasoning have traditionally looked at two types of reasoning processes: *deductive reasoning* and *inductive reasoning*. **Deductive reasoning** involves reasoning from the *general* to the *specific*. In other words, you start with a general rule and apply it to particular cases. For example, you might *deduce* that because studying leads to good grades, your friend Melissa, who makes good grades, must also study hard.

Inductive reasoning, on the other hand, is the opposite. When using inductive reasoning, one reasons from the *specific* to the *general*. Here the object is to begin with specific instances and to discover what general rule fits all these instances. For example, as children, we may have noticed time and time again that our classmates who did well were also those who seemed to study the most, so we induced that studying hard leads to good grades. We used these specific instances to help us *induce* the rule that studying hard leads to good grades.

We hope you see the parallels between inductive reasoning and the *scientific method* that psychologists use to conduct research (Chapter 1). When conducting studies to test theories, psychologists try to induce the general rules that explain mental processes and behavior. Once these rules have been induced, they can then be applied to individual situations to help deduce, or predict, how people and animals are likely to behave. This, of course, does not mean that reasoning is just for scientists. Deductive and inductive reasoning are equally important in everyday life. Effective reasoning can be a very important aspect of making good decisions in our lives.

Decision Making: Outcomes and Probabilities

Decision making involves choosing from among several alternatives. We must first choose a course of action before we can implement a solution to the problem. As part of the problem-solving process, the decisions we make can have serious implications for our lives. Decisions about what subject to major in, whom to date, and where to invest your money are just some of the life-altering decisions you might have to make in your lifetime. Given the importance of the decision-making process, researchers have been looking at *how* we make decisions.

Two factors that influence our decisions are the perceived *outcomes* of our decisions and the *probability* of achieving these outcomes. For example, when you choose a major, you weigh the expected outcomes of the major. How interesting is the subject area to you? What kind of job will it lead to? How difficult will the course work be? What is the pay like in this field? You also temper these judgments with your perception of whether these outcomes will actually occur. There may be high-salaried jobs in your major area, but if you see little chance of actually getting one of them, then you may decide against that major.

Logically, we would seek to make decisions that we believe have a good chance of leading to favorable outcomes. However, our decision-making processes are a bit more complex than this. Another factor that affects our decisions is how the possible courses of action are presented, or *framed* (Kahneman & Tversky, 1984). For example, which of the following options would you choose? Would you choose to take a class in which you had an 80% chance of passing? Or one in which you had a 20% chance of failing? Many people would choose the first option because it is framed positively, even though the chance of succeeding in the course is the same in both cases. Whether you prefer a positively framed option or a negatively framed one is an individual preference. Sometimes we exhibit *loss aversion*, or a tendency to focus on what a certain decision could cost us in terms of potential gain. Other times, we exhibit *risk aversion*, or concern over losing what we already have. Our relative aversions to risk and loss can have implications for some of the decisions we make in life, such as retirement planning (Goldstein, Johnson, & Sharpe, 2008).

Judgments: Estimating the Likelihood of Events

Judgment can be seen as a type of problem solving in which we estimate the probability of an event. If you don't know what the probability of a certain event is, and you need to have this probability to make a decision, what do you do? As with all problems, you can solve this one using either an algorithm or a heuristic. An algorithm would involve somehow looking up or calculating the exact probability of the event's occurring, but this is often neither possible nor practical, as in the case of trying to figure out what the stock market will do in the coming months. So, as we saw before, we tend to rely on heuristics when we make judgments.

JGI/Jamie Grill/Getty Images

Retirement planning involves making many decisions, such as whether to invest your money in stocks or bonds. Stocks are associated with greater risk of losing your money, but they also have a higher historical rate of return on your investment. Bonds are safer, but yield lower historical returns. Which one would you choose? Our choices are likely influenced by our tendency toward risk aversion and loss aversion. Loss-averse people will be more likely to choose stocks, whereas risk-averse people will likely stick to bonds.

The Availability Heuristic

Many people are afraid to fly, even though air travel is statistically safer than traveling by car ("Air Travel Remains Safe," 1999). Why would people be afraid to choose a *safer* form of travel? The answer lies in the manner in which we make judgments about the frequency of events. When we estimate the frequency of events, we heuristically base our judgments on the ease with which we can recall instances of the event in memory. The more easily we can recall a memory for an event, the more frequent we estimate the event to be. This heuristic is called the **availability heuristic** (A. Tversky & Kahneman, 1974).

The availability heuristic explains the previous example of fearing air travel more than driving. Although fatal car accidents occur every day, they are not as widely covered by the media as plane crashes are. A fatal car crash may result in one or a few deaths, but a plane crash usually involves larger numbers of fatalities. Therefore, when a plane goes down, the news coverage is graphic, horrifying, and prolonged. This publicity leaves us with a strong, easily accessible memory for the plane crash. The result is that when we think of ways to travel, we more readily recall memories of plane crashes, and we may mistakenly overestimate the risk associated with air travel (Bahk, 2006). The upshot of this response is that many people fear flying, when they really ought to be more afraid of traveling by car.

The Representativeness Heuristic

We also make heuristic judgments when deciding whether or not an object, event, or person belongs in a particular category by relying on the degree to which the person or thing in question is representative of the category. This tendency, called the **representativeness heuristic**, explains some of the mistakes we make in judgment (A. Tversky & Kahneman, 1974).

For instance, we often ignore the true probability, or *base rate*, of events in favor of our heuristic judgments. In one experiment on the representativeness heuristic, participants were told that a group of 100 people contained 70 engineers and 30 lawyers. They were also given a description of one of the group members—a man—that included the following traits: conservative, ambitious, nonpolitical, likes carpentry, and enjoys solving mathematical puzzles. Then they were asked to judge the probability that he was an engineer or a lawyer. If we were to approach this question logically, we would base our judgment on the base rate and say that there is a 70% chance that the man is an engineer and a 30% chance that he is a lawyer. The

Mario Tama/Getty Images

According to the availability heuristic, the ease with which we can retrieve memories of events from long-term memory biases our judgments of how frequently the event occurs in real life. Seeing news coverage of air disasters like this one leaves us with vivid memories of plane crashes that cause us to overestimate the probability of a plane crash occurring in the future. As a result, air traffic often falls off immediately following a crash, although in general flying is still safer than driving to your destination.

participants, however, did not approach this task logically. Instead, they based their judgments on the representativeness of the description that they were given and ignored the base rate information. As a result, the participants judged that there was a 90% chance that the man was an engineer (Kahneman & Tversky, 1973). Clearly, we often place more confidence in irrational judgments based on heuristics than in rational ones based on more factual probabilities (A. Tversky & Kahneman, 1980).

Heuristics like representativeness can contribute to serious problems such as prejudice. For example, one of the authors once met a man who had little personal contact with African Americans. His exposure to African Americans was mostly limited to watching episodes of the TV show *Cops*, in which he saw many African Americans being arrested for crimes. This limited exposure left the man with the false impression that most African Americans are representative of the category *criminal*. As a result, the man grew uneasy when he encountered any African American—a clear and unfortunate expression of a racial prejudice. Media depictions of people can interact with our tendency to use heuristics like representativeness, making them powerful influences on our judgments of others.

If all this sounds as though humans are incapable of making good judgments, don't despair. This is not the case. Often heuristics do lead to correct judgments. In addition, we do not always behave in a heuristic way. Sometimes we do pay attention to probabilities (Cosmides & Tooby, 1996). Whether we make judgments algorithmically or heuristically is a product of both the situation (Cosmides & Tooby, 1996) and the characteristic way that we as individuals tend to think (Stanovich & West, 1998). When the conditions are right, we do make good and logical judgments. This outcome is especially true when we are making judgments in everyday, real-life situations (J. R. Anderson, 2000). Take a moment to test your knowledge of this section before moving on to learn about language and its relationship to thought.

Let's REVIEW

In this section, we described how people make decisions and judgments and discussed some of the shortcomings of using heuristics. For a quick check of your understanding, try answering the following questions at increasing levels of difficulty.

1. When we make decisions, we base our decisions in part on _____.

   a. the likely outcomes of the decision

   b. the probability of obtaining certain outcomes

   c. our aversion to risk and loss

   d. all of the above

2. The frequency of memorable events is likely to be _____ due to the _____.

   a. underestimated; availability heuristic

   b. overestimated; availability heuristic

   c. underestimated; representativeness heuristic

   d. overestimated; representativeness heuristic

3. Of the 100 people in Harry's psychology class, 60 are education majors and 40 are psychology majors. Yet when Harry first met a classmate named Sally, he guessed that there was a 90% chance that she was a psychology major because she had a poster of Sigmund Freud on her dorm room wall. Harry likely based his judgment on _____.

   a. the base rate   c. representativeness

   b. an algorithm   d. availability

ANSWERS 1. d; 2. b; 3. c

IS LANGUAGE IMPORTANT TO MORE THAN COMMUNICATION?

LEARNING OBJECTIVES

What Should You Know?
- Describe how children acquire language.
- Explain the usefulness of language.
- Describe current research on the issue of nonhuman language.

Our capacity for **language** is one of the most spectacular human abilities. No other species has such a well-developed, syntactical verbal system for representing its world. As you learned in Chapter 2 (see p. 64), *Broca's* and *Wernicke's areas* are specialized structures in the left hemisphere of the human brain that help us produce and comprehend speech. We put these brain areas to good use in that we use words in just about every aspect of our lives. As we have seen, much of our knowledge is represented in memory using words. Without words, our ability to mentally represent our world, solve problems, and make decisions would be drastically altered. Imagine trying to learn psychology without using any language! When you think about it, it is truly remarkable that Ildefonso was able to do as well as he did in the world before he was introduced to language. Luckily, most of us are introduced to language at a much younger age than Ildefonso was.

How Humans Acquire Language

Some researchers and philosophers have proposed that humans are born with an innate tendency to acquire language (R. Cattell, 2006; Chomsky, 1957). According to this view, we are born with a *language acquisition device (LAD)*, or a biological makeup that gives us an innate knowledge of the syntax of a language (Chomsky, 1965). A *poverty of stimulus argument* is often used to support the idea of an LAD. According to this argument, children across the world are not uniformly exposed to enough language and language coaching to account for the speed and uniformity with which they tend to learn language (Behme & Deacon, 2008). Therefore, language acquisition must be partially innate.

Yet, some disagree with this idea of innate language, believing instead that children are natural problem solvers, and language is a means of solving one of their greatest problems—the need to communicate with others (see Helmuth, 2001). Others argue that the *poverty of stimulus argument* underestimates children's true exposure to early language (Behme & Deacon, 2008).

A complicating factor in settling this debate is that it is practically impossible to isolate the effects that *nature* and *nurture* have on language development. **How can we determine if children are born with innate knowledge of language (nature), when nearly all children in the world are immediately exposed to language after birth (nurture)?** When children begin speaking (at about 1 year), it could be due to some innate, biological mechanism, or it could be that they learned to speak from interacting with others who use language. Teasing apart the relative contributions of nature and nurture in language development is complex.

So the debate over the existence of an LAD continues. In the end, whatever science reveals about the nature of language development, our theories will have to account for some interesting uniformities in language development. Regardless of the culture, language seems to develop in children at about the same age and in the same sequence of stages, which are discussed next.

Cooing and Babbling: Baby Steps to Learning One or More Languages

Most of us acquire our first language beginning in the first couple of years of life. Research indicates that newborns from birth to 1 month are capable of categorizing vowel sounds in an adult-like manner (Alderidge, Stillman, & Bower, 2001), and by about 2 months, infants begin **cooing**. Cooing involves making vowel sounds, such as "ooo" and "ah." By 4 months, infants begin to engage in **babbling**, which adds consonant sounds to the vowel sounds they emitted during cooing. For example, an infant might repeat the sound "ka, ka, ka" over and over. Infants' first babbles are very similar across cultures, but this commonality soon changes (Stoel-Gammon & Otomo, 1986). By 7 months, infants begin to emit babbles that contain sounds that are part of the language they have been exposed to in their environment. In this fashion, the infant's language system apparently tunes itself to the language or

language a well-developed, syntactical verbal system for representing the world

cooing the vowel sounds made by infants beginning at 2 months

babbling the combinations of vowel and consonant sounds uttered by infants beginning around 4 months

languages that the infant hears on a regular basis. By 1 year, children's babbling contains the sounds and intonations of their native language (Levitt & Utmann, 1992).

Perhaps because the infant's language system appears to tune itself to the sounds of the language the child hears, the age at which we are exposed to a second language is a powerful predictor of our eventual fluency in that language (Petitto, 2009). Children who grow up in *bilingual* households, where adults speak two languages to the children, tend to acquire both languages at high levels of proficiency. But, this does not mean that a child cannot learn a second language later in life. A child who is not exposed to a second language until elementary school can still develop near-native proficiency in the language (Hakuta, 1999). However, from childhood to adulthood, it seems to become steadily more difficult for us to become bilingual. For example, an adolescent who is just beginning to learn Spanish may never speak Spanish as fluently as a child who began learning Spanish in elementary school (Hakuta, Bailystok, & Wiley, 2003). Therefore, if true bilingualism is desired, it is best to begin learning the second language as early as possible.

But what if the child is not exposed to any language, as was the case with Ildefonso? With no exposure to spoken language (because they are unable to hear), deaf infants fail to emit language-like babbling (Eilers & Oiler, 1994). Therefore, deaf infants do not progress to learn a spoken language the way hearing children do. What about learning written language or sign language? How do deaf children fare here? Unfortunately, many deaf children are developmentally delayed when it comes to learning any form of language because most have hearing parents. If parents do not already know and use sign language, they will not provide the necessary stimulation for their deaf infant to naturally acquire sign language in the same way the infant would have acquired a spoken language. We saw this in Ildefonso's case, in which his parents did not know a sign language and, worse, considered him a "dummy." Even when deaf children are later taught to sign, they may not catch up developmentally and often struggle in school and in social relationships. Interestingly, these developmental delays are not seen in deaf children of deaf parents (Bornstein, Selmi, Haynes, Painter, & Marx, 1999; Strong & Prinz, 2000). It appears that when deaf children are exposed to sign language from infancy, they tend to acquire sign language in a manner that is analogous to language development in hearing children.

Once a child achieves the stage of babbling the basic sounds, or **phonemes**, of her native tongue, the next step in language development is learning to communicate. At around 12 months, children begin trying to communicate with others. This communication is often based on gestures before it is based on words. For example, a child may point at a toy that he wants. When parents learn to interpret these *preverbal gestures*, communication is accomplished. As they catch on to their child's preverbal gestures, parents often verbalize the meaning of the gesture for the child. Parents say things like, "Oh, do you want this toy?" This verbalization of the child's intention allows the child to begin to learn **morphemes**, or the smallest sounds in a language that have meaning. As a result, by the end of the first year or so, children begin to speak their first words.

From "Mama" and "Dada" to Full Conversations

A child's first words are usually the names of familiar objects, people, actions, or situations, ones with which they have had a great deal of contact. Typically, these words are *Dada, Mama, hi, hot,* and the like. During the first 6 months or so of speech, children utter only one word at a time, and often they convey tremendous meaning with these one-word sentences. For example, the utterance "Milk!" may stand for "I want some milk, please!" Interestingly, as Ildefonso began to learn his first language, there were some similarities between his early sign language and the speech of a child who is just learning to speak. Just as in young children, the first words Ildefonso learned tended to be concrete nouns, like *cat* and *table*, and these words would often convey whole sentences of meaning. One example of this was the word *green.* For Ildefonso, who first came to the United States as an undocumented worker, *green* stood for anything that had to do with the U.S. Border Patrol because U.S. Border Patrol uniforms and trucks are green. So Ildefonso attached a great deal of meaning to the word *green* when he finally learned it (Schaller, 1995, pp. 64, 93). Similar overuse of a word is also seen in young children.

phoneme the smallest unit of sound in a language

morpheme the smallest unit of sound that has meaning in a language

Young children may exhibit **overextension** in their language, using one word to symbolize all manner of similar instances. For instance, the word *dog* may be used to symbolize any animal. During this period, the opposite problem may also occur when children exhibit **underextension** of language. In this situation, children inappropriately restrict their use of a word to a particular case, such as when a child uses the word *dog* to refer only to the family pet.

By the time children reach 20–26 months, they begin to combine words into two-word sentences in what is called **telegraphic speech**. Telegraphic speech is often ungrammatical, but it does convey meaning, such as "Doggie bad," meaning "The dog was bad." From here, children rapidly acquire vocabulary and the grammatical rules of the language, such as word order in a sentence and tense. By age 6, the average child has an impressive vocabulary of around 10,000 words and a fairly competent mastery of grammar (Tager-Flusberg, 2005).

As children's vocabularies grow, so does their understanding of **grammar**, or the rules that govern the sentence structure in their language. From the simple subject–verb combinations of telegraphic speech, English-speaking children progress to more complex subject–verb–object sentences between ages 2 and 3. Children who speak other languages adopt the relevant grammatical patterns of their native language. As children develop throughout the preschool years, their knowledge and use of grammar becomes increasingly complex. By age 4 or 5, children can use most of the grammatical structures of their native language (Tager-Flusberg, 2005).

As children develop better vocabularies and acquire the grammatical rules of language, they exercise these abilities during social interactions with others. It's during these social interactions with peers and adults that children begin to learn **pragmatics**, or the rules of conversation operating in their culture. Pragmatics may include rules about turn taking, eye contact, tone of voice, and so on, during conversation.

These hard-earned linguistic abilities will be very valuable to the child, as they are to us all. Let's take a closer look at what, exactly, language does for us.

Andersen Ross/PhotoLibrary

As babies are exposed to their first language, they progress from cooing to babbling to telegraphic speech to full sentences and, finally, to conversations that follow the pragmatics of their specific culture.

The Function of Language in Culture and Perception

It is not difficult to see that language affects us in many ways. Obviously, one of language's main functions is to facilitate communication. We use language to describe our world, our thoughts, and our experiences to others. And, as our world continues to change and evolve so does our language. We develop new words (for example, *Googling*). Other words and phrases drop from common use (for example, *She had the vapors*). Even sentence structure changes with time (for more, see the ● TECHNOLOGY AND BEHAVIOR box, p. 282). Regardless of the form of our language, one of the most important functions of language is to bring us together.

Language and the Development of Culture

Because language brings us together and allows us to share ideas and experiences, language also plays a role in the development of *culture*. Russian psychologist Lev Vygotsky (1896–1934) noted the influence of language in the development of culture in his *sociocultural theory* (Vygotsky, 1934/1987; see also Chapter 9). According to sociocultural theory, older and more knowledgeable members of a society pass on the values, beliefs, and customs of their culture to children by telling the children stories and by engaging in conversations with them. The children store these dialogues in their memory and later use this knowledge to guide their behavior.

Perhaps you can identify how your own elders used language to pass along the elements of your particular culture. Have you ever found yourself saying things that you have heard your parents say before? Do you still celebrate holidays with the traditions your parents and grandparents shared with you as a child? If you have children of your own, do you ever tell them

overextension when a child uses one word to symbolize all manner of similar instances (e.g., calling all birds *parakeet*)

underextension when a child inappropriately restricts the use of a word to a particular case (e.g., using the word *cat* to describe only the family pet)

telegraphic speech two-word sentences that children begin to utter at 20–26 months

grammar the rules that govern sentence structure in a particular language

pragmatics the rules of conversation in a particular culture

TECHNOLOGY and BEHAVIOR

OMG! ARE TEXTING AND TWITTERING RUINING OUR LANGUAGE? :(

One of the most talked about influences on language today is the growing use of SMS (short message services), or texting. If you Twitter, text, or IM, you are part of an expanding segment of the population that is finding creative ways to express themselves in 140–160 characters or less. Texting and the abbreviated language of text messages became popular in many European countries in the late1990s, a couple of years before they became commonplace in the United States (Crystal, 2008). Yet, the United States quickly caught up, and by 2007, Americans sent a whopping 362 billion texts (CTIA, 2010).

As texting and Twittering have become larger parts of our lives, many people have been quick to suggest that the abbreviated language used in these technologies is having a harmful effect on language. Some social commentators and educators have claimed that texting is keeping kids from learning spelling, grammar, and writing skills (e.g., Stephens, 2008). Yet, others argue that fears about the negative influence of texting on language are largely exaggerated and unsupported by scientific data (e.g., Crystal, 2008).

There is scientific evidence to suggest that certain *textisms*, or abbreviations commonly used in SMS (such as CUL8R for *see you later*), are becoming absorbed into everyday English (McWilliam, Schepman, & Rodway, 2009). But, haven't we always used abbreviations in English? After all, even the middle-aged and seniors are likely to know what RSVP, XOXO, and FYI represent.

British linguist David Crystal also points out that despite the apparent prevalence of textisms, they do not make up the bulk of the language used in SMS applications. Rather, most SMS communications are largely composed of conventional words and phrases that are peppered with textisms here and there. Crystal also points out that although trillions of text messages are sent worldwide each year, this number pales in comparison to the number of conventional, grammatically correct communications we are exposed to each year (Crystal, 2008).

Furthermore, the assumption that texting may hinder children's literacy has also been called into question. In Britain, researchers found a positive correlation between children's ability to use textisms and their ability to read words. Preteen children, who used more textisms while writing text messages, were also able to read more words on a vocabulary test relative to children who used fewer textisms in their text messages (Plester, Wood, & Joshi, 2009). Of course, such a correlation does not prove that texting directly improves literacy. Yet, it does suggest that we shouldn't be quick to blame all the educational and literacy problems we see on texting—at least not without scientific data to support this position.

The spirited debate on the relative merits and dangers of textisms in language will likely continue for some time. For right now, a good piece of advice is to always use language that is appropriate to the setting and the audience with whom you are communicating. Textisms are great for Twitter, IM, and texting. Conventional language that uses grammatically correct sentences and proper spelling is more appropriate for academic and professional settings. Turning in a college paper or submitting a résumé replete with textisms may create an unfavorable impression in the reader and is likely to result in a poor grade or a lost job opportunity!

© Stock Connection/SuperStock

Can texting change a culture's language?

stories from your childhood? Most of us can relate to these examples of Vygotsky's ideas on language and culture. Although we can readily see how language facilitates the transmission of culture from generation to generation, how language affects our cognitive processes is the subject of much more debate. **Does the language we speak affect the way we view the world?** In the next section, we'll take a look at this interesting issue.

Linguistic Relativity: Language Directs Our Thoughts

One of the most intriguing theories about language came from an unlikely source. Benjamin Whorf was a Connecticut fire insurance inspector whose unusual hobby was *linguistics*, or the study of language. After intensive studies of the languages of Native Americans, Whorf became convinced that one's language could directly determine or influence one's thoughts (Whorf, 1956). This notion has since come to be called the **Whorfian hypothesis** or the **linguistic relativity hypothesis** (for a review, see Tohidian, 2009).

In its strictest definition, the linguistic relativity hypothesis states that one's language determines one's thoughts and one's perception of the world. According to this view, people who have different native languages think differently and perceive the world in a different light. Whorf claimed that differences among languages make it impossible to express all thoughts equally in all languages. Therefore, you can think and see the world only in terms of the language that you know. Your language determines what you think and how you perceive the world. For example, Whorf claimed that Eskimos have many different words for *snow*, but in English we have only the word *snow*. Because of this vocabulary difference, Whorf argued, Eskimos perceive snow and think about snow in ways that English speakers cannot.

The strict form of Whorf's linguistic relativity hypothesis has not withstood the tests of science. Careful examination of Eskimo languages and English offer little reason to believe that Eskimos and English speakers necessarily perceive and think about snow differently. As it turns out, Eskimos do not have a tremendous number of words for *snow* (L. Martin, 1986; Pullman, 1989), and English speakers have multiple words to describe snow (for example, *powder, slush, sleet*; see ● TABLE 7.2). Furthermore, researchers have found that despite significant differences in language, cognitive processing of information is often very similar across cultures.

In one study, English speakers were compared to members of the Dani culture, a nonindustrialized culture from New Guinea. The Dani have only two words to describe different colors—*mili* for cool, dark colors and *mola* for bright, warm colors—whereas English speakers have many color names. Despite this difference, the Dani performed similarly to English speakers when they were asked to memorize a list of made-up names for different colors. Both the Dani and the English speakers found it easier to remember the made-up names that were associated with basic colors, such as red and blue, than those associated with unusual colors, such as saffron and magenta (Rosch, 1973b). This result is not what the linguistic relativity hypothesis would predict. If the strong form of the linguistic relativity hypothesis were true, the Dani should have performed differently than the English speakers on this memory task because their limited vocabulary for colors would have affected the way they perceived and thought about the colors in the experiment.

The Modern View: Language Influences Our Thoughts

Although the strict version of the linguistic relativity hypothesis has not been supported, there is reason to think that a modified, or less rigid, interpretation of the Whorfian hypothesis may hold true. The less rigid version states that instead of language *determining* thought processes, language merely *influences* them. For example, when Spanish speakers were compared to Mayan speakers, differences were seen in their ability to remember colors. Furthermore, these memory differences were related to how easy it is to verbally label colors in Spanish and Mayan (Stefflre, Castillo-Vales, & Morley, 1966). It appears that how easily you can label a color in your language does affect your memory for that color.

It is also likely that language can influence our perception of the world. In one study involving the sorting of color samples, participants who spoke Setswana were more likely to

TABLE 7.2

● **Different Words for Snow**
Contrary to Whorf's hypothesis, like the Eskimo, English speakers do have several words for snow.

ESKIMO	ENGLISH
qanuk: "snowflake"	snowflake
qanir: "to snow"	snow
kanevvluk: "fine snow/rain particles"	snowfall
muruaneq: "soft deep snow"	powder
pirta: "blizzard, snowstorm"	blizzard, snowstorm
nutaryuk: "fresh snow"	powder
qengaruk: "snow bank"	snowbank

Whorfian hypothesis/linguistic relativity hypothesis the theory that one's language can directly determine or influence one's thoughts

group blues and greens together than were those who spoke English or Russian. This finding was attributed to the fact that in Setswana, one word describes both blue and green colors (I. R. L. Davies, 1998).

Furthermore, researchers have shown that adults can be trained to categorize colors in novel ways; for example, people can learn to categorize many very similar hues of blue into novel categories based on a set of rules defined by the experimenter (Özgen & Davies, 2002). Because training can modify how we perceive and categorize color, these data indicate that there is no universal means of categorizing color information in human memory. The boundaries of our categories for color are not entirely based on the physical properties of light. The idea that all humans do not necessarily categorize color the same way is an important premise of the linguistic relativity hypothesis.

Language may also make certain thoughts more difficult than others. For example, in the Kiriwina language of Papua New Guinea, the word *mokita* means "the truth that everybody knows but nobody speaks." Although English speakers can understand the idea represented in this phrase, it is not likely that we would use this idea in everyday thought or conversation due to its awkwardness. For speakers of Kiriwina, thinking about *mokita* is not awkward (E. Hunt & Agnoli, 1991), because this commonly used and succinct word is part of their vocabulary.

Language in Other Species: Are We the Only Speakers?

Are humans the only animals to use language? For centuries, humans believed that they alone had the ability to use language. It was assumed that only the advanced human mind was capable of dealing with the complexities of a language. Remarkably, this assumption has been called into question. Although it is very controversial, today some researchers believe that some other animals may possess linguistic abilities (e.g., Hillix & Rumbaugh, 2004; Savage-Rumbaugh, Rumbaugh, & Fields, 2006).

In looking at the linguistic abilities of other species, we first have to make a distinction between *language* and *communication*. Language is a system of communication that has a set vocabulary and a set structure, or grammar. For instance, English sentences generally follow a subject–verb–object pattern:

Billy [subject] threw [verb] the ball [object].

Although many languages reverse the order of the verb and the object, most of the world's languages place the subject at the beginning of the sentence (Ultan, 1969).

Languages also differ with respect to the placement of adjectives and adverbs. In Spanish and French, adjectives usually follow the noun they modify, but in English adjectives precede the noun. The Spanish phrase *caballo blanco* translates to "horse white" in English. As you can see, each language has its own set of rules. In contrast to the structure and order of language, communication can be very unstructured. All that is required in a communication system is that your meaning be conveyed to others. By this definition, Ildefonso could communicate via pantomime before he even knew that language existed.

There is little argument that animals can communicate. For example, a rooster will emit an alarm cry to warn other chickens of danger (Marler, Duffy, & Pickert, 1986). Young chimpanzees use physical gestures to communicate with other chimpanzees (Tomasello, Call, Nagell, Olguin, & Carpenter, 1994). King penguins use vocalizations to find their mates when they are in a large group or colony (Lengagne, Jouventin, & Aubin, 1999). And domestic dogs respond to specific play signals of their owners (Rooney, Bradshaw, & Robinson, 2001). It appears that many species have evolved specific means of communicating with other species members, but does this ability of some animals to communicate equate with the capacity for language?

Bonobos: Matata and Kanzi

Some of the best evidence for animal language comes from studies done on Bonobo chimpanzees. Bonobos, also known as pygmy chimpanzees, are perhaps our closest genetic relatives, even more closely related to us than the common chimpanzee. During the 1980s, researcher Sue Savage-Rumbaugh and others attempted to teach English to a Bonobo named Matata. Because Bonobos do not have vocal cords that produce humanlike speech, they cannot actually speak. To get around this problem, the researchers used a special computer keyboard during the language training. On the surface of the keyboard were pictures, and when a picture was pressed, a computer-generated voice spoke the name of the object in the picture. Using this keyboard, Savage-Rumbaugh tried to teach Matata the meaning of certain words, but Matata did not catch on well. After 2 years of training and more than 30,000 research trials, Matata learned to use only six of the pictures on the keyboard (S. M. Wise, 2000, p. 223).

Although the experiments with Matata failed to show that Bonobos could learn English, there was a remarkable and unexpected outcome of the research. While Matata was being trained to use the keyboard, her infant stepson, Kanzi, was observing what was going on. Although Savage-Rumbaugh and her colleagues never attempted to teach Kanzi to use the keyboard, he picked up this skill on his own (Savage-Rumbaugh, McDonald, Sevcik, Hopkins, & Rupert, 1986). By age 2-1/2, Kanzi had begun to use some of the symbols his mother was trying to learn on the keyboard. When experimenters gave up trying to teach Matata to use the keyboard, they separated her from Kanzi. The day Matata left, Kanzi approached the keyboard and began to use it to make requests and express himself. In fact, he used it a total of 120 times on that first day (S. M. Wise, 2000).

Much like a young child, Kanzi appeared to have learned some vocabulary just by observing language being used around him. Kanzi's acquisition of language seemed to occur quite naturally (Shanker, Savage-Rumbaugh, & Taylor, 1999). For example, a patch of wild strawberries grew outside Kanzi's laboratory, and when he discovered them, Kanzi began to eat them. He overheard researchers referring to them by the word *strawberries* and soon appeared to understand what the word *strawberries* meant. After apparently learning the meaning of the word *strawberries*, Kanzi would head for the berry patch whenever he heard someone speak the word (Savage-Rumbaugh, 1987).

Overall, Kanzi's use of language is quite impressive. He uses the keyboard to make requests, such as to visit another chimpanzee named Austin. If he is told that he cannot visit because it's too cold to go outside, Kanzi modifies his request to ask to see a picture of Austin on TV (Savage-Rumbaugh, 1987). Furthermore, Kanzi seems to be able to respond to very unusual and novel requests, such as "Put the pine needles in the refrigerator" or "Put the soap on the ball."

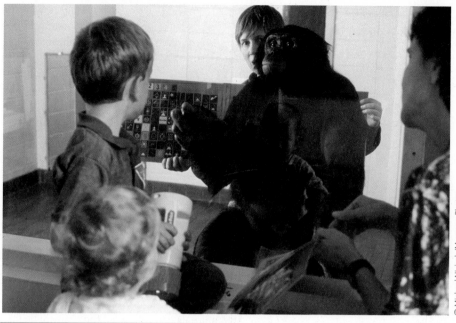

As an infant, Kanzi learned to use a language keyboard like this one to communicate with humans just by watching researchers who were working with his mother, Matata.

© Michael Nichols/Magnum Photos

Talking Parrots and Dolphins

Language abilities have been shown in species other than the Bonobos as well. Researcher Irene Pepperberg (1993, 1999) has had some success in training an African gray parrot named Alex to speak some English. Unlike the Bonobo, a parrot has the physical ability to produce speech as well as comprehend it. After years of training, Alex was able to speak some words in English, and he could identify the shape, color, and material of many objects (Pepperberg, 1991).

Dolphins have also shown some linguistic promise. Researcher Louis Herman and his colleagues have had some success in training dolphins to understand a language that the researchers created. This created language is based on gestures, but it has a set vocabulary in which certain gestures stand for certain words, and a specific set of grammatical rules

Although controversial, studies of animals like Alex challenge the presumption that language is a solely human attribute.

© Rick Friedman/Corbis

that dictate how gestures can be combined into phrases. One of the dolphins, named Phoenix, was shown to follow a complex sequence of instructions delivered in this gestured language (Herman & Uyeyama, 1999). Furthermore, another dolphin, Ake, seemed to notice when the grammatical laws of the language had been violated (Herman, Kuczaj, & Holder, 1993).

Can Other Animals Really Use Language?

As impressive as the linguistic abilities of Kanzi, Alex, Ake, and Phoenix are, not everyone is convinced that animals truly have the capacity for language. Some argue that these animals are merely highly trained (Pinker, 1994). Skeptics propose that rather than actually using language, the animals are engaging in trained behaviors that they hope will lead to some reward. Certainly, Alex, Ake, and Phoenix were trained to use language, but what about Kanzi, who was never trained to use language? He learned it on his own during his early years, just as children learn language (Shanker et al., 1999).

Another criticism of animal language research directly questions the linguistic abilities of animals. Some argue that animal language researchers have not adequately demonstrated that animals can follow all the grammatical and syntactical rules of human language (Kako, 1999). Animal language researchers counter that their critics have unfairly focused on the linguistic abilities that animals lack and have largely ignored the linguistic abilities that animals *do* have (Shanker et al., 1999).

You can see that this is a very passionate debate—as well it should be, for there is a great deal at stake here. If we ultimately determine that animals do have linguistic capacities, then we may have to reconsider what separates humans from the rest of the animal kingdom. This possibility brings up a whole host of questions concerning animals and the manner in which we treat them in human society (Wise, 2000). For example, if some animals have linguistic capacities, what does that say about their intelligence in comparison to ours? And do we have the ethical right to perform experiments on animals that are so similar to ourselves? These are questions that we may have to tackle in the near future. For the moment, the jury is still out on the issue of language in animals.

Let's REVIEW

In this section, we covered many aspects of language, including how we acquire language, what it does for us, and the debate over language as a purely human attribute. For a quick check of your understanding, try answering the following questions at increasing levels of difficulty.

1. Babies begin _____ when they begin to make _____ sounds.

   a. cooing; consonant
   b. babbling; vowel
   c. cooing; vowel and consonant
   d. babbling; vowel and consonant

2. Which of the following people would be the *most* likely to agree with the statement "Language facilitates the development of culture"?

   a. Lev Vygotsky
   b. Benjamin Whorf
   c. Sue Savage-Rumbaugh
   d. Stephen Kosslyn

3. Emmanuel grew up in Haiti, where he learned to speak Haitian Creole. Speaking Haitian Creole is least likely to influence Emmanuel's _____.

   a. speech
   b. memory
   c. perception
   d. sensation

ANSWERS 1. d; 2. a; 3. d

WHAT IS INTELLIGENCE AND HOW DO WE MEASURE IT?

What makes a person intelligent? Is it earning good grades? Knowing how to survive in the wilderness? Knowing how to make large amounts of money in the stock market? Having social skills? What do you think? How do *you* define intelligence? Today, many psychologists view **intelligence** broadly as having abilities that allow you to adapt to your environment and behave in a goal-directed way. But over the years, psychologists have found that precise definition of intelligence is not as easy as it may seem, and our conception of intelligence has undergone several revisions in the history of psychology. Equally challenging has been finding ways of measuring intelligence.

Measuring Intelligence by Abilities and IQs

One of the first people to study the measurement of intelligence was British psychologist Sir Francis Galton (1822–1911). Galton, who was a cousin to Charles Darwin, claimed that intelligence is an inherited trait that is correlated with having superior physical abilities. As such, he believed that intelligence could be measured by measuring traits like reaction time, eyesight, and so on. However, early studies failed to find much support for Galton's ideas (Schultz & Schultz, 2000), and they soon fell out of favor. Researchers, such as Alfred Binet and Lewis Terman, soon began to focus on the more cognitive aspects of intelligence and on developing tests to measure and quantify mental abilities.

Alfred Binet: Measuring Intelligence by Measuring Cognitive Abilities

Although Francis Galton was influential in starting psychologists thinking about ways to measure intelligence, the modern intelligence test is credited to Alfred Binet (1857–1911). In 1904, the French government appointed Alfred Binet and psychiatrist Théodore Simon to a commission charged with developing a means of measuring the intelligence of French schoolchildren. The ultimate goal of this project was to give the government a process for identifying children who were mentally deficient so that these children could be placed in special education programs.

Binet saw intelligence as our capacity to *find and maintain a purpose, adapt our strategy to reach that purpose,* and *evaluate the strategy so it can be adjusted as necessary* (Terman, 1916). In essence, Binet suggested that having intelligence makes one a good problem solver. As such, Binet aimed to develop an intelligence test that focused on the assessment of general cognitive abilities—specifically, the individual's attention, judgment, and reasoning (Binet & Simon, 1905).

Binet prepared a set of 30 tasks that measured these skills and arranged them in order of difficulty. He placed the easiest questions first and the hardest questions last, and then he administered the test to the schoolchildren. Not surprisingly, the brighter students could answer more of the questions than the not-so-bright students could. Also, not surprisingly, the older children tended to answer more questions correctly than the younger children. In fact, Binet noticed that the brighter younger children could sometimes answer correctly as many questions as the average child of an older age. For example, a very smart 6-year-old might be able to answer as many questions as the average 10-year-old child could. So Binet began to quantify children's intelligence in terms of **mental age**, or the age that reflects a child's mental abilities in comparison to the "average" child. In Binet's scheme, a mental age that exceeds one's chronological age indicates above-average intelligence, and a mental age that is below a child's actual age indicates a below-average level of intelligence. Binet's concept of mental age became the foundation for the very familiar IQ score, and his test became the basis for modern intelligence tests.

Lewis Terman: The Intelligence Quotient and the Stanford-Binet

In 1916, Stanford psychologist Lewis Terman completed an American revision of the intelligence test that Binet and Simon had developed. Terman translated the test into English and

intelligence abilities that enable you to adapt to your environment and behave in a goal-directed way

mental age the age that reflects the child's mental abilities in comparison to the average child of the same age

refined and added some test items. He named his version of the test the Stanford Revision of the Binet-Simon Scale, which became known as the Stanford-Binet. Perhaps his most significant contribution to the test was to introduce an **intelligence quotient**, or **IQ score**, as the measure of an individual's intelligence. An IQ score is calculated as follows:

$$IQ = (MA/CA) \times 100$$

where

$$MA = \text{mental age}$$

and

$$CA = \text{chronological, or actual, age}$$

Using the concept of an IQ, a person of average abilities has, by definition, an IQ of 100 or, in other words, a mental age equal to her or his actual age. IQs over 100 indicate above-average intelligence, and IQs below 100 indicate below-average intelligence.

The Stanford-Binet has undergone four major revisions since 1916 and is still in wide use. The most recent edition, the Stanford-Binet Intelligence Scales, 5th edition (SB5), was released in 2003. However, a modern IQ test developed by psychologist David Wechsler (1896–1981) and first released in 1939 has greatly challenged the popularity of the Stanford-Binet.

David Wechsler's Intelligence Scales

Wechsler (1939) developed an intelligence test in response to shortcomings he saw in the Stanford-Binet. Wechsler objected to the fact that the Stanford-Binet test tried to sum up intelligence in a single score. He believed that one number could not adequately express something as complex as intelligence. Furthermore, Wechsler objected to the use of the mental age concept for adults (R. M. Kaplan & Saccuzzo, 1989). After all, would you necessarily expect a 40-year-old to correctly answer more questions than a 35-year-old? The concept of mental age doesn't apply as well to adults as it does to children because adults do not change as much from year to year as children do. Therefore, mental age has little significance in adulthood.

To correct these problems, Wechsler developed an intelligence test that yields scores on individual *subscales* that measure different mental abilities. Furthermore, instead of using mental age to determine IQ, Wechsler's tests compare a participant's performance to the average person's performance to determine IQ. The Wechsler tests are devised so that an average person's performance on the test results in an IQ of 100. Using this number as a benchmark, people who score above average on the test are given IQ scores above 100, and people who perform below average are given IQ scores below 100. Most people can expect to score near this average IQ, somewhere in the range of 85–115 (● FIGURE 7.8).

Today there are three separate Wechsler intelligence tests. The Wechsler Pre-school and Primary Scale of Intelligence (WPPSI-III) is administered to children ages 2-1/2–7. The Wechsler Intelligence Scale for Children, 4th edition (WISC-IV) is used for children ages 6–16. And the Wechsler Adult Intelligence Scale, 4th edition (WAIS-IV) is used for people ages 16–90.

The WAIS-IV consists of 11 subtests that measure various verbal and performance abilities (see ● THE BIG PICTURE REVIEW, p. 289). Performance on these subtests is used to calculate an overall IQ score as well as separate index scores for *verbal comprehension*, *perceptual reasoning*, *working memory*, and *processing speed*. The design of the WAIS-IV makes it flexible. Testers can administer any of the indexes alone (for example, only measure perceptual reasoning) or all of them together to obtain the overall IQ score.

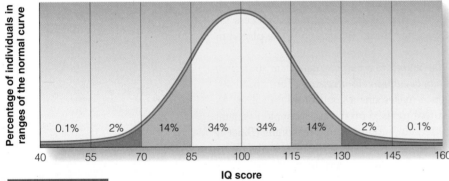

FIGURE 7.8

● **The Normal Distribution of IQ Scores** IQs tend to be normally distributed across the population. This means that when a frequency distribution of IQ scores is plotted, it forms a bell-shaped curve, with most people scoring an average of 100 on the IQ test and very few scoring extremely high or low.

intelligence quotient (IQ score)
one's mental age divided by one's chronological age times 100

 *review*

The Wechsler Adult Intelligence Scale (WAIS-IV) and Its Subscales

NOTE: The test items shown are examples—they do not appear in the actual test.

CONTENT AREA	EXPLANATION OF TASKS/QUESTIONS	EXAMPLES OF A POSSIBLE TASK/QUESTION
Verbal Comprehension		
Vocabulary	Define the meaning of the word.	What does **persistent** mean? What does **archaeology** mean?
Information	Supply generally known information.	Who is Hillary Clinton? What are six New England states?
Similarities	Explain how two things or concepts are similar.	In what ways are an ostrich and a penguin alike? In what ways are a lamp and a heater alike?
Perceptual Reasoning		
Block design	Use patterned blocks to form a design that looks identical to a design shown by the examiner.	Assemble the blocks on the left to make the design on the right.
Matrix reasoning	Fill in the missing cell in a matrix with a picture that would logically complete the matrix.	Which of these figures would complete the logical sequence in this matrix?
Visual puzzles	Construct a figure from a series of puzzle pieces.	Which of these pieces go together to make this puzzle?
Working Memory		
Digit span	Listen to a series of digits (numbers), then repeat the numbers either forward, backward, or both.	Repeat these numbers backward: "9, 1, 8, 3, 6."
Arithmetic	Mental manipulation of arithmetical concepts.	How many 52-cent candy bars can you buy with a five-dollar bill?
Processing Speed		
Symbol search	When given an array of symbols, find the specified symbol and circle it.	Circle the ♣ in the following array: ♣ ψ Δ λ ♦ ⊗ ℑ ♣ θ / ♣ θ Δ λ ♥ ⊕ Σ ℑ • / Δ ♣ λ ♦ ♥ ℑ ≅ ψ ♦
Digit symbol	When given a key matching particular symbols to particular numerals, copy a sequence of symbols, transcribing from symbols to numerals, using the key.	Look carefully at the key. In the blanks, write the correct numeral for the symbol below each symbol. ○ □ ⊗ ◇ ⊖ = 1 2 3 4 5

Chip Somodevilla/Getty Images

This award winner may owe her success, in part, to high levels of intelligence. An average IQ is 100. If a person scores at a higher than average level of performance for her age, her IQ score will be above 100.

reliability the degree to which a test yields consistent measurements of a trait

validity the degree to which a test measures the trait that it was designed to measure

cultural bias the degree to which a test puts people from other cultures at an unfair disadvantage because of the culturally specific nature of the test items

Testing the Test: What Makes a Good Intelligence Test?

So far, we have looked at two widely accepted tests that psychologists and educators use to measure intelligence. These are but two of a great many tests that have been devised to measure intelligence and other psychological traits. When choosing which test to administer or when interpreting the scores yielded by these tests, we have to ask, "Is this a good test?" If psychologists never worried about the quality of their measurements, they could well find themselves making many faulty judgments about the people they measure. Think about it—how would you feel if someone gave you an IQ test and then told you that your score would determine whether or not you got a job? Wouldn't you want some assurance that the test actually reflected your true intellectual ability? Most of us would. So how do psychologists ensure that their tests are good measures of people's abilities?

Before a test is used to make decisions about anyone's life, the test itself must be tested and evaluated (in Chapter 13, we will see that this requirement is also true of personality tests). Psychologists must be assured that the test is both *reliable* and *valid* before it can be put into widespread use. The **reliability** of a test refers to the degree to which the test yields consistent measurements over time. Although intelligence can change over time, it usually does so very slowly. In general, if you are intelligent today, you will be intelligent 6 months from now. So, if we use a test to measure your IQ today and then again in 6 months, the scores should be comparable. This doesn't mean that the test has to yield *exactly* the same score, but the scores should be close.

The simplest way to assess the reliability of a test is to look at the *test–retest reliability* of the test in an experimental setting. To do this, the test is administered to a large group of people, and their scores are computed. Then later, after 6 months or a year, the test is readministered to the same people, and their new scores are computed. If the test is reliable, the two sets of scores should correlate. If they do not correlate, the test should not be used because measuring IQ with an unreliable test is a lot like trying to measure distance with an elastic ruler. The scores will keep changing, and you will not be able to determine which, if any, of the scores are correct.

Establishing the reliability of an intelligence test is very important, but the **validity** of the test is an equally important characteristic. Validity is the degree to which the test measures what it was designed to measure. In the case of an intelligence test, one must show that the test actually measures intelligence.

Psychologists often assess the validity of their tests by assessing *predictive validity*. To establish predictive validity, we must show that scores on the test reliably predict future behavior. For example, if we expect that intelligence is related to doing well in school, then scores on a *valid* IQ test should predict who does well in school—and who does not. To assess for our test's validity, we would test a large number of students and then correlate their IQ scores with their high school GPA. If our test is valid, IQ and GPA should correlate. If they do not, the IQ test is not a valid predictor of academic success, and it should not be used as such.

You might be thinking that validity seems like a trivial issue. After all, if you create an IQ test that asks people questions that seem to require intelligence to answer, won't the test tell you who is smart and who is not? As it turns out, it is quite easy to devise tests that are invalid. For example, questions that require specific cultural knowledge may not assess the intelligence of people unfamiliar with that culture—even though they may be very intelligent (c.f., Helms, 2006). This validity problem is referred to as **cultural bias**. Some people have argued that intelligence tests are often biased and invalid for cultural minority members (C. R. Reynolds & Brown, 1984).

TRY THIS DEMONSTRATION

To illustrate this point, try to answer the following sample IQ test question.

Choose the term that best completes this analogy:

Chayote is to soup as scissors are to _____.

     a. a drawer   b. paper   c. tools   d. cutting

Was the answer immediately apparent to you? If you are from a culture that is not familiar with the word *chayote*, which is a type of squash eaten in some Latin American cultures, you might not realize that you put scissors *into* a drawer the way you put chayote *into* soup. Does this mean you are unintelligent? Of course not—but an incorrect answer would count against you if it were on an IQ test. Some people contend that IQ tests can't help reflecting the cultural values, language, and knowledge of the people who develop them, and there-fore all IQ tests carry some form of cultural bias (Greenfield, 1997). We should always keep in mind that IQ tests do not measure all human abilities, and our cultural environment can affect our performance on these tests (Sternberg, 1997b).

The Nature of Intelligence: The Search Continues

Back in the early 1900s, when psychologists were busily trying to measure intelligence, psychological historian E. G. Boring noted that "intelligence is what the tests test" (quoted in Gardner, 1999, p. 13). By this, Boring meant that psychologists had placed a great deal of emphasis on developing tests to measure intelligence, but they had not spent adequate time exploring what intelligence actually is.

Intelligence as a Single Factor

A century ago, British statistician Charles Spearman argued that because test scores of separate mental abilities (e.g., verbal skills, mathematical ability, deductive reasoning skills) tend to correlate, there must be one general level of intelligence that underlies these separate mental abilities (Spearman, 1904). Spearman referred to this **generalized intelligence** as *g*. In Spearman's view, one's level of *g* would determine how well he or she functioned on any number of cognitive tasks. This idea of intelligence as a single, unitary factor helped lead to the rapid expansion of intelligence testing in schools, the workplace, and the military. But Spearman's notion that intelligence is a single factor would soon be challenged.

Intelligence as a Collection of Abilities

Is intelligence really a single factor? Can't a person be smart in some areas, but not in others? By the 1930s, some theorists were beginning to challenge the idea of a single intelligence. The notion of *g* fell from favor as psychologists proposed theories that described intelligence as a set of abilities rather than a single trait. One of the earliest of these theories came from psychologist L. L. Thurstone (1938), who argued that intelligence was made up of seven distinct mental abilities. These were reasoning, associative memory, spatial visualization, numerical fluency, verbal comprehension, perceptual speed, and word fluency. Others would eventually propose as many as 120 different factors underlying intelligence (Guilford, 1967).

However, not everyone was convinced that intelligence was made up of many different factors. In the 1960s, Raymond Cattell (1963) revived the idea of *g* when he argued that Thurstone had been wrong in his interpretation of his data. Raymond Cattell proposed that *g* does exist, but in two different forms, which he called *crystallized intelligence* and *fluid intelligence*. **Crystallized intelligence** refers to our accumulation of knowledge. For example, your knowledge of psychology is part of your crystallized intelligence. **Fluid intelligence**

generalized intelligence (*g*) Charles Spearman's notion that there is a general level of intelligence that underlies our separate abilities

crystallized intelligence abilities that rely on knowledge, expertise, and judgment

fluid intelligence abilities that rely on information-processing skills such as reaction time, attention, and working memory

refers to the speed and efficiency with which we learn new information and solve problems. For instance, the higher your fluid intelligence, the more quickly you will learn the material in this chapter. As a result, both fluid and crystallized intelligence are related to educational attainment across the lifespan (Kaufman, Kaufman, Liu, & Johnson, 2009).

There is both good and bad news when it comes to our levels of fluid and crystallized intelligence over a lifetime. The evidence shows that crystallized intelligence can continue to grow well into late adulthood (Horn, Donaldson, & Engstrom, 1981), but fluid intelligence tends to decrease across adulthood (Schaie, 1994). The degree to which we retain these abilities throughout life is affected by our environment and our physical well-being, although environment is much more important in the case of crystallized intelligence (Horn, 1982). We'll discuss this finding in more detail when we describe cognitive changes in adolescence and adulthood in Chapter 9.

As you can see, there has been much disagreement as to exactly what intelligence is, and this debate is likely to continue for some time. Today, many psychologists still favor the idea of a generalized intelligence, especially those psychologists who focus on its measurement (Gardner, 1999, p. 14). However, other psychologists have gone on to develop newer theories that conceptualize intelligence as a multifaceted set of abilities, or *intelligences*. Next, we will take a look at two of the most popular and influential of these modern theories.

A New Spin: Howard Gardner's Multiple Intelligences

In the early 1980s, Harvard psychologist Howard Gardner proposed a theory of intelligence that views humans as possessing many different intelligences (Gardner, 1983). According to Gardner, an intelligence is "a biopsychological potential to process information that can be activated in a cultural setting to solve problems or create products that are of value in a culture" (Gardner, 1999, pp. 33–34). This definition emphasizes the fact that intelligence allows us to function efficiently in our own environment, and it also highlights the fact that different cultures and environments place different demands on our intelligence.

For example, in the United States today, we might consider the ability to understand and predict fluctuations in the stock market as a sign of intelligence. In an unindustrialized, nomadic culture, however, the ability to seek out a source of water may be a more highly valued intelligence. After carefully considering the different human abilities that allow us to function in our environment, Gardner developed a strict set of criteria for identifying an intelligence (Gardner, 1999). Using these criteria, Gardner has identified nine different intelligences and allowed for the possibility that more may someday be identified (Gardner, 2004). Gardner's theory of **multiple intelligences** is summarized in ● TABLE 7.3.

As you look at Table 7.3, can you see that you have more of some types of intelligence and less of others? Most of us do not possess equal levels of all types of intelligence. Rather, we each have our own strengths and weaknesses. Therefore, Gardner doesn't have much use for tests that seek to measure one's generalized intelligence. For Gardner, it is far more important to look at a person's intelligence *profile*—his or her level of ability across the different types of intelligence.

Robert Sternberg's Triarchic Theory of Intelligence

Psychologist Robert Sternberg has taken an approach somewhat similar to Howard Gardner's. Like Gardner, Sternberg rejects the usefulness of trying to measure a single, generalized intelligence. However, Sternberg doesn't subscribe to the idea that we possess many separate intelligences. Sternberg considers some of Gardner's intelligences as *talents* that some people possess. For example, it's hard to see why musical intelligence would be important in many cultures. Even if you have little or no musical ability, you could still function very well in many cultures, including American society. However, in the United States and many other cultures, the ability to think logically would be very important to your survival and well-being.

Sternberg suggests that *successful intelligence*, or intelligence that helps us function in our world, is composed of three types of cognitive abilities. Accordingly, Sternberg calls his theory the **triarchic theory of intelligence** (Sternberg, 1985, 1997a). According to the triarchic theory, intelligence is composed of analytical, practical, and creative abilities that help us adapt successfully to our environment.

multiple intelligences the idea that we possess different types of intelligence rather than a single, overall level of intelligence

triarchic theory of intelligence a theory that proposes that intelligence is composed of analytical, practical, and creative abilities that help us adapt to our environment

TABLE 7.3

● **Gardner's Multiple Intelligences**

INTELLIGENCE	DESCRIPTION	EXAMPLES
Linguistic	The ability to learn and use languages	An author has a good command of language and can express ideas well in written form.
Spatial	The ability to recognize and manipulate patterns of space	A surveyor is very good at judging distances. A seamstress designs a pattern for a jacket.
Logical-mathematical	The ability to attack problems in a logical manner, solve mathematical problems, and in general exhibit scientific thought	A psychologist can develop and test theories in a scientific manner. A physician examines a patient and makes a diagnosis.
Musical	The ability to perform, compose, and appreciate music	A songwriter can create unique melodies and perform them.
Bodily-kinesthetic	The ability to use one's body to solve problems and create products	A gymnast can perform intricate maneuvers on the balance beam.
Interpersonal	The ability to understand the intentions, motivations, and desires of others	A manager is good at working with others and can inspire others to perform at their optimal level.
Intrapersonal	The ability to understand oneself	A student knows what she wants in terms of her career and future life, and she uses this information to choose an appropriate major.
Naturalistic	Paying attention to nature and understanding environmental issues	A homemaker recycles her trash and avoids using household cleaners that are harmful to the environment.
Existential	Being concerned with "ultimate" issues; seeking higher truths	A philosophy student ponders the meaning of life.

From Intelligence Reframed: Multiple Intelligences for the 21st Century *by Howard Gardner (New York: Basic Books/Perseus, 1999). Reprinted by permission of BASIC BOOKS, a member of Perseus Books Group.*

Analytical intelligence is seen in our ability to use logic to reason our way through problems. Going back to our earlier example, if your car breaks down on exam day, you would use your analytical powers to generate possible solutions to this dilemma. Analytical intelligence is also important as we implement and evaluate problem-solving strategies. For example, analytical intelligence allows us to evaluate whether or not a particular problem-solving strategy is working well.

Practical intelligence is our ability to adapt to our environment. This is the type of intelligence that we see in people who have a great deal of common sense. People who are high in practical intelligence exhibit savvy. They know how to function efficiently within their environment. For example, a Central American farmer may be able to predict the weather by noticing changes in the environment. Or someone who lives in New York City may be very good at finding the quickest way across town during rush hour. Both of these people, although they possess very different skills, exhibit practical intelligence.

Keep in mind that behaviors and skills may be intelligent in some environments, but not in others. The skills that Ildefonso used to survive in his world may be very different from the skills you use. Nonetheless, he exhibited practical intelligence in the way in which he survived without language in a language-rich world.

Creative intelligence is our ability to use our knowledge of the world in novel situations. For example, suppose you found yourself in a foreign culture where you did not know the language or the customs. Would you be able to function? People who are high in creative intelligence can adapt what they know about the world to meet the unique demands of new situations. For instance, you might use the pantomime skills you learned while playing charades to help you communicate with those whose language you do not speak or understand. Creative intelligence is also seen when people break out of *mental sets* to solve problems in unique ways. For example, in the earlier story of the author using her cell phone to locate her purse, we saw an example of creative intelligence.

Daniel Goleman's Theory of Emotional Intelligence

Yet another way of conceptualizing intelligence comes from psychologist Daniel Goleman. In his best-selling book *Emotional Intelligence*, Goleman (1995) argues that a concept of intelligence that is based solely on cognitive abilities is too limiting. He notes that even people with relatively high IQs can fail to succeed in life and sometimes do things that appear to be downright unintelligent. For example, a gifted student with a perfect score on the SAT may turn out to be a poor college student who takes 10 years to earn a degree (Goleman, 1995). According to Goleman, the reason for this discrepancy is that many times our actions are guided not by our intellectual abilities, but by our emotions. Goleman contends that just as some of us are intellectually gifted, some of us are endowed with emotional prowess—an ability he calls *emotional intelligence*.

In Goleman's view, emotional intelligence includes awareness of your own emotional states, accurate assessment of your own abilities, self-confidence, self-control, trustworthiness, conscientiousness, the ability to adapt to changes, innovation or creativity, achievement motivation, commitment to completing goals, initiative or self-motivation, and a sense of optimism (Goleman, 1998; Petrides, Furnham, & Martin, 2004). In other words, an emotionally intelligent person is a confident self-starter who is ethical and adaptable—the kind of person who sets a goal and works toward it without letting minor obstacles derail his or her progress. With this sort of determination, confidence, and ability to adapt, a person with only an average IQ might be able to go far. Likewise, a bright person with low emotional intelligence might become overwhelmed with self-doubt or lack of motivation and, as a result, fail to perform well in life.

Today, the concept of emotional intelligence is sparking interest among researchers and in the workplace (Yunker & Yunker, 2002). For instance, Goleman and his colleagues have suggested that one way to increase effective leadership in the corporate world is to teach personnel to achieve higher levels of emotional intelligence (Goleman, Boyatzis, & McKee, 2002).

With an eye toward such practical applications, researchers John Mayer, Peter Salovey, and David Caruso have developed a test of emotional intelligence, the *Mayer-Salovey-Caruso Emotional Intelligence Test*, or *MSCEIT*. The MSCEIT measures four different aspects of emotional intelligence: perceiving emotions accurately, using emotions to facilitate thought, understanding emotions, and managing emotions in oneself and others (J. D. Mayer, Salovey, Caruso, & Sitarenios, 2003). In one study, MSCEIT scores were found to be positively correlated with measures of social competence in relationships with friends—but only for men. Men who scored low in emotional intelligence were found to engage in more behaviors that were harmful to their friendships than men who scored high in emotional intelligence. No such correlation was found for women (Brackett, Rivers, Shiffman, Lerner, & Salovey, 2006). At this time, the meaning of this finding is unclear, and there are doubts about the validity of the MSCEIT as a measure of emotional intelligence (R. D. Roberts et al., 2006). Researchers still have much work to do before we fully understand the nature of emotional intelligence and its importance to the everyday lives of men and women.

So, What Is Intelligence After All?

As you can see from our discussions, there has always been a great deal of controversy over the nature of intelligence. Over the years, people have argued for viewing intelligence as a single factor (Spearman, 1904), as a combination of mental abilities (e.g., R. Cattell, 1963; Sternberg, 1985), or as a number of independent multiple intelligences (Gardner, 1999). So who is correct? At this time, we cannot say for sure, and the controversy is likely to continue. We will all have to wait and see what researchers will uncover about intelligence in the years to come.

The issue of *what* intelligence is has certainly stimulated a great deal of debate among researchers, but another issue has captured the attention of the public even more. Where does intelligence come from—our genes or our environment?

Let's
REVIEW
In this section, we discussed intelligence. We looked at ways psychologists attempt to test, measure, and define intelligence. For a quick check of your understanding, try answering the following questions at increasing levels of difficulty.

1. Which psychologist proposed that we possess many intelligences?

   a. Robert Sternberg   c. Howard Gardner

   b. Francis Galton   d. James Cattell

2. _____ is to *accurate* as _____ is to *consistent*.

   a. Valid; reliable   c. Unbiased; valid

   b. Reliable; valid   d. Valid; unbiased

3. One day, Sabrina's front door started squeaking at the hinges. She was out of the spray lubricant that she would normally use for this purpose, so she went to her kitchen and got a bottle of cooking oil. She dabbed a bit of the corn oil on the hinge, and the squeak went away. Sabrina *best* exhibits a high level of _____ intelligence.

   a. analytical   c. practical

   b. existential   d. creative

ANSWERS 1. c; 2. a; 3. d

LEARNING OBJECTIVE

What Should You Know?

- Describe the nature versus nurture debate as it applies to intelligence.

INDIVIDUAL DIFFERENCES IN INTELLIGENCE: WHY ARE WE ALL SO UNIQUE?

All of us differ to some degree in the level of intelligence (or intelligences) that we have. Some of us may score an average IQ of 100. And, others may score substantially higher or lower on traditional IQ tests. For example, a person is often considered *gifted* if she has an IQ of 130 or greater and also outperforms her peers on certain intellectual tasks, such as academics, creative tasks, or artistic tasks (National Association for Gifted Children [NAGC], 2010). On the other hand, a person is considered to be *developmentally delayed* if he has an IQ score below 70 and also experiences difficulties in everyday functioning (American Psychiatric Association, 1994). **What determines where we fall on the intelligence continuum?**

Nature, Nurture, and IQ

Like all our individual characteristics, intelligence may be examined in the context of the *nature–nurture debate* (see Chapter 2), and this debate is never more contentious than when it's applied to the issue of intelligence. The argument over whether intelligence is due primarily to genetic factors (the nature side of the debate) or to environmental influences (the nurture side) has led to heated and emotional debate in our society. Most recently, this debate was brought into the public eye with the publication of *The Bell Curve* (Herrnstein & Murray, 1994). The title of this book refers to the fact that IQ scores tend to follow a normal distribution, which is shaped like a bell (see Figure 7.8, p. 288). In *The Bell Curve*, the authors argued that intelligence is primarily encoded in our genes and that environmental influences do little to change it. This extreme position was largely denounced by scholars (Gardner, 1999), but the public became engaged in heated discussions about the merits of this position as well as the implications of the authors' claims. Of particular concern was the implication that some minority groups may be genetically inferior with respect to intelligence. Though the authors never stated that minorities were genetically inferior, this conclusion appeared to follow from their arguments and the data that have been collected on IQ differences across racial groups.

Generally speaking, studies have shown that *average* IQ scores tend to vary across racial groups in America. As a group, African Americans tend to score about 10 to 15 points lower on IQ tests than European Americans, who are in turn outscored, on average, by Asian Americans (Nisbett, 1995; Rushton & Jensen, 2005). If we are to believe the message of *The Bell Curve*, the inference would be that these differences exist mostly because of genetic inheritance. Furthermore, some may be tempted to conclude that if these differences are genetically based, then any attempt to raise children's IQ scores by improving their environment would be a waste of time and money. It is this sort of offensive assertion that has kept the debate on race, genetics, and intelligence ignited for decades (see Rushton & Jensen, 2005, and Sternberg, Grigorenko, & Kidd, 2005, for thorough reviews of the research from opposing points of view).

Twin Studies and the Nature or Nurture of Intelligence

To answer questions about the relative contributions of nature and nurture, researchers often focus on twin studies. **Twin studies** compare specific traits between pairs of **identical twins** (twins who share 100% of their genetic code) and pairs of nonidentical or **fraternal twins** (twins no more genetically related than other siblings). If identical twins have a similar trait more often than fraternal twins do, a genetic basis for the trait is implied. In contrast, if identical twins and fraternal twins do not differ in similarity, there is less support for the existence of a genetic influence on the trait. Other valuable comparisons include comparing identical twins raised in different environments to identical twins raised in the same household. Dissimilarities between identical twins reared together and identical twins raised apart would be a powerful argument for environmental influence on the trait being measured. In doing such comparisons, psychologists can isolate the influence of nature and nurture on the development of specific traits.

Overall, the results of twin studies (and other studies) on the inheritance of traits in families have not supported the strong nature claims made in *The Bell Curve*. Rather, the results of studies on intelligence indicate that genetics accounts for about 50% of the variability (or differences) in intelligence that is seen in people; the remaining 50% of the variability is the result of environmental influence (Bouchard, 2004). Thus, the *interactionist* perspective on intelligence—that intelligence seems to stem from both our genes and our environment— is the best-supported position on intelligence (Chipuer, Rovine, & Polmin, 1990; Polmin, 1994). It is just as likely that racial differences in IQ are due to environmental differences as genetic ones.

An impoverished environment may contribute to lesser performance on IQ tests for a number of reasons. Poorer parents cannot afford educational toys, good schools, computers, and so on, for their children. Poorer parents may themselves not be highly educated and therefore may be less able to stimulate their children in the ways that highly educated parents can. Poverty-stricken children may not receive adequate nutrition and medical care, and this deficiency may affect neural development. A stronger argument can be made by looking at what happens when poorer minority children are placed in a different environment. One study (E. G. J. Moore, 1986) showed that African American children who were placed in affluent European American families as infants had, on average, IQs that were above average for *European American* children by the time they had reached middle school.

It is also worth noting that there is more variability in intelligence *within* racial groups than there is *between* racial groups. In other words, the range of IQ scores among European Americans or among African Americans is wider than the average difference between these groups.

Interpreting Intelligence Studies

Data like these seriously question the notion that intelligence is primarily an inherited characteristic. Furthermore, we all would do well to keep in mind that *group* characteristics do not predict individual characteristics. For instance, let's say that through some magic we could tell you with 100% accuracy that the class average on your next psychology exam will be a

twin studies research that compares specific traits of identical and fraternal twins to ascertain the relative contributions of genes and environment to our characteristics

identical twins twins that developed from a single fertilized egg and share 100% of their genes

fraternal twins twins that developed from two separate fertilized eggs and are no more genetically similar than normal siblings

71. Does this mean that you are going to earn a 71? Not at all—you could earn *any* grade on the exam. You might earn a 95. There is no way to predict your performance based on the class average. The same is true of IQ scores. Even if, for whatever reason, the average IQ for a minority group is higher or lower than the average IQ in the majority group, we cannot predict what an individual minority member's IQ will be. It is a mistake to assume that an individual minority member has a lower IQ based on data that were obtained from a group of people. It would be equally wrong to assume that a majority member would necessarily have a comparatively high IQ. When we make assumptions about individuals based on group characteristics, and we ignore individual characteristics, we are engaging in a *prejudice*. We will have more to say about prejudice in Chapter 11 when we look at social psychology. For now, let's take a look at another controversial area of intelligence research—the question of whether men and women differ in intelligence.

Gender and Intellectual Abilities: Are We Really All That Different?

Just as we saw in our discussion on race and IQ, data are at times open to different interpretations. One area in which the interpretation of data has been varied and sometimes contentious is in the study of how gender relates to intellectual abilities. Beliefs or stereotypes about male and female intellectual abilities abound. For example, in the United States (and many other cultures), people tend to believe that men are better at math and women are better at verbal tasks. Another common stereotype is that men are more logical than women and women are more emotional than men. But stereotypes are just our perceptions or beliefs. Are there truly gender differences in intelligence?

The answer to this question has proved to be somewhat complicated. Over the last several decades, many researchers have investigated the issue of gender differences in intelligence, and often their results have been difficult to interpret (Galliano, 2003). In part, the confusion has to do with how individual researchers have defined specific abilities. For example, to evaluate mathematical ability, you could look at a person's ability to solve equations, the speed with which he or she can solve word problems, whether the person succeeds in math classes, and so on. Another problem is that studies that fail to find predicted gender differences are often not published. Therefore, if we look only at published studies that do show gender differences in intelligence, we may falsely conclude that gender differences are more prevalent than they actually are (Galliano, 2003).

After examining the available research, many psychologists have concluded that men and women do not differ in general intelligence, or *g* (Halpern & LeMay, 2000). On the other hand, some gender differences have been indicated with respect to specific multiple intelligences. We have summarized some of these suspected differences in ● TABLE 7.4. Keep a few things in mind as you read this table. First, many gender differences are small (e.g., Galliano, 2003; Hyde, Fenneman, & Lamon, 1990). Second, finding such differences often depends on how they were measured. For example, females tend to earn better grades in math classes, but males tend to do better on standardized tests of mathematical ability (Hyde & McKinley, 1997). Third, gender differences can vary by culture, age, and race. For instance, in Thailand girls outperform boys in math, but in France boys do better than girls (Galliano, 2003). And in the United States, male superiority on math SAT scores occurs only among European Americans (N. M. Robinson, Abbott, Berninger, & Busse, 1996). Finally, gender differences are at times a product of bias in the tests used to measure different abilities. For example, David Share and Phil Silva (2003) found that in a sample of New Zealand students, boys were more likely to be labeled as having reading disabilities because of a statistical bias in the way that reading disability scores were calculated.

Given these types of idiosyncrasies in the data, it is difficult to conclude that there are broad-based, global differences between men and women when it comes to intelligence. Despite the lack of clarity concerning the differences, it is fairly clear that we tend to believe the stereotypes we have about men's and women's abilities. Belief in these stereotypes has been well documented in studies that ask men and women to assess their own intellectual abilities. For example, in one study, Adrian Furnham and colleagues found that parents tended to estimate their sons' IQs as being higher than their daughters', indicating that they

TABLE 7.4

● **Gender Differences on Some Cognitive Tasks**

TASKS ON WHICH WOMEN OFTEN HAVE HIGHER AVERAGE SCORES	TASKS ON WHICH MEN OFTEN HAVE HIGHER AVERAGE SCORES
Verbal Tasks	**Visual Memory Tasks**
verbal fluency	mental rotation tasks
synonym generation	
spelling	
anagrams	
reading comprehension	
writing	
foreign languages	
tongue twisters	
knowledge about literature	
Perceptual Tasks	**Spatial Tasks**
searching for letters within lines of text	making judgments about moving objects—for
detecting touch, taste, odor, and sound at low	example, judging how far away a moving object is
levels of intensity	
Motor Skill Tasks	**Motor Skill Tasks**
fine motor skill tasks like tracing the mirror image	motor skills that involve aiming, such as throwing
of a stimulus on a piece of paper	a baseball or darts
Academic Performance	**Knowledge Areas**
most subject areas at school	general knowledge
	knowledge about math, geography, and science
	Fluid Reasoning Tasks
	mechanical reasoning
	scientific reasoning
	quantitative reasoning
	proportional reasoning
	verbal analogies

Source: Adapted from Halpern, 1996.

had more confidence in their sons' overall intelligence, or *g*. When asked to rate their children on specific multiple intelligences, the parents tended to rate their sons higher on mathematical and spatial intelligence and their daughters higher on verbal and musical intelligences (Furnham, Reeves, & Budhani, 2002).

These biases also seem to extend to how we view our own levels of intelligence. In cultures as diverse as the United States, Poland, Argentina, China, Iran, New Zealand, and Slovakia, men's self-ratings of intelligence are higher than women's (see Furnham, Wytykowska, & Petrides, 2005, for a review). Men also rate themselves as having lower levels of emotional intelligence (Petrides, Furnham, & Martin, 2004), better general knowledge, and more skill on tasks of visual perception (Pallier, 2003). Studies like these seem to suggest that both men and women have (perhaps misguidedly) bought into the commonly held stereotypes about their respective abilities. This self-assessment can be problematic. If a woman believes that she is less intelligent, this perception may lower her performance (Chamorro-Premuzic & Furnham, 2004). Furthermore, even if she performs well, stereotypes like these can be the basis for prejudice and discrimination—topics that we will discuss more in Chapter 11.

Let's REVIEW

In this section, we discussed the controversy concerning influences that affect an individual's level of intelligence. For a quick check of your understanding, try answering the following questions at increasing levels of difficulty.

1. Identical twins share what percentage of their genes?

   a. 10%   c. 50%

   b. 25%   d. 100%

2. Being male is correlated with better _____ .

   a. spatial abilities   c. academic performance

   b. verbal fluency   d. fine motor skill tasks

3. Jared is a 25-year-old African American man. Based on the research on intelligence, what do you know about Jared's individual level of intelligence?

   a. He has an IQ of 100 or greater.   c. He has an IQ between 85 and 115.

   b. He has an IQ of 85 or lower.   d. We don't know what his IQ is.

ANSWERS 1. d; 2. a; 3. d

STUDYING the CHAPTER

KEY TERMS

cognition (264)
knowledge (265)
thinking (265)
mental representation (265)
cognitive map (267)
concept (268)
superordinate category (269)
basic level category (269)
subordinate category (269)
formal concept (269)
natural concept (270)
prototype (271)
exemplar (271)
well-structured problem (272)
algorithm (272)

heuristic (272)
ill-structured problem (273)
insight (274)
creativity (274)
functional fixedness (274)
mental set (275)
incubation (275)
reasoning (276)
deductive reasoning (276)
inductive reasoning (276)
decision making (276)
judgment (277)
availability heuristic (277)
representativeness heuristic (277)

language (279)
cooing (279)
babbling (279)
phoneme (280)
morpheme (280)
overextension (281)
underextension (281)
telegraphic speech (281)
grammar (281)
pragmatics (281)
Whorfian hypothesis/linguistic relativity hypothesis (283)
intelligence (287)
mental age (287)

intelligence quotient (IQ score) (288)
reliability (290)
validity (290)
cultural bias (290)
generalized intelligence (g) (291)
crystallized intelligence (291)
fluid intelligence (291)
multiple intelligences (292)
triarchic theory of intelligence (292)
twin studies (296)
identical twins (296)
fraternal twins (296)

LEARNING CHALLENGE

Now that you have studied the chapter, assess your comprehension of the material by answering the following questions. Then use the key at the end to determine if your understanding is at the basic, intermediate, or advanced level. For a more comprehensive assessment of your learning, please see your student study guide and your Psychology CourseMate (www.cengagebrain.com).

TEST YOURSELF!

1. _____ is the way in which we use and store information in memory.

   a. Thinking

   b. Reasoning

   c. Cognition

   d. Judgment

2. The concept of *knowledge* is most closely related to which of the following concepts?

   a. mental representation
   b. decision making
   c. judgment
   d. problem solving

3. A cognitive map is best described as a mental representation of _____.

   a. a sound
   b. the environment
   c. a picture
   d. a thought

4. Studies of _____ provide the strongest evidence that we do not store all the details of visual stimuli in the visual images we store in memory.

   a. mental rotation
   b. image scanning
   c. cognitive maps
   d. reasoning

5. Which of the following is the most superordinate category?

   a. food
   b. vegetable
   c. chocolate bar
   d. candy

6. Which of the following is the best example of a natural concept?

   a. car
   b. mammal
   c. tool
   d. woman

7. A(n) _____ is the most typical member of a category.

   a. exemplar
   b. prototype
   c. natural concept
   d. formal concept

8. Which of the following concepts is most closely associated with the concept of *correctness*?

   a. prototype
   b. heuristic
   c. algorithm
   d. creativity

9. After days of trying to determine how to stop his garden hose from leaking, Jordan suddenly realizes that he can tape a sleeve of bicycle inner tube over the hole in the hose. Jordan's solution represents an instance of _____.

   a. functional fixedness
   b. mental sets
   c. well-structured problem solving
   d. insight

10. A period of time during which you do not think about a problem is called _____.

   a. a mental set
   b. incubation
   c. insight
   d. divergent thinking

11. Which of the following represents a correct chronological sequence of language development?

   a. phonemes, cooing, telegraphic speech, pragmatics
   b. pragmatics, phonemes, cooing, telegraphic speech
   c. babbling, cooing, telegraphic speech, pragmatics
   d. babbling, morphemes, telegraphic speech, pragmatics

12. According to current research on language, which of the following statements is *not* true?

   a. Language plays a role in the transmission of culture from one generation to the next.
   b. Language determines the types of thoughts we have and how we perceive the world.
   c. Language can influence our memory, thoughts, and perceptions.
   d. Language is a system of communication with a set vocabulary and structure or grammar.

13. According to Lewis Terman, if 7-year-old Alberto has an IQ of 114, his mental age is approximately _____.

   a. 6 years
   b. 7.5 years
   c. 8 years
   d. 9 years

14. Mina has a very clear understanding of herself. She has an accurate understanding of her strengths and weaknesses. She knows what she likes and doesn't like, and she knows what she wants from life. Mina is likely very high in which type of intelligence?

   a. analytical
   b. intrapersonal
   c. emotional
   d. b and c

15. _____ intelligence tends to decrease with age.

   a. Fluid
   b. Generalized (g)
   c. Emotional
   d. Interpersonal

Scoring Key

Below are the answers and the associated point values for each of the Learning Challenge questions. Circle the associated points for each question that you answered correctly. To obtain your Learning Challenge Score, add up the points you circled and write the total in the blank.

1. C, 1 pt   **3.** B, 1 pt   **5.** A, 2 pts

2. A, 2 pts   **4.** C, 3 pts   **6.** C, 3 pts

7. B, 1 pt   **10.** B, 1 pt   **13.** C, 3 pts

8. C, 2 pts   **11.** D, 2 pts   **14.** D, 3 pts

9. D, 3 pts   **12.** B, 2 pts   **15.** A, 1 pt

Learning Challenge Score _____

(27–30) Congratulations! You scored at the advanced level. You are well on your way to mastering the material. Take the next step by answering the questions in your Student Study Guide or your Psychology CourseMate (www.cengagebrain.com).

(21–26) You are almost there! You scored at the intermediate level. Review the material you missed before moving on to answer the questions in your Student Study Guide or your Psychology CourseMate (www.cengagebrain.com).

(20 and below) You are on your way, but you're not there yet! You scored at the beginner level. It appears that you need to carefully review the chapter to improve your mastery of the material.

USE IT OR LOSE IT: APPLYING PSYCHOLOGY

1. What abilities define our concept of an intelligent person in the United States? What abilities do you think would define the concept of an intelligent person in rural Africa?

2. Make a case for why one would want to use heuristics for solving problems and making decisions and judgments.

3. Give an original example of an ill-structured and a well-structured problem.

4. Describe the stages that children go through as they develop language and give an example of each. If you wanted to raise a bilingual child, how do you think you could best accomplish this?

5. Examine the theories of multiple intelligences that you read about in this chapter. Are there any types of intelligence that you feel were overlooked in these theories? Why or why not?

CRITICAL THINKING FOR INTEGRATION

1. How could Lev Vygotsky's idea (see Chapter 9) of the zone of proximal development be useful to child caregivers who wish to improve a child's language development?

2. Presume that someday we finally do provide conclusive evidence that animals have linguistic abilities. How do you think this would change psychology and other sciences?

3. Given what you have learned about language, intelligence, and psychology in general, what advice would you give a

first-time parent who is concerned about raising the best child he or she can?

4. Damage to which areas of the brain would be most likely to impair a person's ability to use language? Would this damage also affect the person's problem-solving skills? Explain.

5. How could cultural bias in intelligence testing facilitate the development or maintenance of racial prejudices?

CHAPTER STUDY RESOURCES

Student Study Guide

To help organize your learning, work through Chapter 7 of the *What Is Psychology? Student Study Guide*. The study guide includes learning objectives, a chapter summary, fill-in review, key terms, a practice test, and activities.

CengageNOW

Go to **www.cengage.com/login** to link to CengageNOW, your online study tool. First take the Pre-Test for this chapter to get your personalized study plan, which will identify topics you need to review and direct you to online resources. Then take the Post-Test to determine what concepts you have mastered and what you still need work on.

CourseMate

Access an interactive eBook, chapter-specific interactive learning tools, including flashcards, quizzes, videos, and more in your Psychology CourseMate, available at **CengageBrain.com**.

Aplia   aplia

Aplia™ is an online interactive learning solution that helps you improve comprehension—and your grade—by integrating a variety of tools such as video, tutorials, practice tests, and interactive eBook. Founded by a professor to enhance his own courses, Aplia provides automatically graded assignments with detailed, immediate explanations on every question, and innovative teaching materials. More than 1,000,000 students like you have used Aplia at over 1,800 institutions. Aplia should be purchased only when assigned by your instructor as part of your course.

The case of Ildefonso, a languageless man, high-lights the interconnected nature of *language*, *thought*, and *intelligence*. These cognitive abilities are essential to our everyday functioning because they allow us to perceive and understand our world, solve problems, and communicate with others.

COGNITION, LANGUAGE, AND INTELLIGENCE: HOW DO WE THINK?

THINKING: HOW DO WE REPRESENT OUR WORLD?

- **Cognition** is the way in which we store and use information.
- Our **knowledge** comprises the mental representations of the world that we have stored in long-term memory.
- **Thinking**, or the use of knowledge to accomplish a goal, involves two broad classes of mental representation—those based on sensory aspects and those based on the meaning of the object.
- Visual images are powerful **mental representations** that allow us to remember a person's face or a map of a town.
- **Cognitive maps** are mental representations of geographical information.
- **Concepts** are mental categories that contain related bits of knowledge and are organized around the meaning of the information they represent.
- We tend to organize our knowledge into three levels of categorization: the general, broad, **superordinate category**; the **basic level category**; and the **subordinate category**, which is the most specific.
- We acquire **formal concepts** as we learn the rigid rules that define certain categories of things, but **natural concepts** develop naturally as we live our lives and experience the world.
- A **prototype** is our concept of the most typical member of a category—in essence, a summary of all members of that category.
- **Exemplars** are stored representations of actual category members we have experienced.

PROBLEM SOLVING: WHERE DOES OUR THINKING GET US?

- An **algorithm** is a method of solving a particular problem that always leads to the correct solution. A **heuristic** is a shortcut, or rule of thumb, that may or may not lead to the solution of a problem.
- **Insight** occurs when we find a new way of looking at a problem that leads to a sudden understanding of how to solve it.
- **Creativity** involves the ability to combine mental elements in new and useful ways.
- **Functional fixedness** is the limitation of being able to see objects only in their familiar roles.
- A **mental set** is a tendency to habitually use the methods of problem solving that have worked for you in the past.
- **Incubation**, or a period of not thinking about a problem, sometimes helps us to solve the problem.

ARE WE ALWAYS LOGICAL WHEN REASONING, MAKING DECISIONS, OR MAKING JUDGMENTS?

- We engage in **reasoning** when we draw conclusions that are based on certain assumptions about the world. **Deductive reasoning** involves reasoning from the general to the specific, whereas **inductive reasoning** involves reasoning from the specific to the general.

- **Decision making** involves choosing among several alternatives and is often part of the problem-solving process.

- Framing, or how possible courses of action are presented, can affect our decisions.

- Two mental shortcuts that can be useful but that can also lead to mistakes are the **availability** and the **representativeness heuristics**.

JGI/Jamie Grill/Getty Images

IS LANGUAGE IMPORTANT TO MORE THAN COMMUNICATION?

- Human **language** is a well-developed, syntactical, verbal system for representing the world.

- Scientists debate the idea that humans are born with an innate language acquisition device—a programmed capacity for language.

- Research indicates that infants generally proceed from **cooing** to **babbling** to **morphemes** on their road to language skills. By the time a child is approximately 2 years old, he or she begins to combine words into two-word sentences, in what is called **telegraphic speech**. Soon after, children learn the rules of **grammar** and **pragmatics** for their language.

- One theory, known as the **Whorfian hypothesis** or the **linguistic relativity hypothesis**, suggests that one's language determines one's thoughts and perceptions of the world. A more widely held view is that language influences, rather than determines, our thoughts.

- Although animals communicate, it is hotly debated whether they have the capacity for language.

© Helen King/Corbis

WHAT IS INTELLIGENCE AND HOW DO WE MEASURE IT?

- Many modern psychologists broadly view **intelligence** as those abilities that allow you to adapt to your environment and behave in a goal-oriented way.

- Alfred Binet established the measurement of **mental age** that reflected a child's mental abilities compared to those of the "average" child at a specific age.

- Stanford psychologist Lewis Terman revised Binet's testing procedures and introduced the **intelligence quotient**, or **IQ score**, which divided one's mental age by one's chronological age.

- The adult version of David Wechsler's test (WAIS-IV) yields a full-scale IQ score (FSIQ) and four index scores: verbal comprehension, perceptual reasoning, working memory, and processing speed.

- Intelligence tests are frequently criticized for having a **cultural bias**.

- The idea of mental ability as a single unitary factor is known as **generalized intelligence**, or *g*.

- **Crystallized intelligence** refers to our accumulation of knowledge, whereas **fluid intelligence** refers to the speed and efficiency with which we learn new information and solve problems.

- Some theorists argue that we have **multiple intelligences**. Examples are Robert Sternberg's **triarchic theory** and Howard Gardner's theory of multiple intelligences.

- Daniel Goleman's theory of emotional intelligence argues that emotions are also an important component of successful living.

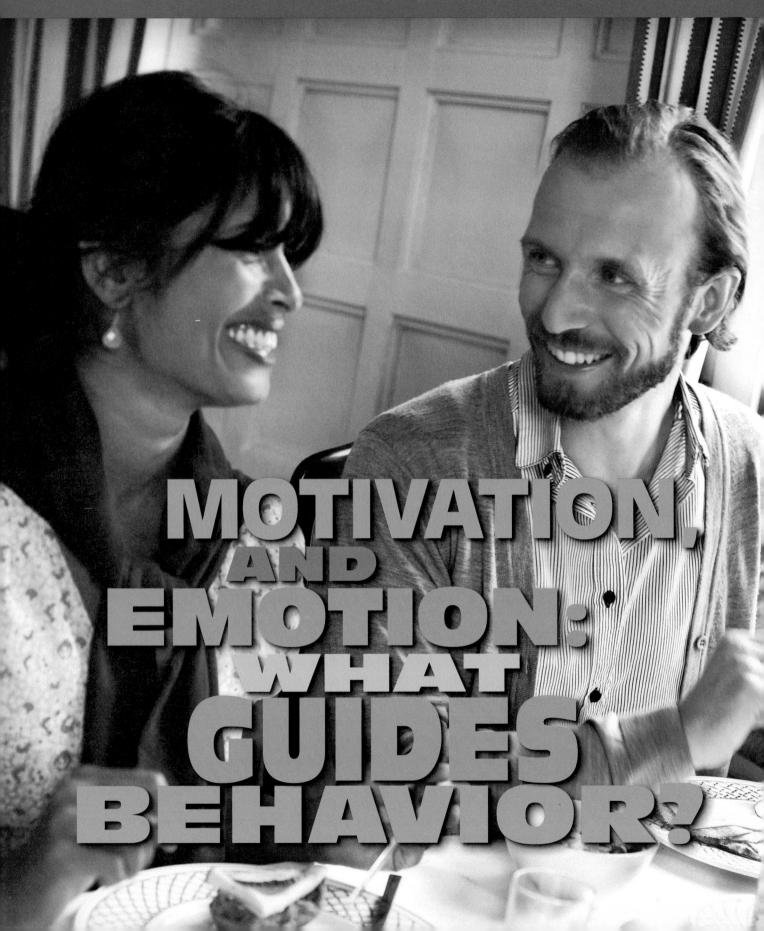

CHAPTER 8

MOTIVATION, AND EMOTION: WHAT GUIDES BEHAVIOR?

THE BIG PICTURE

What Happens When Motives Go Astray?

You have obviously started to read this chapter in your psychology text—good for you! Because we teach psychology and we wrote this book, we think that this activity is worthwhile. But what are *your* reasons for reading this chapter? What has *motivated* you to read it at this moment? Do you want to earn a good grade on an upcoming exam? Do you want to learn more about motivation, the subject of this chapter? What is it that is driving you right now?

When we are *motivated*, we are driven to engage in some form of behavior. Just as something motivated you to start to read this chapter, every day we are motivated to do many different things. For example, we are motivated to eat, drink, attend school, go to work, interact with family and friends, and so on. In psychological terms, a **motive** is the tendency to desire and seek out positive incentives or rewards and to avoid negative outcomes (Atkinson, 1958/1983; McClelland, 1987). When we experience the motive of hunger, we eat to avoid this aversive feeling. We are motivated to study because we want the feelings of pride and the opportunities for advancement that accompany academic success. We drink to quench our thirst, and so on.

Because we are generally motivated to avoid pain and other aversive states, our motives often serve to protect us. Without the motivation to eat, we could suffer from malnutrition or even starvation. Without thirst, we would face dehydration, and so on. Our motives tend to direct our behavior in ways that benefit us—but there are exceptions to this rule. Sometimes our motivations are in conflict, and we can end up being motivated to engage in behaviors that are detrimental to our well-being. Our case studies for this chapter tell the tales of two such people whose motives were at odds with one another.

For Marya Hornbacher, competing motives to eat and to starve herself have characterized her lifelong battle with eating disorders—a battle she chronicles in *Wasted*, her beautifully written autobiography (Hornbacher, 1998). For Toren Volkmann, the motive to drink alcohol was at odds with his motive to succeed in life. In the eye-opening *From Binge to Blackout* (Volkmann & Volkmann, 2006), Toren and his mother detail the devastating toll that teenage alcoholism can take on a family.

Marya was born into a chaotic family. Her parents were caring, but they were also very self-absorbed. They fought constantly and often burdened Marya with their marital problems. Her mother was cold and distant; her father was overly intrusive and gave Marya little room for privacy. Despite the chaos at home, Marya was a very bright and

Jonas Ingerstedt/Getty Images

305

Marya Hornbacher has struggled with eating disorders for much of her life. She chronicles her struggle in this well-written and moving memoir, *Wasted*.

motive a tendency to desire and seek out positive incentives or rewards and to avoid negative outcomes

bulimia nervosa a mental health disorder in which a person alternately binges on large quantities of food and then engages in some inappropriate compensatory behavior to avoid weight gain

anorexia nervosa a mental health disorder in which a person has an intense fear of gaining weight, even though he or she is actually underweight. This irrational fear motivates the person to lose unhealthy amounts of weight through self-starvation.

talented child. She was driven to succeed in life, but she was also plagued by fears of inadequacy. At only 9 years old, she already felt as if she had no control over much of her life.

The one area where Marya did feel she had some control was her own body and what she put into it. At this young age, Marya was already obsessed with her body, which she hated. Insecurity over her appearance led her to experience negative emotions, such as anxiety and fear, in many situations. To calm her anxieties and gain a sense of control in her life, Marya began to experiment with **bulimia nervosa**. Bulimia nervosa is an eating disorder in which people *binge* on large quantities of food and then engage in some inappropriate compensatory behavior to avoid weight gain. These compensatory behaviors may include self-induced vomiting, or *purging*; abuse of laxatives or diuretics (water pills); enemas; fasting; or excessive exercise. In the beginning, Marya would come home from school and eat anything she could get her hands on. Bingeing seemed to calm the anxiety, but these binges caused Marya to gain some weight—something she dreaded. One day, on a whim, she stuck her fingers down her throat and vomited the bag of corn chips she had just eaten. At first, the purging was infrequent, but soon it became a constant obsession. It was the only way Marya knew to fill the emotional void in her life, and she sank further and further into bulimia nervosa.

During junior high school, Marya began moving toward **anorexia nervosa**, an eating disorder in which people have an intense fear of gaining weight, even though they are actually underweight. This irrational fear motivates the person to lose unhealthy amounts of weight through self-starvation. Marya now concentrated on precise control of her daily eating, attempting to eat as little as possible while exercising intensely. As a result, she rapidly lost weight. But no matter how much weight she lost, it was never enough to make Marya happy, and soon she was in serious trouble. At age 18, Marya was near death when she was hospitalized at the astounding weight of 52 pounds. Marya had a choice to make. She could die, or she could find a way to fight her way back from bulimia and anorexia. She decided to fight.

Marya worked hard to gain control of her behavior and her life. At age 24, she was diagnosed with *bipolar disorder*, a mental health disorder characterized by extreme mood swings (see Chapter 14). Bipolar disorder may help explain why Marya felt so overwhelmed by life that she sought refuge in obsessively controlling her body. With the help of therapy, Marya did learn to better control her behavior. She is now married and is a successful author. But, Marya can never erase the damage that years of starvation and bingeing and purging did to her body. She cannot have children. She has a heart murmur, and she has lost 25% of her heart muscle. These lingering conditions could potentially impact her future health.

Like Marya, Toren Volkmann showed much promise as a child. He was smart, athletic, and charming. Toren seemed to be an average teenager. He did well in school and had many friends. When Toren was caught experimenting with alcohol and drugs during high school, his parents thought this behavior was just normal teenage rebellion. They lectured him on the dangers of substance abuse, punished him accordingly, and thought the problem was fixed. However, Toren's use of alcohol increased when he went off to college. During his freshman year, he was reprimanded many times for inappropriate use of alcohol on campus. Yet he still managed to do well in his classes. With Toren bringing home good grades, his parents did not think that his problems with alcohol could be very serious. What they didn't know—what Toren didn't even know—was that he was already an alcoholic. When Toren graduated from college, he set off to fulfill his dream of becoming a Peace Corps volunteer in Paraguay, only to have this dream derailed by alcohol.

At 24, Toren had been drinking heavily for almost 9 years. He was physically dependent on alcohol and would suffer debilitating withdrawal symptoms when he tried to stop. He would shake. He suffered from memory loss and blackouts. He couldn't sleep or eat. In short, he could not function. Toren had no choice but to inform the Peace Corps that he had a problem with alcohol. They responded by immediately sending him back to the United States for treatment—a move that may well have saved his life.

Back in the United States, Toren underwent inpatient treatment for his alcoholism that involved medically supervised detoxification and psychotherapy. After treatment, he spent 6 months living in a halfway house, which allowed him to transition back into society and remain sober. As for Marya, successful treatment does not mean that Toren is completely free of his destructive motives. Like most recovering alcoholics, he lives one day at a time in his quest to remain sober.

Marya's and Toren's stories illustrate the devastating effects of having one's motives go astray. What would motivate anyone to deliberately starve herself? Why would someone abandon his dreams to drink himself into a stupor? To answer these questions, we will first look at the roles that motivation and emotion play in our everyday lives. By understanding the forces that drive normal behaviors such as eating and drinking, we may gain some understanding of what goes wrong in cases like Marya's and Toren's. Let's begin by taking a look at some of the ways psychologists have conceptualized the process of motivation over the years.

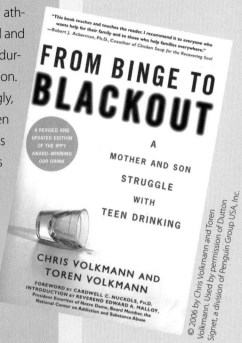

By the time he was 20, years of heavy drinking had left Toren Volkmann physically dependent on alcohol and unable to fulfill his dreams. Toren and his mother, Chris, detail his recovery from alcoholism in *From Binge to Blackout*.

WHAT IS MOTIVATION?

Over the years, psychologists have viewed motivation in several different ways—as *instincts* that direct our behavior, as uncomfortable biological states called *drives* that motivate us to find ways to feel better, as the desire to maintain an optimal level of *arousal* in our body, or as *incentives* that guide us to seek reward from the world. However, none of these theories seems to fully explain all aspects of motivation. Today psychologists do not expect any single theory to explain all our motivations. Instead, we recognize that each of these theories has its strengths and weaknesses. Let's take a closer look at these different theories of motivation.

Motivation as Instinct

One of the earliest views on motivation was one that was heavily influenced by the work of Charles Darwin and the theory of natural selection (Chapter 2; Darwin, 1859/1936). Back in the 1800s, American psychologist William James proposed that motives are, in fact, genetically determined **instincts** that have evolved in humans because they support survival and procreation (James, 1890/1950). According to William James, instincts are impulses from within a person that direct or *motivate* that person's behavior.

Over time, the idea that motives are inborn instincts gradually fell out of favor with psychologists. One problem with James's view was that the list of proposed instincts kept getting longer and longer. Taken to its logical extreme, instinct theory could be used to argue that all behavior is due to instinct. Furthermore, it is impossible to determine whether many of the proposed instincts are truly inborn. Many of our so-called instincts may result from learning.

Motivation as a Drive

Instinct theory was followed by **drive reduction theories** of motivation. According to the drive reduction approach, motivation stems from the desire to reduce an uncomfortable internal state, called a **drive**, that results when our needs are not fulfilled (Hull, 1943). For instance, when we do not have enough food in our system, we feel the uncomfortable state of *hunger*, which *drives* us to eat until we have taken in the food that our bodies require. Then, when we have taken in enough food, the hunger drive dissipates, and we stop eating. In this fashion, our drives can help us survive by creating what psychologists call a *drive state*, which ensures that we will be motivated to meet our biological needs.

Primary drives, such as the need for food, water, and warmth, motivate us to maintain certain bodily processes at an internal state of equilibrium, or **homeostasis**. Obviously, it would be desirable for us to take in just the right amount of food and water, to sleep just enough, and to maintain our body temperature at 98.6 degrees. Without the motivation from drives, we would not keep our bodies at homeostasis because we would not know when to eat, sleep, drink, and so on. But what causes a drive state in the first place?

Primary drives begin in the body when the brain recognizes that we are lacking in some biological need. The brain recognizes need based on the *feedback* that it receives from the body's systems and organs. One type of feedback system is called a **negative feedback loop** (● FIGURE 8.1). Negative feedback loops are information systems in the body that monitor the level of a bodily process and adjust it up and down accordingly. A good analogy for a negative feedback loop is the action of a thermostat. In your home, you set the thermostat at a desired level, and the thermostat monitors the air temperature and

instinct innate impulse from within a person that directs or motivates behavior

drive reduction theory theory of motivation that proposes that motivation seeks to reduce internal levels of drive

drive an uncomfortable internal state that motivates us to reduce this discomfort through our behavior

primary drive a drive that motivates us to maintain homeostasis in certain biological processes within the body

homeostasis an internal state of equilibrium in the body

negative feedback loop a system of feedback in the body that monitors and adjusts our motivation level so as to maintain homeostasis

Sam Bloomberg-Rissman/Blend Images/Getty Images

According to the instinct theory of motivation, it is instinct that motivates us to do things like clean our homes. What do you think? Are you driven by instinct to clean your home? Or is this an example of a learned motive?

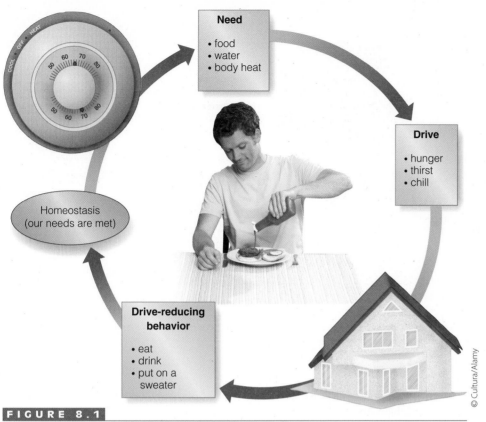

FIGURE 8.1

● **Negative Feedback Loops** Negative feedback loops maintain homeostasis in our bodies by monitoring certain physiological conditions (e.g., glucose levels and fluid levels). When levels drop too low, feedback from the body tells the brain to increase motivation (e.g., hunger or thirst). When levels are too high, feedback from the body tells the brain to decrease motivation.

compares it to that set level. If the room gets too cold, the heater turns on. If the room gets too warm, the heater turns off. Many primary drives in the body work in the same fashion.

The idea that motivation in the form of primary drives serves to maintain homeostasis makes a great deal of sense. Without primary drives, our biological needs would likely not be met, and we might not survive. **But how well does the idea of drive explain some of our other motivations?** For example, does drive reduction theory explain academic achievement motivation, or motivation to be loved? To help explain what motivates those behaviors not directly related to survival, drive reduction theorists developed the notion of **secondary drives**, or drives that motivate us to perform behaviors that are not directly related to biological needs.

Secondary drives are presumed to develop as we begin to associate things like achievement with satisfaction of primary drives—for example, receiving a candy bar for doing well in school satisfies hunger. As a result, we may also become more motivated to achieve academically. ● FIGURE 8.2 shows a list of secondary needs that were identified by psychologist Henry Murray back in the 1930s (H. A. Murray, 1938). According to some psychologists, the need to fulfill certain secondary drives differs from person to per-

secondary drive learned drive that is not directly related to biological needs

According to drive reduction theory, we are motivated to eat when our body sends feedback signals to the brain indicating that our energy supplies are running low. This need for fuel sets up a primary drive state, which motivates us to eat so that we can reduce our hunger.

Achievement (the need to achieve success in life)	**Affiliation** (the need to be close to others)
Counteraction (the need to overcome one's fears and failures)	**Rejection** (the need to reject those you do not like)
Abasement (the need to admit inferiority)	**Defendance** (the need to defend oneself against others)
Narcissism (the need to be self-absorbed)	**Nurturance** (the need to be nurturing and care for others)
Autonomy (the need to be independent)	**Succorance** (the need to have others care for you)
Understanding (the need to understand one's world)	**Sex** (the need to engage in sexual relations)
Play (the need to have fun)	**Blamavoidance** (the need to avoid being blamed or rejected by others)
Sentience (the need to seek out experiences that are pleasing to the senses)	**Aggression** (the need to be aggressive and to fight)
Order (the need to be neat and organized)	**Dominance** (the need to control your environment and the people in it)
Harmavoidance (the need to avoid pain and harm to oneself)	**Exhibition** (the need to have others notice you)
Infavoidance (the need to avoid humiliation and embarrassment)	**Deference** (the need to defer to others)

Hill Street Studios/Getty Images

FIGURE 8.2

● **Murray's Needs** Psychologist Henry Murray developed a list of secondary needs, or drives, that motivate us beyond our primary drives of hunger, thirst, and so on. *Source: H. A. Murray, 1938.*

son, like any other personality characteristic. For example, some people may be more or less motivated to achieve than others.

The concept of motivation as a means of reducing drives seems to make more sense for primary drives than for secondary drives, but even here it is not without its faults. There are times when drive reduction theory cannot explain certain aspects of our biological motives. For example, what about overeating? Think about a typical holiday meal in your family. At holiday dinners, do you eat only enough food to satisfy your primary drive of hunger? We bet not. How many times have you eaten until you felt ill because it was a special occasion? If our sole motivation for eating were drive reduction, we would not "pig out" in instances like these. Likewise, Marya's story goes against the predictions of drive reduction theory, which cannot easily explain why she refused to eat even though her body was screaming for her to satisfy its primary biological needs.

Drive reduction theories also fail to account for times when we seem to be motivated to *increase* the tension or arousal levels in our bodies. For instance, when you decide to ride a roller coaster at an amusement park or to skydive, what possible drive could these behaviors lower? Activities such as these do not appear to reduce any of our primary drives. Rather, the sole purpose of these activities seems to be to *arouse* us physiologically. Clearly, we will have to conceptualize motivation in some other way to account for these types of behavior.

Arousal Theory of Motivation

The **arousal theory** of motivation states that each of us has a level of physiological arousal at which we operate best, an *optimal* level of arousal. In general, we perform best on tasks when we are moderately aroused (● FIGURE 8.3); too much or too little arousal generally weakens performance (Arent & Landers, 2003; Hebb, 1955). Therefore, each of us is motivated to seek out arousal when we find ourselves underaroused and to reduce our arousal level when we are overaroused.

Although most of us perform best at moderate levels of arousal, some people seem to crave arousal, seeking out higher levels of arousal than the rest of us. In fact, sometimes they seek out levels of arousal that the rest of us would find *aversive*. For example, think of adventurers who handle dangerous animals, climb skyscrapers without protective gear, or bungee-jump off bridges. Many of us wouldn't try these activities even if we were *paid* to! So what

arousal theory a theory of motivation that states that we are motivated to seek out activities that allow us to perform at our optimum level of arousal

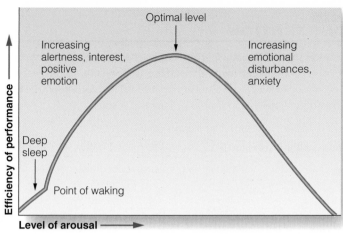

General relationship between performance and arousal level

FIGURE 8.3

● **Performance as a Function of Arousal**
Our best performance often occurs at moderate levels of arousal. You would likely do your best on an exam if you were neither too sleepy nor too anxious.

motivates some people to habitually seek out such arousing activities? Some people are what psychologists call **sensation seekers**; they habitually tend to seek out high levels of physiological arousal by engaging in intensely stimulating experiences (Zuckerman, 1978, 1994). Some sensation seekers pursue daring activities such as mountain climbing, skydiving, and fast driving, whereas others may be stimulated by engaging in problem behaviors such as drug use, aggression, and delinquency (Lynne-Landsman, Graber, Nichols, & Botvin, 2010).

One theory that seeks to explain the causes of sensation seeking looks at biological differences in the brains of sensation seekers. Psychologist Marvin Zuckerman found that sensation seekers tend to have low levels of a substance called *monoamine oxidase* (*MAO*; Zuckerman & Kuhlman, 2000). MAO is an enzyme that breaks down neurotransmitters such as serotonin, dopamine, and norepinephrine (Chapter 2). One of these neurotransmitters, dopamine, seems to be responsible for motivating us to obtain rewards. The low level of MAO in the brains of sensation seekers may mean that they experience more dopamine activity than other people. Without MAO to break it down, the dopamine would remain in the synapse longer, continuing to stimulate the neuron. This increased dopamine action may be related to the sensation seeker's motivation to experience reward from intense arousal.

sensation seeker a person who by trait tends to seek out arousing activities

According to psychologist Marvin Zuckerman, some people are sensation seekers who are motivated to engage in highly energizing and stimulating activities such as skydiving and extreme sports. Sensation seekers may have lower levels of MAO in their brains, which causes them to have higher levels of some neurotransmitters, such as dopamine, that motivate them to seek out higher levels of arousal and reward.

TRY THIS DEMONSTRATION

Are you a sensation seeker? To get a feel for your level of sensation seeking, take the questionnaire in ● FIGURE 8.4. Just keep in mind that this questionnaire is a brief version of the full Zuckerman Sensation Seeking Scale (Zuckerman, 1994). Therefore, your true level of sensation seeking may differ from that indicated by your test results.

Measuring sensation seeking

Answer "true" or "false" to each item listed below by circling "T" or "F." A "true" means that the item expresses your preference most of the time. A "false" means that you do not agree that the item is generally true for you. After completing the test, score your responses according to the instructions that follow the test items.

T F   1. I would really enjoy skydiving.
T F   2. I can imagine myself driving a sports car in a race and loving it.
T F   3. My life is very secure and comfortable—the way I like it.
T F   4. I usually like emotionally expressive or artistic people, even if they are sort of wild.
T F   5. I like the idea of seeing many of the same warm, supportive faces in everyday life.
T F   6. I like doing adventurous things and would have enjoyed being a pioneer in the early days of this country.
T F   7. A good photograph should express peacefulness creatively.
T F   8. The most important thing in living is fully experiencing all emotions.
T F   9. I like creature comforts when I go on a trip or vacation.
T F 10. Doing the same things each day really gets to me.
T F 11. I love snuggling in front of a fire on a wintry day.
T F 12. I would like to try several types of drugs as long as they didn't harm me permanently.
T F 13. Drinking and being rowdy really appeals to me on weekends.
T F 14. Rational people try to avoid dangerous situations.
T F 15. I prefer figure A to figure B.

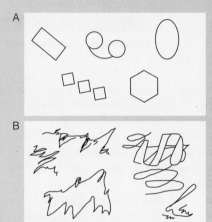

Give yourself 1 point for answering "true" to the following items: 1, 2, 4, 6, 8, 10, 12, and 13. Also give yourself 1 point for answering "false" to the following items: 3, 5, 7, 9, 11, 14, and 15. Add up your points, and compare your total to the following norms: 11–15, high sensation seeker; 6–10, moderate sensation seeker; 1–5, low sensation seeker. Bear in mind that this is a shortened version of the Sensation Seeking Scale and that it provides only a rough approximation of your status on this personality trait.

FIGURE 8.4

● **Brief Sensation-Seeking Questionnaire** *Source: A. F. Grasha & D. S. Kirschenbaum (1986). Adjustment and competence: Concepts and applications. St. Paul, MN: West Publishing. Reprinted by permission of Anthony F. Grasha.*

Self-Determination Theory of Motivation

Perhaps jumping out of airplanes and skiing off mountainsides is not your cup of tea. The idea that humans have different types of motivation is part of a broad theory of motivation called **self-determination theory** (Deci & Ryan, 2008). According to self-determination theory, humans need to feel *competent* (skilled), *autonomous* (in control of our own behavior), and *related* (or connected) to others. As we live our lives, actively trying to meet these needs, we will at times experience *autonomous motivation* and *controlled motivation*. When we are autonomously motivated, we are self-motivated to engage in a behavior. For example, you might study for an exam because you want to do well on the exam. When we experience controlled motivation, our behavior is externally regulated. For example, you may study for an exam because you want to please your professor.

These examples show the power that **incentives** have to motivate us into action (J. W. Atkinson, 1958/1983). You can think of incentives as goals or desires that you wish to satisfy or fulfill. For example, someone who desires money will be motivated to engage in behaviors that will likely lead to obtaining money, such as taking a job or buying lottery tickets. Incentives can be either *intrinsic* (coming from within us) or *extrinsic* (coming from outside us).

self-determination theory a theory of motivation that emphasizes the fact that as we pursue the fulfillment of basic needs, we are motivated by different types of motivation that come from both our self and the outside world

incentive a goal or desire that we are motivated to fulfill

Intrinsic incentives, such as wanting to make a good grade to please yourself, provide **intrinsic motivation** for behavior whereas extrinsic incentives, such as wanting to please others or desiring monetary rewards, provide **extrinsic motivation** for behavior (Deci & Ryan, 1985).

People differ in their orientation toward either an intrinsic or an extrinsic motivation. Some of us tend to be more motivated by intrinsic rewards in life, such as a sense of accomplishment and pride. Others of us tend to be more motivated by extrinsic rewards, such as grades and money. Which motivates you more? Although all of us are motivated at times by both intrinsic and extrinsic motives, some studies suggest an advantage to having a more intrinsic orientation. For example, research has indicated that intrinsically motivated college students are less likely to use drugs and alcohol (Rockafellow & Saules, 2006; Shamloo & Cox, 2010). And, intrinsic motivation has been shown to predict success in sticking to an exercise program (Teixeira et al., 2010) and doing well in school (Lepper, Corpus, & Iyengar, 2005). It appears that intrinsic rewards, such as a sense of accomplishment, are more likely to keep us working hard for success.

The self-determination theory of motivation states that many of us are motivated by extrinsic rewards such as money, material goods, and praise from others.

Nisian Hughes/Getty Images

Maslow's Hierarchy of Needs

Imagine that you have to miss lunch because you don't have time to stop and eat. On this particular day, you have a paper to write, an exam to study for, and a long list of algebra problems to finish. As you sit down to study, you find that several different motives are all trying to influence your behavior at the same time. You need to study, you are hungry, you are sleepy because you did not sleep well last night, and you really want to go to the movies with your friends. Which of these motives will win? What will your *first* course of action be in this situation? Will you eat, study, go to the movies, or fall asleep? We often find ourselves pulled in different directions by our motives. **Are some types of motives inherently stronger than others?** Perhaps.

Psychologist Abraham Maslow (1908–1970) recognized that in certain circumstances, some motives have greater influence over our behavior than others do. Maslow conceptualized both our physiological and psychological motives as different classes of *needs* to which we assign different levels of priority. These different classes form a **hierarchy of needs**, in which the lower-level needs have the first priority (Maslow, 1970). Maslow's hierarchy of needs is usually presented as a pyramid, as shown in ● FIGURE 8.5.

The lowest level of Maslow's hierarchy—the base of the pyramid—is our *physiological needs*. Maslow theorized that we seek to satisfy such basic needs as hunger, thirst, and need for warmth before we are motivated to satisfy any of our other needs. If our physiological needs are met, then our next level of concern is satisfying *safety* and *security needs*, such as having a safe place to live. At the next level, Maslow identified *belongingness* and *love needs*—the motivation to be with others, to be loved, and to be appreciated by others. At the next levels we would seek to successively satisfy our *esteem needs*, *cognitive needs*, and *aesthetic needs* (see Figure 8.5 for descriptions).

If we meet our aesthetic needs, we may seek to move to even higher levels, toward self-fulfillment. At these levels, motives include the need for **self-actualization**, or the motivation to reach our full potential, and the need for *transcendence*, the motivation to achieve spiritual fulfillment. Abraham Maslow had little hope that the average person would actually reach the self-fulfillment level. He believed that most people are unable to fulfill enough of the needs at the lower and middle levels of the pyramid, but that some of us do satisfy enough of our lower-level needs to at least try for self-actualization and transcendence.

intrinsic motivation motivation that comes from within the person

extrinsic motivation motivation that comes from outside the person

hierarchy of needs Maslow's theory that humans are motivated by different needs, some of which take precedence over others

self-actualization the need to reach our full potential as a human being

● **Maslow's Hierarchy of Needs**

Source: A. Maslow, "Hierarchy of Needs," from Motivation and Personality. *Copyright © 1954 by Harper and Row Publishers, Inc. Reprinted by permission of Pearson Education, Inc., Upper Saddle River, NJ.*

Transcendence

Self-actualization needs: to find self-fulfillment and realize one's potential

Aesthetic needs: symmetry, order, and beauty

Cognitive needs: to know, understand, and explore

Esteem needs: to achieve, be competent, and gain approval and recognition

Belongingness and love needs: to affiliate with others, be accepted, and belong

Safety needs: to feel secure and safe, out of danger

Physiological needs: hunger, thirst, and so forth

At first glance, Maslow's hierarchy seems to make sense. If you are starving, you will probably be less concerned with whether or not people love you and more concerned with finding food. Unfortunately, there is not much evidence to support Maslow's hierarchy of needs (Soper, Milford, & Rosenthal, 1995). In fact, we often seem to behave in ways that contradict Maslow's notion that we must fulfill lower needs before we can be concerned with higher-order needs. For instance, Marya's behavior did not fit Maslow's theory very well. She denied herself food, a physiological need, even as she pursued higher-level needs of belongingness and love. Likewise, Toren pursued belongingness and esteem needs as a Peace Corps volunteer even as his physiological and safety needs were imperiled by his drinking. Even if you argue that Marya's and Toren's behavior was abnormal and therefore should be expected to deviate from Maslow's hierarchy, there are many cases of "normal" people pursuing higher-level needs even though they have not yet met lower-level needs. Have you ever gone without sleep to pursue some other activity, such as studying for an exam? In that case, you were motivated by esteem needs even though your physiological needs had not been met! Likewise, the research also indicates that when we have satisfied our needs at a certain level of the hierarchy, we do not always move up to the next level and attempt to satisfy those needs (D. T. Hall & Nougaim, 1968).

Despite the lack of empirical support for Maslow's hierarchy, the theory is still used widely in the field of business—especially in the area of marketing (Soper et al., 1995). There, some have found ways to apply certain elements of Maslow's theory. For example, the idea that people are motivated by different needs may affect the way a manager deals with employees (Antonioni, 2003; Buhler, 2003) or the way that a firm markets a particular product. For example, after the September 11 attacks in 2001, some advertisers marketed products based on their *dependability*, hoping this quality would resonate with a public that was feeling insecure (DeJoseph, 2003).

According to Abraham Maslow, few of us will ever fulfill enough of our lower-level needs to actually reach the level of self-actualization. During her lifetime, Mother Teresa appeared to have reached the levels of self-actualization and transcendence. Similarly, singer Bono of the group U2 appears to be striving for self-actualization, spending much of his time engaged in humanitarian causes.

Andrew Gombert/Landov

Tim Graham/Getty Images

Another application of Maslow's hierarchy is in the evaluation of people under care in institutional settings (Timonen & O'Dwyer, 2009) or hospice (Zalenski & Raspa, 2006). In these settings, caregivers evaluate which of Maslow's needs are being met (or not met) for each client and adjust their caregiving in an attempt to move the client as high on the hierarchy as possible.

We have seen that there are many different ways to look at motivation. However, whether you view motivation as an instinct, a drive, a need, or an incentive, one thing is certain: Motivation is what catalyzes our behavior and moves us into action.

Let's REVIEW

In this section, we defined motivation and discussed some of the theoretical perspectives on motivation. For a quick check of your understanding, try answering the following questions at increasing levels of difficulty.

1. Which of the following approaches to motivation is most closely aligned with Darwin's theory of evolution?

   a. drive theory
   b. instinct theory
   c. incentive approaches
   d. Maslow's hierarchy of needs

2. Which of the following is the best example of intrinsic motivation?

   a. studying hard to earn an A on an exam
   b. staying late at work to earn overtime
   c. cleaning your house because you enjoy a tidy home
   d. dressing up for a job interview because you want to make a good impression

3. Which of the following approaches to motivation assumes that motivation can come from outside the person?

   a. instinct theory
   b. drive theory
   c. self-determination theory
   d. none of the above

ANSWERS 1. b; 2. c; 3. c

HUNGER AND THIRST: WHAT MAKES US EAT AND DRINK?

Eating is one of our most fundamental activities, basic to survival. To protect us from starvation, the motivation to eat remains strong even when we have competing or conflicting motivations. At the height of her anorexia, Marya Hornbacher still had motivation to eat. As hard as she tried to stamp out her desire to eat, she was unable to completely eliminate eating from her daily routine (Hornbacher, 1998). Because of her persistent motivation to eat, Marya survived, albeit just barely, despite her disorder. Marya's case shows us the primal strength of our motivation to eat. But, what is it in our bodies that initiates the hunger that motivates us to eat?

Hunger and Feedback in the Body

Hunger is a motive that helps us maintain homeostasis in the body, as we explained in the section on primary drives. The goal of hunger is to motivate us to eat when our bodies need fuel. As such, we should feel hungry when we are lacking fuel and nutrients, but we should *not* feel the motivation to eat when we have enough fuel and nutrients in our bodies. Recall that hunger works on a *negative feedback loop* system (see Figure 8.1). Like a thermostat, our brain turns our hunger on and off in order to maintain homeostasis in our bodies.

LEARNING OBJECTIVES

What Should You Know?

- Describe the feedback our bodies use to regulate hunger.
- Explain what is known about why some people become obese.
- Describe bulimia, anorexia, and binge eating disorder and explain their possible causes.
- Describe the feedback in the body that leads to thirst.

Homeostatic regulation of hunger explains why we seem to have a **set point**, or a weight that our body naturally attempts to maintain. Having a set point may be one reason why the vast majority of people who lose weight tend to regain it. When the body loses weight, the person's hunger increases, the person eats more, and the weight is regained. Although having a set point makes dieting very difficult, experiencing increased hunger when we fall below our set point also protects us from starvation. In environments where people struggle to find enough to eat, this extra motivation may make them work harder to obtain enough food to survive.

To motivate us to eat enough food to maintain homeostasis and thereby our set point, our brain must receive accurate and reliable feedback from the rest of our body. Where in the body does this feedback about the current status of our body's fuel supply originate?

Hunger Feedback From the Gut

If you ask the average person on the street why he feels hunger, he will probably say something about feeling hungry when his stomach is empty. One of the first places psychologists looked for clues to hunger was the stomach. The stomach and intestines form much of our *gastrointestinal tract* or *gut*, where food is digested and nutrients are absorbed into the bloodstream.

When our stomachs become empty, the walls of the stomach contract, and these contractions appear to stimulate hunger. Additionally, the stomach releases a hormone called **ghrelin** that sends strong hunger signals to the brainstem and hypothalamus (Suzuki, Simpson, Minnion, Shillito, & Bloom, 2010). Just as the stomach signals hunger, it may also play a role in telling our brains when it is time to stop eating. When we eat, our stomach's walls must distend to expand the volume of the stomach and allow room for the food we eat. When we have eaten enough and our stomachs are full, this distention of the stomach is one source of feedback that signals to our brains that it is time to stop eating (J. A. Deutsch, 1990; Xu, Sun, Lu, Tang, & Chen, 2008).

The amount of food in our stomach is only one source of feedback that regulates hunger. The quality of the food we eat is also important. After eating nutritious food, ghrelin levels fall while **peptide YY**, a hunger suppressant, is released by the gut. As ghrelin falls and peptide YY increases, hunger diminishes. Studies show that the balance of proteins, carbohydrates, fats, and other nutrients we eat directly affect post-meal levels of ghrelin and peptide YY. For example, a high-protein, low-carbohydrate meal promotes patterns of ghrelin and peptide YY release that are more conducive to weight loss than high-carbohydrate or high-fat meals do (El Khoury, El-Rassi, Azar, & Hwalla, 2010; Lomenick, Melguizo, Mitchell, Summar, & Anderson, 2009).

Another chemical that is important in hunger regulation is **cholecystokinin (CCK)**, a hormone released by the small intestines in response to eating. CCK appears to shut off hunger. A rat that is injected with CCK will drink less milk than a rat that has not been injected with CCK (Canova & Geary, 1991). Likewise, the presence of CCK in the bloodstream decreases human hunger (Holt, Brand, Soveny, & Hansky, 1992; Lassman et al., 2010). However, the level of hunger that we experience is due to more than just the amount of CCK in our bloodstream. How much food we have recently eaten also seems to influence hunger. In one experiment, participants ate either 100 or 500 grams of soup and were then given either CCK or a placebo substance. Afterward, they were allowed to eat a meal. The dependent variable in the study was how much the participants ate of the meal that followed the soup. The results showed that the amount eaten was a function of both the amount of soup the participants had eaten earlier and whether or not they had received the CCK. Participants who had eaten the larger amount of soup (500 grams) and received the CCK tended to eat less at the meal. But for participants who had eaten only 100 grams of soup, the CCK did not reduce the amount of food eaten at the meal. It appears that if we have not taken in enough food, CCK by itself may not be enough to stop our hunger and our eating (Muurahainen, Kisileff, Lachaussee, & Pi-Sunyer, 1991).

Hunger Feedback From the Endocrine System

The endocrine system also plays a role in regulating hunger. **Glucose** is the form of sugar that our bodies burn for energy, and **glycogen** is the form of starch that we store along with fatty

set point the theory that our body has a particular weight that it seeks to maintain

ghrelin a hunger-stimulating hormone produced by the stomach

peptide YY a hormone released in the gut that reduces hunger

cholecystokinin (CCK) a hormone released by the small intestines that plays a role in hunger regulation

glucose the form of sugar that the body burns as fuel

glycogen a starchy molecule that is produced from excess glucose in the body; it can be thought of as the body's stored energy reserves

acids. Made in the pancreas, the hormone *insulin* can increase feelings of hunger because insulin facilitates the movement of glucose from the blood into our cells, where it is metabolized (cf. M. I. Grossman & Stein, 1948). When glucose moves into the cells, blood levels of glucose drop, so we begin to dip into our glycogen reserves, and hunger is initiated. In this indirect way, insulin can produce feelings of hunger.

Foods that cause a rapid increase in blood sugar, called *high glycemic* foods, do not keep our hunger satisfied for very long. This occurs because the body pumps out a large amount of insulin to counteract the rapid increase in blood sugar, resulting in a subsequent drop in blood glucose levels, which causes hunger (Bornet, Jardy-Gennetier, Jacquet, & Stowell, 2007). So, if you are looking for a snack and want to feel full for longer, choose a low glycemic food (for example, an apple) over a high glycemic food (for example, sweetened apple sauce).

Hunger Feedback From the Liver

The liver is another source of feedback for hunger. Our liver has the capacity to help regulate hunger by monitoring the levels of glucose and glycogen in our body. When we have excess glucose in our body, we convert it into glycogen and then store it for future use. The liver determines our energy requirements by monitoring our levels of glucose and glycogen. If the liver detects that we are converting glucose into glycogen, indicating that we have too much fuel in our bodies, it will send signals to the brain to shut off hunger. On the other hand, if the liver notices that glycogen is being turned back into glucose, indicating that we are dipping into our energy reserves, it will send signals to the brain to initiate hunger.

Our bodies are able to dip into our reserves at the same time that the liver is signaling us to begin eating so we have a sufficient supply of glucose on hand. If we had to wait for our bodies to metabolize glucose from the new food we take in to feel hunger, we'd run out of glucose before we could digest our food.

Hunger Feedback From Fat Cells

Fat cells may provide yet another source of feedback for hunger regulation. Fat cells store our fuel reserves, swelling up as the liver converts excess glucose into glycogen and fatty acids. When we need to use our reserves, the fatty acids are mobilized out of the fat cells and converted back into glucose, which our bodies then burn as fuel. We need to have some reserves of energy stored in our fat cells, but we do not want to have too much fat in reserve. **So how does the body maintain just enough fat, without becoming obese?**

One possible answer lies in the fat cells themselves. Fat cells make and secrete a chemical called **leptin**. When fat cells release leptin into the bloodstream, it travels to the brain, where it is picked up by receptors near the brain's *ventricles* (the fluid-filled cavities in the brain) and in the *hypothalamus* (McGregor et al., 1996). Leptin is thought to inform the brain about the level of fat reserves available. For example, when the brain senses high leptin levels, this may indicate that a large number of fat cells are full of fat reserves. Therefore, we do not need to take in more fuel, and our hunger may be reduced. In support of this hypothesis, researchers have found that mice that are bred to be genetically fat will lose weight if they are given injections of leptin (Pelleymounter et al., 1995).

Unfortunately, we are a long way from understanding the exact role of leptin in motivating human eating. For example, researchers are currently investigating the role that the neurotransmitter *dopamine* plays in mediating leptin action in the brain (Benoit et al., 2003). Some studies suggest that leptin amplifies the effects of signals from CCK and other gut chemicals in the brain (Blevins & Baskin, 2010). Currently, there is no body of evidence to support the notion that losing weight is as simple as taking a few tablets of leptin.

Hunger Regulation in the Brain

The brain, of course, plays a significant role in our eating behavior. It receives and processes signals from the stomach about contractions and distention, from the gut about what we have eaten, from the liver about the glucose–glycogen balance, and from fat cells' secretion of leptin. The brain may also directly monitor our energy supplies. There appear to be specialized *glucoreceptors* in the hypothalamus that measure glucose levels in the bloodstream

leptin a hormone released by fat cells in the body that plays a role in hunger regulation

(Burdakov, Luckman, & Verkhratsky, 2005). If an animal is given a substance that makes its hypothalamus unresponsive to glucose, the animal goes on an eating binge (Miselis & Epstein, 1970). Disabling the hypothalamus's glucoreceptors tricks the brain into thinking that the body is critically low on fuel. The brain then signals extreme hunger to quickly replenish the body's glucose.

Further clues about the role of the hypothalamus in hunger regulation come from animal studies in which surgical lesions are made in the brain. By destroying part of the hypothalamus and observing the effect that this destruction has on behavior, psychologists have uncovered some clues about the role that the different parts of the hypothalamus play in both initiating and stopping eating.

Early studies on hunger control in the brain suggested that part of the hypothalamus, the **lateral hypothalamus**, or **LH**, is an "on switch" for hunger. When the LH is destroyed in a rat, the rat stops eating. As a result, the rat loses weight and eventually dies. Without the LH, the rat simply starves to death (Teitelbaum & Stellar, 1954), indicating that the LH turns *on* hunger. However, further study has shown that it is an oversimplification to interpret the LH as an "on switch" for hunger. When the LH is disabled, an animal does not lose its appetite forever. If a rat is force-fed for long enough after having had its LH destroyed, the rat will eventually get some of its appetite back. The rat's appetite will not be as great as it was prior to losing its LH, but the rat will eat, particularly very tasty foods (Teitelbaum & Epstein, 1962).

Another bit of evidence that suggests hunger is regulated outside the LH comes from studies using **neuropeptide Y**, the most powerful hunger stimulant known (Gibbs, 1996). When an animal is injected with neuropeptide Y, its strongest effect occurs outside the LH (Leibowitz, 1991). It stands to reason that if the LH were the primary "on switch" for hunger, then this powerful stimulant would have its strongest effect in the LH, but this does not appear to be the case, suggesting that there is an even more important "on switch" for hunger elsewhere in the brain.

Today, researchers recognize that many different neural circuits in the hypothalamus are involved in regulating hunger and that the hypothalamus communicates with the brainstem and higher cortical areas in turning on our hunger motive (Suzuki et al., 2010). We no longer believe in the concept of a single "on switch" for hunger in the brain.

The mechanisms through which the brain turns off our hunger are similarly complex. Early studies suggested that the **ventromedial hypothalamus**, or **VMH**, plays a role in creating a feeling of *satiety*, or lack of hunger. Rats that have had their VMH destroyed will begin to eat ravenously and will gain enormous amounts of weight (● FIGURE 8.6). If the VMH were the rat's only satiety center, or hunger "off switch," then destroying its VMH should make the rat eat continuously until it dies. But this doesn't happen. A rat without a VMH will eat a great deal of food and gain a great deal of weight, but after a certain amount of weight gain, its appetite will level off and the rat will then eat only enough food to maintain its new, higher weight. It's as if losing the VMH changes the rat's set point. In other words, the weight that the rat's body tries to maintain through homeostatic regulation has been shifted upward to a new, higher weight.

These and other studies indicate that satiety is not merely due to VMH action. In fact, it is now believed that the VMH may affect satiety only indirectly. When the VMH is destroyed, the autonomic nervous system's control over insulin release is disturbed (Bray, Inoue, & Nishizawa, 1981). The result is an increased release of insulin into the bloodstream, which produces great hunger, increased eating, and obesity (Valensi et al., 2003). Loss of the VMH doesn't remove a satiety center but, rather, causes disturbances in the nervous system that result in increased eating and fat storage.

We have learned that hunger regulation in the brain depends on the intricate communication among several different brain structures. There does not appear to be a single "on" or "off" switch for hunger (B. M. King, 2006). Rather, hunger seems to be regulated by a complex network of feedback to the brain from various sources in the body as well as by direct signaling in the brain (Suzuki et al., 2010).

We have presented some of the abundant evidence for physiological controls on our eating (see ● THE BIG PICTURE REVIEW). **But,** is our eat-

lateral hypothalamus (LH)   a region of the hypothalamus once thought to be the hunger center in the brain

neuropeptide Y   the most powerful hunger stimulant known

ventromedial hypothalamus (VMH)   a region of the hypothalamus that plays an indirect role in creating a feeling of satiety

© Richard Howard

FIGURE 8.6

● **A Mouse With a Lesion in the Ventromedial Hypothalamus (VMH)** This mouse had its ventromedial hypothalamus damaged. As a result, the mouse has eaten more than normal and gained a great deal of weight. But this mouse will not eat itself to death. Rather, it will now eat just enough to maintain this new, higher set-point weight.

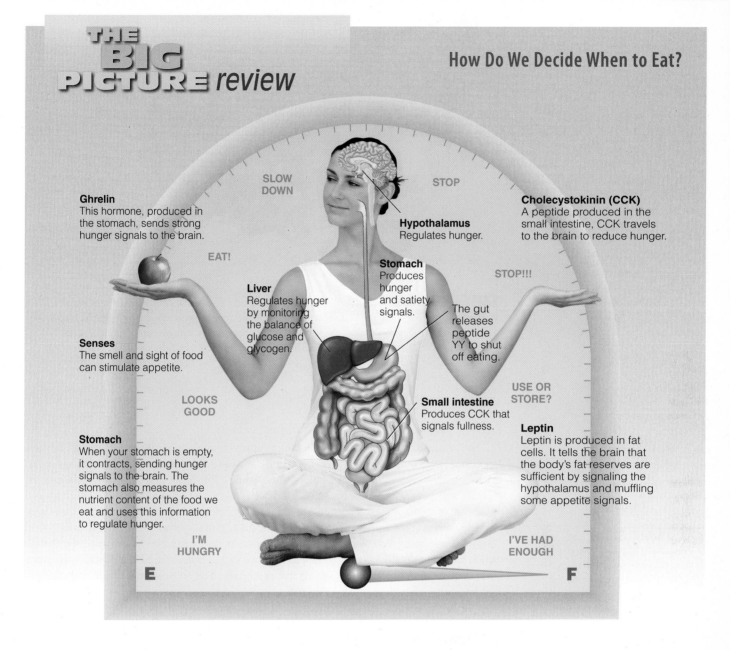

THE BIG PICTURE *review*

How Do We Decide When to Eat?

Ghrelin
This hormone, produced in the stomach, sends strong hunger signals to the brain.

Hypothalamus
Regulates hunger.

Cholecystokinin (CCK)
A peptide produced in the small intestine, CCK travels to the brain to reduce hunger.

Liver
Regulates hunger by monitoring the balance of glucose and glycogen.

Stomach
Produces hunger and satiety signals.

The gut releases peptide YY to shut off eating.

Senses
The smell and sight of food can stimulate appetite.

Small intestine
Produces CCK that signals fullness.

Leptin
Leptin is produced in fat cells. It tells the brain that the body's fat reserves are sufficient by signaling the hypothalamus and muffling some appetite signals.

Stomach
When your stomach is empty, it contracts, sending hunger signals to the brain. The stomach also measures the nutrient content of the food we eat and uses this information to regulate hunger.

SLOW DOWN · STOP · EAT! · STOP!!! · LOOKS GOOD · USE OR STORE? · I'M HUNGRY · I'VE HAD ENOUGH · E · F

ing motivated entirely by hunger and the drive to maintain homeostasis of our energy supplies? It is not. If it were, we would not see some of the behaviors we see in the real world. For example, Marya's bulimic and anorectic behaviors, hunger strikes for political reasons, and rampant obesity defy explanations of hunger as a simple physiological process of homeostatic regulation. Our eating behavior can apparently be modified by other sources of feedback that have little to do with maintaining homeostasis.

Culture and Consumerism: Do You Have to Be Hungry to Eat?

Have you ever eaten until you felt as if you were going to burst? Have you ever eaten a big bag of popcorn at the movies just minutes after you finished a very large meal? If so, your behavior has shown that eating is often more than just satisfying biological needs. Recently, psychologists have begun to discriminate between *intuitive eating*, or eating that is motivated by physiological hunger and satiety feedback, and eating that is motivated by emotional and situational cues that have little connection to energy requirements (Avalos & Tylka, 2006). For example, the smell of popping popcorn at a theater can make you want to eat popcorn, even shortly after you've had a full meal. Or you may be tempted to indulge in a treat after a stressful day at work when you see an ad for pizza or ice cream on TV.

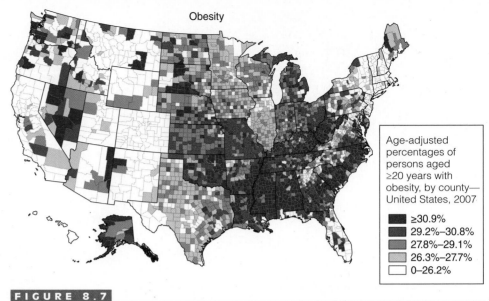

Obesity

Age-adjusted percentages of persons aged ≥20 years with obesity, by county— United States, 2007

■ ≥30.9%
■ 29.2%–30.8%
■ 27.8%–29.1%
■ 26.3%–27.7%
□ 0–26.2%

FIGURE 8.7

● **The Obesity Epidemic in the United States** In the United States, almost one third of all adults are obese. This map shows the percentage of obese people county by county throughout the United States. The highest concentrations of obese people (shown in black) seem to be in the southern states. The reasons for this epidemic are the subject of much debate, but it is likely that several causes are at work—including genetic, lifestyle, and diet factors.

obese having a body mass index of 30 or over

FIGURE 8.8

● **Calculating Your BMI** This chart shows how to calculate your own body mass index (BMI). To do so, you will need a calculator, your weight in pounds, and your height measured in inches.

Body mass index (BMI) = (weight in pounds × 703) ÷ (height in inches)²	
Multiply your weight in pounds by 703 _____ × 703 = _____	Example 155 lbs × 703 = 108,965
Multiply your height in inches by itself (squared) _____² = _____	68 × 68 [inches] = 4,624
Divide the first number by the second: $$\frac{\text{_____}}{\text{Weight} \times 703} \div \frac{\text{_____}}{\text{Height squared}} = \frac{\text{_____}}{\text{BMI}}$$	$$\frac{108,965}{4,624} = 23.6 \text{ BMI}$$

BMI	Weight status
below 18.5	Underweight
18.5–24.9	Normal
25.0–29.9	Overweight
30.0 and above	Obese

Such eating occurs for reasons other than supplying fuel for our bodies. In many cultures, food and feasting are an integral part of cultural customs. This is especially true in the United States, where our holiday celebrations—including Christmas, Thanksgiving, Halloween, Hanukkah, Easter, Passover, Kwanzaa, and New Year's Eve—are all associated with special foods in large quantities. The same holds true for more personal celebrations—birthdays, weddings, reunions, and even funerals. Americans and many other peoples around the world use food and eating to celebrate. This connection between joy and food can lead to eating when we do not really need to. Whereas intuitive eating is associated with lower body mass in college women (Tylka, 2006), eating that is motivated by emotion and situational cues can lead to a major health concern—obesity.

Obesity: Nature and Nurture, Again

Americans are obsessed with weight. Collectively we spend millions and millions of dollars each year on diets, exercise equipment, diet pills, and gym memberships, yet roughly two thirds of all Americans are considered *overweight* and almost a third are **obese** (● FIGURE 8.7). Sadly, among children ages 9–19, 16% are considered overweight (R. M. Kaplan, 2007). One way to define *overweight* and *obesity* is to look at the *body mass index* (*BMI*; ● FIGURE 8.8). A BMI of 25 or higher indicates overweight, and a BMI of 30 or more indicates obesity (Centers for Disease Control, 2010a). BMIs over 30 are correlated with higher incidences of many diseases, including type II diabetes, heart disease, and some cancers (Kopelman, 2000). In light of these problems, the government-funded Medicare program now considers obesity a disease ("Medicare to Fund Obesity Treatment," 2004). **Why then, despite our great concern over the issues of weight and health, are so many of us losing the battle of the bulge?**

Behavioral Factors in Obesity

Poor diet is one reason that some people gain weight. Simply put, consuming more calories than you can burn leads to weight gain. But given the negative feedback loop systems we've described, why would one eat too much? One culprit is the high-fat diet common in many Western cultures. A typical fast-food lunch can contain a whole day's worth of fat and calories. Coupled with a lack of exercise, this diet leads to weight gain in many people. Another factor comes from the way our society views food. As we mentioned earlier, we tend to eat for reasons that have little to do with maintaining homeostasis. Many of us use food as a means of dealing with emotions, such as eating when we are lonely, sad, or nervous (Konttinen, Männistö, Sarlio-Lähteenkorva, Silventoinen, & Haukkala, 2010). This *emotional eating* may be one of the factors involved in weight gain for some people, but emotional distress has not been clearly shown to be a general cause of obesity. Studies examining the correlation between obesity and anxiety or depression have yielded mixed results (for example, Gadalla, 2009; McElroy et al., 2004; Papelbaum, Moreira, Gaya, Preissler, & Coutinho, 2010). However, the prejudices that overweight people experience can lead some of them to suffer low self-esteem (Friedman & Brownell, 1996).

Culture and Weight-Based Prejudice

Curiously, prejudice toward obese people is a cultural phenomenon. Americans abhor fat. The media negatively depicts overweight people (Ata & Thompson, 2010). Overweight Americans are often ridiculed, socially isolated, and even discriminated against in the workplace. Shockingly, studies have shown that even health care professionals who specialize in the treatment of obesity sometimes demonstrate negative attitudes toward overweight people. In one study, health care professionals, including psychologists, were found to have used words such as *lazy* and *stupid* to refer to overweight persons (M. Schwartz, O'Neal Chambliss, Brownell, Blair, & Billington, 2003). Similarly, researcher Kristen Davis-Coelho and her colleagues found that some members of the American Psychological Association displayed a negative bias in their perceptions of overweight versus normal weight women. This tendency to perceive overweight people less favorably was most evident in younger and less experienced mental health care professionals (Davis-Coelho, Waltz, & Davis-Coelho, 2000).

Prejudice against obese people seems to also extend to children. In fact, studies have shown that children's prejudice against other overweight children has grown significantly since the 1960s. This trend is very unfortunate because children who are teased by their peers for being overweight are at higher risk for having a negative self-image, fewer friends, and increased likelihood of suicide (see DeAngelis, 2004).

This negative attitude about obesity is not worldwide, however. For example, one of the authors once had an overweight friend from Iceland. After living in the United States for a few years, the friend observed that although there were fewer obese people in her native country, she was treated more normally there than she was in the United States, where so many people are overweight. In yet other cultures, such as the African country of Mauritania, overweight women are valued for their beauty—so much so that young girls are often force-fed to make them obese. Because of health concerns, we do not advocate intentionally creating obesity in anyone. However, such cultural differences suggest that just as our perceptions of beauty and weight vary cross-culturally, so do our levels of prejudice against people who are overweight.

Keep this situation in mind when you read about stereotypes and prejudices in Chapter 11. Although some prejudices may be tolerated in a culture, they still exact a human toll on their victims. A little later in this chapter, we will see that our cultural fear of fat may also play a role in the development of certain eating disorders.

The Battle of the Bulge: Why Is Dieting So Hard?

Because of health concerns and social pressure, many people spend a good deal of their time dieting. When following a weight loss diet, the idea is to decrease your caloric intake so that the body will burn up its reserves of fat. Unfortunately, depriving yourself of food is also one reason that most diets fail. When we reduce our caloric intake to the point that we begin to lose weight, our bodies try to counteract the diet. Recall that our motivation to eat is designed to keep us from starving. When we begin to draw on our fat reserves while dieting, our body

Which of these meals would you rather eat? Unhealthy eating habits contribute to obesity and health problems in many people.

takes steps to avoid "starvation." At first, we may feel increased hunger as our body tries to avoid burning up fat reserves by urging us to eat. Later, our **basal metabolic rate**—the rate at which we burn energy in our bodies when resting—may drop as the body tries to conserve energy, again in order to avoid burning up its fat reserves. The drop in metabolic rate may offset the reduction in calories on the diet, with the result being little or no weight loss. Even more discouraging is the fact that our metabolism may drop even lower with each successive diet we go on (Brownell, 1988). This consequence means that the more you diet, the harder it may become to lose weight. Our bodies appear inclined to fight against weight loss and to maintain our typical, or set point, weight.

There are psychological factors in dieting, too. Depriving yourself of food often leads to bingeing on food. It appears that when a dieter strays from his diet program, he feels as if he might as well *really* go off the diet (Spencer & Fremouw, 1979). In one study, researchers surveyed shoppers to determine if they had recently lost weight. On the basis of the surveys, the investigators classified the shoppers as those who had deliberately lost weight on a diet, those who passively lost weight without dieting, and controls who had not recently lost weight. Then, the researchers analyzed what the shoppers had purchased by looking at their receipts. Compared to those who had passively lost weight and the control participants, the deliberate dieters were found to have purchased more meat, dairy, and sweets and fewer fruits and vegetables. These results are consistent with the notion that depriving oneself leads to greater motivation to eat later (Paradis & Cabanac, 2008).

People who restrain their eating are most at risk for this bingeing when they are emotionally aroused. Emotional distress can make a dieter slip off his or her diet (Ruderman, 1985), but so can positive emotions (Cools, Schotte, & McNally, 1992). Whether one is happy or sad, it seems that dieting makes eating binges more likely. **So how does one succeed in losing weight?** The recipe for dieting success involves two factors. First, you have to make permanent changes in your eating behavior. "Dieting" is forever, and it is probably a mistake to think of losing weight as dieting. Some suggest that we should focus on teaching people to become more intuitive in their eating—to eat when hungry, but not eat when our bodies do not require energy (Outland, 2010). When hungry, it's generally better to focus on eating healthy, balanced meals that are lower in calories than on how many pounds you can lose in a week. The best way to lose weight is to do it *slowly*. People don't typically gain 15 pounds in a week, so why should we expect to lose weight that fast?

The second aspect of successful weight loss is exercise. Cultural changes that reduce physical activity, such as driving to work or school, sedentary jobs, television, and computer games, are also major contributing factors to the growing obesity epidemic. Any weight loss plan that does not include exercise is likely to fail. Exercise not only burns extra calories and causes weight loss, it also increases your metabolism. Recall that when we diet, our body adjusts its metabolic rate downward. You can help keep your metabolism higher by exercising, which will lead to a more permanent weight loss as your set point moves to a lower weight. So next time you see an advertisement for some miracle diet that allows you to eat all you want without exercising and still promises to safely take off 10 pounds a week, save your money and possibly your health. There are no quick fixes when it comes to shedding pounds. Even people who undergo *gastric bypass* surgery to drastically reduce the size of their stomach must adhere to a strict diet regimen and make lifestyle changes to achieve and sustain long-term weight loss (L. H. Powell, Calvin, & Calvin, 2007). See the ● TECHNOLOGY AND BEHAVIOR feature for a new way to incorporate exercise into your life.

Biological Factors in Obesity: Are Some of Us Born to Be Heavy?

Given that so many people have a difficult time achieving permanent weight loss, some scientists have questioned whether obesity is always a simple matter of eating too much and exercising too little. Are some people actually predisposed to being overweight? Yes, indeed.

basal metabolic rate the rate at which we burn energy in our bodies when resting

TECHNOLOGY and BEHAVIOR

CAN EXERGAMING HELP US WIN THE BATTLE OF THE BULGE?

These days it seems as though we rely more and more on technology to help us lead our everyday lives and entertain us during leisure time. Where would we be without our remote controls, cell phones, Internet connections, video games, GPS systems, and so on? Some have criticized our use of some of these devices, particularly computer games, as contributing to an increasingly sedentary lifestyle that has consequently played a role in the obesity epidemic. After all, sitting at the computer does not burn a lot of calories.

Although some studies have failed to support the idea that overall frequency of gaming is related to body mass index (Ballard, Gray, Reilly, & Noggle, 2009; Wack & Tantleff-Dunn, 2009), there may still be some cause for concern. For example, some researchers have found that the amount of time one spends gaming in a single sitting is positively correlated with body mass index (BMI), and it is also negatively correlated with the amount of exercise one gets (Ballard et al., 2009). Remember that exercise is important for good health even if you are not overweight.

In light of the obesity epidemic, many manufacturers are trying to find ways to use technology to improve our health. Many weight loss companies have online tools to help clients manage their diet and exercise regimens. Most large restaurant chains have their products' nutritional information posted online to aid in meal planning. There are health management programs that you can buy for handheld computer devices. And, one of the most exciting inventions has been the Nintendo Wii and the rise of a new type of computer gaming—exergaming.

Exergaming uses interactive devices like the Wii to combine the fun of video gaming with physical exercise. Can tools like this get more exercise back into our lives and help us win the battle of the bulge? To date, there has not been adequate research to address this question (Daley, 2009). However, preliminary research has suggested that people do enjoy exergaming.

Even people who have identified themselves as being sedentary tend to have positive attitudes toward playing these types of electronic exercise games (M. J. Klein & Simmers, 2009).

Results like these are encouraging because liking an activity can provide intrinsic motivation for performing that activity. And, although playing games on the Wii does not burn as many calories as performing the real-life versions of the sport (Daley, 2009), exergaming does burn more calories than sitting still. More studies are needed to determine if long-term exergaming can result in significant health gains and for which people (young, old, male, female, and so on) any potential gains seem most likely. For now, at least we have a new way to entertain ourselves—one that we can hope will also prove to be good for us.

Fabrice Lerouge/PhotoLibrary

Exercise is essential to weight loss because building lean muscle mass helps increase your metabolic rate and lower your set point. One interesting new development is the rise of a new type of gaming, called exergaming. Exergaming uses devices like the Nintendo Wii to involve the players in bodily movements that approximate those executed when engaging in the real-life activity. Time will tell if this new technology is helpful in getting more exercise back into the lives of sedentary people—especially children.

ELI ELI/PhotoLibrary

Genetics play a role in obesity for some overweight people. So-called thrifty genes that lead to low metabolic rates or efficient digestive systems may cause some overweight people to gain weight even though they eat and exercise at the same levels as their thin counterparts.

Some obese people suffer from biological conditions that predispose them to gaining extra weight. One biological reason for obesity is having a *low metabolic rate.* People differ with respect to how much energy is required to run their bodies. Some people have high metabolic rates and require large amounts of fuel; others have low metabolic rates and require relatively little energy to survive. A person with a very low metabolic rate who eats the same number of calories and exercises just as much as a person with a normal metabolic rate will still gain more weight than the normal person will. Over time, this weight gain could lead to obesity (Friedman, 1990).

Ironically, having a low metabolic rate isn't always a disadvantage. In fact, across our evolutionary history, a low metabolic rate was probably a decided advantage. Our ancestors had to hunt and forage for enough food to eat. Those early humans who required less energy to survive probably had an easier time finding enough food to meet their needs. Therefore, those with low metabolic rates probably survived better and procreated more than their counterparts with high metabolic rates. This advantage could have led to some members of our modern society having "thrifty genes" that conserve energy, but it may have also led to obesity in a world in which hunting and gathering high-calorie foods is as simple as a trip to the grocery store or fast-food drive-through. So far, scientists have not found direct genetic evidence to support the thrifty gene hypothesis (Prentice, 2009), but some interesting observations can be found when examining what happens to cultures that adopt a high-fat, American-style diet.

For example, ethnic Hawaiians have the shortest life span of any ethnic group on the Hawaiian Islands. As a group, ethnic Hawaiians show high rates of high blood pressure, diabetes, obesity, and cholesterol. One major culprit in these health problems appears to be the fat-heavy American diet they have taken on. When ethnic Hawaiians return to their native diet of sweet potatoes, taro root, breadfruit, fish, chicken, and vegetables, their health significantly improves. In one study, after only 21 days of eating their native diet instead of the typical American diet, Hawaiians showed significant drops in blood pressure, weight, and cholesterol (Shintani, Hughes, Beckham, & O'Connor, 1991). Perhaps many native Hawaiians are biologically unsuited to eat the American diet. The same may be true of many other obese Americans.

Another biological factor is how our body extracts nutrients from food. When we eat, we lose some of the nutritive content of the food because of the inefficiency of our digestive system. As a result, some of the nutrients will be expelled as waste. Some obese people may have digestive systems that can extract and use more of the nutritive content in the food they eat. This increased efficiency can cause an obese person to gain weight from eating the same diet as someone who is not obese because her body retains more nutrients—and therefore more calories—in foods (Tsai & Coyle, 2009).

Another possibility is that obese people may automatically convert some of the nutrients they eat into fat (Friedman, 1990; Tsai & Coyle, 2009). This conversion would leave fewer calories immediately available to be burned as fuel, and the person would be motivated to eat more. A portion of any extra food eaten would also be automatically converted into fat. This vicious cycle would ensure that the person continued to eat more food than necessary and that too much of that food would be stored as fat. As you can see, for some people, gaining excess weight is not a simple matter of self-control or poor habits.

Obesity is a problem for many people, exposing them to social ridicule and discrimination as well as health risks. Despite our awareness of these problems, obesity has risen in America over the past several decades—especially among children. Although the trend toward obesity in the United States appears to be slowing down (Flegal, Carroll, Ogden, & Curtin, 2010), the overall number of obese people in the United States is a major health concern. Obesity is not, however, the only problem that involves eating. Our chapter case study of Marya Hornbacher illustrates the devastating toll that eating disorders, or mental illnesses that are associated with eating, can take on a person's health and life. Why would anyone be motivated to binge, purge, or starve the way that Marya did? We'll examine the answer to this question as we take a closer look at eating disorders.

Eating Disorders: Bulimia Nervosa, Anorexia Nervosa, and Binge Eating Disorder

Marya's eating disorder formally began while she was still in grade school, but the seeds of Marya's problems were there long before her disorder emerged. From early childhood, Marya had an unhealthy preoccupation with her body, its size, and its shape, as well as an unhealthy feeling of not having any control over her troubled home life. These factors are part of the unhealthy mix that seems to give rise to eating disorders.

Bulimia Nervosa

Marya's eating disorders began with the onset of *bulimia*. As we described at the start of this chapter, bulimia is an eating disorder that is characterized by alternating bouts of *bingeing* and inappropriate compensatory behaviors such as *purging*, fasting, or excessive exercise. People who are bulimic gorge on large quantities of food, sometimes as much as 20,000 calories at a time; then they either go on a very rigid starvation diet or purge the food from their system (Schlesier-Stropp, 1984). Purging is achieved by self-induced vomiting or the abuse of laxatives to help move food quickly through the digestive tract before the body can absorb its nutrients.

One of the authors once met a girl with bulimia who spent an entire semester's tuition on a 2-week cycle of bingeing and purging. She would go out at night and travel from one drive-through restaurant to another buying large quantities of tacos, hamburgers, and other fast food. She would take the food back to her dorm room, where she would quickly eat all of it and then purge it through vomiting. Luckily, this 2-week binge probably saved her life. When she was unable to explain the missing tuition money, her parents insisted she enter a treatment program. After intense treatment, she regained some measure of normalcy in her eating behavior.

Like this woman, the typical victim of bulimia is a young female who is of average to slightly-above-average weight. Approximately 1.4–1.9% of American women suffer from bulimia (see Wade, 2007), and the bulimic behavior is especially likely among female college students (A. S. Cain, Epler, Steinley, & Sher, 2010). Bulimia can be a socially isolating disorder. A college student who spends her evenings gathering up large quantities of food and bingeing and purging usually does so alone. In Marya's memoir *Wasted*, she speaks frequently of the steps she took to hide her disorders and of how isolated she felt from everyone around her (Hornbacher, 1998). Aside from its social toll, bulimia can sometimes be fatal. The frequent purging of food can lead to dehydration and electrolyte imbalances, which can lead to serious cardiac problems and other problems like the hole in Marya's esophagus.

Given the devastating toll that bulimia can take on one's life, what would motivate anyone to engage in bulimic behavior? At this time, no one can say for sure why people become bulimic. However, many people with bulimia are troubled by low self-esteem and depression (Perez, Joiner, & Lewisohn, 2004). Those with bulimia tend to be perfectionists who have negative views of their bodies. They tend to have grown up in families that were troubled in some way (Bardone, Vohs, Abramson, Heatherton, & Joiner, 2000). All these things were true of Marya. In her case, it appeared that her bulimic behavior was in some way a response to the chaos of her home life. By rigidly controlling her body, she felt a tiny bit more in control of her life. Unfortunately, Marya could never control her body well enough to feel actually happy, and her bulimic behavior turned into full-blown *anorexia nervosa*.

Anorexia Nervosa

As we discussed in the opening case study, *anorexia nervosa* is an eating disorder that is characterized by self-starvation, intense fear of gaining weight, and a distorted body image. Estimates of the percentage of the female population in the United States with anorexia range

Anorexia nervosa is a devastating disorder in which people are motivated to drastically restrict their eating while simultaneously increasing their level of exercise. The result is extreme weight loss, but this weight loss is never enough to please the anorectic. Anorectics like this woman still look in the mirror and feel that they need to lose more weight.

Wirelmage/Getty Images

● **Too Thin?** Many models and actresses are very thin. The steady parade of these women in the media may have contributed to the increase in eating disorders that began in the 1980s and 1990s.

from 0.12% to 2.0% (Wade, 2007). Unlike people suffering from bulimia, those with anorexia can be easily spotted by their very low body weight. An anorectic can weigh even less than the 52 pounds that Marya weighed during the height of her illness, and 5–10% of anorectics die as a result of the disorder (G. T. Wilson, Grilo, & Vitousek, 2007). The most bizarre aspect of anorexia is that even at a life-threateningly low weight, a person with anorexia can look in the mirror and *see* herself as fat (J. E. Grant & Phillips, 2004). Even when others easily recognized Marya's obvious anorexia, she was convinced that she still looked as "fat" as she always did—even though she had never been what most people would call fat (Hornbacher, 1998).

Most individuals with anorexia are females from middle- and upper-class families in industrialized countries. Anorexia is rarely found in men, and it is less common in cultures that hold a fuller-figured woman up as the standard of beauty. It appears that one of the contributing factors in the development of anorexia is societal pressure on young women to be very thin—unrealistically thin. If you pick up just about any American fashion magazine or watch just about any American television show, you will find that most of the females depicted are thin—very thin. Sometimes they actually look anorectic (● FIGURE 8.9). Many television stars and models wear size 0 or 2 clothes, whereas many American women wear size 10 or 12 (or larger). If you do the math, you'll see that many American women fall short of the standard of beauty depicted in the media. What do you do if you are a young girl who aspires to look like the actors you see on TV, and a healthy diet and exercise do not allow you to meet your goals? Some girls take drastic steps to reach their "ideal" body image, and anorexia may be the result.

Researchers have found wide cultural variations in women's perceptions of their ideal body image. For example, in one study that compared U.S., Israeli, Spanish, and Brazilian women, the American women were found to be the least satisfied with their bodies (Joliot, 2001). And, a whopping 74.5% of American women report that concerns about their body shape and weight had interfered with their happiness (Reba-Harrelson et al., 2009). This finding is significant because in cultures that portray beautiful women as being somewhat plumper—for example, in Jamaica (D. E. Smith & Cogswell, 1994) or even in American culture prior to the 1970s—anorexia is uncommon. Pre-1970s, women who were considered beautiful were considerably heavier than those who are considered beautiful today. For example, Marilyn Monroe was considered to be the standard of beauty in the 1950s and early 1960s, and before her, Mae West—these two women were not the ultrathin models of today (● FIGURE 8.10). Obviously, most American girls do *not* become anorectic despite being bombarded with images of very thin women. **Why then do some become anorectic whereas others do not?**

At one time, anorexia was thought to be correlated with ethnicity. Because the thin standard of female beauty is most frequently portrayed as a White woman in American culture, many predicted that White women would suffer greater pressure to be unrealistically thin and therefore suffer from higher rates of anorexia. Indeed, studies conducted in the 1980s seemed to confirm this hypothesis. However, this correlation seems to have changed. A recent study conducted in the United States did not find White women to have more symptoms and predictors of eating disorders than Black, Hispanic, and Asian women. The authors concluded that ethnic women have caught up to White women in this domain and are equally susceptible to risk factors for eating disorders such as dissatisfaction with one's body (H. Shaw, Ramirez, Trost, Randall, & Stice, 2004; see also Wade, 2007).

Other characteristics that do seem to be correlated with anorexia include perfectionism (Davies, Liao, Campbell, & Tchanturia, 2009) and faulty thinking about food (for example, thinking one should never eat carbohydrates; Steinhausen & Vollrath, 1993), as well as certain biochemical abnormalities (Ferguson & Pigott, 2000). Additionally, many people suffering from eating disorders also suffer from *personality disorders*—characteristic, maladaptive ways of dealing with the world (see Chapter 14; Marañon, Echeburúa, & Grijalvo, 2004). We do not yet know if these are *causal* factors or merely factors that *correlate* with eating disorders. Another piece of the puzzle may be genetics (Keel & Klump, 2003).

Some have argued that genes for anorexia evolved to allow our ancestors to survive famine by helping them to ignore food while migrating to better environments (Guisinger, 2003).

FIGURE 8.10

● **How the American Standard of Female Beauty Has Changed Over Time** Standards of beauty in the United States have changed over time, and they also differ across cultures. In the 1930s, Mae West was considered an icon of feminine beauty. In the 1950s and early 1960s, it was Marilyn Monroe. Today, thin women like Angelina Jolie are the standard of beauty.

In cultures like Jamaica, Fiji, and Mexico, the standard of beauty leans toward heavier women. Cultures such as these have far lower rates of eating disorders than the United States.

Indeed, there is evidence to support the idea of a genetic basis for anorexia. If one identical twin is anorectic, the other twin's chances of becoming anorectic are drastically increased. However, having a fraternal twin with anorexia only modestly increases one's chances of developing anorexia (Holland, Sicotte, & Treasure, 1988). This pattern of results supports the existence of a genetic predisposition to anorexia. At present, it appears that both bulimia and anorexia may result from a complex mix of cultural factors, personality characteristics, environmental issues, and biological factors.

Binge Eating Disorder

Although bulimia and anorexia nervosa are both incapacitating illnesses, they are not the most common eating disorders (see Stice, Telch, & Rizvi, 2000; Wade, 2007). **Binge eating disorder** is a mental health disorder characterized by recurrent episodes of binge eating, such as those seen in bulimia nervosa, but without regular use of the inappropriate compensatory measures that those with bulimia employ to avoid weight gain. Because binge eaters do not compensate for their overeating, they may be overweight. As we've already seen, obesity and being overweight are at epidemic levels in the United States. Just how many obese and overweight people suffer from binge eating disorder is not precisely known at this time. However, one estimate suggests that up to 30% of people who seek professional treatment for weight control may meet the criteria for this disorder (M. J. Brody, Walsh, & Devlin, 1994; see ● TABLE 8.1).

binge eating disorder a mental health disorder characterized by recurrent episodes of binge eating, as in bulimia nervosa, but without regular use of compensatory measures to avoid weight gain

TABLE 8.1

● **A Summary of the Diagnostic Criteria for Bulimia Nervosa, Anorexia Nervosa, and Binge Eating Disorder**

BULIMIA NERVOSA

- Recurrent episodes of bingeing in which the person eats unusually large amounts of food. The person must have the sense of being unable to control his or her eating during these binges.
- Recurrent inappropriate compensatory behavior aimed at preventing weight gain (e.g., purging; enemas; misuse of laxatives, diuretics, or other medicines; fasting; excessive exercise).
- Bingeing and inappropriate compensatory behaviors must both occur, on average, twice a week for a period of at least 3 months.
- Self-evaluation is unduly influenced by one's body shape or weight.
- These behaviors do not occur exclusively during episodes of anorexia nervosa.

ANOREXIA NERVOSA

- Refusal to maintain a minimally normal body weight (usually defined as 85% of the normal weight for one's height).
- Intense fear of gaining weight, even though underweight.
- A disturbed perception of one's body weight or shape, denial of the seriousness of one's low weight, or undue influence of one's body weight or shape on his or her self-evaluation.
- In females, having missed at least three consecutive menstrual periods.

BINGE EATING DISORDER

- Recurrent episodes of binge eating (as defined for bulimia nervosa) without regularly engaging in inappropriate compensatory behaviors to avoid weight gain.

Thirst

As we have seen, the hunger motive drives us to take in food to meet our nutritional requirements. Yet for most of us a typical meal will include both food and a beverage. Does this mean that hunger motivates us to eat *and* drink? It appears not. Maintaining homeostasis of our fluid level is made possible by another motive—thirst, which is in some ways a more important motivation than hunger. If deprived of food and water, we would die from dehydration before we starved to death.

To function well, our bodies must have enough fluid. Fluid is critical because it allows ions to travel into and out of cells. As we saw in Chapter 2, ions such as potassium and sodium are absolutely essential to the functioning of the nervous system. If we were to become dehydrated, these ions would not be able to flow across the cell membranes during the firing of neural impulses, which could mean nervous system collapse and death. In fact, you can live for quite some time without food, but you would not be able to live 1 week without water. Even those with anorexia like Marya, who may go for days without eating, must take in fluids regularly.

Given that water is so crucial to survival, how do you know when you are thirsty? Many people would say that thirst is a feeling of having a parched throat or a dry mouth. Certainly, these characteristics are indicative of thirst, but just as the stomach plays only a partial role in the sensation of hunger, the mouth and throat play only a partial role in thirst. Even people who have had their larynx (part of the throat containing the vocal cords) removed still feel thirst and still drink (Miyaoka, Sawada, Sakaguchi, & Shingai, 1987).

To understand thirst, you must first understand where the body stores fluids. Fluid that is stored inside cells is called **intracellular fluid**. Fluid that is stored in the spaces between cells is called **extracellular fluid**. To maintain optimum fluid levels, the brain's hypothalamus monitors the levels of intracellular and extracellular fluid in and around its neurons. If we eat a salty meal, the sodium concentration in our extracellular fluid increases, which causes intracellular fluid from inside the hypothalamic neurons to cross the cell membrane into the extracellular space. This action dilutes, or lowers, the sodium content of the extracellular fluid, but it also decreases the pressure inside the hypothalamic neurons. When this transition begins, and the hypothalamic neurons begin to lose their intracellular fluids, the hypothalamus signals thirst to motivate fluid intake (Memmler, Cohen, & Wood, 1992). Another mechanism of thirst comes from cells that monitor the body's extracellular fluid levels outside the brain.

© Neal Preston/Corbis

Dehydration results in the loss of extracellular fluid in our bodies. This loss of fluid causes a drop in blood pressure that signals the brain to initiate thirst. This athlete will likely feel tremendous thirst, which will motivate her to replace the fluids she has lost through sweating.

intracellular fluid the fluid found inside the cells of the body and that is used to regulate thirst

extracellular fluid the fluid found in the spaces between the cells of the body and that is used to regulate thirst

As we sweat, exhale, and urinate, we lose fluid from our extracellular fluid. As we become dehydrated, this loss of fluid causes a drop in blood volume and a corresponding drop in blood pressure. Specialized *pressure receptors* in the heart, kidneys, and blood vessels detect this slight drop in blood pressure, and they send signals to the brain that will eventually initiate thirst. These pressure receptors also signal the start of measures to conserve the water that is already inside our body (Pinel, 1997).

Let's REVIEW

In this section, we discussed eating disorders, obesity, and healthy motivation to eat and drink. For a quick check of your understanding, try answering the following questions at increasing levels of difficulty.

1. Which of the following is the hormone that the small intestines release to shut off hunger?

a. insulin
b. CCK

c. leptin
d. serotonin

2. A friend of yours was recently in a car accident and suffered damage to his ventromedial hypothalamus. What effect would you expect this damage to have on your friend's behavior?

a. He will likely stop eating.
b. He will likely die.
c. He will likely gain a great deal of weight.

d. He will likely gain a great deal of weight, but then he will lose the pounds and return to his normal weight.

3. You just ran a 10-mile marathon. This exercise would most likely result in which of the following?

a. loss of intracellular fluid in the hypothalamus, causing thirst
b. loss of extracellular fluid in the hypothalamus, causing thirst
c. a decrease in CCK levels in the bloodstream, causing hunger
d. a decrease in ghrelin in the bloodstream, causing hunger

ANSWERS 1. b; 2. c; 3. a

LEARNING
OBJECTIVE

What Should You Know?

• Describe the role that motivation may play in substance abuse behavior.

WHY ARE SOME PEOPLE MOTIVATED TO ABUSE DRUGS?

For the most part, our motives help us survive. Motives such as hunger and thirst are essential to life because they help maintain homeostasis in our bodies. But not all motives are helpful. Obviously, in the case of anorexia and bulimia the motivation to stop eating or to purge what you have eaten is detrimental to the body's health and well-being. But there are other disorders in which our motives are destructive—for example, substance abuse. Why would someone like Toren Volkmann, who had such a bright future, become so dependent on alcohol that he could no longer function?

You may recall from Chapter 4 that caffeine, nicotine, and alcohol are the three most widely used psychoactive substances. Many people struggle with substance abuse problems such as drug addiction, alcoholism, smoking, inhalant use, and even caffeine addiction. In fact, substance abuse disorders are some of the most common mental disorders in the general population. Roughly 40% of college students drink heavily at least once every 2 weeks (O'Leary Tevyaw, Borsari, Colby, & Monti, 2007). Like Toren, some of these students will develop alcoholism. Males have close to a 35% chance of being diagnosed with a substance disorder in their lifetime, and females have nearly a 20% chance (R. C. Kessler et al., 1994). In addition, 8% of people age 12 and older have engaged in illicit drug use in the past month (Centers for Disease Control, 2009b). These are *high* numbers.

© JGI/Jamie Grill/Blend Images/Corbis

Substance abuse is a form of destructive motivation that causes problems in many people's lives. Understanding people's motivation to begin abusing substances is a complicated matter, but it is clear that tolerance and physical dependence can motivate them to continue abusing substances once they have started.

● **An Opponent-Process View of Drug Taking** Notice how the body tries to counteract the effects of the depressant by increasing its baseline level of arousal.

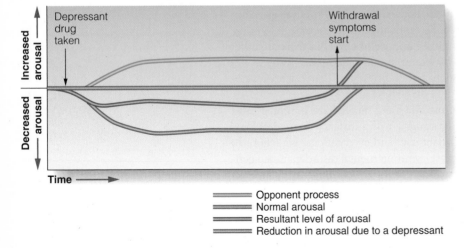

What makes substance abuse such a common problem? It is hard to say what motivates people to abuse substances in the first place, but many sociological and psychological factors have been shown to correlate with drug use. These include exposure to drugs, low self-esteem, boredom, and depression. One perspective on drug taking is that of *operant conditioning* (Chapter 5). In operant conditioning terms, drugs can be seen as both *positive* and *negative reinforcers*. Drugs can be positive reinforcers by producing feelings of pleasure and euphoria. You'll recall from Chapter 4 that users often report pleasurable feelings as part of a drug-induced altered state of consciousness. So the drugs may have initial appeal for some because they produce these pleasurable feelings, however temporary. The pleasurable effects of alcohol were one of the reasons Toren persisted in drinking; he found drinking fun—for a while.

On the flip side, some people take drugs so that they don't feel bad. For people who are in physical or psychological pain, drugs can act as negative reinforcers, removing their discomfort. When you think about it, this is the purpose behind many *legal* drugs. We take aspirin to stop the pain of a headache. Some substance abusers take drugs to lessen or stop the pain of low self-esteem, bad relationships, or depression.

Although it is difficult to come up with a theoretical explanation for taking drugs in the first place, it is easier to explain why someone would continue to take them. In fact, one theory of motivation, called **opponent-process theory**, provides an elegant explanation of continued drug use (R. L. Solomon, 1980; Koob & Le Moal, 2008). (Note that this theory is not the same opponent-process theory covered in Chapter 3 related to color vision.) Opponent-process theory proposes that when a person takes a drug repeatedly, the body attempts to counteract the effects of the drug by engaging in an *opponent process*. For example, with a stimulant drug, the opponent process will *decrease* the user's physiological arousal to counteract the drug's arousal effects. If the drug is a depressant, then the opponent process will *increase* the user's physiological arousal to counteract the drug's effects. The problem is that the body's opponent process is slow to start, and the effect lasts longer than the drug does. As you can see in ● FIGURE 8.11, the opponent process is still going strong after the effects of the drug have worn off. Without the drug to balance out the opponent process, the user starts to feel unpleasant **withdrawal** symptoms that are opposite to the drug's effects. In other words, coming down from depressants will make the person feel anxious, and coming down from stimulants will make people feel depressed.

Because withdrawal symptoms are uncomfortable and aversive, the user will be *motivated* to continue taking the drug because it has become a negative reinforcer that can remove the withdrawal symptoms. Removal of the withdrawal symptoms is reinforcing—so operant conditioning ensures that the user will be more likely to take drugs the next time withdrawal symptoms occur—which will be shortly after the drug begins to wear off. Do you recognize the vicious circle of **physical dependence** here? The opponent-process mechanism in the body ensures that withdrawing from the drug will produce aversive symptoms, which is just another way of saying that the opponent process creates a physical dependence on the drug.

To make matters worse, opponent processes also cause drug **tolerance**, or the phenomenon of needing more and more of a drug to get the same "high" after repeated drug use. Tolerance develops as the user continues to take the drug in order to avoid withdrawal. The opponent process keeps adjusting the body's state to offset the drug, and as time goes on, the opponent process gets stronger and stronger. In other words, the body tries more intently to counteract the drug. The net effect is that it takes larger and larger doses of the drug to achieve the effect that the user once got from the initial dose. ● FIGURE 8.12 shows the strengthening of the opponent process as the user develops a tolerance to a depressant. If this user were to stop taking the depressant, the jitters would set in. This is exactly what happened to Toren—shakiness, anxiety, insomnia, and an inability to concentrate whenever he tried to stop drinking.

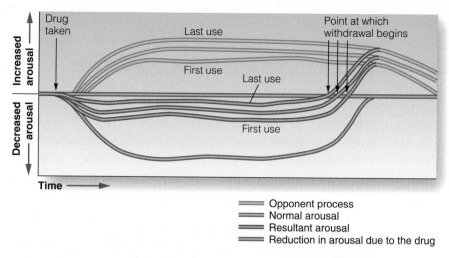

FIGURE 8.12

● **An Opponent-Process View of Physical Dependence on a Drug** Notice how successive doses of the depressant force the body to successively increase its baseline level of arousal. This is how physical dependence on a drug develops.

Not everyone develops physical dependence and tolerance at exactly the same rate, however. For instance, human and animal studies suggest that females may develop physical dependence on certain drugs—including alcohol and cocaine—more quickly than males (Carroll, Morgan, Lynch, Campbell, & Dess, 2002; Lynch, Roth, & Carroll, 2002). Recent research has also suggested that people with a family history of alcoholism may be at higher risk for developing alcoholism because they more easily develop a tolerance to alcohol (Chapter 4). In fact, they begin to develop tolerance to alcohol within a few hours of starting to drink (Morzorati, Ramchandani, Flury, Li, & O'Connor, 2002). This early tolerance may encourage them to drink larger and larger amounts of alcohol, resulting in physical dependence.

A family history of heavy drinking was one of Toren Volkmann's risk factors for alcoholism. Another was the age at which he began drinking—before age 16. Some data suggest that adolescents are at higher risk of becoming dependent on alcohol than adults are. Alcohol dependence is highest among people ages 18–29 (Hasin & Grant, 2004), and having symptoms of alcohol dependence in high school strongly predicts alcohol dependence in one's college years (Grekin & Sher, 2006).

There is growing evidence that heavy drinking during adolescence can damage the brain as well. One study found that adolescents who drank heavily had smaller than average hippocampal regions, which are critical to the ability to form new memories (Chapter 6; Bellis et al., 2000). Other researchers used fMRI technology to scan the brains of young women and found that those who had abused alcohol since adolescence exhibited less brain function during a memory task than did women who had no history of alcohol abuse (Tapert et al., 2001). Take a look at these dramatic scans in ● WHAT'S HAPPENING IN YOUR BRAIN?

In addition to incurring possible brain damage, people who become severely alcoholic develop tolerance that can be so severe that withdrawal from alcohol is physically dangerous. Longtime alcoholics may have to drink large amounts of alcohol in order to feel drunk, and they may need to drink just to feel *normal*. Because alcohol is a central nervous system (CNS) depressant, the opponent process for alcohol causes arousal of the CNS. An alcoholic who tries to quit drinking "cold turkey" risks being in a state of having a *hyperaroused* CNS because the opponent process will still be in effect—with or without more alcohol. This can result in hallucinations, tremors, seizures—and even death. Withdrawal from long-term alcohol abuse should be done under the supervision of a physician who can control the withdrawal so as to avoid these problems. During treatment, Toren was given tranquilizing drugs to help him avoid the dangers of withdrawal from alcohol. Given the dangers of substance abuse and the vicious cycle of physical dependence that can trap users, it is best to avoid abusing drugs in the first place.

opponent-process theory a theory of motivation that states that the body will counteract the effects of ingested drugs by adjusting its arousal level in a direction opposite that of the drug's effect

withdrawal an unpleasant physiological state that results when one stops taking a drug to which he or she has built up a tolerance

physical dependence a condition that occurs when a person is motivated to continue taking a drug because to stop taking the drug would result in painful withdrawal symptoms

tolerance a condition in which after repeated use, more of a drug is needed to achieve the same effect

WHAT'S HAPPENING
IN YOUR BRAIN?

ALCOHOL ABUSE AND THE ADOLESCENT BRAIN

There is growing evidence that heavy drinking during adolescence can damage the brain. These fMRI images compare brain activity in two 20-year-old women while they engaged in tasks such as reading a map, doing math problems, and working puzzles. The woman on the left is healthy. The woman on the right has been alcohol dependent since adolescence. Notice that the alcohol-dependent woman has much less brain activity (shown in pink, red, and yellow) compared to the healthy woman. Researchers believe that this lack of brain activity may indicate brain damage.

Source: Tapert et al., 2001.

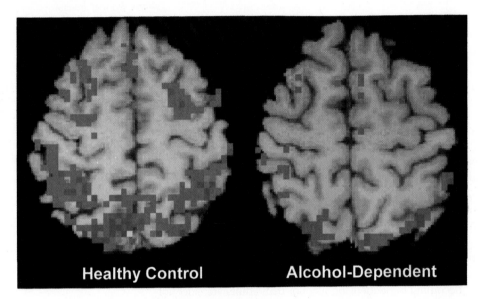

Healthy Control   Alcohol-Dependent

Note differences in back of brain

Let's
REVIEW
In this section, we discussed the destructive side of motivation in looking at why some people are motivated to abuse drugs and other substances. For a quick check of your understanding, try answering the following questions at increasing levels of difficulty.

1. _____ ensure(s) that drug users will need to take higher and higher doses of their preferred drug to experience the feeling of their first high.

   a. Tolerance
   b. Instincts
   c. Secondary drives
   d. Both b and c

2. Craig is trying to stop drinking coffee. For the last year, Craig has consumed a full pot of strong coffee on a daily basis, but today he has not had any coffee at all. How would you expect Craig to be feeling?

   a. anxious and jittery
   b. sluggish and tired
   c. alert and refreshed
   d. none of the above

3. Opponent-process theory can explain all of the following, except _____.

   a. why people begin taking drugs
   b. why people continue to take drugs
   c. why drug addictions are hard to kick
   d. why withdrawal symptoms differ for different drugs

ANSWERS 1. a; 2. b; 3. a

WHAT IS EMOTION?

What is an emotion? If you ask people that question, you will get a variety of answers. Most will probably say that emotions are *feelings*. Some will give examples, such as *happiness, sadness,* or *anger*, but few will be able to produce a good definition of what an emotion actually is. Even psychologists have had trouble defining what is meant by an emotion. One definition is that an **emotion** is a complex reaction to some internal or external event that involves physiological reactions, behavioral reactions, facial expressions, cognition, and affective responses (cf. Lazarus, 1991). For example, let's imagine that you are walking through the woods and you hear some rustling up ahead. You look up to see a large bear in your path. This event would likely cause an emotional reaction of *fear*. Your experience of fear would have several aspects to it:

Physiological reactions: Your heart rate would increase, your respiration would increase, your pupils would dilate, and your muscles would tense.
Behavioral reactions: You might freeze in your tracks. You might run (an unwise choice in this situation). You might yell at the bear.
Facial expressions: Fear would show on your face. If someone were to observe you at this moment, they would likely recognize that you were afraid.
Cognition: You might think about the TV show you saw on bears last week and what the experts said that you should do in this situation. You might wonder if this is a female bear with cubs just out of sight in the brush. You might think about the danger that faces you should the bear charge.
Affective responses: You would have some subjective reaction to this situation. For example, "I am scared," "I am terrified," or—if you are an animal lover—"I'm thrilled!"

As you can see, emotions are complex. Perhaps that is why psychologists have had a difficult time defining exactly what an emotion is. Another confusing aspect of emotion is that emotion is very similar to motivation. In fact, emotions can produce motivation (e.g., Zaalberg, Manstead, & Fischer, 2004). In our previous example, your fear of the bear might motivate you to run or to yell at the bear. **So what separates emotions from motivation? What makes** *fear* **different from** *hunger*? One unique element is the **affective component of emotion**, the subjective experience of what you are *feeling* that fills your consciousness during the emotion. When you are scared, you *know* that you are scared because you *feel* the affective state of fear. This affective quality of emotion allows us to clearly know when we are feeling an emotion.

Emotions can also be distinguished from motivation in that they are usually (but not always) sparked by things outside our bodies. For instance, when we see a tragic movie, we may feel sad. Or when we see a baby, we may feel happy. Motivation, on the other hand, often comes from some internal source—hunger may be initiated by low blood sugar or thirst by low blood pressure. Motives tend to be sparked by a specific need or goal, but emotions can be elicited by many stimuli. For instance, many things can make us happy, but only a few conditions will lead to hunger.

Although psychologists have struggled with the concept of emotion, several notable theories of emotion have been set out over the years. Let's take a look at some of them now.

The James-Lange Theory of Emotion

American psychologist William James and Danish physiologist Carl Lange each proposed one of the earliest theories of emotion at approximately the same point in history (James, 1884). Their theory, now called the **James-Lange theory** of emotion, states that emotion *is equal to* the pattern of physiological arousal that the person experiences during an emotion. In short, emotion is a physiological response to some stimulus. In our example of meeting the bear in the woods, from the James-Lange point of view, the emotion you feel is the pattern of physical and physiological reactions you have as you see the bear. The increased heart rate, the increased respiration, the running—these constitute the emotion of fear that you would experience in this situation.

How would you feel if you came across a bear while hiking in the woods?

emotion a complex reaction to some internal or external event that involves physiological reactions, behavioral reactions, facial expressions, cognition, and affective responses

affective component of emotion the subjective experience of what you are feeling during the emotion

James-Lange theory a theory of emotion that defines an emotion as a unique pattern of physiological arousal

Shane Keyser/MCT/Landov

According to the James-Lange theory of emotion, this woman is experiencing anger because her body has reacted with a characteristic pattern of physiological changes in response to this event.

Walter Cannon's Criticisms of the James-Lange Theory

The James-Lange view of emotion has had many critics. One important critic was Walter Cannon, who noted that for the James-Lange theory to adequately explain emotion there would have to be a different bodily response for *each* emotion we experience. Because emotion equals a physiological and bodily response in the James-Lange view, the only way to discriminate among emotions would be if there were different physical reactions for each emotion. Walter Cannon doubted that this was true and, in fact, offered three good reasons to doubt the James-Lange view of emotion (W. B. Cannon, 1927). His first criticism, which we just mentioned, is that the physiological experience of emotion does not appear to vary from emotion to emotion to the degree that would be necessary to distinguish one emotion from another based purely on our physiological reaction. For example, anger doesn't feel very different from terror—both involve increased heart rate, muscle tension, and so forth.

Second, Cannon argued that the physiological, bodily aspect of emotion sometimes follows our subjective experience of the emotion. For example, we may know that we are afraid *before* we feel our heart pounding and our muscles tensing. In the James-Lange view, there can be no emotion before there is a physiological response.

Cannon's third criticism was that artificially created physiological responses do not give rise to emotions. For example, drinking a lot of coffee may increase your physiological arousal, but it does not cause you to experience fear, excitement, love, or any other emotion. If emotion were nothing more than a physiological response, it would stand to reason that artificially caused physiological responses would also cause emotional responses.

In light of these criticisms, Cannon proposed that emotion does not originate in the body; rather, it originates in the brain. According to Cannon, when you see a bear in the woods, your fear is not due to the increased heart rate and rapid breathing you experience. Instead, when you see the bear, your brain causes you to feel fear. You may even be aware that you are afraid *before* you become aware of your rapidly beating heart and your panting breath. Cannon's explanation of emotion was later extended by a man named Philip Bard, and today this theory is called the **Cannon-Bard theory** of emotion.

New Support for the James-Lange Theory

Of Cannon's three criticisms, by far the most compelling criticism was the first one—that physiological responses are too similar to allow us to adequately discriminate among the many emotions we feel. For many years this criticism was seen as a fatal blow to the James-Lange theory. Things change, however, and in the 1990s, some new evidence gave the James-Lange theory new life. By the 1990s, psychologists had new tools for studying bodily reactions. In addition to precisely measuring heart rate, researchers could now measure minute changes in skin temperature, in brain function, and in the electrical conductivity of the skin that indicate small changes in the moisture of the skin. With these measurement techniques, it was now possible to examine the physiological response that accompanies emotions in greater detail than was possible in Walter Cannon's time.

Using measures such as these, researchers have been able to show that some emotions do indeed involve differing patterns of autonomic nervous system arousal (for a review, see Kreibig, 2010) and other bodily reactions. In one clever study (Levenson, Ekman, & Friesen, 1990), participants were asked to make facial expressions for the emotions of fear, anger, happiness, disgust, sadness, and surprise and to hold these expressions for 10 seconds. While the participants held these expressions, their physiological reactions were measured very precisely. Just as the James-Lange theory predicts, there were slight but noticeable differences in heart rate, skin temperature, and other physiological reactions for the different emotions. Although all the emotions caused changes in heart rate and skin temperature, it was the *degree* of change that separated the emotions from one another (● Figure 8.13).

Cannon-Bard theory a theory of emotion that states that emotions originate in the brain, not the body

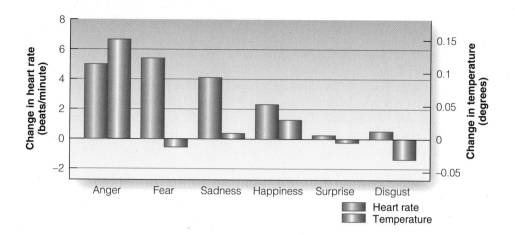

FIGURE 8.13
● **Physiological Changes for Six Different Emotions** Note the varying degrees of change for these different emotions. *Source: Levenson, Ekman, & Friesen, 1990.*

These results indicate that there may be some merit to the James-Lange approach, but they do not necessarily support the entire theory. These results do not address Walter Cannon's other two criticisms—that physiological reactions sometimes follow our awareness of emotions and that artificially created arousal does not seem to directly cause the experience of emotion. Even if patterns of physiological arousal do help us discriminate among emotions, there still may be other factors involved in the experience of emotion. One of these factors could be feedback from our faces.

The Facial Feedback Hypothesis

You may have noticed that in the experiment we just described, the researchers induced the different emotions in an unusual way (Levenson et al., 1990): having the participants make and hold facial expressions of the desired emotion for 10 seconds. In other words, they induced the emotional state through the facial expression of the emotion. How does this work? **Doesn't the emotion come** *before* **the facial expression?** Well, maybe not entirely, according to the **facial feedback hypothesis** (D. N. McIntosh, 1996). This theory proposes that our experience of an emotion is affected by the feedback our brain gets from our facial muscles. Thus, smiling can influence us to feel happy, and frowning can influence us to feel bad. In one study, participants were asked to smell and rate a series of odors while either smiling or frowning. Consistent with the facial feedback hypothesis, they rated the smells more positively when they were smiling and less positively when they were frowning (Kraut, 1982). Based on this and other studies (e.g., Soussignan, 2002; Davis, Senghas, & Ochsner, 2009), it appears as if the configuration of your facial muscles does influence your mood. But why would this be true?

One possibility is that the configuration of your facial muscles affects the blood flow to your brain, which in turn affects the temperature of your brain. Certain configurations, such as frowns, may change blood flow to the brain, increasing the temperature of the brain. Other facial configurations, such as smiles, may result in blood flow changes that decrease the brain's temperature. Brain temperature, in turn, may affect the release of certain neurotransmitters that affect mood. As wild as this idea sounds, there is some evidence to support it. In one study, a group of participants was asked to read a story that contained words that forced them to repeatedly hold their mouths in a position that was similar to smiling (Zajonc, Murphy, & Inglehart, 1989). A different group of participants was asked to read a story that did not contain such words. Both stories were of similar emotional tone. As the participants read the stories, the temperature of their forehead was measured, providing a crude measure of their brain's internal temperature.

After they had read the stories, the participants were asked to rate the stories for pleasantness. As the facial feedback hypothesis would predict, those who read the story that forced them to use their facial

facial feedback hypothesis a theory of emotion that states that our emotional state is affected by the feedback our brain gets from facial muscles

According to the facial feedback hypothesis, smiling sends signals to the brain that actually make your mood more positive. Next time you are feeling upset, give it a try. Put a smile on your face—maybe it will make you feel better.

muscles in a manner consistent with a smile rated their story more positively than the other participants rated theirs. Furthermore, when researchers looked at the participants' forehead temperatures, those who read the story that forced them to approximate a smile had lower forehead temperatures.

Although researchers have been able to correlate blood flow patterns in the brain with positive and negative emotional states (Hoshi et al., 2009), there are no other published accounts of researchers who have replicated the link between emotion and brain temperature using more precise measurements of temperature. Until we have corroborating evidence, we cannot be certain that facial feedback is indeed mediated by blood flow and brain temperature.

The Schachter-Singer Two-Factor Theory of Emotion

So far, the theories of emotion we have looked at see emotion in physiological terms. Certainly physiological responses and facial expressions are part of an emotional experience—but what about cognition? **Do our thoughts play a role in our emotions?** Some theorists, including psychologists Stanley Schachter and Jerome Singer, believe that they do. Their **two-factor theory** of emotion states that emotions are a product of both physiological arousal and cognitive interpretations of this arousal. Schachter and Singer agreed with Walter Cannon that we do not have a separate pattern of physiological arousal for each emotion we experience; rather, when we experience an emotion, we experience a diffuse and general physiological arousal. We then use the situational context to help us cognitively interpret the meaning of this arousal. This cognitive interpretation leads to the experience of an emotion. Going back to our example of the bear in the woods, when we see the bear, we become aroused and our heart begins to beat faster. Next, we interpret why we are reacting this way, given the context of the situation. Because we are faced with a potentially dangerous wild animal, our arousal is likely to be interpreted as stemming from fear. Therefore, we label our emotional experience as one of fear.

In one of their studies, Schachter and Singer (1962) gave participants an injection of epinephrine, a stimulant that causes increased heart rate, respiration, and nervousness. Some of the participants were accurately informed about what to expect from the injection. Others were not. Instead, they were told that the injection was a harmless shot that would produce no symptoms. After receiving the injection, all the participants were asked to wait in a room with another participant. But the "participants" in the waiting room were *confederates*, or actors playing a part in the experiment. In one condition, the confederate acted angry. He complained, stomped his feet, and eventually left the waiting room in a huff. In the other condition, the confederate acted happy. He appeared joyful, tossed paper airplanes, and generally acted a bit silly.

The dependent variable in the experiment was the mood of the study participants *after* their time in the waiting room with the confederate. Schachter and Singer reasoned that the mood of the informed participants would not be influenced by the mood of the confederate. Because the informed participants would interpret their arousal as being due to the drug and not due to some emotional state, there was no reason for their mood to be influenced by the confederate. On the other hand, Schachter and Singer predicted that the mood of the uninformed participants would indeed be influenced by the mood of the confederate. Because they did not have a ready (cognitive) explanation for their arousal, the uninformed participants would look to the situation to help them interpret their reactions. If the confederate was happy, the participants would interpret their arousal as part of a positive emotional state. If the confederate was angry, then the participants would interpret their arousal as part of a negative emotional state.

The results confirmed Schachter and Singer's predictions. The mood of the informed participants was not influenced by the confederate's mood, but the confederate did influence the mood of the uninformed participants. The uninformed participants who waited with the angry confederate reported feeling angrier than did the informed participants. The uninformed participants who waited with the happy confederate reported feeling happier than did the informed participants. It appears that the uninformed participants used the situation to help them figure out their own emotions.

two-factor theory a theory of emotion that states that emotions result when we cognitively interpret our physiological reactions in light of the situation

Although Schachter and Singer produced experimental evidence to support their theory, the two-factor theory has not stood the test of time well. Decades of research on the two-factor theory show that there is little reason to believe that emotions require physiological arousal or that emotions can come from labeling unexplained physiological arousal (Reisenzein, 1983). Despite doubts about the two-factor theory, Schachter and Singer's contribution to the study of emotion is significant. They introduced the idea that cognition plays an important role in emotion, and many theorists recognize that thoughts are part of the emotional experience.

Lazarus's Cognitive-Mediational Theory of Emotion

According to Richard Lazarus (1995, 2006), cognition is the most important part of emotion. Lazarus's **cognitive-mediational theory** of emotion states that our *cognitive appraisal* of a situation determines what emotion we will feel in the situation. Going back to the bear example, if you see a bear in the woods one day after having seen a show on TV about some hikers who were killed by a bear, you would likely feel a lot of fear. On the other hand, you might feel less fear on encountering the bear if your only knowledge of bears came from a TV show about a boy and his pet bear. According to cognitive-mediational theory, your appraisal of the situation determines your specific emotion.

For example, when Marya went home for Thanksgiving dinner, she viewed the family meal as a threatening situation in which she would gain weight. As a result of this appraisal, she felt anxiety where many of us would feel joy. Differing appraisals are one reason different people react with different emotions in the same situation. Cognitive-mediational theory also suggests that the best way to cope with our emotions is by controlling how we perceive situations in life. For instance, a student who perceives that she received a poor grade because the teacher doesn't like her will likely get angry. A calmer student may simply see the grade as a challenge to work harder and not get mad. Teaching yourself to appraise events like this as opportunities and not as threats may help you become a happier, more successful student.

Although it is clear that cognitive appraisals do influence our emotional states (e.g., van-Reekum, Johnstone, Etter, Wehrle, & Scherer, 2004), not everyone agrees that cognition is an essential part of emotion. Robert Zajonc has argued that we can have an emotional reaction to something that is completely independent of our thoughts. In one study, Zajonc (1980) showed English-speaking participants Japanese ideographs (the symbols of the Japanese language). Each ideograph was presented either frequently or infrequently. Later, the participants were asked to rate their preference for ideographs. Despite having no knowledge about the meaning of the ideographs, the participants showed a clear preference for some of them. They preferred the ideographs that they had seen more frequently to the ones they had seen infrequently. Zajonc called this phenomenon of preferring things to which we have had the most exposure the **mere exposure effect**. He reasoned that because the participants did not know the meaning of the ideographs, their emotional reactions to them could not have been influenced by cognition. Rather, their emotions were purely physiological. We will examine the mere exposure effect again in Chapter 11 when we look at its implications for romantic attraction.

Communicating Emotions: Culture, Gender, and Facial Expressions

Imagine that you have traveled to a place where you do not speak the local language at all. You do not recognize any of the words being spoken all around you. In fact, you can't even tell how many words are being spoken in each sentence, because they all seem to run together as the people speak. You are all alone in this place, and you have to survive somehow. How will you communicate with these people? Perhaps you will try to use pantomime to communicate with someone, but how will you choose *which* person? How will you tell if a particular person is likely to react kindly to your attempts at communication? One way would be to read the emotional expression on the person's face. Does she look happy? Does he look angry? This could be a crucial source of information for you. But what about the cultural differences in this situation? Can we read the emotional expressions of someone from an unfamiliar culture? This is another question psychologists have tried to answer.

cognitive-mediational theory a theory of emotion that states that our cognitive appraisal of a situation determines what emotion we will feel in the situation

mere exposure effect the idea that the more one is exposed to something, the more one grows to like it

TRY THIS DEMONSTRATION

Look at the pictures in ● FIGURE 8.14. Can you identify the emotions that these people are feeling? These pictures represent the facial expressions of what psychologists call *basic emotions*. **Basic emotions** are defined as emotions that all humans are thought to have, regardless of cultural background. The idea behind basic emotions is that the capacity for these emotions is genetically programmed in us as a result of evolution. Many psychologists believe that anger, happiness, fear, and sadness are basic emotions, but there is disagreement about what other emotions might be basic. Some add disgust, shame, interest, surprise, and anxiety to the list (A. J. Turner & Ortony, 1992). But others do not. Furthermore, some believe that basic emotions can blend together to give us more complex emotions like guilt, pride, and disappointment (Plutchik, 1984). So, were you able to accurately identify the facial expressions? From left to right they are: *happiness, anger, sadness, surprise, disgust,* and *fear.*

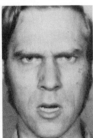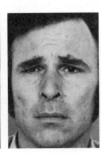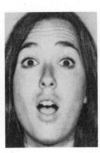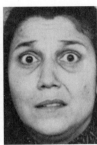

FIGURE 8.14

● **Can You Identify These Emotions?** *Source: Ekman & Friesen, 1984.*

Paul Ekman (1973) showed pictures like these to people from Argentina, Brazil, Chile, Japan, and the United States, and then asked participants to identify the emotions being expressed. He found that people were pretty much able to identify the emotions regardless of their culture, although some emotions appeared to be more universal than others. Happiness appeared to be the easiest emotion to identify. People from the different cultures disagreed the most when identifying fear and anger. Other studies have shown that fear and surprise are also easily confused, but curiously women are better at discriminating between these emotions. This may be due to women's greater concern for relating to others and an increased tendency for women to look at other people's faces (McAndrew, 1986).

In addition to facial expression, we also seem to be able to discern the basic emotions from the sounds that we make. Recently, Ekman and colleagues found that Western and Namibian participants were both good at detecting basic emotions in each other's nonverbal vocalizations, such as laughs and screams that transcend language barriers (Sauter, Eisner, Ekman, & Scott, 2010). Further support for the notion of basic emotion comes from researchers using neuroimaging technologies to show that specific and distinct patterns of neural activity in the brain are linked to the basic emotions (Duan, Dai, Gong, & Chen, 2010; Vytal & Hamann, 2009).

Yet, researchers have found that people from different cultures have different **display rules** governing when it is and isn't appropriate to show certain emotions. For example, in the United States, it would be considered inappropriate for a man to display fear or sadness

basic emotions a proposed set of innate emotions that are common to all humans and from which other, higher-order emotions may derive

display rules rules that guide the appropriate expression of emotion within a specific culture

during a business meeting. And, if an Arab man is insulted, he must respond with a display of extreme anger to avoid dishonor (see Heine, 2008). Furthermore, people from different cultures may have slightly different ways of displaying basic emotions through facial expressions—somewhat similar to how speakers of the same language can have different *accents* or *dialects*. In one study, participants from Quebec and Gabon were asked to pose facial expressions for several different emotions. Their expressions were carefully coded by the experimenters, who found that Quebecois and Gabonese participants used slightly different facial muscles to express the same emotions. Furthermore, these *dialects* of facial expressions seemed to account for the errors that participants made in judging each other's facial expressions. As you might expect, participants tended to make more errors when judging the facial expressions from the other culture that had the strongest facial *accents* because they were the more idiosyncratic (Elfenbein, Beaupre, Levesque, & Hess, 2007).

Does the fact that some emotions result in characteristic physiological patterns and translate fairly well across cultures guarantee that these emotions are *basic* emotions? Perhaps not. Some cultures list "basic" emotions that may be recognizable to people from other cultures but would not be considered by those people to be basic emotions in their culture. Hindus list *peace, wonder, amusement,* and *heroism* as basic emotions (Hejmadi, Davidson, & Rozin, 2000). Americans may be able to feel these emotions and recognize them in others, but may not consider them to be basic emotions. For reasons like these, some people have begun to question whether basic emotions truly exist (Ortony & Turner, 1990).

Whether or not we humans have basic emotions, an even more open question is this: If we do have basic emotions, what are they? Regardless of whether basic emotions exist, emotions are powerful tools of communication. A smile can signal friendliness to many people—regardless of background or culture.

Let's REVIEW

In this section, we defined emotion and discussed some theories of emotion. We also looked at how humans tend to show emotions through facial expressions. For a quick check of your understanding, try answering the following questions at increasing levels of difficulty.

1. Which of the following is not typically thought of as a basic emotion?

a. fear   c. pride

b. sadness   d. happiness

2. Mohammed and Betty are each stuck in a traffic jam. Mohammed remains calm, but Betty begins to get very angry. Which theory of emotion best explains Mohammed's and Betty's different emotions in this situation?

a. cognitive-mediational theory   c. facial feedback theory

b. two-factor theory   d. James-Lange theory

3. The fact that people, regardless of cultural heritage, show distinct patterns of neurological and physiological activation in the body when experiencing happiness and sadness supports which theory of emotion?

a. James-Lange theory   c. cognitive-mediational theory

b. Ekman's theory of basic emotion   d. a & b

ANSWERS 1. c; 2. a; 3. d

STUDYING the CHAPTER

KEY TERMS

motive (305)
bulimia nervosa (306)
anorexia nervosa (306)
instinct (308)
drive reduction theory (308)
drive (308)
primary drive (308)
homeostasis (308)
negative feedback loop (308)
secondary drive (309)
arousal theory (310)
sensation seeker (311)
self-determination theory
   (312)

incentive (312)
intrinsic motivation (313)
extrinsic motivation (313)
hierarchy of needs (313)
self-actualization (313)
set point (316)
ghrelin (316)
peptide YY (316)
cholecystokinin (CCK) (316)
glucose (316)
glycogen (316)
leptin (317)
lateral hypothalamus (LH)
   (318)

neuropeptide Y (318)
ventromedial hypothalamus
   (VMH) (318)
obese (320)
basal metabolic rate (322)
binge eating disorder (327)
intracellular fluid (328)
extracellular fluid (328)
opponent-process theory
   (330)
withdrawal (330)
physical dependence (330)
tolerance (330)
emotion (333)

affective component of emotion (333)
James-Lange theory (333)
Cannon-Bard theory (334)
facial feedback hypothesis
   (335)
two-factor theory (336)
cognitive-mediational theory
   (337)
mere exposure effect (337)
basic emotions (338)
display rules (338)

LEARNING CHALLENGE

Now that you have studied the chapter, assess your comprehension of the material by answering the following questions. Then use the key at the end to determine if your understanding is at the basic, intermediate, or advanced level. For a more comprehensive assessment of your learning, please see your student study guide and your Psychology CourseMate (www.cengagebrain.com).

TEST YOURSELF!

1. Which of the following researchers viewed motives as instincts?

   a. Paul Ekman
   b. William James
   c. Henry Murray
   d. Marvin Zuckerman

2. If Janel were given a drug that blocks MAO action in her brain, what effect would this likely have on her?

   a. She would experience more negative emotions.
   b. She would lose some of her motivation for everyday activities.
   c. She would become more motivated to engage in exciting activities.
   d. She would become hungrier and consume larger amounts of food.

3. Wanting to do well in school to make your parents proud is an example of _____.

   a. extrinsic motivation
   b. intrinsic motivation
   c. a primary drive
   d. an instinct

4. Which of the following needs is highest on Maslow's hierarchy of needs?

   a. esteem
   b. aesthetic
   c. transcendence
   d. cognitive

5. Which of the following chemicals is a hunger stimulant in the body?

   a. CCK
   b. ghrelin
   c. peptide YY
   d. leptin

6. If you were trying to develop a new weight loss drug, which of the following effects would you *not* want the drug to have in the body?

   a. Increase the brain's sensitivity to leptin.
   b. Decrease the stomach's production of ghrelin.
   c. Block the release of peptide YY in the gut.
   d. Stimulate receptors in the stomach that indicate stomach distention.

7. Of the following conditions, which one has the least in common with binge eating disorder?

   a. anorexia nervosa
   b. bulimia nervosa
   c. obesity
   d. ventromedial hypothalamic lesions

8. Which of the following people is most likely to experience prejudice due to being overweight?

  a. Ama from Iceland
  b. Marta from Mexico
  c. Fatima from Mauritania
  d. Sandy from the United States

9. Kyle was injured in a car crash and lost a lot of blood. Knowing what you know about motivation and emotion in the body, which of the following would you most expect to see in Kyle?

  a. He would become thirsty.
  b. He would become hungry.
  c. He would become less thirsty.
  d. He would become less hungry.

10. The idea that our body tries to physiologically counteract the drugs we put into it is a statement of _____.

  a. drive theory
  b. cognitive-mediational theory
  c. two-factor theory
  d. opponent-process theory

11. Eddie has been drinking several cups of coffee a day for most of his life. Susanna rarely drinks coffee. If Eddie and Susanna both have a cup of coffee tonight, what will likely happen?

  a. Eddie will sleep normally, but Susanna will not due to caffeine tolerance.
  b. Susanna will sleep normally, but Eddie will not due to caffeine tolerance.
  c. Eddie and Susanna will both sleep normally due to caffeine tolerance.
  d. Neither Eddie nor Susanna will sleep normally due to caffeine tolerance.

12. According to opponent-process theory, withdrawal from Valium (a central nervous system depressant) is likely to cause what type of symptoms?

  a. depression
  b. lack of energy
  c. anxiety
  d. sleepiness

13. Ali and Manuel are hiking in the woods when they are startled by a rattlesnake. Ali's pulse rate increases by 10% as a result. Manuel's pulse rate increases by 23%. Which of the following interpretations of this event is most consistent with the James-Lange theory of emotion?

  a. Ali has more experience with snakes; therefore he is less afraid.
  b. Manuel is more out of shape, and he attributed some of the exertion he felt on the hike to fear when he saw the snake.
  c. Ali was smiling at the time they spotted the snake and consequently felt less fear.
  d. Ali and Manuel are experiencing different emotions.

14. According to Paul Ekman's theory of basic emotions, if you are traveling to a country where you do not speak the language, you can expect that people will be most likely to understand how you are feeling when you are _____.

  a. sad
  b. happy
  c. frightened
  d. angry

15. The fact that we tend to experience positive feelings for things that we have had a great deal of contact with is referred to as the _____ effect.

  a. basic emotion
  b. cognitive-mediation
  c. mere exposure
  d. opponent-process

Scoring Key

Below are the answers and the associated point values for each of the Learning Challenge questions. Circle the associated points for each question that you answered correctly. To obtain your Learning Challenge Score, add up the points you circled and write the total in the blank.

1. B, 1 pt	**6.** C, 3 pts	**11.** A, 2 pts
2. C, 3 pts	**7.** A, 3 pts	**12.** C, 2 pts
3. A, 2 pts	**8.** D, 2 pts	**13.** D, 3 pts
4. C, 1 pt	**9.** A, 3 pts	**14.** B, 2 pts
5. B, 1 pt	**10.** D, 1 pt	**15.** C, 1 pt

Learning Challenge Score _____

(27–30) Congratulations! You scored at the advanced level. You are well on your way to mastering the material. Take the next step by answering the questions in your Student Study Guide or your Psychology CourseMate (www.cengagebrain.com).

(21–26) You are almost there! You scored at the intermediate level. Review the material you missed before moving on to answer the questions in your Student Study Guide or your Psychology CourseMate (www.cengagebrain.com).

(20 and below) You are on your way, but you're not there yet! You scored at the beginner level. It appears that you need to carefully review the chapter to improve your mastery of the material.

USE IT OR LOSE IT: APPLYING PSYCHOLOGY

1. Assume that you are a scientist who is trying to develop a new appetite suppressant pill for weight loss. Given your understanding of hunger, what kind of an effect would you want your pill to have on a person's body?

2. What would life be like if humans did not have the capacity for emotion?

3. What types of jobs would be suitable for people high in sensation seeking? Which jobs would be good for those low in sensation seeking? Explain.

4. Sabina was cut off in traffic on the way home from work, nearly causing her to have a serious accident. Immediately on arriving home, Sabina finds that her husband has left a dirty towel on the bathroom floor, something Sabina dislikes. What predictions would Schachter and Singer make about Sabina's emotional reaction to finding the dirty towel? Explain.

5. Pretend that you are in charge of developing a campaign to prevent eating disorders in teenage girls. What type of campaign would you develop?

CRITICAL THINKING FOR INTEGRATION

1. How can the theory of natural selection (Chapter 2) explain destructive behaviors such as eating disorders and drug abuse?

2. Given your understanding of physiology (Chapter 2), what impact do you think emotion has on our health?

3. What role do you think the four types of learning (Chapter 5) plays in drug abuse? Explain.

4. How might theories of motivation and emotion help explain romantic attraction (Chapter 11)?

CHAPTER STUDY RESOURCES

Student Study Guide

To help organize your learning, work through Chapter 8 of the *What Is Psychology? Student Study Guide*. The study guide includes learning objectives, a chapter summary, fill-in review, key terms, a practice test, and activities.

CengageNOW

Go to **www.cengage.com/login** to link to CengageNOW, your online study tool. First take the Pre-Test for this chapter to get your personalized study plan, which will identify topics you need to review and direct you to online resources. Then take the Post-Test to determine what concepts you have mastered and what you still need work on.

CourseMate

Access an interactive eBook, chapter-specific interactive learning tools, including flashcards, quizzes, videos, and more in your Psychology CourseMate, available at **CengageBrain.com**.

Aplia

aplia

Aplia™ is an online interactive learning solution that helps you improve comprehension—and your grade—by integrating a variety of tools such as video, tutorials, practice tests, and interactive e-book. Founded by a professor to enhance his own courses, Aplia provides automatically graded assignments with detailed, immediate explanations on every question, and innovative teaching materials. More than 1,000,000 students like you have used Aplia at over 1,800 institutions. Aplia should be purchased only when assigned by your instructor as part of your course.

MOTIVATION, AND EMOTION: WHAT GUIDES BEHAVIOR?

The stories of Marya Hornbacher and Toren Volkmann show us that motivation and emotion are complex, intertwined processes that have the power to direct our behavior in many ways. Motivation and emotion can be adaptive in helping us survive, but at times they can also be problematic. Better insight into the processes of motivation and emotion will not only help people like Marya and Toren recover, it may also help the rest of us better reach our goals in life.

A **motive** is the tendency to desire and seek out positive incentives and rewards and to avoid negative outcomes.

WHAT IS MOTIVATION?

- William James believed that motives tend to be inborn **instincts**.
- According to the **drive reduction theory**, **primary drives** maintain **homeostasis**.
- The **arousal theory** of motivation suggests that each of us has an optimal level of arousal.
- According to the **self-determination theory**, as we pursue the fulfillment of basic needs, we are motivated by different types of motivation provided by **intrinsic** and **extrinsic** motives.
- Abraham Maslow proposed a **hierarchy of needs** in which some needs take priority over others.

Transcendence

Self-actualization needs: to find self-fulfillment and realize one's potential

Aesthetic needs: symmetry, order, and beauty

Cognitive needs: to know, understand, and explore

Esteem needs: to achieve, be competent, and gain approval and recognition

Belongingness and love needs: to affiliate with others, be accepted, and belong

Safety needs: to feel secure and safe, out of danger

Physiological needs: hunger, thirst, and so forth

Chuck Karcher/Jupiter Images

HUNGER AND THIRST: WHAT MAKES US EAT AND DRINK?

ELI ELI/PhotoLibrary

- Receptors in the stomach monitor the intake of food and contractions of the stomach, and signal the brain when to make us hungry or to shut off hunger.
- Liver cells, gut hormones, fat cells, and glucoreceptors in the hypothalamus all play a role in signaling hunger or shutting it off.
- External cues such as advertisements and the sight or smell of food can also trigger hunger.
- **Obesity** can be caused by biological factors, such as a slow metabolism, as well as by a number of behavioral factors, including a poor diet, excessive food intake, and emotional eating.
- **Anorexia nervosa** is a serious eating disorder that involves extreme concern about gaining weight and reduction in caloric intake that leads to drastic weight loss.
- **Bulimia nervosa** involves bingeing on food followed by purging or drastic reduction in caloric intake to rid the body of the extra calories.
- The body uses two mechanisms to regulate and signal thirst: a drop in **intracellular fluid** pressure, and a drop in **extracellular fluid** pressure.

© Neal Preston/Corbis

WHY ARE SOME PEOPLE MOTIVATED TO ABUSE DRUGS?

- Many factors correlate with substance abuse: exposure to drugs, low self-esteem, boredom, and depression.

- The **opponent-process theory** of motivation holds that the body counteracts the effects of a drug with an opposite physiological reaction, resulting in **withdrawal** symptoms, growing **tolerance** for the drug, and **physical dependence**.

© JGI/Jamie Grill/Blend Images/Corbis

WHAT IS EMOTION?

© Renee Lynn/Corbis

- Components of **emotion** include physiological reactions, behavioral reactions, facial expressions, cognition, and **affective** response.

- The **James-Lange theory** of emotion proposes that emotion can be understood as a physiological response to some stimulus.

- The **Cannon-Bard theory** of emotion holds that emotion is the brain responding to some stimulus or situation, then prompting an emotional reaction.

- In the **facial feedback hypothesis**, the experience of an emotion is affected by the feedback the brain receives from muscles in the face. Thus, smiling can influence us to feel happy, and frowning can influence us to feel bad.

- The Schachter-Singer **two-factor theory** of emotion states that emotions are a product of both physiological arousal and cognitive interpretations of this arousal.

- The **cognitive-mediational theory** states that our cognitive appraisal of a situation determines what emotion we will feel in the situation; thus, different people react with different emotions in the same situation.

- Ekman's theory of **basic emotions** states that certain emotions such as happiness, sadness, anger, fear, surprise, and disgust are universal human emotions that are found across all cultures. Yet, **display rules** govern the expression of emotions, including basic emotions, across cultures.

 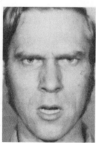    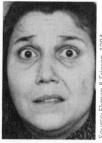

Source: Ekman & Friesen, 1984.

HOW DO PEOPLE GROW, CHANGE, AND DEVELOP?

THE BIG PICTURE

The Changes and Challenges of Life

In previous chapters we have focused on specific psychological processes such as biology, learning, and memory. This chapter expands on these topics by applying them to people as they undergo development throughout the lifespan. **Development** consists of changes in behavior and abilities. In this chapter, we will see that human development is complicated. Physical changes are occurring along with emotional, social, and mental (or cognitive) development. At the same time, social forces (such as people around us) and our environment affect these processes. Our chapter case study powerfully illustrates these mutually influential forces. It is the life story of Hongyong Lee, as told by her granddaughter Helie Lee in *Still Life with Rice* (1996). As you read about the challenges she faced, think about those changes that have already affected your development. At the same time, consider and imagine what challenges may still be ahead of you. Is the person you are today capable of surviving the journey through adulthood?

Hongyong Baek was born in Korea in 1912, the second of four children and the first daughter of wealthy parents. She was strong and willful and curious to conquer life. As was the custom for Korean girls, at the age of 9, Hongyong began daily lessons in virtue, womanhood, and managing a household. She preferred the household lessons as they were "something I could touch, see, and use freely," but her headstrong temperament often incurred her mother's wrath and discipline. She understood obedience, but the idea of chastity was difficult to grasp. For example, when her mother told her to protect her "private parts," she thought her mother meant her knees, because she was constantly being told to keep her knees covered. At age 12 when she started to menstruate, her mother told her it was a woman's curse. Ashamed, she hid in her room fearing that everyone would know.

Unwed at 22, Hongyong feared she was too plain and clumsy to marry. She prayed to Buddha for a husband; without one she was considered a burden on her family. A marriage was arranged, to 19-year-old Dukpil Lee. Hongyong now belonged to another man's family. To her surprise, Hongyong's husband encouraged her to share her ideas and opinions, and her affection for him grew. She gave birth to a boy, Yongwoon, fulfilling her most important wifely duty by giving her husband a son. Over the next 15 years, Hongyong bore four more children, two daughters and two sons.

© Masterfile

(continued)

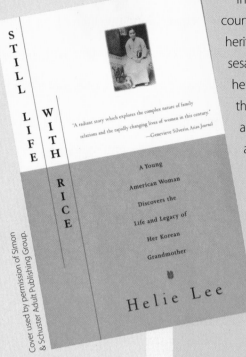

In 1939, as Hongyong gloried in the role of wife and mother, civil unrest in her country, long occupied by the Japanese, grew. Not wanting to lose their Korean heritage, the Lee family went to China. At Hongyong's suggestion, they started a sesame oil business. The business prospered, but Hongyong grew bored. Against her husband's wishes, she began to smuggle opium. Soon they had more money than they could spend. However, her husband spent more time away from her and had affairs with other women. Hongyong's insecurities about her appearance resurfaced. To keep her husband's attention, they opened a restaurant to entertain the most prominent and powerful people in China.

In her 30s, Hongyong was plagued with health problems. She discovered the ancient art of *ch'iryo*, a healing technique in which the flesh is pinched and slapped in order to improve blood circulation. Hongyong used *ch'iryo* to improve her health and treated herself and her children daily.

In 1945, Americans dropped the atomic bomb on Japan, and the Japanese surrendered Korea. The Lee family returned to North Korea, which was quickly occupied by Korean communists. Most of the family's land and money were confiscated. As her husband turned to alcohol, Hongyong converted to Christianity and developed a thirst for knowledge. She questioned her reason for living, learned how to read and write, and gave away what little riches they had left.

In 1950, the Korean War erupted at the 38th parallel. Because of her religion, Hongyong was imprisoned for "treasonous" activities. She spent 30 days in an overcrowded prison cell. Her daughter Dukwah dodged bombs and gunfire to bring her baby sister Dukhae to be breastfed by Hongyong every day. Once she was released, Hongyong knew her family would not be safe unless they went to South Korea.

Hongyong watched her husband leave, and then bid farewell to her eldest son. Unable to bear the waiting, Hongyong packed up her children to cross the Taedong River. Thousands of other refugees had the same idea. During the crossing, Hongyong and her baby were trampled. Once across, Hongyong prepared to bury her baby. Miraculously, Dukhae was still breathing, although barely. With frozen feet, empty bellies, and little energy, the family continued to walk, hoping to find shelter and peace. At one point, Hongyong was so exhausted that she wanted to leave Dukhae under a tree to die. Because the baby was practically dead, Hongyong thought to sacrifice her in hopes that the rest of the family would survive. But Dukwah refused to leave her sister, and the two women took turns carrying her.

Amid exploding bombs, throngs of people, and piles of wreckage, the Lee family made it to Seoul, 2 weeks before the South Korean borders closed. Hongyong found her husband in a refugee camp, but her eldest son, Yongwoon, never appeared. The agony was too much for Hongyong. For 8 months, she was a living ghost, ignoring her husband and children, forgetting to pray. She sat on a crate all day, staring into space, barely eating or sleeping. Her husband took care of the children and made ends meet

development changes in behavior or abilities or both

by selling gum and cigarettes. Finally, Hongyong's two sisters found her and took in the entire family.

Just as their lives were returning to some sort of normalcy, Hongyong's husband contracted diphtheria. She watched him die and vowed to find her way back to God. Just shy of 40 years old, she was now a widow. She again questioned her purpose in life and turned back to her *ch'iryo*. As her patients' health improved, more clients came looking for her services. Her hands could not keep up with the demand, so she developed an internship program to train other women in the art of *ch'iryo*.

As Hongyong's practice expanded, her children grew, went to college, married, and had children. She enjoyed being a grandmother and doted on her grandchildren with affection. As her 60th birthday approached, Hongyong waved goodbye to her daughter and granddaughters, as they emigrated to the United States. Eight years later, Hongyong bid farewell to Korea and emigrated to America herself, but she never stopped searching for her eldest son. After 40 years, she finally received news. He was alive! He had been caught behind the lines in North Korea. At 80 years of age, Hongyong finally achieved peace of mind.

Hongyong's story illustrates the sometimes dramatic kinds of turning points that shape development. A multitude of forces help or hinder our development: the love or ridicule of others, our ability to deal with death, our quest to find personal meaning in our lives, to name just a few. By understanding the physical, cognitive, and social aspects of development, you will be able to appreciate the many forces that make each child, teenager and adult unique—just as Hongyong's journey makes her tale one of a kind. We hope this understanding will lead to more productive and enjoyable interactions with the people around you.

DEVELOPMENT: HOW DOES IT ALL BEGIN?

LEARNING OBJECTIVES

What Should You Know?

- Explain the nature–nurture issue.
- Identify and describe the three stages of prenatal development—germinal, embryonic, and fetal—and explain the importance of a positive prenatal environment.

Why do psychologists study development? Psychologists study development in order to understand the changes that humans experience from conception to the end of life. Because this period covers such a large time span, developmental psychologists typically further specialize by limiting their investigations to a particular age group such as infancy, childhood, adolescence, or adulthood. Within any one of these age stages, psychologists may focus on different aspects of development: physical, cognitive, social, or personality development. One developmental psychologist may study how language develops in infants while another may research how peer pressure affects drug use in adolescents.

Nature–Nurture Revisited: Biology and Culture

Recall from Chapter 1 that psychology seeks to describe, predict, control, and explain behavior. If psychologists can accomplish these goals, then we can promote healthy development and prevent or alter maladaptive patterns of development. For example, if we understand how children think, we can then create appropriate educational environments, thus

Both nature and nurture influence every aspect of development.

Alison Wright/Photo Researchers, Inc

maximizing each child's potential. Understanding the dynamics of peer pressure during adolescence may suggest strategies to reduce drug use, delinquency, and teenage pregnancy. Stories like Hongyong's illustrate the importance of understanding more fully how stressors such as war, miscarriage, or a spouse's alcoholism affect people's development. Knowing about developmental processes, therefore, has numerous real-world applications.

However, explaining developmental changes is not easy. Think about all the variables that can potentially influence how a person grows and changes. What factors may have played a role in Hongyong's development? In addition to a unique biological foundation (genetics), every person is also influenced by a multitude of environments: family, school, friends, neighborhoods, religion, and culture. The potential contribution of these factors to development has become a central issue for developmental psychologists. Recall from Chapter 2 that this is referred to as the **nature–nurture issue**. Psychologists are interested in how much one's biology, or *nature*, contributes to a person's development versus how much one's environment and culture, or *nurture*, influence this process.

Genetics, or *nature*, influences almost every aspect of development, from personality and physical development to cognitive processes such as language development and intelligence (Bouchard, 2004; Gottlieb, Wahlsten, & Lickliter, 1998; Davis et al., 2009; R. J. Rose, 1995). *Nurture* is the total effect of all the external environmental events and circumstances that influence your development. It includes your family, friends, how others perceive and behave toward you, events that happen to you, television programs that you watch, music that you listen to, the customs and rituals of your ethnic background, your gender, your culture, your schooling, and so on.

Recall that it is not really a case of nature *or* nurture. Rather, it is the *interaction* of these two forces that influences behavior. Genes may moderate the influence of environmental forces; gene pathways may be altered by the environment (Champagne & Mashoodh, 2009; S. W. Cole, 2009). As you read about the various types of development that we experience, keep this nature–nurture issue in mind, as the influences of nature and nurture interact in a complex fashion.

Changes in the Prenatal Period

nature–nurture issue the degree to which biology (nature) or the environment (nurture) contributes to one's development

What happens during prenatal development? From the outside, all we see is a woman with a swollen belly who walks with a waddle. Any woman who has been pregnant has

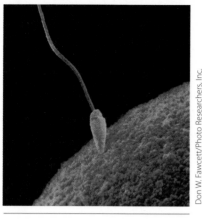

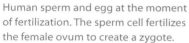

Human sperm and egg at the moment of fertilization. The sperm cell fertilizes the female ovum to create a zygote.

Don W. Fawcett/Photo Researchers, Inc.

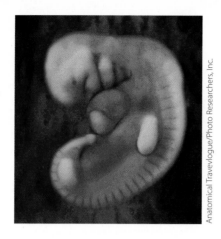

Anatomical Travelogue/Photo Researchers, Inc.

Micro-MRI, reconstructed with 3-D imagery, actual size of embryo 4.0 mm. The image depicts a human embryo during its 4th week of development. Age is calculated from the day of fertilization. In this image, the fusing tubes of the heart are highlighted in red. Early growth of the cardiovascular system begins during the 3rd week when blood vessels form and continues into the following weeks of development. Image from the book *From Conception to Birth: A Life Unfolds.*

experienced having some people want to touch her stomach or to treat her more delicately because of her "condition." Both tendencies speak to our fascination with the developments going on inside.

As we saw in Chapter 2, all the genetic material for development is inherited from your biological parents at the time of conception. The male sperm cell, containing 23 single chromosomes, fertilizes the female ovum, which also contains 23 single chromosomes, to create a fertilized egg, called a **zygote**, that has 23 pairs of chromosomes. Over the next 38 to 40 weeks, the average gestation period for a human, the zygote will experience dramatic changes as it evolves into a baby. So many changes occur during this time that scientists divide the prenatal period into three stages: the *germinal* or *zygotic stage*, the *embryonic stage*, and the *fetal stage*.

The first 14 days after conception are the **germinal stage** of development. The major characteristic of this stage is cell division. Following conception, the zygote starts to replicate itself and divide. This process ensures that all the cells of the organism contain the same genetic material. The zygote divides into 2 cells, which then replicate and divide again,

zygote   a fertilized egg

germinal stage   the first stage of prenatal development, from conception to 14 days

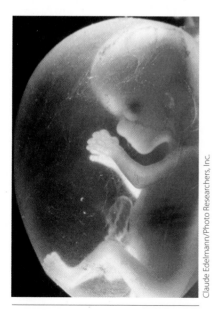

Claude Edelmann/Photo Researchers, Inc.

At 14 weeks, the fetus's lungs and external sex organs have developed.

Neil Bromhall/Photo Researchers, Inc.

View of a 5-month-old (20-week) male fetus holding his hand over his mouth. By this time the fetus appears completely human, with fully developed lips, eyelids, eyebrows, external ears, fingers, and toes. There is not much subcutaneous fat on the limbs or face, and the weight of the fetus by the end of the 5th month is still less than 500 grams. Fetal movements can now usually be felt by the mother.

creating a 4-cell organism. The cells continue replicating and dividing, and around the 5th day after conception the zygote has become a 100-cell organism, called a *blastocyst*. During this process of cell division, the mass of cells also travels down the fallopian tube to the uterus. On approximately the 9th day after conception, the blastocyst implants itself in the lining of the uterine wall. Cell division continues through the 2nd week.

The **embryonic stage** covers development of the organism, now called an *embryo*, from the 3rd through the 8th week. After the blastocyst attaches to the uterine wall, its outside cells develop into the support structures: the placenta, umbilical cord, and amniotic sac. The inner cells become the embryo.

The major characteristic of the embryonic period is the formation and development of the major organs and systems. Cells start to specialize into bone, muscle, and body organs. All the major biological systems—the cardiovascular system, the digestive system, the skeletal system, the excretory system, the respiratory system, and the nervous system—are forming. Given the importance of these systems for survival and well-being, the embryonic stage is perhaps the most precarious stage of prenatal development. Most miscarriages and genetic defects surface during this stage. The embryo's development may also be harmed by outside environmental factors, producing devastating effects. We will return to these topics in a moment.

By the end of the embryonic stage, all basic bodily structures and systems have formed. About 4 weeks after conception, the heart is beating, the spinal cord is forming, the liver is producing red blood cells, and ovaries or testes have formed (but the embryo's sex is not apparent by ultrasound until between 12 and 18 weeks). Although only an inch long, the embryo already looks human. Facial features, such as the eyes, lips, nose, and jaw, have taken shape. Short stubs represent arms and legs, and the beginnings of fingers and toes are apparent.

The third prenatal development period, the **fetal stage**, begins the 9th week after conception. From now until birth, the organism is referred to as a *fetus*. The major characteristic of the fetal stage is continued growth and maturation. The fetus grows larger and starts to move. By 14 weeks, the fetus can kick, open its mouth, swallow, and turn its head. Its lungs and external sex organs have developed. By the end of the 6th month (24 weeks), the organs are sufficiently formed such that the fetus has reached *viability*—the possibility of surviving outside the womb (but only in a neonatal intensive care unit). During the last 3 months, the fetus is responsive to sound, light, and touch.

From the union of a single sperm cell and egg, the fetus has undergone significant and complex changes over the course of 40 weeks. However, not all zygotes experience these changes. About half of all fertilized eggs die and are miscarried, usually before the woman knows she is pregnant. Of pregnancies that the mother knows about (because of a missed menstrual cycle), approximately 10 to 20% end in miscarriage, making miscarriage quite common (Mortensen, Sever, & Oakley, 1991).

The Importance of a Positive Prenatal Environment

The support structures of the intrauterine environment are designed to protect the developing organism. However, internal and external forces can still interfere with this natural defense system and cause birth defects.

When internal chromosomal abnormalities are present at conception, their effects typically arise during the embryonic stage. For example, **Down syndrome** results from an extra 21st chromosome. Babies with Down syndrome are characterized by distinct facial features (such as almond-shaped eyes or a flat nose) and are more likely to experience heart defects and varying degrees of intellectual disability. Medical tests can identify the presence of Down syndrome and hundreds of other inherited genetic disorders so that parents can prepare themselves or terminate the pregnancy (Rappaport, 2008). This possibility highlights the importance of regular prenatal consultations with a physician.

Birth defects may also be caused by outside environmental forces. Any environmental agent that has the potential to harm the embryo is referred to as a **teratogen**. It may be a drug that the mother takes such as cocaine or alcohol, a disease such as German measles

embryonic stage the second stage of prenatal development, lasting from the 3rd through the 8th week

fetal stage the third stage of prenatal development from the 9th week through the 9th month

Down syndrome a genetic birth disorder resulting from an extra 21st chromosome, characterized by distinct facial features and a greater likelihood of heart defects and intellectual disability

teratogen an environmental substance that has the potential to harm the developing organism (rubella), or chemicals that the mother inhales such as cleaning fluids. All these substances have the potential to cause birth defects. The critical factor seems to be *when* the mother is exposed to these agents. These **sensitive periods** emphasize the complex interplay of nature and nurture on development. Certain organs and systems are more vulnerable to the effects of teratogens during particular stages of prenatal development (● FIGURE 9.1). Notice that the most severe effects are more likely to occur during the embryonic stage of development. Because a woman usually does not discover that she is pregnant until the embryo is already formed and developing, she may unknowingly expose her developing baby to harm.

Women who use any type of drug during pregnancy can potentially affect their babies. Women who smoke during pregnancy reduce the flow of oxygen to the fetus; their babies tend to be irritable, have respiratory problems, and have lower birth weight (B. M. Lester, Andreozzi, & Appiah, 2004; Rosenblith, 1992). Women who drink alcohol heavily during pregnancy put their unborn children at risk for **fetal alcohol syndrome (FAS)**. Children with FAS tend to have low birth weight and brain abnormalities and to exhibit limb, head, and facial deformities. FAS is the leading cause of intellectual disability (Ikonomidou et al., 2000; Niccols, 1994; N. K. Young, 1997). Even moderate drinking can affect the embryo's brain development, resulting in lowered levels of intellectual functioning later (J. M. Kraft, 1996). Prenatal alcohol exposure has also been linked to an increased risk of low birth weight and poorer visual acuity in infancy (Carter et al., 2005; Mariscal et al., 2006).

sensitive period in prenatal development, a time when genetic and environmental agents are most likely to cause birth defects

fetal alcohol syndrome (FAS) a birth condition resulting from the mother's chronic use of alcohol during pregnancy that is characterized by facial and limb deformities and intellectual disability

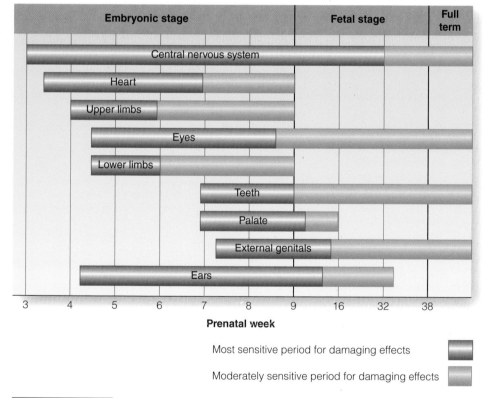

● **Sensitive Periods and Effect on Prenatal Development** The darker bars indicate the most sensitive period for certain organs and structures, and the lighter bars indicate lessened vulnerability. Sensitivity is greatest during the embryonic period, although some structures remain vulnerable throughout the prenatal period. *Adapted from K. L. Moore and T. V. N. Persaud,* Before We Are Born: Essentials of Embryology and Birth Defects. *Philadelphia: Saunders. Copyright © 1998 Elsevier Science (USA). All rights reserved. Reprinted by permission.*

Illegal drugs also produce damaging effects. If the mother is a heroin addict, the baby will be born addicted and have to undergo withdrawal. Crack or cocaine babies are often born premature, underweight, and irritable, and tend to have poor feeding habits (Frank et al., 2002; Inciardi, Surratt, & Saum, 1997).

Prenatal exposure to teratogens may also have long-term effects. Children exposed to drugs during pregnancy tend to be more impulsive, be less adaptable, and evidence more behavioral problems later in life than children whose mothers did not use drugs during pregnancy (Espy, Riese, & Francis, 1997). In southern Japan, adults whose mothers took in high levels of methylmercury (found in fish) during pregnancy have shown accelerated rates of aging (Newland & Rasmussen, 2003).

Prescription and over-the-counter medicines may also influence fetal development. For example, one study (D. K. Li, Liu, & Odouli, 2003) indicates that using nonsteroidal anti-inflammatory drugs (NSAIDs) during pregnancy may contribute to miscarriage. Read the warning labels on any over-the-counter medication and you will see that pregnant women are cautioned to seek a doctor's advice before using any medicine. Whatever the mother takes in during her pregnancy or breastfeeding, so does the baby.

Proper nutrition and a healthy lifestyle are paramount for pregnant women. These factors increase the chances of producing a healthy newborn who is better prepared to face the developmental and life challenges ahead. These challenges include the enormous changes that occur in infancy and childhood—our next topic of discussion.

Let's REVIEW

In this section, we reviewed the nature–nurture issue, described prenatal development, and emphasized the importance of a positive prenatal environment. For a quick review, try answering the following questions at increasing levels of difficulty.

1. Loretta is in her 5th month of pregnancy. What stage of development is her unborn child in?

a. germinal

b. zygote

c. embryonic

d. fetal

2. Studying identical twins to assess the degree to which they are similar provides evidence for the _____ side of a key developmental issue.

a. nature

b. nurture

c. development

d. learning

3. Which of the following is *most* characteristic of the germinal stage of prenatal development?

a. cell division

b. viability

c. birth defects

d. formation of major body systems

ANSWERS 1. d; 2. a; 3. a

LEARNING OBJECTIVE

What Should You Know?

• Describe major physical changes that infants and children experience as their brains and bodies develop.

HOW DO INFANTS AND CHILDREN DEVELOP PHYSICALLY?

What physical changes do infants and children experience? The average **neonate**, or newborn up to 28 days old, enters the world 20 inches long, weighing 7 pounds. One year later, the average infant is 29 inches long and will have tripled in weight, emphasizing how rapidly babies grow during infancy. Physical growth and developmental changes result from the complex interaction of the forces of nature and nurture. Our genes lay the foundation for how tall we grow and how our body fat is distributed. The environmental factors of nutrition,

neonate a newborn during the first 28 days of life

health care, and lifestyle also influence our height and build. A similar interplay of nature and nurture is seen in brain and motor development.

Brain Development

What is your very first childhood memory? How old were you then? Most people do not recall events in infancy or before 3 years old. This lack of memory may be related to the development of the nervous system. At birth, an infant's brain has billions of neurons, but the connections between the neurons are very limited, and myelin (see Chapter 2) is incomplete. Experience and learning, however, mix with heredity to shape brain development. Neural pathways grow rapidly, and by the time a child is 3 years old, 1,000 trillion synapses have formed (Garlick, 2003). A 2-month-old has very few neural connections compared to the billions a 2-year-old has. More experience plus increased activity equals more neural connections.

During childhood and early adolescence, the brain prunes and discards unnecessary connections, reducing the total number of synapses (Cook & Cook, 2005; Seeman, 1999; P. M. Thompson et al., 2000). Those connections that are used repeatedly become permanent, whereas those that are used infrequently or not at all are unlikely to survive (Greenough et al., 1993). This discovery has altered researchers' thinking on infant care and early education. Providing stimulating age-appropriate activities fosters and strengthens brain development. Impoverished environments weaken neural connections—fewer connections are made, and unexercised connections are likely to be discarded.

A young child's brain is highly *plastic*, or changeable, and very dense with neurons when compared to adults' brains. If a certain area of the brain is damaged in infancy, other areas of the brain can compensate by reorganizing neural connections (Kolb, 1989; Rakic, 1991). However, there are individual inherited differences in this process; some brains may be better able to adapt than others (Garlick, 2002). As children age, the brain is less able to change and adapt because neural connections have already been formed and in some cases discarded, although some plasticity remains throughout adulthood (Huttenlocher, 2002). For example, children who are rarely spoken to or read to in their early years are more likely to have difficulty mastering language skills. Similarly, young children have an easier time learning a second language than do adolescents and adults, whose brains are less malleable (J. S. Johnson & Newport, 1991). The plasticity and density of the brain ensures a child's best chance of adapting to his or her environment. This adaptation also is evident in the development of children's motor skills.

Reflexes and Motor Development

Infants are born relatively helpless creatures. They cannot feed themselves and are unable to walk. Infants do have certain sensory abilities, a good set of lungs that enable them to cry, and a set of *reflexes*, all of which biologically prepare them to get the help they need to survive.

A **reflex** is an *automatic* response to a particular stimulus. Reflexes enable infants to learn about their environment, thus establishing important neural connections for *voluntary* motor behaviors. Hence, reflexes serve as the foundation for behaviors such as walking, eating, crying, smiling, and grasping. For example, infants are born with a sucking reflex. They will automatically suck on any object that touches their lips. Infants also have a *rooting reflex*. When you touch the side of infants' cheeks, they will turn in that direction and open their mouth. These two reflexes teach infants how to use their mouths to get food. Infants are also born with a grasping reflex. When an object is placed on their palm, they will automatically grasp it. From this reflex, infants learn to handle items with their hands, an ability referred to as *prehension*. Their brains and bodies learn, through grasping, the necessary skills that will later be used to write with a pen, play a musical instrument, tie their shoes, or give a parent a hug.

Infants are also biologically prepared to communicate, despite lacking formal language skills. A crying reflex—automatically crying when distressed—alerts the caretaker to the infant's needs. In a matter of weeks, the baby learns to use crying to get the caretaker's

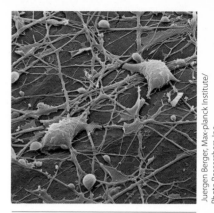

Juergen Berger, Max-planck Institute/ Photo Researchers, Inc.

Synaptic connections proliferate during infancy and early childhood. The brain then selectively prunes and discards unused connections during childhood and early adolescence.

reflex an automatic response to a specific environmental stimulus

attention. Luckily, infants are also born with a smiling reflex to use when they are pleased (which also serves as positive reinforcement for their caregivers). This reflex evolves into a *social smile* during the second month of life, when the infant smiles at everybody. Infants' smiles then become more discriminating by 6 months of age, when infants reserve their smiles for familiar voices and faces.

Reflexes also initiate *locomotive* ability, or the ability to move around. Crawling and stepping reflexes prepare the brain and body for motions involved in pulling oneself up, crawling, and walking. These abilities develop in much the same sequence for all infants around the world, evidence of our genetic heritage. However, experience may speed up this process and lack of opportunities may slow it down (E. Thelen, 1995).

By age 2, most infants are walking, running, and getting into everything. However, motor development, the changes in a child's body activities, does not end there. As children age, gross motor skills become more proficient. **Gross motor skills** refer to behaviors that involve large muscle groups such as the biceps or quadriceps. These include running, walking, jumping, and hopping. This proficiency is apparent when you watch a toddler, a preschooler, and an 8-year-old run. The toddler waddles and is unsteady on her feet. The preschooler is more coordinated compared to the toddler, but less fluid and not as fast as the 8-year-old.

gross motor skills motor behaviors involving the large muscles of the body

---

TABLE 9.1

● **Motor Milestones in Infancy and Early Childhood**

3 MOS. © Leila Cutler/Alamy	• Lifts head and chest when lying on stomach • Grasps rattle • Waves arms • Kicks legs
2 YRS. © Clayton Sharrard/PhotoEdit	• Drinks from a straw • Tosses a ball • Feeds self with a spoon • Bends over without falling
6 MOS.	• Reaches for and grasps objects • Helps hold a bottle • Shakes a rattle • Sits with little support • Rolls over
3 YRS.	• Puts on shoes • Dresses self with help • Kicks a ball • Hops on one foot • Pedals • Climbs
1 YR. © Laura Dwight/PhotoEdit	• Sits alone • Crawls and pulls self up • Uses finger to point • Grasps objects with thumb and index finger
4 YRS. © David Young-Wolff/PhotoEdit	• Runs, jumps, hops, and skips • Brushes teeth • Jumps over objects • Catches, bounces, and throws a ball
18 MOS.	• Pulls and pushes objects • Turns pages in a book • Scribbles • Stacks a few blocks • Walks and runs stiffly
5 YRS.	• Rides a bicycle with training wheels • Balances on one foot • Cuts with scissors • Jumps rope • Copies simple designs • Capable of swimming and skating

Note: The motor milestones listed here represent average age of attainment. Children's achievement of these motor milestones is highly variable.

Similar changes occur in **fine motor skills**, which involve small muscle groups. Fine motor skills include such activities as writing, using utensils, and playing a musical instrument. Toddlers and preschoolers are less adept at tasks involving fine motor skills, but as the school years approach, children become much more proficient. ● TABLE 9.1 details average age ranges for specific gross and fine motor skills achieved in infancy and early childhood. Notice that the achievement of a particular task lays the foundation for attaining the subsequent, more difficult task. In other words, babies must be able to sit up before they can crawl. Children must walk before they learn to jump rope.

As you can see, enormous changes occur in physical development all through the infant and childhood years. The same magnitude of change characterizes cognitive development, or how children think, which we'll turn to next.

fine motor skills motor behaviors involving the small muscles of the body

Let's REVIEW
In this section, we described the physical development of infants and children. For a quick review, try answering the following questions at increasing levels of difficulty.

1. Which of the following infants is *most* likely to have the fewest neural connections?

a. a 1-month-old   c. a 3-month-old

b. a 2-month-old   d. a 4-month-old

2. Children in preschool learn how to use scissors in order to help develop their _____ skills.

a. gross motor   c. reflex

b. fine motor   d. locomotive

3. The rooting reflex is to eating as the grasping reflex is to _____.

a. locomotion   c. gross motor skills

b. crawling   d. prehension

ANSWERS: 1. a; 2. b; 3. d

LEARNING OBJECTIVES

What Should You Know?
- Describe the perceptual abilities of infants and how these abilities develop in the first weeks and months of life.
- Compare and contrast Piaget's and Vygotsky's theories of cognitive development.
- Compare and contrast Kohlberg's and Gilligan's theories of moral reasoning.

HOW DO INFANTS AND CHILDREN DEVELOP COGNITIVELY?

How do infants and children think? Television shows, movies, and comic strips capitalize on the unique way in which children develop cognitively. What is it about children's thinking that makes adults laugh? This section reviews psychological research into how infants first learn to conceptualize the world and how this thinking changes as they proceed through childhood. We will start with perceptual development.

Perceptual Development

Infants are hard to study. They sleep most of the time, and they can't talk much. We can't remember what it's like to be an infant. Researchers must therefore study infants when they are awake and active, and devise clever ways to measure what infants know. The best way to gather information about what infants can and cannot perceive seems to be to measure certain behaviors and see how those behaviors change under particular conditions. For example, researchers may measure how long an infant spends looking at a stimulus or how long an infant sucks when exposed to different sounds. As researchers create more precise ways of measuring infant behavior, we are discovering that infants know a lot more than we once believed.

Vision

Babies are very nearsighted at birth. Objects need to be close in order for babies to see them, and even then, the objects look blurry. In addition, a baby's eyes lack *convergence*, or the ability to focus both eyes on an object. This may be why newborns typically look cross-eyed in photographs. However, as the structure of the eyes and the neural connections in the brain mature, babies attain visual convergence.

Newborns show a preference for looking at complex, high-contrast stimuli. If given a choice of various complex visual stimuli, infants will spend most of their time looking at faces (Pascalis & Kelly, 2009; Turati, 2004; Turati & Simion, 2002; Valenza et al., 1996). This preference is adaptive, as it helps foster a social bond with the primary caretaker. By 3 months old, a baby can tell the difference between its primary caretaker's face and that of a stranger and more easily recognizes faces from her own race (Bar-Haim et al., 2006; Burnham, 1993; D. J. Kelly et al., 2007; Sangrigoli & de Schonen, 2004). Infants also have more difficulty processing male faces than female faces (Ramsey-Rennels & Langlois, 2006).

TRY THIS
DEMONSTRATION

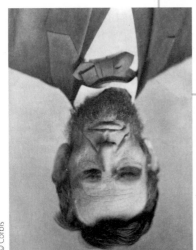

© Corbis

Our brains are predisposed to recognize a face, and this predisposition is present in babies. Look closely at the upside-down image of Lincoln on this page before looking at it right side up. Notice anything? Even when presented with an inverted portrait, we ignore the distortions and recognize that it is a face. When you look at Lincoln's portrait right side up you notice all the distortions.

Depth Perception

During their first year, infants develop depth perception. In a classic experiment conducted in 1960, researchers Eleanor Gibson and Richard Walk created an apparatus called a "visual cliff" (see photo on p. 359). They then observed at what age infants would or would not cross over the surface where it appeared to drop off. Infants as young as 6 months of age hesitated when approaching this perceived cliff. Again, we see that biology prepares us for developmental challenges. Babies acquire depth perception at about the same time they become mobile. Because depth perception and body coordination may not yet be developed in some infants, it is extremely important to never leave a baby unattended on a bed, a changing table, or any other elevated surface. Immature depth perception, as well as inadequate body control, makes it more likely that infants will fall and hurt themselves.

Hearing

Unborn babies react to sounds in the intrauterine environment at around the 20th week. A mother's voice is one of those sounds, which may explain why babies are likely to recognize their mothers' voices soon after birth (L. S. Black et al., 2004; DeCasper & Fifer, 1980). Infants can locate the direction of sounds. They readily learn the difference between similar consonant sounds, such as /d/ and /p/, and appear to remember simple speech sounds a day after hearing them (Swain, Zelazo, & Clifton, 1993). Research suggests that these abilities to discriminate sounds and familiar voices from unfamiliar ones may also be present in fetuses (Draganova et al., 2007; Kisilevsky et al., 2003; Lecanuet, Manera, & Jacquet, 2002).

Babies prefer soft and rhythmic sounds, which explains why they enjoy lullabies so much. They prefer most to listen to voices, specifically the rising tones used by women and children (J. W. Sullivan & Horowitz, 1983) and the exaggerated, high-pitched sounds typically used in baby talk. These preferences are an advantage to social interactions with caretakers. Infants do not like loud noises, which may explain why some children become classically conditioned to fear thunderstorms or the vacuum cleaner (see Chapter 5).

Eleanor Gibson and Richard Walk's visual-cliff apparatus tests depth perception in infants.

The Other Senses

Taste, touch, and smell are other ways that infants gather meaning from their environment. Infants' taste buds are functional at birth, and infants prefer sweet tastes. This, too, is advantageous because breast milk is sweet. Think about that—you come into the world preferring the food that you're going to be given! Infants are also born with an acute sense of smell. As soon as 3 days after birth, breastfed infants can discriminate the smell of their own mother from that of an unfamiliar female (Cernoch & Porter, 1985; Porter, 1999).

Infants are also very responsive to touch. Touching and caressing infants stimulates their growth and can improve brain development and cognitive development (A. Diamond & Amso, 2008). In one study, two groups of premature infants were given the same neonatal care with one exception—half the infants were routinely massaged, and the other half were not. Those receiving the massages gained weight faster, developed faster neurologically, and were therefore able to leave the hospital sooner than those in the control group (T. M. Field et al., 1986). Today, it is standard practice to encourage parents of preterm babies to hold them often. Holding and touching infants also fosters their social development.

Infants' perceptual abilities allow them to gather much-needed information from the environment—how their caretakers look, sound, and smell; where the food is; and what sounds contribute to language. From these beginnings, infants develop the abilities to know, think, and remember, a process called **cognition**. Perhaps no one has advanced our understanding of children's thinking more than Jean Piaget, whose ideas and research are presented next.

Piaget's Theory of Cognitive Development

While scoring intelligence tests for the French government, Swiss psychologist Jean Piaget (1896–1980) noticed common error patterns in children of the same age. He wondered why children routinely got certain answers wrong and what it was about children's thinking that led them to reach the same kinds of erroneous conclusions. To satisfy his curiosity, Piaget interviewed and observed infants and children, including his own, to discover and describe the changes in thinking that occur in childhood. Piaget gave children certain tasks to perform, observed their problem-solving strategies, and then asked them how they came to their conclusions.

cognition the ability to know, think, and remember

Piaget observed children's problem-solving strategies to describe the changes in thinking that they experience.

From these observations and interviews, Piaget (1929, 1952) developed a theory about how children acquire their mental abilities. His theory traces the shifts in thinking from infants' reflexes to a teenager's reasoning abilities. He believed that cognition advances in a series of distinct stages and that how a preschooler thinks differs dramatically from how an elementary school student thinks. Three concepts central to his theory are *schema*, *assimilation*, and *accommodation*.

Schema, Assimilation, and Accommodation

To Piaget, any mental idea, concept, or thought is a **schema**. We form these schemas based on our experiences of the world. For example, a baby may have a sucking schema—"Is this object suckable?"—or a mother schema—"Does this person fit with my cognitive framework of mother?" A preschooler may have the schema "The sun follows me wherever I go." Adults' schemas may be very simple—"A key will start a car"—or more complex, such as individual ideas of justice, morality, or love.

Piaget believed that our brains are biologically programmed to seek understanding of our world. So we form schemas to fit with our perceptions of the world. When we achieve this fit, so that our cognitions correspond with the environment, we have *mental equilibrium*. For example, an infant may grab her pacifier, put it in her mouth, and suck it—an experience that confirms her schema that a pacifier is suckable. However, when there is not a fit between our schemas and the world, we experience *mental disequilibrium*, an uncomfortable state that we are motivated to get rid of so our mental harmony can be restored. For example, an infant may grab a fistful of sand at the beach and put it in his mouth and determine it is not suckable, and therefore not suck on sand in the future. The processes of assimilation and accommodation explain how we use existing schemas and create new ones to fit our experiences and thereby maintain mental equilibrium.

Assimilation is the process by which we apply an existing schema to our understanding of the environment. For example, a young child is traveling in a car with her parents. As they pass an open field, the child sees some cows. The only schema the child has for a four-legged animal is "dog." So the child points and says, "Doggies!" The parents may correct the child—"No, those are called cows"—but she may persist in calling them "doggies" because that is her framework for understanding four-legged animals. The child has assimilated her experience of "cow" into her existing schema of "dog." However, many times our existing schemas will not fit our new experiences. At times like these, the process of accommodation takes center stage.

Accommodation is the process we use to change or modify our existing schemas—or even create new ones—to adapt to some change in the environment. For example, suppose the child in the previous example sees a dog and a cow side by side. The differences in the animals cannot be ignored and will create disequilibrium in the child's mental state. In this situation, she may come to call the new animal "cow." Her existing schema for four-legged animals has now been modified. The child will go through the same process when she sees a horse, a cat, or a hippopotamus.

According to Piaget, assimilation and accommodation create shifts in mental thinking that allow the child to progress through four stages of cognition: *sensorimotor, preoperational, concrete operational*, and *formal operations* (1952; summarized in ● THE BIG PICTURE REVIEW). Each stage has characteristics that permit the child to conceptualize the world in a unique fashion. Let's look at each stage.

Piaget's Stages of Cognition

During the first cognitive stage, the **sensorimotor stage**, from birth to 2 years, Piaget suggested that infants acquire knowledge through their senses and through their motor abilities—hence the name *sensorimotor*. For example, infants quickly recognize and prefer to look at their mothers' faces. Similarly, infants use their hearing to form schemas of what certain utterances mean, establishing the foundation for language. Taste, touch, and smell are also used to gather information and to form schemas as infants explore objects with their hands, mouths, and feet. We also saw that infant reflexes help establish schemas for later voluntary behaviors such as grasping, sitting, crawling, and walking.

schema a mental idea, concept, or thought

assimilation the process by which an existing schema is used to understand something new in the environment

accommodation the process by which a schema is changed, modified, or created anew in order to understand something new in the environment

sensorimotor stage Piaget's first stage of cognitive development, in which infants learn schemas through their senses and motor abilities

© Bill Anderson/Photo Researchers, Inc.

THE BIG PICTURE *review*

Characteristics of Piaget's Stages of Cognitive Development

STAGE	AGE	CHARACTERISTICS OF STAGE
Sensorimotor	Birth–2 years	Infants initially use reflexes and then acquire knowledge through their senses and their motor abilities. Babies begin to have mental representations as evidenced by object permanence.
Preoperational	2–6 or 7 years	Young children actively use symbols to represent the world. These mental representations may be egocentric and illogical due to children's limited experience and because they focus on only one feature of an object or situation.
Concrete Operations	6 or 7–11 or 12 years	The child can reason in a logical way provided such reasoning is within her realm of experience as she understands different perspectives. Conservation abilities become evident.
Formal Operations	12 years–adult	The adolescent can reason in a logical and abstract way.

Piaget believed that during this stage infants can only form schemas of objects and actions that are in their immediate perception—in other words, what they currently see, hear, or touch. They learn by doing and by acting on objects. They lack the ability to represent an object when it is not present. For infants, it is truly "out of sight, out of mind," according to Piaget. The baby thinks of his pacifier when it is present by manipulating it with his mouth or hands. An infant can think about her "blankie" only when it is present. If these objects are not present, they no longer exist for the infant. However, as the infant grows and the brain matures, babies begin to have mental representations. One sign of this milestone is *object permanence*.

Object permanence is the understanding that an object continues to exist even when it is not present. We can see this in infants' behavior when they start to search for hidden objects. For example, Piaget would show a baby an interesting toy and then cover it. Before the age of 6 months, infants would not search for the toy, lacking the understanding that the toy still existed. The infant could not keep a mental representation of the object and its location in mind. However, by 8 months, infants will begin to search for the toy, suggesting the beginnings of object permanence. This ability steadily improves through 24 months, when infants will search long and hard for hidden objects, indicating that they have fully achieved object permanence.

Although Piaget accurately described the process of object permanence in infancy, he may have underestimated infants' abilities. Current research suggests that infants as young as 1 month old (Kaye & Bower, 1994) and infants 3 to 5 months old have a rudimentary understanding of object permanence and that they gradually develop stronger mental representations of objects through experience (Baillargeon & DeVos, 1992; Bremner, Bryant, & Mareschal, 2006; S. P. Johnson, Amso, & Slemmer, 2003; Ruffman, Slade, & Redman, 2005; Shinskey & Munakata, 2005; Wang, Baillargeon, & Brueckner, 2004). Moreover, abilities that Piaget observed in infants 18 months of age are now being seen as early as 6 to 8 months of age, depending on the testing method (Hayne & Rovee-Collier, 1995; Mareschal, 2000).

Once infants acquire object permanence, they are on their way to **symbolic thinking**. This ability is the understanding that an object can be represented with symbols such as gestures or language (Ganea et al., 2007). For example, a toddler may imitate the sound or walk of a monkey even when there is no monkey in sight. This ability to use symbols propels the child to the second stage of cognitive development: the preoperational stage.

object permanence the understanding that an object continues to exist even when it is not present

symbolic thinking the understanding that an object can be represented with a symbol such as bodily gestures or language

© Laura Dwight/Photo Edit

Lacking the ability of conservation, young children are likely to believe that the amount of liquid has changed when it is poured into the thinner, taller glass. They believe the taller, thinner glass has more liquid.

During the **preoperational stage**, from about age 2 to age 6 or 7, preschoolers and young schoolchildren are actively acquiring and using symbols (DeLoache, 2001). Being able to use symbols opens up a new world to the preschooler. It is the foundation of a child's language development. A word symbolizes or stands for an object that may or may not be present. A child's vocabulary and understanding of language dramatically increases during these years. For example, when a parent asks, "Do you want some juice?" the preoperational child knows what juice is and may even go to the refrigerator to get it. Young children's pretend play also demonstrates their use of symbols, such as using a stick to represent a sword or taking on family roles when they play "house." However, the child's new ability to symbolize objects is still illogical and does not always make sense to adults. For example, a child may believe that a switch turns on ocean waves or that there are monsters hiding under the bed.

The illogical thinking of preschoolers is due to cognitive limitations that include *centration* and *egocentrism*. **Centration** occurs when the child focuses on only one feature or aspect of an object. For instance, a child who sees a man with long hair or an earring may conclude that the man is a woman. She focuses on one feature, the man's hair length, and this man's hair length fits with her schema for females. For preschoolers, if it looks like a duck, it is a duck. They have difficulty distinguishing between appearance and reality. Centration so dominates children's thinking at this stage that they do not realize that something can remain the same if its appearance changes, an ability called **conservation**.

In classic experiments, Piaget tested preschoolers and school-age children's conservation abilities (see photo). Children were shown two equal-sized glasses containing the same amount of liquid. In front of the child, Piaget poured the liquid from one of the glasses into a taller, thinner glass. Children were then asked whether the glasses had equal amounts of liquid or whether one glass had more liquid than the other. Children in the preoperational stage were most likely to reply that the tall, thin glass had more because they were focused on the height of the liquid in the tall glass. It looked as though it had more, so it must have more. For preschoolers at a party, then, adults should be aware that it must *look* as though the children all have the same amount of cake or punch. Otherwise the preschoolers will think they are receiving different amounts—which can create havoc!

An additional limitation to the preschooler's thinking is **egocentrism**, or the belief that everyone else thinks as you do. For example, when one of the authors was playing hide-and-seek with her then 3-year-old son, he hid in his room in the corner. His face was turned into the wall, much like a child who is sent to stand in a corner for misbehaving. On entering the room, the author said, "I see you." Her son replied, "No, you don't." From her son's perspective, he could not see his mother; therefore she could not see him. Preschoolers believe that others see things as they do, and therefore think as they do, a finding that has been repeatedly replicated using a range of different methods (Wellman, Cross, & Watson, 2001).

Although adults may find it frustrating, the illogical thinking of a preschooler lends an almost magical quality to their thought processes. For example, they believe in monsters, bad-dream catchers over their beds to prevent nightmares, the tooth fairy, imaginary friends, and fantasy. However, current research suggests that here, too, Piaget's ideas probably underestimate children's thinking abilities. Egocentrism, centration, and the inability to tell the difference between appearance and reality do not *always* characterize preschoolers' thoughts (J. M. Jenkins & Astington, 1996; L. S. Siegel & Hodkin, 1982). Rather, these limitations are sometimes present in children's thinking and gradually fade as the child matures and develops more logical thought processes.

preoperational stage Piaget's second stage of cognitive development, characterized by the use of symbols and illogical thought

centration the act of focusing on only one aspect or feature of an object

conservation the understanding that an object retains its original properties even though it may look different

egocentrism the belief that everyone thinks as you do

During Piaget's third cognitive stage, **concrete operations**, from about age 6 or 7 through age 12, schoolchildren become logical thinkers. They no longer center on one feature or facet of an object as the preschooler did, and their conservation abilities improve (● FIGURE 9.2). Children realize that although the tall, thin glass looks as though it has more liquid, in reality the glasses have equivalent volume. Changes in these abilities force the child to recognize that previous beliefs may be mistaken, so accommodation occurs. It also brings about a reduction in egocentrism as the child can now consider the perspectives of others. This enables empathy, persuasion, and a sense of humor to develop. For example, school-age children can now consider that a word may have more than one meaning. This play on words is evident in their use of knock-knock jokes:

Knock knock.
Who's there?
Dwayne.
Dwayne who?
Dwayne the bathtub, I'm dwowning!

At this age, children who believed in the existence of Santa Claus may begin to question that belief as certain facts just don't add up. For example, if it takes the family 8 hours to travel to a different state for a vacation, how can Santa Claus travel around the world in one night? Given Santa Claus's plump physique, how can he fit down a chimney half his size? What if you don't have a chimney? The child's questioning reflects the desire to clear up these contradictory schemas and restore mental equilibrium.

concrete operations Piaget's third stage of cognitive development, characterized by logical thought

FIGURE 9.2

● **Piaget's Conservation Experiments**
Mastery of conservation tasks begins gradually during the concrete operations stage. Children typically master conservation of number by age 6 or 7. Conservation of area may not be grasped until age 8 or 9.

Typical tasks used to measure conservation		Typical age of mastery
	**Conservation of number** Two equivalent rows of objects are shown to the child, who agrees that they have the same number of objects.	
	One row is lengthened, and the child is asked whether one row has more objects.	6–7
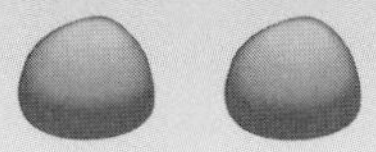	**Conservation of mass** The child acknowledges that two clay balls have equal amounts of clay.	
	The experimenter changes the shape of one of the balls and asks the child whether they still contain equal amounts of clay.	7–8
	**Conservation of length** The child agrees that two sticks aligned with each other are the same length.	
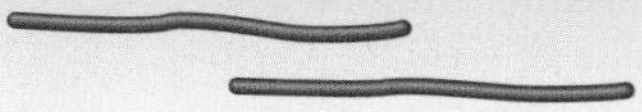	After moving one of the sticks to the left or right, the experimenter asks the child whether the sticks are of equal length.	7–8
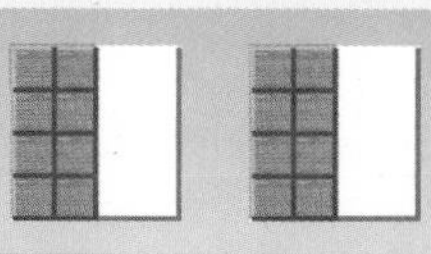	**Conservation of area** Two identical sheets of cardboard have wooden blocks placed on them in identical positions; the child confirms that the same amount of space is left on each piece of cardboard.	
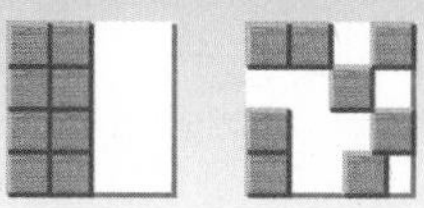	The experimenter scatters the blocks on one piece of cardboard and again asks the child whether the two pieces of cardboard have the same amount of unoccupied space.	8–9

Although the concrete operational child thinks more logically, these schemas are limited to actual experience or concrete objects and situations. School-age children have difficulty reasoning abstractly about what may be or what could be without being able to test their ideas in an observable way. This is why hands-on activities and class demonstrations of abstract ideas for school subjects such as geometry and science are necessary in elementary and middle school. Notice that Hongyong preferred the household lessons as they were "something I could touch, see, and use freely." When told to protect her "private parts," Hongyong thought her mother meant her knees because she was constantly being told to keep her knees covered. Being able to think about situations that are not present occurs in the final stage of Piaget's theory, *formal operations*.

According to Piaget, as children approach their teenage years, they may achieve the final cognitive stage, **formal operations**. They are no longer limited to concrete objects and situations; they can now engage in abstract reasoning. Teenagers can imagine and hypothesize what *may* be. This ability expands their horizons. They are able to understand more abstract, scientific, and mathematical concepts. They can imagine potential careers and envision future consequences for current behavior.

Piaget's Influence on Cognitive Development

Piaget's theory revolutionized our understanding of children's thinking abilities and stimulated much research in cognition. The changes in thinking that Piaget proposed do not always proceed according to the precise stages and timetable he originally suggested (Haith & Benson, 1998). Children's mental abilities develop at different ages. Nurture, culture, or experience can facilitate growth and change in these abilities. However, Piaget very accurately described the *sequence* in which these changes occur, even in diverse societies (Dasen, 1994; Lourenco & Machado, 1996). One final criticism of Piaget's theory is that it overlooks the important effects of culture on cognitive development. The ideas of Lev Vygotsky explore this connection between culture and cognition.

Vygotsky's Theory of Cognitive Development: Culture and Thinking

Lev Vygotsky (1896–1934) was a Russian psychologist whose ideas have influenced how psychologists and educators think about children's cognitive development and have provided an alternative to Piaget's theory (John-Steiner & Mahn, 1996). In contrast to Piaget's emphasis on the internal origin of schemas, Vygotsky (1978, 1986) emphasized that mental processes begin externally with our social interactions with others. For example, babies smile at caretakers or toddlers raise their arms to signal that they want to be picked up. A child internalizes these mental processes to create a cognitive framework for understanding the world. Young children often talk to themselves as they play, a behavior Vygotsky called **private speech**. For Vygotsky, private speech represents an internal monitor that guides the child's actions. Private speech, or self-talk, as it is sometimes called, is common among preschoolers, and peaks around 5 to 7 years of age. Around 9 years of age these spoken words are internalized as silent lip movements. Eventually, children just think the thoughts rather than saying them. However, private speech can return at any age when we are confused or having difficulties in problem solving. Such inner speech cues and guides our thinking. Much research supports Vygotsky's ideas on private speech, even in deaf children using sign language (Berk & Spuhl, 1995; Bivens & Berk, 1990; Diaz & Berk, 1992; Kelman, 2001). It makes sense, therefore, to allow and even encourage children to use private speech to talk or sign themselves through a problem.

According to Vygotsky, because cognition is so intimately tied to our social interactions, culture has a profound influence on our mental processing. The language, measurement systems, rituals, beliefs, and technology of a culture both limit and support certain ways of thinking (Tomasello, 2000). For instance, if your language does not have a word to capture an idea or expression, it is difficult to imagine or understand that concept. Similarly, children who have the opportunity to read books, use the Internet, travel, and attend cultural events will be more capable of conceptualizing ideas than will children without such tools. According to

formal operations Piaget's final stage of cognitive development, characterized by the ability to engage in abstract thought

private speech Vygotsky's term describing the behavior of young children who talk to themselves to guide their own actions

Vygotsky emphasized the importance of culture and social interactions in his theory of cognitive development.

Vygotsky, cognitive development does not occur in fixed stages as Piaget theorized. Rather, cognitive development may proceed in any number of directions, depending on our culture, social interactions with others, and the environment we live in (see Chapter 7).

Representing concepts is not achieved simply by having these tools. Conceptual thinking is taught to children by parents, teachers, siblings, coaches, and other important people in their lives. This instruction is most helpful when it is within a child's **zone of proximal development (ZPD)**—the gap between what a child can already do and what he or she is not yet capable of doing without help. Through collaborative interaction, the adult initially guides and supports the child's efforts to master a task. The less able a child is to do a task, the more direction and guidance an adult must give. The adult then gradually minimizes the guidance and support until the child can do the task alone, in a process called **scaffolding**. For example, when a child is learning to ride a bicycle, an adult first supports the child on the bicycle and walks or runs alongside as the child pedals. When the child seems ready, less support is given until the child is riding on his or her own. It is through these interactions with others that children internalize strategies, reasoning skills, and problem-solving abilities, according to Vygotsky. For this reason, Vygotsky believed that children's cognitive development benefits most when they interact with people who are more capable or advanced in their thinking than the children are.

Moral Reasoning: How We Think About Right and Wrong

How do people distinguish right from wrong, and how does their thinking about right and wrong change as they grow? Consider the following situation. An automatic teller machine (ATM) dispenses $10,000 to you and there is no way that this error would ever be discovered. You keep the money, but you donate half of it to the soup kitchen in your town. Should you have kept the money? How did you decide what to do? Your answer to this situation would provide clues to psychologists about your level of **moral reasoning**, or how you distinguish right from wrong. Two well-known theories on moral development include Lawrence Kohlberg's Stages of Moral Reasoning and Carol Gilligan's Ethic of Care.

Kohlberg's Theory of Moral Reasoning

Lawrence Kohlberg (1927–1987), a student of Piaget's, developed moral dilemmas or situations like the one we posed to you, and then asked participants to detail what the main character should do and why. Kohlberg was interested not so much in whether the participant believed the person's action to be right or wrong, but *why* the participant judged the person's action as right or wrong. After analyzing data from thousands of participants, Kohlberg created a theory of how people morally reason and the changes in this reasoning that they experience as they develop (Kohlberg, 1969; Kohlberg, Levine, & Hewer, 1983). Kohlberg proposed that our moral reasoning develops in six stages, which he arranged in three levels: preconventional, conventional, and postconventional (● TABLE 9.2). As you read through the description of Kohlberg's theory, consider your answers to the ATM dilemma.

At the *preconventional level* of reasoning, children make decisions about right or wrong based on their ability to avoid punishment or to gain rewards. For example, it is wrong to take the money because you may get caught and then punished. It is right to take the money because you can use it and no one will find out about it. Recall that at this age, children are egocentric and have difficulty understanding the nature of rules. Consequently, children are centered on the immediate consequences of their actions.

zone of proximal development (ZPD) according to Vygotsky, the gap between what a child is already able to do and what he or she is not yet capable of doing without help

scaffolding a process in which adults initially offer guidance and support in helping a child to reason, solve a problem, or master a task; as the child becomes more proficient and capable, the adult helps less and less until the child can master the task on his or her own

moral reasoning how you decide what is right and what is wrong

TABLE 9.2
● **Kohlberg's Stages of Moral Reasoning**

PRECONVENTIONAL LEVEL (MOST CHILDREN)
Stage 1: Obedience and Punishment Orientation. Children obey rules to avoid punishment. "Taking a cookie without asking is wrong because you get a timeout."
Stage 2: Naively Egoistic Orientation. Children view morally right action as that which increases their personal rewards and meets their needs. "You scratch my back, and I'll scratch yours."
CONVENTIONAL LEVEL (MOST ADOLESCENTS AND ADULTS)
Stage 3: Good Boy/Good Girl Orientation. Moral rightness is based on maintaining the approval and/or avoiding the disapproval of others such as family and friends. "I will return the rest of the money so my parents won't be disappointed in me."
Stage 4: Law and Order Orientation. Moral rightness is based on following the rules or laws of the society. Exceptions to the rules are not allowed. "Stealing is wrong because it is against the law."
POSTCONVENTIONAL LEVEL (SOME BUT NOT ALL ADULTS)
Stage 5: Contractual/Legalistic Orientation. Exceptions to rules can now be considered, as the protection of individual rights is emphasized over societal laws. "I confessed to the crime, but I was not read my rights, so the confession does not stand."
Stage 6: Universal Principles Orientation. Individuals develop their own set of universal principles that guide their judgments of right and wrong across all situations and all societies. "All people, regardless of skin color, should have access to education."

With the ability to think logically and to understand another person's perspective, children at the *conventional level* of reasoning can now understand rules and expectations that others may have for them. Therefore, their moral reasoning is based on the standards of the group or society. They believe behaviors are right or wrong because they gain the approval or avoid the disapproval of parents, teachers, or peers. You may not take the money because you are afraid your parents would find out and be disappointed in you, or you may take the money to gain acceptance from your friends. Do you remember pleading with your parent(s) to let you participate in an activity with a friend? If your friend's parent(s) let him or her participate, you probably asked why you couldn't, too. At this level, children can appreciate society's rules or laws for moral behavior. However, because they lack the ability to reason abstractly, children apply these laws to every situation and every person very rigidly. Exceptions based on circumstances are not considered.

At the *postconventional level* of moral reasoning, people base their judgments of right or wrong on contractual or universal principles of morality. The person can appreciate extenuating circumstances and realizes that external standards handed down from society cannot always be applied to all the situations in the same manner. The person develops internal standards of right and wrong to guide moral behavior. These abstract principles may include the Golden Rule (Do unto others as you would have them do unto you) or values such as respecting the dignity of all persons regardless of race, creed, or culture. You may not take the money because you did not earn it and because you may be financially hurting someone else. Consider the moral values evidenced by Martin Luther King Jr.; Dr. King lived in a society in which "separate but equal" was the law of the land. It was mandated that Blacks and Whites use separate restrooms, attend different schools, sit in different locations on public transport, and eat in different sections of a restaurant. Yet Dr. King believed that this segregation was immoral, that regardless of a person's skin color, all people should be treated the same and have equal access to public facilities—a universal principle (Stage 6 in Table 9.2) that was self-chosen.

Kohlberg's theory has stimulated much research—as well as much criticism and controversy (Narvaez, 2010). Kohlberg-like studies in 27 cultures support Kohlberg's stage sequence of moral reasoning. People typically move through these stages in the way that Kohlberg proposed (Damon, 1999; Helwig, 1997; L. J. Walker, 1989; L. J. Walker & Taylor, 1991). By adulthood, most people have progressed to conventional moral reasoning, but few people move on to postconventional reasoning, especially the highest stage. Postconventional reasoning emphasizes the individual rights that each person in a society should be afforded. Such reasoning may apply more to people from Western cultures. In other parts of the world, moral systems tend to emphasize the group in regulating values (Haidt, 2008; Snarey, 1995). Another area in which Kohlberg's theory has been criticized is that of gender, a controversy initiated by a student of Kohlberg's, Carol Gilligan.

Dr. Martin Luther King Jr.'s level of moral reasoning was extraordinary; few others have reached Kohlberg's highest level of moral reasoning.

© Bettmann/Corbis

Gilligan's Theory: Gender and Moral Reasoning

Are there gender differences in moral reasoning? Carol Gilligan was assigned to code participants' responses according to the three levels theorized by Kohlberg. While she was involved in this task, Gilligan believed she noticed differences between male and female responses. To her, it seemed that male responses consistently received rankings of higher stages than the responses of females. Were males more morally developed, or were the differences due to the criteria of moral reasoning that were being used? Gilligan hypothesized that males and females do not judge right and wrong in the same manner. She believed that Kohlberg's model emphasized the male perspective on moral reasoning more than the female view.

In her book *In a Different Voice* (1982), Gilligan speculated that males and females focus on different principles for deciding what is right and wrong. Males tend to be more focused on concepts of fairness and justice. Females are more likely to emphasize concern, care, and relations with others in making judgments about right and wrong. Gilligan asserts that women's focus on caring is a different, but not a less valid, basis for moral reasoning.

Research evaluating gender differences in moral reasoning has not strongly supported Gilligan's claims. On hypothetical dilemmas, *both* males and females emphasize themes of justice and caring in their responses (Jadack et al., 1995; Jaffee & Hyde, 2000; L. J. Walker, 1995). Thus, moral reasoning may be based on justice or caring independent of gender (Jorgensen, 2006).

Let's REVIEW

In this section, we described the cognitive development of infants and children. For a quick review, try answering the following questions at increasing levels of difficulty.

1. Which of the following stimuli would an infant most prefer to listen to?

  a. a thunderstorm
  b. a car honking
  c. a dog barking
  d. a human voice

2. Simone sees a military tank on the highway and calls it a "truck." According to Piaget, Simone is engaging in _____.

  a. disequilibrium
  b. private speech
  c. assimilation
  d. accommodation

3. Kayla, a 4-year-old, shares her toys with June so that June will also share her toys. Kayla is operating at what level of Kohlberg's theory?

  a. preconventional
  b. preoperational
  c. conventional
  d. postconventional

ANSWERS: 1. d; 2. c; 3. a

HOW DO INFANTS AND CHILDREN DEVELOP PSYCHOSOCIALLY?

A close connection between nature and nurture also influences a child's social and personality development. Children come into the world with a biological tendency to behave in a certain way. How parents and others respond to these behaviors can influence the child's personality as well as the relationships the child develops with others. We explore these issues as we look at the topics of temperament, attachment, and Erik Erikson's theory of psychosocial development.

Temperament: The Influence of Biology

Babies come into the world showing a general disposition to behave in certain ways in response to their surroundings. These differences are believed to be due more to the child's biological makeup than to his or her environment, especially because the child has not yet been exposed to any environment other than the womb. These differences at birth in behavioral style are referred to as **temperament**. In pioneering research, Stella Chess and Alexander Thomas (Chess & Thomas, 1984; Thomas & Chess, 1977, 1986) gathered information on numerous infant behaviors such as

- General activity level
- General mood
- Ability to establish a regular pattern of eating and sleeping
- Likelihood of approaching or withdrawing from new people and new situations
- Ability to adapt to changes from their normal routine

From observing babies' tendencies on these variables, three temperamental styles of behavior emerged: easy infants, difficult infants, and slow-to-warm-up infants.

LEARNING OBJECTIVES

What Should You Know?

- Define temperament and distinguish among the three temperamental styles of infants.
- Describe behaviors that indicate that an attachment has been formed and distinguish among different attachment patterns.
- Describe the three parenting styles that Baumrind documented.
- Describe Erikson's theory of psychosocial development as it applies to infants and children.

temperament a person's general pattern of attention, arousal, and mood that is evident at birth

As the label implies, *easy infants* are generally in a good mood, establish a regular pattern of eating and sleeping, readily approach new objects and people, and adapt readily to changes in their routines. *Difficult infants*, in contrast, show more intense negative emotions such as crying. They have a more irregular pattern of eating and sleeping and are not as likely to approach new people and situations. Parents may even call such babies "colicky." *Slow-to-warm-up infants* are in between these two extremes. They are not as negative in response as difficult infants, but it takes them some time to adapt to new situations.

How does an infant's temperament influence parenting? Imagine that you have just become a parent and that your baby's temperament is easy. How would you feel about yourself as a parent? Your self-esteem would probably be very high and positive. Now consider the opposite situation—your baby has a difficult temperament. How would you feel as a parent? You would probably feel less capable. A child's temperament and the parents' responses to this temperament influence the parent–child bond called *attachment*. As we saw in the opening case study, Hongyong's temperament was described as willful and strong. Which temperament style do you think she fit?

Attachment: Learning About Relationships

How does a bond form between an infant and a caretaker? **Attachment**, the emotional tie between the infant and the primary caretaker, is usually firmly established by 8 to 9 months. Initially, psychologists believed that feeding provided the basis for building the attachment relationship: the baby feels connected to the primary caretaker because the parent satisfies the infant's hunger. However, animal research by Harry Harlow in the 1950s changed the way we view the attachment process today.

The Nature of Attachment

In a classic study, Harlow and Zimmerman (1959) wanted to investigate the nature of attachment. They used infant rhesus monkeys as subjects because ethical principles would prohibit such a study with human infants. They designed two artificial monkeys to act as surrogate mothers for the babies. One of the "surrogate mothers" was covered with a soft terry cloth fabric. The other "surrogate mother" was made of wire and had a feeding tube attached. The researchers wanted to see which "surrogate mother" the infants preferred. The infant monkeys went to the wire "surrogate mother" for food, but they clung to and spent most of their time with the cloth-covered "surrogate mother." This showed that feeding was not the reason the monkeys attached; rather, it was the close, warm contact that facilitated this bond. Establishing close, warm contact through holding and caressing facilitates attachment. Human infants can easily attach to multiple people and objects, including fathers, grandparents, siblings, and teddy bears.

How can we tell whether an infant has formed an attachment? The attachment bond is readily seen in specific infant behaviors by the end of the first year. For example, most babies reserve certain behaviors for their parents. The infants smile when the parent approaches them, raise their hands toward the parent to be picked up, and nestle closer when the parent holds them. Two additional signs of attachment include *separation anxiety* and *stranger anxiety*. **Separation anxiety** is a fear the infant expresses when separated from the primary caretaker. This distress normally appears at about 6 or 7 months of age and peaks at about 14 to 18 months. Separation anxiety

attachment the emotional bond between caretaker and infant that is established by 8 or 9 months

separation anxiety the fear an infant expresses when separated from the major caretaker

Harlow's studies showed that close, warm contact facilitates the attachment bond.

Courtesy of Harlow Primate Lab, U. of Wisconsin (both)

gradually becomes less frequent and less intense throughout the toddler and preschool years. However, it is not uncommon for even older children to become anxious and fearful when separated from their parents for a long period (Thurber, 1995). In **stranger anxiety**, the infant becomes distressed when approached by unfamiliar people. Stranger anxiety typically appears between 8 and 10 months of age. It may intensify through the end of the first year, but usually subsides over the second year. Therefore, it is not unusual for a 1- or 2-year-old to cry or cling to a parent when approached by a doctor, an unfamiliar relative, or a new babysitter.

Attachment Patterns

Although most infants will establish an attachment with a caregiver by the end of the first year, the quality of these attachments is not necessarily the same from infant to infant. Mary Ainsworth and her colleagues (Ainsworth et al., 1978) designed a research tool called the *strange situation* procedure to try to measure qualitative differences in infant attachments. In the strange situation, infants and their parents are placed in an unfamiliar playroom. The infant's behavior is observed and measured as certain events occur. For example, does the baby explore the new situation and the toys when left in the playroom with the parent? How does the infant behave when a stranger enters the room? What is the baby's response when the parent leaves the room? What is the infant's reaction when the parent returns?

Observations of infants under these circumstances uncovered several patterns, or styles, of attachment. Ainsworth and others (Ainsworth et al., 1978; Hesse & Main, 2006; Main & Solomon, 1990) described four patterns of attachment: secure, avoidant, resistant, and disorganized/disoriented.

- *Secure attachment.* Infants who are securely attached use the parent as a supportive base from which to operate and explore. They explore the toys while in the new situation, paying attention to any new strangers who may enter the room. They may or may not cry when the parent leaves, but this emotional upset quickly subsides once the parent returns.
- *Avoidant attachment.* Infants who show avoidant attachment appear to ignore the parent. They pay the parent little attention. They do not appear to be distressed when the parent leaves, and they show little emotional response when the parent reappears.
- *Resistant attachment.* Infants who display resistant attachment resemble a "clinging" baby. They remain close to the parent and do not actively explore the new situation. They show extreme distress when the parent leaves and appear to be angry when the parent returns. They may hit and push at the parent and are less easily consoled.
- *Disorganized/disoriented attachment.* Infants showing disorganized attachment seem confused or disoriented. They look away from the parent while being comforted and have a blank facial expression after being calmed by the parent.

Although most children worldwide appear to have secure attachments to their caretakers (van Ijzendoorn & Kroonenberg, 1988), we must be cautious in interpreting the "insecure" patterns of attachment. Different child-rearing practices and cultural attitudes influence how we interact with our children, and these interactions as well as the larger social context appear to influence attachment. In some countries, children's independence is encouraged; in other countries, a closeness with the caretaker is emphasized. However, these same styles of attachment have generally emerged when infants are observed in natural, nonexperimental surroundings (Vaughn et al., 1992), suggesting that these styles of attachment are common worldwide.

How does attachment influence development? Many psychologists endorse the notion that the quality of this first attachment relationship lays the foundation for the quality of all other relationships with friends and romantic partners. Research supports this reasoning to a certain degree. Securely attached infants are more likely to become curious, resilient, and self-controlled preschoolers. Such children are more likely to persist in problem-solving tasks, do well in school, and interact more skillfully with their peers during the school years (Elicker, Englund, & Sroufe, 1992; Jacobsen & Hofmann, 1997; Kerns et al., 2007; J. A. Simpson et al., 2007).

However, being securely attached at an early age does not guarantee an absence of problems later. Moreover, research has not been able to consistently document a negative or

stranger anxiety the distress an infant expresses when faced with unfamiliar people

unfavorable picture of development for the other attachment patterns. Some studies suggest that insecurely attached infants are more prone to behavioral and adjustment problems in their social relations with others, whereas other studies do not (Fagot & Kavanaugh, 1990; C. E. Hamilton, 2000; Hill-Soderlund & Braungart-Rieker, 2008; B. O. Rothbaum et al., 1995). Bonds with individuals other than the caretaker can compensate for insecure attachments at home. Moreover, given the number of variables that can influence attachment, an early pattern of insecure attachment does not guarantee a lifelong pattern of insecure relationships. As family circumstances improve, so too may the quality of the attachment. Similarly, social relationships *after* infancy must also be considered when we evaluate children's psychological adjustment.

Does child care have a negative effect on attachment? Child care alone does not contribute to insecure attachments. Rather it is the quality of the primary caretaker–infant relationship and the quality of the child-care center that most influence infant attachment. When a baby receives sensitive caregiving from the parent and from a high-quality child-care center, an infant's emotional development is enhanced. However, if a parent is stressed from juggling full-time work and child-care responsibilities, is depressed, or is otherwise unavailable to the infant, or if the baby spends long hours in a child-care center, or if the child-care center is of poor quality, then an infant may be at risk for adjustment problems (NICHD Early Child Care Research Network, 2002, 2006).

Parenting Styles

Parents' responses to their infants and children also influence the parent–child relationship. Diana Baumrind (1967, 1971) investigated these responses by observing parents' interactions with their children. From her observations, three styles of parenting emerged.

Authoritarian parents tend to exhibit a high level of control and a low level of affection toward their children. They set high expectations for their children but without communicating the reasons behind their expectations. "It's my way or the highway" would be a characteristic attitude of authoritarian parents. The children are not included in discussions of family issues, rules, or roles. They are to do what they are told. If they do not obey, force and physical punishment are used to ensure compliance. Baumrind found that children from authoritarian households tended to be more withdrawn, anxious, and conforming than other children.

Authoritative parents tend to exhibit moderate control and are warm toward their children. Authoritative parents are least likely to spank or hit their children. Rules—and the consequences for violating them—are established in a democratic manner, and children are included in family discussions. Reasonable expectations and demands are made of the children, and the children respond accordingly. Baumrind found that parents who use this style of parenting tended to have competent, happy, and self-confident children. It appears to be the most effective approach to parenting. Although Baumrind's sample was predominantly restricted to European Americans, these benefits of authoritative parenting have also been found to apply to several U.S. ethnic groups including African Americans, Korean Americans, Chinese Americans, and Hispanic Americans (Abar, Carter, & Winsler, 2009; Cheah et al., 2009; H. Kim & Chung, 2003; Querido, Warner, & Eyberg, 2002; Steinberg et al., 1992).

Permissive parents tend to show warmth and affection to their children, but have very little control over them. Discipline is lax. Children make their own decisions even when they may not be capable of doing so. Very few demands are made of the children in terms of rules or chores. Baumrind found that children of permissive parents tended to be the most immature. They were disobedient, lacked impulse control, and were most likely to be rebellious.

Now reflect on your parents for a moment. Do they *cause* you to act a certain way? Perhaps not. Recall that these are correlations and that causal connections cannot be made from correlational data. A parent–child relationship is not a one-way street. Children's temperaments influence the way parents treat them just as much as parents' responses influence the development of their children. Moreover, other variables such as the quality of the parents' relationship or the level of family functioning can influence how parents and children interact (Caldera & Lindsey, 2006; Schoppe-Sullivan et al., 2007). How a child develops socially and

authoritarian parent a parenting style characterized by high levels of control and low levels of affection

authoritative parent a parenting style characterized by moderate levels of control and affection

permissive parent a parenting style characterized by moderate levels of affection but low levels of control

emotionally will depend in part on the *goodness of fit* between the child's temperament and his or her surrounding social relationships, including those with parents (Bradley & Corwyn, 2008; Chess & Thomas, 1984; Kochanska, 1995; Reiss, 2005; Roisman & Fraley, 2006; Stright, Gallagher, & Kelley, 2008).

Consider a difficult infant with a permissive parent. Emotional outbursts may be met with attempts to "bribe" the baby into calming down, with little effort made to help the infant begin to handle being upset. The result may be immaturity and defiance that are likely to persist into childhood, causing additional problems in the family, school environment, and then the work world. Adolescents who have serious behavior problems are more likely to have had parents who could not manage their behavior (Dwairy, 2004; Maziade et al., 1990). Consider a difficult infant with an authoritarian parent. The parent will in all likelihood become increasingly frustrated with the difficult child's propensity to test the limits. Physical punishment or other consequences may continually escalate, leading to even further withdrawal or depression in a child or rebellion, anger, and hostility in an adolescent (Muris et al., 2004). The bad fit under these circumstances may result in the persistence of the difficult temperament.

In most cases, a difficult child needs a firm but loving hand, a parent who will adapt to the child's temperament—an authoritative parent. This parenting style will provide a good fit between the child and his or her environment. The difficult child will receive patience and reasonable limits within an atmosphere of warmth and caring. In such an environment, the difficult temperament may not be as evident in childhood or adulthood. The good fit between the child's temperament and the parent's style will result in a healthy parent–child relationship. Positive "nurturing" can modify the "nature" portion of a difficult temperament.

© Simon Marcus/Corbis

Parents who are warm and moderate in control are more likely to have competent and happy children.

Erikson's Stages of Psychosocial Development: The Influence of Culture

After studying child-rearing practices in several cultures, Erik Erikson (1902–1994) believed that all children have the same basic psychological and emotional needs that must be provided by their cultures or social environments—hence the name *psychosocial*. Erikson (1963, 1968, 1980) believed that children and adults progress through eight stages, or developmental crises. At each stage, the environment and the person's responses to the environment influence the development of either a healthy or an unhealthy personality characteristic. At each stage, the person incorporates a new quality into his or her personality. Resolving earlier stages with healthy outcomes makes it easier to resolve later stages with positive outcomes. An unhealthy resolution of a stage can have potential negative effects throughout life, although damage can sometimes be repaired at later stages. Four of Erikson's eight stages pertain to the childhood years and are discussed here. The other four stages focus on the adolescent and adult years and are discussed later in the chapter. ● THE BIG PICTURE REVIEW summarizes all eight stages.

For Erikson, the child-rearing practices of a culture fulfill basic psychological and emotional needs to influence healthy personality development.

Archives of the History of American Psychology, University of Akron, Akron, Ohio

1. *Trust versus mistrust.* This stage occurs during the first year of life, when infants are totally dependent on others in their environment to meet their needs. An infant whose needs are met is more likely to develop trust in others than one whose needs are not met. Developing a sense of trust also fosters the development of a secure attachment.

2. *Autonomy versus shame and doubt.* From 1 to 3 years of age, toddlers struggle with separating from the primary caretaker. They must negotiate an appropriate balance between autonomy, or independence, and dependence. If people in the toddler's environment belittle the child's efforts at independence or encourage dependence by being overly protective, then Erikson believed the child will be more likely to develop shame and doubt.

3. *Initiative versus guilt.* Erikson believed that during the preschool years (ages 3–6), children's environments encourage the development of either initiative or guilt.

THE BIG PICTURE *review*

Erikson's Stages of Psychosocial Development

AGE	STAGE	DEVELOPMENTAL CHALLENGE
Birth–1 year	Trust versus mistrust	Sense of security
1–3 years	Autonomy versus shame and doubt	Independence
3–6 years	Initiative versus guilt	Trying new things
6–12 years	Industry versus inferiority	Sense of mastery and competence
Adolescence	Identity versus role confusion	Sense of self, personal values and beliefs
Young adulthood	Intimacy versus isolation	Committing to a mutually loving relationship
Middle adulthood	Generativity versus stagnation	Contributing to society through one's work, family, or community service
Late adulthood	Ego integrity versus despair	Viewing one's life as satisfactory and worthwhile

When children develop initiative, they are motivated to take the first step, to start something on their own, and to be ambitious. Preschoolers are actively exploring their environments through trial and error. At the same time, they start to understand that others have expectations for their behavior, and they learn to read people's reactions to their explorations. From these explorations and observations, they begin to develop schemas of what they "ought to do." If these schemas conflict with what others in their environment expect from them, guilt may develop. Hongyong's natural curiosity encouraged a sense of initiative. Yet this initiative at a later age was discouraged because it violated cultural expectations of how a female should behave.

4. *Industry versus inferiority.* During the elementary school years (ages 6–12), children receive a great deal of feedback on their performance. They are in school 6 hours a day, where they receive a steady stream of information on their abilities. Their papers may have stars, red marks, or numbers on them. Children may be grouped according to ability. Because children this age can think logically, they can compare their performance on a task with that of their peers. In this way, they form opinions about which activities make them feel industrious, masterful, or competent, as well as ideas about activities or tasks that make them feel inferior or less capable of performing.

According to Erikson, cultures and social environments influence psychosocial development in children and adults by meeting or not meeting basic psychological and emotional needs.

© Gideon Mendel/Corbis

According to Erikson, by the time children approach adolescence, their personality has been shaped by the resolution of each of these developmental challenges. How the child resolves these issues has encouraged the development of either a healthy or a not so healthy personality.

Let's REVIEW

In this section, we described the psychosocial changes that infants and children undergo as they develop. For a quick review, try answering the following questions at increasing levels of difficulty.

1. Diana Baumrind's research suggests that which parenting style is most effective?

a. permissive
c. authoritative

b. authoritarian
d. indulgent

2. In the strange situation procedure, a baby who clings to the mother while she is present and who shows extreme distress when the mother leaves would be exhibiting which style of attachment?

a. secure
c. confused

b. avoidant
d. resistant

3. A toddler who shows a resistant attachment pattern may have the most difficulty resolving which of the following psychosocial stages?

a. trust versus mistrust
c. initiative versus guilt

b. autonomy versus shame/doubt
d. optimism versus anxiety

ANSWERS: 1. c; 2. d; 3. b

LEARNING OBJECTIVE

What Should You Know?

- Describe the physical changes that occur in adolescence and adulthood including puberty, brain changes, aging, and changes in reproductive capacity.

HOW DO ADOLESCENTS AND ADULTS DEVELOP PHYSICALLY?

Development is not limited to the childhood years; changes continue during the adult years, too. In adulthood, however, these changes are much more variable than in childhood. Here we describe the physical changes that characterize adolescence and adulthood. As in childhood, both nature and nurture influence our development.

During adolescence and adulthood we both peak and decline in terms of our physical development. How much and how rapidly we decline are very much influenced by both nature and nurture. Genes affect how we age, but so do the degree to which we exercise mind and body and the experiences we have as we age. What we think of as aging is an incremental and gradual process, but growing into our sexual maturation can be abrupt and actually quite dramatic. We are referring, of course, to the onset of *puberty*.

Puberty: Big Changes, Rapid Growth

Puberty is the process of sexual maturation. These developmental changes involve overall body growth and maturation of sex characteristics that enable people to sexually reproduce. Puberty generally occurs 2 years earlier in girls than in boys, with an average onset at age 10 in females and age 12 for males, but the timing of puberty varies greatly from one person to another and from one culture to another (Parent et al., 2003; F. P. Rice, 1992). Over the past 100 years, the age at which puberty begins has dropped in the United States, Western Europe, and Japan. Even within the United States, African American and Hispanic girls tend to enter puberty a year earlier, on average, than European American girls (Butts & Seifer, 2010; Kaplowitz et al., 1999).

What physical changes do adolescents experience? A growth spurt shortly after age 10 for girls and after age 12 for boys adds almost 10 inches in height and about 40 pounds in

puberty the process of sexual maturation

weight to the average body through adolescence. Girls' hips broaden relative to their shoulders, and boys' shoulders widen relative to their hips. Both sexes gain muscle and fat during puberty; however, girls gain more fat and boys gain more muscle. Because these changes are abrupt and uneven at times, early adolescence is regarded as an especially awkward phase of development (Malina, 1990).

In addition to overall growth, puberty includes internal and external signs of sexual maturity, caused by the release of sex hormones. In girls, sex hormones cause the breasts, ovaries, uterus, and vagina to mature, and initiate the start of their first menstrual cycle, or **menarche**. Pubic hair and underarm hair also develop. In boys, sex hormones cause the penis, scrotum, and testes to mature. These changes are accompanied by the growth of body hair and a deepening of the voice as the larynx enlarges. On average, males and females complete the process of puberty within 4 to 5 years (M. D. Wheeler, 1991). ● FIGURE 9.3 summarizes the physical changes that boys and girls experience during puberty.

How do adolescents react to the physical changes of puberty? Puberty has a definite emotional and psychological impact, particularly on the adolescent's self-image and mood. Typically, adolescents' reactions to these physical changes are mixed, but if they are prepared for the upcoming changes and have a supportive family, psychological adjustment to puberty is better (S. M. Moore, 1995; Mrug et al., 2008; Omar, McElderry, & Zakharia, 2003). As we saw in the opening case study, Hongyong's lack of knowledge and understanding of these changes made puberty confusing for her. Many adults attribute teenagers' moodiness to "raging hormones." Higher hormone levels may influence teenagers' moods, but it is also likely that teenagers' emotions influence hormone levels (Adam, 2006; Nottelmann et al., 1990). Teenagers often juggle multiple activities such as school, sports, clubs, band, or part-time work while interacting with varying groups of people—teachers, peers, family, coworkers, or coaches. Regulating their emotions and expectations within these different interactions and activities can be stressful and result in moodiness.

The timing of puberty also has a psychological impact on the self-image of an adolescent, one that differs for boys and girls. For boys who mature early, the growth in stature and muscle brings with it a better self-image and body image than for boys who mature later. However, early-maturing boys report somewhat more stress than late-maturing boys (Huddleston & Ge, 2003). Early-maturing females experience more adjustment difficulties and are more likely to smoke and drink alcohol during adolescence and to do less well in school than are those who mature later (Bratberg et al., 2005; Ge, Conger, & Elder, 1996; Ge et al., 2006; Graber, Brooks-Gunn, & Warren, 2006; Tanner-Smith, in press; Waylen & Wolke, 2004). Girls whose breasts develop early may find the attention they receive hard to cope with and fraught with pressures to become sexually active when they may

menarche a girl's first menstruation

FIGURE 9.3

● **Physical Changes in Adolescent Males and Females During Puberty**
Hormonal changes during puberty cause the development of sexual characteristics. These include physical changes to the organs directly involved in reproduction.

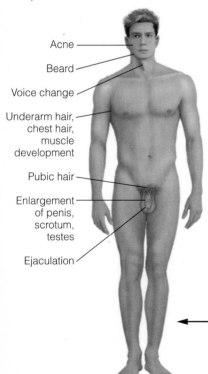

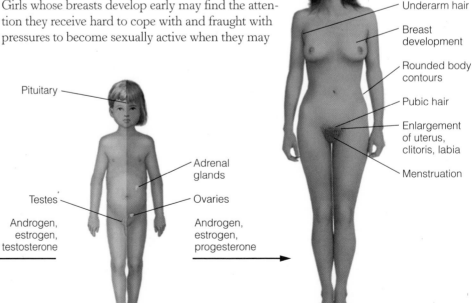

not be ready cognitively and emotionally to do so. Girls who develop later are better adjusted to these changes because the pressure to become sexually active occurs at an older age, when their cognitive abilities are better able to handle such pressures. Long-term studies suggest that the effects of early versus late maturation in puberty may be short-lived, except for early-maturing girls. At age 24, early-maturing girls report poorer family and peer relationships, lower life satisfaction, and higher rates of depression compared to other females (Graber et al., 2004).

Brain Changes in Adolescence and Adulthood

In addition to pubertal changes, a tremendous amount of brain development takes place during adolescence and into early adulthood. Medical technology such as magnetic resonance imaging (MRI and fMRI; see Chapter 2) has allowed researchers to examine teenage brains. These studies indicate dynamic changes in brain anatomy throughout adolescence and into early adulthood (Ashtari et al., 2007; Galvan et al., 2007). These changes appear to start at the back of the brain and move toward the front, as you can see in ● WHAT'S HAPPENING IN YOUR BRAIN? Part A (p. 376). The number of neurons and the complexity of their connections increase in the cerebellum. Recall that the cerebellum is necessary for balance, muscle tone, and performance of motor skills. The amygdala is more active in teens than in adults and is larger in males (Baird et al., 1999; Durston et al., 2001). As we saw in Chapter 2, the amygdala regulates our emotional reactions. Nerve fibers in the corpus callosum—the band of nerves that connects the two cerebral hemispheres—also thicken before and during puberty (Thompson et al., 2000).

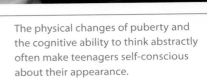

The physical changes of puberty and the cognitive ability to think abstractly often make teenagers self-conscious about their appearance.

Just prior to puberty there appears to be a second wave of overproduction of cortical gray matter—the tissue that covers the outside of the cerebral hemispheres and that appears gray because of the absence of myelin on the axons (Durston et al., 2001; Giedd et al., 1999; Sowell et al., 2001). The brain then prunes these connections as it did earlier in life—keeping the connections that are used while those that are not used wither away. This is illustrated in Part B of What's Happening in Your Brain? This gray matter growth spurt predominates in the prefrontal cortex—the area that plays a major role in cognitive processes such as problem solving, judgment, reasoning, impulse control, and the planning and execution of behavior. This is among the latest brain areas to mature, not reaching adult dimensions until the early 20s (Casey, Giedd, & Thomas, 2000; Giedd, 2004).

Do these brain changes cause teenagers' behavior? It is possible that the changes in the cerebellum may explain why young teens tend to be more physically uncoordinated and awkward than older teens and adults. The immaturity of the prefrontal cortex may explain why teenagers' judgment and reasoning may not always be sound. However, correlation does not mean causation (Chapter 1). Structural changes in the brain correlate with teenage behavior, but that does not mean they *cause* the behavior. Brain data do not take into account environmental and cultural factors such as parenting, peer pressure, the influence of the media, and other factors that contribute to brain processing. Adolescents all over the world experience roughly the same process of brain development, yet teenagers in different cultures and environments do not all behave the same way. However, we do know that teenagers and young adults have continued opportunity to develop their brains through activities in which they participate. Exercising their minds by reading, doing mathematics, and playing sports or music will strengthen neural connections. Research on changes in the adolescent brain also may help us understand why teenagers think differently than adults—a topic we will discuss shortly.

Is the brain completely developed at adolescence? No. As you can see in Part C of What's Happening in Your Brain?, the brain not only continues to grow and develop throughout our

WHAT'S HAPPENING IN YOUR BRAIN?

Part A: Changes in the Adolescent Brain

Changes in the adolescent brain generally start at the back of the brain and move toward the front. Hence the areas of the brain that are most involved in problem solving, planning, and critical thinking are the last areas to mature.

Prefrontal Cortex
Regulates attention span and impulse control; involved in problem solving, critical thinking and empathy. One of the last brain areas to mature.

Frontal Lobe
Organizes and plans, and controls some movements.

Amygdala
Part of limbic system involved in emotion and aggression. Highly active in young adolescents.

Cerebellum
Structure that coordinates fine muscle movement and balance. Complexity and number of neurons increases in adolescence.

Pituitary Gland
"Master" gland that regulates other endocrine glands. Very active during puberty.

Spinal Cord
Responsible for transmitting information between brain and rest of body; handles simple reflexes.

Part B: Neural Growth and Pruning

During early adolescence, new neural connections are formed. In a process called pruning, those that are used will be strengthened, whereas those that are not wither away. Hence engaging in stimulating and interesting activities during adolescence is good for our brains. (From *Time*, May 10, 2004. Reprinted with permission.)

Nerve Proliferation...
By age 11 for girls and 12 for boys, the neurons in the front of the brain have formed thousands of new connections. Over the next few years most of these links will be pruned.

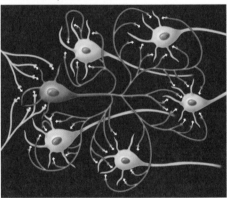

...and Pruning
Those that are used and reinforced—the pathways involved in language, for example—will be strengthened, while the ones that aren't used will die out.

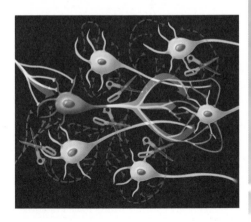

Part C: Injury and Recovery

The brain is highly plastic and adaptable. The photo on the left shows ABC News correspondent Bob Woodruff's skull in January 2006, two days after being hit by an insurgent bomb in Iraq. The photo below shows him a year later, after extensive surgery and rehabilitation.

Courtesy of the Woodruff Family

AFP/Getty Images

entire lives but it can recover from serious injury. Bob Woodruff, a news correspondent in Iraq, was severely injured when rocks and debris were lodged in his head and neck during an insurgent bombing. After extensive surgery and rehabilitation, he recovered sufficiently from his injuries to return to reporting. Under normal conditions, stem cells in some regions of the brain continuously generate neurons throughout life (Schmidt-Hieber, Jonas, & Bischof-berger, 2004). Cortical white matter (neural tissue containing myelin) matures throughout the lifespan as well (Asato et al., 2010; Bava et al., 2010). The brain remains highly plastic—able to adapt in response to new experiences such as new jobs, marriage, divorce, children, new friends, and financial responsibilities.

Physical Changes From Early to Later Adulthood

What physical changes do we experience in adulthood? We hit our biological prime during early adulthood when all major biological systems reach full maturation. Both women and men peak during their late 20s and early 30s in terms of physical strength, stamina, coordination, dexterity, and endurance (Whitbourne, 1996). These abilities gradually decline in middle and late adulthood.

A similar process occurs in our sensory abilities. Visual acuity, or the ability to focus vision, peaks in our early 20s and remains fairly high until middle adulthood. As we age, we lose the ability to focus on close objects (*presbyopia*), so that reading glasses or bifocals may become necessary in middle or late adulthood. Age-related hearing loss is also not uncommon among older adults, especially for high-pitched tones such as a distant telephone or a doorbell. However, people's senses of taste, smell, and touch remain fairly stable until late adulthood.

We see additional signs of the aging process in people's physical appearance as they approach their 40s and 50s. The skin starts to show wrinkles, and the hair may thin and turn gray. Weight gain is likely as metabolism slows, causing noticeable "love handles" or a "pot belly." Then, as people approach their 60s, they typically begin to lose weight and muscle, which may result in a sagging of the skin (Haber, 1994). The compression of vertebrae combined with a loss of bone tissue results in a loss of height as people age.

Although many physical abilities decline over the adult years, it is not clear that these declines are inevitable. As we discuss in more detail in Chapter 12, lifestyle factors such as poor diet, smoking, drinking alcohol, and lack of exercise contribute to the decline in physical functioning for some people. Moreover, culture markedly influences the way we think about aging and our expectations of our physical abilities in middle and later adulthood. In Western cultures such as the United States, becoming old is associated with being frail, useless, and ill, so that many people attempt to push back the aging process. Yet in countries such as Brazil, China, Japan, and Russia, where older people are more valued, aging is viewed more positively and is perceived as a time to look forward to rather than to dread (Gardiner, Mutter, & Kosmitzki, 1998). People with positive perceptions of aging engage in more preventive health behaviors such as exercising and tend to live longer (B. R. Levy & Myers, 2004; B. R. Levy et al., 2002). Across the world, many older people, despite changes in physical functioning, still lead active lifestyles (Baltes, 1997). As people age, they can usually continue their daily activities by making some adjustments and allowing themselves more time.

Gender and Reproductive Capacity

Our reproductive capacity also changes during the adulthood years. Women's fertility steadily decreases from age 15 to age 50 (McFalls, 1990; Rowe, 2006). Sometime around age 50, on average, women undergo changes associated with the process of **menopause**. Menopause signals the end of a woman's childbearing years. Her body produces less and less estrogen, affecting the number of eggs that are released from the ovaries. Eventually ovulation and menstruation stop altogether. Decreasing levels of estrogen also cause the breasts and the uterus to shrink. The vaginal walls produce less lubrication, which may make sexual intercourse somewhat painful.

Although men do not experience a "male menopause," they too undergo hormonal changes after age 60 termed *andropause* (Finch, 2001; Whitbourne, 2001). They gradually produce fewer male hormones as they age, which lowers the concentration of sperm in the

menopause the period when a female stops menstruating and is no longer fertile

semen and results in hair loss on the legs and face. However, men are still capable of producing offspring into their 70s, 80s, and 90s.

Despite these reproductive changes, older adults continue to have active and satisfying sex lives (R. T. Michael et al., 1994). For example, in one national survey of U.S. adults between the ages of 57 and 85, 73% of 57- to 64-year-olds reported regular sexual activity, more than half of the 65- to 74-year-olds reported regular sexual activity, and 26% of the 75- to 85-year-olds reported regular sexual activity (Lindau et al., 2007).

Because many cultures equate "looking old" with being unattractive, especially for women, middle age and later life may not seem very appealing. However, despite the effects of aging, almost 70% of people over 65 report being in good to excellent health (Hobbs, 1996). Although older adults may not be pleased with certain aspects of physical aging, they are no less content with their lives. Happiness and contentment perhaps have more to do with people's ability to adjust to these changes than with the changes themselves.

Let's REVIEW

In this section, we described the physical changes that adolescents and adults experience as they develop. For a quick review, try answering the following questions at increasing levels of difficulty.

1. Which of the following is *not* a physical change associated with puberty in males?

   a. growth of the testes
   b. voice change
   c. widening hips
   d. broadening shoulders

2. Andre, a 65-year-old man, is likely to experience all of the following as the result of aging *except:*

   a. weight loss
   b. thinning of the hair
   c. loss in visual acuity
   d. faster reaction time

3. Which one of the following lists the brain structures in the correct order in which they change (from earliest to latest) in adolescence?

   a. cerebellum, prefrontal cortex, amygdala
   b. cerebellum, amygdala, prefrontal cortex
   c. prefrontal cortex, cerebellum, amygdala
   d. amygdala, prefrontal cortex, cerebellum

ANSWERS: 1. c; 2. d; 3. b

LEARNING OBJECTIVES

What Should You Know?

● Compare and contrast formal operations and postformal thought in adolescence and adulthood.

● Describe changes in memory and mental abilities in adulthood.

HOW DO ADOLESCENTS AND ADULTS DEVELOP COGNITIVELY?

Adolescence and adulthood are also marked by changes in the way that we think. Consider how Hongyong's thoughts and focus changed over time. Initially, as a young adolescent, her concerns and thoughts predominantly centered around herself. With her marriage, her focus expanded to include her husband's and her family's views on herself. Then, as she grew older, she became more accepting of others. This section examines these changes in cognition.

Formal Operations Revisited

How do teenagers think? As we saw earlier in this chapter, children think and reason in ways that are qualitatively different from the thinking of adolescents and adults. Similarly, teenagers do not necessarily think like adults, but they are beginning to practice the reasoning skills and the ability to think outside themselves that characterize later cognitive development.

Recall that Piaget (1952) proposed that teenagers begin to think abstractly during the formal operations stage. This ability to reason abstractly allows them to imagine what could be and to hypothesize about future events and future outcomes. As a result, adolescents experience what they believe are—and often really are—tremendous insights into how things could be rather than how they are. This phenomenon is often labeled the *idealism of youth* (Elkind, 1984, 1998). Adolescents believe that they have the answers to problems such as world hunger or conflicts. This mental ability also helps adolescents in discovering who they are as individuals—a topic that will be detailed later in this chapter.

Formal operational thinking also allows teenagers to tackle more challenging academic subjects (science, geometry, calculus) that rely on abstract visualization and reasoning powers. It also enables adolescents to argue more effectively, a power that may not be seen positively by their parents! They are more capable of suggesting hypothetical scenarios ("What if . . .") to justify their position, making them more effective debaters (Elkind, 1984, 1998). However, along with this ability to think abstractly comes the return of *egocentrism.*

Egocentrism in adolescence involves teenagers' imagining what others must be thinking. However, teens believe that other people are concerned with the same things they are. Because adolescents' ideas focus mainly on themselves, they believe that others are equally concerned about them (Elkind & Bowen, 1979). For example, a teen with a pimple on his face may imagine that his peers and teachers are thinking only about the pimple on his face. Recall how Hongyong hid in her room ashamed that everyone would know that she was menstruating. Teenagers may not ask or answer questions in class because they are so sure that everyone is talking about them and thinking about them. They are newly and acutely aware of their own being. Because teens believe that others are focused on them, they behave as if they are on stage—playing to an audience—a phenomenon referred to as the **imaginary audience** (Elkind, 1984, 1998). They may laugh especially loud or behave dramatically because of their belief that they are being constantly watched. Although the imaginary audience and egocentrism are most associated with the teenage years, they may still be somewhat present later in life as young adults choose clothing, jobs, or interests to impress an audience that is largely imaginary (Frankenberger, 2000; Schwartz, Maynard, & Uzelac, 2008).

Another feature of adolescents' thought that relates to egocentrism is the **personal fable** (Elkind, 1984, 1998). Teenagers develop the "personal fable" that they are special and unique, that their thoughts and feelings cannot be adequately understood by others (Elkind, 1994). Reflect back on your first love. When that relationship broke up, you may have felt as if no one in the world could identify with what you were feeling. You may have hated hearing your peers and

The ability to reason abstractly allows teenagers to successfully tackle complex academic topics.

Teenagers' egocentrism leads them to believe that they are constantly being watched by others.

parents try to cheer you up with phrases such as "There are other fish in the sea" or "This too shall pass." You thought they were insensitive, or at least totally useless and beside the point. How could they understand what you were going through? The story you tell yourself is that this person, who is the only person in the world for you, has now gone away, and your life will never be happy again. This is one personal fable common in adolescence.

Personal fables may contribute to adolescent risk taking. Because teenagers feel that they are special and unique, they often feel that their own risks are less than those of their peers. For example, they may engage in unprotected sexual intercourse, believing that they won't be the ones to contract a sexually transmitted infection or conceive a child. They may experiment with drugs, believing that they will not become addicted. In their minds, addiction happens to other people. However, recent research suggests that this *optimistic bias* is no more prevalent in adolescents than it is in adults (Reyna & Farley, 2006). Moreover, research by L. R. Vartanian (2000, 2001) suggests that both the imaginary audience and the personal fable are biased views of adolescent social cognition that have not been empirically validated.

Although formal operational thinking is often perceived as the hallmark of adolescent thinking, this does not mean that *all* adolescents think abstractly in this way. Cross-cultural research (Hollos & Richards, 1993; Rogoff & Chavajay, 1995) suggests that the development of formal operational thinking is very much influenced by experience and culture. If abstract thought is necessary to "get by" in one's society or for a particular task, then humans may learn it. This thinking is more likely to be found in youths who are formally educated and in societies with more specialized and technical occupations (Flieller, 1999). In addition to Piaget's stage of formal operations, research has documented that adolescents think in other ways that are qualitatively different from adults. One such discovery is from research studies on *postformal thought*.

Postformal Thought

Suppose you were in the same situation as Hongyong. You are traveling in the middle of a war with a baby strapped to your back and three young children. Your baby's survival is questionable because she has been crushed by the crowds, and all of you are tired, hungry, and cold. Her added weight makes it difficult for you to walk, especially because you have been traveling for days with little food or water. What do you do? Would you, like Hongyong, consider leaving the baby under a tree in the hope of ensuring the survival of the rest of your family? Or would you, like Dukwah, insist that the baby continue to be carried? Is there a right or a wrong answer?

When situations like this are presented to adolescents and adults, differences emerge in their thinking. Adolescents may be capable of imagining such a dilemma because of their abstract abilities, but often this reasoning is in terms of black or white, right or wrong, good or bad—what is called **dualistic thinking** (W. G. Perry, 1981). They tend to believe that there is only one solution. However, as people enter adulthood, they are more capable of **relativistic thinking**, the idea that in many situations there is not necessarily one right or wrong answer. As adults we become aware that sometimes solutions and answers are relative to the situation or to the people in the situation. In Hongyong's dilemma, for example, adults typically would consider additional situational aspects such as how much farther the family has to travel, whether the younger children can help carry the baby, and the likelihood of the mother's surviving if she continues to carry the baby. The adolescent, thinking dualistically, may still believe the adult can do everything—carry the baby, lead the family, and reach safety.

Numerous research investigations support the notion that relativistic thinking represents a qualitative change beyond formal operations (P. M. King & Kitchener, 1994; Sinnott, 1998). In this context, it has been termed **postformal thought**. It is characterized by the appreciation that a correct solution or answer may vary from situation to situation and that there may be multiple solutions, each equally viable, to a given problem.

Changes in Memory and Mental Abilities

Does memory get worse as we age? Are we all destined to become forgetful and feeble-minded simply as a function of age? No, not really, but changes in memory do occur as we age.

imaginary audience the belief held by adolescents that everyone is watching what they do

personal fable the belief held by adolescents that they are unique and special

dualistic thinking reasoning that divides situations and issues into right and wrong categories

relativistic thinking the idea that in many situations there is not necessarily one right or wrong answer

postformal thought the idea that a correct solution (or solutions) may vary, depending on the circumstances

Specific memory processes that have been investigated include attention, reaction time, working memory, and the retrieval of information.

Research on attention has focused on how capable young and old people are of performing several tasks at one time. If the two tasks are relatively easy or familiar to the person, young people and older adults perform equally well. However, if the difficulty of the tasks increases or the tasks become less familiar to the individual, younger adults usually perform better (Georgiou-Karistianis et al., 2006; Stine-Morrow & Soederberg Miller, 1999; Zimmerman et al., 2006). This may explain why it is relatively easy for an older adult in your family to prepare a holiday meal for a large gathering of people; the multiple tasks involved in such an endeavor are familiar and automatic. However, the same individual may experience confusion or difficulty when faced with the numerous tasks involved in playing a new board game.

In the area of reaction time, or the speed with which a person can respond, similar results have emerged. We know from hundreds of studies that there appears to be an age-related slowing in reaction time starting at age 25. However, the rate at which one's reaction time slows is very much influenced by the nature of the task. If older adults are experienced in the task or given the opportunity to practice, the differences are less noticeable (Kail & Salthouse, 1994). Working memory, which has a limited capacity, seems to play a role as well. Young adults excel at encoding and storing vast amounts of details. After age 60, adults perform less well at these tasks (Salthouse, 1994). These findings suggest that as we get older, working memory appears to decline (A. D. Smith, 1996). The exact reason for this decline is unclear. Some research suggests that the answer may lie in the slower functioning of the nervous system (Chaytor & Schmitter-Edgecombe, 2004; M. K. Johnson et al., 2004; Rypma et al., 2005). Other research suggests that older adults use less effective memory strategies to keep information active in working memory (Paxton et al., 2006; Salthouse & Siedlecki, 2007; A. D. Smith & Earles, 1996). We must also consider such factors as motivational, educational, and lifestyle differences between younger and older adults who participate in such research. Younger adults may be in school or performing varied tasks in a demanding job (Luszcz, Bryan, & Kent, 1997) whereas older adults are often less involved in cognitively demanding activities. Differences such as these could account for differences in memory performance.

Research into differences in memory retrieval is also difficult to interpret. As we saw in Chapter 6, *recognition* involves identifying the correct answer from a list of correct and incorrect choices. *Recall* involves generating the correct answer on your own from the information that you remember. Over the adulthood years, recognition abilities remain strong. However, recall abilities decrease as we age, and these differences become quite large from early to late adulthood (● FIGURE 9.4; Balota, Dolan, & Duchek, 2000; Grady, 2000; Murphy et al., 2007; Verhaeghen, Marcoen, & Goosens, 1993).

What happens to other mental abilities in adulthood? The most comprehensive research to date, undertaken by Schaie (1983, 1994, 1996; Schaie & Willis, 2000), reveals that patterns of aging differ for different mental abilities. Recall from Chapter 7 that there are two broad categories of skills called *fluid* intelligence and *crystallized* intelligence.

Fluid intelligence, which develops during early childhood, relies heavily on processing skills such as reaction time, attention, and working memory. It is presumed to be based primarily on nature or biology, peaking when brain maturity has been reached (S. Li et al., 2004). Within the category of fluid intelligence, some mental abilities remain stronger than others. For example, perceptual speed and numeric ability tend to decline in one's late 20s and early 30s. Yet fluid skills such as spatial orientation and inductive reasoning remain strong and steady through one's 50s,

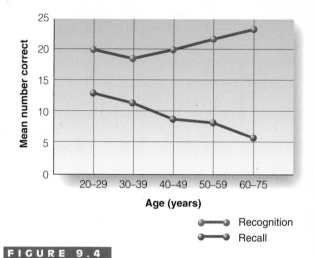

FIGURE 9.4

● **Recognition and Recall Changes as a Function of Age** Over the adulthood years, recognition abilities remain strong. However, recall abilities decrease as we age, probably as a result of both nature and nurture.

fluid intelligence abilities that rely on information-processing skills such as reaction time, attention, and working memory

Although recall abilities may decrease as we age, remaining cognitively active will minimize such memory changes.

Nick Dolding/Getty Images

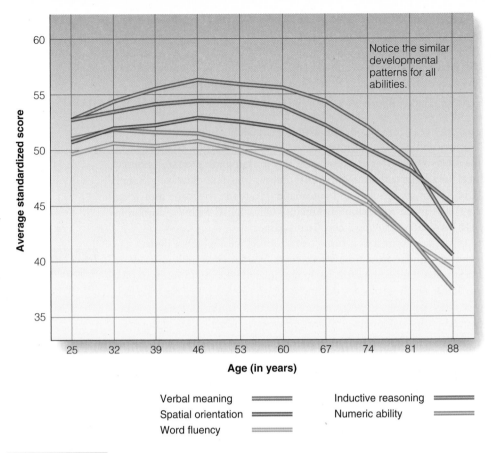

FIGURE 9.5

● **Age Trends in Mental Abilities** In his ongoing study of mental abilities, Schaie (1983, 1994, 1996) has documented that most mental abilities remain strong through early and middle adulthood. Eighty percent showed no declines by age 60, and almost two thirds were still stable through age 80. *From "The Course of Adult Intellectual Development," by K. W. Schaie, 1994,* American Psychologist, 49, 304–313. *Copyright © by the American Psychological Association. Reprinted by permission of the author.*

declining after that (Bucur & Madden, 2010; Salthouse, 2004). **Crystallized intelligence**, in contrast, involves the use of knowledge, expertise, and good judgment. Crystallized intelligence depends more on nurture or experience, such as educational background and occupational expertise. These abilities increase into adulthood and then decline somewhat after one's mid-60s (S. Li et al., 2004; Salthouse, 2004; van Hooren et al., 2007; Willis & Schaie, 1999). Crystallized skills include vocabulary, verbal memory, and responses to social situations. These age-related trends in mental abilities are summarized in ● Figure 9.5.

Many factors other than age shape how well we function mentally. Poor health, diseases, and prescription medications contribute to a rapid decline in mental abilities. Older adults can benefit cognitively from regular physical exercise (Colcombe & Kramer, 2003). A mentally inactive lifestyle is also a potential factor in cognitive decline and Alzheimer's disease (Schaie, 1996; R. S. Wilson & Bennett, 2003). The motto "Use it or lose it!" seems most appropriate in this context. Doing crossword puzzles, watching *Jeopardy,* and continuing to read, travel, or participate in educational pursuits are all activities that help sustain cognitive functioning (Hertzog et al., 2008; Stine-Morrow et al., 2007).

In conclusion, memory loss and declines in mental abilities are *not* inevitable in adulthood. Many of us will continue to perform well in cognitive functioning through our 50s and 60s. When we do show declines, it is more likely to be in late adulthood and on skills that require speed or on unfamiliar tasks. Good health, an active lifestyle, and continuing education are key factors for maintaining those cognitive skills most relevant to our daily activities.

crystallized intelligence abilities that rely on knowledge, expertise, and judgment

Let's REVIEW

In this section, we described the cognitive changes that adolescents and adults experience as they develop. For a quick review, try answering the following questions at increasing levels of difficulty.

1. The idea that a correct solution (or solutions) may vary depending on the circumstances is called _____.

   a. dualistic thinking
   b. egocentrism
   c. postformal thought
   d. recognition memory

2. When at the mall with her friends, Maria acts as if everyone is watching her. Maria's behavior is an example of _____.

   a. egocentrism
   b. imaginary audience
   c. idealism
   d. personal fable

3. Which one of the following mental abilities shows the least amount of decline after age 25?

   a. inductive reasoning
   b. numeric ability
   c. perceptual ability
   d. reaction time

ANSWERS: 1. c; 2. b; 3. a

What Should You Know?
- Detail Erikson's psychological transitions in adolescence and adulthood.
- Describe the varieties of social relations in adolescence and adulthood.
- Describe the new roles and responsibilities of being a parent.
- Explain the stages of career choice, the predictable changes people experience in occupational development, and the factors that influence adjustment to retirement.

How Do Adolescents and Adults Develop Psychosocially?

How people's individuality and character develop and change in adolescence and adulthood and how people navigate their social environment are challenging research areas in contemporary psychology. Erik Erikson sees adolescence and adulthood as a process of building, modifying, and sustaining a personal identity. This identity is influenced by our social relationships as well as the world of work.

Erikson's Stages of Adolescence and Adulthood

Recall Erikson's psychosocial stages of development (The Big Picture Review, p. 372) in which children, adolescents, and adults face developmental events that establish their individuality. Successfully mastering each stage strengthens the person's capacity to confront and negotiate the next stages. Here we examine the four stages Erikson attributed to the adolescent and adult years.

Identity Versus Role Confusion: Know Who You Are

How does an adolescent figure out who he or she is? For Erikson (1956, 1958, 1959), adolescence represents the integration and summation of the previous crises of childhood into an appropriate *identity*. It is a time when teenagers must figure out who they are and what they believe in, what their values are, and how they may be similar to or different from peers and parents. This search for personal identity is thought to be very much influenced by both the biological changes of puberty and the newly acquired cognitive ability of abstract reasoning. Teenagers begin to imagine what they want to be and experiment with new roles and responsibilities as they figure out their personal identity. For example, teenagers may try out different styles of clothing or listen to many types of music. They may join different peer groups or try out different college courses to explore various career options. Sometimes adolescents and young adults become so involved in constantly trying out new roles that they fail to form a stable identity. Erikson referred to this condition as *role confusion*.

Building on Erikson's work, James Marcia (1966, 1968) chose two variables that he believed accurately reflected the process of attaining an identity: exploration and commitment. *Exploration* involves activities geared toward discovering and testing out the roles an adolescent is

Exploration

		Present	Absent
Commitment	**Present**	**Identity achievement** (successful achievement of a sense of identity)	**Identity foreclosure** (unquestioning adoption of parental or societal values)
	Absent	**Identity moratorium** (active struggling for a sense of identity)	**Identity diffusion** (absence of struggle for identity, with no obvious concern about it)

FIGURE 9.6

● **Marcia's Four Identity Statuses** According to Marcia (1966, 1968), the presence or absence of exploration and commitment define four conditions of identity formation. *Adapted from "Identity in Adolescence," by J. E. Marcia, 1980. In J. Adelson (Ed.),* Handbook of Adolescent Psychology, *pp. 159–187. Copyright © 1980 by John Wiley & Sons, Inc. Adapted by permission of John Wiley & Sons, Inc.*

diffusion according to Marcia, an identity status in which the individual has not explored or committed to any personal values

moratorium according to Marcia, an identity status in which the individual actively explores personal values

foreclosure according to Marcia, an identity status in which the individual prematurely commits to personal values before exploration is complete

Participating in career fairs allows students to explore identity options.

© Kim Kulish/Corbis

considering. *Commitment* involves actions that reflect a loyalty to a particular role choice. Marcia developed a typology of possible "normal" conditions or states of identity formation, referred to as *identity statuses* (● FIGURE 9.6).

Initially, the teen has minimally explored identity issues and has not yet committed to any personal values. Marcia called this **diffusion**. For example, middle and high school youth may not yet be focused on what they will do for a living or even whether they will go to college. In the second state, **moratorium**, the teenager begins exploring and experimenting with different roles. However, the teen does not make a commitment to a personal identity. This moratorium phase is often accompanied by uncertainty and anxiety. For example, in our experience as college professors, we often find students quite anxious about making a career choice. There are so many options, courses, and activities to explore that students often feel overwhelmed and agitated. Students may feel that by taking one career path, they automatically cut off other possibilities.

Sometimes the uncertainty of establishing an identity is too great, and the person makes a decision prematurely, before exploration is complete, and enters **foreclosure**. The person has made a commitment to an identity that may not be stable over the rest of his or her life. It is a way to avoid or reduce the anxiety of the moratorium phase and is most likely to occur when parents, teachers, or peers offer little support for the teenager's indecision or pressure the teenager to make a specific decision. For example, a student may choose to pursue a medical career because this is what his or her parents expect. Foreclosure in and of itself is not bad, but it makes the person more likely to become disenchanted with his or her choice at some future point, which may result in dramatic personal change years later.

The final identity status, **achievement**, occurs when adolescents have explored enough to be confident and comfortable with their identity decisions. They have developed a coherent personal position and a commitment based on adequate exploration of who and what they are. For example, after taking a variety of college courses, a young man may decide that what interests him most is the field of nursing. He enjoys working with people and feels capable of the scientific and mathematical reasoning involved in such a choice. He declares nursing as his major despite the tough competition he will face to get into a nursing program. Across cultures and even within diverse U.S. ethnicities, people who have achieved identity tend to be more mature and more competent in relationships than people in the other three identity statuses (Marcia, 1993; D. L. Newman, 2005; Seaton, Scottham, & Sellers; 2006; Yip, Seaton, & Sellers, 2006).

Even when a teen fully attains an identity, his or her identity is not permanently etched in stone. Rather, adolescence represents a time when the core of our identity is established. We continue to refine and modify our identity as we transition to adult roles and responsibilities (Marcia, 2002). However, in industrialized nations, the time between the teenage years and when one assumes adult responsibilities is not as short as it used to be. This added length has resulted in a new transitional phase of development from one's late teens to one's mid-20s referred to as **emerging adulthood**.

Emerging adulthood prolongs identity development as young people pursue education, travel, explore various career paths, and experiment with varying love relationships (Arnett, 2007). Emerging adulthood does not occur for all young people. In many non-Western cultures there is no delay between the teen years and adult roles; young people work, get married, and raise families in adolescence or soon after (UNICEF, 2009). Even in Western nations like the United States that have postponed adult roles, a transitional period of emerging adulthood is not possible for young people with limited economic resources or little education or for those who experience early parenthood (Cohen et al., 2003).

Intimacy Versus Isolation: Connect With Others

In Erikson's model, successful resolution of the identity crisis prepares the young adult for the next developmental crisis: *intimacy versus isolation*. Having formed a stable identity, the person is now prepared to make a permanent commitment to a partner. Intimacy requires that people refine and modify their identity to accommodate the values and interests of another. In successfully meeting this challenge, neither partner's identity would be sacrificed. For Erikson, *intimacy* is characterized by cooperation, tolerance, and an acceptance of others' different views and values. This secure sense of intimacy may be expressed through marriage or long-term romantic partnerships, through close friendships, or through work relationships. Some people may lose their sense of identity—or fear losing it—and therefore be reluctant to connect with others. Erikson referred to this state as *isolation*. Isolated individuals are easily threatened by close relations with others and hesitate to establish close ties. They are more defensive in the relationships they do form, and they have less tolerance for the varying views and opinions of others.

Consider Hongyong and Dukpil's relationship. They met for the first time when they were joined in marriage, but were fortunate to build an intimate relationship. They confided in one another and valued each other's opinions. They each deferred to the other when the other had more interest or expertise on the subject. Hongyong forgave Dukpil and accepted him despite his infidelities and drinking. He accepted her despite her willfulness and conversion to Christianity. They were tolerant of one another.

Generativity Versus Stagnation: Make the World a Better Place

According to Erikson, resolving the intimacy versus isolation stage prepares adults for the developmental crisis of the middle adulthood years: *generativity versus stagnation*. This stage of development has to do with our feeling that we have made significant and meaningful contributions to our society. Middle adulthood is often the time when people become aware of their mortality. They recognize that their time here on Earth is limited. As a result, they then begin to think about their accomplishments and effect on society. Erikson believed that if a middle-aged adult feels that he or she has contributed something worthwhile to society, then a sense of *generativity* has been achieved. Marriage, long-term relationships, child rearing, career accomplishments, and service to the community may all contribute to this sense of having lived a productive life (Westermeyer, 2004). Generativity is associated with positive personality characteristics and life satisfaction (B. E. Peterson & Duncan, 2007). On the

achievement according to Marcia and Erikson, an identity state in which a commitment to personal values that have been adequately explored is attained

emerging adulthood the transitional period between late adolescence and the mid-20s when young people have left adolescence but have not yet assumed adult roles and responsibilities

For many, having a family and raising children provides a sense of having lived a productive life.

© Ed Bock/Corbis

© John Henley/Corbis

For older adults, reminiscing about their experiences provides a sense of integrity and life satisfaction.

other hand, middle-aged adults who conclude that they have contributed very little to improve society will experience *stagnation*, a sense of failure, and an absence of meaningful purpose in life.

People cope with feelings of stagnation in a variety of ways. Some remain disenchanted and bitter. Others attempt to change their lives to regain a sense of generativity and identity. Society often perceives such attempts as a *midlife crisis*. Yet, the number of people who actually experience such dramatic shifts in their life structure is actually quite small (Wrightsman, 1988, 1994). For example, in a 12-year study of people over age 40, Sadler (2000) found that a significant number of middle-aged adults are productive, enjoy their close relationships, and have begun to take risks. They experience what Sadler calls a "second growth" in midlife, characterized by enjoyment of life as Hongyong found with her *ch'iryo* practice.

Integrity Versus Despair: No Regrets

At the end of the life span, adults begin to review their lives and judge their satisfaction with the choices they have made and the direction that their lives have taken. Erikson believed that the issue facing people in their 60s and beyond was *integrity versus despair*. When this evaluation is generally positive and satisfying, individuals have achieved a sense of *integrity*, which allows them to face their eventual death without fear or regret. However, if this life review results in dissatisfaction and a sense of regret over roads not taken, the person is more likely to experience *despair* or hopelessness stemming from the knowledge that one cannot relive one's life. In such a case, the person may become fearful of death.

Social Relations in Adolescence and Adulthood

Hongyong followed the prescribed social roles for her time and for her culture. She did not socialize with boys or date, and her parents arranged her marriage. Despite her husband's infidelities, she never considered divorce. She and her husband expected to have children. If they did not, they would have been viewed as abnormal. Although in many cultures such prescribed social roles may still be the norm, in Western societies, today's adolescents and adults express intimacy in relationships in a wide range of lifestyles, including dating, marriage, cohabitation, divorce, and parenthood. Online social networking has also emerged as a way to expand relationships, as discussed in the ● TECHNOLOGY AND BEHAVIOR box.

Dating and Singlehood

Most teens date at some point in adolescence. Yet, regular dating has declined in recent years. For example, in 2000, 82% of high school seniors reported dating compared to 72% in 2008 (Bachman, Johnston, & O'Malley, 2001, 2009). However, this difference could reflect a change in teens' language. Nowadays, young people more often talk of "hanging out" or "going together" rather than dating (B. C. Miller & Benson, 1999). In these initial romantic relationships, young people look for social support, affection, and someone who has similar interests (B. B. Brown, 2004; W. A. Collins & van Dulmen, 2006). Males rate the attractiveness of a potential partner as especially important, whereas females rate the attractiveness and social status of a potential partner as important factors in who to date (Ha, Overbeek, & Engels, 2010).

Dating or "going together" serves several functions for teenagers. Besides being an outlet for fun and recreation, dating gives teenagers a chance to learn how to cooperate and compromise with people in a variety of situations (Lambeth & Hallett, 2002). For example, choosing a movie or a restaurant entails listening to the other person's wishes and then resolving any differences. Teens can discover more about themselves and how others' needs may differ from their own. Sexual experimentation may also be involved (C. A. Sanderson & Can-

TECHNOLOGY and BEHAVIOR

THE COSTS AND BENEFITS OF ONLINE SOCIAL NETWORKING

Facebook, Twitter, instant messaging, chat rooms, web blogs, and e-mails—the modern world provides more ways to socially connect than ever before. Online social networking is increasingly embraced by today's young people to post information and photos about themselves and communicate with others. Social life is 24/7; people can connect before they get together in person, after their interactions are over, into the wee hours of the morning, and when they first wake up. What characterizes online social relationships, and are there benefits and negative consequences to online social networking?

Initial studies demonstrated a negative relationship between social connectedness and Internet use (Kraut et al., 1998; Mesch, 2001; Nie, 2001). Social connectedness refers to one's relationships with others. Young adults who had higher Internet use were more likely to report lower levels of social connectedness and well-being. These studies, however, were conducted when Internet social networking was not widespread and "cool" and the Internet was more often being used to *form* social relationships. Today, young adults are more likely to use social networking sites to *maintain* existing relationships and reconnect with old ones as opposed to establishing new ones. Although one recent study (Schiffrin et al., 2010) continued to find an association between Internet use and decreased well-being, most research has found that when online communication is used to maintain existing relationships, it demonstrates a positive association with social connectedness, self-esteem, and well-being (Baker & Moore, 2008; Bessiere et al., 2008; Kraut et al., 2002; Valkenburg & Peter, 2007; Valkenburg, Peter, & Schouten, 2006). Online social networking may be especially appealing to certain individuals such as those with higher levels of social or dating anxiety (Stevens & Morris, 2007) and young adults who report higher levels of shyness (Orr et al., 2009; Sheeks & Birchmeier, 2007).

Why might online social networking have a beneficial effect? Several explanations have been offered. Online communication stimulates self-disclosure, or the willingness to reveal personal information about oneself (Christofides, Muise, & Desmarais, 2009; Tidwell & Walther, 2002; Valkenburg & Peter, 2009a), and enhanced self-disclosure increases the quality of existing friendships. For males especially, online self-disclosure may be easier than in face-to face interactions (Schouten, Valkenburg, & Peter, 2007). However, increased self-disclosure is not the only possible explanation for the positive effect of online social networking. Young adults who report higher well-being and happiness typically also report having high-quality friendships. It may be that young people who are already socially competent are using another tool—the Internet—to stay in touch with friends. Online communication may also result in more positive interactions with others or more frequent interactions with others—both of which may enhance the quality of friendships (Valkenburg & Peter, 2009b).

Although online social networking may enhance positive relationships with existing friends, it can also have serious consequences. One such risk is cyberbullying, or the use of communication technology to harm others (Mesch, 2009; Twyman et al., 2010). Kowalski and Limber (2007) sampled over 3,000 middle-school students and found that 11% had been cyberbullied at least once in the last couple of months. A web-based survey of over 1,000 high school students found that 72% of respondents reported at least one incident of online bullying (Juvonen & Gross, 2008). Other potential negative consequences of online social networking result from the personal information that young people disclose on their profile pages. Legal and educational institutions, current employers, and potential employers are increasingly using social networking sites in the hiring process, to monitor student and employee behavior, or as evidence in legal cases (Cain, 2008). Yet, young people often don't monitor the types of information they place on their profiles. For example, in one study of Facebook use by medical students, 70% of these users posted pictures with alcohol (Thompson et al., 2008). A selection of MySpace pages of 16- and 17-year-olds revealed that 47% contained information on drug use and sexual activity (Moreno, Parks, & Richardson, 2007). Social network users also put themselves at risk for identity theft and sexual solicitation. Online social networking can help young people maintain and strengthen social ties, but it also has the potential for bringing unintentional problems to young people's privacy and safety.

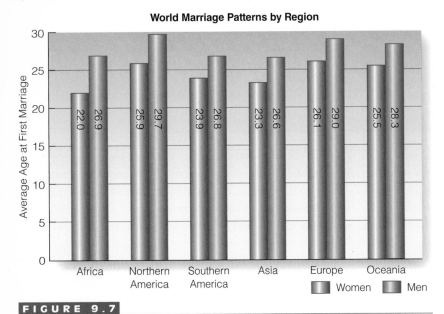

World Marriage Patterns by Region

Average Age at First Marriage

Region	Women	Men
Africa	22.0	26.9
Northern America	25.9	29.7
Southern America	23.9	26.8
Asia	23.3	26.6
Europe	26.1	29.0
Oceania	25.5	28.3

☐ Women ☐ Men

FIGURE 9.7

● **World Trends in Age at First Marriage for Men and Women** Worldwide, the average age when men and women first marry is rising, resulting in a larger number of singles in young adulthood. *Source: United Nations, 2003.*

tor, 1995; Smetana, Campione-Barr, & Metzger, 2006). Dating and romantic relationships during adolescence pave the way for establishing adult intimate relationships.

What do adult lifestyles look like? It is typical to start one's adulthood as unmarried—and the number of young single adults is growing. In 2009, about 55% of 20- to 34-year-olds and 17% of 35- to 44-year-olds had never married (U.S. Census Bureau, 2010). Among African American women, 38% remain unmarried into their late 30s, compared to 17% of Hispanic, 12% of Asian, and 12% of European American women (Teachman, Tedrow, & Crowder, 2000; U.S. Census Bureau, 2010). Worldwide, young adults are delaying marriage (● FIGURE 9.7). In the United States, the average age for first marriages is 28.1 for men and 25.9 for women; in 1980, it was 24.7 for men and 22 for women (U.S. Census Bureau, 2010). Being single allows young adults a chance to explore different types of friendships and relationships as well as to continue refining and defining their identities in emerging adulthood. Young single adults also may be moving or traveling as part of building careers, which can make it harder to start or maintain a relationship.

Cohabitation

Some adults choose to live together, or *cohabit*, with an intimate partner, one with whom they enjoy a sexual relationship. Cohabitation rates have been increasing steadily over the past 20 years in the United States. Currently, 6.7 million unmarried opposite-sex couples live together (U.S. Census Bureau, 2010). Yet these unions tend to be short-lived. About half of cohabiting couples either get married or break up within a year (Bumpass & Lu, 2000; Lichter, Qian, & Mellott, 2006). The increased rate of cohabiting couples is not unique to the United States—an even higher level exists in many other countries, such as Sweden and Denmark (Seltzer, 2001). However, cohabitation is rarer in more traditional societies. It is frowned on in Asian societies and severely discouraged in Islamic societies.

Couples cohabit for various reasons. Many gay and lesbian couples cohabit because their states' laws do not recognize civil unions or marriages. Heterosexual couples may feel that cohabiting before marriage will give them the opportunity to see whether they are truly compatible before undertaking the serious commitment of marriage. Some couples cohabit after divorce as an alternative to remarriage (S. L. Brown, Lee, & Bulanda, 2006; Coleman, Ganong, & Fine, 2000). However, couples who marry after cohabitation tend to be less satisfied with their marriages and are more likely to get divorced (Berrington & Diamond, 1999; Bramlett & Mosher, 2002; Bumpass & Lu, 2000; DeMaris & Rao, 1992; D. R. Hall & Zhao, 1995; Rhoades, Stanley, & Markman, 2009; Thomson & Colella, 1992).

Dating gives teenagers a chance to learn how to cooperate and compromise with people in a variety of situations.

Maria Teijeiro/Getty Images

Before we jump to causal conclusions from this correlation, let's examine this finding more closely. People who choose to live together tend to be less conventional, be less religious, come from lower income levels, and be more open to the idea of divorce than couples who do not live together before marriage (Axinn & Barber, 1997; Cohan & Kleinbaum, 2002; DeMaris & MacDonald, 1993; Smock, 2000). These factors, rather than cohabitation itself, may put a couple at greater risk for divorce. In countries in which cohabitation is more widespread (such as in Europe), premarital cohabitation is *not* associated with an elevated risk for divorce (Liefbroer & Dourleijn, 2006; Teachman, 2003).

Marriage: Adaptation, Satisfaction, and Gender Differences

More than 95% of Americans choose to get married at some point in their lives (U.S. Census Bureau, 2010). Survey research indicates that married couples in the United States are as happy today as they were 20 years ago (Amato et al., 2003). Yet 60% of marriages worldwide are arranged (Mackay, 2000). Up to 90% of marriages are arranged in India (Toledo, 2009), and in Japan, 25 to 30% of marriages are still arranged (Applbaum, 1995). Parents, relatives, and friends choose marriage partners based on their finances, family values, social status, and perceived compatibility with the potential bride or groom (Batabyal, 2001).

More than 95% of people in the United States choose to get married at some point in their lives.

Marriage, like any other lifestyle choice, involves adaptation. A new role as spouse has been added, and people must adjust to living as a couple rather than as an individual. Researchers have found that many aspects of the marital relationship change after the first year. The "I love you's" become less frequent, sexual activity becomes less frequent, and couples spend more time performing daily chores and tasks together rather than talking and having fun. Despite these changes, many couples continue to report satisfaction in their marital relationships.

What makes a marriage work? Research has discovered many factors that are related to marital satisfaction. For example, when both people are similar in family background, social class, education, and religion, couples report more satisfying relationships (Gaunt, 2006). Couples who wait to marry until after age 20 are more likely to report happier marriages than those who marry before age 20. Warm and positive extended family relationships, supportive spouse behavior, a willingness to sacrifice, and secure financial circumstances also increase the chances of a satisfying marital relationship (Bramlett & Mosher, 2002; Karney & Bradbury, 2005; Rank, 2000; Stanley et al., 2006). Perhaps the biggest detriments to a satisfying long-term relationship are boredom, negative comments, contempt, defensiveness, and criticism (Gottman, 1999a, 1999b; Levenson, Carstensen, & Gottman, 1993; Robles & Kiecolt-Glaser, 2003; Russell & Wells, 1994; Tsapelas, Aron, & Orbuch, 2009).

Research also shows some interesting gender differences in marital satisfaction. Although married people report greater life satisfaction than single people (Holt-Lunstad, Birmingham, & Jones, 2008; Myers, 2000), husbands typically report higher marital satisfaction than wives (Schumm, Webb, & Bollman, 1998). For example, Corra and colleagues (2009) investigated trends in marital happiness from 1973 to 2006 and found that Whites and husbands reported greater marital happiness than Blacks and wives. Marriage is associated with better physical and mental health for men (Levenson et al., 1993; Kaslow, Hansson, & Lundblad, 1994; Read & Grundy, in press). Health advantages for married women are more likely when the marriage is characterized as highly satisfying (L. C. Gallo, Troxel, Kuller et al., 2003; L. C. Gallo, Troxel, Matthews, & Kuller, 2003). Today, more married women are employed, but they still perform the majority of household tasks and have more responsibility for child rearing than married men (Bianchi et al., 2000; University of Michigan, 2008). In dual-earner couples, wives average almost 3 times as many hours per week on household tasks as their husbands (Coltrane, 2001; Starrels, 1994). Given these circumstances, it is not surprising that when divorce does occur, it is more likely to be initiated by the female (Amato & Rogers, 1997).

Divorce

About 1 in 5 adults will at some time in their lives experience divorce. First marriages that end in divorce last, on average, about 8 years (Kreider, 2005). Divorce rates are higher among couples who do not have children, who marry at a young age, or whose parents divorced (Amato & DeBoer, 2001; Faust & McKibben, 1999; Kurdek, 1993; Shulman et al., 2001). Divorce rates are also higher among African Americans (10.6%) and Whites (9.8%) than among Hispanics (7.5%) and Asians (4.2%), and higher among lower-income couples than higher-income couples (Rank, 2000; U.S. Census Bureau, 2010).

What changes does divorce bring? Like other lifestyle changes, divorce brings with it stresses and adaptations that the couple and the family must negotiate. Typically, divorce is preceded by a period of conflict and dissatisfaction (Lucas, 2005). Emotional, economic, legal, and practical difficulties follow. What was once one household must now be divided into two. If there are children involved, custody arrangements must be made. Identities are reshaped and redefined as the couple mentally shifts from thinking in terms of "us" to "me." Friendships with other couples may fade. Simultaneously, each member of the couple is resolving feelings of anger, rejection, disappointment, or loneliness (Amato, 2000). Given these changes, it is not surprising that divorced people are more likely to report higher levels of psychological distress or experience physical health problems (Hughes & Waite, 2009; Lillard & Panis, 1996; Lorenz et al., 1997; Lorenz et al., 2006). Perhaps for these reasons, many divorced adults, especially young people, choose to marry again. It is more common for men to remarry than for women (Kreider, 2005).

Divorce also affects the family. Previous styles of parenting may change, as the custodial parent must assume more responsibility for disciplining the children. The noncustodial parent may become more permissive because he or she spends less time with the children. Children experience many of the same emotions as their parents, such as loss, grieving for the family that was, and anger that their parents were not able to make the marriage work. As a result, they are more likely to misbehave. Children of divorce may be more aggressive, disrespectful, disobedient, withdrawn, or moody, and school performance may deteriorate, at least over the short term (Lansford, 2009). Their misbehavior makes it even more difficult for parents to be effective. Studies suggest that it is this breakdown in parenting and children's exposure to marital conflict both prior to and following a divorce that are most detrimental to a child's development (Amato, 1993; Amato & Booth, 1996; Erel & Burman, 1995). Hence, a two-parent household filled with strife and discord is as difficult for a child as the experience of divorce (Booth & Amato, 2001; P. T. Davies & Cummings, 1998; Harold et al., 1997; Lansford, 2009).

Parenting

At one time marriage was synonymous with becoming a parent, but that is not necessarily the case today. With increasing numbers of birth control options available, parenthood is more of a choice today than it used to be. About 15% of U.S. adults ages 40 to 44 in 2009 had never had a child (U.S. Census Bureau, 2010). At the same time, more single women and cohabiting couples are having or adopting children (Manning, 2001; Teachman et al., 2000; U.S. Census Bureau, 2010). For those who choose to have children, parenthood becomes another life transition that includes adaptation to new roles and responsibilities.

How does parenthood change one's life? Although most prospective parents look forward to the birth of their child, children radically change people's lives. With the joy and elation of a newborn baby comes less sleep, leisure time, and time spent together as a couple. Financial planning is a must; it will cost about $204,000 to raise one child born in 2007 over the next 17 years—and that's not including college expenses (Paul, 2008).

Parenting may bring changes in gender roles and the division of labor in the home. Such changes may increase or decrease marital satisfaction.

Barbara Peacock/Getty Images

Life becomes a juggling act as the couple tries to keep an eye on all the responsibilities of work and family at the same time. Although fathers today are more involved in child care and housework than ever before (Coley, 2001), couples become more traditional in their gender roles following the birth of a child (Katz-Wise, Priess, & Hyde, 2010). Mothers, even working mothers, are more likely to become the primary caregiver of the child as the man intensifies his role as provider (C. P. Cowan & Cowan, 2000; F. M. Deutsch, 2001; Haas, 1999). Fathers earn, on average, two thirds of the family income (C. Lewis, 2000). The male breadwinner model not only is a reality but is evident in young men's expectations about their future roles as fathers (Edley & Wetherell, 1999). Many teenagers equate being a man with "having a job" and "defending the family" rather than with being a good father (C. Lewis, 2000). Even in dual-earner couples, women generally carry the major share of household and child-care responsibilities, especially on weekdays and when children are in infancy (F. M. Deutsch, 2001; Laflamme, Pomerleau, & Malcuit, 2002). Fathers are more likely to share equal responsibility for child care and domestic chores on the weekends (Auster & Ohm, 2000). Fathers spend more time with children than do mothers in television viewing, outdoor play, and teaching sports (Yeung et al., 2001).

Does this mean that men don't care about or want to be involved with their children? Absolutely not! The cultural stereotype of men as breadwinners is very powerful. Moreover, our society tends to see men as workers first and fathers second. Fathers work more hours, have fewer days off, and are less likely to take off for family tasks or activities than mothers (J. A. Levine & Pittinsky, 1997). Fathers are also less likely to choose part-time work or use parental leave options (Kitterod & Kjeldstad, 2002). When fathers are involved with their children in ways that affect their work role, they experience more stress and role conflict, and report being more dissatisfied with their work lives (J. O. Berry & Rao, 1997). Hence, there is a high level of stress associated with being an involved father. Yet, the most involved fathers report being more satisfied with their lives (Eggebeen & Knoester, 2001).

Other variables also influence life satisfaction following the birth of a baby. For example, the baby's temperament (see p. 367) may create less or more stress on new parents (Schoppe-Sullivan et al., 2007). Difficult babies who cry all the time are more of a challenge than babies who are quiet or who are generally cheerful. The parent makes a difference, too. Generally, older parents who have waited longer after marrying to have children are better able to adjust to parenthood (Belsky & Rovine, 1990; Umberson et al., 2005). Younger couples who have children right away are adjusting to marriage at the same time that they are coping with being new parents. The levels of income, spousal support, and support from extended family and friends also increase or decrease the amount of stress that comes with parenting (Levy-Shiff, 1994).

As the child grows older, the demands of parenting do not ease up. Parents adjust their styles of discipline to meet the new challenges their children pose as they grow older and become established (O'Brien, 1996). As the child enters middle school, parenthood may become even more stressful, and marital satisfaction tends to hit an all-time low (FIGURE 9.8; Cui & Donnellan, 2009; Kurdek, 1999; Waldron-Hennessey & Sabatelli, 1997). Parent–child conflicts increase as adolescents achieve formal operational abilities and begin defining their own identity (Steinberg & Morris, 2001). At the same time, parents, who are typically middle-aged at this time, may also be evaluating and questioning the direction of their own lives. As a

FIGURE 9.8

● **Marital Satisfaction and Stages of Parenting** First documented by Rollins and Feldman (1975) and later replicated in many studies, the graph shows the percentage of husbands and wives who said their marriage was going well "all the time" at various stages while raising children. *Adapted from Boyd C. Rollins and Harold Feldman, "Marital Satisfaction Over the Family Life Cycle,"* Journal of Marriage and the Family, 32 *(February), 25. Copyrighted 1975 by the National Council on Family Relations, 3989 Central Ave., N.E., Suite 550, Minneapolis, MN 55421. Reprinted by permission.*

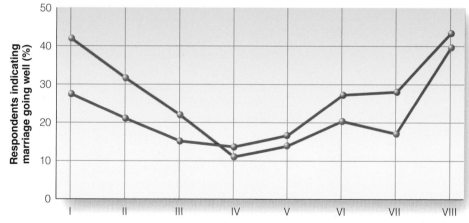

Stage I: Beginning families
Stage II: Child-bearing families
Stage III: Families with preschool children
Stage IV: Families with school-aged children

Stage V: Families with teenagers
Stage VI: Families as launching centers
Stage VII: Families in the middle years
Stage VIII: Aging families

Wives
Husbands

result of this conflict and tension, parents may relinquish some control and move toward more shared decision making with their teenagers. Fortunately, most parents survive their children's adolescent years and look forward to unleashing their offspring on society!

Once the last child has left the family home for college or has moved out to be on her own, parents are left with what is referred to as the *empty nest*. Parents may be lonely at times and feel that a major chapter in their family life is over. The parents are also aware of their own aging. Yet this stage represents lots of opportunity, too. Most parents, especially women, enjoy the changes brought about by the empty nest. Marital satisfaction tends to increase, and women generally feel better about themselves as the stress and responsibilities of parenthood decrease (Gorchoff, John, & Helson, 2008; White & Edwards, 1990).

So what happens to parents if their children don't leave—or if they come back because of divorce, limited finances, or extended schooling? This situation is more common today, when 25–30% of young adults in the United States live with their parents into their late 20s (Gitelson & McDermott, 2006; R. Ward, Logan, & Spitze, 1992). This phenomenon is referred to as the *full nest*, or the *boomerang generation*. It is more common among Hispanic Americans, African Americans, and Asian Americans, perhaps because of the greater emphasis on family closeness in these ethnic groups (Arnett, 2004). If these young adults act responsibly, going to school or working, parents appear to adjust well. However, some parents do find living with their young adult children stressful (Gitelson & McDermott, 2006; Treas & Lawton, 1999; White & Rogers, 1997).

We see, then, that children complicate the lives of adults. Parenthood tends to correlate with lower rates of marital satisfaction and higher levels of stress. Despite these negative effects, most parents don't regret the experience. Children also bring many joys and experiences that enrich their parents' lives.

Adult Development and the World of Work

What do you want to be when you grow up? As a child, you have been asked this question thousands of times, with the expectation that you will answer it with some type of career choice. What we do for a living, or what we hope to do for a living, becomes an integral part of our identity. It may also determine who we socialize with and where we live. **How, then, do people decide on a career?**

According to one model (Ginzberg, 1972, 1984), children first enter a stage of career choice referred to as the *fantasy stage*. At this stage, children dream about what they want to be, such as a teacher, race car driver, or nurse. These wishes are often consistent with the child's developing self-image (Gottfredson, 1996). For Hongyong, this image was prescribed by her culture: she was to be a good wife and mother. Teenagers then enter a second stage, called the *tentative stage*. Adolescents consider such factors as interests (what they like to do), capacities (what they are good at), and values (what they believe to be important, such as money, power, or prestige). However, because adolescents aren't involved in the actual work world, these decisions may not be based on the realities of the job market. Once teens enter the workforce or enroll in college, career selections are narrowed in the *realistic stage* as they learn about the job opportunities in a specific field, the educational requirements, and the outlook for their profession.

What developmental changes do people experience in their careers? With a clear vision of what we want to do, how do we carry out this dream, and what modifications do we make along the way? For five decades, Donald Super (1957, 1976, 1980, 1991) addressed such issues, outlining a progression of career development.

In early adolescence, as teenagers form their identities, they experiment with how various career options fit with their ideas of who they are and what they want to be. During this *crystallization phase*, potential career options are reduced to a few choices. For example, a teenager who views himself as outgoing, quick thinking, and motivated may imagine himself in a marketing or law career. Teenagers and young adults further explore career options by testing prospective career choices in the *specification phase*. For example, a young woman who is considering becoming a doctor may volunteer at a hospital or take a part-time job in a physician's office to determine whether medicine fits her interests and abilities. Although somewhat older, Hongyong explored her talents as an entrepreneur through the sesame oil business, as an opium madam, and as a restaurant owner.

Young people enter the workforce and begin to learn about jobs firsthand in the *implementation phase*. The young adult learns both the actual tasks of the job and job-related skills such as getting along with coworkers, getting to work on time, and responding to authority figures. The reality of the work may not meet the person's initial expectations. For example, a teacher's aide may discover that working with children 6 hours a day is not what he expected it to be. Everyone experiences this sort of *reality shock* in some form. However, it is the degree of reality shock that typically determines our willingness to stay on a particular career path. For this reason, the implementation phase can be quite unsettling and unstable. Young adults may find themselves changing jobs frequently as they attempt to adjust their expectations to the realities of a particular career.

When a young adult decides on a specific occupation, he or she enters the *establishment phase*. Career expectations continue to be adjusted as the person settles into an occupation and advances in his or her career. Today, however, it is unlikely that this establishment will be with one company or on one career path (Cascio, 1995). The establishment phase may also be more characteristic of men's career pathways. Women's careers may be interrupted during these years for childbearing and child rearing (Betz, 1993; Ornstein & Isabella, 1990; Preston, 2005). For Hongyong, the establishment phase came with her *ch'iryo* practice. She knew this was what she wanted to do.

During middle adulthood, career development is characterized by a *maintenance phase*. Although some people may question their career choices and opt for a career change, most middle-aged adults strengthen their commitment to their careers and are more likely to find personal meaning from their work. This personal meaning more often focuses on internal factors such as job satisfaction and contentment than on external factors such as salary and benefits (Warr, 1994).

Workers enter the *deceleration phase* when they begin planning for their upcoming retirement. Older adults consider such things as finances, where they want to live, and how they want to spend their retirement years. When people stop working full-time, the *retirement phase* begins. Most Americans choose to retire sometime in their 60s and look forward to retirement living (Gendell & Siegel, 1996). As with other developmental processes that we have discussed, retirement is a process of adjustment that is influenced by many factors (J. E. Kim & Moen, 2001, 2002; Lowis, Edwards, & Burton, 2009; Price & Balaswamy, 2009; Reitzes & Mutran, 2004; van Solinge & Henkens, 2005):

- *Health.* Ill health often causes retirement rather than the other way around. In this case, people may have difficulty adjusting to retirement because they were forced to retire or because they did not imagine living their retirement years with health problems.
- *High work involvement.* Older adults may adjust less positively to retirement if their career represented a significant part of their identity. Others may find it difficult to give up the predictable pattern of their jobs for a less structured way of life.
- *Control over the decision to retire.* People who voluntarily decide to retire are more likely to report positive adjustment to retirement than people who are forced to retire because of ill health or mandatory retirement age.
- *Finances.* Those who have the financial resources to live comfortably following retirement perceive less stress than do those of more limited means.
- *Social support.* Retirees who are married or who have other social support networks report more positive adjustment to retirement than those with fewer social ties.

During the establishment phase, young adults settle into an occupation or a career.

Older adults generally adapt well to the new role of retiree.

Older adults generally adapt well to retirement. The size of their social networks and frequency of social contacts remain stable. Life satisfaction and mental health are not reduced, and retirees' activity patterns don't change much either (Bosse, Spiro, & Kressin, 1996; Gall, Evans, & Howard, 1997; Hansson et al., 1997; Palmore et al., 1985). Yet, the transition to retirement is not always easy. Like many of the developmental changes we have discussed, it is a new life stage that requires personal adjustment.

Let's
REVIEW
In this section, we detailed the psychosocial changes of adolescence and adulthood. As a quick check of your understanding, try answering the following questions at increasing levels of difficulty.

1. Which of the following is *false* in regard to social relations in adulthood?

  a. Cohabitation rates have increased over the past decade.

  b. People are older at first marriage now than in the past.

  c. Singlehood is associated with better mental and physical health for males.

  d. Divorced people are more likely to experience physical health problems.

2. Tess is a college freshman taking pre-med courses because her parents have always wanted her to be a doctor. She has never considered any other career choice. Marcia would characterize Tess's career identity as _____.

  a. foreclosed   c. diffused

  b. achieved   d. moratorium

3. Jerome is considering what his interests are, what he likes to do, and what he is good at in trying to arrive at a career choice. Which stage of career choice would Jerome fit best?

  a. fantasy stage   c. realistic stage

  b. tentative stage   d. maintenance stage

ANSWERS: 1. c; 2. a; 3. b

LEARNING OBJECTIVE

What Should You Know?

- Describe how people cope psychologically with their own impending death and the death of their loved ones.

HOW DO PEOPLE COPE WITH DEATH AND DYING?

Hongyong Lee witnessed many people's deaths due to war, disease, and starvation. She also personally grieved for the lives of her unborn children, her father, her brother, and her husband. What do people experience psychologically when they know they will die? How do they cope with such news? What do survivors experience? How may others help survivors navigate the storm of grief? Psychologists are also interested in these issues of the last life stage.

Death is a process rather than a point in time. Decades ago it was a process that took place at home, with family members present. Today, it is more likely to occur in a hospital or medical facility, surrounded by doctors, nurses, and machines. In our society, death is more removed from our everyday experiences. As a result, when we face death, we and our families are often unprepared for it. Nevertheless, loss is an inevitable part of our development. Knowing what happens when a loved one is dying and how people respond to the death of a loved one may better prepare us for this final journey.

Reactions to Death: Kübler-Ross's Stages

How do people face death? If you were told today that you only had 6 months to live, how would you react? Elisabeth Kübler-Ross (1926–2004) (1969, 1974), a pioneer researcher on death and dying, interviewed more than 200 terminally ill people to address this question. She wanted to investigate any predictable emotional and psychological changes that people might experience as they confront their own death. From her research, she noted five reactions that may characterize dying people: denial, anger, bargaining, depression, and acceptance.

When people first learn that they have a terminal illness, a typical reaction is *denial*. They behave as if they have not just been told that they are going to die. For example, they may insist on a second or third medical opinion. Others may continue in their normal activities, behaving as if they had never received this news. Denial is an effective coping strategy that allows the person time to come to terms with impending death.

As denial dwindles, it is replaced by the emotional reaction of *anger*. People lash out at loved ones and medical personnel over the unfairness of death. "Why me?" may be a common response during this stage. Looking for others to blame may also be an expression of this anger.

Following denial and anger, some dying people may also express emotions indicative of *bargaining*. They attempt to strike a deal for more time with the doctors, God, or the universe. For example, a man may want to live just long enough to see his daughter get married. Another person may bargain to make it through a particular holiday. These bargains may be unrealistic and impossible to fulfill.

People who are dying may become *depressed*, or extremely sad, when denial, anger, and bargaining fail to delay the progress of their illness. They may lose interest in their usual activities or refuse to participate. This depression may be one way for those who are near the end of life to mourn their own death.

The final emotional state described by Kübler-Ross is *acceptance*. A peace and calm characterize the dying as they face the end of life. They may separate themselves from all but a few of their loved ones as they prepare for life's ending.

© Ken Ross

Elisabeth Kübler-Ross pioneered research on death and dying that noted the emotional reactions terminally ill patients experience.

Research confirms the legitimacy of Kübler-Ross's reaction stages (Kalish, 1985; Samarel, 1995; D. C. Smith, 1993). However, not every dying person experiences all these reactions. Moreover, not all dying persons go through these reactions in the same order. Death, like many other developmental processes, is influenced by a variety of factors, including one's personality and coping style, the type of support received from family members and health professionals, and the nature of the terminal illness. Yet Kübler-Ross's model is useful for understanding the emotions of dying people and for supporting anyone suffering from loss. People may also experience similar reactions when they face a divorce, unemployment, or the impending death of a loved one.

Hongyong experienced many of these emotions as she wondered over the fate of her son and watched her husband die. At first, she denied the possibility that her son was dead or that her husband's illness was fatal. She turned away in anger from her religion when her son did not appear at the refugee camp. Her depression was so intense that she ignored her living children. But as time went by, she slowly accepted her husband's death as well as not knowing the fate of her son.

Bereavement and Grief: How We Respond to Death

How do we cope with the death of a loved one? When a loved one dies, bereavement and grief follow. **Bereavement** is the experience of losing a loved one; **grief** is our emotional reaction to that loss. Just as death is a highly personal experience, so too is grief. However, research on bereaved people has identified common themes and emotional reactions within three phases: impact/shock, confrontation, and accommodation/acceptance (Bowlby, 1980; Parkes, 1986, 1991; Rando, 1995).

Most people's first reaction to the loss of a loved one is shock. This *impact phase* may include disbelief on hearing that a loved one has died. It may feel as if a numbness has settled within one's body or mind. This numbness is adaptive, dulling the painful emotions of loss. People in this stage may perform such actions as picking out a casket, making arrangements for a funeral or a burial, and even calling friends and relatives to inform them of the death, as

bereavement the experience of losing a loved one

grief one's emotional reaction to the death of a loved one

if in a dream. This shock is particularly intense if the person's death was sudden. Think about the emotional numbness and body aches that Hongyong experienced when she thought that her son was dead. She operated as if she were in a fog, a living ghost.

Deep despair and agony may soon follow the numbness and shock in the *confrontation phase*. Uncontrollable weeping, anxiety, and feelings of guilt and anger are not uncommon as the grieving person yearns for the loved one to return. The survivor must confront the reality of the loss, and this can be especially painful. The person may have difficulty concentrating, sleeping, and eating. By confronting each wave of despair, the person moves closer to realizing that the loved one is gone.

As the pain of the confrontation phase subsides, the survivors begin to accept the death of the loved one in the *accommodation phase*. The survivors reengage with life, and the memories of the deceased are internalized. People are now able to refocus their emotional energies on normal daily events and relationships with the living.

How long does this grieving process take? A definitive answer is not possible. The course and intensity of these phases differ from person to person. Personality traits, cultural background, and the circumstances surrounding the death of the loved one are all factors that influence one's grief responses. Some people function considerably better after a year or two; others may take several years. Some may never recover, especially from the death of one's child (Klass, 1993; S. S. Rubin, 1993; W. Stroebe & Stroebe, 1993). This may explain Hongyong's 40-year search for her son. Research also suggests that women may be better able to handle grief, as they are more likely than men to seek social support and express their feelings more openly (Rando, 1995; M. S. Stroebe, 1998; W. Stroebe & Stroebe, 1987).

In this chapter, we examined the many different ways in which people develop. We hope that as you read this chapter, you were able to see how nature and nurture interact and influence physical, cognitive, and social aspects of development. As you look through the key terms and visual summary that follow, relate the material to your own life by generating personal examples that illustrate these concepts. Many of these concepts will be reinforced in later chapters as we explore gender and sexuality, social psychology, coping, and personality.

Shock, disbelief, and numbness are common emotional reactions to the loss of a loved one.

Let's REVIEW

In this section, we discussed how people cope with their own impending death and the death of loved ones. For a quick check of your understanding, try answering the following questions at increasing levels of difficulty.

1. Our emotional reaction to the loss of a loved one is called _____.

   a. bereavement
   b. grief
   c. bargaining
   d. reality shock

2. Caryn has just been diagnosed with cancer and has been given 6 months to live. The next week she signs a 2-year lease on a car. Which stage of dying is Caryn most likely in?

   a. acceptance
   b. bargaining
   c. anger
   d. denial

3. The most intense emotional reactions to the loss of a loved one typically occur during which grief phase?

   a. impact
   b. shock
   c. confrontation
   d. accommodation

ANSWERS: 1. b; 2. d; 3. c

STUDYING the CHAPTER

KEY TERMS

development (347)
nature–nurture issue (350)
zygote (351)
germinal stage (351)
embryonic stage (352)
fetal stage (352)
Down syndrome (352)
teratogen (352)
sensitive period (353)
fetal alcohol syndrome (FAS) (353)
neonate (354)
reflex (355)
gross motor skills (356)
fine motor skills (357)

cognition (359)
schema (360)
assimilation (360)
accommodation (360)
sensorimotor stage (360)
object permanence (361)
symbolic thinking (361)
preoperational stage (362)
centration (362)
conservation (362)
egocentrism (362)
concrete operations (363)
formal operations (364)
private speech (364)

zone of proximal development (ZPD) (365)
scaffolding (365)
moral reasoning (365)
temperament (367)
attachment (368)
separation anxiety (368)
stranger anxiety (369)
authoritarian parent (370)
authoritative parent (370)
permissive parent (370)
puberty (373)
menarche (374)
menopause (377)

imaginary audience (379)
personal fable (379)
dualistic thinking (380)
relativistic thinking (380)
postformal thought (380)
fluid intelligence (381)
crystallized intelligence (382)
diffusion (384)
moratorium (384)
foreclosure (384)
achievement (384)
emerging adulthood (384)
bereavement (395)
grief (395)

LEARNING CHALLENGE

TEST YOURSELF!

Now that you have studied the chapter, assess your comprehension of the material by answering the following questions. Then use the key at the end to determine if your understanding is at the basic, intermediate, or advanced level. For a more comprehensive assessment of your learning, please see your student study guide and your Psychology CourseMate (www.cengagebrain.com).

1. Which of the following cognitive abilities *most* characterizes a child in Piaget's preoperational stage of development?

   a. logical thought
   b. conservation
   c. object permanence
   d. egocentrism

2. Environmental substances that can do harm to the developing organism are called _____.

a. chromosomes
b. teratogens
c. critical periods
d. miscarriage

3. Current thinking on the nature–nurture issue suggests that _____.

a. nature is more important than nurture in determining development
b. nurture is more important than nature in determining development
c. neither nature nor nurture is important in determining development
d. nature and nurture interact in determining development

4. According to Erikson, feeling that you have made important contributions to society will lead to a sense of _____.

a. integrity
b. industry
c. generativity
d. identity

5. "Reality shock" is most likely to happen during which phase of career development?

a. specification phase
b. establishment phase
c. implementation phase
d. deceleration phase

6. Jose is a very active toddler who prefers to do things by himself. According to Erikson, Jose appears to be successfully resolving which developmental crisis?

a. trust versus mistrust
b. autonomy versus shame and doubt
c. initiative versus guilt
d. industry versus inferiority

7. Ms. Lucy, the kindergarten teacher, tries her best to coach her students by making each task somewhat more difficult than the last and modeling how best to approach each task. Ms. Lucy's practice is most consistent with _____.

a. scaffolding
b. accommodation
c. assimilation
d. private speech

8. Some students think it is wrong to cheat because it violates the student code of conduct. Such students are operating at the _____ level of moral reasoning.

a. preconventional
b. conventional
c. postconventional
d. preoperational

9. Jamal sees two differently shaped glasses filled with liquid. He recognizes that even though they look different, the glasses hold the same amount of liquid. Piaget would say that Jamal is operating at the _____ stage of cognitive development.

a. sensorimotor
b. preconventional
c. formal operational
d. concrete operational

10. Changes associated with the middle-aged female occur during _____, when fertility steadily decreases.

a. puberty
b. menarche
c. menopause
d. andropause

11. Alicia is an anxious and conforming child. It is most likely that her parents _____.

a. are divorced
b. have an authoritarian parenting style
c. have a permissive parenting style
d. have an authoritative parenting style

12. The development of one's personal values and character is referred to as _____.

a. identity
b. initiative
c. industry
d. integrity

13. How are preschoolers and teenagers similar in their thinking?

a. Both cannot think abstractly.
b. Both have developed conservation abilities.
c. Both are egocentric in their thinking.
d. Teenagers and preschoolers are not similar in their thinking.

14. As a baby, Reece was generally in a good mood, regularly approached new people and situations, and had a regular pattern of sleeping and eating. Reece's temperament is best described as _____.

a. easy
b. avoidant
c. difficult
d. slow-to-warm-up

15. The symptoms of the impact stage are most closely associated with which Kübler-Ross reaction?

a. depression
b. bargaining
c. anger
d. denial

Scoring Key

The answers and the associated point values for each of the Learning Challenge questions follow. Circle the associated points for each question that you answered correctly. To obtain your Learning Challenge Score, add up the points you circled and write the total in the blank.

1. D, 2 pt   **6.** B, 2 pts   **11.** B, 3 pts

2. B, 1 pt   **7.** A, 2 pts   **12.** A, 1 pt

3. D, 1 pt   **8.** B, 3 pts   **13.** C, 3 pts

4. C, 2 pts   **9.** D, 2 pts   **14.** A, 1 pt

5. C, 3 pts   **10.** C, 1 pt   **15.** D, 3 pts

Learning Challenge Score _____

(27–30) Congratulations! You scored at the advanced level. You are well on your way to mastering the material. Take the next step by answering the questions in your Student Study Guide or your Psychology CourseMate (www.cengagebrain.com).

(21–26) You are almost there! You scored at the intermediate level. Review the material you missed before moving on to answer the questions in your Student Study Guide or your Psychology CourseMate (www.cengagebrain.com).

(20 and below) You are on your way, but you're not there yet! You scored at the beginner level. It appears that you need to carefully review the chapter to improve your mastery of the material.

USE IT OR LOSE IT: APPLYING PSYCHOLOGY

1. At what age would you introduce your child to the following games and toys, and why?

a. a board game   d. hide-and-seek
b. building blocks   e. a chemistry set
c. constructing a model spaceship

2. Analyze your parent(s)' style of discipline during your childhood. How would Baumrind classify their parenting style? How well did their style complement your temperament? What impact do you think your parent(s)' style of discipline had on your development? Be specific, and cite examples to support your answer.

3. For each of Erikson's psychosocial stages, detail what specific behaviors may suggest that an individual is having difficulty resolving that particular stage.

4. Imagine that you have just been told that you are going to have a baby. Use your knowledge about infant development to design a nursery for your baby. Create a list of items you'd like to include, such as furniture, toys, and bedding, and describe how you would decorate the walls. Explain your choices in terms of developmental processes.

5. Describe what you feel are benefits to aging and give examples to support your arguments.

6. Use the information in this chapter to analyze your current identity. How have peers and parents influenced how you see yourself? What modifications in your identity do you expect in the coming years?

CRITICAL THINKING FOR INTEGRATION

1. Review the information on memory processing (Chapter 6) and problem solving (Chapter 7). What strategies and activities would Piaget and Vygotsky suggest are best for improving children's memory and problem-solving skills? Would they suggest the same techniques or different ones?

2. Use operant conditioning (Chapter 5) to explain why it might be difficult for older adults to acquire new abilities.

3. Use each of the different psychological perspectives introduced in Chapter 1 to explain career choice in adulthood.

4. How do the aging trends described in this chapter relate to the information on sensation and perception discussed in Chapter 3?

CHAPTER STUDY RESOURCES

Student Study Guide

To help organize your learning, work through Chapter 9 of the *What Is Psychology? Student Study Guide*. The study guide includes learning objectives, a chapter summary, fill-in review, key terms, a practice test, and activities.

CengageNOW

Go to **www.cengage.com/login** to link to CengageNOW, your online study tool. First take the Pre-Test for this chapter to get your personalized study plan, which will identify topics you need to review and direct you to online resources. Then take the Post-Test to determine what concepts you have mastered and what you still need work on.

CourseMate

Access an interactive eBook, chapter-specific interactive learning tools, including flashcards, quizzes, videos, and more in your Psychology CourseMate, available at **CengageBrain.com**.

Aplia

Aplia™ is an online interactive learning solution that helps you improve comprehension—and your grade—by integrating a variety of tools such as video, tutorials, practice tests, and interactive eBook. Founded by a professor to enhance his own courses, Aplia provides automatically graded assignments with detailed, immediate explanations on every question, and innovative teaching materials. More than 1,000,000 students like you have used Aplia at over 1,800 institutions. Aplia should be purchased only when assigned by your instructor as part of your course.

HOW DO PEOPLE GROW, CHANGE, AND DEVELOP?

The life story of Hongyong Lee illustrates the sometimes dramatic kinds of turning points that shape development. **Development** includes changes in physical, emotional, social, and cognitive behavior and abilities over time through an interaction of **nature** (one's biology) and **nurture** (one's environment and culture).

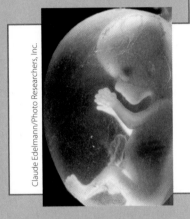

Claude Edelmann/Photo Researchers, Inc.

DEVELOPMENT: HOW DOES IT ALL BEGIN?

- **Germinal stage** (0–14 days): the zygote undergoes rapid cell division and duplication
- **Embryonic stage** (2–8 weeks): major organs and organ systems form
- **Fetal stage** (week 9–birth): body organs and systems more fully develop

HOW DO INFANTS AND CHILDREN DEVELOP PHYSICALLY?

- Infants' and children's brains are highly plastic, or changeable.
- **Reflexes** such as sucking, rooting, and grasping help the infant survive.
- **Gross motor skills** (behaviors that involve large muscle groups) develop and allow the child to run, walk, jump, and hop.
- **Fine motor skills** (involving small muscle groups) develop and aid activities such as writing, using utensils, and playing a musical instrument.

HOW DO INFANTS AND CHILDREN DEVELOP COGNITIVELY?

- According to Jean Piaget:
  - A **schema** (a mental idea or concept) helps the child organize his or her world.
  - **Assimilation** helps children apply a schema to understand their environment.
  - **Accommodation** occurs when existing schemas are changed, modified, or created to adapt to change.
- There are four stages of cognitive development: **sensorimotor stage** (from birth to 2 years), **preoperational stage** (from age 2 to age 6 or 7), **concrete operational stage** (from age 6 or 7 through age 12), and a **formal operational stage** (from the teenage years).
- Lev Vygotsky emphasized that mental processes begin externally and stressed the importance of culture and social interactions in cognitive development.
- Lawrence Kohlberg suggested that **moral reasoning** in children develops at three levels:
  - Preconventional level: avoid punishment or gain rewards
  - Conventional level: the standards of the group or society
  - Postconventional level: contractual and universal principles of morality
- Carol Gilligan proposed gender differences in moral reasoning that have not been supported.

© Laura Dwight/Photo Edit

© Bettmann/Corbis

Courtesy of Harlow Primate Lab, U. of Wisconsin

HOW DO INFANTS AND CHILDREN DEVELOP PSYCHOSOCIALLY?

- Infants generally have one of three **temperament** styles: easy, difficult, or slow-to-warm-up.
- **Attachment** is the emotional tie between the infant and the primary caregiver.
- Diana Baumrind identified three styles of parenting: **authoritarian**, **authoritative**, and **permissive**.
- Psychologist Erik Erikson proposed that the environment and the child's responses to the environment influence the development of either a healthy or an unhealthy personality.

HOW DO ADOLESCENTS AND ADULTS DEVELOP PHYSICALLY, COGNITIVELY, AND PSYCHOSOCIALLY?

- **Puberty** involves maturation of sex characteristics that enable us to reproduce. At around age 50, women experience **menopause** and hormonal changes that eventually bring an end to reproductive capacity.
- During adolescence and throughout life, the brain remains highly plastic, allowing us to adapt to changing conditions.
- Teenagers tend to be **egocentric**, believing that others are concerned with the same things that they are.
- **Postformal thought** is characterized by an appreciation that the correct solution or answer may vary from situation to situation.
- Remaining cognitively active helps adults avoid steep declines in memory.
- Erik Erikson considered adolescence the key stage for developing identity although he believed adults continued to develop when they established intimacy, generativity, and integrity.
- Adolescent and adult relationships are expressed in a wide range of lifestyles, including dating, cohabitation, marriage, divorce, and parenthood.
- Finding satisfying work and holding a job are part of adult development. Career choice develops through fantasy, tentative, and realistic stages.

© Susan Van Etten/Photo Edit

Greg Ceo/Getty Images

HOW DO PEOPLE COPE WITH DEATH AND DYING?

- Death is a process rather than a point in time and is an inevitable part of our development.
- Elisabeth Kübler-Ross, a researcher on death and dying, identified five reactions that may characterize people who know they are dying: denial, anger, bargaining, depression, and acceptance.

© Mark Richards/Photo Edit

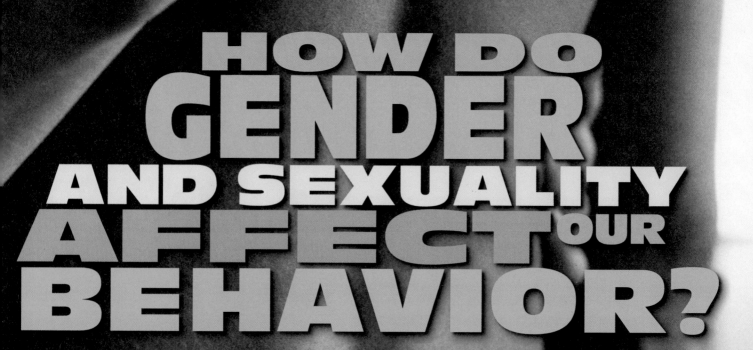

HOW DO GENDER AND SEXUALITY AFFECT OUR BEHAVIOR?

THE BIG PICTURE | How Do We Develop a Gender and Sexual Identity?

The previous chapter outlined the developmental changes that we experience as we progress from infancy to older adulthood. This chapter extends that discussion by looking more specifically at the influence of gender and sexuality on our behavior. Our biological sex and our feelings about it are key aspects of our social development. **Sex** refers to our biological makeup, starting with our chromosomes (XX for female, XY for male) and proceeding to our internal and external genitalia. **Gender** refers to the experience of being male or female. It represents how we think and feel about ourselves in terms of our anatomical sex. By age 3, most toddlers can identify whether they are male or female. This is one of the first steps in establishing our **gender identity**, the personal experience of being male or female. **Sexuality** includes the ways we experience and express ourselves as sexual beings. This includes our sexual behaviors and experiences as well as our sexual attitudes, feelings, and beliefs. Often, gender and sexuality become intertwined within the social and cultural context of a particular time and place, as the following case study illustrates.

In 1993, award-winning poet Maya Angelou read her poem "On the Pulse of the Morning" at President Bill Clinton's inauguration. This honor brought Maya Angelou and her work to national prominence. Although she had been publishing her work since the early 1970s, with the inaugural address, Maya Angelou became a household name. By the late 1990s, Maya Angelou was one of America's most famous African American women. This fame was well deserved, for her accomplishments are quite impressive. She has published numerous best-selling books, in addition to having a successful career as a mother, college professor, poet, singer, actor, playwright, magazine editor, and civil rights activist.

Born Marguerite Johnson in 1928 in St. Louis, Missouri, Maya spent much of her childhood living with her brother, Bailey, and her grandmother after her parents separated. They lived in the small, rural town of Stamps, Arkansas, where the family ran a small general store. Her grandmother's loving care provided Maya with an exceptional female role model. Although life with her grandmother was stable and loving, Maya would periodically go live with her mother. During one of these stays, Maya

© Masterfile

© 1983 by Random House, Inc. Used by permission of Bantam Books, a division of Random House, Inc.

was raped at age 8 by her mother's boyfriend. Maya's uncles beat the man to death. Without access to professional counseling, Maya was pretty much left on her own to deal with and recover from this tragedy. Believing her confession of the rape led to the man's death, Maya coped by not speaking. She was voluntarily mute until she was almost 13 years old, but amazingly she did recover.

Even without such a tragedy, Maya's life was not destined to be an easy one. As she entered adolescence, she was continually confronted with the limitations that society attempted to place on a Black woman. She felt physically plain and self-conscious about her 6-foot frame. Yet her brother Bailey reminded her that size had nothing to do with being female. Like many adolescents, Maya felt the desire to explore the romantic side of life. In doubt about her sexual orientation, Maya had sex with a young man whom she scarcely knew in order to find out whether she was a lesbian. She simply asked the most popular boy in town if he wanted to have sex with her. She found the experience awkward and unromantic. And, as for many young people, these explorations led to some very grown-up problems. At 16, Maya became pregnant; she gave birth three weeks after graduating from high school. Her son, Guy, became the focus of her life.

For an unwed African American woman, raising a child in the 1940s was no easy feat. Poverty, racism, and sexism were constant obstacles, and the attitudes that many held about Black women led to discrimination in the workplace. Back then, a Black woman could look forward to a career as a maid or a cook, but she would not normally be permitted to hold more prestigious positions. On one occasion, Maya was denied a job as a telephone operator even though she passed the operator's exam with flying colors. The company instead offered her a job they deemed more appropriate for a Black woman—busing tables in the company cafeteria (Angelou, 1974). Maya also danced in a strip joint. She didn't have to strip, though, because she barely wore anything to begin with. Her costume consisted of two sequins and a feather.

During young adulthood, Maya went through a series of relationships with men. Unfortunately for her, however, these relationships often did not fulfill her conception of what a romantic relationship was all about. She wrote of her dreams as a young woman: "Like most young women, I wanted a man, any man to give me a June Allyson screen-role life with sunken living room, cashmere-sweater sets, and I, for one, obviously would have done anything to get that life" (Angelou, 1974, p. 192).

Maya grew up with the idea that the female had to be the weak person in a relationship. She believed it would be heaven to find a husband who told her what to think and how to act. Maya's desire for a fairy-tale romance was not very realistic in the 1940s, and it is still unrealistic today. Nonetheless, it drove her to enter into several doomed relationships with married or abusive men. She was tricked by one lover into becoming a prostitute and managed a house of prostitution in order to earn him money. She married an African diplomat and moved to Egypt for two years, where she observed

sex our biological makeup, starting with our chromosomes (XX for female, XY for male) and proceeding to our internal and external genitalia

gender the experience of being male or female

gender identity one's personal experience of being male or female

sexuality the ways we express ourselves as sexual beings

that "a woman is less important than the water buffalo." She wanted to work while she was there, but her husband said it would be impossible in Egypt because nice women did not work. Maya got a job anyway, writing for an English newsweekly. All the other journalists were male, and the idea of having a woman work there, let alone a female boss, was ridiculous.

Maya Angelou's life experiences beautifully illustrate the powerful connections between gender, sexuality, and behavior. Her feelings about her femininity and sexuality influenced her sexual behavior, resulting in an unplanned pregnancy. Her ideas and attitudes about appropriate male and female gender roles influenced the jobs she took as well as the success of her romantic relationships. Being abused at such a young age also probably influenced her ideas about herself, men, and sexuality.

As you read this chapter, keep Maya's story in mind and the complex relationship between gender and sexuality, and attempt to understand how each has made you who you are today. You may not have thought that so many different types of experiences related to gender and sexuality could lie beneath Maya Angelou's many accomplishments and achievements. Yet gender and sexuality greatly influence who we are, what we do, the decisions we make, and how we interact with others. Only by examining such topics more closely can we see their subtle yet enormous influence on our behavior.

Frederick M. Brown/Getty Images

Despite a history of sexual abuse and gender discrimination, Maya Angelou is an accomplished author, poet, educator, and civil rights activist.

HOW DO WE DEVELOP OUR GENDER IDENTITY AND DO MALES AND FEMALES DIFFER?

This section details the biological, psychological, and social components of gender. We will start with *sexual differentiation*, or the biological process by which males and females develop their sexual anatomy. We will then turn our attention to gender-role development and see how nature and nurture influence our gender identity. We will examine how the genders differ in cognitive abilities and personality. Understanding gender identity will allow us to explore its influence on sexual behavior later in this chapter.

Sexual Differentiation: How Do We Develop Our Sexual Anatomy?

Sexual differentiation is the process by which males and females develop their sexual anatomy. This process begins in the womb during the embryonic stage of prenatal development (Chapter 9). The first determination of gender begins at conception with sex chromosomes.

sexual differentiation the process by which males and females develop their sexual anatomy

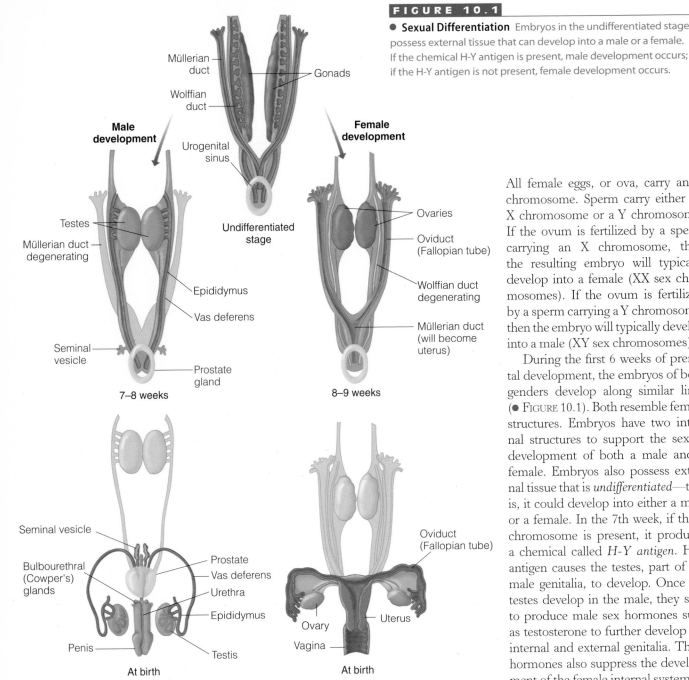

● **Sexual Differentiation** Embryos in the undifferentiated stage possess external tissue that can develop into a male or a female. If the chemical H-Y antigen is present, male development occurs; if the H-Y antigen is not present, female development occurs.

Male development

Müllerian duct

Wolffian duct

Testes

Müllerian duct degenerating

Epididymus

Vas deferens

Seminal vesicle

Prostate gland

7–8 weeks

Gonads

Urogenital sinus

Undifferentiated stage

Female development

Ovaries

Oviduct (Fallopian tube)

Wolffian duct degenerating

Müllerian duct (will become uterus)

8–9 weeks

Seminal vesicle

Bulbourethral (Cowper's) glands

Penis

At birth

Prostate

Vas deferens

Urethra

Epididymus

Testis

Ovary

Vagina

At birth

Oviduct (Fallopian tube)

Uterus

All female eggs, or ova, carry an X chromosome. Sperm carry either an X chromosome or a Y chromosome. If the ovum is fertilized by a sperm carrying an X chromosome, then the resulting embryo will typically develop into a female (XX sex chromosomes). If the ovum is fertilized by a sperm carrying a Y chromosome, then the embryo will typically develop into a male (XY sex chromosomes).

During the first 6 weeks of prenatal development, the embryos of both genders develop along similar lines (● FIGURE 10.1). Both resemble female structures. Embryos have two internal structures to support the sexual development of both a male and a female. Embryos also possess external tissue that is *undifferentiated*—that is, it could develop into either a male or a female. In the 7th week, if the Y chromosome is present, it produces a chemical called *H-Y antigen*. H-Y antigen causes the testes, part of the male genitalia, to develop. Once the testes develop in the male, they start to produce male sex hormones such as testosterone to further develop the internal and external genitalia. These hormones also suppress the development of the female internal system.

In the absence of the Y chromosome, no H-Y antigen is produced, which causes ovaries to develop. The relative absence of male sex hormones also prompts the development of female internal and external sexual organs and suppresses the development of the internal male system. Consequently, if something were to go wrong such that a genetic male (XY) embryo did not secrete H-Y antigen or male sex hormones, female internal and external sexual organs would develop (Federman, 1994).

Can a person develop both male and female sexual anatomy? Yes. Hormonal errors make it possible for a person to develop both fully formed testicular and ovarian tissue, referred to as **hermaphroditism**. However, true hermaphroditism is quite rare (Krstic et al., 2000). More common than hermaphroditism is pseudohermaphroditism. A **pseudohermaphrodite** develops ambiguous internal or external sexual anatomy because of prenatal hormonal errors. For example, a genetic female may have developed ovaries along with an enlarged clitoris that resembles a small penis. Conversely, a genetic male may be born with

hermaphrodite a person who develops both fully formed testicular and ovarian tissue

pseudohermaphrodite a person who develops ambiguous internal or external sexual anatomy

undescended testes and feminized genitals, including a vagina. Today people with ambiguous sex characteristics are commonly referred to as *intersexed*.

The process of sexual differentiation results in a person being labeled as male or female at birth. This gender label then sets the stage for gender-role development, which we turn to next.

Gender and Gender-Role Development

By 2 or 3 years old, children know whether they are a boy or a girl and can label the gender of others. These labels then provide a framework for understanding what clothes, toys, colors, jobs, and behaviors are "appropriate" for each sex. Thus, children at a very early age are processing and developing schemas about **gender roles**, or society's expectations for how a female and a male should behave (Leaper & Friedman, 2007). For example, one day one of the authors was driving in her car with her then 4-year-old son. She asked him what he wanted to do when he got older. He replied, "I want to be a firefighter and drive a fire truck." Her son then asked her what she wanted to be when she was older and suggested that she might also want to consider being a firefighter like him. His mother stated, "It would be cool to drive a fire truck." He replied, "Oh, no, Mommy, you can't drive the fire truck. Only boys can drive fire trucks." His mother replied, "Well, who is driving this car?" "You are, Mommy," the young boy replied. "And am I a boy or a girl?" his mother questioned. "You're a girl," he replied. "And girls can't drive fire trucks." For him, males had received the label of fire truck drivers, and flexibility in this rule was not allowed.

Gender permanence or constancy is the knowledge that our assigned gender will not change. Typically, children under the age of 6 years do not yet understand that their gender is permanent (De Lisi & Gallagher, 1991; Szkrybalo & Ruble, 1999). Recall that at this age children focus on only one aspect of a situation or an object. If one of your features or behaviors looks like that of a male, then you are a male. If the feature fits with the child's concept of a female, then you are a female. Consequently, if a little boy puts on his mother's dress, he may believe that he is now a girl.

How do children learn gender roles? The process by which a child develops gender roles and comes to label specific behaviors and activities as either masculine or feminine is not completely understood. Psychologists currently endorse Sandra Bem's (1981) **gender-schema theory**, a perspective that combines elements of social learning theory and cognitive development. Gender-schema theory suggests that the social learning processes of modeling and reinforcement work together with a child's developing mental abilities to facilitate the child's understanding of gender (C. L. Martin & Halverson, 1981, 1987). From a very early age, children are keen observers of their environment. They see which behaviors men and women engage in, and which of those behaviors are reinforced or punished. With these observations, children actively construct schemas on gender behaviors. These schemas then guide children's decisions about how they and others should behave (C. L. Martin & Ruble, 2010).

The schemas for gender-role behavior are culturally defined and vary from society to society. In many cultures, traditional gender roles are emphasized for children (Shiraev & Levy, 2010). Males are seen as aggressive, unemotional, and dominant whereas females are seen as passive and emotional. Yet within U.S. society, one's ethnic background may convey different gender stereotypes. For example, traditional Hispanic American gender roles stress the faithful, self-sacrificing female who is subordinate to her husband and is seen as the preserver of family and tradition. The male is strong, dominant, and the head of the household who is responsible for the safety and honor of the family (McNeill et al., 2001; Reid & Bing, 2000). Among African Americans, females assume the dominant role in the family. Strong extended family bonds and high levels of adaptability in gender roles are emphasized (Reid & Bing, 2000). Asian Americans value group solidarity. For females, family obligations are expected to be of higher priority than

gender roles society's expectations for how males and females should behave

gender permanence the understanding that one's gender will not change

gender-schema theory the idea that gender roles are acquired through modeling and reinforcement processes that work together with a child's mental abilities

Young children lack gender permanence, the knowledge that our assigned gender does not change. Playing dress-up allows them to explore the gender roles of the other sex.

© Ellen Pastorino

individual achievement, and males are seen as dominant (Pyke & Johnson, 2003). How are such expectations conveyed? We turn to the influence of nature and nurture.

Nature and Nurture Influences on Gender-Role Behavior

Psychologists have explored the extent to which gender-role behavior is due to nature and nurture. For example, research suggests that many gender differences appear across cultures and in other species, such as the preference to develop same-sex friendships, the higher level of activity and physical aggressiveness in males, and toy preferences (Beatty, 1992; Hassett, Siebert, & Wallen, 2008; C. L. Martin & Ruble, 2010). For example, Hassett et al. (2008) found that male rhesus monkeys showed consistent preference for wheeled toys while the female rhesus monkeys tended to show a broader range of toy preferences. These findings suggest that gender differences may in part be influenced by hormonal or genetic differences between males and females, particularly during prenatal development. Females prenatally exposed to high levels of male hormones show increased male-typical play and aggression (Auyeung et al., 2009; Drea, 2009). On the other hand, the child's environment is filled with messages about gender. These messages come from parents, teachers, peers, and the larger society and illustrate the powerful impact of nurture on gender behavior (Bussey & Bandura, 1999).

Parents are the first source of information for babies on gender. Very early in infancy, babies learn to respond differently to their mothers and fathers, suggesting that schemas for gender roles are already developing. For example, on seeing the mother approach, babies are more likely to relax their bodies, showing lowered heart and respiration rates. When seeing the father approach, babies' heart and respiration rates increase, and they open their eyes wide (Pruett, 2000). **Do the babies' behaviors reflect actual differences in parental behaviors?**

In many ways, sons and daughters are treated similarly (Lytton & Romney, 1991). Mothers and fathers encourage both sons and daughters to be independent. Parents are equally warm to their children regardless of gender. Both mothers and fathers have high educational aspirations for their children and value achievement in both their sons and daughters (Paulson & Sputa, 1996; Spera, Wentzel, & Matto, 2009). Yet, daughters experience more parental involvement with their education than do sons, and girls perceive their parents as more encouraging of higher education than do boys (Carter & Wojtkiewicz, 2000; Reynolds & Burge, 2008). However, in the area of science achievement (a traditionally male-stereotyped activity), parents were more likely to believe that science was less interesting and more difficult for their daughters, even when there were no differences in the children's interest or science grades (Tenenbaum & Leaper, 2003). In addition, most parents expect their children to play with gender-appropriate toys. Boys play with guns, cars, blocks, and balls. Girls are expected to play with dolls and tea sets and to enjoy activities such as playing dress-up, house, and school. Parents assign different household chores to their sons and daughters. Girls wash the dishes and do chores inside the house such as vacuuming and dusting. Boys take out the trash

Parents' interactions with their children influence their developing schemas of gender roles.

and do outdoor chores such as mowing the lawn, washing cars, and cleaning out the garage. Fathers are much more likely to hold to these gender stereotypes and tend to be less accepting of cross-gender behaviors, especially in their sons (Lytton & Romney, 1991; O'Bryan, Fishbein, & Ritchey, 2004).

Parents who are less likely to hold these gender expectations tend to have children who are less gender-typed (Warner & Steel, 1999; S. D. Witt, 1997). Moreover, children who *see* their parents behave in a less stereotypical fashion—moms taking out the trash or dads performing household tasks—also tend to be less gender-typed (P. J. Turner & Gervai, 1995). Parents, however, are not the only ones who influence children's gender roles. Once children begin school, teachers and peers influence gender schemas as well.

Are boys and girls treated differently in the classroom? Research suggests that *gender bias* exists in many classrooms (Stromquist, 2007). Gender bias is the favoring of one gender over the other because of different views of male and female roles. Boys tend to receive both more positive and more negative attention from teachers and are called on more often (Einarsson & Granstrom, 2004; S. Jones & Dindia, 2004; Swinson & Harrop, 2009). Teachers are also more likely to accept wrong answers from girls, encourage boys to try harder when they make errors, and see boys as more clever (D. D. Horgan, 1995; Skelton, 2006). Teachers also tend to stereotype mathematics as a male domain even when boys and girls perform similarly (Keller, 2001; Tiedemann, 2002). Even when it comes to career counseling, boys are more likely to be encouraged to enter higher-status professions in math and science, such as engineering, whereas girls are encouraged to pursue education, nursing, and social work (D. Sadker, 2000).

Children's notions about gender are also reinforced within their peer groups, starting as early as 3 years old. Same-sex peers praise the child for engaging in gender-appropriate behaviors. Children who engage in gender-inappropriate behavior may be teased, laughed at, and even isolated from the group. Boys are particularly critical of same-sex peers who engage in "girlish" behavior, resulting in harsher punishment for their activities (G. D. Levy, Taylor, & Gelman, 1995; A. J. Rose & Smith, 2009).

Society in general also contributes to children's gender stereotypes. Fast-food chains offer boy and girl toys with their children's meals. Some toy stores still have aisles marked "Boys" and "Girls." Many television shows still hold to traditional gender stereotypes (Aucoin, 2000). Males appear more frequently and tend to be the dominant characters. Male characters on children's shows are more likely than female characters to engage in active tasks such as climbing or riding a bike. Females are more often depicted as passive, dependent, and emotional. Many of the female characters on television are not employed. When they do have jobs, they are often stereotypical ones such as teachers, nurses, and secretaries (A. C. Huston & Wright, 1998; Signorielli & Bacue, 1999). Analyses of television advertisements in over 20 countries paint a similar picture. Women are more likely to be the user of the product while men are more often portrayed as the wise, knowledgeable expert. Women appear more often in domestic roles selling body care and household cleaning products and appear less often in occupational settings. Men are rarely shown in private residences or with children in the background (Furnham & Paltzer, 2010; Nassif & Gunter, 2008). Children who watch television frequently may adopt these gender-role stereotypes.

Society encourages boys and girls to develop stereotypical gender schema by prescribing what are appropriate "boy" and "girl" toys.

© David Young-Wolff/PhotoEdit, Inc.

Gender Identity: The Influence of Nature and Nurture

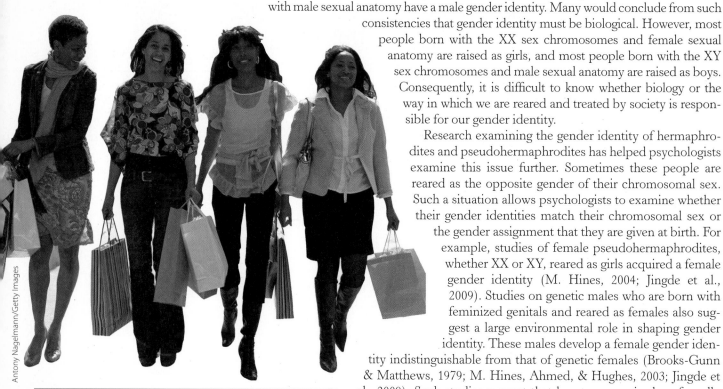

How do we come to think of ourselves as either male or female? For most of us, our gender identity is consistent with our sex chromosomes and sexual anatomy. Most XX individuals with female sexual anatomy have a female gender identity, and most XY individuals with male sexual anatomy have a male gender identity. Many would conclude from such consistencies that gender identity must be biological. However, most people born with the XX sex chromosomes and female sexual anatomy are raised as girls, and most people born with the XY sex chromosomes and male sexual anatomy are raised as boys. Consequently, it is difficult to know whether biology or the way in which we are reared and treated by society is responsible for our gender identity.

Research examining the gender identity of hermaphrodites and pseudohermaphrodites has helped psychologists examine this issue further. Sometimes these people are reared as the opposite gender of their chromosomal sex. Such a situation allows psychologists to examine whether their gender identities match their chromosomal sex or the gender assignment that they are given at birth. For example, studies of female pseudohermaphrodites, whether XX or XY, reared as girls acquired a female gender identity (M. Hines, 2004; Jingde et al., 2009). Studies on genetic males who are born with feminized genitals and reared as females also suggest a large environmental role in shaping gender identity. These males develop a female gender identity indistinguishable from that of genetic females (Brooks-Gunn & Matthews, 1979; M. Hines, Ahmed, & Hughes, 2003; Jingde et al., 2009). Such studies suggest that how we are raised profoundly influences our gender identity.

Most people have a gender identity that matches their assigned sex.

In other investigations, chromosomal females born with masculine-looking external genitalia were treated with minor surgery or hormone therapy and raised as girls. Yet many identified themselves as tomboys, expressed more cross-gender behavior than the female control group, and were less comfortable with a feminine gender identity (Money & Ehrhardt, 1972; Zucker et al., 1996; Slijper et al., 1998). These studies underscore the impact of biological factors in shaping our gender identity.

transsexual a person whose gender identity is opposite to his or her chromosomal sex

In addition, some people are born of one chromosomal sex but identify with the other gender, a condition referred to as transsexualism. A **transsexual** is a person whose gender identity is opposite to his or her chromosomal sex. Transsexuals often feel as if they were born in the wrong body. An anatomical male may feel that she is a woman, or an anatomical female may feel that he is a man. Many transsexuals undergo sex reassignment procedures that may include hormone therapy, living as the preferred gender, genital surgery, or a combination of these so that their anatomical sex is consistent with their gender identity (Sohn & Bosinski, 2007).

Only child of legendary performers Sonny and Cher, Chaz Bono recently underwent reassignment procedures, transitioning from Chastity to Chaz so that his assigned sex would match his gender identity.

So where does that leave us in understanding gender identity? As we have seen, gender identity is a complex process involving biological and environmental roots. Sex chromosomes, hormones, and sexual anatomy intertwine with social influences and life experiences early on in our development to shape our sense of femaleness or maleness.

Gender Differences: Do Males and Females Think and Act Differently?

Do men's and women's behavior differ? Given that males and females arise from similar tissue, you may not be surprised to learn that males and females are more similar than they are different (Hyde, 2007). Just as one particular female may differ from one specific male, there are also wide differences among females and wide differences among males. Yet, consistent gender differences have been found between men and women in the areas of cognitive abilities and personality.

Cognitive Abilities

Society tends to endorse the notion that males do better at some tasks whereas females excel at others. Such attitudes may foster expectations about what a particular male or female can or cannot do. For example, we saw that Maya Angelou was denied a job as a telephone operator and told not to work at all in Egypt because of sexist stereotypes concerning what a female can do. **Are there differences in males' and females' cognitive abilities?** Let's look at what the research suggests.

On average, girls speak earlier than boys, yet boys eventually catch up. However, boys are more often diagnosed with autism, stuttering, and learning disabilities, such as dyslexia and attention deficit disorder with hyperactivity (P. Cohen et al., 1993; Wallentin, 2009). Boys also tend to lag behind girls on tests of reading comprehension and writing (Halpern, 2004; Halpern et al., 2007; Hedge & Nowell, 1995; Hoff-Sommers, 2000).

The research detailing gender differences in math abilities is also quite complex. The stereotype is that males do better in math than females. So it might surprise you to learn that females get higher grades in math classes at all grade levels (Halpern et al., 2007). At the end of high school, males tend to outperform females on the math portion of the SAT (Byrnes & Takahira, 1993; Halpern et al., 2007). More specifically, males do better on math items requiring spatial skills or multiple solutions (A. M. Gallagher et al., 2000). Females do better than males on algebra problems when the cognitive strategy to solve the problem is similar to language-processing strategies (Gallagher, Levin, & Cahalan, 2002; Halpern et al., 2007). Yet these findings may be misleading because more at-risk females than at-risk males take the SAT. Being *at risk* means you are more likely to come from a low-income home or have parents who never graduated from high school or attended college; hence at-risk students are more likely to score lower on the SAT. In addition, males are more variable in their mathematical ability. That is, males outnumber females at both the very high and very low levels of mathematical ability (Halpern et al., 2007; Lohman & Lakin, 2009). Because fewer at-risk males take the SAT (Hoff-Sommers, 2000), the males who do take the test are more likely to be better students and may not fairly represent all males.

In the area of visuospatial skills, it appears that males have the advantage (Halpern, 2004; Halpern et al., 2007; Voyer, Voyer, & Bryden, 1995). Between the ages of 4 and 5, males excel at tasks that require visuospatial processing. Visuospatial tasks include the ability to follow a map, construct a puzzle, build a piece of equipment, or play a video game. This male spatial advantage is more evident among males from higher socioeconomic backgrounds (Levine et al., 2005). Such differences may arise from biological factors. Several studies have documented an early emergence of a gender difference in mental rotation, favoring males as young as 3 to 4 months old (D. S. Moore & Johnson, 2008; Quinn & Liben, 2008). Yet, boys spend more time on these types of activities than girls do, emphasizing the role of learning (C. S. Green & Bavelier, 2007). For example, when women who were non–video game players received 10 hours of training with an action video game, they made substantial gains in mental rotation skills (Feng, Spence, & Pratt, 2007).

© Ellen Pastorino

Playing video games may enhance males' spatial skills.

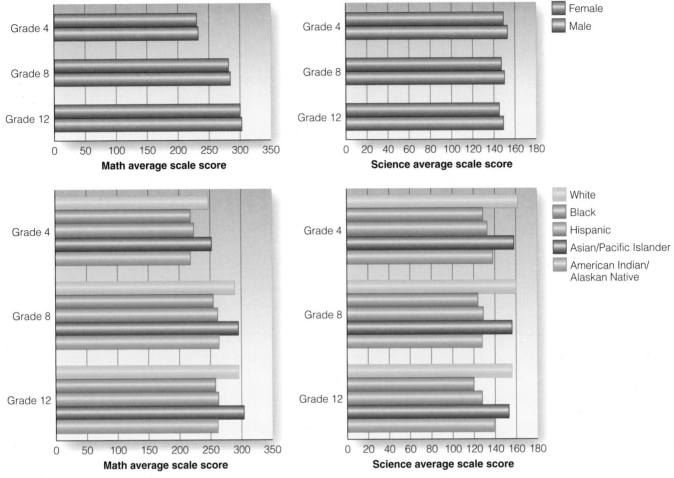

Note: Math scores range from 0 to 500. Science scores range from 0 to 300.

● **Average Math and Science Scores in Grades 4, 8, and 12 by Sex and Ethnicity** Males and females do not differ significantly in their performance on national math and science scores. Ethnic differences are more significant. *Source: U.S. Department of Education, National Center for Education Statistics, National Assessment of Educational Progress (NAEP), 2009.*

When we examine national averages for math and science scores for males and females in grades 4, 8, and 12, we can see that the gender differences are small and insignificant (● FIGURE 10.2). More readily apparent are the ethnic differences in national math and science scores. European Americans and Asian/Pacific Islanders perform significantly better than African American, Hispanic or Latino, and American Indian/Alaska Native groups. These ethnic differences in math and science performance are more striking than male/female differences.

A similar picture emerges when looking at college completion rates (● FIGURE 10.3; U.S. Department of Commerce, 2009). From 1996 through 2009, gender differences across all ethnicities are quite small. More notable are the ethnic differences in college completion rates. European Americans have significantly higher completion rates than African Americans and Hispanic Americans. European Americans have almost twice the college completion rate of African Americans and Hispanic Americans. Looking at total male and female numbers may obscure such significant ethnic differences.

Although more women complete college compared to men, a college degree in no way ensures equal pay for women. One year after college graduation, women earn on average 80% of what men do, and this gap in pay widens over time (● FIGURE 10.4). This gender wage gap is made worse by traditional gender roles. For example, men who hold traditional gender roles are likely to earn more than men who hold more egalitarian gender roles (a belief in gender equality); women who hold more traditional gender roles tend to earn less than women with more egalitarian roles (Judge & Livingston, 2008).

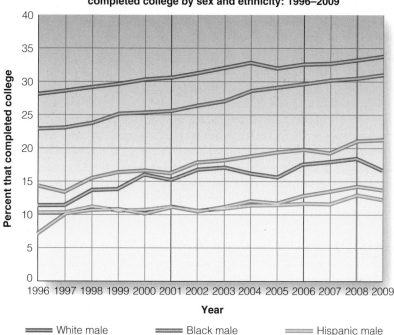

Percentage of 25- to 29-year-old high school completers that completed college by sex and ethnicity: 1996–2009

Percent that completed college (y-axis: 0 to 40)

Year (x-axis: 1996–2009)

- ══ White male
- ══ White female
- ══ Black male
- ══ Black female
- ══ Hispanic male
- ══ Hispanic female

FIGURE 10.3

● **College Completion Rates by Sex and Ethnicity** The ethnic disparity in college completion rates between European Americans and African Americans and Hispanic Americans is more pronounced than the gender differences. *Source: U.S. Department of Commerce, Current Population Survey (CPS), 1996–2009.*

FIGURE 10.4

● **The Gender Pay Gap** Despite equal or higher college completion rates, women on average earn 80% of what men do one year after college graduation, and this gap widens over time. *Source: American Association of University Women Analysis of Current Population Survey data.*

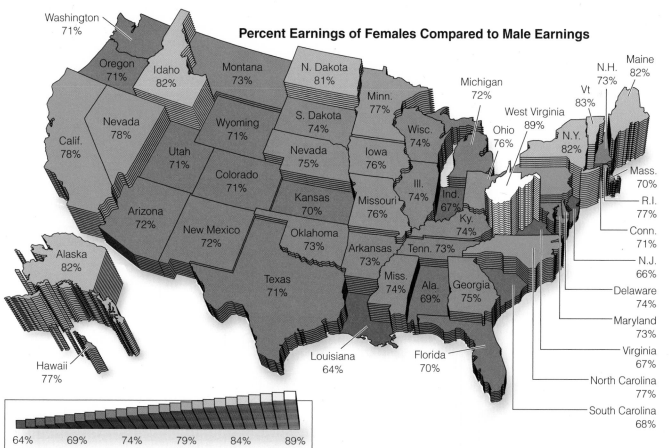

Percent Earnings of Females Compared to Male Earnings

Washington 71%
Oregon 71%
Idaho 82%
Montana 73%
N. Dakota 81%
Minn. 77%
Michigan 72%
N.H. 73%
Maine 82%
Vt 83%
West Virginia 89%
Ohio 76%
N.Y. 82%
Nevada 78%
Wyoming 71%
S. Dakota 74%
Wisc. 74%
Calif. 78%
Utah 71%
Nevada 75%
Iowa 76%
Ill. 74%
Mass. 70%
Colorado 71%
Kansas 70%
Missouri 76%
Ind. 67%
R.I. 77%
Arizona 72%
Ky. 74%
Conn. 71%
New Mexico 72%
Oklahoma 73%
Arkansas 73%
Tenn. 73%
N.J. 66%
Alaska 82%
Delaware 74%
Texas 71%
Miss. 74%
Ala. 69%
Georgia 75%
Maryland 73%
Virginia 67%
Hawaii 77%
Louisiana 64%
Florida 70%
North Carolina 77%
South Carolina 68%

64%   69%   74%   79%   84%   89%

SW Productions/Getty Image

From the age of 2, males are more physically aggressive than females.

Personality Factors

Psychologists have also examined the influence of gender on personality. Such research suggests that females are more extraverted, anxious, trusting, and nurturing than males. Males tend to be more assertive and tough-minded and to have higher self-esteem than females (Feingold, 1994; Kling et al., 1999). However, many of these results have been found using samples of college students who are predominantly White. Such differences may not apply equally to all U.S. ethnic groups. For example, the gender gap in self-esteem, although small among Whites, is almost nonexistent in Blacks (Hyde, 2007).

Interesting gender differences have also been found in the area of *aggression*, or the intention to hurt or harm someone. Aggression can be overt and physical, such as physically injuring someone, or it may be verbal or relational, such as spreading a rumor or making someone a social outcast through gossip or exclusion from a group. Males tend to engage in more overt aggression than females (Archer, 2004; Whiting & Edwards, 1988), but females tend to engage in more relational aggression than males (N. R. Crick, Casas, & Ku, 1999; Murray-Close, Ostrov, & Crick, 2007). Thus, both males and females behave aggressively, but the form in which the aggression is expressed tends to be different. This difference also conforms to gender stereotypes. We expect males to be more physical and females to be more verbal. Gender roles also have an influence on the sexual behavior we expect in males and females, our next topic of discussion.

Let's REVIEW

This section detailed sexual differentiation, gender-role development, gender identity, and gender differences. For a quick check of your understanding, try answering the following questions at increasing levels of difficulty.

1. Which chemical is most responsible for the prenatal sexual differentiation of males and females?

   a. estrogen
   b. testosterone
   c. H-Y antigen
   d. anti-testosterone

2. Consuelo dresses and acts like a girl. She feels that she is female. This describes Consuelo's _____.

   a. gender role
   b. gender identity
   c. sexuality
   d. gender typing

3. Which of the following statements about gender-role development is *false*?

   a. At 3 years old, toddlers can label their gender.
   b. At 4 years old, preschoolers have gender permanence.
   c. At 6 years old, children have gender roles.
   d. At 8 years old, children have gender permanence.

ANSWERS 1. c; 2. b; 3. b

LEARNING OBJECTIVE

What Should You Know?

• Detail changes in sexual attitudes and behaviors gathered through the survey method over the past 50 years.

WHAT SEXUAL BEHAVIORS AND ATTITUDES DO PEOPLE REPORT?

As we have seen, gender roles govern many aspects of male and female behavior. They direct how we expect males and females to dress, the toys they select, how or what they should play, and what tasks they should excel at or not perform well. These expectations also influence our ideas about appropriate sexual behavior in males and females. Recall Maya Angelou's conception of what a romantic relationship was all about and how her expectations led to many doomed relationships. Such cultural and societal norms, together with biology, produce some interesting gender differences in the sexual behavior and attitudes of men and women.

In the 1930s and 1940s, Indiana psychologist Alfred Kinsey and his team (1948, 1953) began a mammoth project of interviewing more than 10,000 Americans about their sexual behavior. This survey research represented the first comprehensive picture of sexual behavior and attitudes in the United States. Other national surveys on sexual behavior soon followed, including the National Health and Social Life Survey (Laumann et al., 1994); the Pfizer Global Study of Sexual Attitudes and Behaviors to assess behaviors, attitudes, and beliefs in 28 countries (Pfizer, 2002), and the National Social Life, Health, and Aging Project (NSHAP) aimed at understanding sexual behavior and health among older women and men (Waite et al., 2009). Because not everyone is willing to disclose what they consider to be one of the most intimate aspects of their life—namely, sexual behavior—none of these surveys is truly representative of the entire population. However, they do offer our best approximation of the sexual attitudes, behaviors, and beliefs of men and women, married and single, young and old, in the world today. Such an approximation will hopefully further our understanding of human sexuality.

Alfred Kinsey was a pioneer in surveying Americans' sexual attitudes and behaviors.

Masturbation and Sexual Fantasy

Masturbation, or sexual self-stimulation, is a sexual behavior that historically has been condemned as physically, mentally, and morally harmful (Hodges, 2005). Despite such negative attitudes, most surveys across many cultures indicate that most people masturbate at some time. Generally, men masturbate more frequently than women (Petersen & Hyde, 2010). For example, data from the National Health and Social Life Survey found that among 18- to 60-year-olds, 61% of the men and 38% of the women reported that they had masturbated during the previous 12 months (Das, 2007). Research in the United States has found a large gender difference in masturbation among college students—college men masturbate 3 times more frequently than college women do (Hyde & Oliver, 2000; I. M. Schwartz, 1999). In a British survey of 16- to 44-year-olds, 73% of the men and 37% of the women reported masturbating in the month prior to the interview (Gerressu et al., 2008). An analysis of survey respondents ages 20–59 in urban China (Das, Parish, & Laumann, 2009) found that 13% of the women and 35% of the men reported masturbating in the preceding year.

Married people and some ethnic groups also report low rates of masturbation. For example, Laumann et al. (1994) found that 57% of the married men and 37% of the married women in the sample reported that they had masturbated in the preceding year, but among African Americans, only 40% of the men and 32% of the women had done so. Gail Wyatt (1997), a sex therapist who has been researching Black sexuality for more than 15 years, has found that 83% of African American women reported not masturbating during childhood. Asian American women have been found to masturbate significantly less than non-Asian women (Meston, Trapnell, & Gorzalka, 1996). Research has also found that education appears to influence rates of masturbation. In both genders, people with more education report more frequent masturbation (Gerressu et al., 2008; Laumann et al., 1994).

Survey research has also investigated the sexual fantasies of adults. A **sexual fantasy** is a mental thought or image that is arousing to a person. Sexual fantasy may be used during or outside of sexual activity. Many people believe that those who engage in sexual fantasy have deficient sex lives, but survey research suggests that this is not the case. Such research shows that the majority of adults and college students engage in sexual fantasies from time to time and that men tend to have more frequent sexual fantasies than women (Hicks & Leitenberg, 2001; D. S. Strassberg & Lockerd, 1998). For example, in one national survey, 54% of

masturbation sexual self-stimulation

sexual fantasy a mental thought or image that is sexually arousing to a person

men and 19% of women said that they thought about sex at least once a day (Laumann et al., 1994). Men's fantasies tend to involve different partners and more varied activities than women's. They generally include visualizing more body parts, specific sex acts, and themes of dominance (Leitenberg & Henning, 1995; Zurbriggen & Yost, 2004). Engaging in different sexual positions, having an aggressive sexual partner, and receiving oral sex are common sexual fantasies for men. Women's sexual fantasies tend to be more romantic than men's. Common sexual fantasies among women include sex with a current partner, reliving a past sexual experience, and engaging in different sexual positions (Maltz & Boss, 2001). Young adults high in spirituality and religiosity tend to have less frequent sexual fantasies (Ahrold et al., in press).

Sex With a Partner

Sex survey research has also asked adult men and women about their attitudes and behaviors in regard to sexual intercourse, oral sex, premarital sex, extramarital sex, and number of sexual partners. Many of these findings are consistent with stereotypical gender roles. That is, we expect women to suppress their sexuality more than men do. We expect females to be responsible for limiting, restricting, and controlling sexual activity, and we expect men to pursue sex. Much of the research supports these expectations. For example, men want sex more than women. They think about sex more often, have more frequent sexual fantasies, and desire more sex partners than women (Laumann et al., 1994; Leitenberg & Henning, 1995; Lindau & Gavrilova, 2010; L. C. Miller & Fishkin, 1997; Peplau, 2003). Men are somewhat more likely to engage in extramarital sex, and when they do stray, they tend to seek out more partners than women do (Wiederman, 1997).

Men tend to be more in favor of casual sex than women (Knox, Sturdivant, & Zusman, 2001; Oliver & Hyde, 1993; Petersen & Hyde, 2010). In college students it is a fairly common occurrence and is engaged in more so between friends than with strangers (Welsh, Grello, & Harper, 2006). Males are typically ready for sex earlier in a relationship than females. Women expect more time spent together before starting to have sex and are less likely to consent to sex after having known someone for only a short time (L. L. Cohen & Shotland, 1996). Women are more likely to endorse the attitude of a *double standard*—the notion that certain sexual acts are okay for a man but not for a woman. Women also report more negative attitudes and feelings about sex, such as anxiety and guilt, than men do (Eisenman & Dantzker, 2006; Geer & Robertson, 2005; Oliver & Hyde, 1993). Even though only about a third of today's adolescents express positive attitudes toward premarital sex, the majority of them indicate that they would engage in sexual intercourse before marriage (P. D. Martin et al., 2003).

Which person do you perceive more negatively? Society tends to view highly sexualized men more positively than highly sexualized women.

Men report an average of 7 female sex partners in their lifetime whereas women report an average of 4 male sex partners in their lifetime (Fryar et al., 2007). Such findings suggest that men have a stronger desire for sex and a larger sex drive than women (Baumeister, Catanese, & Vohs, 2001). However, such a conclusion must be qualified by the profound influence of socialization experiences and social pressure on women's sexuality. In the United States, as well as in many other societies, males are allowed greater sexual freedom than females. Highly sexual American women are often frowned upon or stigmatized and experience challenges in their lives because of their sexuality (Blumberg, 2003). Moreover, both males and females may simply be more likely to report attitudes and behaviors that are consistent with gender stereotypes. For example, in one study, M. G. Alexander and Fischer (2003) found no gender differences in self-reported sexual behavior when the participants believed that lying could be detected. However, when the participants believed that the researcher could not view their responses, gender differences were greater.

How often do adults engage in sexual intercourse? In Pfizer's global study on sexual behavior (2002), more than half of adults in 29 countries reported engaging in sexual intercourse over the past 12 months (● FIGURE 10.5). These rates tend to be higher for males than for females (● FIGURE 10.6). Worldwide, the average for frequency of sexual activity is about once a week (● FIGURE 10.7; Pfizer, 2002).

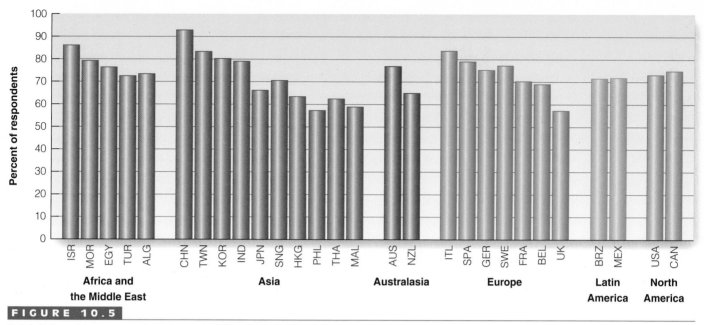

● **Adult Sexual Intercourse Over the Last 12 Months in 29 Countries** Across 29 countries, the majority of adults report having had sexual intercourse in the last 12 months. *Copyright © 2002 Pfizer, Inc. All rights reserved.*

Research has also investigated the frequency of other forms of sexual expression, including oral and anal sex. Survey research indicates that oral sex has increased in acceptance among young people and that for many people first experience with oral sex and sexual intercourse occur closely together (Lindberg, Jones, & Santelli, 2008). In one national survey of 15- to 19-year-old teens, 54% of females and 55% of males reported engaging in oral sex (Lindberg et al., 2008). In another national survey of young adults ages 18–26 who were in a sexual relationship for at least 3 months, 80% reported engaging in oral sex (Kaestle & Halpern, 2007). Oral sexual experience tends to increase with age and is more prevalent among Whites and married couples (Brewster & Tillman, 2008; Leichliter et al., 2007; Lindberg et al., 2008). Anal sex also is becoming more common and is practiced by heterosexual and bisexual men and women, gay men, and lesbians. Data from the National Survey of Family Growth found that one third of heterosexual men and women between the ages of 15 and 44 reported at least one experience with anal sex (Leichliter et al., 2007).

Much of the survey research that has been presented in this section concerns males and females in adulthood. Yet sexual behavior occurs throughout the life span, as our next topic highlights.

Sexuality in Youth and Age

Even before you were born, you were a sexual being with the capacity for sexual pleasure and response. Male fetuses have erections, and boys are often born with erections or experience them during the first few weeks of life. Baby girls can have vaginal lubrication and clitoral erections within the first 24 hours after birth (Eisenberg et al., 2008). However, do not

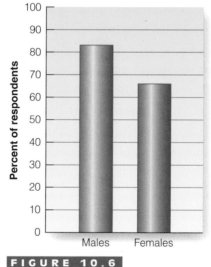

● **Male and Female Sexual Intercourse Over the Last 12 Months** Across 29 countries, males are more likely to report that they have had sexual intercourse over the last 12 months. *Copyright © 2002 Pfizer, Inc. All rights reserved.*

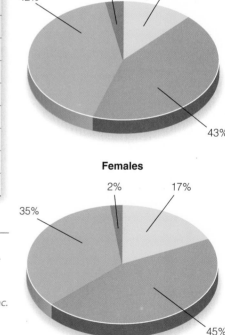

- Less than once per month
- Less than once per week
- 1–6 times per week
- Once a day, or more

● **Frequency of Sexual Intercourse** Worldwide, among those who have had sex in the last 12 months, adult males and females report similar levels of sexual activity. *Copyright © 2002 Pfizer, Inc. All rights reserved.*

Children are naturally curious about and interested in the body.

© Cassy Cohen/PhotoEdit, Inc

interpret a capacity for sexual response as an "interest" in sex as experienced by adults. Typically, infants and young children engage in sexual activity for the pleasure of it. It feels good, and they are naturally curious about their own bodies and those of others. Babies explore their bodies and quickly learn that self-stimulation is pleasurable.

During the preschool years, self-stimulatory behavior may continue. Young children are also likely to be interested in seeing adults and other children nude or undressing. They may hug, cuddle, or kiss other children and are curious about other children's genitals, so that instances of "I'll show you mine if you'll show me yours" may occur (Friedrich et al., 1998). By the time children start school, sexual behaviors decrease as children become more modest and develop better self-control. Yet it is still normal sexual behavior for children between the ages of 6 and 9 to touch their own genitals and try to see others nude or undressing. Touching others' genitals, buttocks, or breast area or "playing doctor" may also take place (Kaeser, DiSalvo, & Moglia, 2001).

Preadolescents grow increasingly self-conscious about their bodies. Yet, mutual display of the genitals or mutual masturbation is quite common. These sexual behaviors are often within their genders and are simply exploration (Leitenberg, Greenwald, & Tarran, 1989). Heterosexuals' interest in the other gender gradually increases as they approach puberty, when surges in sex hormones heighten the sex drive.

Among adolescents, the frequency of masturbation increases, especially among males (A. M. Smith, Rosenthal, & Reichler, 1996). Sexual experimentation is common among both virgins and nonvirgins (Woody et al., 2000). For example, Janet Rosenbaum (2009) compared adolescents who had taken a virginity pledge before they were 15 years old with adolescents of similar religiosity and sexual attitudes who had not taken a virginity pledge. Five years after the pledge, she found that the groups did not differ in premarital sex, sexually transmitted diseases, anal sex, oral sex, age of first sexual intercourse, and number of sex partners. The main difference that she did find between the two groups was that the pledgers were *less* likely to have used birth control than the nonpledgers.

In 2007, 47.8% of high school students in the United States reported having had sexual intercourse. In ninth grade, 38% of males and 27% of females report that they have engaged in sexual intercourse. By twelfth grade, 62% of males and 66% of females have had sexual intercourse (Gavin et al., 2009). African American and Hispanic boys have higher rates of sexual activity than European American boys, and African American girls have higher rates than Hispanic and European American girls (D. K. Eaton et al., 2006; Gavin et al., 2009). Yet the age at which teenagers become sexually active is similar across Canada, France, Great Britain, Sweden, and the United States (Alan Guttmacher Institute, 2001).

Sexual activity among adolescents is very episodic, perhaps because teenagers do not consistently have an available venue for sexual activity. It should not be surprising, therefore, that youths who are unsupervised for 30 or more hours per week have higher rates of sexual activity than youths who are unsupervised for 5 hours a week or less (D. A. Cohen et al., 2002).

Moreover, teenagers who view more sexual content on television are more likely to engage in sexual activities such as "making out" and oral sex, and are also more likely to engage in sexual intercourse earlier, than teenagers who view less sexual content on television (R. L. Collins et al., 2004).

Society tends to equate sexuality with young adults and see older adults as sexless. Yet the needs for intimacy and pleasure continue throughout life. Although sexual activity may decline as we progress through adulthood, a significant proportion of older people remain sexually active. Many older people engage in intercourse, oral sex, and masturbation. And like young adults, sexual activity varies with age and gender. For example, in one national sample of U.S. adults, 73% of 57- to 64-year-olds, 53% of 65- to 74-year-olds, and 26% of 75- to 85-year-olds reported being sexually active (Lindau et al., 2007). Among adults ages 57 to 85 years, males are more likely than females to be sexually active and interested in sex (Lindau & Gavrilova, 2010; Lindau et al., 2007; Waite et al., 2009). Although poor health and the physical changes that accompany

A significant proportion of older people remain sexually active.

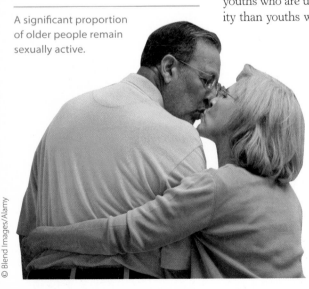

© Blend Images/Alamy

aging may produce less energy and desire for sex, the biggest obstacle to enjoying sexual pleasure in later adulthood appears to be social, rather than physical. The availability of sex partners diminishes as partners or spouses die, and because they live longer than men, women are less likely than men to have a sexual partner (DeLamater & Karraker, 2009; Lindau et al., 2007; Waite et al., 2009). Gender differences in sexual activity are greatest among the 75–85-year-old age group with 39% of men and 17% of women reporting sexual activity (Lindau & Gavrilova, 2010). Yet with Americans now living longer, there is no reason to forgo satisfying and pleasurable sexual relationships into one's 80s and beyond.

Let's REVIEW

This section detailed survey research on the sexual attitudes and behaviors of males and females. For a quick check of your understanding, try answering the following questions at increasing levels of difficulty.

1. Which of the following is a consistent finding in sex survey research?

   a. Men desire more sex partners than women do.

   b. Women have more frequent sexual fantasies than men.

   c. Women want sex more than men do.

   d. Women are more likely to engage in extramarital sex than men.

2. Masturbation is _____.

   a. more common among women than among men

   b. more common among married people than among single people

   c. more common among European Americans than among African Americans

   d. more common among older people than among younger people

3. Which of the following statements is *true*?

   a. Infants are capable of having orgasms.

   b. Mutual masturbation among children is common.

   c. A significant proportion of older adults remain sexually active.

   d. All of the above statements are true.

ANSWERS 1. a; 2. c; 3. d

WHAT CAUSES SEXUAL ORIENTATION?

A more controversial topic in sexuality is **sexual orientation**—one's sexual attraction for members of the same or other sex, or both. Many people never question their sexual orientation, whereas others may be in doubt as they grapple with the developmental task of establishing their identity in adolescence (Chapter 9). Recall how such confusion led Maya Angelou to engage in sexual intercourse, resulting in a teenage pregnancy. There are several types of sexual orientation. **Heterosexuals** are attracted to members of the other sex, **homosexuals** are attracted to members of the same sex, **bisexuals** are attracted to members of both sexes, and **asexuals** have little to no attraction to either sex. However, sexual orientation is not as fixed as these terms suggest. Heterosexuality and homosexuality more often represent endpoints on a broad spectrum of behaviors that Kinsey and his colleagues (Kinsey, Pomeroy, & Martin, 1948) identified as a continuum of sexual orientation (● FIGURE 10.8). Sexual orientation also may change over time, with women reporting greater change in orientation than men (Kinnish, Strassberg, & Turner, 2005). Let's take a look at some aspects of sexual orientation, possible causes of it, and current attitudes toward gay males and lesbians.

sexual orientation one's sexual attraction for members of the same and/or other sex

heterosexual one who is sexually attracted only to members of the other sex

LEARNING OBJECTIVE

What Should You Know?
- Distinguish between sexual orientation and sexual behavior, and analyze the research investigating the causes of sexual orientation.

homosexual one who is sexually attracted only to members of the same sex

bisexual one who is sexually attracted to members of both sexes

asexual one who has little to no attraction to either sex

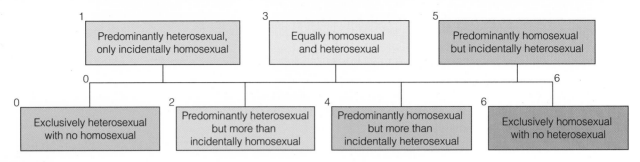

FIGURE 10.8

● **Kinsey's Continuum of Sexual Orientation** Sexual orientation may be expressed along a continuum of behaviors. *Source: Adapted from Kinsey et al., 1948, p. 638.*

homophobia prejudicial attitudes against homosexuals and homosexuality

Fearing discrimination and prejudice due to his sexual orientation, Ricky Martin waited years before coming out as gay.

Sexual Orientation and Sexual Behavior

Do people's sexual orientations predict their sexual behavior? When speaking of sexual orientation, one must be careful to distinguish between attraction and behavior. Sexual orientation is not simply a matter of with whom you have sex. A man could be married to a woman, never have had sex with a man, but still be gay because he is truly attracted only to men. A woman could have sex with other women but still consider herself to be heterosexual. Kinsey's studies (1948, 1953) revealed that 37% of men and 13% of women had had at least one same-sex sexual encounter, but not all of these people identified themselves as gay males or lesbians. If this sounds confusing, it is. When trying to determine just how many people are homosexual, bisexual, asexual, or heterosexual, researchers have had some problems (Savin-Williams, 2006). Kinsey and his colleagues (1948) estimated that roughly 3% of the general population is exclusively homosexual. Nearly 50 years later the rate of homosexuality was estimated at 4–6% for males and 2–4% for females (LeVay, 1996). The U.S. Census Bureau's American Community Survey (2009) estimates that same-sex couples represent less than 1% of American households. Data on 17 southern states estimated that 6% of adult men have sex with men (Lieb et al., 2009). Varying definitions of homosexuality and the negative attitudes that many hold about homosexuality make it difficult to get accurate data. It could well be that some people are reluctant to admit their true sexual feelings because they fear reprisals or they themselves feel stigmatized by their sexuality.

Attitudes Toward Gay Males and Lesbians: Differing Views Across the World

American attitudes toward gay men and lesbians have become somewhat less negative over the last few decades. Television shows such as *Modern Family*, *Glee*, *Brothers and Sisters*, and *The L Word* suggest that the public is becoming more comfortable with homosexuality. Several U.S. cities have openly gay mayors. Some corporations now extend employee benefits to same-sex couples. In 1973 the American Psychiatric Association eliminated homosexuality from its list of mental illnesses, and in 1980 dropped it from its *Diagnostic and Statistical Manual* (*DSM*; discussed in Chapter 14). Moreover, based on evidence that gay and lesbian relationships are influenced by the same set of variables that influence heterosexual marriages, the American Psychological Association passed a resolution declaring it unfair and discriminatory to deny same-sex couples legal access to civil marriage (APA, 2004).

But **homophobia**, or prejudice against homosexuals, has not disappeared. The Netherlands, Belgium, Spain, Canada, and South Africa are the only countries that allow same-sex marriage. In the United States, Massachusetts became the first state to legalize same-sex marriage in 2004. Other states vary in their legal recognition of same-sex relationships. Gays and lesbians do not have the same legal protection against discrimination as other minority groups in the United States, and gays and lesbians continue to be the victims of hate crimes. Hate crime offenses based on sexual orientation have risen each year since 2005 (FBI, 2008). Gay, lesbian, and bisexual adults report more childhood abuse, more partner abuse, and more sexual assault experiences than heterosexual adults, with males reporting more victimization than females (Balsam, Rothblum, & Beauchaine, 2005). Approximately 80% of gay, lesbian, and bisexual youth report verbal abuse (D'Augelli, Grossman, & Starks, 2006; L. Meyer, 1999).

In an effort to reduce such hatred, President Obama in 2009 signed into law the Matthew Shepard and James Byrd Jr. Hate Crimes Prevention Act in honor of two men who had died as a result of hate crimes.

Many religions condemn homosexual behavior as immoral. It is quite possible to turn on the television to see a preacher warning of the dangers of homosexual sin. Others see homosexuality as a mental illness that should be cured. However, there is little evidence to support the view that homosexuality is a mental health problem. Gay males and lesbians are no less well adjusted than their heterosexual counterparts (Weinrich, 1994). Same-sex couples are also quite similar to heterosexual couples on many relationship variables. They are just as committed in their romantic relationships as heterosexual couples and have positive views of their relationships (Roisman et al., 2008). Same-sex couples actually report more positive feelings toward their partners and less conflict than heterosexual married couples (Balsam et al., 2008). Moreover, decades of research show that children of gay and lesbian parents do not differ in adjustment or development when compared to children raised by heterosexual couples (C. J. Patterson, 2006).

Curiously, the negative attitudes that many Americans hold toward gays and lesbians are not shared by all cultures. In fact, many cultures openly accept homosexuality as a natural part of life. One study of 190 societies across the world found that approximately two thirds of the world's societies accepted homosexuality (Ford & Beach, 1951). A historical study of 225 Native American tribes found that more than half of them accepted male homosexuality and 17% accepted female homosexuality (W. Pomeroy, 1965). Why do some people abhor homosexuality or see it as a mental illness, whereas others see it as a normal variation of human sexuality? Perhaps these differing points of view stem from beliefs about what causes sexual orientation.

The Matthew Shepard and James Byrd Jr. Hate Crimes Prevention Act is in honor of two men who died of hate crimes—Matthew Shepard, a gay college student who was beaten and tied to a fence in Wyoming; and James Byrd Jr., an African American who was dragged behind a pickup truck for 3 miles in Texas.

Sexual Orientation: The Influence of Biology and the Environment

What causes one's sexual orientation? One common mistake that people make when trying to answer this question is to confuse sexual orientation with gender. Gender is the collection of personality traits that your society typically associates with either males or females. Gender is not the same thing as sexual orientation. For instance, a gay male may be very masculine or very feminine. Likewise, a heterosexual woman may be either masculine or feminine. In other words, not all feminine men are gay, and not all masculine women are lesbians.

Having said that, there is some indication in the research that early gender-related behavior may be a predictor of later sexual orientation *for some*. Some studies have shown that gender-nonconforming behavior (masculine behavior in girls, feminine behavior in boys) during childhood is correlated with later homosexuality in both men and women (Rieger, Gygax, & Bailey, 2008). Be careful about how you interpret these findings, though. Not all boys who prefer feminine activities became gay, nor do all girls who prefer masculine activities become lesbian. In fact, in one study, approximately half of the adult gay male participants had a

Gay men and lesbians face many prejudices in today's society. Yet their relationships are influenced by the same variables that influence heterosexual relationships.

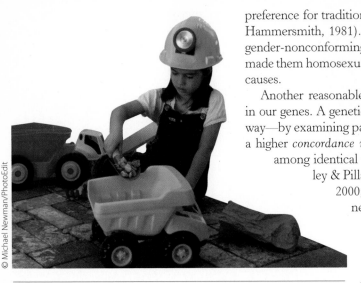

© Michael Newman/PhotoEdit

There is no evidence that cross-gender toy selection causes a homosexual orientation.

preference for traditionally masculine activities in childhood (A. R. Bell, Weinberg, & Hammersmith, 1981). Also, even if some gays and lesbians showed a preference for gender-nonconforming activities in childhood, this does not indicate that the activities made them homosexual. It is just as likely that their homosexuality stemmed from other causes.

Another reasonable question is to ask whether homosexuality could be encoded in our genes. A genetic link for homosexuality has been investigated in the traditional way—by examining pairs of identical and fraternal twins who are gay. Such studies find a higher *concordance rate* (percentage of pairs in which both twins are homosexual) among identical twins than fraternal twins (Bailey, Dunne, & Martin, 2000; Bailey & Pillard, 1991). A similar pattern was found for females (Bailey et al., 2000; Bailey et al., 1993). Such findings suggest a hereditary component in sexual orientation in some people.

Other investigations have found that gay men have a greater number of older brothers than heterosexual men—a phenomenon called *the fraternal birth order effect* (Blanchard, 2004, 2008; Blanchard & Lippa, 2007; Blanchard et al., 1998; Ridley, 2003; Schwartz et al., 2010). *The maternal immune hypothesis* suggests that some mothers may become increasingly immune to prenatal male hormones. In other words, their bodies produce more antibodies to such male hormones, creating a different prenatal hormonal environment that may affect succeeding male fetuses. However, this hypothesis does not explain female homosexuality or other patterns of male and female sexual orientation (Francis, 2008; Whitehead, 2007). Research also has found that homosexuals have a greater chance of being left-handed than heterosexuals, an attribute that is believed to be established prior to birth (Lippa, 2003). Such findings suggest that prenatal factors are related to sexual orientation (Rahman, 2005).

In conclusion, data indicate a strong biological role in sexual orientation. However, as of this moment, no one can say for sure just what causes our sexual orientation. The continuum of sexual orientation is in all likelihood related to the interaction among biological, psychological, and environmental forces that results in different pathways for every person. In any case, the causes of sexual orientation are likely to remain a controversial and emotional issue for some time to come.

Let's REVIEW

This section described sexual orientation. For a quick check of your understanding, try answering the following questions at increasing levels of difficulty.

1. Which is *true* about homosexuality?

   a. Some cultures fully accept homosexual behavior.

   b. Homosexuality is condemned in many religions.

   c. Homosexuality is likely influenced by both genetics and environment.

   d. All of the above are true.

2. Which of the following is *true* about gender and sexual orientation?

   a. They are the same thing.

   b. They are unrelated.

   c. They may be related for some people.

   d. Sexual orientation causes gender.

3. Paul has been married for 5 years to Lisa. However, Paul is primarily sexually attracted to men and not to women. What is Paul's sexual orientation?

   a. heterosexual   c. bisexual

   b. homosexual   d. both a and b

ANSWERS 1. d; 2. c; 3. b

WHAT HAPPENS DURING SEXUAL AROUSAL?

LEARNING OBJECTIVE

What Should You Know?

- Explain the biological and psychological components of sexual desire, and outline the phases of the sexual response cycle in men and women.

What is sexual arousal, and what factors contribute to sexual arousal in humans? **Sexual arousal** is a heightened state of sexual interest and excitement. Like many other behaviors that we have discussed, it is influenced by our biology as well as our learning experiences and cultural expectations. This section details the factors that influence our desire to engage in sexual activity and describes the cycle of physical processes and events that occur during sexual activity.

Sexual Desire: A Mixture of Chemicals, Thoughts, and Culture

Sexual desire is our motivation and interest in engaging in sexual activity. It is the first step in experiencing sexual arousal. Biological and psychological processes influence sexual desire. The physical desire to have sex, or **libido**, is affected by three chemicals: *testosterone, dopamine,* and *oxytocin.*

In mammals, **estrogens** are female hormones that regulate the female animal's desire to mate. Female animals' estrogen levels increase dramatically during a period called *estrus* ("being in heat"), in which the female is receptive to males' attempts to mate with her. Estrus coincides with ovulation in the female. During ovulation, the female's egg (or eggs) matures, so that it can be fertilized by the male sperm during mating. If fertilization does not occur, the female will pass out of estrus, and she will shed the egg along with the lining of her uterus during *menstruation.* If a pregnancy is going to occur, estrus is when it will happen. Therefore, it is in both the male and female animals' best interest to mate during estrus. To ensure that mating will occur, estrus is usually marked by some physical change in the female that signals to males of the species that she is in estrus and ready to mate. For example, many female chimpanzees have sexual swelling, or engorgement, of the external female genitals that indicate to male chimpanzees that it is time to mate.

Humans are a bit different from other mammals in that for a human, there is no defined period of estrus. **Ovaries** are organs that produce eggs and estrogen in a woman's body. Human females can mate at any time in the menstrual cycle, and although female estrogen levels do fluctuate during the menstrual cycle, estrogen is not closely related to human female libido. In humans, the hormone that seems to govern libido is **testosterone**. Testosterone is part of a class of male hormones called androgens. Although testosterone is a male hormone, it is also found in females (likewise, males have estrogen). In males, the **testes** produce testosterone (in addition to sperm). In women, it is produced by the adrenal glands that sit above the kidneys. Adequate testosterone levels seem to be important in maintaining sexual desire. If testosterone levels fall too low, both males and females experience disinterest in sex. Conversely, sexual intercourse raises testosterone levels so having sex may increase desire. Male libido peaks in one's adolescence and 20s when testosterone levels are highest. Postmenopausal women who take testosterone in middle age experience increased sexual desire (Davis et al., 2008; Kingsberg, 2007). Many women also report more sexual desire around ovulation when testosterone levels rise (Van Goozen et al., 1997).

Dopamine, a brain neurotransmitter that produces feelings of pleasure and reward, also influences sexual desire as it can stimulate the release of testosterone. Men and women who are depressed and who take antidepressant medication that increases dopamine experience an increase in sexual desire. Conversely, antidepressant medication that increases the neurotransmitter serotonin tends to dampen sexual desire (Pfaus, 2009).

Oxytocin, another hormone, is most known for its role during labor and lactation, facilitating birth and breastfeeding in female mammals. Oxytocin is now believed to also play a role in adult attachment. It is released when the nipples or genitals are stimulated and during orgasm and is believed to contribute to the sense of closeness one feels after sexual activity with a romantic partner (Fisher, 2004). However, the relationship among oxytocin, dopamine, and testosterone is a complex one. At times, testosterone levels can increase or inhibit oxytocin production; at other times oxytocin can increase or inhibit testosterone production. Dopamine can increase oxytocin; high levels of oxytocin can inhibit dopamine production. As you can see, the chemical nature of sexual desire is quite complicated.

Some female mammals show visible signs when they are receptive to mating.

sexual arousal a heightened state of sexual interest and excitement

sexual desire one's motivation and interest in engaging in sexual activity

libido one's physical desire, or drive, to have sex

estrogens a class of female hormones that regulate many aspects of sexuality

ovaries the organs in a female's body that produce eggs, or ova

testosterone a male hormone that plays a role in many aspects of sexuality, including sexual desire

testes the organs in a male's body that produce both sperm and testosterone

erogenous zones areas of the skin that are sensitive to touch

excitement phase the first stage of the sexual response cycle in which males get erections and females produce vaginal lubrication

plateau phase the second stage of the sexual response cycle in which excitement peaks

orgasm phase the third stage of the sexual response cycle in which the pelvic and anal muscles contract

FIGURE 10.9

● **The Sexual Response Cycle** Masters and Johnson identified three basic patterns of response in females. A female may experience one or more orgasms (A); an extended plateau with no orgasm (B); or a rapid rise to orgasm with a quick resolution (C). Males show less variability in their sexual responses because of the refractory period. *From Human Sexual Response by W. H. Masters and V. E. Johnson. Copyright © 1966 Little, Brown & Co. Reprinted by permission of Lippincott, Williams & Wilkins.*

Are chemicals the sole cause of sexual desire? No. Sexual desire is not merely a function of chemicals in our bodies. Our senses, our thoughts, and our culture also influence human sexual desire. Visual cues can increase or decrease sexual desire. Erotic photographs or movies may be a sexual turn-on to some, but not to others. Seeing a sexual partner nude or in sexy lingerie may be stimulating for some. Such visual stimulation seems to have a greater effect on men than on women (Reinisch, 1991). Sounds, such as a partner's voice or romantic music, may be appealing to some. Research also suggests that our sense of smell may play a role in sexual arousal (K. N. Stern & McClintock, 1998). For some it may be the scent of a particular cologne or perfume, whereas for others it may be natural body scents such as sweat. When fertile or at midcycle, women prefer the scent of males who have more masculine-looking faces. Similarly, men find the scent of women who are ovulating especially attractive (Gangestad, Thornhill, & Garver-Apgar, 2005). Men exposed to the scent of an ovulating woman are also more likely to subsequently display a higher level of testosterone than men exposed to the scent of a nonovulating woman or a control scent (S. L. Miller & Maner, 2010). Such findings suggest an evolutionary role of our sense of smell in sexual desire. However, people vary greatly in the types of smells they find arousing.

Our sense of touch plays a more direct role in sexual desire. Because nerve endings are unevenly distributed throughout the body, some areas of the skin are more sensitive to touch than others. These areas, called **erogenous zones**, include the genitals, buttocks, breasts, armpits, ears, navel, mouth, and the inner surfaces of the thighs. However, areas that may be highly stimulating to one person may produce a negative reaction in another. Hence, our preferences in reaction to touch differ.

Many of the differences in our reactions to sensory cues exist because we all think differently about what should or should not be sexually stimulating. Such expectations may be learned or reflect the larger influence of gender roles and culture on our behavior. For instance, in the United States we emphasize cleanliness and the masking of natural body odors with perfumes and deodorants. Americans may learn to regard such odors as more sexually appealing than body sweat. These learned experiences and cultural influences, along with biology, shape our sexual desire. Once we are willing to engage in sexual activity, a predictable cycle of physical responses occurs, which we detail in the next section.

The Sexual Response Cycle

What physical changes do we experience during sexual activity? In the 1960s, William Masters, a gynecologist, and Virginia Johnson, a nurse, were the first researchers to directly observe and measure the sexual responses of men and women engaged in a variety of activities. Electronic sensors were placed on the bodies of the participants to directly measure physical responses. The participants were also interviewed in detail about their experiences. The information gathered in this study, subsequently published in Masters and Johnson's *Human Sexual Response* (1966), described the common physical changes that we experience in our sexual encounters. The model includes four successive phases: *excitement, plateau, orgasm,* and *resolution* (● FIGURE 10.9). Men and women were remarkably similar in their physical responses.

Female Sexual Response

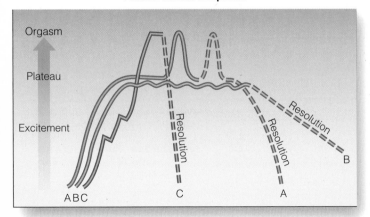

Male Sexual Response

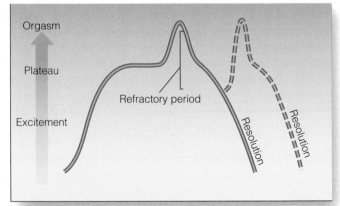

During the **excitement phase**, men and women experience an increase in heart rate and blood pressure. The nipples may become erect, and blood flow is increased to the genital area. Males experience penile erection, and the scrotal sac thickens. Females produce vaginal lubrication, and the inner two thirds of the vagina expand. The clitoris, the female sex organ that is extremely sensitive to sensation, swells. During the **plateau phase**, excitement peaks and remains somewhat constant. Breathing becomes rapid, and blood pressure and heart rate continue to rise. Men experience a full penile erection, and the testes are fully elevated. A few droplets of fluid that can contain sperm may appear at the tip of the penis. In women, the inner part of the vagina expands fully, and the uterus becomes elevated. The clitoris shortens and withdraws.

During the **orgasm phase**, breathing, blood pressure, and heart rate peak. Contractions of the pelvic muscles and the anal sphincter produce the sensation of orgasm. Certain parts of the brain are activated and deactivated (Georgiadis et al., 2006), as shown in ● WHAT'S HAPPENING IN YOUR BRAIN? Muscles throughout the body may spasm. In the male, the internal bodily contractions propel seminal fluid through the penis, causing ejaculation. Hence, in the male, the orgasm phase consists of two processes: orgasm and ejaculation. However, males' and females' subjective experience of orgasm is actually quite similar (Mah & Binik, 2002; Vance & Wagner, 1976). Men and women describe the experience in much the same way.

Masters and Johnson pioneered field research on the sexual response of males and females.

WHAT'S HAPPENING IN YOUR BRAIN?

THE FEMALE ORGASM

When a woman is having an orgasm (top panel of photos), the parts of the brain that govern fear and anxiety are switched off. There is decreased blood flow to the frontal part of the brain. The cerebellum becomes extra active, probably because of its involvement in the muscular contractions of orgasm. Curi-ously, when a woman is imitating an orgasm by performing contractions of the pelvic muscles (bottom panel of photos), the motor cortex—conscious part of the brain—is activated.

Source: Georgiadis et al., 2006.

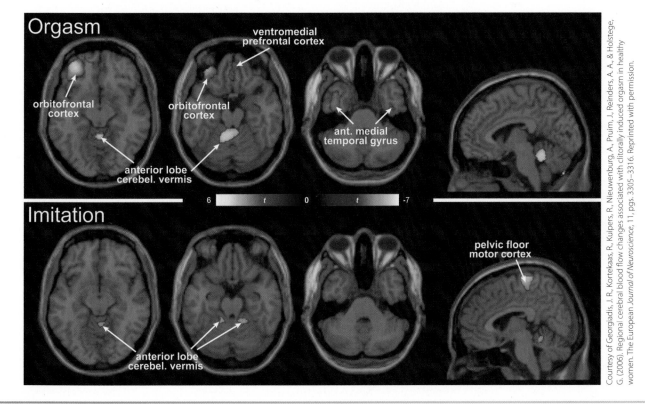

Courtesy of Georgiadis, J. R, Kortekaas, R, Kuipers, R., Nieuwenburg, A., Pruim, J., Reinders, A. A., & Holstege, G. (2006). Regional cerebral blood flow changes associated with clitorally induced orgasm in healthy women. The European *Journal of Neuroscience*, 11, pgs. 3305–3316. Reprinted with permission.

The sexual response cycle concludes with the **resolution phase**, in which the body returns to its prearoused state. Breathing, heart rate, and blood pressure return to normal. The male loses his erection, and in the female the vagina, clitoris, and uterus return to their normal size and position. Yet a distinct gender difference occurs in sexual response during the resolution phase. Unlike women, men experience a **refractory period**, or a time during which they are physically incapable of experiencing another orgasm or ejaculation. This measure of time increases as men age. For an adolescent male, the refractory period may last only a few minutes, whereas for men over age 50, it may last from several minutes to a day. Because women do not undergo a refractory period, they can more easily be rearoused after orgasm, leading some women to experience repeated or multiple orgasms. Hence, compared to males, who experience refractory periods of varying lengths, there is greater variability in the female sexual response pattern (Figure 10.9; Masters, Johnson, & Kolodny, 1993).

Masters and Johnson's research was pivotal in describing the successive physical changes that occur during sexual response. This knowledge, along with our understanding of sexual desire, has been extremely important in helping people who experience sexual problems, our next topic of discussion.

Let's REVIEW

This section described sexual desire and outlined the phases of the sexual response cycle. For a quick check of your understanding, try answering the following questions at increasing levels of difficulty.

1. Which is true of animals, but not of humans?

   a. Testosterone regulates sex drive.   c. Mating occurs only during estrus.

   b. Menstruation follows ovulation.   d. Hormones influence sexual behavior.

2. While dancing with his girlfriend, Malik notices that he has an erection. Malik is in which stage of the sexual response cycle?

   a. excitement   c. orgasm

   b. plateau   d. resolution

3. Males and females differ most strongly in their sexual response during which phase?

   a. excitement   c. orgasm

   b. plateau   d. resolution

ANSWERS 1. c; 2. a; 3. d

resolution phase the final stage of the sexual response cycle in which the body returns to its prearoused state

refractory period a time during the resolution phase in which males are incapable of experiencing another orgasm or ejaculation

LEARNING OBJECTIVE

What Should You Know?

- Discriminate between the various sexual dysfunctions and paraphilias, and explain the role of nature and nurture in causing these disorders.

sexual disorder a persistent sexual problem that causes a person a great deal of distress and interferes with his or her ability to function sexually

sexual dysfunction a persistent problem with sexual desire, arousal, or satisfaction

WHAT IS A SEXUAL DISORDER?

What is a sexual disorder, and how do I know if I have one? Many people experience sexual problems from time to time. The Pfizer Global Study of Sexual Attitudes and Behaviors (2002) reported that 42% of men and 47% of women in 29 countries had experienced sexual difficulties over the past year (● FIGURE 10.10). However, when these problems become persistent, cause a great deal of distress, and interfere with a person's ability to function, they are called **sexual disorders**. This section describes two broad categories of sexual disorders: *sexual dysfunctions* and *paraphilias*. We will also consider a relatively new phenomenon: Internet sexual addictions.

Sexual Dysfunctions: Problems in Sexual Desire or Response

The previous section outlined aspects of sexual desire and detailed the phases of the sexual response cycle. **Sexual dysfunction** is a disorder characterized by a problem with sexual desire, arousal, or satisfaction. Sexual dysfunctions are grouped into four categories related to desire and the stage of sexual response affected. They include *disorders of sexual desire and arousal, orgasmic disorders,* and *sexual pain disorders.* Much of the research has been focused on heterosexual couples so less is known about patterns of sexual dysfunction in homosexual or bisexual people.

Disorders of Sexual Desire

Disorders of sexual desire involve a lack of interest in or an aversion to sexual activity. **Should I always want to have sex?** No. It is normal to have occasional disinterest in sexual activity. For instance, you may want to watch television or sleep instead of having sex. Sexual desire in the same person varies from day to day, month to month, and year to year. However, when such disinterest is persistent and causes personal unhappiness, it may represent a disorder of sexual desire. Two main sexual desire disorders are *hypoactive sexual desire disorder* and *sexual aversion disorder.*

Hypoactive sexual desire disorder is characterized by a persistent disinterest in sex, sexual fantasy, and sexual activities (American Psychiatric Association, 2000a). It is a sexual difficulty experienced by both men and women, but across cultures it is far more common among women (Bach, Wincze, & Barlow, 2001; Laumann, Paik, & Rosen, 1999; Laumann et al., 2005; Sytsma & Taylor, 2001). It is the most common sexual difficulty reported by women (R. D. Hayes et al., 2006). Studies have found that approximately 24–43% of women complain of low desire in the previous year (Segraves & Woodard, 2006). As we have seen, sexual desire is affected by both biological and psychological processes. Hypoactive sexual desire disorder may result from hormone deficiencies, from anxiety involving fears of pleasure or of a lack of control, or from previous negative sexual experiences and trauma such as rape or childhood sexual abuse (DiLillo, 2001; Gracia et al., 2007; Maurice, 2005). Additional conditions that may inhibit desire include stress and depression (Johannes et al., 2009). Medications that are used to control anxiety, depression, or high blood pressure also may dampen sexual desire.

Sexual aversion disorder is characterized by a persistent disgust and aversion toward sexual activity (American Psychiatric Association, 2000a). Such individuals may avoid genital contact. Sexual aversion disorder is less common than lack of desire (Spark, 2000). Its cause appears to be more influenced by psychological factors such as a history of sexual trauma, especially for women (Kingsberg & Janata, 2003). A history of erectile problems in men can cause sexual aversion.

Disorders of Sexual Arousal

During excitement, the first stage of the sexual response cycle, males get erections and females produce vaginal lubrication. Such excitement is necessary to facilitate sexual activity. People with sexual arousal disorders experience persistent difficulty in these responses, or they lack the feelings of sexual excitement that normally accompany sexual arousal (American Psychiatric Association, 2000a). Disorders of sexual arousal include *male erectile dysfunction* and *female sexual arousal disorder.*

Male erectile dysfunction (ED) is characterized by the persistent inability to attain or sustain an erection sufficient to complete sexual activity (American Psychiatric Association, 2000a). More than 50% of U.S. men between the ages of 40 and 70 experience some degree of erectile dysfunction (I. Goldstein et al., 1998). Similar numbers are reported among men in Egypt, suggesting that occasional erectile failure occurs worldwide in middle-aged and older men (Seyam et al., 2003). African American and

Sexual difficulties reported include:
- Lacked interest
- Did not find sex pleasurable
- Reached climax too quickly
- Experienced physical pain
- Had trouble achieving/maintaining erection (males)
- Had trouble becoming lubricated (females)

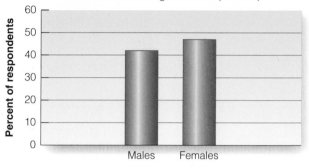

FIGURE 10.10

● **Sexual Difficulties Lasting More Than 2 Months in the Last Year** Men and women across the world experience sexual problems from time to time. If the problem persists, causes distress, and interferes with a person's ability to function, it is called a sexual disorder. *Copyright © 2002 Pfizer, Inc. All rights reserved.*

hypoactive sexual desire disorder a persistent disinterest in sex and sexual activities

sexual aversion disorder a persistent disgust and aversion toward sexual activity

male erectile dysfunction the persistent inability to attain or sustain an erection sufficient to complete sexual activity

One of the most commonly reported sexual dysfunctions is low sexual desire.

Hispanic American men have a higher prevalence of erectile dysfunction than White men (Kupelian et al. 2008). However, these ethnic differences appear to be more due to socioeconomic differences between the groups. Erectile dysfunction also is higher in Asian cultures than Western countries (Laumann et al., 2005).

Erectile dysfunction tends to increase with age, yet all healthy males experience difficulty in getting or sustaining an erection from time to time. Such occasional problems may be due to fatigue, stress, alcohol use, or a short-term illness. If a man begins to fear that such occurrences will continue, he is more likely to suffer from *performance anxiety*, or the fear that he will not be able to perform sexually. Such performance anxiety may cause further instances of erectile failure, leading to erectile dysfunction (Bancroft et al., 2005). Other psychological factors that may contribute to erectile dysfunction include poor self-esteem, depression, and problems in a relationship (Bach et al., 2001). However, chronic problems of erectile dysfunction typically stem from physical causes such as diabetes, prostate surgery, obesity, cardiovascular problems, or multiple sclerosis (Heidelbaugh, 2010). These physical problems impair blood flow to the penis that results in an erection (Bacon et al., 2003; I. Goldstein, 1998; Leland, 1997). Prescription drugs such as antianxiety medication, antidepressants, and heart medication may also impair erectile functioning (Morales, 2003). The regular use of psychoactive drugs such as alcohol, nicotine, heroin, morphine, marijuana, or cocaine can lead to erectile failure as well (Nelson, 1988; Spark, 2000; Weiss & Mirin, 1987).

Female sexual arousal disorder is characterized by persistent difficulty in becoming sexually excited or sufficiently lubricated in response to sexual stimulation (American Psychiatric Association, 2000a). About 20% of U.S. women report difficulties with lubrication or arousal during sexual activity (Laumann et al., 1999), yet 30% of women worldwide experience female sexual arousal disorder (Safarinejad, 2008). Like erectile dysfunction, female sexual arousal disorder can have physical causes related to a lack of blood flow to the genital area (B. Graber, 1993). Any neurological or hormonal problem that interferes with vaginal lubrication can lead to diminished sexual excitement. For example, during menopause (Chapter 9) it is common for women to experience vaginal dryness at times due to the decreased levels of estrogen in their bodies. Prescription medications and illicit drug use also may dampen sexual excitement. However, in many cases female sexual arousal disorder may stem from psychological factors, such as depression, anger, anxiety, a history of sexual trauma, or ineffective sexual stimulation (Johannes et al., 2009; Laurent & Simons, 2009; Morokoff, 1993).

Orgasmic Disorders

Three sexual disorders relate to the orgasm phase of the sexual response cycle: *female orgasmic disorder*, *male orgasmic disorder*, and *premature ejaculation*. **Orgasmic disorder**, which can occur in males and females, is characterized by a lack of orgasm or a persistent delay in reaching orgasm despite adequate stimulation. Approximately 4–9% of men report an inability to ejaculate during sexual intercourse (Laumann et al., 1999). Some may be able to ejaculate by masturbating or through oral sex, but cannot climax during sexual intercourse. About 25% of women report difficulty in reaching orgasm, whereas 5–10% of women report suffering from orgasmic dysfunction, more commonly younger women (Laumann et al., 1999; Spector & Carey, 1990). Laumann and his colleagues (1994) found that African American men and women reported higher rates of orgasmic difficulty than European American men and women. Across cultures, Southeast Asian women reported the highest prevalence of orgasmic disorder (Laumann et al., 2005). Physical causes of orgasmic disorder may include any disease, condition, or drug that interferes with neural control of ejaculation or that causes damage to the pelvic muscles. Orgasmic disorders also may be related to psychological causes such as depression, anxiety, previous negative sexual experiences, or ineffective sexual stimulation (Johannes et al., 2009; Laurent & Simons, 2009; Swaby & Morgan, 2009). Some women report a fear of "letting go" that may interfere with orgasm (Tugrul & Kabakci, 1997).

Premature ejaculation is characterized by persistent or recurrent ejaculation with minimal sexual stimulation before the person wishes it (American Psychiatric Association, 2000a). It is a fairly common male sexual dysfunction, occurring in men of all ages and back-

female sexual arousal disorder persistent difficulty in becoming sexually excited or sufficiently lubricated in response to stimulation

orgasmic disorder a lack of orgasm or a persistent delay in reaching orgasm despite adequate stimulation

premature ejaculation persistent or recurrent ejaculation with minimal sexual stimulation before the person wishes it

grounds (Bettocchi et al., 2008). Roughly 28% of European American males and 34% of African American males reported reaching climax too soon during the past year (Laumann et al., 1994). In contrast to the other sexual dysfunctions, less is known about definitive causes of premature ejaculation. In the past, premature ejaculation was attributed to the inability of the male to employ self-control strategies when he is reaching the threshold of ejaculation (H. S. Kaplan, 1974). However, current research fails to show that men who experience premature ejaculation are less accurate than other men in gauging their sexual arousal (Kinder & Curtiss, 1988; D. S. Strassberg et al., 1990). For some men, performance anxiety may result in reaching orgasm too fast. They are so anxious about performing that they fail to pay attention to their level of sexual arousal (McCarthy, 2001; M. O'Leary, 2003). Current research aims at understanding the neurobiological and psychosocial components of premature ejaculation (Broderick, 2006).

Sexual Pain Disorders

The last category of sexual dysfunctions includes the sexual pain disorders of *dyspareunia* and *vaginismus*. **Dyspareunia**, or painful sexual intercourse, can affect both men and women, although women more frequently report it. For example, Laumann and his colleagues (2005) found that in Western countries roughly 3–5% of men reported pain during sex within the past year. In contrast, 12–15% of women reported experiencing pain during sex in the past year. Among gay men, 14% report pain during anal sex (Damon & Simon Rosser, 2005). Dyspareunia may result from physical causes such as genital and vaginal infections, pelvic inflammatory disease (PID), or allergic reactions to spermicides, condoms, or diaphragms. The most common cause of pain in women is inadequate vaginal lubrication. Psychological factors such as depression or anxiety about sex may also be involved in sexual pain in women. Such feelings inhibit vaginal lubrication and tighten the vaginal muscles, making penile penetration uncomfortable.

In women, dyspareunia can sometimes lead to vaginismus. **Vaginismus** involves involuntary contractions of the vaginal muscles, making penetration painful and sometimes impossible. Approximately 5–17% of women experience vaginismus (Reissing, Binik, & Khalife, 1999). It may develop in response to sexual trauma or a medical condition such that the woman comes to fear vaginal penetration (J. G. Beck, 1993; Koehler, 2002; Lagana et al., 2001; Weijmar Schultz & Van de Wiel, 2005).

Paraphilias: Sexually Aroused by an Object or Situation

Another broad category of sexual disorders is the **paraphilias**. They involve sexual arousal in response to an unusual object, situation, or nonconsenting person. Such disorders include *voyeurism, exhibitionism, fetishism, transvestism, pedophilia, sexual sadism,* and *sexual masochism.*

Fetishism and transvestism are noncoercive paraphilias. That is, they do not exploit others in order to achieve sexual gratification. Being sexually aroused by inanimate objects characterizes **fetishism**. Clothing, such as women's lingerie and high-heeled shoes, and certain materials, such as leather or silk, are common fetish objects. A person with a fetish may compulsively fantasize about such objects in order to become sexually aroused or may act on such fantasies by stroking such an object during masturbation. The majority of those who engage in fetishism are male (Brotto & Klein, 2007). In **transvestism** (often referred to as *transvestic fetishism*), a person is sexually aroused by wearing clothing of the opposite gender. The typical transvestite is a heterosexual, married male (Docter & Prince, 1997; Wheeler, Newring, &

Thomas Hoeffgen/Getty Images

A person with a fetish is sexually aroused by an inanimate object.

dyspareunia a disorder characterized by painful sexual intercourse

vaginismus a disorder in females characterized by involuntary contractions of the vaginal muscles making penetration painful or impossible

paraphilia sexual arousal in response to an unusual object, situation, or nonconsenting person

fetishism a paraphilia characterized by sexual arousal by inanimate objects

transvestism a paraphilia in which a person is sexually aroused by wearing clothing of the other gender

In sexual sadism and masochism, sexual arousal and satisfaction are associated with giving and receiving pain or humiliation.

© PBNJ Productions/Blend Images/Corbis

Draper, 2008). Transvestites are more likely than other people to be the oldest or only child and report closer relationships with their mothers than with their fathers (Schott, 1995). **Is a female impersonator a transvestite?** Not necessarily. The distinguishing feature is whether the person cross-dresses in order to achieve sexual arousal. Many female impersonators cross-dress for entertainment purposes and therefore would not be considered transvestites.

Voyeurism, exhibitionism, and pedophilia are coercive paraphilias. That is, they involve achieving sexual arousal and gratification at the expense of another without his or her permission. **Voyeurism** involves repeated urges to observe unsuspecting strangers who are naked, disrobing, or engaged in sexual activity (American Psychiatric Association, 2000a). It is normal for people to get aroused while watching erotic materials or their sexual partners disrobe. Such people know that they are being observed. In contrast, the voyeur watches people who do not know that they are being observed. Voyeurs may risk physical injury by hiding in a tree or on a rooftop. They generally put themselves in risky situations in which they may be discovered. Such risk appears to increase their sexual arousal. Most voyeurs are heterosexual males who started their voyeuristic activities before they were 15 years old. They may have limited social skills and problems with intimacy (Lavin, 2008).

In **exhibitionism**, a person is sexually aroused by fantasies involving exposing his genitals to some unsuspecting individual. He may or may not act on these fantasies yet feel a compulsion to do so. **Are strippers or exotic dancers exhibitionists?** Not typically. Strippers remove their clothing to excite others sexually in order to earn a living, as Maya Angelou did as a single mother. They do not remove their clothing in front of unsuspecting people to arouse themselves. Those who engage in exhibitionism are primarily men, and most victims are female (W. Murphy & Page, 2008).

Pedophilia involves a person who is sexually aroused by fantasies of or engaging in sexual activity with a prepubescent child. Most pedophiles are heterosexual men attracted to young girls (W. Cole, 1992; J. Murray, 2000). However, all sex offenders are not pedophiles, and not all pedophiles sexually molest children. A pedophile may have fantasies about engaging in sexual activity with children but never act on those desires. If they do act on their compulsions, pedophiles may victimize children of the same gender, opposite gender, or both. Sexual abuse is extremely damaging to children. Its effects are discussed in more detail later in this chapter.

In sexual sadism and sexual masochism, pain becomes connected with sexual pleasure. **Sexual sadism** refers to a situation in which a person achieves sexual satisfaction by inflicting pain or humiliation on a sex partner. **Sexual masochism** involves the desire to be humiliated or receive pain in order to attain sexual pleasure (American Psychiatric Association, 2000a). Sexual sadists and sexual masochists often form consenting sexual relationships based on *sadomasochism (S & M)*. S & M participants may be heterosexual, bisexual, or gay (Nordling et al., 2006). They may engage in elaborate rituals involving dominant and submissive roles such as master and slave. Of all the paraphilias, women are most likely to engage in sexual masochism, but male masochists still outnumber female masochists (American Psychiatric Association, 2000a).

voyeurism a paraphilia in which one is sexually aroused by observing unsuspecting strangers who are undressing or engaged in sexual activity

exhibitionism a paraphilia in which one is sexually aroused by the fantasies or the behavior of exposing his or her genitals to some unsuspecting person

pedophilia a paraphilia in which one is sexually aroused by fantasies of or engaging in sexual activity with a prepubescent child

sexual sadism a paraphilia in which a person achieves sexual satisfaction by inflicting pain or humiliation on a sex partner

sexual masochism a paraphilia in which a person desires to be humiliated or receive pain in order to attain sexual pleasure

TECHNOLOGY and BEHAVIOR

INTERNET SEXUAL ADDICTIONS

Sex sites are among the most widely visited areas on the Internet. At least 30% of Internet users report visiting a sexually oriented website (A. Cooper, 2003). Many people surf sex sites out of curiosity. Yet a growing number are starting to surf the Net solely as a sex outlet, to the exclusion of everything else, and therapists report an increasing number of clients with cybersex-related issues (P. D. Goldberg et al., 2008). Such behavior interferes with a person's ability to function and therefore is seen as problematic. An Internet sex addict surfs sex sites for at least several hours each day; the person may masturbate to these images or engage in online sex with someone in a chat room (A. Cooper et al., 2000). The seemingly infinite number of Internet sex sites hooks the person in much the same way as drug addiction. And like drug addiction, Internet sex addiction can have negative effects on one's family and life (Bird, 2006; A. Cooper, 2002; Landau, Garrett, & Webb, 2008; Woodward, 2003). Partners of Internet sex addicts feel ignored and abandoned as the addicts neglect family and friends to pursue their compulsion. The compulsion may be so strong that Internet sex addicts use workplace computers to surf Internet sex sites, putting their careers and jobs at risk as many workplaces have established policies against online sex surfing. For example, in one study (A. Cooper, Safir, & Rosenmann, 2006), of more than 3,000 people who reported online sexual activities, 18.5% reported engaging in online sexual activities at work. Clearly, future research is needed to define, understand, and effectively treat people with Internet sexual addictions.

© vario images GmbH & Co.KG/Alamy

The Internet has opened up a whole new universe to satisfy people's curiosity about sex. However, this activity becomes problematic when a person spends all day surfing sex sites to the exclusion of family, friends, and usual activities.

Let's REVIEW

This section described sexual disorders. For a quick check of your understanding, try answering the following questions at increasing levels of difficulty.

1. Andrew persistently gets sexually aroused by cross-dressing. Andrew would be considered a(n) _____.

a. transsexual

b. female impersonator

c. exhibitionist

d. transvestite

2. Since Mona's rape, she has been repulsed by the thought of engaging in sexual activity. Mona would most likely be diagnosed with _____.

a. hypoactive sexual desire

b. sexual aversion disorder

c. orgasmic disorder

d. inhibited excitement

3. Which of the following is considered a noncoercive paraphilia?

a. pedophilia

b. exhibitionism

c. fetishism

d. voyeurism

ANSWERS 1. d; 2. b; 3. c

What Is Sexual Coercion?

We saw in the previous section that certain paraphilias are coercive because the sexual behavior is directed at nonconsenting persons. Now we'll expand that discussion by looking at other sexual behaviors that are coercive. **Sexual coercion** involves behaviors that are nonconsenting, abusive, or forcible, such as *sexual harassment*, *sexual abuse*, and *rape*.

Sexual Harassment: Unwelcome Comments, Gestures, or Contact

Sexual harassment includes the repeated use of unwanted verbal comments, gestures, or physical contact of a sexual nature against another person that interferes with his or her work performance, creates a hostile or offensive work environment, or both. The victim of sexual harassment may be made to feel that tolerating such behavior is a condition of employment, promotion, or satisfactory evaluation. Although both men and women can commit sexual harassment, fewer complaints are filed by men, and the majority of these involve same-sex harassment. For example, of all the sexual harassment complaints filed in 2009, only 16% were filed by men (Equal Employment Opportunity Commission, 2010). Similar results have been found when investigating sexual harassment complaints in the military (Magley et al., 1999).

Obvious forms of sexual harassment include demands for sexual favors in order to maintain a job. However, many forms of sexual harassment are subtle, such as unwanted sexual comments, jokes, or gestures. Sexual harassment is further complicated by the fact that the recipient must find such behavior unwelcome. One person may be offended by such behavior whereas another may not. For example, in a study by Woodzicka and LaFrance (2001), the researchers described to female participants a situation in which a male interviewer asked a female job applicant several questions that involved mild sexual harassment, such as "Do you have a boyfriend?" The women were asked how they would respond in such a situation. Many women reported that they would object to such behavior in a clear and overt way. However, when the researchers staged an actual interview, advertising a job and employing a

sexual coercion sexual behaviors that
are nonconsenting, abusive, or forcible

sexual harassment the repeated use
of unwanted verbal comments, gestures,
or physical contact of a sexual nature
against another person that interferes
with his or her work performance

Many forms of sexual harassment
are subtle, such as unwanted sexual
gestures, and the recipient must find
such behavior unwelcome.

© Morgan David de Lossy/Corbis

male confederate to conduct interviews, women's actual behaviors were quite different. They did not object or leave the interview, but more frequently avoided the questions. Moreover, the researchers had to hire a second male confederate because some of the women found the first confederate to be charming. They did not perceive his behavior as sexual harassment.

Sexually harassing behaviors are highly dependent on the reaction and perceptions of the recipient. Men are more likely than women to misperceive friendliness as sexual interest (Farris et al., 2008) which then leads to behavior that women find inappropriate. Moreover, behaviors perceived as sexually harassing to a woman are more often perceived as flattering to men (Lastella, 2005).

Despite increased awareness about sexual harassment, such behavior continues to go unreported. Many who experience sexual harassment choose to ignore the behavior or avoid the person (Barringer, 1993; Magley, 2002; Menard et al., 2003). However, if you are being sexually harassed, a direct, businesslike response to communicate that the behavior is offensive or unwanted is appropriate. People differ in their perceptions of what constitutes sexually offensive behavior, but if a person is told that his (or her) behavior is offensive and still continues the behavior, that person can no longer claim he or she did not know the behavior was objectionable. For repeated instances of sexual harassment, victims may file a complaint. Organizations and companies are required by law to respond to such complaints. It is best to have written documentation of sexually harassing behavior, including when and where it occurred, as well as any witnesses who can substantiate the complaint.

Child Molestation and Sexual Abuse: Short- and Long-Term Effects

What is child sexual abuse? *Sexual abuse* is any sexual activity between an adult and a child. Even if children cooperate in sexual activity with an adult, they are legally incapable of consenting to such activity. Maya Angelou's rape at the age of 8 constitutes child sexual abuse. Sexual abuse may include fondling, kissing, oral sex, and anal or vaginal intercourse. The prevalence of child sexual abuse is difficult to determine because many cases go unreported (Hebert et al., 2009; Maletzky, 1998; Ulibarri, Ulloa, & Camacho, 2009). However, prevalence rates of child sexual abuse across 21 countries range from 3% to 29% for males and 7% to 36% for females (Fieldman & Crespi, 2002; Finkelhor, 1994; Pereda et al., 2009; Valente, 2005). Sexual abuse occurs across all racial, ethnic, and economic categories (Alter-Reid et al., 1986). However, African American and Latina females report more child sexual abuse than Asian or European American females (Amodeo et al., 2006; Newcomb, Munoz, & Carmona, 2009; Ulibarri et al., 2009; Ullman & Filipas, 2005a). The average age of sexual abuse ranges from 6 to 12 years for girls and from 7 to 10 years for boys (Knudsen, 1991).

Who sexually abuses children? Although children are often taught during the preschool years about "stranger danger," in roughly 75–80% of cases, the child knows the molester (J. Murray, 2000). It is estimated that in 10–50% of sexual abuse cases, the perpetrators are family members (Ulibarri et al., 2009; Waterman & Lusk, 1986). Initially, the child may trust the abuser and comply. Although many sexually abused children are molested only once, repeated acts of abuse are more common when a family member is the abuser (Dube & Hebert, 1988). In such instances of repeated abuse, affectionate fondling and kissing may progress to genital touching or oral sex, and then to penetration (anal or vaginal) over the course of the person's childhood (Waterman & Lusk, 1986). Children may fear retaliation by the molester if they tell, or they may believe they are to blame for the sexual abuse. The majority of child sexual abusers are heterosexual males (J. Murray, 2000). However, the number of female child sexual abusers may be higher than research has noted as males are less likely to report child sexual abuse than females (Boroughs, 2004; Hebert et al., 2009; Newcomb et al., 2009).

What are the effects of being sexually abused? They include both short- and long-term physical and psychological effects (Finkelhor, 1990). Physically, children may suffer genital injuries, experience sleep problems, contract sexually transmitted infections, or develop stomachaches and headaches in an attempt to cope with the abuse. Psychologically, sexually abused children may externalize or internalize their distress. External behavioral changes include "acting out," such as tantrums, aggressive behavior, or drug use. Other children may respond by becoming withdrawn or depressed, internal behaviors of distress. Maya Angelou internalized her distress by not speaking for 5 years. Although the effects of sexual abuse on males and females are quite similar, boys tend to engage in more external behavior, whereas girls are more likely to internalize their distress (Ullman & Filipas, 2005b). In adolescence, child sexual abuse survivors may become prematurely sexually active or promiscuous.

The long-term effects of sexual abuse may continue into adulthood in the form of mood and anxiety disorders, eating disorders, suicide attempts, and drug abuse (Bebbington et al., 2009;

Sexual abuse can have devastating effects on a child's self-image.

© Dan Lamont/Corbis

Buzi et al., 2003; Cheasty, Clare, & Collins, 2002; McLaughlin et al., 2010; Ullman, Najdowski, & Filipas, 2009). Being betrayed by a trusted family member or friend may lead to difficulty in forming intimate relationships, as well as negative attitudes about sex and sexual dysfunctions in adulthood (DiLillo, 2001; Maltz, 2002; Swaby & Morgan, 2009; Vandeusen & Carr, 2003). Children who are sexually abused are often maltreated in other ways and may be subject to problem-filled family environments. Children who are exposed to multiple forms of maltreatment often display more emotional and behavioral problems into adulthood (Kim-Cohen & Gold, 2009; Shaffer, Huston, & Egeland, 2008). However, many adult survivors go on to establish healthy lives and loving adult relationships (Banyard & Williams, 2007). This success in no way minimizes the pain of experiencing child sexual abuse, but it does offer hope. Maya Angelou's many accomplishments, achievements, and experiences are a rich illustration of such resilience.

Rape: Forcing Sex on Someone

Another type of sexual coercion is rape. **What is rape?** Although the legal definition of rape varies from state to state, generally **rape** involves the threat or use of force to obtain sex. Surveys suggest that between 17% and 28% of women and 3% of men in the United States are raped at some time in their lives (Tjaden & Thoennes, 2006). Therefore, although men can be raped, too, the majority of rape victims are women (Houry, Feldman, & Abbott, 2000). Women of all ages, races, and social classes are raped. However, younger women are more likely to be raped than older women, and American Indian/Alaska Native women are more likely to be raped than women from other backgrounds (Tjaden & Thoennes, 2006; U.S. Department of Justice, 2005).

Across college campuses, approximately 3% of women experience an attempted or completed rape during a typical college year (B. S. Fisher, Cullen, & Turner, 2000). However, as with child sexual abuse, these numbers may seriously underestimate the actual number of rapes. Women may fear rejection by their families or fear revenge from the offender. Men and women may feel that they will be humiliated by the criminal justice system or assume that they will not be believed and the offender will go free (Sable et al., 2006). Many women may not even define the incident as rape, especially if it took place within a relationship. Yet women are more likely to be raped, injured, or killed by their current or former partner than by other types of assailants (Campbell et al., 2003)

rape the threat or use of force to obtain sex

Attitudes and Beliefs About Rape

Among college students, males and Asian Americans tend to show greater agreement with statements that are supportive of rape (Devdas & Rubin, 2007; Lee et al., 2005). Other studies find that people who hold more traditional gender roles are also more likely to be tolerant of rape and less tolerant of rape victims (Burgess, 2007; Simonson & Subich, 1999). Their belief that "real" men are sexual aggressors who need to overcome a woman's resistance may make them more accepting of violence against women.

Many people also believe a number of myths about rape, such as that "the way women dress, they are just asking to be raped," or that "deep down inside, women want to be raped" (Maurer & Robinson, 2008). Believing such myths further condones rape. Although both men and women are susceptible to rape myths, studies find that men show a greater acceptance of these myths than do women, even after receiving rape education classes that are designed to challenge such views (Burgess, 2007; Franiuk, Seefelt, & Vandello, 2008; Nagel et al., 2005). Where do such attitudes and beliefs stem from? Many believe that reinforcing aggression and competition in males from a very early age socializes males into a sexually dominant role such that they see interpersonal relationships and sex as adversarial (Burgess, 2007; Stock, 1991). Such socialization experiences are evident when we examine date rape.

TRY THIS DEMONSTRATION

Take a look at the statements in ● TABLE 10.1. Indicate whether you agree or disagree with each statement.

TABLE 10.1

● **Attitudes That Support Rape**

DO YOU AGREE WITH ANY OF THE FOLLOWING STATEMENTS?
A man sees sex as an achievement or notch on his belt.
Rape really occurs only when a man has a weapon.
Deep down, a woman likes to be whistled at on the street.
If a woman is heavily intoxicated, it is okay to have sex with her.
Women frequently cry false rape.
In a woman, submissiveness equals femininity.
In a man, aggressiveness equals masculinity.
A prostitute cannot be raped.
Some women ask to be raped and may enjoy it.
Any woman could prevent rape if she wanted to.
The victim often provokes rape.
If a woman says "no" to having sex, she means "maybe" or even "yes."

Note: If you agree with any of the statements, you are endorsing an attitude that helps create a climate that justifies rape and blames the victim.

Date Rape

One commonly held belief about rape is that strangers commit it. However, most women are raped by men they know, not strangers (Howard et al., 2003; Maston, 2010). This particular type of rape is referred to as *acquaintance rape*. Among college women who experience a rape or an attempted rape, the majority knew the person who assaulted them. Nine out of ten of the perpetrators were ex-boyfriends, classmates, friends, or coworkers (B. S. Fisher et al., 2000). Although acquaintance rapes are just as likely to be reported as stranger rapes (Maston, 2010), they are more often treated as "misunderstandings" than as violent crimes. Such interpretations are especially likely in the case of **date rape**, one form of acquaintance rape.

date rape a form of acquaintance rape in which a person is forced or threatened to engage in sexual activity with a social escort

Date rape occurs within a context in which sexual relations could occur as the person has voluntarily agreed to spend time with the other.

Unlike stranger rape, date rape occurs within a context in which sexual relations could occur. The woman has voluntarily agreed to spend time with this man. Moreover, she may have consented to some sexual activity, such as kissing or fondling, but not to sexual intercourse. In such instances, a charge of date rape often comes down to a case of her word against his. If she has consented to a series of acts such as sharing dinner, accompanying him to his hotel room or apartment, and perhaps even kissing, her word is less likely to be persuasive to a jury. However, if a woman says no, a man should take no for an answer.

U.S. college women report high rates of forced sexual behavior in dating relationships (Hines, 2007). Men who commit date rape tend to believe that acceptance of a date indicates a willingness to engage in sexual intercourse. If a woman is willing to return home with him, the man may interpret this behavior as a signal of sexual interest. Recall that men are more likely than women to misinterpret friendliness as sexual interest (Farris et al., 2008). Date rapists are also more likely to interpret resistance as "playing hard to get" or not wanting to appear "too easy." Date rape is most likely to occur in the early stages of dating rather than on the first date, and it is more likely to occur when the couple has had too much alcohol (Hensley, 2002; Lawyer et al., 2010). To deter unwanted sexual advances, it is important for women to be very clear and direct about their sexual wishes. Even more important is for men to examine their attitudes toward sexual activity within a dating relationship.

Let's REVIEW

In this section we discussed sexual coercion—including sexual harassment, child sexual abuse, and rape. For a quick check of your understanding, try answering the following questions at increasing levels of difficulty.

1. The repeated use of unwanted verbal comments, gestures, or physical contact of a sexual nature against another person that interferes with his or her work performance is called _____.

   a. sexual abuse   c. date rape
   b. sexual assault   d. sexual harassment

2. Which of the following individuals is *least* likely to blame a victim of rape?

   a. a male holding less-traditional gender-role stereotypes
   b. a male holding more-traditional gender-role stereotypes
   c. a male who believes that men are expected to be sexually aggressive
   d. a female who believes that women frequently cry false rape

3. Which of the following statements about childhood sexual abuse is *true*?

   a. Males are sexually abused at a higher rate than females.
   b. In the majority of child sexual abuse cases, the perpetrator is unknown to the child.
   c. Sexual abuse occurs across all racial, ethnic, and economic categories.
   d. Male sexual abuse victims are more likely to internalize their distress, whereas female sexual abuse victims are more likely to externalize their distress.

ANSWERS 1. d; 2. a; 3. c

© Bob Daemmrich/PhotoEdit

What Are Sexually Transmitted Infections and Who Is at Risk?

Sexually transmitted infections (STIs) are infections that are passed from one person to another, usually through sexual contact. However, some STIs may be spread by nonsexual contact as well as from a mother to her unborn child. Every day we hear news accounts of the spread of AIDS and the HIV virus. Yet AIDS and the HIV virus are not the only types of STIs, many of which are more widespread, especially in the United States.

Prevalence of STIs: Will I Get an STI?

The Centers for Disease Control and Prevention (CDC, 2008b) estimates that more than 19 million people in the United States become infected each year, and almost half of them are young people between the ages of 15 and 24 (Weinstock, Berman, & Cates, 2004). The United States has one of the highest rates of STIs in the industrialized world. At least 1 in 4 Americans will contract an STI by the age of 21 (Feroli & Burstein, 2003).

Why are STIs so widespread? One reason is that younger people today are more likely to engage in sexual intercourse. Almost half of new cases of STIs occur among teenagers and young adults, who may not use condoms or may use them infrequently, or in women "on the pill" using oral contraceptives, which do not prevent STIs (R. Crosby & Danner, 2008; Feroli & Burstein, 2003). A second reason is that many STIs often have no symptoms, so they are unknowingly passed from one person to the next. A third reason is the social stigma attached to those infected with an STI. Such negative perceptions may prevent people from openly discussing their conditions with medical personnel, partners, and other loved ones.

Risk Factors: Age, Gender, Ethnicity, and Behavior

Who is most at risk for getting an STI? Anyone who is sexually active risks contracting an STI. However, women, teenagers, and some ethnic groups are more likely to have an STI in the United States. Men and women between the ages of 15 and 25 are most at risk (Calvert, 2003; R. Crosby & Danner, 2008). Young people are at increased risk because they engage in many high-risk sexual behaviors, such as having multiple partners and engaging in unprotected sexual intercourse. Women are at higher risk for contracting an STI than are men because the warm, moist environment of the vagina renders women more susceptible to infection (Bolton et al., 2008). Younger women are especially vulnerable as viruses and bacteria can more easily invade immature cervical cells than mature ones (Farley et al., 1997; Parker-Pope, 2002). According to data from the Centers for Disease Control and Prevention (CDC, 2008b), higher rates of STIs are found among all ethnic minority populations except Asians/Pacific Islanders when compared to European Americans.

Engaging in certain sexual behaviors also puts one at a higher risk for contracting an STI. High-risk sexual behaviors include oral–genital sex without a condom or dental dam, semen in the mouth, and vaginal or anal intercourse without a condom (Hatcher et al., 1994). Men who have sex with men are more likely to engage in these high-risk sexual behaviors, and the incidence of STIs in this population has been growing (Brooks et al., 2008). Sex with multiple partners also increases one's chances of contracting an STI. Moreover, some STIs are contracted through nonsexual means. Certain forms of drug use increase the risk, as sharing contaminated needles can directly transmit organisms such as HIV. An infected pregnant woman also risks transmitting the infection to her unborn child and causing serious birth defects.

STIs can cause irreparable damage. The financial cost to our health-care system is enormous. Left untreated, STIs can cause pelvic inflammatory disease (PID), chronic pelvic pain, and infertility in women (CDC, 2008b; Eng & Butler, 1997). They can also result in arthritis, heart problems, brain damage, and even death. The human cost to partners, families, and infected persons is incalculable. It's a cost that does not necessarily have to be paid, as many STIs are easily treated and prevented.

sexually transmitted infection (STI) an infection that is passed from one person to another primarily through sexual contact

Is this couple at risk for an STI?

Stuart McClymont/Getty Images

Types of STIs: Bacterial, Viral, and Parasitic

There are three basic categories of STIs: bacterial infections, viral infections, and parasitic infections.

Bacterial infections include *chlamydia*, *gonorrhea*, and *syphilis*. Bacteria are microorganisms or germs that can quickly reproduce and cause disease in the body. Chlamydia, gonorrhea, and syphilis are transmitted primarily through vaginal, anal, or oral sexual activity. If present in the vagina, these infections also can be transmitted from a mother to a newborn during delivery. An unusual discharge, sore, or painful urination are common symptoms of these infections. However, many men and women show no symptoms during the early stages and therefore do not seek treatment until more serious symptoms develop. Antibiotics are typically used to treat bacterial infections (Cates, 1998).

Viral infections include *genital herpes*, *genital human papillomavirus* (HPV), and *HIV/AIDS*. Viruses are incapable of reproducing on their own. They invade a normal cell and direct that cell to make new viral copies. These copies then invade other healthy cells, causing infection. Many of the symptoms of these infections can be treated, but the virus remains in the body and is yours for life.

Most people with genital herpes or HPV do not initially develop symptoms or health problems. When symptoms do occur in genital herpes, noticeable sores appear. About 1 in 6 people between the ages of 14 and 49 are infected with genital herpes (CDC, 2010b). Similarly, most people who become infected with any of the more than 40 strains of HPV do not know they have it. However, certain types of HPV can cause genital warts, small bumps, or groups of bumps, usually in the genital area. Approximately 20 million people in the United States are currently infected with HPV. It is estimated that at least 50% of sexually active men and women will get infected with HPV at some point in their lives, making it the most common sexually transmitted infection (STI) in the United States (CDC, 2008b). A controversial vaccine can be administered to young females to protect them from four types of HPV that cause most cervical cancers and genital warts. The vaccine also protects males against two HPV types that cause most genital warts.

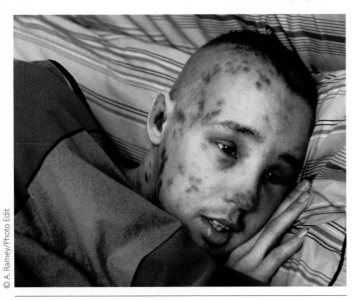

© A. Ramey/Photo Edit

AIDS is a sexually transmitted virus that remains with you for life.

Being HIV-positive means that a person has been infected with the human immunodeficiency virus (HIV). In HIV/AIDS, the HIV attacks the immune system, resulting in mild flu-like symptoms that may then disappear for years before developing into a full-blown case of AIDS. Although symptoms may not be present, a person still carries the virus and is therefore capable of transmitting it to a partner during sexual activity. HIV/AIDS can also be contracted through the exchange of contaminated blood or passed to a fetus during pregnancy or to an infant during breastfeeding.

It is estimated that more than 1 million people are currently living with HIV in the United States (Glynn & Rhodes, 2005). Males account for more than 74% of all HIV/AIDS cases among adolescents and adults. People with HIV tend to come from lower socioeconomic groups, are more likely to be less educated, are more likely to be gay and bisexual men, and are more likely to be African American (CDC, 2008a). However, anyone—regardless of age, income, race, or sexual orientation—can contract this potentially deadly disease. Treatment to suppress HIV/AIDS infection typically consists of a steady regime of antiretroviral drugs. This treatment slows the disease's progression and has significantly decreased the number of HIV- and AIDS-related deaths (Crum et al., 2006; Venkatesh, Biswas, & Kumarasamy, 2008).

Parasitic infections include *pubic lice* and *scabies*. A parasite lives off another organism or host to survive. Pubic lice, or "crabs," survive by feeding on human blood. Scabies are tiny mites that burrow under the skin and lay eggs. Both infections can be spread through sexual contact or by contact with infested towels, linens, or clothing. The most common symptom is intense itching in the genital area. Parasitic infections are typically treated with a solution that kills the lice or mites and their eggs. It is important to carefully reexamine the body 4 to 7 days after treatment to ensure that all the eggs have been killed. Towels, linens, and cloth-

Eye of Science/Photo Researchers, Inc.

Pubic lice are often called "crabs" because of the organism's resemblance to a crab.

ing also need to be treated to prevent reinfection. ● THE BIG PICTURE REVIEW shows the main types of sexually transmitted infections, modes of transmission, symptoms, and treatment.

In this chapter, we examined the influence of gender and sexuality on our behavior. Just as we saw in the chapter on development, gender and sexuality are influenced by the

THE BIG PICTURE review

Sexually Transmitted Infections

STI	TRANSMISSION MODES	SYMPTOMS	TREATMENTS
Bacterial			
Chlamydia	Vaginal, oral, or anal sexual activity, or from an infected mother to her newborn during a vaginal birth	In females: frequent and painful urination, lower abdominal pain, and vaginal discharge. In males: burning or painful urination, and slight penis discharge. However, many people show no symptoms.	Antibiotics
Gonorrhea	Vaginal, oral, or anal sexual activity, or from an infected mother to her newborn during a vaginal birth	In females: increased vaginal discharge, burning urination, or irregular menstrual bleeding (many women show no early symptoms). In males: yellowish, thick penile discharge, or burning urination.	Antibiotics
Syphilis	Vaginal, oral, or anal sexual activity, or by touching an infected chancre or sore	A hard, round, painless chancre or sore appears at site of infection within 2 to 4 weeks.	Penicillin or other antibiotics for penicillin-allergic patients.
Viral			
Genital Herpes	Vaginal, oral, or anal sexual activity	Painful, reddish blisters around the genitals, thighs, or buttocks, and for females on the vagina or cervix. Other symptoms may include burning urination, flu-like symptoms, or vaginal discharge in females.	No cure, although certain drugs can provide relief and help sores heal.
HPV	Vaginal, oral, or anal sexual activity	Some strains cause painless warts to appear in the genital area or anus; other strains may cause abnormal cell changes in the cervix	Cryotherapy (freezing), acid burning, or surgical removal of warts
HIV/AIDS	Sexual contact, infusion with contaminated blood, or from mother to child during pregnancy, childbirth, or breastfeeding.	May develop flu-like symptoms that may disappear for many years before developing full-blown AIDS. AIDS symptoms include fever, weight loss, fatigue, diarrhea, and susceptibility to infection.	No cure; treatment includes a combination of antiretroviral drugs
Parasites			
Pubic Lice	Sexual contact or contact with infested linens or toilet seats	Intense itching in hairy regions of the body, especially the pubic area	Prescription shampoos or nonprescription medications
Scabies	Sexual contact or contact with infested linens or toilet seats	Intense itching, reddish lines on skin, welts, and pus-filled blisters in affected area	Prescription shampoos

interaction between nature and nurture. Our biology, in the form of anatomy, hormones, and susceptibility to infections, plays a role in our sexual behaviors and expressions. However, this biology is strongly influenced by our attitudes, learning experiences, and cultural expectations. Gender and sexuality influence how others perceive us and behave toward us. In the next chapter, we will take a broader look at this topic by examining social psychology and the influence that others have on our behavior.

Let's REVIEW

This section described sexually transmitted infections. For a quick check of your understanding, try answering the following questions at increasing levels of difficulty.

1. Which of the following sexual behaviors is low risk for contracting an STI?
   a. semen in the mouth
   b. vaginal intercourse while the woman is "on the pill"
   c. sex with multiple partners
   d. oral sex with a dental dam or condom

2. Which of the following STIs can be transmitted in the absence of sexual contact?
   a. gonorrhea   c. scabies
   b. genital herpes   d. syphilis

3. Pedro has experienced an intense, burning sensation during urination and a thick, yellowish penile discharge. Pedro most likely has which STI?
   a. gonorrhea   c. genital warts
   b. genital herpes   d. syphilis

ANSWERS 1. d; 2. c; 3. a

STUDYING the CHAPTER

KEY TERMS

sex (403)
gender (403)
gender identity (403)
sexuality (403)
sexual differentiation (405)
hermaphrodite (406)
pseudohermaphrodite (406)
gender roles (407)
gender permanence (407)
gender-schema theory (407)
transsexual (410)
masturbation (415)
sexual fantasy (415)
sexual orientation (419)
heterosexual (419)

homosexual (419)
bisexual (419)
asexual (419)
homophobia (420)
sexual arousal (423)
sexual desire (423)
libido (423)
estrogens (423)
ovaries (423)
testosterone (423)
testes (423)
erogenous zones (424)
excitement phase (425)
plateau phase (425)
orgasm phase (425)

resolution phase (426)
refractory period (426)
sexual disorder (426)
sexual dysfunction (426)
hypoactive sexual desire
    disorder (427)
sexual aversion disorder
    (427)
male erectile dysfunction
    (ED) (427)
female sexual arousal
    disorder (428)
orgasmic disorder (428)
premature ejaculation (428)
dyspareunia (429)

vaginismus (429)
paraphilia (429)
fetishism (429)
transvestism (429)
voyeurism (430)
exhibitionism (430)
pedophilia (430)
sexual sadism (430)
sexual masochism (430)
sexual coercion (432)
sexual harassment (432)
rape (434)
date rape (435)
sexually transmitted
    infection (STI) (437)

TEST
YOURSELF!

LEARNING CHALLENGE

Now that you have studied the chapter, assess your comprehension of the material by answering the following questions. Then use the key at the end to determine if your understanding is at the basic, intermediate, or advanced level. For a more comprehensive assessment of your learning, please see your student study guide and your Psychology CourseMate (www.cengagebrain.com).

1. One's personal experience of being male or female is called _____.

   a. gender
   b. gender identity
   c. sex
   d. sexuality

2. Belinda's baby is genetically a male (XY) that did not secrete H-Y antigen during prenatal development. What is the most likely outcome of this baby's internal and external genitalia?

   a. Both the internal and external genitalia will be male.
   b. Both the internal and external genitalia will be female.
   c. The internal genitalia will be male and the external genitalia will be female.
   d. The internal genitalia will be female and the external genitalia will be male.

3. Which of the following has been found in regard to males' and females' cognitive abilities?

   a. Males outperform females on verbal tasks.
   b. Females outperform males on spatial tasks.
   c. Males outperform females on math tests through the school years.
   d. Females outperform males on math tests through the school years.

4. Sabrina has a partner and two kids. What do we know about Sabrina's sexual orientation?

   a. She is homosexual.
   b. She is heterosexual.
   c. She is bisexual.
   d. We cannot tell from this information.

5. In humans, the hormone that governs libido is _____.

   a. testosterone for males and estrogen for females
   b. estrogen for males and testosterone for females
   c. testosterone for both males and females
   d. estrogen for both males and females

6. Male and female sexual response cycles differ most significantly in which stage?

   a. resolution
   b. plateau
   c. orgasm
   d. excitement

7. Amber has persistent difficulty in becoming sexually aroused and sufficiently lubricated in response to sexual stimulation. Amber most likely would be diagnosed with _____.

   a. sexual aversion disorder
   b. orgasmic disorder
   c. sexual arousal disorder
   d. dyspareunia

8. Which of the following is more likely to be a sexual fantasy for a man than for a woman?

   a. sex with a current partner
   b. receiving oral sex
   c. reliving a past sexual experience
   d. both a and c

9. Which of the following is the biggest obstacle to enjoying sexual pleasure in later adulthood?

   a. availability of sexual partners
   b. less desire for sex
   c. less energy for sex
   d. inability to get aroused

10. Research on the causes of homosexuality suggests _____.

   a. it is due to the types of toys you played with as a child
   b. it is due to genetics only
   c. it is a personal choice that is not influenced by biology
   d. it is due to a combination of biological and environmental factors

11. Date rape is most likely to occur _____.

   a. on the first date
   b. after a long time dating
   c. in the early stages of dating
   d. when the couple is sober

12. Mark is sexually aroused by wearing lacy bras and underwear. Mark would most likely be diagnosed with _____.

   a. transvestism
   b. fetishism
   c. sadism
   d. pedophilia

13. The long-term effects of sexual abuse may include _____.

   a. depression
   b. eating disorders
   c. suicide attempts
   d. all of the above

14. Who is most at risk for getting an STI?

    a. young males

    b. young females

    c. older males

    d. older females

15. Which of the following is a viral sexually transmitted infection?

    a. herpes

    b. gonorrhea

    c. syphilis

    d. chlamydia

Scoring Key

Below are the answers and the associated point values for each of the Learning Challenge questions. Circle the associated points for each question that you answered correctly. To obtain your Learning Challenge Score, add up the points you circled and write the total in the blank.

1. B, 1 pt   **6.** A, 2 pts   **11.** C, 1 pt

2. B, 3 pts   **7.** C, 2 pts   **12.** A, 2 pts

3. D, 2 pts   **8.** B, 3 pts   **13.** D, 1 pt

4. D, 2 pts   **9.** A, 3 pts   **14.** B, 1 pt

5. C, 3 pts   **10.** D, 1 pt   **15.** A, 3 pts

Learning Challenge Score _____

(27–30) Congratulations! You scored at the advanced level. You are well on your way to mastering the material. Take the next step by answering the questions in your Student Study Guide or your Psychology CourseMate (www.cengagebrain.com).

(21–26) You are almost there! You scored at the intermediate level. Review the material you missed before moving on to answer the questions in your Student Study Guide or your Psychology CourseMate (www.cengagebrain.com).

(20 and below) You are on your way, but you're not there yet! You scored at the beginner level. It appears that you need to carefully review the chapter to improve your mastery of the material.

USE IT OR LOSE IT: APPLYING PSYCHOLOGY

1. Spend an hour watching television shows aimed at children, playing children's video games, or using computer programs developed for children. What messages, schemas, or concepts will children acquire from these sources? How might these messages influence their ideas about gender? In your opinion, are these messages appropriate for children? Explain.

2. Explain how your gender identity has influenced your sexual attitudes and behaviors.

3. Examine the gender differences in the prevalence of sexual dysfunctions and paraphilias, and develop a gender theory to account for these differences.

4. Research your state's laws on same-sex marriage and adoption. What companies in your area recognize same-sex partnerships in their benefits packages? Do you agree or disagree with these policies and laws? Defend your position.

5. How does one's gender identity impact one's definition of sexual harassment or rape? What general attitudes about males and females facilitate harassment and rape? Which attitudes would decrease sexual coercion?

6. If one of your children were born a hermaphrodite, would you raise the child as a boy or as a girl? Why did you choose that gender?

CRITICAL THINKING FOR INTEGRATION

1. How might operant conditioning (Chapter 5) influence children's understanding of gender? In your opinion, are males and females reinforced for the same behaviors? Do they receive the same reinforcers? Similarly, are males and females punished for the same behaviors? How do their punishments differ? How might differences in reinforcers and punishers influence gender typing in males and females?

2. Explain the development of fetishism in classical conditioning terms (Chapter 5).

3. Review the milestones of adolescent development presented in Chapter 9. How might these physical, cognitive, and social processes explain why teenagers may be more likely to develop a sexually transmitted infection? Develop several strategies for reducing STIs in the teenage population.

4. Create a chart or graph that details how the brain (Chapter 2) integrates sensory (Chapter 3), hormonal (Chapter 2), and learning information (Chapter 5) to produce human sexual desire.

CHAPTER STUDY RESOURCES

Student Study Guide

To help organize your learning, work through Chapter 10 of the *What Is Psychology? Student Study Guide*. The study guide includes learning objectives, a chapter summary, fill-in review, key terms, a practice test, and activities.

CengageNOW

Go to **www.cengage.com/login** to link to CengageNOW, your online study tool. First take the Pre-Test for this chapter to get your personalized study plan, which will identify topics you need to review and direct you to online resources. Then take the Post-Test to determine what concepts you have mastered and what you still need work on.

CourseMate

Access an interactive eBook, chapter-specific interactive learning tools, including flashcards, quizzes, videos, and more in your Psychology CourseMate, available at **CengageBrain.com**.

Aplia

aplia

Aplia™ is an online interactive learning solution that helps you improve comprehension—and your grade—by integrating a variety of tools such as video, tutorials, practice tests, and interactive e-book. Founded by a professor to enhance his own courses, Aplia provides automatically graded assignments with detailed, immediate explanations on every question, and innovative teaching materials. More than 1,000,000 students like you have used Aplia at over 1,800 institutions. Aplia should be purchased only when assigned by your instructor as part of your course.

HOW DO GENDER AND SEXUALITY AFFECT OUR BEHAVIOR?

Gender and sexuality are influenced by the interaction between nature and nurture. Our biology plays a role in our sexual behaviors and expressions. However, as powerfully illustrated by Maya Angelou's life, this biology is strongly influenced by our attitudes, learning experiences, and cultural expectations.

HOW DO GENDER AND SEXUALITY AFFECT OUR BEHAVIOR?

- **Gender** refers to the state of being male or female.
- **Gender identity** represents our personal experience of being male or female.
- **Sexuality** includes the ways we experience and express ourselves as sexual beings.

SW Productions/Getty Image

HOW DO WE DEVELOP OUR GENDER IDENTITY AND DO MALES AND FEMALES DIFFER?

- Gender is determined by sex chromosomes we receive at conception and by hormonal influences on prenatal development.
- **Gender-schema theory** describes how social learning and reinforcement work with one's mental abilities to foster an understanding of gender.
- Gender differences in verbal abilities are quite small. Females tend to get better grades in math than males at all grade levels, but males outperform females on the math portion of the SAT. Males seem to have an advantage in visuospatial skills.
- Females tend to be more extraverted, anxious, trusting, and nurturing than males. Males tend to be more assertive and tough-minded and to have higher self-esteem than females. Males tend to be more physically aggressive, and females tend to engage in more relational aggression.

Antony Nagelmann/Getty Images

WHAT SEXUAL BEHAVIORS AND ATTITUDES DO PEOPLE REPORT?

- Surveys indicate that most people **masturbate** at some time. Generally, men masturbate more frequently than women.
- The majority of adults engage in **sexual fantasies** from time to time, with men tending to have more frequent sexual fantasies than women.
- Men report wanting sex more often and thinking about sex more often than women. Men also tend to be more favorable toward casual sex and are somewhat more likely to engage in extramarital sex than women.
- The worldwide average for frequency of sexual activity is about once a week; cross-cultural research reports a similar pattern worldwide.

© Michael Keller/Corbis

- Oral sex has increased in acceptance among young people. Oral sex is more common among men, married people, and college-educated people.

Kate M. Deloma/PhotoEdit

WHAT CAUSES SEXUAL ORIENTATION?

- **Sexual orientation** is not simply a matter of with whom you have sex. Survey research reveals that some people may have same-sex sexual encounters but not consider themselves to be gay or lesbian.

- **Heterosexuals** are attracted to members of the other sex. **Homosexuals** are attracted to members of the same sex. **Bisexuals** are attracted to members of both sexes. **Asexuals** have little or no attraction to either sex.

- **Homophobia**, or prejudice against homosexuals, has not disappeared. In the United States, many gay, lesbian, and bisexual youth are verbally or physically abused, yet not all cultures hold negative attitudes toward gays and lesbians.

- Research suggests that biological and environmental factors both play a role in sexual orientation.

WHAT HAPPENS DURING SEXUAL AROUSAL?

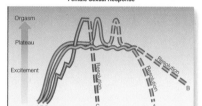

Female Sexual Response / Male Sexual Response

- **Sexual desire** is influenced by hormones, sensory cues, and cultural attitudes about what is sexually appealing.

- Masters and Johnson's research detailed the physical changes experienced during sexual activity in four phases: **excitement**, **plateau**, **orgasm**, and **resolution**.

WHAT IS A SEXUAL DISORDER?

Carol Ford/Getty Images

- Many people experience sexual problems from time to time. When such a problem persists, causes distress, and interferes with one's functioning, it is called a **sexual disorder**.

- A **sexual dysfunction** is characterized by a problem with sexual desire, arousal, or satisfaction.

- **Paraphilias** involve sexual arousal in response to an unusual object (**fetishism**), a nonconsenting person (such as **voyeurism**), or a situation (such as **sexual sadism**).

WHAT IS SEXUAL COERCION?

- **Sexual coercion** is behavior that is nonconsenting, abusive, or forcible in nature.

- **Sexual harassment** is the repeated use of unwelcome verbal comments, gestures, or physical contact of a sexual nature against another person that interferes with his or her work performance.

- Any sexual activity between an adult and a child is sexual abuse, even if the child cooperates in the sexual activity.

- **Rape** generally involves the threat or use of force to obtain sex. The majority of rape victims are women. All ages, races, and social classes are involved, but younger women are more likely to be raped than older women.

WHAT ARE SEXUALLY TRANSMITTED INFECTIONS AND WHO IS AT RISK?

Eye of Science/Photo Researchers, Inc.

- **Sexually transmitted infections (STIs)** are passed from one person to another primarily through sexual contact. One in four Americans will contract an STI by the age of 21.

- Young people are at greater risk for contracting STIs because they are more likely to engage in high-risk sexual behaviors.

- Bacterial infections include chlamydia, gonorrhea, and syphilis. An unusual discharge, sore, or painful urination are common symptoms of these infections.

- Viral infections include genital herpes, HPV, and HIV/AIDS. The symptoms of these infections can be treated, but the virus remains in the body for life.

- Parasitic infections such as pubic lice and scabies can be spread through sexual contact or by contact with infested clothing. The most common symptom is intense genital itching.

SOCIAL PSYCHOLOGY: HOW DO WE UNDERSTAND AND INTERACT WITH OTHERS?

THE BIG PICTURE

How Do We Navigate Our Social World?

Humans are social animals. We may spend our lives in one place, interacting with the same community of people. We may live in broader social circles, interacting with an ever-changing sea of diverse people. But, we all interact. And, these interactions have the power to change us.

For Rose Mahoney, interacting with people from different cultures has certainly been life changing. In 1999, Rose, who took up rowing in Maine, decided to row a 7-foot rowboat up the Nile River in Egypt. It was, in part, the challenge and the danger that compelled Rose to attempt the 120-mile trip from Aswan and Qena—completely alone.

Almost immediately, Rose realized that the most difficult part of her trip would not be the physical labor involved in rowing 120 miles, the relentless heat, or the threat of Nile crocodiles. Rather, the most difficult part of the trip would be the clash of cultural values she would experience along the way.

Cultural norms are the rules that guide the behavior of people living in that culture. Egyptian norms vary substantially from those in the United States. And, although many Egyptians are used to interacting with Western tourists, some cultural beliefs and norms are deeply engrained in all of us. One cultural area in which Egyptian norms differ from Western norms is that of gender roles. In the United States, it is not unusual for women to travel alone, engage in physically demanding tasks, or even work in traditionally male-dominated jobs (for example, firefighting). When Rose rowed alone in the bays of Maine, she was not violating cultural norms. In Egypt, things were different.

Rose found that in Muslim Egypt, it was not acceptable for women to dress in revealing clothes, speak openly about sexuality, explore the countryside alone, or engage in strenuous activities. Egyptian society expected women to remain close to home, cooking, cleaning, and caring for children. Muslim men were expected to respect their wives and protect them from the outside world.

In Rose's estimation, Western women were viewed as a separate class of people. They were not viewed as the equal of Egyptian women. For example, it was not uncommon for Egyptian men to come up to Rose on the street and declare that they would like to have sex with her or tell her that they loved her—things they would never have

Phil Boorman/Getty Images

CHAPTER OUTLINE

- Attitudes: Why Do We Change Our Minds?

- How Do We Form Impressions of Others?

- Prejudice: Why Can't We All Just Get Along?

- What Attracts Us to Others?

- Groups and Group Influence: Are Two Heads Better Than One?

- Compliance and Obedience: Can Others Change Our Behavior?

- Aggression: What Makes Us Hurt Others?

- Helping Behavior: Will You, or Won't You?

Rose Mahoney realized her dream of rowing up the Nile River despite experiencing a clash of cultures along the way.

dreamt of saying to an Egyptian woman. Yet, Western women were also not viewed as the equal of Egyptian men (or any men, for that matter). In Egypt, Rose was freer than an Egyptian woman, but not as free as a man. And this was a problem for Rose's plan to row the Nile.

In Aswan, Rose found that no one would sell her a boat. The idea that a woman would want to row on the Nile was viewed as crazy. Many a boat owner offered to take Rose up the river in his sailboat (called a *felucca*), but no one would sell her a boat to make the trip alone. Then Rose met a sympathetic captain named Amr Khaled.

Amr was a Nubian felucca captain who barely made his living ferrying tourists up the Nile. As a Nubian, Amr was viewed by many Egyptians as being culturally more African than Egyptian. In Egypt, being of Nubian descent meant that Amr was frequently viewed as being inferior. Perhaps it was his perceived status as an outsider that made Amr sympathetic to Rose's dream.

Amr agreed to allow Rose to use his boat for the 3-day journey from Aswan to Edfu, but only if she would agree to let him follow her in his felucca to ensure her safety. Rose agreed but did not tell Amr that she planned to buy a boat in Luxor (just north of Edfu) and continue alone to Qena. For 3 days, Rose rowed alone while Amr trailed behind, and at night, she slept in safety on the felucca.

Occasionally people on shore would realize that Rose was a woman, and astounded, they would desperately yell at her and motion her to shore. Sometimes, they would run along the shore after her—seeing a woman in Rose's position was that incredible to them.

After reaching Edfu, Rose parted from Amr and went on to Luxor. In Luxor, the Egyptians were much more accustomed to dealing with Western tourists and their non-Egyptian ways. To Rose's surprise, she did not have much trouble purchasing a boat—after concocting a story about how she was buying the boat as a present for her imaginary husband! Then, under cover of darkness to avoid the police (Westerners need a permit to boat on the Nile), she set off for Qena.

This was Rose's dream—to row totally alone up the Nile. Yet, she was very nervous. Without Amr to protect her, Rose now felt very vulnerable. To help avoid detection, she wrapped a shirt around her head to hide her hair and appear more like a man. At night, she anchored in secluded coves.

One night, Rose awoke to find a man named Mahmoud and his children in a boat alongside her own. Startled, Rose became afraid. Mahmoud jumped into her boat and began asking many questions of Rose. Was she alone? Whose boat was this? Could he row her upriver to the next town? When polite refusal of his offer did not dissuade him, Rose became afraid. She knew that many Egyptian men viewed Western women as being rich and sexually promiscuous. Rose feared that he was going to rob or attack her. So, she forcefully ordered him out of her boat and quickly rowed away. But, to her horror, Mahmoud dropped off his sons and chased after her.

After a 10-minute chase up the river, Rose stopped rowing, got out her knife, and resolved to kill Mahmoud if he caught up to her and tried anything. When he arrived, she demanded to know what he wanted—was it money? Hearing this, Mahmoud said that he needed 10 pounds (approximately 3 dollars). Rose threw him a 20-pound note and waited for the attack. But, he didn't attack. He told her that he loved America and that he loved her. He thanked her for her generosity and then rowed away yelling his thanks until his voice drifted away on the wind.

After safely arriving in Qena, Rose realized that she had probably misread Mahmoud. In her fear and defensiveness, she perceived danger, yet Mahmoud had not behaved any differently than most of the Egyptian men that Rose had met. He was inquisitive and insistent. Yet, he had not demanded anything, and he never touched her. He was probably just hoping to earn a small tip. Later, in the book she wrote about her trip, *Down the Nile* (Mahoney, 2007), Rose reflected on how in the few days she was with Amr, she had come to know him and value him as a friend. Yet, in her brief encounter with Mahmoud, her perceptions of him had been dominated by prejudice and fear rather than his actual behavior. Like Rose, sometimes we form careful impressions of others, and other times we behave rashly and prejudicially. But, why?

Questions like this are the focus of **social psychology**, the study of how we think and behave in social situations. Because humans are social animals who spend much of their time in the company of others, the study of social psychology encompasses many different topic areas. One area, **social cognition**, investigates the ways in which we think (cognition) about ourselves and others—for example, how do we form prejudices about people, make judgments about others, or become attracted to others? Another area of social psychology, called **social influence**, deals with the ways in which other people influence our behavior—for example, can others make us do things that we know we shouldn't be doing? As we go through this chapter, we will be looking at these types of questions. We hope that you will see that understanding how we think and behave in social situations has great practical significance to all our lives.

social psychology the branch of psychology that studies how we think and behave in social situations

social cognition the area of social psychology that deals with the ways in which we think about other people and ourselves

social influence pressures placed on us by others to change our behavior or our beliefs or both

ATTITUDES: WHY DO WE CHANGE OUR MINDS?

Attitudes are evaluative judgments that integrate what we know and how we feel about people, places, or things (Crano & Prislin, 2006). We all have attitudes about a multitude of things. Our attitudes represent the ways in which we have sized up the contents of our world. So where do our attitudes come from? As with all of our beliefs, we acquire attitudes through *learning*. We learn to like certain things and to dislike others as a result of the same processes you learned about in Chapter 5: *classical conditioning, operant conditioning,* and *observational learning.*

Classical Conditioning of Attitudes

Recall that classical conditioning is often responsible for the development of certain learned *emotional* and *physiological* responses in humans. Because classical conditioning has the power to change the way we *feel* about certain stimuli, it also has the power to influence our attitudes toward these stimuli (● FIGURE 11.1). In short, classical conditioning can explain the gut-level emotional and physiological aspects of our attitudes. For example, if you watch a commercial for mouthwash that makes you laugh and feel good, you may later experience positive emotions (CR) when you see the mouthwash (CS) in the store. Because we often purchase things that make us feel good, classical conditioning can be a powerful advertising tool (R. P. Grossman & Till, 1998).

US → → → UR NS → → US → → UR CS → → → CR

Mom shows fear.   Child is afraid.

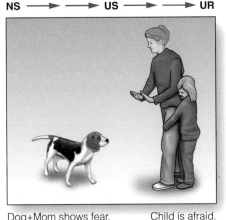
Dog+Mom shows fear.   Child is afraid.

Dog   Child is afraid.

FIGURE 11.1

● **Classical Conditioning of a Negative Attitude Toward Dogs** For a young child, a fear response in her mother (US) will naturally cause fear in the child (UR). On the other hand, the sight of a dog will not reliably elicit fear in a small child. Therefore, the dog is initially a neutral stimulus (NS). When the sight of the dog (NS) is repeatedly paired with a fear response in the mother (US), the child can easily acquire a conditioned fear of dogs (CR) that is elicited by the mere sight of a dog (CS).

attitudes evaluative judgments that integrate what we know and how we feel about people, places, or things

Operant Conditioning of Attitudes

Recall that in operant conditioning an initial, random behavior is strengthened if it results in reward and weakened if it results in punishment. Operant conditioning can affect the development of attitudes in at least two ways. First, if you are rewarded for having certain attitudes, the attitude will be strengthened. But if you are punished for having certain attitudes, the attitude will be weakened.

A second way that operant conditioning can influence the development of attitudes is through the consequences of our direct interaction with the objects of our attitude. For example, suppose a friend convinces you to try a dish with lots of very hot habanero peppers at a new Jamaican restaurant. When you taste the dish, it burns your mouth so badly that your eyes water. As a result of this experience, you acquire a less favorable attitude toward eating habanero peppers, because you found doing so to be punishing. The next time you visit the Jamaican restaurant, your behavior will also likely change—you'll order one of the blander dishes.

Observational Learning, or Modeling of Attitudes

Recall from Chapter 5 that in observational learning we learn by watching the actions of others. We pay attention to how someone or something else behaves, and we store a mental representation of that behavior. Later, we may retrieve that mental representation from long-term memory. At that point, we may or may not choose to actually execute the behavior.

Take a minute to think about your attitudes and the attitudes of those who are closest to you. How do your attitudes compare to theirs? If you are like most people, you will find that overall your attitudes are quite similar to those of your parents (Rohan & Zanna, 1996) and those around you (K. Kowalski, 2003). There will, of course, be some notable differences, but overall we tend to be more like those we love when it comes to attitudes. In fact, such similarity in attitudes is a factor in attraction, which we'll discuss later in this chapter.

We learn attitudes the way that we learn everything in life—through experience. As Rose traveled up the Nile, she developed both positive and negative attitudes about Egyptian men. For example, Rose did not want Amr to follow her boat, but after 3 days they developed a friendship. Although they may change, at any moment our attitudes have the power to affect what we know, how we feel, and how we behave toward just about everything we encounter in our lives. **But is this always the case—do our attitudes always predict our behavior?**

Whether we like it or not, we often take on the attitudes of our parents through social learning.

© Mark Richards/Photo Edit

The Link Between Attitudes and Behavior

Have you ever laughed at a joke that you didn't find funny? Tell a friend that you liked her new outfit, even though you didn't? Or, behave in any manner that contradicts one of your own attitudes? If so, your behavior is not unusual. Social pressures and other influences often make us behave in ways that go against our attitudes. This lack of *attitude–behavior consistency* has intrigued researchers because it seems so counterintuitive and illogical.

If social pressures can make it difficult for us to behave consistently with our attitudes, what factors will make it *more* likely that we will behave in ways that are consistent with our attitudes? Answers to this question have great practical value in society. For instance, under what circumstances might people's positive attitudes toward safer sex actually lead them to engage in protected sex? When might political attitudes accurately predict voting behavior? And in which situations can a company assume that consumer attitudes toward its products will actually translate into sales? Researchers have been diligently trying to answer such questions. ● TABLE 11.1 describes variables that have been shown to influence attitude–behavior consistency.

Given that our attitudes develop through experience and that once in place they influence our behavior at least part of the time, many psychologists are interested in how attitudes can be changed. This information also has great practical value. If we knew how to change attitudes, we might be able to reverse social problems such as prejudice and alcoholism. These and other pragmatic concerns have fueled a great deal of research on attitude change.

Cognitive Consistency and Attitude Change

Throughout our lifetime, our attitudes will change as we acquire new knowledge and have different experiences. For example, a favorable attitude toward a particular restaurant may change if you read in the paper that the restaurant failed its last health inspection. In light of this new information, the old attitude may be discarded in favor of a less favorable one. In this example, the attitude change was motivated from *within* the attitude holder. The change was not the result of a concerted effort on the part of others. It was motivated more by your desire to maintain what psychologists refer to as **cognitive consistency**, or the desire to avoid

cognitive consistency the idea that we strive to have attitudes and behaviors that do not contradict one another

TABLE 11.1

● **Factors That Affect Attitude–Behavior Consistency**

FACTOR	EXAMPLE
If your attitude about the object is low in ambivalence, the attitude will be a better predictor of behavior.	Feeling completely positive about spinach (rather than having mixed feelings about spinach) increases your chance of eating it.
If the cognitive and affective aspects of the attitude are both positive (or both negative), the attitude will be a better predictor of behavior.	Both enjoying spinach and knowing that it is good for you increase the chance that you will eat it.
Attitudes that are quickly and automatically retrieved from long-term memory are better predictors of behavior.	If the first thing you think of when ordering dinner is your love of spinach, you are more likely to order it.
Attitudes that have been stable over time are likely to be better predictors of behavior.	If you have loved spinach since early childhood, you are more likely to continue eating it than you would be if you only recently developed a liking for spinach.
Attitudes that are certain are better predictors of behavior.	If you are very sure about your love of spinach, you are more likely to eat it than you would be if you were not very certain about liking spinach.
Attitudes that are learned through direct experience with the attitude object are likely to be better predictors of behavior.	If you first learned to love spinach by actually eating it, you are more likely to eat it again.

Adapted from Cooke & Sheeran (2004).

cognitive dissonance theory
a theory that predicts that we will be motivated to change our attitudes or our behaviors or both to the extent that they cause us to feel dissonance, an uncomfortable physical state

Because smoking is inconsistent with being health conscious, this person is likely to experience dissonance that may lead to attitude or behavior change.

contradictions among our attitudes and behaviors (Festinger, 1957). Cognitive consistency theories (Festinger, 1957; Heider, 1946) propose that humans find it uncomfortable when there is an inconsistency among their attitudes or between their attitudes and their behavior. Most of us believe that we are intelligent, logical beings. The attitude of being intelligent and logical would be inconsistent with an attitude that an unhealthy restaurant is a good place to eat. So you adjust your attitude concerning the restaurant to avoid such an inconsistency. But why does inconsistency make us uncomfortable and therefore motivate attitude change?

One explanation of how cognitive inconsistency motivates attitude change is **cognitive dissonance theory** (Festinger, 1957). According to cognitive dissonance theory, inconsistencies among attitudes or between attitudes and behavior cause an unpleasant physical state called *dissonance*. Think of dissonance as a state of unease much like being hungry or being anxious. It stems from the realization that we have behaved in a way that is contrary to our self-concept (Aronson, 1998). Because dissonance makes us feel bad, we are motivated to stop this unpleasant feeling, which can lead to attitude or behavior change or both (Joule & Azdia, 2003). For example, a health-conscious person who smokes is likely to experience dissonance because smoking is inconsistent with being health conscious. Once the person experiences dissonance, she may be motivated to stop the dissonance by removing the inconsistency.

In general, there are three ways to remove the inconsistencies that cause dissonance. First, she can change her behavior (stop smoking). Second, she can change her attitudes (decide that she is not health conscious after all). Or third, she can remove the inconsistency by bringing new beliefs and attitudes to bear on the situation (convince herself that smoking has never really been *proven* to cause health problems). Any of these three methods will reduce the dissonance felt by the person and restore a state of *consonance*, in which there is no inconsistency among attitudes and behavior.

In this fashion, cognitive dissonance theory can explain certain aspects of how we change and grow as human beings. Recall the story of Rose and the night Mahmoud jumped into her boat. Initially, Rose's attitude toward Mahmoud was very negative. She feared him to the point of being prepared to kill him. Later, her attitude softened, but why? Perhaps Rose's initial attitude was dissonant with some of her other attitudes. If Rose saw herself as a confident world traveler and a good woman who was open to experiencing and valuing people from other cultures, then her initial dislike and fear of Mahmoud might have produced dissonance. After all, confident world travelers are not timid people who are terrified without significant provocation by the people they encounter. As such, Rose's reassessment of her attitude toward Mahmoud may have been motivated by her desire to reduce the dissonance and once again see herself as an independent woman.

Cognitive dissonance theory can also potentially explain some of our odder behaviors. For example, when you pay a high price for goods, it tends to make you like them more. You figure that only an idiot would pay top dollar for junk, and being an idiot is dissonant with seeing yourself as an intelligent person, so you convince yourself that the goods are worth the price you paid. Cognitive dissonance theory also predicts that going through painful or embarrassing initiations to join certain groups, such as fraternities and sororities, actually makes you like these groups more (Aronson & Mills, 1959). It appears that during painful rituals, dissonance is aroused because smart, independent people do not allow others to abuse them for no good reason. Further, it appears that the only way to reduce the dissonance you feel following the abuse is to convince yourself that the pain of the ritual was justified because it allowed you to gain entry into an especially attractive group. Even a smart, independent person may be willing to suffer for a good cause.

Although cognitive dissonance theory predicts that severe initiations will lead to increased attraction to the group, some studies have questioned whether this actually happens in the real world. In one study, researchers found that all initiations to student organizations increased attraction for the group—regardless of the severity of the initiation. The researchers attributed this increase in attraction to the group to the interaction, or *affiliation*, the group members had with other group members during the initiation (Lodewijkx & Syroit, 2001). Curiously, in a follow-up study, the researchers found that when participants expected to experience a threatening initiation, their tendency to affiliate increased and they were even more inclined to be attracted to the group. But, this effect was only found for males. For females, anticipating a severe initiation did not enhance affiliation and subsequent attraction to the group (Lodewijkx, van Zomeren, & Syroit, 2005). Whether the attraction we feel is a result of dissonance or affiliation, belonging to groups is important to many of us. We will talk more about the power of groups when we discuss social influence.

Keep in mind that attitude change through dissonance does not usually involve attempts on the part of others to cause attitude change. Attitude change through dissonance is motivated from *within* the individual experiencing the attitude change. When another person or persons attempt to change our attitudes, we are facing the powers of **persuasion**.

Persuasion and Attitude Change

In addition to changing our own attitudes, we all encounter situations in which others directly attempt to change the way we think and feel about an attitude object. Every day we face persuasive attempts from friends, family members, politicians, the media, and advertisers. By some estimates, the average American encounters a whopping 3,000 advertisements per day (Stanton, 2004)! With all of these persuasive attempts being hurled at us on a daily basis, understanding the process of persuasion becomes almost a necessity.

Obviously, not all of the persuasive attempts we are subjected to actually produce attitude change. We do not become loyal to every product we see advertised on TV. We do not vote for every political candidate we hear speak. So just what makes persuasion successful—or what makes it fail? One very important factor in the effectiveness of persuasion is the type of *cognitive processes* that we engage in during the persuasive attempt. The degree to which we analyze persuasive arguments can influence whether or not those arguments are effective in changing our attitudes (Petty & Cacioppo, 1986; Wegener & Carlston, 2005). When we process on the **central route to persuasion**, our attention is *centered* on the arguments we are hearing, and we carefully and critically evaluate the logic of these arguments. On the central route, we will only be persuaded by arguments with which we cannot find logical fault. On

persuasion a type of social influence in which someone tries to change our attitudes

central route to persuasion a style of thinking in which the person carefully and critically evaluates persuasive arguments and generates counterarguments; the central route requires motivation and available cognitive resources

the other hand, when we process on the **peripheral route to persuasion**, our attention is not wholly focused on the arguments. Rather, the arguments are more *peripheral* to our attention, and as a result, we do not attempt to critically evaluate them. On the peripheral route, we are likely to be persuaded by superficial aspects of the arguments such as the likability of the person making them.

Other variables also affect the success of persuasion. These variables fall into three categories: variables associated with the *communicator* of the message, variables associated with the persuasive *message* itself, and variables associated with the *audience* that receives the persuasive message.

Communicator Variables

We tend to be most persuaded when the person communicating the message to us is attractive (Eagly & Chaiken, 1975), appears to be credible (Hovland & Weiss, 1951; Tormala, Briñol, & Petty, 2007), and appears to be expert (Petty, Cacioppo, & Goldman, 1981). We are also most persuaded when the communicator does not appear to be trying to persuade us—unless he or she is attractive, in which case persuasion is still likely (Messner, Reinhard, & Sporer, 2008). This is one reason that advertisers hire well-respected, attractive actors and actresses to sell their products. They know that we will be more likely to be persuaded because we place our trust in such people—especially if we are processing on the peripheral route (Petty et al., 1981).

Message Variables

The logic of the persuasive arguments has its greatest impact when we are processing on the central route, for it is here that we can truly appreciate the goodness of the argument (see Petty & Briñol, 2008). In addition, we are more likely to be persuaded if the communicator effectively presents both the pros (why we should accept the arguments) and cons (why we might not accept the arguments) of the proposal. Of course, for a two-sided argument to be effective, the communicator must be able to effectively argue against the reasons for not accepting the proposal (A. E. Crowley & Hoyer, 1994). The superiority of two-sided arguments over one-sided arguments (only the pros) occurs in part because we tend to trust a communicator who is willing to openly discuss the drawbacks of a proposal.

Audience Variables

Effective persuasion is heavily dependent on who is being persuaded. In general, all of us are easier to persuade on the peripheral rather than the central route to persuasion. However, individual differences among us can also influence whether or not we are persuaded. Variables such as intelligence (Rhodes & Wood, 1992), self-esteem (Petty, Fabrigar, & Wegener, 2003), and mood (Sanaktekin & Sunar, 2008) can all impact our tendency to be persuaded. Yet, after decades of research, it is impossible to make blanket statements about the effect these variables have on persuasion because our individual differences interact in a complex fashion with other variables, such as the route we are processing on (Petty & Briñol, 2008). As such, under the right circumstances both high or low levels of intelligence, self-esteem, or positive emotion can all lead to high or low persuasion.

peripheral route to persuasion a style of thinking in which the person does not carefully and critically evaluate persuasive arguments or generate counterarguments; the peripheral route ensues when one lacks motivation or available cognitive resources or both

Attractiveness of a communicator can be one factor that makes you more likely to accept his arguments. This is especially true when you are processing on the peripheral route to persuasion.

Neal Hamberg/Bloomberg News /Landov

Let's
REVIEW In this section, we covered ways in which we acquire and change our attitudes. For a quick check of your understanding, try answering the following questions at increasing levels of difficulty.

1. On the _____ route to persuasion, we are not likely to critically evaluate persuasive arguments.

a. central

b. peripheral

c. algorithmic

d. shortest

2. Which of the following variables is likely to have the greatest impact on persuasion?

a. attractiveness of the communicator

b. the one- or two-sidedness of the arguments

c. the route the audience is processing on

d. the intelligence of the audience

3. Thelma recently discovered that her favorite actress supports a radical political group that Thelma despises. According to cognitive dissonance theory, what is *most* likely to happen in this situation?

a. She will begin to like the actress more.

b. She will begin to like the actress less.

c. She will begin to dislike the political group more.

d. Her attitudes toward the actress and the group will not change.

ANSWERS 1. b; 2. c; 3. b.

HOW DO WE FORM IMPRESSIONS OF OTHERS?

LEARNING OBJECTIVE

What Should You Know?

● Describe how we form impressions about ourselves and others, and explain the attribution process.

One of the most important aspects of social cognition is **impression formation**, or how we understand and make judgments about others. When Rose met Amr for the first time, she had to decide what type of man he was. Would he be like many of the men she had met on her trip—intrusive and mocking of her? Or would he be kind and sympathetic? Why is it so important to know what other people are like? In short, if we have a good understanding of other people's traits and abilities, we can predict how they will behave in certain situations. This allows us to guide our own behavior in social situations. When Rose determined that Amr was kind, she was able to relax around him. Without some understanding of others, social interactions would be much more awkward and uncertain.

The Attribution Process

It appears that one of our basic social cognitive tendencies is to try to explain the behavior of ourselves and others, but just how do we make such judgments? **How do you determine the traits and characteristics of someone you've just met?** If you're thinking that we pay attention to what the person says and does, you're correct. When we judge a person, we observe his or her behavior, and then we attempt to determine the cause of this behavior (Heider, 1958). This process of assigning cause to behavior is called **attribution**. For example, imagine that you enter a local café and see a man yelling at a woman in the corner booth. Witnessing his outburst, you would likely try to determine why the man is yelling. Is it because he is an aggressive person? Or did the woman somehow provoke this type of outburst in an otherwise kind man? Questions like these may pass through your mind as you watch the scene unfold.

In this example, we can attribute the man's behavior to one of two types of causes. We can attribute the behavior to his traits, abilities, or characteristics, in which case we are making a **trait attribution**. Or we may attribute the behavior to something in the environment, in

impression formation the way that we understand and make judgments about others

attribution the act of assigning cause to behavior

trait attribution an attribution that assigns the cause of a behavior to the traits and characteristics of the person being judged

which case we are making a **situational attribution**. If we make a trait attribution about the yelling man, we assume that he is yelling because he is an aggressive person. If we make a situational attribution, we assume that something happened in the environment that caused the man to yell. Perhaps his female companion just told him that she has been unfaithful. Maybe she just spilled hot coffee in his lap. Note that when we make a situational attribution, we do *not* attribute the man's behavior to his personality.

Heuristics and Biases in Attribution

situational attribution an attribution that assigns the cause of a behavior to some characteristic of the situation or environment in which the behavior occurs

fundamental attribution error our tendency to overuse trait information when making attributions about others

Ideally, we would weigh all the available evidence before making either a trait attribution or a situational attribution. Unfortunately, the realities of the world do not always allow us to make careful, analytic attributions. Humans are *cognitive misers*, meaning that we try to conserve our cognitive resources whenever we can (S. T. Fiske & Taylor, 1991). We have seen evidence of our miserliness in earlier discussions. As we saw in Chapter 7, when we need to quickly solve a problem, we often use shortcuts, or *heuristics*. Heuristics may lead to quick answers, but they do not always lead to accurate answers. People have been shown to employ several time-saving heuristics while making attributions, and these shortcuts often lead to errors and biases in the attribution process.

Fundamental Attribution Error

TRY THIS DEMONSTRATION

Hugh Laurie of *House*	George Lopez of *Lopez Tonight*	Eva Longoria of *Desperate Housewives*	Tyra Banks of *America's Next Top Model*
Trait:	Trait:	Trait:	Trait:
Trait:	Trait:	Trait:	Trait:
Trait:	Trait:	Trait:	Trait:
Confidence rating:	Confidence rating:	Confidence rating:	Confidence rating:

Look at the photos in ● FIGURE 11.2 and follow the instructions. What type of personality traits did you list for these people? How confident were you in these judgments? Now ask yourself this question: What evidence do I have that these people actually possess these personality traits? If you're like most people, your perceptions of these celebrities are based on the roles they play on TV. Most of us assume that their behavior on TV is indicative of their personality traits in real life. Did you? If so, what situational explanations for these people's TV behavior did you fail to take into account? Did you take into account that on TV, these celebrities are acting? Did you think about the fact that even "reality shows" involve someone directing the actors' behavior and the actors are aware that they are being watched by millions of people? Probably not. The bottom line is that

FIGURE 11.2

● **What Do You Think About These Celebrities?** Take a look at these well-known celebrities. Would you like to be friends with these people? What kind of people do you think they are? In the space below each photo, write down the traits that you think these people possess. Then rate your confidence in the accuracy of these judgments using the following scale: 1 = not at all confident that your judgment is correct; 10 = very confident that your judgment is correct.

unless you've spent time with these celebrities in real life, you've never really seen their natural behavior; therefore, it's somewhat illogical to draw firm conclusions about their personality traits. If you did just that, don't feel bad. Similar results have been found in the lab (Tal-Or & Papirman, 2007). In fact, the general tendency to rely on trait attributions and to discount situational explanations of behavior is so common that it is called the **fundamental attribution error.**

Why we tend to engage in the fundamental attribution error is not entirely clear (Landridge & Butt, 2004). Perhaps it reflects our preference to know more about a person's traits than about a person's environment. After all, the goal of forming attributions is to understand the person, not the environment (E. E. Jones, 1979). Another explanation is that when we view someone in a social setting, we tend to focus our attention on the person and his or her behavior, paying less attention to the situation (Heider, 1958). If we don't pay much attention to the situation, we are unlikely to give situational factors much weight when making our attributions.

Engaging in the fundamental attribution error varies with the degree to which our culture emphasizes individual behavior over group behavior. Some cultures, such as those in North America and Western Europe, are **individualistic cultures**, emphasizing the behavior and success of individuals rather than groups. Some other cultures, such as those in India and Japan, are **collectivistic cultures**, emphasizing the behavior and success of groups more than individuals (Triandis, 1994). Research has shown that people from individualistic cultures are more likely to engage in the fundamental attribution error (I. Choi & Nesbitt, 1998). Presumably, the Western focus on the individual accounts for this difference in attribution, but more research needs to be done to pinpoint the difference between individualistic and collectivistic cultures.

Actor/Observer Bias

What kind of attributions do we make when we are examining our own behavior? What if you found yourself yelling at a companion in a café? How would you attribute your own behavior? Would you be as likely to label yourself as a mean person as you would the man in the previous example? Probably not. When we observe our own behavior, we tend to take situational factors more into account than we do for others. This tendency has been called the **actor/observer bias** because we make different attributions as *actors* in a situation than we make as *observers* of others (I. Choi & Nesbitt, 1998; E. E. Jones & Nesbitt, 1971). The actor/observer bias predicts that you are more likely to weigh situational influences on your own behavior when making an attribution. Perhaps your companion angered you, or perhaps you had a bad day at work. It's unlikely that you would attribute your own behavior to a mean personality.

The actor/observer bias may seem self-serving, but this is not always the case. You would also be more likely to attribute a classmate's unexpected A on an exam to his or her traits than you would your own unexpected A. In this case, the actor/observer bias predicts that you would consider situational causes, such as an easy exam, more for yourself than for others. So why do we treat ourselves differently from others when it comes to attribution?

One potential reason for the actor/observer bias stems from the way we perceive our own behavior versus the behavior of others. When we are the actor, we cannot literally see our own behavior, and our attention is generally focused outward on the environment. But when we are the observer, our attention is generally focused on the other person's behavior. Therefore, because we are relatively unaware of our own behavior and very aware of the environment, we are more likely to consider situational factors in making attributions for ourselves (M. D. Storms, 1973).

The actor/observer bias may also stem from the different knowledge we have about ourselves and other people (Eisen, 1979). When we are making attributions about our own behavior, we are usually very aware of the way in which the environment influences it. Because we do not typically know other people's thoughts, we usually do not know how other people perceive the situation and whether it indeed influences their behavior.

The differences in knowledge and perspective that underlie the actor/observer bias explain how people can have differing interpretations of shared events. For example, research done in the aftermath of Hurricane Katrina shows that the actor/observer bias played a role in creating the many differing opinions of who was to blame for the tragedy (Martinko, Breaux, Martinez, Summers, & Harvey, 2009). For example, a citizen may conclude that a public official's curt demeanor during a press conference means he is uncaring. On the other hand, the official may view his own curtness as being due to the stress of the situation.

individualistic culture a culture, like many Western cultures, in which individual accomplishments are valued over group accomplishments

collectivistic culture a culture, like many Asian cultures, in which group accomplishments are valued over individual accomplishments

actor/observer bias our tendency to make the fundamental attribution error when judging others, while being less likely to do so when making attributions about ourselves

Self-Serving Bias

Although the actor/observer bias does not stem from a desire to enhance one's self-esteem, this does not mean that we never seek to make ourselves look better. At times, we do make attributions that are designed to make us feel good about ourselves. The **self-serving bias** refers to our tendency to make trait attributions for our successes and situational attributions for our failures (D. T. Miller & Ross, 1975). For example, if you wanted to feel good about the A on your next psychology exam, you would likely attribute this grade to your ability or your study habits. However, if you were to fail your next psychology exam (and we hope that you do not!), you might protect your self-esteem by attributing your grade to some situational factor, such as an unfair exam or the fact that your roommate interfered with your studying.

Most people, regardless of age, gender, or culture, engage in the self-serving bias (Mezulis, Abramson, Hyde, & Hankin, 2004). The major reason for the self-serving bias appears to be our desire to feel good about ourselves (J. D. Brown & Rogers, 1991; Trafimow, Armendariz, & Madsen, 2004). This bias helps protect our self-esteem, although it can also cause problems if we become too self-serving. For instance, not taking responsibility for our failures can lead others to like us less (Carlston & Shovar, 1983).

As we have seen in this section, we often take shortcuts, or heuristics, when making attributions about others. Heuristics may save time, but often they lead to incorrect attributions and judgments. As we will see in the next section, our tendency to use mental shortcuts can also lead to bigger problems, including prejudice and discrimination.

Let's REVIEW

In this section, we discussed how we form impressions of ourselves and others. For a quick check of your understanding, try answering the following questions at increasing levels of difficulty.

1. Our tendency to overuse trait attributions and to ignore the situational influences on behavior is known as the _____.

   a. fundamental attribution error
   b. self-serving bias
   c. social desirability bias
   d. actor/observer bias

2. Jasper was quick to assume that Susan was intelligent when he saw that she earned an A on her last psychology exam. However, when Jasper earned an A on his history test, he was not so quick to assume that he was intelligent. Which of the following biases in social cognition best explains Jasper's behavior?

   a. the fundamental attribution error
   b. the self-serving bias
   c. the social desirability bias
   d. the actor/observer bias

3. If you conducted a cross-cultural study of attribution in Japan, Israel, New Zealand, and El Salvador, which of the following behaviors would you most expect to see in people from all these countries?

   a. The tendency to assume that people's behavior is indicative of their traits.
   b. The tendency to examine the situational causes of their own behavior and not to do this as much for others.
   c. The tendency to attribute their successes to their traits and their failures to situational factors.
   d. All of these tendencies would vary from culture to culture.

ANSWERS 1. a; 2. d; 3. c

self-serving bias our tendency to make attributions that preserve our own self-esteem; for example, making trait attributions for our successes and situational attributions for our failures

PREJUDICE: WHY CAN'T WE ALL JUST GET ALONG?

Prejudices based on race, gender, sexual orientation, age, religion, country of origin, and other perceived differences still hamper many people's ability to live a productive and happy life. People have been harassed and belittled, lost jobs, and even been killed because of prejudice. In 2008, the FBI reported a total of 7,783 incidents of hate crimes. Most of these incidents were motivated by racial prejudice, with religious prejudice and prejudice based on sexual orientation the next most frequent motives for hate crimes (Federal Bureau of Investigation [FBI], 2009a).

Besides violent crimes and crimes against property, there are subtler forms of discrimination. One study found that African American loan applicants in Columbus, Ohio, were more likely to have their loan applications denied when they were trying to buy homes in White neighborhoods than when they attempted to secure financing for homes in Black neighborhoods (Holloway, 1998). And despite gains in equal rights over the last several decades, women have still not achieved equal status in the workforce, academia, or the government (see Blackwell, Snyder, & Mavriplis, 2009; Cheung & Halpern, 2010; Sanchez-Hucles & Davis, 2010). Prejudice remains a serious social problem. Because prejudice poses a threat to all of us, understanding where prejudice comes from is essential.

We can view prejudice as an extension of normal cognitive processes, in that prejudices are attitudes that develop like all other attitudes. At the same time, prejudices are unique because they are especially problematic and divisive attitudes that can cause upheaval in a society. As we look at the development of prejudice, we will examine the similarities between normal cognition and prejudiced thought.

Stereotypes, Prejudice, and Discrimination

You will recall from Chapter 6 that as we acquire knowledge about the world, we store that information in generalized knowledge structures called *schemata*. Schemata reside in our long-term memory and allow us to more efficiently encode, store, and retrieve information (Fiske & Taylor, 1991). When we form a schema for a particular group of people, that schema is referred to as a **stereotype**. All of us have stereotypes for the various groups of people we encounter in life. Our stereotypes allow us to make assumptions about others and to have certain expectations about how others will behave. For example, when you walk into your local library, you have some idea of what to expect from the people working there because you have a stereotype for librarians stored in your long-term memory. Without stereotypes, we would find it difficult to predict the behavior of others, and every social interaction would be a new experience for us. Every time you walked into a library, you would have to relearn what a librarian is like. In the terminology of developmental psychology (Chapter 9), without stereotypes we would not be able to *assimilate* in social situations. If you were to find yourself in a situation in which you had no stereotypes to guide your behavior, such as meeting someone from a culture that you knew nothing about, you would likely feel unsure of yourself and not know what to do.

So if stereotypes are generally helpful to us, how do they become the prejudices that cause problems in a society, such as the racism and other forms of bias that many people must endure? One way to conceptualize a prejudice is as a stereotype gone awry. A stereotype can be thought of as the *cognitive* component of an attitude (Aronson, Wilson, & Akert, 2005). In other words, a stereotype is the knowledge you have stored in memory about some group of people. Stereotypes become problematic when we generically apply them to all members of a group without regard to those individuals' unique characteristics. Furthermore, when a stereotype contains biased and negative information about a particular group of people, the stereotype begins to look like a prejudice (e.g., Chory-Assad & Tamborini, 2003). Finally, when a biased, negative stereotype becomes coupled with a negative *affective* or emotional reaction toward all (or most) people belonging to that group, a **prejudice** results.

Fear is one emotion that seems to be associated with prejudice. Researchers have found that holding prejudicial beliefs is correlated with experiencing increased activity in the brain's

stereotype a schema for a particular group of people

prejudice a largely negative stereotype that is unfairly applied to all members of a group regardless of their individual characteristics

WHAT'S HAPPENING IN YOUR BRAIN?

A CLOSER LOOK AT PREJUDICE

Using fMRI technology, researchers have found that White participants who held prejudices against Blacks experienced more activation in the left amygdala of the brain (circled in green) while viewing pictures of unfamiliar Blacks than they did when viewing pictures of unfamiliar Whites. Because the amygdala is responsible for processing emotion, especially fear, these findings suggest that prejudices may be associated with fearing certain out-group members.

Source: Phelps, E. A., O'Connor, K. J., Cunningham, W. A., Funayama, E. S., Gatenby, J. C., Gore, J. C., et al. (2000). Performance on indirect measures of race evaluation predicts amygdala activation. Journal of Cognitive Neuroscience, 12, 729–738.

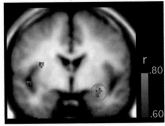

© 2000 The MIT Press. Reprinted with permission.

fear center, the amygdala, when viewing a picture of a member of the group against which one is prejudiced (Cunningham, Raye, & Johnson, 2004; Phelps et al., 2000). For a closer look at these findings, see the ● WHAT'S HAPPENING IN YOUR BRAIN? feature.

In the mind of the prejudiced person, all members of a particular group are disliked and labeled as having negative characteristics, regardless of their individual qualities. Additionally, prejudice can affect how the prejudiced person *behaves* toward others. Too often, prejudice motivates people to treat others poorly. **Discrimination** is the behavioral expression of a prejudice. During Rose's time in Egypt, she was frequently treated as if she were incompetent. Many times, she was told that she could not do something, simply because she was a woman. In the United States, discrimination often takes more subtle forms.

Psychologists Samuel Gaertner and John Dovidio (1986, 2005) have argued that racial prejudice in the United States now takes the form of **aversive racism**. According to this theory, European Americans, who outwardly support equality and fairness, may still feel negative emotions in the presence of African Americans. These negative emotions are *aversive* and may motivate the person to discriminate against or avoid interaction with minority members. Other researchers have proposed that aversive racism may be even more likely in stressful situations because stress may heighten these aversive feelings. For example, European Americans were found to be slower to help African Americans during a severe emergency than they were to help other European Americans, but equally likely to help African and European Americans during a minor emergency (Kunstman & Plant, 2008). These results suggest that racism is still present, although more subtle, and that stressful situations may increase the chance of discrimination occurring.

Stereotype Threat: The Self-fulfilling Nature of Prejudice

Knowing that prejudice and discrimination exist makes life difficult for people who are the objects of negative stereotypes. How would you be affected if you knew that many people in the world held negative stereotypes about you? Psychologist Claude Steele proposes that some victims of prejudice end up reinforcing certain aspects of the prejudices held against them because of a phenomenon called **stereotype threat**. Stereotype threat exists when a person fears that others will judge her not on her own qualities, but rather on prejudicial stereotypes held about the group(s) to which she belongs (C. M. Steele, 1997). Understandably, this fear can lead to considerable anxiety in minorities because of the negative nature of the prejudices they face.

In educational settings, females often suffer stereotype threat when performing scientific and mathematical tasks (Good, Woodzicka, & Wingfield, 2010; Keller & Dauenheimer, 2003). For example, normally high-achieving females tend to have lower scores on mathematics problems, but higher scores on verbal tasks, when they are asked to perform these tasks in an environment where they are outnumbered by men (Inzlicht & Ben-Zeev, 2000). In

discrimination the behavioral expression of a prejudice

aversive racism a proposed form of subtle racism in which European Americans feel aversive emotions around African Americans, which may lead European Americans to discriminate against African Americans

stereotype threat a phenomenon in which fears of being discriminated against elicit stereotype-confirming behaviors

this situation, females presumably become aware of the negative stereotypes that many people hold—that men are better at math—and the fear of being perceived to be mathematically inept (stereotype threat) then impairs their math performance. Females are not stereotyped as being poor at verbal tasks, so there is no stereotype threat for verbal tasks, and females exhibit no impairment in performance even when they are outnumbered by males. Stereotype threat can thus become a self-fulfilling prophecy, in which a woman behaves in a manner that actually reinforces negative stereotypes about females (Keller & Dauenheimer, 2003).

Stereotype threat has also been shown to impair African Americans' academic performance (e.g., C. M. Steele & Aronson, 1995), and may contribute to some African Americans' experience of *disidentification* with certain aspects of European American culture. For example, if young African Americans experience stereotype threat in school (they perceive that others expect them to fail), one way they may protect themselves emotionally is by devaluing education. If one feels that academic achievement is not important, then failing at academics is not damaging to his or her self-esteem (Steele, 1997). Unfortunately, this perception not only prevents the disidentified person from achieving academically, it may also place pressure on those African Americans who do wish to pursue academic success. If your friends devalue your dreams, you must either abandon your plans or distance yourself from your friends—both of which can be painful. One thing is certain—as long as negative stereotypes persist, it's a safe bet that many people will suffer as a result.

Learning to Be Prejudiced

Like other attitudes, prejudices can develop through the processes of classical conditioning, operant conditioning, and observational learning (Duckitt, 1992). As you can see in ● THE BIG PICTURE REVIEW, these types of learning allow prejudices to develop and also be passed from parent to child and from person to person within a culture. The experiences we have with other groups of people, the models we are exposed to (K. Kowalski, 2003), and the rewards and punishments we receive in life all have the power to mold our stereotypes and prejudices.

How easily prejudices can be learned was dramatically demonstrated in one of the most famous classroom exercises ever done on prejudice. In the 1970s, grade-school teacher Jane Elliot decided to teach her third-grade class an important lesson about prejudice. One day in class, Elliot told her students that she had recently heard that scientists had determined that brown-eyed people were inferior to blue-eyed people. She told the class that brown-eyed people were less intelligent, trustworthy, and nice than the "superior" blue-eyed people.

© Mark Peterson/Corbis

This child is likely to adopt the prejudices of her parents due to modeling.

THE BIG PICTURE review

Learning to Be Prejudiced

TYPE OF LEARNING	SITUATION	OUTCOME
Classical conditioning	Marlita is robbed at knifepoint (US) by a White man (CS). During the attack, she feels terror and anger (UR/CR).	After the attack, Marlita feels anger and terror when she sees White men. She has been classically conditioned to feel negative emotions in response to White men.
Operant conditioning	Bobby makes fun of some girls at his school. He calls them "stupid crybabies" (behavior). All of Bobby's friends laugh when they see him behaving this way (reward).	Bobby is more likely to make fun of girls in the future because in the past he has been rewarded for doing so. His friends have operantly conditioned his prejudiced, discriminatory behavior.
Observational learning	From a young age, Jackie hears her mother frequently say that men are sloppy, stubborn, insensitive creatures.	Jackie is likely to model her mother's prejudices and adopt her mother's belief that men are sloppy, stubborn, and insensitive.

To make the group differences very salient, Elliot had all the brown-eyed children wear brown cloth collars over their clothing so they could be immediately identified as members of the "inferior" group of students.

Within hours of her announcement concerning eye color, Elliot had created a strong prejudice in her classroom. The blue-eyed children made fun of the brown-eyed children. The blue-eyes called the brown-eyes names, ostracized them, and in general treated them cruelly. A fight even occurred on the playground as a result of the prejudice. In less than a day, Elliot turned a peaceful, egalitarian classroom into a hotbed of prejudice and discrimination (Monteith & Winters, 2002) based on meaningless eye color distinctions.

Elliot's demonstration shows how easily we can learn prejudice from others, especially those people that we admire, such as teachers, parents, and peers. What other situations contribute to the development of prejudices?

Intergroup Dynamics and Prejudice

We all belong to certain groups: families, schools, clubs, states, countries, religions, and races. These groups and the roles we play in them help define who we are as individuals (e.g., Gergen & Gergen, 1988). Because we tend to identify with the groups to which we belong, we also tend to prefer the groups of which we are members.

In-Group Bias: Us Versus Them

We tend to like the people in our group a little more than we like the people who are not members. In other words, we exhibit an **in-group bias** (Hewstone, Rubin, & Willis, 2002). We tend to like our family members a little more than strangers. We like those who attend our school more than those who do not. We have a bias toward liking our country's citizens a little more than foreigners.

Think of the groups of spectators at a sporting event. Each group sits on its team's side, and at times the rivalry between the two sides erupts into name-calling and even violence. If these same people met under other conditions in which their team affiliations were not obvious, such as at the grocery store or library, do you think they would be as likely to call each other names and fight? Probably not. Why do we sometimes allow our group affiliations to bias how we feel about and treat others? It appears to boil down to self-esteem.

We apparently derive some of our self-esteem from the groups of which we are members. One way to enhance self-esteem is by belonging to a group we perceive as good and desirable. For example, if you perceive your religion as being the *best* religion, then belonging to this religious group increases your self-esteem. Unfortunately, one way to perceive your particular group as being good is to believe that other groups are not as good (Tajfel, 1982). When our group succeeds at something, we tend to be especially proud (Cialdini et al., 1976). In the absence of meaningful victory, we still tend to view our in-group members as superior to **out-group** members (Brewer, 1979; Molero, Navas, Gonzalez, Aleman, & Cuadrado, 2003; Tajfel, 1982).

Furthermore, if we encounter an out-group that we really don't like, we may commit the *ultimate attribution error* and be more likely than we would with our own in-group to attribute the out-group members' successes to situational causes and their failures to their traits (Pettigrew, 2001). For example, if an out-group member gets a promotion at work, we may attribute that success to luck or favoritism from the boss. On the other hand, if an out-group member is reprimanded at work, we may attribute this to poor job performance or work ethic. With our own in-group, we would be more likely to make self-serving attributions—for example, he earned the promotion, and she was unfairly reprimanded by an overbearing boss. Although we do not always make the ultimate attribution error (for example, Khan & Liu, 2008), when we do, it is an example of prejudice toward out-group members.

Another aspect of in-group bias is the **out-group homogeneity bias,** or the tendency to perceive out-group members as being all alike (Linville, Fischer, & Salovey, 1989). The old phrase "they all look alike" in reference to a minority group is a clear expression of the out-group homogeneity bias. Individual characteristics are perceived not to differ much from

in-group bias our tendency to favor people who belong to the same groups that we do

out-group a group that is distinct from one's own and so usually an object of more hostility or dislike than one's in-group

out-group homogeneity bias our tendency to see out-group members as being all alike

the stereotype that defines the group. So once we have knowledge about one member of an out-group, we tend to apply it to all people in that group (Quattrone & Jones, 1980). Out-group homogeneity paves the way for prejudice in that if we have a negative encounter with one out-group member, we will expect similar encounters with other out-group members.

Intergroup Conflict and Prejudice: The Dark Side of Competition

Realistic-conflict theory (R. A. Levine & Campbell, 1972) proposes that competition among groups for resources motivates the development of prejudice. In the United States, immigrants are often the targets of prejudice because they are perceived as coming here "to steal jobs away from hard-working Americans" (Esses, Dovidio, Jackson, & Armstrong, 2001). Minority out-group members often play the role of **scapegoat**, those blamed for society's problems, when times are hard (Allport, 1954/1979). In modern America, as you might expect, racial prejudice most often exists when groups are in direct competition for the same jobs (G. Simpson & Yinger, 1985).

Possibly the most famous study ever conducted on conflict and prejudice is Muzafer Sherif's Robber's Cave experiment (Sherif, Harvey, White, Hood, & Sherif, 1961). Sherif and his colleagues conducted this experiment in a naturalistic setting, a summer boys' camp at Robber's Cave State Park in Oklahoma (hence the experiment's nickname). The participants were normal, healthy, middle-class, White, Protestant, 11- to 12-year-old boys who attended Boy Scout camp at the park. Prior to participation in the camp, the boys were all strangers to one another.

As they arrived at the camp, the boys were randomly assigned to one of two cabins, Eagles' cabin or Rattlers' cabin. The cabins were situated fairly far apart to ensure that the two groups would not have much contact with each other. The boys in each group lived together, ate together, and spent much of their time together. Under these conditions of isolation from each other, the Eagles and the Rattlers became separate, tight-knit in-groups.

Once each group bonded, the experimenters had the Eagles and Rattlers compete with each other in sporting events. The winning group would get prizes that 12-year-old boys find attractive, such as pocketknives. The losers got nothing for their efforts except defeat. As a result of this competition, the Eagles and the Rattlers began to call each other names, sabotage each other's cabins and belongings, and even engage in physical violence against one another. In short, the Eagles hated the Rattlers, and the Rattlers hated the Eagles. A prejudice based on the relatively meaningless distinctions of being Eagles or Rattlers was fully developed in the boys. When the prejudice between the Eagles and Rattlers reached the point of physical violence, the experimenters stopped the competition between the boys and sought ways to reduce the prejudice that had developed. But how do you remove a prejudice once it has formed?

Does Social Contact Reduce Prejudice?

One of Sherif's strategies to reduce prejudice was to increase noncompetitive contact between the Eagles and the Rattlers (e.g., watching movies together). In fact, the idea that contact between groups is enough to reduce prejudice, the so-called **contact hypothesis**, has been around for quite some time (Lee & Humphrey, 1943, cited in Allport, 1954/1979). If people from different in-groups see a lot of each other, won't they realize that the prejudices they hold about one another are unfounded and abandon them?

As Sherif found out, mere contact did not reduce prejudice between the Eagles and Rattlers. One problem with trying to reduce prejudice through intergroup contact is that prejudice can work to reduce contact (Binder et al., 2009). When thrown together, the Eagles and Rattlers self-segregated to avoid contact with each other. A drive through any big city shows that self-segregation is fairly common. Neighborhoods are often well defined on the basis of ethnicity and race—even though people are legally free to live where they choose.

Yet, when meaningful contact between groups does occur, prejudice can be reduced. Contact that meets the criteria spelled out in ● TABLE 11.2 is especially effective (Pettigrew & Tropp, 2006).

realistic-conflict theory the theory that prejudice stems from competition for scarce resources

scapegoat an out-group that is blamed for many of society's problems

contact hypothesis the theory that contact between groups is an effective means of reducing prejudice between them

TABLE 11.2

● Reducing Prejudice: Contact That Works

THESE CONDITIONS MAKE IT MORE LIKELY THAT CONTACT WILL WORK TO REDUCE PREJUDICE.
The different groups must have a common, superordinate goal that requires everyone's effort to achieve.
The different groups must work shoulder to shoulder on an equal playing field to accomplish the goal.
The groups must cooperate during the contact.
The norms governing the contact situation must promote harmony and mutual respect.

Source: Allport (1954/1979); Pettigrew & Tropp (2006).

After experimenting with increased contact between the Eagles and the Rattlers, Sherif and his colleagues (1961) did find a way to reduce the prejudice between the two groups of boys. The key was a special type of contact, one that involved *cooperative contact*. Sherif and his colleagues created superordinate goals for the Eagles and the Rattlers. A **superordinate goal** is a goal that both groups want to accomplish but cannot without the help of the other group. For instance, the researchers disrupted the water supply that both groups used by tampering with the water pipes. To reestablish water to the camp, the Eagles and Rattlers had to work together to find the source of the trouble. While they were trying to solve their mutual problem, the Eagles and Rattlers did not seem to have much time to hate one another. In another instance, a food supply truck broke down, and the two groups had to work together to push-start the truck. Without their combined efforts, both groups would have gone hungry. After a series of such contacts, the prejudice between the groups began to dissolve, perhaps because the Eagles and Rattlers now saw themselves as part of the same in-group—the group that was trying to find food and water. Without clear lines between the boys, there was no basis for in-group or out-group bias or prejudice. The researchers noted that friendships began to form between individual Eagles and Rattlers, and as a whole, the Rattlers and Eagles began to cooperate, spend time together, and even share their money. The prejudice that was once so virulent was dramatically reduced (Sherif, 1966).

superordinate goal a goal that is shared by different groups

Superordinate goals are an effective means of reducing prejudice. These people are likely to see themselves as members of the same in-group as they work together and as a result, they are likely to experience less prejudice for one another.

© Jeff Greenberg/PhotoEdit

Effective Contact in the Jigsaw Classroom

Psychologist Gordon Allport (1954/1979) outlined some aspects of contact that he believed were necessary for the reduction of prejudice (see Table 11.2). Although subsequent research has found that these conditions are not necessary for reducing prejudice, they do substantially enhance the effectiveness of intergroup contact (Pettigrew & Tropp, 2006). One practical application of these conditions is called a *jigsaw classroom* (Aronson, 2000). A jigsaw classroom is one in which students from diverse cultural groups are asked to work together on a project in a cooperative way. Each child is responsible for a different piece of the project, which forces the children to be interdependent. Because they must rely on each other, the children begin to focus more on the tasks at hand and less on their differences. According to psychologist Elliot Aronson (2000), research on the outcomes of jigsaw classrooms consistently indicates that as participants begin to identify as members of the same in-group, prejudice and hostility among the children are reduced, and self-esteem and academic performance are increased. These findings further underscore the message of the Robber's Cave experiment—that cooperation rather than competition can best work to lower prejudice in the world.

We have seen that prejudices can affect the judgments we make about other people. When we attribute negative characteristics to people simply because they belong to a certain social group, we are behaving prejudicially. Our prejudices can, in turn, affect the way we treat other people.

Regardless of whether we base our impressions on a prejudice or on actual behavior, we tend to want to spend more time with people we *like*. In the next section, we'll discuss what attracts us to others.

Let's REVIEW

In this section, we discussed prejudice and ways to reduce it. For a quick check of your understanding, try answering the following questions at increasing levels of difficulty.

1. Our tendency to view out-group members as being all alike is known as _____.

a. out-group prejudice

b. out-group bias

c. out-group homogeneity bias

d. out-group stereotype

2. The research on prejudice suggests that knowing that out-group members hold prejudices about you will likely make you _____.

a. more likely to behave in ways that confirm those prejudices

b. perform better to prove them wrong

c. desire to be accepted by the out-group

d. develop extremely negative prejudices about the out-group

3. Kelly is a manager at a firm that has been troubled by considerable prejudice between its male and female employees. Kelly wants to institute a program that will reduce the level of prejudice between the sexes. Which of the following plans has the best chance of working?

a. Make sure that each department is staffed with both men and women.

b. Have a "battle of the sexes" to see which sex can outperform the other on the job.

c. Form work teams to solve company problems, and make sure that the teams contain both male and female members.

d. Threaten to fire anyone who says or does anything prejudicial, and post this message around the workplace to ensure that everyone knows about the policy.

ANSWERS 1. c; 2. a; 3. c

What Should You Know?

● Describe the factors affecting attraction: exposure, proximity, similarity, balance, and physical attractiveness.

proximity geographical closeness

balance theory the theory that when we are attracted to people who do not share our attitudes, we feel dissonance, which motivates us to change in some way to reduce this dissonance

Students who sit in proximity to each other in the classroom are more likely to be friends or lovers.

© Bill Aron/PhotoEdit

WHAT ATTRACTS US TO OTHERS?

The attitudes that we form about a person determine whether or not we will be attracted to this person as a friend or as a romantic partner. The affective component of the attitudes we hold about someone is particularly important. If a person produces positive emotional reactions in us, we are much more likely to find him or her attractive. Think about the people closest to you. How do you *feel* about your best friend, your family, and your significant others? We are betting that most of you generally feel positive emotions about those you love. Most of us do. When it comes to attraction, the most important question is this: **What makes us feel good about another person?**

Proximity

One early finding in the area of attraction concerns the exposure we have to certain people and how this exposure affects our feelings of attraction for them. Recall from Chapter 8 that the more often we see a person or an object, the more we tend to like it. This trend, called the *mere exposure effect* (A. Y. Lee, 2001; Zajonc, 1968), also seems to play a role in interpersonal attraction. Many studies have shown that we tend to be friends and romantic partners with those who live and work close to us (Clarke, 1952; Festinger, 1951; Festinger, Schachter, & Back, 1950; Ineichen, 1979; Segal, 1974). The more **proximity**, or geographical closeness, we have to someone in our daily lives, the more exposure we have to him or her, and the more we tend to like that person. For example, within an apartment building, the closer a person's apartment is to yours, the higher the probability that you will be friends with that person (Festinger, 1951). Attraction to those who live and work nearby seems to hold across cultures as well. Studies have found evidence supporting a relationship between proximity and liking in both Africa (Brewer & Campbell, 1976) and France (Maisonneuve, Palmade, & Fourment, 1952).

Similarity

There are two old adages about the people we tend to choose as friends or romantic partners. One is "Birds of a feather flock together," and the other is "Opposites attract." You probably know some couples who demonstrate both views of attraction. But what does the average person look for? **Do we want someone who is similar to us, or are we looking for someone who is different to complement our personality?**

Research on this issue indicates that, indeed, "Birds of a feather flock together." When choosing a romantic partner, we tend to gravitate to people who are of similar age, socioeconomic status, education, intelligence, race, religion, attitudes, power, and physical attractiveness to ourselves (Brehm, 1992; Browning, Kessler, Hatfield, & Choo, 1999; Hendrick & Hendrick, 1983). Furthermore, similarity seems to predict attraction across a variety of cultures, including Mexico, India, and Japan (D. Byrne et al., 1971). Similarity also seems to be a factor in the friends we choose (Kandel, 1978; T. M. Newcomb, 1961; K. H. Rubin, Lynch, Coplan, Rose-Krasnor, & Booth, 1994).

One possible explanation for the influence of similarity on attraction is **balance theory**, which is related to cognitive dissonance theory (Heider, 1958). Balance theory states that when we like someone who does not like the things we like, we experience an *imbalance* that causes dissonance. As we saw earlier, dissonance motivates change that restores consonance. To restore consonance

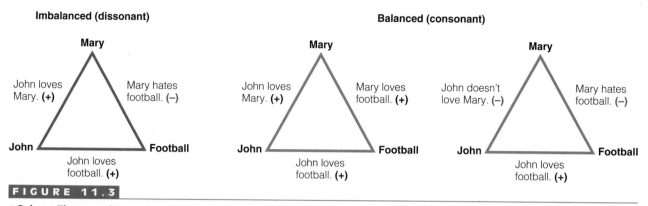

FIGURE 11.3

● **Balance Theory and Attraction: Two Ways of Restoring Consonance** John and Mary are attracted to each other. Unfortunately, John loves football, and Mary hates it. If John can convince Mary to love football, he is back in balance. If John can't convince Mary, he may decide he doesn't love her after all.

in this case, we would have to either change the other person's attitudes or change our own attitudes (● FIGURE 11.3). Because it is easier to change our own opinions, we may stop liking that person in order to restore consonance. Therefore, we tend to like those who are similar to us, and liking leads to attraction.

Self-esteem may also play a role in our preference for similar others. In an interesting study, researchers compared North American and Japanese college students' attraction to similar and dissimilar others. They found that although both cultural groups were attracted to similarity, the effect was much stronger for the North American participants. Yet, when the researchers accounted for differences in self-esteem between the groups (Japanese tend to have lower self-esteem than Westerners), the attraction to similarity seen across the groups became more comparable. This finding suggests that being attracted to similar others may be motivated in part by a desire to maintain high self-esteem. After all, valuing similar others is, in a way, valuing one's self (Heine, Foster, & Spina, 2009).

Physical Attractiveness

One of the first things we notice about a potential romantic partner is his or her physical attractiveness. Although standards of physical attractiveness vary across cultures (● FIGURE 11.4), it is an important factor in determining our attraction to others. In a classic study that examined physical attractiveness and attraction in a blind-date scenario, physical attractiveness was the *only* factor found to predict whether a person wanted to go out on a second date (Walster, Aronson, Abrahams, & Rottman, 1966).

More recent studies suggest that in romantic situations, such as speed dating, physical attractiveness is important for both men and women (Luo, 2009). Yet, men seem to place particular emphasis on how attractive their potential romantic partners are (S. K. Green, Buchanan, & Heuer, 1984; Jonason, 2009). This special emphasis that men place on physical attractiveness seems to hold for both homosexual and heterosexual men. Heterosexual and homosexual women, on the other hand, place more importance on the psychological and social characteristics of their potential partners. For example, heterosexual women place more emphasis on a man's social status when choosing a mate (Alterovitz & Mendelsohn, 2009). It seems that although physical attractiveness is important to women, it is not the *most* important aspect of a partner (Deaux & Hanna, 1984).

Although we may be attracted to good-looking people, we tend to become romantically involved with people whose level of physical attractiveness is comparable to our own. This tendency, called the **matching hypothesis,** is seen in both dating and married couples (Zajonc, Adelmann, Murphy, & Neidenthal, 1987). Matching is so pervasive that we actually expect to date people at our same level of attractiveness (Montoya, 2008).

Interestingly, the influence of physical attractiveness on romantic relationships seems to be mirrored in our same-sex friendships. The matching hypothesis predicts that our same-sex friends will be, on average, about as attractive as we are (McKillip & Reidel, 1983). And although both men and women seem to choose their friends on the basis of their physical

matching hypothesis the theory that we are attracted to people whose level of physical attractiveness is similar to our own

FIGURE 11.4

●**Cultural Differences in Physical Attractiveness** Standards of physical attractiveness can vary across cultures. All of these people would be considered attractive in their respective cultures. Which of these people do you find attractive?

attractiveness, again men place more emphasis on this characteristic than do women (Berscheid, Dion, Walster, & Walster, 1971; Feingold, 1988; Perlini, Bertolissi, & Lind, 1999). The importance of physical attractiveness in social relationships isn't surprising in light of findings that we tend to perceive attractive people more positively than unattractive people (Lemay, Clark, & Greenberg, 2010). For example, attractive people are perceived to be more interesting, sociable, kind, sensitive, and nurturing than unattractive people (Dion, Berscheid, & Walster, 1972).

What Makes a Person Attractive?

The old adage that beauty is in the eye of the beholder holds some truth. Across the cultures of the world, there are large variations in what is perceived to be attractive (see Figure 11.4). Yet, within this diversity are some universal elements of attractiveness. In an interesting study, researchers found that babies as young as 2 months old looked longer at attractive faces than they did at unattractive ones (Langlois et al., 1987), indicating that they preferred the attractive faces. Because it is hard to imagine that 2-month-old babies have had time to *learn* to be biased toward attractive people, these findings suggest that we are born with an instinctive preference for good-looking faces. Perhaps this instinct has evolved in humans because certain features that are found in attractive people, such as clear skin, symmetry of features, or typical features, indicate good genes and good health (Bronstad, Langlois, & Russell, 2008; Gangestad, Thornhill, & Yeo, 1994; Montagu, 1986). In terms of natural selection and evolution (see Chapter 2), it makes sense for us to be sexually attracted to people who are healthy and therefore able to facilitate our ability to produce offspring.

Yet, pure attraction is not the only reason that we are drawn to others. Sometimes our desire to be with others serves a purpose other than sex and reproduction. In the next section, we will further explore our social nature by examining some of the reasons we are driven to be with others in the form of social groups.

Let's REVIEW

In this section, we discussed what attracts us to others. For a quick check of your understanding, try answering the following questions at increasing levels of difficulty.

1. Which of the following is not likely to affect your choice of a romantic partner?

    a.   your level of self-esteem

    b.   your cultural background

    c.   your level of attractiveness

    d.   All of these will affect your choice.

2. According to the matching hypothesis, you are *most* likely to end up in a romantic relationship with _____.

    a.   someone who shares your attitudes

    b.   someone who is about as attractive as you are

    c.   someone you live near

    d.   someone with symmetrical facial features

3. The balance theory of attraction links which two concepts?

    a.   dissonance and similarity

    b.   similarity and proximity

    c.   physical attractiveness and self-esteem

    d.   mere exposure and proximity

ANSWERS 1. d; 2. b; 3. a

LEARNING OBJECTIVES

What Should You Know?

*   Describe the factors that affect our tendency to conform to the norms of a group, and how this conformity affects group decision making.

*   Describe the phenomena of social facilitation and social loafing.

GROUPS AND GROUP INFLUENCE: ARE TWO HEADS BETTER THAN ONE?

Think about the groups to which you belong. Can you identify those that you freely chose to join and those that you were forced into by circumstance? For example, many of us choose to spend time with particular groups of friends, but we are born into our families. Psychologists who study the formation of groups suggest several potential explanations (Baumeister & Leary, 1995; Paulus, 1989). One reason is that group membership can fulfill *social needs*, such as the need for companionship and a sense of belonging. Being a group member can also provide a sense of *security*. The safety we feel in a group may allow us to take risks that we would not face alone (E. S. Park & Hinsz, 2006). Furthermore, groups can give members a sense of *social identity*. We often define ourselves in part by the groups to which we belong—for example, as members of a baseball team. Finally, people may join groups to gain *information* and to ensure the *achievement of goals*. For example, your authors are both psychologists, and we belong to several organizations for psychologists. We joined these groups to learn more about psychology and to achieve our goals of becoming better teachers of psychology. As students, perhaps you have already joined groups for the same reasons. Study groups, clubs, and preprofessional organizations all help students learn more and achieve career-related goals.

Regardless of why we join a group, once we do join, the group and its collective members then have the power to influence our behavior. **What gives groups the power to change how we behave?**

Social Forces Within Groups: Norms and Cohesiveness

Groups are characterized by the expectations and attitudes of their members. One way that the expectations of group members manifest themselves is through the formation of group **norms**. Norms are the laws that guide the behavior of group members. Norms can be explicitly stated rules or unwritten expectations that members have for behavior within the group. Norms tell us how to dress, how to behave, how to interact with each other, and so on. Virtually every group has its own unique set of norms—each family, culture, workplace, and group of friends may have different expectations for how its members should behave. For

norm an unwritten rule or expectation for how group members should behave

We are likely to conform to the norms of groups because we do not wish to be ostracized or ridiculed.

UPI Photo/Bill Greenblatt/Landov

an example of how norms can vary across ethnic groups in the United States, take a look at
● TABLE 11.3.

Violating the norms of a group can cause distress. What would happen if you had to go to class in your bathing suit after someone robbed your gym locker? Would you be comfortable as you sat in class in this attire? Most of us would find this type of situation stressful, but why?

In general, we do not like to break the norms of the groups to which we belong. When we do, we may face several unpleasant consequences. Group members may ridicule us or try to persuade us to change our behavior, or—perhaps most threatening—we might be thrown

TABLE 11.3

● **Some Cross-Cultural Differences in Norms Governing Conversation in the United States**

CULTURE NORM	NATIVE AMERICAN CULTURE	EUROPEAN AMERICAN CULTURE	ASIAN AMERICAN CULTURE	AFRICAN AMERICAN CULTURE	HISPANIC AMERICAN CULTURE
Level of eye contact	Direct eye contact is seen as invasive and disrespectful.	Direct eye contact is generally expected—especially when being spoken to.	Direct eye contact that lasts more than a second or two is considered disrespectful—especially with one's superiors.	Direct eye contact is expected and prolonged during speaking, but less when listening.	Direct eye contact is often viewed as disrespectful—especially when one is being spoken to.
Level of emotion displayed	Conversations are often unemotional and dispassionate.	Highly emotional, animated conversation is not preferred in public settings.	Controlling one's display of emotion is very important.	Conversations are often passionate and animated.	Conversations that take place among Hispanics only may be very emotional and animated. Conversations that occur in ethnically mixed settings tend to be more low-key.
Level of gesture use	In daily conversation, gesture use tends to be restrained.	Moderate gesture use is typical.	Gesture use is restrained. Asian Americans tend to use fewer gestures than European Americans.	Frequent and large gestures are the norm.	Moderate to high use of gestures is typical.

Comma Image/Jupiter Images

© PYMCA/Alamy

© Masterfile

Source: Adapted from C. E. Elliott (1999), Cross-cultural communication styles. *Available online at http://www.awesomelibrary.org/ multiculturaltoolkit-patterns.htm*

out or ostracized from the group. In her book, Rose Mahoney explains that when she said goodbye to Amr, she really wanted to hug him. But, to do so would have violated Egyptian social norms. Rose settled for shaking Amr's hand because hugging him in public would have likely led to unpleasant consequences for both of them.

Recall that groups often fulfill social needs and give us a sense of security and identity. Because of these benefits, we often value our group memberships and wish to protect them. The degree to which members wish to maintain membership in the group is referred to as **cohesiveness**. In groups in which members tend to have very positive attitudes about their membership in the group, cohesiveness is high, and the group tends to be close-knit. When cohesiveness is high, the pressure we feel to meet group norms is also high. This means that as our attraction for certain groups increases, so does the influence these groups have over us. The more we value our membership in a group, the less willing we are to risk losing that membership. Therefore, group cohesiveness helps ensure **conformity** within a group as group members modify their behavior to avoid breaking the group's norms (Crandall, 1988; Latané & L'Herrou, 1996; Schachter, 1951).

Conformity Within a Group

One of the most influential psychologists to formally study the process of conformity was Solomon Asch. During the 1950s, Asch conducted a series of classic experiments on conformity and the factors that make us more or less likely to conform in a given situation. Asch (1951) had male participants engage in a perceptual task with eight other men. The participants were unaware that the eight other men in the experiment were *confederates*, or actors posing as participants. Each participant, along with the eight confederates, was shown a series of lines and asked to match the length of a test line to one of three other comparison lines (● FIGURE 11.5). The experiment was set up so that the confederates made their judgments first. The participant heard all of the confederates in turn choose—aloud—the wrong line (in this case, the 6-1/4-inch line). By the time the true participant's turn came, he had heard all the others choose what was clearly the wrong line. A norm had formed in the group, the norm of choosing the wrong line. The *dependent variable* in Asch's study was whether the participant would conform to the norm by selecting the wrong line or whether he would go with his own perception and choose the correct comparison line.

What do you think Asch found? What would you have done in this situation? In fact, Asch found that 74% of his participants conformed at least once during the experiment. Apparently, many people can be easily made to conform. Only 26% of the participants consistently stood by their convictions and refused to conform.

Resisting Conformity

Asch's next step was to ask whether certain situations made it easier or harder to resist the pressure to conform. In a variation of the first experiment, Asch had one of the confederates choose the correct line, whereas the other seven were instructed to choose the incorrect line. In this situation, the participant had one ally, or partner, and the *unanimity* of the confederates was destroyed. Did this make the participants less likely to conform? Under these conditions, Asch found that conformity dropped significantly. Having even one person back us up against the majority seems to give us more courage to break the norms of a group. It seems there truly is strength in numbers. If having one person on our side gives us strength, how many people must oppose us before we yield? This was the next question Asch tackled.

Asch varied the number of confederates in the procedure to test the effect that the size of the *majority group* (the members who conform to the norm) has on the conformity of the *minority* (those members opposed to the norm—in this case, the participant). In this variation, Asch tested participants in groups with 1, 2, 3, 4, 8, and 16 confederates who all chose the wrong comparison line. By manipulating the *independent variable* of majority group size, or number of confederates, Asch was able to examine its effects on the *dependent variable* of conformity. Asch's results for this variation are rather surprising. He found that 3 majority members were enough to produce maximum conformity in a participant. A majority of 16 produced no more conformity than a majority of 3. More recent research, however, has questioned these findings. Newer evidence suggests that conformity may continue to increase

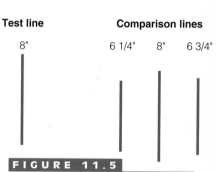

Test line	Comparison lines		
8"	6 1/4"	8"	6 3/4"

FIGURE 11.5

● **The Asch Procedure for Testing Conformity (after Asch, 1951)** In Asch's study, 74% of the subjects conformed and chose the 6-1/4-inch line as the match for the comparison line after hearing the confederates make this obviously incorrect choice.

cohesiveness the degree to which members of a group value their group membership; cohesive groups are tight-knit groups

conformity behaving in accordance with group norms

TABLE 11.4

● **Factors That Affect Conformity**

FACTOR	EFFECT ON CONFORMITY
Majority group size	As majority group size increases to three members, conformity increases.
Unanimity of the group	Unanimity increases conformity. One dissenter can dramatically reduce conformity.
Anonymity	When we are anonymous, we are much less likely to conform.
Cohesiveness of the group	As cohesiveness increases, so does conformity.
Self-esteem	Those high in self-esteem are less likely to conform.
Gender	Due to differences in their areas of expertise, males and females conform at equal rates but in different situations.
Knowledge/confidence about the issue at hand	The more expert we are about the issue or task at hand, the less likely we are to conform.
Tendency to feel anxious in social situations	People who tend to feel anxious in social situations are more likely to conform.
The need to be individuated, or individualistic and nonconforming	Those who tend to feel the need to not conform are less likely to actually conform.

normative conformity conformity that occurs when group members change their behavior to meet group norms but are not persuaded to change their beliefs and attitudes

Nonconformists seem to enjoy breaking the norms of the majority group.

up to a majority group size of 8 and perhaps more (Bond & Smith, 1996). How many friends would it take to get you to see a movie that you don't really want to see?

A final variable examined in Asch's study was the effect of *anonymity* on conformity. If the participant was allowed to make his judgments in private, rather than in public, would this affect conformity? Asch tested this by running experimental conditions that allowed participants to record their judgments on paper rather than choosing a comparison line out loud (they still had knowledge of how the majority had voted, however). Under these conditions, conformity dropped to nearly zero. It appears that anonymity provides us the security we need to not conform to group norms.

Since Asch's original experiments, others have studied the factors that affect conformity in groups. ● TABLE 11.4 summarizes the particular influence of some of these factors. **It's obvious that we conform in many situations, but why are we so willing to conform?**

Explaining Conformity

After conducting his experiments, Asch *debriefed* the participants—he told them about the deception in the experiment. As part of this debriefing, Asch asked participants why they had chosen the wrong line. In general, Asch received two types of answers.

Some participants indicated that they chose the wrong line even though they knew it was wrong. This type of conformity, involving a change of behavior to fit a norm but no real attitude change or persuasion, is called **normative conformity**. The primary motive for normative conformity seems to be a desire to fit in with the group and be liked by others. This desire is one reason that cohesiveness tends to increase conformity. When we like being in the group, we want others to like us as well (Sakari, 1975). Research has shown that people in cultures that value individualism (such as the United States) are less likely to conform than are people from cultures that place more value on being part of a group (such as Japan; Bond & Smith, 1996). Yet, knowing a person's country of origin may not necessarily predict his or her level of conformity in all situations. For example, in a recent study, Japanese college club members were not found to conform more than Americans (Takano & Sogon, 2008). And, although being from a collectivistic culture, such as Japan, is related to increased conformity in face-to-face interactions, it did not predict conformity in online interactions among Japanese participants (Cinnirella & Green, 2007).

Wanting to be liked was not the only reason that Asch's participants conformed. Some reported that they chose the wrong line because they became convinced that it was the correct choice. These participants were actually persuaded by the majority group. Recall that persuasion leads to attitude change. The way these participants perceived the lines and what they believed to be true about the lines changed as a function of the majority opinion. The majority opinion *informed* these participants of what the correct choice was. For this reason, conformity that results in actual attitude change is referred to as **informational conformity**. Informational conformity is heightened when people are unsure of their opinions and insecure about their abilities (Cacioppo & Petty, 1980).

The Dark Side of Conformity: The Stanford Prison Experiment

In 1971, Stanford University psychologist Phillip Zimbardo set out to conduct an experiment on the effects of a prison setting on the behavior of prisoners and guards. Twenty-four healthy male participants were randomly assigned to play the role of either a prisoner or a guard in a mock prison set up in the basement of a campus building. All participants wore uniforms appropriate to their roles as guards or prisoners. The prisoners wore prison uniforms and were referred to by serial numbers rather than their names. The guards had dark sunglasses, wore khaki uniforms, and carried clubs.

The experiment was slated to last 2 weeks, with the prisoners remaining in the "prison" for the entire experiment. Within days, some very disturbing behavior began to emerge. The men assigned to play the guards became abusive toward the mock prisoners. The men assigned to play the prisoners became docile and depressed, allowing the so-called guards to abuse and manipulate them. The mock guards hooded the prisoners, called them names, and subjected them to a host of demeaning, humiliating activities. Their behavior got so out of hand that Zimbardo had to cancel the experiment before the end of the first week (Zimbardo, 1972).

Why would 24 healthy young men begin to behave abusively in such a short time? A great deal of their behavior stemmed from the fact that they were isolated from the outside world and the norms of society. Within the prison-like setting, a new set of norms sprang up—ones that called for the guards to be abusive and the prisoners to be submissive. Another factor at work is **deindividuation**. In deindividuation, a person's behavior becomes controlled more by external norms than by the person's own internal values and morals. In short, the roles that the men were playing became stronger determinants of their behavior than their own attitudes and beliefs. Several factors aided the deindividuation process:

- All participants wore uniforms, which heightened their anonymity.
- All participants were "playing" a role.
- The guards hid behind dark glasses, which heightened their anonymity.
- The prisoners were referred to by numbers, not names, which made them seem less human.
- The experiment was conducted in a basement, away from the outside world and its norms.
- There was no strong leader who argued for fair treatment of the prisoners.

When deindividuation occurs, dangerous things can happen. All it takes is one person to begin behaving badly, and even good people may blindly conform to this new norm of behavior. See the ● TECHNOLOGY AND BEHAVIOR box for a new twist on this phenomenon.

informational conformity
conformity that occurs when conformity pressures actually persuade group members to adopt new beliefs or attitudes or both

deindividuation a state in which a person's behavior becomes controlled more by external norms than by the person's own internal values and morals

The Stanford Prison Experiment showed us that when we lose track of our own internal values and beliefs, we become deindividuated, and our behavior comes under the control of the group's norms. When deindividuated, we may find ourselves doing things we never thought we would do.

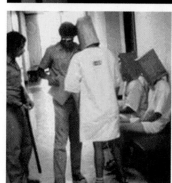
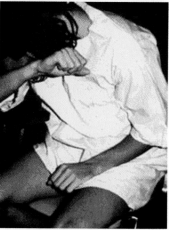

© Philip Zimbardo

TECHNOLOGY and BEHAVIOR

WHAT IS A FLASH MOB?

Social networking sites such as Facebook, MySpace, and Twitter have become enormously popular. They provide a fun way to stay connected with friends, family, and even customers. Some have found a new use for these sites and the Internet in general—to create unique social gatherings called flash mobs. The object of a flash mob is to get a large number of people to converge on a public place to engage in some unifying act (for example, having a pillow fight or dancing). Although the origin of flash mobs is complex, they seem to have begun as a mixture of social experiment and performance art. Two of the best known flash mobs are the 2006 silent disco, in which thousands of people converged on London subway stations to dance to the music on their iPods, and the 2008 World Pillow Fight Day, in which thousands of people in cities around the world had a simultaneous pillow fight. By posting notices of these flash mob events on social networking sites, organizers are able to reach millions of potential participants.

Sometimes, these events are just for fun. Other times, they are politically motivated. For example, we found a recent posting urging people to bring a quart of oil to the Lincoln Memorial in Washington, D.C., and dump it into the reflecting pool at noon on May 23, 2010, to protest the recent British Petroleum oil spill in the Gulf of Mexico (Flashmob.com, 2010). Whether politically motivated or just for fun, flash mobs have the capacity to get out of hand if deindividuation occurs in the crowd. Philadelphia has recently seen several instances of flash mobbing in which young people gathered downtown, only to have these gatherings turn into riots that caused destruction and led to felony charges for some participants (Graham, 2010).

When online sites are used for flash mobbing, the results can be unpredictable and uncontrollable. Organizers have no way of controlling how many people will show up. And, once the crowd has gathered, it has the potential to deindividuate. Then, all it takes is a few people to begin acting out (for example, throwing things) to change the norms of the group and lead to rioting. If you choose to participate in a flash mob, be mindful of your own moral values, keep your own behavior in check, and keep an eye on the crowd for sudden changes.

Organizers of flash mobs may hope to have fun, create art, or make a political statement; however, the potential for deindividuation and unintended consequences, such as rioting, exists in these large gatherings.

Reuters/Johannes Eisele/Landov

Working in Groups: Productivity and Decision Making

Have you ever heard the saying, "Many hands make light work"? Or, "Two heads are better than one"? Such sayings extol the virtues of working in groups. Do we really accomplish more when we are part of a group?

In the late 1800s, psychologist Norman Triplett observed that people seem to perform tasks faster when they perform in the presence of others. For example, bicyclers seem to ride faster when riding along with other cyclists than they do when riding alone (Triplett, 1898). This enhanced performance when others are present is called **social facilitation**. Over the last century, social facilitation has been demonstrated in humans and many other species across a wide variety of situations (see Aiello & Douthitt, 2001).

But, do we always perform better when others are around? Not always. For example, when we perform unfamiliar or complex tasks, having others around is likely to impede performance (Zajonc, 1965). For many of us, giving a speech is an example of an unfamiliar task that becomes more daunting when others are present. And, many of us can think of times when we "choked" in front of others despite the fact that we could recite our speech perfectly when alone. Today, *social facilitation theories* seek to explain the complex interplay of situational, task, and personality factors that result in either our enhanced or impaired performance in front of others (Aiello & Douthitt, 2001).

Having an audience can affect performance, but what happens when we are working *with* others? How does working toward a common goal affect individual performance? Unfortunately, sometimes **social loafing** occurs when group members fail to work as hard as they would if they were working alone (Harkins, 1987). Social loafing occurs, in part, because group members perceive that others will not hold them accountable for their individual performance (Pearsall, Christian, & Ellis, 2010). For example, if everyone receives the same grade for a group project, some members may be tempted to slack off in the hope that other members will pick up the slack. One way to reduce social loafing is to encourage individual effort and teamwork by rewarding group members for both the quality of the group's output and their individual performance (Pearsall, Christian, & Ellis, 2010).

So, many hands only *sometimes* make light work. What about cognitive processes? Are two heads better than one? We often seek out others when we have important decisions to make. We form committees to set policy for organizations. We choose juries to try court cases. The assumption is that important decisions are best placed in the hands of many. Ironically, psychological research indicates that in some instances our faith in the wisdom of groups may be misplaced. Group decisions are not necessarily better, more effective, or more logical than decisions made by individuals.

One factor that can contribute to poor group decisions is known as **groupthink**. Groupthink occurs when a group fixates on one decision and members assume that it must be the correct one, without carefully examining other alternatives (Janis, 1982). When groupthink occurs, the group does not weigh all of the options, often resulting in disastrous decisions. The following are four unfortunate historical examples of groupthink that have had dire consequences.

- *World War II.* In September 1938, Adolph Hitler demanded that parts of Czechoslovakia be given to Germany. In a hastily ordered conference held at Munich in October 1938, European leaders, including Germans, British, French, and Italians, decided to give in to Hitler even though it was apparent that Hitler was gaining the strength needed to fight an aggressive world war (Duiker & Spielvogel, 2004; Janis, 1982).
- *The Bay of Pigs.* In 1961, President John F. Kennedy committed the United States to the Bay of Pigs invasion of Cuba in an attempt to overthrow Fidel Castro's regime. It was an utter failure that almost led to the placement of Soviet nuclear missiles in Cuba and an escalation of the Cold War between the Soviet Union (present-day Russia) and the United States (Duiker & Spielvogel, 2004; Janis, 1982).
- *The Vietnam War.* In the mid-1960s, President Lyndon B. Johnson and his advisers decided to escalate U.S. involvement in Vietnam despite the growing lack of public support and intelligence reports that advised against it. The result was a disastrous, unwinnable conflict (Duiker & Spielvogel, 2004; Janis, 1982).

social facilitation performing better on a task in the presence of others than you would if you were alone

social loafing when group members exert less effort on a group task than they would if they were performing the task alone

groupthink a situation in which a group fixates on one decision, and members blindly assume that it is the correct decision

● *The Challenger Disaster.* In 1986, NASA decided to launch the space shuttle *Challenger* despite troubling data from engineers indicating that O-rings on the rocket booster could fail. The result was an explosion that claimed the lives of all aboard and brought intense public and governmental scrutiny of NASA.

What factors increase the likelihood of groupthink? *Group isolation, group cohesiveness, strong dictatorial leadership,* and *stress within the group* have all been implicated as factors that promote groupthink (Janis, 1985). Sometimes groups must work in isolation because the issues they are dealing with are secret or confidential. This was likely the case in most of the four historical examples of groupthink you just read. An isolated group is unable to get information from or call on outside sources. Therefore, members are able to consider only solutions that are generated within the group. Because the group cannot consider all possible solutions, some potentially good solutions may be overlooked, and groupthink is more likely.

Group cohesiveness also contributes to groupthink. As we have seen, when a group is very cohesive, members highly value their membership in the group. When this is the case, the group's norms become powerful influences on the members' behavior. In a cohesive group, members may be hesitant to voice their objections to the prevailing group attitude because they do not want to "rock the boat." When members hesitate to voice objections, groupthink becomes more likely because potentially poor decisions are not adequately critiqued and rejected (Packer, 2009).

For the same reason, a dictatorial group leader would also facilitate groupthink. When members are afraid to disagree with a leader, they tend to go along with the leader's position, and groupthink is more likely (Shafer & Crichlow, 1996). If a group wants to make good decisions, thoughtful critique of all ideas should be encouraged rather than discouraged in the group.

A final reason for groupthink is stress. When a group is making decisions under some form of duress, members may not behave in as logical a manner as they would if they were not stressed. Time pressure is one such stressor that can contribute to groupthink. When a group has a very short time in which to generate a solution to some problem, members are less likely to be able to examine all possible options, and groupthink is made more likely. Take a minute to think about the historical examples of groupthink. Which of the preceding factors do you think contributed to groupthink in these cases?

Let's REVIEW

In this section, we explored groups and how they influence us. For a quick check of your understanding, try answering the following questions at increasing levels of difficulty.

1. When we change our behavior to meet the norms of a group, we have engaged in _____.

   a. deindividuation
   b. compliance
   c. dissonance
   d. conformity

2. Which of the following is an example of conformity?

   a. donating to a charity after receiving a request for funding in the mail
   b. driving 55 mph in a 45 mph zone
   c. wearing fashionable clothes
   d. cleaning the bathroom because your roommates ask you to clean it

3. What do groupthink and deindividuation have in common?

   a. They both involve persuasion.
   b. They both are more common in individualistic cultures.
   c. They both involve dissonance.
   d. They both involve conformity.

ANSWERS 1. d; 2. c; 3. d

COMPLIANCE AND OBEDIENCE: CAN OTHERS CHANGE OUR BEHAVIOR?

Imagine that you answer the phone one evening and hear a telemarketer on the other end. After she identifies herself as a telemarketer, she asks you to contribute to the local police organization. How would you respond to her request? Would you agree to contribute, or would you refuse? Would you be polite, or would you hang up on her? Now compare this situation with a similar one. This time, you answer the phone and hear a police officer on the other end. After identifying herself as a local officer, she asks you to contribute to the police organization. Would you be *more* inclined to agree to the officer's request? Many people would, but why? What makes these two situations different?

One difference is the source of the request. A police officer represents an authority figure to many people. Many of us would perceive a request coming from an authority figure to be more of a demand. On the other hand, we are less likely to be intimidated by a telemarketer, and therefore we would likely perceive her request as just that, a simple request. Although the difference may appear subtle, it has great implications for how we respond to these situations. Although it's true that we often give in to simple requests, we are even more likely to give in to demands that come from perceived authority figures. Because we respond differently to requests and demands, psychologists have traditionally made a distinction between situations involving these different types of social influence. In psychological terminology, yielding to a simple request is called **compliance**, and giving in to a demand is called **obedience**. Let's begin by taking a closer look at some of the situations in which we are pressured to comply.

Compliance Techniques

Compliance situations are very common in life. For instance, salespeople try to get us to agree to buy their products. Doctors ask us to follow their instructions. Our significant others ask us to do household chores. Given that pressures to comply are inescapable, psychologists are interested in identifying compliance techniques that seem to work well. They also seek to understand why these techniques produce high rates of compliance. Psychologists are not the only people interested in understanding compliance. Marketers and other professionals also want to understand compliance so that they can create more effective campaigns for changing public behavior. For example, research on direct mail (e.g., catalog) marketing often centers on effective use of compliance techniques (e.g., Weyant, 1996), whereas other researchers study how compliance techniques enhance health-promoting behaviors, such as committing to a weight loss program (Nyer & Dellande, 2010). It's a good idea for us to become familiar with compliance techniques because others will be using them on us.

Foot-in-the-Door Compliance

Suppose a friend asks to borrow a dollar, and you comply. Later, if that same friend asks to borrow $5, would it be harder to refuse the request because you had previously lent him the dollar? Research on compliance suggests that it would. Once a person gets a foot in the door, so to speak, by getting us to comply with a small request, it seems to open the way to getting us to comply with another, larger request. In a classic experiment on **foot-in-the-door compliance**, researchers approached some homes and asked the person answering the door to sign a petition to promote safe driving. The researchers also selected other homes in the neighborhood to participate in the study but did not approach them at this time. Two weeks later, the researchers returned to the neighborhood and approached the homes they had previously visited as well as the homes that were not visited on the first day. This time, the researchers asked if they could put up a huge billboard that said "Drive Carefully" in the front yard. The data showed that those people who had complied with the first request to sign the petition were most likely to comply with the request for the billboard (Freedman & Fraser, 1966). Similarly, researchers in Israel found that people who had previously signed a petition for a specific charity were more likely to agree to donate money to the charity at a

compliance yielding to a simple request

obedience yielding to a demand

foot-in-the-door compliance increasing compliance by first asking people to give in to a small request, which then paves the way for compliance with a larger request

© James Shaffer/PhotoEdit

Compliance techniques, like foot-in-the-door, door-in-the-face, and reciprocity, can be used to increase demonstrations of political support.

later date (Schwarzwald, Bizman, & Raz, 1983). It appears that giving in to a small request paves the way for us to give in to a larger request.

Why does foot-in-the-door compliance work? One explanation for this technique's effectiveness is that our general desire to behave in a consistent fashion makes it hard for us to refuse subsequent requests. When you give in to the initial small request, your self-image changes ever so slightly. Having already complied, you are now the type of person who complies with requests made by this person or group. Because your self-image has changed, you now feel compelled to behave consistently with this new self-image. Recall that to not act in accordance with one's attitudes would likely produce *dissonance*. So when the person or group makes a subsequent request, to deny it would mean going against one's self-image and perhaps feeling dissonance. Therefore, compliance is more likely. When a clever manipulator gets a person to give in on a small matter, it does indeed usually seem to lead to future compliance (Cialdini, 2001; Girandola, 2002).

Door-in-the-Face Compliance

The opposite of the foot-in-the-door approach also seems to lead to high rates of compliance. In this technique, called **door-in-the-face compliance**, a very large request is followed by a smaller target request. For example, researchers asked college students whether they would agree to commit to volunteering 2 hours a week for the next 2 years in a program to help juvenile delinquents. As you might guess, all the students declined. Then the researchers asked if the students would be willing to volunteer to take the juveniles to the zoo for a couple of hours. A full 50% of the students agreed to take the trip to the zoo *after* they had refused to volunteer weekly. This number was significantly higher than the 17% of students in a control group who agreed after being asked only whether they would take the trip to the zoo (Cialdini, Vincent, Catalan, Wheeler, & Darby, 1975). It appears that if we figuratively "slam the door" in the face of a person's request, we are more likely to comply if she makes a more reasonable request later. Why should this be the case?

There are several explanations for door-in-the-face compliance. One centers on the *perceptual contrast* between the two requests. After the extremity of the first request, the second, smaller request may seem more reasonable to you than if it had been the only request you received. Research shows that perceptual contrast explains part, but not all, of door-in-the-face compliance (Cialdini et al., 1975).

Another explanation for door-in-the-face compliance centers on **reciprocity**, a very strong norm in many cultures (Mowen & Cialdini, 1980). Reciprocity is a norm in which we expect others to reciprocate our behaviors. For example, if you do something nice for someone else, you expect that the person will, in turn, do something nice for you. If you are cruel to another, then you do not expect the person to be especially kind toward you. This notion of reciprocity explains in part why we feel more obligated to comply in a door-in-the-face situation than with a single request. In a door-in-the-face situation, after you refuse the initial request, the requester then concedes the initial position and makes a more reasonable request. Because the requester has made a concession, we feel as though we must reciprocate and also make a concession. The easiest way to do this is to comply with the second request. If we don't make this concession, then we may feel as if we are breaking an important social norm.

A third explanation of door-in-the-face compliance is emotional. Some researchers (e.g., O'Keefe & Figge, 1997) propose that when we turn down the initial large request, we feel negative emotions, such as guilt. Because we do not enjoy feeling bad, we look for a way

door-in-the-face compliance increasing compliance by first asking people to give in to a very large request and then, after they refuse, asking them to give in to a smaller request

reciprocity a strong norm that states that we should treat others as they treat us

to reduce these negative emotions. With the opportunity to comply when a second, more reasonable request is presented, we are more likely to comply to relieve our guilt and make ourselves feel better (Millar, 2002).

The research on compliance shows that we are fairly likely to give in to simple requests from others. What happens when others do more than make a simple request—how do we respond to demands for obedience?

Obedience

In the aftermath of the Holocaust, the people of the world were astounded and horrified as the details of the Nazis' destruction became public. Many people found the grisly details of the death camps incomprehensible. What kind of person would carry out orders to send thousands of defenseless men, women, and children to die in gas chambers? Were the Nazis successful in their attempt to commit genocide because they recruited legions of sadistic, criminally insane people to do their bidding in the death camps? Or, is it possible that the *average* person could be influenced to hurt others if an authority figure gave orders to do so? This is the question Stanley Milgram at Yale University set out to answer in a series of famous experiments on obedience during the 1960s.

To test his ideas about obedience and the average person, Stanley Milgram ran an ad in a New Haven, Connecticut, newspaper that solicited participants for an experiment that would investigate the role of punishment in learning. In actuality, the experiment would measure the participants' willingness to obey an order to administer a very painful electric shock to another person. The participants weren't told this until *after* the experiment was over. As far as the participants knew, they were participating in a study on learning, not obedience.

In all, 40 men participated in Milgram's first study (Milgram, 1963). These men ranged from 20 to 50 years of age, and they represented a variety of professions, including teachers, engineers, and postal clerks. All of the men were paid $4.50 (approximately $32 in today's money) for their participation *before* the experiment began.

When they arrived at the lab, the participants were told that they would be playing the role of a teacher in the experiment. As the teacher, their job would be to administer electric shocks, using an apparatus that delivered shocks ranging from 15 volts to 450 volts, to a participant playing the role of the learner (● FIGURE 11.6). The learner was supposed to learn a list of words, and the teachers were told that the purpose of the experiment was to see whether the shocks would improve the learner's rate of learning. In actuality, the learner was a confederate, an actor who only pretended to be shocked, but the participants did not know this until after the experiment ended.

During the procedure, the experimenter stood slightly behind the seated "teacher." Throughout the experiment, the teacher and learner communicated via an intercom system, but they did not have visual contact. The teacher was instructed to read a list of words to the learner over the intercom, and then to listen as the learner recalled the words from memory. Every time the learner made a mistake, the teacher was told to deliver a shock to the learner by flipping one of the switches on the apparatus. The procedure began with the 15-volt switch, and the teacher was instructed to move progressively up the scale toward the 450-volt switch as the learner made more and more mistakes.

Stanley Milgram was primarily interested in seeing how far up the scale the teachers would go before they refused to obey orders to shock the learner further. At the 300-volt mark, the learner began to pound on the wall as if in great pain, protesting the continued shocking. At this point, most participants began to question the experimenter as to whether they should continue to shock the learner, who was obviously in pain. The teachers began to show clear signs of distress, including shaking, stuttering, sweating, nervous laughter, and biting their lips and fingernails. The teachers often protested verbally and indicated that they didn't feel good about continuing to shock the learner.

In response to such displays and protests, the experimenter calmly prodded the participants to continue with the procedure. The experimenter never yelled. He never made verbal

Obedience © 1965, Stanley Milgram

FIGURE 11.6

● **The Apparatus Used by Milgram in His Famous Obedience Studies** How far would you go before you refused to obey?

or physical threats. He never threatened to take away their $4.50. The experimenter merely requested that the participants continue following orders. The strongest statement by the experimenter was, "You have no other choice, you must go on" (Milgram, 1963, p. 374).

After the 315-volt mark, the learner fell completely silent and unresponsive, as if he had lost consciousness or was injured. Because the learner missed all the words on the trial by not responding, the experimenter instructed the teacher to continue delivering the shocks. At this point, it is likely that the teacher believed that he was being asked to shock an injured—or even unconscious—man. What would you do in this situation? What do you think the teachers did? Did they confirm Milgram's hypothesis that the average person is willing to follow orders even when it means hurting others? Or do you think they rebelled and refused to obey?

The results of Milgram's study were nothing short of shocking. A full 65% of the teachers continued to shock the learner all the way up to the 450-volt mark. Despite believing the learner to be ill or worse, most of the teachers continued to follow the experimenter's orders. Even Stanley Milgram was surprised by his findings. Prior to the experiment, Milgram had surveyed psychology students and behavioral science professionals to get a feel for how many participants they thought would go all the way to 450 volts (Milgram, 1963, 1974). Most people believed that only 1–3% would. The results showed, of course, a very different picture. More than half did go all the way to 450 volts, and no participant refused to obey before the 300-volt mark had been reached! ● FIGURE 11.7 shows the distribution of maximum shock intensities delivered by the teachers (Milgram, 1963).

Are these results for real? Would the average person really go all the way to 450 volts? As you might imagine, Milgram's findings generated a great deal of skepticism. Some people questioned whether the participants in Milgram's (1963) study were abnormal in some

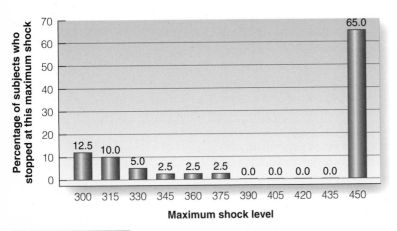

FIGURE 11.7

● **Maximum Shocks Delivered to the Learner by Milgram's Participants**

Twenty-six out of the 40 participants went all the way to the 450-volt level!

Based on Table 2, p. 376, "Behavioral Study of Obedience" by Stanley Milgram in Journal of Abnormal and Social Psychology, 67, pp. 371–378, © 1963. Used by permission.

way. To answer such skepticism and to further investigate the variables that affect the rate of obedience, Milgram repeated his procedure with different participants. He replicated the study in another town (Bridgeport, Connecticut) and found similar results (Milgram, 1965). Milgram also conducted the study using female participants and again found high rates of obedience (Milgram, 1974).

Other researchers have since replicated Milgram's findings. High school students were found to be even *more* willing to obey orders (Rosenhan, 1969). Cross-cultural research in other Western cultures has also yielded high rates of obedience using Milgram's procedure (Triandis, 1994). Unfortunately, it seems as though Milgram's results were not flukes. So, what accounts for our tendency to obey orders to hurt others?

Factors That Affect Obedience

One factor that contributed to the high rate of obedience in the Milgram studies was the presence of a perceived *authority figure*. During the procedure, the experimenter, dressed in a lab coat and looking official, stood close by the participant and issued orders to deliver the shocks. Authority figures work in two ways to ensure obedience. First, the fact that the authority figure is ultimately in charge may seem to relieve the person following orders from responsibility for his actions. A person can always tell himself that he was only following orders. Second, the presence of official-looking authority figures tends to intimidate us, and we are therefore more likely to obey their orders (Bushman, 1988).

In later experiments, Milgram found that he could reduce obedience in his participants by increasing the physical distance between the experimenter and the teacher. If the experimenter was not physically present to watch the teacher's behavior, the teachers were much less likely to obey the orders to shock the participant (see ● TABLE 11.5).

TABLE 11.5

● **Some Experimental Conditions in Milgram's Experiments and Their Resultant Rates of Obedience**

EXPERIMENTAL MANIPULATION	PERCENTAGE OF PARTICIPANTS WHO OBEYED ALL THE WAY TO THE 450-VOLT LEVEL
The learner was seated in the same room with the teacher.	40%
The teacher had to hold the learner's hand down on the shock plate.	30%
The experimenter delivered his orders by telephone instead of in person.	27.5%
The teacher was tested with two *confederates* who pretended to be participants also playing the role of teacher. Halfway through the experiment, the two confederates refused to shock the learner any further.	10% of participants continued to obey after the confederates refused to further shock the learner.
The teacher was tested with two *confederates* who pretended to be participants also playing the role of teacher. One of the confederates was the one who actually flipped the switch to shock the learner. The real participant only played an auxiliary role in shocking the learner.	92.5%
Female participants played the role of teacher.	65%

Source: Milgram, 1965.

Another reason for the high rates of obedience in Milgram's studies is the *timing of the requests* made by the experimenter. When the participants arrived at the lab, they very quickly found themselves faced with orders from an authority figure to shock another human being. Because the orders began almost immediately after the participants arrived, they did not have much time to think about their actions. As we saw earlier, when we do not have time to think things through, we are more susceptible to persuasive attempts.

Another factor that contributed to high rates of obedience was the fact that the shock levels were increased incrementally. In essence, Milgram's procedure was a textbook example of foot-in-the-door compliance in action. The first orders were for the teachers to deliver a 15-volt shock, a mere tingle compared to the final shock level of 450 volts. Few people would have qualms about following an order to deliver an almost painless shock, so why not obey? What the participants did not know was that by obeying the order to deliver the 15-volt shock, they were paving the way for their own obedience to further orders to shock the learner. Every time the participants obeyed an order to shock, it became harder for them to refuse to continue. Some have likened this type of incremental obedience to standing on a **slippery slope**. Once you begin to obey, it's like beginning to slide down the slope. The farther you go, the more momentum you gain, and the harder it is to stop obeying. If Milgram's procedure had begun with an order to deliver the potentially dangerous shock of 450 volts, it is unlikely that he would have obtained such high rates of obedience.

A final factor that affects obedience is the **psychological distance** we feel between our actions and the results of those actions. In Milgram's first experiment (Milgram, 1963), the teacher could not see the learner during the procedure. In this type of condition, psychological distance is large, meaning that it was relatively easy for the teachers to not think about the consequences of their actions. If you don't think about the consequences of your actions, then you don't have to consciously come to terms with and take responsibility for those actions. This allows you to obey even in situations in which your actions may harm others.

As you read about Stanley Milgram's research, you may have found yourself troubled by what you read. Certainly Milgram provided the world with disturbing evidence of our willingness to obey authority figures. Based on Milgram's findings, it would appear that the average person has the capacity to obey orders even when doing so hurts others. Some researchers have termed this type of obedience **destructive obedience**, to distinguish it from obedience that does not lead to harming others. In many instances, obedience is a good thing. For instance, we want people to obey the laws of our society; otherwise, chaos would ensue. Therefore, you should not conclude from Milgram's studies that all obedience is bad.

slippery slope the use of foot-in-the-door compliance in an obedience situation to get people to obey increasing demands

psychological distance the degree to which one can disassociate oneself from the consequences of one's actions

destructive obedience obedience to immoral, unethical demands that cause harm to others

Were Milgram's Studies Ethical?

Another aspect of Milgram's work that may have bothered you is the obvious discomfort Milgram inflicted on his research participants. As we mentioned earlier, during the procedure, his participants exhibited many stress-related behaviors. Their obvious discomfort indicated that they did, in fact, believe that they were hurting the learner. Milgram's use of *deception* to convince his participants that they were hurting another person has been heavily criticized by other psychologists (e.g., Baumrind, 1964).

Milgram did **debrief** his participants afterward, explaining that they had never actually hurt the learner and that the purpose of the experiment was to study obedience, not learning. Recall our discussion of ethics in psychological research from Chapter 1 and the ethical mandate that all human participants in psychological experiments should leave the experiment in at least as good a condition as they were in prior to the experiment. Critics maintain that the participants left the Milgram studies knowing that they were capable of hurting another human being simply because they were told to do so. This is not a very positive thing to learn about oneself. Additionally, critics have asserted that exposing participants to the trauma of the procedure itself was an ethical violation of their rights (Baumrind, 1964). Today, at most universities in the United States, it would be virtually impossible to get approval to do an experiment such as Milgram's because of the possible ethical problems associated with it. Modern psychologists are extremely protective of the rights of research participants.

Despite the criticisms, Milgram's work remains one of the most powerful statements ever made about human behavior. Aside from demonstrating our obedience to authority, Milgram's work brings up some important and perhaps frightening questions about basic human nature. For instance, how can psychologists explain the tendency of some people to behave aggressively? We will look at this issue next. Don't get too depressed, though. Humans also have great capacity for goodness. Before this chapter is finished, we will also look at the positive side of human nature.

Let's REVIEW

In this section, we examined the social influence that occurs in compliance and obedience. For a quick check of your understanding, try answering the following questions at increasing levels of difficulty.

1. In Milgram's original experiment, what percentage of participants went all the way to 450 volts when "shocking" the learner?

a. 35%

b. 55%

c. 65%

d. 75%

2. You want your friend to lend you $50. If you want to use the door-in-the-face compliance technique to ensure that your friend will comply with your request, what should you do?

a. First ask for $1,000 before asking for the $50.

b. First ask for $10 before asking for the $50.

c. Wash your friend's car before you ask for the $50.

d. Tell your friend that you will pay the money back in 1 week.

3. Which of the following would be least likely to help a manager get her employees to follow a company policy to fill out their time sheets in triplicate?

a. reminding employees that she is the boss before telling employees of the policy

b. first asking employees to fill out the time sheets in duplicate

c. telephoning the employees to tell them to fill out the time sheets in triplicate

d. staying in the room while employees fill out the time sheets

debriefing after an experiment, participants are fully informed of the nature of the study

ANSWERS 1. c; 2. a; 3. c

AGGRESSION: WHAT MAKES US HURT OTHERS?

Psychologists define *aggression* as an action that is intended to cause harm to another person who does not want to be harmed (Baron & Richardson, 1992; Brehm, Kassin, & Fein, 2002; Huesmann, 1994). Aggressive acts can be classified as *instrumental* or *hostile*. **Instrumental aggression** is aimed at achieving some goal. For example, a child may hit a playmate to distract her so the child can grab her toy. **Hostile aggression** is motivated solely by a desire to hurt others. For example, a bully may punch another child on the playground just to see the child cry.

Although both types of aggression are widespread in many cultures, the overall prevalence of aggression varies across cultures. Among developed countries, the United States is considered to be an aggressive society (c.f. Osterman et al., 1994). Pick up a major American metropolitan newspaper any day of the week, and you will see abundant evidence of this conclusion in the daily crime reports. In 2009, New York City, Los Angeles, Atlanta, and Dallas reported a combined total of 29,588 violent crimes (FBI, 2010).

Besides the almost daily reports of violent crime in the United States, it appears that even noncriminals have aggression on their minds. Researchers surveyed 312 college students at a U.S. university about whether they had ever thought about killing someone. Fully 73% of male students and 66% of female students reported that they had (Kenrick & Sheets, 1993)! What could account for such numbers? Could aggressive feelings be more natural than we like to think?

Biological Theories of Aggression: The Role of Sex Hormones, Neurotransmitters, and Brain Damage

It has been widely documented that among many species, including humans, males tend to be more aggressive than females (e.g., Sysoeva, Kulikova, Malyuchenko, Tonevitskii, & Ivanitskii, 2010). In 2008, males accounted for 81.7% of those arrested for all violent crimes (FBI, 2009b). Because males have more of the hormone testosterone in their bodies, researchers have long suspected that testosterone and aggressive behavior are related. But the research on the relationship between aggression and testosterone has yielded a somewhat confusing picture. Sometimes higher levels of testosterone are associated with higher levels of aggression in animals (G. C. Wagner, Bueving, & Hutchinson, 1980), and sometimes they are not (A. H. Eaton & Resko, 1974). Likewise, human studies sometimes show a correlation between high testosterone levels and aggression (see Book, Starzyk, & Quinsey, 2001), and sometimes they fail to find a clear relationship (Coccaro, Beresford, Minar, Kaskow, & Geracioti, 2007).

A Possible Role for Serotonin

Perhaps the reason that testosterone levels alone do not always predict aggressiveness is that testosterone interacts with other chemicals in the body. For instance, recent research has found that testosterone interacts with levels of serotonin in the body (Kuepper et al., 2010).

It has been widely suggested that serotonin plays a role in the regulation of aggressive behavior (Libersat & Pflueger, 2004). Researchers measured levels of the neurotransmitter serotonin in the bloodstream of three groups of people: survivors of suicide attempts, people institutionalized since childhood for aggressive behavior, and a normal control group (Marazzitti et al., 1993). They found that the suicide survivors and the aggressive patients had *lower* levels of serotonin than those in the normal control group. And, animal studies link exposure to aggression to a loss of receptors in the brain for serotonin (Suzuki, Han, & Lucas, 2010).

instrumental aggression aggression used to facilitate the attainment of one's goals

hostile aggression aggression that is meant to cause harm to others

Instrumental aggression is aimed at achieving some goal. This child is being aggressive to obtain a toy.

© Barbara Stitzer/PhotoEdit

Low levels of serotonin are associated with diseases such as *obsessive-compulsive disorder*, in which the person has difficulty controlling his or her behavior and feels compelled to repeat certain actions (see Chapter 14). If we extend this thinking to the relationship between serotonin and aggression, we can speculate that people with lower levels of serotonin may have difficulty in controlling their aggressive impulses toward themselves (as in suicide) and toward others (as in the institutionalized patients). However, more research is needed before any firm conclusions can be drawn about the role of serotonin in aggression.

Childhood Abuse and Aggression

Another connection between biology and aggression comes from research into the backgrounds of incarcerated criminals. Beginning in the 1980s, psychiatrist Dorothy Otnow Lewis began interviewing murderers in an attempt to discover whether they had experienced physical abuse as children (D. O. Lewis, 1992). During the interviews, Lewis discovered that an overwhelming majority of these murderers had suffered extreme abuse during childhood. In particular, many had suffered severe head injuries as a result of the abuse, which led Lewis and her colleagues to hypothesize that the murderers' aggressive tendencies may have resulted from brain damage (D. O. Lewis, Picus, Feldman, Jackson, & Bard, 1986; D. O. Lewis, Yeager, Blake, Bard, & Strenziok, 2004).

More recent research seems to reinforce Lewis's notions. It is now thought that childhood abuse and neglect are related to the development of several brain abnormalities. Using some of the techniques for studying the brain that we discussed in Chapter 2 (such as EEG, MRI, and fMRI), researchers have found that childhood abuse and neglect correlate with having structural abnormalities in the amygdala, hippocampus, corpus callosum, left frontal lobe, left temporal lobe, and cerebellum (Teicher, 2002).

Virtually no one would disagree that an end to child abuse would be good for society. Aside from a possible link between the physical damage caused by child abuse and later aggression, psychologists have other reasons to fear the destructive influence of child abuse. An aggressive model, such as an aggressive, punitive parent or a violent TV character, can teach a child to be aggressive.

Learning Theories of Aggression

In Chapter 5, we described Albert Bandura's *Bobo doll* experiments, in which children who watched an adult model beat up a plastic Bobo doll were likely to mimic the model's aggression when later left alone with the doll (Bandura, Ross, & Ross, 1963). After being exposed to an *aggressive model*, the children acquired new and aggressive behaviors. Many psychologists believe that aggression is often learned through this type of *observational learning*.

However, exposure to violence and aggression may promote more than just modeling of aggressive behavior. Such exposure may actually influence the cognitive, emotional, and behavioral responses we have to events in our daily lives. One model of aggression, the *cognitive neoassociation theory*, proposes that cues present during an aggressive event can become associated in memory with the thoughts and emotions experienced during that event (C. A. Anderson & Bushman, 2002; Berkowitz, 1990). For example, if you see many instances (real or televised) in which people use guns to shoot and hurt those who have humiliated them, you may begin to associate concepts from these events in your memory. You may begin to associate guns with anger, hurt, fear, and humiliation—or conflict with shooting. Because these concepts become tightly linked in memory, activation of one of them can *prime* (Chapter 6) other related concepts and cause them to become active. In other words, merely seeing a gun may cause you to have aggressive thoughts. Being humiliated may activate feelings of anger and the desire to use a gun to retaliate against those who hurt you. Indeed, research participants have been shown to have aggressive thoughts after simply being shown pictures of weapons (C. A. Anderson, Benjamin, & Bartholow, 1998).

If our behavior is heavily influenced by the cues we perceive to be associated with aggression and violence, then the nature of such perceptions is very important. Given that many of our ideas about the world are influenced by the media, it is worthwhile to ask the question, Does television portray violence and its consequences accurately?

Violence and Television

TV has been shown to portray many aspects of life unrealistically, including marriage (Segrin & Nabi, 2002), the medical profession (Chory-Assad & Tamborini, 2001), and violence. One study reported a total of 2,126 antisocial acts in 65.5 hours of so-called reality television programming, or shows that are supposed to document real life, such as *Cops*. The problem is that these "reality shows" do not give an accurate picture of real life. They portray acts of aggression at rates that are far above the actual rates at which they occur in U.S. society (Potter et al., 1997).

And, the children are watching. According to the Nielsen Company, children ages 2 to 5 watch 32 hours of television a week, and children 6 to 11 watch 28 hours a week ("Study Reinforces," 2009). By the time a child reaches age 18, she will have witnessed some 200,000 acts of televised violence, of which 16,000 will have been murders (APA, cited in Muscari, 2002). And, Saturday morning children's programming exposes children to 20–25 acts of violence per hour (Kaiser Family Foundation, 2006). Even more disturbing is that many televised acts of aggression are ones in which the aggressor experiences no negative repercussions for his or her actions. In 1996, a report sponsored by the National Cable Television Association indicated that perpetrators go unpunished in 73% of all violent scenes on TV and that only 16% of all violent acts on TV portrayed long-term negative consequences of violence for the victim. These false impressions may increase the likelihood that children will actually model the behavior they see on TV (Bandura, 1965; Hogben, 1998).

Situations That Promote Aggressive Behavior

When are you most likely to behave aggressively? Are there circumstances in which you might behave in a physically aggressive manner toward another? What would it take? One key factor in aggression appears to be frustration. According to the **frustration-aggression hypothesis** (Dollard, Doob, Miller, Mowrer, & Sears, 1939), when we become frustrated, we activate a motive to harm other people or objects. These motives are likely to be directed at those people or objects that we perceive to be the source of our frustration. For example, most physically abusive parents never *intend* to threaten or harm their children. But in the

frustration-aggression hypothesis
the idea that frustration causes aggressive behavior

Is this child learning to be aggressive as he watches television?

© David Young-Wolff/PhotoEdit

heat of the moment some parents take out their frustration on their children. Parents in high-stress situations—such as extreme poverty—who do not have good coping skills are most at risk for becoming abusive (Garbarino, 1997). Recall from Chapter 8 that motives drive and catalyze behavior. Consequently, when we are frustrated, our chances of behaving aggressively increase. Therefore, during stressful, frustrating situations, we have to be on guard for possible aggressive behavior in ourselves and in others.

Let's
REVIEW In this section, we explored the nature of aggression. For a quick check of your understanding, try answering the following questions at increasing levels of difficulty.

1. Which neurotransmitter has been implicated as possibly playing a role in aggressive behavior?

a. testosterone

c. dopamine

b. serotonin

d. estrogen

2. Road rage incidents are more likely to occur in heavy traffic. This fact can best be explained as due to the increase in _____ that occurs among drivers in heavy traffic.

a. frustration

c. fear

b. fatigue

d. anxiety

3. If you were trying to develop a drug to reduce aggressiveness, what would you have that drug do?

a. decrease serotonin receptors in the brain

c. increase serotonin action in the body

b. increase free testosterone in the body

d. both a and b

ANSWERS 1. b; 2. a; 3. c

LEARNING
OBJECTIVE
What Should You Know?
● Describe helping behavior and the factors that influence helping, including the bystander effect.

HELPING BEHAVIOR: WILL YOU, OR WON'T YOU?

By now you might be thinking that humans are pretty rotten creatures. We seem to be easily biased against others, easily influenced by others, aggressive, and even easily convinced to do real harm to others. In fact, humans are often very generous as well. Sometimes we even demonstrate **altruism**, or a willingness to help others without considering any possible benefit for ourselves. Just as we have the capacity for violence, we also have the capacity for kindness and compassion.

The Murder of Kitty Genovese

As was the case with the study of obedience, the psychological study of altruism, or **helping behavior**, was prompted by a tragedy, the murder of Kitty Genovese in New York City on March 13, 1964. Kitty Genovese, age 28, was returning to her apartment in Queens at 3:20 a.m. when she was approached and stabbed by a man in a prolonged assault that lasted 30 minutes. During the attack, Kitty's screams were heard by 38 of her neighbors. Tragically, the neighbors' reactions did not lead to Kitty getting the help she needed, and Kitty died from her injuries. A *New York Times* article that reported the murder claimed that although 38 people witnessed Kitty's murder, none of them called the police until after she was dead (Gansberg, 1964). As you might imagine, people reacted with shock and outrage to this news. Further reports of interviews with some of the witnesses only fanned the flames. Some of the witnesses explained their inaction by saying, "I didn't want to get involved." Even a man who did call the police first called a friend for advice because he was so afraid of getting involved (Mohr, 1964).

Today, some people allege that these early reports misrepresented some of the facts of the case and overstated the witnesses' apathy. For example, many of the witnesses may not have been in a position to actually see the attack and may have only heard some commotion on the street. It is also possible that some witnesses may have tried to call the police immediately

altruism helping another without being motivated by self-gain

helping behavior another term for altruism

after Kitty was attacked but for unknown reasons the calls were ineffective (De May, 2006). Perhaps we will never know exactly how the 38 witnesses, many of whom have since passed away, actually responded that night. However, what is certain is how the public *perceived* the situation back in 1964. The perception that 38 witnesses were apathetic raised many questions. Why didn't the witnesses do more to help Kitty? Are most people so callous and unconcerned that they would let someone die right before their eyes without lifting a finger to help?

Soon after Kitty's murder and the uproar that followed, researchers Bibb Latané and John Darley (1969) set out to find answers to these questions. They found that apathy or lack of concern is *not* the reason that people fail to help in situations like the Genovese murder. They also discovered that deciding whether or not to help someone is not necessarily a single decision, nor is it a simple decision to make. You must first *notice* that something out of the ordinary is occurring. Second, you must correctly *interpret* the situation as one that requires your aid. It is very possible that some of those who heard Kitty Genovese's cries did not realize that they were anything other than the normal sounds of a New York City street at night. Third, you must feel that you have a *responsibility* to intervene in the situation. Some of the 38 witnesses may have believed that someone else was coming to Kitty Genovese's aid. Fourth, you must decide *how to help* the person in distress. If you don't know what to do, you cannot offer help to someone in need. And, finally, you must *implement* your helping strategy and actually help the person in need.

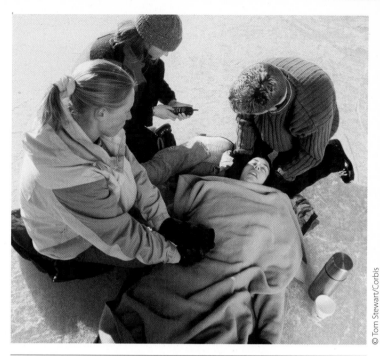

Humans do often come to the aid of others.

The Bystander Effect

Because deciding to help is a multistep process, failure can occur at any of the five steps. Early studies of helping behavior focused on responsibility and the thought processes that might contribute to one person feeling responsible to help another in need. Latané and Darley hypothesized what they called the **bystander effect**. As the number of bystanders *increases* in an emergency situation, the probability that any one of the bystanders will actually intervene *decreases*.

To test their theory, Latané and Darley conducted a number of experiments (Latané & Darley, 1969). In one study, participants worked on a questionnaire either alone or in the presence of two other people. Halfway through the questionnaire, smoke began to filter into the room through a wall vent, as if there were a fire nearby. The dependent variable in the study was whether or not the participant got up to investigate the source of the smoke and how quickly he or she did so. The results of this experiment supported the idea of the bystander effect. When participants were in the room alone, 75% of them got up to investigate the source of the smoke. When there were two other people in the room (confederates who ignored the smoke), only 10% of the participants got up to investigate. It appears that even when you may be helping yourself, the presence of other bystanders can reduce your tendency to help. Why would this be the case?

Explaining the Bystander Effect

One explanation for the bystander effect is **diffusion of responsibility**, or the idea that all bystanders *equally* share the responsibility for helping in an emergency. Each of the 38 witnesses would have borne only a fraction of the responsibility for helping Kitty Genovese. As the number of bystanders *decreases*, the amount of responsibility any one bystander bears *increases*. When you are the only witness, you bear all of the responsibility for helping. So what can you do if you need help and there are several bystanders present? You can reduce the bystander effect by clearly identifying one bystander and requesting his or her help. By singling out one person, you eliminate the diffusion of responsibility, placing all of the responsibility on that one person. Remembering this could save your life someday.

bystander effect the idea that the more witnesses there are to an emergency, the less likely any one of them is to offer help

diffusion of responsibility the idea that responsibility for taking action is diffused across all the people witnessing an event

TABLE 11.6

● **Variables That Affect Helping Behavior**

VARIABLE	DESCRIPTION
Level of bystander's hurry	A bystander who is in a hurry is less likely to stop and help someone in distress.
Bystander's relationship to other bystanders	When bystanders are friends, they are more likely to help a stranger in need.
Relationship between victim and bystander	A bystander who knows the victim is more likely to help.
Bystander's perceived ambiguity	If the situation is ambiguous, a bystander will tend to see it as a nonemergency and therefore be less likely to help.
Bystander's fear for own safety	If a bystander is afraid of being harmed, he or she is less likely to help.
Bystander's prejudice against the victim or belief that the victim is an out-group member	A bystander who is prejudiced against the victim or sees the victim as an out-group member is less likely to help.
Victim's level of dependency	A bystander is more likely to help a victim he or she perceives to be dependent—for example, a child.
Victim's responsibility for own plight	A bystander is less likely to help if he or she perceives the emergency to be the victim's own fault.
Bystander's belief in the *just-world hypothesis* (the belief that people get what they deserve in life).	Belief in a just world is correlated with an increased tendency to blame victims for their own plight and consequent reluctance to help them.

Diffusion of responsibility is not the only factor that prevents people from helping others. Another possible explanation for a bystander's failure to help is **pluralistic ignorance**, or the failure of a group of witnesses to perceive there is a problem that requires their help (Latané & Darley, 1969). When the witnesses saw the others doing nothing to help Kitty, this lack of action and excitement on the part of the other witnesses may have caused the individual witnesses to inaccurately perceive that Kitty did not need help (Sexton, 1995). In other words, when we see that others are not interpreting a situation as an emergency, we are less likely to interpret the situation as an emergency, and therefore we are less likely to help.

A New Twist on the Bystander Effect: Taking Care of Our Own

Researchers now believe that the number of witnesses to an emergency is only one factor that influences helping. Several other variables that have been shown to influence helping behavior are summarized in ● TABLE 11.6. As you read through Table 11.6, you'll notice that, unfortunately, not all people are equally likely to receive help.

As we have already seen, whether or not a victim receives help may be influenced by the degree to which the bystander sees the victim as belonging to the bystander's in-group. Mark Levine and Kirstien Thompson (2004) tested a *social categorization theory* of helping behavior, which predicts that you are most likely to help others when you perceive that they belong to the same in-group as you do. Levine and Thompson used British research participants who belonged to two major in-groups—being British and being part of the European Union (EU). The participants were randomly divided into two groups: a British identity group and a European identity group. In the British group, participants were reminded of their British identity when the researchers placed a color copy of the British flag on the cover of their research questionnaire. In the European identity group, participants were reminded of their European identity with a picture of the European Union flag on the cover of their questionnaire. These flags served to make the participants focus on particular aspects of their own in-group membership (i.e., being British or European). The questionnaires that were attached to the cover sheets contained two scenarios that described natural disasters (floods and earthquakes) in Europe and in South America. After reading about the disasters in these places, the participants were asked to rate their willingness to give financial support to the victims of the disasters.

Consistent with the social categorization theory, Levine and Thompson found that the British identity group did not differ with respect to its willingness to help Europeans or South Americans, presumably because both types of victims were perceived as out-group members. The European identity group, however, was found to be more willing to help victims of the European disaster (in-group members) and less willing to aid the South Americans (out-group members). And most interestingly, the European identity group was more willing than the British identity group to help victims of a European disaster. Although Britain is part of the EU, when participants were led to focus on their "Britishness," people from other countries in Europe were less likely to be perceived as in-group members; as a result, the British identity participants were less willing to help European victims.

What's important in this study is that the same place and people (Europeans in Europe) can be defined as an in-group or an out-group simply by manipulating which aspect of the bystander's identity (British or European) is activated in memory. Britain is a part of the EU, and as such the British belong to the same in-group as Europeans. But when it comes to helping, it appears that actual group membership is not as important as *perceived* group member-

pluralistic ignorance the idea that we use the behavior of others to help determine whether a situation is really an emergency requiring our help; if no one else is helping, we may conclude that help isn't needed

ship. We are most likely to help victims from our in-group when we have reason to focus on the fact that we are indeed members of the same group. In other words, we do tend to take care of our own, but who we perceive to be "our own" can vary across situations.

The results of this experiment may have implications for all of us. If we are more willing to help people who belong to our own in-groups, then one way to facilitate helping might be to encourage people to see others as belonging to their in-group. Ultimately, if we all perceived ourselves to be members of the "human" in-group, we might see a lot less war and a great deal more cooperation in the world.

When People Choose to Help

Although help did not come for Kitty Genovese, there are many examples of situations in which people have come forward to help total strangers. During 2010, when earthquakes devastated portions of Haiti and Chile, people from all over the world rushed to help with donations of time, money, and supplies. When the I-35 bridge across the Mississippi River in Minneapolis collapsed on August 1, 2007, many bystanders rushed to help pull people from the trapped vehicles and debris. In the aftermath of Hurricane Katrina, which devastated the Gulf Coast on August 29, 2005, many ordinary citizens rushed to help the thousands of victims. As these examples indicate, we do not always think of ourselves first, and we frequently are motivated to help others in need. **But must we behave like superheroes or run into burning buildings to exhibit altruism?** Of course not.

Altruism takes many forms. For example, Amr could have made a good deal of money selling his old rowboat to Rose. Instead, he accepted only a small fee and spent several days trailing her on the Nile, just to ensure her safety. One of the authors used to work with two women who regularly grew their hair long so that they could cut it off and send it to a charity that makes wigs for women undergoing chemotherapy. And millions of people across the world contribute time and money to innumerable charities and prosocial organizations. Many of us find simple, everyday means of helping others lead better lives.

Culture and Helping Behavior

When it comes to collectivistic and individualistic cultures, where would you expect to find higher rates of helping behavior? At first glance, the logical choice seems to be that collectivistic cultures would exhibit higher altruism because of their collective focus. But is this the case? Markus Kemmelmeier and colleagues (2006) argued that within the United States, people who strongly identify with being American will also identify with the ideal of American individualism. Thus, a person who feels very bonded to fellow Americans may also be very individualistic. Using this logic, Kemmelmeier's team predicted that within the United States, states that exhibit stronger individualistic tendencies would also exhibit higher rates of volunteerism and charitable giving. And, that is exactly what they found. Individualistic states were more helpful than the collectivistic states. If you are curious about where your state falls on the collectivistic–individualistic dimension, take a look at ● Table 11.7.

The belief that cities are cold-hearted places was also challenged by *New York Times* reporter Susan Orr Braudy (2003). Braudy examined the ways that New Yorkers exhibit altruism on a daily basis. Her analysis of what she called "urban altruism" is especially uplifting because she easily found numerous examples of human kindness in the same city that failed to aid Kitty Genovese more than 40 years ago. Her examples include a doctor who helped homeless people get access to social services, an antiques dealer who spontaneously helped a woman who was short on cash buy a gift for her friend, and an apartment dweller who spent days watching over a fellow tenant who she feared might become suicidal. In his or her own way, each of these people exhibited concern for the well-being and comfort of others with little concern for personal interests—in other words, *altruism*. Despite tragedies like the Kitty Genovese murder, it does appear that humans are generally concerned with the welfare of

TABLE 11.7

● **State Rankings on the United States Collectivism Index**

RANK	STATE	RANK	STATE
1	Hawaii	26	Arizona
2	Louisiana	27	Alaska
3	South Carolina	28	Rhode Island
4	Mississippi	29	West Virginia
5	Maryland	30	Michigan
6	Utah	31	Wisconsin
7	Virginia	32	Massachusetts
8	Georgia	33	Missouri
9	California	34	Ohio
10	New Jersey	35	Maine
11	Texas	36	New Hampshire
12	Alabama	37	Oklahoma
13	Indiana	38	Idaho
14	North Carolina	39	Vermont
15	Tennessee	40	Minnesota
16	Delaware	41	Iowa
17	Arkansas	42	Kansas
18	Florida	43	Washington
19	New York	44	North Dakota
20	Kentucky	45	Colorado
21	Pennsylvania	46	South Dakota
22	Nevada	47	Wyoming
23	Illinois	48	Nebraska
24	New Mexico	49	Oregon
25	Connecticut	50	Montana

Note: Higher rank numbers indicate more individualism (e.g., Montana was the most individualistic state). Source: Vandello & Cohen (1999).

others. When we fail to help, it is usually not out of a sense of apathy or cruelty, but rather out of misunderstanding, confusion, or fear (Latané & Darley, 1969).

Let's REVIEW

In this section, we discussed altruism, or helping behavior. For a quick check of your understanding, try answering the following questions at increasing levels of difficulty.

1. What did Latané and Darley conclude about the witnesses in the Kitty Genovese murder case?

   a. Many of the witnesses were uncaring people, and that is why they failed to help.

   b. The witnesses were not really witnesses; they did not actually see or hear Kitty being attacked.

   c. Many of the witnesses did not help because they assumed that someone else would help.

   d. Fear was the best explanation for why the witnesses did not help.

2. If you are ever the victim of an accident, and there are many witnesses, what should you do to help ensure that one of the witnesses helps you?

   a. Scream for help.

   b. Remain quiet so as not to scare the witnesses.

   c. Single out one of the witnesses, and request that he or she help you.

   d. Yell "Fire!"

3. Recently, Susann was sitting in her office when the fire alarms in her building went off. To her amazement, everyone seemed to ignore the sirens, and no one evacuated the building until security forced them to leave. Which of the following best explains their reluctance to leave the building?

   a. diffusion of responsibility   c. apathy

   b. pluralistic ignorance   d. a lack of conformity

ANSWERS 1. c; 2. c; 3. b

STUDYING the CHAPTER

KEY TERMS

social psychology (449)
social cognition (449)
social influence (449)
attitudes (450)
cognitive consistency (451)
cognitive dissonance
   theory (452)
persuasion (453)
central route to persuasion
   (453)
peripheral route to
   persuasion (454)
impression formation (455)
attribution (455)

trait attribution (455)
situational attribution (456)
fundamental attribution
   error (456)
individualistic culture (457)
collectivistic culture (457)
actor/observer bias (457)
self-serving bias (458)
stereotype (459)
prejudice (459)
discrimination (460)
aversive racism (460)
stereotype threat (460)
in-group bias (462)

out-group (462)
out-group homogeneity
   bias (462)
realistic-conflict theory (463)
scapegoat (463)
contact hypothesis (463)
superordinate goal (464)
proximity (466)
balance theory (466)
matching hypothesis (467)
norm (469)
cohesiveness (471)
conformity (471)
normative conformity (472)

informational
   conformity (473)
deindividuation (473)
social facilitation (475)
social loafing (475)
groupthink (475)
compliance (477)
obedience (477)
foot-in-the-door
   compliance (477)
door-in-the-face
   compliance (478)
reciprocity (478)
slippery slope (481)

psychological distance (481)
destructive obedience (481)
debriefing (482)
instrumental aggression (483)

hostile aggression (483)
frustration-aggression
    hypothesis (485)

altruism (486)
helping behavior (486)
bystander effect (487)

diffusion of responsibility
    (487)
pluralistic ignorance (488)

LEARNING CHALLENGE

TEST YOURSELF!

Now that you have studied the chapter, assess your comprehension of the material by answering the following questions. Then use the key at the end to determine if your understanding is at the basic, intermediate, or advanced level. For a more comprehensive assessment of your learning, please see your student study guide and your Psychology CourseMate (www.cengagebrain.com).

1. _____ is most closely related to the concept of compliance.

   a. Cohesiveness
   b. Reciprocity
   c. Altruism
   d. Deindividuation

2. A(n) _____ is a schema for a group of people.

   a. norm
   b. attribution
   c. bias
   d. stereotype

3. _____ is most closely related to the concept of persuasion.

   a. Normative conformity
   b. Informational conformity
   c. Obedience
   d. Compliance

4. Which of the following things would you not want to do if you were trying to get an audience to process your persuasive arguments on the peripheral route to persuasion?

   a. Throw a great deal of information at the audience in a short span of time.
   b. Try to distract the audience in some way.
   c. Use illogical arguments.
   d. All of the above would ensure that the audience processes peripherally.

5. _____ could be thought of as the self-serving bias applied to groups.

   a. The fundamental attribution error
   b. The ultimate attribution error
   c. The actor-observer bias
   d. The matching hypothesis

6. When you pass an exam, you attribute your success to your ability, but when you fail an exam, you attribute your failure to the professor's failure to teach you well. You are engaging in the_____.

   a. fundamental attribution error
   b. ultimate attribution error
   c. actor-observer bias
   d. self-serving bias

7. During a flash mob, you have to be most concerned about the occurrence of _____.

   a. prejudice
   b. discrimination
   c. dissonance
   d. deindividuation

8. Johnny, an African American man, has a flat tire on the side of the road and no one stops to help him despite heavy traffic on the road. Johnny's failure to receive help could be due to _____.

   a. aversive racism
   b. pluralistic ignorance
   c. diffusion of responsibility
   d. all of the above

9. The fact that prejudice tends to increase during hard economic times is best explained by _____.

   a. aversive racism
   b. in-group/out-group bias
   c. out-group homogeneity bias
   d. realistic-conflict theory

10. As a group becomes more cohesive, what happens?

   a. Conformity in the group increases.
   b. Decision making in the group improves.
   c. The out-group homogeneity bias reduces.
   d. Both a and b occur.

11. Joan loves science fiction movies so much that she regularly attends conventions for sci-fi fans. Robert is a filmmaker who makes romantic comedies exclusively. Both are good-looking, smart, and funny, but when Joan and Robert go on a blind date, they are not attracted to each other. Which of the following cannot explain the lack of attraction between Joan and Robert?

   a. the matching hypothesis
   b. cognitive dissonance theory
   c. balance theory
   d. similarity

12. According to the _____, exposure to out-group members will reduce prejudice.

   a. mere exposure effect
   b. contact hypothesis
   c. matching hypothesis
   d. balance theory

13. The _____ predicts that we are less likely to get help from a crowd of people than we would be if there was only one witness to our plight.

  a. pluralistic ignorance effect
  b. bystander effect
  c. balance theory
  d. aversive racism effect

14. Another name for the slippery slope is _____.

  a. door-in-the-face compliance
  b. foot-in-the-door compliance
  c. reciprocity
  d. hostile aggression

15. Aggression has been linked to _____.

  a. testosterone
  b. serotonin
  c. gender
  d. all of the above

Scoring Key

Below are the answers and the associated point values for each of the Learning Challenge questions. Circle the associated points for each question that you answered correctly. To obtain your Learning Challenge Score, add up the points you circled and write the total in the blank below.

1. B, 2 pts	**6.** D, 2 pts	**11.** A, 3 pts
2. D, 1 pt	**7.** D, 2 pts	**12.** B, 1 pt
3. B, 2 pts	**8.** D, 3 pts	**13.** B, 1 pt
4. C, 3 pts	**9.** D, 2 pts	**14.** B, 1 pt
5. B, 3 pts	**10.** A, 3 pts	**15.** D, 1 pt

Learning Challenge Score _____

(27–30) Congratulations! You scored at the advanced level. You are well on your way to mastering the material. Take the next step by answering the questions in your Student Study Guide or your Psychology CourseMate (www.cengagebrain.com).

(21–26) You are almost there! You scored at the intermediate level. Review the material you missed before moving on to answer the questions in your Student Study Guide or your Psychology CourseMate (www.cengagebrain.com).

(20 and below) You are on your way, but you're not there yet! You scored at the beginner level. It appears that you need to carefully review the chapter to improve your mastery of the material.

USE IT OR LOSE IT: APPLYING PSYCHOLOGY

1. Given what you have learned about obedience and compliance, what precautions would you urge people to take if they wanted to make themselves less vulnerable to requests and demands from others?

2. Pretend you have just been appointed to a committee at your place of work. Your mission is to develop a strategic plan that will take your company beyond the 21st century. What precautions would you take to ensure that your group does not develop groupthink?

3. Pretend you are an advertising account executive working for a new client. Using your knowledge of persuasion, design a television ad campaign to sell a new type of dishwashing detergent called Squeeky Clean Suds. Then justify to your client why your plan should be successful.

4. Pretend you are a community leader in a racially divided community. Design a program to reduce racial tensions among your community's citizens. Then explain why your plan should work.

5. Watch two television shows that feature male and female characters, one modern show and one older show from prior to the 1990s. What gender stereotypes are portrayed in these two shows? How do the shows differ in their depiction of male and female roles? Do these differences reflect changes in our culture over the past 50 years?

6. Keep a log of the attributions you make in a single day. How often did you use the heuristics discussed in this chapter? How often did you engage in careful attributions?

7. Find an article from a major metropolitan newspaper that discusses an instance in which someone committed an act of altruism. Then find an article that describes an emergency in which no one came to the aid of the victim. Compare and contrast the two situations in terms of the variables that affect helping behavior. Do these situations fit with what you have learned about helping behavior? If not, how do they differ?

CRITICAL THINKING FOR INTEGRATION

1. Give examples, not cited in the text, of how the learning theories from Chapter 5 (i.e., classical conditioning, operant conditioning, and observational learning) can contribute to the development of a prejudice.

2. Given what you have learned about developmental psychology in Chapter 9, when would you expect to see prejudice develop in children? Explain your answer.

3. Use what you learned in Chapter 1 to design an experiment to test the matching hypothesis.

4. Use what you learned in Chapter 1 to design an experiment to test the hypothesis that bystanders will be less likely to help a victim who they perceive to be responsible for his own plight.

CHAPTER STUDY RESOURCES

Student Study Guide

To help organize your learning, work through Chapter 11 of the *What Is Psychology? Student Study Guide*. The study guide includes learning objectives, a chapter summary, fill-in review, key terms, a practice test, and activities.

CengageNOW

CENGAGENOW

Go to **www.cengage.com/login** to link to CengageNOW, your online study tool. First take the Pre-Test for this chapter to get your personalized study plan, which will identify topics you need to review and direct you to online resources. Then take the Post-Test to determine what concepts you have mastered and what you still need work on.

CourseMate

Access an interactive eBook, chapter-specific interactive learning tools, including flashcards, quizzes, videos, and more in your Psychology CourseMate, available at **CengageBrain.com**.

Aplia

aplia

Aplia™ is an online interactive learning solution that helps you improve comprehension—and your grade—by integrating a variety of tools such as video, tutorials, practice tests, and interactive e-book. Founded by a professor to enhance his own courses, Aplia provides automatically graded assignments with detailed, immediate explanations on every question, and innovative teaching materials. More than 1,000,000 students like you have used Aplia at over 1,800 institutions. Aplia should be purchased only when assigned by your instructor as part of your course.

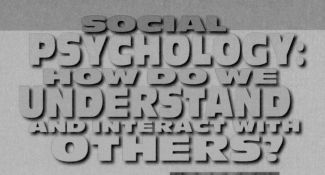

SOCIAL PSYCHOLOGY: HOW DO WE UNDERSTAND AND INTERACT WITH OTHERS?

The story of Rose Mahoney's 120-mile trip up the Nile River in Egypt highlights some of the intricacies of social interaction and how these interactions can change us. **Social psychology**, the study of how we think and behave in social situations, seeks to clarify the principles of human interaction. Two subfields of social psychology are **social cognition**, the study of how we think about ourselves and others, and **social influence**, the study of how others affect our behavior.

ATTITUDES: WHY DO WE CHANGE OUR MINDS?

- **Attitudes** are evaluative beliefs that contain affective, behavioral, and cognitive components.
- Attitudes develop through learning processes including classical conditioning, operant conditioning, and observational learning or modeling.
- Attitude-behavior consistency is affected by many factors, such as the accessibility of the attitude in memory.
- Dissonance results from a lack of **cognitive consistency**, and it motivates us to change either our attitudes or our behavior.
- **Persuasion** occurs when someone makes a direct attempt to change our attitudes.
- We tend to be most persuaded by people who appear to be attractive, credible, and expert.
- Typically, people are easier to persuade when they are processing on the **peripheral route** rather than the **central route**.

© Colin Young-Wolff/Photo Edit

HOW DO WE FORM IMPRESSIONS OF OTHERS?

- In forming impressions of others, we make **trait** or **situational attributions** when we assign cause to their behavior.
- The **fundamental attribution error** is the tendency to discount situational explanations during attribution.
- The **actor/observer bias** and the **self-serving bias** are two other sources of mistaken or biased attributions.

Neal Hamberg/Bloomberg News /Landov

© Jeff Greenberg/PhotoEdit

PREJUDICE: WHY CAN'T WE ALL JUST GET ALONG?

- **Prejudices** are negatively biased **stereotypes** that are applied to all members of a social group regardless of the members' individual characteristics.
- Like most attitudes, prejudices are learned.
- Intergroup dynamics such as **in-group bias** and **out-group homogeneity bias** often play a role in prejudice.
- **Aversive racism** is most likely to occur in stressful situations.

- The **contact hypothesis** states that mere contact between in-group and out-group members can reduce prejudice. Cooperative contact and **superordinate goals** have been shown to be more effective in reducing prejudice.

WHAT ATTRACTS US TO OTHERS?

- Some of the factors that affect our attraction to others include **proximity**, similarity of their attitudes and characteristics to ours, physical attractiveness, and cultural standards of beauty.

GROUPS AND GROUP INFLUENCE: ARE TWO HEADS BETTER THAN ONE?

- **Conformity** is the tendency to behave in ways that are consistent with the **norms** or expectations of a group.

- In **normative conformity**, we conform just to avoid breaking norms. In **informational conformity**, we conform because we are persuaded by conformity pressure to believe the group's stance is correct.

- **Social facilitation** occurs when we perform better in the presence of others, but sometimes working with others can lead to **social loafing** as group members decrease their effort.

- **Groupthink** occurs when groups working under conditions of isolation, high cohesiveness, stress, and dictatorial leadership make poor decisions after failing to examine all possible solutions to a problem.

© Anthony Redpath/Corbis

- **Compliance** is giving in to a simple request.

- In **foot-in-the-door compliance**, one is more likely to yield to a second, larger request after having already complied with a first, smaller request.

- In **door-in-the-face compliance**, one is more likely to yield to a second, smaller request after having refused an earlier, large request.

- **Reciprocity**, or feeling obligated to return others' favors, is a major reason we comply.

COMPLIANCE AND OBEDIENCE: CAN OTHERS CHANGE OUR BEHAVIOR?

- **Obedience** is giving in to a demand. Factors that make us more likely to obey orders, even when they direct us to behave destructively, include the following:

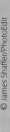

© James Shaffer/PhotoEdit

  - the presence of an authority figure
  - the foot-in-the door compliance of the **slippery slope**
  - **psychological distance**

AGGRESSION: WHAT MAKES US HURT OTHERS?

- Aggression is causing harm or injury to someone who does not wish to be harmed.

- **Instrumental aggression** is goal-directed aggression, while **hostile aggression** is aimed solely at hurting others.

- Potential causes of aggression include high levels of testosterone, a lack of serotonin, brain damage caused by child abuse, observational learning or modeling the aggression of others, cognitive neoassociation theory, and the **frustration-aggression hypothesis**.

© Barbara Stitzer/PhotoEdit

HELPING BEHAVIOR: WILL YOU, OR WON'T YOU?

- **Helping behavior**, or **altruism**, is the tendency to help others in need with little concern for our own gain.

- One of the factors affecting helping behavior is the **bystander effect**, in which **diffusion of responsibility** reduces your chance of obtaining help when there are many witnesses. **Pluralistic ignorance** may also ensure that we do not correctly perceive the situation as an emergency.

- Group membership and culture also impact our tendency to help. We are more likely to help those from our own group, and, at least in the United States, individualism predicts more helping.

© Tom Stewart/Corbis

CHAPTER 12

HEALTH, STRESS, AND COPING: HOW CAN YOU CREATE A HEALTHY LIFE?

THE BIG PICTURE

What Can Psychology Tell Us about Health?

In this chapter we'll explore the field of **health psychology**. Health psychologists study how people's behavior influences their health for better and for worse. In this regard, health is seen as a result of the interaction among biological, psychological, and social forces (Brannon & Feist, 2004; S. E. Taylor, 2003). We present the topics of stress, coping, and health. Because all of us cope with stress on a daily basis, this chapter offers much psychological research that will be relevant to your day-to-day living. It will help you realize how some of your personal habits, thoughts, or daily actions may be unhealthy, and hopefully will encourage you to live a healthier, longer life! Consider the following case.

Ellen, a 19-year-old college student, was looking forward to her spring break. She had decided to travel home to Florida to enjoy the beach, sunshine, and her family, a welcome diversion from midterm exams and the hassles of college life. On the third day of her vacation, her father, Edward, arrived home at his usual time and excitedly announced that he had great news—he had just found out that he was going to live!

Ellen was confused. What did he mean? Edward explained that over the past 4 months he had seen some medical specialists because he had been experiencing abdominal pain and weight loss. The doctors had discovered that he had cancer—specifically, a blood cancer called leukemia. Luckily, though, it was a treatable form of leukemia. Ellen was shocked by the news. Her father was only 53 years old. His parents had lived into their 80s, and his brother and sisters were in their 60s. None of them had experienced any significant health problems, let alone a cancer diagnosis. He had no family history of any form of cancer. Ellen reflected on all she knew about her father. Perhaps the clues to his illness could be found there.

Edward was born in 1930 in the Bronx, New York. His childhood was unremarkable, and he experienced no major medical illnesses or injuries other than frequent sinus difficulties. At 18, he received an appointment to the U.S. Naval Academy. After graduation, Edward entered the Marine Corps, was sent to Korea, and became involved in negotiating the trading of POWs.

Out of the Marine Corps and back in the United States, Edward started working for an electronics company. About the same time, he met Joan Cantelmo on a blind date. She was a recent graduate of Duquesne University and now a fifth-grade teacher. The couple fell in love and after 6 months got engaged. Once married, Edward climbed the

CHAPTER OUTLINE

- What Is Stress? Stress and Stressors
- The Stress Response: How Does the Body React?
- How Can I Cope With Stress?
- Does Your Personality Influence Your Health?
- What Behaviors Promote Health and Well-being?

© Rob Wilkinson/Alamy

497

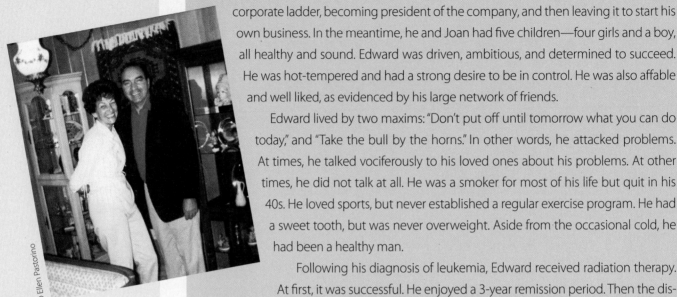

Perhaps because of advances in medical knowledge, or perhaps because of differences in their personalities or coping styles, Joan fared much better than Edward.

© Ellen Pastorino

corporate ladder, becoming president of the company, and then leaving it to start his own business. In the meantime, he and Joan had five children—four girls and a boy, all healthy and sound. Edward was driven, ambitious, and determined to succeed. He was hot-tempered and had a strong desire to be in control. He was also affable and well liked, as evidenced by his large network of friends.

Edward lived by two maxims: "Don't put off until tomorrow what you can do today," and "Take the bull by the horns." In other words, he attacked problems. At times, he talked vociferously to his loved ones about his problems. At other times, he did not talk at all. He was a smoker for most of his life but quit in his 40s. He loved sports, but never established a regular exercise program. He had a sweet tooth, but was never overweight. Aside from the occasional cold, he had been a healthy man.

Following his diagnosis of leukemia, Edward received radiation therapy. At first, it was successful. He enjoyed a 3-year remission period. Then the disease changed in form to non-Hodgkin's lymphoma, a cancerous growth of white blood cells in the lymph system. Edward received chemotherapy, but this time the therapy did not help. Ellen watched her father resume smoking and lose all his usual drive and ambition. Eventually, he gave up hope of beating the cancer. Not surprisingly, within months, at 56 years of age, Edward died. It was a devastating blow to Ellen and her family. All of them had relied on his guidance, tutelage, and strength. After a period of grieving, Ellen's family learned to cope with his passing.

Sadly, Ellen and her family received a second blow 10 years later. Joan, Ellen's mother, was diagnosed with the same form of cancer! She was given 5 years to live. Joan was also a smoker, but she was an avid bowler and was optimistic that she could beat the cancer. For the next 8 years, she led a high-quality life, mostly unimpeded by the disease. She died quietly in her sleep just 2 months shy of her 71st birthday. Perhaps because of advances in medical knowledge, or perhaps because of differences in their personalities or coping styles, Joan fared much better than Edward. Their daughter Ellen is one of the authors of this textbook.

Edward's illness serves as a prime example of the complex relationship between behavior and health. Health psychologists examine how a person's behavior, thoughts, personality, and attitudes influence his or her health for better and for worse. They try to understand the nature of stress and how one's perception of stress and coping styles may influence the effect of stress on the body. This knowledge can help us understand Edward's illness. It also helps us recognize the complex interplay between our behavior and our health.

health psychology the subfield of psychology that investigates the relationship between people's behaviors and their health

What Should You Know?
● Define stress, and identify stressors and conflict situations.

WHAT IS STRESS? STRESS AND STRESSORS

You are running late for school and your car breaks down—today of all days, when you have a major project due in one class and a midterm in another. Or maybe you're a working parent, trying to get the kids off to school in the morning, when your youngest can't find her shoes and the dog just got into the garbage. Perhaps you have just fallen in love and have decided to make the relationship more serious. Or maybe you have grown dissatisfied with your relationship and are contemplating ending it. All these situations have one thing in common. They all include *stress*, an inevitable and unavoidable fact of life.

Stress can be defined as any event or environmental stimulus (stressor) that we respond to because we perceive it as challenging or threatening. This definition implies three aspects to stress. First, we all encounter stressors—stimuli in our lives that we perceive as challenges or threats, such as traffic, an approaching midterm exam, or a hurricane. Second, our reactions to these stressors include bodily reactions. Third, by perceiving and then reacting, we cope with the challenges or threats (successfully or not, as we will see). This chapter explores these three aspects of stress.

What are stressors? Let's first look at different types of stressors. Briefly reflect on an ordinary day in your life. There are probably many events or stimuli that you perceive as provoking or annoying: a long line at the fast-food drive-through, a confrontation with your boss, or having several errands to run in a limited amount of time. There probably have also been events in your life that you found to be particularly trying or traumatic, such as the death of a loved one, dealing with an unplanned pregnancy, or being fired from your job. Stressors come in all shapes and sizes. Psychological research classifies these stressors into four types:

● Major life events
● Catastrophes
● Daily hassles
● Conflict

Let's take a look at how each of these stressors is defined.

Life Events: Change Is Stressful

How do we know which events in our life qualify as major, rather than minor, stressors when they all *feel* stressful? Believe it or not, psychologists have tried to measure this difference. Pioneering research by Thomas Holmes and Richard Rahe in 1967 set out to measure the impact of particular stressors on people's health. They asked a large sample group to rate **life events**, or changes in one's living, both good and bad, that require us to adjust to them. In other words, which life events did the respondents perceive as more stressful? From these ratings, Holmes and Rahe developed the Social Readjustment Rating Scale (SRRS), reprinted in ● TABLE 12.1.

stress any event or environmental stimulus (stressors) that we respond to because we perceive it as challenging or threatening

life event a change in one's life, good or bad, that requires readjustment

TABLE 12.1

● Holmes and Rahe's Social Readjustment Rating Scale

RANK	LIFE EVENT	LIFE CHANGE UNITS	RANK	LIFE EVENT	LIFE CHANGE UNITS
1	Death of spouse	100	23	Son or daughter leaving home	29
2	Divorce	73	24	Trouble with in-laws	29
3	Marital separation	65	25	Outstanding personal achievement	28
4	Jail term	63	26	Spouse begins or stops work	26
5	Death of a close family member	63	27	Begin or end school	26
6	Personal injury or illness	53	28	Change in living conditions	25
7	Marriage	50	29	Revision of personal habits	24
8	Fired at work	47	30	Trouble with boss	23
9	Marital reconciliation	45	31	Change in work hours or conditions	20
10	Retirement	45	32	Change in residence	20
11	Change in health of family member	44	33	Change in school	20
12	Pregnancy	40	34	Change in recreation	19
13	Sex difficulties	39	35	Change in church activities	19
14	Gain of new family member	39	36	Change in social activities	18
15	Business readjustment	39	37	Take out loan less than $20,000	17
16	Change in financial state	38	38	Change in sleeping habits	16
17	Death of a close friend	37	39	Change in number of family get-togethers	15
18	Change to different line of work	36	40	Change in eating habits	15
19	Change in number of arguments with spouse	35	41	Vacation	13
20	Take out mortgage or loan for major purchase	31	42	Christmas	12
21	Foreclosure of mortgage or loan	30	43	Minor violation of the law	11
22	Change in responsibilities at work	29			

Reprinted with permission from T. H. Holmes & R. H. Rahe (1967), "The Social Readjustment Rating Scale," in the Journal of Psychosomatic Research, *Vol. 11, No. 2, pp. 213–218. Copyright © 1967 Elsevier Science.*

Note: In Holmes and Rahe's Social Readjustment Rating Scale, each major life event is assigned a numerical value. The higher the number, the more stressful the life event is perceived to be. Add up the life change units for all those events you have experienced in the past year. Then compare your total to the standards indicated in the text.

Life events, both good and bad, can be perceived as stressful and require us to adjust to them.

Digital Vision/Getty Images

Holmes and Rahe assigned each major life event a numerical value, referred to as a *life change unit*. The higher the number, the more stressful this life event was rated by Holmes and Rahe's sample. Notice that Edward and his family experienced several stressors that fall at the top of this list. Being diagnosed with cancer, a personal illness, was a major stressor for Edward. Experiencing the death of a loved one was a major stressor for Ellen and her family. Notice too that the life events on the scale include positive as well as negative changes—for example, marriage, a new family member, and outstanding personal achievement. However, it is not just experiencing one of these events that is at issue. Rather, it is reacting to several of these events within a year that Holmes and Rahe found may influence one's health.

TRY THIS
DEMONSTRATION

Take a moment to look at the Social Readjustment Rating Scale (Table 12.1). Add up the life change units for all those events you have experienced in the last year. Compare your total to the standards devised by Holmes and Rahe:

0–150	No significant problems
150–199	Mild life crisis
200–299	Moderate life crisis
300 or more	Major life crisis

Holmes and Rahe (1967) found that the higher people scored on the SRRS, the more prone they were to illness. Of those who scored within the mild life crisis range, 37% had experienced deteriorated health. This figure rose to 51% for those whose scores indicated they were experiencing a moderate life crisis, and 79% for those in the major life crisis range. Follow-up studies have supported Holmes and Rahe's findings (Gruen, 1993; Scully, Tosi, & Banning, 2000). If you scored high on the scale, you may want to consider adjusting your lifestyle in ways that reduce your chances of becoming ill. However, keep in mind that these are correlations, and as we discussed in Chapter 1, correlation does not mean causation. Life events do not directly cause illness, but they may make a person more vulnerable to illness and disease.

Subsequent research (Pearlin, 1993) evaluating Holmes and Rahe's scale indicates that the impact of these life changes is not simply a matter of how many of them one experiences. We need to take several other variables into account, including:

- The voluntary or involuntary nature of the life change
- How desirable or undesirable the life change is perceived to be
- Whether the life change is scheduled or unscheduled

For example, Edward's cancer diagnosis can be considered involuntary because he did not choose to get ill (although he did choose to smoke) and undesirable as a threat to his life. It was unscheduled because he did not foresee (even in his family's history) his susceptibility to cancer. Consider as another example a couple about to break up. Typically, the partner who initiates the breakup feels less stress after she has informed her significant other of her decision. In this context, the breakup is seen as voluntary, desirable, and scheduled. At the same time, her partner may experience increased stress, as the dissolution of the relationship is involuntary (not of the partner's choosing), undesirable, and unscheduled. As these examples illustrate, the amount of stress one experiences when faced with life changes may vary across people. We can consider Holmes and Rahe's scale a rough index of how susceptible one may be to illness, given the number of major stressors the person encounters.

You may have noticed that the scale has very few life events that are likely to be experienced by college students and younger people. The SRRS has been criticized for not adequately defining stress events among younger age groups. Yet research supports the notion that major changes, such as the breakup of a relationship, academic pressure, or even college itself, may influence the health of college students (Crandall, Preisler, & Aussprung, 1992). This connection is important because perceived stress also seems to predict how well students perform academically. High levels of perceived stress in college students correlate with lower grade point averages (Lloyd et al., 1980; Maville & Huerta, 1997). For example, in a survey of college students (American College Health Association [ACHA], 2006), stress was the most frequent reason given for academic problems. You may find that the Undergraduate Stress Questionnaire (● TABLE 12.2) includes more of the stressors that you typically face than does Holmes and Rahe's SRRS. It was specifically designed to measure life event stress in college students. Undergraduates who have experienced more of these life events are more likely to report more physical symptoms and are less likely to report a positive mood (Crandall et al., 1992). It may therefore provide a more accurate assessment of your stress level and hence your susceptibility to illness.

TABLE 12.2

● Undergraduate Stress Questionnaire

Have any of the following stressful events happened to you at any time during the past semester? If any has, check the space next to it. If an item has not occurred, leave it blank. Stressful life events are listed in descending order of severity. Students with more checkmarks are more likely to need health care than students with fewer checkmarks.

___ 1. Death (family member or friend)	___ 42. Crammed for a test
___ 2. Had a lot of tests	___ 43. Feel unorganized
___ 3. It's finals week	___ 44. Trying to decide on major
___ 4. Applying to graduate school	___ 45. Feel isolated
___ 5. Victim of a crime	___ 46. Parents controlling with money
___ 6. Assignments in all classes due the same day	___ 47. Couldn't find a parking space
___ 7. Breaking up with boy/girlfriend	___ 48. Noise disturbed you while trying to study
___ 8. Found out boy/girlfriend cheated on you	___ 49. Someone borrowed something without your permission
___ 9. Lots of deadlines to meet	___ 50. Had to ask for money
___ 10. Property stolen	___ 51. Ran out of ink while printing
___ 11. You have a hard upcoming week	___ 52. Erratic schedule
___ 12. Went into a test unprepared	___ 53. Can't understand your professor
___ 13. Lost something (especially wallet)	___ 54. Trying to get into your major or college
___ 14. Death of a pet	___ 55. Registration for classes
___ 15. Did worse than expected on test	___ 56. Stayed up late writing a paper
___ 16. Had an interview	___ 57. Someone you expected to call did not
___ 17. Had projects, research papers due	___ 58. Someone broke a promise
___ 18. Did badly on a test	___ 59. Can't concentrate
___ 19. Parents getting a divorce	___ 60. Someone did a "pet peeve" of yours
___ 20. Dependent on other people	___ 61. Living with boy/girlfriend
___ 21. Having roommate conflicts	___ 62. Felt need for transportation
___ 22. Car/bike broke down, flat tire	___ 63. Bad haircut today
___ 23. Got a traffic ticket	___ 64. Job requirements changed
___ 24. Missed your menstrual period and waiting	___ 65. No time to eat
___ 25. Thoughts about future	___ 66. Felt some peer pressure
___ 26. Lack of money	___ 67. You have a hangover
___ 27. Dealt with incompetence at the Registrar's Office	___ 68. Problems with your computer
___ 28. Thought about unfinished work	___ 69. Problem getting home when drunk
___ 29. No sleep	___ 70. Used a fake ID
___ 30. Sick, injury	___ 71. No sex in a while
___ 31. Had a class presentation	___ 72. Someone cut ahead of you in line
___ 32. Applying for a job	___ 73. Checkbook didn't balance
___ 33. Fought with boy/girlfriend	___ 74. Had a visit from a relative and entertained him/her
___ 34. Working while in school	___ 75. Decision to have sex on your mind
___ 35. Arguments, conflict of values with friends	___ 76. Spoke with a professor
___ 36. Bothered by not having family's social support	___ 77. Change of environment (new doctor, dentist, etc.)
___ 37. Performed poorly at a task	___ 78. Exposed to upsetting TV show, book, or movie
___ 38. Can't finish everything you need to do	___ 79. Got to class late
___ 39. Heard bad news	___ 80. Holiday
___ 40. Had confrontation with an authority figure	___ 81. Sat through a boring class
___ 41. Maintaining a long-distance boy/girlfriend	___ 82. Favorite sports team lost

Source: C. S. Crandall et al., "*Measuring Life Event Stress in the Lives of College Students: The Undergraduate Stress Questionnaire (USQ)*," in Journal of Behavioral Medicine, *15(6), pp. 627–662,* © 1992. Reprinted with kind permission of Springer Science and Business Media.

Catastrophes: Natural Disasters and Wars

Unexpected traumatic events or catastrophes that almost all people perceive as threats also qualify as stressors. Catastrophes may affect one's physical and psychological health. After catastrophic events such as tsunamis, earthquakes, hurricanes, tornadoes, or fires, people are generally more likely to experience depression or anxiety (Brende, 2000; J. R. T. Davidson, 2000; Dewaraja & Kawamura, 2006; Neria, Nandi, & Galea, 2008; Weems et al., 2007).

We have for a long time recognized the stress of war on soldiers, as evidenced by the various names we have given to the pattern of symptoms that soldiers experience when they return. It was called *shell shock* in World War I, *battle fatigue* in World War II, and *posttraumatic stress disorder* (*PTSD*) following the Vietnam War and Operation Desert Storm. Soldiers experienced nightmares, flashbacks, and vivid memories as they relived their war experiences. They evidenced intense startle responses to loud noises and had difficulty concentrating and getting along with others. Rape victims report similar physical and psychological symptoms that may meet the criteria for what is referred to as *rape trauma syndrome*, more evidence that unexpected events may take their toll on one's health. Traumatic events and catastrophes are often involuntary, undesirable, and somewhat unscheduled in that we typically don't have a lot of time to prepare for them, so it is relatively easy to see how they may influence our health and well-being. We'll discuss PTSD in more detail in Chapter 14.

Do catastrophes or traumatic events always affect health negatively? Not necessarily. Over the last decade, research has documented a potential positive effect of stressful life experiences for *some* people, referred to as *posttraumatic growth* or *benefit-finding*. People report that these events have changed their lives in positive ways, such as forging stronger relationships with others, emphasizing enjoyment in life, and producing positive changes in health behaviors (Bower, Moskowitz, & Epel, 2009). Perhaps a severe life-threatening event provides an opportunity for some people to reevaluate their lives and prompts them to initiate positive changes.

Jean-Phillipe Ksiazek/AFP/Getty Images

Unexpected traumatic events also cause stress and can affect one's physical and psychological health.

Daily Hassles: Little Things Add Up!

When psychologists evaluate the relationship between stress and health, they not only measure life changes and analyze the influence of catastrophes, they also evaluate the impact of everyday irritations and frustrations. These **daily hassles** also appear to play a role in our health. At times these irritants add to the stress of major life changes and catastrophic events, such as the daily planning for a wedding or getting stuck in traffic during an evacuation due to a natural disaster. But for most of us, the routine annoyances and frustrations we experience on a daily basis are stressful in themselves. Can you think of any examples of daily hassles? Waiting in lines, experiencing a lack of money, losing your keys, or having fights with loved ones may be a few that come to mind. Such daily hassles may in fact be the most significant source of stress, placing a great burden on our immediate health and well-being and on our relationships (Lazarus, 1990; Repetti, Wang, & Saxbe, 2009; S. M. Roberts, 1995; Ruffin, 1993). As daily hassles increase, our physical and mental health decrease (Chamberlain & Zika, 1990; D. B. O'Connor et al., 2008; Sim, 2000). However, whether we perceive these frustrations as stressful is of prime importance in determining our susceptibility to illness. Some people easily shrug off these annoyances, whereas others find them particularly perturbing.

daily hassles the everyday irritations and frustrations that individuals face

Everyday irritations and frustrations increase our stress level and can influence our health.

Gender, race, age, socioeconomic status, and education seem to influence our perception of stress from daily hassles (Almeida, 2005; H. Taylor, 2002). Women are more likely than men to perceive stress from concerns about money, having too many things to do, health issues, and having trouble relaxing. In general, younger people report more daily hassles in their lives than older people. Those with more money and more education also report lower levels of perceived stress from daily hassles than those with lower income and less education. Although people who make more money and have more education may lead full and hectic lives, they generally perceive that they have more control over their lives and report having more fun. They are less likely to experience hassles concerning health, illness of a family member, trouble relaxing, problems at work, and exposure to excessive noise than are people with less education and lower incomes. Racial differences also appear in reports on daily hassles. African Americans are more likely than Hispanic or European Americans to report economic issues, exposure to noise, feeling lonely, and invasion of personal privacy as frequent day-to-day hassles. Hispanic Americans are more likely than European or African Americans to report problems with aging parents as a hassle of daily living.

Prejudice and discrimination is a unique source of stress for members of minority groups (R. Clark et al., 1999; D'Anna, Ponce, & Siegel, 2010; Okazaki, 2009; V. L. Thompson, 1996; D. C. Watkins et al., 2007). For example, in a study by Klonoff and Landrine (1999), 95% of the 520 African American respondents reported experiencing some form of racial discrimination in the past year that they perceived as stressful. Other research indicates that Hispanic, Asian, and Arab Americans also experience discrimination and perceive it as stressful (Bernstein et al., in press; Jackson, Williams, & Torres, 1997; McClure et al., 2010; Padela & Heisler, 2010). Homosexuals and bisexuals face more lifetime and day-to-day experiences with discrimination than do heterosexuals (Huebner & Davis, 2007; Mays & Cochran, 2001).

The interpretation of others' behaviors as discriminatory increases stress in some people. For example, Kimberly King (2005) asked African American female college students to imagine that they overheard European American males make negative comments about them. The participants who reported the most stress were those who assumed that the negative evaluations had to do with race or gender or both. Another study found that having adequate coping resources to deal with racism reduces stress from discrimination (Bynum, Burton, & Best, 2007).

The anticipation of being discriminated against may also be a source of stress for members of minority groups. They worry that their behavior will be interpreted in a way that confirms negative stereotypes (C. M. Steele, 1997). If they try to behave in a way that does not conform to these stereotypes, they may then be ridiculed by members of their own group for "selling out" or "acting White" (Contrada et al., 2000). All these situations are potentially stressful. Researchers are just beginning to evaluate the potential ill effects of such stress on people's physical and mental health (e.g., Pieterse & Carter, 2007; Rich-Edwards et al., 2001; D. R. Williams et al., 1997). Such research illustrates the impact that our interactions with others can have on our physical and mental well-being.

Conflict: Approach and Avoidance

Conflict, or having to choose between two or more needs, desires, or demands, can also place stress on us. Should you take the required science course or the required math course? Should you wear the blue or the gray suit to the job interview? Whether we perceive these options as positive or negative results in four basic forms of conflict (● FIGURE 12.1).

1. *Approach–approach conflicts.* The easiest conflict to resolve, and therefore the conflict that is accompanied by the least amount of perceived stress, is the **approach–approach conflict**, in which a person must choose between two likable, or positive, events. Choosing between seeing an old friend who is passing through town or going out with some-

conflict having to choose between two or more needs, desires, or demands

approach–approach conflict a situation in which a person must choose between two likable events

Approach-Approach Conflict

Choosing a Movie

The new Johnny Depp movie | The new Will Smith movie

Avoidance-Avoidance Conflict

Choosing a Vegetable

Eating okra | Eating beets

Approach-Avoidance Conflict

Getting a pet

Cuddly companion | Clean up messes

Multiple Conflicts

Choosing a job

Job 2

Choosing a job

Job 1

Choosing a job

Job 3

PhotoDisc

one you've been hoping would ask you out is an example of an approach–approach conflict. A more stressful approach–approach example could be liking and being challenged in your job and being offered another attractive and challenging position in the same company. In this type of conflict you really can't lose because both options are favorable.

2. *Avoidance–avoidance conflicts.* The opposite of the approach–approach conflict is the **avoidance–avoidance conflict**, in which a person has to choose between two undesirable, or negative, events. You can think of this type of conflict as a Catch-22 situation. For example, do you spend the morning in line to register your car, or do you get your car towed because the registration has expired? Because both options in an avoidance–avoidance conflict are unappealing, many people remain undecided and inactive, or "frozen." They don't do anything. Consequently, avoidance–avoidance conflicts are accompanied by a greater degree of perceived stress than are approach–approach conflicts.

3. *Approach–avoidance conflicts.* Another stressful conflict to resolve is the **approach–avoidance conflict**, in which a person is faced with a desire or need that has both positive and negative qualities. He or she is drawn to the situation because of its positive features (approach), but is also repelled by and would rather not experience the negative aspects of the situation (avoidance). Edward's decision to receive radiation treatment, followed 3 years later by chemotherapy treatment, had elements of an approach–avoidance conflict. The positive qualities of such treatments are the increased chances of survival. The major side effects, which most of us would like to avoid, include extreme fatigue, nausea, hair loss, loss of taste, and a high susceptibility to viruses and bacteria, which means avoiding situations in which there may be a lot of people. These side effects may lessen one's quality of life, a consideration particularly for those who are terminally ill. Or think of a home fire with your dog trapped inside the burning structure. You don't want to lose your lifelong friend and therefore want to save the dog, but attempting to do so may put your own life at risk. As with avoidance–avoidance conflicts, these situations may immobilize people so that they cannot make a decision or resolve the conflict, which leads to the experience of stress.

4. *Multiple conflicts.* In real life, many conflicts involve several alternatives, each with both positive and negative features. These **multiple approach–avoidance conflicts** can contribute to the amount of stress we feel. In deciding which college to attend, you may have been faced with several choices. Each school may have had its good points and bad points (distance from home, tuition cost, program of studies, social life). Deciding on a major or a career, choosing between two job offers, and deciding which house or car to

FIGURE 12.1

● **Four Common Conflict Situations**
In an approach–approach conflict, a person must choose between two appealing choices—in this example, two movies one would like to see. In an avoidance–avoidance conflict, a person must choose between two undesirable choices—in this example, two disliked vegetables. In an approach–avoidance conflict, a person faces a decision that has both positive and negative features—in this example, owning a pet that cuddles yet also makes messes. Multiple conflicts involve several choices that have both positive and negative qualities—in this example, choosing among three jobs.

avoidance–avoidance conflict
a situation in which a person must choose between two undesirable events

approach–avoidance conflict
a situation in which a person is faced with a need that has both positive and negative aspects

multiple approach–avoidance conflict a situation that poses several alternatives that each have positive and negative features

buy are other examples of multiple conflicts. This may account for *buyer's remorse*, which some people experience after making a major purchase. They bought, or approached, an item because of its attractive features but afterward felt regret as they contemplated the item's negative features or alternatives that they should have considered more seriously.

Let's REVIEW

In this section, we defined stress and described four types of stressors. For a quick review, try answering the following questions at increasing levels of difficulty.

1. Getting stuck in traffic on your way to a job interview is an example of a _____.

   a. daily hassle
   b. major life event
   c. catastrophe
   d. stress response

2. Which of the following does the Social Readjustment Rating Scale consider the most stressful major life event?

   a. a jail term
   b. death of a spouse
   c. divorce
   d. pregnancy

3. You go to the dentist and find out that you have to get a tooth extracted. The only time the dentist can schedule your appointment is at the same time as a traffic court appointment. This situation is an example of a(n) _____.

   a. approach–approach conflict
   b. approach–avoidance conflict
   c. avoidance–avoidance conflict
   d. multiple conflict

ANSWERS 1. a; 2. b; 3. c

LEARNING OBJECTIVES

What Should You Know?

- Discuss the role of appraisal in the stress response.
- Explain how the body responds to stress and how that response influences immunity to disease.

primary appraisal our initial interpretation of an event as either irrelevant, positive, or stressful

Do you perceive an oral presentation as a threat or a challenge? A primary appraisal of threat will make you feel more stressed than viewing it as a challenge.

© Tony Freeman/PhotoEdit

THE STRESS RESPONSE: HOW DOES THE BODY REACT?

Now that we have looked at the types of stressors that may influence health, we will examine the second feature of stress: the reactions that accompany stress. This analysis will further your understanding of the relationship between stress and health.

Appraisal: Assessing Stress

How does stress start? We all experience stressors, especially daily hassles. We all wait in lines, sit in traffic, and pay bills. Yet not all of us interpret these events as equally stressful. Some people view giving blood as less stressful than others. You may feel excited about giving a speech, whereas others cringe at the same prospect. Therefore, the first step in experiencing stress is how you think about or interpret an event or situation. Our initial interpretation of an event is called **primary appraisal** (Lazarus, 1991, 1993). Primary appraisal can be irrelevant, positive, or stressful.

If your primary appraisal of an event is *irrelevant*, you interpret the situation as unrelated to your happiness or safety. For example, the number of students in a particular course you are taking may not make a difference to you one way or another. Class size may be appraised as not relevant to your performance in the class, and therefore viewed as not stressful. Primary appraisals also can be *positive*. For example, you may take a class in which there is a small number of students and view this situation as something good. However, when we appraise a situation as *stressful*, we believe it will require a great deal of our emotional and psychological resources. For example, you may view a small class size as stressful if you fear speaking in front of a group and you are expected to participate in class discussion.

Our primary appraisal of an event as stressful can lead to positive or negative emotions that either increase or decrease our perceived stress levels (Barlow, 2002). How much stress we experience will depend on whether we see the situation as a threat, a harm, or a challenge. If we appraise a stressful event as *threatening*, we believe that the situation will cause us some harm in the future. When we interpret an event in this manner, we typically feel fear, anxiety, or anger—negative emotions that increase our stress levels and decrease our performance (Gildea, Schneider, & Shebilske, 2007). For example, having to give an oral presentation on a project later in the term may be perceived as threatening by a student. He may fear negative evaluations by the professor or other students or be anxious that his voice will crack or that he will stammer. If we appraise an event as *harmful*, we believe it will do us some damage or injury. For example, one of the authors of your textbook appraised putting holiday lights up on her house as stressful because she believed that getting on the roof of her house would lead to injury. Again, such appraisals typically lead to feelings of fear and anxiety that increase our feelings of stress. However, situations can also be appraised as *challenging*, as a means toward personal growth or personal gain. For example, taking a new job may be appraised as an opportunity for career growth, or getting married may be appraised as an opportunity to deepen and expand the nature of an intimate relationship. Challenge appraisals typically elicit positive emotions such as excitement and are therefore perceived as less stressful.

Not all primary appraisals break down easily into the categories of threat, harm, or challenge. A situation or event may involve a combination of appraisals. For example, starting a relationship, finding a job, or having a baby are complex situations that may involve appraisals of both threat and challenge. Also, the appraisal process is a personal one. Not everyone appraises the same situation in the same manner. For example, some students may perceive course exams as threats, whereas other students may see them as challenges. Yet for everyone, primary appraisal is the first step in experiencing stress. Once you appraise a situation or event as stressful, your body changes to deal with the stressor.

general adaptation syndrome (GAS) the general physical responses we experience when faced with a stressor

Selye's General Adaptation Syndrome: The Body's Response to Stress

How does our body respond to stress? Many of us recognize stressful situations because of the bodily reactions that accompany them. For example, if you perceive giving a speech as a stressor, when faced with doing so, you may feel shaky, perspire more, feel your heart race, or even experience difficulty breathing. You may experience these same reactions when accepting an award or before an important job interview. These reactions are a part of a general bodily pattern termed the **general adaptation syndrome (GAS**; Selye, 1976). ● FIGURE 12.2 shows the GAS as three phases that we all experience when we perceive a stressor in the environment: an initial *alarm reaction*, *resistance*, and *exhaustion*.

Alarm Reaction

The **alarm reaction** consists of those bodily responses that are immediately triggered when we initially appraise an event as stressful. It is much like the car alarm that goes off the moment an intruder tries to open the car door. In the body, this response involves activation of the nervous system and the endocrine system (● FIGURE 12.3).

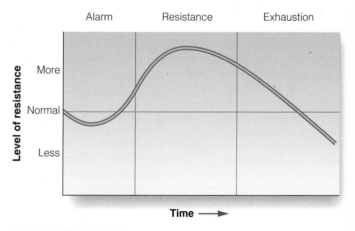

FIGURE 12.2

● **General Adaptation Syndrome** According to Hans Selye, the biological stress response consists of three phases. In the alarm reaction, the body releases chemicals to deal with a stressor. These chemicals lower the body's resistance. In the resistance stage, the body shores up additional resources to cope with the stressor. If the stressor persists, the body enters the exhaustion stage in which bodily resources dwindle, and we function at less than normal. Wear and tear on the body begin.

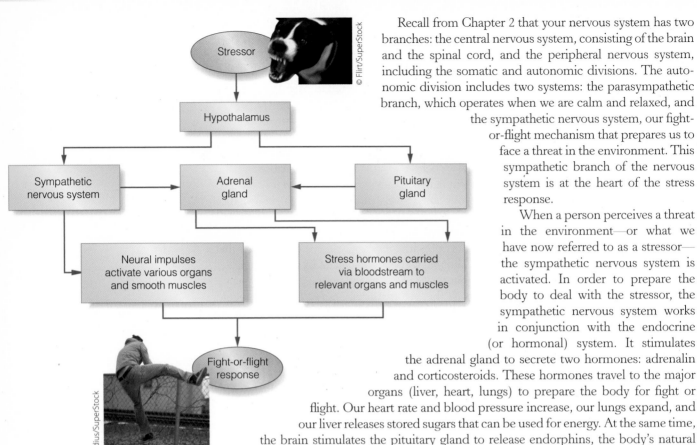

FIGURE 12.3

● **Biological Pathway of the Stress Response** When we perceive an event as stressful, the hypothalamus in the brain activates two systems: the sympathetic branch of the nervous system and the pituitary gland of the hormonal system. The nervous system sends neural messages to the major glands and muscles to prepare for fight or flight. At the same time, neural messages activate the adrenal gland to secrete the stress hormone adrenalin. The pituitary gland sends hormonal messages to the adrenal gland to secrete the stress hormones corticosteroids. The combined effects of these stress hormones prepare our bodies to face stressors.

alarm reaction the first phase of the general adaptation syndrome, characterized by immediate activation of the nervous and endocrine systems

resistance stage the second phase of the general adaptation syndrome, in which the nervous and endocrine systems continue to be activated

Recall from Chapter 2 that your nervous system has two branches: the central nervous system, consisting of the brain and the spinal cord, and the peripheral nervous system, including the somatic and autonomic divisions. The autonomic division includes two systems: the parasympathetic branch, which operates when we are calm and relaxed, and the sympathetic nervous system, our fight-or-flight mechanism that prepares us to face a threat in the environment. This sympathetic branch of the nervous system is at the heart of the stress response.

When a person perceives a threat in the environment—or what we have now referred to as a stressor—the sympathetic nervous system is activated. In order to prepare the body to deal with the stressor, the sympathetic nervous system works in conjunction with the endocrine (or hormonal) system. It stimulates the adrenal gland to secrete two hormones: adrenalin and corticosteroids. These hormones travel to the major organs (liver, heart, lungs) to prepare the body for fight or flight. Our heart rate and blood pressure increase, our lungs expand, and our liver releases stored sugars that can be used for energy. At the same time, the brain stimulates the pituitary gland to release endorphins, the body's natural painkillers. The body continues to expend these resources for as long as the stressor persists. Once the stressor passes, the brain turns off the sympathetic nervous system, which in turn shuts off the release of these stress hormones, and the body returns to its parasympathetic mode of calm and relaxation. However, if the stressor continues, the body enters the resistance stage.

Resistance Stage

During the **resistance stage**, the body continues its efforts to cope with the stressor. The sympathetic nervous system and endocrine system continue to be activated. However, the bodily reactions associated with resistance are less intense than the alarm reaction, as the body's resources begin to dwindle. When the body has drained its resources and energy is no longer available, we enter the exhaustion stage.

Exhaustion Stage

It is during the **exhaustion stage** that wear and tear on the body begins. High levels of adrenalin and corticosteroids in the body over a prolonged period of time damage the heart and lessen the effectiveness of the immune system. The result is that you become more vulnerable to heart disease, ulcers, high blood pressure, and colds and flus (S. Cohen, 1996; Doctor & Doctor, 1994; Kiecolt-Glaser et al., 2002; G. E. Miller & Blackwell, 2006; V. H. Rice, 2000). Excessive and prolonged exposure to stress hormones may also produce headaches, backaches, indigestion, constipation, diarrhea, fatigue, insomnia, mood swings, and muscle tension (R. Chou et al., 2007; De Benedittis, Lorenzetti, & Pieri, 1990; J. M. Nash & Thebarge, 2006).

Stress and the Immune System: Resistance to Disease

As we have seen, our body's reaction to stress, particularly during the exhaustion phase, can influence the effectiveness of our immune system. Researchers' interest in the connection between the immune system and stress generated a new field of study called **psychoneuroimmunology** that investigates the connections among psychology (behaviors, thoughts, emotions), the nervous system, and immune system functioning. The immune system is our body's best defense against illness because it destroys and fights bacteria, viruses, and other foreign substances that may invade our bodies. If this system is impaired, as in the case of prolonged stress, we are more prone to illness and disease (Kiecolt-Glaser, 2009; Webster Marketon & Glaser, 2008).

How does stress affect our immune system? The corticosteroids and endorphins that are released into our body during the stress response actually reduce and dampen the activity of our immune system. This effect is referred to as **immunosuppression**. Consequently, turning on our stress response, which ensures our ability to survive immediate danger, comes at the expense of our immune system, our long-term survival mechanism.

Much research supports the notion that stress suppresses the functioning of the immune system, which then increases the chances of developing infections such as the common cold (C. Anderson, 2003; S. Cohen, Tyrrell, & Smith, 1991; Kiecolt-Glaser et al., 2002; V. H. Rice, 2000). During final exam time and other periods of academic pressure, students show a weakened immune system (Chandrashekara et al., 2007; D. G. Gilbert et al., 1996; Jemmott et al., 1985). This effect may explain why you catch a cold or are more likely to experience allergies and sinus infections during finals week or when you have several projects or papers due at the same time. Immunosuppression also occurs in both men and women following the death of a spouse or partner (Beem et al., 1999; Schleifer et al., 1983) and in people going through separation and divorce (Kiecolt-Glaser et al., 2003). People who are caregivers for someone with a terminal disease or dementia experience chronic stress that also results in immunosuppression (Damjanovic et al., 2007; Kiecolt-Glaser et al., 1995; Vitaliano et al., 1998; Vitaliano, Young, & Zhang, 2004). Lower socioeconomic status and family chaos are related to higher stress hormones in children, which may increase their risk of later health problems (Chen, Cohen, & Miller, 2010).

More serious, though, is the correlation among stress, the immune system, and cancer. Most people's initial reaction to a cancer diagnosis is panic, anger, or depression—emotions that activate the stress response and momentarily retard immune system functioning (Ader, 2001). Moreover, our response and attitude toward having cancer may influence the eventual spread and fatality of the disease. For example, emotional distress in breast cancer patients is associated with a lower survival rate (Luecken & Compas, 2002; R. H. Osborne et al., 2004). Patients who express their emotions about the disease—both positive and negative—tend to have a higher chance of survival than patients who hold in their emotions (Lehto et al., 2006; P. Reynolds et al., 2000; Temoshok, 1992). Similarly, cancer patients with an optimistic attitude who are determined to beat the disease often outlive patients with a less positive attitude (C. S. Carver et al., 2000; S. Gilbert, 1998; Shen, McCreary, & Myers, 2004). Notice that this research does not say that stress *causes* cancer but, rather, that stress may influence the rate at which cancer cells grow. If your immune system is functioning at reduced levels during times of stress, it is less available to fight these life-threatening cells.

To illustrate, let's use these research findings to analyze the opening case study. The initial diagnosis of cancer may have made Edward's body even more susceptible to the growth of cancer cells. His attitude and inability to express his feelings about the illness may have hampered his body's defense against the cancer. Consequently, Edward's ultimate decline over a 3-year period may have been related to his reactions to the cancer diagnosis, which in turn impaired the functioning of his immune system. These research findings also may account for Joan's eventual cancer diagnosis. Being widowed at a relatively young

exhaustion stage the third and final phase of the general adaptation syndrome, in which bodily resources are drained, and wear and tear on the body begins

psychoneuroimmunology field of study that investigates the connections among psychology (behaviors, thoughts, emotions), the nervous system, and immune system functioning

immunosuppression the reduction in activity of the immune system

Caring for a loved one is a highly stressful experience that can reduce the effectiveness of our immune system and make us more vulnerable to illness.

age may have increased her susceptibility to cancer. However, Joan's reaction to the illness was much different from her husband's. She was more optimistic and hopeful about beating the cancer than he was. This attitude may account for why she developed a milder form of cancer and survived longer with generally the same type of illness.

We are by no means saying that surviving or not surviving cancer is totally up to the individual. The onset, course, and magnitude of cancer in patients are influenced by variables that include one's genetics, the type of cancer, when it is detected, social support, and the treatments available. Our attitude about developing cancer and receiving cancer treatment is only one factor among many to consider when examining the connection between stress and health. Moreover, there is virtually no scientific evidence that our mental state *causes* cancer or that our mental state *cures* cancer.

We don't yet understand the exact relationship between stress, cancer, and immune system functioning. Some research suggests that low to moderate stress can *enhance* immune system functioning (Bosch et al., 2001; Dhabhar et al., 1995). Current studies also speculate that chronic stress leads to an imbalance in our immune system, in which some immune responses are suppressed while others are enhanced; it is this disruption of the normal balance in our immune system that increases our vulnerability to illness and disease (Robles, Glaser, & Kiecolt-Glaser, 2005; Segerstrom, 2007). Moreover, the exact nature of our physical response to stress depends on the specific stressors and our cognitive appraisals of those stressors (Kemeny, 2003). We look to future research to fill in the blanks and make our knowledge more complete.

Let's REVIEW

In this section we discussed how we appraise stress, the body's response to stress, and the relationship between stress and the functioning of our immune system. As a quick review, try answering the following questions at increasing levels of difficulty.

1. Immunosuppression refers to _____.
   a. the activation of the immune system when we are faced with a stressor
   b. a reduction in the activity of the immune system
   c. the immune system's ability to survive immediate danger
   d. the release of endorphins and corticosteroids to help the immune system function

2. You are more vulnerable to illness during which stage of Selye's stress response model?
   a. alarm reaction   c. rejuvenation
   b. resistance   d. exhaustion

3. The first step in experiencing stress is _____.
   a. the alarm reaction   c. primary appraisal
   b. resistance   d. exhaustion

ANSWERS 1. b; 2. d; 3. c

LEARNING OBJECTIVES

What Should You Know?
- Distinguish between problem-focused and emotion-focused coping styles.
- Indicate adaptive ways to manage stress.

HOW CAN I COPE WITH STRESS?

How do we cope with stress? Think of the exam or exams you will take for this course. Does your body evidence the telltale signs of the stress response when thinking about your exam? What do you do when faced with stress like this? Are you likely to react emotionally, becoming very anxious and worrying about what the test will be like? Are you likely to tackle the stressor directly, focusing all your energy on studying and preparing for the exam? Or do you simply ignore your stress, hoping for a miracle such as postponement or cancellation of the exam? Maybe you experience some or all of these reactions.

Whatever you do to manage an event or stimulus that you perceive as threatening is part of **coping**. How we cope with stress influences the way stress affects us. We will discuss two

coping the behaviors that we engage in to manage stressors

broad types of strategies for coping: *problem-focused coping* and *emotion-focused coping* (Folkman & Lazarus, 1988). You may use one or both types of coping when you're faced with a stressor. Each has its benefits and costs (Lazarus & Folkman, 1984; Roth & Cohen, 1986).

Problem-Focused Coping: Change the Situation

Problem-focused coping is aimed at controlling or altering the environment that is causing the stress. Let's say, for example, that you are working while going to school and your boss just increased your work hours. You now feel that you don't have enough time for school or your social life. A problem-focused approach to coping with this increased workload may include finding another job without as many required hours or reducing the number of credit hours you are taking in school. Both these strategies are aimed at changing the situation to reduce the amount of perceived stress. One benefit of either of these problem-focused coping strategies would be elimination of the perceived stressor. At the same time, you benefit by experiencing more control over your environment, which may also enhance your self-esteem. However, it is also possible that you have misdiagnosed the problem, which is a cost of problem-focused coping. Maybe the number of work hours isn't affecting your college work so much as your motivation or your social schedule is. You may actually increase your long-term level of stress by choosing an inappropriate course of action. For example, reducing your college hours increases the time it will take to complete your college education. Alternately, changing jobs may result in lower wages, making it more difficult to pay for your education.

Generally, problem-focused coping tends to be most useful when we feel that we can actually do something about a situation (Folkman & Moskowitz, 2000). Under these circumstances, problem-focused coping is more likely to lead to a more positive health outcome (Largo-Wight, Peterson, & Chen, 2005; Penley, Tomaka, & Wiebe, 2002; M. C. Smith & Dust, 2006). However, when we do not feel that a situation is controllable, we often rely more on emotion-focused coping strategies (Lazarus, 1993).

Emotion-Focused Coping: Change Your Reaction

Emotion-focused coping is aimed at controlling your internal, subjective, emotional reactions to stress. You alter the way you feel or think in order to reduce stress. Stressors activate a variety of emotions, including anxiety, worry, guilt, shame, jealousy, envy, and anger. Because these emotions are usually experienced as unpleasant, we are motivated to reduce or avoid them. For example, suppose that a young woman is anticipating the arrival of her partner at a party where they planned to meet, and he is already an hour late. The stress of this situation not only activates the physical sensations that we have discussed previously but also triggers emotional reactions. She may be angry with him because she feels that he is purposely ignoring her. She may take her anger out on a friend, or she may turn all her emotional energy into being the life of the party. Conversely, she may experience anxiety and worry, fearing that something harmful has happened to him. When he arrives, she may express her anger by complaining about his lateness or by ignoring him altogether, or she may be especially loving and attentive. Either way, her coping behavior is directed at reducing the emotions that she is experiencing.

We attempt to lessen the effects of these emotions in two ways: by engaging in *cognitive reappraisal* and by using psychological *defense mechanisms*. **Cognitive reappraisal** is an active and conscious process in which we alter our interpretation of the stressful event. In the previous example, the young woman has appraised her partner's lateness in a negative

problem-focused coping behaviors that aim to control or alter the environment that is causing stress

emotion-focused coping behaviors aimed at controlling the internal emotional reactions to a stressor

cognitive reappraisal an active and conscious process in which we alter our interpretation of a stressful event

Taking your anger out on someone to relieve stress is an example of emotion-focused coping.

Jetta Productions/Getty Images

manner (he's ignoring her or something bad has happened to him). These appraisals have led to feelings of anger and anxiety. She can reappraise or reinterpret his lateness in a more realistic manner—he got caught in traffic or he had to work late. These reappraisals are less likely to lead to emotional distress. Thus, cognitive reappraisal can be an emotionally constructive way of coping with a stressful event (Mauss et al., 2007; Ray, Wilhelm, & Gross, 2008). In one study, positive reappraisal even led to less immunosuppression during a chronic stress period (Koh et al., 2006).

A more automatic and unconscious way in which we lessen the effects of our emotions is by using **defense mechanisms**. Sigmund Freud was one of the first theorists to identify psychological defense mechanisms. You will learn more about Freud's ideas on personality and coping in Chapter 13. For now, what is relevant is that Freud suggested that coping strategies are employed unconsciously to allow us to reduce our anxiety and maintain a positive self-image and self-esteem. Because of these features, we now consider these defense mechanisms emotion-focused coping strategies. We use them to avoid or reduce the emotions associated with a stressor, but they do not necessarily eliminate the source of stress. For example, you might use the defense mechanism of *displacement* to deal with your anger toward a boss, a parent, or a significant other. You take your anger out on a friend by yelling at her or on an object by throwing it against the wall. Afterward, you may *feel* better, but it does not resolve the issue that made you angry in the first place. The stressor is still present and may resurface again in the future.

Everyone uses defense mechanisms from time to time. Some of these defense mechanisms are adaptive. Directing your anger into a more constructive activity such as washing your car is more productive than hurting someone else (see sublimation in ● TABLE 12.3). Other defense mechanisms, especially when we use them to excess, can prevent us from developing effective ways of coping. For example, the student who fails to study for a test may decide that his roommate who watches television is at fault. Such a defense on the part of the student does not promote an adaptive way of coping with failure. The more common defense mechanisms are displayed in Table 12.3. See if you can identify the defense mechanisms that you tend to use.

defense mechanisms unconscious, emotional strategies that are engaged in to reduce anxiety and maintain a positive self-image

TABLE 12.3

● **Common Defense Mechanisms**

DEFENSE MECHANISM	DEFINITION	EXAMPLES
Denial	Refusing to accept or acknowledge the reality of a situation or idea	Going out partying the night before an exam denies how this behavior will affect your exam performance. Having unprotected sex denies the possibility of experiencing an unwanted pregnancy or contracting an STI.
Rationalization	Devising a plausible reason or motive to explain one's behavior	You rationalize your excessive consumption of alcohol by saying it makes you more sociable or improves your personality.
Reaction Formation	Engaging in a behavior or attitude that is at the opposite extreme of one's true motive or impulse	A young boy pulls the ponytail of the girl sitting in front of him, behaving aggressively to cover up the opposite emotion—liking her. After seeing someone at the mall whom you dislike, you approach and say warmly, "Hi. How have you been? You look great!"
Regression	Returning to an earlier stage of development in one's behavior, thinking, or attitudes	Adults who throw tantrums, pout, or whine are engaging in childlike behaviors. An older child may react to the birth of a sibling by wetting the bed or sucking her thumb again.
Sublimation	Directing emotions into an activity that is more constructive and socially acceptable	Some people exercise or clean their room when they are angry or upset. Others direct their emotions into writing, sculpting, playing music, or painting.
Repression	Excluding wishes, impulses, ideas, or memories from consciousness	A person may forget the details of an accident, crime, or other situation associated with trauma or harm.
Projection	Attributing one's own ideas, feelings, or attitudes to other people	You accuse another student of brown-nosing the professor when in reality it is you who engage in this behavior. A person in a relationship may accuse his partner of wanting to date other people when this is his own desire.
Displacement	Directing emotions toward a less-threatening source	You yell at your partner after an argument with your boss. An athlete throws objects or kicks the bench after a missed play.

The use of defense mechanisms involves costs and benefits. The main reason we use them is to restore our self-image. We also benefit because defense mechanisms reduce anxiety. They may also give us the confidence to handle additional stressors. However, the benefits of defense mechanisms are typically outweighed by the costs. Defense mechanisms often inhibit our ability to resolve a problem. Using our emotions to cope with stressors may impede our functioning in other daily activities—yelling at our friends too often may drive them away. Most important, using defense mechanisms keeps us in a state of unawareness as to the true source of any stress-related symptoms. Given these disadvantages, why do we continue to use defense mechanisms? Basically, they are easier and produce quicker results in reducing our feelings of anxiety. Unfortunately, these advantages are often at the expense of our well-being as we may experience more distress and negative mood over the long run (Littleton et al., 2007; O'Brien, Terry, & Jimmieson, 2008).

Managing Stress

What are effective ways to manage stress? A discussion of stress would by no means be complete without detailing effective means by which to handle or manage stress. Because stress affects our health, considerable research has addressed what strategies may reduce our risk of illness and disease. These techniques all focus on changing one or more aspects of the stress response: your physical reactions, your emotional reactions, your thoughts or appraisal of events (cognitive), and your responses (behavioral). Many of these methods address both problem-focused and emotion-focused coping.

Physical Methods of Stress Management

Physical methods of stress management focus on managing the body's fight-or-flight mechanism. As we have seen, the stress response entails the activation of the sympathetic nervous system, which makes our bodies tense and prepared to respond to a threatening situation. In the face of chronic stress, we reach exhaustion, having depleted the body's resources. This exhaustion can lead to immunosuppression and increased risk of illness. However, when we are able to release this tension, we allow the body to replenish its resources, and these ill effects are less likely to occur. Releasing physical tension can be achieved in several ways.

- *Exercise.* Some form of regular aerobic exercise, such as swimming, walking, running, or dancing, can be an effective strategy for reducing physical stress reactions (Anshel, 1995; Langreth, 2000; Stear, 2003). Exercise reduces negative emotions such as depression and anxiety that we often feel in response to stress (Brugman & Ferguson, 2002; Long & van Stavel, 1995). Exercise raises energy levels, strengthens the heart, and lowers muscle tension. We sleep more soundly after exercise and also feel better as the body increases its production of natural mood elevators like serotonin and endorphins (Chapter 2).
- *Use biofeedback.* Until the 1960s, most scientists believed that the bodily reactions involved in the stress response were totally involuntary—not under our control. In the past 40 years, several electronic devices have been created that can measure and record these bodily changes. Referred to as **biofeedback**, training on these devices can increase your awareness of bodily reactions and may enable you to increase control over them. Biofeedback training has been somewhat successful for people experiencing migraine and tension headaches (Buse & Andrasik, 2009; Landy, 2004; McGrady, Bush, & Grubb, 1997; Rokicki et al., 1997), asthma (Lehrer et al., 2002), incontinence (Ozturk et al., 2004), and hypertension (Moravec, 2008).
- *Relax.* One of the most successful nonchemical ways to manage stress is through the application of relaxation techniques. Such methods may include **progressive relaxation training**, in which you learn to alternately tense and then relax each muscle group of the body in a systematic fashion. This activity gives you

biofeedback an electronic device that measures and records bodily changes so that an individual can monitor and control these changes more effectively

progressive relaxation training a stress management technique in which a person learns how to systematically tense and relax muscle groups in the body

Biofeedback training helps you manage stress by making you aware of your bodily reactions to perceived stressors, then teaching you to use this awareness to control your stress reactions.

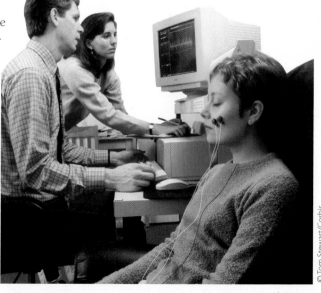

an awareness of when and where you feel tension when you're under stress. You then learn to manage and control the tension that you feel by relaxing on command. Other relaxation techniques may include regular massages, meditation, yoga, deep breathing exercises, engaging in a hobby, or listening to music.

Relaxing the body breaks up the stress response, moderates its intensity, and helps the body return to homeostasis (Stoyva & Budzynski, 1974). Daily use of relaxation procedures is effective in lessening symptoms of asthma, insomnia, headaches, rheumatoid arthritis, high blood pressure, chronic pain conditions, intestinal problems, and chronic anxiety (Astin, 2004; Benson, 1996; Fumal & Schoenen, 2008; Lebovits, 2007; McCallie, Blum, & Hood, 2006; Meissner, Blanchard, & Malamood, 1997; Ostelo et al., 2007; Smyth et al., 2001).

Emotional Methods of Stress Management

Emotional methods of stress management center on our connections with others. Being connected with others helps us manage our emotions of worry and anxiety that often accompany feelings of stress. Two examples include social support and spirituality.

● *Develop social support.* Having friends, a shoulder to cry on, or someone to discuss an issue or trying event with are all examples of **social support**—having close and positive relationships with others. Social support buffers the effects of stress (S. Cohen et al., 2003; E. Diener & Seligman, 2004; Shields, 2004; Uchino, 2009; Wills & Fegan, 2001). Family stability, a partner's support, or simply having friends to confide in is related to a longer life span as well as a longer survival rate for those with cancer or heart disease (Antoni & Lutgendorf, 2007; S. Cohen & Janicki-Deverts, 2009; Hawkley & Cacioppo, 2007; Krantz & McCeney, 2002; Shen et al., 2004). Even giving social support to others appears to buffer the effects of stress (S. L. Brown et al., 2003). Social support also may act to decrease the release of stress hormones and reverse stress-induced immune responses (Eisenberger et al., 2007; Koh et al., 2006; Pressman et al., 2005; Uchino, Cacioppo, & Kiecolt-Glaser, 1996).

How does social support reduce stress? We don't yet understand exact causal mechanisms for the relationship between social support and health. Perhaps a social network promotes more self-disclosure and expression of feelings, which makes us feel better (R. M. Kowalski, 1996; Lepore, Ragan, & Jones, 2000). Perhaps being loved and liked enhances self-esteem and encourages a sense of purpose and optimism toward life. A biobehavioral model suggests that a hormone called *oxytocin* is released in response to some stressors that prompts us to seek out others, which helps us weather stress (S. E. Taylor, 2006). Social support may provide a combination of these effects. Only future research will tell.

social support having close and positive relationships with others

---

Having close relationships with others helps us weather stress.

Leonora Hamill/Getty Images

● *Be spiritual.* Spiritual faith, prayer, church or temple membership, and strong value systems promote physical health and well-being (Hawks et al., 1995; McCullough et al., 2000; W. R. Miller & Thoresen, 2003; L. H. Powell, Shahabi, & Thoresen, 2003). Spirituality often means having a purpose in life, self-awareness, and connectedness with self, others, and a larger community. Religiousness is typically defined as participation in an institutionalized doctrine. For example, several studies have found that prayer and spirituality are associated with reduced symptoms of distress in cancer patients (Laubmeier, Zakowski, & Bair, 2004; E. J. Taylor & Outlaw, 2002). Religiousness and spirituality have also been shown to be significantly associated with reduced symptoms in people with serious mental illness (Corrigan et al., 2003). One study found a relationship between prayer and better health, but only among less educated and, to a lesser extent, lower-income people (Banthia et al., 2007).

How do religion and spirituality promote health? We don't yet know the reason for these associations. Religion, spirituality, and health are correlated. We cannot conclude that religiousness or spirituality causes better health. Which, if any, specific religious or spiritual factors enhance health and well-being remains unclear. Many of the studies have significant methodological flaws, and they define religion and spirituality in an assortment of ways (P. C. Hill & Pargament, 2003; Sloan & Bagiella, 2002). As more sound research is conducted, psychologists will be able to uncover the distinct contribution of religion and spirituality to health and well-being.

Cognitive Methods of Stress Management

Another group of stress management techniques focuses on changing how we think about or appraise our situations. We can reduce the effects of stress by using our cognitions either to promote relaxation or to change the way we view the world.

The stress management technique of guided imagery involves using your mind to achieve a state of relaxation. Whenever you feel stressed, you focus on a pleasant, calming environment like the image shown here to relieve bodily tensions and promote relaxation.

- *Imagine a calm environment.* **Guided imagery** is a technique in which you learn to use your mind to achieve a state of relaxation. You imagine that you are in a safe, pleasant, calming environment, perhaps walking along a beach or in a forest. You maintain your focus on this image as you feel the tensions associated with stress leave your body. Similar to progressive relaxation, you become trained to automatically summon this image when you feel stressed. Guided imagery is effective in managing chronic pain and headaches (Lebovits, 2007; Tsao & Zeltzer, 2005). For some people, guided imagery is just as effective as the relaxation techniques discussed previously (Astin, 2004). Can you think of your own image, scene, or memory that would provide these benefits for you? How does your body feel as you think about it?

- *Meditate.* **Meditation** in the form of yoga, Zen, or transcendental meditation also may reduce tension and anxiety caused by stress (Andresen, 2000; Grossman et al., 2004; Paul, Elam, & Verhulst, 2007). These practices are mental exercises in which people consciously focus their attention to heighten awareness and bring their mental processes under more control. Meditation appears to decrease heart rate, respiration, and oxygen consumption (Carrington, 1993; Tang et al., 2009). Some studies have also found that meditation can improve mood, lessen tiredness, and enhance immune system responses (Fan et al., 2010; Solberg, Halvorsen, & Holen, 2000). Isolating the key element common to the different meditation practices may help us draw more solid conclusions on the specific health benefits of meditation (Xiong & Doraiswamy, 2009).

guided imagery a technique in which you focus on a pleasant, calming image to achieve a state of relaxation when you feel stressed

meditation mental exercises in which people consciously focus their attention to heighten awareness and bring their mental processes under more control

Yoga helps manage stress by exercising the body, promoting relaxation, and clearing the mind.

- *Be optimistic.* Simply expecting good things to happen may influence your health. For example, in a study on first-year law students, those students who endorsed optimistic beliefs, such as believing they could succeed and having confidence about their abilities, had better immune system functioning across the semester than did students with a more pessimistic outlook (Segerstrom & Sephton, 2010). Optimists report lower stress levels and have fewer stress-related physical complaints (Finkelstein et al., 2007; C. Peterson, 2000; C. Peterson & Bossio, 2001; Pritchard, Wilson, & Yamnitz, 2007). Cancer and heart disease patients with an optimistic attitude often show a better response to treatment than patients with a less positive attitude (C. S. Carver et al., 2000; Shen et al., 2004). Focusing on the half of the glass that is full is better for your health than focusing on the half that is empty.

Behavioral Methods of Stress Management

In addition to changing your thoughts, physical reactions, and emotional responses, you can engage in certain behaviors that reduce the influence of stress on your health.

© Picturequest/Jupiter Images

Laughter promotes relaxation, which helps manage stress levels.

- *Laugh.* Laughter promotes relaxation, which may explain why good-humored people perceive less stress when faced with life's challenges (Lefcourt, 2001; Lefcourt & Davidson-Katz, 1991). Laughter may buffer stress by reducing blood pressure, increasing deep breathing, boosting the immune system, increasing feelings of well-being, and raising energy levels (M. P. Bennett et al., 2003; Christie & Moore, 2005). Any one or all of these factors may be responsible for the positive health effects.

- *Manage your time wisely.* Many of us experience stress because we feel that there is not enough time to accomplish all the tasks, errands, and work that we have established for ourselves. One way to minimize the stress resulting from such pressures is to organize your time better. Keeping a daily planner or formal time schedule to record your obligations, commitments, and deadlines for study, work, and leisure activities can ease tension. Remembering to schedule time with loved ones (social support), time for exercise, and time to simply relax will provide further ammunition against stress. Writing out a formal time schedule also allows you to evaluate the number and importance of your commitments. Prioritizing your activities and possibly reducing their number illustrates problem-focused coping strategies. Be sure to schedule *enough* time for activities, factoring in travel time (and traffic). One of the most common time management mistakes that college students make is not allowing enough time to study all the assigned material (Buehler, Griffin, & Ross, 1994). The key to effective time management is to treat each responsibility—whether work, study, or play—as a serious commitment.

- THE BIG PICTURE REVIEW summarizes the techniques that can be used to reduce the effects of stress. How many do you use? Could you use more of them? By using these methods, you have the opportunity to reduce the ill effects of stress on your health right now, as well as the cumulative effect of stress on your body in the future. However, if you sometimes feel that you cannot manage the stress in your life, or you aren't coping well with your stressors, then it may be time to seek professional help. Chapter 15 describes the different types of mental health professionals who can help us cope more effectively.

Let's REVIEW

In this section we distinguished between problem-focused and emotion-focused coping and described some stress management techniques. For a quick review, try answering the following questions at increasing levels of difficulty.

1. Organizing your time better would be best classified as a(n) _____ coping skill.

   a. problem-focused   c. avoidance-focused

   b. emotion-focused   d. encounter-focused

2. It is common for young children to react to the birth of a sibling by regressing to earlier behaviors such as sucking their thumb again or wanting to feed from a bottle. Such behaviors exemplify _____ coping skills.

   a. problem-focused   c. avoidance-focused

   b. emotion-focused   d. encounter-focused

3. Which of the following is the *least* effective stress management technique?

   a. guided imagery   c. defense mechanisms

   b. physical exercise   d. relaxation techniques

ANSWERS 1. a; 2. b; 3. c

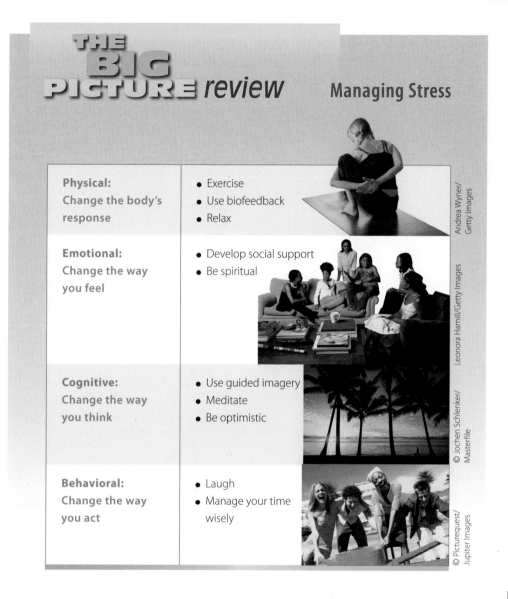

THE BIG PICTURE *review* — Managing Stress

Physical: Change the body's response	• Exercise • Use biofeedback • Relax
Emotional: Change the way you feel	• Develop social support • Be spiritual
Cognitive: Change the way you think	• Use guided imagery • Meditate • Be optimistic
Behavioral: Change the way you act	• Laugh • Manage your time wisely

Andrea Wyner/Getty Images

Leonora Hamill/Getty Images

© Jochen Schlenker/Masterfile

© Picturequest/Jupiter Images

LEARNING OBJECTIVE

What Should You Know?
● Discuss the relationship between personality and health.

DOES YOUR PERSONALITY INFLUENCE YOUR HEALTH?

Think about Edward from the opening case study. Is it possible that his personality made him more susceptible to disease? If so, which particular features of his personality do you think might be critical? Health psychologists have also been interested in how personality influences our health. A number of personality dimensions have been related to health—specifically, to the functioning of our cardiovascular and immune systems (Segerstrom, 2000; T. W. Smith, 2006). We consider three such avenues of research here: the *Type A personality*, *learned helplessness*, and the *hardy personality*.

Type A Personality: Ambition, Drive, and Competitiveness

Take a moment to look at ● TABLE 12.4. Which of these descriptions more accurately reflects your personality? Would you consider yourself more of a **Type A personality**, a person who is aggressive, competitive, and driven to achieve? Or do you characterize yourself as more of a **Type B personality**, a person who is more relaxed, easygoing, patient, and flexible? Or do you consider yourself more like a **Type C personality**, a relatively new category describing a person who is cautious, careful, and overly patient and nice, and who avoids conflict and suppresses negative emotions such as anger? Edward probably fit the Type A description more than the Type B or Type C. Could this have been a possible factor in his illness?

Type A personality a personality that is aggressive, ambitious, and competitive

Type B personality a personality characterized by patience, flexibility, and an easygoing manner

Type C personality a personality that is cautious, serious, sensitive to criticism, and results oriented and that suppresses negative emotions such as anger

TABLE 12.4

● **The ABCs of Personality: Which Type Are You?**

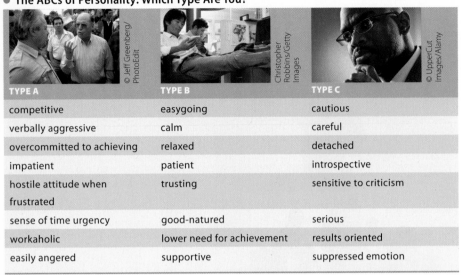

TYPE A	TYPE B	TYPE C
competitive	easygoing	cautious
verbally aggressive	calm	careful
overcommitted to achieving	relaxed	detached
impatient	patient	introspective
hostile attitude when frustrated	trusting	sensitive to criticism
sense of time urgency	good-natured	serious
workaholic	lower need for achievement	results oriented
easily angered	supportive	suppressed emotion

At one time, having a Type A personality was considered a risk factor for heart disease. Cardiologists Meyer Friedman and Ray Rosenman (1974) were the first to examine the connection between personality and heart disease. They suspected that personality or behavior patterns might play a role in the lives of men who were more likely to develop heart disease or more likely to die from a heart attack. To test their idea, the researchers gathered a sample of 3,000 men between the ages of 35 and 59 with no known health problems. Each man was interviewed, and based on his behavior during the interview, each was designated a Type A personality, a Type B personality, or somewhere in between. A label of Type A or Type B was given to those men who very much exemplified those traits listed in Table 12.4. The majority of the sample fell somewhere in between, but in comparing the two types, Friedman and Rosenman found that over the next decade those with Type A personalities were 2 to 3 times more likely to suffer a heart attack. Keep in mind that the majority of the sample could not easily be categorized as either Type A or Type B.

Friedman and Rosenman's landmark study stimulated additional research on how personality factors may place people at risk for disease. However, subsequent research on the connection between Type A personality and the risk of heart disease has not been able to replicate these results (Booth-Kewley & Friedman, 1987; T. Q. Miller et al., 1991). Given the broad definitions of Type A and Type B personalities, this disparity should not be surprising, especially when Friedman and Rosenman themselves had difficulty in classifying their sample. Later research attempted to isolate which specific aspects of the Type A personality might predispose a person to heart problems. The key features include anger, mistrust, and hostility. People who are frequently angry, suspicious, bitter, antagonistic, and distrustful of others seem more likely to experience heart-related health problems and have a shorter life span (Denollet, 1993; Krantz & McCeney, 2002; T. Q. Miller et al., 1996; B. W. Roberts et al., 2007; T. W. Smith et al., 2004; J. E. Williams et al., 2000; R. Williams, 1993). People with a Type A personality who do not show these specific behaviors appear to be no more at risk for heart disease than their Type B counterparts.

Research continues to investigate the precise relationship between hostility, anger, and heart disease. For example, perhaps the culprit is the increased stress level and lack of social support that goes along with being a hostile person (Helmers et al., 1995). Efforts to modify Type A behavior as a means of reducing repeat heart attacks have achieved modest success (Friedman et al., 1984; Nakano, 1996). Yet in one follow-up study of patients who had already experienced heart attacks, although Type A behavior was associated with a greater probability of a second heart attack, Type B behavior was associated with a greater probability of death (Catipovic-Veselica et al., 2001). Such a finding argues against modifying Type A behavior following a heart attack. Our U.S. culture highly values achievement and competition, fostering emotions such as anger and pride. In contrast, collectivist cultures (see Chapter 11) such as Japan encourage engaging emotions such as friendliness and guilt. Expressing anger rather than suppressing it may in some instances be associated with a feeling of well-being, especially in cases where one's anger in a situation is justifiable (Kitayama, Mesquita, & Karasawa, 2006). One's culture may teach this behavior pattern of expressing anger at a very early age, which makes it difficult to change before people develop heart disease.

Research on the Type C or cancer-prone personality has proceeded in a similar fashion. That is, at one time having a Type C personality was suggested as a major factor in the development of cancer, specifically breast cancer in women (see Scheier & Bridges, 1995, for review). However, subsequent research suggests that it is the suppression or denial of anger, one specific aspect of the Type C personality, that may put a woman more at risk for breast cancer. There is little evidence for a so-called cancer-prone personality; yet a modest to weak relationship has been found between not expressing one's negative emotions and the risk of breast cancer (Bleiker et al., 2008; Bleiker et al., 1996; Butow et al., 2000; McKenna et al., 1999).

Learned Helplessness: I Can't Do It

Do you believe that you have no control over stressful life events? Do you believe that even your best efforts will result in failure? When you blame yourself for any failure you experience, are you more likely to attribute your failure to a specific factor—you're just not good at soccer—or to a more global feature—you're just too uncoordinated to do any athletic activity? These questions illustrate the key features of a personality factor called **learned helplessness**, in which people develop a passive response to stressors based on their exposure to previously uncontrolled, negative events.

Learned helplessness was first demonstrated in dogs in a psychological laboratory (Seligman & Maier, 1967). The dogs were placed in a cage that was equipped with an electrified grid. When the dogs received a shock they could not escape from, after repeated trials, the dogs' escape responses slowly decreased. Recall from Chapter 5 that this decrease in responding is called *extinction*. Even when they were later given the opportunity to escape the shock, the dogs remained in the cage. The dogs had learned to be helpless. Experiments using human participants (not using shock) have produced similar results (Hiroto, 1974; W. R. Miller & Seligman, 1975). Consequently, when previous experiences lead you to believe that you cannot "fix" the problems facing you, you may approach new situations with this perceived lack of control and passively endure whatever comes your way (Dweck, Chiu, & Hong, 1995; C. Peterson, Maier, & Seligman, 1993). You are likely to view stressors as threats rather than as challenges. As a result, your levels of stress increase, and you are more likely to develop stress-related physical illnesses (Overmier, 2002; S. L. Stern, Dhanda, & Hazuda, 2009; G. S. Stern, McCants, & Pettine, 1982).

Research supports the notion that college students who feel helpless are less likely to persist and more likely to give up easily; as a result, they earn poor grades and report unhappiness (Fazio & Palm, 1998; McKean, 1994). Adults and adolescents who react to stress by feeling at a loss to do anything about the situation are more prone to depression and other stress problems (C. Diener et al., 2009; Haack et al., 1996; Waschbusch et al., 2003). Learned helplessness has also been documented in children with a history of reading failure (Fowler & Peterson, 1981). It can develop in elderly people in nursing homes who are not given choices about their daily activities and routines (Seligman, 1989). In all these situations, the *expectation* of failure and lack of control is what influences one's perceived level of stress, one's subsequent response to stress, and ultimately, one's mental and physical health. In analyzing the opening case study, it is possible that once Edward was told that his disease was no longer manageable, he adopted an attitude of learned helplessness. This attitude may have contributed to the continued spread of the disease.

The Hardy Personality: Control, Commitment, and Challenge

Do you view stressors as challenges or as threats? For example, if you try out for the tennis team one year and don't make it, do you try out again the next year, or do you simply give up? Do you stay committed to the pursuit of your goals and values? If you fail an exam, do you get help, or do you just assume that you'll never understand the material and withdraw from the class? Do you believe that your actions

learned helplessness a passive response to stressors based on exposure to previously uncontrolled, negative events

If you fail an exam, do you get help, or do you just assume that you'll never understand the material and withdraw from the class? Expecting to fail and believing you have no control over the outcome of events are key qualities of learned helplessness.

Digital Vision/Getty Images

influence the outcome of a situation? Your answers to these questions outline three factors that appear to be related to health: challenge, commitment, and control.

● The tendency to see life as a series of *challenges*
● A sense of personal *commitment* to self, work, family, and other values
● A perception of *control* over life and work

The "three Cs" taken together were labeled by psychologists Salvatore Maddi and Suzanne Kobasa (1984) as the **hardy personality**.

This term resulted from Kobasa's (1982) research on upper-level executives and attorneys who had experienced considerable stress over a 3-year period. Those who exemplified hardy traits were less likely to get ill during this time of stress. Even Type A people who scored high on measures of hardiness were less likely to get ill than Type A people who scored low on hardiness. This result led Kobasa to conclude that hardiness traits may decrease stress levels, thereby decreasing one's chances of developing illness.

Psychological research confirms that hardy people seem to be unusually resistant to stress (Bonanno, 2004; Maddi, 2005). They endorse a positive worldview in which stressors are appraised as challenges rather than threats, so they feel less potential harm from them. Notice that these qualities are in direct contrast to learned helplessness. This positive attitude appears to promote more problem-focused coping, enabling such people to handle conflict better and be more willing to rely on the help of others when weathering stress (Maddi et al., 2006; Scheir & Carver, 1992). Hardy people also report higher levels of personal satisfaction with their work (Rush, Schoel, & Barnard, 1995) and show greater immune system responses to bacteria (Dolbier et al., 2001).

 Taken together, what does all this research on personality tell us? First, we can recognize that how one expresses negative emotions such as anger and hostility can influence one's health. Frequent anger and hostility as well as suppressing one's negative emotions do not promote good health. Similarly, negative cognitions such as expecting failure or a lack of control do not appear to be good for our health. In contrast, the "three Cs" of hardiness—a sense of control, being comfortable with challenge, and maintaining commitment—appear to be most beneficial to our ability to deal with stress and therefore most advantageous to our health.

hardy personality a personality, high in the traits of commitment, control, and challenge, that appears to be associated with strong stress resistance

After surviving a shark attack in which she lost her left arm, Bethany Hamilton still perceives life as a challenge. She overcame her debilitating injury and has returned to surfing. She exemplifies the three traits of a hardy personality.

David Gregerson/Sport
Studio Photos/Getty Images

Let's
REVIEW In this section we detailed research investigating the relationship between personality and health. As a quick review, try answering the following questions at increasing levels of difficulty.

1. Donald is described by his friends as easygoing, calm, and patient. Donald would most likely be classified as a _____.

   a. Type A personality
   b. Type B personality
   c. hardy personality
   d. learned helplessness personality

2. After working on a project for more than 3 years, Zilmarie is told by her boss to redesign the project in a new way. Zilmarie considers such a task a challenge and commits herself to the new project with gusto. Zilmarie is probably high on which personality dimension?

   a. Type A personality
   b. Type B personality
   c. Hardiness
   d. Learned helplessness

3. Which of the following personality factors has been strongly linked to depression and other stress problems?

   a. Type A traits
   b. Type B traits
   c. Hardiness
   d. Learned helplessness

ANSWERS 1. b; 2. c; 3. d

WHAT BEHAVIORS PROMOTE HEALTH AND WELL-BEING?

LEARNING OBJECTIVES

What Should You Know?
- Identify health-defeating and health-promoting behaviors.
- Identify the five factors that contribute to happiness and well-being.

Health psychologists also examine lifestyle and environmental factors that may play a role in our susceptibility to illness and disease. Considerable research has examined voluntary lifestyle behaviors that put us at higher risk for illness and disease. However, health is also a positive state that can be fostered by lifestyle choices. Consistent with this view, research over the past decade in the field of *positive psychology* describes those factors that contribute to happiness and well-being (Ruark, 2009; Wallis, 2005).

HEALTH-DEFEATING BEHAVIORS

We already have seen that high levels of stress may increase our chances of illness. Some of these events may or may not be under your control. Health psychologists define **health-defeating behaviors** as those behaviors that increase the chance of illness, disease, or death. They include risky behaviors such as driving and texting, carrying a weapon, or being a passenger in a car with a driver who is under the influence of drugs or alcohol. Risky behaviors endanger your health because you place yourself in a situation in which you have a higher risk of physical injury. Many of the leading causes of death are related to unsafe health practices associated with behavior and lifestyle (see ● TECHNOLOGY AND BEHAVIOR and ● FIGURE 12.4). The top three leading causes of death—heart disease, cancer, and stroke—have been linked to personal habits that damage our health. We will examine behavior patterns, usually engaged in over a long period of time, that *are* controllable and seriously put your health at risk. These behaviors include alcohol consumption, smoking, and unsafe sex practices that can lead to contracting HIV.

health-defeating behaviors behaviors that increase the chance of illness, disease, or death

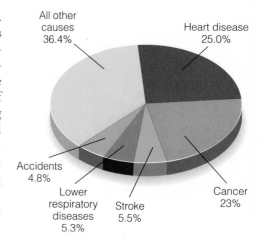

FIGURE 12.4

● **Leading Causes of Death in the United States** In 2007, heart disease, cancer, stroke, respiratory diseases, and accidents were the top five causes of deaths in the United States. The top two causes of death, heart disease and cancer, were the same for males and females and for Whites, Blacks, and American Indians; for Asian/Pacific Islanders, cancer was the leading cause of death with heart disease second. Many of these deaths could have been prevented by engaging in better health practices. *Source: National Vital Statistics Report, Vol. 58, No. 1, August 19, 2009.*

TECHNOLOGY and BEHAVIOR

TECHNOLOGY'S HEALTH EFFECTS

Technology has the potential for great benefit and great harm to our health. On the plus side, social networking sites, e-mail, and text messaging can reduce loneliness and offer companionship and social support that can help combat stress and improve well-being (Barker, 2009; L. H. Shaw & Gant, 2002). The Internet provides instant access to health information and resources that can reduce stress and worry. Fitness video games offer a fun, enjoyable, and often inexpensive way to remain physically active. However, being inundated with constant communication 24/7 creates stress and can make it more difficult to relax. Feeling like you are being left out of a social loop can create social anxiety. People may disengage from loved ones and pay more attention to the person on the phone or on the computer than to the people who are actually present. The Internet may produce information overload or give contradictory or unreliable health information that creates stress and worry (Abbott, 2010).

Texting while driving is a health-defeating behavior because it increases one's chances of injury or death.

© fStop/SuperStock

However, there are more serious, adverse health effects of technology use. After prolonged cell phone use, people may notice aching, burning, numbness, or tingling in the forearm and hand called "cell phone elbow" (Darowish, Lawton, & Evans, 2009). It is associated with people who use their cell phones for extended periods while holding their neck crooked and elbow bent. It can aggravate a painful and disabling condition called cubital tunnel syndrome, or the compression of the ulnar nerve near the elbow. Similarly, irritation and compression of the median nerve in the wrist, known as carpal tunnel syndrome, can result from repetitive work such as uninterrupted computer typing and frequent mouse use, depending on the frequency of use and wrist position of the user (Rempel, Keir, & Bach, 2008). Excessive texting uses short little motions that do not effectively use the muscles. This action can lead to painful cramping in the thumbs, hands, or joints, popularly called "Blackberry thumb" or "teenager tendonitis" (Gordon, 2008). Staring at computer or cell phone screens for long periods can lead to dry eyes, eye irritation, redness, blurred vision, and eye strain, a condition referred to as computer vision syndrome and which can cause headaches, pain, and fatigue (Blehm et al., 2005). Perhaps one of the most dangerous behaviors that has resulted from technology is an increase in distracted driving.

In 2008 almost 6,000 people were killed and a half million were injured in crashes related to driver distraction (National Highway Traffic Safety Administration [NHTSA], 2009). People do not turn off their connection to the outside world when they get into their cars. Yet, our brain is not capable of fully concentrating on two things simultaneously. Text messaging and conversing on either a handheld or hands-free cell phone while driving slows reaction time more than being drunk or high (Drews et al., 2009; Strayer, Drews, & Crouch, 2006). Text messaging also takes drivers' eyes off the road for the longest time compared to drivers using a cell phone and those not using a phone. Drivers who are text messaging also show more missed lane changes as well as variability in lane position and following distances (Hosking, Young, & Regan, 2009). Driving safely is keeping your eyes and your mind on the road. Text messaging while driving compromises both.

Alcohol

Recall from Chapter 4 the specific effects that alcohol has on the body and brain. These effects can be seen within a larger context by detailing the social and physical ramifications of alcohol abuse on people's health and well-being. Consider that the majority of manslaughter convictions, assaults, and domestic violence incidents involve alcohol. Nearly half of all U.S. highway deaths involve alcohol. Fetal alcohol syndrome (FAS), caused by a mother's excessive ingestion of alcohol during pregnancy, is the leading cause of mental retardation (J. Adler & Rosenberg, 1994). In one survey (Johnston et al., 2009), 27% of high school seniors admitted being drunk in the past month, despite being underage. For college men and women, the rate is even higher.

Alcohol abuse not only leads to social problems but also is associated with major health problems including heart disease, stroke, cancer, liver disease, memory blackouts, and erectile dysfunction in males. These statistics convey the drastic impact that alcohol abuse has on our nation's health and suggest that alcohol should be used only in moderation, if at all.

In the United States, drinking alcohol is often marketed as part of having fun. Yet the majority of manslaughter convictions, assaults, and intimate partner violence incidents involve alcohol use.

Smoking

Another easily preventable behavior is cigarette smoking. Recall from Chapter 4 that nicotine affects several neurotransmitters in the brain that act as stimulants, increasing arousal, feelings of pleasure and reward, and metabolic rate, which is why smokers tend to be thinner than nonsmokers. However, in high doses, nicotine causes vomiting, diarrhea, sweating, and dizziness. Most first-time users report nausea and dizziness from smoking cigarettes. Yet users quickly develop nicotine dependence and cravings for cigarettes that correlate with activity in specific brain regions (Rose et al., 2007), as shown in ● WHAT'S HAPPENING IN YOUR BRAIN?

WHAT'S HAPPENING IN YOUR BRAIN?

BRAIN AREAS RELATED TO CIGARETTE CRAVINGS

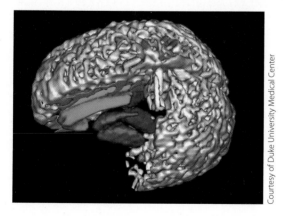

PET scans of smokers studied at Duke University revealed three specific brain areas that appear to control nicotine dependence and cigarette cravings. In blue is the thalamus, a part of the brain critical to calming down when stressed. In red is the striatum, a region associated with feelings of pleasure and reward. In green is the anterior cingulated cortex, a part of the brain vital to self-control and concentration.

Who smokes? Smokers differ from nonsmokers on several variables. In some developing countries, smoking is the norm. In the United States, smoking has declined over the past 30 years, yet 1 in 5 adults over the age of 18 still smoke (Centers for Disease Control and Prevention [CDC], 2009a). The percentage of current smokers in the United States is higher for men (23%) than for women (18%); higher for American Indian/Alaska Natives (27%), African Americans (22%), and Whites (21%) than for Hispanic/Latino Americans (15%) and Asian Americans (11%); and lower among adults age 65 and older, perhaps because many longtime smokers die (CDC, 2009a; Pleis & Lethbridge-Ceiku, 2007). Level of education and income level also differentiate smokers from nonsmokers, with people living below poverty level and people with lower levels of education having higher smoking rates (Wetter et al., 2005).

Why do people smoke? Many adolescents experiment with smoking in middle and high school. In 2008, 9% of 12- to 17-year-olds were current cigarette smokers (Substance Abuse and Mental Health Services Administration [SAMHSA], 2009). Many of these young people are aware of the health hazards associated with smoking, yet they begin anyway. Smoking initiation is related to both biological and environmental factors. On the side of biology, there is considerable evidence that specific genes and gene combinations are involved in smoking and nicotine dependence (Erblich et al., 2005; Kremer et al., 2005; Ling et al., 2004). However, social pressure also contributes to smoking. For example, peer pressure is often cited as a reason why young people start smoking (Hayes & Plowfield, 2007). Seeing their favorite celebrities or music idols smoke, or even watching movies in which many characters smoke, also glamorizes smoking (Cin et al., 2007; Distefan, Pierce, & Gilpin, 2004; Heatherton & Sargent, 2009; Pierce, 2005). For this reason, many antismoking programs are aimed at teenagers because this seems to be the prime age when smoking begins. Health officials have determined that the cost of treating the health problems associated with smoking far outweighs the cost of prevention programs.

Unsafe Sex and the Risk of HIV

Several years ago, Christine, a young European American woman in her early 20s, had just experienced an intense breakup of a long-term relationship. The next time she saw her ex-boyfriend, he was on a talk show describing how he was coping with an illness. As it turned out, he was HIV-positive. This was news to Christine! She was devastated but had the personal strength and wisdom to get tested. Sadly, the news was not good. Christine had contracted the AIDS virus. This is a true story. The woman referred to as Christine is a childhood friend of one of your authors.

Since the discovery of the AIDS (acquired immune deficiency syndrome) virus in the late 1970s, health psychologists have been concerned with the number of people who engage in unsafe sex. As we saw in Chapter 10, sexually active people who have multiple partners, engage in oral sex without using a condom or dental dam, or have sexual intercourse without using a condom, increase their risk of becoming HIV-positive. HIV-positive means that a person has been infected with the human immunodeficiency virus (HIV). Communicable through blood, semen, breast milk, or vaginal fluids, this virus steadily destroys your immune system. Engaging in unprotected sex even within a monogamous relationship can be risky. If either partner is an intravenous drug user or has had multiple sexual partners in the past in which unsafe sex has occurred, the risk of being HIV-positive is also increased. But note that you cannot contract AIDS through casual contact such as hugging.

Health-Promoting Behaviors

Health psychologists define **health-promoting behaviors** as those that decrease the chance of illness, disease, or death. Throughout this chapter we have indicated behaviors that you can engage in that are related to better physical and psychological functioning. Three additional behaviors that benefit the body and mind include *physical activity, eating healthy,* and *getting enough sleep.* Regular physical activity, healthful eating, and a good night's sleep promote a longer and healthier life.

Physical Activity

Rates of inactivity are highly prevalent in our society. Consider that in 2007 only one third of high school students met recommended levels of physical activity. However, 25% of stu-

health-promoting behaviors
behaviors that decrease the chance of illness, disease, or death

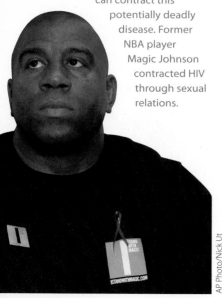

AIDS/HIV does not discriminate. Anyone—regardless of age, gender, wealth, race, or sexual orientation—can contract this potentially deadly disease. Former NBA player Magic Johnson contracted HIV through sexual relations.

AP Photo/Nick Ut

dents played video or computer games or used a computer for something other than school work for more than 3 hours per day on an average school day, and 35% of students watched television 3 or more hours per day on an average school day (CDC, 2008d). A *sedentary*, or inactive, lifestyle compromises one's health.

The good news is that any increase in physical activity improves health. This activity may include taking the stairs instead of the elevator at school or at work; parking farther away from stores when shopping; or walking or biking to campus instead of driving. However, moderate physical activity for at least 30 minutes a day is recommended by most health experts. Moderate physical activity includes walking briskly, swimming, cycling, or jogging—aerobic activities that stimulate heart and lung functioning.

Regular physical activity plays an important role in people's health. In addition to combating stress, physical activity helps us live longer, improves psychological health, and positively affects memory and cognition (A. Collins et al., 2009; D. C. Lee et al., in press; K. N. Williams & Kemper, 2010). Engaging in regular physical activity also protects against cardiovascular disease, some kinds of cancer, and bone density loss, and can help manage weight control (Bassuk & Manson, 2010; Slattery et al., 2010). Regular exercise is one of the most critical elements in any weight-loss program. Another important factor is eating right.

Eating Right

As we saw in Chapter 8, poor diet and overeating are just two of the many factors that contribute to the obesity epidemic in the United States. Being overweight or obese is associated with a higher risk of several types of health problems, such as diabetes, sleep apnea, migraine headaches, heart disease, and some cancers. It also shortens one's lifespan (K. F. Adams et al., 2006). Healthful eating when combined with physical activity can decrease one's risk of disease and death.

Eating right involves decisions about (1) what to eat, (2) when to eat, and (3) how much to eat. First, it means choosing foods that are nutritious and healthy. Nutritious foods are high in vitamins, minerals, and fiber, such as fruits, vegetables, and grains. Processed foods and foods high in sugar, salt, oil, or fat (like fast food) increase cholesterol, which contributes to the development of heart problems (Phelan et al., 2009). One should strive to eat well-balanced meals that meet one's nutritional needs and include a variety of foods from each of the major food groups.

Eating right also means eating breakfast. Skipping breakfast is one of the biggest nutritional mistakes that people make. Breakfast is your first chance to refuel your body to prepare it for the day's activities. Regularly eating a healthy breakfast is associated with increased attention span, less risk of chronic diseases, and living a longer life (Hoyland, Dye, & Lawton, 2009; Schoenborn, 1986). Eating a healthy breakfast also makes us less likely to overeat later in the day.

How much should I eat? An exact amount cannot be given as each person's appropriate food intake will depend on many factors including age, gender, height, and physical activity level, to name a few. However, most people overeat—not the good stuff like fruits and vegetables, but, rather, foods that lack nutrition and put one more at risk for weight gain and health disorders. People excessively consume salty snacks, cookies, candy, and sugary beverages (D. A. Cohen et al., 2010). The growth in the fast-food and soda industries as well as the increase in restaurant portion sizes encourage increased food consumption. Combined with low levels of physical activity, overeating results in weight gain. Maintaining an appropriate weight requires that people expend as many calories as they take in.

Getting Enough Sleep

As we saw in Chapter 4, most adults and teenagers require at least 8 hours of sleep a night, although few of us achieve this. Yet, getting enough sleep enhances your immune system and your mood. With the appropriate amount of sleep, your immune system is stronger (Lange et al., 2006; Motivala & Irwin, 2007). When you deprive your body of sleep, your natural immune responses are reduced (Irwin et al., 2003; Murphy & Delanty, 2007). The right amount of sleep also enhances mood as sleep activates chemicals that influence your emotions and mood. If you are deprived of sleep, you are more likely to be irritable, cranky, and unhappy, in addition to being tired (Durmer & Dinges, 2005; Murphy & Delanty, 2007). Sleep offers many benefits to our functioning and ensures that we will be healthy, alert, and happy.

Happiness and Well-Being

Healthy living promotes happiness and life satisfaction. So, it is fitting to end this chapter by investigating what makes people happy. Research typically measures happiness by asking people how satisfied they are with their lives. This evaluation is referred to as *subjective well-being*. People who score high on measures of subjective well-being live longer and have healthier lives (Chida & Steptoe, 2008; J. Xu & Roberts, 2010). Those factors that contribute to happiness nicely summarize many of the health behaviors that this chapter has explored (E. Diener & Biswas-Diener, 2008):

- *Social relationships:* People who are happy have close, strong, and positive relationships with others. Higher well-being is associated with social rather than solitary pursuits and involves meaningful conversations with others (Mehl et al., 2010). Strong ties increase subjective well-being and help moderate the ill effects of stress.
- *Cognitive patterns:* People think in ways that contribute to happiness. Happy people view stressors as opportunities rather than as threats, are optimistic in their outlook on life, and remember positive experiences rather than dwelling on negative ones.
- *Temperament:* Good and bad events happen to everyone and affect levels of happiness. Yet, individuals differ in their ability to adapt to these events. Those who bounce back from negative events by using positive emotions to cope can more easily reset their point of being happy to the same or a new adjusted level. This ability may stem from inherited differences in temperament and thereby be greatly influenced by genetics.
- *Wealth:* Can money buy happiness? Only to a certain extent. In poor societies, people who have more money report higher levels of happiness. However, once people rise above poverty level in terms of wealth, money doesn't buy more happiness. Moreover, valuing money above relationships, love, and personal satisfaction is negatively associated with happiness.
- *Culture:* One's feeling of happiness is also influenced by the values that characterize one's society. Cultural norms dictate whether happiness is important and what constitutes a good life. Individualistic cultures endorse the value of personal happiness whereas collectivistic cultures value group identity. Not surprisingly, East Asians and Asian Americans

People who are happy are healthier and live longer.

Soul/Getty Images

report lower levels of happiness than Europeans and European Americans (Wirtz et al., 2009). The World Values Survey of 97 countries found Denmark to be the happiest nation. Freedom of choice, social acceptance, and standard of living were all factors that influenced a nation's happiness level. Not surprisingly, people in war-torn nations report less happiness and well-being than do people in stable countries (Inglehart et al., 2008).

Future research will help us discover more about the nature of happiness and life satisfaction. This knowledge will enable health psychologists to continue their efforts at understanding stress, preventing illnesses, and promoting lifelong well-being.

This chapter explored the topics of stress, coping, and health—topics that are bound to be relevant to you. For a moment, reflect on what your life is like. How do you look for your age, what activities comprise your daily routine, and what is your health like? Examine the ways in which you handle stress. Do you spend a significant amount of your time watching television, drinking alcohol, smoking, exercising, getting together with friends, or using drugs? Detail any stress-related symptoms such as headaches, backaches, muscle tension, anxiety, or upset stomach that you have experienced over the past year. How might your coping style be influencing your health? Analyze your personality and lifestyle. Are there any improvements that you could make in these areas that would enhance your health? Addressing these issues in this manner will help you master the material. It is our hope that it will also cause you to pause for a moment to contemplate how your health might be improved, for today and for the future.

Let's
REVIEW
In this section we examined behaviors that put us at higher risk for illness and disease, and those that have been linked to healthier living. For a quick review, try answering the following questions at increasing levels of difficulty.

1. Which of the following is *not* a health-promoting behavior?

   a. Viewing stressors as challenges rather than as threats
   b. Perceiving events as controllable
   c. Relying exclusively on one defense mechanism for coping
   d. Engaging in problem-focused coping

2. Which of the following would be considered a safe sex practice?

   a. Engaging only in oral sex
   b. Using a condom when having sexual intercourse
   c. Having multiple sexual partners
   d. Having unprotected sex only within a monogamous relationship

3. Which of the following people is most likely to report being the happiest?

   a. Haifa, who is extremely wealthy, has a few close friends, and focuses on negative experiences
   b. Sam, who is moderately wealthy, optimistic, and adapts well to negative events
   c. Agustin, who is moderately wealthy, optimistic, and lives in a war-torn nation
   d. All of these would report similar levels of happiness.

ANSWERS 1. c; 2. b; 3. b

STUDYING the CHAPTER

KEY TERMS

health psychology (497)
stress (499)
life event (499)
daily hassles (503)
conflict (504)
approach–approach
   conflict (504)
avoidance–avoidance
   conflict (505)
approach–avoidance
   conflict (505)

multiple approach–avoidance
   conflict (505)
primary appraisal (506)
general adaptation syndrome
   (GAS) (507)
alarm reaction (507)
resistance stage (508)
exhaustion stage (508)
psychoneuroimmunology
   (508)
immunosuppression (509)

coping (510)
problem-focused coping
   (511)
emotion-focused coping
   (511)
cognitive reappraisal (511)
defense mechanisms (512)
biofeedback (513)
progressive relaxation
   training (513)
social support (514)

guided imagery (515)
meditation (515)
Type A personality (517)
Type B personality (517)
Type C personality (517)
learned helplessness (519)
hardy personality (520)
health-defeating behaviors
   (521)
health-promoting behaviors
   (524)

LEARNING CHALLENGE

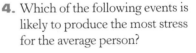

Now that you have studied the chapter, assess your comprehension of the material by answering the following questions. Then use the key at the end to determine if your understanding is at the basic, intermediate, or advanced level. For a more comprehensive assessment of your learning, please see your student study guide and your Psychology CourseMate (www.cengagebrain.com).

1. Which of the following is *not* considered a major life event?

   a. marriage
   b. losing your job
   c. buying a home
   d. being late to work

2. Cecilia feels stressed from her full-time job and taking care of her two children. Cecilia finds a more flexible job that allows her to spend more time with her children. Which style of coping does Cecilia's behavior illustrate?

   a. emotion-focused
   b. problem-focused
   c. defensive
   d. both a and c

3. Which one of the following behaviors promotes health and well-being?

   a. perceiving events as controllable
   b. engaging in defense mechanisms
   c. expecting failure
   d. All of these help your health.

4. Which of the following events is likely to produce the most stress for the average person?

   a. losing your job after months of talk about a buyout
   b. losing your job without any warning
   c. quitting your job to look for a different line of work
   d. keeping your job after others have lost their jobs due to downsizing

5. Ryan can't decide which of two sound speakers to buy with his birthday money. Ryan is experiencing a(n) _____.

   a. approach–avoidance conflict
   b. approach–approach conflict
   c. avoidance–avoidance conflict
   d. multiple approach–avoidance conflict

6. Matresha is driving when a van pulls out in front of her and almost causes a car accident. Matresha's heart begins to pound and her blood pressure shoots up. Matresha is likely in the _____ phase of the general adaptation syndrome.

   a. alarm
   b. resistance
   c. exhaustion
   d. final

7. April recently lost her high-paying job. While talking to a friend about her job loss, April says that she is looking forward to finding a job in a new field. April appears to be exhibiting the hardy trait of _____.

   a. challenge
   b. commitment
   c. control
   d. resistance

8. Which of the following is not a helpful means of managing stress?

   a. exercise
   b. relaxation techniques
   c. talking to friends
   d. throwing away your planner

9. Jariel is a workaholic. He never takes a vacation. He won't even speak to friends and family on the phone when they call him at work. He is often angry and impatient with others. What type of personality does Jariel appear to have?

   a. Type A
   b. Type B
   c. Type C
   d. a hardy personality

10. The two leading causes of death in the United States are _____.

   a. accidents and stroke
   b. respiratory diseases and cancer
   c. accidents and heart disease
   d. heart disease and cancer

11. Tom views his new job as a positive and challenging change. Tom's appraisal of stress in this situation is most likely to elicit the emotion of _____.

   a. anger
   b. fear
   c. excitement
   d. anxiety

12. Lucinda believes she has no control over what happens to her. She expects failure and often feels stressed out. What type of personality does Lucinda appear to have?

   a. learned helplessness
   b. Type A personality
   c. Type B personality
   d. Type C personality

13. Which of the following is an accurate statement concerning the relationship between stress and the immune system?

   a. Stress always decreases the effectiveness of our immune system.
   b. Stress always increases the effectiveness of our immune system.
   c. If stress disrupts normal immune system functioning, we increase our vulnerability to illness and disease.
   d. If stress disrupts normal immune system functioning, we decrease our vulnerability to illness and disease.

14. When Alexandra gets in a fight with her partner, she stomps her feet, covers her ears, and refuses to listen. Alexandra's behavior best illustrates the defense mechanism called _____.

   a. regression
   b. repression
   c. reaction formation
   d. displacement

15. Health-defeating behaviors _____.

   a. are not controllable
   b. are engaged in over a short period of time
   c. make us more susceptible to illness and disease
   d. All of these are true.

Scoring Key

Below are the answers and the associated point values for each of the Learning Challenge questions. Circle the associated points for each question that you answered correctly. To obtain your Learning Challenge Score, add up the points you circled and write the total in the blank below.

1. D, 1 pt	**6.** A, 2 pts	**11.** C, 3 pts
2. B, 2 pts	**7.** A, 3 pts	**12.** A, 2 pts
3. A, 1 pt	**8.** D, 1 pt	**13.** C, 3 pts
4. B, 3 pts	**9.** A, 2 pts	**14.** A, 3 pts
5. B, 2 pts	**10.** D, 1 pt	**15.** C, 1 pt

Learning Challenge Score _____

(27–30) Congratulations! You scored at the advanced level. You are well on your way to mastering the material. Take the next step by answering the questions in your Student Study Guide or your Psychology CourseMate (www.cengagebrain.com).

(21–26) You are almost there! You scored at the intermediate level. Review the material you missed before moving on to answer the questions in your Student Study Guide or your Psychology CourseMate (www.cengagebrain.com).

(20 and below) You are on your way, but you're not there yet! You scored at the beginner level. It appears that you need to carefully review the chapter to improve your mastery of the material.

USE IT OR LOSE IT: APPLYING PSYCHOLOGY

1. What defense mechanisms do you think are more often employed by people who engage in health-defeating behaviors? Provide examples to illustrate and support your answer.

2. Look once again at the opening case study. Given that Edward did not have a family history of cancer, what specific behaviors and stressors do you think might have contributed to the development of his illness?

3. Using your own behavior, give an example of each of the following defense mechanisms: projection, denial, reaction formation, displacement, and sublimation.

4. Using your own behavior, give an example of each of the conflict situations discussed in this chapter. How did you respond to each of these situations? Indicate whether your response reflected a problem-focused coping strategy or an emotion-focused coping strategy.

5. Develop a formal time schedule to better manage your time. First create a chart showing all the hours in a day and all the days of the week. Block out all those times that are already committed, such as sleeping, class time, work, and daily chores. Now allocate a specific amount of time to study for your classes and to exercise. Follow this plan for a week to see whether you need to make any modifications. Provide an analysis of your time use.

CRITICAL THINKING FOR INTEGRATION

1. Review the four types of learning detailed in Chapter 5. How can these theories be used to explain why people smoke or engage in unsafe sex practices?

2. After reviewing the processes of memory in Chapter 6, suggest how learned helplessness may be a process of memory.

3. What obstacles or aids to problem solving (Chapter 7) may be connected to maladaptive and adaptive forms of coping?

4. Combining information from Chapters 4, 8, and 12, develop an anti-alcohol campaign that addresses the effects of alcohol (Chapter 4), the motivating forces behind using alcohol (Chapter 8), and the effects that alcohol has on one's health (Chapter 12).

5. Given that pregnancy is a stressor, how might women best cope with the immediate changes associated with pregnancy and childbirth, as well as the transition to parenthood (Chapter 9)? What might be indicators of maladaptive coping patterns during pregnancy?

6. Review the cognitive changes that take place in adolescence (Chapter 9). How might adolescent cognitive development account for teenagers' willingness to engage in health-defeating behaviors?

Student Study Guide

To help organize your learning, work through Chapter 12 of the *What Is Psychology? Student Study Guide*. The study guide includes learning objectives, a chapter summary, fill-in review, key terms, a practice test, and activities.

CengageNOW

Go to **www.cengage.com/login** to link to CengageNOW, your online study tool. First take the Pre-Test for this chapter to get your personalized study plan, which will identify topics you need to review and direct you to online resources. Then take the Post-Test to determine what concepts you have mastered and what you still need work on.

CourseMate

Access an interactive eBook, chapter-specific interactive learning tools, including flashcards, quizzes, videos, and more in your Psychology CourseMate, available at **CengageBrain.com**.

Aplia

Aplia™ is an online interactive learning solution that helps you improve comprehension—and your grade—by integrating a variety of tools such as video, tutorials, practice tests, and interactive e-book. Founded by a professor to enhance his own courses, Aplia provides automatically graded assignments with detailed, immediate explanations on every question, and innovative teaching materials. More than 1,000,000 students like you have used Aplia at over 1,800 institutions. Aplia should be purchased only when assigned by your instructor as part of your course.

HEALTH, STRESS, AND COPING: HOW CAN YOU CREATE A HEALTHY LIFE?

Health psychologists study how people's behavior influences their health for better and for worse. This knowledge can help us understand the biological, psychological, and social factors that influenced the health of Edward and Joan Pastorino.

WHAT IS STRESS? STRESS AND STRESSORS

- **Stress** is any event or environmental stimulus (stressor) that we respond to because we perceive it as challenging or threatening.

- Significant **life events**, such as the death of a loved one or a new job, are major stressors. Everyday frustrations—called **daily hassles**—are less serious stressors, but can have a negative effect on health.

- **Conflict** also produces stress.

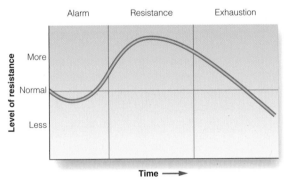

Digital Vision/Getty Images

© Bubbles Photolibrary/Alamy

Jean-Phillipe Ksiazek/AFP/Getty Images

THE STRESS RESPONSE: HOW DOES THE BODY REACT?

- If our initial interpretation or **primary appraisal** of an event is one of stress, we may view it as a threat, as harmful, or merely as a challenge.

- Our body responds to stress in a three-phase **general adaptation syndrome**:

  - The **alarm reaction** consists of those bodily responses, including the nervous system and endocrine system, that are immediately triggered when we initially appraise an event as stressful.

  - In the **resistance stage**, the body continues to cope with the stressor, but the bodily reactions are less intense than during the alarm reaction.

  - In the **exhaustion stage**, wear and tear on the body begins, causing serious damage if stress continues over an extended period of time.

- The corticosteroids and endorphins that are released into our body during the stress response actually dampen the activity of our immune system (**immuno-suppression**), making us more vulnerable to health problems.

Alarm | Resistance | Exhaustion

Level of resistance

More

Normal

Less

Time ⟶

HOW CAN I COPE WITH STRESS?

- **Coping** is how we manage a threatening event or stimulus.

- **Problem-focused coping** controls or alters the environment that caused the stress. It is most useful when we feel that we can do something about the stressor.

- **Emotion-focused coping** controls our internal, subjective, emotional responses to stress. We alter the way we feel or think in order to reduce stress.

© Picturequest/Jupiter Images

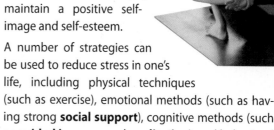

Andrea Wyner/Getty Images

- **Defense mechanisms** are unconscious coping strategies that allow us to reduce our anxiety and maintain a positive self-image and self-esteem.

- A number of strategies can be used to reduce stress in one's life, including physical techniques (such as exercise), emotional methods (such as having strong **social support**), cognitive methods (such as **guided imagery** and **meditation**), and behavioral methods (such as laughter and time management).

DOES YOUR PERSONALITY INFLUENCE YOUR HEALTH?

- A person with a **Type A personality** is aggressive, competitive, and driven to achieve; a person with a **Type B personality** is relaxed, easygoing, patient, and flexible; a person with a **Type C personality** is careful and patient and suppresses negative emotions such as anger. The Type A personality trait of hostility is related to a higher incidence of heart disease.

- **Learned helplessness** is when you believe that you have no control over stressful life events. You view stressors as threats, your level of stress increases, and you are more likely to develop stress-related illnesses.

- The **hardy personality** is resistant to stress; it includes characteristics such as
  - A tendency to see life as a series of *challenges*
  - A sense of personal *commitment* to self, work, family, and other values
  - A perception of *control* over one's life and work

WHAT BEHAVIORS PROMOTE HEALTH AND WELL-BEING?

Soul/Getty Images

- **Health-defeating behaviors**, such as alcohol and substance abuse, smoking, driving recklessly, and engaging in unsafe sex, increase the chance of illness, disease, or death.

- **Health-promoting behaviors** decrease the chance of illness, disease, or death.

- Regular physical activity and healthful eating promote a longer and healthier life. Happiness is related to a strong social support network, an optimistic outlook, economic resources, temperament, and cultural values.

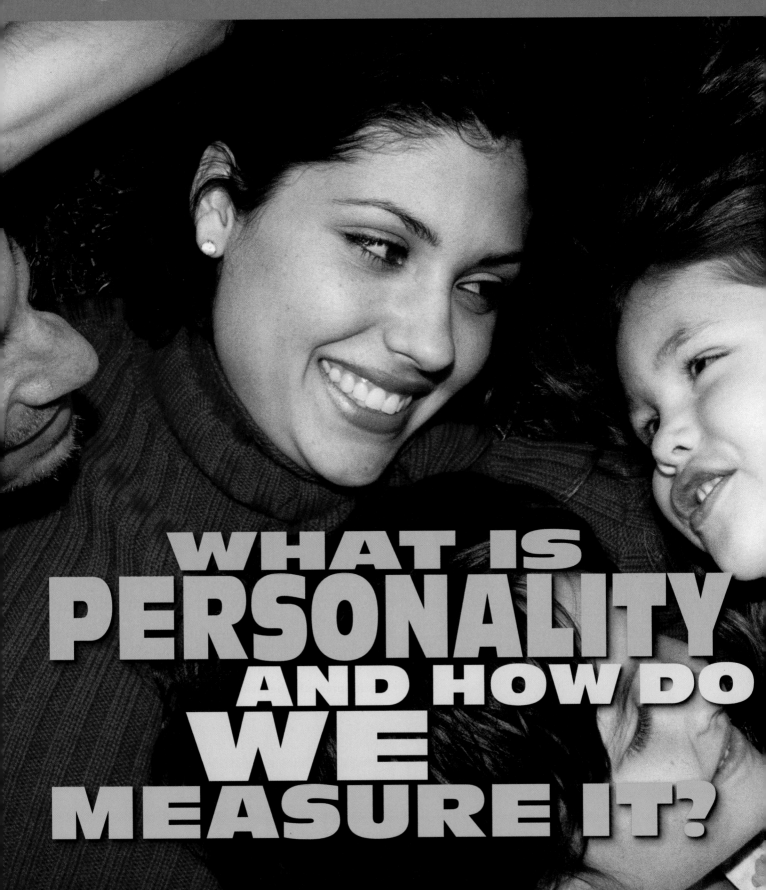

CHAPTER 13

WHAT IS PERSONALITY AND HOW DO WE MEASURE IT?

THE BIG PICTURE | How Can We Understand Personality?

This chapter and the following two cover what you probably originally thought psychology was all about: the unique and sometimes strange qualities of our behavior. This chapter's topic is **personality**, or the unique collection of attitudes, emotions, thoughts, habits, impulses, and behaviors that define how a person typically behaves across situations.

The material in this chapter will remind you of theories we have covered throughout this textbook, and the four perspectives on personality introduced in this chapter will be revisited in the next two chapters as well. Understanding how different perspectives explain the formation of personality will help you understand psychologists' explanations for why some people respond to difficulty by becoming depressed or anxious—material addressed in the next chapter. Similarly, the four personality perspectives presented here are the basis for many of the treatment methods discussed in Chapter 15.

In his memoir *The Color of Water: A Black Man's Tribute to His White Mother* (1996), James McBride describes the different personalities in his large family. His remarkable mother, Rachel, grew up an Orthodox Jew in Virginia during the Great Depression. Rachel's father owned a general store that served mainly poor, rural African Americans, yet he was blatantly racist. At the age of 21, despite her parents' protests, Rachel married Andrew McBride, an African American from New York. Andrew and Rachel settled in Harlem and established their own family. Andrew died before their eighth child, James, was born in 1957. Rachel then married Hunter Jordan, also an African American, and they added four more children to the family. These 12 African American Jewish children grew up in cramped quarters in Brooklyn and Queens, yet all went to college; they became doctors, teachers, and scientists.

This family stood out at a time when interracial marriage was rare. It also contained a lively mix of personalities. Rachel was intensely private, and mistrustful and suspicious of all authority figures. She had a strict, no-nonsense approach to parenting and to life in general. She was hardworking and religious, and she insisted that all of her children work hard in school. Hunter Jordan, the only father James ever knew, had quite the opposite personality. He was easygoing, quiet, and tough, yet open-minded. He was a methodical worker with abundant patience. He was a suave and handsome man who worked hard and drank hard. He was rarely angry, and he never worried about anything.

© Trinette Reed/Corbis

Tiziana Fabi/AFP/Getty Images

In *The Color of Water: A Black Man's Tribute to His White Mother* (1996), James McBride describes the different personalities in his large family.

Rachel's 12 children made for a hectic household of interesting and diverse personalities. For example, Dennis, the eldest son, was an artist and a straight-A student in his childhood. In college, he became an active civil rights proponent. Richie was a tenor sax player, creative yet absentminded, and considered more of a free spirit by his siblings. He went on to become a chemist. Rosetta, the eldest daughter, was intelligent and bossy and went to Howard University on a full scholarship. Helen, another sister, was pretty, talkative, and obstinate. Helen played the piano and was accepted to and briefly attended several music and art schools before eventually obtaining a nursing degree.

Like his siblings, James was cute, smart, and musically talented. In other ways, James was quite different from them. As a child, he recalls being "shy, passive, and quiet." He spent a lot of time reading or talking to imaginary friends. By the age of 10, James became secretive, angry, and very fearful—fearful in particular that his friends would discover that his mother was White. His stepfather died when James was 14, and his personality appeared to change completely. He failed all his subjects at school and became a truant. He joined a soul band, smoked marijuana, and began drinking heavily. He and his friends broke into cars, shoplifted, and even mugged older women. Fortunately, at age 16 James realized that his behavior needed to change. The family moved to Delaware, and James made a fresh start. He gave up pot smoking and drinking but remained interested in music. He graduated from Oberlin College and received a master's degree in journalism from Columbia University. He currently describes himself as a Black man with something of a Jewish soul.

We can see just within this one family a complex and rich array of personalities. There were similarities and differences. All the children were creative and artistic either in music, writing, or the arts. They were all excellent students. Some were more outgoing and independent, whereas others were more quiet and unassuming. Perhaps your family is similarly varied, seeming like a cast of actors put together for an off-Broadway play! How can we understand these similarities and differences in personality? That is the focus of this chapter as we explore this critical question: **How do we get our personalities, and how stable—or changeable—are they?**

Some of us are slow to anger, whereas others become angry quickly. Some people look for opportunities to be the star, whereas others shrink from the limelight. Where does this unique way of responding come from? Psychologists do not agree on a single, specific answer to this question—personality is difficult to define, difficult to measure, and influenced by many factors (Schultz & Schultz, 2005).

Four dominant perspectives have emerged to explain our personalities: the *psychoanalytic approach*, the *trait approach*, the *social cognitive approach*, and the *humanistic approach*. Each attempts to provide answers to different questions about personality. For example, some approaches focus more on the factors that influence our personalities. Others concentrate more on explaining the causes or problems of personality development, or how we can reach our fullest potential. No single theoretical approach can explain all facets of personality development in all people. Each perspective has its advantages and disadvantages. The disadvantages prompted development of other perspectives to explain personality, whereas the advantages demonstrate the contributions to the field of psychology and, specifically, to our understanding of personality.

As we describe each major perspective, consider your own ideas about personality and how they differ from or are similar to each approach. Do you think that you inherit your personality or that it is formed from your experiences? Do you think that your behavior is influenced by your unconscious? Do you think that people strive to be all that they can be? Examining such ideas will allow you to connect the material to your values, experiences, and current way of thinking.

personality the unique collection of attitudes, emotions, thoughts, habits, impulses, and behaviors that define how a person typically behaves across situations

psychoanalytic perspective a personality approach developed by Sigmund Freud that sees personality as the product of driving forces within a person that are often conflicting and sometimes unconscious

conscious level the level of consciousness that holds all the thoughts, perceptions, and impulses of which we are aware

THE PSYCHOANALYTIC APPROACH: HOW DOES THE UNCONSCIOUS INFLUENCE PERSONALITY?

The **psychoanalytic perspective** on personality originated with Sigmund Freud. We introduced his approach to understanding behavior in Chapter 1. Recall that Freud practiced medicine, specializing in "nervous diseases." However, soon after beginning private practice, Freud moved away from physical explanations of nervous disorders and focused more on investigating psychological causes of these disorders. His ideas about personality were based on case studies of his patients, his reading of literature, and his own self-analysis. Freud saw personality as the product of driving forces within a person that were often conflicting and sometimes unconscious. As we saw in Chapter 4, Freud believed that dreams were one of the ways these unconscious forces expressed themselves. Freud's theory is unique in that it strongly emphasizes unconscious aspects of personality. How does Freud explain personality?

Freud's Levels of Awareness

Freud (1940/1964) proposed that human personality operates at three different levels of awareness or consciousness and that each level of awareness influences behavior. Freud viewed consciousness as being like an iceberg (● FIGURE 13.1). When we look at behavior, all we usually see is the tip of the iceberg, or the **conscious level**: the thoughts, perceptions, and explanations of behavior of which the person is aware. The major portion of the iceberg, according to Freud, is below the surface. These impulses, memories, and thoughts are unseen but have a huge impact on personality. Because so large a portion of one's personality lies below the surface of consciousness, or awareness, Freud believed any explanation of personality and behavior must focus on these unconscious forces. We must look not only at what is showing above the surface but, even more important, at all that goes on beneath the surface of consciousness.

The psychoanalytic perspective on personality originated with Sigmund Freud. Freud saw personality as the product of driving forces within a person that were often conflicting and sometimes unconscious.

Hulton Archive/Getty Images

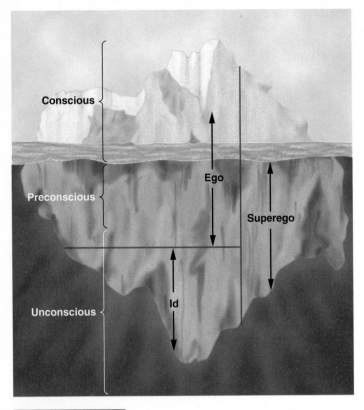

FIGURE 13.1

● **Iceberg Analogy of Freud's Levels of Awareness** In Freud's "iceberg" analogy of the mind, the id and parts of the ego and superego are submerged below the water in the unconscious. Parts of the ego and superego also operate in the conscious and preconscious.

preconscious level the level of consciousness that holds thoughts, perceptions, and impulses of which we could potentially be aware

unconscious level the level of awareness that contains all the thoughts, perceptions, and impulses of which we are unaware

Unconscious id impulses drive babies to cry for food.

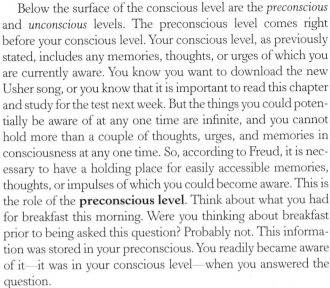

George Doyle/Getty Images

Below the surface of the conscious level are the *preconscious* and *unconscious* levels. The preconscious level comes right before your conscious level. Your conscious level, as previously stated, includes any memories, thoughts, or urges of which you are currently aware. You know you want to download the new Usher song, or you know that it is important to read this chapter and study for the test next week. But the things you could potentially be aware of at any one time are infinite, and you cannot hold more than a couple of thoughts, urges, and memories in consciousness at any one time. So, according to Freud, it is necessary to have a holding place for easily accessible memories, thoughts, or impulses of which you could become aware. This is the role of the **preconscious level**. Think about what you had for breakfast this morning. Were you thinking about breakfast prior to being asked this question? Probably not. This information was stored in your preconscious. You readily became aware of it—it was in your conscious level—when you answered the question.

The **unconscious level** contains all those thoughts, impulses, memories, and behaviors of which you are unaware. However, although you are unaware of them, they always influence your behavior. Consider the 4-year-old boy who stops his parents from hugging or inserts himself between them to prevent them from kissing. He is not aware that this behavior stems from a need or wish to bond with his mother, yet it is still influencing his behavior.

In summary, Freud believed consciousness had three levels: the conscious, preconscious, and unconscious. As Freud saw it, these unconscious and conscious forces do exist and are the energy behind one's personality.

Freud's Structure of Personality

How did Freud believe the energy of one's personality is distributed? To Freud (1940/1964), human personality is an energy system comprised of three major personality structures: the *id*, the *ego*, and the *superego*. At birth, all of the energy of the personality is contained within a structure called the **id**. The id is an unconscious energy force that seeks pleasure and gratification. Hungry infants cry for food or because they are wet or tired. The id operates according to the **pleasure principle**; it drives people to feel good and to maximize pleasure and gratification. Freud saw the impulses driving the id as primarily sexual and aggressive in nature. In this way, he viewed humans as very similar to animals—unconsciously and selfishly motivated by basic sexual and aggressive instincts. Such basic instincts ensure and promote the survival of the individual, and therefore the survival of the species as a whole. When we grow and begin to interact with our environment, we realize that our demands cannot always be immediately fulfilled. For example, when a baby's cry for food is not met every time, the baby has encountered reality. As such, part of the energy of the id becomes directed to the ego.

The **ego**, the second personality structure, acts as a negotiator between the instinctual needs of the id and the demands of membership in human society. Children learn that their id demands can be fulfilled only when they behave appropriately. The ego operates according to the **reality principle**. It realizes that the desires of the id can be met only by successfully dealing with the environment, by finding appropriate or attainable means by which to fulfill id impulses. Suppose a 4-year-old wants something to eat. Does he immediately cry like a baby? Not typically. The 4-year-old with a functioning ego knows that there are more appropriate and acceptable ways of getting something to eat. He will probably ask for something to eat and be willing to wait (at least for a little while) for his caregiver to prepare it for him. We see the ego functioning in the child's ability to delay his desire for food, for example.

But the ego's job is still to fulfill the instinctual demands of the id—the unseen force beneath the tip of the iceberg (see Figure 13.1).

As the child continues to grow, parents and other important people impart their values and standards of behavior to the child. Parents convey the right and wrong ways to feel, think, and behave. The child incorporates these standards as the energy of the personality further divides into a third personality structure. The **superego** typically emerges during the resolution of the phallic stage (discussed shortly) and represents your moral conscience. Your superego judges the rightness or wrongness of your actions. When you have the sense that you did something wrong, your superego is talking. The moral directives of the superego must also be taken into account by the ego. Just like id demands, superego demands must be met realistically by the ego in order to function in society.

The energy that these three personality components use cannot be cut apart. For Freud, personality is a dynamic, or active, process. The id, ego, and superego are not fixed entities but, rather, parts of our personality that serve different functions. A healthy personality will have developed a strong ego that appropriately releases and controls instinctual energy. However, problems may arise in personality functioning if id energy or superego energy overwhelms the functioning of the ego.

To Freud, all adult behaviors are a reflection of the interplay among these three structures (● FIGURE 13.2). When examining behavior, we see only the functioning of the ego, but this ego is simultaneously being influenced by the unconscious demands of the id and the superego. *Freudian slips* help explain this interaction. A Freudian slip is the expression of an unconscious impulse from the id before the ego controls the impulse. The ego may then state that it did not mean to say something and corrects the slip to conform to socially approved behavior. For example, one might say to a rival businessperson at a meeting, "Would you like to hit in this chair?" instead of "Would you like to sit in this chair?" and then quickly

Mel Yates/Getty Images

It is a child's superego that drives feelings of guilt after wrongdoing.

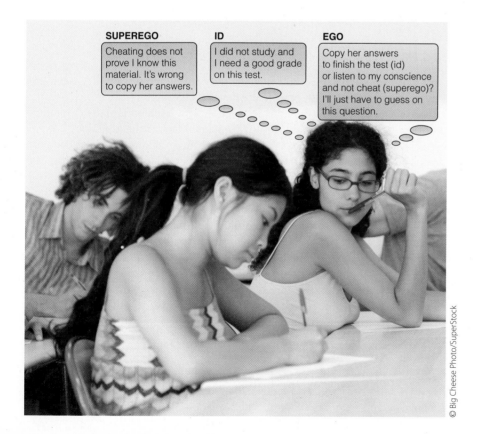

SUPEREGO

Cheating does not prove I know this material. It's wrong to copy her answers.

ID

I did not study and I need a good grade on this test.

EGO

Copy her answers to finish the test (id) or listen to my conscience and not cheat (superego)? I'll just have to guess on this question.

© Big Cheese Photo/SuperStock

FIGURE 13.2

● **Freud's Personality Structures**
According to Freud, adult behavior results from the interaction among the three personality structures of the id, ego, and superego.

id the unconscious part of the personality that seeks pleasure and gratification

pleasure principle the basis on which the id operates; to feel good and maximize gratification

ego the conscious part of the personality that attempts to meet the demands of the id in a socially appropriate way

reality principle the basis on which the ego operates; finding socially appropriate means to fulfill id demands

superego the part of the personality that represents your moral conscience

correct the error. Freud would state that what "slipped out" was meant; it just hadn't yet been socially screened by the ego. An older sibling may hit a younger sibling and claim that she did not mean to do it. Freud would state that the aggressive impulse was meant indeed, just not caught in time by the functioning ego.

To Freud, every behavior you engage in—including supposed errors or mistakes—has meaning or can be analyzed within the context of these three interacting personality structures. For example, suppose you are attracted to someone. What is your id telling you to do? It would urge you to go for it! Just do it, seek what gives you pleasure. Meanwhile, what will the demands of your superego be? We learn that we must respect the rights and bodies of others. Your ego must now balance these opposing demands in a socially appropriate way. The ego might prompt you to strike up a conversation or hang out with the person. These are just two ways a healthy ego might resolve the demands of the id and superego in this situation.

You can see that the demands of the id and the superego are often in direct opposition to one another. This internal conflict sometimes overwhelms the ego, creating anxiety. The ego handles this anxiety by using **defense mechanisms** (A. Freud, 1936). Defense mechanisms, discussed in Chapter 12, protect the ego by reducing the anxiety it feels when faced with the conflicting demands of the id and the superego. We all make use of these *coping mechanisms*, as they are now familiarly called. We tend to use those defense mechanisms that have been previously reinforced or that successfully reduce anxiety. For example, if you *rationalized* behavior as a child, you probably continue to use this defense mechanism as an adult.

Consider our chapter case story. From a psychoanalytic perspective, James McBride's truancy and delinquency would be related to his efforts to cope with his stepfather's death. Emotionally, James would feel anger at this loss. It is normal to feel anger when a loved one dies, to be mad at him or her for leaving and abandoning us. We cannot direct our anger toward its true source because the person is dead. We may also feel it is wrong to be angry with someone we love. So James's superego would attempt to squelch his anger, but the energy of those feelings would still need an outlet. James's ego satisfied both the id and the superego by taking his anger out on others, using the defense mechanism of *displacement* (see p. 512).

Differences in personality, then, arise from internal energy conflicts among the id, ego, and superego (called *intrapsychic conflicts*). Freud further believed that personality is shaped by differences in how we resolve psychosexual stages of development.

Freud's Psychosexual Stages of Development

What are psychosexual stages, and how do they influence personality development? According to Freud (1940/1964), personality develops through a series of five psychosexual stages. These stages represent a complex interaction between natural shifts of pleasure from one part of the body to another and the environmental factors that influence how we handle these sexual desires. From birth through adolescence, children must resolve numerous unconscious conflicts that arise from sexual pleasure associated with stimulation of certain body parts, or what Freud called *erogenous zones*. For example, the infant nursing (from the mother's breast or from a bottle) derives a great deal of sensual pleasure from the feel of the nipple on his or her lips and the satisfaction of hunger the milk brings. However, the pleasure received from any erogenous zone must be balanced with parental restrictions or permissiveness placed on one's behavior. This creates an internal struggle, or "conflict," that significantly influences the resulting personality. Freud uses the term *psychosexual* to refer to the psychological significance of these sexual drives in the formation of a healthy personality. Because environmental circumstances vary in terms of how we are parented or how we respond to these socialization experiences, the result is individual differences in personality. Let's take a brief look at each of Freud's psychosexual stages.

Oral stage

The **oral stage** lasts from birth until approximately 18 months of age. The mouth, tongue, and lips are the erogenous zones, or focus of pleasure. Babies receive pleasure from sucking, licking, biting, and chewing.

defense mechanisms processes used to protect the ego by reducing the anxiety it feels when faced with the conflicting demands of the id and the superego

oral stage Freud's first psychosexual stage of development, which occurs during the first year of life, in which the handling of the child's feeding experiences affects personality development

anal stage Freud's second psychosexual stage, which occurs from approximately 18 months to 3 years of age, in which the parents' regulation of the child's biological urge to expel or retain feces affects personality development

phallic stage Freud's third psychosexual stage of development, which occurs between 3 and 6 years of age, in which little boys experience the Oedipus complex and little girls the Electra complex

Oedipus complex in the male, an unconscious sexual urge for the mother that develops during the phallic psychosexual stage

Electra complex in the female, an unconscious sexual urge for the father that develops during the phallic psychosexual stage

latency stage Freud's fourth psychosexual stage of development, which occurs from around age 6 to puberty, in which the child's sexuality is suppressed due to widening social contacts with school, peers, and family

Anal stage

The **anal stage** lasts from approximately 18 months to 3 years. The anus and rectum are the erogenous zones. Freud viewed production of feces in particular as a creative act. The toddler typically feels quite proud of them, either holding them in or spreading them around. How the parent then responds to this or how the parent attempts to control this production through toilet-training practices is the key to adequately resolving this stage.

Phallic stage

During the **phallic stage**, from 3 to 6 years of age, the genitals are the primary erogenous zones, and children receive pleasure from self-stimulation. This stage is particularly important for personality development as it represents the time when the **Oedipus complex** and the **Electra complex** occur. Freud believed that at this age, young children develop unconscious sexual urges for the parent of the other sex. The child wants to bond with the parent of the other sex as the child sees the parents bonding. Using the terms *Oedipus* and *Electra* from two ancient Greek tragedies, Freud believed that at this psychosexual stage little boys unconsciously fall in love with their mothers and experience hostile feelings toward their fathers much as Oedipus (unknowingly) married his mother and killed his father. Like Electra, little girls unconsciously fall in love with their fathers and feel jealousy toward their mothers.

For example, children at this age may prevent their parents from hugging or be jealous of the parents' spending time alone together. Children then resolve these complexes by identifying with and behaving more like the same-sex parent. The child incorporates the values and standards of the same-sex parent, thus ending the rivalry. The child's psychic energy is then redirected to the growth of the superego (discussed earlier). A young boy may start to imitate the way his father eats, or a young girl may mimic the way her mother brushes her hair.

Parents' toilet-training practices influence a toddler's attempt to resolve the anal psychosexual stage, according to Freud.

Latency stage

The **latency stage** occurs from age 6 until puberty. During the latency stage, sexual impulses are pushed into the background. The child's energy focuses on other demands of the environment, most noticeably school and peer relations. Sexuality reappears at puberty as reflected in the final psychosexual stage, the genital stage.

Genital stage

The **genital stage** occurs during puberty. The genitals again become the source of pleasure, as the adolescent must revisit the sexual urges that first appeared during the phallic stage. Recall that during the phallic stage, children developed unconscious attractions to the other-sex parent. Recognizing now that the love for the parent cannot be fulfilled, the adolescent seeks resolution of the genital stage by transferring this love to an other-sex mate. Consequently, for Freud, adult heterosexual intimate relations reflect the unconscious desire to choose a mate in the image of one's other-sex parent. If during the phallic stage the child develops unconscious attractions to the same-sex parent, then during the genital stage, homosexual intimate relations arise from transferring love to a same-sex partner.

A daughter's imitation of her mother reflects the youngster's attempt to resolve the negative emotions of the Electra complex, according to Freud.

As Freud saw it, children develop through these predictable stages that are primarily sexual but are psychologically significant in forming a healthy personality. Successfully resolving these stages entails receiving an optimal amount of gratification at each stage—not too much and not too little. A child who receives too much satisfaction at one stage may be reluctant to move on to the next stage. Too little satisfaction may result in frustration for the child, who may continue to seek gratification instead of moving on. These examples of inadequate resolution of a stage result in what Freud called a *fixation*. Those who fixate at one stage remain stuck, and their personalities remain immature or underdeveloped. Part of the psychic energy of the personality remains focused on the concerns of this stage.

For Freud, problems in adult personality reflect these unresolved issues or fixations from childhood. For example, a person whose oral urges were not adequately satisfied in infancy

genital stage Freud's final psychosexual stage of development, which occurs during puberty, in which sexual energy is transferred toward peers of the other sex (heterosexual orientation) or same sex (homosexual orientation)

According to Freud, the genital stage of psychosexual development unconsciously motivates teens to interact with potential sexual partners.

© Adrian Sherratt/Alamy

Hulton Archive/Getty Images

Carl Jung divided the unconscious into the personal unconscious (forgotten memories and repressed experiences) and the collective unconscious (the collected images and ideas from the earliest development of the human psyche).

would develop an *oral fixation*. An oral fixation might be expressed in the adult behaviors of overeating, nail biting, constantly chewing on pens or pencils, or boasting. More serious behaviors reflecting oral fixations include smoking, alcoholism, and binge eating. Fixation at the anal stage may express itself in the adult personality as *anal-retentiveness* or *anal-expulsiveness*. Being overly neat, stingy, or orderly (anal-retentive) or being excessively sloppy, generous, or carefree (anal-expulsive) both result from inadequate resolution of the anal stage. These are just two examples of how fixations might manifest themselves in an adult personality.

Neo-Freudians: Alfred Adler, Karen Horney, and Carl Jung

Freud's work created much controversy among professionals in the developing field of psychology. Many physicians and psychologists were initially intrigued by Freud's ideas but had their differences with aspects of his theory and eventually separated from Freud. These *neo-Freudians* agreed with Freud that unconscious conflicts were important to understanding personality, but they placed less emphasis on the role of the instinctual impulses of sex and aggression in motivating behavior. We have already introduced one neo-Freudian, Erik Erikson, whose theory of psychosocial development we discussed in Chapter 9. His eight stages detailed the influence of the environment on the developing ego over the life span. Three other examples of neo-Freudian theories are presented here, in the ideas of Carl Jung, Alfred Adler, and Karen Horney.

Carl Jung and the Collective Unconscious

Carl Jung was a student of Freud's who came to reject his ideas about personality, particularly the sexual aspects of Freud's theory. Like Freud, Jung

© Sony Pictures/courtesy Everett Collection

personal unconscious according to Jung, the part of the unconscious that consists of forgotten memories and repressed experiences from one's past

The persona and shadow archetypes are evident in Spiderman's latest adventure as good and evil do battle within Peter Parker.

maintained that personality was a function of the interplay between conscious and unconscious processes. However, Jung (1917/1966) divided the unconscious into the *personal unconscious* and the *collective unconscious*. The **personal unconscious**, much like Freud's unconscious, consisted of forgotten memories and repressed experiences. The **collective unconscious** (C. G. Jung, 1967) is universal to all people of all time periods and cultures. The collective unconscious represents the collected images and ideas from the earliest development of the human psyche. In particular, the collective unconscious includes **archetypes**, mental representations or symbols of themes and predispositions to respond to the world in a certain way. According to Jung, two of the major archetypes of the personality are the *anima* and the *animus*, the female and male aspects of each person. Among the other archetypes Jung identified are the *persona* and the *shadow*. The persona is the appearance we present to the world, the role or character we assume when relating to others, such as the martyr, the rebel, or the teacher. The shadow includes those negative tendencies or qualities of the self that a person tries to deny or hide from the world. Jung's emphasis on the collective unconscious and his belief that spiritual and religious drives are just as important as sexual ones are issues that continue to draw attention. He also stressed the importance of enduring personality traits such as introversion and extraversion (discussed shortly).

Alfred Adler and the Inferiority Complex

Alfred Adler also began as a student of Freud's but disagreed with Freud's emphasis on aggressive and sexual urges as the major force in personality development. Adler (1928) believed that it is the child's desire to overcome feelings of helplessness and to master the environment that directs behavior. In the world of adults, children are small and helpless and feel inadequate and weak. Children have to be bathed by a parent and hold a parent's hand when crossing a street. These feelings of inferiority motivate the child—and later the adult— toward achievement. For Adler, personality develops from our attempts to compensate for inferiority feelings. Moderate feelings of inferiority will result in constructive achievement and creative growth, but deep feelings of inferiority will impede positive growth and development and result in an *inferiority complex*.

Adler also emphasized the importance of birth order as a factor in personality development. He argued that firstborns, middle-borns, and youngest children grow up in differing family environments and are not necessarily treated the same by parents. These different experiences are likely to affect personality development. Adler's ideas have resulted in hundreds of studies on the effects of birth order. These studies have generally not found any reliable relationships between birth order and personality (Abdel-Khalek & Lester, 2005; J. R. Harris, 2000). Yet people generally believe that birth order affects personality, which may then actually encourage those in various birth ranks to differ in their personalities (Herrera et al., 2003).

Karen Horney and Basic Anxiety

Although Karen Horney agreed with Freud on the significance of early childhood in personality development, she rejected his belief that this development arose from instinctual conflicts. Instead, Horney (1937, 1939) suggested that family environments and disturbances in early relationships lead to **basic anxiety**, or a feeling of helplessness in children. Children cope with this basic anxiety by pursuing love, power, prestige, or detachment. Horney further argued, in contrast to Freud, that culture plays a larger role

Children's small stature and dependence on parents create inferiority feelings that motivate them toward achievement, according to Adler.

Alfred Adler believed that it is the child's desire to overcome feelings of helplessness and to master the environment that directs behavior.

collective unconscious according to Jung, the part of the unconscious that contains images and material universal to people of all time periods and cultures

archetypes according to Jung, mental representations or symbols of themes and predispositions to respond to the world in a certain way that are contained in the collective unconscious

basic anxiety according to Horney, the feeling of helplessness that develops in children from early relationships

Karen Horney argued that culture plays a larger role in personality development than does biology and suggested that family environments and disturbances in early relationships lead to basic anxiety in children. Children cope with this basic anxiety by pursuing love, power, prestige, or detachment.

More than 50 years after his death, Freud appeared on the cover of *Time* magazine, a testament to his influence on Western culture.

in personality development than do biology and instinct. For Horney, personality is not merely the result of psychosexual conflicts, as Freud would argue, but, rather, is influenced by all the events and people in the culture that make a child feel unsafe and unloved, giving rise to basic anxiety.

Contributions and Criticisms of the Psychoanalytic Approach

Freud's contributions to psychology have been immense (Erwin, 2002). He is regarded as one of the most influential thinkers of the 20th century (Gedo, 2002). His presence is still felt among the general public through literature, arts, and the movies. For example, in 1993, 54 years after his death, Freud appeared on the cover of *Time* magazine. His theory on dreams stimulated much research on the nature of sleep. His notion of defense mechanisms was extensively elaborated on by his daughter, Anna Freud, and his focus on coping and well-being sparked interest and research in health psychology. His ideas are evident in tests designed to measure personality (discussed later in this chapter) and in therapy approaches to help people with psychological problems (Chapter 15). Freud's basic notion of the unconscious influencing our behavior also has merit (Bargh & Morsella, 2008; Gedo, 2002; Greenwald & Draine, 1997; Kihlstrom, 1993; Westen, 1999). How many of us can say that we know why we have engaged in every single behavior we have ever produced? Isn't it possible that there are unconscious forces influencing our behavior?

Furthermore, Freud was one of the first to see the importance of early development in later adult behavior (Gedo, 2002). In the early 1900s, children were seen as mini-adults. People did not believe as strongly as we do now that how infants and children are treated influences their adult behavior. Although we know that infancy and childhood experiences do not *determine* adult behavior, as Freud asserted, his emphasis on the importance of these early years was a critical departure from accepted beliefs at that time. Through his psychosexual stages, Freud placed much emphasis on explaining the developmental nature of personality, probably more so than any other theorist. His views on sexuality and the impact of culture on sexuality continue to influence research (Hartmann, 2009; Person, 2005).

Freud's perspective has been criticized on several counts. First, many believe that Freud placed too much emphasis on sexual and aggressive instincts. His perspective shines very little light on environmental and social conditions that may affect personality functioning. We have just discussed that many neo-Freudians diverged from Freud on this point, creating alternate views of the ego and personality that take our interactions with others into account (J. Horgan, 1996). His ideas and themes have also been attacked for his focus on male development and perpetuation of the idea of male superiority (Person, 1990).

Much more problematic are Freud's method of data collection and the fact that his theories cannot be readily tested experimentally (Crews, 1996). His theories are based almost entirely on case study research and his own self-analysis. His observations may not have been objective, and his case studies involved patients who were diagnosed with nervous disorders. What his patients told him may not have been accurate, and their statements were not corroborated by other sources. These issues make it difficult to generalize Freud's observations. Scientifically testing Freud's theoretical concepts is also quite challenging. Measuring the unconscious is impossible if participants are unaware of these impulses. It is equally difficult to measure psychosexual stages of development. For this reason, we cannot prove that Freud's theory is true, but we also cannot disprove it. Thus, it remains a possible explanation of personality functioning, though not as popular as it was in the past. Freud's ideas have not been supported by data from other cultures, possibly because his theories reflect the Western cultural value of individualism. They may not apply in collectivist cultures that emphasize the importance of the group (Matsumoto, 1994).

Let's REVIEW

In this section, we outlined the psychoanalytic perspective on personality. For a quick check of your understanding, try answering the following questions at increasing levels of difficulty.

1. The psychoanalytic perspective emphasizes the influence of _____ on personality.

    a. unconscious desires
    b. traits
    c. self-actualization
    d. environmental factors

2. Maria often feels guilty when she engages in even the slightest offensive behavior. Freud would say that Maria has a strong _____.

    a. id
    b. ego
    c. superego
    d. collective unconscious

3. One of the major criticisms of Freud's theory concerns its _____.

    a. overemphasis on environmental and cognitive factors in explaining behavior
    b. difficulty in being experimentally tested and validated
    c. emphasis on the unconscious
    d. assumption that all people are good

ANSWERS 1. a; 2. c; 3. b.

THE TRAIT APPROACH: HOW DO OUR GENES INFLUENCE PERSONALITY?

A second major perspective on personality is called the **trait approach**. The trait approach, like the psychoanalytic approach, focuses on internal aspects of personality. Whereas the psychoanalytic approach attempts to explain personality by focusing on unconscious forces, the trait perspective attempts to describe personality and emphasizes its biological aspects. Trait theory assumes that we all have internal **traits**, or tendencies to behave in a certain way across most situations. These traits remain relatively stable as we age and explain why people generally behave the same way across a variety of situations. Yet because people differ in the degree to which they possess various traits, we develop unique personalities. We will describe four major approaches to understanding these personality traits in the theories of Gordon Allport, Raymond Cattell, and Hans Eysenck and in the five factor theory.

LEARNING OBJECTIVES

What Should You Know?

*   Define trait and compare the various trait approaches to understanding personality (Allport, Cattell, Eysenck, and the five factor theory). Indicate the strengths and weaknesses of the trait approach.
*   Discuss genetic contributions to personality, and address whether personality is consistent and stable over time.

Gordon Allport's Trait Theory

Psychologist Gordon Allport (1961) believed that three types of traits help us understand a person's uniqueness: *central traits*, *secondary traits*, and *cardinal traits*. **Central traits** include those tendencies we have across most situations; they are the core qualities your friends would

trait approach a personality perspective that attempts to describe personality by emphasizing internal, biological aspects of personality called traits

trait tendency to behave in a certain way across most situations

central traits according to Allport, those tendencies we have to behave in a certain way across most situations

Stan Honda/AFP/Getty Images

At a sporting event, passionate fans may express behaviors that they do not ordinarily exhibit—a secondary trait, according to Allport.

© Courtesy of Cattell Family

Using factor analysis, Raymond Cattell (1905–1998) reduced the number of core personality traits to 16 basic traits, referred to as source traits.

secondary traits according to Allport, the tendencies we have that are less consistent and describe how we behave in certain situations

cardinal traits according to Allport, those dominant elements of our personalities that drive all of our behaviors

surface traits basic traits that describe people's personalities, according to Cattell

source traits universal tendencies that underlie and are at the core of surface traits, according to Cattell

state if they were asked to describe you. For example, if you are friendly in most situations, then friendly would be considered a central trait. Similarly, if your sister is generally shy most of the time, then shyness would be considered a central trait for her. We all have central traits, yet the actual qualities that are considered central traits may differ from person to person. In the McBride family, we saw examples of different central traits: Dennis, Rosetta, and Helen were generally outgoing, whereas James was quieter.

Secondary traits describe how we behave in certain situations; they are tendencies that are less consistent and more situation-specific. Many of us behave aggressively in certain situations, such as when we are frustrated or when we see others behave aggressively. In these specific situations, aggression is an example of a secondary trait. However, for someone who is aggressive across most situations, aggression would be an example of a central trait. Again, we all have secondary traits, but whether a specific quality is considered a secondary trait may differ from person to person.

Cardinal traits describe how we behave across all situations. Allport considered these a very basic and dominant element of our personalities—but he had difficulty in finding cardinal traits in all people that he studied. Consequently, the validity of cardinal traits became suspect. Recall from Chapter 5 on learning and Chapter 11 on social psychology the powerful effect the environment can have on our behavior. This effect often makes us behave differently across situations.

Allport's goal in describing traits was to understand the behavior of a specific individual. Other research focused on identifying and understanding core or universal traits that direct the behavior of people in general, relying heavily on the use of statistics. This inquiry set the stage for Raymond Cattell's statistical analysis of personality traits.

Raymond Cattell's Factor Analytic Trait Theory

Raymond Cattell (1943) attempted to document relationships among traits using a sophisticated statistical technique called *factor analysis*. In contemporary factor analysis, data are entered into a computer. The computer is then asked to find shared qualities among the data and to group these shared relationships into factors. For example, suppose we perform a factor analysis on soups. All the ingredients for all soups are entered into the computer database. The computer is then instructed to generate a list of any shared ingredients among all the soups. If it finds a shared "quality" among them—perhaps salt or water was in every soup—then these items would be called soup factors. Psychologists can do the same thing with personality traits. All traits that are used to describe people are entered into a computer, and then the computer is instructed to find any shared qualities or factors. In this way, Cattell reduced the number of personality traits that could be used to describe all people.

Cattell's research (1965) originally yielded 36 **surface traits** that could describe personality. He hypothesized that there must be common underlying factors that account for the 36 surface traits. Cattell referred to these qualities or dimensions as **source traits**. Source traits are basic, broad, and relatively universal tendencies at the core of our personalities. We may differ in the amount or quality of these traits, but they are present in everyone's personality to some degree. For example, two of Cattell's source traits include emotional stability and apprehension (● TABLE 13.1). Someone who is not emotionally stable and is high in apprehension would evidence neuroticism, a surface trait that includes several related behaviors such as anxiety, fear, and indecision that stem from source traits. Through subsequent analysis and research, Cattell identified 16 source traits (see Table 13.1). However, Cattell's 16 source traits did not easily lend themselves to research. Research led by British psychologist Hans Eysenck would further reduce the number.

Hans Eysenck Narrows the Traits

Building on Cattell's factor analytic studies, Eysenck and Rachman (1965) found two factors that they believed measured people's key characteristics: *introversion/extraversion* and *emotional stability/neuroticism* (● FIGURE 13.3). Introversion and extraversion define where a person's energy is directed. **Introversion** means that the person's energy is directed inward. This tendency could include being rigid, reliable, sober, or controlled. **Extraversion** means that the person's energy is directed outward. This tendency could include being easygoing, lively, or excitable. *Emotional stability* and *neuroticism* refer to control over one's emotions. Being even-tempered, calm, or a leader are traits that include more control over emotions and represent **emotional stability**, whereas moody and touchy describe traits that represent **neuroticism**. We all are somewhere on the introversion/extraversion scale and somewhere on the emotional stability/neuroticism continuum; we just differ in the degree to which we express the two factors. (see ● Figure 13.3)

In the 1970s, Eysenck in collaboration with his wife, Sybil Eysenck, added a third dimension called *psychoticism* to the model (Eysenck & Eysenck, 1969, 1976). **Psychoticism** includes tendencies toward recklessness, disregard for common sense and cultural norms, inconsideration, hostility, anger, and impulsivity. Eysenck originally characterized impulsivity as a dimension of extraversion. However, once the dimension of psychoticism was added, he moved this trait from extraversion to psychoticism. Eysenck's three factor model of personality is referred to as the PEN (Psychoticism, Extraversion, Neuroticism) model (● TABLE 13.2).

Eysenck (1967, 1982, 1991) proposed that variations in these personality characteristics were partly due to genetics. Specifically, Eysenck suggested that introverts inherit the tendency toward higher levels of physical arousal than extraverts. Introverts are more likely to avoid social situations because such experiences will elevate their arousal and lead to overstimulation and discomfort. Hence, they are more likely than extraverts to turn inward and become introverted.

Research has generally supported Eysenck's theory; several studies confirm that introverts tend to show higher levels of physical arousal than extraverts (Beauducel, Brocke, & Leue, 2006; Bullock & Gilliland, 1993; LeBlanc, Ducharme, & Thompson, 2004). Research by Kumari and colleagues (2004) has even documented a relationship between extraversion scores and changes in fMRI signals from rest, as shown in the ● WHAT'S HAPPENING IN YOUR BRAIN? feature.

TABLE 13.1

● **Cattell's 16 Personality Factors**

FACTOR	DESCRIPTION (Extremes of each factor from low to high levels)	
Warmth	Reserved	Warm
Reasoning	Less intelligent	More intelligent
Emotional Stability	Easily upset	Emotionally stable
Dominance	Submissive	Dominant
Liveliness	Serious	Expressive
Rule Consciousness	Nonconforming	Conforming
Social Boldness	Shy	Venturesome
Sensitivity	Tough-minded	Sensitive
Vigilance	Trusting	Suspicious
Abstractedness	Practical	Imaginative
Privateness	Open	Shrewd
Apprehension	Unworried	Worried
Openness to Change	Conservative	Experimenting
Self-reliance	Dependent	Self-sufficient
Perfectionism	Undisciplined	Precise
Tension	Relaxed	Tense

TABLE 13.2

● **Eysenck's PEN Model**

PSYCHOTICISM	EXTRAVERSION	NEUROTICISM
Aggressive	Sociable	Anxious
Assertive	Irresponsible	Depressed
Impulsive	Expressive	Guilt feelings
Manipulative	Active	Moody
Tough-minded	Dominant	Obsessive
Hostile	Lack of reflection	Tense

FIGURE 13.3

● **Eysenck's Trait Theory** British psychologist Hans Eysenck arrived at two universal traits using factor analysis. The stable–unstable axis defines one's emotionality; the introverted–extraverted axis defines the degree to which a person's energy is directed inward or outward. The traits in each quadrant indicate where they are placed with respect to these two factors. *(From H. J. Eysenck and S. Rachman, "The Causes and Cures of Neurosis." Copyright © 1965 Reproduced by permission from EdiTS Publishers, San Diego, CA. All rights reserved.)*

introversion personality traits that involve energy directed inward, such as being calm or peaceful

extraversion personality traits that involve energy directed outward, such as being easygoing, lively, or excitable

emotional stability having control over one's emotions

neuroticism the degree to which one is emotionally unstable

psychoticism the degree to which one is hostile, nonconforming, impulsive, and aggressive

WHAT'S HAPPENING IN YOUR BRAIN?

BRAIN ACTIVITY AND INTROVERSION/EXTRAVERSION

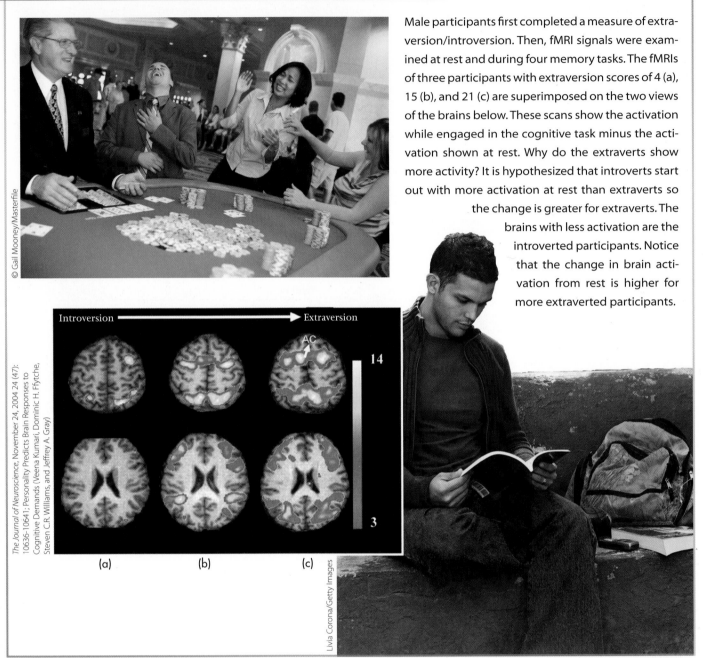

Male participants first completed a measure of extraversion/introversion. Then, fMRI signals were examined at rest and during four memory tasks. The fMRIs of three participants with extraversion scores of 4 (a), 15 (b), and 21 (c) are superimposed on the two views of the brains below. These scans show the activation while engaged in the cognitive task minus the activation shown at rest. Why do the extraverts show more activity? It is hypothesized that introverts start out with more activation at rest than extraverts so the change is greater for extraverts. The brains with less activation are the introverted participants. Notice that the change in brain activation from rest is higher for more extraverted participants.

The Journal of Neuroscience, November 24, 2004 24 (47): 10636–10641; Personality Predicts Brain Responses to Cognitive Demands (Veena Kumari, Dominic H. Ffytche, Steven C.R. Williams, and Jeffrey A. Gray)

Introversion → Extraversion

AC

14

3

(a)   (b)   (c)

© Gail Mooney/Masterfile

Livia Corona/Getty Images

The Five Factor Trait Theory

Currently, the most widely accepted trait theory derived from factor analysis is Paul Costa and Robert McCrae's (1992) **five factor theory**. This theory proposes five core dimensions that can be measured along a continuum in all people:

● *Openness*: the degree to which one is thoughtful and rational in considering new ideas. People who score high in openness tend to be imaginative, creative, and curious and to prefer variety; those who score low in openness prefer routine and are more narrowminded in their ideas and experiences.

five factor theory Costa and McCrae's trait theory that proposes five core dimensions to personality: openness, conscientiousness, extraversion, agreeableness, and neuroticism

- *Conscientiousness*: the degree to which one is aware of and attentive to other people, to the details of a task, or to both. People who are high in conscientiousness tend to be hardworking, ambitious, reliable, and self-controlled, whereas individuals low in this dimension are more often described as unreliable, lazy, and spontaneous.
- *Extraversion*: the degree to which one's energy is directed inward or outward. People high in extraversion are talkative and sociable and prefer to be around others. At the other end of the continuum are people low in extraversion (introverts), who are quiet, reserved, and comfortable on their own.
- *Agreeableness*: the degree to which one gets along well with others. Being easygoing and trusting are traits characteristic of one high in agreeableness. At the other end of the spectrum are people who are unfriendly, antagonistic, and suspicious (low agreeableness).
- *Neuroticism*: the degree to which one is emotionally stable or unstable. People high in neuroticism are temperamental, worrisome, and pessimistic. People who score low on this factor tend to be more even-tempered and calm.

These five dimensions appear in all cultures, suggesting that these five factors may represent universal personality components (Katigbak et al., 2002; McCrae & Costa, 1998; Yamagata et al., 2006). An easy way to remember the five factors is with the acronym OCEAN. Each letter in OCEAN stands for one of the five factors: O = openness, C = conscientiousness, E = extraversion, A = agreeableness, and N = neuroticism. See how the five factor theory applies to online game players in the ● TECHNOLOGY AND BEHAVIOR feature on page 550.

● THE BIG PICTURE REVIEW compares the four trait theories. Notice that the main difference in these theories is the number of basic traits that are proposed. Allport's theory proposes 3, Eysenck's theory proposes 3, Cattell's theory proposes 16, and Costa and McCrae's model proposes 5. A question that follows from these theories is this: **Where do these traits come from?**

Genetic Contributions to Personality

The trait perspective assumes that people have internal dispositions to behave consistently across situations. Thus, some researchers have speculated that we inherit some aspects of our personalities. Recall that newborn infants do show differences in behavior that we refer to as temperament (see Chapter 9), that these temperamental differences appear strongly related to genes (Braungart et al., 1992), and that they are quite stable over time (Jaffari-Bimmel et al., 2006; Majdandzic & van den Boom, 2007; McCrae et al., 2000; Rothbart, Ahadi, & Evans, 2000). In one study, children's temperament type at age 3 was strongly correlated with their behavioral style at age 26 (Caspi et al., 2003). It seems possible that other characteristics or personality dispositions are also inherited.

Some studies have found that children's personality test scores moderately correlate with those of their parents and siblings (M. H. Davis, Luce, & Kraus, 1994). But what does this finding mean? It could be that you are hot-tempered because you have inherited your

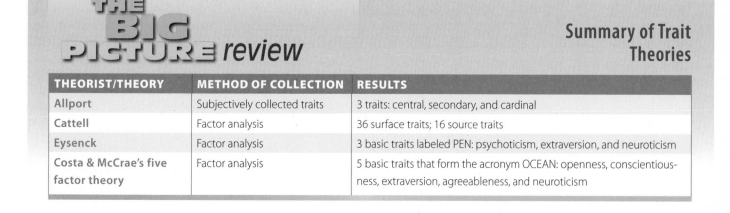

THE BIG PICTURE *review*

Summary of Trait Theories

THEORIST/THEORY	METHOD OF COLLECTION	RESULTS
Allport	Subjectively collected traits	3 traits: central, secondary, and cardinal
Cattell	Factor analysis	36 surface traits; 16 source traits
Eysenck	Factor analysis	3 basic traits labeled PEN: psychoticism, extraversion, and neuroticism
Costa & McCrae's five factor theory	Factor analysis	5 basic traits that form the acronym OCEAN: openness, conscientiousness, extraversion, agreeableness, and neuroticism

TECHNOLOGY and BEHAVIOR

PERSONALITY AND ONLINE GAME PLAY

Millions of people around the globe play online games. For many it is a major leisure activity and may be preferred over watching TV, going to the movies, or reading books. Much of the research has focused on adolescents and on the more negative aspects of online gaming such as the effect of playing aggressive and violent games and excessive game play. Yet, relatively little research has examined the characteristics of adults who play online games and the relationship between personality traits and online gaming.

Who are adult online gamers? Most studies have found that the majority of online gamers are White males in their 20s and 30s (Griffiths, Davies, & Chappell, 2003, 2004; D. Williams, Yee, & Caplan, 2008). However, one study found no gender difference among people who play games on the Internet, people who use the Internet but not for gaming, and people who do not use the Internet (Youn, Lee, & Doyle, 2003). Although online gamers typically have some college experience or above-average education and income, non-gaming Internet users have a higher socioeconomic level (Youn et al., 2003).

Are certain people more attracted to online gaming than others? Some personality traits are associated with gaming. Online gamers tend to be more impulsive and higher in sensation seeking and risk-taking (Mehroof & Griffiths, 2010; Youn et al., 2003). Online gamers report higher levels of openness, conscientiousness, and extraversion than nonplayers (L. S. Chen, Tu, & Wang, 2008; Teng, 2008). Those gamers that get most immersed in games tend to be higher in openness to experience, neuroticism, and extraversion (Weibel, Wissmath, & Mast, 2010). These personality traits tend to work well in the gaming environment. Taking risks and being open to new activities and tasks are necessary skills in the online gaming world and are often rewarded. Similarly, people high in extraversion may be more comfortable working online with others to achieve game objectives than are less extraverted people. Many online gamers report achievement and the social aspect of the game as the most important factors in playing (H. Cole & Griffiths, 2007; Griffiths et al., 2004; D. Williams et al., 2008). Playing on teams also necessitates conscientiousness or the knowledge of other people's needs. Online gamers also report that gaming alleviates negative feelings and stress (Hussain & Griffiths, 2009). Hence, some people's personality traits may attract them to the nature of online gaming, enhance their pleasure while playing, and motivate them to keep playing online games. Given online gaming's relative newness, future research may shed more light on the personality characteristics of online game players.

quick temper from your mother or father. However, your temper might also be due to being exposed to your parent's temper. It may upset you and make you temperamental in response, or you may be modeling your parent's behavior—or both. It is not possible to tell exactly where environmental influences end and genetic ones begin when children share genes and a family environment. To unravel such a puzzle, adoption and twin studies are used.

One way to study genetic contributions—the nature side of personality—is to look at children who are adopted. Because adopted children have no genes in common with their adoptive family members, any similarities in personality characteristics between these children and their adoptive parents are likely due to learning or modeling. On the other hand, because these children have genes in common with their biological parents but do not share a family environment, any similarities to them are likely due to genetics. These research studies have found more personality similarities between adoptive children and their biological parents (G. Carey & DiLalla, 1994). These findings suggest a strong genetic component to personality.

Another method for investigating the contribution of genes—or nature—is to study identical twins (W. Johnson et al., 2009). Research on identical twins provides even more compelling evidence that at least some personality tendencies may be inherited (Bouchard, 2004; A. Weiss, Bates, & Luciano, 2008). Identical twins reared in separate environments appeared to show remarkable similarities in behavior years later when they were reunited (Bouchard et al., 1990; Holden, 1980; Lykken et al.,1992). One of the more famous separated pairs is James Springer and James Lewis, known as the "Jim twins." Both drove Chevrolets and chain-smoked Salem cigarettes. They both worked as sheriff's deputies and listed stockcar racing, carpentry, and mechanical drawing as interests and hobbies (Holden, 1980). Studies have found more similarities between the personalities of identical twins than of nonidentical twins (D. M. Buss, 1995; Plomin et al., 2001; Saudino et al., 1995). Such evidence indicates a significant genetic role in the personalities that we exhibit. Perhaps such research can explain why all of Rachel McBride's children were creative in some way and academically successful—maybe aspects of their intelligence and creativity were inherited.

© Ashley Cooper/Alamy

Studies have found more similarities between identical twins' personalities than between nonidentical twins' personalities, indicating a significant genetic role in the personalities that we exhibit.

Other research on the heritability of personality traits has focused on gene markers that direct our neurotransmitter functioning and how these gene markers influence behavior. For example, as we saw in Chapter 2, the neurotransmitter serotonin is associated with regulating behavior, mood, and thought processes. Low serotonin activity has been linked to traits such as aggression and impulsivity. Low serotonin activity can be caused by a multitude of factors, including how we think about our environment or ourselves. However, increasing evidence indicates that serotonin responsivity may be partly genetically determined (Lesch & Merschdorf, 2000; Manuck et al., 2000; Twitchell et al., 1998). Several studies have found an association between the *serotonin transporter gene* and anxiety-related personality traits (B. D. Greenberg et al., 2000; Hayden et al., 2007; Jang et al., 2001; Melke et al., 2001; Osher, Hamer, & Benjamin, 2000; Sen, Burmeister, & Ghosh, 2004; Sen et al., 2004). This gene influences the levels of serotonin in the brain and may account for differences in anxiety levels from person to person.

Other studies have investigated the relationship between a *dopamine receptor gene* and the personality trait of novelty seeking (Jonsson, Burgert et al., 2003; Jonsson, Ivo et al., 2002; Katsuragi et al., 2001; Munafo et al., 2008; Schinka, Letsch, & Crawford, 2002). No consistent significant relationships have emerged from these studies. There has also been little success in attempting to link neurotransmitter gene regions with infant temperaments (Garpenstrand et al., 2002; Lakatos et al., 2003; L. A. Schmidt et al., 2009).

Such results suggest a complex interaction between biology, environment, and personality. Human behavior is the product of many genes working simultaneously, together with multiple environmental and developmental events (Ebstein et al., 2002; Hamer, 2002). Unraveling these connections and influences will keep scientists very busy in the years ahead.

Stability and Change in Personality

Has your personality changed over time, or do you still show the same tendencies that you did when you were a child? The trait approach not only assumes that traits are inherited; it also assumes that these internal tendencies are consistent and stable over time. What does the research indicate? Research does support the stability of *some* personality traits over the course of adulthood. However, age, culture, and gender are important when considering stability and change in personality.

The Influence of Age, Culture, and Gender on Personality

After the age of 30, changes in personality traits are smaller than in childhood and young adulthood (Costa & McCrae, 1997; B. W. Roberts & DelVecchio, 2000; B. W. Roberts, Walton, & Viechtbauer, 2006; Terracciano, Costa, & McCrae, 2006). Evidence on the stability of traits prior to age 30 is quite complex. As a part of the developmental process, children, adolescents, and young adults experiment with new identities and ways of behaving. They may adopt new values and attitudes or revise existing ones (McAdams & Olson, 2010). Changes in personality, therefore, are more frequent during these periods. Some studies suggest that at least for some traits, there is a consistency from childhood to adulthood (B. W. Roberts, Caspi, & Moffitt, 2001). For example, McCrae and colleagues (2002) found stability in the traits of extraversion, agreeableness, and conscientiousness from age 12 to age 18. Hampson and Goldberg (2006) found stability for the traits of extraversion and conscientiousness from elementary school to midlife. Shiner, Masten, and Roberts (2003) found modest continuity in academic conscientiousness and agreeableness from childhood to adulthood. Another study (R. W. Robins et al., 2001) found consistency in the five factor personality traits when following the same people from the beginning to the end of their college years.

Age differences in personality have also been investigated in other cultures, and a similar picture has emerged. Data from Germany, Britain, Spain, Italy, Portugal, Croatia, Turkey, South Korea, and the Czech Republic are consistent with findings on the five factor model of personality in U.S. samples (McCrae et al., 1999, 2000). Older men and women in these cultures also tended to be lower in extraversion and openness to experience and higher in agreeableness and conscientiousness. Such findings appear to support the universality of some personality traits. These societies differ dramatically in language, culture, and historical experiences from one another and from the experiences of most people in the United States. Yet the cultural differences seemed to have little impact on age differences in personality traits.

Cultures also differ markedly in how they define themselves and in which traits they find most admirable. Recall from Chapter 11 that individualistic cultures such as the United States, Canada, Western Europe, and Australia emphasize individual behavior, whereas collectivistic cultures such as India and Japan emphasize group behavior. Such cultural orientations also influence how we see ourselves. People from individualistic cultures are more likely to use personal traits to describe themselves. People from collectivistic cultures are more likely to describe themselves in a social context, citing their group memberships and social activities (Gardiner, Mutter, & Kosmitzki, 1998). This cultural difference makes it difficult to assess similarities in traits across cultures.

Although some research has indicated a consistency in personality traits in adulthood and across cultures, other research suggests substantial *changes* in personality even during the course of adulthood. People generally become more conscientious, agreeable, and emotionally stable, slightly less open to experience, and less extraverted across adulthood (Carducci, 2009; Ludtke, Trautwein, & Husemann, 2009; Ravenna, Jones, & Kwan, 2002; B. W. Roberts & Mroczek, 2008; Roberts, Walton, & Viechtbauer, 2006; Scollon & Diener, 2006; Srivastava et al., 2003). Many people also become more *androgynous*, exhibiting both male and female traits, as they age (M. Fiske, 1980). Even McCrae and colleagues' (1999, 2000) cross-cultural research did not find consistency across all of the five factor traits.

Gender differences in personality traits also show evidence of both stability and change. Across cultures and for both college-age and adult samples, women report themselves to be higher in neuroticism, extraversion, agreeableness, conscientiousness, and openness to feelings, whereas men report themselves higher in assertiveness and openness to ideas (Costa, Terracciano, & McCrae, 2001; Schmitt et al., 2008). Yet these personality traits varied more within each gender than they did between genders. Gender differences in neuroticism and extraversion also become smaller over time as men and women age (Carducci, 2009; Srivastava et al., 2003). Moreover, the research demonstrates that not all people change at the same rate over their lives. Some people's traits may be stable whereas other people's traits may change (Mroczek & Spiro, 2003; Roberts & Mroczek, 2008; Small et al., 2003). Why personality change occurs for some people and not others is a question that continues to be researched.

The Influence of the Environment on Traits

Situational factors also influence the stability and consistency of traits. Many of us display the same trait (behave the same way) when faced with similar circumstances—that is, when the environmental cues are the same. However, when the situation is different, our behavior may change. This relationship among traits, situations, and behavior is referred to as the **person–situation interaction** (Mischel & Shoda, 1995). For example, the students of one of the authors of this textbook are always surprised to hear that she has a fear of public speaking. They see her speak every week in class with little anxiety. They know that she has been teaching for more than 20 years. From such knowledge, they predict that she would not fear public speaking in other situations, such as at a research conference or at a community function. But in these different situations, she is extremely anxious, panicked, and nauseated at the thought of speaking in front of a group. The cues of the two different situations evoke different behaviors and reactions. Thus, our traits do not always predict how we will behave across different situations.

How do psychologists reconcile these seemingly contradictory findings? Psychologists recognize that personality is both stable *and* changeable. Some traits are probably more consistent across the life span and from culture to culture, whereas others are more easily influenced by one's society, gender, environment, and daily situations (Fleeson, 2004). Such flexibility enables individuals to face developmental changes and challenges throughout their lives.

person–situation interaction the influence of the situation on the stability of traits; when in the same situation, we display similar behavior, but when the situation is different, behavior may change

Contributions and Criticisms of the Trait Approach

The trait perspective has contributed to our understanding of personality by providing psychologists with a common vocabulary to describe people's personalities. Because this common language facilitates communication within the field, the trait approach has been particularly useful in the area of personality assessment, a topic we will turn to shortly. Knowing a person's tendencies or traits also helps psychologists predict future behavior. These predictions, however, will be influenced by the nature of the situation (J. A. Johnson, 1997). The assumptions of the trait perspective—that traits are internal and stable—have also fueled research investigating the biological aspects of personality and the consistency and stability of personality traits across the life span.

However, the objective of personality research is to uncover how we differ from one another. Although the trait perspective does a good job of *describing* people's personalities, it is criticized for not *explaining* why we behave in a particular way (Digman, 1997; Funder, 1993). Critics further argue that the trait approach portrays personality too simplistically and fails to reflect its complexity and depth (J. A. Block, 1995; Epstein, 1994; Gladwell, 2004). Can everyone really be reduced to 3, 5, or 16 dimensions? Can we cleanly divide personality into biological and environmental components without taking into account the complex interactions among them? We have also seen the trait perspective's shortcomings in predicting people's behavior across different situations (Wiggins, 1997). This outcome should not be surprising, though, given the powerful influence of situational forces on behavior.

Often our personality interacts with our environment. A behavior we display in one context (texting on our cell phone when the teacher is not looking) may not be the same behavior we exhibit at other times (being studious and engaged when the teacher is attentive).

Let's
REVIEW In this section, we presented the trait approach to personality and discussed genetic aspects of personality and its stability over time. For a quick check of your understanding, try answering the following questions at increasing levels of difficulty.

1. The trait perspective emphasizes the influence of _____ on personality.

   a. unconscious impulses
   b. internal tendencies

   c. self-actualization
   d. environmental factors

2. Terrence is outgoing in most situations. Allport would describe this tendency in Terrence as a _____.

   a. source trait
   b. secondary trait

   c. cardinal trait
   d. central trait

3. Which of the following is *not* considered one of the "big five" traits of personality?

   a. achievement
   b. extraversion

   c. conscientiousness
   d. agreeableness

ANSWERS 1. b; 2. d; 3. a

social cognitive approach a personality perspective that emphasizes the influence of one's thoughts and social experiences in formulating personality

reciprocal determinism according to Bandura, the constant interaction among one's behavior, thoughts, and environment determines personality

THE SOCIAL COGNITIVE APPROACH: HOW DO THE ENVIRONMENT AND OUR THOUGHTS INFLUENCE PERSONALITY?

The **social cognitive approach** sees personality as influenced by both the environment and one's thoughts. Whereas Freud focused on how unconscious forces influence behavior and the trait perspective investigates internal dispositions, the social cognitive approach looks at the characteristic ways a person perceives and interprets events in the environment. For example, the person who assumes that others are unlikely to treat her fairly is more likely to have a quarrelsome personality than a person who tends to assume that things generally happen for the best. These patterns of thoughts are established through our interactions with and observations of other people. Two examples of this approach are Albert Bandura's *reciprocal determinism* and Julian Rotter's *locus of control* theory.

Reciprocal Determinism: Albert Bandura's Interacting Forces

Albert Bandura (1986) speculates that personality is the product of three interacting forces: *environment*, *behavior*, and *thoughts*. Bandura called the constant interaction among these three factors **reciprocal determinism** (● FIGURE 13.4). We choose to place ourselves in certain environments, and these environments then influence our behavior and the way we think. However, the way we think—our attributions, goals, values, and perceptions—may guide which environments we choose to be in as well as the behavior we exhibit (Dweck, 2008). Our behavior, in turn, may change the environment as well as the way we think. All three variables influence one another in a reciprocal manner.

For example, when we were children, we were placed in a family environment that modeled specific child-rearing techniques. We tend to think that everything we experienced in our home was normal and that these same experiences occurred everywhere else. We tend to think that everyone else grew up with the parental discipline style we had. If we have not learned anything different, we tend to behave in the same way toward our own children. The family environment and our understanding of the way we were raised have now influenced our own parenting behavior.

Bandura speculates that personality is the product of reciprocal determinism, or the mutual interaction among one's environment, behavior, and thoughts.

Archives of the History of American Psychology, University of Akron, Akron, Ohio

A critical cognitive element in this interplay is what Bandura (1997) termed **self-efficacy**, or one's expectation of success in a given situation. Self-efficacy can differ among different domains in one's life. People with high self-efficacy in a certain domain believe that they will be successful in that domain. Approaching a situation with this belief is more likely to result in actual success. On the other hand, people with low self-efficacy in a particular domain are more likely to approach a task believing that they won't succeed at it. This mind-set then decreases their chance of succeeding by causing them to give up too easily or not even really try in the first place.

Returning to our previous example, if you believe that you will be a successful parent by using the same discipline techniques that your parents used with you, you will be more likely to use such measures. If such practices are successful—in other words, your children behave as you would like—you feel even better as a parent. However, if you do not believe that you will be a successful parent, you may constantly change the methods you use to discipline your children. Such inconsistency will make it even more likely that your children will not behave the way you want, which only reinforces your lack of confidence in your parenting ability.

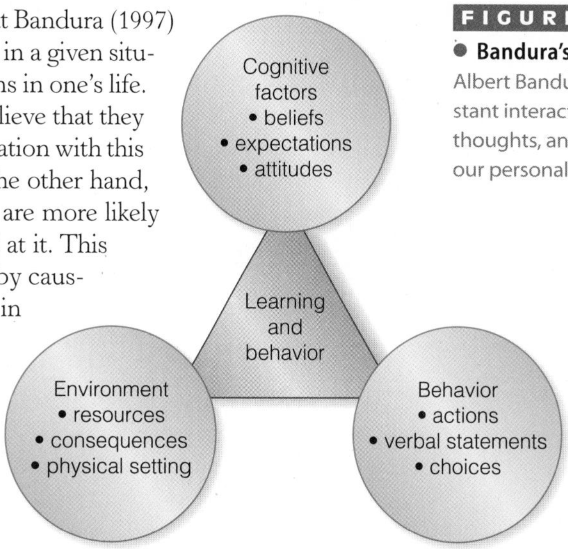

Julian Rotter's Locus of Control: Internal and External Expectations

Julian Rotter provides another example of a social cognitive approach to personality. His theory (Rotter, 1982) is referred to as **locus of control**, or *location of control*. Rotter believes that we all have expectations regarding how much control we have over the outcome of an event. These expectations fall on a continuum from internal to external. For example, you probably enter the testing room on exam day already expecting to do well, average, or poorly on the exam. This is your expectation of the event. Some people attribute the outcome of an event to internal forces, such as hard work. If you expect to do well on an exam because you studied hard, you are exhibiting an *internal locus of control*. As an "internal," you are attributing the outcome of the event to factors within your control. However, other people attribute the outcome of an event to external forces, such as good luck, fate, or environmental factors. If you believe you will do well on the exam because the course or test is easy or because the professor likes you, these expectations demonstrate an *external locus of control*. As an "external," you attribute the outcome to factors outside your control. Not surprisingly, internals demonstrate higher academic achievement than externals. Externals tend to believe that only fate or the luck of a sympathetic teacher will get them a good grade, and so they do not study as much as internals (Schultz & Schultz, 2005).

Rotter suggests that these varying expectations of control lead to differences in personality. Think about voting behavior. Would an internal or external type be more likely to vote? Externals are more likely to believe that forces outside their control determine elections, so they are less likely to vote. Internals, on the other hand, are more likely to believe that their votes count and will influence who is elected. Therefore, they are more likely to vote. Think about your health. Who would be more likely to exercise regularly and maintain a healthy lifestyle? Externals are more likely to attribute their weight, health, or medical condition to fate. "What will be, will be" could be their motto. They feel that when their time is up, it's up and nothing

FIGURE 13.4

● **Bandura's Reciprocal Determinism** Albert Bandura speculates that the constant interaction between our behavior, thoughts, and environment determines our personalities.

Cognitive factors
• beliefs
• expectations
• attitudes

Learning and behavior

Environment
• resources
• consequences
• physical setting

Behavior
• actions
• verbal statements
• choices

self-efficacy the expectation that one has for success in a given situation

locus of control the expectation of control we have over the outcome of an event; an internal locus expects some degree of personal control, whereas an external locus expects little personal control

People who vote believe that their one voice makes a difference—an example of an internal locus of control.

Rob Crandall/Jupiter Images

can change it. Internals, however, believe that they can control their health and are therefore more likely to exercise, follow doctors' directions, get regular checkups, and eat wisely, behaviors that actually contribute to better health (Phares, 1991; Strickland, 1989).

In examining the opening case study, Bandura's and Rotter's social cognitive perspectives would explain the McBride personalities as expressions of an internal locus of control and a strong sense of self-efficacy. Rachel's insistence that her children work hard in school could have influenced her children's subsequent academic achievement. Her determination to be treated fairly modeled to her children high self-efficacy and an internal locus of control. The children adopted these attitudes, leading to their own successes and fights for equality.

Contributions and Criticisms of the Social Cognitive Approach

The social cognitive approach has made major contributions to the field of psychology. By detailing the cognitive processes such as thinking, expectations, and other mental events that influence our behavior, it has expanded our conceptualization and understanding of personality. This knowledge in turn has stimulated an enormous amount of research focusing on how environmental and cognitive factors influence behavior. Our knowledge of memory, attributions, and problem solving stem directly from this perspective, which easily lends itself to research, specifically experimental testing. Objectively measuring social and cognitive processes is easier than measuring unconscious forces or biological tendencies. Despite these contributions, the social cognitive approach has been criticized for not addressing biological, unconscious, and emotional factors that influence personality (Liebert & Spiegler, 1998). It also has been criticized for not detailing the exact nature of personality development.

Let's
REVIEW In this section, we described social cognitive approaches to personality. For a quick check of your understanding, try answering the following questions at increasing levels of difficulty.

1. The social cognitive perspective emphasizes the influence of _____ on personality.

   a. unconscious impulses
   b. internal tendencies
   c. self-actualization
   d. patterns of thoughts

2. Juanita believes that finding a job is a matter of being in the right place at the right time. Rotter would classify Juanita as having _____.

   a. low self-efficacy
   b. low determinism
   c. an internal locus of control
   d. an external locus of control

3. Dylan is sure he will do poorly on his next psychology exam. Dylan often thinks this way in regard to his academic studies. Bandura would say that Dylan has _____.

   a. low self-esteem
   b. low self-efficacy
   c. an internal locus of control
   d. reciprocal determinism

ANSWERS 1. d; 2. d; 3. b

humanistic approach a personality perspective that emphasizes the individual, personal choice, and free will in shaping personality; assumes that humans have a built-in drive toward fulfilling their own natural potential

LEARNING OBJECTIVE

What Should You Know?
• Define self-actualization, and describe how the humanistic views of Maslow and Rogers propose that it can be achieved. Indicate the strengths and weaknesses of the humanistic approach.

THE HUMANISTIC APPROACH: HOW DOES FREE WILL SHAPE PERSONALITY?

The fourth and final personality perspective we will discuss is the humanistic approach. Humanistic psychology viewed itself as a "third force" in American psychology, following behavioral and psychoanalytic views. The **humanistic approach** emphasizes the individual, personal choice, and free will in shaping personality. The individual is seen as an active participant in his or her growth as a person. The humanistic view further assumes that humans have a built-in drive toward fulfilling their own natural potential. The attainment of this potential is referred to as **self-actualization**. Two well-known humanistic theorists have charted somewhat different paths to achieving self-actualization. One is Abraham Maslow, whose hierarchy of needs theory was introduced in Chapter 8. The other is Carl Rogers and his self theory.

Abraham Maslow and the Hierarchy of Needs Theory

Recall from Chapter 8 that Maslow (1968, 1970, 1971) believed that the pathway to achieving self-actualization was in the form of a hierarchy, with physical or biological needs at the bottom and more psychological or social needs at the top. According to Maslow, a person must satisfy lower-level needs before higher-level needs can be attained. At the bottom of the hierarchy are basic physiological needs, such as the need for food and water. Without food and water, we cannot proceed to the next rung of the ladder. At this next level, safety becomes the concern: the need to be free from harm and to feel secure. Once this safety need is met, the person focuses on psychological needs, such as feeling a sense of belongingness (the need to fit in), feeling esteem or respect from others, and meeting cognitive and aesthetic needs. Once these needs have been satisfied, self-actualization can be attained.

How do self-actualized people differ from people at other need levels? Maslow estimated that only 1 person in 10 operates from self-actualized needs. Research on individuals who Maslow believed were self-actualized, such as Eleanor Roosevelt, Walt Whitman, and Albert Einstein, has revealed certain personal qualities or attributes (Maslow, 1971), listed in ● TABLE 13.3. Read through this list of qualities. What general impression do you get about self-actualized people? Although it may seem attractive to be self-actualized, many people perceive self-actualized individuals as proud and stubborn. Fortunately, these evaluations would not affect the well-being of a truly actualized personality.

Unfortunately, Maslow's hierarchy does not explain why some people would deprive themselves of lower food and safety needs in favor of higher needs, such as esteem or self-actualization. For example, Mohandas Gandhi voluntarily fasted in protest of English rule over India. He fasted again in protest of the civil wars following independence from English rule and was assassinated shortly thereafter. Nelson Mandela preferred to remain imprisoned in South Africa for many years rather than to lose his right to criticize the apartheid government. Salman Rushdie was forced into exile under threat from an Islamic *fatwah* and other death threats he received for publishing *The Satanic Verses*, a critique of life in Islamic countries. Perhaps Maslow's hierarchy is too simple a view of personality (Neher, 1991). Another view of self-actualization is Carl Rogers' self theory.

Carl Rogers and Self Theory

Carl Rogers (1942, 1951, 1961, 1970, 1980) believed that understanding human personality required an understanding of how people view themselves and how they interpret events around them. He believed that human beings naturally strive for fulfillment and enhancement, a basic motive that he referred to as the **actualizing tendency**.

Rogers' proposed actualizing tendency is set at birth and moves the infant to recognize that she is separate from the mother and is an independent being. The infant begins to experience the self as "I" or "me." This self gradually evolves into the person's self-concept. **Self-concept** is our perception or image of our abilities and our uniqueness. At first one's self-concept is very general and changeable, as in the 4-year-old who describes herself as a girl with brown hair or the 3-year-old who states in one moment that he is happy but five minutes later that he is sad. As we grow older, these self-perceptions become much more organized, detailed,

TABLE 13.3
● **Characteristics of a Self-actualized Person**
· Perceives reality accurately
· Accepts self, others, and nature
· Tends to be autonomous
· Is more concerned with problem solving than with self
· Is spontaneous, engaged, and alive
· Deeply cares about and identifies with all people
· Possesses a nonhostile sense of humor
· Values solitude and feels at ease when alone
· Shares deep, loving bonds with only a few people
· Renews appreciation of life's basic elements
· Accepts democratic values
· Has a strong ethical sense
· Tends to be creative
· Frequently has peak experiences or feels ecstatic, harmonious, and one with the world; is filled with beauty and good

Source: Adapted from Maslow, 1970.

People who meet the criteria for self-actualization, such as Mother Teresa, might actually deprive themselves of lower-level needs, such as food or shelter.

Carl Rogers believed that understanding human personality requires an understanding of how people view themselves and how they interpret events around them.

self-actualization the fulfillment of one's natural potential

actualizing tendency according to Rogers, the natural drive in humans to strive for fulfillment and enhancement

self-concept one's perception or image of his or her abilities and uniqueness

and specific. For example, a 15-year-old is more likely to describe himself in terms of his academic abilities, athletic abilities, social abilities, and talents. For example, he may say, "I'm a decent second baseman, I'm a B student, and I have a lot of friends."

Underlying Rogers' actualizing tendency is an *organismic valuing process*. Experiences that maintain or enhance the person are valued and, therefore, preferred and liked. Experiences that do not maintain or enhance the person are not valued and, therefore, are rejected (Sheldon, Arndt, & Houser-Marko, 2003). An infant's valuing process is direct and simple. We know as infants what we like and what we dislike. We value food because it reduces the sensation of hunger. We value being held in a parent's arms because it makes us feel secure. However, such an internal evaluation of our values is soon influenced by our interactions with others and our basic need for love and acceptance.

As children, we come to realize that other important people in our lives (such as parents, teachers, siblings, or other relatives) also place value on our experiences. They communicate to us the "right" and "wrong" ways to think, feel, and behave. Because we desire their love and affection, we incorporate these messages into our valuing process. Experiences that meet these imposed values tend to be incorporated into our self-concept. For example, if a parent has communicated to a child that good grades are valued and the child gets good grades, the child may describe herself as a good student. A child may come home every day reporting on how well she did in school. This accomplishment gives the child the opportunity to gain acceptance and love from the parent. On the other hand, suppose the child does not get good grades at school. This child may hide test scores from parents for fear of being rejected and unloved. This example illustrates the enormous influence of others' standards and values on our self-concepts. We may no longer listen to our own internal valuing system but pay more attention to the views and values of loved ones. Our worth and regard are now judged on the basis of the imposed opinions, judgments, and values of others, rather than our own internal organismic valuing process. We have come to see ourselves as others see us.

What determines the degree to which we "listen" to, or incorporate, these parental and other outside norms and standards? For Rogers, it is the degree of **unconditional positive regard**, or acceptance and love with no strings attached that we receive from others. Our good points as well as bad points are accepted. People accept us and love us for who we are. This acceptance does not mean that a person's *actions* always receive approval. For example, suppose a youngster kicks the dog because the dog chewed a cherished toy. A parent can express displeasure at the child's actions, yet let the child know that the angry behavior is understood and that the child is still loved by the parent despite the behavior. However, if the parent attacks the child's self, calling the child "bad," the parent has now communicated *conditional* positive regard. The child will believe that feeling angry is wrong because feeling angry will lose her parent's love and acceptance. In other words, unconditional positive regard communicates respect for a person's thoughts and feelings.

It isn't easy to be always accepting of a person's thoughts and feelings, and it is impossible to experience complete unconditional positive regard. Parents naturally have expectations about how their children will think and behave. However, if a child, especially during the early years of life, experiences unconditional positive regard, he is less likely to lose contact with the organismic valuing process established at birth. In this way, the child grows into an adult who chooses to act, feel, or think on the basis of his inner evaluations, taking into consideration the effect of his behavior on others. For Rogers, this outcome represented a healthy personality. On the other hand, if a child experiences primarily conditional positive regard dur-

unconditional positive regard
acceptance and love of another's thoughts and feelings without expecting anything in return

The approval (or disapproval) we receive from others influences our self-concept, according to Rogers.

© Jeff Greenberg/PhotoEdit

ing her early years, she is more likely to develop a self-concept that is based on how others see her and disregard the inner guiding voice in her behavior. Such people think, act, or behave in a certain way in hope of ensuring the continued love and acceptance of others. They believe that if they don't meet certain self-imposed expectations, then their parents will not love them anymore. These perceptions, whether accurate or not, impede our ability to fulfill our potential, according to Rogers. In such situations, healthy development of the personality is hindered, and psychological discomfort may occur (Assor, Roth, & Deci, 2004).

Let's take one more look at the McBride family from a humanistic perspective. Growing up Black with a White mother during a time of racial discrimination, the civil rights movement, and integration potentially influenced the McBride children's perception of reality and their evaluations of their self-concepts. For example, James expresses his struggle in reconciling his Black identity with his mother's Whiteness and Jewish background. Others' opinions and judgments affected his view of himself. Moreover, the McBrides' everyday struggle to fulfill basic biological and security needs may have influenced the attainment of higher psychological needs.

Contributions and Criticisms of the Humanistic Approach

Many humanistic ideas have been incorporated into individual, family, and group therapy approaches, as we will see in Chapter 15. The humanistic approach has encouraged many people to become more aware of themselves and their interactions with others. However, the humanistic perspective has been criticized for its seemingly naïve and optimistic view of behavior. It assumes that all people are good and are motivated toward good in attaining self-actualization. Critics argue that all people are not necessarily good and pure in their intentions. They believe that humanists underestimate the capacity for evil in some individuals (Coffer & Appley, 1964; Ellis, 1959). Equally problematic is the difficulty in validating through experiments many of the humanistic concepts such as actualizing tendency, organismic valuing process, and unconditional positive regard (Burger, 2004). The major source of data for Rogers' self theory has been under scrutiny as well, as it was derived from clients' self-statements. How reliable and valid are such statements? It's possible that clients did not always present their "true" selves to Rogers and that as a listener Rogers was biased. As a result, humanistic psychology has not become as major a force in psychology as Maslow once hoped, although many consider the emergence of *positive psychology* (see Chapter 12) a rebirth of humanistic goals and the perspective's enduring legacy (E. Diener, Oishi, & Lucas, 2003).

Let's REVIEW

In this section, we presented the humanistic view of personality. For a quick check of your understanding, try answering the following questions at increasing levels of difficulty.

1. The humanistic perspective emphasizes the influence of _____ on personality.

   a. unconscious impulses

   b. internal tendencies

   c. an actualizing tendency

   d. environmental and cognitive factors

2. SuLing was recently mugged. Since the mugging, she has been suspicious and paranoid. She locks her doors at night and suffers from nightmares. Maslow would attribute SuLing's behavior to _____.

   a. esteem needs

   b. safety needs

   c. belongingness needs

   d. biological needs

3. Which of the following is not an element of Carl Rogers' personality theory?

   a. unconditional positive regard

   b. esteem needs

   c. organismic valuing process

   d. self-concept

ANSWERS 1. c; 2. b; 3. b

reliability the degree to which a test yields consistent measurements of a trait

validity the degree to which a test measures the trait that it was designed to measure

personality inventory objective paper-and-pencil self-report form that measures personality on several dimensions

HOW IS PERSONALITY MEASURED?

We have detailed four approaches to personality. Each perspective tends to employ certain tools to measure or assess personality. As with any tool or measuring device, it is important that the test be *reliable* and *valid*. **Reliability** refers to the consistency of a measurement tool. If we were to assess your height as an adult with a tape measure, we would want to get a consistent "reading" every time we measured your height. Personality tests also need to be reliable, or yield similar results over time. This reliability will not be perfect as we are not consistent in our behavior at all times. However, personality tests should report similar trends if they are reliable.

Measurement tools like personality tests also need to be valid. **Validity** refers to the ability of a test to measure what it says it is measuring. If a test states that it is measuring your intelligence and it does so by measuring your foot size, this test would not be valid. There is no relationship between foot size and intelligence. Notice that this test would be reliable (that is, yield a consistent measure from time to time), but it does not measure what we think of as intelligence. Therefore, personality tests should measure what we believe personality to be.

Each of the four major perspectives has developed its own way of measuring personality. These measures include *personality inventories, projective tests, rating scales,* and *clinical interviews.* See if you can identify the psychological perspective that correlates with each type of test.

TABLE 13.4

● **Sample MMPI-2 Items**

I have trouble with my bowel movements.	T F
I do not sleep well.	T F
At parties, I sit by myself or with one other person.	T F
A lot of people have it in for me.	T F
In school, I was frequently in trouble for acting up.	T F
I am anxious most of the time.	T F
I hear strange things that others do not hear.	T F
I am a very important person.	T F

Minnesota Multiphasic Personality Inventory (MMPI-2) a personality inventory that is designed to identify problem areas of functioning in a person's personality

projective test a less structured and subjective personality test in which an individual is shown an ambiguous stimulus and is asked to describe what he or she sees

Rorschach inkblot test a projective personality test consisting of 10 ambiguous inkblots in which a person is asked to describe what he or she sees; the person's responses are then coded for consistent themes and issues

Thematic Apperception Test (TAT) a projective personality test consisting of a series of pictures in which the respondent is asked to tell a story about each scene; the responses are then coded for consistent themes and issues

Personality Inventories: Mark Which One Best Describes You

Personality inventories are objective paper-and-pencil self-report forms. You are typically asked to indicate how well a statement describes you or to answer true or false to a specific statement. For example, in college settings many students have completed the *Myers-Briggs Personality Inventory.* This test details an individual's personality on four different dimensions. In clinical settings, the most frequently used personality inventory is the **Minnesota Multiphasic Personality Inventory (MMPI-2)**.

The MMPI-2 is a 567-item, true–false questionnaire that takes about 1 hour to complete. The questions describe a wide range of behaviors (● TABLE 13.4). The purpose of the MMPI-2 is to identify problem areas of functioning in a person's personality. It is organized into 10 groups of items, called *clinical scales.* These scales measure patterns of responses associated with specific psychological disorders such as depression, paranoia, and schizophrenia. A person's response patterns are reviewed to see whether they resemble the pattern of responses from groups of people who have specific mental health disorders. Interpreting the MMPI-2 involves comparing the test taker's responses to those of the "norming" population.

As part of its construction, the MMPI-2 was given to thousands of people, called a *norming group.* Individuals in the norming group included people who had no psychological disorders and people who had particular disorders. In this way the test constructors could see how frequently someone without the disorder would respond "true" to these items and how frequently someone with the psychological disorder would respond "true." The first group established the average, or "normal," number of items for each of these clinical scales, whereas the second group gave an indication of what would be considered problematic functioning. A psychologist is interested in examining any areas of your personality that fall outside the normal range. These areas would be considered problem areas of your personality and might suggest issues for therapy.

One of the main problems with self-report measures such as the MMPI-2 is the test taker's honesty or truthfulness. For this reason, the MMPI-2 also contains four *validity scales* to assess the truthfulness of the individual's responses. Given the nature and description of personality inventories such as the MMPI-2, which personality approach do you think is most closely connected to it? The correct answer is the trait approach. Notice how the MMPI-2 measures 10 different traits. ● FIGURE 13.5 provides an example of an MMPI-2 personality profile.

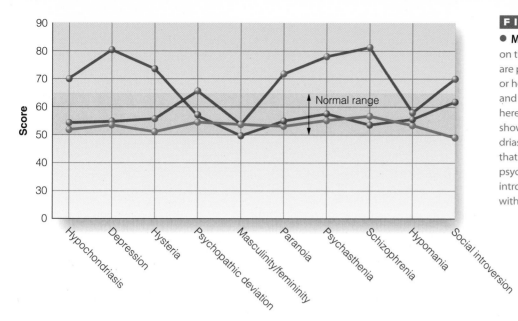

FIGURE 13.5

● **MMPI-2 Personality Profiles** Scores on the 10 clinical scales of the MMPI-2 are plotted to show a client where his or her behavior is in the normal range and where it is abnormal. Presented here are three participants: one that shows elevated scores on hypochondriasis, depression, and hysteria; one that shows elevated scores on paranoia, psychasthenia, schizophrenia, and social introversion; and one that shows scores within the normal range on all 10 scales.

Projective Tests: Tell Me What You See

Another type of tool to measure personality, the **projective test**, is less structured compared to the personality inventory. When taking this test, you are shown an ambiguous image and then asked to describe what you see or to tell a story about the picture. Children may be asked to draw pictures and describe what they have drawn. Such tests rely on the idea that whatever stories, motives, or explanations are offered by the person reflect his or her own issues and concerns, projected onto the image.

One of the most famous projective tests is the **Rorschach inkblot test**. The Rorschach test consists of 10 inkblots on cards. As each card is presented, you indicate what images you see. Your responses are then coded according to specific guidelines to decrease subjectivity and enhance the validity of the results. A sample card is shown in ● FIGURE 13.6.

Another widely used projective test is the **Thematic Apperception Test (TAT)**. In the TAT, you are shown images that are not as ambiguous as inkblots yet still allow for a variety of interpretations. You are asked to tell a story about the image, and your responses are then coded for any consistent themes, emotions, or issues. A sample TAT image is depicted in ● FIGURE 13.7. After being shown this image, a client might relate the following story: "It's a picture of a young man who has been waiting several hours at a park for his partner to arrive. He is tired, anxious, and angry. He is hoping that nothing bad has happened to his partner. He is also hoping that he wasn't stood up."

The purpose of projective tests is similar to that of personality inventories. Psychologists want to pinpoint healthy and unhealthy areas of functioning in the person. However, unlike personality inventories, projective tests are derived from the psychoanalytic perspective; the images and stories described are thought to reflect underlying unconscious urges and desires. The images also may symbolically represent the core issues and concerns of the individual. For example, suppose a person sees a rabbit in one of the

FIGURE 13.6

● **Sample Rorschach Inkblot** After being shown an inkblot like this one, the person indicates what he or she sees on the card.

FIGURE 13.7

● **Sample Thematic Apperception Test (TAT) Card** In taking the TAT, a person is asked to tell a story about a scene such as this one.

Rorschach inkblots. It is probably not that rabbits are an issue for the individual, but rather what rabbits symbolically represent, such as fertility, or anxiety and fear about pregnancy or childbearing. Because projective tests are more subject to the interpretation of the clinician than are personality inventories, coding systems have been devised to decrease variation in interpretation. However, research suggests that they are less reliable than objective tests in measuring personality (Aiken, 1996; Lilienfeld, Wood, & Garb, 2000; T. B. Rogers, 1995). Projective tests are most useful for identifying themes in a person's life or for delineating an individual's problem-solving style.

Rating Scales and Direct Observation

A third type of tool used by psychologists to measure personality is the *rating scale*. Rating scales are formatted similarly to checklists. You check off the statements or behaviors that most apply to you. A sample from a child behavior rating scale is depicted in ● TABLE 13.5 (on facing page). Because the person being evaluated may not answer the statements truthfully, teachers, parents, partners, and clinicians can also complete rating scales on the person being evaluated. These alternate perspectives minimize the self-distortions that are associated with self-report instruments.

Psychologists may also rely on directly observing a client's behavior and interactions with others to assess personality. Closely watching how you behave in particular situations can be helpful in determining what happens before and after your responses. Such information is particularly important to clinicians who favor a social-cognitive approach and who want to understand the social or environmental factors that may be influencing problem behavior.

TRY THIS DEMONSTRATION

Psychologists may find rating scales on self-esteem and self-concept useful to understanding how a person perceives reality and the degree to which one's real self is congruent with one's ideal self. Take a moment to complete the self-esteem scale provided in ● TABLE 13.6.

TABLE 13.6

● Rosenberg Self-Esteem Scale

Below is a list of statements dealing with your general feelings about yourself. If you Strongly Agree, circle SA. If you Agree with the statement, circle A. If you Disagree, circle D. If you Strongly Disagree, circle SD.

		STRONGLY AGREE	AGREE	DISAGREE	STRONGLY DISAGREE
1.	I feel that I'm a person of worth, at least on an equal plane with others.	SA	A	D	SD
2.	I feel that I have a number of good qualities.	SA	A	D	SD
3.	All in all, I am inclined to feel that I am a failure.	SA	A	D	SD
4.	I am able to do things as well as most other people.	SA	A	D	SD
5.	I feel I do not have much to be proud of.	SA	A	D	SD
6.	I take a positive attitude toward myself.	SA	A	D	SD
7.	On the whole, I am satisfied with myself.	SA	A	D	SD
8.	I wish I could have more respect for myself.	SA	A	D	SD
9.	I certainly feel useless at times.	SA	A	D	SD
10.	At times I think I am no good at all.	SA	A	D	SD

Scoring:

For items 1, 2, 4, 6, 7: Strongly Agree = 3; Agree = 2; Disagree = 1; Strongly Disagree = 0

For items 3, 5, 8, 9, 10: Strongly Agree = 0; Agree = 1; Disagree = 2; Strongly Disagree = 3

The scale ranges from 0 to 30, with 30 indicating the highest score possible. There are no discrete cutoff points for high and low self-esteem. Higher scores indicate more positive feelings toward the self while lower scores indicate more negative feelings toward the self.

Source: M. Rosenberg (1989), Society and the adolescent self-image (Middletown, CT: Wesleyan University Press).

TABLE 13.5

● Sample Rating Scale

Child Behavior Checklist

Below is a list of items that describe children and youth. For each item that describes your child now or within the past 6 months, please circle the 2 if the item is very true or often true of your child. Circle the 1 if the item is somewhat or sometimes true of your child. If the item is not true of your child, circle the 0. Please answer all items as well as you can, even if some do not seem to apply to your child.

0 = Not True (as far as you know)   1 = Somewhat or Sometimes True   2 = Very True or Often True

0 1 2 1. Acts too young for his/her age	0 1 2 33. Feels or complains that no one loves him/her
0 1 2 2. Drinks alcohol without parents' approval (describe):	0 1 2 34. Feels others are out to get him/her
_____	0 1 2 35. Feels worthless or inferior
_____	0 1 2 36. Gets hurt a lot, accident-prone
0 1 2 3. Argues a lot	0 1 2 37. Gets in many fights
0 1 2 4. Fails to finish things he/she starts	0 1 2 38. Gets teased a lot
0 1 2 5. There is very little he/she enjoys	0 1 2 39. Hangs around with others who get in trouble
0 1 2 6. Bowel movements outside toilet	0 1 2 40. Hears sounds or voices that aren't there (describe):
0 1 2 7. Bragging, boasting	
0 1 2 8. Can't concentrate, can't pay attention for long	_____
0 1 2 9. Can't get his/her mind off certain thoughts, obsessions (describe):	0 1 2 41. Impulsive or acts without thinking
	0 1 2 42. Would rather be alone than with others
_____	0 1 2 43. Lies or cheats
_____	0 1 2 44. Bites fingernails
0 1 2 10. Can't sit still, restless, or hyperactive	0 1 2 45. Nervous, high-strung, or tense
0 1 2 11. Clings to adults or too dependent	0 1 2 46. Nervous movements or twitching (describe):
0 1 2 12. Complains of loneliness	
0 1 2 13. Confused or seems to be in a fog	_____
0 1 2 14. Cries a lot	0 1 2 47. Nightmares
0 1 2 15. Cruel to animals	0 1 2 48. Not liked by other kids
0 1 2 16. Cruelty, bullying, or meanness to others	0 1 2 49. Constipated, doesn't move bowels
0 1 2 17. Daydreams or gets lost in his/her thoughts	0 1 2 50. Too fearful or anxious
0 1 2 18. Deliberately harms self or attempts suicide	0 1 2 51. Feels dizzy or lightheaded
0 1 2 19. Demands a lot of attention	0 1 2 52. Feels too guilty
0 1 2 20. Destroys his/her own things	0 1 2 53. Overeating
0 1 2 21. Destroys things belonging to his/her family or others	0 1 2 54. Overtired without good reason
0 1 2 22. Disobedient at home	0 1 2 55. Overweight
0 1 2 23. Disobedient at school	0 1 2 56. Physical problems without known medical cause:
0 1 2 24. Doesn't eat well	0 1 2 a. Aches or pains (*not* stomach or headaches)
0 1 2 25. Doesn't get along with other kids	0 1 2 b. Headaches
0 1 2 26. Doesn't seem to feel guilty after misbehaving	0 1 2 c. Nausea, feels sick
	0 1 2 d. Problems with eyes (*not* if corrected by glasses) (describe):
0 1 2 27. Easily jealous	
0 1 2 28. Breaks rules at home, school, or elsewhere	_____
0 1 2 29. Fears certain animals, situations, or places, other than school (describe):	_____
	0 1 2 e. Rashes or other skin problems
_____	0 1 2 f. Stomachaches
_____	0 1 2 h. Other (describe):
0 1 2 30. Fears going to school	_____
0 1 2 31. Fears he/she might think or do something bad	_____
0 1 2 32. Feels he/she has to be perfect	

A clinical interview typically takes place during the first meeting between the client and the clinician. The focus is on identifying as clearly as possible the difficulty in functioning that the person is experiencing.

Clinical Interviews

One tool used by most clinical psychologists is the **clinical interview**. This interview typically takes place during the first meeting between the client and the clinician and involves the clinician asking the client questions to identify the client's difficulty in functioning. The format and length of the interview, as well as the questions that are asked during the interview, may differ from clinician to clinician. These differences again relate to the alternate views on personality that were discussed in this chapter. For example, a clinician who favors the social cognitive approach is more likely to ask specific questions about social situations and patterns of thoughts. This clinician may want to know what the client was thinking about before, during, and after a particular behavior occurred. A humanist is more likely to focus on the client's interpretation and perception of reality. The focus of any clinical interview, however, is to identify as clearly as possible the difficulty in functioning that the person is experiencing. This difficulty is often given a name, or diagnosis. The exact nature of these diagnoses is the subject of the next chapter.

This chapter presented four different views of personality: the psychoanalytic perspective, the trait approach, the social cognitive perspective, and the humanistic approach. Rather than debating which of these perspectives is "right," many psychologists prefer instead to see these viewpoints as complementary. Just as a photographer may take the same picture from many different angles, psychologists, too, like to understand personality from varying viewpoints. When taken together, these theories provide a much more complex and richer view of the forces that make us unique than any single perspective could. Understanding these theoretical approaches will also help you grasp the concepts in our next chapter as we move on to consider abnormal behavior.

Let's REVIEW

In this section, we detailed the various methods psychologists use to measure personality. For a quick check of your understanding, try answering the following questions at increasing levels of difficulty.

1. When one goes to a clinical psychologist, the first session is most likely to involve _____.

   a. personality testing
   b. a physical examination
   c. hypnosis
   d. a clinical interview

2. Tamara goes to see a clinical psychologist. The psychologist asks her to look at some vague pictures and report what she sees. Most likely Tamara is taking a _____.

   a. personality inventory
   b. projective test
   c. rating scale
   d. clinical interview

3. The major disadvantage of self-report instruments, such as the MMPI-2, is _____.

   a. the subjective interpretation of the results by the clinician
   b. the respondents may not tell the truth
   c. the scoring criteria are very vague and unreliable
   d. there are no norms to compare one's responses against

ANSWERS 1. d; 2. b; 3. b

clinical interview the initial meeting between a client and a clinician in which the clinician asks questions to identify the difficulty in functioning that the person is experiencing

Zigy Kaluzny/Getty Images

STUDYING the CHAPTER

LEARNING CHALLENGE

TEST YOURSELF!

Now that you have studied the chapter, assess your comprehension of the material by answering the following questions. Then use the key at the end to determine if your understanding is at the basic, intermediate, or advanced level. For a more comprehensive assessment of your learning, please see your student study guide and your Psychology CourseMate (www.cengagebrain.com).

1. Which perspective suggests that human beings naturally strive for fulfillment and enhancement?

   a. psychoanalytic perspective
   b. trait perspective
   c. humanistic perspective
   d. social cognitive perspective

2. Meera's friends describe her as warm and giving across most situations. According to Allport, warm and giving are _____ of Meera's.

   a. central traits
   b. secondary traits
   c. cardinal traits
   d. primary traits

3. Which personality perspective emphasizes genetic contributions to personality?

   a. psychoanalytic perspective
   b. trait perspective
   c. humanistic perspective
   d. social cognitive perspective

4. Even though her mother told her not to, Gretchen had a second piece of chocolate cake. Which personality structure, according to Freud, motivated Gretchen's behavior?

   a. superego
   b. ego
   c. id
   d. the preconscious

5. Defense mechanisms are used to handle intrapsychic conflict between which two personality structures?

   a. id and ego
   b. id and superego
   c. ego and superego
   d. the ego and the preconscious

6. The Oedipus and Electra complexes occur during which psychosexual stage?

   a. phallic
   b. latency
   c. anal
   d. genital

7. Which of the following individuals will most likely undergo the most personality change in the future?

a. Carver, a 30-year-old
b. Tracy, a 15-year-old
c. Gene, a 45-year-old
d. Winston, a 60-year-old

8. Melinda believes that her hard work and determination have led to her successful career. According to Rotter, Melinda has a(n) _____.

a. positive self-concept
b. external locus of control
c. internal locus of control
d. overactive superego

9. You take a personality test in which you are asked to look at vague drawings and tell a story about what you see. Most likely you are taking which of the following personality tests?

a. MMPI-2
b. aptitude test
c. self-esteem scale
d. TAT

10. Your long-term memories most likely reside in which level of consciousness?

a. unconscious
b. subconscious
c. preconscious
d. conscious

11. Wally is described as hostile, impulsive, and aggressive. According to Eysenck, Wally is high in _____.

a. extraversion
b. neuroticism
c. openness
d. psychoticism

12. Marley is in high school and very much wants to be a part of the in-crowd. According to Maslow, Marley is trying to fulfill _____ needs.

a. physical
b. safety
c. belongingness
d. esteem

13. Donny's mother is very upset when Donny's grades slip below a B. Donny feels that he must make good grades in order to receive his mother's love and acceptance. According to Rogers, Donny perceives _____ from his mother.

a. unconditional positive regard
b. conditional positive regard
c. actualizing tendency
d. self-actualization

14. Shanique takes a personality test in which she is asked to count to ten and identify pictures of animals. This personality test most lacks _____.

a. validity
b. reliability
c. consistency
d. norming

15. Which of the following is not a contribution of the psychoanalytic perspective?

a. stimulated research on sleep and dreaming
b. stimulated research on coping and health
c. created personality tests and therapy approaches
d. stimulated experimentation on learning and perception

Scoring Key

Below are the answers and the associated point values for each of the Learning Challenge questions. Circle the associated points for each question that you answered correctly. To obtain your Learning Challenge Score, add up the points you circled and write the total in the blank.

1. C, 1 pt	**6.** A, 3 pts	**11.** D, 2 pts
2. A, 2 pts	**7.** B, 1 pt	**12.** C, 1 pt
3. B, 1 pt	**8.** C, 2 pts	**13.** B, 2 pts
4. C, 1 pt	**9.** D, 2 pts	**14.** A, 3 pts
5. B, 3 pts	**10.** C, 3 pts	**15.** D, 3 pts

Learning Challenge Score _____

(27–30) Congratulations! You scored at the advanced level. You are well on your way to mastering the material. Take the next step by answering the questions in your Student Study Guide or your Psychology CourseMate (www.cengagebrain.com).

(21–26) You are almost there! You scored at the intermediate level. Review the material you missed before moving on to answer the questions in your Student Study Guide or your Psychology CourseMate (www.cengagebrain.com).

(20 and below) You are on your way, but you're not there yet! You scored at the beginner level. It appears that you need to carefully review the chapter to improve your mastery of the material.

USE IT OR LOSE IT: APPLYING PSYCHOLOGY

1. Which theory of personality do you find most compelling, and why?

2. Using one of the personality perspectives discussed in this chapter, analyze the personality of a favorite television or movie character.

3. How has your personality changed over the years? How has it remained the same? What theory or theories can best explain these changes and consistencies?

4. How would you go about constructing a personality test? How does this construction relate to your perspective on personality?

5. Try to describe your personality in detail from each of the perspectives discussed in this chapter.

CRITICAL THINKING FOR INTEGRATION

1. Review the theories of motivation discussed in Chapter 8. How do they correlate with the views on personality discussed in this chapter?

2. In Chapter 11, we discussed behaviors such as conformity, aggression, and helpfulness in relation to the effect that others have on our behavior. How would the psychoanalytic perspective explain such behaviors? How would they be explained from the humanistic perspective?

3. Discuss how memory (Chapter 6), problem solving (Chapter 7), and intelligence (Chapter 7) relate to personality.

CHAPTER STUDY RESOURCES

Student Study Guide

To help organize your learning, work through Chapter 13 of the *What Is Psychology? Student Study Guide*. The study guide includes learning objectives, a chapter summary, fill-in review, key terms, a practice test, and activities.

CengageNOW

Go to **www.cengage.com/login** to link to CengageNOW, your online study tool. First take the Pre-Test for this chapter to get your personalized study plan, which will identify topics you need to review and direct you to online resources. Then take the Post-Test to determine what concepts you have mastered and what you still need work on.

CourseMate

Access an interactive eBook, chapter-specific interactive learning tools, including flashcards, quizzes, videos, and more in your Psychology CourseMate, available at **CengageBrain.com**.

Aplia

aplia

Aplia™ is an online interactive learning solution that helps you improve comprehension—and your grade—by integrating a variety of tools such as video, tutorials, practice tests, and interactive eBook. Founded by a professor to enhance his own courses, Aplia provides automatically graded assignments with detailed, immediate explanations on every question, and innovative teaching materials. More than 1,000,000 students like you have used Aplia at over 1,800 institutions. Aplia should be purchased only when assigned by your instructor as part of your course.

WHAT IS PERSONALITY AND HOW DO WE MEASURE IT?

Personality is the unique collection of attitudes, emotions, thoughts, habits, impulses, and behaviors that defines how a person typically behaves across situations. The McBride family illustrated a rich array of personalities that were influenced by a multitude of forces: unconscious motives, heredity, cognitions, the environment, and self-concepts. It is all of these forces rather than just one that constitutes our personality.

THE PSYCHOANALYTIC APPROACH: HOW DOES THE UNCONSCIOUS INFLUENCE PERSONALITY?

- Emphasizes unconscious aspects of personality. It proposes that personality operates at the **conscious**, **preconscious**, and **unconscious** levels.

- According to Freud, personality is comprised of the unconscious **id** that operates according to the **pleasure principle**, the conscious **ego** that operates according to the **reality principle**, and the moral directives of the **superego**.

- For Freud, personality develops through a series of five psychosexual stages (**oral**, **anal**, **phallic**, **latency**, **genital**) that represent a complex interaction between natural sexual urges and our socialization experiences.

- Neo-Freudians such as Jung, Adler, and Horney placed less emphasis on the role of the instinctual impulses in motivating behavior.

Hulton Archive/Getty Images

THE TRAIT APPROACH: HOW DO OUR GENES INFLUENCE PERSONALITY?

- Attempts to describe personality by identifying the internal **traits**, or tendencies that we have across most situations.

- Allport classified traits into three types: **central**, **cardinal**, and **secondary** traits.

- Cattell's factor analysis of traits yielded 16 **source traits** that could be measured in everyone. Eysenck proposed three universal traits in his PEN model: **psychoticism**, **extraversion**, and **neuroticism**.

- Costa and McCrae's **five factor theory** proposes five core universal traits: openness, conscientiousness, extraversion, agreeableness, and neuroticism (OCEAN).

- Research suggests a complex interaction between genes and the environment in producing personality. Some traits remain stable over the course of adulthood, but situational factors also influence the consistency of traits.

© Ashley Cooper/Alamy

Are You Getting THE BIG PICTURE?

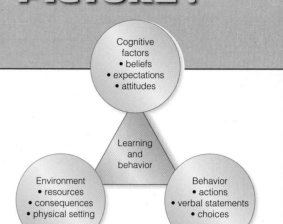

THE SOCIAL COGNITIVE APPROACH: HOW DO THE ENVIRONMENT AND OUR THOUGHTS INFLUENCE PERSONALITY?

- Evaluates environmental and cognitive factors that influence personality.

- Bandura's **reciprocal determinism** speculates that personality is due to the constant interaction between one's environment, one's behavior, and one's thoughts. A critical cognitive element is **self-efficacy**, or the expectation one has for success in a given situation.

- Rotter believes that one's **locus of control**, or one's expectations of whether the outcome of an event is due to internal or external forces, influences personality.

- The **social cognitive approach** is comprehensive, has many applications, and is easily tested experimentally.

THE HUMANISTIC APPROACH: HOW DOES FREE WILL SHAPE PERSONALITY?

© Roger Ressmeyer/Corbis

- Emphasizes one's drive toward uniqueness and **self-actualization**.
- Maslow believed that the pathway to self-actualization lies in fulfilling a hierarchy of needs, with physical needs at the bottom and psychological needs at the top.
- Rogers' self theory emphasizes how one's **self-concept**, or perception of self, is influenced by the standards and values of others, most notably the degree to which we perceive and receive **unconditional positive regard** from others.
- The **humanistic approach** promotes self-awareness and positive interactions with others, and its ideas have been incorporated into several therapy approaches.

HOW IS PERSONALITY MEASURED?

- Tools that assess personality should be **reliable** and **valid**.
- **Personality inventories** such as the **MMPI-2** are objective paper-and-pencil self-report forms that can reliably detail a person's traits if answered honestly.
- **Projective tests** such as the **Rorschach inkblot test** and the **Thematic Apperception Test** are less structured tests in which a person is shown an ambiguous image and asked to describe it. A person's responses are believed to reflect underlying unconscious concerns, according to the psychoanalytic perspective.
- Psychologists may also use rating scales and direct observation to measure behaviors and interactions with others.
- The focus of the **clinical interview** is to identify the difficulty in functioning that a person is experiencing.

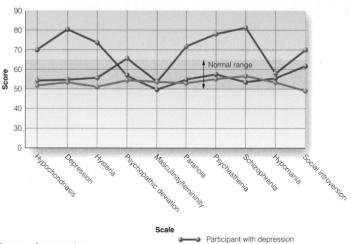

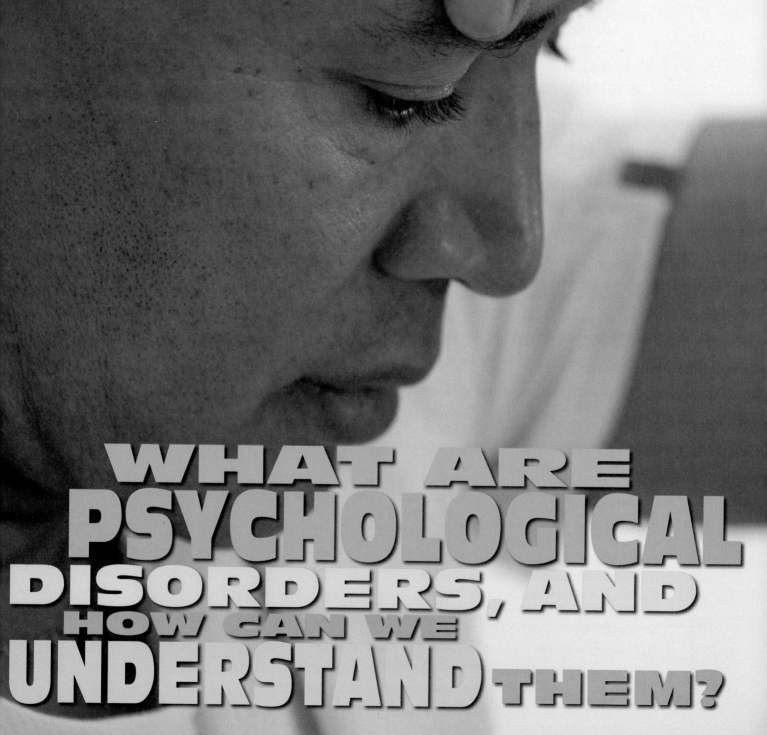

CHAPTER 14

WHAT ARE PSYCHOLOGICAL DISORDERS, AND HOW CAN WE UNDERSTAND THEM?

THE BIG PICTURE

How Does a Beautiful Mind Go Awry?

The previous chapter on personality detailed four main perspectives for understanding how we each develop our own unique way of behaving and operating in our environment. This chapter extends that discussion by examining how at times our behavior may make it difficult for us to function.

Consider the following personal stories:

J. K. Rowling, best-selling author of the Harry Potter books, thought of killing herself when her first marriage fell apart. She had moved back to Great Britain with her baby daughter and was living in a cramped apartment, barely able to make ends meet. She woke each morning expecting to find her little girl dead. She was deeply unhappy and felt that life was colorless. Fortunately, she sought therapy that helped her recover. The hooded creatures called the Dementors that torment the characters in her novel *The Prisoner of Azkaban* are reportedly based on Rowling's depressive feelings ("Author Rowling considered suicide," 2008). Is depression always this dark?

Nathaniel Ayers is an extraordinary musician. At 19, as a promising classical bass student, he was one of the few Black students accepted into the Juilliard School (for performing artists) in 1970. However, soon his behavior became bizarre. His grades dropped, he was angry with fellow students and teachers for no apparent cause, and he was no longer neat and well-groomed. At times he was coherent while at other times his conversation was a jumble of disorganized speech. Finally, he was picked up by the police and taken to Bellevue Hospital to be evaluated for mental illness. He moved back to his hometown of Cleveland, where he tried medication and shock therapy, but neither helped. He drifted away to live on the streets, eventually making it to California. His life was originally highlighted in the *Los Angeles Times* by newspaper columnist Steve Lopez and then in the film *The Soloist*. How can we understand his struggles?

Howie Mandel, well-known stand-up comedian, actor, and host of the game show *Deal or No Deal*, has an obsession with germs and cleanliness. He does not shake hands with people anymore and prefers instead a fist bump, as he cannot get rid of the thought that he will get that person's germs on his hands and feel compelled to wash his hands continuously with scalding water. He likewise avoids doorknobs and toilet

© John Lund/Marc Romanelli/Blend I/Blend Images/Corbis

(continued)

handles, using his elbows or knees to manipulate lids, faucets, and doors. He has a seemingly normal life with his wife and three children. He can hug, kiss, and touch, but he has issues with hands and airborne germs. He frequently uses masks and gloves, especially when those around him cough or sniffle. Why does he feel this way?

These are all real people and real stories illustrating difficulty in functioning. Each of them has been diagnosed with a mental health disorder. This chapter outlines several major categories of mental health disorders and explains the symptoms necessary to be diagnosed with a particular disorder. For each type of disorder, we will consider the possible reasons why a person behaves this way. Although the research presented may seem overwhelming at times, keep in mind that these explanations are closely tied to topics with which you are already familiar. For example, many of the symptoms of mental health disorders are physical in nature, focusing on brain functioning, neurotransmitters, hormones, and genetics—biological factors that were introduced in Chapter 2. Many of the symptoms also focus on psychological concepts such as learning, cognition, personality, and emotions—again, topics that have been addressed in previous chapters. Furthermore, we will see that certain disorders are more common among certain segments of the population. Your familiarity with previous discussions on gender, race, and culture will assist you in understanding the influence of these social factors on mental health.

Author J. K. Rowling experienced depression before writing her Harry Potter novels.

In his new book, *Here's the Deal: Don't Touch Me* (2009), Howie Mandel, comedian and actor, describes living with obsessive-compulsive disorder.

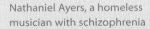

Nathaniel Ayers, a homeless musician with schizophrenia

WHAT MAKES BEHAVIOR ABNORMAL, AND HOW PREVALENT IS ABNORMAL BEHAVIOR?

LEARNING OBJECTIVE

What Should You Know?
- Identify the criteria that psychologists use for determining abnormal behavior.

What is abnormal behavior? Psychologists primarily use four main criteria when distinguishing normal from abnormal behavior.

1. *Statistical infrequency.* If we judge normal as what most people do, then one criterion that may be used to gauge abnormality is engaging in a behavior a lot less frequently than others. For example, it is considered crucial for survival to ingest a minimum amount of food per day. People who engage in this behavior a lot less than most people—as in the case of people with anorexia—would qualify as abnormal. Persons with autism engage in social communication far less than most people. As such, their behavior may be considered abnormal. Statistical infrequency can also include engaging in a behavior that most people do not. For example, believing that you are from another planet or galaxy is a thought that most people do not have. It represents an unusual, or statistically infrequent, thought and therefore may be judged as abnormal. However, there are problems with using the criterion of statistical infrequency. For example, only one person holds the record for running a mile the fastest; this person is certainly atypical but not necessarily abnormal.

2. *Violation of social norms.* Another measure of abnormality is to assess whether the behavior *violates social norms* of how people are supposed to behave. However, it is extremely important to emphasize that social norms vary widely across cultures, within cultures, and across historical times. What is considered socially acceptable in San Francisco may be considered unacceptable in Keokuk, Iowa. Similarly, what was deemed unacceptable in the 1950s may be considered acceptable today. For example, changing views on homosexuality in part influenced the American Psychiatric Association to remove homosexuality from its list of psychological disorders in 1973. Because social norms vary so widely, judging the abnormality of behavior on this criterion alone is especially problematic.

3. *Personal distress.* This criterion focuses on whether a behavior causes great *personal distress* to the individual. Often people seek treatment when a behavior causes such suffering. J. K. Rowling sought help after experiencing suicidal thoughts. Problems can also arise from judging a behavior by this criterion alone, however. A person may murder one or more people and not be distressed by such behavior, although it causes great harm to others.

4. *Level of impairment.* Because each of these criteria by itself is not adequate in defining abnormality, many psychologists find that combining them and assessing whether a behavior *interferes with a person's ability to function and/or causes oneself or others distress* may best explain abnormality (Wakefield, 1992). By using this broader criterion, we can see that all three of the people described in the opening section were clearly engaging in abnormal behavior.

Prevalence of Abnormal Behaviors

An estimated 26% of Americans 18 and older will suffer from a diagnosable mental disorder in any given year (R. C. Kessler, Chiu, Demler, & Walters, 2005). Lifetime prevalence estimates are quite a bit higher, with more than half of U.S. adults meeting the criteria for a mental health disorder at some time in their lives (NCS-R, 2007; see ● FIGURE 14.1). And yet, this may be a conservative estimate (Moffitt et al., 2009). Mental disorders are the leading

Autism is a developmental disorder marked by impaired communication.

© Michael Macor/San Francisco Chronicle/Corbis

FIGURE 14.1

● **Lifetime Prevalence of Psychological Disorders** More than half of U.S. adults will be diagnosed with a psychological disorder at some time in their lives. *(Source: National Comorbidity Survey Replication data. Table 1. Updated 2007. http://www.hcp.med.harvard.edu/ncs).*

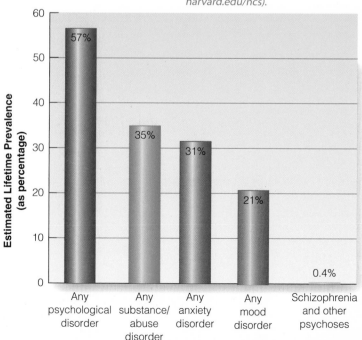

FIGURE 14.2

● **Prevalence of Depression, Anxiety, Substance Abuse, and Antisocial Personality Disorder in Women and Men**
Males and females differ in the types of psychological disorders they are more likely to experience. *(Source: National Comorbidity Survey Replication data. Table 1. Updated 2007. http://www.hcp.med.harvard.edu/ncs).*

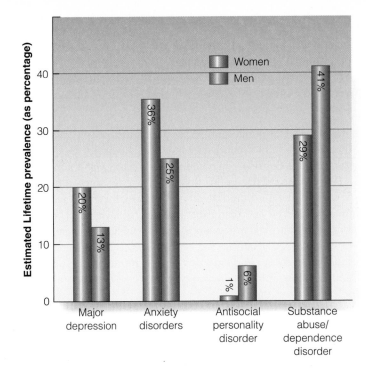

cause of disability in the United States and Canada for people between the ages of 15 and 44 (World Health Organization, 2004). Although there is little overall gender difference in the lifetime risk of a psychological disorder, males and females do show differences in the types of psychological disorders they are more likely to experience (NCS-R, 2007; see ● FIGURE 14.2). Consequently, it is likely that you or someone close to you will at some time experience a mental health disorder.

Let's REVIEW In this section, we looked at the criteria that psychologists use to distinguish abnormal from normal behavior. For a quick check of your understanding, try answering the following questions at increasing levels of difficulty.

1. Judging abnormality by social norms is especially problematic because social norms _____.

   a. may be atypical or rare, but not abnormal
   b. cause great distress to the individual
   c. interfere with a person's ability to function
   d. vary widely across and within cultures

2. Susan enjoys eating garbage when she is hungry. By which criterion can Susan's behavior be considered abnormal?

   a. danger to others
   b. violates social norms
   c. personal distress
   d. all of the above

3. What is the likelihood that you or someone close to you will be diagnosed with a psychological disorder sometime in your life?

   a. 15%
   b. 26%
   c. 57%
   d. 75%

HOW DO WE EXPLAIN ABNORMAL BEHAVIOR? PERSPECTIVES REVISITED

Why do people behave abnormally? Since the beginning of time, doctors and philosophers have tried to understand *why* people exhibit abnormal behavior. For example, during the Stone Age, abnormal behavior was attributed to possession by evil spirits. Treating someone who was possessed might entail drilling holes in the person's skull, a process called *trephining*, in order to allow the evil spirits to escape (Selling, 1940). Although some cultures today continue to emphasize spiritual causes of abnormality, Western cultures predominantly lean toward three main models or approaches for understanding abnormal behavior: *biological theories*, *psychological theories*, and *social* or *cultural theories*.

Biological Theories: The Medical Model

Biological theories attribute abnormal behavior to some physical process: genetics, an imbalance in hormones or neurotransmitters, or some brain or bodily dysfunction. The biological perspective can be traced back to ancient China, Egypt, and Greece. Because these early philosophies saw psychological disorders as similar to physical diseases, this perspective became known as the **medical model**, and the concept of mental illness was born. The medical model and the notion of mental illness persist today. Physicians and psychiatrists generally believe that psychological disorders are the result of biological disturbances. As such, they can be diagnosed, treated, and cured in much the same way as other physical illnesses. For example, antidepressant medications are used to treat substance abuse and eating disorders as well as depression. Other biological treatments (covered in more detail in the next chapter) include electroconvulsive therapy and neurosurgery (psychosurgery).

© John Verano

One historical method of treating abnormal behavior entailed drilling a hole in a person's skull, a process called trephining, in order to allow evil spirits to escape.

Psychological Theories: Humane Treatment and Psychological Processes

Psychological theories attribute abnormal behavior to internal or external stressors. Beginning in the 1700s, dissatisfaction with the treatment of those with mental illness led many to believe that dignity, tranquility, rest, and relaxation would restore normal functioning to the mentally ill. Such efforts led to more humane treatment of the mentally ill and opened the door to the exploration of psychological processes that underlie mental illness. You will recall from the previous chapter on personality that four predominant perspectives resulted, which we briefly review here.

The Psychoanalytic Perspective

This perspective attributes abnormal behavior to unresolved unconscious conflicts. According to Freud, psychological disorders result from the conflict between the unconscious sexual and aggressive instinctual desires of the id and the outward demands of society. Newer theories, referred to as *psychodynamic* theories, developed by Freud's followers such as Alfred Adler and Karen Horney, downplay the role of sexual and aggressive instincts and instead emphasize the role of the ego and interpersonal relationships in maintaining or restoring psychological health.

The Social Learning Perspective

Learning theorists (particularly B. F. Skinner and his successors) explain abnormal behavior as a result of the same learning processes that produce normal behavior—classical conditioning, operant conditioning, and social learning. A person's responses to stimuli in the environment and the consequences of these behaviors are what lead to abnormal behavior. For example, Howie Mandel learned to respond with fear to germs in his environment. Avoiding the germs with surgical masks or gloves reinforced his fear because this behavior reduced his

medical model perspective that views psychological disorders as similar to physical diseases; they result from biological disturbances and can be diagnosed, treated, and cured like other physical illnesses

anxiety about germs—a positive consequence. Thus, a person's past learning and modeling along with current experiences can explain psychological disorders.

The Cognitive Perspective

This perspective emphasizes the role of thoughts, expectations, assumptions, and other mental processes in abnormal behavior. For example, anxiety results from irrational assumptions or from believing that negative outcomes will occur despite one's best efforts. Think about the little voice inside of you that comments on your behavior. Does it encourage you to do well, or does it criticize you for your stupidity? Is it possible that such internal messages influence your behavior? The cognitive perspective maintains that they do.

The Humanistic Perspective

Humanists like Carl Rogers see abnormal behavior as resulting from a distorted perception of the self and reality. When people lose touch with their personal values and their sense of self, or when they fail to fulfill their basic biological and psychological needs, they cannot attain self-actualization. Instead, they experience personal distress and maladaptive behavior.

Sociocultural Theories: The Individual in Context

Sociocultural theories emphasize social or cultural factors that may play a role in psychological disorders. Such a perspective argues that internal biological and psychological processes can be understood only in the context of the larger society and culture that shape and influence people's behavior. Abnormal behavior, therefore, can be fully understood only when social factors such as age, race, gender, social roles, and socioeconomic status are taken into account. In addition, social conditions such as poverty, discrimination, and environmental stressors must be looked at when evaluating abnormal behavior.

Consider the increasing prevalence of eating disorders in industrialized countries such as the United States, Europe, Jordan, Asia, and the United Arab Emirates over the past decade (Chisuwa & O'Dea, 2010; Mousa et al., 2010; Stunkard, 1997; Thomas, Khan, & Abdulrahman, 2010). In developing cultures, eating disorders are uncommon. This difference may stem in part from the cultural differences in ideal body images. The ideal shape, especially for women, has become progressively thinner over the last decade in industrialized countries. In other, less developed countries, heavier bodies are seen as more beautiful (C. V. Wiseman et al., 1992). Even within the United States and Europe, ethnic and socioeconomic differences in the rates of eating disorders are apparent. Eating disorders appear to be more prevalent among those in the upper- and middle-income levels than among people from lower-income levels. However, the higher prevalence may reflect the fact that people with higher incomes can afford to get treatment whereas people with lower incomes cannot. In addition, European American and Asian American females have a higher incidence of eating disorders (particularly anorexia nervosa) than do African American or Hispanic American females (Cummins & Lehman, 2007; J. E. Pate et al., 1992). Again, such differences may be related to differences in cultural values concerning attractiveness and beauty. African American and Hispanic American cultures tend to hold a more voluptuous and rounded ideal of feminine beauty than does the European American or Asian American culture. Hence, European American and Asian American women may be more susceptible to starving themselves to attain the thinner ideal image of attractiveness (Gluck & Geliebter, 2002; Osvold & Sodowsky, 1993; A. Roberts et al., 2006). However, the thin ideal of beauty has spread, and weight-related concerns and behaviors are prevalent among adolescents in the United States regardless of their ethnic/racial background (Gentile et al., 2007; Kronenfeld et al., 2010; McKnight Investigators, 2003; Neumark-Sztainer et al., 2002). These results highlight how social factors such as gender, ethnicity, and income level as well as cultural ideals and expectations may influence behavior.

Musical artist and actress Mariah Carey received much negative media attention when she gained weight, illustrating how the thin ideal of beauty is spreading across U.S. ethnic groups.

Kevin Winter/Getty Images for AFI

A Biopsychosocial Model: Integrating Perspectives

Which viewpoint explains abnormal behavior? Despite decades of research, no single theory or perspective is correct. In the upcoming sections we'll explore several theories that have been helpful in understanding the causes of specific psychological disorders. However, it is only by integrating all the perspectives that our explanations of abnormality become comprehensive. We often hear in the popular press and in television commercials that a psychological disorder such as depression or anxiety is caused by "a specific gene" or "a chemical imbalance." But such reports are too simplistic to explain the complexity of mental illness. Most psychological disorders result from a combination of biological, psychological, and social factors (hence the name of the *biopsychosocial* model); they do not have just one cause.

For example, as we will soon see, people diagnosed with major depression often show changes in brain chemistry—a biological factor. They also are likely to engage in a negative pattern of thinking, which is a cognitive symptom that we would characterize as a psychological factor. In addition, major depression is more likely to be diagnosed in women—a sociocultural factor. Current research in psychology focuses on understanding how these forces operate together, much like the way pieces of a jigsaw puzzle fit together.

Let's REVIEW

In this section, we reviewed perspectives on explaining abnormal behavior. For a quick check of your understanding, try answering the following questions at increasing levels of difficulty.

1. The medical model is also known as the _____ perspective.

   a. psychoanalytic

   b. supernatural

   c. biological

   d. cognitive

2. Environmental conditions such as poverty, discrimination, and violent crime are most likely to be considered important causes of abnormal behavior by which perspective?

   a. psychoanalytic

   b. sociocultural

   c. learning

   d. supernatural

3. Dr. Kwan believes that Ken's abnormal behavior has resulted from a distorted sense of self and a loss of personal values. Dr. Kwan is adopting which perspective?

   a. humanistic

   b. psychoanalytic

   c. learning

   d. cognitive

ANSWERS 1. c; 2. b; 3. a

HOW ARE DIAGNOSES MADE? THE *DSM* MODEL

LEARNING OBJECTIVE

What Should You Know?
- Describe the nature of the *DSM* model, and identify its strengths and weaknesses.

How do psychologists diagnose people's abnormal behaviors? In 1952 the American Psychiatric Association (APA) published a book listing the symptoms that must be shown in order for a person to be diagnosed with a specific psychological disorder. More than 50 years later, the **Diagnostic and Statistical Manual of Mental Disorders (DSM)** is in its fourth edition, published in 1994. In 2000, the APA did a text revision (TR) to clarify the diagnosis of some psychological disorders. This most recent edition, known as the *DSM-IV-TR*, lists specific and concrete criteria for diagnosing nearly 400 disorders in children, adolescents, and adults. It also indicates the length of time that a person must show these symptoms to qualify for a diagnosis. These criteria require that the symptoms interfere with the person's ability to function, adopting the maladaptive criterion that we discussed at the start of this chapter and that is accepted by many professionals today. However, the current version of the *DSM* does not speculate as to the causes of the individual's behavior—it is *atheoretical*. This atheoretical position underscores the complex nature of the causes of mental illness.

Diagnostic and Statistical Manual of Mental Disorders (DSM) a book published by the American Psychiatric Association (APA) that lists the criteria for close to 400 mental health disorders

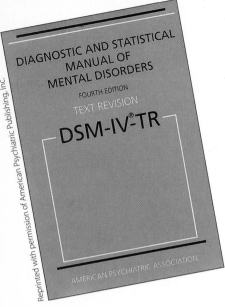

The *Diagnostic and Statistical Manual of Mental Disorders (DSM)* describes the specific symptoms that must be present in order for someone to be diagnosed with a specific mental health disorder.

A Multidimensional Evaluation

With the third edition of the *DSM*, published in 1980, clinicians began to evaluate patients along five dimensions or *axes*, listed in ● TABLE 14.1. Axis I represents conditions that impair a person's ability to function. It includes 15 major categories of mental disorders, such as anxiety and eating disorders. These disorders are the focus of this chapter and are listed in ● TABLE 14.2. Axis II represents lifelong conditions that interfere with the person's ability to function, including any personality disorder or mental retardation. Axis III indicates any medical or physical conditions that the person is experiencing. It is important for the clinician to be aware of medical issues because they may be related to a person's mental health. For example, a woman might be depressed because of recent diagnosis and treatment for breast cancer. Knowledge of medical conditions is also important when considering appropriate treatment options, especially if medication will be prescribed. Axis IV indicates any psychosocial or environmental stressors facing the person. These may include school problems, work problems, housing problems, economic problems, physical or sexual abuse, legal problems, or lack of adequate social support. For instance, a person may be anxious over losing a job and concerned about paying the bills. Again, such information will assist the clinician in understanding the client's behavior as well as in forming feasible treatment options. Axis V rates (on a scale of 1 to 100) the person's current level of functioning on a global level, taking into account all the previously mentioned psychological, social, and medical conditions. This number communicates to others the degree of impairment in the person's overall functioning. The multiaxial system of the *DSM* attempts to provide as comprehensive a picture as possible of a person's behavior.

How Good Is the *DSM* Model?

How *reliable* and *valid* is the *DSM* model? Recall from Chapter 13 that *reliability* refers to the consistency of a measurement system. We would expect two different clinicians to give a similar judgment or a consistent rating when presented with the same symptoms. Different clinicians should make a similar diagnosis when presented with the same individual, and similar diagnoses should be made when different people exhibit the same symptoms.

Validity refers to how well a rating system does what it was intended to do and refers to the accuracy of the test. We would expect that the *DSM* model should be accurate in diagnosing people who are having difficulty functioning. In addition, it should be accurate in the label it applies to a person's condition. People who are depressed should be diagnosed as depressed, and people addicted to drugs should be diagnosed as having a substance abuse problem.

TABLE 14.1

● *DSM-IV-TR* Diagnostic Axes

	Axis I
Clinical disorders	Major categories of mental disorders, including depression, anxiety disorders, phobias, amnesia, substance abuse, and schizophrenia (see Table 14.2).
	Axis II
Personality disorders; mental retardation	Lifelong conditions that negatively affect a person's ability to function. Divided into two major classes: *mental retardation* and *personality disorders* (see Table 14.7).
	Axis III
General medical conditions	Physical problems or conditions—such as cancer diagnosis and treatment, diabetes, and arthritis—that may influence the person's mental health and that must also be considered when medication is prescribed.
	Axis IV
Psychosocial and environmental problems	*Psychosocial* problems might include problems holding a job or staying in school, or lack of social support. *Environmental* problems might include physical or sexual abuse, or experiencing a traumatic event.
	Axis V
Global assessment of functioning	A numerical scale for evaluating the person's level of functioning. A rating of 90 indicates a person who is functioning very well in all areas of life, has minimal symptoms, if any, and is experiencing only everyday problems. At a rating of 50, a person shows serious symptoms or one or more problems with relationships, work, or school, including possible suicidal thoughts and obsessional behavior.

Reprinted with permission from the Diagnostic and Statistical Manual of Mental Disorders, Fourth Edition, Text Revision, Copyright 2000. American Psychiatric Association.

TABLE 14.2

● *DSM-IV-TR* Axis I Major Categories of Mental Disorders

AXIS I MAJOR CATEGORY	SOME INCLUDED DISORDERS		EXAMPLES
Disorders usually first diagnosed in infancy, childhood, or adolescence	• Learning disorders • Pervasive developmental disorders • Disruptive behavior and attention deficit disorders	• Tic disorders • Communication disorders	Attention deficit disorder, autism, enuresis (bedwetting), stuttering, difficulty in academic skills
Delirium, dementia, amnesia, and other cognitive disorders	• Deliria • Dementias	• Amnesic disorders	Delirium (due to a general medical condition or substance induced), dementia (Alzheimer's), amnesia (due to a general medical condition or substance induced)
Substance-related disorders (see Chapter 4)	• Alcohol use disorders • Cocaine use disorders • Inhalant use disorders	• Polysubstance use disorders	Alcoholism, cocaine or crack addiction, use of inhalants (sniffing glue or paint)
Schizophrenia and other psychotic disorders (see Table 14.6)	• Schizophrenia • Delusional disorder • Brief psychotic disorder (1 major symptom of psychosis that lasts less than 1 month; often in reaction to a stressor)	• Psychotic disorder due to a general medical condition	Paranoid type, catatonic
Mood disorders	• Depressive disorders • Bipolar disorders	• Substance-induced mood disorder	Major depressive disorder, dysthymic disorder, bipolar disorder, cyclothymic disorder
Anxiety disorders (see Big Picture Review)	• Panic disorder • Agoraphobia without history of panic disorder • Specific phobia (simple phobia)	• Obsessive-compulsive disorder • Posttraumatic stress disorder	Generalized anxiety disorder Panic disorder without agoraphobia, acrophobia
Somatoform disorders (see Table 14.5)	• Conversion disorder • Hypochondriasis	• Body dysmorphic disorder • Pain disorder	
Dissociative disorders (see Table 14.4)	• Dissociative amnesia • Dissociative fugue disorder	• Dissociative identity disorder	
Sexual and gender identity disorders (see Chapter 10)	• Sexual dysfunction • Paraphilias	• Gender identity disorder	Sexual aversion disorder, male erectile disorder, fetishism, pedophilia
Eating disorders (see Chapter 8)	• Anorexia nervosa	• Bulimia nervosa	Binge eating disorder
Sleep disorders (see Chapter 4)	• Primary sleep disorders	• Dyssomnia not otherwise specified	Sleepwalking disorder, narcolepsy, primary insomnia
Factitious disorders	• Factitious disorder (deliberately faking a physical or psychological disorder)		
Impulse control disorders not elsewhere classified	• Kleptomania (recurrent failure to control the urge to steal things that are not needed)	• Pyromania (recurrent failure to control the urge to set fires) • Pathological gambling	
Adjustment disorder	• Adjustment disorder with anxiety • Adjustment disorder with disturbance of conduct (maladaptive reactions to a known stressor such	as a family crisis that begins within 3 months of the stressor but does not last longer than 6 months)	
Other conditions that may be a focus of clinical attention	• Medication-induced movement disorders • Relational problems	• Problems related to abuse or neglect	Parent–child relational problem, occupational problem, borderline intellectual functioning

Reprinted with permission from the Diagnostic and Statistical Manual of Mental Disorders, *Fourth Edition, Text Revision, Copyright 2000. American Psychiatric Association.*

TECHNOLOGY and BEHAVIOR

INTERNET ADDICTION: A PSYCHOLOGICAL DISORDER?

As the American Psychiatric Association prepares for the release of the *DSM-V* sometime in 2013, one major controversy centers around whether it should include a new disorder called "Internet Addiction Disorder." Since the publication of the *DSM-IV* in 1994, Americans' use of the Internet has grown dramatically (see ● Figure 14.3). In 1997, 18% of U.S. households had access to the Internet compared to over 60% in 2007 (U.S. Census Bureau, 2007). People use the Internet for a variety of activities, including paying bills online, shopping, visiting chat rooms, participating in virtual worlds, gaming, gambling, stock-trading, and viewing pornography. So when does Internet use become an addiction?

Although not yet a formal *DSM* diagnosis, commonly proposed diagnostic criteria for Internet addiction include uncontrollable use of the Internet and excessive preoccupation or urges regarding computer use that results in impairment or distress, often harming relationships and one's ability to carry out normal responsibilities (Beard, 2005; Beard & Wolf, 2001; Block, 2008; Shaw & Black, 2008)

Conceptually, the description of Internet addiction has been based on the definition of impulse control and substance abuse disorders. For example, in both Internet addiction and impulse control disorders like pathological gambling, people experience high levels of anxiety and cannot resist the impulse to engage in the behavior despite endangering significant relationships, their job, or educational pursuits. Like substance abuse disorders, Internet addiction is characterized by tolerance, cravings, and withdrawal symptoms.

Estimates of how many people may have an Internet addiction vary widely. A recent random telephone survey of U.S. adults reported an estimate of 1% (Aboujaoude et al., 2006). Yet in Asian countries where computer use and Internet cafés are more widespread, estimates are higher. For instance, the South Korean government estimates 2.1% of children between the ages of 6 and 19 have Internet addiction (Choi, 2007). Surveys of college and high school students show Internet addiction rates ranging from 5.9% in Taiwan to 10.6% in China with a higher incidence rate among males (Chou & Hsiao, 2000; Lam, Peng, Mai, & Jing, 2009; Wu & Zhu, 2004). However, many of these surveys are hampered by sample bias and other methodological concerns that occur with self-report data.

Although U.S. studies on characteristics of people with Internet addictions are scarce, research on Taiwanese and Chinese adolescents and young adults indicates that high social anxiety, poor peer interactions, and an external locus of control may make youth more vulnerable to Internet addiction (Chak & Leung, 2004; Liu & Kuo, 2007).

FIGURE 14.3

● **Percentage of U.S Households With Internet Use at Home**
(Source: U.S. Census Bureau, Current Population Survey, November 1997, 2000, 2001, 2003, 2007).

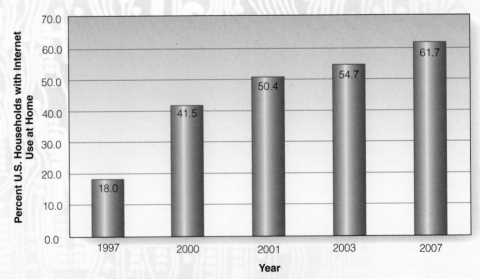

Source: U.S. Census Bureau, Current Population Survey, November 1997, 2000, 2001, 2003, 2007

The numerous revisions of the *DSM* have attempted to improve its reliability and validity. As a result, the reliability and validity for many of the Axis I clinical disorders are very high (T. A. Brown et al., 2001; Foa & Kozak, 1995; Hasin et al., 2006; Lahey et al., 2004). However, the reliability of Axis II personality disorders is considered extremely low, calling into question the validity of diagnosing the personality disorders (L. A. Clark, 2007; Falkum, Pedersen, & Karterud, 2009; Jablensky, 2002; Livesley, Jang, & Vernon, 1998; Widiger, 2003; Zanarini et al., 2000). Future revisions of the *DSM* model will need to address such inadequacies. The preparatory work for the next edition of the *DSM* (*DSM-V*) has begun, and it is due to be published in 2013. Internet addiction as a possible disorder is discussed in ● Technology and Behavior (facing page).

Having a standard system such as the *DSM* does not guarantee an accurate diagnosis. Making diagnostic judgments will always involve some subjectivity and personal bias on the part of the clinician, as people's symptoms often do not fit neatly into one category. Biases having to do with gender, race, or culture—whether conscious or unconscious—can also skew a diagnosis. For example, females are more likely to be diagnosed with personality disorders that are characterized by emotionality and dependence on others—behaviors that conform to negative stereotypes of the female gender role. Similarly, males are more likely to be diagnosed with personality disorders that are characterized by hostility and control of others—behaviors that conform to negative stereotypes of the male gender role. It has been argued that these gender differences in the frequency of personality disorders result from gender biases in diagnosis (Hartung & Widiger, 1998; Jane et al., 2007; Skodol & Bender, 2003; Widiger, 1998; Widiger & Chaynes, 2003).

Critics of the *DSM* model also point out the possible negative effects of labeling someone with a psychological disorder (Baumann, 2007; Grover, 2005). A diagnostic label may serve as a *self-fulfilling prophecy*, encouraging a person to behave in a way that is consistent with the disorder. Others in the person's environment may also treat the person in a way that encourages the symptoms of the disorder. We as a society tend to treat people with any diagnostic label negatively, perhaps increasing their maladaptive functioning through prejudice and discrimination. Such negative treatment may persist even after the person's behavior returns to normal (Rosenhan, 1973; Szasz, 1987).

The *DSM* model is not perfect and can provide only a general description of the problem a person is experiencing. It does not consider the uniqueness of each individual, nor can it tell us how this person will behave in the future. Yet, the *DSM* provides a useful framework and a common language for clinicians and researchers. Its multiaxial system offers more information to help clinicians identify appropriate treatments, and its standardized vocabulary allows researchers to more effectively study the underlying causes of psychological disorders. Keep in mind the advantages and criticisms of the *DSM* system as we review some of the more prevalent and more interesting mental health disorders, starting with the anxiety disorders.

Let's REVIEW

In this section, we presented the general structure of the *DSM* model and reviewed its strengths and weaknesses. For a quick check of your understanding, try answering the following questions at increasing levels of difficulty.

1. The *DSM* model relies mainly on which criterion of abnormality?

   a. statistical infrequency
   b. violation of social norms
   c. inability to function
   d. mental insanity

2. The purpose of the *DSM* is to _____.

   a. explain the causes of mental disorders
   b. describe the symptoms of mental disorders
   c. indicate the frequency of mental disorders
   d. prescribe treatment methods for mental disorders

3. Which of the following is not information gained by using the multiaxial system of the current *DSM*?

   a. presence of mental retardation
   b. degree of social support
   c. medical conditions
   d. a prediction of future behavior

ANSWERS 1. c; 2. b; 3. d

WHAT ARE ANXIETY DISORDERS? IT'S NOT JUST "NERVES"

What is abnormal anxiety? We all experience some anxiety from time to time. Many students are anxious when they have to make an oral presentation. Other people are nervous when they have to meet new people or fly in an airplane. In these examples, however, the anxiety tends to decrease once the situation is over. People with **anxiety disorders** are different in that they experience chronic anxiety that seriously interferes with their ability to function. Howie Mandel, whom we introduced at the beginning of this chapter, is a prime example of a person with an anxiety disorder.

Components of the Anxiety Disorders

Typically, anxiety disorders can be characterized by four components: *physical*, *cognitive*, *emotional*, and *behavioral*. These components interact powerfully, creating an unpleasant experience of fear or dread, although there may not be a specific fear-producing stimulus present.

The *physical* components of anxiety include dizziness, elevated heart rate and blood pressure, muscle tension, sweating palms, and dry mouth. These physical symptoms stem from the activation of the sympathetic nervous system (see Chapter 2). The hormonal system is also activated as adrenalin is released into the bloodstream. Recall that this occurrence is referred to as the fight-or-flight response. This fight-or-flight response occurs every time we perceive a threat in our environment.

People with anxiety disorders have concerns that are unrealistic and out of proportion to the amount of harm that could occur. *Cognitive* components of anxiety may include worrying, fearing loss of control, exaggerating (in one's mind) the danger of a situation, exhibiting paranoia, or being extremely wary and watchful of people and events. These thoughts may lead to *emotional* reactions such as a sense of dread, terror, panic, irritability, or restlessness. These thoughts and emotions propel the person to behave in ways meant to cope with the anxiety.

Coping with abnormal anxiety may include *behaviors* such as escaping or fleeing from the object or situation; behaving aggressively; "freezing," which results in being unable to move; or avoiding the situation in the future. Again, these symptoms are so intense that they disrupt the quality of the person's life.

Types of Anxiety Disorders

Approximately 19% of Americans over 18 years of age are diagnosed with an anxiety disorder in a given year (NCS-R, 2007). We will discuss five anxiety disorders: *generalized anxiety disorder*, *panic disorder*, *phobic disorder*, *obsessive-compulsive disorder*, and *posttraumatic stress disorder* (see ● FIGURE 14.4).

anxiety disorder a disorder marked by excessive apprehension that seriously interferes with a person's ability to function

generalized anxiety disorder (GAD) an anxiety disorder characterized by chronic, constant worry in almost all situations

FIGURE 14.4

● **Prevalence of Anxiety Disorders in a Given Year** Among adults 18 years of age or older, social and specific phobias are the most commonly diagnosed disorders in any given year because the age of onset for the phobias is typically earlier than that for other anxiety disorders. *(Source: National Comorbidity Survey Replication data. Table 2. Updated 2007. http://www.hcp.med.harvard.edu/ncs).*

Generalized Anxiety Disorder (GAD)

Some people are anxious all the time in almost all situations. These individuals may be diagnosed with **generalized anxiety disorder (GAD)**. Symptoms of GAD include excessive anxiety, worry, and difficulty in controlling such worries. The person may be easily fatigued, restless, and irritable, and may experience difficulty concentrating or sleeping (American Psychiatric Association, 2000a). People with GAD chronically worry not only about major issues, such as which car or house to buy, their children's health, or their job performance, but also about minor issues, such as being late or wearing the right outfit. It is estimated that about 3% of American adults experience GAD in any given year (R. C. Kessler, Chiu et al., 2005). European

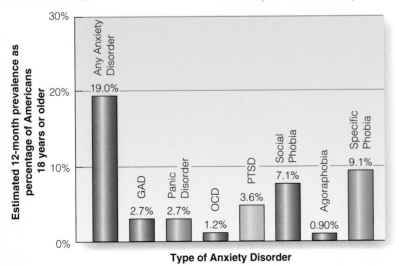

Estimated 12-month prevalence as percentage of Americans 18 years or older

Type of Anxiety Disorder

Any Anxiety Disorder 19.0%
GAD 2.7%
Panic Disorder 2.7%
OCD 1.2%
PTSD 3.6%
Social Phobia 7.1%
Agoraphobia 0.90%
Specific Phobia 9.1%

Americans are at higher risk of GAD than are African Americans and Hispanic Americans (Breslau et al., 2006).

Panic Disorder

Imagine that you are attending a party given by a good friend. When you arrive at the party, a feeling of panic suddenly overwhelms you. Your heart begins to pound, you hear ringing in your ears, your skin feels tingly and numb, and it becomes harder and harder to breathe. These are common symptoms that occur during a *panic attack*, a short but intense episode of severe anxiety. As many as 30–40% of young adults in the United States report occasional panic attacks that do not interfere with their daily functioning (Ehlers, 1995; N. J. King et al., 1993). However, when panic attacks are more common and a person begins to fear having panic attacks, to the extent that it interferes with the ability to function, a diagnosis of **panic disorder** may be given (American Psychiatric Association, 2000a).

It is estimated that between 1.5% and 4% of people will develop panic disorder at some time in their lives (American Psychiatric Association, 2000a). It typically develops in late adolescence or early adulthood and is twice as common in women as in men (Craske & Barlow, 2001; R. C. Kessler, Berglund et al., 2005). European Americans tend to have a higher prevalence rate of panic disorder than do African Americans, Hispanic Americans, and Asian Americans (Breslau et al., 2006; A. Y. Zhang & Snowden, 1999).

People with panic disorder often feel so overwhelmed by the feelings of panic that they think they are having a heart attack or a seizure. They may believe that they are "going crazy" or going to die, and many seek medical attention to find out what is wrong with them. The panic attacks may occur frequently or only sporadically. Most people with panic disorder cannot identify any specific thing that might have triggered the attack. However, when a panic attack occurs, the same situation may then trigger a future attack. Fear of having another panic attack may lead to **agoraphobia**, or a fear of being in places from which escape may be difficult or where help may not be available if one were to experience panic. People affected with agoraphobia avoid any place—the mall, the grocery store, or the movie theater—in which they believe a panic attack may occur. Such fears can leave people housebound for years. At least 75% of those who suffer from agoraphobia are women (Barlow, 2002). Note that people without panic disorder can experience agoraphobia (W. W. Eaton & Keyl, 1990), which is then characterized as a phobic disorder, our next topic of discussion.

For many college students, taking a test is an anxiety-producing event.

Image Source/Getty Images

panic disorder an anxiety disorder characterized by intense fear and anxiety in the absence of danger that is accompanied by strong physical symptoms

agoraphobia an excessive fear of being in places from which escape might be difficult or where help might not be available if one were to experience panic

TABLE 14.3
● **Common Specific Phobias**

PHOBIA NAME	FEAR
Acrophobia	Heights
Aerophobia	Flying
Agoraphobia	Crowds or open spaces
Aichmophobia	Needles
Arachnophobia	Spiders
Astraphobia	Storms, thunder, lightning
Aviophobia	Airplanes
Claustrophobia	Closed spaces
Cynophobia	Dogs
Dentophobia	Dentists
Gephyrophobia	Crossing bridges
Hematophobia	Blood
Hydrophobia	Water
Microphobia	Germs or contamination
Nyctophobia	Darkness
Ophidophobia	Snakes
Pathophobia	Disease
Phonophobia	Public speaking
Pyrophobia	Fire
Thanatophobia	Death
Xenophobia	Strangers
Zoophobia	Animals

phobic disorder an anxiety disorder characterized by an intense fear of a specific object or situation

specific phobia a persistent fear and avoidance of a specific object or situation

social phobia an irrational, persistent fear of being negatively evaluated by others in a social situation

obsession a recurrent thought or image that intrudes on a person's awareness

compulsion repetitive behavior that a person feels a strong urge to perform

obsessive-compulsive disorder (OCD) an anxiety disorder involving a pattern of unwanted intrusive thoughts and the urge to engage in repetitive actions

Phobic Disorders

All of us have fears. Some of us get anxious when we think of or see a snake or a spider. Others may fear public speaking or eating in public. As children, we may have been afraid of the dark or the dentist. These are common fears. However, when our fears become so intense that they cause severe anxiety, possibly even panic attacks that interfere with our ability to function, then a diagnosis of **phobic disorder** is made (American Psychiatric Association, 2000a). We have already mentioned one type of phobic disorder, *agoraphobia*. Two other types of phobic disorders are *specific phobias* and *social phobias*.

Specific phobias involve a persistent fear and avoidance of a specific object or situation—animals, heights, bridges—or other specific stimuli. They are one of the most common disorders worldwide, affecting approximately 9% of American adults (NCS-R, 2007), 4% of the general population in Mexico (Medina-Mora et al., 2005), 2.7% in Japan (Kawakami et al., 2005), and 7.7% across several European countries (ESEMed/MHEDEA, 2004). ● TABLE 14.3 describes a few of the hundreds of specific phobias that have been identified. Specific phobias typically begin in childhood (Kessler, Berglund et al., 2005).

Social phobias include an irrational, persistent fear of being negatively evaluated by others in a social situation. A person with a social phobia (also called *social anxiety disorder*) may have an extreme fear of embarrassment or humiliation. This disorder may include fear of public speaking, fear of eating or undressing in front of others, or fear of using public restrooms. It is estimated that 12% of American adults will experience a social phobia at some time in their lives (Ruscio et al., 2008). American actress Scarlett Johansson is just one of many celebrities who has reported experiencing "stage fright," a social phobia. Although she does not experience stage fright while making movies, public appearances make her extremely anxious and prevented her from acting on Broadway until recently. Social phobias tend to develop in the early preschool years and in adolescence and are somewhat more likely to develop in women than in men (A. J. Lang & Stein, 2001; Kessler, Berglund et al., 2005; Turk, Heimberg, & Hope, 2001). African Americans and Hispanic Americans tend to have a lower lifetime risk of social phobias than do European Americans (Breslau et al., 2006). Lifetime risk of social phobias tends to be more common in developed countries than in developing countries (D. J. Stein et al., 2010).

People with phobic disorders typically recognize that their fears are irrational, but they cannot stop the overwhelming anxiety they feel when faced with the feared object or situation.

Obsessive-Compulsive Disorder (OCD)

Obsessions are recurrent thoughts or images that intrude on a person's consciousness or awareness. **Compulsions** are repetitive behaviors that a person feels a strong urge to perform. All of us experience intrusive thoughts and strong urges. For example, on your way to school or work, the thought pops into your head that you left the stove on, and you start worrying about a house fire. What do you do? Many of us feel compelled to turn the car around to check that everything is okay. However, what if this scenario occurred every time you got in the car, and you felt compelled to check each time? In such a case, you might be diagnosed with **obsessive-compulsive disorder (OCD)**.

Obsessive-compulsive disorder is an anxiety disorder in which a person experiences recurrent obsessions or compulsions that he or she feels cannot be controlled (American Psychiatric Association, 2000a). The person recognizes that these thoughts or behaviors are irrational, yet cannot seem to control them. Obsessions often center on dirt and contamination, doing harm to oneself or others, sexual thoughts, or repeated doubts (such as not having locked the house). Common compulsions include cleaning, checking, counting things, or arranging and straightening things in a particular fashion. The compulsions are often performed with the hope of preventing the obsessive thoughts or making them go away. However, performing these "rituals" provides only temporary relief. Not performing the rituals increases the person's anxiety. Howie Mandel's constant obsessions with germs made him compulsively wash his hands with scalding water over and over again or avoid shaking hands or touching items and people with his hands.

Recurrent obsessions cause great personal distress, and the compulsions can be time-consuming and in some cases harmful—as when a person washes his or her hands so frequently that they bleed. It is estimated that between 1% and 3% of individuals will develop OCD at some time in their lives, and in the United States, the rates are higher among European Americans than among Hispanic Americans and African Americans (Hewlett, 2000; R. C. Kessler, Chiu et al., 2005; A. Y. Zhang & Snowden, 1999).

Posttraumatic Stress Disorder (PTSD)

Another type of anxiety disorder is **posttraumatic stress disorder (PTSD)**. PTSD develops after exposure to a terrifying event or ordeal in which grave physical harm occurred or was threatened. Traumatic events may include:

● Violent personal assaults such as rape, physical abuse, or sexual abuse
● Natural or human-caused disasters such as an earthquake, a hurricane, a terrorist attack, a bombing, or an outbreak of an infectious disease
● Military combat
● Events that anyone might experience—the sudden, unexpected death of a loved one or witnessing a violent crime or a deadly traffic accident

A diagnosis of PTSD requires that the person repeatedly reexperience the ordeal in the form of distressing memories, nightmares, frightening thoughts, or flashback episodes, especially when exposed to situations that are similar to the original trauma. For example, a car backfire might trigger a flashback to a combat trauma or being the victim of an armed robbery. Anniversaries of the event also can trigger symptoms. In addition, people diagnosed with PTSD may experience emotional numbness or withdrawal from themselves or others such that they lose interest in usual activities or are regarded as distant and emotionally unavailable. Finally, people with PTSD are always on guard and alert to any real or imagined potential threats in their environments—showing *hypervigilance*, having difficulty concentrating, or having difficulty sleeping (American Psychiatric Association, 2000a). They may experience depression, anxiety, irritability, or outbursts of anger; physical symptoms such as headaches, dizziness, or chest pain; or feelings of intense guilt. For some people, such symptoms can seriously disrupt the ability to work or to meet social, professional, and family obligations.

Approximately 3.5% of U.S. adults are diagnosed with PTSD in a given year (R. C. Kessler, Chiu et al., 2005). More than twice as many females as males experience PTSD following exposure to a trauma, typically sexual assault (J. R. T. Davidson, 2000; Tolin & Foa, 2006). Women's higher PTSD risk has been attributed to a number of variables that reinforce the biopsychosocial nature of mental health disorders. For example, sex differences in the responses of the *amygdala*, the brain structure that mediates fear, have been documented (Hamann, 2005). Moreover, women are more likely to perceive threat and loss of control than are men—psychological factors that may influence the risk of PTSD (Olff et al., 2007). Women are more likely to be victims of sexual abuse and experience these traumas at younger ages than men—social factors that also play a role in PTSD (Cortina & Kubiak, 2006; Olff et al., 2007; Tolin & Foa, 2006).

Soldiers (male or female) are also at high risk for developing PTSD, as military conflict is a source of trauma. About 19% of Vietnam veterans developed PTSD at some point after the war (Dohrenwend et al., 2006). After two decades of conflict in Afghanistan, 42% of Afghan participants in a national population-based survey reported PTSD symptoms (Cardozo et al., 2004). Studies of U.S. military personnel in Iraq also indicate problems in mental health, most notably PTSD (Felker et al., 2008; Hoge et al., 2004; Milliken, Auchterlonie, & Hoge, 2007).

Research on the mental health effects of the September 11 attacks revealed a remarkable

posttraumatic stress disorder (PTSD) an anxiety disorder, characterized by distressing memories, emotional numbness, and hypervigilance, that develops after exposure to a traumatic event

Exposure to a natural disaster such as the January 2010 earthquake in Haiti can lead to the development of PTSD.

Anatoli Zhdanov/UPI/Landov

degree of PTSD, at least initially (Calderoni et al., 2006; Grieger, Fullerton, & Ursano, 2004; Lating et al., 2004). A comprehensive mental health screening of more than 11,000 rescue and recovery workers and volunteers at the World Trade Center revealed that more than 20% of the participants experienced symptoms of PTSD and 13% met the diagnostic criteria for PTSD (Centers for Disease Control and Prevention [CDC], 2004b). Years later, many of these individuals are faring better; however, people who were directly exposed to the attacks are more likely to have persistent symptoms of PTSD (Bonanno et al., 2006; Laugharne, Janca, & Widiger, 2007).

Similar statistics emerged following Hurricane Katrina's effects on the U.S. Gulf Coast in 2005. More than 19% of people from the largest employer in New Orleans evidenced PTSD symptoms 6 months after the hurricane (Desalvo et al., 2007). ● The Big Picture Review summarizes the anxiety disorders that we have discussed.

Explaining Anxiety Disorders

What causes anxiety disorders? Research on people with anxiety disorders suggests biological, psychological, and sociocultural factors that may contribute to such behavior, underscoring the biopsychosocial nature of psychological disorders presented at the beginning of the chapter.

Biology and the Brain

The functioning of several neurotransmitters has been linked to anxiety disorders. For example, abnormal activity of norepinephrine, serotonin, or GABA may be involved in panic attacks (C. J. Bell & Nutt, 1998; Charney et al., 2000; Goddard et al., 2010). Abnormal activity of GABA has been linked to people with GAD while problems in serotonin regulation have been suggested as a cause for OCD and PTSD (Kuzelova, Ptacek, & Milan, 2010; Mellman et al., 2009; Saxena et al., 1998).

Anxiety disorders tend to run in families, suggesting a genetic link. Children of parents with anxiety disorders have a greater risk for anxiety disorders than do children of parents with no psychological disorders (Micco et al., 2009). Even relatives (siblings, aunts, uncles) of a person with an anxiety disorder are more likely to have one compared with relatives of someone without a disorder (Hanna, 2000). Twin and family studies have found high heritability especially for panic disorder and OCD (Biederman et al., 2001; Grados, Walkup, &

THE BIG PICTURE review

Symptoms of the Main Anxiety Disorders

DISORDER	SYMPTOMS
Panic Disorder	Abrupt experiences of unexpected intense fear accompanied by physical symptoms such as heart palpitations, shortness of breath, or dizziness that interfere with a person's functioning.
Phobic Disorder	Persistent fear of a specific object or social situation that is excessive and unreasonable and interferes with a person's ability to function.
Posttraumatic Stress Disorder	Exposure to a traumatic event during which one feels helplessness or fear followed by recurrent and intrusive memories or nightmares of the event, avoidance of stimuli associated with the event, numbing of emotions, and increased arousal that impair the person's functioning.
Obsessive-Compulsive Disorder	A pattern of recurrent, persistent, intrusive thoughts or images followed by repetitive behaviors or mental acts that a person feels driven to perform to reduce stress or to prevent some event from happening. The thoughts or behaviors are time-consuming and interfere with the person's functioning.
Generalized Anxiety Disorder	Excessive worry for at least 6 months about a number of events accompanied by physical symptoms, such as muscle tension, mental agitation, and irritability that impair a person's functioning.

Walford, 2003; Hettema, Neale, & Kendler, 2001; Mosing et al., 2009; Nicolini et al., 2009; Scherrer et al., 2000). Specific chromosomal regions have been identified that may play a role in anxiety disorders, but specific genes have not yet been identified (S. J. Kim, Lee, & Kim, 2005; Politi et al.,2006).

Studies on animals and humans have focused on specific brain areas that are involved in anxiety and fear (LeDoux, 1998; Lonsdorf et al., 2009; Rosen, 2004; Rosen & Donley, 2006). As stated previously, our fear response is coordinated by the amygdala, a small structure deep inside the brain that also plays a role in our emotional memories (LaBar, 2007). Neuroimaging research on individuals with GAD shows difficulty in regulating an area of the brain that lessens the activity of the amygdala. As a result, the amygdala becomes overactive, and the person experiences a heightened level of anxiety and difficulty in regulating emotions (Etkin et al., 2010). Similarly, neuroimaging studies on people with PTSD suggest dysfunction in the amygdala that may contribute to their emotional and memory-related symptoms (Kolassa & Elbert, 2007; Liberzon et al., 1999; Rauch, Shin, & Phelps, 2006; Rogers et al., 2009; Shin, Rauch, & Pitman, 2006). Specifically, people who have PTSD show overactivity in the amygdala, as depicted in ● WHAT'S HAPPENING IN YOUR BRAIN?

Research on OCD suggests abnormal functioning of a part of the forebrain called the *striatum* (Choi et al., 2007). For example, in one study (Rauch et al., 1997), PET scans of individuals with OCD showed different brain circuitry in the striatum when performing a cognitive task than did the PET scans of people without OCD. Other research suggests that an overactive monitoring system in the brain is related to the symptoms of OCD (Gehring, Himle, & Nisenson, 2000; Ursu et al., 2003).

WHAT'S HAPPENING IN YOUR BRAIN?

PTSD AND THE BRAIN

Mike Goldwater/Getty Images

Brain Activation in PTSD in Response to Trauma-related Stimuli, by Israel Liberzon et al., *Biological Psychiatry*, vol. 45, 821, © 1999 by the Society of Biological Psychiatry. Reprinted with permission of the Society of Biological Psychiatry.

PTSD patients

Healthy individuals

Vets without PTSD

The amygdala is thought to play a role in the emotion of fear and in memory formation. The brain images shown here suggest that in people with PTSD this brain area produces an exaggerated response that may contribute to their emotional and memory-related symptoms. Vietnam veterans with PTSD (shown in the top scans) have exaggerated responses in their amygdala (marked with red arrows) after hearing combat sounds reminiscent of the trauma that gave rise to their PTSD symptoms. Healthy individuals and veterans without PTSD do not have this intense amygdala response, as shown in the middle and lower brain scans.

Psychological Factors

Psychological factors also help in explaining anxiety disorders. The psychoanalytic perspective suggests that anxiety is linked to unresolved unconscious conflicts. For example, Freud would attribute GAD to a weak ego, which is unable to handle the natural conflict between the id and the superego. Typically, the ego does this by using defense mechanisms. Consequently, if a person feels anxious all the time, the ego—with its defense mechanisms—must not be doing its job. Freud (1909) also suggested that phobias result when unconscious anxiety is displaced onto a symbolic object or situation. Fear of being abandoned may express itself as a fear of the dark. Similarly, Freud attributed the obsessions and compulsions of OCD to symbolic manifestations of unconscious conflicts.

The social learning perspective suggests that phobias are learned in the same way that Watson and Rayner were able to condition Little Albert to fear a white rat (see Chapter 5; A. P. Field, 2006). A neutral stimulus (the phobic object) gets paired with a stimulus that naturally elicits fear. So, when a thunderstorm gets paired with a loud noise (thunder) that naturally evokes fear, we learn to be fearful of thunderstorms.

Conditioning processes also may play a role in panic disorder. Neutral stimuli that are present during an initial panic attack may then become conditioned stimuli that trigger panic symptoms on subsequent occasions. These conditioned stimuli are then thought to generalize to other neutral stimuli resulting in a variety of cues that evoke panic symptoms (Lissek et al., 2010).

Direct experience is not always necessary to develop an anxiety disorder. For example, we may acquire fears simply by observing or hearing about others' negative experiences (Kelly & Forsyth, 2007; Kleinknecht, 1991). How many of us have come face-to-face with a demon? But after seeing the movie *Paranormal Activity*, we may be more fearful when we hear unexplained noises in our home. We now associate an unexpected noise with a mysterious force that wants to do us harm. We may sleep with the lights on or sleep at someone else's house to avoid possible disaster. Avoiding the noises reduces our anxiety but only makes us more fearful the next time anything unusual occurs in our home.

Reinforcement also helps explain compulsions. If you engage in a certain behavior following an anxiety-provoking obsession, your anxiety is often reduced. The next time the obsession occurs, you feel more compelled to engage in the behavior so that you can reduce your anxiety (Barlow, 2002). Learning and conditioning theories have also been useful in understanding PTSD. Sights, sounds, or images of the trauma all become conditioned stimuli that trigger the fear reaction.

Cognitive research suggests that our thinking processes play a role in developing an anxiety disorder. In particular, people who perceive situations and objects as uncontrollable, unpredictable, dangerous, and disgusting are more vulnerable to anxiety disorders (Armfield, 2006; Bryant & Guthrie, 2005). People with anxiety disorders also tend to process negative information rather than positive or neutral information about an event (Fox, Cahill, & Zougkou, 2010). For example, studies show that people with panic disorder sometimes misinterpret their bodily sensations, thinking they are beginning a panic attack. Their negative and catastrophic thinking then heightens their anxiety (Barlow, 2000; Craske & Barlow, 2001). People diagnosed with GAD tend to anticipate that something bad will happen to them and that they will feel out of control. While driving in a car, they may worry that they will get lost or in an accident. These worries become constant and almost automatic in their thought processes (A. T. Beck, 1997; Riskind et al., 2000).

We may acquire fears by observing others' negative experiences either in real life or through media portrayals.

Blumhouse Productions/The Kobal Collection

3:08:26 AM

Research has found that the shattering of certain basic assumptions about life may bring on PTSD. An unpredictable trauma—such as a rape, an earthquake, or an automobile accident—may make us question our assumptions that the world is safe and just and that events happen for a reason. It dispels our illusion of control and invincibility and our assumption that bad things only happen to bad people (Janoff-Bulman, 1992; Terr, 1983). Some research suggests that people with OCD are less able to turn off the intrusive, negative obsessions that we all experience from time to time (Salkovskis et al., 1997).

Carl Rogers (1959) and other humanists attribute anxiety to an unrealistic self-image, although this idea has not been extensively researched. An unrealistic self-image results in being overly critical of oneself and setting unrealistic standards for acceptance by others. Because neither the standards nor the self-image can ever be attained, anxiety results.

Sociocultural Factors

Sociocultural factors must also be considered when explaining anxiety disorders. For example, in cultures experiencing rapid social change or war, people are more likely to exhibit anxiety symptoms than are people in more stable countries (Compton et al., 1991). Similarly, people who have been abused as children or who have had other previous traumatic or stressful experiences are more likely to develop anxiety disorders (J. G. Green et al., 2010; Hyman & Rudorfer, 2000; McLaughlin et al., 2010; Widom, 1999). In the United States, African Americans and Hispanic Americans have a lower lifetime risk of anxiety disorders than do European Americans (Breslau et al., 2005). This lower lifetime risk is even more pronounced at lower levels of education, suggesting that perhaps some protection against anxiety disorders develops in childhood for these disadvantaged groups (Breslau et al., 2006). However, African Americans who do develop anxiety disorders are more likely to have more persistent symptoms than are European Americans (Breslau et al., 2005). Women are also more likely than men to be diagnosed with an anxiety disorder (NCS-R, 2007). This gender difference has been attributed to several factors: women's relative lack of power in society; differences in gender-role socialization, making it acceptable for women to report fear (Arrindell et al., 2003); differences in coping styles; and the greater likelihood that women will be victims of violence, crime, or abuse. More research will have to examine the role of gender and culture in anxiety disorders before we fully understand their influence.

Let's REVIEW

In this section, we described the main anxiety disorders and detailed our current understanding of what causes them. For a quick check of your understanding, try answering the following questions at increasing levels of difficulty.

1. Which of the following is *not* an anxiety disorder?

a. panic disorder

b. phobic disorder

c. obsessive-compulsive disorder

d. schizophrenia

2. Marilu is anxious and nervous all the time. She constantly worries over her family, her job, and her schoolwork. Which anxiety disorder *best* describes Marilu's behavior?

a. panic disorder

b. generalized anxiety disorder

c. phobic disorder

d. obsessive-compulsive disorder

3. Learning theories suggest that obsessive-compulsive disorder is the result of _____.

a. reinforcement processes

b. faulty cognitions

c. low self-esteem

d. unconscious impulses

ANSWERS 1. d; 2. b; 3. a

LEARNING
OBJECTIVE

What Should You Know?

• Describe the nature of dissociative and somatoform disorders.

DISSOCIATIVE AND SOMATOFORM DISORDERS: OTHER FORMS OF ANXIETY?

Dissociative and somatoform disorders are quite rare in the general population, but often are of the most interest to students. Here we outline the general nature of these disorders and the psychological factors that may play a role in their development.

TABLE 14.4
• Types of Dissociative Disorders

DISORDER	MAJOR FEATURES
Dissociative identity disorder	Separate multiple personalities in the same individual.
Dissociative fugue disorder	Person unexpectedly travels away from home and assumes a new identity with amnesia of previous identity.
Dissociative amnesia	Memory loss of important personal information. Not due to organic problems or brain injury.
Depersonalization disorder	Frequent episodes in which the person feels detached from own mental state or body.

Dissociative Disorders: Flight or Multiple Personalities

To *dissociate* means to break or pull apart. Thus, the **dissociative disorders** involve a loss of awareness of some part of our self, our surroundings, or what is going on around us. Mild dissociative experiences are common (Aderibigbe, Bloch, & Walker, 2001; Hunter, Sierra, & David, 2004; C. A. Ross, 1997). For instance, have you ever driven somewhere and on arrival did not remember driving there? Have you ever missed a part of a conversation but can tell from the speaker's demeanor that you appeared to have been listening the whole time? Have you ever appeared attentive in class while you were daydreaming about your plans for the weekend? All of these are common, everyday dissociative experiences.

However, when loss of awareness becomes more extreme, a diagnosis of a dissociative disorder may apply. Such extreme dissociation is typically linked to severe stress or a series of emotionally traumatic events (Classen, Koopman, & Spiegel, 1993; Isaac & Chand, 2006; Kihlstrom, 2001; Spiegel, 1997). • TABLE 14.4 provides a brief description of the dissociative disorders listed in the *DSM-IV-TR*. Here we will confine our discussion to two: *dissociative fugue disorder* and *dissociative identity disorder*.

In 2006 a 57-year-old husband and father of two left work at his New York law firm and disappeared. Six months later he was found living under a new name in a homeless shelter in Chicago. He didn't know who he was or where he came from. During the same year, another man left his Washington home to visit a friend in Canada who was dying from cancer. Four days later, he was walking around Denver asking people for help because he didn't know who he was. Both of these men were diagnosed with *dissociative fugue disorder* (J. Brady, 2007).

Dissociative fugue disorder involves one or more episodes of amnesia in which a person is unable to recall some or all of his or her past and is confused about his or her identity. A new identity may be formed in which the person suddenly and unexpectedly travels away from home (American Psychiatric Association, 2000a). In this fugue (meaning "flight") state the person appears normal. He or she may adopt a new name, identity, and residence and engage in normal social interactions. The fugue state may last hours, weeks, or months. However, at some point confusion about one's identity or the return of the original identity may surface, leading to personal distress. Once the person has returned to the prefugue identity, he or she may or may not remember what happened during the fugue state, which may cause additional confusion and distress.

Although no specific cause is known for dissociative fugue, its onset is typically related to a stressful or traumatic event such as a natural disaster, war experience, or unbearable stress at work or at home (Putnam, 2000). It is a relatively uncommon disorder with only an estimated 0.2% prevalence in the general population (American Psychiatric Association, 2000a).

Dissociative identity disorder (DID), formerly called multiple personality disorder, involves the existence of two or more separate personalities in the same individual (American Psychiatric Association, 2000a). Although dissociative identity disorder is rare, it has become well known through the media. Movies such as *Identity*; *Me, Myself and Irene*; and *Sybil* attest to the public's fascination with this disorder.

The separate personalities—referred to as *alters* (for alternate personalities)—may or may not be known to the "core," or "host," personality—the person who asks for treatment. Each personality has its own perceptions, thoughts, mannerisms, speech characteristics, and ges-

dissociative disorder a disorder marked by a loss of awareness of some part of one's self or one's surroundings that seriously interferes with the person's ability to function

dissociative fugue disorder a disorder marked by episodes of amnesia in which a person is unable to recall some or all of his or her past and is confused about his or her identity; a new identity may be formed in which the person suddenly and unexpectedly travels away from home

dissociative identity disorder (DID) a disorder in which two or more personalities coexist within the same individual; formerly called multiple personality disorder

tures. Each alter appears to have a specific function. For example, one alter may arise to deal with romantic relationships, whereas another alter deals with academic work. The alter personalities may be of different ages, gender, or ethnicities. The majority of people diagnosed with DID are women (American Psychiatric Association, 2000a).

Frequent blackouts or episodes of amnesia are common in people with dissociative identity disorder. They may notice money missing from their bank accounts that they don't remember spending or find objects in their home that they do not recognize. Self-mutilating behavior is also common in people with this disorder. They may repeatedly burn or cut themselves and have a history of suicide attempts (Foote et al., 2008; C. A. Ross, 1997). Often they have been previously diagnosed with other disorders such as major depression, PTSD, substance abuse disorder, or schizophrenia, especially if they have reported hearing voices (Ellason, Ross, & Fuchs, 1996; R. J. Loewenstein & Putnam, 2004).

One striking similarity among people with DID is their backgrounds. Almost all have reported experiencing chronic, horrific childhood physical or sexual abuse or both at the hands of family members (Coons, 1994; Ellason et al., 1996; Putnam et al., 1986). Many clinicians believe that in an attempt to cope with such trauma, these people defensively dissociate, developing alter personalities that can protect them from experiencing such events in life or in memory. People with DID have a high level of hypnotic susceptibility (Kihlstrom, Glisky, & Angiulo, 1994). Thus, the ability to dissociate may have become an effective coping mechanism early in life.

Some psychologists question the validity of the dissociative identity disorder (Kihlstrom, 2005; Piper & Merskey, 2004). There has been a great increase in the number of reported cases since 1980 (American Psychiatric Association, 2000a). Only one third of a sample of U.S. psychiatrists believed DID should have been included in the *DSM-IV* (Pope et al., 1999). Verifying the claims of amnesia and blackouts is difficult, and people with DID have often been diagnosed with other psychological disorders (Kluft, 1999; Loewenstein & Putnam, 2004). Some believe that DID may represent an extreme form of posttraumatic stress disorder (Butler et al., 1996). Future research may help us better understand the nature of this disorder.

Somatoform Disorders: Hypochondriasis, or Doctor, I'm Sure I'm Sick

Somatic means "related to the body." The **somatoform disorders** involve physical complaints for which there is no apparent physical cause. The physical symptoms are real to the person, but physicians can find no medical reason why the individual is experiencing such symptoms. For example, a person may complain of constant hip pain. Numerous medical tests are completed, but there is no apparent physical cause for the hip ache. Because no physical cause can be found, it is assumed that psychological distress underlies the physical problem. ● TABLE 14.5 describes the somatoform disorders listed in the *DSM-IV-TR*. Our discussion in this section will focus on one of them, *hypochondriasis*.

In **hypochondriasis**, a person believes that he or she has a serious medical disease despite evidence to the contrary (American Psychiatric Association, 2000a). Many of us know someone who we think is a hypochondriac because that person frequently complains about physical ailments. However, people with hypochondriasis are convinced that they have a disease, not just one or two specific symptoms. People with hypochondriasis may undergo extensive medical testing by several doctors to confirm the existence of their disease. When a doctor suggests that they may have a psychological problem,

somatoform disorder a disorder marked by physical complaints that have no apparent physical cause

hypochondriasis a somatoform disorder in which the person persistently worries over having a disease, without any evident physical basis

TABLE 14.5

● **Types of Somatoform Disorders**

DISORDER	MAJOR FEATURES
Conversion disorder	Loss of functioning in some part of the body, but no physical cause can be found.
Somatization disorder	Long history of physical complaints affecting several areas of the body. The person has sought medical attention, but no physical cause can be found.
Pain disorder	Long history of pain complaints. The person has sought medical attention, but no physical cause can be found.
Hypochondriasis	Persistent worry over having a physical disease. The person frequently seeks medical attention, but no physical disease can be found.
Body dysmorphic disorder	Extreme preoccupation and obsession with a part of the body that is believed to be defective. The person makes elaborate attempts to conceal or change the body part.

Somatoform disorders involve physical complaints with no apparent physical cause. Numerous medical tests may be completed, but no physical cause can be found for the patient's complaint.

© David Young-Wolff/PhotoEdit

people with hypochondriasis are likely to seek out another physician rather than seek psychological treatment (Kirmayer & Looper, 2007). People with hypochondriasis often have a family history of depression or anxiety (Escobar et al., 1998), leading some researchers to speculate that hypochondriasis is an intense form of health anxiety related to panic disorder and obsessive-compulsive disorder (Abramowitz & Moore, 2007; Braddock & Abramowitz, 2006). It is estimated that 4.5 to 7.7% of people have hypochondriasis during any one year (Creed & Barsky, 2004).

Let's REVIEW

In this section, we described the nature of the dissociative and somatoform disorders. For a quick check of your understanding, try answering the following questions at increasing levels of difficulty.

1. Dissociative disorders involve _____.
   a. the disintegration of one's personality
   b. physical symptoms without any physical cause
   c. a splitting off of one's conscious mind
   d. a numbness or paralysis in some part of the body

2. Alphonsia has recurrent abdominal pain. Her doctors have conducted numerous medical tests and can find no physical cause for her symptom. Alphonsia appears to have a _____.
   a. personality disorder   c. dissociative disorder
   b. somatoform disorder   d. depressive disorder

3. What do the dissociative and somatoform disorders have in common?
   a. They both occur more frequently in men than in women.
   b. They both involve a preoccupation with the body.
   c. They both include a loss of identity.
   d. They both may represent alternate expressions of anxiety.

ANSWERS 1. c; 2. b; 3. d

LEARNING OBJECTIVES

What Should You Know?

- Distinguish between the symptoms of unipolar and bipolar depressive disorders, and discuss our current understanding of the causes of mood disorders.
- Detail common misconceptions that people hold about suicide.

WHAT CHARACTERIZES MOOD DISORDERS? BEYOND THE BLUES

A third major category of disorders described in the *DSM-IV-TR* is mood disorders. **Mood disorders** involve a significant change in a person's emotional state. This change may include feeling depressed or extremely elated for an extended time. Following anxiety disorders, mood disorders are one of the more common psychological disorders, affecting approximately 9.5% of adult Americans in a given year (R. C. Kessler, Chiu et al., 2005). But don't we all get blue from time to time?

How does clinical depression differ from normal periods of sadness? As we will see, the main distinctions are (1) the length of time a person experiences the mood change and (2) whether the conditions and events around the person are consistent with the mood change. For example, many of us experience sadness, but typically this period of sadness lasts only a few days. In clinical depression, the mood change is persistent and interferes significantly with a person's ability to function. Also, normal periods of sadness are usually brought on by environmental events—the loss of a loved one, the breakup of a relationship, or a disappointment in one's life. People with clinical depression are sad over a longer period, in the absence of such external events or long after most people would have adjusted to such changes. Mood disorders can be devastating to personal relationships and to the ability to work or go to school. Many people think that the symptoms are not "real" and that the person

mood disorder a disorder marked by a significant change in one's emotional state that seriously interferes with one's ability to function

should be able to "snap out of it." These inaccurate beliefs may cause shame, which discourages people from seeking appropriate treatment. Recall J. K. Rowling's period of deep sadness that indicated a mood disorder. We will discuss two basic types of mood disorders: *unipolar depression* and *bipolar depression*.

Unipolar Depressive Disorders: Pervasive Sadness

Unipolar depressive disorders involve a variety of physical, cognitive, emotional, and behavioral symptoms. The *DSM-IV-TR* indicates two categories of unipolar depressive disorder: *major depression* and *dysthymic disorder*.

A diagnosis of **major depression** requires that a person experience either extreme sadness (referred to as **dysphoria**) or loss of interest or pleasure in one's usual activities (referred to as **anhedonia**) plus at least four other symptoms of depression for a period of at least 2 weeks. These symptoms must be severe enough that they interfere with the person's ability to function but not be due to a general medical condition or the death of a loved one (American Psychiatric Association, 2000a). In addition to the emotional symptoms of dysphoria and anhedonia, people diagnosed with major depression must show at least three of the following symptoms nearly every day during the 2-week period:

Major depression is marked by physical, behavioral, and cognitive symptoms, in addition to depressed mood.

Physical and Behavioral Symptoms
- Change in sleep patterns—sleeping either too much (hypersomnia) or too little (insomnia)
- Change in appetite—eating either too much (resulting in weight gain) or too little (resulting in weight loss)
- Change in motor functioning—either moving slowly and sluggishly or appearing agitated in movement
- Fatigue, or loss of energy

Cognitive Symptoms
- Inability to concentrate or pay attention
- Difficulty in making decisions
- Feelings of hopelessness, pessimism, and helplessness
- Exaggerated feelings of worthlessness or guilt
- Thoughts of suicide
- Delusions (believing something that is not true) and hallucinations (perceiving things that are not there) with depressing themes

Major depression may occur as a single episode or as repeated episodes over the course of years. Some episodes may be so severe that the person requires hospitalization, especially in the presence of frequent suicide attempts or delusional thinking. Looking back on J. K. Rowling's behavior and emotional state, we see that she had many of the symptoms of major depression. She felt deeply sad and worthless and had suicidal thoughts.

Dysthymic disorder is a less severe but more chronic form of major depression. The person seems sad and downcast over a longer time. A diagnosis of dysthymic disorder requires the symptom of depressed mood plus at least two other symptoms of depression for a period of at least 2 years. Dysthymic disorder generally begins in childhood, adolescence, or early adulthood (American Psychiatric Association, 2000a). Typically, the symptoms of dysthymic disorder are not severe enough to require hospitalization. However, most people with dysthymic disorder eventually experience a major depressive episode (D. N. Klein, Lewinsohn, & Seeley, 2001; Regier et al., 1993).

Worldwide, major depression is the leading cause of disability (C. J. Murray & Lopez, 1996; World Health Organization, 2004). In the United States, 17% of adults will experience an acute episode of depression at some time in their lives, and 6% will experience more

major depression a mood disorder involving dysphoria, feelings of worthlessness, loss of interest in one's usual activities, and changes in bodily activities such as sleep and appetite that persists for at least 2 weeks

dysphoria an extreme state of sadness

anhedonia absence of pleasure from one's usual activities

dysthymic disorder a mood disorder that is a less severe but more chronic form of major depression

chronic depression (R. C. Kessler, Chiu et al., 2005). Depression also appears to be related to age and gender. Although major depression can develop at any age, the average age of onset is 32 (R. C. Kessler, Berglund et al., 2005). People between 15 and 24 years of age are at high risk for experiencing a major depressive episode, whereas 45- to 54-year-olds experience the lowest rates of depressive episodes (Blazer et al., 1994; R. C. Kessler et al., 2003). Women are twice as likely as men to experience both mild and more severe depression, a difference found in many different countries and ethnic groups and across adult age groups (Bradley & Hopcroft, 2007; Culbertson, 1997; Ebmeier, Donaghey, & Steele, 2006; R. C. Kessler et al., 2003; Nolen-Hoeksema, 2002; Weissman & Olfson, 1995; D. R. Williams et al., 2007). Although African Americans and Hispanic Americans have a lower lifetime risk for a major depressive disorder, when they do experience one, it tends to be more chronic and severe (Breslau et al., 2005, 2006; D. R. Williams et al., 2007). Curiously, major depression is reported at very low rates (0.8%) for Asian Americans (Jackson-Triche et al., 2000). Unfortunately, many people with depression never receive treatment. In one study, only 51% of participants who met the criteria for major depression during the prior year received some type of treatment for it. African Americans and Mexican Americans were least likely to receive any care (Gonzalez et al., 2010).

Bipolar Depressive Disorders: The Presence of Mania

A second major group of mood disorders is the bipolar depressive disorders. The *DSM-IV-TR* indicates two categories of bipolar depressive disorders: *bipolar disorder* and *cyclothymic disorder.*

Bipolar disorder involves a shift in mood between two states, or *poles.* One of these shifts is to a depressed state, with symptoms similar to those of major depression. The person feels sad, lacks self-worth, and may show changes in sleeping and eating over a 2-week period. The second mood change is to the opposite extreme—to a "high" or euphoric state, called **mania**. During a manic state, people feel elated and have high self-esteem, have a decreased need for sleep, are more talkative than usual, and are highly distractible. Much energy is directed at achieving goals, although many projects may be started and few finished. People in this state have an inflated sense of self, feeling confident and able to accomplish anything. This may result in delusional thinking or hallucinations. Also, their boundless energy often results in more impulsive and risk-taking behaviors. When such symptoms of mania and depression interfere with a person's ability to function, a diagnosis of bipolar disorder is appropriate (American Psychiatric Association, 2000a).

Cyclothymic disorder is a less severe but more chronic form of bipolar disorder. In cyclothymic disorder, a person alternates between milder periods of mania and more moderate depression for at least 2 years (American Psychiatric Association, 2000a). The person functions reasonably well during the mild mania but is likely to be more impaired during the depressive phase.

Bipolar disorders are less common than unipolar disorders, with 2.6% of adult Americans experiencing an episode of bipolar disorder at some time in their lives (R. C. Kessler, Chiu et al., 2005; Lewinsohn, Klein, & Seeley, 2000). Men are just as likely as women to be diagnosed with bipolar disorder. The median age of onset for bipolar disorder is late adolescence and early adulthood (Angst & Sellaro, 2000; R. C. Kessler, Berglund, et al., 2005). Asian Americans also have significantly lower rates of bipolar disorder than do other ethnic groups (A. Y. Zhang & Snowden, 1999).

Suicide Facts and Misconceptions

Our descriptions of depressive disorders include suicidal thoughts as one symptom of depression. In 2008, 3.7% of adults age 18 or older had serious thoughts of suicide in the past year, with over 1 million adults attempting suicide (Substance Abuse and Mental Health Services Administration [SAMHSA], 2009b). Research suggests that nearly 90% of all people who commit suicide have some diagnosable mental disorder, commonly a depressive disorder or a substance abuse disorder (National Institute of Mental Health [NIMH], 2002; Wulsin,

bipolar disorder a mood disorder characterized by both depression and mania

mania a period of abnormally excessive energy and elation

cyclothymic disorder a mood disorder that is a less severe but more chronic form of bipolar disorder

Vaillat, & Wells, 1999). In 2007, suicide was the eleventh leading cause of death in the United States (higher than homicide). Among 25- to 34-year-olds, it was the second leading cause of death; among 35- to 44-year-olds, it was the fourth leading cause of death. Among 15- to 24-year-olds, suicide was the third leading cause of death. However, these rates are probably grossly underestimated given the negative stigma attached to suicide in the United States (CDC, 2009c; Kung et al., 2008; Xu, Kochanek, & Tejada-Vera, 2009). Women are two to three times more likely than men to *attempt* suicide, but four times as many men actually kill themselves, in part because of the means chosen (CDC, 2009c; Denning et al., 2000; Hoyert et al., 2006; Kung et al., 2008). Men tend to shoot, hang, or stab themselves. Women are more likely to choose less lethal means, such as drug overdoses. This gender difference appears in many countries across the world (Weissman et al., 1999; Welch, 2001) except China, where more women commit suicide than men (Phillips, Li, & Zhang, 2002). As seen in ● FIGURE 14.5, in the United States, Whites and American Indian/Alaska Natives have higher rates of suicide than other ethnic groups (CDC, 2009c; Kung et al., 2008). Because many of us will encounter or already have encountered someone who is suicidal, let's take a moment to dispel some of the more common misconceptions concerning suicide.

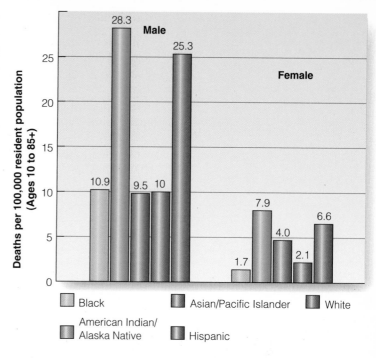

FIGURE 14.5

● **U.S. Death Rates for Suicide by Gender and Ethnicity in 2006**
Although women attempt suicide more often, men across all ethnic groups are more likely to commit suicide. *Source: Centers for Disease Control and Prevention (CDC). (2009c). Web-based Injury Statistics Query and Reporting System (WISQARS). Fatal Injury Reports. Atlanta, GA: National Center for Injury Prevention and Control.*

Misconception #1: People who talk of suicide will not kill themselves.

Although most people who talk of suicide do not go on to attempt suicide, people who commit suicide typically have expressed their intentions at some time to family members or friends before their attempt (Ortega & Karch, 2010; Shneidman, 1987). They may have talked about "going away" or be preoccupied in general with the notion of death. Therefore, any talk of suicide should be taken seriously. A person who is suicidal should not be left alone. You may need to contact a mental health professional, call 911, or call a suicide crisis hotline in your area.

Misconception #2: If you ask someone who is depressed whether he or she has thoughts of suicide, it will only plant the idea of suicide in his or her head.

Asking direct questions about a person's plan for suicide is the only way to assess the person's risk for committing suicide. Bringing up the subject can also give the person an opportunity to talk about his or her problem. People who have a concrete plan in mind for when or how they will end their life are more likely to attempt suicide than those whose plans are less specific (D. C. Clark et al., 1989; SAMHSA, 2009b).

Misconception #3: People who have unsuccessfully attempted suicide will not try again.

In the United States from 2003 to 2007 among women age 15–44 who committed suicide, 37% had a history of suicide attempts (Ortega & Karch, 2010). Similarly, among adolescents, a previous history of suicide attempts is the single best predictor of future suicide attempts and completions (Lewinsohn, Rohde, & Seeley, 1994). Therefore, a previous suicide attempt puts adolescents and young adult and middle-aged women in particular at a higher risk for future suicide attempts.

Misconception #4: A better mood means the risk of suicide is gone.

Suicide does not typically happen when a person is in the depths of a deep depression. Rather, suicide attempts are more likely to occur when people with depression have energy and can think more clearly and make decisions. This energy and clearer thinking make it appear to loved ones that the person is getting better and is therefore at a lower risk of suicide, when sometimes a better mood can indicate an increased risk of suicide.

Misconception #5: Only people who are depressed attempt suicide.

Although suicidal thoughts are a symptom of depression, people with other serious psychological disorders, including bipolar disorder, substance abuse disorder, and schizophrenia are also at risk for suicide (Foote et al., 2008; Statham et al., 1998; Tsuang, Fleming, & Simpson, 1999). According to findings from the WHO World Mental Health Surveys, the strongest predictors of suicide attempts in developed countries are mood disorders whereas in developing countries they are substance use, PTSD, and impulse control disorders (Nock et al., 2009). Though overall women attempt suicide more often, males who are depressed are especially at risk, with a rate four times higher than that for women who are depressed (NIMH, 2007). A number of other events and situations also increase one's risk of suicide, including economic hardship, serious illness, problems with a partner or the loss of a relationship, childhood sexual or physical abuse, and the presence of a firearm in the home (Crosby, Cheltenham, & Sacks, 1999; Enns et al., 2006; Fergusson, Horwood, & Lynskey, 1996; S. J. Kaplan et al., 1997; Karch et al., 2009; McHolm, MacMillan, & Jamieson, 2003; Ortega & Karch, 2010; Welch, 2001). Suicide occurs among people who have psychological disorders as well as those who face environmental stressors. The majority of suicide attempts are expressions of extreme distress and helplessness, not just "harmless" bids for attention.

Explaining Mood Disorders

What causes mood disorders? Not surprisingly, research has identified biological, psychological, and sociocultural factors that may contribute to mood disorders. Again, this finding highlights the biopsychosocial nature of psychological disorders.

Biological Factors: Genes, Neurotransmitters, and Stress Hormones

One biological factor indicated as a cause in mood disorders is our genes. The evidence from family history studies and twin studies suggests that mood disorders may be genetically transmitted, especially in the case of bipolar disorder. For example, first-degree relatives (parent, child, or sibling) of persons with bipolar disorder are much more likely to develop the disorder than are relatives of people without the disorder (Perlis et al., 2006; Saunders et al., 2008). Similarly, if an identical twin is diagnosed as having bipolar disorder, the other identical twin has a higher probability of developing the disorder than if they were fraternal twins (MacKinnon, Jamison, & DePaulo, 1997; McGuffin et al., 2003; Wallace, Schneider, & McGuffin, 2002; Winokur et al., 1995). In one twin study, the heritability of bipolar disorder was estimated to be as high as 93% (Kieseppa et al., 2004).

The evidence for genetic factors in major depression is less clear. The trend toward genetic transmission is present, particularly in women, but it is not as strong as the evidence in bipolar disorders (Abkevich et al., 2003; Bierut et al., 1999; Ebmeier et al., 2006; Mosing et al., 2009; P. F. Sullivan, Neale, & Kendler, 2000). Specific regions of chromosomes have been identified that may contribute to susceptibility to depression and bipolar disorder, but a specific gene mechanism has not yet been identified (Hayden & Nurnberger, 2006; Holmans et al., 2007; Kuzelova et al., 2010; D. F. Levinson et al., 2007).

The malfunctioning of certain neurotransmitters has also been linked to mood disorders, specifically serotonin and norepinephrine (Carver, Johnson, & Joormann, 2009; Goddard et al., 2010; Soares & Mann, 1997; Thase, Jindal, & Howland, 2002). Antidepressant drugs that act on serotonin and norepinephrine to relieve the symptoms of depression seem to offer evidence for the role of these neurotransmitters in depression. Similarly, abnormalities in the neurotransmitters norepinephrine, dopamine, and glutamate have been investigated as possible factors for bipolar disorder (Carlson et al., 2006; Cousins, Butts, & Young, 2009; Dixon & Hokin, 1998; Keck, McElroy, & Arnold, 2001). Dysfunction in the serotonin system may also account for the depressive phase of bipolar disorder (Oquendo et al., 2007).

The connection between depression and hormones has also been studied. Hormones regulate such functions as sleep, appetite, sexual desire, and pleasure. Symptoms of depression relate to these bodily functions (McClung, 2007). Of particular interest to psychologists is the link between stress hormones and depression. When stress hormones are released, they tend to inhibit the activity of brain neurotransmitters that are related to mood. Hence, repeated activation of the hormonal stress system may lay the groundwork for depression (Arborelius et al., 1999; Gillespie & Nemeroff, 2007). Excessive levels of stress hormones have been linked to the shrinkage of certain brain areas that may also be related to depression (Sapolsky, 2000b; Sheline, 2000).

Research is also investigating how connections in the brain between the cortex and the limbic system may be associated with depressive symptoms (Gotlib & Hamilton, 2008; Jacobs, 2004; Jacobs, van Praag, & Gage, 2000). Helen Mayberg and her colleagues (1997; 1999; 2005) have demonstrated a consistent relationship between depression and dysfunction in an area of the brain's cortex called the *subgenual cingulate*, also known as Brodmann's area 25 (Dobbs, 2006; Drevets, Savitz, & Trimble, 2008). Overactivity in this area allows negative emotions to overwhelm the thinking part of the brain. Additional evidence for this brain region's role in depression comes from treatment studies. Effective antidepressant treatment reduces abnormal activation in this area in people who are depressed (Fu et al., 2004). Using electrodes to reduce activity in this area has also been moderately successful in alleviating symptoms in people with treatment-resistant depression (symptoms that do not respond to at least one trial of antidepressant medication) (Hamani et al., 2009; Mayberg et al., 2005).

Because of the connection between neurotransmitter dysregulation and depressive conditions, more recent investigations have focused on genes that regulate the activity of brain neurotransmitters, specifically serotonin. However, the results of such studies indicate a complex relationship between genes, neural activity, and depression (Dannlowski et al., 2007; J. B. Kraft et al., 2007; Kuzelova et al., 2010; Rao et al., 2007; Vergne & Nemeroff, 2006). Bipolar disorder presents a similar complex picture with multiple factors—genes, brain functioning, neurochemistry—implicated in its development. Future technologies may assist us in sorting out the precise relationship between biology and mood disorders.

Psychological Factors: Abandonment, Learned Helplessness, and Negative Thinking

Psychological factors also help in explaining mood disorders, especially depression. For example, psychoanalytic theory suggests that depression is linked to unresolved childhood issues of abandonment, rejection, and loss. Freud (1917) believed that depression was a symbolic expression of anger. A child who perceives that he or she has been abandoned or rejected by loved ones is afraid to express anger outwardly. Instead, the child redirects this anger onto the self, resulting in self-blame, self-hatred, and other symptoms of depression. As the child enters adolescence and adulthood and forms new relationships, these feelings of abandonment and separation may resurface. When they do, the person falls into another depression.

Some research is consistent with this view. A history of early adverse experiences such as insecure attachments, abuse, separations, and losses can make one vulnerable to depression (J. G. Green et al., 2010; Hammen, 2005; Heim, Plotsky, & Nemeroff, 2004; McLaughlin et al., 2010; Vergne & Nemeroff, 2006; Weissman, Markowitz, & Klerman, 2000). People who are depressed do show low self-esteem, and some do have difficulty expressing anger (Bromberger & Matthews, 1996; Klein et al., 2002). While it is possible that early feelings of abandonment and rejection may lead to unresolved anger that results in depression, it is also possible that such early stressful life events may adversely affect brain chemistry and immune system responses that contribute to depression (Hennessy, Schiml-Webb, & Deak, 2009).

Social learning theories suggest that mood disorders are related to *lower levels of positive reinforcement, learned helplessness*, and *ruminative coping styles*. Peter Lewinsohn's (1974) theory of depression links depression to a reduction in the number of positive reinforcers we receive from others. This reduction is more likely in people with poor social skills. Imagine for a moment that you pass an acquaintance on your campus, someone who is in one of your courses. As you pass by, what do you do? Most people nod, say hello, or express some form of acknowledgment; this is a social skill. Imagine further that the classmate fails to respond, continues walking, and does not reciprocate your casual greeting. What happens the next time that you walk by this person? In all likelihood, you will ignore the person, giving her or him no positive reinforcement. As this example illustrates, people with poor social skills or those who tend to withdraw receive less positive reinforcement from others. Lewinsohn suggests that such a pattern may result in depression.

Another psychological explanation of depression is **learned helplessness**, which involves the belief that you cannot control the outcome of events or what is going to happen (see Chapter 12). Therefore, you do not respond even when your response could lead to success. Initial evidence for learned helplessness came from studies in which dogs were administered controllable shock, uncontrollable shock, or no shock (Overmier & Seligman, 1967; M. E. P. Seligman & Maier, 1967). The dogs in the controllable shock situation had to learn to jump a barrier in order to turn off the shock. They quickly learned this behavior. The dogs in the uncontrollable shock situation could not turn off the shock. Later, when the dogs who had been in the uncontrollable shock situation were given the opportunity to jump the barrier to avoid the shock, they failed to respond. They had learned to be helpless and just sat there taking the shock *even when they could escape it.* Such research suggests that people who are depressed may respond similarly—they do not take steps to solve or even prevent problems when such action could be helpful because they believe that life is uncontrollable (Ilgen & Hutchison, 2005).

Research by Susan Nolen-Hoeksema and her colleagues (Nolen-Hoeksema, 2001, 2002; Nolen-Hoeksema, Larson, & Grayson, 1999; Nolen-Hoeksema et al., 2007; Nolen-Hoeksema, Wisco, & Lyubomirsky, 2008) indicates that coping styles play a role in depression. People who are depressed are more likely to engage in what is called a **ruminative coping style**. To ruminate means to focus on your thoughts. People who are depressed spend a lot of time thinking about their depression and why they are depressed. They tend not to do anything about their depression or its causes but rather remain focused on repetitively analyzing their feelings and concerns. This focus makes it more likely that they will become more severely depressed and also stay depressed longer. Many studies support an association between rumination and vulnerability to depression (Aldao, Nolen-Hoeksema, & Schweizer, 2010; Donaldson & Lam, 2004; Huffziger, Reinhard, & Kuehner, 2009; Hong, 2007; Ito et al., 2006; Jones et al., 2009; McIntosh, Gillanders, & Rodgers, 2010; McLaughlin, Borkovec, & Sibrava, 2007).

Cognitive research highlights the role of negative thinking patterns and attributions in the development of mood disorders. If you have ever been around someone who is "down," or depressed, you realize that his or her thoughts tend to be pessimistic and negative. People who are depressed are more likely to engage in negative thinking errors, called **cognitive distortions**, according to classic research by Aaron Beck (1967, 1976). For example, people who are depressed tend to reject positive experiences and focus only on the negative aspects of a situation. To help you understand negative thinking errors, try the following demonstration.

TRY THIS
DEMONSTRATION

Before you go to bed tonight, write down how you feel generally—for example, happy, sad, or stressed. Tomorrow, carry a pad of paper around with you all day. Every time you have a positive thought or experience, write it down. At the end of the day, again write down how you feel generally. It is likely that noting positive feelings all day will create a more positive overall feeling. If we had asked you to note negative thoughts for an entire day, how do you think that would affect your outlook on your day?

For people with depression, a negative worldview applies to their perceptions of themselves, the world, and the future. Beck believes that these people engage in such a negative view so automatically that they may not even realize their errors in thinking. J. K. Rowling believed that she was worthless, that her baby daughter would die, and that life was meaningless. Such a negative worldview could have contributed to her bout of depression.

Research on the *attributions* that people who are depressed make further supports Beck's model. An attribution is an explanation of why an event happened (see Chapter 11). People who are depressed tend to attribute negative environmental events to factors within themselves (Alloy, Abramson, & Francis, 1999; C. Peterson & Seligman, 1984). For instance, failing an exam is interpreted to mean that one is stupid, will always be stupid, and will probably fail more exams. A relationship breakup is interpreted to mean that one is not lovable and will always be unlovable. These negative attributions and cognitive distortions appear related to depressed mood (Abramson et al., 2002; Gibb et al., 2004; M. T. Moore & Fresco, 2007).

learned helplessness the belief that one cannot control the outcome of events

ruminative coping style the tendency to persistently focus on how one feels without attempting to do anything about one's feelings

cognitive distortion thought that tends to be pessimistic and negative

Recently, Aaron Beck (2008) has suggested that early adverse experiences combined with biological vulnerabilities (genetics and neurochemistry) may influence the development of these cognitive deficits in people who are depressed. The negative cognitions then influence the interpretation and processing of future stressors as well as neurochemistry, creating a vicious cycle of biopsychosocial factors and the maintenance of depression.

Sociocultural Factors

Sociocultural factors must also be considered when explaining mood disorders. Depression is more likely among people of lower social status (Blazer et al., 1994), especially those from adverse neighborhoods (Cutrona, Wallace, & Wesner, 2006). A considerable body of research also documents a consistent relationship between major stressful life events and the onset of depression especially among people who are genetically predisposed to depression (Caspi, Sugden, et al., 2003; J. G. Green et al., 2010; Hammen, 2009; Monroe & Reid, 2009; S. E. Taylor et al., 2006; Wilhelm et al., 2006). For example, J. K. Rowling's depression occurred following her separation from her first husband. Explaining such differences is further complicated by the worldwide gender difference in depression. As we have noted, women are more likely to be diagnosed with depression than are men.

Gender and Depression

Biological, psychological, and social forces that are unique to women may explain their higher vulnerability to depressive disorders (see ● FIGURE 14.6; Gorman, 2006; Mazure, Keita, & Blehar, 2002). We have already seen that the genetic risk of depression appears stronger in women than in men. Research has also investigated—over many years and many studies—the relationship between the female ovarian hormones (estrogen and progesterone) and mood in an effort to understand pathways to depression. However, it is not as simple as saying ovarian hormones cause depression. Symptoms of depression do not appear to correspond to changes in levels of estrogen and progesterone across the menstrual cycle (Steiner & Born, 2000). Rather, research suggests that women's estrogen and progesterone levels may influence the functioning of the neurotransmitter serotonin, which plays a central role in mood. However, researchers don't yet understand the precise actions by which estrogen and progesterone influence serotonin functioning (Hughes et al., 2009; Lu et al., 2003; G. Parker & Brotchie, 2004; Steiner, Dunn, & Born, 2003).

Psychological forces unique to women must also be considered when examining gender differences in depression. For example, females are more likely than males to engage in a ruminative coping style (C. E. Li, DiGiuseppe, & Froh, 2006; Lopez, Driscoll, & Kistner, 2009; Nolen-Hoeksema, 2001; Papadakis et al., 2006). That is, women tend to focus on how they feel and to fret about their feelings. Even co-rumination, or excessively talking about problems with friends, while offering women social support, can also amplify or increase one's depressive symptoms (Byrd-Craven et al., 2008; Rose, Carlson, & Waller, 2007). In contrast, men are more likely to engage in some activity to take their minds off their feelings, to withdraw, or to abuse drugs. As Nolen-Hoeksema and her colleagues (Nolen-Hoeksema, Larson, & Grayson, 1999) put it, "Women think and men drink." Women are also more likely to have an interpersonal orientation that puts them at risk for depression (Mazure et al., 2002). Relationships are more important to a woman's sense of self-worth than they

FIGURE 14.6

● **Women and Depression** Biological, psychological, and sociocultural forces unique to women may explain their higher vulnerability to depressive disorders.

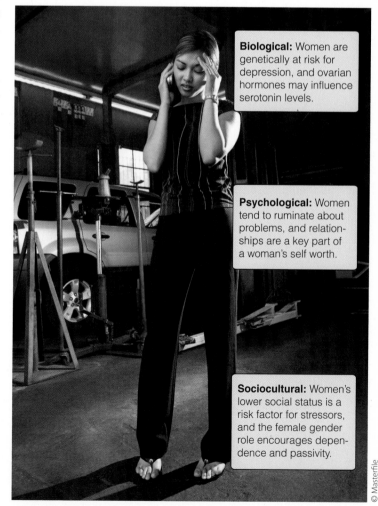

Biological: Women are genetically at risk for depression, and ovarian hormones may influence serotonin levels.

Psychological: Women tend to ruminate about problems, and relationships are a key part of a woman's self worth.

Sociocultural: Women's lower social status is a risk factor for stressors, and the female gender role encourages dependence and passivity.

© Masterfile

are to a man's. As a result, women are more likely to silence their own demands in order to maintain a positive relationship and are more likely to place their needs secondary to those of others. This relational style may also predispose women to depression.

Tied to these biological and psychological factors are the social circumstances that women face. Women are at a disadvantage in society: they earn less and have less power than men. They report less satisfaction with work and family and are more likely to be victims of violence, discrimination, abuse, and poverty (Klonoff, Landrine, & Campbell, 2000; Koss & Kilpatrick, 2001). Negative life events such as these foster feelings of uncontrollability and helplessness, perceptions that are intimately connected to mood disorders (Browne, 1993; Fitzgerald, 1993; Ilgen & Hutchison, 2005). Traditional gender roles also discourage women from being masterful, independent, and assertive and encourage them to be dependent and passive. These prescribed roles may increase women's feelings of uncontrollability and helplessness (Barlow, 2002).

Although rates of major depression are higher in women, approximately 13% of U.S. men will experience a major depressive disorder at some time in their lives (NCS-R, 2007). We have also seen that men are at a much higher risk for committing suicide than are women. Yet, some men may not express the symptoms of depression in the same manner as women. Although men may report the physical symptoms of depression—fatigue, sleep problems, and loss of interest in their usual activities—men are less likely to cry and express sadness and are more likely to hide their feelings, be irritable, lash out at others, and abuse alcohol. Male gender-role socialization encourages men to be strong and in control, which may discourage them from admitting and expressing emotional distress (Cochran & Rabinowitz, 2000; Pollack, 1998).

For both men and women, depression is a complex behavior affected by biological, psychological, and sociocultural variables. Each of us probably has *some* biological vulnerability to mood disorders. However, social and psychological factors may act to protect us from such vulnerability, or, alternatively, make us more likely to express this vulnerability. For J. K. Rowling, a number of ingredients may have combined to contribute to her depression. She had recently given birth, perhaps changing her biochemistry; she had just experienced numerous stressful life events, including the dissolution of her marriage, parenthood, moving to a new place, and financial struggles; she is female; and she engaged in cognitive distortions. Similarly, a unique combination of factors may determine for each one of us whether we will become depressed. Research continues to explore the exact role these factors play. People's lives depend on it.

Let's REVIEW

In this section, we outlined the major types of mood disorders and described our current understanding of their causes. For a quick check of your understanding, try answering the following questions at increasing levels of difficulty.

1. Research on depression has found that people who are depressed are more likely to _____.

   a. engage in negative thinking
   b. engage in rumination
   c. believe they have little control over events
   d. all of the above

2. Maria has been sad for 3 weeks. She can't sleep, eat, or concentrate and is constantly crying. She has lost interest in her usual activities. Maria would most likely be diagnosed with which disorder?

   a. bipolar depression
   b. manic depression
   c. major depression
   d. cyclothymic disorder

3. Which of the following statements about suicide is true?

   a. People who talk of suicide are often just looking for attention and will not kill themselves.
   b. Among adolescents, previous suicide attempts are a predictor of future attempts.
   c. A better mood means the risk of suicide is gone.
   d. Only people who are depressed commit suicide.

ANSWERS 1. d; 2. c; 3. b

WHAT IS SCHIZOPHRENIA? DISINTEGRATION

LEARNING
OBJECTIVE

What Should You Know?
● Identify and describe the symptoms of schizophrenia, discriminate between the types of schizophrenia, and discuss our current understanding of the causes of schizophrenia.

Schizophrenia is a chronic, disabling psychological disorder that affects roughly 1–2% of the general population worldwide (Ho, Black, & Andreasen, 2003). It involves the disintegration of one's personality.

Is schizophrenia the same thing as multiple personalities? No. Multiple personalities (now called dissociative identity disorder, as previously discussed) involve the existence of several *intact* personalities within a person. In schizophrenia, the one personality is no longer intact, or held together and connected. If we think of someone's personality as a related set of cognitive, emotional, perceptual, and motor behaviors, then in schizophrenia we see the disconnection among these personality elements. As these elements lose their connections with one another, the person loses his or her connection with reality. This results in impaired functioning. Nathaniel Ayers, whose story appeared in the beginning of the chapter, is an example of someone with schizophrenia.

Onset, Gender, Ethnicity, and Prognosis

Symptoms of schizophrenia typically appear in adolescence or young adulthood. In some cases, the symptoms come on gradually; in others, they appear more abruptly. Schizophrenia affects men and women with equal frequency, although it typically appears earlier in men than in women. Men tend to develop the disorder in their late teens or early 20s, and women are generally affected in their 20s or early 30s (American Psychiatric Association, 2000a; L. N. Robins & Regier, 1991). This gender difference may be related to hormonal and sociocultural factors. The hormone estrogen may protect women by lessening abnormal brain development associated with schizophrenia (Canuso & Pandina, 2007). In addition, women's higher social competence and more extensive social networks may delay the onset of the disorder (Combs & Mueser, 2007). Perhaps because of the earlier onset, men with schizophrenia tend to be more chronically impaired (J. M. Goldstein & Lewine, 2000; Ho et al., 2003).

Schizophrenia is diagnosed more often in African Americans and Asian Americans. However, this difference may be due to racial bias and cultural insensitivity (American Psychiatric Association, 2000a; Barnes, 2004; Bresnahan et al., 2007). Lifetime prevalence rates of schizophrenia are lower among Hispanics than among Whites (A. Y. Zhang & Snowden, 1999). Schizophrenia also is more prevalent in lower socioeconomic groups (Escobar, 1993; Kirkbride et al., 2007).

Most people with schizophrenia suffer throughout their adult lives, losing opportunities for careers and relationships (Harrow et al., 1997). Several factors contribute to this suffering: the negative stigma that a schizophrenia diagnosis brings, the lack of public understanding, and inaccurate media portrayals of people with schizophrenia as criminally violent. Most people with schizophrenia are not violent toward others but are withdrawn and prefer to be

schizophrenia a severe disorder characterized by disturbances in thought, perceptions, emotions, and behavior

Schizophrenia is a severe psychological disorder marked by disordered thoughts, perceptions, emotions, and/or motor behavior, as depicted in this drawing by someone with schizophrenia.

© Jean-Michel Girand/Photo Researchers, Inc.

left alone (Steadman et al., 1998). Although there currently is no cure, a diagnosis of schizophrenia does not necessarily mean progressive deterioration in functioning, as most people believe. Rather, for reasons not yet understood, schizophrenic symptoms and episodes tend to decline as a person ages, with 20–30% of people with schizophrenia showing only minor impairment 20 or 30 years later (Breier et al., 1991; W. W. Eaton et al., 1998; Jablensky, 2000). However, recovery is very much related to social factors such as economic and social support. Most people with schizophrenia continue to experience difficulties throughout their lives. Nathaniel Ayers, now 58, continues to spend his days on the street and his nights at a private shelter for the homeless who are mentally ill. Refusing to take new medications that treat schizophrenia, he continues to experience difficulty in functioning.

Symptoms of Schizophrenia

Schizophrenia may express itself in many forms, depending on which symptoms are present. People diagnosed with schizophrenia show two or more of the following symptoms nearly every day during a 1-month period with continued disturbance for at least 6 months. These symptoms are not due to substance use or a medical condition and interfere with the person's ability to function. Symptoms of schizophrenia fall into two broad categories: positive and negative symptoms.

Positive Symptoms

Positive symptoms of schizophrenia represent an excess or distortion of normal functions. They include *delusions, hallucinations, disorganized speech,* and *grossly disorganized* or *catatonic behavior.*

- **Delusions** are thoughts and beliefs that the person believes to be true but that have no basis in reality. We all carry some false beliefs, but the delusions of schizophrenia are typically less believable and more unusual. For example, *persecutory delusions* involve beliefs about being followed or watched, usually by agents of authorities such as the FBI or the government. *Grandiose delusions* involve beliefs about being a famous or special person. For instance, a person with schizophrenia may believe that he is Julius Caesar or the president of France. People with schizophrenia may also hold *delusions of reference* (believing that others are talking about them) or *delusions of thought control* (believing that their thoughts are controlled by another person or force).

- People who are diagnosed with schizophrenia also may experience **hallucinations** in which the person sees, hears, tastes, smells, or feels something that others do not perceive. In schizophrenia, hearing voices or other sounds (called *auditory hallucinations*) is the most common altered perception, followed by *visual hallucinations* (seeing things that aren't there). The hallucinations may tell the person to perform certain acts or may be frightening in nature.

- The speech of individuals with schizophrenia is often disorganized in a variety of ways that impair effective communication (American Psychiatric Association, 2000a). **Disorganized speech** (*formal thought disorder*) involves a lack of associations between ideas and events. Because the ideas of people with schizophrenia lack connection, we refer to this disconnection as *loose associations.* Their ideas seem unrelated to one another, and their speech is often characterized as a *word salad* (words seem tossed together without any apparent syntax or organization). They may be saying a lot, but what they say is not communicating anything to the receiver. Nathaniel Ayers's conversations on several occasions were totally incoherent, suggesting the presence of disorganized speech.

- **Disorganized behavior** may also characterize some people with schizophrenia. This may take the form of unusual, odd, or repetitive behaviors and gestures. Head banging, finger flapping, or tracing a pattern over and over again are examples. Childlike silliness, inappropriate sexual behavior (such as public masturbation), or difficulty maintaining hygiene may be present. Some people with schizophrenia may show an absence of all motor behaviors, remaining totally motionless and rigid for hours on end and resisting efforts to be moved. Such behavior is referred to as a **catatonic stupor**. Alternatively, other people with schizophrenia may show **catatonic excitement**, in which they are suddenly agitated, fidgety, shouting, swearing, or moving around rapidly.

delusion a thought or belief that a person believes to be true but in reality is not

hallucination perceiving something that does not exist in reality

disorganized speech a symptom of schizophrenia in which one's speech lacks association between one's ideas and the events that one is experiencing

disorganized behavior a symptom of schizophrenia that includes inappropriate or unusual behavior in a situation such as silliness, catatonic excitement, or catatonic stupor

catatonic stupor a disorder in motor behavior involving immobility

catatonic excitement a disorder in motor behavior involving excited agitation

In catatonic schizophrenia, the person may remain in a "posed" position for hours on end.

Grunnitus Studio/Photo Researchers, Inc.

Negative Symptoms

Negative symptoms of schizophrenia represent a restriction or absence of normal functions. These include *blunted affect*, *alogia*, and *avolition* (American Psychiatric Association, 2000a). Approximately 25% of persons with schizophrenia display these symptoms (Ho et al., 2003).

- Affect, in psychological terms, refers to expressing emotions. Some people with schizophrenia show **blunted affect**, or a lack of emotional expression. They appear passive with immobile facial expressions. Their vocal tone does not change even when the conversation is emotional in tone. They do not respond to events in their environment with any emotion.
- **Alogia**, also called *poverty of speech*, refers to decreased quality or quantity of speech, or both. The person with schizophrenia gives brief and empty replies.
- **Avolition** is the inability to follow through on one's plans. A person with schizophrenia may seem apathetic, sitting for long periods of time, showing little interest in her or his usual activities.

Many people with schizophrenia exhibit both positive and negative symptoms. The *DSM-IV-TR* recognizes five subtypes of schizophrenia, classified according to which symptoms are most prevalent. These five types—*paranoid*, *disorganized*, *catatonic*, *undifferentiated*, and *residual schizophrenia*—are described in ● TABLE 14.6. People with schizophrenia who show predominantly positive symptoms tend to have a less severe course of schizophrenia and respond better to medication. For instance, positive symptoms predominate in *paranoid schizophrenia*, which may partly explain why people with paranoid schizophrenia tend to have a more favorable prognosis than do those with other types of schizophrenia (Fenton & McGlashan, 1994; Kendler et al., 1994). Such findings have led researchers to believe that positive symptoms of schizophrenia may have a different cause than negative symptoms. So let's look at our current understanding of the development of schizophrenia.

Explaining Schizophrenia: Genetics, the Brain, and the Environment

What causes schizophrenia? To date, biological factors account for the strongest evidence in the development of schizophrenia, although environmental factors must also be considered. It is likely that environmental conditions interact with biological factors to make a person either more or less susceptible to the illness. Biological research has focused on three main areas: genetics, brain abnormalities, and the malfunctioning of specific neurotransmitters in the brain. Environmental research has focused on prenatal and development factors, as well as the role of family and the environment.

TABLE 14.6
● *DSM-IV-TR* Types of Schizophrenia

TYPE	MAJOR FEATURES
Catatonic schizophrenia	Extreme behavior in either dimension: total unresponsiveness to the environment (stupor) or excessive motor activity (agitated excitement)
Disorganized schizophrenia	Speech and behavior are disorganized or difficult to understand; inappropriate emotions such as giggling constantly for no apparent reason, and repetitive, purposeless, or silly behavior
Paranoid schizophrenia	Delusions of grandeur or persecution, hallucinations that may be of a frightening nature. May exhibit anxiety and/or argumentativeness.
Undifferentiated schizophrenia	Schizophrenic symptoms present but does not meet criteria for other subtypes
Residual schizophrenia	Only negative symptoms are present or prior positive symptoms have lessened in severity or frequency

Reprinted with permission from the Diagnostic and Statistical Manual of Mental Disorders, *Fourth Edition, Text Revision, Copyright 2000. American Psychiatric Association.*

blunted affect a lack of emotional expression

alogia decreased quality and/or quantity of speech

avolition the inability to follow through on one's plans

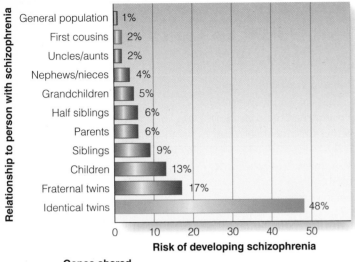

Genes shared

▨ 12.5% 3rd-degree relatives	▨ 25% 2nd-degree relatives
▨ 50% 1st-degree relatives	▨ 100% Identical twins

FIGURE 14.7

● **Risk of Schizophrenia and Genetic Relatedness** The incidence of schizophrenia in the general population is 1–2%. However, the more closely one is genetically related to a person with schizophrenia, the higher the risk of developing the disorder. *(Source: Reprinted by permission of Irving I. Gottesman)*

A Strong Genetic Factor

Family, twin, and adoption studies have routinely demonstrated a high heritability of schizophrenia (Levy et al., 2010; NIMH Genetics Workgroup, 1998; Parnas et al., 1993). As ● FIGURE 14.7 shows, although the incidence of schizophrenia in the general population is 1–2%, the more genetically similar a person is to someone with schizophrenia, the more likely he or she will also develop the disorder (Cardno & Gottesman, 2000). In identical twin pairs, if one twin develops schizophrenia, the other twin has about a 48% chance of developing the disorder. However, in fraternal twins (who are not genetically identical), the probability is only 17%. Adoption studies show a similar pattern (Heston, 1966; Kety et al., 1994; Tienari et al., 2003). Adopted children who have biological parents with schizophrenia are 10 times more likely to develop the disorder than are adopted children whose biological parents are not diagnosed with schizophrenia.

Despite these results, it is unlikely that a single gene is responsible for the illness; if it were, the heritability rates would be higher. Research has therefore moved toward exploring several chromosomal regions that may work together to increase a person's vulnerability to schizophrenia, as well as altered gene expressions that may give rise to brain abnormalities (Nicodemus et al., in press; N. Norton, Williams, & Owen, 2006; Rapoport et al., 2005; Shi et al., 2009; Walker & Tessner, 2008). The exact nature of these pathways has yet to be identified and detailed.

Another genetic explanation for schizophrenia stems from the association between advanced paternal age and an increased risk of schizophrenia. That is, some people with schizophrenia are more likely to have had older fathers (45 years or older) at birth. Such an association has led to the hypothesis that mutations in male sperm cells (that are more likely to occur as a male ages) may be in part a genetic mechanism for schizophrenia in at least some people (Byrne et al., 2003; Dalman & Allebeck, 2002; Malaspina et al., 2001; Torrey et al., 2009).

The Brain: Neurotransmitters and Structural Abnormalities

A second area of research on the development of schizophrenia looks at neurotransmitters. It was originally believed that schizophrenia was caused by excess activity of the neurotransmitter dopamine in the brain. The drugs that are prescribed for schizophrenia, called *phenothiazines*, reduce dopamine activity in the brain and are typically more effective in reducing the positive symptoms of schizophrenia. However, many people with schizophrenia do not respond to treatment with phenothiazines. One of the newest drugs used to treat schizophrenia, called *clozapine*, does not block the same dopamine receptors as the phenothiazines, clearly indicating that dopamine is involved, but in a more complex way (Conklin & Iacono, 2002). Researchers continue to investigate the exact role of dopamine in the development of schizophrenia (Howes & Kapur, 2009).

Other research suggests a potential role for the neurotransmitter glutamate (Coyle, 2006; Goff & Coyle, 2001). Drugs such as PCP and ketamine (see Chapter 4) that block the action of glutamate can cause normal participants to exhibit cognitive impairments and negative symptoms similar to those found in people with schizophrenia (Deakin et al., 2008). Current research is focused on how glutamate and dopamine dysfunction may interact to contribute to the development of schizophrenia (Javitt, 2007; Stahl, 2007; Stone, Morrison, & Pilowsky, 2007). Obviously, the relationship between neurotransmitters and schizophrenia remains a complex one.

Abnormalities in certain brain structures have also been investigated for their links to schizophrenia. The most consistent abnormality found in people with schizophrenia is enlarged ventricles (Andreasen et al., 1990; Lieberman et al., 2001; Zorrilla et al., 1997). A

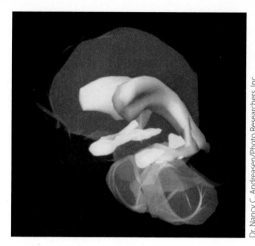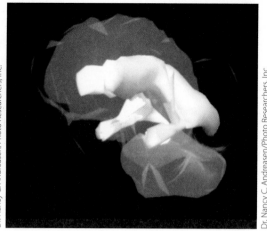

The most consistent brain abnormality that has been found in people with schizophrenia is enlarged ventricles. Shown here are 3-D magnetic resonance images (MRIs) of a brain of a person with schizophrenia (*right*) and the brain of a person without schizophrenia (*left*). The hippocampus (yellow, at center) is shrunken and the fluid-filled ventricles (white) enlarged in the brain of a person with schizophrenia.

ventricle is a fluid-filled cavity in the brain. Enlarged ventricles reduce the overall size of the brain, which in turn may contribute to the development of schizophrenia (Wright et al., 2000). Brain dysfunction in the frontal and temporal lobes has also been implicated in the development of schizophrenia (Mitelman et al., 2005; Weinstein, Woodward, & Ngan, 2007; Wolf et al., 2007). The frontal lobe is responsible for language, emotions, and social behavior, and the temporal lobe plays an important role in memory. The symptoms of schizophrenia (disordered speech, blunted affect, and catatonic behavior) are associated with these brain areas.

Prenatal and Developmental Factors

How do people with schizophrenia develop these neurochemical or brain abnormalities? In addition to possible hereditary factors, these abnormalities have been linked to birth complications and the mother's exposure to prenatal viruses (A. S. Brown et al., 2004; T. D. Cannon, 1998; Goldstein et al., 2000; Mednick et al., 1998), although many other causes could exist. A genetic predisposition to schizophrenia interacts with prenatal environmental agents such as a maternal virus or poor nutrition, causing changes in normal brain development. Then, as the brain reaches maturation (during adolescence), a natural trimming away of brain synapses occurs. It is hypothesized that in people with schizophrenia, the brain trims away too many synapses, resulting in the expression of the disorder in the teenage years. Symptoms of schizophrenia are particularly likely to appear if the person has a strong genetic disposition or if environmental circumstances have encouraged the expression of the disorder in those with even a mild genetic link (Fatemi & Folsom, 2009; McGlashan & Hoffman, 2000; Rapoport et al., 2005).

The Role of Family and Environment

What environmental and psychological factors appear to contribute to the onset and course of schizophrenia? Two critical factors appear to be family support and exposure to stressful living conditions. Studies on the families of people with schizophrenia have found that the quality of family communications and interactions may either encourage or discourage the onset of schizophrenia in people who are genetically at high risk. The quality of family interactions may also influence whether future psychotic episodes are triggered. Families that are critical, harsh, hostile, and poor communicators may make a high-risk person more susceptible to the disorder (Butzlaff & Hooley, 1998; Hooley & Hiller, 1998). Chronic stress from living a low-income lifestyle or within a family with poor communication also appears to influence future relapses (Dohrenwend et al., 1987; Norman & Malla, 1993; Ventura et al., 2000). Although it appears that family and lifestyle do not *cause* schizophrenia, they are especially critical factors in people's susceptibility to the disorder and must be taken into account when designing prevention or treatment programs for those with schizophrenia.

Let's
REVIEW In this section, we described the symptoms and types of schizophrenia and outlined our current understanding of the factors that play a role in its development. For a quick check of your understanding, try answering the following questions at increasing levels of difficulty.

1. The most consistent brain abnormality found among people with schizophrenia is _____.
   a. a small frontal lobe
   b. a small temporal lobe
   c. enlarged ventricles
   d. an enlarged frontal lobe

2. People with _____ schizophrenia show predominantly positive symptoms, such as delusions and hallucinations.
   a. disorganized
   b. catatonic
   c. paranoid
   d. undifferentiated

3. Loose associations, poverty of content, and word salad characterize which symptom of schizophrenia?
   a. disorganized speech
   b. catatonic stupor
   c. delusions
   d. flat affect

ANSWERS 1. c; 2. c; 3. a

LEARNING OBJECTIVE

What Should You Know?
• Describe the nature of personality disorders.

CAN A PERSONALITY BE DISORDERED? MALADAPTIVE PATTERNS OF BEHAVIOR

Recall from our discussion on the *DSM* model that the **personality disorders** are represented on Axis II (see Table 14.1). They consist of lifelong or longstanding patterns of malfunctioning. All of us have personality "quirks." Some people may be excessively neat. Others may be somewhat suspicious and mistrustful of others. Still others may appear to be conceited or selfish. However, these traits do not necessarily qualify someone for a personality disorder. In personality disorders, the person's behavior (1) is maladaptive to self or others and (2) has been stable across a long period and across many situations, typically since adolescence or early adulthood.

People with personality disorders also can be diagnosed with any of the clinical disorders previously discussed, and they typically seek treatment for these clinical disorders or because someone else has a problem with their behavior and encourages them to undergo therapy. Individuals with a personality disorder often don't see a problem with their behavior and, therefore, seldom seek treatment on their own. It is estimated that as many as 14% of adults in the United States meet the criteria for at least one personality disorder (B. F. Grant et al., 2004). The list of personality disorders is long, and space considerations prohibit a discussion of all of them, but we give a brief description of the *DSM* personality disorders in ● TABLE 14.7. Here we will confine our discussion to two: *antisocial personality disorder* and *borderline personality disorder*.

Antisocial Personality Disorder: Charming and Dangerous

People who are impulsive and disregard the rights of others without showing any remorse or guilt are diagnosed with **antisocial personality disorder** (American Psychiatric Association, 2000a). A person with this disorder is commonly referred to as a psychopath. People who have antisocial personalities are callous and malicious, blame others for their problems, and frequently have difficulty maintaining social relationships. They can also be superficially charming and sociable, typically in order to manipulate others into doing what they want. Such antisocial behavior has often been present since childhood or adolescence (Loney et al., 2007). Serial murderers such as Charles Manson, Gary Gilmore, Andrew Cunanan, and Ted Bundy come to mind when thinking about antisocial personality disorder, as they have

personality disorder a disorder marked by maladaptive behavior that has been stable across a long period and across many situations

antisocial personality disorder a personality disorder marked by a pattern of disregard for and violation of the rights of others with no remorse or guilt for one's actions

TABLE 14.7

● Types of Personality Disorders

DISORDER	MAJOR FEATURE
Paranoid personality disorder	Excessive suspicion and mistrust of others.
Schizoid personality disorder	Lack of desire to form close relationships with others; emotional detachment and coldness toward others.
Schizotypal personality disorder	Considered a mild version of schizophrenia. The person shows inappropriate social and emotional behavior, and unusual thoughts and speech.
Antisocial personality disorder	Chronic pattern of impulsive behavior; violates rights of others and does not show remorse or guilt for actions.
Borderline personality disorder	Instability in mood, self-concept, and interpersonal relationships.
Histrionic personality disorder	Intense need for attention; always wants to be the center of attention; excessively dramatic behavior; rapidly changing moods.
Narcissistic personality disorder	Preoccupation with own sense of importance and view of self as above others; typically ignores the needs and wants of others.
Avoidant personality disorder	Intense and chronic anxiety over being negatively evaluated by others, so avoids social interactions.
Dependent personality disorder	Excessive need to be cared for by others; denies own thoughts and feelings and clings to others.
Obsessive-compulsive personality disorder	Pattern of rigid and perfectionist behavior; preoccupied with details, rules, order, and routine; experiences upset when routine is disrupted. (This is *not* the same as the anxiety disorder OCD.)

received much media attention. It is one of the more common personality disorders, and men are 5 times more likely than women to be diagnosed with this disorder (Cloninger, Bayon, & Przybeck, 1997; B. F. Grant et al., 2004).

People with antisocial personality disorder are more often sent to prison than to treatment. Does this mean that all criminals have antisocial personality disorder? No. Although antisocial behavior is highly correlated with criminal behavior, not all criminals are antisocial. One of the key features distinguishing the two is the lack of remorse and guilt for one's actions. A person can commit armed robbery yet afterward regret his actions. The antisocial person does not experience such regret or remorse. People with antisocial personality disorder may not be violent. They may be "con artists," and more of them may live outside of prison than in it. They may function successfully in business, politics, or entertainment (Stout, 2005).

What causes antisocial personality disorder? Some research suggests biological factors. Twin studies, adoption studies, and family studies support a genetic influence (G. Carey & Goldman, 1997; Hicks et al., 2004; Moffitt, 2005). For example, family members of people with antisocial personality disorder have higher rates of the disorder than the general population. Other research suggests low levels of the neurotransmitter serotonin (Moffitt et al., 1998); deficits in brain areas that control impulsivity, attention, and decision making (B. Henry & Moffitt, 1997; Kiehl et al., 2006; Raine, 2008); elevated levels of the hormone testosterone (van Honk & Schutter, 2007); and low arousal of the nervous system (Raine, 1997; Raine et al., 2000). However, psychological and social variables cannot be ruled out. People with antisocial personality disorder often experience conflict-filled childhoods. Their parents may be neglectful, inconsistent in discipline, harsh, hostile, or less warm. As a result, they often learn to expect such treatment from others and adopt a mistrustful and aggressive stance toward others (N. R. Crick & Dodge, 1994; Dishion & Patterson, 1997; Feinberg et al., 2007). In all likelihood, a complex interplay between gene–environment processes best explains the development of antisocial personality disorder (Caspi et al., 2002; Fowles & Dindo, 2009; Moffitt, 2005; Raine, 2008; van Goozen, Fairchild, & Harold, 2008).

WANTED BY THE FBI

Andrew Phillip Cunanan
Unlawful Flight to Avoid Prosecution - Murder

Race: White; Sex: Male; Height: 5'9" - 5'11"; Weight: 160-185 lbs.
Date of Birth: 8/31/69; Hair: Brown (short); Eyes: Brown; Wears glasses and/or contact lenses
CAUTION: CONSIDER ARMED AND DANGEROUS
Please contact the nearest FBI office if you have any information
on Andrew Phillip Cunanan.

Andrew Cunanan murdered famous clothes designer Gianni Versace after killing several others. He was described by many as a charming and bright young man.

Borderline Personality Disorder: Living on Your Fault Line

Borderline personality disorder (BPD) is characterized by instability in moods, interpersonal relationships, self-image, and behavior (American Psychiatric Association, 2000a). This key feature of instability often disrupts people's relationships, career, and identity. Their unstable emotions result in intense bouts of anger, depression, or anxiety that may occur for

borderline personality disorder (BPD) a personality disorder marked by a pattern of instability in mood, relationships, self-image, and behavior

hours or for a day. Their unstable self-concepts are reflected in extreme insecurity at some times and exaggerated feelings of importance at other times. This instability may prompt frequent changes in goals, jobs, friendships, and values because people with borderline personalities lack a clear definition of themselves. They have little idea of who they are. Their interpersonal relationships are also characterized by instability. They may admire, idealize, and cling to loved ones at first, but when conflict occurs, feelings of abandonment and rejection surface, and their feelings quickly turn to anger and dislike. They then seek out new friends or loved ones, and the cycle repeats itself. People with this disorder often feel unworthy, bad, or empty inside. At times of extreme insecurity and depression, self-injury and suicide attempts are common (Black et al., 2004; Soloff et al., 1994).

People with BPD are often diagnosed with other clinical disorders such as major depression, substance abuse, or anxiety (Weissman, 1993). It is estimated that approximately 2% of the population will be diagnosed with BPD at some point in their lives, and it is diagnosed more often in women than in men (M. Swartz et al., 1990). Extensive mental health services are often needed to treat people with BPD.

Research on what causes borderline personality disorder has focused on biological, psychological, and social factors. Low levels of serotonin are related to impulsive behaviors (Ni et al., 2007; Siever & Koenigsberg, 2000). Difficulty in regulating emotions may be related to abnormal brain functioning (R. J. Davidson, Jackson, & Kalin, 2000; Davidson, Putnam, & Larson, 2000; L. M. Williams et al., 2006). However, many people with BPD report a history of abuse, neglect, or separation as young children, making environment a probable factor (Bornovalova et al., 2006; Zanarini & Frankenburg, 1997). For example, in one study (Zanarini, 2000), a large percentage of patients with BPD had reported being sexually abused. Such social stressors may impede normal attachment patterns, identity development, and the ability to express appropriate emotions.

In this chapter, we have outlined 6 of the 13 major categories of psychological disorders listed in the *DSM-IV-TR*. Each disorder meets the criterion of abnormality endorsed at the beginning of the chapter—inability to function. Although research continues into the exact origins of each disorder, we have seen that in many cases, a person's biological vulnerability appears to combine with psychological and sociocultural factors—learning experiences, thinking patterns, family interactions, cultural attitudes, gender roles—to trigger the onset of the disorder. Many people with psychological disorders seek help in the form of therapy. So keep the symptoms of these disorders in mind. It will assist you in mastering the material of the next chapter, as we explore the different therapies psychologists and psychiatrists use to treat psychological disorders.

Let's
REVIEW
In this section, we described the nature of personality disorders, in particular antisocial and borderline personality disorders. For a quick check of your understanding, try answering the following questions at increasing levels of difficulty.

1. Personality disorders are represented on which axis of the *DSM*?

a. Axis I   c. Axis III

b. Axis II   d. Axis IV

2. Felicia is extremely insecure and lacks a clear sense of identity. She often clings to new friends and then hates them a month later. She has an intense fear of abandonment and rejection. Felicia's behavior best fits which personality disorder?

a. narcissistic   c. borderline

b. antisocial   d. paranoid

3. Personality disorders _____.

a. do not coexist with clinical disorders such as depression or anxiety

b. generally appear in early or middle adulthood

c. are stable patterns of malfunctioning

d. do not pose any threat to others

ANSWERS 1. b; 2. c; 3. c

STUDYING the CHAPTER

KEY TERMS

medical model (575)
Diagnostic and Statistical Manual of Mental Disorders (DSM) (577)
anxiety disorder (582)
generalized anxiety disorder (GAD) (582)
panic disorder (583)
agoraphobia (583)
phobic disorder (584)
specific phobia (584)
social phobia (584)
obsession (584)

compulsion (584)
obsessive-compulsive disorder (OCD) (584)
posttraumatic stress disorder (PTSD) (585)
dissociative disorder (590)
dissociative fugue disorder (590)
dissociative identity disorder (DID) (590)
somatoform disorder (591)
hypochondriasis (591)
mood disorder (592)

major depression (593)
dysphoria (593)
anhedonia (593)
dysthymic disorder (593)
bipolar disorder (594)
mania (594)
cyclothymic disorder (594)
learned helplessness (598)
ruminative coping style (598)
cognitive distortion (598)
schizophrenia (601)
delusion (602)
hallucination (602)

disorganized speech (602)
disorganized behavior (602)
catatonic stupor (602)
catatonic excitement (602)
blunted affect (603)
alogia (603)
avolition (603)
personality disorder (606)
antisocial personality disorder (606)
borderline personality disorder (BPD) (607)

LEARNING CHALLENGE

Now that you have studied the chapter, assess your comprehension of the material by answering the following questions. Then use the key at the end to determine if your understanding is at the basic, intermediate, or advanced level. For a more comprehensive assessment of your learning, please see your student study guide and your Psychology CourseMate (www.cengagebrain.com).

1. Allison can't help feeling sad most of the time. It upsets her that she can't be happy and seem "normal." Allison's behavior best fits which criterion of abnormality?

   a. violation of social norms
   b. personal distress
   c. danger to others
   d. all of the above

2. Which psychological disorder is characterized by a persistent fear and avoidance of a specific object or situation?

   a. phobic disorder
   b. conversion disorder
   c. major depression
   d. schizophrenia

3. Dr. Sanchez believes that mental illness is the result of unresolved, unconscious conflicts. Dr. Sanchez views mental illness from the _____ perspective.

   a. social learning
   b. biological
   c. psychoanalytic
   d. cognitive

TEST YOURSELF!

4. Abdul was involved in a four-car pileup on the interstate 8 months ago. Since then, he has been having nightmares and flashback episodes of the accident. He has difficulty concentrating and has withdrawn from his family and friends. Abdul is most likely to be diagnosed with which anxiety disorder?

   a. panic disorder
   b. posttraumatic stress disorder
   c. phobic disorder
   d. generalized anxiety disorder

5. Which of the following neurotransmitters has *not* been linked to anxiety disorders?

   a. GABA
   b. norepinephrine
   c. serotonin
   d. acetylcholine

6. Last week, Tyrone had little sleep but felt confident, exhilarated, and excessively happy. He talked fast and felt that he could accomplish anything. Now his energy has evaporated. He sleeps most of the time, feels worthless, and lacks his usual vitality. Tyrone would most likely be diagnosed with which disorder?

   a. major depression
   b. bipolar disorder
   c. dysthymic disorder
   d. unipolar depressive disorder

7. Dysthymic disorder is a less severe but more chronic form of _____.

   a. major depression
   b. bipolar disorder
   c. dysphoria
   d. apathy

8. Schizophrenia has been linked most strongly to which neurotransmitter?

   a. dopamine
   b. GABA
   c. serotonin
   d. acetylcholine

9. Some clinicians question the validity of dissociative identity disorder and suggest that it represents an extreme form of which disorder?

   a. phobic disorder
   b. panic disorder
   c. generalized anxiety disorder
   d. posttraumatic stress disorder

10. Men are more likely than women to be diagnosed with _____.

   a. anxiety disorders
   b. antisocial personality disorder
   c. major depression
   d. schizophrenia

11. A young woman was found by police wandering the streets alone and confused. She asked the police to help her discover her identity. This woman is most likely to be diagnosed with which psychological disorder?

   a. dissociative fugue disorder
   b. hypochondriasis
   c. agoraphobia
   d. borderline personality disorder

12. Which psychological disorder is characterized by delusions, hallucinations, incoherent thought and speech, and inappropriate emotions?

   a. dissociative identity disorder
   b. schizophrenia
   c. panic disorder
   d. bipolar depression

13. Which personality disorder is characterized by instability in moods, interpersonal relationships, self-image, and behavior?

   a. histrionic
   b. narcissistic
   c. antisocial
   d. borderline

14. Which of the following information is not gathered by the five axes of the current *DSM*?

   a. medical conditions
   b. causes of the disorder
   c. personality disorders
   d. environmental factors

15. Social learning theorists emphasize the role of _____ in explaining psychological disorders.

   a. thoughts
   b. cultural processes
   c. unrealistic self-images
   d. reinforcement processes

Scoring Key

Below are the answers and the associated point values for each of the Learning Challenge questions. Circle the associated points for each question that you answered correctly. To obtain your Learning Challenge Score, add up the points you circled and write the total in the blank.

1. B, 2 pts	**6.** B, 2 pts	**11.** A, 2 pts
2. A, 1 pt	**7.** A, 3 pts	**12.** B, 1 pt
3. C, 2 pts	**8.** A, 3 pts	**13.** D, 1 pt
4. B, 2 pts	**9.** D, 3 pts	**14.** B, 1 pt
5. D, 3 pts	**10.** B, 1 pt	**15.** D, 3 pts

Learning Challenge Score _____

(27–30) Congratulations! You scored at the advanced level. You are well on your way to mastering the material. Take the next step by answering the questions in your Student Study Guide or your Psychology CourseMate (www.cengagebrain.com).

(21–26) You are almost there! You scored at the intermediate level. Review the material you missed before moving on to answer the questions in your Student Study Guide or your Psychology CourseMate (www.cengagebrain.com).

(20 and below) You are on your way, but you're not there yet! You scored at the beginner level. It appears that you need to carefully review the chapter to improve your mastery of the material.

USE IT OR LOSE IT: APPLYING PSYCHOLOGY

1. Create a facility that would best address the treatment and care of people with schizophrenia.

2. What behaviors do you believe would be considered abnormal in every culture and society (present and past) and in all situations? Are these behaviors symptoms of any of the disorders discussed in this chapter? How does this list help or hinder psychologists' understanding of abnormality?

3. Which disorders would people be most likely and least likely to seek treatment for, and why? How might this search differ by gender, age, or ethnicity?

4. After reading this chapter, what factors appear to be most linked to mental illness? Is there anything that can be done to remove such factors from our society?

5. Which mental health disorders do you think you are most at risk for, and why? Be sure to consider biological, psychological, and sociocultural factors in formulating your response.

CRITICAL THINKING FOR INTEGRATION

1. How might memory processes (Chapter 6) be linked to the development of anxiety disorders?

2. How might gender (Chapter 10) explain the gender differences in the prevalence of anxiety and depressive disorders? Describe what might be the attributional process (Chapter 11) for individual success and failure of a person with an anxiety or depressive disorder. How might these individuals judge the behavior of others? Provide examples to support your ideas.

3. Refer to the section on research methods in Chapter 1. In a study on schizophrenia, how might the presence of various types of schizophrenia in your sample complicate a study's conclusions? How could more valid research on the origin of schizophrenia be conducted? What might make your solution difficult to implement?

CHAPTER STUDY RESOURCES

Student Study Guide

To help organize your learning, work through Chapter 14 of the *What Is Psychology? Student Study Guide*. The study guide includes learning objectives, a chapter summary, fill-in review, key terms, a practice test, and activities.

CengageNOW

Go to **www.cengage.com/login** to link to CengageNOW, your online study tool. First take the Pre-Test for this chapter to get your personalized study plan, which will identify topics you need to review and direct you to online resources. Then take the Post-Test to determine what concepts you have mastered and what you still need work on.

CourseMate

Access an interactive eBook, chapter-specific interactive learning tools, including flashcards, quizzes, videos, and more in your Psychology CourseMate, available at **CengageBrain.com**.

Aplia

aplia

Aplia™ is an online interactive learning solution that helps you improve comprehension—and your grade—by integrating a variety of tools such as video, tutorials, practice tests, and interactive eBook. Founded by a professor to enhance his own courses, Aplia provides automatically graded assignments with detailed, immediate explanations on every question, and innovative teaching materials. More than 1,000,000 students like you have used Aplia at over 1,800 institutions. Aplia should be purchased only when assigned by your instructor as part of your course.

WHAT ARE PSYCHOLOGICAL DISORDERS, AND HOW CAN WE UNDERSTAND THEM?

Psychologists use several criteria, including statistical infrequency, violation of social norms, and personal distress, to define abnormal behavior. However, abnormality is best explained when a behavior interferes with a person's ability to function. We have seen that in many cases, a person's biological vulnerability appears to combine with psychological and sociocultural factors, to trigger the onset of abnormal behavior. Such an interaction of variables is helpful in understanding why people like J. K. Rowling, Nathaniel Ayers, and Howie Mandel behaved the way they did.

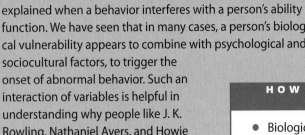

HOW DO WE EXPLAIN ABNORMAL BEHAVIOR? PERSPECTIVES REVISITED

- Biological theories suggest that mental illness is a disease resulting from physical causes.

- Psychological theories propose that psychological factors lead to abnormal behavior.

- Sociocultural theories suggest that environmental stressors and social factors such as age, race, gender, and culture influence abnormal behavior.

- Psychological disorders result from a combination of biological, psychological, and social factors (biopsychosocial model). They do not have just one cause.

HOW ARE DIAGNOSES MADE? THE DSM MODEL

- The **Diagnostic and Statistical Manual of Mental Disorders (DSM)**, currently in its fourth edition, is an atheoretical, multiaxial system that details specific criteria for a diagnosis of a mental health disorder.

- Labeling someone with a mental health disorder can have negative effects as it may encourage the person to behave in a way that is consistent with the disorder.

DIAGNOSTIC AND STATISTICAL MANUAL OF MENTAL DISORDERS
FOURTH EDITION
TEXT REVISION
DSM-IV-TR
AMERICAN PSYCHIATRIC ASSOCIATION

Reprinted with permission of American Psychiatric Publishing, Inc.

WHAT ARE ANXIETY DISORDERS? IT'S NOT JUST "NERVES"

- **Anxiety disorders** include physical, cognitive, emotional, and behavioral components.

- **Generalized anxiety disorder** is characterized by excessive anxiety, worry, and difficulty in controlling such worries.

- **Panic disorder** is characterized by recurrent panic attacks or the persistent fear of having a panic attack.

- A persistent fear of a specific object or social situation comprises **phobic disorder**.

- In **obsessive-compulsive disorder**, a person experiences recurrent **obsessions** or **compulsions** that cannot be controlled.

Image Source/Getty Images

- **Posttraumatic stress disorder** develops after exposure to a terrifying event. The person experiences distressing memories, nightmares, thoughts, or flashback episodes of the event that interfere with functioning.

- Potential causes of anxiety disorders include:

  - Biological factors such as genetics, neurotransmitter imbalances, and abnormal brain functioning

  - Psychological factors such as conditioning, maladaptive cognitions, and an unrealistic self-image

  - Social factors such as rapid social change, stress, low social status, and gender

Are You Getting THE BIG PICTURE?

DISSOCIATIVE AND SOMATOFORM DISORDERS: OTHER FORMS OF ANXIETY?

- **Dissociative disorders** are characterized by a loss of awareness of some part of our self.

- In **dissociative fugue disorder,** a person unexpectedly travels away from home and may assume a new identity with amnesia of the previous identity. In **dissociative identity disorder,** separate multiple personalities exist in the same person. Both disorders are believed to be related to severe stress or a series of emotionally traumatic events.

- **Somatoform disorders** are characterized by physical complaints or symptoms with no apparent physical cause, as in **hypochondriasis.** Psychological distress appears to underlie the physical complaints of these disorders.

WHAT CHARACTERIZES MOOD DISORDERS? BEYOND THE BLUES

- **Mood disorders** are characterized by a significant change in one's emotional state over an extended period.

- In unipolar depression, the person experiences extreme or chronic sadness (**dysphoria**) or loss of pleasure (**anhedonia**).

- **Bipolar disorder** involves a shift in mood between two states: sadness and **mania**.

- Potential causes of mood disorders include:

  - Biological factors such as genetics, neurotransmitter imbalances, and hormones

  - Psychological factors such as unresolved issues of loss and rejection, low positive reinforcement, **learned helplessness**, **ruminative coping style**, **cognitive distortions**, and pessimistic attributions

  - Social factors such as lower social status, stressful life events, and gender

Benelux Press/Getty Images

WHAT IS SCHIZOPHRENIA? DISINTEGRATION

Grunnitus Studio/Photo Researchers, Inc.

- **Schizophrenia** is a chronic mental health disorder characterized by positive symptoms (**delusions, hallucinations, disorganized speech, catatonic stupor** or **catatonic excitement**) and negative symptoms (**blunted affect, alogia, avolition**).

- Types of schizophrenia include paranoid, disorganized, catatonic, undifferentiated, and residual.

- Potential causes of schizophrenia are primarily biological, including genetics, dopamine and glutamate activity, and abnormal brain functioning. However, family support and interactions and stressful living conditions may influence the course of the disorder.

CAN A PERSONALITY BE DISORDERED? MALADAPTIVE PATTERNS OF BEHAVIOR

- The **personality disorders** consist of longstanding patterns of malfunctioning typically evident in childhood or adolescence.

- People who disregard the rights of others without showing any remorse or guilt are diagnosed with **antisocial personality disorder**.

- **Borderline personality disorder** is characterized by instability in moods, interpersonal relationships, self-image, and behavior.

- Personality disorders are related to biological factors (genetics, neurotransmitters, abnormal brain functioning) and psychosocial factors (inconsistent parenting practices, gender, conflict-filled childhood).

WANTED BY THE FBI

Andrew Phillip Cunanan
Unlawful Flight to Avoid Prosecution - Murder

Race: White; Sex: Male; Height: 5'9" - 5'11"; Weight: 160-185 lbs.
Date of Birth: 8/31/69; Hair: Brown (short); Eyes: Brown; Wears glasses and/or contact lenses
CAUTION: CONSIDER ARMED AND DANGEROUS
Please contact the nearest FBI office if you have any information on Andrew Phillip Cunanan

AP Photo/FB

CHAPTER 15

WHAT THERAPIES ARE USED TO TREAT PSYCHOLOGICAL PROBLEMS?

THE BIG PICTURE

The Ups and Downs of Life

The previous chapter outlined major psychological disorders such as depression, anxiety, and schizophrenia. It included the main symptoms of these disorders as well as our current understanding of what causes such problems. This chapter extends that discussion by examining the ways in which we treat those disorders. As such, this chapter nicely represents the big picture of psychology as we review many of the concepts and issues we have introduced throughout this textbook.

This chapter explores the principal approaches to therapy common today. **Therapy** consists of techniques that are used to help people with psychological or interpersonal problems. All therapies attempt to change a person's behavior. But the techniques that are used differ, because each therapy approach stems from one of the main theoretical perspectives introduced in the first chapter and explained in more detail in subsequent chapters.

What is the experience of therapy like? It varies considerably from person to person, from approach to approach, and from therapist to therapist. To illustrate, consider for a moment the following story.

At 18 years old, Emily should have been care-free and excited about life. She should have been going to college and discovering or nurturing her talents and ambitions. But that is not Emily's story. Before the age of 17, Emily had been to at least five therapists, and her world centered around mental health institutions. In Emily's words, "I was formed by therapy, absorbing its influence in ways that would require most of my life to raise to consciousness" (Gordon, 2000, p. 29).

Dr. V. was her first therapist when Emily was in the eighth grade. Emily was sent to Dr. V. following an incident at school in which she angrily chased another student with what school administrators described as an intention to inflict physical harm. In these therapy sessions, Emily would lie down on a couch while Dr. V. remained silent in a chair. Not knowing what to do, Emily remained silent as well, listening to Dr. V. steadily scribbling on a notepad. After a year, Emily's family moved, and she was sent to see Dr. H. There, Emily sat on a couch, and Dr. H. remained silent in a nearby chair, knitting a sweater. After a year of listening to the click-clacking of knitting needles, therapy with Dr. H. was terminated. Given the amount of money involved and Emily's lack of progress, this outcome should not be surprising.

Tetra Images/Getty Images

Needless to say, Emily's problems continued. She was kicked out of several private schools for misbehavior and truancy. At 16, against her parents' orders, Emily attended an unchaperoned party. Her father found her there with a boy in a dark room, kissing and groping one another. Her father dragged her out of the party and drove her home. Furious with her parents, Emily broke an aspirin jar and, using a piece of the glass, scratched her wrists in a half-hearted suicide attempt. Her parents sent her to see another therapist, Dr. G.

Therapy with Dr. G. was different from what Emily had experienced before. She sat facing him and was encouraged to talk freely about her dreams and problems while Dr. G. looked for themes threaded through her discussions. She saw Dr. G. on and off through her high school years. After she again attempted suicide at age 18, Dr. G. recommended an inpatient facility for Emily. She was placed in the highly regarded Austen Riggs treatment center in Massachusetts. She was diagnosed as having an anxiety problem with borderline personality trends. She stayed at Riggs for 3 years, 1 year as an inpatient and another 2 years as an outpatient in residential apartments.

As an inpatient, Emily was told when to eat and sleep, and she attended group meetings. If she did not get her work jobs done or go to bed at the appropriate time, she lost privileges. She received medication at regular intervals. Her first therapist in the hospital was considerably different from her previous therapists. He took walks with Emily, drank wine with her and her roommate, and on one occasion put his arm around her waist. Emily knew he was becoming inappropriately attached to her, and so she searched for a new therapist. She was fortunate enough to find Dr. Leslie Farber.

Dr. Farber's approach seemed radically different. He emphasized the presence of will in human behavior, and he communicated to Emily that he believed in her and her value. He shared with Emily anecdotes about his own life that were similar to her experiences and feelings. He treated her with warmth and understanding rather than aloofness or pity. He challenged her personal beliefs and highlighted her negative self-remarks. Through many years and many therapy sessions, Dr. Farber helped Emily "recover" her life.

As you can see, Emily experienced various forms of therapy and interacted with many different types of therapists. Her "therapeutic journey," detailed in her book *Mockingbird Years: A Life In and Out of Therapy* (2000), highlights the various forms of therapies and how therapists are a crucial variable in determining the effectiveness of therapy.

This chapter examines the nature of these various types of therapy, explaining the techniques used in each approach, how they are conducted, and analyzing their effectiveness in treating people with mental health disorders. We will begin by defining therapy, examining who is qualified to give it, and addressing when it is appropriate for a person to seek therapy.

therapy techniques that are used to help people with psychological or interpersonal problems

WHAT IS THE NATURE OF THERAPY?

Mental health professionals today use two broad forms of therapy to help people who are having difficulty functioning: *psychotherapy* and *biomedical therapy*. As we have seen, Emily received both. **Psychotherapy** is the use of psychological principles and techniques to treat the symptoms of psychological disorders, such as depression, or to treat interpersonal problems, such as troubled relationships. Psychotherapy is a general term that encompasses hundreds of different forms of therapy. However, all psychotherapies are based on the central assumption that underlying psychological factors, such as emotions, cognitions, behavior, or relationships, are at the root of interpersonal problems and psychological disorders.

In contrast, **biomedical therapy** uses medications or other medical interventions to treat the symptoms of mental health problems. Biomedical therapy assumes that biological factors, such as abnormal brain functioning or chemistry, are at the root of mental illness. As we saw in the previous chapter on psychological disorders, both assumptions are supported by substantial research. Many people receive therapy that combines both psychological and biomedical approaches.

Who Is Qualified to Give Therapy?

Trained professionals administer psychotherapy and biomedical therapy. A variety of educational and experiential backgrounds characterize psychotherapists (● TABLE 15.1). These include clinical psychologists, psychoanalysts, licensed counselors or social workers, and marital or family therapists. Many of these professionals were highlighted when we discussed careers in psychology in Chapter 1. A master's degree is the minimum educational requirement for any of these professions, and some require doctorate-level degrees. Many therapists receive training in specialty areas or in specific forms of psychotherapy. For example, a psychoanalyst is trained in Freud's methods of treatment. Therapists' backgrounds often include internships in which they have been supervised in administering treatment. In addition, most states require licensing or certification, or both, of mental health professionals.

LEARNING OBJECTIVE

What Should You Know?
● Identify when a person should consider seeking therapy, who is qualified to give therapy, and the ethical standards that psychotherapists must follow.

psychotherapy the use of psychological principles and techniques to treat mental health disorders

biomedical therapy the use of medications or other medical interventions to treat mental health disorders

TABLE 15.1

● Types of Mental Health Professionals

PROFESSION	EDUCATION	TRAINING
Clinical Psychologist	• College degree • Graduate school in clinical psychology to earn a doctorate (PhD or PsyD; requires 5–8 years after college degree)	Supervised research and/or training in psychotherapy techniques, psychological testing, and the diagnosis of psychological disorders
Counseling Psychologist	• College degree • Graduate school in counseling psychology or education to earn a doctorate (PhD or EdD; requires 4–6 years after college degree)	Supervised training in assessment, counseling, and therapy techniques
Licensed Professional Counselor	• College degree • Graduate school to earn a master's degree in counseling (requires 3–5 years after college degree)	Supervised training in assessment, counseling, and therapy techniques
Licensed Social Worker	• College degree • Graduate school in social work to receive a master's degree (MSW; requires 3–5 years after college degree)	Supervised training in a social service agency or a mental health center; may or may not include training in psychotherapy
Couple or Family Therapist	• College degree • Graduate school to receive a master's degree in counseling, psychology, or social work (requires 3–5 years after college degree)	Supervised training in family and couple therapy; may also include training in individual psychotherapy methods
Psychiatrist	• College degree • Medical school to receive a medical degree (MD or DO) and then specialize in psychiatry (requires 5–10 years after college degree)	Training in the diagnosis and prevention of mental health disorders with a focus on psychopharmacology; may include training in psychotherapy methods

In contrast, only licensed psychiatrists or other medical doctors can legally administer biomedical therapies. A degree in psychiatry requires completion of medical school before specializing in psychiatry. For the most part, a psychiatrist is the only mental health professional who can prescribe medication. However, the right of clinical psychologists to administer medications is currently the subject of a hot debate. For example, the state of New Mexico passed legislation allowing prescription privileges for clinical psychologists who have completed additional training.

Ethical Standards for Psychotherapists

Are there any rules that mental health professionals must follow when administering therapy? Yes. In addition to being adequately trained and educated, mental health professionals are required to behave ethically and according to certain professional standards when conducting treatment. These are not legal statutes but, rather, standards established by the American Psychological Association (APA, 2002) indicating how psychotherapists should behave toward their clients. Violations of these standards should be reported to professional review boards that oversee the licensing of psychotherapists. Four essential ethical principles are *competent treatment*, *informed consent*, *confidentiality*, and *appropriate interactions*.

Competent Treatment and Informed Consent

The primary responsibility of the clinician toward a client is to provide *appropriate and adequate treatment*. Such a guideline prevents clinicians from merely warehousing clients in a treatment center, a practice that was common in previous decades and centuries. When providing treatment, psychotherapists must get *informed consent* from their clients. This guideline involves fully informing clients of the nature of treatment and the details of their participation, including any potential side effects or consequences of treatment. These requirements are especially critical if any experimental types of treatment will be used.

Confidentiality

Psychotherapists must respect the *confidentiality* of their communications with clients. They do not repeat to family members or friends any client discussions that occur within the context of therapy. Consultations with other professionals are permitted only when the client has agreed. Using client stories or experiences in a published work is not permitted without the express permission of the client. This requirement ensures trust within the therapist–client relationship.

However, there are exceptions to this guideline. One exception occurs when the therapist believes that the client should be committed to a treatment facility. In this circumstance, the therapist will have to break confidentiality to convince a court that the client is a danger to him- or herself or to others. Another exception to maintaining confidentiality occurs when others might be in danger. For example, if during therapy a client expresses violent intent toward another person, therapists are legally required to inform the potential victim of this potential harm. In addition, if a therapist suspects child abuse, partner abuse, or elder abuse, he or she is legally required to report such cases to the appropriate authorities.

Appropriate Interactions

Therapists must *interact appropriately* with clients for successful therapy to occur. For example, psychotherapists are forbidden from becoming sexually or romantically involved with any client and are not to socialize with their clients either. Psychotherapists do not drink alcohol with their clients or engage in intimate demonstrations of affection such as an arm around the waist. The behavior of Emily's first therapist in the hospital was inappropriate and therefore unethical. Psychotherapists are not to go into business with clients or establish any other form of social relationship that would impede the course of therapy. Unfortunately, when therapists are depicted in movies and on television, they often do not maintain these ethical standards. Such media portrayals confuse the public as to the appropriate behavior of therapists.

When Does One Need to Consider Psychotherapy?

Why do people want psychotherapy? People seek psychotherapy for a variety of reasons. Many come to therapy because they are in distress from one of the many psychological disorders discussed in the previous chapter. Their behavior is maladaptive, or they are experiencing difficulty in functioning in everyday life. They may be dealing with depression, extreme anxiety, or schizophrenia. Others who seek treatment have a history of mental illness and exhibit significant symptoms of a disorder. Some people are legally mandated to receive therapy by the court system. People with severe mental illness are at an economic disadvantage because they are more likely to be uninsured, so many do not receive adequate mental health care (McAlpine & Mechanic, 2000).

You do not have to be diagnosed with a psychological disorder in order to benefit from psychotherapy. Millions of people seek professional help to cope with other life problems. For example, couples and families in conflict may consider counseling to deal with their troubled relationships. People who have experienced major life transitions such as divorce, unemployment, retirement, or the death of a loved one may seek therapy to help them adjust to these changes. People are more likely to receive therapy if they have medical insurance and are educated. Females are also more likely than males to seek therapy (Olfson & Pincus, 1996; Roy-Byrne et al., 2009; see ● FIGURE 15.1).

When should therapy be considered? Consider therapy if you feel helpless, sad, blue, or anxious for a prolonged period or if such feelings do not improve despite several efforts to change them. You also may want to consider therapy if you are having difficulty carrying out your everyday activities. Therapy may also be useful if you want to make decisions differently, improve the functioning of important relationships, or change your life to feel more satisfied.

How do you find a therapist? Talk to family and friends for recommendations, consult your local or state psychological association, or inquire at your community mental health center. Your church, temple, mosque, physician, or local college may also be useful resources for finding a therapist. Given the hundreds of psychotherapy approaches, which one should you choose? The next five sections of this chapter describe the main psychotherapy approaches. After reading about them, you may find that you are more comfortable with the philosophy, goals, and techniques of some over others. This information will assist you in understanding the nature of therapy, and in choosing a therapist if the need ever arises.

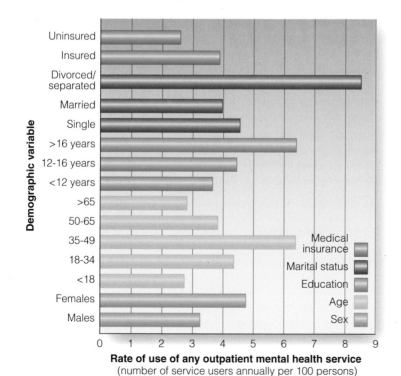

Rate of use of any outpatient mental health service
(number of service users annually per 100 persons)

FIGURE 15.1

● **Who Uses Therapy?** People are more likely to enter therapy if they have medical insurance and are educated. Therapy is also more likely to be used by people who are divorced or separated, people between the ages of 35 and 49, and females. *Source: Olfson & Pincus, 1996.*

Let's
REVIEW

In this section, we detailed who is qualified to give therapy, the ethical standards that psychotherapists must follow when giving therapy, and when one should consider psychotherapy. As a quick check of your understanding, try answering the following questions at increasing levels of difficulty.

1. Psychotherapy should be considered when _____.

    a. you get in trouble with your boss

    b. you are having difficulty functioning in some aspect of your life

    c. you have physical problems

    d. all of the above

2. Which of the following professionals is most likely to administer medication as a form of therapy?

    a. clinical psychologist   c. biological psychologist

    b. social worker   d. psychiatrist

3. Michael is seeing a social worker to help him with his interpersonal problems. Michael is undergoing _____.

    a. psychiatric counseling   c. psychotherapy

    b. medical treatment   d. biomedical therapy

ANSWERS 1. b; 2. d; 3. c

LEARNING OBJECTIVE

What Should You Know?

• Describe the aim of psychoanalytic therapies, and distinguish between traditional and modern psychoanalysis.

WHAT IS PSYCHOANALYSIS?
UNCOVERING UNCONSCIOUS CONFLICTS

As we have seen from previous chapters, Sigmund Freud originally developed the psychoanalytic approach based on his ideas about different levels of consciousness and personality formation. Recall that Freud theorized that each of us has an unconscious level that contains desires, urges, thoughts, and memories of which we are unaware or that have been repressed or hidden. These unconscious conflicts psychologically threaten the functioning of the ego by causing us distress and anxiety. Over the years, we continue to defend our ego by erecting more barriers to keep these conflicts hidden.

Freud assumed that symptoms of psychological disorders stem from these unresolved unconscious issues. Consequently, the goal of psychoanalytic therapies is to change maladaptive behavior by uncovering unconscious conflicts so that clients can gain *insight* into the real source of their problems (Wolitzky, 1995). Freud named this approach **psychoanalysis**. Professionals who administer this type of therapy are called *psychoanalysts*. Here we will describe two forms of psychoanalysis: *traditional psychoanalysis* and the more *modern psychodynamic approach*.

Traditional Psychoanalysis

What do psychoanalysts do? In traditional psychoanalysis as developed by Freud, the client lies down on a couch and talks about his or her concerns. It is the psychoanalyst's job to listen carefully and attentively to the client and discover what unconscious conflicts, themes, or concerns may be affecting the person. The first two therapists that Emily went to adopted this approach. Uncovering unconscious conflicts is not an easy task. Therefore, the psychoanalyst uses several methods to help clients gain insight and uncover critical issues from their pasts (Freud, 1949). These methods include *free association, dream analysis, interpretation, resistance,* and *transference*.

psychoanalysis a method of therapy formulated by Freud that focuses on uncovering unconscious conflicts that drive maladaptive behavior

Free association involves talking freely about a subject without censoring any thoughts. The client is fully awake and is asked to talk about a specific topic. The client says whatever comes to mind. The psychoanalyst makes very few comments during free association, instead focusing on important themes or issues that may be revealed.

Dream analysis is a tool that some psychoanalysts use to reveal unconscious conflicts (Pesant & Zadra, 2004). Dreams do not directly represent unconscious conflicts; rather, they are comprised of symbols that reflect these underlying unconscious impulses (see Chapter 4). It is the psychoanalyst's job to decipher the true meaning, or *latent content*, of these dreams and thereby reveal important unconscious issues. Recall that one of Emily's therapists was very interested in the content of her dreams and would attempt to find the themes embedded within them.

Free association and dream content provide the psychoanalyst with information on the unconscious workings of the client's mind. The psychoanalyst can then make interpretations to the client. **Interpretations** are the psychoanalyst's views on the themes and issues that may be influencing the client's behavior. These interpretations may help the client gain insight into his or her problems. However, if the client is not psychologically ready to deal with these issues, he or she may resist these interpretations.

Resistance occurs when a client behaves in such a way as to deny or avoid certain topics or issues. A client may resist a psychoanalyst's interpretation because it is too close to the truth and therefore creates anxiety. Clients may miss appointments or arrive late as a way of resisting the revealing nature of the therapy session. Clients may laugh or joke about topics that are actually quite painful for them. These resistant behaviors provide the psychoanalyst an additional clue to the unconscious conflicts affecting the client.

The process of **transference** also provides a clue to a client's unconscious conflicts. Freud (1949) believed that at some point during therapy, a client would unconsciously react to the therapist as if the therapist were his or her parent, friend, sibling, or romantic partner. Freud termed this unconscious reaction *transference* because the client was unknowingly transferring feelings and emotions toward a loved one onto the therapist. The psychoanalyst can explore such instances of transference to reveal how the dynamics of clients' relationships may be influencing their behavior.

Traditional psychoanalysis was a dominant treatment approach through the 1950s. However, uncovering unconscious conflicts often took years and called for as many as five sessions per week. This long-term nature of traditional psychoanalysis made it increasingly impractical and expensive for the average person and for the growing involvement of the health insurance industry. The development of other psychotherapies as well as the advent of drug therapy (discussed later) also led to a decrease in the popularity of traditional psychoanalysis (Henry et al., 1994). Hence, psychoanalysis was forced to move in a new direction.

Modern Psychoanalysis

Modern psychoanalysis, often referred to as **psychodynamic therapy**, or *short-term dynamic therapy*, is evident in many different forms. Such therapies are consistent with the views of Freud and the psychoanalytic approach. They continue to rely on the therapist's interpretations of the client's feelings and behavior and on identifying instances of transference and resistance. However, modern psychoanalysis tends to focus less on the client's past. Current problems and the nature of interpersonal relationships are seen as more important in improving the client's behavior. The therapist also plays a more direct role, rapidly interviewing and questioning the client to uncover unconscious issues and themes in a shorter time. Then the therapist and client agree to focus on a limited set of problems that are seen as causing the client the most trouble. Modern psychoanalysis tends to be more short term,

In psychoanalysis, the patient lies down on a couch away from the therapist so that the patient may freely associate and express whatever comes to mind.

© Jose Luis Pelaez, Inc./Corbis

free association a technique in psychoanalysis in which the client says whatever comes to mind

dream analysis a technique in psychoanalysis in which the therapist examines the hidden symbols in a client's dreams

interpretation the psychoanalyst's view on the themes and issues that may be influencing the client's behavior

resistance a process in psychoanalysis whereby the client behaves in such a way as to deny or avoid sensitive issues

transference a process in psychoanalysis in which the client unconsciously reacts to the therapist as if the therapist were a parent, friend, sibling, or lover

psychodynamic therapy modern psychoanalysis delivered in a shorter time that focuses less on the client's past and more on current problems and the nature of interpersonal relationships

lasting no more than a few months, and appears to be effective in improving clients' symptoms (Blagys & Hilsenroth, 2000; Blatt & Shahar, 2004; Cortina, 2010; Crits-Christoph, 1992; Leichsenring & Leibing, 2007; S. Reynolds et al., 1996; Schottenbauer et al., 2008).

Let's REVIEW

In this section, we detailed the aim of psychoanalytic therapies and described traditional and modern psychoanalysis. As a quick check of your understanding, try answering the following questions at increasing levels of difficulty.

1. The goal of psychoanalysis is to change behavior by _____.

   a. uncovering unconscious conflicts so that the client can gain insight into the source of his or her problems
   b. uncovering negative cognitive patterns that impede the client's ability to function
   c. examining environmental conditions and how they influence the client's responses
   d. providing the client with unconditional support and love so that he or she makes adaptive and healthy behavioral choices

2. Modern psychoanalysis differs from traditional psychoanalysis in that _____.

   a. it is shorter in duration
   b. it is focused less on the client's past and more on present relationships and issues
   c. the therapist is more direct
   d. all of the above

3. Song often arrives late for her psychoanalysis appointment and sometimes forgets her appointments altogether. Her psychoanalyst might interpret Song's behavior as a sign of _____.

   a. transference   c. resistance
   b. interpretation   d. free association

ANSWERS 1. a; 2. d; 3. c

What Should You Know?
● Describe humanistic therapy approaches.

WHAT IS HUMANISTIC THERAPY? EMPATHIZING TO EMPOWER

As we have just seen, problems with psychoanalysis forced it to move in a new direction that resulted in briefer psychodynamic therapies that were still connected to the ideas of Freud. However, some psychoanalysts departed radically from these views and developed different forms of therapy. One example is humanistic therapy.

The *humanistic approach* focuses less on unconscious forces and more on the conscious actions we take in controlling our behavior. Even though Dr. Farber was a trained psychoanalyst, his belief in Emily's value and his emphasis on her free will exemplify this humanistic perspective. In Emily's words:

> Dr. Farber was both far humbler than his more conventional colleagues and far bolder. He was humbler because he approached his patients as a whole human being. . . . He was bolder because . . . he committed himself to a risky, open-ended friendship and to all the claims of responsibility that friendship entails. (Gordon, 2000, p. 125)

Humanists believe that behavior is driven not by unconscious impulses but by how we interpret the world and our awareness of our feelings. The only way to understand a person's behavior, therefore, is to connect with and understand the person's worldview. Humanism further assumes that people will naturally strive toward personal growth and achievement of their full potential when raised in a positive and accepting environment. When a person holds distorted perceptions or lacks self-awareness, psychological problems arise, preventing the person from becoming self-actualized. Yet people are capable of healing themselves, if only the right environment is provided. The therapist's role is to create this safe environment for self-exploration and facilitate the journey toward self-fulfillment (L. S. Greenberg & Rice, 1997). One of the most influential and best known of the humanistic therapies is *client-centered therapy*.

Client-Centered Therapy

Disillusioned with the goals, methods, and assumptions of psychoanalysis, Carl Rogers (1902–1987) developed a different therapy approach that exemplifies the humanistic perspective. Whereas Freud saw the analyst as all-knowing and responsible for client change, Rogers believed that the therapist should serve more as a facilitator or coach to help move the client in the direction of change. Such a viewpoint resulted in **client-centered therapy**, or *person-centered therapy*. As the names imply, in client-centered therapy, the focus and direction of therapy comes from the person, or client. The client decides what to talk about, without interpretation or judgment from the therapist.

What does a client-centered therapist do? According to Rogers (1951, 1980, 1986), the therapist creates a positive and accepting environment to facilitate self-awareness and personal growth by providing three key characteristics: *empathy*, *genuineness*, and *unconditional positive regard*.

In humanistic therapy, therapist and client sit face-to-face as they work together in solving the client's problems.

Empathy: Understanding the Client

Are you a good listener? Do friends and family frequently confide in you? If so, then maybe you possess empathy. According to Rogers, **empathy** is the ability to understand a client's feelings and thoughts without being judgmental. The therapist does not express disapproval toward the client but rather indicates understanding of the client's feelings. Conveying empathy involves actively listening to the client—making eye contact, nodding as the client speaks, and assuming an interested and attentive pose. Empathy also involves *reflection*. The therapist restates, repeats, or summarizes the thoughts and feelings that he or she hears the client express. Reflected statements communicate to the client the active attention of the therapist and mirror the client's perceptions and views of reality. Consider this example of empathy and reflection from Irvin Yalom's work, *Love's Executioner and Other Tales of Psychotherapy* (1989):

> Client: I believe he is intentionally trying to drive me to suicide. Does that sound like a crazy thought?
>
> Therapist: I don't know if it's crazy, but it sounds like a desperate and terribly painful thought. (p. 29)

Notice in this example that the therapist does not judge the client's thoughts as crazy and reflects the emotions underlying the statement of suicide. Ideally, empathy and reflection will help clients see themselves and their problems more clearly, promoting a realistic self-image and greater self-acceptance.

Genuineness: Sharing Thoughts, Feelings, and Experiences

A second key therapist quality in client-centered therapy is genuineness. **Genuineness** is the ability to openly share one's thoughts and feelings with others. The therapist expresses his or her true feelings and thoughts to the client and does not hide behind the mask of being the "professional," "doctor," or authority figure. The therapist self-discloses a fair amount to the client, which allows the client to see the therapist as a real, living person. Such disclosure also creates an open environment that promotes trust and an honest expression of thoughts and feelings. Rogers believed that such an environment would model to the client how relationships can be built on a foundation of trust and honesty. Emily learned such a lesson from Dr. Farber. His genuineness made her believe he truly cared about her well-being.

client-centered therapy a humanistic psychotherapy approach formulated by Carl Rogers that emphasizes the use of empathy, genuineness, and unconditional positive regard to help the client reach his or her potential

empathy the ability of a therapist to understand a client's feelings and thoughts without being judgmental

genuineness the ability of a therapist to openly share his or her thoughts and feelings with a client

Unconditional Positive Regard: Valuing the Client

The third key quality in client-centered therapy, unconditional positive regard, was introduced in the chapter on personality (Chapter 13). Recall that Rogers defined **unconditional positive regard** as the ability to accept and value a person for who he or she is, regardless of his or her faults or problems. Rogers believed that receiving unconditional positive regard in one's childhood is a key factor in healthy personality adjustment. A therapist who offers unconditional positive regard to a client does not indicate shock, dismay, or disapproval to any client statements. Instead, the therapist communicates caring and respect toward the client regardless of what the client says. This does not mean that the therapist has to personally *agree* with everything the client states. Rather, the therapist's job is to reflect the client's feelings and thoughts in order to further the client's self-knowledge and enable the client to solve problems in his or her own way. Unconditional positive regard enables the client to believe that he or she has value and is competent at making decisions. Such attitudes foster self-confidence and self-acceptance that lead to healthier growth choices.

For Rogers, a therapist who demonstrates all three qualities—empathy, genuineness, and unconditional positive regard—establishes a positive and nurturing environment. A person feels accepted, understood, and valued. These feelings help the client self-explore a more realistic self-image and perception of the world. This in turn removes the obstacles to personal growth so that self-actualization can be realized.

Do these therapist qualities actually have an effect on changing people's behavior? Each quality by itself does not appear to help clients change (Beutler, Machado, & Neufeldt, 1994). Yet when used together, they lead to more promising results, emphasizing the importance of a positive client–therapist relationship. Compared to no-treatment control groups, people in client-centered therapy do change their behavior (L. S. Greenberg & Rice, 1997; C. E. Hill & Nakayama, 2000). Compared to more structured therapy approaches, client-centered therapy is equally effective (L. S. Greenberg, Elliot, & Lietaer, 1994; Stiles et al., 2008; Stiles et al., 2006). However, it may not be appropriate for people who are seriously distressed (Bohart, 1990).

unconditional positive regard the ability to accept and value a person for who he or she is, regardless of his or her faults or problems

Let's REVIEW

In this section, we described humanistic approaches to therapy. As a quick check of your understanding, try answering the following questions at increasing levels of difficulty.

1. The goal of humanistic therapy is to change behavior by _____.

    a. uncovering unconscious conflicts so that the client can gain insight into the source of his or her problems
    b. uncovering negative cognitive patterns that impede the client's ability to function
    c. examining environmental conditions and how they influence the client's responses
    d. providing the client with a safe environment for self-exploration and facilitating the journey toward self-fulfillment

2. Which of the following is *not* one of the elements used in client-centered therapy to help the client achieve self-fulfillment?

    a. genuineness   c. unconditional positive regard
    b. free association   d. empathy

3. Marcos is receiving client-centered therapy. His therapist openly shares his thoughts and feelings with Marcos, relating his own experiences that are similar to those of Marcos. Marcos' therapist is exhibiting which quality of client-centered therapy?

    a. genuineness   c. unconditional positive regard
    b. reflection   d. empathy

What Should You Know?
● Describe the aim of behavior therapy approaches, and explain how they operate through classical or operant conditioning processes.

WHAT IS BEHAVIOR THERAPY? LEARNING HEALTHIER BEHAVIORS

Psychoanalytic and humanistic therapies focus on internal reflection by the client. Self-understanding through self-exploration is vital for psychological health. In contrast, **behavior therapy** focuses directly on changing current problem behaviors rather than delving into the client's past.

What do behavior therapists do? Behavior therapies, also called *behavior modification*, consist of techniques and methods that use learning principles to change problem behavior. Chapter 5 described the learning processes of classical conditioning and operant conditioning. The behavioral perspective relies on these principles to modify behavior. Recall that the *behavioral perspective* assumes that behavior is a result of environmental variables such as stimuli and consequences in the environment. It further assumes that people learn maladaptive behavior in the same way that they learn adaptive behavior. So, changing behavior involves changing the environmental circumstances that seem to elicit negative behavior. Learning principles that focus on *extinction* are used to stop disruptive behaviors. Similarly, learning principles that focus on *shaping* or acquiring behaviors are used to replace undesirable behaviors with more adaptive ones.

Behavior therapy can take many forms. Here we discuss two broad categories of behavior therapy: *classical conditioning techniques* and *operant conditioning techniques*.

Classical Conditioning Techniques

Some behavior therapies rely on the principles of classical conditioning outlined in Chapter 5. Briefly, classical conditioning occurs when stimuli in the environment become associated so that both produce the same response. For example, as a child, one of the authors was bitten by a dog twice within a 2-year period. In both instances, the dog was a German shepherd. Following those incidents, she developed an intense fear of large dogs. Her dog-biting experiences became associated with pain, so that now she feared pain from all large dogs and routinely avoided them. Her fear was a learned behavior. Behavior therapy would focus on having her unlearn her response to dogs. Typically this is achieved through *counterconditioning*. Counterconditioning involves replacing an undesirable behavior (such as fear) with a positive and pleasurable one (Chapter 5). An early example of counterconditioning was an experiment by Mary Cover Jones (1924) in which she treated a 3-year-old's fear of rabbits. The child, Peter, sat at a distance from a caged rabbit while eating one of his favorite foods. The cage was gradually moved closer to Peter until he was able to play with the rabbit and not experience any fear. Jones had countered Peter's negative emotional reaction of fear with a positive one of pleasure from the food. Two behavior therapy counterconditioning techniques are *systematic desensitization* and *aversion therapy*.

Systematic Desensitization: Relax and Have No Fear

One effective tool for treating phobias and anxiety is systematic desensitization (Wolpe, 1958). **Systematic desensitization** involves replacing a fear or anxiety response with an incompatible response of relaxation. Anxiety and relaxation are *competing responses*. You cannot feel both at the same time; you can only feel one or the other. So the aim of systematic desensitization is to have a client learn how to relax and then slowly and systematically introduce the feared object, situation, or thought while the client maintains this state of relaxation.

Systematic desensitization is accomplished in three basic steps. First, the client is trained in *progressive muscle relaxation*. This method involves alternately tensing and relaxing different muscle groups, beginning with the head and working down to the toes, so that the client learns to distinguish when muscles are tense and when they are relaxed.

behavior therapy therapy that applies the principles of classical and operant conditioning to help people change maladaptive behaviors

systematic desensitization a behavior therapy technique in which a client is desensitized to a fear in a gradual, step-by-step process

Behavior therapy helps people unlearn negative or distressful responses like a fear of large dogs.

TRY THIS DEMONSTRATION

Try systematic relaxation training on your own. Close your eyes and take deep breaths for a minute. Then tighten your jaw muscles and clench your teeth. Hold the tension for a few moments and then relax and take several deep breaths. Do the same for your eyes, forehead, neck, and shoulders, alternating between tensing your muscles and then relaxing them. You will be pleasantly surprised by how a few minutes of this procedure can reduce tension.

anxiety hierarchy outlines, according to the degree of fear, the threatening images elicited by a feared object or situation; the outline starts with the least frightening images and progresses to the most distressing

FIGURE 15.2

● **Sample Anxiety Hierarchy** An anxiety hierarchy like the one shown here is used during systematic desensitization. This hierarchy was developed for a woman who had a fear of heights. *From K. E. Rudestam, Methods of Self Change: An ABC Primer, © 1980 Wadsworth. Reprinted with permission of the author.*

Once the client has learned progressive relaxation, in the second step the client and therapist develop an anxiety hierarchy. An **anxiety hierarchy** (● FIGURE 15.2) outlines, according to the degree of fear, the threatening images elicited when the client is faced with the feared object or situation. The hierarchy starts with the least frightening images and progresses to the most distressing.

In the third step, progressive relaxation and the anxiety hierarchy are combined. Relaxation is paired with each item in the hierarchy. As the client becomes able to imagine a feared situation and remain relaxed, the next item in the hierarchy is addressed. Over several therapy sessions, this systematic process continues until the client has become desensitized to all items in the hierarchy.

You may be skeptical at this point, unconvinced that thinking about a feared stimulus is similar to actually encountering the object or situation. This skepticism is somewhat warranted, so once the client has mastered the mental images, behavior therapists can extend systematic desensitization to a simulated or actual environment. For many fears, this is when systematic desensitization is most effective (Antony & Barlow, 2002; Menzies & Clark, 1993). For example, flight simulators can be used to help desensitize people to a fear of flying. Combining systematic desensitization with the actual situation, called *in vivo exposure*, is also a very effective tool in treating a variety of anxiety disorders (Choy, Fyer, & Lipsitz, 2007; Follette & Hayes, 2000; Gould et al., 1997).

An Anxiety Hierarchy for Systematic Desensitization	
Degree of fear	
5	I'm standing on the balcony of the top floor of an apartment tower.
10	I'm standing on a stepladder in the kitchen to change a light bulb.
15	I'm walking on a ridge. The edge is hidden by shrubs and treetops.
20	I'm sitting on the slope of a mountain, looking out over the horizon.
25	I'm crossing a bridge 6 feet above a creek. The bridge consists of an 18-inch-wide board with a handrail on one side.
30	I'm riding a ski lift 8 feet above the ground.
35	I'm crossing a shallow, wide creek on an 18-inch-wide board, 3 feet above water level.
40	I'm climbing a ladder outside the house to reach a second-story window.
45	I'm pulling myself up a 30-degree wet, slippery slope on a steel cable.
50	I'm scrambling up a rock, 8 feet high.
55	I'm walking 10 feet on a resilient, 18-inch-wide board which spans an 8-foot-deep gulch.
60	I'm walking on a wide plateau, 2 feet from the edge of a cliff.
65	I'm skiing an intermediate hill. The snow is packed.
70	I'm walking over a railway trestle.
75	I'm walking on the side of an embankment. The path slopes to the outside.
80	I'm riding a chair lift 15 feet above the ground.
85	I'm walking up a long, steep slope.
90	I'm walking up (or down) a 15-degree slope on a 3-foot-wide trail. On one side of the trail the terrain drops down sharply; on the other side is a steep upward slope.
95	I'm walking on a 3-foot-wide ridge. The slopes on both sides are long and more than 25 degrees steep.
100	I'm walking on a 3-foot-wide ridge. The trail slopes on one side. The drop on either side of the trail is more than 25 degrees.

Virtual reality computer technology also can be used to simulate a feared situation. Virtual reality bridges the gap between imagining feared stimuli in a therapist's office and in vivo exposure in the field by simulating a feared situation. The client wears a head-mounted display with small video monitors and stereo earphones that integrate visual and auditory cues to immerse the client in a computer-generated virtual environment. For example, a person with a fear of flying may be exposed to stimuli that simulate sitting in a plane and hearing the plane's engines revving for takeoff. A person with a fear of public speaking may experience simulation of standing at a podium. The therapist can control the images the client receives while monitoring heart rate, respiration, and skin temperature to assess the client's fear responses during the session (Bender, 2004).

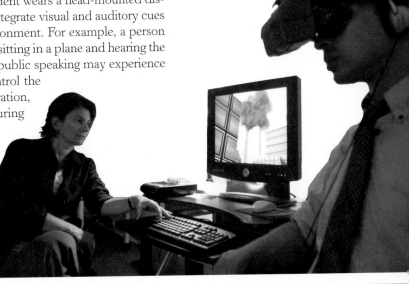

Virtual reality technology provides an effective treatment for people who have a fear of heights and of flying (Krijn et al., 2004; B. O. Rothbaum et al., 1995; B. O. Rothbaum et al., 1996; Wiederhold et al., 2002). It also has had some success in treating driving phobia (J. Wald & Taylor, 2003), social phobia (Klinger et al., 2005), fear of public speaking (P. L. Anderson et al., 2005; S. R. Harris, Kemmerling, & North, 2002), panic disorders (Botella et al., 2004; de Carvalho, Freire, & Nardi, 2010), and posttraumatic stress disorder (J. G. Beck et al., 2007; Difede & Hoffman, 2002; McLay et al., 2010). However, to date, the results of such research are not conclusive.

Virtual reality exposure therapy allows clients to experience their fears in a simulated, nonthreatening environment.

Aversion Therapy: We Won't Do Something If We Dislike It

Do you bite your nails? As a child, did you suck your thumb? Did loved ones try to get you to stop such behaviors? Many parents put a foul-tasting or spicy liquid such as Tabasco sauce on their child's nails or thumb to stop nail-biting or thumb-sucking. These parents unknowingly are performing *aversion therapy*, another example of a behavior therapy that relies on counterconditioning principles. **Aversion therapy** involves pairing an unpleasant stimulus (foul or spicy taste) with a specific undesirable behavior such as biting one's fingernails. Ideally, the aversive stimulus becomes associated with the undesirable response so that the person is less likely to engage in the response again.

Aversive conditioning occurs frequently in everyday life. Food poisoning is a prime example. If a particular food has ever made you sick, normally it will be months or even years before you touch that food again. The food (stimulus) becomes associated with being sick (response) so that you avoid it at all costs. Therapists use this knowledge to treat a variety of undesirable habits and behaviors. For example, an aversion therapy method for treating alcoholism involves taking a drug called Antabuse (D. S. Cannon & Baker, 1981). Antabuse interacts with alcohol, causing nausea and vomiting. If a person with alcohol dependence drinks while using Antabuse, it makes him or her ill. The unwanted stimulus (alcohol) becomes associated with the response of feeling ill and nauseated. The person with alcoholism learns to avoid alcohol in order to avoid the associated unpleasant response. Unfortunately, the person with alcohol dependence can also simply avoid taking the medication, thereby nullifying the effectiveness of the procedure. In clinical trials, Antabuse has demonstrated mixed results in helping people abstain from alcohol use. Yet, when Antabuse is given under supervision and in conjunction with a drug that specifically reduces alcohol cravings, its effectiveness is improved (Barth & Malcolm, 2010; B. A. Johnson, 2008; Krampe & Ehrenreich, 2010; Suh et al., 2006). Aversion therapy also has been effective in eliminating a variety of other behaviors, including compulsive hair pulling, gambling, smoking (tobacco, marijuana, or crack cocaine), and maladaptive sexual behaviors such as pedophilia (child molestation) and fetishism (sexual arousal to objects) (Emmelkamp, 1994; Laws, 2001).

At this point, you may be disturbed by the knowledge that therapists use such unpleasant procedures in treatment. Keep in mind, though, that therapists are ethically bound to get informed consent from clients. Clients are informed of the procedure and must agree before

aversion therapy a type of therapy that uses classical conditioning to condition people to avoid certain stimuli

such a method can be used. An alternative form of aversion therapy is called **covert sensitization therapy**. In this procedure, graphic imagery is used to create unpleasant associations with specific stimuli. For example, a person who smokes cigarettes may have to repeatedly imagine black and diseased lungs when faced with a cigarette as a stimulus.

Operant Conditioning Techniques

Whereas the counterconditioning techniques of systematic desensitization and aversion therapy rely on classical conditioning principles, some behavior therapies rely on the principles of operant conditioning outlined in Chapter 5. Briefly, operant conditioning focuses on the consequences of a behavior. It assumes that reinforced behavior will be maintained and that punished behavior will be extinguished. For instance, in the previous example in which your author developed a fear of large dogs, recall that following the dog-biting episodes she responded by avoiding large dogs. The consequence of this response was reinforcing—it reduced her fear. She learned that the next time she encountered a large dog, avoiding it would quickly rid her of any anxiety. This example illustrates how consequences can maintain problem behaviors.

Changing undesirable behavior, therefore, involves changing the consequences of a behavior. These changes can be accomplished in a variety of ways (Thorpe & Olson, 1997):

1. *Positive reinforcement.* Positive reinforcement is used to encourage or maintain a behavior. For example, every time a child complies with a parental request, verbal praise follows. After the child's compliance increases, verbal praise need not occur every single time.
2. *Nonreinforcement and extinction.* To discourage unwanted behavior, any reinforcers of the behavior are removed. For instance, to discourage a child from throwing tantrums at home, the child's parents ignore the behavior so that no attention (even negative attention, such as a reprimand) reinforces the behavior. If a reinforcer does not follow a behavior, the behavior will occur less frequently. Eventually the behavior will be eliminated or extinguished. However, keep in mind that often the unwanted behavior will increase before it goes away because a person is expecting the reinforcer. The child's tantrums will be longer or more frequent in an attempt to get a reaction from the parents. Misbehavior may also continue because all subtle forms of reinforcers have not been eliminated. For example, consider what happens when the same child acts up in school. Although the teacher may scold or reprimand the child, the child still receives a form of attention, and therefore the behavior may not subside. Even if the teacher ignores the child's misbehavior, classmates may reinforce the behavior by laughing and paying attention to him or her.
3. *Punishment.* Sometimes punishment is used to decrease undesirable behaviors. Recall that punishment occurs when an undesired behavior is immediately followed by a negative or aversive consequence such as loss of a privilege. But also remember the side effects of punishment. It can produce negative emotions, such as anger or fear, or negative behaviors, such as avoidance. For these reasons, punishment is used sparingly.
4. *Shaping.* Recall from Chapter 5 that shaping involves positively reinforcing each successive attempt at a behavior. It is used to teach a person new, desired behaviors. For example, shaping may be used to teach children with autism how to speak. If the child makes a "t" sound to say *toy*, this attempt is rewarded. Shaping has also been successfully used to teach people with intellectual disabilities self-help skills, such as washing their face or brushing their teeth.
5. *Token economy.* Recall from Chapter 5 that a **token economy** involves rewarding people with tokens, or symbolic rewards, for desired behavior. Because not everyone is influenced by the same reward, tokens—such as chips, points, or stars—are given each time a person engages in a desired behavior. These tokens can then be exchanged for a variety of reinforcers such as food, privileges, goods, phone time, and so on.

You may recall having had a treasure chest or goody box in elementary school. Students who had acquired a certain number of points or tokens could visit the prize box at the end of the week. Today, your consumer behavior may be unknowingly reinforced by a token economy. Many credit card companies offer points for purchases. These points can then be exchanged for a variety of merchandise. Airlines do the same thing with frequent flyer points. Their aim is to increase your consumption of their services.

covert sensitization therapy a milder form of aversion therapy in which graphic imagery is used to create unpleasant associations with specific stimuli

token economy a behavioral therapy technique in which people are rewarded with tokens for desired behavior; the tokens can then be exchanged for what is reinforcing to the individuals

The same principle can be used in hospitals, halfway houses, prisons, drug abuse treatment centers, and other institutional settings. People earn tokens for desired behavior and constructive activities, and then exchange them for passes, free time, meals, access to television, or private rooms. Recall that Emily's behavior in Riggs treatment center was monitored in this fashion. To receive privileges, she had to get her work jobs done and go to bed at the appropriate time. In some institutions, patients may lose or be charged tokens for undesired behavior such as fighting, noncompliance, or not completing their chores. A token economy can be a very effective tool for children with intellectual disabilities and autism, and for managing behavior in a group setting (C. D. Adams et al., 2002; Comaty, Stasio, & Advokat, 2001; Matson & Boisjoli, 2009; Morisse et al., 1996; Mottram & Berger-Gross, 2004; Petry et al., 2004; M. A. Sullivan & O'Leary, 1990).

Although the behavior therapies have been very successful in treating a variety of psychological and behavioral problems, particularly in children, they do not address the thoughts and perceptions that often accompany behavior. For this reason, behavioral strategies have been increasingly used in conjunction with cognitive therapy (K. G. Wilson, Hayes, & Gifford, 1997), our next topic of discussion.

Let's REVIEW

In this section, we described behavior therapy approaches and the ways in which classical and operant conditioning techniques are used to change behavior. For a quick check of your understanding, try answering the following questions at increasing levels of difficulty.

1. Behavior therapies change behavior by _____.

   a. uncovering unconscious conflicts so that the client can gain insight into the source of his or her problems

   b. uncovering negative cognitive patterns that impede the client's ability to function

   c. examining and then changing the environmental circumstances that seem to elicit negative behavior

   d. providing the client with a safe environment for self-exploration and facilitating the journey toward self-fulfillment

2. Celia goes to a therapist to try to reduce her fear of driving. The therapist teaches Celia how to relax and then has her imagine those aspects of driving that make her fearful while maintaining her relaxed mode. Celia is most likely undergoing _____.

   a. aversion therapy   c. systematic desensitization

   b. a token economy   d. client-centered therapy

3. Which of the following is *not* a therapy approach based on the principles of operant conditioning?

   a. a token economy   c. positive reinforcement

   b. shaping   d. aversion therapy

ANSWERS 1. c; 2. c; 3. d

LEARNING OBJECTIVE

What Should You Know?

● Describe the aim of cognitive therapy approaches, and distinguish between rational-emotive therapy and Beck's cognitive therapy.

WHAT IS COGNITIVE THERAPY? THINKING THROUGH PROBLEMS

What do cognitive therapists do? We saw in Chapter 14 that many psychological problems such as anxiety and depression may stem from negative and distorted thought patterns. *Cognitive therapies* focus on changing these maladaptive patterns of thinking and perceiving, and replacing them with more adaptive ways of interpreting events. Two of the most widely used cognitive therapies are Albert Ellis's *rational-emotive therapy* and Aaron Beck's *cognitive therapy*.

Courtesy of Ellis Institute

Albert Ellis developed rational-emotive therapy to deal with clients' faulty or irrational beliefs that lead to self-defeating behaviors such as anxiety, depression, or anger.

TABLE 15.2

● Examples of Irrational Assumptions

1. I must be loved by or approved of by everyone.
2. I must be competent and achieving in all things I do; otherwise I am worthless.
3. Some people are bad and should be severely blamed and punished for it. I should be extremely upset over the wrongdoings of others.
4. It is awful and upsetting when things are not the way I would like them to be.
5. Unhappiness is caused by external events, and I cannot control my bad feelings and emotional reactions.
6. If something unpleasant happens, I should dwell on it.
7. Avoiding difficulties, rather than facing them, will make you happy.
8. Always rely on someone who is stronger than you.
9. Your past will indefinitely affect your present life.
10. There is a perfect solution for every problem, and it is awful and upsetting if this solution is not found.

rational-emotive therapy a cognitive therapy approach created by Albert Ellis that focuses on changing the irrational beliefs that people hold that are believed to impede healthy psychological functioning

cognitive therapy a therapy created by Aaron Beck that focuses on uncovering negative automatic thought patterns that impede healthy psychological functioning

cognitive distortion distorted thinking patterns, such as overgeneralization or all-or-none thinking, that according to Aaron Beck lead to depression, anxiety, and low self-esteem

Ellis's Rational-Emotive Therapy

Developed by Albert Ellis (1973, 1995), **rational-emotive therapy** is based on the premise that many psychological problems stem from how people think about and interpret events in their lives. It is not the actual event that causes the emotional upset, but rather the person's *interpretation* of the event that results in emotional distress. Specifically, rational-emotive therapy identifies the client's faulty or irrational beliefs that lead to self-defeating behaviors, anxiety, depression, anger, or other psychological problems. Several studies support Ellis's notion that people who think more irrationally evidence more psychological distress (Nieuwenhuijsen et al., 2010; A. Solomon et al., 2003; Taghavi et al., 2006; Ziegler & Leslie, 2003; Ziegler & Smith, 2004).

Ellis identified common irrational beliefs (1991) that often impede people's functioning, as listed in ● TABLE 15.2. Identifying such irrational beliefs is the first step in rational-emotive therapy. For example, one client may have an excessive need for approval because she believes that she "must be loved by everyone." Another client may irrationally believe that there is a "right" solution for every problem and become frustrated or depressed because a problem recurs. Once these beliefs have been identified, the therapist challenges their validity. The therapist confronts and disputes these fallacies in a logical and persuasive manner, pushing the client to recognize that such beliefs are irrational and unhealthy. The therapist might make statements such as "What evidence do you have to support this belief?" or "In what other ways could this evidence be interpreted?" Additionally, the client may be asked "What is the worst thing that could happen?" and "If that happened, what could you do?" Asking such questions forces the client to consider alternative viewpoints, face his fears and anxieties, and explore possible problem-solving methods. After a client's irrational beliefs have been recognized and refuted, they can then be replaced with more realistic and rational beliefs. These beliefs may be reflected in such statements as "Not everyone will like me, but that is okay and not a measure of my worth" or "There are several ways to solve a problem, and if I fail I can try another approach."

Rational-emotive therapy is a very direct and confrontational approach. Admitting that our way of thinking is irrational and unhealthy and radically changing our interpretation of events in our lives is not an easy task. Yet despite these obstacles, rational-emotive therapy has generally been effective in treating depression, social phobias, and other anxiety disorders (David et al., 2008; Gould et al., 1997; Lewinsohn et al., 1990; L. A. Robinson, Berman, & Neimeyer, 1990; Sava et al., 2009).

Beck's Cognitive Therapy

A second illustration of focusing on thought patterns in therapy is Aaron Beck's **cognitive therapy**. Noticing that many of his clients who were depressed expressed a negative view of themselves and the world almost habitually, Beck turned his attention to the role cognitions play in emotional distress. He developed a cognitive therapy based on the principle that distorted thinking in the form of **cognitive distortions** and negative, automatic thought patterns lead to depression, anxiety, and low self-esteem (A. T. Beck et al., 1979). For example, do you ever make critical remarks to yourself such as "Oh, I am so stupid" or "I am such an idiot"? Such personal negative statements depress mood and lower self-esteem. Beck believed that such maladaptive patterns could be identified and changed, resulting in more adaptive behavior. ● TABLE 15.3 illustrates some of the more common cognitive distortions that Beck identified in people who are depressed.

Beck's cognitive therapy is not as confrontational in its approach as rational-emotive therapy. Rather, Beck (1991) saw the client and therapist as a collaborative team, working together to identify and evaluate the accuracy and biases of the client's thought patterns. At first, the therapist teaches the client how to recognize and keep track of her negative auto-

TABLE 15.3

● **Examples of Cognitive Distortions**

COGNITIVE ERROR	DESCRIPTION	EXAMPLE
All-or-nothing thinking	Seeing each event as completely good or bad, right or wrong, a success or a failure	"If I don't get this job, I am a failure."
Arbitrary inference	Concluding that something negative will happen or is happening even though there is no evidence to support it	"My neighbor did not say hello to me. She must be mad at me."
Disqualifying the positive	Rejecting positive experiences	"Anyone can paint. It's no big deal."
Emotional reasoning	Assuming that negative emotions are accurate without questioning them	"I feel fat, so I must be fat."
Labeling	Placing a negative, global label on a person or situation	"I can't do anything right, so why should I try?"
Magnification and minimization	Overestimating the importance of negative events and underestimating the impact of positive events	"In my job evaluation, my boss said I need to work on my time management skills. She only said I was a productive worker and good team manager to be nice."
Overgeneralization	Applying a negative conclusion of one event to other unrelated events and areas of one's life	"I messed up on my math test, so I won't do well in history or Spanish. I should drop out of school."
Personalization	Attributing negative events to oneself without reason	"My parents are in a bad mood because they have an idiot for a son."
Selective abstraction	Focusing on a single, irrelevant, negative aspect of a situation, while ignoring the more relevant and important aspects of the situation	"It doesn't matter that I got a raise and promotion. I have to go to work an hour earlier."

matic thoughts such as "I never do anything right" or "I always fail at whatever I do." The therapist and client then test the validity or accuracy of these thoughts. For example, a client may be asked to list all the tasks assigned to him in a week and then indicate whether each task was completed. The therapist hopes that such an exercise will not only point out the inaccuracy of the client's beliefs but also train him how to evaluate negative automatic thoughts in the future. We saw that as a part of therapy, Dr. Farber would often highlight Emily's negative thought patterns as a way of improving her self-image.

Cognitive therapy, like rational-emotive therapy, has been very effective in treating depression and anxiety disorders (David et al., 2008; Gibbons et al., 2010; Resick et al., 2002; Wampold et al., 2002). In some studies, it has been just as effective as drugs (Abramowitz, 1997; Gould et al., 1997; Sava et al., 2009). More importantly, clients who have adopted new and more adaptive patterns of thinking are less likely to become depressed in the future—a benefit that drugs cannot provide (G. A. Fava et al., 1996; Jarrett et al., 2001; Teasdale et al., 2001).

Currently, the elements of cognitive therapy are often combined with the techniques of behavioral therapy (discussed previously), called *cognitive-behavior therapy (CBT)*. CBT has been shown to be highly effective in treating anxiety and depression (T. B. Baker, McFall, & Shoham 2008; Hofmann & Smits, 2008; McEvoy & Nathan, 2007; P. J. Norton & Price, 2007) and a variety of other disorders, including eating disorders and substance abuse (T. B. Baker et al., 2008; Dobson, Backs-Dermott, & Dozois, 2000; Pike, Devlin, & Loeb, 2004; U. Schmidt et al., 2007).
● THE BIG PICTURE REVIEW of the psychotherapy approaches will help you contrast their goals and therapeutic techniques.

Courtesy of Beck Institute for Cognitive Therapy and Research

Aaron Beck developed cognitive therapy based on the principle that distorted thinking and negative, automatic thought patterns lead to depression, anxiety, and low self-esteem.

Psychotherapy Approaches

PSYCHOLOGICAL PERSPECTIVE	THERAPY APPROACHES	THERAPY GOALS	THERAPY TECHNIQUES
Psychoanalytic	Traditional psychoanalysis and modern psychodynamic therapy	Insights and resolution regarding unconscious conflicts	Free association, dream analysis, interpretation
Humanistic	Client-centered therapy	Acceptance of genuine self and personal growth	Genuineness, empathy, and unconditional positive regard
Behavioral/Learning	Behavior modification	Eliminate maladaptive behaviors and acquire adaptive behaviors	Systematic desensitization, aversion therapy, shaping, reinforcement, extinction, token economy
Cognitive	Rational-emotive therapy, cognitive therapy	Reduce negative thinking and irrational beliefs; develop more realistic thinking	Challenge irrational beliefs, record negative automatic thoughts

Let's REVIEW In this section, we detailed the aim of cognitive therapy approaches and described rational-emotive therapy and cognitive therapy. For a quick check of your understanding, try answering the following questions at increasing levels of difficulty.

1. The goal of cognitive therapy approaches is to change behavior by _____.

   a. uncovering unconscious conflicts so that the client can gain insight into the source of his or her problems
   b. uncovering negative cognitive patterns that impede the client's ability to function
   c. examining and then changing the environmental circumstances that seem to elicit negative behavior
   d. providing the client with a safe environment for self-exploration and facilitating the journey toward self-fulfillment

2. The cognitive therapies have been most effective in treating which type of disorders?

   a. schizophrenia   c. mood
   b. personality disorders   d. autism

3. Svetlana goes to a therapist who focuses on her negative automatic statements. Svetlana is most likely undergoing what type of therapy?

   a. rational-emotive therapy   c. systematic desensitization
   b. cognitive therapy   d. client-centered therapy

ANSWERS 1. b; 2. c; 3. b

LEARNING OBJECTIVE

What Should You Know?

• Describe the advantages and disadvantages of group therapy approaches.

WHAT HAPPENS IN GROUP THERAPY?

The psychotherapies we have described so far focus on a one-to-one relationship between a client and a therapist. This technique is known as *individual psychotherapy*. However, therapy can be administered to many people at one time with one or more therapists, in a process called **group therapy**. Group therapy approaches are often used in psychiatric facilities, group homes, the military, addiction centers, and mental institutions. They are also frequently offered by community mental health centers and outpatient treatment programs. Emily attended many group meetings, not only at the hospital as an in-patient but also as an outpatient at the community center. Group therapy often centers on one type of problem (such as addiction or depression) or is offered for a specific type of client (such as women who have been battered, teenagers, or sex offenders). Group therapy may be administered by any of the different types of professionals discussed at the beginning of this chapter.

The Benefits of Group Therapy

Is group therapy better than individual therapy? Group therapy has several distinct advantages over individual therapy (Dies, 1993; Yalom & Leszcz, 2005). First, group therapy tends to be less expensive than individual therapy. The cost of one or more therapists is shared by several people. However, clients do receive less one-on-one or individualized treatment in a group therapy setting. Second, group therapy offers therapists a view into the client's

social interactions with others. Because many people receive therapy to address interpersonal problems, group therapy offers a safe mini-environment in which to explore new social behaviors or to understand how our interactions with others may be impeding our psychological health. Group therapy also enables clients to recognize that they are not the only ones struggling with difficulties. Group members can offer acceptance, trust, and support for someone who is having problems. They can offer ideas or suggestions for solving problems and can learn from one another. Studies on group therapy have found it to be generally comparable in outcomes to individual psychotherapy (Forsyth & Corazzini, 2000; Nevonen & Broberg, 2006).

Jon Bradley/Getty Images

Group therapy can be a less-expensive alternative to individual psychotherapy.

The Nature and Types of Group Therapy

Group therapy, like individual psychotherapy, can take many forms. Any one of the four approaches previously described can be used for treating groups of people (Alonso & Swiller, 1993). For example, group behavior therapy can be used to reduce people's fear of flying. Group psychoanalysis or group cognitive therapy can be adapted to work with people who are depressed or to improve interpersonal relations. Humanistic group therapy may be conducted to encourage positive self-regard among its participants. Three unique forms of group therapy are *family therapy*, *couple therapy*, and *self-help groups*.

Family Therapy: The Whole System

In **family therapy**, the family unit is the group. Often families come to therapy with an "identified patient," such as a misbehaving or rebellious teenager. Yet the focus of family therapy is not on the functioning of the individual but, rather, on the functioning of the family as a whole system. The goal of family therapy is to create balance and restore harmony within the family system to improve its functioning. If one person in the family is having problems, these problems are seen as a symptom of disharmony within the family unit (Lebow & Gurman, 1995).

group therapy therapy that is administered to more than one person at a time

family therapy therapy that focuses on creating balance and restoring harmony to improve the functioning of the family as a whole system

Think of your own family for a moment. All members of a family have roles, expectations, or labels placed on them, usually at a very young age. One member of the family may be considered "the brain." Another family member may be viewed as "the peacemaker." These roles are not spoken but rather are communicated through our interactions with our family members. If a family member does not conform to his or her assigned role, then the rest of the family system will be disrupted. Many times we try to make family members behave in a way that is consistent with our expectations of their perceived roles. Do you ever feel that your family does not know the "real" you? Have you ever tried to step out of your assigned role, only to find family members so concerned or shaken by your new behavior that it is easier to just go back to your old pattern of behaving? If so, you have experienced the power of the family system.

Family therapists view the "identified patient" as merely the focus for problems in the family system. Thus, they explore and analyze the interactions and communications between family members. They address sources of conflict and note how unspoken rules or expected roles may be interfering with healthy family functioning. Recall Emily's case presented at the beginning of this chapter. Although Emily never underwent family therapy, in her book she acknowledges how a family therapist might have viewed her situation: "A family therapist would have identified me as the family scapegoat, the child designated to 'act out' the conflicts between my tense, driven father and my incipiently alcoholic mother" (Gordon, 2000, p. 63).

Couple Therapy: Improving Communication

Couple therapy focuses on improving communication and intimacy between two people in a committed relationship. The unspoken rules that couples use to communicate, and the ways in which they miscommunicate are identified and addressed. The couple therapist then replaces ineffective or unhealthy patterns of communicating with more adaptive ones (Gurman & Jacobson, 2002). For example, each partner is encouraged to paraphrase what the other has said to confirm that the correct message has been heard. Criticism and derogatory labels or names are discouraged. These are just two examples of the "new rules" therapists suggest to improve communication and intimacy within couples.

Self-Help Groups: Helping Each Other Cope

Self-help groups are comprised of people who share the same problem and meet to help one another. Self-help groups differ from other forms of group therapy in that they are organized and led by nonprofessionals. Self-help organizations are becoming increasingly popular. It

couple therapy therapy that focuses on improving communication and intimacy between two people in a committed relationship

self-help group group comprised of people who share the same problem and meet to help one another

---

The goal of family therapy is to improve the functioning of the family system.

© Nancy Sheehan/Photo Edit

is estimated that as many as 20 million people belong to one of these groups and that perhaps 2–3% of the U.S. population is involved in a self-help group at any one time (Borkman, 1997). In one study of Michigan and Massachusetts psychiatrists, 75% reported referring clients with depression to a self-help group (T. J. Powell, Silk, & Albeck, 2000). Self-help groups can be found for anything from addictions and eating disorders to people who have undergone a medical procedure such as a mastectomy or open heart surgery. The main purpose of these groups is to offer social support and help one another cope, but they often provide useful information and advice as well.

The format and purpose of self-help groups vary widely. For example, group meetings may be highly structured or conducted more loosely. Many self-help groups adopt a 12-step program format originated by the well-known Alcoholics Anonymous (AA). Such a format includes admitting that you have a problem and that you are powerless over the problem. It encourages people to seek strength from a "greater power," to admit shortcomings, and to make amends to people they have harmed. Although such 12-step programs are not therapy, mental health professionals often encourage clients to participate in such groups to receive additional emotional support and encouragement. Such groups can increase a patient's adherence to treatment and reduce the severity of psychological symptoms (Depression and Bipolar Support Alliance, 2002; Kaskutas, 2009; Magura et al., 2002). Some research suggests that self-help groups can be just as effective as therapy with a mental health professional (Christensen & Jacobson, 1994). However, research has been unable to specify what elements of self-help groups make them effective or what types of people they benefit most.

AP Photo/Steve Pope

Self-help groups offer social support and encouragement to group members.

Let's REVIEW

In this section, we discussed the advantages and disadvantages of group therapy approaches. For a quick check of your understanding, try answering the following questions at increasing levels of difficulty.

1. Which of the following is *not* an advantage of group therapy approaches?

   a. less expensive
   b. more individual attention
   c. focus on interpersonal interactions
   d. none of the above

2. Many self-help groups, such as Alcoholics Anonymous and Narcotics Anonymous, assume that _____ is a critical factor in improving one's psychological health.

   a. social support
   b. physical health
   c. financial status
   d. medication

3. The goal of family therapy is to _____.

   a. fix the person with the most problems
   b. improve communication between the parents
   c. create harmony and balance within the family unit
   d. understand the past problems of the family

ANSWERS 1.b; 2.a; 3.c

LEARNING
OBJECTIVE

What Should You Know?
• Examine the effectiveness of psychotherapy and the factors that contribute to effective therapy.

EFFECTIVE PSYCHOTHERAPY: WHAT TREATMENTS WORK?

After reading about all these different forms of psychotherapy, you may be asking yourself, "Does psychotherapy work? And if it does work, which approach is the best?" Researchers analyzing the effectiveness of therapy have asked themselves similar questions. As we shall soon see, the answers to these questions are neither simple nor straightforward. Many factors influence and contribute to the effectiveness of therapy.

Which Type of Psychotherapy Is Best?

To answer the question "Does psychotherapy work?" research typically compares clients who are receiving therapy with clients who are receiving a placebo treatment or no treatment at all. Such studies have generally shown that psychotherapy has positive effects and is better than a placebo treatment or no treatment at all. They also suggest that the different approaches—psychodynamic, humanistic, behavioral, and cognitive—produce relatively equivalent results in terms of client improvement (Asay & Lambert, 1999; T. B. Baker et al., 2008; Chambless & Ollendick, 2001; Kopta et al., 1999; Lambert & Bergen, 1994; Nathan, Stuart, & Dolan, 2000; L. A. Robinson et al., 1990; M. L. Smith & Glass, 1977; M. L. Smith, Glass, & Miller, 1980; Wampold et al., 1997; Westen & Bradley, 2005). This finding has been termed the *Dodo Bird verdict* after the Dodo Bird in *Alice and Wonderland* who, following the race, stated, "Everyone has won, and all must have prizes." The Dodo Bird verdict implies that it doesn't matter which therapy approach a therapist uses because all are equivalent in effectiveness. Other research suggests that certain forms of therapy work better for certain types of disorders (Chambless & Ollendick, 2001; Crits-Christoph, 1997; Engels, Garnefski, & Diekstra, 1993; Lambert & Bergen, 1994). For example, panic disorder may respond best to cognitive-behavior therapy, whereas phobias may respond best to behavioral methods (L. B. Allen et al., 2010; Chambless & Ollendick, 2001; Hollon & Beck, 1994; M. E. P. Seligman, 1995)

Some evidence shows that psychotherapy can even alter the functioning of the brain. For example, A. L. Brody and colleagues (1998) took PET scans of persons with obsessive-compulsive disorder before and after receiving 2 months of behavioral therapy. As you can see in the ● WHAT'S HAPPENING IN YOUR BRAIN? feature, metabolic activity of the brain decreased in the patients following treatment. Excessive activity in certain areas of the brain may in part explain the intrusive and uncontrollable obsessions that inundate people with this disorder. It appears that psychotherapy, like medication, can reduce these faulty signals. Neuroimaging studies on people with other psychological disorders (panic disorder, major depression, phobic disorder, PTSD) have also documented changes in brain metabolism following psychotherapy treatment (Beauregard, 2007; Dichter, Felder, & Smoski, 2010; Felmingham et al., 2007; Frewen, Dozois, & Lanius, 2008; Kennedy et al., 2007).

WHAT'S HAPPENING IN YOUR BRAIN?

PSYCHOTHERAPY AND THE BRAIN

Psychiatric News, May 7, 2004—Volume 39, Number 9, p. 34. © 2004 American Psychiatric Association. Reprinted with permission.

PRE   POST

These are PET scans of a person with obsessive-compulsive disorder who responded to behavior therapy. The scans on the left were taken before treatment (pre); the scans on the right were taken after 2 months of therapy (post). Brain activity decreases on the right suggest an effect of psychotherapy on the brain as there are fewer hot areas (red and yellow).

Such mixed results underscore the complexity of conducting research on therapy effectiveness. First, think about the selection of participants for such a study. It is hard to find people who all have the same disorder to the same degree. Such differences in symptoms introduce potential sampling problems into the research. Next, think about the administration of the independent variable. In an experiment, therapists would be trained to deliver a very specific type of therapy. To ensure consistency among therapists, deviations from these methods would not be allowed. As you might imagine, this is much different from the way treatment is administered in the real world (Chambless & Hollon, 1998). In addition, it is difficult to design a "no treatment" control group. Add to these issues the problem of defining what a good outcome is and how it will be measured (the dependent variable; Hollon, 1996; Westen & Bradley, 2005). Do we rely on the therapist's judgment of improvement, the client's self-report of well-being, or some other measure? How long should the client be free of symptoms for treatment to be considered effective? Although you may not feel that such research questions are important to you, the results of such studies are important to health insurance companies. They use this research to determine the most cost-effective and efficient means of treatment. Consequently, outcome research may indirectly affect you or a loved one in the future as the competition between therapies increases.

Perhaps a more appropriate question to ask about therapy is "Which treatment is most effective for this person, with this problem, under these circumstances?" Such a personalized approach to treatment is becoming more common as many therapists are adopting an *eclectic approach* to treatment (Kopta et al., 1999). An **eclectic therapy approach** involves an integrated and diverse use of therapeutic methods. For example, *Eye Movement Desensitization and Reprocessing (EMDR)* therapy is an eclectic treatment approach used primarily for people who have experienced trauma. It includes elements of psychodynamic, cognitive, behavioral, and client-centered approaches.

Developed by Francine Shapiro (1991), EMDR therapy is designed to reduce distress from traumatic memories. In a multi-phase treatment approach, the client's distressing memories are identified along with specific behaviors and positive beliefs the client will need to cope with future stressful situations. The client focuses on the most vivid image of the trauma and related negative beliefs, emotions, and physical sensations while simultaneously attending to another stimulus for 20 to 30 seconds. Moving one's eyes back and forth is the most commonly used dual attention stimulus, but tapping one's fingers or listening to auditory tones in one ear and then the other are also used. The client is directed to notice whatever thoughts, feelings, or images come to mind. This process is repeated numerous times until the client's distress is reduced. The client then focuses on the positive belief while engaging in the dual attention task for several sets (Shapiro, 2001).

EMDR therapy is effective at reducing posttraumatic stress symptoms when compared to no-treatment control groups (Kemp, Drummond, & McDermott, 2010; Rodenburg et al., 2009). It is recommended by the American Psychiatric Association as an effective treatment for trauma (American Psychiatric Association, 2004). It appears to be just as effective as cognitive-behavioral therapy (Bisson et al., 2007; Ponniah & Hollon, 2009; G. H. Seidler & Wagner, 2006) and more effective than medication (van der Kolk et al., 2007) in reducing symptoms of PTSD. However, fewer studies have tested the effectiveness of EMDR and sample sizes are small, raising methodological concerns about the data (Hertlein & Ricci, 2004). Further study of EMDR therapy's effectiveness is warranted.

Factors That Contribute to Effective Psychotherapy

Although research has provided mixed results on the question "Which psychotherapy is most effective?" evidence suggests that all successful psychotherapies share certain common elements, even when the specific methods used differ greatly. Over the last decade, the term **therapeutic alliance** has surfaced to describe the interactive and collaborative relationship between the client and the therapist. The nature and development of this relationship influence the effectiveness of therapy (Barber et al., 2000; Kozart, 2002; D. J. Martin, Garske, & Davis, 2000; J. C. Watson, Schein, & McMullen, 2010).

Therapists contribute to a successful alliance in many ways. First, they establish a positive relationship with the client. This relationship involves creating an atmosphere of mutual respect and trust. Clients who trust their therapist are more likely to believe that they will

eclectic therapy approach therapy that incorporates an integrated and diverse use of therapeutic methods

therapeutic alliance the interactive and collaborative relationship between the client and the therapist

benefit from therapy. The clients, therefore, are more likely to engage in the therapy process by revealing important information about themselves and by trying the new skills, behaviors, or techniques that the therapist suggests. Second, effective therapists are empathetic and warm, evidencing a caring attitude toward the client and the ability to listen (Beutler et al., 1994; Crits-Christoph et al., 1991; Teyber & McClure, 2000). Third, successful therapists offer an explanation or interpretation of why the client is having a problem and encourage clients to confront painful emotions (Garfield, 1992; Ingram, Hayes, & Scott, 2000; Snyder et al., 2000).

Effective therapists are also sensitive to any cultural differences between them and their clients (Yutrzenka, 1995). Given that most providers of psychological services come from the majority culture and clients may be members of minority cultures, it is important to the success of therapy that therapists acknowledge and understand the experiences and values of diverse ethnocultural populations in the United States (P. B. Pedersen, 2002). If the cultural differences between a client and a therapist are wide, empathy and trust are more difficult to achieve (Draguns, 2002).

Therapists working with Native Americans, for example, must be aware of the specific traditions and customs of the tribes, villages, or communities where the mental health services will be provided, as Native Americans comprise many different groups with different languages, traditions, and orientations. Moreover, Native American clients may have a view of "counselor" that differs from the typical therapist–client relationship. They may view therapists as "healers" and therefore seek counseling for a multitude of issues such as financial problems, spiritual guidance, or the problems of other family members, as Native Americans tend to be very family-oriented (Trimble & Thurman, 2002). For example, alcohol treatment approaches for Native Americans that incorporate spirituality as well as sensitivity to cultural issues seem to enhance the effectiveness of treatment (Garrett & Carroll, 2000).

Similarly, therapists need to understand several basic cultural values that may be operating when working with Asian American populations. For example, high respect for and obedience to one's parents is a strong value that may influence Asian Americans to comply with family wishes rather than their own desires. Such a value illustrates the Asian American emphasis on consensus, belongingness, and togetherness rather than the U.S. model of individualism. Asian Americans tend to value self-control and inconspicuousness and avoid being the center of attention or asserting themselves (Maki & Kitano, 2002). However, as with other cultural groups, Asian Americans differ widely among themselves. Therefore a therapist should be careful not to overemphasize traditional cultural expectations just because of the client's ethnicity.

Given such considerations, does successful therapy depend on the therapist and client sharing the same racial or ethnic background? Not necessarily. However, research suggests that a good match between the therapist's and client's beliefs and value systems is of prime importance (Gamst et al., 2000). Training and research in multicultural counseling are necessary for many therapists to achieve such sensitivity and knowledge (Vega et al., 2007). The need for such sensitivity has encouraged academic programs in the United States to incorporate training on multicultural issues into their curricula. Some states require psychologists to complete such training before they can become licensed. Until cultural differences are understood, ethnic minorities—a growing segment of the U.S. population—will continue to receive inadequate mental health services.

Therapist characteristics are not the only determinant of a successful alliance. Client attitudes and behaviors also make a difference (Garfield, 1994; Kwan, Dimidjian, & Rizvi, 2010; Leon, Kopta, Howard, & Lutz, 1999). Clients who are motivated and committed to therapy tend to experience more positive results. Those who are actively involved in the therapy process and optimistic about the benefits of therapy also fare better. Moreover, clients who can express their feelings and thoughts and who are more psychologically mature experience more gains from therapy. Clients who have no previous history of psychological disorders also tend to benefit more. The social environment of the client is also important. Clients who have supportive loved ones and stable, rather than chaotic, living conditions tend to benefit more from therapy.

Notice that none of these characteristics is specific to any one of the therapy approaches we have described. So if you or a loved one is in need of a therapist, it is important to find a therapist and an approach that make you comfortable. Believing in the therapist and his or her approaches will establish a positive therapeutic alliance, thereby enhancing the effectiveness of your therapy.

The ● TECHNOLOGY AND BEHAVIOR feature explores a modern approach to delivering therapy.

TECHNOLOGY and BEHAVIOR

COMPUTER TECHNOLOGY AND CYBERTHERAPY

In recent years, the rapid development of computer technology and the Internet has started to influence psychotherapy (C. B. Taylor & Luce, 2003). Computer-based programs can now be used to administer psychological assessments such as the MMPI-2. Personal digital assistants (PDAs) can be used to collect data from clients on their thoughts, behaviors, and mood, allowing clinicians to analyze a client's behavior across many situations. Effective computer programs have been developed to reduce symptoms in people with anxiety, depressive, and substance dependence disorders (K. M. Carroll et al., 2008; Cavanagh et al., 2009; Kenardy et al., 2003; B. Klein et al., 2010; Proudfoot, 2004; Selmi et al., 1990). Videoconferencing can provide clients who live too far away a link to therapists. These are just some of the computer tools that can enhance the delivery of psychotherapy.

Are there online psychological services? You bet! The Internet has produced psychological treatment by e-mail, real-time online counseling, professionally assisted chat rooms, self-help groups, and mental health information and education sites. However, Internet-based interventions present a number of professional and ethical issues (Hsiung, 2001; Humphreys, Winzelberg, & Klaw, 2000; Spriggs, 2009). Online psychological services lack the close, personal contact of face-to-face interactions. Establishing a therapeutic alliance is more difficult when you cannot hear the tone of someone's voice or read his or her body language and facial expressions. "Cybershrinks" may or may not have adequate training or be appropriately licensed (J. W. Bloom, 1998). Client confidentiality is of great concern because information on the Internet can be easily accessed. Moreover, the effectiveness of these programs has not been demonstrated. Studies on Internet-based treatments for grief and anxiety suggest improved client functioning (Hirai & Clum, 2005; Richards, Klein, & Carlbring, 2003; B. Wagner, Knaevelsrud, & Maercker, 2006). Yet controlled studies are needed to evaluate all the benefits and disadvantages of these new communication tools (K. M. Griffiths, Calear, & Banfield, 2009). At this time, technology and the Internet appear to be valuable resources that can be added to traditional psychotherapy (Castelnuovo et al., 2003). However, caution should be exercised if they are the only type of treatment used.

© Artiga Photo/Corbis

Videoconferencing can provide mental health services to people who live a long distance away such as in large rural areas.

Let's REVIEW

In this section, we detailed the effectiveness of psychotherapy and described those factors that contribute to effective therapy. As a quick check of your understanding, try answering the following questions at increasing levels of difficulty.

1. Which of the following is an element associated with successful therapy?

   a. free association

   b. chaotic living conditions of the client

   c. being forced to receive therapy

   d. a positive therapist–client relationship

2. An eclectic approach to therapy refers to _____.

   a. an integrated and diverse use of therapeutic methods

   b. a reliance on free association and interpretation

   c. a mutual bond of respect and warmth between the therapist and client

   d. deepening the client's knowledge of psychology

3. Which of the following statements about the effectiveness of psychotherapy is *true*?

   a. Cognitive therapy is considerably more effective than other forms of therapy.

   b. Psychoanalysis is considerably more effective than other forms of therapy.

   c. The main types of therapy appear to be equally effective.

   d. Receiving therapy appears to be no more effective than no therapy.

ANSWERS 1. d; 2. a; 3. c

WHAT ARE THE BIOMEDICAL THERAPIES?

Now that we have described psychological treatments for psychological disorders, it is time to turn our attention to biomedical approaches. The two dominant biomedical approaches are *drug therapy* and *electroconvulsive therapy* (ECT). Far less used, but still a dramatic last resort, is *psychosurgery*.

Drug Therapies

The most common form of biomedical therapy is psychopharmacology, or prescribing medications for psychological disorders.

Today, the most common biomedical therapy used to treat mental health problems is medications. Recall that medications must be prescribed by physicians and psychiatrists who have extensive training in **psychopharmacology**, or the use of drugs to treat mental health problems. Medications are generally not prescribed by psychologists. As with any prescribed medication, side effects can occur and must be considered in any treatment plan. Medication cannot cure a psychological disorder. Rather, it reduces the symptoms of the disorder while the person is taking the medication. Often, therefore, medications are prescribed jointly with psychotherapy. The medication stabilizes the person sufficiently so that psychological issues can be addressed. Here we present the major types of medications that are prescribed for specific psychological disorders.

Antianxiety Drugs

As the name implies, **antianxiety medications** are sedatives prescribed to reduce tension and anxiety (● TABLE 15.4). The best-known antianxiety drugs are the *benzodiazepines* such as Valium, Ativan, and Xanax. These medications reduce tension, relax the muscles, and promote sleep by depressing the central nervous system. They influence the functioning of three neurotransmitters: GABA, serotonin, and

© Brian Pieters/Masterfile

TABLE 15.4

● **Antianxiety Drugs**

GENERIC NAME	TRADE NAME	COMMON SIDE EFFECTS
BENZODIAZEPINES		
Alprazolam	Xanax	Dizziness, drowsiness, low blood pressure, blurred vision
Chlordiazepoxide	Librium	Dizziness, drowsiness, low blood pressure, blurred vision
Diazepam	Valium	Dizziness, drowsiness, low blood pressure, blurred vision
Lorazepam	Ativan	Dizziness, drowsiness, memory problems, weakness, unsteadiness
Oxazepam	Serepax	Dizziness, drowsiness, headache, memory problems, nervousness
Temazepam	Restoril	Dizziness, drowsiness, fatigue, headache, nausea, nervousness
Triazolam	Halcion	Headache, tiredness, drowsiness
NONBENZODIAZEPINE		
Buspirone	BuSpar	Dizziness, headache, depression, insomnia, nervousness, numbness, tremors, nausea, dry mouth, diarrhea, constipation, heart palpitations, sore throat, blurred vision, nasal congestion, muscle pain and weakness, rash, sweating

norepinephrine. They are fast-acting drugs, calming feelings of anxiety within an hour or so. These medications are useful in treating people who are diagnosed with generalized anxiety disorder, panic disorder, posttraumatic stress disorder, agoraphobia, and insomnia (Barlow, 2002; Greenblatt, Harmatz, & Shader, 1993; Nardi et al., 2010).

What are the side effects of antianxiety medications? The benzodiazepines are highly addictive if taken over a long period. People quickly build up a tolerance to these medications, requiring higher and higher dosages to achieve a reduction in anxiety. If dependence does occur, the person must be gradually weaned from the drug because abrupt withdrawal can be life threatening. Withdrawal symptoms can include tremors, irritability, insomnia, tingling sensations, a return of intense anxiety, and in rare cases even seizures and paranoia.

A second drawback of taking benzodiazepines is the effect on cognitive and motor functioning. As a depressant drug, the benzodiazepines reduce coordination, alertness, and reaction time (van Laar, Volkerts, & Verbaten, 2001). These impairments can affect a person's ability to drive a car or perform tasks at work or school. These effects are even more severe when alcohol is used with these medications.

Finally, *relapse rates* for patients taking benzodiazepines are high. This means that many patients taking these drugs experience the anxiety symptoms again when they discontinue treatment or are taken off the drugs. The drugs appear to provide only short-term relief from anxiety symptoms. Long-term benefits are more likely when benzodiazepine treatment is combined with cognitive-behavioral therapies (D. A. Spiegel, 1998).

Because of the disadvantages of benzodiazepine treatment, a nonbenzodiazepine drug, called *buspirone* (trade name BuSpar), is sometimes prescribed to treat anxiety, particularly generalized anxiety disorder (Asnis et al., 2004; Chessick et al., 2006; Mokhber et al., 2010; Rickels et al., 2000; Varley & Smith, 2003). A modest success, buspirone has a lower risk of dependence, but it takes considerably longer for the drug to reduce anxiety. The person must take this medication for several days or weeks before a noticeable reduction in anxiety symptoms is achieved.

Antipsychotic Drugs

Over the centuries, many medical treatments had been unsuccessful in treating psychotic symptoms, especially in people diagnosed with schizophrenia. Such treatments included brain surgery (lobotomy), insulin injections, and shock treatment. Because these treatments were ineffective, most people with schizophrenia were merely warehoused in mental hospitals. Then, in the 1950s, *chlorpromazine* (trade name Thorazine) was discovered to be an effective drug in treating psychosis, or a loss of touch with reality. As Thorazine and the numerous drugs that followed, such as Mellaril and Haldol, were the first drugs to effectively reduce psychosis for some people, they are referred to as *conventional* or *first-generation* antipsychotic medications. **Antipsychotic medications** are major tranquilizers prescribed

psychopharmacology the use of medications to treat mental health problems

antianxiety medications minor tranquilizers such as Valium that are prescribed to reduce tension and anxiety

antipsychotic medications major tranquilizers such as Haldol that are prescribed to relieve psychotic symptoms such as delusions and hallucinations

to relieve psychotic symptoms such as agitation, delusions, disordered thinking, and hallucinations (● TABLE 15.5). They may be prescribed for people with schizophrenia, bipolar depression, or major depression when such individuals have lost touch with reality. These drugs appear to work by reducing the action of the neurotransmitter dopamine in the brain (Sanyal & vanTol, 1997). Recall that dopamine has long been suspected as a major link in understanding psychotic behavior.

Although conventional antipsychotic drugs dramatically decreased the number of patients in mental hospitals for several decades, they are effective for only 60% of persons who try them (American Psychiatric Association, 2000b). They are more effective in treating the positive symptoms of schizophrenia—such as delusions (false beliefs) and hallucinations (hearing voices)—than the negative symptoms such as blunted affect (lack of emotional reactions), alogia (poverty of speech), and avolition (lack of motivation) (see Chapter 14). The conventional antipsychotic medications also have significant side effects, including sleepiness, dry mouth, blurred vision, weight change, drooling, constipation, sexual dysfunction, and depression. Motor side effects also occur, including tremors, spasms, frozen facial expressions, and motor agitation, causing people with schizophrenia to pace. These motor side effects often look like Parkinson's disease. This should not be surprising given that Parkinson's disease has been related to a reduced functioning of dopamine in the brain, precisely the effect of conventional antipsychotic medications.

Long-term use of such drugs can lead to an irreversible motor disorder called **tardive dyskinesia** that involves involuntary motor movements of the mouth, tongue, and face. People experiencing this side effect may repeatedly smack their lips, stick out their tongues, puff out their cheeks, or make other odd facial movements. It is estimated that this serious side effect occurs in 15–20% of people with long-term use of conventional antipsychotic drugs (Chakos et al., 1996; Morgenstern & Glazer, 1993).

Newer drugs, called *atypical antipsychotics* or second-generation antipsychotics, have renewed hope of successfully treating schizophrenia. These drugs influence the action of serotonin and dopamine in the brain and cause less serious side effects. They are effective in reducing both the positive and negative symptoms of schizophrenia (Buchanan et al., 1998; Lieberman et al., 2003; Lindenmayer et al., 2007; Macfadden et al., 2010; Stahl, 2001a, 2001b). Side effects include sedation, nausea, headaches, seizures, dizziness, and an increased risk

tardive dyskinesia a possible long-term side effect of antipsychotic medications involving involuntary motor movements of the mouth, tongue, and face

TABLE 15.5

● Antipsychotic Drugs

GENERIC NAME	TRADE NAME	COMMON SIDE EFFECTS
CONVENTIONAL ANTIPSYCHOTICS		
Chlorpromazine	Thorazine	Low blood pressure, dry mouth, nausea, vomiting, constipation, rash, pseudoparkinsonism, tardive dyskinesia, headache
Fluphenazine	Prolixin	Low blood pressure, dry mouth, nausea, vomiting, constipation, rash, drowsiness, headache, pseudoparkinsonism, tardive dyskinesia
Haloperidol	Haldol	Low blood pressure, dry mouth, nausea, vomiting, constipation, rash, drowsiness, headache, pseudoparkinsonism, tardive dyskinesia
Thioridazine	Mellaril	Dry mouth, nausea, vomiting, constipation, rash, pseudoparkinsonism, tardive dyskinesia, headache
ATYPICAL ANTIPSYCHOTICS		
Aripiprazole	Abilitat	Drowsiness, insomnia, agitation, anxiety, headache, nausea
Clozapine	Clozaril	Sedation, salivation, dizziness, headache, tremors, sleep problems, fever, sweating, confusion, fatigue, insomnia, drooling, constipation, nausea, abdominal discomfort, vomiting, diarrhea, low blood pressure, hypertension, urinary abnormalities
Olanzapine	Zyprexa	Agitation, constipation, dizziness, dry mouth, increased appetite/weight, indigestion, low blood pressure upon standing, sleepiness, tremor, weakness
Quetiapine	Seroquel	Abdominal pain, constipation, diminished and/or uncontrollable movement, dizziness, drowsiness, dry mouth, excessive muscle tone, headache, indigestion, low blood pressure upon standing, nasal inflammation, neck rigidity, rapid or irregular heartbeat, rash, tremor, weakness
Risperidone	Risperdal	Drowsiness, insomnia, agitation, anxiety, headache, pseudoparkinsonism, tardive dyskinesia, nausea, constipation
Ziprasidone	Geodon	Accidental injury, constipation, cough, diarrhea, dizziness, drowsiness, dry mouth, headache, indigestion, involuntary muscle contractions, muscle tightness, nausea, rash, stuffy and runny nose, upper respiratory infection, vision problems, vomiting, weakness

of sleep apnea (Rishi et al., 2010), but for people who do not respond to conventional antipsychotic medications, these newer drugs can be a lifesaver. As a result, they have become the most commonly used antipsychotic drugs in clinical practice. Examples of such drugs include *clozapine, risperidone,* and *aripiprazole* (see Table 15.5). Atypical antipsychotic medications may also be useful in the treatment of bipolar disorder (Vieta & Goikolea, 2005) and dementia-related behaviors (Daiello, 2007).

Antidepressants

Antidepressants are prescribed to alter mood and alleviate the symptoms of major depression. Antidepressants have also been effective in treating people with obsessive-compulsive disorders, panic disorders, eating disorders, and cigarette cravings (Barlow, 2002). As shown in ● TABLE 15.6, there are three main classes of antidepressants: *tricyclics, MAO inhibitors,* and *selective serotonin reuptake inhibitors (SSRIs).*

Tricyclics Tricyclic antidepressants, such as Tofranil and Elavil, elevate mood and reduce the symptoms of depression by influencing the action of norepinephrine and serotonin in the brain (Stahl, 1998). However, it takes from 4 to 8 weeks on such medication before noticeable relief from depression occurs. Tricyclics are effective in relieving depressive symptoms in 60–85% of people who are depressed (Arroll et al., 2005; Fawcett, 1994; Guze & Gitlin, 1994). As with any drug, tricyclics have a number of side effects, including dry mouth, weight gain, dizziness, blurred vision, constipation, and sexual dysfunction. The tricyclics can also be fatal in overdose amounts, which is why they are seldom prescribed to patients who are suicidal.

MAO Inhibitors The monoamine oxidase (MAO) inhibitors are a class of antidepressants that elevate mood by increasing the monoamine neurotransmitters in the brain (Stahl, 1998). They are just as effective as the tricyclic antidepressants but are less frequently prescribed

antidepressants medications prescribed to alleviate the symptoms of depression, eating disorders, and some anxiety disorders

TABLE 15.6
● Antidepressant Drugs

GENERIC NAME	TRADE NAME	COMMON SIDE EFFECTS
TRICYCLIC ANTIDEPRESSANTS		
Amitriptyline	Elavil	Dizziness, drowsiness, constipation, dry mouth, water retention, low blood pressure, hair loss, blurred vision
Desipramine	Norpramin Pertofrane	Dizziness, drowsiness, dry mouth, low blood pressure, headache, increased appetite/weight, nausea, tiredness, unpleasant taste
Doxepin	Adepin Sinequan	Dizziness, drowsiness, diarrhea, dry mouth, water retention, low blood pressure, blurred vision
Imipramine	Tofranil	Dizziness, drowsiness, diarrhea, dry mouth, water retention, low blood pressure
Nortriptyline	Aventyl Pamelor	Dizziness, drowsiness, constipation, dry mouth, water retention, low blood pressure, blurred vision
MAO INHIBITORS		
Phenelzine	Nardil	Dizziness, drowsiness, change in appetite, low blood pressure, constipation, dry mouth, headache, liver problems, sexual problems, sleep disturbances, stomach and intestinal problems, water retention, weight gain
Tranylcypromine	Parnate	Dizziness, drowsiness, dry mouth, diarrhea, change in appetite, insomnia, nausea, rapid or irregular heartbeat, water retention, weakness, weight loss
SELECTIVE SEROTONIN REUPTAKE INHIBITORS (SSRIs)		
Fluoxetine	Prozac	Headache, insomnia, drowsiness, tremor, dizziness, fatigue, poor concentration, abnormal dreams, agitation, nausea, diarrhea, dry mouth, change in appetite, constipation, cramps, vomiting, flatulence, sweating, rash, nasal congestion, cough, heart palpitations, muscle pain, decreased sexual desire, urinary frequency
Paroxetine	Paxil	Nausea, prolonged sleepiness, headache, dry mouth, constipation, dizziness, insomnia, diarrhea, sweating
Sertraline	Zoloft	Insomnia or prolonged drowsiness, dizziness, headache, tremor, fatigue, male sexual dysfunction, diarrhea, nausea, constipation, change in appetite, dry mouth, vomiting, flatulence
OTHER ANTIDEPRESSANTS		
Bupropion	Wellbutrin, Zyban	Headache, agitation, dizziness, confusion, insomnia, tremors, hypertension, nausea, vomiting, dry mouth, constipation, menstrual irregularities, rash, sweating, blurred vision, weight loss or gain

because of their more serious side effects (M. Fava & Rosenbaum, 1995). These include lowered blood pressure, liver damage, and weight gain. These drugs also interact with substances high in an amino acid called *tyramine*. Tyramine is present in common foods such as cheese, smoked meats, and chocolate, liquids such as beer and wine, and even over-the-counter medications. This interaction can produce a sudden rise in blood pressure that is potentially fatal. You may have noticed the caution statements on the back of any over-the-counter cold medication stating that it is not to be used by a person who is taking an MAO inhibitor. Yet MAO inhibitors may be more effective in the treatment of severe depression than the newer antidepressants, which are the SSRIs discussed next (G. Parker et al., 2001).

Selective Serotonin Reuptake Inhibitors (SSRIs) Currently, the most frequently prescribed antidepressant medications are the **selective serotonin reuptake inhibitors (SSRIs)** such as Prozac and Zoloft. Recall from Chapter 2 that reuptake is the process whereby the neurotransmitters that are left over in the synapse of the neuron are recycled back into the presynaptic neuron. SSRIs elevate mood by leaving the neurotransmitter serotonin in the synapse longer. SSRIs are just as effective as the other classes of antidepressants (Arroll et al., 2005; Gartlehner et al., 2005; Mulrow et al., 2000; Thase, 2003; Thase et al., 2002) and have several advantages.

The side effects of SSRIs are less severe and are not fatal in overdose. These include increased nervousness, headaches, insomnia, nausea, stomach cramps, decreased sexual drive, and sexual dysfunction (S. Fisher, Kent, & Bryant, 1995; Michelson et al., 2000). Some of these side effects may diminish after a few weeks of treatment, however. As stated previously, the SSRIs are useful in treating other disorders besides depression, including anxiety disorders, eating disorders, and substance abuse, especially alcohol dependence (Abramowitz, 1997; Barlow & Durand, 2005; C. J. Bell & Nutt, 1998; Lenze et al., 2009; D. J. Stein et al., 2003; van Apeldoorn et al., 2010). For all these reasons, the SSRIs are quite popular. Other antidepressants, such as Zyban and Wellbutrin, that are similar to the SSRIs but influence the norepinephrine and dopamine systems, are also being prescribed (Stahl, 1998). These antidepressants do not decrease one's sexual drive and are therefore sometimes used in combination with SSRI drugs to optimize one's therapeutic response (elevate mood) while lessening the sexual side effects (Leuchter et al., 2008; Zisook et al., 2006).

However, antidepressant medication has been associated with an increased risk of suicidal thoughts and behaviors in children and adolescents, especially in the first few months of treatment (FDA Public Health Advisory, 2004). In 2004, the Food and Drug Administration directed that manufacturers of antidepressants include a "black box" warning—the FDA's strongest—on all antidepressant medication for children and adolescents.

Antimanics

The **antimanic medications** are prescribed to alleviate manic symptoms of bipolar disorder. The first mood-stabilizing drug approved by the FDA was **lithium**, a naturally occurring mineral salt. Lithium has the advantage of controlling both manic and depressive symptoms in people with bipolar disorder, although it is far more effective in treating mania (Amsterdam & Shults, 2010; Barondes, 1993; Kahn, 1995; Nivoli, Murru, & Vieta, 2010; Young et al., 2010). For this reason, people with bipolar disorder may be prescribed antidepressant drugs in addition to lithium to stabilize their moods. Lithium achieves its effect by influencing several neurotransmitters in the brain: glutamate, serotonin, and dopamine (Dixon & Hokin, 1998; Lenox & Manji, 1995). It is taken even when people have no symptoms of mania to prevent future manic episodes.

Research on the effectiveness of lithium treatment is challenging as there is extreme variability in people's absorption of lithium. Some people absorb lithium rather quickly and can therefore tolerate only small dosages, whereas others absorb the chemical more slowly. Lithium dosage amounts, therefore, vary considerably from one person to the next. Too little lithium can lead to manic episodes, whereas too much can lead to lithium poisoning, involving vomiting, nausea, slurred speech, and impaired muscle coordination. For any one person, the difference between the correct, or "therapeutic," amount of lithium and a toxic amount is a very fine line. For this reason, lithium levels must be carefully monitored in people with bipolar disorder.

selective serotonin reuptake inhibitor (SSRI) a type of antidepressant drug that inhibits the reuptake of the neurotransmitter serotonin, thereby improving mood

antimanic medications drugs that are prescribed to alleviate manic symptoms of bipolar disorder

lithium a naturally occurring mineral salt prescribed to control manic symptoms in people with bipolar disorder; it influences several neurotransmitters in the brain, including glutamate, serotonin, and dopamine

What are the side effects of lithium? Lithium, like all the drugs discussed so far, also has side effects, including nausea, vomiting, diarrhea, blurred vision, reduced concentration, weight gain, and increased risk of diabetes and kidney problems (Maj et al., 1997). It can also lead to birth defects if taken by pregnant women during their first trimester.

For those people with bipolar disorder who do not respond to lithium or who cannot tolerate its side effects, other drug options are available. For example, *anticonvulsant drugs* such as carbamazepine (Tegretol) and valproate (Depakote) are effective in treating severe mania and produce fewer side effects than lithium. Valproate, approved by the FDA to treat mania in 1995, has recently overtaken lithium as the most frequently prescribed mood-stabilizing drug. However, the anticonvulsant drugs are less effective than lithium in preventing suicide (Goodwin & Goldstein, 2003; Thies-Flechtner et al., 1996; Tondo & Baldessarini, 2009). Moreover, there is some evidence that valproate may lead to adverse hormone changes in women who begin taking the drug before age 20 (Vainionpaa et al., 1999). The anticonvulsant drugs can also cause birth defects when taken by pregnant women. Yet, when compared to placebo, both lithium and the anticonvulsant drugs have been shown to be effective treatments for bipolar disorder (Bowden et al., 2003; Bowden et al., 2010; Calabrese et al., 2005; J. F. Goldberg, 2007; Keck & McElroy, 2002). Drugs called *calcium channel blockers* have proven effective in treating manic symptoms in some cases (Goodnick, 2000; N. A. Levy & Janicak, 2000; Post et al., 1998; Wisner et al., 2002; Yingling et al., 2002). Although their effectiveness is uncertain, these drugs are advantageous in that they have fewer side effects and do not lead to birth defects when taken by pregnant women. When a person with bipolar disorder experiences a manic state that progresses to the point of psychosis, antipsychotic medications (discussed previously) may be prescribed.

The effectiveness of medications for treating bipolar disorder is further complicated by patient compliance (Sachs & Rush, 2003). Some people with bipolar disorder miss the euphoric feelings of the manic state and, against the advice of their physicians, go off their medications when they are feeling better. They often believe that they can control their symptoms without medication. For example, in one large study of patients with bipolar disorder receiving treatment in VA settings, almost 50% did not take their medications as prescribed (Sajatovic et al., 2007). Unfortunately, manic symptoms often return, thus requiring a recalibration of appropriate medication levels (Cookson, 1997).

Electroconvulsive Therapy (ECT)

Before the birth of drug therapy in the 1950s, the most common form of biomedical therapy consisted of administering electrical shocks to the brains of patients to induce seizures. This procedure, called **electroconvulsive therapy (ECT)**, was a routine therapy approach used on people with schizophrenia. It was believed that producing a seizure would calm the hallucinations, agitation, and delusions that people with schizophrenia experience. In fact, ECT was not effective in treating people with schizophrenia. However, for reasons that aren't clear, it can be effective in treating people with severe depression.

How is ECT administered? Although still highly controversial, ECT today consists of a series of treatments, usually performed in a hospital, in which electrical current is passed through the brain, causing a seizure. After administration of anesthesia and a muscle relaxant, metal electrodes are placed on the head of the now unconscious patient. A current of 70–130 volts is passed through one side of the brain for roughly one-half second. A seizure occurs, causing the patient to have muscle tremors for about 1 minute. Violent convulsions do not occur because of the administration of the muscle relaxant prior to the procedure. The patient undergoes this procedure about every other day for 6 to 12 sessions. It is a quick and painless medical procedure.

Many students are appalled and even frightened by ECT. It seems so archaic and primitive. These are natural and common reactions. However, keep in mind that ECT is not the first treatment for depression, but rather a last resort. It is administered to patients who are depressed and are not responding to psychotherapy or drug therapy and remain in a severely depressed state. These patients may be suicidal or even psychotic. For these patients, ECT may be the only form of treatment that is effective (Nemeroff, 2007).

electroconvulsive therapy (ECT)
a series of treatments in which electrical current is passed through the brain, causing a seizure; used to alleviate severe depression

Electroconvulsive therapy (ECT) is a last-resort treatment option administered to patients who are depressed and are not responding to psychotherapy or drug therapy and remain in a severely depressed state.

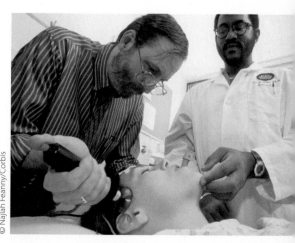

© Najlah Feanny/Corbis

Is ECT effective? Yes. ECT is effective for 50–80% of people who are severely depressed, and it is very effective in treating psychotic depression (Coryell, 1998; Damm et al., in press; Kellner et al., 2010; Maxmen & Ward, 1995; Merkl, Heuser, & Bajbouj, 2009; G. Parker et al., 2001). It also relieves depression faster than drug therapy. Most patients improve within a few days.

How does ECT work? It is not currently understood how ECT lifts depression. It is speculated that the seizure may alter the functioning of brain structures, of neurotransmitters in the brain, or both (M. K. O'Connor, 1993; Yatham et al., 2010). Identifying the precise effect of shock on all brain functions is rather like finding a needle in a haystack, and research continues to investigate the power of ECT on depression.

What are the side effects of ECT? ECT does have its drawbacks. It can lead to cognitive impairments, such as memory loss, learning difficulties, or disturbances in verbal abilities. A second concern in using ECT is the high relapse rate. As many as 85% of ECT patients relapse into depression. This relapse may occur as soon as 4 months after treatment. Thus, the effects of ECT seem to be short-lived (C. Swartz, 1995). Despite ECT's short-term effectiveness, these concerns—as well as people's fears about administering electrical shock to the brain—continue to make ECT a very controversial treatment approach. Given this controversy, research is currently investigating more focused brain stimulation techniques that have the same effectiveness as ECT but without the risks and side effects (Holtzheimer & Nemeroff, 2006).

Psychosurgery

Another dramatic last resort for the treatment of psychological disorders is psychosurgery. **Psychosurgery** involves surgically altering the brain to alleviate symptoms in someone with a mental health disorder. First introduced in the 1940s and 1950s, probably the best-known psychosurgery is the *prefrontal lobotomy*, in which the neurons connecting the frontal lobe to the rest of the brain were surgically disconnected. However, with the rise and success of drug therapies, psychosurgery declined considerably, as lobotomies were generally ineffective and produced seizures and a loss in intellectual functioning (Swayze, 1995).

Is psychosurgery still used today? Yes. Many neurosurgeons continue to use psychosurgery for treating people with mental illness who do not respond to conventional biomedical or psychological treatments. Today, psychosurgery methods are more precise, thanks to recent improvements in surgical techniques. For example, a neurosurgeon may lesion (destroy) a small target area of the brain to reduce symptoms of obsessive-compulsive disorder. Research suggests that approximately 25–30% of patients who have undergone this procedure improve significantly (Baer et al., 1995; Dougherty et al., 2002; Jenike et al., 1991; Read & Greenberg, 2009; Shah et al., 2008). Since 1993, neurosurgeons have been implanting deep brain stimulators in people who have Parkinson's disease (Benabid et al., 2001). It is the most commonly practiced surgical treatment for this disease, improving motor function by at least 60%, leading to a significant improvement in the quality of life for people with Parkinson's (Ashcan et al., 2004). Deep brain stimulation for treatment-resistant depression and severe obsessive-compulsive disorder also shows promising results (Hamani et al., 2009; Huff et al., 2010; Mayberg et al., 2005; Read & Greenberg, 2009; Shah et al., 2008). Yet keep in mind that such operations are performed very infrequently and only as a last resort. Psychosurgery continues to be a controversial biomedical technique (C. A. Anderson & Arciniegas, 2004).

This chapter outlined the major types of psychotherapies and biomedical therapies. We have seen that each therapeutic approach stems from one of the main psychological perspectives introduced in the beginning of this textbook: biological, psychoanalytic, cognitive, behavioral, and humanistic. We also have seen that therapy is generally effective, regardless of the specific techniques endorsed. Of course, the effectiveness of therapy will be directly related to the characteristics of the therapist and the client as was illustrated by Emily and Dr. Farber's relationship.

We hope that you have enjoyed your journey through psychology. Moreover, we hope that you have found the material relevant to your life. Being aware of the complex interaction among biological, psychological, and social variables will further your understanding of not only your behavior but the behavior of those around you. Good luck!

psychosurgery a biomedical treatment approach involving neurosurgery to alleviate symptoms in someone with a mental health disorder

Let's REVIEW

In this section, we described biomedical approaches to therapy, including drug therapies, electroconvulsive therapy, and psychosurgery. For a quick check of your understanding, try answering the following questions at increasing levels of difficulty.

1. Electroconvulsive therapy is most effective for the treatment of _____.

a. schizophrenia

b. panic attacks

c. severe depression

d. bipolar disorder

2. Prozac is what type of antidepressant drug?

a. SSRI

b. MAO inhibitor

c. tricyclic

d. benzodiazepine

3. Which of the following is the most serious side effect of taking conventional antipsychotic medication?

a. rebound anxiety

b. physical dependence

c. hallucinations

d. tardive dyskinesia

ANSWERS 1. c; 2. a; 3. d

STUDYING the CHAPTER

LEARNING CHALLENGE

Now that you have studied the chapter, assess your comprehension of the material by answering the following questions. Then use the key at the end to determine if your understanding is at the basic, intermediate, or advanced level. For a more comprehensive assessment of your learning, please see your student study guide and your Psychology CourseMate (www.cengagebrain.com).

1. Most psychotherapists hold at least a _____ degree and in most states hold an appropriate license or certificate.

a. bachelor's

b. associate's

c. master's

d. doctorate

TEST YOURSELF!

2. Which of the following are exceptions to the ethical guideline of confidentiality?

    a. when the therapist believes the client is a danger to herself
    b. when a client expresses violent intent toward another
    c. if a therapist suspects some type of abuse
    d. all of the above

3. _____ uses techniques such as free association and dream analysis to uncover hidden conflicts.

    a. Psychoanalysis
    b. Cognitive therapy
    c. Behavior therapy
    d. Client-centered therapy

4. Which psychotherapy would use systematic desensitization to treat a person with a phobic disorder?

    a. psychoanalysis
    b. cognitive therapy
    c. behavior therapy
    d. client-centered therapy

5. Dr. Ramon expresses genuineness and empathy to her client. Dr. Ramon is most likely engaging in _____.

    a. psychoanalysis
    b. cognitive therapy
    c. behavior therapy
    d. client-centered therapy

6. Dr. Andrews reinforces appropriate client behavior and ignores inappropriate behavior. Dr. Andrews is engaging in _____.

    a. psychoanalysis
    b. cognitive therapy
    c. behavior therapy
    d. client-centered therapy

7. Dr. Shu reflects her client's thoughts and feelings so that she can better understand the client's problems. Dr. Shu is engaging in _____.

    a. behavior modification
    b. client-centered therapy
    c. rational-emotive therapy
    d. free association

8. Which type of therapy pairs an unpleasant stimulus with a problem behavior in the hope of reducing the behavior's occurrence?

    a. aversion therapy
    c. token economy
    b. systematic desensitization
    d. client-centered therapy

9. Dr. Tyler teaches his client how to recognize negative automatic thought patterns. Dr. Tyler is engaging in _____.

    a. rational-emotive therapy
    b. systematic desensitization
    c. cognitive therapy
    d. psychodynamic therapy

10. Dr. Mendel encourages Maurice to paraphrase what his partner says to confirm that he has understood the comment. It is most likely that Maurice is engaged in _____.

    a. psychoanalysis
    b. family therapy
    c. couple therapy
    d. drug therapy

11. Dr. Garfield and his client have an interactive and collaborative relationship, commonly referred to as a(n) _____.

    a. eclectic approach
    b. therapeutic alliance
    c. psychotherapeutic effect
    d. transference

12. Which of the following is a disadvantage of cybertherapy?

    a. increases client confidentiality
    b. provides clients who live far away from therapists access to psychological services
    c. lacks the close, personal contact of face-to-face interactions
    d. none of the above

13. Antipsychotic medications affect which neurotransmitter?

    a. serotonin
    b. glutamate
    c. GABA
    d. dopamine

14. Craig has been diagnosed with PTSD. His psychiatrist has prescribed the benzodiazepine Xanax to help Craig function. Which of the following are side effects that Craig may experience from taking this medication?

    a. dizziness and drowsiness
    b. tardive dyskinesia
    c. fluid retention and rash
    d. kidney problems

15. Which of the following medications has been associated with an increased risk of suicidal thoughts and behaviors in children and adolescents?

    a. Valium
    b. Lithium
    c. Paxil
    d. Haldol

Scoring Key

Below are the answers and the associated point values for each of the Learning Challenge questions. Circle the associated points for each question that you answered correctly. To obtain your Learning Challenge Score, add up the points you circled and write the total in the blank.

1. C, 1 pt	**6.** C, 2 pts	**11.** B, 1 pt
2. D, 1 pt	**7.** B, 2 pts	**12.** C, 1 pt
3. A, 1 pt	**8.** A, 3 pts	**13.** D, 3 pts
4. C, 3 pts	**9.** C, 2 pts	**14.** A, 3 pts
5. D, 2 pts	**10.** C, 2 pts	**15.** C, 3 pts

Learning Challenge Score _____

(27–30) Congratulations! You scored at the advanced level. You are well on your way to mastering the material. Take the next step by answering the questions in your Student Study Guide or your Psychology CourseMate (www.cengagebrain.com).

(21–26) You are almost there! You scored at the intermediate level. Review the material you missed before moving on to answer the questions in your Student Study Guide or your Psychology CourseMate (www.cengagebrain.com).

(20 and below) You are on your way, but you're not there yet! You scored at the beginner level. It appears that you need to carefully review the chapter to improve your mastery of the material.

USE IT OR LOSE IT: APPLYING PSYCHOLOGY

1. Compare and contrast psychoanalysis and client-centered therapy. What qualities do they have in common? What are their major differences?

2. Which psychotherapy approach do you find the most appealing, and why? Which psychotherapy approach do you find the least appealing, and why?

3. What can the critical components of therapy effectiveness teach us about resolving our own problems? How might these components be useful in group therapy approaches?

4. What are the advantages and disadvantages of using medication to treat mental health problems?

5. Think about a behavior or problem that you have had or are having. Choose a behavior therapy method to change this behavior. What would the behavior and the method be, and how would you go about changing the behavior?

CRITICAL THINKING FOR INTEGRATION

1. Design an experiment (Chapter 1) that would test the effectiveness of a drug therapy versus a psychotherapy. Be sure to carefully define your dependent measure of effectiveness.

2. Refer to the conditioning of Little Albert's fear of a white rat in Chapter 5, and design a therapy approach to reduce Albert's fear.

3. How might some of the psychotherapy techniques described in this chapter promote problem-focused coping styles in response to stress (Chapter 12)?

CHAPTER STUDY RESOURCES

Student Study Guide

To help organize your learning, work through Chapter 15 of the *What Is Psychology? Student Study Guide*. The study guide includes learning objectives, a chapter summary, fill-in review, key terms, a practice test, and activities.

CengageNOW

Go to **www.cengage.com/login** to link to CengageNOW, your online study tool. First take the Pre-Test for this chapter to get your personalized study plan, which will identify topics you need to review and direct you to online resources. Then take the Post-Test to determine what concepts you have mastered and what you still need work on.

CourseMate

Access an interactive eBook, chapter-specific interactive learning tools, including flashcards, quizzes, videos, and more in your Psychology CourseMate, available at **CengageBrain.com**.

Aplia

aplia

Aplia™ is an online interactive learning solution that helps you improve comprehension—and your grade—by integrating a variety of tools such as video, tutorials, practice tests, and interactive eBook. Founded by a professor to enhance his own courses, Aplia provides automatically graded assignments with detailed, immediate explanations on every question, and innovative teaching materials. More than 1,000,000 students like you have used Aplia at over 1,800 institutions. Aplia should be purchased only when assigned by your instructor as part of your course.

Therapy consists of techniques that are used to help people with psychological or interpersonal problems. Emily Gordon's story highlights the various forms of therapies and how therapists are a crucial variable in determining the effectiveness of therapy.

WHAT THERAPIES ARE USED TO TREAT PSYCHOLOGICAL PROBLEMS?

WHAT IS THE NATURE OF THERAPY?

- **Psychotherapy** is administered by clinical psychologists, licensed counselors, social workers, or therapists.
- Psychotherapists abide by ethical standards of confidentiality, competent treatment, informed consent, and appropriate interactions.
- You should consider therapy if you feel helpless, sad, or nervous for a prolonged period of time or if such feelings do not improve despite several efforts to change them.

Nancy Sheehan/Photo Edit

© Tom Stewart/Corbis

WHAT ARE THE MAIN TYPES OF PSYCHOTHERAPY?

- Traditional **psychoanalysis** has clients gain insight into the real source of their problems.
- Modern **psychodynamic therapy** also relies on the therapist's **interpretations** of the client's feelings and behaviors but places more emphasis on current problems and interpersonal relations and less on the client's past.
- Humanistic therapy such as **client-centered therapy** connects with and understands the client's worldview. The therapist offers **genuineness**, **empathy**, and **unconditional positive regard** to encourage self-exploration and self-fulfillment.
- **Behavior therapies** use learning principles to change maladaptive behavior. In classical conditioning therapies such as **systematic desensitization**, virtual reality technology, and **aversion therapy**, the client's responses to stimuli are changed. Operant conditioning therapies use techniques such as shaping, extinction, positive reinforcement, and **token economies** to change behavior.
- In cognitive therapies, maladaptive patterns of thinking and perceiving are replaced with more adaptive ways of interpreting events. In **rational-emotive therapy**, the therapist confronts, questions, and challenges the validity of the client's irrational beliefs. In **cognitive therapy**, the therapist identifies and tracks negative automatic thoughts and has the client test the accuracy of these **cognitive distortions**.

WHAT HAPPENS IN GROUP THERAPY?

- The goal of **group therapy** is to improve the functioning and interactions among individuals, families, couples, or other groups.

- Group therapy tends to be less expensive than individual therapy and offers a safe mini-environment in which to explore new social behaviors or to understand how our interactions with others may be impeding our psychological health.

Jon Bradley/Getty Images

EFFECTIVE PSYCHOTHERAPY: WHAT TREATMENTS WORK?

© Jose Luis Pelaez, Inc./Corbis

- Generally, the different psychotherapy approaches produce relatively equivalent results in terms of client improvement.

- A personalized approach to treatment is becoming more common as many therapists adopt an **eclectic therapy approach** that involves an integrated and diverse use of therapeutic methods.

- The effectiveness of modern delivery methods of therapy such as cybertherapy has not been demonstrated.

WHAT ARE THE BIOMEDICAL THERAPIES?

- **Biomedical therapies** are administered by psychiatrists and other medical professionals.

- The most common biomedical therapy is **psychopharmacology**, or the use of medications to treat mental health problems. Drug therapies influence brain neurotransmitters to alter behavior.

  - **Antianxiety medications** are prescribed to reduce tension and anxiety.

  - **Antipsychotic medications** are prescribed to relieve psychotic symptoms such as agitation, delusions, disordered thinking, and hallucinations.

  - **Antidepressants** are prescribed for mood and anxiety disorders, eating disorders, and substance dependence.

  - **Antimanic medications** are used primarily to treat mania.

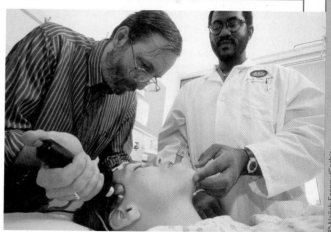

© Najlah Feanny/Corbis

- More controversial biomedical therapies include **electroconvulsive therapy (ECT)** and **psychosurgery**. In ECT, a seizure is created in the brain to treat severe depression. Psychosurgery involves surgically altering the brain to alleviate severe symptoms of Parkinson's disease and obsessive-compulsive disorder.

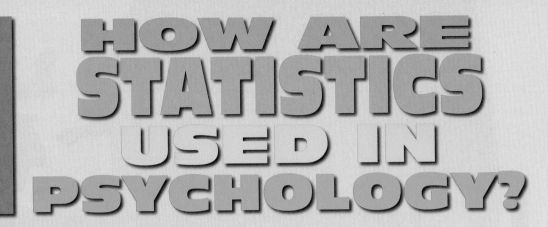

LEARNING OBJECTIVES

What Should You Know?

- Define the terms data and statistics, and explain how they are used in science.

- Describe the different types of graphs and distributions used in statistical analyses, including frequency distributions, frequency polygons, histograms, and scatter plots.

- Calculate and interpret the different measures of central tendency and variability used in statistics—the mean, median, mode, range, sample variance, and standard deviation.

- Explain what a normal and standard normal distribution are.

- Calculate and interpret a *z* score and the correlation coefficient.

data information gathered in scientific studies

statistics a type of applied mathematics used to describe data and test hypotheses

graph a visual depiction of data

frequency distribution a graph of data that plots the frequency of data points on the *y*-axis and the data points themselves on the *x*-axis

frequency polygon a line graph that is used to illustrate a frequency distribution

histogram a bar graph that is used to illustrate a frequency distribution

How Do Psychologists Use Statistics to Describe Data?

As you learned in Chapter 1, psychology is the scientific study of behavior and mental processes. Psychologists develop hypotheses about behavior and mental processes and then test these hypotheses using experiments, case studies, surveys, naturalistic observations, or other research methods. In the course of their research, psychologists collect a variety of information, or **data**, from their research participants.

Imagine that you are a health psychologist interested in whether the legal drinking age in a country affects the rate of underage drinking in that society. More specifically, you might ask questions like these: "Does having a lower legal drinking age encourage drinking among 15-year-olds? And if so, does the legal drinking age equally affect both male and female 15-year-olds?" To see whether such relationships exist, you must first collect data on the number of 15-year-olds who drink in particular countries along with each country's legal drinking age (see ● TABLE A.1).

Take a moment to look at the data in Table A.1. By just looking at the table, can you tell whether a relationship exists between the percentage of 15-year-old students who drink and a country's minimum legal drinking age? If you cannot, you are in good company—it's impossible to tell from just a table whether the data support one's hypothesis. Instead, psychologists must use a type of applied mathematics, called **statistics**, to describe and analyze their data. Only then can a researcher determine what the data say about her hypothesis.

Graphs: Depicting Data Visually

Take another look at the data in Table A.1. Where would you start if you wanted to see whether the legal drinking age is related to drinking rates among 15-year-olds? Well, have you ever heard that *a picture is worth a thousand words*? One way to start would be to create a **graph**, or pictorial representation of the data. Psychologists use many different types of graphs to help describe their data. One of the more common graphs is a **frequency distribution**. A graph of a frequency distribution is a two-dimensional illustration that plots how frequently certain events occur. For example, it might be useful to see how many countries have set certain minimum drinking ages. This information could be depicted using several types of graphs to illustrate the frequency distribution, but two of the more common ones are **frequency polygons** (a line graph) and **histograms** (a bar graph). ● FIGURES A.1a and A.1b show the frequency distribution of legal drinking age depicted with both a frequency polygon and a histogram. By looking at these graphs, we can see that most of these selected governments have set their minimum drinking age below 21, most commonly at 18.

An even more useful type of graph for this investigation would be a **scatter plot**. In a scatter plot, two variables are plotted as a function of each other. For example, we could plot the percentage of 15-year-old drinkers as a function of the country's minimum drinking age. ● FIGURE A.2a shows such plots for males and females. By looking at the scatter plots in Figure A.2a, you can get a *very crude* picture of the relationship between drinking age and the rate of underage drinking at age 15. Looking at Figure A.2a, as the minimum drinking age decreases, does the rate of underage drinking increase? Do these data confirm or discount our hypothesis that lowering the drinking age encourages underage drinking? Although it is true that countries with a minimum drinking age of 16 or younger have relatively high levels of underage drinking, there are also a number of countries with a minimum drinking age of 18 that have even higher levels of underage drinking by 15-year-olds. Similarly, ● FIGURE A.2b seems to show that male and female rates of drinking are related. It appears that as more males drink, more females also engage in drinking—but if you look closely at the scatter plot, this isn't always true. Therefore, these plots only give us a crude picture of the relationship between our variables. It's impossible to say for sure whether our hypotheses about teenage drinking have merit by simply looking at these plots. To truly examine our hypothesis, we will have to delve deeper into our statistical analysis.

TABLE A.1

● Percentage of Students Who Report Drinking Alcohol Weekly at Age 15, Selected Countries

COUNTRY	MINIMUM LEGAL DRINKING AGE	MALES (%)	FEMALES (%)
Austria	16	39	23
Belgium	16	38	22
Canada	18	22	22
Czech Republic	18	32	17
Denmark	15	46	38
England	18	47	36
Estonia	18*	21	10
Finland	18	11	8
France	16	31	15
Germany	16	29	22
Greece	16*	52	31
Greenland	18	13	10
Hungary	16	29	11
Ireland	18	27	12
Israel	18	26	10
Latvia	18	28	12
Lithuania	21	16	9
Northern Ireland	18	33	20
Norway	18	16	12
Poland	18	20	8
Portugal	16	29	9
Russia	18	28	24
Scotland	18	37	33
Slovakia	18	32	16
Sweden	18	17	11
Switzerland	16	19	9
United States	21	23	15
Wales	18	53	36

Source: Except where noted, data taken from Kaul, C. (2002). Statistical Handbook on the World's Children (p. 447). Westport, CT: Oryx Press.
These data retrieved November 6, 2003, from http://www2.potsdam.edu/alcohol-info/LegalDrinkingAge.html#worlddrinkingages

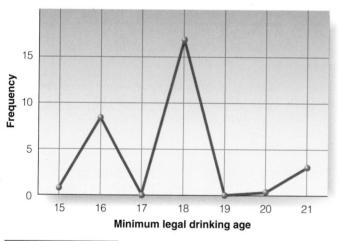

FIGURE A.1a

● **Frequency Distribution (Shown Using a Frequency Polygon) for the Minimum Drinking Age in the 28 Countries Listed in Table A.1**

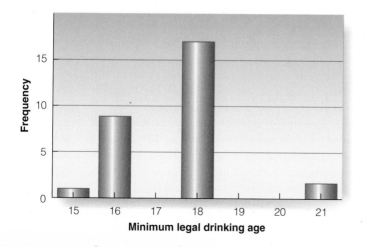

scatter plot a graph of data that plots pairs of data points, with one data point on the *x*-axis and the other on the *y*-axis

FIGURE A.1b

● **Frequency Distribution (Shown Using a Histogram) for the Minimum Drinking Age in the 28 Countries Listed in Table A.1**

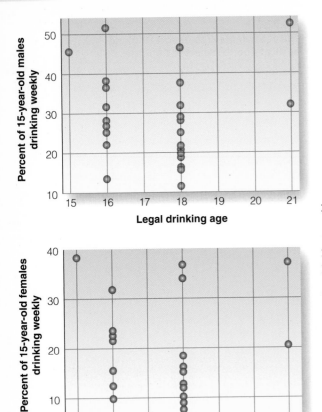

FIGURE A.2a

● Scatter Plots for Male and Female Drinking at Age 15 as a Function of Minimum Legal Drinking Age for the 28 Selected Countries

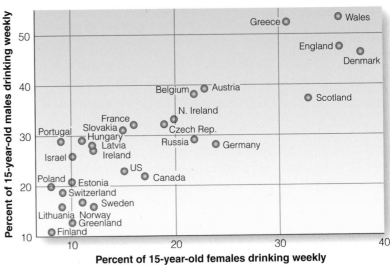

FIGURE A.2b

● Scatter Plot of the Percentage of Males and Percentage of Females Who Drink Alcohol Weekly at Age 15 for the 28 Selected Countries

Measures of Central Tendency: Means, Medians, and Modes

To get to the heart of the matter, we are going to have to use **descriptive statistics**. Descriptive statistics are numerical values that are calculated on the data to summarize and describe the data as a whole. For example, you could calculate the percentage of the 28 countries that have a minimum drinking age of 18 or higher. This percentage would be 19 of the 28 countries, or 67.9%. Or you could calculate the percentage of countries with a minimum drinking age under 18 in which more than 25% of their male sample indicate that they drink weekly (i.e., 8 out of 9 countries, or 88.9%). Although such percentages can sometimes be helpful, there are other, better statistical methods to use in this situation.

Some of the most useful descriptive statistics are those that describe the average, or most typical, entry in a data set; in other words, a statistic that shows what a *typical* country's legal drinking age is. These measures are collectively referred to as **measures of central tendency** in that they tell us something about the center of the frequency distribution (i.e., what minimum drinking age is most common, or most typical). Look again at Figures A.1a and A.1b. What do you think is the most common minimum drinking age? To answer this question, we have three different measures of central tendency: the *mean, mode,* and *median*.

The **mean** is synonymous with the average of a distribution. To calculate the mean, you add up all the data points (for example, the minimum drinking age in each country) and divide the total by the number of data points (such as the number of countries being evaluated). This formula can be expressed with the following equation:

$$\overline{X} = \Sigma X / N$$

descriptive statistics statistics that are calculated to summarize or describe certain aspects of a data set

measures of central tendency descriptive statistics that describe the most central, or typical, data points in the frequency distribution

mean a descriptive statistic that describes the most average, or typical, data point in the distribution

Where

$\overline{X}$ is the symbol for the mean

Σ is a mathematical symbol that means to sum up the items that follow it

X = the individual data points in the distribution

N = the total number of data points or scores in the distribution

The calculation of the average minimum drinking age and the average percentages of males and females that drink weekly at age 15 is shown in ● TABLE A.2.

Another measure of central tendency is the **median**, or the score that is at the center of the frequency distribution of the scores. To find the median, you must first list all the scores in ascending order (smallest to largest). Once this is done, simply find the score that is at the center of this ordered list of scores. The calculation of the median legal drinking age is shown in ● FIGURE A.3. As you can see in Figure A.3, the median and the mean are not the same number. This shows one advantage of the median over the mean. The mean is highly affected by unusual scores, or **outliers**, in the distribution. In this case, one country, Denmark, has an unusually low drinking age of 15. Although Denmark's minimum drinking age of 15 does not differ that much from the other countries that set their limit at 16, Denmark is the only country to set the age this low, and this outlying score works to lower the mean somewhat. However, because the median is simply the center score of the distribution, it is unaffected by unusual scores. So, whereas the mean drinking age is 17.5, the median drinking age is somewhat higher at 18.

When a distribution contains outliers, the median is the better choice for measuring central tendency. This is especially true in situations in which the outliers are even more outlying than those in our drinking-age example. For instance, assume that in a class of 10 students, 9 students score a 75 on an exam, and 1 student scores a 15. The mean for the class would be 69, but the median would be 75. That's a difference of over half a letter grade between these two measures of central tendency, with the median more accurately reflecting how most of the students scored on the exam.

TABLE A.2

Average Minimum Drinking Age and Average Percentage of Students Who Report Drinking Alcohol Weekly at Age 15, Selected Countries

COUNTRY	MINIMUM LEGAL DRINKING AGE	MALES (%)	FEMALES (%)
Austria	16	39	23
Belgium	16	38	22
Canada	18	22	17
Czech Republic	18	32	19
Denmark	15	46	38
England	18	47	36
Estonia	18*	21	10
Finland	18	11	8
France	16	31	15
Germany	16	29	22
Greece	16*	52	31
Greenland	18	13	10
Hungary	16	29	11
Ireland	18	27	12
Israel	18	26	10
Latvia	18	28	12
Lithuania	21	16	9
Northern Ireland	18	33	20
Norway	18	16	12
Poland	18	20	8
Portugal	16	29	9
Russia	18	28	24
Scotland	18	37	33
Slovakia	18	32	16
Sweden	18	17	22
Switzerland	16	19	9
United States	21	23	15
Wales	18	53	36
Σx	491	814	498
$X = \Sigma X/N$	491/28 = 17.5	814/28 = 29.1	498/28 = 17.8

Source: Except where noted, data taken from Kaul, C. (2002). Statistical Handbook on the World's Children (p. 447). Westport, CT: Oryx Press.
These data retrieved November 6, 2003, from http://www2.potsdam.edu/alcohol-info/LegalDrinkingAge.html#worlddrinkingages

---

First take all of the minimum legal drinking ages for the countries and list them in ascending order:

15, 16, 16, 16, 16, 16, 16, 16, 16, 18, 18, 18, 18, 18,
18, 18, 18, 18, 18, 18, 18, 18, 18, 18, 18, 18, 21, 21

Now find the score at the center of this distribution. In this case, because there is an even number of scores ($N = 28$) the center of this distribution would be between the 14th and 15th score in the list. Therefore, to find the median or X_{50}, we would average the 14th and 15th score:

$$(18 + 18)/2 = 18$$
$$X_{50} = 18$$

FIGURE A.3

● Calculation of the Median Legal Drinking Age

median A descriptive statistic that identifies the center of the frequency distribution; 50% of the scores are above and 50% are below this point in the distribution

outliers unusual data points that are at the extremes of the frequency distribution and either far above or below the mean

The final measure of central tendency is the **mode**, or the most *frequent* score in the distribution. If you look again at Figure A.1a (or Figure A1.b), you will see that the most frequent, or most common, drinking age is 18. Therefore, like the median, the mode is also 18. The mode is an especially useful measure of central tendency when the data being examined are not numerical (e.g., the most typical car color in the student parking lot).

Measures of central tendency tell us something about the most representative scores at the center of the frequency distribution, but they do not tell us anything about the range, or breadth, of the scores in the distribution. To determine this characteristic of the distribution, we will have to look at *measures of variability*.

Measures of Variability: Analyzing the Distribution of Data

Variability refers to the degree to which the individual scores of the distribution tend to *differ* from the central tendency of the distribution. In other words, variability measures how spread out the frequency distribution is. Look back at Figure A.1a. As we just saw, the mean drinking age is 17.5. As you would expect, most of the scores in the frequency distribution are clustered around 18, but that does not mean that *all* the scores are close in value to 18. Some scores are as low as 15, and some are as high as 21. Measures of variability tell us about the degree to which these more extreme scores differ from the mean. The simplest measure of variability is the **range** of the distribution, or the difference between the highest and lowest scores in the distribution. In this case, the range of drinking ages would be $21 - 15 = 6$ years.

Although the range is a measure of variability, it is fairly crude in that it doesn't really tell us how much the average score differs from the mean. Another measure of variability, called **sample variance**, takes into account the difference between the individual scores of the distribution and the mean of the distribution. The first step to calculating the sample variance is to calculate the mean of the distribution. The next step is to calculate the **sum of squares** of the distribution. The term *squares* refers to the difference between each score in the distribution (X) and the mean of the distribution ($\overline{X}$), with this difference being taken to the second power. So, the sum of squares (SS) can be calculated using the following equation:

$$SS = \Sigma(X - \overline{X})^2$$

The sample variance of a distribution is the sum of squares divided by the total number of data points in the distribution. Once you have calculated the SS, the sample variance (S^2) is simply calculated by the following formula:

$$S^2 = \Sigma(\overline{X} - X)^2/N$$

Another measure of variability is the **standard deviation** (S), or the square root of the sample variance:

$$S = \sqrt{\Sigma(X - \overline{X})^2/N}$$

All three measures of variability indicate the degree to which the scores in the distribution are *dispersed*. The higher these measures are, the more dispersion, or spread, there is among the scores. Although it may be difficult to see why you would want to know the variability of a distribution, one reason is that you can use the standard deviation as a ruler, or guideline, for judging how atypical or typical a score in the distribution is. To see how this works, take a look at ● FIGURE A.4. Figure A.4 shows the calculation of the standard deviation for the male drinking percentages across the 28 countries. As you can see, the standard deviation for the distribution of male drinking scores is 11.03. We can use the standard deviation to gauge how unusual a specific score in the distribution is; that is, how far away, or outlying, a specific score is from the mean score. Using the standard deviation and the mean of the distribution, we can calculate a **z score**. A z score expresses the degree to which an individual score differs from the mean of the distribution in terms of the standard deviation of the distribution.

$$Z = (X - \overline{X})/S$$

For example, in Germany, 29% of 15-year-old males drink weekly. This means that Germany's score would be:

$$Z = (29 - 29.1)/11.03 = -.009$$

mode a measure of central tendency that identifies the most common, or frequent, score in the distribution

range a measure of variability that is the difference between the high score and the low score of the distribution

sample variance a measure of variability that shows on average how much the scores vary from the mean

sum of squares the sum of the squared errors, or deviations, from the mean for the scores in the distribution; the numerator of the sample variance equation

standard deviation a measure of variability equal to the square root of the sample variance; often used to gauge the degree to which an individual score deviates from the mean of a distribution

z score a measure of relative standing that measures the distance of a score from the mean of the distribution in standard deviation units

normal distribution a bell-shaped, symmetric frequency distribution

standard normal distribution a bell-shaped, symmetric distribution ($\overline{X} = 0$; and $S = 1$) for which we know the exact area under the curve

correlation coefficient the average product of **z** scores calculated on pairs of scores; describes the degree to which the scores in the pairs are linearly related

Germany's z score indicates that the percentage of German 15-year-old boys who drink is far less than one standard deviation below the mean of 29.1 for all of the 28 countries (● FIGURE A.5). This means that compared to the other countries, Germany has only a slightly below average percentage of 15-year-old boys who drink. Drinking among German 15-year-old males is pretty typical for the countries sampled.

On the other hand, look at the figure reported for Wales. In Wales, 53% of the 15-year-old males surveyed were drinking. Wales's z score of 2.17 indicates that its score of 53% is more than 2 standard deviations above the mean. This figure indicates that Wales's experience is not very typical of the average country's experience with male underage drinking at age 15. Wales seems to have a bigger problem with this issue than the average country does, but is this deviation from the mean enough of a problem to worry about? To answer this question, we have to assess the probability that a given country would have a particular percentage of its young men drinking alcohol on a weekly basis. Luckily, we might be able to do this.

Many variables, such as height, weight, IQ, and so on, have a **normal distribution**. In other words, if you measured these characteristics for a very large number of people and plotted them in a frequency distribution, the resulting graph would be bell-shaped and symmetrical (● FIGURE A.6). If we assume that drinking behavior is normally distributed, then we can also assume that if we calculated the z scores for all of the different countries and plotted them in a frequency distribution, that distribution of z scores would also be a normal distribution, with $\overline{X} = 0$ and $S = 1$. When a distribution of z scores is normal in shape, it is referred to as the **standard normal distribution**. The great thing about the standard normal distribution is that we know exactly what percentage of the distribution falls between any two scores (again, see Figure A.6). As you can see from Figure A.6, 68.26% of the z scores should be within the range of z scores from -1 to $+1$, whereas only .26% of the scores will be above a z score of $+3$ or below a z score of -3. This means that the probability that Wales would have a z score of $+2.17$ or higher is on the order of a mere 1.5%. So, indeed, Wales seems to have some possible cause for concern here because the number of 15-year-old males consuming alcohol on a weekly basis is unusual compared to other countries.

The Correlation Coefficient: Measuring Relationships

Look again at Figure A.2b, the scatter plot for underage drinking in males and females from the 28 countries. Do you notice anything interesting about this scatter plot? Don't the data points of the scatter plot tend to fall along a line that slopes up to the right of the graph? Doesn't this pattern seem to indicate that there might be a linear relationship between the percentage of 15-year-old males and females drinking alcohol in a country? As one sex drinks more, doesn't the other seem to generally follow suit? To examine the degree to which such a relationship might exist, psychologists would use yet another statistic to describe these data—the **correlation coefficient**. Simply put, the correlation coefficient measures the degree to which pairs of data points fall along a straight line on a scatter plot. The formula for the correlation coefficient is:

$$r = (\Sigma_{z_x z_y})/N$$

Country N = 28	X = Percent of 15-Year-Old Males Drinking	X − $\overline{X}$ = X − 29.1	(X − $\overline{X}$)² = (X − 29.1)²
Austria	39	9.9	98.01
Belgium	38	8.9	79.21
Canada	22	− 7.1	50.41
Czech Republic	32	2.9	8.41
Denmark	46	16.9	285.61
England	47	17.9	320.41
Estonia	21	− 8.1	65.61
Finland	11	−18.1	327.61
France	31	1.9	3.61
Germany	29	− .1	.01
Greece	52	22.9	524.41
Greenland	13	−16.1	259.21
Hungary	29	− .1	.01
Ireland	27	− 2.1	4.41
Israel	26	− 3.1	9.61
Latvia	28	− 1.1	1.21
Lithuania	16	−13.1	171.61
Northern Ireland	33	3.9	15.21
Norway	16	−13.1	171.61
Poland	20	− 9.1	82.81
Portugal	29	− .1	.01
Russia	28	− 1.1	1.21
Scotland	37	7.9	62.41
Slovakia	32	2.9	8.41
Sweden	17	−12.1	146.41
Switzerland	19	−10.1	102.01
United States	23	− 6.1	37.21
Wales	53	23.9	571.21
	$\Sigma X = 814$		$\Sigma(X − \overline{X})^2 =$ 3407.88
	$\overline{X} = \Sigma X/N =$ 814/28 = 29.1		$S^2 = \Sigma(X − \overline{X})^2 / N =$ 3407.88/28 = 121.71
			$S = \sqrt{\Sigma(X − \overline{X})^2 / N} =$ $\sqrt{121.71} = 11.03$

Legend: $\overline{X}$ = the mean; S^2 = the sample variance; S = the standard deviation; Σ = a symbol that means sum up the items that follow; N = the total number of scores or data points

FIGURE A.4

● Calculation of the Standard Deviation for the Percentage of Males Drinking Weekly at Age 15

FIGURE A.5

● **Z Scores for Germany and Wales**
The average or mean percentage of 15-year-old males who drank was 29.1% and the standard deviation was 11.03 across the 28 countries. This figure shows the individual z scores for the percentage of 15-year-old males drinking in Germany and Wales. Z scores indicate how many standard deviations away from the mean a particular score falls. As you can see, Germany has a slightly below average percentage of 15-year-old male drinkers, with a raw score of 29% and a z score of −.009. Wales is quite a bit above average in its underage drinking, with a raw score of 53% and a z score of 2.17.

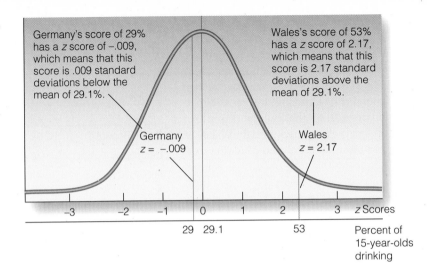

FIGURE A.6

● **The Standard Normal Distribution of Z Scores** The standard normal distribution is a symmetric, bell-shaped distribution of z scores with $\overline{X} = 0$ and $S = 1$. The z score is the number of standard deviations from the mean that the score is.

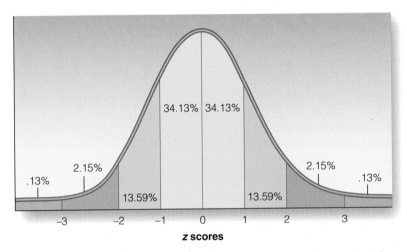

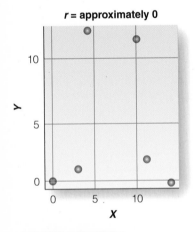

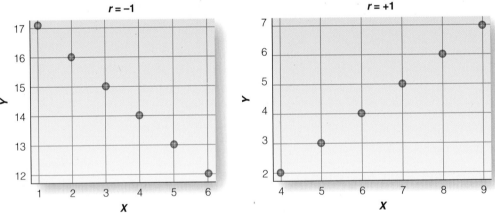

FIGURE A.7

● **Depictions of Different Values of the Correlation Coefficient, r**

Where:

r = the correlation coefficient

z_x = the z score for one of the variables in a pair

z_y = the z score for the other variable of the pair

N = the total number of pairs of scores

The correlation coefficients that can be calculated with this formula will have a possible range of $-1 \leq r \leq +1$. See ● FIGURE A.7 for an interpretation of these values. As you can see from Figure A.7, as r approaches either −1 or +1, the linear relationship between the two variables is stronger. An r value of zero indicates no linear relationship between the two vari-

Country	Percent of 15-yr-old Males Drinking	z score for Percent of Males Drinking	Percent of 15-yr-old Females Drinking	z score for Percent of Females Drinking	$z_{male}z_{female}$
Austria	39	.90027	23	.56263	.50652
Belgium	38	.80961	22	.45464	.36808
Canada	22	−.64098	17	−.08531	.05468
Czech Republic	32	.26564	19	.13067	.03471
Denmark	46	1.53490	38	2.18251	3.34994
England	47	1.62557	36	1.96652	3.19671
Estonia	21	−.73164	10	−.084125	.61549
Finland	11	−1.63826	8	−1.05724	1.73203
France	31	.17498	15	−.30130	−.05272
Germany	29	−.00635	22	.45464	−.00289
Greece	52	2.07888	31	1.42657	2.96565
Greenland	13	−1.45694	10	−.84125	1.22565
Hungary	29	−.00635	11	−.73326	.00465
Ireland	27	−.18767	12	−.62527	.11734
Israel	26	−.27833	10	−.84125	.23415
Latvia	28	−.09701	12	−.62527	.06066
Lithuania	16	−1.18495	9	−.94924	1.12481
Northern Ireland	33	.35630	20	.23866	.08504
Norway	16	−1.18495	12	−.62527	.74091
Poland	20	−.82230	8	−1.05724	.86937
Portugal	29	−.00635	9	−.94924	.00602
Russia	28	−.09701	24	.67063	−.06506
Scotland	37	.71895	33	1.64255	1.18091
Slovakia	32	.26564	16	−.19330	−.05135
Sweden	17	−1.09429	11	−.73326	.80240
Switzerland	19	−.91296	9	−.94924	.86663
United States	23	−.55032	15	−.30130	.16581
Wales	53	2.16954	36	1.96652	4.26644
				$\Sigma\, z_{male}z_{female} =$ 24.403	
				$r = \Sigma\, z_{male}z_{female}\, /\, N$ $= 24.403/28 = .8715$	

Recall that the formula for a z score is: $z = (X - \bar{X})/S$, where $\bar{X}$ = the mean and S = the standard deviation.

FIGURE A.8

● Calculation of the Correlation Coefficient for the Percentage of Males and Females Who Drink Alcohol Weekly in 28 Select Countries

ables. Positive *r* values indicate a *direct* (or positive) relationship between the variables—in other words, one variable increases with the other. Negative *r* values indicate an *indirect* (or inverse) relationship between the variables—in other words, one variable increases whereas the other decreases.

So let's return to our question of a relationship between the percentage of males and females in a country who at age 15 drink weekly. ● FIGURE A.8 shows the calculation of the correlation coefficient for these data. As you can see, there is a strong positive correlation (*r* = .8715) between the percentage of males and females who drink alcohol weekly at age 15. This makes sense, because one might expect many of the factors that influence male underage drinking in a country to influence females similarly. One might think that one of these factors would be the legal drinking age in the country—that countries with a younger drinking age would have a higher percentage of 15-year-olds drinking alcohol illegally.

The data, however, do not fully support this hypothesis. In our sample, the correlation between legal drinking age and the percentage of males drinking at 15 is $r = -.412$. This moderately negative correlation indicates that countries with a lower legal drinking age tend to have higher rates of males drinking illegally at age 15. However, such a clear relationship for females was not found. Therefore, we can conclude that having a lower drinking age is *related* to higher rates of drinking at age 15 for males only. Recall from Chapter 1 that correlation does not imply causation here. We cannot say that a lower drinking age *causes* males to drink at 15. We can only say that the two variables are related in a linear fashion.

LEARNING OBJECTIVE

What Should You Know?

• Explain the logic behind inferential statistics, hypothesis testing, and statistical significance.

How Do Statistics Help Psychologists Draw Conclusions?

Inferential statistics are statistics that psychologists use to test hypotheses and draw conclusions about their data. In short, inferential statistics help psychologists judge whether observed differences in their data are large enough to be **significant**, or meaningful. To illustrate this issue, let's look at the difference in the average rate of drinking for males and females across the 28 countries (see Figures A.2a and A.2b). The mean percentage of males drinking at 15 is 29.1%, but the mean percentage of females who report drinking at 15 is only 17.8%. Thus, it appears that males and females are not equally likely to drink at age 15. But is this difference ($29.1 - 17.8 = 11.3$) large enough to convince us that males really differ from females in their underage drinking? Is it possible that these data are merely a fluke or coincidence? How big a difference must we see between the sexes before we can say that our results are *significant*? These are the questions that inferential statistics tackle for us.

The first step to understanding inferential statistics is to understand the nature of hypotheses. In all studies that use inferential statistics, the researcher sets forth two hypotheses. The first one, called the **null hypothesis (H$_0$)**, is a statement of what the researcher does *not* believe to be true about the variables. The second one, called the **alternative hypothesis (H$_1$)**, is a statement of what the researcher *does* believe to be true about the variables. In our example, these hypotheses would be:

$$H_0: \mu_{males} = \mu_{females}$$

$$H_1: \mu_{males} \neq \mu_{females}$$

Where

μ_{males} = the mean percentage of males drinking in the entire population of all 15-year-old males

$\mu_{females}$ = the mean percentage of females drinking in the entire population of all 15-year-old females

inferential statistics statistics that psychologists use in hypothesis testing to tell them when they should reject or accept their hypotheses about the population

significant results are considered significant when we find that there is a very small chance (usually less than 5%) of finding our results given the assumption that our null hypothesis is true

null hypothesis (H$_0$) the hypothesis that contains a statement of what we do *not* believe is true about our variables in the population

alternative hypothesis (H$_1$) the hypothesis that contains a statement of what we do believe is true about our variables in the population

So, in other words, we do *not* believe that the rate of drinking is the same for males and females across the world at age 15. Rather, we believe that 15-year-old males drink at a different rate than 15-year-old females. Although it may seem odd, the way that scientists proceed from this point is to try to show that the null hypothesis is correct. Rather than directly testing the notion set forth in the alternative hypothesis, we will instead test the hypothesis that contains the statement of what we do *not* believe to be true about our variables. So for the moment, we will assume that there is no difference between the rates of drinking for males and females at age 15. We will analyze our data to see whether they support this notion or whether we must reject this null hypothesis in favor of the alternative hypothesis that at age 15, males and females do indeed differ in their rates of drinking alcohol.

To test the null hypothesis, we must determine the probability of finding our results (that 29.1% of males and 17.8% of females drink), given the *assumption* that there is no real difference between the males and females when it comes to drinking at age 15. This is where a standard distribution comes in handy. If we can calculate a statistic on our data for which we know the distribution and the probabilities of obtaining certain values of the statistic, then

LEARNING CHALLENGE

In this appendix, we described how psychologists use statistics to describe data and test hypotheses. For a quick check of your understanding, try answering the following questions.

1. _____ are bits of knowledge gathered in scientific studies.

   a. Statistics
   b. Data
   c. Hypotheses
   d. Correlations

2. If we want to know if a person's height is a good predictor of his shoe size, which statistic(s) would be the most useful?

   a. the mean
   b. the mode
   c. the correlation coefficient
   d. a *z* score

3. If you want to describe the most common pet in America, after surveying 20,000 people to determine the type(s) of pet(s) they own, you should calculate the _____ of your data.

   a. mean
   b. median
   c. mode
   d. variance

4. A small company employs 10 people. At this company, three employees earn $20,000 a year, four employees earn $17,000, two employees earn $21,000, and the president earns $210,000 a year. Which of the following measures of central tendency is the most appropriate measure for accurately depicting the typical salary at this company?

   a. mean
   b. median
   c. mode
   d. variance

5. The mean of the standard normal distribution is equal to _____.

   a. 0
   b. 2
   c. 3
   d. −1

6. Which of the following statistics would be most useful for describing how the grades in a psychology course differ across the students in the class?

   a. mean
   b. sample variance
   c. correlation coefficient
   d. *z* score

7. A *z* score of 2.66 means that the raw score in question is _____ the mean of the distribution.

   a. 1.33 standard deviations below
   b. 1.33 standard deviations above
   c. 2.66 standard deviations below
   d. 2.66 standard deviations above

8. Assuming that IQ scores are normally distributed, what percentage of the population can be expected to score 2 or more standard deviations above the mean on an IQ test?

   a. 2.28%
   b. 5.36%
   c. 8.77%
   d. 52.35%

9. The hypothesis that psychologists actually test is called the _____ hypothesis.

   a. true
   b. null
   c. alternative
   d. testable

10. A(n) _____ distribution is a bell-shaped, symmetric frequency distribution.

   a. normal
   b. histogram
   c. scatter plot
   d. frequency polygon

Answers:

1. b	**5.** a	**9.** b
2. c	**6.** b	**10.** a
3. c	**7.** d	
4. b	**8.** a	

APPENDIX B

HOW DO WE APPLY PSYCHOLOGY IN THE WORKPLACE?

KATHY A. HANISCH, Iowa State University

WHAT IS I/O PSYCHOLOGY AND WHY IS IT IMPORTANT TO YOU?

You have applied for a job, submitted your résumé, and taken a series of tests. You have been interviewed by your potential supervisor and given a tour of the company. You now find yourself sitting across from the co-owners, who have just offered you a position. They tell you that their organization is a great place to work. As evidence, they tell you that no one has quit in the last 5 years and that employees are rarely absent. They also tell you that they have flexible policies. You can work whatever hours you like and take vacation whenever you want. And if you decide to work for them, you'll have access to spending cash as well as keys to the company.

You try to maintain your composure. You'd heard interesting things about this company, but didn't really believe them. Finally, the co-owners ask you what you are worth, indicating they will pay you whatever you wish. Now you're really dumbfounded and wonder what the catch is, but sit quietly while they talk about other issues. Does this sound too good to be true? Wouldn't this be ideal?

Almost this exact scenario played out in an organization owned and managed by an Oakland appliance dealer in the 1970s. His name was Arthur Friedman, and he had decided to change how he ran his business. Art, as reported in the *Washington Post* (Koughan, 1975), announced at one of his staff meetings that employees could work the hours they wanted, be paid what they thought they were worth, take vacation time when they wanted, and help themselves to petty cash if they were in need of spending money. New employees would be allowed to set their own wages too. As you might imagine, the employees weren't sure how to take this news. It was reported that no one said anything during the meeting when Art first described his plan (Koughan, 1975).

When asked why he was changing his business practices, Art replied, "I always said that if you give people what they want, you get what you want. You have to be willing to lose, to stick your neck out. I finally decided that the time had come to practice what I preached" (Koughan, 1975). In the final analysis, Art's experiment worked. The organization was profitable. Friedman signed union contracts without reading them (the employees didn't need a union with Art in charge). Employees didn't quit, they didn't steal from the company, and they were rarely absent. Net profits increased, and the company was a success. The employees realized that to make the organization work and remain in business, they had to be reasonable in their requests and behavior (Koughan, 1975).

A present-day company with some enticing work perks is SAS, the largest privately held software company. In 2010, *Fortune* magazine rated it the number one company to work for. Included among its many perks are 90% coverage of the health care premium, unlimited sick days, free health care with an on-site medical center that has a $4.5 million budget (it still saves the company $5 million a year; Kaplan, 2010), subsidized child care and cafeteria, free fitness center, swimming pool, and summer camps for employees' children. In addition SAS has an on-site billiards hall, sauna, manicurist, and hair salon, and offers massages. The company also has picnics and other family events (which employees and their families want to attend) as well as snacks (fruit, donuts, and M&Ms) on different days. In addition to these benefits, SAS rewards innovation and risk-taking while supporting the growth of its employees both personally and professionally (www.sas.com).

Organizations like SAS and Art Friedman's company are interesting because of how they deal with their employees and how that treatment affects the employees' behaviors. Psychologists who study people's behavior at work using psychological principles are called *industrial and organizational psychologists*, and their field of study is **industrial and organizational (I/O) psychology.** I/O psychologists study employee selection, performance appraisal, training, job design, communication, work stress, motivation, leadership, groups and teams, organizational culture/climate, human factors, job attitudes, well-being, and work behavior. This appendix will introduce you to the field of I/O psychology. You will experience many of the topics discussed here when you seek, obtain, and keep a job.

Adam Berry/Bloomberg via Getty Images

Jim Goodnight has been the CEO of SAS since incorporation in 1976. His organization was rated #1 by Forbes in 2010.

industrial and organizational (I/O) psychology the study of people's behavior at work using psychological principles

INDUSTRIAL AND ORGANIZATIONAL PSYCHOLOGY
Work in Our Lives

You have learned about work since you were a small child. You may have asked where your mother was going when she took you to day care or why your father left the house before 8 a.m. and did not return until after 5 p.m. You likely "played" at different jobs by dressing up as an astronaut, a firefighter, a teacher, a chef, or a construction worker. As you got older, other information about work may have come from your friends, other family members, school, and the media. In high school, more education and a part-time job may have given you additional details about the meaning of work. As you pursue a college degree, you may

Courtesy of K. Hanisch

Electrical workers!

receive information about the work and jobs available in your chosen field through classes, internships, or other job or research experiences.

Work is an important part of life for many people. We often ask people we meet what they "do," which translates into "What is your job and whom do you work for?" Many people identify with their work because they spend so much of their waking lives at work. Work is important because it provides many of the things people need and value. Income from work provides us with the money necessary to satisfy our basic needs for food, shelter, and security (for example, health care or retirement income), while the "leftover" money provides us with discretionary funds to use as we see fit. These funds may be used to buy a round of golf, an iPad, or a fancy place to live; to support charities or attend athletic or fine art performances; or to save for college. Essentially, money, typically from work, provides us with a standard of living that varies from person to person depending on our income and how we choose to spend it. In addition, work provides much more. It provides a source of social interactions and friendships, independence, a sense of accomplishment, satisfaction, a reason to get up in the morning, happiness, a sense of identity, recognition, and prestige (see ● TABLE B.1).

Although most researchers and practitioners agree that money and recognition are nearly universal motivators (R. E. Clark, 2003), many of the things we value or seek from work vary from person to person. For example, the prestige of a job may not be important to you, but it might be important to your best friend. Perhaps you will want your work to provide you with a sense of accomplishment or be a source of social interactions, while those attributes may not be valued by your friend. It is important to understand what you want from your work as well as what a job can provide.

From an employer's perspective, it is useful to determine what employees want because satisfied employees will be more likely than dissatisfied employees to work to meet organizational goals. Part of a supervisor's job is to ascertain what employees value because those values can be used to motivate employees to perform well in their jobs.

Types of Jobs

There are many types of work, in many types of jobs, in many different organizational settings. These settings include multinational conglomerates; public and private companies; nonprofits; federal, state, and local government organizations; and home businesses.

People in the United States work a variety of schedules, from extended workweeks (45–99 hours) to standard workweeks (35–44 hours) to part-time workweeks (fewer than 35 hours). Some people, such as police officers, medical personnel, and factory workers, because of the nature of their jobs, work shifts other than the typical 8 a.m. to 5 p.m. workday. Others are offered flexible working schedules that best fit their lives as long as they work the required number of hours and accomplish the work. Telecommuting is becoming more and more popular with the increase in appropriate technology. Some people work for virtual organizations that use communication technologies to outsource the majority of their functions.

Regardless of the type of job or your work schedule, you will likely spend most of your waking hours in some type of employment for many years. Many people spend their weekends working, too. Because work is critical to

TABLE B.1
● Jobs With the Highest and Lowest Prestige (2009)*

JOB DESCRIPTION	PERCENTAGE RATING JOB AS HIGH PRESTIGE
Highest Prestige	
Firefighter	62%
Scientist	57%
Doctor	56%
Nurse	54%
Teacher	51%
Military Officer	51%
Lowest Prestige	
Real Estate Agent/Broker	5%
Accountant	11%
Stockbroker	13%
Actor	15%

*It is interesting to note that some of the professions with the highest prestige (firefighter, nurse, teacher) are not considered high-paying jobs while some of those with the least prestige (actor, stockbroker, real estate agent) are associated with fame or high earning potential or both. It appears that the polled individuals do not equate money and fame with high prestige; they appear to be unique concepts. Source: www.harrisinteractive.com

who we are and what we do, studying the psychological principles and some of the topics examined by I/O psychologists will provide you with information that may be useful to you in your future careers.

Let's REVIEW

In this section, we provided an introduction to industrial and organizational psychology and highlighted the importance of work in our lives. As a quick check of your understanding, try answering the following questions at increasing levels of difficulty.

1. Nearly all people value _____ and _____ from their work.

   a. money; prestige
   b. prestige; social interactions
   c. money; recognition
   d. satisfaction; prestige

2. Which of the following would an I/O psychologist be *least* likely to study?

   a. leadership
   b. life satisfaction
   c. employee selection
   d. performance appraisal

3. SAS offers many enticing work perks. CEO Jim Goodnight chooses to do this primarily because _____.

   a. it makes inconveniences easy to deal with so employees can focus on their work
   b. most other companies offer these same perks
   c. he wanted SAS to be rated the number one company to work for in 2010
   d. there is a powerful employee union at SAS

ANSWERS 1. c; 2. b; 3. a

LEARNING OBJECTIVE

What Should You Know?
● Describe how employers decide which job applicants to hire.

SELECTING EMPLOYEES
The Hiring Process

Industrial and organizational psychologists first became involved in the process of selecting employees when the U.S. government needed help selecting and placing officers and soldiers in World War I (Aamodt, 2010). Psychologists used mental ability tests to determine who would become officers and who would be in the infantry. The process many employers now use to hire employees is very detailed, typically consisting of five components: job analysis, testing, legal issues, recruitment, and the selection decision.

Job Analysis

Job analysis is the identification of the critical elements of a job. I/O psychologists have helped devise effective strategies for determining three basic aspects of any job: (1) What tasks and behaviors are essential to the job? (2) What knowledge, skills, and abilities are needed to perform the job? And (3) What are the conditions (such as stress, safety, and temperature) under which the job is performed? A job analysis can be conducted in many ways. An analyst (an I/O psychologist, human resources employee, manager, or outside consultant) may interview current employees, have them complete questionnaires, observe people in the job, or talk to people knowledgeable about the job (Gael, 1988).

The information from a job analysis is used in many types of personnel functions. These include employee selection, performance appraisal, training, and human resources planning. Within the hiring process, job analysis is used to write job descriptions; to determine what tests might be used to assess the relevant knowledge, skills, and abilities of job applicants; and to assist in meeting legal requirements that affect the selection process.

job analysis identification of the critical elements of a job, including tasks, skills required, and working conditions

Testing

You are familiar with tests and taking tests. **Tests** are defined here as the measurement of carefully chosen samples of behavior. These include the standard paper-and-pencil tests used to measure specific skills or abilities in a class, or more general abilities as in the SAT or ACT. They also include personality assessments such as conscientiousness and honesty tests. In addition, work samples, in which applicants do a replica of the work they will be asked to do on the job, are useful tests. Tests are vital to the success of organizations. They are used to ascertain differences between people. The goal of these tests is to help employers choose the person best suited for the job and the organization. Regardless of the type of test or how it is administered, the reliability and validity of a test are very important (see Chapter 7).

Another type of test is the employee interview. Nearly all organizations use some type of interview in their selection of employees (Salgado, Viswesvaran, & Ones, 2003), even though interviews are often viewed as subjective and worthless. More than 85 years of research has provided evidence regarding when interviews are useful and when they are not.

Selection interviews can be broadly classified as unstructured and structured. **Unstructured interviews** are informal and unplanned. They are conducted by an untrained interviewer, with random questions and no scoring key. **Structured interviews** are conducted by a trained interviewer. They have standardized questions, a specific question order, and a predetermined scoring or answer key. Some typical questions asked during an unstructured interview are listed in ● TABLE B.2. Examples of structured interview questions are listed in ● TABLE B.3. Structured interviews, based on a job analysis, have greater reliability and validity than unstructured interviews (Huffcutt & Arthur, 1994).

Legal Issues

One of the most important pieces of legislation regarding employment, and specifically the hiring of employees, is **Title VII of the Civil Rights Act of 1964** (Equal Employment Opportunity Commission, 2002). Title VII "prohibits discrimination based on race, color, religion, sex, and national origin," known as the "Big 5." Providing protection for people comprising the Big 5 helps to ensure that they have equal employment opportunities. Exceptions to this provision include national security, seniority systems, and bona fide occupational qualifications (BFOQs). BFOQs permit organizations to discriminate in hiring persons in a protected class if the qualification is determined to be reasonably necessary to the operation of the business. For example, women can be discriminated against when hiring someone to model men's swimwear, and vice versa. It is reasonably necessary to the marketing and selling of swimwear that organizations hire men to model male swimwear and women to model female swimwear; sex is a BFOQ. It is not reasonably necessary, however, that a secretary in a church who does secretarial work and not church or religious work believe in the same religion as the church that employs him; religion in this case could not be used as a BFOQ.

test the measurement of a carefully chosen sample of behavior

unstructured interview informal, unplanned interview conducted by an untrained interviewer using random questions and no scoring key

structured interview interview conducted by a trained interviewer using standardized questions, a specific question order, and a predetermined scoring or answer key

Title VII of the Civil Rights Act of 1964 law that prohibits discrimination based on race, color, religion, sex, and national origin

---

TABLE B.2
● Typical Unstructured Interview Questions

1. What are your weaknesses?
2. Why should we hire you?
3. Why do you want to work here?
4. What are your goals?
5. Why did you leave (or why are you leaving) your job?
6. When were you most satisfied in your job?
7. What can you do for us that other candidates can't?
8. What are three positive things your last boss would say about you?
9. What salary are you seeking?
10. If you were an animal, which one would you want to be?

Source: C. Martin, 2006, Monster.com.

TABLE B.3
● Structured Behavior-Based Interview Questions

1. Tell me in specific details about a time when you had to deal with a difficult customer.
2. Give me an example of a time when you had to make a decision without a supervisor present.
3. Give me a specific example of when you demonstrated your initiative in an employment setting.
4. Give me an example of a time when you had to work with a team.
5. Describe a time when you had to be creative at solving a problem.

Source: Adapted from The Job Centre, Niagara College Canada, 2005, http://jobs.niagarac.on.ca/.

It is important for employers to abide by laws that protect people against discrimination because the costs of litigation can be very high, both monetarily and in terms of an organization's reputation. This protection applies to discrimination based not only on the Big 5, covered under the Civil Rights Act, but on other characteristics such as age (Age Discrimination in Employment Act) and disability (Americans with Disabilities Act). Employment law in the United States is meant to protect and provide equal opportunities for all individuals.

Legal issues in employment vary in different countries, however. The advertisement shown in ● FIGURE B.1 for a bookkeeper in Johannesburg would not be legal in the United States. It specifies that the applicant must be female, which would be illegal under Title VII of the Civil Rights Act. It also specifies age 40 or older, which would be illegal in some states that protect younger individuals against age discrimination. U.S. federal law prohibits discrimination based on age once a person reaches the age of 40 (Age Discrimination in Employment Act). The employer is seeking an older woman, which is likely not related to expected job performance; people younger than 40 could perform just as well in the job of a bookkeeper.

Employment legislation offers fair treatment for people looking for a job. In the United States, organizations with several employees are required to abide by the employment laws. These laws make the U.S. job market fairer than in many other countries.

Recruitment

The process organizational managers use to identify potential employees for a job is called **recruitment**. Depending on the job, a manager or owner may recruit from inside the company or seek someone outside the organization. The owner or manager may advertise on the company website or on a site for specific types of jobs. In addition, websites like monster.com and careerbuilder.com link potential employees and employers in a variety of jobs and locations. Other recruitment sources include newspapers, radio and television advertisements, trade magazines, professional publications, and employee referrals.

recruitment the process organizations use to identify potential employees for a job

---

FIGURE B.1

Bookkeeper - Johannesburg East

Expiry Date: 2010-07-02

Location: Johannesburg East

Category: Banking and Financial Services

Job Type: Permanent

Salary: R8000.00 to R10000.00 MONTHLY COST TO COMPANY

Apply Now!

Minimum Education: National Diploma (NQF5)

Required Experience: 3 Years

Job Details:

We are urgently looking for a 40 year or older lady to perform full bookkeeping duties.

We will consider the candidate with an accounting degree or diploma in bookkeeping. She must have a Pastel Partner, Pastel Evolution experience and also be able to work on books to trial balance.

Duties:
Invoicing
Full
Creditors
Cashbook
Pettycash
Management
Reports

Software Proficiency:
Microsoft Excel: Intermediate
Microsoft Word: Intermediate
Pastel Partner: Intermediate
Pastel Evolution: Basic

© Louis Quail/Corbis

Research indicates that employees recruited through inside sources such as employee referrals or rehires work for the organization longer and have better job performance than those recruited through outside sources including advertisements, employment agencies, or recruiters (Zottoli & Wanous, 2000). Studies have supported the idea that those recruited using inside sources receive more accurate information about the job than those recruited through external sources (Conrad & Ashworth, 1986; McManus & Baratta, 1992). In effect, the new employees receive realistic job previews.

A survey of the 50 best small and medium organizations to work for in the United States found that 92% use employee referrals and that more than 30% of all hires were referred by a current employee (A. Pomeroy, 2005). Because of their effectiveness, some companies provide rewards to employees who recommend an applicant who is hired. These rewards include cash, vacations, and prizes such as televisions and free house cleaning services for a year (R. Stewart, Ellenburg, Hicks, Kremen, & Daniel, 1990). Typically, the new employee must work for the organization a set period of time before the referring employee can receive the award (R. Stewart et al., 1990). SAS Canada offers a bonus up to $8,000 for a successful employee referral (http://www.eluta.ca/top-employer-sas-canada).

After applicants have submitted either a résumé or an application, someone from the organization such as the human resources manager or supervisor will determine which applicants should be considered further. In that process, he or she may make telephone inquiries of previous employers or other references and conduct criminal background checks.

A growing phenomenon is employers' use of social networking sites such as Facebook, LinkedIn, MySpace, and Twitter to learn about and even seek job candidates. In a 2009 CareerBuilder survey, 45% of employers reported that they use social networking sites in their selection process while 11% plan to start using them. On these sites employers have found promising candidates reporting on their own drug use, sexual exploits, and drinking, as well as posting inappropriate photographs and bad-mouthing their previous employer (Haefner, 2009). In addition to identifying risky behavior patterns, managers are using social networking sites to determine whether applicants would fit in well with the company culture and to evaluate their professionalism (Hargis, 2008). Some of the information job applicants thought would only be viewed by their peers is making its way into the public arena, with future employers and relatives viewing the information without the posters' knowledge.

Making the Decision

When selecting employees, employers are looking for a good match between the employee and the organization. They would like to match the requirements for excellent performance in the job with the person's knowledge, skills, abilities, personality, and motivation for the job. They attempt to accomplish this by using the different types of tests discussed earlier.

Researchers have posited two groups of factors that determine an employee's performance in a job. They are the "**can-do**" and the "**will-do**" **factors** (N. Schmitt, Cortina, Ingerick, & Wiechmann, 2003). "Can-do" factors suggest what an employee is capable of doing on the job if he is working to the best of his ability. Personality factors such as conscientiousness and need for achievement as well as integrity have been classified as important "will-do" factors in performance (N. Schmitt et al., 2003). "Will-do" factors suggest the time and effort an employee is willing to exert for the organization. A person's "can-do" and "will-do" factors may change as she moves from organization to organization. Once a person is selected, the important process of being accepted and socialized into the organization at all levels, including a work group or team, begins.

can-do factors factors that determine the maximum performance an employee can exhibit

will-do factors factors that determine the normal or typical performance by an employee

Let's REVIEW

In this section, we discussed the process of employee selection, which consists of five components, including job analysis, testing, legal issues, recruitment, and the decision of whom to hire. As a quick check of your understanding, try answering the following questions at increasing levels of difficulty.

1. Asking employees to describe their job is one way of conducting a _____.

   a. job evaluation   c. performance appraisal

   b. job analysis   d. job review

2. Zachary is usually a conscientious and hardworking employee, but the company has hired a new boss who is really lazy and doesn't motivate his employees. It is likely that Zachary's _____ will be compromised in this situation.

   a. try-to factors   c. can-do factors

   b. will-do factors   d. must-do factors

3. Alexander, a television reporter, wants access to the women's locker room right after the basketball game to conduct interviews with the team members. The women's team lets female reporters in to interview them, but wants Alexander to wait until after they have showered and changed because they think he is too critical in his reporting style. Alexander argues he needs to be treated the same as the female reporters. What would be the likely outcome if this issue goes before a court?

   a. The team would win because sex is a BFOQ in this case.

   b. The team members would win because they can discriminate against Alexander because they don't like his reporting style.

   c. Alexander would win because the team members can't discriminate against him because they don't like his reporting style.

   d. Alexander would win because sex is not a BFOQ in this case.

ANSWERS 1. b; 2. b; 3. d

SOCIALIZING EMPLOYEES: CULTURE, GROUPS, LEADERSHIP, AND PERFORMANCE APPRAISAL

What Should You Know?

- Describe how new employees become adapted to their work and organization.

When you report for your first day of work in an organization, there will be many things you will need to learn to be successful in your job. The process of learning these things is called **organizational socialization**, which has been defined as "the process by which organizational members become a part of, or are absorbed into, the culture of the organization" (Jablin, 1982, p. 255). Organizational socialization consists of people learning how the organization operates by using information provided by management, coworkers, observation, and company handbooks or memos.

Nowadays, electronic communication is an important part of how employees are socialized (Flanagin & Waldeck, 2004). Employees communicate through e-mail, texting, company websites, chat groups, and blogs. Job applicants also use these resources to learn about the organization before submitting their applications, and employers often screen job applicants through some of these same mediums.

Often, one of the first things an employee encounters on the job is new employee orientation training that focuses on the goals and expectations of the organization. These clearly help to set the expectations and culture of the organization. Other common types of training in organizations are diversity and harassment training. These training programs are usually required company-wide to ensure that all employees are aware of the policies of the organization; they also are used by organizations to try to prevent and correct harassment problems in an attempt to limit liability in harassment complaints (Equal Employment Opportunity Commission, 2010).

organizational socialization
the process by which members of an organization become a part of, or are absorbed into, the culture of the organization

Supervisors and coworkers are also important sources of socialization information. **Mentoring** is a form of training in which a current and often long-term employee (the mentor) is paired with a new employee. The mentor's role is to help the new employee adapt to the job by assisting with advice or resources. The mentor may provide information about how the organization works, career advancement opportunities, and how performance is evaluated. Good mentoring helps new employees become successful on the job and learn the formal and informal rules of the organization (Aamodt, 2010).

Research indicates that both mentors and those they mentor often benefit from the relationship. For example, in one study of health care employees, it was found that those who were mentored reported higher salaries, greater promotion rates, and more positive career success than those who did not receive mentoring (T. D. Allen, Lentz, & Day, 2006). Employees who have been mentored experience more effective socialization and better compensation, advancement, career satisfaction, job satisfaction, job involvement, and organizational commitment than those with no mentoring (Greenhaus, 2003).

"We've worked hard to create a corporate culture that is based on trust between our employees and the company."

—Jim Goodnight, SAS CEO

(http://www.sas.com/jobs/corporate/index.html)

Organizational Culture and Climate

Organizational culture includes the shared assumptions and beliefs of the organization. These cognitions then influence the **organizational climate**, or actions and behaviors of the people in the group or organization (Schein, 1985). These behaviors are considered the norm for the organization; they represent the "normal behaviors" expected from its members. Because culture and climate generally operate in unison, our discussion will refer to these elements collectively as *culture* (Ostroff, Kinicki, & Tamkins, 2003). Organizational culture is important because it lets employees know what is expected of them and affects how they think and behave. Culture is often determined by the founders of the organization and may be modified over time by the successes and failures of an organization. See ● FIGURE B.2 for factors that affect organizational culture.

Some organizations like SAS have cultures that appear to have been successful from the start as suggested by low turnover and organizational profitability. There have been several case studies of organizations that have successfully changed their culture from poor to better or great. Remember Art Friedman from the beginning of this appendix? Art Friedman allowed his employees to set their own wages and decide the hours they worked; he also required employees to belong to the union. After Friedman made these changes, employee grumbling stopped (Koughan, 1975). The organizational culture changed, resulting in better morale, increased productivity, and employee longevity. No one wanted to quit working in a culture where the employees got to make their own decisions that affected the organization's bottom line. Finding an organizational culture that fits your working style will have consequences for your attitudes, performance, and tenure in an organization. Work teams and the leadership of an organization have a large influence on the culture of an organization.

Groups and Teams

Work teams and **groups** can be defined as two or more employees who have common goals, have tasks that are interdependent, interact socially, and work on relevant organizational tasks within specific requirements and rules (Kozlowski & Bell, 2003). Just as there can be a culture in an organization, groups or teams also exhibit cultures that may encourage or discourage certain types of work-related behaviors and attitudes. These cultures then form the basis for the socialization of new group or team members.

---

mentoring the pairing of a current and often long-term employee (the mentor) with a new employee

organizational culture the shared cognitive assumptions and beliefs of an organization

organizational climate the behavioral norms of an organization

work teams/groups two or more employees who together perform organizationally relevant tasks, share one or more common goals, interact socially, exhibit task interdependencies, and maintain and manage boundaries within an organizational context

FIGURE B.2

Several factors affect the organizational culture of an organization.

- Amplified by behaviors of leaders
- Evident in the behaviors of individuals and groups
- Embedded in a network of organizational practices
- Organizational Culture
- Visible in the 'way that work gets done' on a day-to-day basis
- Shared beliefs, values and assumptions held by members of an organization

Although most organizations provide formal means of socializing new employees (for example, new employee orientation training), the group or team dynamics have immediate and direct effects on employees' socialization (N. Anderson & Thomas, 1996). The outcomes of organization socialization and work group socialization may be different. Teams may have leaders or may be self-managing. Self-managing teams tend to show better productivity, an increase in work quality, improved quality of life for employees, decreased absenteeism, and decreased turnover than teams with leaders (S. G. Cohen & Ledford, 1994). When teams fail, often the failure is linked to the team leader, who may be too autocratic, wielding too much power or influence. As a result the team does not realize the autonomy and control levels it needs to be successful (G. L. Stewart & Manz, 1995).

Leadership

"Leadership is the art of getting someone else to do something you want done because he wants to do it."

—*Dwight D. Eisenhower*

Leadership has many definitions, including one person influencing another person or a team toward a goal (Bryman, 1996). Leadership has received a lot of research attention in industrial/organizational psychology. Yet it is still difficult to describe how to make or select the ideal or best leader. Many theories exist, and most have been useful in helping us understand what makes a good leader and how to improve leadership style.

Personality plays a role in many leadership theories. Certainly, it is an important aspect of successful or unsuccessful leaders. Kirkpatrick and Locke's (1991) review suggests that drive, honesty and integrity, self-confidence, cognitive abilities, and knowledge are associated with successful leaders. Leaders with poor cognitive abilities and social skills and those who are indecisive, low in self-confidence and self-esteem, dishonest, and lacking in ambition tend to be less successful (R. E. Kaplan, Drath &, Kofodimos, 1991).

Art Friedman's integrity likely made him a successful leader. He decided to give employees what he would want, providing them with the capabilities to make major decisions that could either make or break the organization. In his case, he created a self-managing group that had no need for external assistance from unions or other entities. As a result, Friedman demonstrated the transformational leadership approach (Bass, 1990). **Transformational leadership** is characterized by high ethical standards, inspirational motivation, intellectual stimulation, and individual consideration—all clearly evident in Arthur Friedman's leadership style.

Jim Goodnight, the CEO of SAS, has the philosophy that you should "treat employees like they make a difference and they will" (www.sas.com/jobs/corporate/index.html). Undoubtedly, his philosophy is working because SAS, even with the economic turbulence of the past several years, has continued to grow and has remained profitable. Other indicators include the company's number one ranking in 2010 by *Forbes* magazine, employee turnover of 2% in 2009 compared to the software industry average of 22%, and an employee average of only 2 sick days per year (there is no limit). Jim Goodnight wants a balanced work and personal life for his employees so they work 35-hour workweeks with many of them setting their own hours. He wants his employees to work well during their 7-hour days so his company tries to take care of inconveniences by having many services on-site (e.g., fitness center, day care, cafeteria, medical center). Employees rave about how great it is to work at SAS (Kaplan, 2010).

Leaders today must contend with information-based team environments requiring the capacity for sifting large amounts of information coming from computer networks (Avolio, Kahai, & Dodge, 2000). The widely varying working environments that result from global competition require leaders to be adaptable (Mann, 1959), capable of handling stress (D. Goleman, 1998), knowledgeable about competitors and products (Kirkpatrick & Locke, 1991), and able to solve complex problems quickly (Zaccaro, Mumford, Connelly, Marks, & Gilbert, 2000). Leaders in organizations today also need to be concerned with human resources planning (the hiring and maintenance of an employee workforce) and the

Amy Sussman/Getty Images for Discovery Communications

Oprah Winfrey is a modern-day charismatic leader. She is probably best known as host of the Oprah Winfrey Show. In addition, she has started multiple charity groups, donating millions of dollars across the globe.

leadership a social influence process in which a person steers others toward a goal

transformational leadership characterized by high ethical standards, inspirational motivation, intellectual stimulation, and individual consideration

appropriate evaluation of employee performance to ensure their organizations will be competitive and profitable in the ensuing years.

Performance Appraisal

Performance appraisals are the evaluations or reviews of employees' performance. Employees should continually be told about their job performance, both the good and the bad, by their employers. Formal employee performance appraisals are times for management to systematically evaluate employee performance and productivity on the job, set performance goals, and directly convey information about the culture of the organization (see Fletcher & Perry, 2001, for a review of research and future trends in performance appraisal). Performance reviews are important for many reasons, including (1) determining areas of employees' work needing improvement and areas to be complimented, (2) effectively managing employee raises and promotions, (3) dealing with unproductive employees in a fair and appropriate manner that may include termination, and (4) assisting in workforce planning that may be particularly important in difficult economic times, but should be done routinely to have the best employees in the organization.

Performance reviews vary in terms of their frequency, with some organizations evaluating new employees after 30 or 60 days after hire while others evaluate new employees' performance 3 or 6 months after hire. Once an employee has been working for an organization for one year, most organizations formally evaluate performance annually or semi-annually (Aamodt, 2010). A typical performance review consists of some type of carefully developed form that is filled out by the supervisor of the employee; some organizations have both the employee and the employer fill out the same form to allow them to compare their views of the employee's performance. This is followed by a meeting between the manager and employee to discuss the employee's performance. This meeting should be held in a neutral, distraction-free location with an appropriate amount of time for discussion.

Because the performance review will often clearly define the most important components of employees' jobs and help shape the culture of the organization, it is recommended that employers provide performance appraisal forms to new employees when they are hired or on their first day of work. This will send a clear message to the employees about the work that is valued by the organization and about whether they will be evaluated according to criteria set by management (this may suggest a more collaborative or cooperative culture) or will be appraised relative to their coworkers (this may suggest a more competitive culture). It is in the best interest of both the employer (for performance management) and the employee (as a road map to success) that the job performance requirements be known at the time of hire. Once employees are hired who can complete the work tasks and be effective in the organization (that is, they have the ability to do the job), then their attitudes become important because their attitudes will directly influence their work behaviors.

Performance review meetings should be conducted in a distraction-free, neutral location with a prepared and trained employer.

performance appraisals the evaluations or reviews of employees' job performance

Let's REVIEW

Let's REVIEW In this section, we discussed employee socialization within an organization and its work groups. Leadership and the type of work group will affect employees' job performance, which should be reviewed in successful organizations. As a quick check of your understanding, try answering the following questions at increasing levels of difficulty.

1. Spencer, a new employee of the company, has learned most of the behaviors required to do his job effectively. This would illustrate that Spencer has learned the _____ of the organization.

   a. organizational climate

   b. organizational culture

   c. transformational culture

   d. transformational climate

2. Performance reviews are important because they _____.

   a. help define the culture of the organization

   b. provide employees needed information on their job performance

   c. aid employers in determining the type of training needed by their employees

   d. all of the above

3. Carol is part of a successful self-managing team in an organization that produces handcrafted furniture. Compared to her coworkers in traditional-leader teams, Carol and her work team should have _____.

   a. better productivity, lower work quality, and a decrease in absenteeism

   b. an increase in work quality, decrease in work quantity, and better quality of life

   c. an increase in absenteeism, lower work quality, and higher work quantity

   d. better productivity, better work quality, and a better quality of life

ANSWERS 1. a; 2. d; 3. d

ATTITUDES AND BEHAVIORS AT WORK

LEARNING OBJECTIVE

What Should You Know?

- Describe the impact of employees' attitudes on their behaviors at work.

One of the most important factors influencing whether you will be motivated to do a good job hinges on your attitudes at work (see Chapter 11). The causes and consequences of work attitudes have been extensively researched. Some of the outcomes of attitudes include volunteering for a project, helping out a coworker, quitting, absenteeism, tardiness, early retirement, and performance.

Attitudes at Work

Attitudes at work are many and varied. In general, you can be satisfied or dissatisfied with the tasks and conditions at work, the people in your work environment, and the rewards you get from work. Employee satisfaction is important because it has been shown to be related to employee behaviors at work (Hanisch, 1995). Two of the most commonly studied work attitudes are job satisfaction and organizational commitment.

Job Satisfaction

The positive or negative feelings associated with a job define **job satisfaction** (Thurstone, 1931). Some of the ways organizations can create satisfied employees include flexible working hours, professional growth opportunities, interesting work (Hackman & Oldham, 1976), autonomy, job security, a good supervisor, good benefits, competitive pay, opportunities for promotion (Cranny, Smith, & Stone, 1992), respect, recognition, and being part of something or being included. It is important to note that what makes one worker satisfied may not make another worker satisfied. For some people, interesting work is paramount. Others place higher emphasis on having coworkers they like. Still others feel that the pay and benefits they receive are most important. Virtually all employees value recognition (some acknowledgment of their work), respect, and being part of the organization. These rewards are all inexpensive

attitudes at work satisfaction with the work itself, pay and benefits, supervision, coworkers, promotion opportunities, working conditions, and job security

job satisfaction the positive or negative affect associated with a job

and typically require very little time to implement. Just as in selection, a match between what you want and what the organization can provide will result in a successful outcome for both parties.

TRY THIS DEMONSTRATION

Fill out the JDI Work on Present Job scale (● TABLE B.4). One measure often used to assess employee work attitudes, and specifically different facets of job satisfaction, is the Job Descriptive Index (JDI; P. C. Smith, Kendall, & Hulin, 1969). This index has been improved upon based on years of research (e.g., Balzer et al., 1997; Hanisch, 1992). The JDI measures five facets of satisfaction: Work on Present Job, Supervisor, Coworkers, Present Pay, and Opportunities for Promotion.

TABLE B.4

● Work on Present Job

Think of the work you do at present. How well does each of the following words or phrases describe your job? In the blank beside each word or phrase below, write:

Y for "Yes" if it describes your work

N for "No" if it does *not* describe your work

? if you cannot decide

_____ 1. Fascinating	_____ 10. Useful
_____ 2. Routine	_____ 11. Tiring
_____ 3. Satisfying	_____ 12. Healthful
_____ 4. Boring	_____ 13. Challenging
_____ 5. Good	_____ 14. Too much to do
_____ 6. Creative	_____ 15. Frustrating
_____ 7. Respected	_____ 16. Simple
_____ 8. Uncomfortable	_____ 17. Repetitive
_____ 9. Pleasant	_____ 18. Gives sense of accomplishment

Scoring Key:

1. Y=3, N=0, ?=1;	7. Y=3, N=0, ?=1;	13. Y=3, N=0, ?=1;
2. Y=0, N=3, ?=1;	8. Y=0, N=3, ?=1;	14. Y=0, N=3, ?=1;
3. Y=3, N=0, ?=1;	9. Y=3, N=0, ?=1;	15. Y=0, N=3, ?=1;
4. Y=0, N=3, ?=1;	10. Y=3, N=0, ?=1;	16. Y=0, N=3, ?=1;
5. Y=3, N=0, ?=1;	11. Y=0, N=3, ?=1;	17. Y=0, N=3, ?=1;
6. Y=3, N=0, ?=1;	12. Y=3, N=0, ?=1;	18. Y=3, N=0, ?=1

To interpret your score on the work scale, 27 is considered the neutral value (Balzer et al., 1997). Values considerably higher would be evaluated as very satisfied; values considerably lower would be evaluated as very dissatisfied with the work on your present job.

A recent survey found that listening to music at work leads to higher levels of reported employee satisfaction. About one third of those participating in a Spherion Workplace Snapshot survey conducted by Harris Interactive in 2006 reported they listened to an iPod, MP3 player, or other personal music device while working (www.spherion.com). Seventy-nine percent of the participants reported that listening to music improved their job satisfaction or productivity or both at work. Allowing workers to listen to music may become more and more popular in jobs where music does not interfere with coworkers, safety, or job performance. Having happy workers contributes to an organization's success.

Organizational Commitment

Employee commitment to an organization is related to employee retention within the organization. There are three types of organizational commitment: affective, normative, and continuance (J. P. Meyer & Allen, 1991). Meyer and Allen define **affective commitment** as an

affective commitment an employee's emotional attachment to the organization employee's emotional attachment to the organization that makes the employee want to stay in the organization. **Normative commitment** is based on feelings of obligation. **Continuance commitment** results when an employee remains with a company because of the high cost of losing organizational membership, including monetary (for example, pension benefits) and social (such as friendships) costs. J. P. Meyer and Herscovitch (2001) argue that employees have an organizational commitment profile at any given time in their job, with high or low values on each of the three types of commitment. In other words, an employee may have high scores on normative and continuance commitment, but be lower on affective commitment. Depending on the profile, the employee may engage in different behaviors such as quitting or helping out the organization.

Students may experience these different types of commitment to their college. Affective commitment occurs when a student feels an emotional attachment to her university because she really likes the school, including classes, the football team, and the town. Normative commitment might be evidenced by a student whose parents attended that college and who feels obligated to do the same regardless of whether it is the best school for him. Staying at a college because your friends are there and you have already paid for 2 years would typify acting under continuance commitment. The three levels of commitment could be represented as a commitment profile for a student.

Organizational commitment is related to job satisfaction. Employees who are satisfied with their job are more committed to their organization than are those who are less satisfied (Mueller, Boyer, Price, & Iverson, 1994; Mosedeghrad, Ferlie, and Rosenberg, 2008). Other correlates of organizational commitment include trust in one's supervisor and human resources practices that are supportive of employees (Arthur, 1994). The organizational commitment of Friedman's employees was very high, as evidenced by no turnover in 5 years; the low turnover at SAS also supports strong organizational commitment by its employees.

Employees report their job satisfaction and productivity increase if they are allowed privileges such as listening to music while they work.

Behaviors at Work

Employers want their employees to engage in behaviors that will make them successful in the job because their success helps the organization meet its goals, including earning profits and fulfilling its mission. Employees have control over two aspects of their work: their time and their effort (Naylor, Pritchard, & Ilgen, 1980). Having employees at work instead of late or absent as well as exerting effort while at work are important to performance and productivity. Positive behaviors generally help an organization meet its goals while negative behaviors detract from goal attainment.

Organizational Citizenship Behaviors

Organizational citizenship behaviors (OCBs), or prosocial behaviors, are often described as extra-role behaviors because they are behaviors not specifically required by the job and not usually evaluated during performance reviews. These behaviors go beyond what is expected by the organization (C. A. Smith, Organ, & Near, 1983). Examples include staying late to finish a project, mentoring a new employee, volunteering for work, and helping a coworker. Some reasons why people engage in organizational citizenship behaviors are job satisfaction, high job autonomy, a positive organizational culture, high agreeableness (as a personality dimension; Witt, Kacmar, Carlson, & Zivnuska, 2002), and high conscientiousness (Borman, Penner, Allen, & Motowidlo, 2001). OCBs have positive consequences for the organization and for employees in their day-to-day interactions with others in the organization.

Organizational Withdrawal and Counterproductive Behaviors

Unhappy employees cause problems for organizations because they sometimes engage in behaviors that researchers refer to as **organizational withdrawal** (Hanisch, Hulin, & Roznowski, 1998) and counterproductive behaviors (Sackett & DeVore, 2001). Organizational withdrawal has been defined as behaviors employees use to avoid their work (**work withdrawal**) or their job (**job withdrawal**) (Hanisch, 1995; Hanisch & Hulin, 1990, 1991). Examples of work withdrawal are being absent from work, leaving work early, arriving to work late, missing meetings, and using work equipment for personal use without permission. Examples of job withdrawal are quitting one's job, transferring to another department within an organization, and retiring.

normative commitment commitment to the organization based on feelings of obligation

continuance commitment remaining with an organization because of the high cost (monetary or social or both) of losing organizational membership

organizational citizenship behaviors (OCBs) employee behaviors that go beyond what is expected by the organization

organizational withdrawal work withdrawal or job withdrawal

work withdrawal behaviors employees use to avoid their work (e.g., lateness, absenteeism)

job withdrawal behaviors employees use to avoid their job (e.g., quitting, retiring)

College students are familiar with withdrawal behaviors when it comes to certain college courses. Some classes may fail to keep your attention, and you may find yourself taking a nap in class or texting with a friend during lecture. You may even look for legitimate reasons not to attend class, such as offering to fill in for another employee at work or deciding to attend an optional session for another class.

Counterproductive behaviors, although similar in some ways to withdrawal behaviors, are defined as "any intentional behavior on the part of an organizational member viewed by the organization as contrary to its legitimate interests" (Sackett & DeVore, 2001). An example of a counterproductive behavior would be an intentional violation of safety procedures that puts the employee and the organization at risk. Other examples of counterproductive behavior are theft, destruction of property, unsafe behavior, poor attendance, drug use, and inappropriate physical actions such as attacking a coworker.

Relation Between Attitude and Behavior

Organizational citizenship behaviors are positively related to job satisfaction and organizational commitment. In other words, employees with good attitudes and who feel committed to their organization are more likely to do positive things to assist the organization (LePine, Erez, & Johnson, 2002). Research indicates that those employees who demonstrate organizational citizenship behaviors are less likely to engage in counterproductive behaviors (Dalal, 2006). Researchers have found strong links between job satisfaction and specific withdrawal or counterproductive behaviors such as absenteeism (Hackett, 1989), and even stronger links with job withdrawal (Hanisch & Hulin, 1990).

Employers need to evaluate their work environment and benefit packages and make modifications where necessary to ensure that they have employees who are satisfied and committed. Art Friedman made modifications in the work environment of his organization that resulted in high satisfaction and commitment among his employees. To help with the inconvenience of going to the doctor, SAS built an on-site medical center for employees and their families; there is no charge unless you fail to show up for an appointment (Kaplan, 2010). Employees need to learn how to seek out satisfying work and perks that will result in their commitment to the organization. Satisfaction and commitment facilitate OCBs and decrease withdrawal and counterproductive behaviors. Together the right employee attitudes and behaviors will lead to successful organizational functioning.

counterproductive behaviors
intentional behaviors on the part of an organizational member viewed by the organization as contrary to its legitimate interests

Let's
REVIEW
In this section, we discussed employee attitudes and behaviors at work, focusing on job satisfaction, organizational commitment, withdrawal, and counterproductive behaviors. As a quick check of your understanding, try answering the following questions at increasing levels of difficulty.

1. Quitting one's job would be an example of _____.

a. normative commitment   c. organizational citizenship behavior

b. job withdrawal   d. work withdrawal

2. _____ would be an example of an organizational citizenship behavior while _____ would be an example of a counterproductive behavior.

a. Mentoring a new employee; engaging in safe work practices

b. Being late; staying late to help a coworker

c. Missing a meeting; being late for work

d. Volunteering to serve on a committee; physically attacking your supervisor

3. Gordon's organizational commitment has been decreasing in the last year. Which of the following is Gordon most likely to do if his organizational commitment doesn't improve soon?

a. quit   c. ask for a raise

b. be absent   d. steal from the organization

SUMMARY

This appendix detailed the role of I/O psychologists in the workplace, including job analysis, employee recruitment and selection, organizational culture, performance appraisal, and the effect of employees' work attitudes on their work behaviors.

Now that you have an understanding of the process organizations use to hire successful employees, you have some of the tools necessary to help you in your search for a job. You also learned about the appropriate matches you might strive for in seeking employment that will make your work with an organization fulfilling for both you and the company.

If you enjoyed learning about I/O psychology and think it might be a possible career for you, education and employment opportunities may interest you. Most I/O psychologists earn a master's or doctoral degree from a graduate school. This may take an additional 2 to 5 years beyond a bachelor's degree. Job opportunities are varied and often lucrative. For example, people with master's degrees in I/O psychology may work for an organization in its human resources office or conduct research on the best ways to train its employees. They may also work for the government, be employed in a consulting firm, or start their own consulting firm after obtaining some experience in the workplace. Those who earn a doctoral degree may secure the same types of jobs as those with master's degrees, but will typically be paid more for their expertise. In addition, they may also work for a university or college teaching courses or conducting research on topics of their choosing, or doing both. I/O psychology is an excellent career choice for many students interested in business who wish to have an impact on the work lives of employees.

STUDYING the APPENDIX

KEY TERMS

industrial and organizational
   (I/O) psychology (665)
job analysis (667)
test (668)
unstructured interview (668)
structured interview (668)
Title VII of the Civil Rights
   Act of 1964 (668)
recruitment (669)

can-do factors (670)
will-do factors (670)
organizational
   socialization (671)
mentoring (672)
organizational culture (672)
organizational climate (672)
work teams/groups (672)
leadership (673)

transformational
   leadership (673)
performance appraisals (674)
attitudes at work (675)
job satisfaction (675)
affective commitment (676)
normative commitment (677)
continuance
   commitment (677)

organizational citizenship
   behaviors (OCBs) (677)
organizational
   withdrawal (677)
work withdrawal (677)
job withdrawal (677)
counterproductive
   behaviors (678)

LEARNING CHALLENGE

TEST YOURSELF!

In this appendix, we described I/O psychology and how I/O psychologists impact the work lives of employees. For a quick check of your understanding, try answering the following questions.

1. Industrial and organizational psychologists may be employed in _____.

   a. organizations
   b. universities
   c. government agencies
   d. all of the above

2. On Sharon's first day working for the Campbell Company she will most likely be required to attend  _____.

   a. diversity training
   b. safety training
   c. employee orientation training
   d. job rotation training

3. Mentoring of new employees, in general, has been found to have positive outcomes or consequences for _____.

a. both the mentor and the employee
b. the mentor
c. the employee
d. organizations with autocratic leaders

4. Structured interviews are better than unstructured interviews because they are _____.

a. easier to conduct
b. more valid and reliable
c. liked better by job applicants
d. less time consuming

5. Giving new employees a copy of their performance appraisal forms would be important in helping to _____.

a. determine employees' organizational citizenship behaviors
b. shape the culture and climate of the organization
c. determine employees' organizational withdrawal behaviors
d. alleviate legal concerns about performance reviews

6. SAS has company picnics and provides tickets to rodeos and the circus to help employees with the process of _____.

a. organizational withdrawal
b. organizational socialization
c. organizational transformation
d. organizational productivity

7. Todd stays late to help a coworker who has gotten behind in his work. Todd is exhibiting which type of behavior?

a. work withdrawal
b. productive behavior
c. organizational citizenship behavior
d. job withdrawal

8. The employees of SAS believe they have a great place to work with a fair employer and a trusting environment. In I/O psychology terms, they have a positive _____.

a. organizational culture
b. organizational climate
c. work-group climate
d. transformational leader

9. Don has been offered a position in another company that pays better and is more profitable than his current company. He is having a hard time deciding whether to accept the position because the company has given him a lot of time off to care for his mother. Don's decision-making problem is likely due to his _____.

a. normative commitment
b. occupational commitment
c. affective commitment
d. continuance commitment

10. Howard refers Lucille for a position in his organization. Based on research on employee referral programs, Lucille should _____.

a. be more satisfied with her job
b. be a poor performer
c. file fewer grievances with the company
d. stay longer with the organization

Answers:

1. d	**5.** b	**9.** a
2. c	**6.** b	**10.** d
3. a	**7.** c	
4. b	**8.** a	

USE IT OR LOSE IT: APPLYING PSYCHOLOGY

1. You have been invited to interview with a company. What types of benefits or perks do you want from the job? If the interviewer asked you what you would like for a starting salary, what would you say? How could you make sure you were in line with what the company might be able to pay someone with your education and experience?

2. What types of things are most important to you when seeking a job? Do you value interesting work? Stimulating coworkers? Or is money most important to you? Think about those things you value in a job that will make for a satisfying and successful career, and devise a few strategies to obtain them.

CRITICAL THINKING FOR INTEGRATION

1. The reliability and validity of employment tests (discussed in Chapter 7), as broadly defined in this appendix, are very important. Think about how you would evaluate the validity of a new personality test that an organization wants to use to hire salespeople. What are two different ways that the test's validity could be evaluated?

2. Stress is associated with attitudes, as discussed in Chapter 12. How can employers help to ensure a work environment where stress is manageable? Do you think an organization could completely eliminate work stress for its employees? Would it want to do so?

3. Sexual harassment (discussed in Chapter 10) is an issue many organizations have faced. What are some of the outcomes and consequences of sexual harassment for employers and employees? Do you think sexual harassment is expensive for organizations? If so, in what ways?

GLOSSARY

absolute threshold the minimum intensity of a stimulus at which participants can identify its presence 50% of the time

accommodation Ch. 3: the process through which the lens is stretched or squeezed to focus light on the retina; Ch. 9: the process by which a schema is changed, modified, or created anew in order to understand something new in the environment

acetylcholine (ACh) neurotransmitter related to muscle movement and perhaps consciousness, learning, and memory

achievement according to Marcia and Erikson, an identity state in which a commitment to personal values that have been adequately explored is attained

acquisition the process of learning a conditioned response or behavior

action potential neural impulse fired by a neuron when it reaches −55 mv

activation-synthesis theory suggests that dreams do not have symbolic meaning, but are the by-product of the brain's random firing of neural impulses during REM sleep

actor/observer bias our tendency to make the fundamental attribution error when judging others, while being less likely to do so when making attributions about ourselves

actualizing tendency according to Rogers, the natural drive in humans to strive for fulfillment and enhancement

adrenal cortex outside part of the adrenal gland that plays a role in the manufacture and release of androgens and therefore influences sexual characteristics

adrenal medulla center part of the adrenal gland that plays a crucial role in the functioning of the sympathetic nervous system

affective commitment an employee's emotional attachment to the organization

affective component of emotion the subjective experience of what you are feeling during the emotion

agoraphobia an excessive fear of being in places from which escape might be difficult or where help might not be available if one were to experience panic

alarm reaction the first phase of the general adaptation syndrome, characterized by immediate activation of the nervous and endocrine systems

algorithm a method of solving a particular problem that always leads to the correct solution

all-or-none fashion all action potentials are equal in strength; once a neuron begins to fire an action potential, it fires all the way down the axon

alogia decreased quality and/or quantity of speech

alternative hypothesis (H_1) the hypothesis that contains a statement of what we do believe is true about our variables in the population

altruism helping another without being motivated by self-gain

amplitude a physical property of some energies that corresponds to the height of the wave peaks

amygdala part of the limbic system that plays a role in our emotions of fear and aggression

anal stage Freud's second psychosexual stage, which occurs from approximately 18 months to 3 years of age, in which the parents' regulation of the child's biological urge to expel or retain feces affects personality development

androgens a class of male hormones found in both males and females

anhedonia absence of pleasure from one's usual activities

anorexia nervosa a mental health disorder in which a person has an intense fear of gaining weight, even though he or she is actually underweight. This irrational fear motivates the person to lose unhealthy amounts of weight through self-starvation.

anterograde amnesia a type of amnesia in which one is unable to store new memories in long-term memory

antianxiety medications minor tranquilizers such as Valium that are prescribed to reduce tension and anxiety

antidepressants medications prescribed to alleviate the symptoms of depression, eating disorders, and some anxiety disorders

antimanic medications drugs that are prescribed to alleviate manic symptoms of bipolar disorder

antipsychotic medications major tranquilizers such as Haldol that are prescribed to relieve psychotic symptoms such as delusions and hallucinations

antisocial personality disorder a personality disorder marked by a pattern of disregard for and violation of the rights of others with no remorse or guilt for one's actions

anxiety disorder a disorder marked by excessive apprehension that seriously interferes with a person's ability to function

anxiety hierarchy outlines, according to the degree of fear, the threatening images elicited by a feared object or situation; the outline starts with the least frightening images and progresses to the most distressing

aphasia an impairment of language, most often resulting from brain damage, in which the person may have difficulty producing speech, understanding speech, or both

applied research scientific study to solve a problem

approach–approach conflict a situation in which a person must choose between two likable events

approach–avoidance conflict a situation in which a person is faced with a need that has both positive and negative aspects

archetypes according to Jung, mental representations or symbols of themes and predispositions to respond to the world in a certain way that are contained in the collective unconscious

arousal theory a theory of motivation that states that we are motivated to seek out activities that allow us to perform at our optimum level of arousal

asexual one who has little to no attraction to either sex

assimilation the process by which an existing schema is used to understand something new in the environment

association cortex areas of the cortex involved in the association or integration of information from the motor-sensory areas of the cortex

attachment the emotional bond between caretaker and infant that is established by 8 or 9 months

attention conscious awareness; can be focused on events that are taking place in the environment or inside our minds

attitudes evaluative judgments that integrate what we know and how we feel about people, places, or things

attitudes at work satisfaction with the work itself, pay and benefits, supervision, coworkers, promotion opportunities, working conditions, and job security

attribution the act of assigning cause to behavior

auditory cortex a region of the cortex found in the temporal lobe that governs our processing of auditory information in the brain

auditory nerve the nerve that carries information from the inner ear to the brain

authoritarian parent a parenting style characterized by high levels of control and low levels of affection

authoritative parent a parenting style characterized by moderate levels of control and affection

autobiographical memory memory for our past that gives us a sense of personal history

autonomic nervous system branch of the peripheral nervous system that primarily governs involuntary organ functioning and actions in the body

availability heuristic a heuristic in which we use the ease with which we can recall instances of an event to help us estimate the frequency of the event

aversion therapy a type of therapy that uses classical conditioning to condition people to avoid certain stimuli

aversive racism a proposed form of subtle racism in which European Americans feel aversive emotions around African Americans, which may lead European Americans to discriminate against African Americans

avoidance–avoidance conflict a situation in which a person must choose between two undesirable events

avolition the inability to follow through on one's plans

axon the long tail-like structure that comes out of the cell body of the neuron and carries action potentials that convey information from the cell body to the synapse

babbling the combinations of vowel and consonant sounds uttered by infants beginning around 4 months

balance theory the theory that when we are attracted to people who do not share our attitudes, we feel dissonance, which motivates us to change in some way to reduce this dissonance

basal metabolic rate the rate at which we burn energy in our bodies when resting

basic anxiety according to Horney, the feeling of helplessness that develops in children from early relationships

basic emotions a proposed set of innate emotions that are common to all humans and from which other, higher-order emotions may derive

basic level category the intermediate level of categorization that seems to be the level that we use most to think about our world

basic research scientific study about the specifics of a behavior without concern for its application

basilar membrane the structure in the cochlear duct that contains the hair cells, which transduce sound waves into action potentials

behavior therapy therapy that applies the principles of classical and operant conditioning to help people change maladaptive behaviors

behavioral perspective focuses on external, environmental influences on behavior

behaviorism a psychological perspective that emphasizes the study of observable responses and behavior

bereavement the experience of losing a loved one

binge eating disorder a mental health disorder characterized by recurrent episodes of binge eating, as in bulimia nervosa, but without regular use of compensatory measures to avoid weight gain

binocular depth cues depth cues that utilize information from both eyes

biofeedback an electronic device that measures and records bodily changes so that an individual can monitor and control these changes more effectively

biological/physiological perspective focuses on physical causes of behavior

biomedical therapy the use of medications or other medical interventions to treat mental health disorders

bipolar disorder a mood disorder characterized by both depression and mania

bisexual one who is sexually attracted to members of both sexes

blindspot the point where the optic nerve leaves the retina and where there are no rods or cones

blunted affect a lack of emotional expression

borderline personality disorder (BPD) a personality disorder marked by a pattern of instability in mood, relationships, self-image, and behavior

bottom-up perceptual processing perception that is not guided by prior knowledge or expectations

brightness the intensity of light; it corresponds to the amplitude of the light waves

Broca's area a region in the left frontal lobe that plays a role in the production of speech

bulimia nervosa a mental health disorder in which a person alternately binges on large quantities of food and then engages in some inappropriate compensatory behavior to avoid weight gain

bystander effect the idea that the more witnesses there are to an emergency, the less likely any one of them is to offer help

can-do factors factors that determine the maximum performance an employee can exhibit

Cannon-Bard theory a theory of emotion that states that emotions originate in the brain, not the body

cardinal traits according to Allport, those dominant elements of our personalities that drive all of our behaviors

case study an in-depth observation of one person

catatonic excitement a disorder in motor behavior involving excited agitation

catatonic stupor a disorder in motor behavior involving immobility

causal hypothesis an educated guess about how one variable will influence another variable

cell body the part of the neuron that contains the nucleus and DNA

central executive in the working memory model, the attention-controlling component of working memory

central nervous system (CNS) the brain and the spinal cord

central route to persuasion a style of thinking in which the person carefully and critically evaluates persuasive arguments and generates counterarguments; the central route requires motivation and available cognitive resources

central traits according to Allport, those tendencies we have to behave in a certain way across most situations

centration the act of focusing on only one aspect or feature of an object

cerebellum hindbrain structure that plays a role in balance, muscle tone, and coordination of motor movements

cerebral cortex thin, wrinkled outer covering of the brain in which high-level processes such as thinking, planning, language, interpretation of sensory data, and coordination of sensory and motor information take place

cerebral hemispheres right and left sides of the brain that to some degree govern different functions in the body

cholecystokinin (CCK) a hormone released by the small intestines that plays a role in hunger regulation

chunking a means of using one's limited short-term memory resources more efficiently by combining small bits of information to form larger bits of information, or chunks

circadian rhythm changes in bodily processes that occur repeatedly on approximately a 24- to 25-hour cycle

classical conditioning learning that occurs when a neutral stimulus is repeatedly paired with an unconditioned stimulus; because of this pairing, the neutral stimulus becomes a conditioned stimulus with the same power as the unconditioned stimulus to elicit the response in the person or animal

client-centered therapy a humanistic psychotherapy approach formulated by Carl Rogers that emphasizes the use of empathy, genuineness, and unconditional positive regard to help the client reach his or her potential

clinical interview the initial meeting between a client and a clinician in which the clinician asks questions to identify the difficulty in functioning that the person is experiencing

closure a Gestalt principle of perception that states that when we look at a stimulus, we have a tendency to see it as a closed shape, rather than lines

cochlea the curled, fluid-filled tube that contains the basilar membrane in the inner ear

cognition Ch. 7: the way in which we use and store information in memory; Ch. 9: the ability to know, think, and remember

cognitive consistency the idea that we strive to have attitudes and behaviors that do not contradict one another

cognitive dissonance theory a theory that predicts that we will be motivated to change our attitudes or our behaviors or both to the extent that they cause us to feel dissonance, an uncomfortable physical state

cognitive distortion Ch. 14: thought that tends to be pessimistic and negative; Ch. 15: distorted thinking patterns, such as overgeneralization or all-or-none thinking, that according to Aaron Beck lead to depression, anxiety, and low self-esteem

cognitive map a mental representation of the environment

cognitive perspective focuses on how mental processes influence behavior

cognitive psychology the study of mental processes such as reasoning and problem solving

cognitive reappraisal an active and conscious process in which we alter our interpretation of a stressful event

cognitive therapy a therapy created by Aaron Beck that focuses on uncovering negative automatic thought patterns that impede healthy psychological functioning

cognitive-mediational theory a theory of emotion that states that our cognitive appraisal of a situation determines what emotion we will feel in the situation

cohesiveness the degree to which members of a group value their group membership; cohesive groups are tight-knit groups

collective unconscious according to Jung, the part of the unconscious that contains images and material universal to people of all time periods and cultures

collectivistic culture a culture, like many Asian cultures, in which group accomplishments are valued over individual accomplishments

color blindness a condition in which a person cannot perceive one or more colors because of a lack of specific cones in the retina

compliance yielding to a simple request

compulsion repetitive behavior that a person feels a strong urge to perform

concept mental category that contains related bits of knowledge

concrete operations Piaget's third stage of cognitive development, characterized by logical thought

conditioned response (CR) the response elicited by a conditioned stimulus in a person or animal

conditioned stimulus (CS) a stimulus that elicits a conditioned response in a person or animal

cones the cells of the retina that are sensitive to specific colors of light and send information to the brain concerning the colors we are seeing

confidentiality researchers do not reveal which data were collected from which participant

conflict having to choose between two or more needs, desires, or demands

conformity behaving in accordance with group norms

confounding variable any factor other than the independent variable that affects the dependent measure

conscious level the level of consciousness that holds all the thoughts, perceptions, and impulses of which we are aware

consciousness feelings, thoughts, and aroused states of which we are aware

conservation the understanding that an object retains its original properties even though it may look different

control group the group of participants that do not receive the manipulation that is being tested

constructive memory memory that utilizes knowledge and expectations to fill in the missing details in retrieved memory traces

contact hypothesis the theory that contact between groups is an effective means of reducing prejudice between them

contiguity the degree to which two stimuli follow one another in time

contingency the degree to which the presentation of one stimulus is contingent on the presentation of the other

continuance commitment remaining with an organization because of the high cost (monetary or social or both) of losing organizational membership

continuous reinforcement a schedule of reinforcement in which the person or animal is rewarded for every instance of the desired response

cooing the vowel sounds made by infants beginning at 2 months

coping the behaviors that we engage in to manage stressors

corpus callosum a thick band of neurons that connects the right and left hemispheres of the brain

correlation the relationship between two or more variables

correlation coefficient the average product of z scores calculated on pairs of scores; describes the degree to which the scores in the pairs are linearly related

counterconditioning using classical conditioning to remove an undesired conditioned response in a person or animal

counterproductive behaviors intentional behaviors on the part of an organizational member viewed by the organization as contrary to its legitimate interests

couple therapy therapy that focuses on improving communication and intimacy between two people in a committed relationship

covert sensitization therapy a milder form of aversion therapy in which graphic imagery is used to create unpleasant associations with specific stimuli

creativity the ability to combine mental elements in new and useful ways

crystallized intelligence abilities that rely on knowledge, expertise, and judgment

cue-dependent forgetting a type of forgetting that occurs when one cannot recall information in a context other than the context in which it was encoded

cultural bias the degree to which a test puts people from other cultures at an unfair disadvantage because of the culturally specific nature of the test items

cycle a physical characteristic of energy defined as a wave peak and the valley that immediately follows it

cyclothymic disorder a mood disorder that is a less severe but more chronic form of bipolar disorder

daily hassles the everyday irritations and frustrations that individuals face

dark adaptation the process through which our eyes adjust to dark conditions after having been exposed to bright light

data information gathered in scientific studies

date rape a form of acquaintance rape in which a person is forced or threatened to engage in sexual activity with a social escort

debriefing after an experiment, participants are fully informed of the nature of the study

decay theory a theory of forgetting that proposes that memory traces that are not routinely activated in long-term memory will degrade

decibels (dB) the unit of measure used to determine the loudness of a sound

decision making making a choice from among a series of alternatives

declarative memory a type of long-term memory that encompasses memories that are easily verbalized, including episodic and semantic memories

deductive reasoning reasoning from the general to the specific

defense mechanisms Ch. 12: unconscious, emotional strategies that are engaged in to reduce anxiety and maintain a positive self-image; Ch. 13: processes used to protect the ego by reducing the anxiety it feels when faced with the conflicting demands of the id and the superego

deindividuation a state in which a person's behavior becomes controlled more by external norms than by the person's own internal values and morals

delusion a thought or belief that a person believes to be true but in reality is not

dendrites branchlike structures on the cell body of the neuron that receive incoming signals from other neurons in the nervous system

dependent variable the variable in an experiment that measures any effect of the manipulation

depressants drugs that inhibit or slow down normal neural functioning

dermis the inner layer of the skin that contains most of the touch receptors

descriptive statistics statistics that are calculated to summarize or describe certain aspects of a data set

destructive obedience obedience to immoral, unethical demands that cause harm to others

development changes in behavior or abilities or both

Diagnostic and Statistical Manual of Mental Disorders (DSM) a book published by the American Psychiatric Association (APA) that lists the criteria for close to 400 mental health disorders

diffusion according to Marcia, an identity status in which the individual has not explored or committed to any personal values

diffusion of responsibility the idea that responsibility for taking action is diffused across all the people witnessing an event

discrimination the behavioral expression of a prejudice

dishabituation to begin re-responding to a stimulus to which one had been habituated

disorganized behavior a symptom of schizophrenia that includes inappropriate or unusual behavior in a situation such as silliness, catatonic excitement, or catatonic stupor

disorganized speech a symptom of schizophrenia in which one's speech lacks association between one's ideas and the events that one is experiencing

display rules rules that guide the appropriate expression of emotion within a specific culture

dissociation theory Hilgard's proposal that hypnosis involves two simultaneous states: a hypnotic state and a hidden observer

dissociative disorder a disorder marked by a loss of awareness of some part of one's self or one's surroundings that seriously interferes with the person's ability to function

dissociative fugue disorder a disorder marked by episodes of amnesia in which a person is unable to recall some or all of his or her past and is confused about his or her identity; a new identity may be formed in which the person suddenly and unexpectedly travels away from home

dissociative identity disorder (DID) a disorder in which two or more personalities coexist within the same individual; formerly called multiple personality disorder

distributed practice spreading one's study time across a series of study sessions

door-in-the-face compliance increasing compliance by first asking people to give in to a very large request and then, after they refuse, asking them to give in to a smaller request

dopamine neurotransmitter that plays a role in movement, learning, and attention

double-blind study an experiment in which both the experimenter and the study participants do not know to which group (experimental or control) participants have been assigned

Down syndrome a genetic birth disorder resulting from an extra 21st chromosome, characterized by distinct facial features and a greater likelihood of heart defects and intellectual disability

dream analysis a technique in psychoanalysis in which the therapist examines the hidden symbols in a client's dreams

drive an uncomfortable internal state that motivates us to reduce this discomfort through our behavior

drive reduction theory theory of motivation that proposes that motivation seeks to reduce internal levels of drive

dual coding system a system of memory that encodes information in more than one type of code or format

dualistic thinking reasoning that divides situations and issues into right and wrong categories

duplicity theory proposes that a combination of volley and place theory explains how our brain decodes pitch

dyspareunia a disorder characterized by painful sexual intercourse

dysphoria an extreme state of sadness

dysthymic disorder a mood disorder that is a less severe but more chronic form of major depression

echoic memory sensory memory for auditory information

eclectic approach integrates and combines several perspectives when explaining behavior

eclectic therapy approach therapy that incorporates an integrated and diverse use of therapeutic methods

ego the conscious part of the personality that attempts to meet the demands of the id in a socially appropriate way

egocentrism the belief that everyone thinks as you do

elaborative rehearsal forming associations or links between information one is trying to learn and information already stored in long-term memory so as to facilitate the transfer of this new information into long-term memory

Electra complex in the female, an unconscious sexual urge for the father that develops during the phallic psychosexual stage

electroconvulsive therapy (ECT) a series of treatments in which electrical current is passed through the brain, causing a seizure; used to alleviate severe depression

embryonic stage the second stage of prenatal development, lasting from the 3rd through the 8th week

emerging adulthood the transitional period between late adolescence and the mid-20s when young people have left adolescence but have not yet assumed adult roles and responsibilities

emotion a complex reaction to some internal or external event that involves physiological reactions, behavioral reactions, facial expressions, cognition, and affective responses

emotion-focused coping behaviors aimed at controlling the internal emotional reactions to a stressor

emotional stability having control over one's emotions

empathy the ability of a therapist to understand a client's feelings and thoughts without being judgmental

encoding the act of inputting information into memory

endocrine glands organs of the endocrine system that produce hormones and release them into the bloodstream

endorphins neurotransmitters that act as a natural painkiller

enuresis a condition in which a person over the age of 5 shows an inability to control urination during sleep

epidermis the outer layer of the skin that contains some touch receptors

epigenetics the principle that environmental factors can alter the expression of genes in our bodies without altering the DNA sequence of the gene

episodic memory long-term declarative memory for the events in our lives

erogenous zones areas of the skin that are sensitive to touch

estrogens a class of female sex hormones that regulate many aspects of sexuality and are found in both males and females

evolutionary perspective focuses on how evolution and natural selection influence behavior

excitation when a neurotransmitter binds with the postsynaptic cell and makes it more likely to fire an action potential

excitement phase the first stage of the sexual response cycle in which males get erections and females produce vaginal lubrication

exemplar a mental representation of an actual instance of a member of a category

exhaustion stage the third and final phase of the general adaptation syndrome, in which bodily resources are drained, and wear and tear on the body begins

exhibitionism a paraphilia in which one is sexually aroused by the fantasies or the behavior of exposing his or her genitals to some unsuspecting person

experiment a research method that is used to test causal hypotheses

experimental group the group of participants that receive the manipulation that is being tested

explicit memory the conscious use of memory

extinction the removal of a conditioned response

extinction burst a temporary increase in a behavioral response that occurs immediately after extinction has begun

extracellular fluid the fluid found in the spaces between the cells of the body and which is used to regulate thirst

extraversion personality traits that involve energy directed outward, such as being easygoing, lively, or excitable

extrinsic motivation motivation that comes from outside the person

facial feedback hypothesis a theory of emotion that states that our emotional state is affected by the feedback our brain gets from facial muscles

family therapy therapy that focuses on creating balance and restoring harmony to improve the functioning of the family as a whole system

feature detection theory a theory of perception that proposes the existence of feature detectors or cortical cells that only fire when we see certain visual stimuli such as shapes, colors of light, or movements

feature detectors specialized cells in the visual cortex that fire only when they receive input that indicates we are looking at a particular shape, color, angle, or other visual feature

female sexual arousal disorder persistent difficulty in becoming sexually excited or sufficiently lubricated in response to stimulation

fetal alcohol syndrome (FAS) a birth condition resulting from the mother's chronic use of alcohol during pregnancy that is characterized by facial and limb deformities and intellectual disability

fetal stage the third stage of prenatal development from the 9th week through the 9th month

fetishism a paraphilia characterized by sexual arousal by inanimate objects

figure-ground a Gestalt principle of perception that states that when we perceive a stimulus, we visually pull the *figure* part of the stimulus forward while visually pushing backward the background, or *ground*, part of the stimulus

fine motor skills motor behaviors involving the small muscles of the body

five factor theory Costa and McCrae's trait theory that proposes five core dimensions to personality: openness, conscientiousness, extraversion, agreeableness, and neuroticism

fixed interval schedule a schedule of reinforcement in which the person or animal is rewarded for the first desired response in an *x*th interval of time

fixed ratio schedule a schedule of reinforcement in which the person or animal is rewarded for every *x*th instance of the desired response

flashbulb memory an unusually detailed and seemingly accurate memory for an emotionally charged event

fluid intelligence abilities that rely on information-processing skills such as reaction time, attention, and working memory

foot-in-the-door compliance increasing compliance by first asking people to give in to a small request, which then paves the way for compliance with a larger request

forebrain brain structures including the limbic system, thalamus, hypothalamus, and cortex that govern higher-order mental processes

foreclosure according to Marcia, an identity status in which the individual prematurely commits to personal values before exploration is complete

formal concept concept that is based on learned, rigid rules that define certain categories of things

formal operations Piaget's final stage of cognitive development, characterized by the ability to engage in abstract thought

fraternal twins twins that developed from two separate fertilized eggs and are no more genetically similar than normal siblings

free association a technique in psychoanalysis in which the client says whatever comes to mind

frequency a physical characteristic of energy defined as the number of cycles that occur in a given unit of time

frequency distribution a graph of data that plots the frequency of data points on the y-axis and the data points themselves on the x-axis

frequency polygon a line graph that is used to illustrate a frequency distribution

frequency theory proposes that our brain decodes pitch directly from the frequency at which the hair cells of the basilar membrane are firing

frontal lobe cortical area directly behind the forehead that plays a role in thinking, planning, decision making, language, and motor movement

frustration-aggression hypothesis the idea that frustration causes aggressive behavior

functional fixedness being able to see objects only in their familiar roles

functionalism an early psychological perspective concerned with how behavior helps people adapt to their environment

fundamental attribution error our tendency to overuse trait information when making attributions about others

gamma amino butyric acid (GABA) the body's chief inhibitory neurotransmitter, which plays a role in regulating arousal

gender the experience of being male or female

gender identity one's personal experience of being male or female

gender permanence the understanding that one's gender will not change

gender roles society's expectations for how males and females should behave

gender-schema theory the idea that gender roles are acquired through modeling and reinforcement processes that work together with a child's mental abilities

general adaptation syndrome (GAS) the general physical responses we experience when faced with a stressor

generalizability how well a researcher's findings apply to other individuals and situations

generalized anxiety disorder (GAD) an anxiety disorder characterized by chronic, constant worry in almost all situations

generalized intelligence (g) Charles Spearman's notion that there is a general level of intelligence that underlies our separate abilities

genes strands of DNA found in the nuclei of all living cells

genital stage Freud's final psychosexual stage of development, which occurs during puberty, in which sexual energy is transferred toward peers of the other sex (heterosexual orientation) or same sex (homosexual orientation)

genotype inherited genetic pattern for a given trait

genuineness the ability of a therapist to openly share his or her thoughts and feelings with a client

germinal stage the first stage of prenatal development, from conception to 14 days

Gestalt approach a psychological school of thought originating in Germany that proposed that the whole of a perception must be understood rather than trying to deconstruct perception into its parts

Gestalt psychology an early psychological approach that emphasized how our minds organize sensory stimuli to produce the perception of a whole form

ghrelin a hunger-stimulating hormone produced by the stomach

glial cells brain cells that provide support functions for the neurons and may play a role in regulating neural signaling

glucose the form of sugar that the body burns as fuel

glutamate the chief excitatory neurotransmitter in the brain, found at more than 50% of the synapses in the brain

glycogen a starchy molecule that is produced from excess glucose in the body; it can be thought of as the body's stored energy reserves

good continuation a Gestalt principle of perception that states that we have a preference for perceiving stimuli that seem to follow one another as being part of a continuing pattern

grammar the rules that govern the sentence structure in a particular language

graph a visual depiction of data

grief one's emotional reaction to the death of a loved one

gross motor skills motor behaviors involving the large muscles of the body

group therapy therapy that is administered to more than one person at a time

groupthink a situation in which a group fixates on one decision, and members blindly assume that it is the correct decision

guided imagery a technique in which you focus on a pleasant, calming image to achieve a state of relaxation when you feel stressed

gustation the sense of taste

habituation the tendency of a person or animal to ignore repeated stimuli

hair cells neurons that grow out of the basilar membrane and transduce sound waves into action potentials

hallucination perceiving something that does not exist in reality

hallucinogens drugs that simultaneously excite and inhibit normal neural activity, thereby causing distortions in perception

hardy personality a personality, high in the traits of commitment, control, and challenge, that appears to be associated with strong stress resistance

health psychology the subfield of psychology that investigates the relationship between people's behaviors and their health

health-defeating behaviors behaviors that increase the chance of illness, disease, or death

health-promoting behaviors behaviors that decrease the chance of illness, disease, or death

helping behavior another term for altruism

hermaphrodite a person who develops both fully formed testicular and ovarian tissue

heterosexual one who is sexually attracted only to members of the other sex

heuristic a shortcut or rule of thumb that may or may not lead to a correct solution to the problem

hierarchy of needs Maslow's theory that humans are motivated by different needs, some of which take precedence over others

hindbrain primitive part of the brain that comprises the medulla, pons, and cerebellum

hippocampus part of the brain that plays a role in the transfer of information from short- to long-term memory

histogram a bar graph that is used to illustrate a frequency distribution

homeostasis an internal state of equilibrium in the body

homophobia prejudicial attitudes against homosexuals and homosexuality

homosexual one who is sexually attracted only to members of the same sex

hormones chemical messengers of the endocrine system

hostile aggression aggression that is meant to cause harm to others

hue the color of a light

humanism a psychological perspective that emphasizes the personal growth and potential of humans

humanistic approach a personality perspective that emphasizes the individual, personal choice, and free will in shaping personality; assumes that humans have a built-in drive toward fulfilling their own natural potential

humanistic perspective focuses on how an individual's view of himself or herself and the world influence behavior

hypnosis a state of heightened suggestibility

hypoactive sexual desire disorder a persistent disinterest in sex and sexual activities

hypochondriasis a somatoform disorder in which the person persistently worries over having a disease, without any evident physical basis

hypothalamus part of the forebrain that plays a role in maintaining homeostasis in the body involving sleep, body temperature, sexual functions, thirst, and hunger; also the point where the nervous system intersects with the endocrine system

hypothesis an educated guess

iconic memory sensory memory for visual information

id the unconscious part of the personality that seeks pleasure and gratification

identical twins twins that developed from a single fertilized egg and share 100% of their genes

ill-structured problem a problem for which an algorithm is not known

imaginary audience the belief held by adolescents that everyone is watching what they do

immunosuppression the reduction in activity of the immune system

implicit memory the unconscious use of memory

impression formation the way that we understand and make judgments about others

incentive a goal or desire that we are motivated to fulfill

incubation a period of not thinking about a problem that helps one solve the problem

independent variable the variable in an experiment that is manipulated

individualistic culture a culture, like many Western cultures, in which individual accomplishments are valued over group accomplishments

inductive reasoning reasoning from the specific to the general

industrial and organizational (I/O) psychology the study of people's behavior at work using psychological principles

inferential statistics statistics that psychologists use in hypothesis testing to tell them when they should reject or accept their hypotheses about the population

informational conformity conformity that occurs when conformity pressures actually persuade group members to adopt new beliefs or attitudes or both

informed consent research participants agree to participate after being told about aspects of the study

in-group bias our tendency to favor people who belong to the same groups that we do

inhibition when a neurotransmitter binds with the postsynaptic cell and makes it less likely to fire an action potential

insight a new way of looking at a problem that leads to a sudden understanding of how to solve it

insomnia a sleep disorder in which a person cannot get to sleep or stay asleep or both

instinct innate impulse from within a person that directs or motivates behavior

Institutional Review Board (IRB) a committee that reviews research proposals to ensure that ethical standards have been met

instrumental aggression aggression used to facilitate the attainment of one's goals

intelligence abilities that enable you to adapt to your environment and behave in a goal-directed way

intelligence quotient (IQ score) one's mental age divided by one's chronological age times 100

interactionism perspective that our genes and environmental influences work together to determine our characteristics

interpretation the psychoanalyst's view on the themes and issues that may be influencing the client's behavior

intracellular fluid the fluid found inside the cells of the body and which is used to regulate thirst

intrinsic motivation motivation that comes from within the person

introspection observing one's own thoughts, feelings, or sensations

introversion personality traits that involve energy directed inward, such as being calm or peaceful

ions charged particles that play an important role in the firing of action potentials in the nervous system

James-Lange theory a theory of emotion that defines an emotion as a unique pattern of physiological arousal

job analysis identification of the critical elements of a job, including tasks, skills required, and working conditions

job satisfaction the positive or negative affect associated with a job

job withdrawal behaviors employees use to avoid their job (e.g., quitting, retiring)

judgment the act of estimating the probability of an event

just noticeable difference (jnd) the minimum change in intensity of a stimulus that participants can detect 50% of the time

kinesthesis the ability to sense the position of our body parts in relation to one another and in relation to space

knowledge information stored in our long-term memory about the world and how it works

language a well-developed, syntactical verbal system for representing the world

latency stage Freud's fourth psychosexual stage of development, which occurs from around age 6 to puberty, in which the child's sexuality is suppressed due to widening social contacts with school, peers, and family

latent content according to Freudian theory, the symbolic meaning of a dream

latent learning learning that cannot be directly observed in a person's or animal's behavior

lateral geniculate nucleus (LGN) the part of the thalamus that processes visual information en route to the cortex

lateral hypothalamus (LH) a region of the hypothalamus once thought to be the hunger center in the brain

law of effect a principle discovered by E. L. Thorndike that states that random behaviors that lead to positive consequences will be strengthened and random behaviors that lead to negative consequences will be weakened

leadership a social influence process in which a person steers others toward a goal

learned helplessness Ch. 12: a passive response to stressors based on exposure to previously uncontrolled, negative events; Ch. 14: the belief that one cannot control the outcome of events

learning a relatively permanent change in behavior or behavior potential as a result of experience

lens the part of the eye that lies behind the pupil and focuses light rays on the retina

leptin a hormone released by fat cells in the body that plays a role in hunger regulation

levels-of-processing model a model that predicts that information that is processed deeply and elaboratively will be best retained in and recalled from long-term memory

libido one's physical desire, or drive, to have sex

life event a change in one's life, good or bad, that requires readjustment

light adaptation the process through which our eyes adjust to bright light after having been exposed to darkness

limbic system system of structures including the amygdala and hippocampus that govern certain aspects of emotion, motivation, and memory

lithium a naturally occurring mineral salt prescribed to control manic symptoms in people with bipolar disorder; it influences several neurotransmitters in the brain, including glutamate, serotonin, and dopamine

lock-and-key theory proposes that olfactory receptors are excited by odor molecules in a fashion that is similar to how neurotransmitters excite receptor sites

locus of control the expectation of control we have over the outcome of an event; an internal locus expects some degree of personal control, whereas an external locus expects little personal control

long-term memory (LTM) a system of memory that works to store memories for a long time, perhaps even permanently

long-term potentiation as neurons are repeatedly stimulated, it becomes easier for them to fire action potentials

loudness the psychophysical property of sound that corresponds to the amplitude of a sound wave

maintenance rehearsal repeating information over and over again to keep it in short-term memory for an extended period of time

major depression a mood disorder involving dysphoria, feelings of worthlessness, loss of interest in one's usual activities, and changes in bodily activities such as sleep and appetite that persists for at least 2 weeks

male erectile dysfunction the persistent inability to attain or sustain an erection sufficient to complete sexual activity

mania a period of abnormally excessive energy and elation

manifest content according to Freudian theory, what the dreamer recalls on awakening

massed practice cramming or attempting to learn large amounts of information in a single session of study

masturbation sexual self-stimulation

matching hypothesis the theory that we are attracted to people whose level of physical attractiveness is similar to our own

mean a descriptive statistic that describes the most average, or typical, data point in the distribution

measures of central tendency descriptive statistics that describe the most central, or typical, data points in the frequency distribution

median a descriptive statistic that identifies the center of the frequency distribution; 50% of the scores are above and 50% are below this point in the distribution

medical model perspective that views psychological disorders as similar to physical diseases; they result from biological disturbances and can be diagnosed, treated, and cured like other physical illnesses

meditation mental exercises in which people consciously focus their attention to heighten awareness and bring their mental processes under more control

medulla part of the hindbrain that controls basic, life-sustaining functions such as respiration, heart rate, and blood pressure

melatonin hormone in the body that facilitates sleep

memory consolidation the stabilization and long-term storage of memory traces in the brain

memory traces the stored code that represents a piece of information that has been encoded into memory

menarche a girl's first menstruation

menopause the period when a female stops menstruating and is no longer fertile

mental age the age that reflects the child's mental abilities in comparison to the average child of the same age

mental representation memory traces that represent objects, events, people, and so on, that are not present at the time

mental set the tendency to habitually use methods of problem solving that have worked for you in the past

mentoring the pairing of a current and often long-term employee (the mentor) with a new employee

mere exposure effect the idea that the more one is exposed to something, the more one grows to like it

microsleep brief episode of sleep that occurs in the midst of a wakeful activity

midbrain brain structure that connects the hindbrain with the forebrain

Minnesota Multiphasic Personality Inventory (MMPI-2) a personality inventory that is designed to identify problem areas of functioning in a person's personality

mnemonic device a cognitive procedure or mental trick that is designed to improve one's memory

mode a measure of central tendency that identifies the most common, or frequent, score in the distribution

monocular depth cues depth cues that require information from only one eye

mood disorder a disorder marked by a significant change in one's emotional state that seriously interferes with one's ability to function

moral reasoning how you decide what is right and what is wrong

moratorium according to Marcia, an identity status in which the individual actively explores personal values

morpheme the smallest unit of sound that has meaning in a language

motive a tendency to desire and seek out positive incentives or rewards and to avoid negative outcomes

motor cortex a strip of cortex at the back of the frontal lobe that governs the execution of motor movement in the body

motor (efferent) neurons neurons that transmit commands from the brain to the muscles of the body

multiple approach–avoidance conflict a situation that poses several alternatives that each have positive and negative features

multiple intelligences the idea that we possess different types of intelligence rather than a single, overall level of intelligence

myelin fatty, waxy substance that insulates portions of some neurons in the nervous system

narcolepsy a rare sleep disorder in which an individual falls asleep during alert activities during the day

natural concept concept that develops naturally as we live our lives and experience the world

natural selection cornerstone of Darwin's theory of evolution, which states that genes for traits that allow an organism to be reproductively successful will be selected or retained in a species and genes for traits that hinder reproductive success will not be selected and therefore will die out in a species

naturalistic observation observing behavior in the environment in which the behavior typically occurs

nature–nurture debate/issue the degree to which biology (nature) or the environment (nurture) contributes to one's development

negative correlation a relationship in which increases in one variable correspond to decreases in a second variable

negative feedback loop a system of feedback in the body that monitors and adjusts our motivation level so as to maintain homeostasis

negative punishment weakening a behavior by removing something pleasant from the person's or animal's environment

negative reinforcement strengthening a behavior by removing something unpleasant from the environment of the person or animal

neonate a newborn during the first 28 days of life

nervous system an electrochemical system of communication within the body that uses cells called neurons to convey information

neurons cells in the nervous system that transmit information

neuropeptide Y the most powerful hunger stimulant known

neuroscience science that investigates the relationships between the nervous system and behavior/mental processes

neuroticism the degree to which one is emotionally unstable

neurotransmitters chemical messengers that carry neural signals across the synapse

neutral stimulus (NS) a stimulus that does not naturally elicit an unconditioned response in a person or animal

night terrors very frightening non-REM sleep episodes

nightmare a brief, scary REM dream that is often remembered

non-REM sleep relaxing state of sleep in which the individual's eyes do not move

norepinephrine (NOR) neurotransmitter that plays a role in regulating sleep, arousal, and mood

norm an unwritten rule or expectation for how group members should behave

normal distribution a bell-shaped, symmetric frequency distribution

normative commitment commitment to the organization based on feelings of obligation

normative conformity conformity that occurs when group members change their behavior to meet group norms but are not persuaded to change their beliefs and attitudes

null hypothesis (H_0) the hypothesis that contains a statement of what we do not believe is true about our variables in the population

obedience yielding to a demand

obese having a body mass index of 30 or over

object permanence the understanding that an object continues to exist even when it is not present

observational learning learning through observation and imitation of others' behavior

obsession a recurrent thought or image that intrudes on a person's awareness

obsessive-compulsive disorder (OCD) an anxiety disorder involving a pattern of unwanted intrusive thoughts and the urge to engage in repetitive actions

occipital lobe cortical area at the back of the brain that plays a role in visual processing

Oedipus complex in the male, an unconscious sexual urge for the mother that develops during the phallic psychosexual stage

olfaction the sense of smell

olfactory epithelium a special piece of skin at the top of the nasal cavity that contains the olfactory receptors

operant behavior behavior that operates on the environment to cause some sort of consequence to occur

operant conditioning a type of learning in which the person or animal learns through the consequences of its behavior

opiates painkilling drugs that depress some brain areas and excite others

opponent-process theory Ch. 3: proposes that we have dual-action cells beyond the level of the retina that signal the brain when we see one of a pair of colors; Ch. 8: a theory of motivation that states that the body will counteract the effects of ingested drugs by adjusting its arousal level in a direction opposite that of the drug's effect

optic chiasm the point in the brain where the optic nerve from the left eye crosses over the optic nerve from the right eye

optic nerve the structure that conveys visual information away from the retina to the brain

oral stage Freud's first psychosexual stage of development, which occurs during the first year of life, in which the handling of the child's feeding experiences affects personality development

organizational citizenship behaviors (OCBs) employee behaviors that go beyond what is expected by the organization

organizational climate the behavioral norms of an organization

organizational culture the shared cognitive assumptions and beliefs of an organization

organizational socialization the process by which members of an organization become a part of, or are absorbed into, the culture of the organization

organizational withdrawal work withdrawal or job withdrawal

orgasm phase the third stage of the sexual response cycle in which the pelvic and anal muscles contract

orgasmic disorder a lack of orgasm or a persistent delay in reaching orgasm despite adequate stimulation

orienting reflex the tendency of a person or animal to orient its senses toward unexpected stimuli

out-group a group that is distinct from one's own and so usually an object of more hostility or dislike than one's in-group

out-group homogeneity bias our tendency to see out-group members as being all alike

outliers unusual data points that are at the extremes of the frequency distribution and either far above or below the mean

ovaries the organs in a female's body that produce eggs, or ova

overextension when a child uses one word to symbolize all manner of similar instances (e.g., calling all birds *parakeet*)

overlearning improving memory for material that is already known by continuing to rehearse it

panic disorder an anxiety disorder characterized by intense fear and anxiety in the absence of danger that is accompanied by strong physical symptoms

papillae bumps on the tongue that many people mistake for taste buds

paraphilia sexual arousal in response to an unusual object, situation, or nonconsenting person

parasympathetic nervous system branch of the autonomic nervous system most active during times of normal functioning

parietal lobe cortical areas on the top sides of the brain that play a role in touch and certain cognitive processes

partial reinforcement schedule a schedule of reinforcement in which the person or animal is rewarded for only some instances of the desired response

pedophilia a paraphilia in which one is sexually aroused by fantasies of or engaging in sexual activity with a prepubescent child

peptide YY a hormone released in the gut that reduces hunger

perception the process through which we interpret sensory information

performance appraisals the evaluations or reviews of employees' job performance

peripheral nervous system (PNS) all of the nervous system except the brain and spinal cord

peripheral route to persuasion a style of thinking in which the person does not carefully and critically evaluate persuasive arguments or generate counterarguments; the peripheral route ensues when one lacks motivation or available cognitive resources or both

permissive parent a parenting style characterized by moderate levels of affection but low levels of control

personal fable the belief held by adolescents that they are unique and special

personal unconscious according to Jung, the part of the unconscious that consists of forgotten memories and repressed experiences from one's past

personality the unique collection of attitudes, emotions, thoughts, habits, impulses, and behaviors that define how a person typically behaves across situations

personality disorder a disorder marked by maladaptive behavior that has been stable across a long period and across many situations

personality inventory objective paper-and-pencil self-report form that measures personality on several dimensions

person–situation interaction the influence of the situation on the stability of traits; when in the same situation, we display similar behavior, but when the situation is different, behavior may change

persuasion a type of social influence in which someone tries to change our attitudes

phallic stage Freud's third psychosexual stage of development, which occurs between 3 and 6 years of age, in which little boys experience the Oedipus complex and little girls the Electra complex

phenotype actual characteristic that results from the interaction of the genotype and environmental influences

pheromones airborne chemicals that are released from glands and detected by the vomeronasal organs in some animals and perhaps humans

phobic disorder an anxiety disorder characterized by an intense fear of a specific object or situation

phoneme the smallest unit of sound in a language

phonological loop in the working memory model, the part of working memory that processes the phonological, or sound, qualities of information

photopigments light-sensitive chemicals that create electrical changes when they come into contact with light

physical dependence a condition that occurs when a person is motivated to continue taking a drug because to stop taking the drug would result in painful withdrawal symptoms

pitch the psychophysical property of sound that corresponds to the frequency of a sound wave

pituitary gland master gland of the endocrine system that controls the action of all other glands in the body

place theory proposes that our brain decodes pitch by noticing which region of the basilar membrane is most active

placebo effect a measurable change in participants' behavior due to the expectation or belief that a treatment will have certain effects

plateau phase the second stage of the sexual response cycle in which excitement peaks

pleasure principle the basis on which the id operates; to feel good and maximize gratification

pluralistic ignorance the idea that we use the behavior of others to help determine whether a situation is really an emergency requiring our help; if no one else is helping, we may conclude that help isn't needed

pons hindbrain structure that plays a role in respiration, consciousness, sleep, dreaming, facial movement, sensory processes, and the transmission of neural signals from one part of the brain to another

population of interest the entire universe of animals or people that could be studied

positive correlation a relationship in which increases in one variable correspond to increases in a second variable

positive psychology the study of factors that contribute to happiness, positive emotions, and well-being

positive punishment weakening a behavior by adding something unpleasant to the person's or animal's environment

positive reinforcement strengthening a behavior by adding something pleasant to the environment of the person or animal

postformal thought the idea that a correct solution (or solutions) may vary, depending on the circumstances

postsynaptic neuron the neuron that is receiving the signal at a synapse in the nervous system

posttraumatic stress disorder (PTSD) an anxiety disorder, characterized by distressing memories, emotional numbness, and hypervigilance, that develops after exposure to a traumatic event

pragmatics the rules of conversation in a particular culture

preconscious level the level of consciousness that holds thoughts, perceptions, and impulses of which we could potentially be aware

prediction an expected outcome of how variables will relate

predictive hypothesis an educated guess about the relationships among variables

prejudice a largely negative stereotype that is unfairly applied to all members of a group regardless of their individual characteristics

premature ejaculation persistent or recurrent ejaculation with minimal sexual stimulation before the person wishes it

preoperational stage Piaget's second stage of cognitive development, characterized by the use of symbols and illogical thought

presynaptic neuron the neuron that is sending the signal at a synapse in the nervous system

primacy effect the tendency for people to recall words from the beginning of a list better than words that appeared in the middle of the list

primary appraisal our initial interpretation of an event as either irrelevant, positive, or stressful

primary drive a drive that motivates us to maintain homeostasis in certain biological processes within the body

primary reinforcer a reinforcer that is reinforcing in and of itself

private speech Vygotsky's term describing the behavior of young children who talk to themselves to guide their own actions

proactive interference a type of forgetting that occurs when older memory traces inhibit the retrieval of newer memory traces

problem-focused coping behaviors that aim to control or alter the environment that is causing stress

procedural memory long-term memory for skills and behaviors

progressive relaxation training a stress management technique in which a person learns how to systematically tense and relax muscle groups in the body

projective test a less structured and subjective personality test in which an individual is shown an ambiguous stimulus and is asked to describe what he or she sees

prototype our concept of the most typical member of the category

proximity Ch. 3: a Gestalt principle of perception that states that we tend to group close objects together during perception; Ch. 11: geographical closeness

pseudohermaphrodite a person who develops ambiguous internal or external sexual anatomy

psychoactive drugs substances that influence the brain and thereby the behavior of individuals

psychoanalysis a method of therapy formulated by Freud that focuses on uncovering unconscious conflicts that drive maladaptive behavior

psychoanalytic perspective a personality approach developed by Sigmund Freud that sees personality as the product of driving forces within a person that are often conflicting and sometimes unconscious

psychoanalytic theory Sigmund Freud's view that emphasizes the influence of unconscious desires and conflicts on behavior

psychodynamic perspective focuses on internal unconscious mental processes, motives, and desires that may explain behavior

psychodynamic therapy modern psychoanalysis delivered in a shorter time that focuses less on the client's past and more on current problems and the nature of interpersonal relationships

psychological distance the degree to which one can disassociate oneself from the consequences of one's actions

psychology the scientific study of behavior and mental processes

psychoneuroimmunology field of study that investigates the connections among psychology (behaviors, thoughts, emotions), the nervous system, and immune system functioning

psychopharmacology the use of medications to treat mental health problems

psychophysics the study of how the mind interprets the physical properties of stimuli

psychosurgery a biological treatment approach involving neurosurgery to alleviate symptoms in someone with a mental health disorder

psychotherapy the use of psychological principles and techniques to treat mental health disorders

psychoticism the degree to which one is hostile, nonconforming, impulsive, and aggressive

puberty the process of sexual maturation

punishment the weakening of a response that occurs when a behavior leads to an unpleasant consequence

pupil the hole in the iris through which light enters the eye

quasi-experiment a research study that is not a true experiment because participants are not randomly assigned to the different conditions

random assignment participants have an equal chance of being placed in any condition of the study

range a measure of variability that is the difference between the high score and the low score of the distribution

rape the threat or use of force to obtain sex

rational-emotive therapy a cognitive therapy approach created by Albert Ellis that focuses on changing the irrational beliefs that people hold that are believed to impede healthy psychological functioning

realistic-conflict theory the theory that prejudice stems from competition for scarce resources

reality principle the basis on which the ego operates; finding socially appropriate means to fulfill id demands

reasoning drawing conclusions about the world based on certain assumptions

recall a type of retrieval process in which the probe or cue does not contain much information

recency effect the tendency for people to recall words from the end of a list better than words that appeared in the middle of the list

reciprocal determinism according to Bandura, the constant interaction among one's behavior, thoughts, and environment determines personality

reciprocity a strong norm that states that we should treat others as they treat us

recognition a type of retrieval process in which the probe or cue contains a great deal of information, including the item being sought

reconstructive memory memory that is based on the retrieval of memory traces that contain the actual details of the events that we have experienced

recruitment the process organizations use to identify potential employees for a job

reflex an automatic response to a specific environmental stimulus

refractory period Ch. 2: brief period after a neuron has fired an action potential in which the neuron is inhibited and unlikely to fire another action potential; Ch. 10: a time during the resolution phase in which males are incapable of experiencing another orgasm or ejaculation

reinforcement the strengthening of a response that occurs when the response is rewarded

relativistic thinking the idea that in many situations there is not necessarily one right or wrong answer

reliability the degree to which a test yields consistent measurements of a trait

REM behavior disorder a condition in which normal muscle paralysis does not occur, leading to violent movements during REM sleep

REM rebound loss of REM sleep is recouped by spending more time in REM on subsequent nights

REM sleep active state of sleep in which the individual's eyes move

representativeness heuristic a heuristic in which we rely on the degree to which something is representative of a category, rather than the base rate, to help us judge whether or not it belongs in the category

repression a type of forgetting proposed by Sigmund Freud in which memories for events, desires, or impulses that we find threatening are pushed into an inaccessible part of the mind called the unconscious

resistance a process in psychoanalysis whereby the client behaves in such a way as to deny or avoid sensitive issues

resistance stage the second phase of the general adaptation syndrome, in which the nervous and endocrine systems continue to be activated

resolution phase the final stage of the sexual response cycle in which the body returns to its prearoused state

response an organism's reaction to a stimulus

response set theory of hypnosis asserts that hypnosis is *not* an altered state of consciousness, but a cognitive set to respond appropriately to suggestions. The intent to behave as a "hypnotized person" and the expectation that one will succeed in following the hypnotist's suggestion becomes a response set that triggers the hypnotic response automatically.

resting potential potential difference that exists in the neuron when it is resting (approximately −70 mv in mammals)

reticular formation part of the midbrain that regulates arousal and plays an important role in attention, sleep, and consciousness

retina the structure at the back of the eye that contains cells that transduce light into neural signals

retinal disparity a binocular depth cue that uses the difference in the images projected on the right and left retinas to inform the brain about the distance of a stimulus

retrieval the process of accessing information in memory and pulling it into consciousness

retroactive interference a type of forgetting that occurs when newer memory traces inhibit the retrieval of older memory traces

retrograde amnesia a type of amnesia in which one is unable to retrieve previously stored memories from long-term memory

reuptake process by which unused neurotransmitters are recycled back into the vesicles

rods the light-sensitive cells of the retina that pick up any type of light energy and convert it to neural signals

Rorschach inkblot test a projective personality test consisting of 10 ambiguous inkblots in which a person is asked to describe what he or she sees; the person's responses are then coded for consistent themes and issues

ruminative coping style the tendency to persistently focus on how one feels without attempting to do anything about one's feelings

sample the portion of the population of interest that is selected for a study

sample variance a measure of variability that shows on average how much the scores vary from the mean

saturation the purity of light; pure light or saturated light consists of a single wavelength

scaffolding a process in which adults initially offer guidance and support in helping a child to reason, solve a problem, or master a task; as the child becomes more proficient and capable, the adult helps less and less until the child can master the task on his or her own

scapegoat an out-group that is blamed for many of society's problems

scatter plot a graph of data that plots pairs of data points, with one data point on the *x*-axis and the other on the *y*-axis

schedule of reinforcement the frequency and timing of the reinforcements that a person or animal receives

schema Ch. 6: an organized, generalized knowledge structure in long-term memory; Ch. 9: a mental idea, concept, or thought

schizophrenia a severe disorder characterized by disturbances in thought, perceptions, emotions, and behavior

scientific method a systematic process used by psychologists for testing hypotheses about behavior

secondary drive learned drive that is not directly related to biological needs

secondary reinforcer a reinforcer that is reinforcing only because it leads to a primary reinforcer

secondary traits according to Allport, the tendencies we have that are less consistent and describe how we behave in certain situations

selective serotonin reuptake inhibitor (SSRI) a type of antidepressant drug that inhibits the reuptake of the neurotransmitter serotonin, thereby improving mood

self-actualization Ch. 8: the need to reach our full potential as a human being; Ch. 13: the fulfillment of one's natural potential

self-concept one's perception or image of his or her abilities and uniqueness

self-determination theory a theory of motivation that emphasizes the fact that as we pursue the fulfillment of basic needs, we are motivated by different types of motivation that come from both our self and the outside world

self-efficacy the expectation that one has for success in a given situation

self-help group group comprised of people who share the same problem and meet to help one another

self-serving bias our tendency to make attributions that preserve our own self-esteem; for example, making trait attributions for our successes and situational attributions for our failures

semantic encoding encoding memory traces in terms of the meaning of the information being stored

semantic memory long-term, declarative memory for conceptual information

sensation the process through which our sense organs transduce environmental energies such as light and sound into neural impulses

sensation seeker a person who by trait tends to seek out arousing activities

sensitive period in prenatal development, a time when genetic and environmental agents are most likely to cause birth defects

sensorimotor stage Piaget's first stage of cognitive development, in which infants learn schemas through their senses and motor abilities

sensory memory a system of memory that very briefly stores sensory impressions so that we can extract relevant information from them for further processing

separation anxiety the fear an infant expresses when separated from the major caretaker

serotonin neurotransmitter that plays a role in many different behaviors, including sleep, arousal, mood, eating, and pain perception

set point the theory that our body has a particular weight that it seeks to maintain

sex our biological makeup, starting with our chromosomes (XX for female, XY for male) and proceeding to our internal and external genitalia

sexual arousal a heightened state of sexual interest and excitement

sexual aversion disorder a persistent disgust and aversion toward sexual activity

sexual coercion sexual behaviors that are nonconsenting, abusive, or forcible

sexual desire one's motivation and interest in engaging in sexual activity

sexual differentiation the process by which males and females develop their sexual anatomy

sexual disorder a persistent sexual problem that causes a person a great deal of distress and interferes with his or her ability to function sexually

sexual dysfunction a persistent problem with sexual desire, arousal, or satisfaction

sexual fantasy a mental thought or image that is sexually arousing to a person

sexual harassment the repeated use of unwanted verbal comments, gestures, or physical contact of a sexual nature against another person that interferes with his or her work performance

sexual masochism a paraphilia in which a person desires to be humiliated or receive pain in order to attain sexual pleasure

sexual orientation one's sexual attraction for members of the same and/or other sex

sexual sadism a paraphilia in which a person achieves sexual satisfaction by inflicting pain or humiliation on a sex partner

sexuality the ways we express ourselves as sexual beings

sexually transmitted infection (STI) an infection that is passed from one person to another primarily through sexual contact

shaping using operant conditioning to build a new behavior in a person or animal by rewarding successive approximations of the desired response

short-term memory (STM) a system of memory that is limited in both capacity and duration; in the three stages model of memory, short-term memory is seen as the intermediate stage between sensory memory and long-term memory

signal detection a method of analyzing the relative proportions of hits and false alarms to eliminate the effects of response bias in a participant's detection of a stimulus

significant results are considered significant when we find that there is a very small chance (usually less than 5%) of finding our results given the assumption that our null hypothesis is true

similarity a Gestalt principle of perception that states that we tend to group like objects together during perception

situational attribution an attribution that assigns the cause of a behavior to some characteristic of the situation or environment in which the behavior occurs

Skinner box a device created by B. F. Skinner to study operant behavior in a compressed time frame; in a Skinner box, an animal is automatically rewarded or punished for engaging in certain behaviors

sleep apnea a sleep disorder in which a person stops breathing during sleep

sleep disorder a disturbance in the normal pattern of sleeping

sleepwalking a sleep disorder in which a person is mobile and may perform actions during stage IV sleep

slippery slope the use of foot-in-the-door compliance in an obedience situation to get people to obey increasing demands

social cognition the area of social psychology that deals with the ways in which we think about other people and ourselves

social cognitive approach a personality perspective that emphasizes the influence of one's thoughts and social experiences in formulating personality

social facilitation performing better on a task in the presence of others than you would if you were alone

social influence pressures placed on us by others to change our behavior or our beliefs or both

social loafing when group members exert less effort on a group task than they would if they were performing the task alone

social phobia an irrational, persistent fear of being negatively evaluated by others in a social situation

social psychology the branch of psychology that studies how we think and behave in social situations

social support having close and positive relationships with others

sociocultural perspective focuses on societal and cultural factors that may influence behavior

somatic nervous system branch of the peripheral nervous system that governs sensory and voluntary motor action in the body

somatoform disorder a disorder marked by physical complaints that has no apparent physical cause

somatosensory cortex a strip of the cortex at the front of the parietal lobe that governs our sense of touch

source traits universal tendencies that underlie and are at the core of surface traits, according to Cattell

specific phobia a persistent fear and avoidance of a specific object or situation

split brain a brain with its corpus callosum severed; sometimes done to control the effects of epilepsy in patients who do not respond to other therapies

spontaneous recovery during extinction, the tendency for a conditioned response to reappear and strengthen over a brief period before reextinguishing

standard deviation a measure of variability equal to the square root of the sample variance; often used to gauge the degree to which an individual score deviates from the mean of a distribution

standard normal distribution a bell-shaped, symmetric distribution ($\overline{X} = 0$; and $S = 1$) for which we know the exact area under the curve

statistics a type of applied mathematics used to describe data and test hypotheses

stereotype a schema for a particular group of people

stereotype threat a phenomenon in which fears of being discriminated against elicit stereotype-confirming behaviors

stimulants drugs that speed up normal brain functioning

stimulus any object or event that is perceived by our senses

stimulus discrimination responding only to particular stimuli

stimulus generalization responding in a like fashion to similar stimuli

storage the place where information is retained in memory

stranger anxiety the distress an infant expresses when faced with unfamiliar people

stress any event or environmental stimulus (stressor) that we respond to because we perceive it as challenging or threatening

structuralism an early psychological perspective concerned with identifying the basic elements of experience

structured interview interview conducted by a trained interviewer using standardized questions, a specific question order, and a predetermined scoring or answer key

subliminal when the intensity of a stimulus is below the participant's absolute threshold and the participant is not consciously aware of the stimulus

subordinate category the lowest level of categorization, which contains concepts that are less general and more specific than those at the basic level

substance abuse loss of control over one's drug use

substance dependence a condition in which a person needs a drug in order to maintain normal functioning

sum of squares the sum of the squared errors, or deviations, from the mean for the scores in the distribution; the numerator of the sample variance equation

superego the part of the personality that represents your moral conscience

superordinate category the highest, most general level of a concept

superordinate goal a goal that is shared by different groups

suprachiasmatic nucleus (SCN) a group of brain cells located in the hypothalamus that signal other brain areas when to be aroused and when to shut down

surface traits basic traits that describe people's personalities, according to Cattell

survey a research method that asks a large group of people about their attitudes, beliefs, and/or behaviors

symbolic thinking the understanding that an object can be represented with a symbol such as bodily gestures or language

sympathetic nervous system branch of the autonomic nervous system most active during times of danger or stress

synapse the connection formed between two neurons when the axon bulb of one neuron comes into proximity with the dendrite of another neuron

systematic desensitization a behavior therapy technique in which a client is desensitized to a fear in a gradual, step-by-step process

tardive dyskinesia a side effect of antipsychotic medications involving involuntary motor movements of the mouth, tongue, and face

taste aversion classical conditioning that occurs when a person or animal pairs the experience of nausea with a certain food and becomes conditioned to feel ill at the sight, smell, or idea of the food

taste buds the sense organs for taste that are found between the papillae on the tongue

telegraphic speech two-word sentences that children begin to utter at 20–26 months

temperament a person's general pattern of attention, arousal, and mood that is evident at birth

temporal lobe cortical areas directly below our ears that play a role in auditory processing and language

teratogen an environmental substance that has the potential to harm the developing organism

test the measurement of a carefully chosen sample of behavior

testes the organs in a male's body that produce both sperm and testosterone

testosterone a male hormone that plays a role in many aspects of sexuality, including sexual desire

thalamus part of the forebrain that functions as a sensory relay station in the brain

THC (tetrahydrocannabinol) the active ingredient in marijuana that affects learning, short-term memory, coordination, emotion, and appetite

Thematic Apperception Test (TAT) a projective personality test consisting of a series of pictures in which the respondent is asked to tell a story about each scene; the responses are then coded for consistent themes and issues

theory an explanation of why and how a behavior occurs

therapeutic alliance the interactive and collaborative relationship between the client and the therapist

therapy techniques that are used to help people with psychological or interpersonal problems

thinking the use of knowledge to accomplish some sort of goal

threat simulation theory (TST) suggests that dreaming is an ancient biological defense mechanism that allows us to repeatedly simulate potentially threatening situations so that we can rehearse our responses to these events

three stages model an early model of memory proposing that information is stored in three sequential stages: sensory, short-term, and long-term memory

threshold of excitation potential difference at which a neuron will fire an action potential (-55 mv in mammals)

Title VII of the Civil Rights Act of 1964 law that prohibits discrimination based on race, color, religion, sex, and national origin

token economy Ch. 5: a system of operant conditioning in which participants are reinforced with tokens that can later be cashed in for primary reinforcers; Ch. 15: a behavioral therapy technique in which people are rewarded with tokens for desired behavior; the tokens can then be exchanged for what is reinforcing to the individuals

tolerance a condition in which after repeated use, more of a drug is needed to achieve the same effect

top-down perceptual processing perception that is guided by prior knowledge or expectations

trait tendency to behave in a certain way across most situations

trait approach a personality perspective that attempts to describe personality by emphasizing internal, biological aspects of personality called traits

trait attribution an attribution that assigns the cause of a behavior to the traits and characteristics of the person being judged

transduction the process through which our sense organs convert environmental energies into neural impulses

transference a process in psychoanalysis in which the client unconsciously reacts to the therapist as if the therapist were a parent, friend, sibling, or lover

transformational leadership characterized by high ethical standards, inspirational motivation, intellectual stimulation, and individual consideration

transsexual a person whose gender identity is opposite to his or her chromosomal sex

transvestism a paraphilia in which a person is sexually aroused by wearing clothing of the other gender

triarchic theory of intelligence a theory of emptthat proposes that intelligence is composed of analytical, practical, and creative abilities that help us adapt to our environment

trichromatic theory of color vision the idea that color vision is made possible by the presence of three different types of cones in the retina that react, respectively, to either red, green, or blue light

twin studies research that compares specific traits of identical and fraternal twins to ascertain the relative contributions of genes and environment to our characteristics

two-factor theory a theory of emotion that states that emotions result when we cognitively interpret our physiological reactions in light of the situation

Type A personality a personality that is aggressive, ambitious, and competitive

Type B personality a personality characterized by patience, flexibility, and an easygoing manner

Type C personality a personality that is cautious, serious, sensitive to criticism, and results oriented and that suppresses negative emotions such as anger

unconditional positive regard Ch. 13: acceptance and love of another's thoughts and feelings without expecting anything in return; Ch. 15: the ability to accept and value a person for who he or she is, regardless of his or her faults or problems

unconditioned response (UR) the response that is elicited by an unconditioned stimulus

unconditioned stimulus (US) a stimulus that naturally elicits a response in a person or animal

unconscious level the level of awareness that contains all the thoughts, perceptions, and impulses of which we are unaware

underextension when a child inappropriately restricts the use of a word to a particular case (e.g., using the word *cat* to describe only the family pet)

unstructured interview informal, unplanned interview conducted by an untrained interviewer using random questions and no scoring key

vaginismus a disorder in females characterized by involuntary contractions of the vaginal muscles making penetration painful or impossible

validity the degree to which a test measures the trait that it was designed to measure

variable interval schedule a schedule of reinforcement in which the person or animal is rewarded for the first desired response in an average *x*th interval of time

variable ratio schedule a schedule of reinforcement in which the person or animal is rewarded on average for every *x*th instance of the desired response

ventromedial hypothalamus (VMH) a region of the hypothalamus that plays an indirect role in creating a feeling of satiety

vestibular sense the sense of balance

visible spectrum the spectrum of light that humans can see

visual cortex a region of cortex found at the back of the occipital lobe that processes visual information in the brain

visuospatial sketch pad in the working memory model, the part of working memory that processes the visual and spatial aspects of information

volley theory proposes that our brain decodes pitch by noticing the frequency at which *groups* of hair cells on the basilar membrane are firing

voyeurism a paraphilia in which one is sexually aroused by observing unsuspecting strangers who are undressing or engaged in sexual activity

wavelength a physical property of some energies that corresponds to the distance between the wave peaks

Weber's law a psychophysical formula used to predict the jnd for a given stimulus: $\Delta I / I = k$, where ΔI is the change in the stimulus required to produce a jnd, I is the original intensity of the stimulus, and k is a constant that varies for each of the five senses

well-structured problem problem for which there is a clear pathway to the solution

Wernicke's area a region in the left temporal lobe that plays a role in the comprehension of speech

Whorfian hypothesis/linguistic relativity hypothesis the theory that one's language can directly determine or influence one's thoughts

will-do factors factors that determine the normal or typical performance by an employee

withdrawal an unpleasant physiological state that results when one stops taking a drug to which he or she has built up a tolerance

withdrawal symptoms physical or behavioral effects that occur after a person stops using a drug

work teams/groups two or more employees who together perform organizationally relevant tasks, share one or more common goals, interact socially, exhibit task interdependencies, and maintain and manage boundaries within an organizational context

work withdrawal behaviors employees use to avoid their work (e.g., lateness, absenteeism)

working memory a multifaceted component of long-term memory that contains short-term memory, a central executive, a phonological loop, and a visuospatial sketch pad; the function of working memory is to access, move, and process information that we are currently using

z score a measure of relative standing that measures the distance of a score from the mean of the distribution in standard deviation units

zone of proximal development (ZPD) according to Vygotsky, the gap between what a child is already able to do and what he or she is not yet capable of doing without help

zygote a fertilized egg

REFERENCES

Aamodt, M. G. (2010). *Industrial/Organizational Psychology*: An Applied Approach. California: Thomson Wadsworth.

Abad, V. C., & Guilleminault, C. (2004). Review of rapid eye movement behavior sleep disorders. *Current Neurology Neuroscience Reports, 4*, 157–163.

Abar, B., Carter, K. L., & Winsler, A. (2009). The effects of maternal parenting style and religious commitment on self-regulation, academic achievement, and risk behavior among African-American parochial college students. *Journal of Adolescence, 32*, 259–273.

Abbott, R. (2010). Delivering quality-evaluated healthcare information in the era of Web 2.0: Design implication for Intute: Health and Life Sciences. *Health Informatics Journal, 16*, 5–14.

Abdel-Khalek, A., & Lester, D. (2005). Sibship size, birth order, and personality. *Psychological Reports, 97*, 387–388.

Abkevich, V., Camp, N. J., Hensel, C. H., Neff, C. D., Russell, D. L., Hughes, D. C., et al. (2003). Predisposition locus for major depression at chromosome 12q22-12q23.2. *American Journal of Human Genetics, 73*, 1271–1281.

Aboujaoude, E., Koran, L. M., Gamel, N., Large, M. D., & Serpe, R. T. (2006). Potential markers for problematic Internet use: A telephone survey of 2,513 adults. *CNS Spectrums, 11*, 750–755.

Abramov, I., & Gordon, J. (1994). Color appearance: On seeing red—or yellow, or green, or blue. *Annual Review of Psychology, 45*, 451–485.

Abramowitz, J. S. (1997). Effectiveness of psychological and pharmacological treatments for obsessive-compulsive disorder: A quantitative review. *Journal of Consulting and Clinical Psychology, 65*, 44–52.

Abramowitz, J. S., & Moore, E. L. (2007). An experimental analysis of hypochondriasis. *Behaviour Research and Therapy, 45*, 413–424.

Abrams, D. B., & Wilson, G. T. (1983). Alcohol, sexual arousal, and self-control. *Journal of Personality and Social Psychology, 45*, 188–198.

Abramson, L. Y., Alloy, L. B., Hankin, B. L., Haeffel, G. J., MacCoon, D. G., & Gibb, B. E. (2002). Cognitive vulnerability—stress models of depression in a self-regulatory and psychobiological content. In I. H. Gotlib & C. L. Hammen (Eds.), *Handbook of depression* (pp. 268–294). New York: Guilford Press.

Adam, E. K. (2006). Transactions among adolescent trait and state emotion and diurnal and momentary cortisol activity in naturalistic settings. *Psychoneuroendocrinology, 31*, 664–679.

Adams, C. D., Girolami, P. A., Joseph, K. E., Sauvageot, S. A., & Slater, H. (2002). Use of a token reinforcement system to promote appropriate behavior at a pediatric burn summer camp. *Journal of Burn and Care Rehabilitation, 23*, 297–305.

Adams, J. (1976). *Conceptual blockbusters* (2nd ed.). New York: Norton.

Adams, K. F., Schatzkin, A., Harris, T. B., Kipnis, V., Mouw, T., Ballard-Barbash, R., et al. (2006). Overweight, obesity, and mortality in a large prospective cohort of persons 50 to 71 years old. *New England Journal of Medicine, 355*, 763–778.

Adan, A., & Natale, V. (2002). Gender differences in morningness-eveningness preference. *Chronobiology International, 19*, 709–720.

Ader, R. (2001). Psychoneuroimmunology. *Current Directions in Psychological Science, 10*, 94–98.

Aderibigbe, Y. A., Bloch, R. M., & Walker, W. R. (2001). Prevalence of depersonalization and derealization experiences in a rural population. *Social Psychiatry and Psychiatric Epidemiology, 36*, 63–69.

Adler, A. (1928). *Understanding human nature*. London: Allen & Unwin.

Adler, J., & Rosenberg, D. (1994, December 19). The endless binge. *Newsweek*, p. 72.

Adolphs, R. (2002). Neural systems for recognizing emotion. *Current Opinion in Neurobiology, 12*, 169–177.

Adolphs, R., Tranel, D., & Damasio, A. R. (1998). The human amygdala in social judgment. *Nature, 393*, 470–474.

Aghajanian, G. K. (1994). Serotonin and the action of LSD in the brain. *Psychiatric Annals, 24*, 137–141.

Ahrold, T. K., Farmer, M., Trapnell, P. D., & Meston, C. M. (in press). The relationship among sexual attitudes, sexual fantasy, and religiosity. *Archives of Sexual Behavior*.

Aiello, J. R., & Douthitt, E. A. (2001). Social facilitation from Triplett to electronic performance monitoring. *Group Dynamics: Theory, Research, and Practice, 5*, 163–180.

Aiken, L. R. (1996). *Personality assessment methods and practices* (2nd ed.). Seattle: Hogrefe & Huber.

Ainsworth, M. D., Blehar, M. C., Waters, E., & Wall, S. (1978). *Patterns of attachment*. Hillsdale, NJ: Erlbaum.

Air travel remains safe. (1999, November 5). *Salt Lake City Tribune*, p. A12.

Alan Guttmacher Institute. (2001). Facts in brief: Teenagers' sexual and reproductive behavior, developed countries. Retrieved September 6, 2004, from http://www.agiusa.org/pubs/fb_teens.html

Albouy, G., Sterpenich, V., Balteau, E., Vandewalle, G., Desseilles, M., Dang-Vu, T., et al. (2008). Both the hippocampus and striatum are involved in consolidation of motor sequence memory. *Neuron, 58*, 261–272.

Aldao, A., Nolen-Hoeksema, S., & Schweizer, S. (2010). Emotion-regulation strategies across psychopathology: A meta-analytic review. *Clinical Psychology Review, 30*, 217–237.

Alderidge, M.A., Stillman, R. D., & Bower, T. G. R. (2001). Newborn categorization of vowel-like sounds. *Developmental Science, 4*, 220–232.

Alexander, G. M. (2003). An evolutionary perspective on sex-typed toy preferences: Pink, blue, and the brain. *Archives of Sexual Behavior, 32*, 7–14.

Alexander, M. G., & Fisher, T. D. (2003). Truth and consequences: Using the bogus pipeline to examine sex differences in self-reported sexuality. *Journal of Sex Research, 40*, 27–35.

Allen, L. B., White, K. S., Barlow, D. H., Shear, M. K., Gorman, J. M., & Woods, S. W. (2010). Cognitive-behavior therapy (CBT) for panic disorder: Relationship of anxiety and depression comorbidity with treatment outcome. *Journal of Psychopathology and Behavioral Assessment, 32*, 185–192.

Allen, L. S., & Gorski, R. A. (1991). Sexual dimorphism of the anterior commissure and the massa intermedia of the human brain. *Journal of Comparative Neurology, 312*, 97–104.

Allen, T. D., Lentz, E., & Day, R. (2006). Career success outcomes associated with mentoring others: A comparison of mentors and nonmentors. *Journal of Career Development, 32(3)*, 272–285.

Alloy, L. B., Abramson, L. Y., & Francis, E. L. (1999). Do negative cognitive styles confer vulnerability to depression? *Current Directions in Psychological Science, 8*, 128–132.

Allport, G. W. (1961). *Pattern and growth in personality*. New York: Holt, Rinehart & Winston.

Allport, G. W. (1979). *The nature of prejudice*. Reading, MA: Addison-Wesley. (Original work published 1954)

Almeida, D. M. (2005). Resilience and vulnerability to daily stressors assessed via diary methods. *Current Directions in Psychological Science, 14*, 64–68.

Alonso, A., & Swiller, H. I. (1993). Introduction: The case for group therapy. In A. Alonso & H. I. Swiller (Eds.), *Group therapy in clinical practice* (pp. xxi–xxv). Washington, DC: American Psychiatric Press.

Alter-Reid, K., Gibbs, M. S., Lachenmeyer, J. R., Sigal, J., & Massoth, N. A. (1986). Sexual abuse of children: A review of the empirical findings. *Clinical Psychology Review, 6*, 249–266.

Alterovitz, S. S. & Mendelsohn, G. A. (2009). Partner preferences across the lifespan: Online dating by older adults. *Psychology and Aging, 24*, 513–517.

Alvarez, F. J., Delrio, M. C., & Prado, R. (1995). Drinking and driving in Spain. *Journal of Studies on Alcohol, 56(4)*, 403–407.

Amato, P. R. (1993). Children's adjustment to divorce: Theories, hypotheses, and empirical support. *Journal of Marriage and the Family, 55*, 23–38.

Amato, P. R. (2000). The consequences of divorce for adults and children. *Journal of Marriage and the Family, 62*, 1269–1287.

Amato, P. R., & Booth, A. (1996). A prospective study of divorce and parent–child relationships. *Journal of Marriage and the Family, 58*, 356–365.

Amato, P. R., & DeBoer, D. D. (2001). The transmission of marital instability across generations: Relationship skills or commitment to marriage? *Journal of Marriage and the Family, 63*, 1038–1051.

Amato, P. R., & Rogers, S. J. (1997). A longitudinal study of marital problems and subsequent divorce. *Journal of Marriage and the Family, 59*, 612–624.

Amato, P. R., Johnson, D. R., Booth, A., & Rogers, S. J. (2003). Continuity and change in marital quality between 1980 and 2000. *Journal of Marriage and the Family, 65*, 1–22.

American College Health Association (ACHA). (2006). American College Health Association National College Health Assessment (ACHA-NCHA) spring 2005 reference group data report. *Journal of American College Health, 55*, 5–16.

American Psychiatric Association. (1994). *Diagnostic and statistical manual of mental disorders* (4th ed.). Washington, DC: Author.

American Psychiatric Association. (2000a). *Diagnostic and statistical manual of mental disorders* (4th ed., Text Revision). Washington, DC: Author.

American Psychiatric Association. (2000b). Substance use disorders: Alcohol, cocaine, opiods. In *Practice guidelines for the treatment of psychiatric disorders: Compendium 2000* (pp. 139–238). Washington, DC: Author.

American Psychiatric Association (2004). *Practice guideline for the treatment of patients with acute stress disorder and posttraumatic stress disorder*. Arlington, VA: American Psychiatric Association Practice Guidelines.

American Psychological Association (APA). (1984). *Behavioral research with animals*. Washington, DC: Author.

American Psychological Association (APA). (1997). *Visions and transformations*. Washington, DC: APA's Commission on Ethnic Minority Recruitment, Retention and Training in Psychology.

American Psychological Association (APA). (2000a). *Psychology careers for the twenty-first century*. Washington, DC: Author.

American Psychological Association (APA). (2000b). *Women in academe: Two steps forward, one step back*. Washington, DC: Author.

American Psychological Association (APA). (2002). Ethical principles of psychologists and code of conduct. *American Psychologist, 57*, 1060–1073.

American Psychological Association (APA). (2004). *Resolution on sexual orientation and marriage*. Retrieved

May 2, 2007, from http://www.apa.org/releases/gaymarriage.html

Amodeo, M., Griffin, M. L., Fassler, I. R., Clay, C. M., & Ellis, M. A. (2006). Childhood sexual abuse among Black women and White women from two-parent families. *Child Maltreatment, 11,* 237–246.

Amoore, J. E. (1970). *Molecular basis of odor.* Springfield, IL: Thomas.

Amoranpanth, P. X., Widick, P., & Chatterjee, A. (2009). The neural basis for spatial relations. *Journal of Cognitive Neuroscience.* doi:10.1162/jocn.2009.21322.

Amsterdam, J. D., & Shults, J. (2010). Efficacy and safety of long-term fluoxetine versus lithium monotherapy of bipolar II disorder: A randomized, double-blind, placebo substitution study. *American Journal of Psychiatry, 167,* 792–800.

Anderson, C. (2003). Social stress and support factors in susceptibility to the common cold. *APS Observer, 16,* 37.

Anderson, C. A., & Arciniegas, D. B. (2004). Neurosurgical interventions for neuropsychiatric syndromes. *Current Psychiatry Reports, 6,* 355–363.

Anderson, C. A., Benjamin, A. J., & Bartholow, B. D. (1998). Does the gun pull the trigger? Automatic priming effects of weapon pictures and weapon names. *Psychological Science, 9,* 308–314.

Anderson, C. A., & Bushman, B. J. (2002). Human aggression. *Annual Review of Psychology, 53,* 27–51.

Anderson, J. R. (1974). Verbatim and propositional representation of sentences in immediate and long-term memory. *Journal of Verbal Learning and Verbal Behavior, 13,* 149–162.

Anderson, J. R. (2000). *Cognitive psychology and its applications* (5th ed). New York: Worth.

Anderson, N., & Thomas, H. D. C. (1996). Work group socialization. In M. A. West (Ed.), *Handbook of work group psychology,* (pp. 423–450). Chichester, England: John Wiley & Sons.

Anderson, P. L., Zimand, E., Hodges, L. F., & Rothbaum, B. O. (2005). Cognitive behavioral therapy for public-speaking anxiety using virtual reality for exposure. *Depression and Anxiety, 22,* 156–158.

Andreasen, N. C., Swayze, V. W., Flaum, M., & Alliger, R. (1990). Ventricular abnormalities in affective disorder: Clinical and demographic correlates. *American Journal of Psychiatry, 147,* 893–900.

Andresen, J. (2000). Meditation meets behavioural medicine: The story of experimental research on meditation. *Journal of Consciousness Studies, 7*(11–12), 17–73.

Angelou, M. (1974). *Gather together in my name.* New York: Random House.

Angst, J., & Sellaro, R. (2000). Historical perspectives and natural history of bipolar disorder. *Biological Psychiatry, 48,* 445–457.

Anshel, M. H. (1995). Effect of chronic aerobic exercise and progressive relaxation on motor performance and affect following acute stress. *Behavioral Medicine, 21*(4), 186–196.

Antoni, M. H., & Lutgendorf, S. (2007). Psychosocial factors and disease progression in cancer. *Current Directions in Psychological Science, 16,* 42–46.

Antonioni, D. (2003). Leading with responsibility. *Industrial Management, 45,* 8–15.

Antony, M. M., & Barlow, D. H. (Eds.). (2002). *Handbook of assessment and treatment planning for psychological disorders.* New York: Guilford Press.

APA Center for Psychology Workforce Analysis and Research. (2007a). *2006–07 Faculty Salary Survey.* Retrieved December 26, 2009, from http://www.apa.org/workforce/publications/07-fac-sal/index.aspx

APA Center for Psychology Workforce Analysis and Research. (2007b). *2008 Graduate Study in Psychology.* Retrieved December 26, 2009, from http://www.apa.org/workforce/snapshots/2007/figure-15.aspx.

APA Center for Workforce Studies. (2007). *2007 Doctorate Employment Survey.* Retrieved December 26, 2009, from http://www.apa.org/workforce/publications/07-doc-empl/table-3.pdf.

Applbaum, K. D. (1995). Marriage with the proper stranger: Arranged marriage in metropolitan Japan. *Ethnology, 34,* 37–51.

Appleby, D. (1997). *The handbook of psychology.* New York: Longman.

Araque, A. (2008). Astrocytes process synaptic information. *Neuron Glia Biology, 4,* 3–10.

Arborelius, L., Owens, M. J., Plotsky, P. M., & Nemeroff, C. B. (1999). The role of corticotropin-releasing factor in depression and anxiety disorders. *Journal of Endocrinology, 160,* 1–12.

Archer, J. (2004). Sex differences in aggression in real-world settings: A meta-analytic review. *Review of General Psychology, 8,* 291–322.

Arendt, J. (2006). Melatonin and human rhythms. *Chronobiology International, 23,* 21–37.

Arendt, R. E., Short, E. J., Singer, L. T., Minnes, S., Hewitt, J., Flynn, S., et al. (2004). Children prenatally exposed to cocaine: Developmental outcomes and environmental risks at seven years of age. *Journal of Developmental and Behavioral Pediatrics, 25,* 83–90.

Arent, S. M., & Landers, D. M. (2003). Arousal, anxiety, and performance: A reexamination of the inverted-U hypothesis. *Research Quarterly for Exercise and Sport, 74,* 436–444.

Armfield, J. M. (2006). Cognitive vulnerability: A model of the etiology of fear. *Clinical Psychology Review, 26,* 746–768.

Armitage, R. (1995). The distribution of EEG frequencies in REM and NREM sleepstages in healthy young adults. *Sleep, 18*(5), 334–341.

Arnett, J. J. (2004). *Emerging adulthood: The winding road from the late teens through the twenties.* New York: Oxford University Press.

Arnett, J. J. (2007). Emerging adulthood: What is it and what is it good for? *Child Development Perspectives, 1,* 68–73.

Aronson, E. (1998). Dissonance, hypocrisy, and the self-concept. In E. Harmon-Jones & J. S. Mills, *Cognitive dissonance theory: Revival with revisions and controversies.* Washington, DC: American Psychological Association.

Aronson, E. (2000). The jigsaw strategy. *Psychology Review, 7,* 2.

Aronson, E., & Mills, J. (1959). The effects of severity of initiation on liking for a group. *Journal of Abnormal and Social Psychology, 59,* 177–181.

Aronson, E., Wilson, T. D., & Akert, R. M. (2005). *Social psychology* (5th ed.). Englewood Cliffs, NJ: Prentice Hall.

Arrindell, W. A., Eisemann, M., Richter, J., Oei, T. P. S., Caballo, V. E., van der Ende, J., et al. (2003). Masculinity-femininity as a national characteristic and its relationship with national agoraphobic fear levels: Fodor's sex role hypothesis revitalized. *Behaviour Research and Therapy, 41,* 795–807.

Arroll, B., Macgillivray, S., Ogston, S., Reid, I., Sullivan, F., Williams, B., et al. & Crombie, I. (2005). Efficacy and tolerability of tricyclic antidepressants and SSRIs compared with placebo for treatment of depression in primary care: A meta-analysis. *Annals of Family Medicine, 3,* 449–456.

Arthur, J. B. (1994). Effects of human resource systems on manufacturing performance and turnover. *Academy of Management Journal, 37,* 670–687.

Asato, M. R., Terwilliger, R., Woo, J., & Luna, B. (2010). White matter development in adolescence: A DTI study. *Cerebral Cortex, 20,* 2122–2131.

Asay, T. P., & Lambert, M. J. (1999). The empirical case for the common factors in therapy: Quantitative findings. In M. A. Hubble, B. L. Duncan, & S. D. Miller (Eds.), *The heart and soul of change: What works in therapy* (pp. 33–56). Washington, DC: American Psychological Association.

Asch, S. E. (1951). Effects of group pressure upon modification and distortion of judgments. In H. Guetzkow (Ed.), *Groups, leadership, and men* (pp. 117–190). Pittsburgh: Carnegie.

Ashby, F. G., & Maddox, W. T. (2005). Human category learning. *Annual Review of Psychology, 56,* 149–178.

Ashcan, K., Wallace, B., Bell, B. A., & Benabid, A. L. (2004). Deep brain stimulation of the subthalamic nucleus in Parkinson's disease 1993–2003: Where are we ten years on? *British Journal of Neurosurgery, 18,* 19–34.

Ashtari, M., Cervellione, K. L., Hasan, K. M., Wu, J., McIlree, C., Kester, H., et al. (2007). White matter development during late adolescence in healthy males: A cross-sectional diffusion tensor imaging study. *NeuroImage, 35,* 501–510.

Ashwin, C., Baron-Cohen, S., Wheelwright, S., O'Riordan, M., & Bullmore, E. T. (2007). Differential activation of the amygdala and the "social brain" during fearful face-processing in Asperger syndrome. *Neuropsychologia, 45,* 2–14.

Asnis, G. M., Kohn, S. R., Henderson, M., & Brown, N. L. (2004). SSRIs versus non-SSRIs in post-traumatic stress disorder: An update with recommendations. *Drugs, 64,* 383–404.

Assor, A., Roth, G., & Deci, E. L. (2004). The emotional costs of parents' conditional regard: A self-determination theory analysis. *Journal of Personality, 72,* 47–88.

Astin, J. A. (2004). Mind-body therapies for the management of pain. *Clinical Journal of Pain, 20,* 27–32.

Ata, R. N., & Thompson, J. K. (2010). Weight bias in the media: A review of recent research. *Obesity Facts, 3,* 41–46.

Atkinson, J. W. (1983). Towards experimental analysis of human motivation in terms of motives, expectancies, and incentives. In J. W. Atkinson (Ed.), *Personality, motivation, and action: Selected papers* (pp. 81–97). New York: Praeger. (Original work published 1958)

Atkinson, R. C., & Shiffrin, R. W. (1968). Human memory: A proposed system and its control processes. In K. Spence & J. Spence (Eds.), *The psychology of learning and motivation* (Vol. 2, pp. 89–195). New York: Academic Press.

Aucoin, D. (2000, May 25). Feminist report says "sexist stereotypes" abound in prime time. *Oregonian,* E9.

Auster, C. J., & Ohm, S. C. (2000). Masculinity and femininity in contemporary American society: A reevaluation using the Bem Sex-Role Inventory. *Sex Roles, 43,* 499–528.

Author Rowling considered suicide. (2008). *USA Today.* Retrieved February 13, 2010, from www.usatoday.com/life/people/2008-03-23-rowling-report_N.htm?csp=34

Auyeung, B., Baron-Cohen, S., Ashwin, E., Knickmeyer, R., Taylor, K., Hackett, G., et al. (2009). Fetal testosterone predicts sexually differentiated childhood behavior in girls and in boys. *Psychological Science, 20,* 144–148.

Avalos, L. C., & Tylka, T. L. (2006). Exploring a model of intuitive eating with college women. *Journal of Counseling Psychology, 53,* 486–497.

Avolio, B. J., Kahai, S. S., & Dodge, G. (2000). E-leading in organizations and it implications for theory, research and practice. *Leadership Quarterly, 11,* 615–670.

Axinn, W. G., & Barber, J. S. (1997). Living arrangements and family formation attitudes in early adulthood. *Journal of Marriage and the Family, 59,* 595–611.

Azar, B. (1998). A genetic disposition for certain tastes may affect people's food preferences. *American Psychological Association Monitor* [Online], *29.* Available from http://www.apa.org/monitor/jan98/food.html

Azevedo, F. A., Carvalho, L. R., Grinberg, L. T., Farfel, J. M., Ferretti, R. E., Leite, R. E., et al. (2009). Equal numbers of neuronal and nonneuronal cells make the human brain an isometrically scaled-up primate brain. *Journal of Comparative Neurology, 513,* 532–541.

Bach, A. K., Wincze, J. P., & Barlow, D. H. (2001). Sexual dysfunction. In D. H. Barlow (Ed.), *Clinical handbook of psychological disorders: A step-by-step treatment manual* (3rd ed., pp. 562–608). New York: Guilford Press.

Bachman, J. G., Johnston, L. D., & O'Malley, P. M. (2001). *Monitoring the future: Questionnaire responses from the nation's high school seniors, 2000.* Ann Arbor, MI: Institute for Social Research.

Bachman, J. G., Johnston, L. D., & O'Malley, P. M. (2009). *Monitoring the future: Questionnaire responses from the nation's high school seniors, 2008.* Ann Arbor, MI: Institute for Social Research.

Bacon, C., Mittleman, M., Kawachi, I., Giovannucci, E., Gasser, D., & Rimm, E. (2003). Sexual function in men older than 50 years of age: Results from the health professionals follow-up study. *Annals of Internal Medicine, 139,* 161–168.

Baddeley, A. D. (1986). *Working memory.* Oxford, UK: Clarendon Press.

Baddeley, A. D. (1992). Working memory. *Science, 255,* 556–559.

Baddeley, A. D. (2002). Is working memory still working? *European Psychologist, 7,* 85–97.

Baddeley, A. D., & Hitch, G. J. (1974). Working memory. In G. H. Bower (Ed.), *The psychology of learning and motivation* (Vol. 8, pp. 47–89). London: Academic Press.

Baer, L., Rauch, S. L., Ballantine, T., Martuza, R., Cosgrove, R., Cassem, E., et al. (1995). Cingulotomy for intractable obsessive-compulsive disorder. *Archives of General Psychiatry, 52,* 384–392.

Bagshaw, S. M., Jr. (1985). The desensitisation of chronically motion sick aircrew in the Royal Air Force. *Aviation Space Environmental Medicine, 56,* 1144–1151.

Bahk, C. (2006). College students' perceived risk and anxiety after reading airplane crash news. *Psychological Reports, 99,* 107–110.

Bahrick, H. P. (1984). Semantic memory content in permastore: Fifty years of memory for Spanish learned in school. *Journal of Experimental Psychology: General, 113,* 1–24.

Baillargeon, R., & DeVos, J. (1992). Object permanence in young infants: Further evidence. *Child Development, 62(6),* 1227–1246.

Bailey, J., & Pillard, R. C. (1991). A genetic study of male sexual orientation. *Archives of General Psychiatry, 48,* 1089–1096.

Bailey, J., Dunne, M., & Martin, N. (2000). Genetic and environmental influences on sexual orientation and its correlates in an Australian twin sample. *Journal of Personality and Social Psychology, 78,* 524–536.

Bailey, J., Pillard, R. C., Neale, M. C., & Agyei, Y. (1993). Heritable factors influence female sexual orientation in women. *Archives of General Psychiatry, 50,* 217–223.

Baillieux, H., De Smet, H. J., Dobbeleir, A., Paquier, P. F., De Deyn, P. P., & Mariën, P. (2009). Cognitive and affective disturbances following focal cerebellar damage in adults: A neuropsychological and SPECT study. *Cortex.* Retrieved December 17, 2009, from http://sciencedirect.comhttp://www.sciencedirect.com

Baird, A. A., Gruber, S. A., Fein, D. A., Maas, L. C., Steingard, R. J., Renshaw, P. F., et al. (1999). Functional magnetic resonance imaging of facial affect recognition in children and adolescents. *Journal of the American Academy of Child and Adolescent Psychiatry, 38,* 195–209.

Baker, J. R., & Moore, S. M. (2008). Blogging as a social tool: A psychosocial examination of the effects of blogging. *Cyberpsychology and Behavior, 11,* 747–749.

Baker, T. B., Japuntich, S. J., Hogle, J. M., McCarthy, D. E., & Curtin, J. J. (2006). Pharmacologic and behavioral withdrawal from addictive drugs. *Current Directions in Psychological Science, 15,* 232–236.

Baker, T. B., McFall, R. M., & Shoham, V. (2008). Current status and future prospects of clinical psychology: Toward a scientifically principled approach to mental and behavioral health care. *Psychological Science in the Public Interest, 9,* 67–103.

Ball, E. M. (1997). Sleep disorders in primary care. *Comprehensive Therapy, 23,* 25–30.

Ballard, M., Gray, M., Reilly, J., & Noggle, M. (2009). Correlates of video game screen time among males: Body mass, physical activity, and other media use. *Eating Behaviors, 10,* 161–167.

Balota, D. A., Dolan, P. O., & Duchek, J. M. (2000). Memory changes in healthy older adults. In E. Tulving & F. I. M. Craik (Eds.), *The Oxford handbook of memory* (pp. 395–409). Oxford, UK: Oxford University Press.

Balsam, K. F., Beauchaine, T. P., Rothblum, E. D., & Solomon, S. E. (2008). Three-year follow-up of same-sex couples who had civil unions in Vermont, same-sex couples not in civil unions, and heterosexual married couples. *Developmental Psychology, 44,* 102–116.

Balsam, K. F., Rothblum, E. D., & Beauchaine, T. P. (2005). Victimization over the life span: A comparison of lesbian, gay, bisexual, and heterosexual siblings. *Journal of Consulting and Clinical Psychology, 73,* 477–487.

Baltes, P. B. (1997). On the incomplete architecture of human ontogeny: Selection, optimization, and compensation as foundation of developmental theory. *American Psychologist, 52,* 366–380.

Balthazart, J., & Ball, G. F. (2006). Is brain estradiol a hormone or neurotransmitter? *Trends in Neurosciences, 29,* 241–249.

Balzer, W. K., Kihm, J. A., Smith, P. C., Irwin, J. L., Bachiochi, P. D., Robie, C., et al. (1997). *Users' manual for the Job Descriptive Index (JDI, 1997 revision) and the Job in General Scales.* Bowling Green, OH: Bowling Green State University.

Bancroft, J., Herbenick, D., Barnes, T., Hallam-Jones, R., Wylie, K., & Janssen, E. (2005). The relevance of the dual control model to male sexual dysfunction: The Kinsey Institute/BASRT collaborative project. *Sexual and Relationship Therapy, 20,* 13–30.

Bandura, A. (1965). Influence of model's reinforcement contingencies on the acquisition of imitative responses. *Journal of Personality and Social Psychology, 1,* 589–595.

Bandura, A. (1977). *Social learning theory.* Englewood Cliffs, NJ: Prentice Hall.

Bandura, A. (1986). *Social foundations of thought and action: A social cognitive theory.* Englewood Cliffs, NJ: Prentice Hall.

Bandura, A. (1997). *Self-efficacy: The exercise of control.* New York: W. H. Freeman.

Bandura, A., Grusec, J. E., & Menlove, F. L. (1966). Observational learning as a function of symbolization and incentive set. *Child Development, 37,* 499–506.

Bandura, A., Ross, D., & Ross, S. (1961). Transmission of aggression through imitation of aggressive models. *Journal of Abnormal and Social Psychology, 63,* 575–582.

Bandura, A., Ross, D., & Ross, S. (1963). Imitation of film-mediated aggressive models. *Journal of Abnormal and Social Psychology, 66,* 3–11.

Bangasser, D. A., Waxler, D. E., Santollo, J., & Shors, T. J. (2006). Trace conditioning and the hippocampus: The importance of contiguity. *Journal of Neuroscience, 26,* 8702–8706.

Banich, M. T., & Heller, W. (1998). Evolving perspectives on lateralization of function. *Current Directions in Psychological Science, 74,* 1–2.

Banthia, R., Moskowitz, J. T., Acree, M., & Folkman, S. (2007). Socioeconomic differences in the effect of prayer on physical symptoms and quality of life. *Journal of Health Psychology, 12,* 249–260.

Banyard, V. L., & Williams, L. M. (2007). Women's voices on recovery: A multi-method study of the complexity of recovery from child sexual abuse. *Child Abuse and Neglect, 31,* 275–290.

Barbee, J. G. (1993). Memory, benzodiazepines, and anxiety: Integration of theoretical and clinical perspectives. *Journal of Clinical Psychiatry, 54(*Suppl. 10), 86–101.

Barber, J. P., Connolly, M. B., Crits-Christoph, P., Gladis, L., & Siqueland, L. (2000). Alliance predicts patients' outcome beyond in-treatment change in symptoms. *Journal of Consulting and Clinical Psychology, 68,* 1027–1032.

Bardone, A. M., Vohs, K. D., Abramson, L. Y., Heatherton, T. F., & Joiner, T. E., Jr. (2000). The confluence of perfectionism, body dissatisfaction, and low self-esteem predicts bulimic symptoms: Clinical implications. *Behavior Therapy, 31,* 265–280.

Barger, L. K., Lockley, S. W., & Rajaratnam, S. M., & Landrigan, C. P. (2009). Neurobehavioral, health, and safety consequences associated with shift work in safety-sensitive professions. *Current Neurology and Neuroscience Reports, 9,* 155–164.

Bargh, J. A., & Morsella, E. (2008). The unconscious mind. *Perspectives on Psychological Science, 3,* 73–79.

Bar-Haim, Y., Ziv, T., Lamy, D., & Hodes, R. M. (2006). Nature and nurture in own-race face processing. *Psychological Science, 17,* 159–163.

Barker, V. (2009). Older adolescents' motivations for social network site use: The influence of gender, group identity, and collective self-esteem. *Cyberpsychology and Behavior, 12,* 209–213.

Barlow, D. H. (2000). Unraveling the mysteries of anxiety and its disorders from the perspective of emotion theory. *American Psychologist, 55,* 1247–1263.

Barlow, D. H. (2002). *Anxiety and its disorders: The nature and treatment of anxiety and panic* (2nd ed.). New York: Guilford Press.

Barlow, D. H., & Durand, V. M. (2005). *Abnormal psychology: An integrative approach* (4th ed.). Belmont, CA: Wadsworth.

Barnes, A. (2004). Race, schizophrenia, and admission to state psychiatric hospitals. *Administration and Policy in Mental Health, 31,* 241–252.

Baron, R. A., & Richardson, D. R. (1992). *Human aggression* (2nd ed.) New York: Plenum Press.

Barondes, S. H. (1993). *Molecules and mental illness.* New York: Scientific American Library.

Barringer, F. (1993, June 2). School hallways as gauntlets of sexual taunts. *New York Times,* p. B7.

Barsalou, L. W. (2008). Grounded cognition. *Annual Review of Psychology, 59,* 617–645.

Barth, K. S., & Malcolm, R. J. (2010). Disulfiram: An old therapeutic with new applications. *CNS and Neurological Disorders Drug Targets, 9,* 5–12.

Bartlett, F. C. (1932). *Remembering.* Cambridge, UK: Cambridge University Press.

Bartoshuk, L. M. (2000). Comparing sensory experiences across individuals: Recent psychophysical advances illuminate genetic variation in taste perception. *Chemical Senses, 25,* 447–460.

Bartoshuk, L. M., & Beauchamp, G. K. (1994). Chemical senses. *Annual Review of Psychology, 45,* 419–449.

Bass, B. M. (1990). From transactional to transformational leadership: Learning to share the vision. *Organizational Dynamics* (Winter), 19–31.

Bassuk, S. S., & Manson, J. E. (2010). Physical activity and cardiovascular disease prevention in women: A review of the epidemiological evidence. *Nutrition, Metabolism, and Cardiovascular Diseases, 20,* 467–473.

Batabyal, A. A. (2001). On the likelihood of finding the right partner in an arranged marriage. *Journal of Socio-Economics, 30,* 273–281.

Bates, B. L. (1994). Individual differences in response to hypnosis. In J. W. Rhue, S. J. Lynn, & I. Kirsch (Eds.), *Handbook of clinical hypnosis* (pp. 23–54). Washington, DC: American Psychological Association.

Bauby, J. D. (1997). *The diving bell and the butterfly.* New York: Vintage.

Baumann, A. E. (2007). Stigmatization, social distance and exclusion because of mental illness: The individual with mental illness as a "stranger." *International Review of Psychiatry, 19,* 131–135.

Baumeister, R. F., & Leary, M. R. (1995). The need to belong: The desire for interpersonal attachments as a fundamental human motivation. *Psychological Bulletin, 117,* 497–529.

Baumeister, R. F., Catanese, K. R., & Vohs, K. D. (2001). Is there a gender difference in strength of sex drive? Theoretical views, conceptual distinctions, and a review of relevant evidence. *Personality and Social Psychology Review, 5,* 242.

Baumrind, D. (1964). Some thoughts on ethics of research: After reading Milgram's "Behavioral study of obedience." *American Psychologist, 19,* 421–423.

Baumrind, D. (1967). Child care practices anteceding three patterns of preschool behavior. *Genetic Psychology Monographs, 75,* 43–88.

Baumrind, D. (1971). Current patterns of parental authority. *Developmental Psychology Monograph, 4(1, Pt. 2).*

Bava, S., Thayer, R., Jacobus, J., Ward, M., Jernigan, T. L., & Tapert, S. F. (2010). Longitudinal characterization of white matter maturation during adolescence. *Brain Research, 1327,* 38–46.

Beach, S. R. H., Sandeen, E. E., & O'Leary, K. D. (1990). *Depression: A marital model for etiology and treatment.* New York: Guilford Press.

Beard, K. W. (2005). Internet addiction: A review of current assessment techniques and potential assessment questions. *Cyberpsychology and Behavior, 8,* 7–14.

Beard, K. W., & Wolf, E. M. (2001). Modification in the proposed diagnostic criteria for Internet addiction. *Cyberpsychology and Behavior, 4,* 377–383.

Beardsley, T. (1996, July). Waking up. *Scientific American,* pp. 14, 18.

Beatty, W. W. (1992). Gonadal hormones and sex differences in nonreproductive behaviors. In A. A. Gerall, H. Moltz, & I. L. Ward (Eds.), *Handbook of behavioral neurobiology: Vol 11. Sexual differentiation* (pp. 85–128). New York: Plenum Press.

Beauducel, A., Brocke, B., & Leue, A. (2006). Energetical bases of extraversion: Effort, arousal, EEG, and performance. *International Journal of Psychophysiology, 62,* 212–223.

Beauregard, M. (2007). Mind does really matter: Evidence from neuroimaging studies of emotional self-regulation, psychotherapy, and placebo effect. *Progress in Neurobiology, 81,* 218–236.

Bebbington, P. E., Cooper, C., Minot, S., Brugha, T. S., Jenkins, R., Meltzer, H., et al. (2009). Suicide attempts, gender, and sexual abuse: Data from the 2000 British Psychiatric Morbidity Survey. *American Journal of Psychiatry, 166,* 1135–1140.

Beck, A. T. (1967). *Depression: Clinical, experimental, and theoretical aspects.* New York: Harper & Row.

Beck, A. T. (1976). *Cognitive therapy and the emotional disorders.* New York: International Universities Press.

Beck, A. T. (1991). Cognitive therapy: A 30-year retrospective. *American Psychologist, 46,* 368–375.

Beck, A. T. (1997). Cognitive therapy: Reflections. In J. K. Zeig (Ed.), *The evolution of psychotherapy: The third conference* (pp. 55–67). New York: Brunner/Mazel.

Beck, A. T. (2008). The evolution of the cognitive model of depression and its neurobiological correlates. *American Journal of Psychiatry, 165,* 969–977.

Beck, A. T., Rush, A. J., Shaw, B. F., & Emery, G. (1979). *Cognitive therapy of depression.* New York: Guilford Press.

Beck, J. G. (1993). Vaginismus. In W. O'Donohue & J. H. Geer (Eds.), *Handbook of sexual dysfunctions: Assessment and treatment* (pp. 381–397). Boston: Allyn & Bacon.

Beck, J. G., Palyo, S. A., Winer, E. H., Schwagler, B. E., & Ang, E. J. (2007). Virtual reality exposure therapy for PTSD symptoms after a road accident: An uncontrolled case series. *Behavior Therapy, 38,* 39–48.

Becker, P.M., Schwartz, J.R., Feldman, N.T., & Hughes, R. J. (2004). Effect of modafinil on fatigue, mood, and health-related quality of life in patients with narcolepsy. *Psychopharmacology, 171,* 133–139.

Beem, E. E., Hooijkaas, H., Cleiren, M. H., Schut, H. A., Garssen, B., Croon, M. A., et al. (1999). The immunological and psychological effects of bereavement: Does grief counseling really make a difference? A pilot study. *Psychiatry Research, 85,* 81–93.

Beeman, M. J., & Chiarello, C. (1998). Complementary right- and left-hemisphere language comprehension. *Current Directions in Psychological Science, 74,* 2–8.

Behme, C., & Deacon, S. H. (2008). Language learning in infancy: Does the empirical evidence support a domain specific language acquisition device? *Philosophical Psychology, 21,* 641–671.

Békésy, G. von (1960). *Experiments in hearing.* New York: McGraw-Hill.

Bell, A. R., Weinberg, M. S., & Hammersmith, S. K. (1981). *Sexual preference: Its development in men and women.* Bloomington: Indiana University Press.

Bell, C. J., & Nutt, D. J. (1998). Serotonin and panic. *British Journal of Psychiatry, 172,* 465–471.

Bellis, M. D., Clark, D. B., Beers, S. R., Soloff, P. H., Boring, A. M., Hall, J., et al. (2000). Hippocampal volume in adolescent-onset alcohol use disorders. *American Journal of Psychiatry, 157,* 737–744.

Belsky, J., & Rovine, M. (1990). Patterns of marital change across the transition to parenthood: Pregnancy to three years postpartum. *Journal of Marriage and the Family, 52,* 5–19.

Belsky, J., Woodworth, S., & Crnic, K. (1996). Trouble in the second year: Three questions about family interaction. *Child Development, 67,* 556–578.

Bem, S. L. (1981). Gender schema theory: A cognitive account of sex typing. *Psychological Review, 88,* 354–364.

Benabid, A. L., Koudsie, A., Benazzouz, A., Vercueil, L., Fraix, V., Chabardes, S., et al. (2001). Deep brain stimulation of the corpus luysi (subthalamic nucleus) and other targets in Parkinson's disease. Extension to new indications such as dystonia and epilepsy. *Journal of Neurology, 248*(Suppl. 3), III37–III47.

Bender, E. (2004). Virtual reality treatment combats phobias, PTSD. *Psychiatric News, 39,* 45.

Benham, G., Woody, E. Z., Wilson, K. S., & Nash, M. R. (2006). Expect the unexpected: Ability, attitude, and responsiveness to hypnosis. *Journal of Personality and Social Psychology, 91,* 342–350.

Benjamin, L. T., Jr., Henry, K. D., & McMahon, L. R. (2005). Inez Beverly Prosser and the education of African Americans. *Journal of the History of the Behavioral Sciences, 41,* 43–62.

Bennett, M. P., Zeller, J. M., Rosenberg, L., & McCann, J. (2003). The effect of mirthful laughter on stress and natural killer cell activity. *Alternative Therapies in Health and Medicine, 9,* 38–45.

Bennett, W. I. (1990, December). Boom and doom. *Harvard Health Letter, 16,* 1–3.

Benoit, S. C., McQuade, J. A., Clegg, D. J., Xu, M., Rushing, P. A., Woods, S. C., et al. (2003). Altered feeding responses in mice with targeted disruption of the dopamine-3 receptor gene. *Behavioral Neuroscience, 117,* 46–54.

Benson, H. (1996). *Timeless healing: The power and biology of belief.* New York: Scribner.

Berger, A. M., & Hobbs, B. B. (2006). Impact of shift work on the health and safety of nurses and patients. *Clinical Journal of Oncology Nursing, 10,* 465–471.

Berk, L. E., & Spuhl, S. T. (1995). Maternal interaction, private speech, and task performance in preschool children. *Early Childhood Research Quarterly, 10,* 145–169.

Berkowitz, L. (1990). On the formation and regulation of anger and aggression: A cognitive-neoassociationistic analysis. *American Psychologist, 45,* 494–503.

Bernstein, K. S., Park, S. Y., Shin, J., Cho, S., & Park, Y. (in press). Acculturation, discrimination and depressive symptoms among Korean immigrants in New York City. *Community Mental Health Journal.*

Berrington, A., & Diamond, I. (1999). Marital dissolution among the 1958 British birth cohort: The role of cohabitation. *Population Studies, 53,* 19–38.

Berry, A. K. (2006). Helping children with nocturnal enuresis: The wait-and-see approach may not be in anyone's best interest. *American Journal of Nursing, 106,* 56–63.

Berry, J. O., & Rao, J. M. (1997). Balancing employment and fatherhood: A systems perspective. *Journal of Family Issues, 18,* 386–402.

Berscheid, E., Dion, K., Walster, E., & Walster, G. W. (1971). Physical attractiveness and dating choice: A test of the matching hypothesis. *Journal of Experimental Social Psychology, 7,* 173–189.

Bessiere, K., Kiesler, S., Kraut, R., & Boneva, B. S. (2008). Effects of Internet use and social resources on changes in depression. *Information, Communication, and Society, 11,* 47–70.

Bettocchi, C., Verze, P., Palumbo, R., Arcaniolo, D., & Mirone, V. (2008). Ejaculatory disorders: Pathophysiology and management. *Nature Clinical Practice: Urology, 5,* 93–103.

Betz, N. E. (1993). Women's career development. In F. L. Denmark & M. A. Paludi (Eds.), *Psychology of women* (pp. 627–684). Westport, CT: Greenwood Press.

Beutler, L. E., Machado, P. P., & Neufeldt, S. A. (1994). Therapist variables. In A. E. Bergin & S. L. Garfield (Eds.), *Handbook of psychotherapy and behavior change* (4th ed., pp. 229–269). New York: Wiley.

Bezchlibnyk-Butler, K. Z., & Jeffries, J. J. (Eds.). (1998). *Clinical handbook of psychotropic drugs* (8th ed.). Seattle: Hogrete & Huber.

Bhaskara, R. M., Brijesh, C. M., Ahmed, S., & Borges, R. M. (2009). Perception of ultraviolet light by crab spiders and its role in the selection of hunting sites. *Journal of Comparative Physiology. A. Neuroethology, Sensory, Neural, and Behavioral Physiology, 195,* 409–417.

Bianchi, S. M., Kilkie, M. A., Sayer, L. C., & Robinson, J. P. (2000). Is anyone doing the housework? Trends in the gender division of household labor. *Social Forces, 79,* 191–228.

Biederman, J., Faraone, S. V., Hirschfeld-Becker, D. R., Friedman, D., Robin, J. A., & Rosenbaum, J. F. (2001). Patterns of psychopathology and dysfunction in high-risk children of parents with panic disorder and major depression. *American Journal of Psychiatry, 158,* 49–57.

Bierut, L. J., Heath, A. C., Bucholz, K. K., Dinwiddie, S. H., Madden, P. A. F., Statham, D. J., et al. (1999). Major depressive disorder in a community-based twin sample: Are there different genetic contributions for men and women? *Archives of General Psychiatry, 56,* 557–563.

Binder, J., Zagefka, H., Brown, R., Funke, F., Kessler, T., Mummendey, A., et al. (2009). Does contact reduce prejudice or does prejudice reduce contact? A longitudinal test of the contact hypothesis among majority and minority groups in three European countries. *Journal of Personality and Social Psychology, 96,* 843–856.

Binet, A., & Simon, T. (1905). Méthodes nouvelles pour le diagnotics du niveau intéllectuel des anormaux. *L Année Psychologique, 11,* 191–244.

Bird, M. H. (2006). Sexual addiction and marriage and family therapy: Facilitating individual and relationship healing through couple therapy. *Journal of Marital and Family Therapy, 32,* 297–311.

Bisson, J. I., Ehlers, A., Matthews, R., Pilling, S., Richards, D., & Turner, S. (2007). Psychological treatments for chronic post-traumatic stress disorder. Systematic review and meta-analysis. *British Journal of Psychiatry, 190,* 97–104.

Bitterman, M. E. (2006). Classical conditioning since Pavlov. *Review of General Psychology, 10,* 365–376.

Bivens, J. A., & Berk, L. E. (1990). A longitudinal study of elementary school children's private speech. *Merrill-Palmer Quarterly, 36,* 443–463.

Black, D. W., Blum, N., Pfohl, B., & Hale, N. (2004). Suicidal behavior in borderline personality disorder: Prevalence, risk factors, prediction, and prevention. *Journal of Personality and Disorders, 18,* 226–239.

Black, L. S., deRegnier, R. A., Long, J., Georgieff, M. K., & Nelson, C. A. (2004). Electrographic imaging of recognition memory in 34–38 week gestation intrauterine growth restricted newborns. *Experimental Neurology, 190,* S72–S83.

Blackwell, L. V., Snyder, L. A., & Mavriplis, C. (2009). Diverse faculty in STEM fields: Attitudes, performance, and fair treatment. *Journal of Diversity in Higher Education, 2,* 195–205.

Blagys, M. D., & Hilsenroth, M. J. (2000). Distinctive features of short-term psychodynamic-interpersonal psychotherapy: A review of the comparative psychotherapy process literature. *Clinical Psychology: Science and Practice, 7,* 167–188.

Blanchard, R. (2004). Quantitative and theoretical analyses of the relation between brothers and homosexuality in men. *Journal of Theoretical Biology, 230,* 173–187.

Blanchard, R. (2008). Review and theory of handedness, birth order, and homosexuality in men. *Laterality, 13,* 51–70.

Blanchard, R., & Lippa, R. A. (2007). Birth order, sibling sex ratio, handedness, and sexual orientation of male and female participants in a BBC Internet research project. *Archives of Sexual Behavior, 36,* 163–176.

Blanchard, R., Zucker, K. J., Siegelman, M., Dickey, R., & Klassen, P. (1998). The relation of birth order to sexual orientation in men and women. *Journal of Biosocial Science, 30,* 511–519.

Blane, H. T. (1988). Prevention issues with children of alcoholics. *British Journal of Addiction, 83*(7), 793–798.

Blatt, S. J., & Shahar, G. (2004). Psychoanalysis—with whom, for what, and how? Comparisons with psychotherapy. *Journal of the American Psychoanalysis Association, 52,* 393–447.

Blazer, D. G., Kessler, R. C., McGonagle, K. A., & Swartz, M. S. (1994). The prevalence and distribution of major depression in a national community sample: The National Comorbidity Study. *American Journal of Psychiatry, 151,* 979–986.

Blehm, C., Vishnu, S., Khattak, A., Mitra, S., & Yee, R. W. (2005). Computer vision syndrome: A review. *Survey of Ophthalmology, 50,* 253–262.

Bleiker, E. M., van der Ploeg, H. M., Hendriks, J. H., & Ader, H. J. (1996). Personality factors and breast cancer development: A prospective longitudinal study. *Journal of the National Cancer Institute, 88,* 1478–1482.

Bleiker, E. M., Hendriks, J. H., Otten, J. D., Verbeek, A. L., & van der Ploeg, H. M. (2008). Personality factors and breast cancer risk: A thirteen-year follow-up. *Journal of the National Cancer Institute, 100,* 213–218.

Blevins, J. E., & Baskin, D. G. (2010). Hypothalamic-brainstem circuits controlling eating. *Forum of Nutrition, 63,* 133–140.

Blincoe, L., Seay, A., Zaloshnja, E., Miller, T., Romano, E., Luchter, S., et al. (2002). *The economic impact of motor vehicle crashes, 2000.* Washington, DC: National Highway Traffic Safety Administration.

Block, J. A. (1995). A contrarian view of the five-factor approach. *Psychological Bulletin, 117,* 187–215.

Block, J. J. (2008). Issues for DSM-V: Internet addiction. *American Journal of Psychiatry, 165,* 306–307.

Bloom, F., Nelson, C. A., & Lazerson, A. (2001). *Brain, mind and behavior* (3rd ed.). New York: Worth.

Bloom, J. W. (1998). The ethical practice of WebCounseling. *British Journal of Guidance and Counselling, 26,* 53–59.

Blumberg, E. S. (2003). The lives and voices of highly sexual women. *Journal of Sex Research, 40,* 146–157.

Boden, M. (1988). *Computer models of the mind.* Cambridge, UK: Cambridge University Press.

Boeri, M. W., Sterk, C. E., & Elifson, K. W. (2004). Rolling beyond raves: Ecstasy use outside the rave setting. *Journal of Drug Issues, 34,* 831–860.

Bohart, A. C. (1990). Psychotherapy integration from a client-centered perspective. In G. Lietaer (Ed.), *Client-centered and experiential psychotherapy in the nineties* (pp. 481–500). Leuven, Belgium: Leuven University Press.

Boivin, D. B., Czeisler, C. A., Dijk, D. J., Duffy, J. F., Folkard, S., Minors, D. S., et al. (1997). Complex interaction of sleep-wake cycle and circadian phase modulates mood in healthy subjects. *Archives of General Psychiatry, 54,* 145–152.

Bolton, M., van der Stratesn, A., & Cohen, C. (2008). Probiotics: Potential to prevent HIV and sexually transmitted infections in women. *Sexually Transmitted Diseases, 35,* 214–225.

Bonanno, G. A. (2004). Loss, trauma, and human resilience. *American Psychologist, 59,* 20–28.

Bonanno, G. A., Galea, S., Bucciarelli, A., & Vlahov, D. (2006). Psychological resilience after disaster: New York City in the aftermath of the September 11th terrorist attack. *Psychological Science, 17,* 181–186.

Bond, R., & Smith, P. B. (1996). Culture and conformity: A meta-analysis of studies using Asch's (1952, 1956) line judgment task. *Psychological Bulletin, 119,* 111–137.

Bonne, O., Vythilingam, M., Inagaki, M., Wood, S., Neumeister, A., Nugent, A. C., et al. (2008). Reduced posterior hippocampal volume in posttraumatic stress disorder. *Journal of Clinical Psychiatry, 69,* 1087–1091.

Bonte, M. (1962). The reaction of two African societies to the Mueller-Lyer illusion. *Journal of Social Psychology, 58,* 265–268.

Book, A. S., Starzyk, K. B., & Quinsey, V. L. (2001). The relationship between testosterone and aggression: A meta-analysis. *Aggression and Violent Behavior, 6,* 579–599.

Booth, A., & Amato, P. R. (2001). Parental pre-divorce relations and offspring postdivorce well-being. *Journal of Marriage and the Family, 63,* 197–212.

Booth-Kewley, S., & Friedman, H. S. (1987). Psychological predictions of heart disease: A quantitative review. *Psychological Bulletin, 101,* 343–362.

Bootzin, R. R., & Rider, S. P. (1997). Behavioral techniques and biofeedback for insomnia. In M. R. Pressman & W. C. Orr (Eds.), *Understanding sleep: The evaluation and treatment of sleep disorders* (pp. 315–338). Washington, DC: American Psychological Association.

Borkman, T. J. (1997). A selected look at self-help groups in the U.S. *U.S. Health and Social Care in the Community, 5,* 357–364.

Borman, W. C., Penner, L. A., Allen, T. D., & Motowidlo, S. J. (2001). Personality predictors of citizenship performance. *International Journal of Selection and Assessment, 9,* 52–69.

Born, J., Lange, T., Hansen, K., Molle, M., & Fehm, H. L. (1997). Effects of sleep and circadian rhythm on human circulating immune cells. *Journal of Immunology, 158,* 4454–4464.

Bornet, F. R., Jardy-Gennetier, A. E., Jacquet, N., & Stowell, J. (2007). Glycaemic response to foods: Impact on satiety and long-term weight regulation. *Appetite, 49,* 535–553.

Bornovalova, M. A., Gratz, K. L., Delany-Brumsey, A., Paulson, A., & Lejuez, C. W. (2006). Temperamental and environmental risk factors for borderline personality disorder among inner-city substance users in residential treatment. *Journal of Personality Disorders, 20,* 218–231.

Bornstein, M. H. (1985). On the development of color naming in young children: Data and theory. *Brain and Language, 26,* 72–93.

Bornstein, M. H., & Marks, L. E. (1982, January). Color revisionism. *Psychology Today, 16,* 64–73.

Bornstein, M. H., Selmi, A. M., Haynes, O. M., Painter, K. M., & Marx, E. S. (1999). Representational abilities and the hearing status of child/mother dyads. *Child Development, 70,* 833–852.

Boroughs, D. S. (2004). Female sexual abusers of children. *Children and Youth Services Review, 26,* 481–487.

Bosch, J. A., de Geus, E. J., Kelder, A., Veerman, E. C., Hoogstraten, J., & Amerongen, A. V. (2001). Differential effects of active versus passive coping on secretory immunity. *Psychophysiology, 38,* 836–846.

Bosse, R., Spiro, A., III, & Kressin, N. R. (1996). The psychology of retirement. In R. T. Woods (Ed.), *Handbook of the clinical psychology of aging* (pp. 141–157). Chicester, UK: Wiley.

Bossy-Wetzel, E., Schwarzenbacher, R., & Lipton, S. A. (2004). Molecular pathways to neurodegeneration. *Nature Medicine, 10*(suppl), S2–S9.

Botella, C., Villa, H., Garcia Palacios, A., Quero, S., Banos, R. M., & Alcaniz, M. (2004). The use of VR in the treatment of panic disorders and agoraphobia. *Student Health and Technology Information, 99,* 73–90.

Bouchard, T. J. (2004). Genetic influence on human psychological traits: A survey. *Current Directions in Psychological Science, 13,* 148–151.

Bouchard, T. J., Lykken, D. T., McGue, M., Segal, N. L., & Tellegen, A. (1990). Sources of human psychological differences: The Minnesota study of twins reared apart. *Science, 250,* 223–228.

Boulcott, P., & Braithewaite, V. (2005). Ultraviolet light and visual behavior in the three-spined stickleback, gasterosteus aculeatus. *Physiological and Biochemical Zoology, 78,* 736–743.

Bowden, C. L., Calabrese, J. R., Sachs, G., Yatham, L. N., Asghar, S. A., Hompland, M., et al. (2003). A placebo-controlled 18-month trial of lamotrigine and lithium maintenance treatment in recently manic or hypomanic patients with bipolar I disorder. *Archives of General Psychiatry, 60,* 392–400.

Bowden, C. L., Mosolov, S., Hranov, L., Chen, E., Habil, H., Kongsakon, R., et al. (2010). Efficacy of valproate versus lithium in mania or mixed mania: A randomized, open 12-week trial. *International Clinical Psychopharmacology, 25,* 60–67.

Bower, B. (2003, November 8). Forgetting to remember: Emotion robs memory while reviving it. *Science News, 164,* 293.

Bower, J. E., Moskowitz, J. T., & Epel, E. (2009). Is benefit finding good for your health? Pathways linking positive life changes after stress and physical health outcomes. *Current Directions in Psychological Science, 18,* 337–341.

Bowers, K. S., & LeBaron, S. (1986). Hypnosis and hypnotizability: Implications for clinical intervention. *Hospital and Community Psychiatry, 37,* 457–467.

Bowlby, J. (1980). *Attachment and loss: Vol. 3. Loss, sadness, and depression.* New York: Basic Books.

Bozarth, M. A., & Wise, R. A. (1984). Anatomically distinct opiate receptor fields mediate reward and physical dependence. *Science, 224,* 516–518.

Brackett, M. A., Rivers, S. E., Shiffman, S., Lerner, N., & Salovey, P. (2006). Relating emotional abilities to social functioning: A comparison of self-report and performance measures of emotional intelligence. *Journal of Personality and Social Psychology, 91,* 780–795.

Braddock, A. E., & Abramowitz, J. S. (2006). Listening to hypochondriasis and hearing health anxiety. *Expert Review of Neurotherapeutics, 6,* 1307–1312.

Bradley, D. B., & Hopcroft, R. L. (2007). The sex difference in depression across 29 countries. *Social Forces, 85,* 1483–1507.

Bradley, R. H., & Corwyn, R. F. (2008). Infant temperament, parenting, and externalizing behavior in first grade: A test of the differential susceptibility hypothesis. *Journal of Child Psychology and Psychiatry and Allied Disciplines, 49,* 124–131.

Brady, J. (2007, April). When a brain forgets where memory is. *New York Times.* Retrieved May 13, 2008, from nytimes.com

Brady, S. S., & Matthews, K. A. (2006). Effects of media violence on health-related outcomes among young men. *Archives of Pediatric Adolescent Medicine, 160,* 341–347.

Brainerd, C. J., & Reyna, V. F. (2002). Recollection rejection: How children edit their false memories. *Developmental Psychology, 38,* 156–172.

Bramlett, M. D., & Mosher, W. D. (2002). Cohabitation, marriage, divorce, and remarriage in the United States. *Vital Health Statistics, 23*(22). Hyattsville, MD: National Center for Health Statistics.

Brannon, L., & Feist, J. (2004). *Health psychology: An introduction to behavior and health* (5th ed.). Belmont, CA: Wadsworth.

Bratberg, G. H., Nilsen, T. I., Holmen, T. L., & Vatten, L. J. (2005). Sexual maturation in early adolescence and alcohol drinking and cigarette smoking in late adolescence: A prospective study of 2,129 Norwegian girls and boys. *European Journal of Pediatrics, 164,* 621–625.

Braudy, S. O. (2003, April 13). Small kindness in the big city. *New York Times,* p. 3.

Braungart, J. M., Plomin, R., DeFries, J. C., & Fulker, D. W. (1992). Genetic influence on tester-rated infant temperament as assessed by Bayley's Infant Behavior Record. *Developmental Psychology, 28*(1), 40–47.

Bray, G. A., Inoue, S., & Nishizawa, Y. (1981). Hypothalamic obesity: The autonomic hypothesis and the lateral hypothalamus. *Diabetologia, 20 Supp,* 366–377.

Brehm, S. S. (1992). *Intimate relationships* (2nd ed.). New York: McGraw-Hill.

Brehm, S. S., Kassin, S. M., & Fein, S. (2002). *Social psychology* (5th ed.). Boston: Houghton Mifflin.

Breier, A., Schreiber, J. L., Dyer, J., & Pickar, D. (1991). National Institutes of Mental Health longitudinal study of chronic schizophrenia: Prognosis and predictors of outcome. *Archives of General Psychiatry, 48,* 239–246.

Bremner, A. J., Bryant, P. E., & Mareschal, D. (2006). Object-centered spatial reference in 4-month-old infants. *Infant Behavior and Development, 29,* 1–10.

Brende, J. O. (2000). Stress effects of floods. In G. Fink (Ed.), *Encyclopedia of stress* (Vol. 2, pp. 153–157). San Diego: Academic Press.

Breslau, J., Aguilar-Gaxiola, S., Kendler, K. S., Su, M., Williams, D., & Kessler, R. C. (2006). Specifying race-ethnic differences in risk for psychiatric disorder in a USA national sample. *Psychological Medicine, 36,* 57–68.

Breslau, J., Kendler, K. S., Su, M., Gaxiola-Aguilar, S., & Kessler, R. C. (2005). Lifetime risk and persistence of psychiatric disorders across ethnic groups in the United States. *Psychological Medicine, 35,* 317–327.

Bresnahan, M., Begg, M. D., Brown, A., Schaefer, C., Sohler, N., Insel, B. et al. (2007). Race and risk of schizophrenia in a U.S. birth cohort: Another example of health disparity? *International Journal of Epidemiology, 36,* 751–758.

Brewer, M. B. (1979). In-group bias in the minimal intergroup situation: A cognitive-motivational analysis. *Psychological Bulletin, 86,* 307–324.

Brewer, M., & Campbell, D. T. (1976). *Ethnocentrism and intergroup attitudes: East African evidence.* New York: Halstead.

Brewster, K. L., & Tillman, K. H. (2008). Who's doing it? Patterns and predictors of youths' oral sexual experiences. *Journal of Adolescent Health, 42,* 73–80.

Britt, G. C., & McCance-Katz, E. F. (2005). A brief overview of the clinical pharmacology of "club drugs." *Substance Use and Misuse, 40,* 1189–1201.

Broderick, G. A. (2006). Premature ejaculation: On defining and quantifying a common male sexual dysfunction. *Journal of Sexual Medicine, 3,* 295–302.

Brody, A. L., Saxena, S., Schwartz, J. M., Stoessel, P. W., Maidment, K., Phelps, M. E., et al. (1998). FDG-PET predictors of response to behavioral therapy and pharmacotherapy in obsessive compulsive disorder. *Psychiatry Research: Neuroimaging, 84,* 1–6.

Brody, M. J., Walsh, B. T., & Devlin, M. (1994). Binge eating disorder: Reliability and validity of a new diagnostic category. *Journal of Consulting and Clinical Psychology, 62,* 381–386.

Bromberger, J. T., & Matthews, K. A. (1996). A longitudinal study of the effects of pessimism, trait anxiety, and life stress on depressive symptoms in middle-aged women. *Psychology and Aging, 11,* 207–213.

Bronstad, P. M., Langlois, J. H., & Russell, R. (2008). Computational models of facial attractiveness judgments. *Perception, 37,* 126–142.

Brooks, R., Lee, S., Newman, P., & Leibowitz, A. (2008). Sexual risk behavior has decreased among men who have sex with men in Los Angeles but remains greater than that among heterosexual men and women. *AIDS Education and Prevention, 20,* 312–324.

Brooks-Gunn, J., & Matthews, W. S. (1979). *He and she: How children develop their sex-role identity.* Englewood Cliffs, NJ: Spectrum.

Brotto, L. A., & Klein, C. (2007). Sexual and gender identity disorders. In M. Hersen, S. M. Turner, & D. C. Beidel (Eds.), *Adult psychopathology and diagnosis* (5th ed., pp. 504–570). New York: Wiley.

Brown, A. S., Begg, M. D., Gravenstein, S., Schaefer, C. A., Wyatt, R. J., Brenahan, M. et al. (2004). Serological evidence of prenatal influenza in the etiology of schizophrenia. *Archives of General Psychiatry, 61,* 774–780.

Brown, B. B. (2004). Adolescents' relationship with peers. In R. Lerner & L. Steinberg (Eds.), *Handbook of adolescent psychology* (2nd ed., pp. 363–394). Hoboken, NJ: Wiley.

Brown, J. A. (1958). Some tests of the decay theory of immediate memory. *Quarterly Journal of Experimental Psychology, 10,* 12–21.

Brown, J. D., & Rogers, R. J. (1991). Self-serving attributions: The role of physiological arousal. *Personality and Social Psychology Bulletin, 17,* 501–506.

Brown, R., & Kulik, J. (1977). Flashbulb memories. *Cognition, 5,* 73–99.

Brown, S. L., Lee, G. R., & Bulanda, J. R. (2006). Cohabitation among older adults: A national portrait. *Journals of Gerontology, Series B: Psychological Sciences and Social Sciences, 61,* S71–S79.

Brown, S. L., Nesse, R. M., Vinokur, A. D., & Smith, D. M. (2003). Providing social support may be more beneficial than receiving it: Results from a prospective study of mortality. *Psychological Science, 14,* 320–327.

Brown, T. A., DiNardo, P. A., Lehman, C. L., & Campbell, L. A. (2001). Reliability of DSM-IV anxiety and mood disorders: Implications for the classification of emotional disorders. *Journal of Abnormal Psychology, 110,* 49–58.

Browne, A. (1993). Violence against women by male partners: Prevalence, outcomes, and policy implications. *American Psychologist, 48,* 1077–1087.

Brownell, K. (1988, January). Yo-yo dieting. *Psychology Today, 22,* 22–23.

Browning, J. R., Kessler, D., Hatfield, E., & Choo, P. (1999). Power, gender, and sexual behavior. *Journal of Sex Research, 36,* 342–348.

Brugman, T., & Ferguson, S. (2002). Physical exercise and improvements in mental health. *Journal of Psychosocial Nursing and Mental Health Services, 40,* 24–31.

Bryant, R. A., & Guthrie, R. M. (2005). Maladaptive appraisals as a risk factor for posttraumatic stress: A study of trainee firefighters. *Psychological Science, 16,* 749–752.

Bryman, A. S. (1996). The importance of context: Qualitative research and the study of leadership. *Leadership Quarterly, 7,* 353–370.

Brzezinski, A. (1997). Melatonin in humans. *New England Journal of Medicine, 336,* 186–195.

Buchanan, R. W., Breier, A., Kirkpatrick, B., Ball, P., & Carpenter, W. T. (1998). Positive and negative symptom response to clozapine in schizophrenic patients with and without the deficit syndrome. *American Journal of Psychiatry, 155,* 751–760.

Buckley, K. W. (1989). *Mechanical man: John Broadus Watson.* New York: Guilford Press.

Buckner, J. P., & Fivush, R. (2002). Gendered themes in family reminiscing. *Memory, 8,* 401–412.

Bucur, B., & Madden, D. J. (2010). Effects of adult age and blood pressure on executive function and speed of processing. *Experimental Aging Research, 36,* 153–168.

Buehler, R., Griffin, D., & Ross, M. (1994). Exploring the "planning fallacy": Why people underestimate their task completion times. *Journal of Personality and Social Psychology, 67,* 366–381.

Buehner, M., Mangels, M., Krumm, S., & Ziegler, M. (2005). Are working memory and attention related constructs? *Journal of Individual Differences, 26,* 121–131.

Bueno-Nava, A., Montes, S., DelaGarza-Montano, P., Alfaro-Rodriguez, A., Ortiz, A., & Gonzalez-Pina, R. (2008). Reversal of noradrenergic depletion and lipid peroxidation in the pons after brain injury correlates with motor function recovery in rats. *Neuroscience Letters, 443,* 32–36.

Buhler, P. M. (2003). Managing in the new millennium. *Supervision, 64,* 20–22.

Bullock, W. A., & Gilliland, K. (1993). Eysenck's arousal theory of introversion-extraversion: A converging measures investigation. *Journal of Personality and Social Psychology, 64,* 113–123.

Bumpass, L. L., & Lu, H. H. (2000). Trends in cohabitation and implications for children's family contexts in the United States. *Population Studies, 54,* 29–41.

Burdakov, D., Luckman, S. M., & Verkhratsky, A. (2005). Glucose-sensing neurons of the hypothalamus. *Philosophical Transactions of the Royal Society of London. Series B, Biological Sciences, 360,* 2227–2235.

Burger, J. M. (2004). *Personality* (6th ed.). Belmont, CA: Wadsworth.

Burgess, G. H. (2007). Assessment of rape-supportive attitudes and beliefs in college men: Development, reliability, and validity of the rape attitudes and beliefs scale. *Journal of Interpersonal Violence, 22,* 973–993.

Burnham, D. (1993). Visual recognition of mother by young infants: Facilitation by speech. *Perception, 22,* 1133–1153.

Burt, C. D. B., Kemp, S., & Conway, M. (2008). Ordering the components of autobiographical events. *Acta Psychologica, 127,* 36–45.

Buse, D. C., & Andrasik, F. (2009). Behavioral medicine for migraines. *Neurologic Clinics, 27,* 445–465.

Bush, S. I., & Geer, J. H. (2001). Implicit and explicit memory of neutral, negative emotional, and sexual information. *Archives of Sexual Behavior, 30,* 615–631.

Bushman, B. J. (1988). The effects of apparel on compliance: A field experiment with a female authority figure. *Personality and Social Psychology Bulletin, 14,* 459–467.

Buss, D. M. (1995). Psychological sex differences. *American Psychologist, 50,* 164–168.

Buss, D. M., Larsen, R. J., Westen, D., & Semmelroth, J. (1992). Sex differences in jealousy: Evolution, physiology, and psychology. *Psychological Science, 3,* 251–255.

Buss, D. N. (2009). The great struggles of life: Darwin and the emergence of evolutionary psychology. *American Psychologist, 64,* 140–148.

Bussey, K., & Bandura, A. (1999). Social cognitive theory of gender development and differentiation. *Psychological Review, 106,* 676–713.

Butler, L. D., Duran, R. E. F., Jasiukaitis, P., Koopman, C., & Spiegel, D. (1996). Hypnotizability and traumatic experience: A diathesis stress model of dissociative symptomatology. *American Journal of Psychiatry, 153,* 42–63.

Butow P. N., Hiller, J. E., Price, M. A., Thackway, S. V., Kricker, A., & Tennant, C. C. (2000). Epidemiological evidence for a relationship between life events, coping style, and personality factors in the development of breast cancer. *Journal of Psychosomatic Research, 49,* 169–181.

Buttazzo, G. (2008) Artificial consciousness: Hazardous questions (and answers). *Artificial Intelligence in Medicine, 44,* 139–146.

Butts, S. F., & Seifer, D. B. (2010). Racial and ethnic differences in reproductive potential across the life cycle. *Fertility and Sterility, 93,* 681–690.

Butzlaff, R. L., & Hooley, J. M. (1998). Expressed emotion and psychiatric relapse. *Archives of General Psychiatry, 55,* 547–552.

Buunk, B. P., Angleitner, A., Oubaid, V., & Buss, D. M. (1996). Sex differences in jealousy in evolutionary and cultural perspective: Tests from the Netherlands, Germany, and the United States. *Psychological Science, 7,* 359–363.

Buzi, R., Tortolero, S., Roberts, R., Ross, M., Markham, C., & Fleschler, M. (2003). Gender differences in the consequences of a coercive sexual experience among adolescents attending alternative schools. *Journal of School Health, 73,* 191–196.

Bynum, M. S., Burton, E. T., & Best, C. (2007). Racism experiences and psychological functioning in African American college freshman: Is racial socialization a buffer? *Cultural Diversity and Ethnic Minority Psychology, 13,* 64–71.

Byrd-Craven, J., Geary, D. C., Rose, A. J., & Ponzi, D. (2008). Co-ruminating increases stress hormone levels in women. *Hormones and Behavior, 53,* 489–492.

Byrne, D. (1969). Attitudes and attraction. In L. Berkowitz (Ed.), *Advances in experimental social psychology* (Vol. 4, pp. 35–89). New York: Academic Press.

Byrne, D., Gouaux, C., Griffitt, W., Lamberth, J., Murakawa, N., Prasad, M. B., et al. (1971). The ubiquitous relationship: Attitude similarity and attraction: A cross-cultural study. *Human Relations, 24,* 201–207.

Byrne, M., Agerbo, E., Ewald, H., Eaton, W. W., & Mortensen, P. B. (2003). Parental age and risk of schizophrenia: A case-control study. *Archives of General Psychiatry, 60,* 673–678.

Byrnes, J., & Takahira, S. (1993). Explaining gender differences on SAT-math items. *Developmental Psychology, 29,* 805–810.

Cabeza, R., & Nyberg, L. (2000). Imaging cognition II: An empirical review of 275 PET and fMRI studies. *Journal of Cognitive Neuroscience, 12,* 1–47.

Cacioppo, J. T., & Petty, R. E. (1980). Sex differences in influenceability: Toward specifying the underlying processes. *Personality and Social Psychology Bulletin, 6,* 651–656.

Cain, A. S., Epler, A. J., Steinley, D., & Sher, K. J. (2010). Stability and change in patterns of concerns related to eating, weight, and shape in young adult women: A latent transition analysis. *Journal of Abnormal Psychology, 119,* 255–267.

Cain, J. (2008). Online social networking issues within academic and pharmacy education. *American Journal of Pharmacy Education, 72,* 1–7.

Cain, W. S. (1988). Olfaction. In R. C. Atkinson, R. J. Herrnstein, G. Lindzey, & R. D. Luce (Eds.), *Steven's handbook of experimental psychology* (2nd ed., Vol. 1, pp. 409–459). New York: Wiley.

Calabrese, J. R., Shelton, M.D., Rapport, D.J., Youngstrom, E. A., Jackson, K., Bilali, S., et al. (2005). A 20-month, double-blind, maintenance trial of lithium versus divalproex in rapid-cycling bipolar disorder. *American Journal of Psychiatry, 162,* 2152–2161.

Caldera, Y. M., & Lindsey, E. W. (2006). Coparenting, mother–infant interaction, and infant–parent attachment relationships in two-parent families. *Journal of Family Psychology, 20,* 275–283.

Calderoni, M. E., Alderman, E. M., Silver, E., J., & Bauman, L. J. (2006). The mental health impact of 9/11 on inner-city high school students 20 miles north of Ground Zero. *Journal of Adolescent Health, 39,* 57–65.

Calvert, H. (2003). Sexually transmitted diseases other than human immunodeficiency virus infection in older adults. *Clinical Infectious Diseases, 36,* 609–614.

Campbell, J. C., Webster, D., Koziol-McLain, J., Block, C. R., Campbell, D., Curry, M. A., et al. (2003). *Assessing risk factors for intimate partner homicide.* Washington, DC: National Institute of Justice, U.S. Department of Justice.

Camper, J. (1990, February 7). Drop pompom squad, U. of I. rape study says. *Chicago Tribune,* p.1.

Cannon, D. S., & Baker, T. B. (1981). Emetic and electric shock alcohol aversion therapy: Assessment of conditioning. *Journal of Consulting and Clinical Psychology, 49,* 20–33.

Cannon, T. D. (1998). Genetic and perinatal influences in the etiology of schizophrenia: A neurodevelopmental model. In M. F. Lenzenweger (Ed.), *Origins and development of schizophrenia: Advances in experimental psychopathology* (pp. 67–92). Washington DC: American Psychological Association.

Cannon, W. B. (1927). The James-Lange theory of emotions: A critical examination and an alternative theory. *American Journal of Psychology, 39,* 106–124.

Canova, A., & Geary, N. (1991). Intraperitoneal injections of nanogram CCK-8 doses inhibits feeding in rats. *Appetite,* 17, 221–227.

Canuso, C. M., & Pandina, G. (2007). Gender and schizophrenia. *Psychopharmacology Bulletin, 40,* 178–190.

Caplan, G. A., & Brigham, B. A. (1990). Marijuana smoking and carcinoma of the tongue: Is there an association? *Cancer, 66,* 1005–1006.

Cardno, A. G., & Gottesman, I. I. (2000). Twin studies of schizophrenia: From bow-and-arrow concordances to star wars Mx and functional genomics. *American Journal of Medical Genetics, 97,* 12–17.

Cardozo, B. L., Bilukha, O. O., Crawford, C. A., Shaikh, I., Wolfe, M. I., Gerber, M., et al. (2004). Mental health, social functioning, and disability in post-war Afghanistan. *Journal of the American Medical Association, 292,* 575–584.

Carducci, B. J. (2009). *The psychology of personality: Viewpoints, research, and applications.* Malden, MA: Wiley-Blackwell.

Carey, B. (2007, October 23). An active, purposeful machine that comes out at night to play. *New York Times.*

Carey, B. (2008, December 5). H.M., an unforgettable amnesiac, dies at age 82. *New York Times.* Retrieved December 14, 2009, from http://www.nytimes.com

Carey, G., & DiLalla, D. L. (1994). Personality and psychpathology: Genetic perspectives. *Journal of Abnormal Psychology, 103,* 32–43.

Carey, G., & Goldman, D. (1997). The genetics of antisocial behavior. In D. M. Stoff, J. Breiling, & J. D. Maser (Eds.), *Handbook of antisocial personality disorder* (pp. 243–254). New York: Wiley.

Carlson, P. J., Singh, J. B., Zarate, C. A., Jr., Drevets, W. C., & Manji, H. K. (2006). Neural circuitry and neuroplasticity in mood disorders: Insights for novel therapeutic targets. *NeuroRx, 3,* 22–41.

Carlston, D. E., & Shovar, N. (1983). Effects of performance attributions on others' perceptions of the attributor. *Journal of Personality and Social Psychology, 44,* 515–525.

Carney, C. E., Edinger, J. D., Meyer, B., Lindman, L., & Istre, T. (2006). Daily activities and sleep quality in college students. *Chronobiology International, 23,* 623–637.

Carrington, P. (1993). Modern forms of meditation. In P. M. Lehrer & R. L. Woolfolk (Eds.), *Principles and practice of stress management* (2nd ed., pp. 139–168). New York: Guilford Press.

Carroll, K. M., Ball, S. A., Martino, S., Nich, C., Babuscio, T. A., Nuro, K. F., et al. (2008). Computer-assisted delivery of cognitive behavioral therapy for addiction: A randomized trial of CBT4CBT. *American Journal of Psychiatry, 165,* 793–795.

Carroll, M. E., Morgan, A. D., Lynch, W. J., Campbell, U. C., & Dess, N. K. (2002). Intravenous cocaine and heroin self-administration in rats selectively bred for differential saccharin intake: Phenotype and sex differences. *Psychopharmacology, 161,* 304–313.

Carskadon, M. A., Acebo, C., & Jenni, O. G. (2004). Regulation of adolescent sleep: Implications for behavior. *Annals of the New York Academy of Sciences, 1021,* 276–291.

Carter, R. C., Jacobson, S. W., Molteno, C. D., Chiodo, L. M., Viljoen, D., & Jacobson, J. L. (2005). Effects of prenatal alcohol exposure on infant visual acuity. *Journal of Pediatrics, 14,* 473–479.

Carter, R. S., & Wojtkiewicz, R. A. (2000). Parental involvement with adolescents' education: Do daughters or sons get more help? *Adolescence, 35,* 29–44.

Cartwright, R. D. (1993). Who needs their dreams? The usefulness of dreams in psychotherapy. *Journal of the American Academy of Psychoanalysis, 21,* 539–547.

Carver, C. S., Harris, S. D., Lehman, J. M., Durel, L. A., Antoni, M. H., Spencer, S. M., et al. (2000). How important is the perception of personal control? Studies of early stage breast cancer patients. *Personality and Social Psychology Bulletin, 26,* 139–149.

Carver, C. S., Johnson, S. L., & Joormann, J. (2009). Two-mode models of self-regulation as a tool for conceptualizing effects of the serotonin system in normal behavior and diverse disorders. *Current Directions in Psychological Science, 18,* 195–199.

Carver, L. J., & Bauer, P. J. (2001). The dawning of the past: The emergence of long-term explicit memory in infancy. *Journal of Experimental Psychology: General, 130,* 726–745.

Cascio, W. F. (1995). Whither industrial and organizational psychology in a changing world of work? *American Psychologist, 50,* 928–939.

Casey, B. J., Giedd, J. N., & Thomas, K. M. (2000). Structural and functional brain development and its relation to cognitive development. *Biological Psychology, 54,* 241–257.

Caspi, A., Harrington, H., Milne, B., Amell, J. W., Theodore, R. F., & Moffitt, T. E. (2003). Children's behavioral styles at age 3 are linked to their adult personality traits at age 26. *Journal of Personality, 71,* 495–513.

Caspi, A., McClay, J., Moffitt, T. E., Mill, J., Martin, J., Craig, I. W., et al. (2002). Role of genotype in the cycle of violence in maltreated children. *Science, 297,* 851–854.

Caspi, A., Sugden, K., Moffitt, T. E., Taylor, A., Craig, I. W., Harrington, H., et al. (2003). Influence of life stress on depression: Moderation by a polymorphism in the 5-HTT gene. *Science, 301,* 386–389.

Castelnuovo, G., Gaggioli, A., Mantovani, F., & Riva, G. (2003). From psychotherapy to e-therapy: The integration of traditional techniques and new communication tools in clinical settings. *Cyberpsychology and Behavior, 6,* 375–382.

Cates, W., Jr. (1998). Reproductive tract infections. In R. A. Hatcher et al. (Eds.), *Contraceptive technology* (17th rev. ed., pp. 179–210). New York: Ardent Media.

Catipovic-Veselica, K., Glavas, B., Kristek, J., & Sram, M. (2001). Components of Type A behavior and two-year prognosis of patients with acute coronary syndrome. *Psychological Reports, 89,* 467–475.

Cattell, R. (2006). *An introduction to mind, consciousness and language.* London: Continuum.

Cattell, R. B. (1943). The description of personality: Basic traits resolved into clusters. *Journal of Abnormal and Social Psychology, 38,* 476–506.

Cattell, R. B. (1963). Theory of fluid and crystallized intelligence: A critical experiment. *Journal of Educational Psychology, 54,* 1–22.

Cattell, R. B. (1965). *The scientific analysis of personality.* Baltimore: Penguin.

Cavanagh, K., Shapiro, D. A., Van Den Berg, S., Swain, S., Barkham, M., & Proudfoot, J. (2009). The acceptability of computer-aided cognitive behavioural therapy: A pragmatic study. *Cognitive Behaviour Therapy, 38,* 235–246.

Ceci, S. J. (1995). False beliefs: Some developmental and clinical considerations. In D. L. Schacter (Ed.), *Memory distortions* (pp. 91–125). Cambridge, MA: Harvard University Press.

Centers for Disease Control and Prevention (CDC). (2002). Involvement by young drivers in fatal alcohol-related motor-vehicle crashes—United States, 1982–2001. *Morbidity and Mortality Weekly Report, 51,* 1089–1091.

Centers for Disease Control and Prevention (CDC). (2004a). Alcohol-attributable deaths and years of potential life lost—United States, 2001. *Morbidity and Mortality Weekly Report, 53,* 866–870.

Centers for Disease Control and Prevention (CDC). (2004b). Mental health status of World Trade Center rescue and recovery workers and volunteers—New York City, July 2002–August 2004. *Morbidity and Mortality Weekly Report, 53,* 812–815.

Centers for Disease Control and Prevention (CDC). (2008a). HIV prevalence estimates—2006. *Morbidity and Mortality Weekly Report, 57,* 1073–1076.

Centers for Disease Control and Prevention (CDC). (2008b). *Sexually transmitted disease surveillance, 2008.* Atlanta, GA: Author.

Centers for Disease Control and Prevention (CDC). (2008c). Smoking-attributable mortality, years of potential life lost, and productivity losses—United States, 2000–2004. *Morbidity and Mortality Weekly Report, 57,* 1226–1228.

Centers for Disease Control and Prevention (CDC). (2008d). Youth Risk Behavior Surveillance—United States, 2007. *Morbidity and Mortality Weekly Report, 57,* No. SS-4.

Centers for Disease Control and Prevention (CDC). (2009a). Cigarette smoking among adults and trends in smoking cessation—United States, 2008. *Morbidity and Mortality Weekly Report, 58,* 1227–1232.

Centers for Disease Control and Prevention (2009b). *Health, United States, 2009.* Retrieved May 2, 2010, from http://www.cdc.gov/nchs/data/hus/hus09.pdf#063

Centers for Disease Control and Prevention (CDC). (2009c). Web-based Injury Statistics Query and Reporting System (WISQARS). *Fatal Injury Reports.* Atlanta, GA: National Center for Injury Prevention and Control.

Centers for Disease Control and Prevention (2010a). *Defining overweight and obesity.* Retrieved May 2, 2010, from http://www.cdc.gov/obesity/defining.html

Centers for Disease Control and Prevention (CDC). (2010b). Seroprevalence of herpes simplex virus type 2 among persons aged 14–49 years—United States, 2005–2008. *Morbidity and Mortality Weekly Report, 59,* 456–459.

Cepeda, N. J., Coburn, N., Rohrer, D., Wixted, J. T., Mozer, M. C., & Pashler, H. (2009). Optimizing distributed practice theoretical analysis and practical implications. *Experimental Psychology, 56,* 236–246.

Cermak, L. S., Lewis, R., Butters, N., & Goodglass, H. (1973). Role of verbal mediation in performance of motor tasks by Korsakoff patients. *Perceptual and Motor Skills, 37,* 259–262.

Cernoch, J., & Porter, R. H. (1985). Recognition of maternal axillary odors by infants. *Child Development, 56*(6), 1593–1598.

Cervera, T. C., Soler, M. J., Dasi, C., & Ruiz, J. C. (2009). Speech recognition and working memory capacity in young-elderly listeners: Effects of hearing sensitivity. *Canadian Journal of Experimental Psychology, 63,* 216–226.

Chabris, C. F., & Kosslyn, S. M. (1998). How do the cerebral hemispheres contribute to encoding spatial relations? *Current Directions in Psychological Science, 74,* 8–14.

Chak, K., & Leung, L. (2004). Shyness and locus of control as predictors of Internet addiction and Internet use. *Cyberpsychology and Behavior, 7,* 559–570.

Chakos, M. H., Alvir, J. M., Woerner, M., & Koreen, A. (1996). Incidence and correlates of tardive dyskinesia in first episode of schizophrenia. *Archives of General Psychiatry, 53,* 313–319.

Chamberlain, K., & Zika, S. (1990). The minor events approach to stress: Support for the use of daily hassles. *British Journal of Psychology, 81,* 469–481.

Chambers, D., & Reisberg, D. (1985). Can mental images be ambiguous? *Journal of Experimental Psychology: Human Perception and Performance, 11,* 317–328.

Chambers, D., & Reisberg, D. (1992). What an image depicts depends on what an image means. *Cognitive Psychology, 24,* 145–174.

Chambless, D. L., & Hollon, S. D. (1998). Defining empirically supported therapies. *Journal of Consulting and Clinical Psychology, 66,* 7–18.

Chambless, D. L., & Ollendick, T. H. (2001). Empirically supported psychological interventions: Controversies and evidence. *Annual Review of Psychology, 52,* 685–716.

Chamorro-Premuzic, T., & Furnham, A. (2004). A possible model for understanding the personality–intelligence interface. *British Journal of Psychology, 95,* 249–264.

Champagne, F. A., & Mashoodh, R. (2009). Genes in context: Gene-environment interplay and the origins of individual differences in behavior. *Current Directions in Psychological Science, 18,* 127–131.

Chandrashekar, J., Hoon, M. A., Ryba, N. J. P., & Zuker, C. S. (2006). The receptors and cells for mammalian taste. *Nature, 444,* 288–294.

Chandrashekara, S., Jayashree, K., Veeranna, H. B., Vadiraj, H. S., Ramesh, M. N., Shobha, A., et al. (2007). Effects of anxiety on TNF-a levels during psychological stress. *Journal of Psychosomatic Research, 63,* 65–69.

Charney, D. S., Nagy, L. M., Bremner, J. D., Goddard, A. W., Yehuda, R., & Southwick, S. M. (2000). Neurobiologic mechanisms of human anxiety. In B. S. Fogel (Ed.), *Synopsis of neuropsychiatry* (pp. 273–288). Philadelphia: Lippincott Williams & Wilkins.

Chaves, J. F. (1989). Hypnotic control of clinical pain. In N. P. Spanos & J. F. Chaves (Eds.), *Hypnosis: The cognitive-behavioral perspective* (pp. 242–272). Buffalo, NY: Prometheus Books.

Chaves, J. F. (1994). Recent advances in the application of hypnosis to pain management. *American Journal of Clinical Hypnosis, 37,* 117–129.

Chaytor, N., & Schmitter-Edgecombe, M. (2004). Working memory and aging: A cross-sectional and longitudinal analysis using a self-ordered pointing task. *Journal of the International Neuropsychological Society, 10,* 489–503.

Cheah, C. S., Leung, C. Y., Tahseen, M., & Schuz, D. (2009). Authoritative parenting among immigrant Chinese mothers of preschoolers. *Journal of Family Psychology, 23,* 311–320.

Cheasty, M., Clare, A. W., & Collins, C. (2002). Child sexual abuse: A predictor of persistent depression in adult rape and sexual assault victims. *Journal of Mental Health, 11,* 79–84.

Chen, E., Cohen, S., & Miller, G. E. (2010). How low socioeconomic status affects 2-year hormonal trajectories in children. *Psychological Science, 21,* 31–37.

Chen, L. S., Tu, H. H., & Wang, E. S. (2008). Personality traits and life satisfaction among online game players. *Cyberpsychology and Behavior, 11,* 145–149.

Chess, S., & Thomas, A. (1984). *Origins and evolution of behavior disorders: From infancy to early adult life.* New York: Brunner/Mazel.

Chessick, C. A., Allen, M. H., Thase, M., Batista Miralha da Cunha, A. B., Kapczinski, F. F., de Lima, M. S., et al. (2006). Azapirones for generalized anxiety disorder. *Cochrane Database of Systematic Reviews, 19,* CD006115.

Cheung, F. M., & Halpern, D. F. (2010). Women at the top: Powerful leaders define success as work + family in a culture of gender. *American Psychologist, 65*, 182–193.

Chiang, A. A. (2006). Obstructive sleep apnea and chronic intermittent hypoxia: A review. *Chinese Journal of Physiology, 49*, 234–243.

Chida, Y., & Steptoe, A. (2008). Positive psychological well-being and mortality: A quantitative review of prospective observational studies. *Psychosomatic Medicine, 70*, 741–756.

Chipuer, H. M., Rovine, M. J., & Polmin, R. (1990). LISREL modeling: Genetic and environmental influences on IQ revisited. *Intelligence, 14*, 11–29.

Chisuwa, N., & O'Dea, J. A. (2010). Body image and eating disorders amongst Japanese adolescents: A review of the literature. *Appetite, 54*, 5–15.

Choi, I., & Nesbitt, R. E. (1998). Situational salience and cultural differences in the correspondence bias and actor-observer bias. *Personality and Social Psychology, Bulletin, 24*, 949–960.

Choi, J. S., Kim, S. H., Yoo, S. Y., Kang, D. H., Kim, C. W., Lee, J. M., et al. (2007). Shape deformity of the corpus striatum in obsessive-compulsive disorder. *Psychiatry Research, 155*, 257–264.

Choi, Y. H. (2007). *Advancement of IT and seriousness of youth Internet addiction, in 2007.* International Symposium on the Counseling and Treatment of Youth Internet Addiction. Seoul, Korea: National Youth Commission, p. 20.

Chollar, S. (1989, April). Dreamchasers. *Psychology Today,* pp. 60–61.

Chomsky, N. (1957). *Syntactic structures.* The Hague: Mouton.

Chomsky, N. (1965). *Aspects of the theory of syntax.* Cambridge, MA: MIT Press.

Chory-Assad, R. M., & Tamborini, R. (2001). Television doctors: An analysis of physicians on fictional and non-fictional television programs. *Journal of Broadcasting and Electronic Media, 45*, 499–521.

Chory-Assad, R. M., & Tamborini, R. (2003). Television exposure and the public's perceptions of physicians. *Journal of Broadcasting and Electronic Media, 47*, 197–215.

Chou, C., & Hsiao, M. C. (2000). Internet addiction, usage, gratification, and pleasure experience: The Taiwan college students' case. *Computers and Education, 35*, 65–80.

Chou, K. L. (2009). Specific phobia in older adults: Evidence from the National Epidemiologic Survey on alcohol and related conditions. *American Journal of Geriatric Psychiatry, 17*, 376–386.

Chou, R., Qaseem, A., Snow, V., Casey, D., Cross, J. T., Jr., Shekelle, P., et al. (2007). Diagnosis and treatment of low back pain: A joint clinical practice guideline from the American College of Physicians and the American Pain Society. *Annals of Internal Medicine, 147*, 478–491, W118–W120.

Chou, S. P., Dawson, D. A., Stinson, F. S., Huang, B., Pickering, R. P., Zhou, Y., et al. (2006). The prevalence of drinking and driving in the United States, 2001–2002: Results from the national epidemiological survey on alcohol and related conditions. *Drug and Alcohol Dependence, 83*, 137–146.

Choy, Y., Fyer, A. J., & Lipsitz, J. D. (2007). Treatment of specific phobia in adults. *Clinical Psychology Review, 27*, 266–286.

Christensen, A., & Jacobson, N. S. (1994). Who (or what) can do psychotherapy: The status and challenge of non-professional therapies. *Psychological Science, 5*, 8–14.

Christie, W., & Moore, C. (2005). The impact of humor on patients with cancer. *Clinical Journal of Oncology Nursing, 9*, 211–218.

Christofides, E., Muise, A., & Desmarais, S. (2009). Information disclosure and control on Facebook: Are they two sides of the same coin or two different processes? *Cyberpsychology and Behavior, 12*, 341–345.

Church, R. M., & Black, A. H. (1958). Latency of the conditioned heart rate as a function of the CS-US interval. *Journal of Comparative and Physiological Psychology, 51*, 478–482.

Cialdini, R. B. (2001). *Influence: Science and practice* (4th ed.). Needham Heights, MA: Allyn & Bacon.

Cialdini, R. B., Borden, R. J., Thorne, A., Walker, M. R., Freeman, S., & Sloan, L. R. (1976). Basking in the reflected glory: Three (football) field studies. *Journal of Personality and Social Psychology, 34*, 366–375.

Cialdini, R. B., Vincent, J. E., Catalan, J., Wheeler, D., & Darby, B. L. (1975). Reciprocal concessions procedure for inducing compliance: The door-in-the-face technique. *Journal of Personality and Social Psychology, 31*, 206–215.

Cin, S. D., Gibson, B., Zanna, M. P., Shumate, R., & Fong, G. T. (2007). Smoking in movies, implicit associations of smoking with the self, and intentions to smoke. *Psychological Science, 18*, 559–563.

Cinnirella, M., & Green, B. (2007). Does "cyber-conformity" vary cross-culturally? Exploring the effect of culture and communication medium on social conformity. *Computers in Human Behavior, 23*, 2011–2025.

Clark, D. C., Gibbons, R. D., Fawcett, J., & Scheftner, W. A. (1989). What is the mechanism by which suicide attempts predispose to later suicide attempts? A mathematical model. *Journal of Abnormal Psychology, 98*, 42–49.

Clark, K. B. (1950). *Effect of Prejudice and Discrimination on Personality Development.* Paper written for the White House Mid-Century Conference on Children and Youth.

Clark, K. B., & Clark, M. P. (1950). Emotional factors in racial identification and preference in Negro children. *The Journal of Negro Education, 19*, 341–350.

Clark, L. A. (2007). Assessment and diagnosis of personality disorder: Perennial issues and emerging conceptualization. *Annual Review of Psychology, 58*, 227–257.

Clark, R. E. (2003). Fostering the work motivation of individuals and teams. *Performance Improvement, 42(3)*, 21–29.

Clark, R., Anderson, N. B., Clark, V. R., & Williams, D. R. (1999). Racism as a stressor for African Americans: A biopsychosocial model. *American Psychologist, 54*, 805–816.

Clarke, A. C. (1952). An examination of the operation of residential propinquity as a factor in mate selection. *American Sociological Review, 17*, 17–22.

Classen, C., Koopman, C., & Spiegel, D. (1993). Trauma and dissociation. *Bulletin of the Menninger Clinic, 57*, 178–194.

Clay, R. A. (1996, May). Modern hypnosis wins clinical respect, praise. *APA Monitor.*

Cloninger, C. R., Bayon, C., & Przybeck, T. (1997). Epidemiology and axis I comorbidity of antisocial personality disorder. In D. M. Stoff, J. Breiling, & J. D. Maser (Eds.), *Handbook of antisocial personality disorder* (pp. 12–21). New York: Wiley.

Coccaro, E. F., Beresford, B., Minar, P., Kaskow, J., & Geracioti, T. (2007). CSF testosterone: Relationship to aggression, impulsivity, and venturesomeness in adult males with personality disorder. *Journal of Psychiatric Research, 41*, 488–492.

Cochran, S. V., & Rabinowitz, F. E. (2000). *Men and Depression: Clinical and Empirical Perspectives.* San Diego: Academic Press.

Coffer, C. N., & Appley, M. (1964). *Motivation: Theory and research.* New York: Wiley.

Cohan, C. L., & Kleinbaum, S. (2002). Toward a greater understanding of the cohabitation effect: Premarital cohabitation and marital communication. *Journal of Marriage and Family, 64*, 180–192.

Cohen, D. A., Farley, T. A., Taylor, S. N., Martin, D. H., & Schuster, M. A. (2002). When and where do youths have sex? The potential role of adult supervision. *Pediatrics, 110*, E66.

Cohen, D. A., Sturm, R., Scott, M., Farley, T. A., & Bluthenthal, R. (2010). Not enough fruit and vegetables or too many cookies, candies, salty snacks, and soft drinks? *Public Health Reports, 125*, 88–95.

Cohen, L. L., & Shotland, R. L. (1996). Timing of first sexual intercourse in a relationship: Expectations, experiences, and perceptions of others. *Journal of Sex Research, 33*, 291–299.

Cohen, N. J. (1984). Preserved learning capacity in amnesia: Evidence for multiple memory systems. In L. R. Squire & N. Butters (Eds.), *Neuropsychology of memory* (pp. 83–103). New York: Guilford Press.

Cohen, P., Cohen, J., Kasen, S., Velez, C. N., Hartmark, C., Johnson, J., et al. (1993). An epidemiological study of disorders in late adolescence: I. Age- and gender-specific prevalence. *Journal of Child Psychology and Psychiatry, 6*, 851–867.

Cohen, P., Kasen, S., Chen, H., Hartmark, C., & Gordon, K. (2003). Variations in patterns of developmental transitions in the emerging adulthood period. *Developmental Psychology, 39*, 657–669.

Cohen, S. (1996). Psychological stress, immunity, and upper respiratory infections. *Current Directions in Psychological Science, 5*, 86–90.

Cohen, S., & Janicki-Deverts, D. (2009). Can we improve our physical health by altering our social networks? *Perspectives on Psychological Science, 4*, 375–378.

Cohen, S. G., & Ledford, G. E., Jr. (1994). The effectiveness of self-managing teams: A quasi-experiment. *Human Relations, 47*, 13-43.

Cohen, S., Doyle, W. J., Turner, R., Alper, C. M., & Skoner, D. P. (2003). Sociability and susceptibility to the common cold. *Psychological Science, 14*, 389–395.

Cohen, S., Tyrrell, D., & Smith, A. (1991). Psychological stress and susceptibility to the common cold. *New England Journal of Medicine, 325*, 606–612.

Colado, M. I., O'Shea, E., & Green, A. R. (2004). Acute and long-term effects of MDMA on cerebral dopamine biochemistry and function. *Psychopharmacology* (Berlin), *173*, 249–263.

Colcombe, S., & Kramer, A. F. (2003). Fitness effects on the cognitive function of older adults: A meta-analytic study. *Psychological Science, 14*, 125–130.

Cole, H., & Griffiths, M. D. (2007). Social interactions in massively multiplayer online role-playing gamers. *Cyberpsychology and Behavior, 10*, 575–583.

Cole, S. W. (2009). Social regulation of human gene expression. *Current Directions in Psychological Science, 18*, 132–137.

Cole, W. (1992). Incest perpetrators: Their assessment and treatment. *Psychiatric Clinics of North America, 15*, 689–701.

Coleman, M., Ganong, L., & Fine, M. (2000). Reinvestigating marriage: Another decade of progress. *Journal of Marriage and the Family, 62*, 1288–1307.

Coley, R. L. (2001). (In)visible men: Emerging research on low-income, unmarried, and minority fathers. *American Psychologist, 56*, 743–753.

Colley, A., Ball, J., Kirby, N., Harvey, R., & Vingelen, I. (2002, December). Gender-linked differences in everyday memory performance: Effort makes the difference. *Sex Roles: A Journal of Research, 47*, 577–582.

Collier, G. Hirsch, E., & Hamlin, P. H. (1972). The ecological determinants of reinforcement in the rat. *Physiology and Behavior, 9*, 705–716.

Collins, A., Hill, L. E., Chandramohan, Y., Witcomb, D., Droste, S. K., & Reul, J. M. (2009). Exercise improves cognitive responses to stress through enhancement of epigenetic mechanisms and gene expression in the dentate gyrus. *PLoS One, 4*, e4330.

Collins, A. M., & Quillian, M. R. (1969). Retrieval time from semantic memory. *Journal of Verbal Learning and Verbal Behavior, 8*, 240–248.

Collins, M. W., Field, M., Lovell, M. R., Iverson, G., Johnston, K. M., Maroon, J., et al. (2003). Relationship between postconcussion headache and neuropsychological test performance in high school athletes. *American Journal of Sports Medicine, 31*, 168–173.

Collins, R. L., Elliott, M. N., Berry, S. H., Kanouse, D. E., Kunkel, D., Hunter, S. B., et al. (2004). Watching sex on television predicts adolescent initiation of sexual behavior. *Pediatrics, 114*, 280–289.

Collins, W. A., & van Dulmen, M. (2006). Friendships and romance in emerging adulthood: Assessing distinctiveness in close relationships. In J. J. Arnett & J. L. Tanner (Eds.), *Emerging adults in America: Coming of age in the 21st century* (pp. 219–234). Washington, DC: APA.

Colombres, M., Sagal, J. P., & Inestrosa, N. C. (2004). An overview of the current and novel drugs for Alzheimer's disease with particular reference to anti-cholinesterase compounds. *Current Pharmaceutical Design, 10*, 3121–3130.

Coltheart, M. (1983). Ecological necessity of iconic memory. *Behavioral and Brain Sciences, 6*, 17–18.

Coltrane, S. (2001). Research on household labor: Modeling and measuring the social embeddedness of routine family work. In R. M. Milardo (Ed.), *Understanding families in the new millennium: A decade in review* (pp. 427–452). Minneapolis: National Council on Family Relations.

Comaty, J. E., Stasio, M., & Advokat, C. (2001). Analysis of outcome variables of a token economy in a state psychiatric hospital: A program evaluation. *Research in Developmental Disabilities, 22,* 233–253.

Combs, D. R., & Mueser, K. T. (2007). Schizophrenia. In M. Hersen, S. Turner, and D. Beidel (Eds.), *Adult psychopathology and diagnosis* (5th ed., pp. 234–285). New York: Wiley.

Compton, W. M., Helzer, J. E., Hwu, H., Yeh, E., McEvoy, L., Tipp, J. E., et al. (1991). New methods in cross-cultural psychiatry: Psychiatric illness in Taiwan and the United States. *American Journal of Psychiatry, 148,* 1697–1704.

Conklin, H. M., & Iacono, W. G. (2002). Schizophrenia: A neurodevelopmental perspective. *Current Directions in Psychological Science, 11,* 33–37.

Conrad, M. A., & Ashworth, S. D. (1986). *Recruiting source effectiveness: A meta-analysis and re-examination of two rival hypotheses.* Paper presented at the First Annual Meeting of the Society for Industrial and Organizational Psychology, Chicago, IL.

Conrad, R. (1964). Acoustic confusions in immediate memory. *British Journal of Psychology, 55,* 75–84.

Contrada, R. J., Ashmore, R. D., Gary, M. L., Coups, E., Egeth, J. D., Sewell, A., et al. (2000). Ethnicity-related sources of stress and their effects on well-being. *Current Directions in Psychological Science, 9,* 136–139.

Conway, B. R. (2003). Colour vision: A clue to hue in V2. *Current Biology, 13,* R308–R310.

Conway, B. R. (2009). Color vision, cones, and color-coding in the cortex. *Neuroscientist, 15,* 274–290.

Conway, B. R., & Livingstone, M. S. (2005). A different point of hue. *Proceedings of the National Academy of Sciences of the United States of America, 102,* 10761–10762.

Cook, J. L., & Cook, G. (2005). *Child development: Principles and perspectives.* Boston: Allyn & Bacon.

Cooke, R., & Sheeran, P. (2004). Moderation of cognition-intention and cognition-behaviour relations: A meta-analysis of properties of variables from the theory of planned behaviour. *British Journal of Social Psychology, 43,* 159–186.

Cookson, J. (1997). Lithium: Balancing risks and benefits. *British Journal of Psychiatry, 171,* 113–119.

Cools, J., Schotte, D. E., & McNally, R. J. (1992). Emotional arousal and overeating in restrained eaters. *Journal of Abnormal Psychology, 69,* 390–400.

Coons, P. M. (1994). Confirmation of childhood abuse in child and adolescent cases of multiple personality disorder and dissociative disorder not otherwise specified. *Journal of Nervous and Mental Disease, 182,* 461–464.

Cooper, A. (2003, December). *Cybersex addictions: How to identity and treat the effects of aberrant online sexual pursuits.* Paper presented at the American Society of Professional Education, Portland, OR.

Cooper, A. (Ed.). (2002). *Sex and the Internet.* Philadelphia: Brunner-Routledge.

Cooper, A., Boies, S., Maheu, M., & Greenfield, D. (2000). Sexuality and the Internet: The next sexual revolution. In L. Szuchman & F. Muscarella (Eds.), *Psychological perspectives on human sexuality,* (pp. 519–545). New York: Wiley.

Cooper, A., Safir, M. P., & Rosenmann, A. (2006). Workplace worries: A preliminary look at online sexual activities at the office: Emerging issues for clinicians and employers. *Cyberpsychology and Behavior, 9,* 22–29.

Cooper, L. A., & Shepard, R. N. (1973). Chronometric studies of the rotation of mental images. In W. G. Chase (Ed.), *Visual information processing* (pp. 75–176). New York: Academic Press.

Cooper, M. L., Russell, M., Skinner, J. B., Frone, M. R., & Mudar, P. (1992). Stress and alcohol use: Moderating effects of gender, coping, and alcohol expectancies. *Journal of Abnormal Psychology, 101,* 139–152.

Cooper, Z. D., & Haney, M. (2008). Cannabis reinforcement and dependence: Role of the cannabinoid CB1 receptor. *Addiction Biology, 13,* 188–195.

Coren, S., Ward, L. M., & Enns, J. T. (1999). *Sensation and perception* (5th ed.). Fort Worth, TX: Harcourt Brace.

Corkin, S. (1968). Acquisition of motor skill after bilateral medial temporal-lobe excision. *Neuropsychologia, 6,* 255–265.

Corra, M., Carter, S. K., Carter, J. S., & Knox, D. (2009). Trends in marital happiness by gender and race, 1973 to 2006. *Journal of Family Issues, 30,* 1379–1404.

Corrigan, P. W., McCorkle, B., Schell, B., & Kidder, K. (2003). Religion and spirituality in the lives of people with serious mental illness. *Community Mental Health Journal, 39,* 487–499.

Cortina, L. M., & Kubiak, S. P. (2006). Gender and post-traumatic stress: Sexual violence as an explanation for women's increased risk. *Journal of Abnormal Psychology, 115,* 753–759.

Cortina, M. (2010). The future of psychodynamic psychotherapy. *Psychiatry, 73,* 43–56.

Coryell, W. (1998). The treatment of psychotic depression. *Journal of Clinical Psychiatry, 59*(Suppl. 1), 22–27.

Cosmides, L., & Tooby, J. (1996). Are humans good intuitive statisticians after all? Rethinking some conclusions from the literature on judgment under uncertainty. *Cognition, 58,* 1–73.

Costa, P. T., & McCrae, R. R. (1992). Multiple uses for longitudinal personality data. *European Journal of Personality, 6*(2), 85–102.

Costa, P. T., & McCrae, R. R. (1997). Longitudinal stability of adult personality. In R. Hogan, J. A. Johnson, & S. R. Briggs (Eds.), *Handbook of personality psychology* (pp. 269–290). San Diego, CA: Academic Press.

Costa, P. T., Terracciano, A., & McCrae, R. R. (2001). Gender differences in personality traits across cultures: Robust and surprising findings. *Journal of Personality and Social Psychology, 81,* 322–331.

Council of Europe (2008). *Children and corporal punishment: "The right not to be hit, also a children's right."* CommDH/IssuePaper(2006)1REV. Retrieved February 23, 2010, from https://wcd.coe.int/ViewDoc.jsp?id=1237635

Cousins, D. A., Butts, K., & Young, A. H. (2009). The role of dopamine in bipolar disorder. *Bipolar Disorders, 11,* 787–806.

Cowan, C. P., & Cowan, P. A. (2000). *When partners become parents: The big life change for couples.* Mahwah, NJ: Erlbaum.

Cowan, R. L. (2007). Neuroimaging research in human MDMA users: A review. *Psychopharmacology* (Berlin), *189,* 539–556.

Coyle, J. T. (2006). Glutamate and schizophrenia: Beyond the dopamine hypothesis. *Cellular and Molecular Neurobiology, 26,* 365–384.

Coyle, J. T., Tsai, G., & Goff, D. (2003). Converging evidence of NMDA receptor hypofunction in the pathophysiology of schizophrenia., *Annual New York Academy of Science, 1003,* 318–327.

Craik, F. I. M., & Lockhart, R. S. (1972). Levels of processing: A framework for memory research. *Journal of Verbal Learning and Verbal Behavior, 11,* 671–684.

Crandall, C. S. (1988). Social contagion of binge eating. *Journal of Personality and Social Psychology, 55,* 588–598.

Crandall, C. S., Preisler, J. J., & Aussprung, J. (1992). Measuring life event stress in the lives of college students: The Undergraduate Stress Questionnaire (USQ). *Journal of Behavioral Medicine, 15*(6), 627–662.

Cranny, C. J., Smith, P. C., & Stone, E. F. (1992). *Job satisfaction: How people feel about their jobs and how it affects their performance.* New York: Lexington Books.

Crano, W. D., & Prislin, R. (2006). Attitudes and persuasion. *Annual Review of Psychology, 57,* 345–374.

Craske, M. G., & Barlow, D. H. (2001). Panic disorder and agoraphobia. In D. H. Barlow (Ed.), *Clinical handbook of psychological disorders* (3rd ed., pp. 1–59). New York: Guilford Press.

Crawford, H. J., Brown, A. M., & Moon, C. E. (1993). Sustained attentional and disattentional abilities: Differences between low and highly hypnotizable persons. *Journal of Abnormal Psychology, 102*(4), 534–543.

Creed, F., & Barsky, A. (2004). A systematic review of the epidemiology of somatisation disorder and hypochondriasis. *Journal of Psychosomatic Research, 56,* 391–408.

Crews, F. (1996). The verdict on Freud. *Psychological Science, 7,* 63–68.

Crick, F., & Mitchison, G. (1995). REM sleep and neural nets. *Behavioural Brain Research, 69*(1–2), 147–155.

Crick, N. R., & Dodge, K. A. (1994). A review and reformulation of social information-processing mechanisms in children's social adjustment. *Psychological Bulletin, 115,* 74–101.

Crick, N. R., Casas, J. F., & Ku, H. C. (1999). Relational and physical forms of peer victimization in preschool. *Developmental Psychology, 35,* 376–385.

Crits-Christoph, P. (1992). The efficacy of brief dynamic psychotherapy: A meta-analysis. *American Journal of Psychiatry, 149,* 151–158.

Crits-Christoph, P. (1997). Limitations of the Dodo Bird verdict and the role of clinical trials in psychotherapy research: Comment on Wampold et al. (1997). *Psychological Bulletin, 122,* 216–220.

Crits-Christoph, P., Baranackie, K., Kurcias, J. S., & Beck, A. T. (1991). Meta-analysis of therapist effects in psychotherapy outcome. *Psychotherapy Research, 1,* 81–91.

Crombag, H. S., & Robinson, T. E. (2004). Drugs, environment, brain, and behavior. *Current Directions in Psychological Science, 13,* 107–111.

Crosby, A. E., Cheltenham, M. P., & Sacks, J. J. (1999). Incidence of suicidal ideation and behavior in the United States, 1994. *Suicide and Life-Threatening Behavior, 29,* 131–140.

Crosby, R., & Danner, F. (2008). Adolescents' STD protective attitudes predict sexually transmitted disease acquisition in early adulthood. *Journal of School Health, 78,* 310–313.

Cross, E. S., Mackie, E. C., Wolford, G., & de C. Hamilton, A. F. (2009). Contorted and ordinary body postures in the human brain. *Experimental Brain Research,* doi:10.1007/s00221–00902093-x.

Crowell, T. A., Luis, C. A., Vanderploeg, R. D., Schinka, J. A., & Mullan, M. (2002). Memory patterns and executive functioning in mild cognitive impairment and Alzheimer's disease. *Aging Neuropsychology and Cognition, 9,* 288–297.

Crowley, A. E., & Hoyer, W. D. (1994). An integrative framework for understanding two-sided persuasion. *Journal of Consumer Research, 20,* 561–574.

Crowley, S. J., Acebo, C., & Carskadon, M. A. (2007). Sleep, circadian rhythms, and delayed phase in adolescence. *Sleep Medicine, 8,* 602–612.

Croxford, J. L. (2003). Therapeutic potential of cannabinoids in CNS disease. *CNS Drugs, 17,* 179–202.

Crum, N., Riffenburgh, R., Wegner, S., Agan, B., Tasker, S., Spooner, K., et al. (2006). Comparisons of causes of death and mortality rates among HIV-infected patients: Analysis of the pre-, early, and late HAART (highly active antiretroviral therapy) eras. *Journal of Acquired Immune Deficiency Syndromes, 41,* 194–200.

Crystal, D. (2008). *Txtng the gr8 db8.* Oxford, UK: Oxford University Press.

CTIA (2010). "Text"book wireless safety. Retrieved April 9, 2010, from http://www.ctia.org/consumer_info/safety/index.cfm/AID/10672

Cui, M., & Donnellan, M. B. (2009). Trajectories of conflict over raising adolescent children and marital satisfaction. *Journal of Marriage and the Family, 71,* 478–494.

Culbertson, F. M. (1997). Depression and gender: An international review. *American Psychologist, 52,* 25–31.

Cummins, L. H., & Lehman, J. (2007). Eating disorders and body image concerns in Asian American women: Assessment and treatment from a multicultural and feminist perspective. *Eating Disorders, 15,* 217–230.

Cunningham, W. A., Raye, C. L., & Johnson, M. K. (2004). Implicit and explicit evaluation: fMRI correlates of valence, emotional intensity, and control in the processing of attitudes. *Journal of Cognitive Neuroscience, 16,* 1717–1729.

Cutrona, C. E., Wallace, G., & Wesner, K. A. (2006). Neighborhood characteristics and depression: An examination of stress processes. *Current Directions in Psychological Science, 15,* 188–192.

Cytowic, R. E. (1999). *The man who tasted shapes.* Cambridge, MA: MIT Press.

Daiello, L. A. (2007). Atypical antipsychotics for the treatment of dementia-related behaviors: An update. *Medicine and Health, 90,* 191–194.

Dalal, (2006). A meta-analysis of the relationship between organizational citizenship behavior and counterproductive work behavior. *Journal of Applied Psychology, 90*(6), 1241–1255.

Daley, A. J. (2009). Can exergaming contribute to improving physical activity levels and health outcomes in children? *Pediatrics, 124,* 763–771.

Dalman, C., & Allebeck, P. (2002). Paternal age and schizophrenia: Further support for an association. *American Journal of Psychiatry, 159,* 1591–1592.

Damak, S., Rong, M., Yasumatsu, K., Kokrashvii, Z., Varadarajan, V., Zou, S., et al. (2003). Detection of sweet and umami taste in the absence of taste receptor T1r3. *Science, 301,* 850–851.

Damasio, H., Grabowski, T., Frank, R., Galaburda, A. M., & Damasio, A. R. (1994). The return of Phineas Gage: Clues about the brain from the skull of a famous patient. *Science, 264,* 1102–1105.

Damjanovic, A. K., Yang, Y., Glaser, R., Kiecolt-Glaser, J. K., Huy, N., Laskowski, B., et al. (2007). Accelerated telomere erosion is associated with a declining immune function of caregivers of Alzheimer's disease patients. *Journal of Immunology, 179,* 4249–4254.

Damm, J., Eser, D., Schule, C., Obermeier, M., Moeller, H. J., Rupprecht, R., et al. (in press). Influence of age on effectiveness and tolerability of electroconvulsive therapy. *Journal of ECT.*

Damon, W. (1999). The moral development of children. *Scientific American, 281,* 73–78.

Damon, W., & Simon Rosser, B. R. (2005). Anodyspareunia in men who have sex with men: Prevalence, predictors, consequences and the development of DSM diagnostic criteria. *Journal of Sex and Marital Therapy, 31,* 129–141.

Danhauer, J. L., Johnson, C. E., Byrd, A., & DeGood, L. (2009). Survey of college students on iPod and hearing health. *Journal of the American Academy of Audiology, 20,* 5–27.

D'Anna, L. H., Ponce, N. A., & Siegel, J. M. (2010). Racial and ethnic health disparities: Evidence of discrimination's effects across the SEP spectrum. *Ethnicity and Health, 15,* 121–143.

Dannlowski, U., Ohrmann, P., Bauer, J., Kugel, H., Baune, B. T., Hohoff, C., et al. (2007). Serotonergic genes modulate amygdale activity in major depression. *Genes, Brain and Behavior, 6,* 672–676..

Darowish, M., Lawton, J. N., & Evans, P. J. (2009). Q: What is cell phone elbow, and what should we tell our patients? *Cleveland Clinic Journal of Medicine, 76,* 306–308.

Darwin, C. (1859). *On the origin of species by means of natural selection.* London: John Murray.

Darwin, C. (1936). *On the origin of species by means of natural selection.* New York: Random House. (Original work published 1859)

Das, A. (2007). Masturbation in the United States. *Journal of Sex and Marital Therapy, 33,* 301–317.

Das, A., Parish, W. L., & Laumann, E. O. (2009). Masturbation in urban China. *Archives of Sexual Behavior, 38,* 108–120.

Dasen, P. R. (1994). Culture and cognitive development from a Piagetian perspective. In W. J. Lonner & R. Malpass (Eds.), *Psychology and culture* (pp. 141–150). Boston: Allyn & Bacon.

Dasgupta, A. M., Juza, D. M., White, G. M., & Maloney, J. F. (1995). Memory and hypnosis: A comparative analysis of guided memory, cognitive interviews, and hypnotic hyperamnesia. *Imagination, Cognition, and Personality, 14*(2), 117–130.

D'Augelli, A. R., Grossman, A. H., & Starks, M. T. (2006). Childhood gender atypicality, victimization, and PTSD among lesbian, gay, and bisexual youth. *Journal of Interpersonal Violence, 21,* 1462–1482.

Dauvilliers, Y., Cervena, K., Carlander, B., Espa, F., Bassetti, C., Claustrat, B., et al. (2004). Dissociation in circadian rhythms in a pseudohypersomnia form of fatal familial insomnia. *Neurology, 63,* 2416–2418.

David, D., Szentagotai, A., Lupu, V., & Cosman, D. (2008). Rational emotive behavior therapy, cognitive therapy, and medication in the treatment of major depressive disorder: A randomized clinical trial, posttreatment outcomes, and six-month follow-up. *Journal of Clinical Psychology, 64,* 728–746.

Davidson, J. R. T. (2000). Trauma: The impact of post-traumatic stress disorder. *Journal of Psychopharmacology, 14,* S5–S12.

Davidson, R. J., Jackson, D. C., & Kalin, N. H. (2000). Emotion, plasticity, context, and regulation: Perspectives from affective neuroscience. *Psychological Bulletin, 126,* 873–889.

Davidson, R. J., Putnam, K. M., & Larson, C. L. (2000). Dysfunction in the neural circuitry of emotion regulation: A possible prelude to violence. *Science, 289,* 591–594.

Davidson, S. R., Cook, S. P., & Glisky, E. L. (2006). Flashbulb memories for September 11th can be preserved in older adults. *Aging, Neuropsychology, and Cognition, 13,* 196–206.

Davies, H., Liao, P. C., Campbell, I. C., & Tchanturia, K. (2009). Multidimensional self reports as a measure of characteristics in people with eating disorders. *Eating and Weight Disorders, 14,* e84–91.

Davies, I. R. L. (1998). A study of colour grouping in three languages: A test of the linguistic relativity hypothesis. *British Journal of Psychology, 89,* 433–452.

Davies, P. T., & Cummings, E. M. (1998). Exploring children's emotional security as a mediator of the link between marital relations and child adjustment. *Child Development, 69,* 124–139.

Davis, J. I., Senghas, A., & Ochsner, K. N. (2009). How does facial feedback modulate emotional experience? *Journal of Research in Personality, 43,* 822–829.

Davis, K. C., George, W. H., Norris, J., Schacht, R. L., Stoner, S. A., Hendershot, C. S., et al. (2009). Effects of alcohol and blood alcohol concentration limb on sexual risk-taking intentions. *Journal of Studies on Alcohol and Drugs, 70,* 499–507.

Davis, M., & Egger, M. D. (1992). Habituation and sensitization in vertebrates. In L. R. Squire, J. H. Byrne, L. Nadel, H. L. Roediger, D. L. Schacter, & R. F. Thompson (Eds.), *Encyclopedia of learning and memory* (pp. 237–240). New York: Macmillan.

Davis, M. H., Luce, C., & Kraus, S. J. (1994). The heritability of characteristics associated with dispositional empathy. *Journal of Personality, 60,* 369–391.

Davis, O. S., Haworth, C. M., & Plomin, R. (2009). Dramatic increase in heritability of cognitive development from early to middle childhood: An 8-year longitudinal study of 8,700 pairs of twins. *Psychological Science, 20,* 1301–1308.

Davis, P. J. (1999). Gender differences in autobiographical memory for childhood emotional experiences. *Journal of Personality and Social Psychology, 76,* 498–510.

Davis, S. R., Morequ, M., Kroll, R., Bouchard, C., Panay, N., Gass, M., et al. (2008). Testosterone for low libido in postmenopausal women not taking estrogen. *New England Journal of Medicine, 359,* 2005–2017.

Davis-Coelho, K., Waltz, J., & Davis-Coelho, B. (2000). Awareness and prevention of bias against fat clients in psychotherapy. *Professional Psychology: Research and Practice, 31,* 682–684.

De Benedittis, G., Lorenzetti, A., & Pieri, A. (1990). The role of stressful life events in the onset of chronic primary headache. *Pain, 40*(1), 65–75.

de Fonseca, F., Carrera, M. R. A., Navarro, M., Koob, G. F., & Weiss, F. (1997, June 27). Activation of corticotropin-releasing factor in the limbic system during cannabinoid withdrawal. *Science, 276*(5321), 2050–2054.

De Lisi, R., & Gallagher, A. M. (1991). Understanding gender stability and constancy in Argentinean children. *Merrill-Palmer Quarterly, 37,* 483–502.

De May, J. (2006). A critical review of the March 27, 1964, *New York Times* article that first broke the story. Retrieved July 12, 2007, from http://www .oldkewgardens.com/ss-nytimes-3.html

Deakin, J. F., Lees, J., McKie, S., Hallak, J. E., Williams, S. R., & Dursun, S. M. (2008). Glutamate and the neural basis of the subjective effects of ketamine: A pharmacomagnetic resonance imaging study. *Archives of General Psychiatry, 65,* 154–164.

DeAngelis, T. (2004, January). Size-based discrimination may be hardest on children. *American Psychological Association Monitor on Psychology, 35,* 62.

Deaux, K., & Hanna, R. (1984). Courtship in the personals column: The influence of gender and sexual orientation. *Sex Roles, 11,* 363–375.

de Carvalho, M. R., Freire, R. C., & Nardi, A. E. (2010). Virtual reality as a mechanism for exposure therapy. *World Journal of Biological Psychiatry, 11,* 220–230.

DeCasper, A. J., & Fifer, W. P. (1980). Of human bonding: Newborns prefer their mothers' voices. *Science, 208,* 1174–1176.

de Castro, B. M., Pereira, G. S., Magalhães, V., Rossato, J. I., De Jaeger, X., Martins-Silva, C., et al. (2009). Reduced expression of the vesicular acetylcholine transporter causes learning deficits in mice. *Genes, Brain, and Behavior, 8,* 23–35.

de Castro, J. M. (2002). The influence of heredity on self-reported sleep patterns in free-living humans. *Physiology and Behavior, 76,* 479–486.

Deci, E. L. & Ryan, R. M. (1985). *Intrinsic motivation and self-determination in human behavior.* New York: Plenum Press.

Deci, E. L., & Ryan, R. M. (2008). Self-determination theory: A macrotheory of human motivation, development, and health. *Canadian Psychology, 49,* 182–185.

Degroot, A. B. (2004). The role of the septo-hippocampal system in fear and anxiety. *Dissertation Abstracts International: Section B: The Sciences and Engineering, 65*(1-B), 475.

DeJoseph, J. (2003, December 8). After the fall. *Adweek, 48,* p. 17.

DeLamater, J., & Karraker, A. (2009). Sexual functioning in older adults. *Current Psychiatry Reports, 11,* 6–11.

DeLoache, J. (2001). The symbol-mindedness of young children. In W. W. Hartup & R. A. Weinberg (Eds.), *Child psychology in retrospect and prospect (Vol. 32,* pp. 73–101). Mahwah, NJ: Erlbaum.

DeMaris, A., & MacDonald, W. (1993). Premarital cohabitation and marital instability: A test of the unconventionality hypothesis. *Journal of Marriage and the Family, 55,* 399–407.

DeMaris, A., & Rao, K. V. (1992). Premarital cohabitation and subsequent marital stability in the United States: A reassessment. *Journal of Marriage and the Family, 54,* 178–190.

Dement, W. (1960). The effect of dream deprivation. *Science, 131,* 1705–1707.

Dement, W., & Kleitman, N. (1957). Cyclic variations in EEG during sleep and their relation to eye movements, body motility, and dreaming. *Electroencephalography and Clinical Neurophysiology, 9,* 673–690.

Dement, W., & Vaughan, C. (1999). *The promise of sleep: A pioneer in sleep medicine explains the vital connection between health, happiness, and a good night's sleep.* New York: Delacorte.

Denis, M., & Borst, G. (2006). Variations on the image scanning paradigm: What do they contribute to our knowledge of mental imagery? In V. Tomaso & G. Bottinia (Eds.), *Imagery and spatial cognition: Methods, models and cognitive assessment* (pp. 62–81). Amsterdam, Netherlands: John Benjamins.

Denning, D. G., Conwell, Y., King, D., & Coz, C. (2000). Method choice, intent, and gender in completed suicide. *Suicide and Life-Threatening Behavior, 30,* 282–288.

Denollet, J. (1993). Biobehavioral research on coronary heart disease. *Journal of Behavioral Medicine, 16*(2), 115–141.

Depression and Bipolar Support Alliance. (2002). *National DMDA support groups: An important step on the road to wellness.* Chicago: Author.

Desalvo, K. B., Hyre, A. D., Ompad, D. C., Menke, A., Tynes, L. L., & Muntner, P. (2007). Symptoms of posttraumatic stress disorder in a New Orleans workforce following Hurricane Katrina. *Journal of Urban Health, 84,* 142–152.

DeSteno, D. A., & Salovey, P. (1996). Evolutionary origins of sex differences in jealousy? Questioning the "fitness" of the model. *Psychological Science, 7,* 367–372.

Deutsch, F. M. (2001). Equally shared parenting. *Current Directions in Psychological Science, 10,* 25–28.

Deutsch, J. A. (1990). Food intake. In E. M. Stricker (Ed.), *Handbook of behavioral neurobiology: Vol. 10. Neurobiology of food and fluid intake* (pp. 151–182). New York: Plenum Press.

DeValois, R. L., & DeValois, K. K. (1975). Neural coding of color. In E. C. Carterette & M. P. Friedman (Eds.), *Handbook of perception* (pp. 117–166). New York: Academic Press.

Devdas, N., & Rubin, L. (2007). Rape myth acceptance among first- and second-generation South Asian American women. *Sex Roles, 56,* 701–705.

Dewaraja, R., & Kawamura, N. (2006). Trauma intensity and posttraumatic stress: Implications of the tsunami experience in Sri Lanka for the management of future disasters. *International Congress Series, 1287,* 69–73.

Dhabhar, F. S., Miller, A. H., McEwen, B. S., & Spencer, R. L. (1995). Effects of stress on immune cell distribution. Dynamics and hormonal mechanisms. *Journal of Immunology, 154*(10), 5511–5527.

Diamond, A., & Amso, D. (2008). Contributions of neuroscience to our understanding of cognitive development. *Current Directions in Psychological Science, 17,* 136–141.

Diaz, R. M., & Berk, L. E. (Eds.). (1992). *Private speech: From social interaction to self-regulation.* Hillsdale, NJ: Erlbaum.

Dichter, G. S., Felder, J. N., & Smoski, M. J. (2010). The effects of brief behavioral activation therapy for depression on cognitive control in affective contexts: An fMRI investigation. *Journal of Affective Disorders, 126,* 236–244.

Diekelmann, S., & Born, J. (2010). The memory function of sleep. *Nature Reviews: Neuroscience, 11,* 114–126.

Diener, C., Kuehner, C., Brusniak, W., Struve, M., & Flor, H. (2009). Effects of stressor controllability on psychophysiological, cognitive, and behavioral responses in patients with major depression and dysthymia. *Psychological Medicine, 39,* 77–86.

Diener, E., & Biswas-Diener, R. (2008). *Happiness: Unlocking the mysteries of psychological wealth.* Malden, MA: Blackwell Publishing.

Diener, E., Oishi, S., & Lucas, R. E. (2003). Personality, culture, and subjective well-being: Emotional and cognitive evaluations of life. *Annual Review of Psychology, 54,* 403–425.

Diener, E., & Seligman, M. E. (2004). Beyond money: Toward an economy of well-being. *Psychological Science in the Public Interest, 5,* 1–31.

Dies, R. R. (1993). Research on group psychotherapy: Overview and clinical applications. In A. Alonso & H. I. Swiller (Eds.), *Group therapy in clinical practice* (pp. 473–518). Washington, DC: American Psychiatric Press.

Difede, J., & Hoffman, H. G. (2002). Virtual reality exposure therapy for World Trade Center post-traumatic stress disorder: A case report. *Cyber-psychology and Behavior, 5,* 529–535.

Digman, J. M. (1997). Higher-order factors of the Big Five. *Journal of Personality and Social Psychology, 73,* 1246–1256.

DiLillo, D. (2001). Interpersonal functioning among women reporting a history of childhood sexual abuse: Empirical findings and methodological issues. *Clinical Psychology Review, 21,* 553–576.

Dingfelder, S. F. (2010). How artists see. *Monitor on Psychology, 41,* 40.

Dion, K. K., Berscheid, E., & Walster, E. (1972). What is beautiful is good. *Journal of Personality and Social Psychology, 24,* 285–290.

Dishion, T. J., & Patterson, G. R. (1997). The timing and severity of antisocial behavior: Three hypotheses within an ecological framework. In D. M. Stoff, J. Breiling, & J. D. Maser (Eds.), *Handbook of anti-social personality disorder* (pp. 205–217). New York: Wiley.

Distefan, J.M., Pierce, J.P., & Gilpin, E.A.(2004). Do favorite movie stars influence adolescent smoking initiation? *American Journal of Public Health, 94,* 1239–1244.

Dixon, J. F., & Hokin, L. E. (1998). Lithium acutely inhibits and chronically up-regulates and stabilizes glutamate uptake by presynaptic nerve endings in mouse cerebral cortex. *Neurobiology, 95,* 8363–8368.

Dobbs, D. (2006). Turning off depression. *Scientific American, 17,* 26–31.

Dobson, K. S., Backs-Dermott, B. J., & Dozois, D. J. A. (2000). Cognitive and cognitive-behavioral therapies. In C. R. Snyder & R. E. Ingram (Eds.), *Handbook of psychological change: Psychotherapy processes and practices for the 21st century* (pp. 409–428). New York: Wiley.

Docter, R. F., & Prince, V. (1997). Transvestism: A survey of 1032 cross-dressers. *Archives of Sexual Behavior, 26,* 589–605.

Doctor, R. M., & Doctor, J. N. (1994). Stress. *Encyclopedia of human behavior* (Vol. 4). San Diego, CA: Academic Press.

Dohrenwend, B. P., Levav, I., Shrout, P. E., Link, B. G., Skodol, A. E., & Martin, J. L. (1987). Life stress and psychopathology: Progress on research begun with

Barbara Snell Dohrenwend. *American Journal of Community Psychology, 15,* 677–715.

Dohrenwend, B. P., Turner, J. B., Turse, N. A., Adams, B. G., Koen, K. C., & Marshall, R. (2006). The psychological risk of Vietnam for U.S. veterans: A revisit with new data and methods. *Science, 313,* 979–982.

Dolbier, C. L., Cocke, R. R., Leiferman, J. A., Steinhardt, M. A., Schapiro, S. J., Nehete, P. N., et al. (2001). Differences in functional immune responses of high vs. low hardy healthy individuals. *Journal of Behavioral Medicine, 24,* 219–229.

Dollard, J., Doob, L., Miller, N., Mowrer, O. H., & Sears, R. R. (1939). *Frustration and aggression.* New Haven, CT: Yale University Press.

Dominowski, R. L., & Dallob, P. (1995). Insight and problem solving. In R. J. Sternberg & J. E. Davidson (Eds.), *The nature of insight* (pp. 33–62). Cambridge, MA: MIT Press.

Domjan, M., & Purdy, J. E. (1995). Animal research in psychology: More than meets the eye of the general psychology student. *American Psychologist, 50,* 496–503.

Donaldson, C., & Lam, D. (2004). Rumination, mood, and social problem-solving in major depression. *Psychological Medicine, 34,* 1309–1318.

Doty, R. L. (2001). Olfaction. *Annual Review of Psychology, 52,* 423–447.

Dougherty, D. D., Baer, L., Cosgrove, G. R., Cassem, E. H., Price, B. H., Nirenberg, A. A., et al. (2002). Prospective long-term follow-up of 44 patients who received cingulotomy for treatment of refractory obsessive-compulsive disorder. *American Journal of Psychiatry, 159,* 269–275.

Dow, G. T., & Mayer, R. E. (2004). Teaching students to solve insight problems: Evidence for domain specificity. *Creativity Training Research Journal, 16,* 389–402.

Draganova, R., Eswaran, H., Murphy, P., Lowery, C., & Preissi, H. (2007). Serial magnetoencephalographic study of fetal and newborn auditory discriminative evoked responses. *Early Human Development, 83,* 199–207.

Draguns, J. G. (2002). Universal and cultural aspects of counseling and psychotherapy. In P. B. Pedersen, J. G. Draguns, W. J. Lonner, & J. E. Trimble (Eds.), *Counseling across cultures* (5th ed., pp. 29–50). Thousand Oaks, CA: Sage.

Drea, C. M. (2009). Endocrine mediators of masculinization in female mammals. *Current Directions in Psychological Science, 18,* 221–226.

Drevets, W. C., Savitz, J., & Trimble, M. (2008). The subgenual anterior cingulated cortex in mood disorders. *CNS Spectrums, 13,* 663–681.

Drews, F. A., Yazdani, H., Godfrey, C. N., Cooper, J. M., & Strayer, D. L. (2009). Text messaging during simulated driving. *Human Factors, 51,* 762–770.

Driesen, N. R., & Raz, N. (1995). The influence of sex, age, and handedness on corpus callosum morphology: A meta-analysis. *Psychobiology, 23,* 240–247.

Druckman, D., & Bjork, R. A. (1994). *Learning, remembering, believing: Enhancing human performance.* Washington, DC: National Academy Press.

Dube, R., & Hebert, M. (1988). Sexual abuse of children 12 years of age: A review of 511 cases. *Child Abuse and Neglect, 12,* 321–330.

Duckitt, J. (1992). Psychology and prejudice: A historical analysis and integrative framework. *American Psychologist, 47,* 1182–1193.

Duiker, W. J., & Spielvogel, J. J. (2004). *The world history: Vol. 2. Since 1400* (4th ed.). Belmont, CA: Wadsworth.

Duan, X., Dai, Q., Gong, Q., & Chen, H. (2010). Neural mechanism of unconscious perception of surprised facial expression. *Neuroimage,* doi:10.1016/j.neuroimage.2010.04.021.

Durmer, J. S., & Dinges, D. F. (2005). Neurocognitive consequences of sleep deprivation. *Seminars in Neurology, 25,* 117–129.

Durrence, H. H., & Lichstein, K. L. (2006). The sleep of African Americans: A comparative review. *Behavioral Sleep Medicine, 4,* 29–44.

Durston, S., Hulshoff Pol, H. E., Casey, B. J., Giedd, J. N., Buitelaar, J. K., & van Engeland, H. (2001). Anatomical MRI of the developing human brain: What have we learned? *Journal of the American Academy of Child and Adolescent Psychiatry, 40,* 1012–1020.

Dwairy, M. (2004). Parenting styles and mental health of Palestinian-Arab adolescents in Israel. *Transcultural Psychiatry, 41,* 233–252.

Dweck, C. (2008). Can personality be changed? The role of beliefs in personality and change. *Current Directions in Psychological Science, 17,* 391–394.

Dweck, C. S., Chiu, C., & Hong, Y. (1995). Implicit theories and their role in judgments and reactions: A world from two perspectives. *Psychological Inquiry, 6,* 267–285.

Eagly, A. H., & Chaiken, S. (1975). An attribution analysis of communicator characteristics on opinion change: The case of communicator attractiveness. *Journal of Personality and Social Psychology, 32,* 136–144.

Eaton, A. H., & Resko, J. A. (1974). Plasma testosterone and male dominance in a Japanese macaque (Macca fuscata) troop compared with repeated measures of testosterone in laboratory males. *Hormones and Behavior, 5,* 251–259.

Eaton, D. K., Kann, L., Kinchen, S., Ross, J., Hawkins, J., Harris, W. A., et al. (2006). Youth risk behavior surveillance, United States, 2005. *Morbidity and Mortality Weekly Report, 55,* 1–108.

Eaton, W. W., & Keyl, P. M. (1990). Risk factors for the onset of Diagnostic Schedule/DSM-III agoraphobia in a prospective population-based study. *Archives of General Psychiatry, 47,* 819–824.

Eaton, W. W., Thara, R., Federman, E., & Tien, A. (1998). Remission and relapse in schizophrenia: The Madras longitudinal study. *Journal of Nervous and Mental Disease, 186,* 357–363.

Ebert, P. L., & Anderson, N. D. (2009). Proactive and retroactive interference in young adults, healthy older adults, and older adults with amnestic mild cognitive impairment. *Journal of the International Neuropsychological Society, 15,* 83–93.

Ebbinghaus, H. (1910). *Abriss der psychologie.* Leipzig: Veit & Company.

Ebbinghaus, H. (1913). *Memory: A contribution to experimental psychology* (H. Ruyer & C. E. Bussenius, Trans.). New York: Teachers College, Columbus University. (Original work published 1885)

Ebmeier, K. P., Donaghey, C., & Steele, J. D. (2006). Recent developments and current controversies in depression. *Lancet, 367,* 153–167.

Ebstein, R. P., Zohar, A. H., Benjamin, J., & Belmaker, R. H. (2002). An update on molecular genetic studies of human personality traits. *Applied Bioinformatics, 1,* 57–68.

Edenberg, H. J., & Foroud, T. (2006). The genetics of alcoholism: Identifying specific genes through family studies. *Addiction Biology, 11,* 386–396.

Edley, N., & Wetherell, M. (1999). Imagined futures: Young men's talk about fatherhood and domestic life. *British Journal of Social Psychology, 38,* 181–194.

Eggebeen, D. J., & Knoester, C. (2001). Does fatherhood matter for men? *Journal of Marriage and the Family, 63,* 381–393.

Egner, T., Jamieson, G., & Gruzelier, J. (2005). Hypnosis decouples cognitive control from conflict monitoring processes of the frontal lobe. *Neuroimaging, 27,* 969–978.

Ehlers, A. (1995). A 1-year prospective study of panic attacks: Clinical course and factors associated with maintenance. *Journal of Abnormal Psychology, 104,* 164–172.

Eich, J., Weingartner, H., Stillman, R. C., & Gillin, J. C. (1975). State-dependent accessibility of retrieval cues in the retention of a categorized list. *Journal of Verbal Learning and Verbal Behavior, 14,* 408–417.

Eilers, R. E., & Oiler, D. K. (1994). Infant vocalizations and the early diagnosis of severe hearing impairment. *Journal of Pediatrics, 124,* 199–203.

Einarsson, C., & Granstrom, K. (2004). Gender-biased interaction in the classroom: The influence of gender and age in the relationship between teacher and pupil. *Scandinavian Journal of Educational Research, 46,* 117–127.

Eisen, S. V. (1979). Actor-observer differences in information inference and causal attribution. *Journal of Personality and Social Psychology, 37,* 261–272.

Eisenberg, A., Murkoff, H., Hathaway, S., & Maxel, S. (2008). *What to expect the first year* (2nd ed.). New York: Workman.

Eisenberger, N. I., Taylor, S. E., Gable, S. L., Hilmert, C. J., & Liberman, M. D. (2007). Neural pathways link social support to attenuated neuroendocrine stress responses. *NeuroImage, 35,* 1601–1612.

Eisenman, R., & Dantzker, M. L. (2006). Gender and ethnic differences in sexual attitudes at a Hispanic-serving university. *Journal of General Psychology, 133,* 153–162.

Eiser, A. S. (2005). Physiology and psychology of dreams. *Seminars in Neurology, 25,* 97–105.

Ekman, P. (1973). Cross-cultural studies of facial expression. In P. Ekman (Ed.), *Darwin and facial expression* (pp. 169–222). New York: Academic Press.

Ekman, P., & Friesen, W. V. (1984). *Unmasking the face* (2nd ed.). Palo Alto, CA: Consulting Psychologists Press.

Elfenbein, H. A., Beaupre, M., Levesque, M., & Hess, U. (2007). Toward a dialect theory: Cultural differences in the expression and recognition of posed facial expressions. *Emotion, 7,* 131–146.

Elicker, J., Englund, M., & Sroufe, L. A. (1992). Predicting peer competence and peer relationships in childhood from early parent–child relationships. In R. D. Parke & G. W. Ladd (Eds.), *Family-peer relationships: Modes of linkage* (pp. 77–107). Hillsdale, NJ: Erlbaum.

El Khoury, D., El-Rassi, R., Azar, S., & Hwalla, N. (2010). Postprandial ghrelin and PYY responses of male subjects on low carbohydrate meals to varied balancing proportions of proteins and fats. *European Journal of Nutrition,* doi:10.1007/s00394–010–0108–9.

Elkind, D. (1984). *All grown up and no place to go.* Reading, MA: Addison-Wesley.

Elkind, D. (1994). *A sympathetic understanding of the child: Birth to sixteen* (3rd ed.). Boston: Allyn & Bacon.

Elkind, D. (1998). *All grown up and no place to go.* Reading, MA: Perseus Books.

Elkind, D., & Bowen, R. (1979). Imaginary audience behavior in children and adolescents. *Developmental Psychology, 15,* 38–44.

Ellason, J. W., Ross, C. A., & Fuchs, D. L. (1996). Lifetime axis I and II comorbidity and childhood trauma history in dissociative identity disorder. *Psychiatry, 59,* 255–266.

Ellenbogen, J. M., Hu, P. T., Payne, J. D., Titone, D., & Walker, M. P. (2007). Human relational memory requires time and sleep. *Proceedings of the National Academy of Science, U.S.A., 104,* 7723–7728.

Ellis, A. (1959). Requisite conditions for basic personality change. *Journal of Consulting Psychology, 23,* 538–540.

Ellis, A. (1973, February). The no cop-out therapy. *Psychology Today, 7,* 56–60, 62.

Ellis, A. (1991). *Reason and emotion in psychotherapy.* New York: Carol Publishing.

Ellis, A. (1995). Changing rational-emotive therapy (RET) to rational-emotive behavior therapy (REBT). *Journal of Rational-Emotive and Cognitive Behavior Therapy, 13,* 85–89.

Emery, L., Hale, S., & Myerson, J. (2008). Age differences in proactive interference, working memory, and abstract reasoning. *Psychology and Aging, 23,* 634–645.

Emmelkamp, P. M. (1994). Behavior therapy with adults. In A. E. Bergin & S. L. Garfield (Eds.), *Handbook of psychotherapy and behavior change* (4th ed., pp. 379–427). New York: Wiley.

End, C. M., Worthman, S., Mathews, M. B., & Wetterau, K. (2010). Costly cell phones: The impact of cell phone rings on academic performance. *Teaching of Psychology, 37,* 55–57.

Eng, T. R., & Butler, W. T. (1997). *The hidden epidemic: Confronting sexually transmitted diseases.* Washington, DC: National Academy Press.

Engels, G. I., Garnefski, N., & Diekstra, R. F. W. (1993). Efficacy of rational-emotive therapy: A quantitative analysis. *Journal of Consulting and Clinical Psychology, 61,* 1083–1090.

Enns, M. W., Cox, B. J., Afifi, T. O., De Graaf, R., Ten Have, M., & Sareen, J. (2006). Childhood adversities and risk for suicidal ideation and attempts: A longitudinal population-based study. *Psychological Medicine, 36,* 1769–1778.

Epley, N., Savitsy, K., & Kachelski, R. A. (1999). What every skeptic should know about subliminal persuasion. *Skeptical Inquirer, 23,* 40–45.

Epping-Jordan, M. P., Watkins, S. S., Koob, G. F., & Markou, A. (1998). Dramatic decreases in brain reward function during nicotine withdrawal. *Nature, 393,* 76.

Epstein, S. (1994). Trait theory as personality theory: Can a part be as great as the whole? *Psychological Inquiry, 5,* 120–122.

Equal Employment Opportunity Commission (2002). *Federal laws prohibiting job discrimination questions and answers.* May 24.

Equal Employment Opportunity Commission (2010). *Sexual harassment charges EEOC and FEPAs combined: FY 1997–FY 2009.* Office of Research, Information and Planning: Author.

Erblich, J., Lerman, C., Self, D. W., Diaz, G. A., & Bovbjerg, D. H. (2005). Effects of dopamine D2 receptor (DRD2) and transporter (SLC6A3) polymorphisms on smoking cue-induced cigarette craving among African-American smokers. *Molecular Psychiatry, 10,* 407–414.

Erel, O., & Burman, B. (1995). Interrelatedness of marital relations and parent–child relations: A meta-analytic review. *Psychological Bulletin, 118,* 108–132.

Erikson, E. H. (1956). The problem of ego identity. *Journal of American Psychoanalysis Association, 4,* 56–121.

Erikson, E. H. (1958). *Young man Luther.* New York: Norton.

Erikson, E. H. (1959). Identity and life cycle. Selected papers. *Psychological Issues, 1,* 1–171.

Erikson, E. H. (1963). *Childhood and society* (2nd ed.). New York: Norton.

Erikson, E. H. (1968). *Identity, youth and crisis.* New York: Norton.

Erikson, E. H. (1980). *Identity and the life cycle* (2nd ed.). New York: Norton.

Erwin, E. (Ed.). (2002). *The Freud encyclopedia: Theory, therapy, and culture.* London: Routledge.

Escobar, J. I. (1993). Psychiatric epidemiology. In A. C. Gaw (Ed.), *Culture, ethnicity, and mental illness* (pp. 43–73). Washington, DC: American Psychiatric Press.

Escobar, J. I., Gara, M., Waitzkin, H., Cohen Silver, R., Holman, A., & Compton, W. (1998). DSM-IV hypochondriasis in primary care. *General Hospital Psychiatry, 20,* 155–159.

ESEMed/MHEDEA 2000 Investigators (2004). Prevalence of mental disorders in Europe: Results from the European Study of the Epidemiology of Mental Disorders (ESEMed). *Acta Psychiatrica Scandinavica, 109,* 21–27.

Espy, K. A., Riese, M. L., & Francis, D. J. (1997). Neurobehavior in preterm neonates exposed to cocaine, alcohol, and tobacco. *Infant Behavior and Development, 20,* 297–309.

Essed, N. H., van Staveren, W. A., Kok, F. J., & de Graaf, C. (2007). No effect of 16 weeks flavor enhancement on dietary intake and nutritional status of nursing home elderly. *Appetite, 48,* 29–36.

Esses, V. M., Dovidio, J. F., Jackson, L. M., & Armstrong, T. L. (2001). The immigration dilemma: The role of perceived group competition, ethnic prejudice, and national identity. *Journal of Social Issues, 57,* 389–412.

Etkin, A., Prater, K. E., Hoeft, F., Menon, V., & Schatzberg, A. F. (2010). Failure of anterior cingulated activation and connectivity with the amygdala during implicit regulation of emotional processing in generalized anxiety disorder. *American Journal of Psychiatry, 167,* 545–554.

Eynon, R., Schroeder, M., & Fry, J. (2009). New techniques in online research: Challenges for research ethics. *21st Century Society, 4,* 187–199.

Eysenck, H. J. (1967). *The biological basis of personality.* Springfield, IL: Charles C. Thomas.

Eysenck, H. J. (1982). *Personality, genetics, and behavior: Selected papers.* New York: Praeger.

Eysenck, H. J. (1991). Dimensions of personality: 16, 5 or 3?—Criteria for a taxonomic paradigm. *Personality and Individual Differences, 12,* 773–790.

Eysenck, H. J. (1995). *Genius: The natural history of creativity.* Cambridge, UK: Cambridge University Press.

Eysenck, H. J., & Eysenck, S. B. G. (1969). *Personality structure and measurement.* London: Routledge.

Eysenck, H. J., & Eysenck, S. B. G. (1976). *Psychoticism as a dimension of personality.* London: Hodder and Stoughton.

Eysenck, H. J., & Rachman, S. (1965). *The causes and cures of neurosis: An introduction to modern behavior therapy based on learning theory and the principle of conditioning.* San Diego: Knapp.

Fagot, B. I., & Kavanaugh, K. (1990). The prediction of antisocial behavior from avoidant attachment classifications. *Child Development, 61,* 864–873.

Falkum, E., Pedersen, G., & Karterud, S. (2009). Diagnostic and Statistical Manual of Mental Disorders, Fourth Edition, paranoid personality disorder diagnosis: A unitary or a two dimensional construct? *Comprehensive Psychiatry, 50,* 533–541.

Fan, W., & Yan, Z. (2010). Factors affecting response rates of the web survey: A systematic review. *Computers in Human Behaviour, 26,* 132–139.

Fan, Y., Tang, Y. Y., Ma, Y., & Posner, M. I. (2010). Mucosal immunity modulated by integrative meditation in a dose-dependent fashion. *Journal of Alternative and Complementary Medicine, 16,* 151–155.

Farley, E., Loup, D., Nelson, M., Mitchell, A., Esplund, G., Macri, C., et al. (1997). Neoplastic transformation of the endocervix associated with down regulation of lactoferrin expression. *Molecular Carcinography, 20,* 240–250.

Farris, C., Treat, T. A., Viken, R. J., & McFall, R. M. (2008). Perceptual mechanisms that characterize gender differences in decoding women's sexual intent. *Psychological Science, 19,* 348–354.

Fatemi, S. H., & Folsom, T. D. (2009). The neurodevelopmental hypothesis of schizophrenia, revisited. *Schizophrenia Bulletin, 35,* 528–548.

Faust, K. A., & McKibben, J. N. (1999). Marital dissolution: Divorce, separation, annulment, and widowhood. In M. B. Sussman, S. K. Steinmetz, & G. W. Peterson (Eds.), *Handbook of marriage and the family* (pp. 475–502). New York: Plenum Press.

Fava, G. A., Grandi, S., Zielezny, M., & Rafanelli, C. (1996). Four-year outcome for cognitive-behavioral treatment of residual symptoms in major depression. *American Journal of Psychiatry, 153,* 945–947.

Fava, M., & Rosenbaum, J. F. (1995). Pharmacotherapy and somatic therapies. In E. E. Beckham & W. R. Leber (Eds.), *Handbook of depression* (2nd ed., pp. 280–301). New York: Guilford Press.

Fawcett, J. (1994). Antidepressants: Partial response in chronic depression. *British Journal of Psychiatry, 165*(Suppl. 26), 37–41.

Fazio, N. M., & Palm, L. J. (1998). Attributional style, depression, and grade point averages of college students. *Psychological Reports, 83,* 159–162.

FDA Public Health Advisory. (2004, October 15). *Suicidality in children and adolescents being treated with anti-depressant medications.* Retrieved October 23, 2004, from www.fda.gov/cder/drug/antidepressants/SSRIPHA200410.htm

Federal Bureau of Investigation [FBI] (2008). 2008 hate crime statistics. Retrieved April 17, 2010, from http://www.fbi.gov/ucr/hc2008/index.html

Federal Bureau of Investigation [FBI] (2009a). *Uniform crime reports: 2008 hate crime statistics.* Retrieved May 14, 2010, from http://www.fbi.gov/ucr/hc2008/incidents.html

Federal Bureau of Investigation [FBI] (2009b). *Uniform crime reports: 2008 crime in the United States.* Retrieved May 14, 2010, from http://www.fbi.gov/ucr/2009prelimsem/table_4.html

Federal Bureau of Investigation [FBI] (2010). *Uniform crime reports.* Retrieved May 14, 2010, from http://www.fbi.gov/ucr/2009prelimsem/table_4.html

Federal Communications Commission [FCC] (2004). The history of . . . cell phones. Retrieved December 19, 2009, from http://www.fcc.gov/cgb/kidszone/history_cellphone.html

Federman, D. D. (1994). Life without estrogen. *New England Journal of Medicine, 331,* 1088–1089.

Feinberg, M. E., Button, T. M., Neiderhiser, J. M., Reiss, D., & Hetherington, E. M. (2007). Parenting and adolescent antisocial behavior and depression: Evidence of genotype × parenting environment interaction. *Archives of General Psychiatry, 64,* 457–465.

Feingold, A. (1988). Matching for attractiveness in romantic partners and same-sex friends: A meta-analysis and theoretical critique. *Psychological Bulletin, 104,* 226–235.

Feingold, A. (1994). Gender differences in personality: A meta-analysis. *Psychological Bulletin, 116,* 429–456.

Felker, B., Hawkins, E., Dobie, D., Gutierrez, J., & McFall, M. (2008). Characteristics of deployed Operation Iraqi

Freedom military personnel who seek mental health care. *Military Medicine, 173,* 155–158.
Felmingham, K., Kemp, A., Williams, L., Das, P., Hughes, G., Peduto, A., et al. (2007). Changes in anterior cingulate and amygdala after cognitive behavior therapy of posttraumatic stress disorder. *Psychological Science, 18,* 127–129.
Feng, J., Spence, I., & Pratt, J. (2007). Playing an action video game reduces gender differences in spatial cognition. *Psychological Science, 18,* 850–855.
Fenton, W. S., & McGlashan, T. H. (1994). Antecedents, symptom progression, and long-term outcome of the deficit syndrome in schizophrenia. *American Journal of Psychiatry, 151,* 351–356.
Ferguson, C. P., & Pigott, T. A. (2000). Anorexia and bulimia nervosa: Neurobiology and pharmacotherapy. *Behavior Therapy, 31,* 237–263.
Fergusson, D. M., Horwood, L. J., & Lynskey, M. T. (1996). Childhood sexual abuse and psychiatric disorder in young adulthood II: Psychiatric outcomes of childhood sexual abuse. *Journal of the American Academy of Child and Adolescent Psychiatry, 35,* 1365–1374.
Feroli, K., & Burstein, G. (2003). Adolescent sexually transmitted diseases. *American Journal of Maternal/Child Nursing, 28,* 113–118.
Ferrell, D. (1996, December 16). Scientists unlocking secrets of marijuana's effects. *Los Angeles Times,* p. 3.
Festinger, L. (1951). Architecture and group membership. *Journal of Social Issues, 1,* 152–163.
Festinger, L. (1957). *A theory of cognitive dissonance.* Evanston, IL: Row, Peterson.
Festinger, L., Schachter, S., & Back, K. (1950). *Social pressures in informal groups: A study of human factors in housing.* Stanford, CA: Stanford University Press.
Field, A. P. (2006). Is conditioning a useful framework for understanding the development and treatment of phobias? *Clinical Psychology Review, 26,* 857–875.
Field, T. M., Schanberg, S. M., Scafidi, F., Bauer, C. R., Vega-Lahr, N., Garcia, R., et al. (1986). Tactile/kinesthetic stimulation effects of preterm neonates. *Pediatrics, 77,* 654–658.
Fieldman, J. P., & Crespi, T. D. (2002). Child sexual abuse: Offenders, disclosure, and school-based initiatives. *Adolescence, 37,* 151–160.
Fiellin, D. A., Friedland, G. H., & Gourevitch, M. N. (2006). Opioid dependence: Rationale for and efficacy of existing and new treatments. *Clinical Infectious Diseases, 43*(Suppl.), S173–S177.
Finch, C. E. (2001). Toward a biology of middle age. In M. E. Lachman (Ed.), *Handbook of midlife development* (pp. 77–108). New York: Wiley.
Finkelhor, D. (1990). Early and long-term effects of child sexual abuse: An update. *Professional Psychology: Research and Practice, 21,* 325–330.
Finkelhor, D. (1994). The international epidemiology of child sexual abuse. *Child Abuse and Neglect, 18,* 409–417.
Finkelstein, D. M., Kubzansky, L. D., Capitman, J., & Goodman, E. (2007). Socioeconomic differences in adolescent stress: The role of psychological resources. *Journal of Adolescent Health, 40,* 127–134.
Finn, R. (2003). Antabuse no panacea for alcoholism. *Clinical Psychiatry News, 31,* 6.
Finn, R. (2004, February 15). Functional MRI offers insights into working memory in Alzheimer's (greater whole-brain activation). *Internal Medicine News, 37,* 29.
Fiorentino, L., Marler, M., Stepnowsky, C., Johnson, S., & Ancoli-Israel, S. (2006). Sleep in older African Americans and Caucasians at risk for sleep-disordered breathing. *Behavioral Sleep Medicine, 4,* 164–178.
Fisher, B. S. (2009). The effects of question wording on rape estimates: Evidence from a quasi-experimental design. *Violence Against Women, 15,* 133–147.
Fisher, B. S., Cullen, F. T., & Turner, M. G. (2000). *Are rapes and sexual assault part of college life?* National Institute of Justice Bureau of Justice Statistics. Retrieved September 4, 2004, from http://www.center4policy.org/violencem.html
Fisher, C. A., Hoffman, K. J., Austin-Lane, J., & Kao, T. C. (2000). The relationship between heavy alcohol use and work productivity loss in active duty military personnel: A secondary analysis of the 1995 Department of Defense Worldwide Survey. *Military Medicine, 165,* 355–361.
Fisher, H. E. (2004). *Why we love: The nature and chemistry of romantic love.* New York: Henry Holt.
Fisher, S., Kent, T. A., & Bryant, S. G. (1995). Postmarketing surveillance by patient self-monitoring: Preliminary data for sertraline versus fluoxetine. *Journal of Clinical Psychiatry, 56,* 288–296.
Fiske, M. (1980). Tasks and crises of the second half of life: The interrelationship of commitment, coping, and adaptation. In J. E. Birren & R. B. Sloane (Eds.), *Handbook of mental health and aging* (pp. 337–373). Englewood Cliffs, NJ: Prentice Hall.
Fiske, S. T. & Taylor, S. E. (1991). *Social cognition* (2nd. ed.). New York: McGraw-Hill.
Fitzgerald, L. F. (1993). Sexual harassment: Violence against women in the workplace. *American Psychologist, 48,* 1070–1076.
Flanagin, A. J. & Waldeck, J. H. (2004). Technology use and organizational newcomer socialization. *Journal of Business Communication, 41(2),* 137–165.
Flashmob.com (2010). Pentecost Sunday a BP environmental protest. Retrieved May 15, 2010, from http://www.flashmob.com/
Fleeson, W. (2004). Moving personality beyond the person-situation debate. *Current Directions in Psychological Science, 13,* 83–87.
Flegal, K. M., Carroll, M. D., Ogden, C. L., & Curtin, L. R. (2010). Prevalence and trends in obesity among US adults, 1999–2008. *Journal of the American Medical Association, 303,* 235–241.
Fletcher, C., & Perry, E. L. (2001). Performance appraisal and feedback: A consideration of national culture and a review of contemporary research and future trends. In N. Anderson, D. S. Ones, H. K. Sinangil, & C. Viswesvaran (Eds.), *Handbook of Industrial, Work and Organizational Psychology, 1* (pp. 127–144).
Flieller, A. (1999). Comparison of the development of formal thought in adolescent cohorts aged 10 to 15 years (1967–1996 and 1972–1993). *Developmental Psychology, 35,* 1048–1058.
Fligor, B. J., & Cox, L. C. (2004). Output levels of commercially available portable compact disc players and the potential risk to hearing. *Ear and Hearing, 25,* 513–527.
Foa, E. B., & Kozak, M. J. (1995). DSM-IV field trial: Obsessive-compulsive disorder. *American Journal of Psychiatry, 152,* 90–96.
Fogel, S. M., & Smith, C. T. (2006). Learning-dependent changes in sleep spindles and stage 2 sleep. *Journal of Sleep Research, 15,* 250–255.
Fogel, S. M., Smith, C. T., & Cote, K. A. (2007). Dissociable learning-dependent changes in REM and non-REM sleep in declarative and procedural memory systems. *Behavior and Brain Research, 180,* 48–61.
Folkman, S., & Lazarus, R. (1988). *Manual for the ways of coping questionnaire.* Palo Alto, CA: Consulting Psychologists Press.
Folkman, S., & Moskowitz, J. T. (2000). Stress, positive emotion, and coping. *Current Directions in Psychological Science, 9,* 115–118.
Follette, W. C., & Hayes, S. C. (2000). Contemporary behavior therapy. In C. R. Snyder & R. E. Ingram (Eds.), *Handbook of psychological change: Psychotherapy processes and practices for the 21st century* (pp. 381–408). New York: Wiley.
Foote, B., Smolin, Y., Neft, D. I., & Lipschitz, D. (2008). Dissociative disorders and suicidality in psychiatric outpatients. *Journal of Nervous and Mental Disease, 196,* 29–36.
Ford, C. S., & Beach, F. A. (1951). *Patterns of sexual behavior.* New York: Harper & Row.
Forsyth, D. R., & Corazzini, J. G. (2000). Groups as change agents. In C. R. Snyder & R. E. Ingram (Eds.), *Handbook of psychological change: Psychotherapy processes and practices for the 21st century* (pp. 309–336). New York: Wiley.
Fowler, J., & Peterson, P. (1981). Increasing reading persistence and altering attributional style of learned helpless children. *Journal of Educational Psychology, 73,* 251–260.
Fowles, D. C., & Dindo, L. (2009). Temperament and psychopathy: A dual-pathway model. *Current Directions in Psychological Science, 18,* 179–183.
Fox, E., Cahill, S., & Zougkou, K. (2010). Preconscious processing biases predict emotional reactivity to stress. *Biological Psychiatry, 67,* 371–377.
Francis, A. M. (2008). Family and sexual orientation: The family-demographic correlates of homosexuality in men and women. *Journal of Sex Research, 45,* 371–377.
Franiuk, R., Seefelt, J., & Vandello, J. (2008). Prevalence of rape myths in headlines and their effects on attitudes toward rape. *Sex Roles, 58,* 790–802.
Frank, D. A., Jacobs, R. R., Beeghly, M., Augustyn, M., Bellinger, D., Cabral, H., et al. (2002). Level of prenatal cocaine exposure and scores on the Bayley Scales of Infant Development: Modifying effects of caregiver, early intervention, and birth weight. *Pediatrics, 110,* 1143–1152.
Frankenberger, K. D. (2000). Adolescent egocentrism: A comparison among adolescents and adults. *Journal of Adolescence, 23,* 343–354.
Freedman, J. L., & Fraser, S. C. (1966). Compliance without pressure: The foot-in-the-door technique. *Journal of Experimental Social Psychology, 4,* 195–203.
Freud, A. (1936). *The ego and the mechanisms of defense.* London: Hogarth Press.
Freud, S. (1909). *Analysis of a phobia of a five-year-old boy* (Vol. III). New York: Basic Books.
Freud, S. (1915). Repression. In *Freud's collected papers* (Vol. IV). London: Hogarth.
Freud, S. (1917). Mourning and melancholia. *Collected works.* London: Hogarth Press.
Freud, S. (1943). *A general introduction to psychoanalysis.* New York: Garden City.
Freud, S. (1949). *An outline of psychoanalysis.* New York: Norton.
Freud, S. (1964). An outline of psycho-analysis. In J. Strachey (Ed. and Trans.), *The standard edition of the complete psychological works of Sigmund Freud* (Vol. 23). London: Hogarth Press. (Originally published 1940)
Freud, S. (1980). *The interpretation of dreams* (J. Strachey, Ed. and Trans.). New York: Avon. (Original work published 1900)
Frewen, P. A., Dozois, D. J., & Lanius, R. A. (2008). Neuroimaging studies of psychological interventions for mood and anxiety disorders: Empirical and methodological review. *Clinical Psychology Review, 28,* 228–246.
Fried, C. B. (2008). In-class laptop use and its effects on student learning. *Computers and Education, 50,* 906–914.
Friedman, M. (1990). Body fat and the metabolic control of food intake. *International Journal of Obesity, 14,* 53–67.
Friedman, M., & Brownell, K. D. (1996). A comprehensive treatment manual for the management of obesity. In V. B. Van Hasselt & M. Hersen (Eds.), *Source book of psychological treatment manuals for adult disorders* (pp. 375–422). New York: Plenum Press.
Friedman, M., & Rosenman, R. (1974). *Type A behavior and your heart.* New York: Knopf.
Friedman, M., Thoresen, C. E., Gill, J. J., & Powell, E. (1984). Alteration of Type A behavior and reduction in cardiac recurrences in postmyocardial infarction patients. *American Heart Journal, 108*(2), 237–248.
Friedrich, W. N., Fisher, J., Broughton, D., Houston, M., & Shafran, C. R. (1998). Normative sexual behavior in children: A contemporary sample. *Pediatrics, 101,* E9.
Frielingsdorf, H., Simpson, D. R., Thal, L. J., & Pizzo, D. P. (2007). Nerve growth factor promotes survival of new neurons in the adult hippocampus. *Neurobiology of Disease, 26,* 46–55.
Frings, M., Awad, N., Jentzen, W., Dimitrova, A., Kolb., F. P., Diener, H. C., et al. (2006). Involvement of the human cerebellum in short-term and long-term habituation of the acoustic startle response: A serial PET study. *Clinical Neurophysiology, 117,* 1290–1300.
Fry, C., & Miller, P. (2002). *Victorian drug trends 2001: Findings from the illicit drug reporting system* (IDRS), National Drug and Alcohol Research Centre (NDARC) Technical Report No. 129. Sydney: NDARC, University of New South Wales.
Fryar, C. D., Hirsch, R., Porter, K. S., Kottiri, B., Brody, D. J., & Louis, T. (2007). Drug use and sexual behaviors reported by adults: United States, 1999–2002. *CDC Advance Data from Vital and Health Statistics, 384,* 15pp.
Fu, C. H., Williams, S. C., Cleare, A. J., Brammer, M. J., Walsh, N. D., Kim, J. et al. (2004). Attenuation of the neural response to sad faces in major depression by antidepressant treatment: A prospective, event-related

functional magnetic resonance imaging study. *Archives of General Psychiatry, 61,* 877–889.
Fumal, A., & Schoenen, J. (2008). Tension-type headache: Current research and clinical management. *Lancet Neurology, 7,* 70–83.
Funder, D. C. (1993). Explaining traits. *Psychological Inquiry, 5,* 125–127.
Furnham, A., & Paltzer, S. (2010). The portrayal of men and women in television advertisements: An updated review of 30 studies published since 2000. *Scandinavian Journal of Psychology,* doi:10.1111; 1–21.
Furnham, A., Reeves, E., & Budhani, S. (2002). Parents think their sons are brighter than their daughters: Sex differences in parents' self-estimations and estimations of their children's multiple intelligences. *Journal of Genetic Psychology, 163,* 24–39.
Furnham, A., Wytykowska, A., & Petrides, K. V. (2005). Estimates of multiple intelligences: A study in Poland. *European Psychologist, 10,* 51–59.
Furumoto, L. (1989). The new history of psychology. In I. S. Cohen (Ed.), *The G. Stanley Hall lecture series* (Vol. 9, pp. 5–34). Washington D.C.: American Psychological Association.
Fusari, A., & Molina, J. A. (2009). Sense of smell, physiological ageing and neurodegenerative diseases: II. Ageing and neurodegenerative diseases. *Revista de Neurologica, 49,* 363–369.
Gadalla, T. M. (2009). Association of obesity with mood and anxiety disorders in the adult general population. *Chronic Diseases in Canada, 30,* 29–36.
Gael, S. A. (1988). *The job analysis handbook for business, industry, and government* (Vols. 1 and 2). New York: Wiley.
Gaertner, S. L., & Dovidio, J. F. (1986). The aversive form of racism. In J. F. Dovidio & S. L. Gaertner (Eds.), *Prejudice, discrimination, and racism* (pp. 61–89). San Diego, CA: Academic Press.
Gaertner, S. L., & Dovidio, J. F. (2005). Understanding and addressing contemporary racism: From aversive racism to the common ingroup identity model. *Journal of Social Issues, 61,* 615–639.
Gais, S., Hullemann, P., Hallschmid, M., & Born, J. (2006). Sleep-dependent surges in growth hormone do not contribute to sleep-dependent memory consolidation. *Psychoneuroendocrinology, 31,* 786–791.
Gais, S., Lucas, B., & Born, J. (2006). Sleep after learning aids memory recall. *Learning and Memory, 13,* 259–262.
Galensky, T. L., Miltenberger, R. G., Stricker, J. M., & Garlinghouse, M. A. (2001). Functional assessment and treatment of mealtime behavior problems. *Journal of Positive Behavior Interventions, 3,* 211.
Gall, T. L., Evans, D. R., & Howard, J. (1997). The retirement adjustment process: Changes in the well-being of male retirees across time. *Journal of Gerontology: Psychological Sciences, 52,* P110–P117.
Gallagher, A. M., DeLisi, R., Holst, P. C., McGillicuddy-DeLisi, R., Marley, M., & Cahalan, C. (2000). Gender differences in advanced mathematical problem solving. *Journal of Experimental Child Psychology, 75,* 165–190.
Gallagher, A. M., Levin, J., & Cahalan, C. (2002). *GRE research: Cognitive patterns of gender differences on mathematics admission tests* (ETS Report No. 02-19). Princeton, NJ: Educational Testing Service.
Gallagher, W. (1994). *The power of place.* New York: Harper Perennial.
Gallerani, M., Manfredini, R., Dal Monte, D., Calo, G., Brunaldi, V., & Simona, C. (2001). Circadian differences in the individual sensitivity to opiate overdose. *Critical Care Medicine, 29,* 96–101.
Galliano, G. (2003). *Gender: Crossing boundaries.* Belmont, CA: Wadsworth.
Gallo, L. C., Troxel, W. M., Kuller, L. H., Sutton-Tyrell, K., Edmundowicz, D., & Matthews, K. A. (2003). Marital status, marital quality, and atherosclerotic burden in postmenopausal women. *Psychosomatic Medicine, 65,* 952–962.
Gallo, L. C., Troxel, W. M., Matthews, K. A., & Kuller, L. H. (2003). Marital status and quality in middle-aged women: Associations with levels and trajectories of cardiovascular risk factors. *Health Psychology, 22,* 453–463.
Gallo, U. E., & Fontanarosa, P. B. (1989). Locked-in syndrome: Report of a case. *American Journal of Emergency Medicine, 7,* 581–583.
Gallopin, T., Luppi, P. H., Rambert, F. A., Frydman, A., & Fort, P. (2004). Effect of the wake-promoting agent modafinil on sleep-promoting neurons from the ventrolateral preoptic nucleus: An in vitro pharmacologic study. *Sleep, 27,* 19–25.
Galvan, A. Hare, T., Voss, H., Glover, G., & Casey, B. J. (2007). Risk-taking and the adolescent brain: Who is at risk? *Developmental Science, 10,* F8–F14.
Gamst, G., Dana, R. H., Der-Karaberian, A., & Kramer, T. (2000). Ethnic match and client ethnicity effects on global assessment and visitation. *Journal of Community Psychology, 28,* 547–564.
Ganea, P. A., Shutts, K., Spelke, E. S., & DeLoache, J. S. (2007). Thinking of things unseen: Infants' use of language to update mental representations. *Psychological Science, 18,* 734–739.
Gangestad, S. W., Thornhill, R., & Garver-Apgar, C. E. (2005). Adaptations to ovulation: Implications for sexual and social behavior. *Current Directions in Psychological Science, 14,* 312–316.
Gangestad, S. W., Thornhill, R., & Yeo, R. A. (1994). Facial attractiveness, developmental stability, and fluctuating symmetry. *Ethology and Sociobiology, 15,* 73–85.
Gansberg, M. (1964, March 27). 37 who saw murder didn't call the police: Apathy at stabbing of Queens woman shocks inspector. *New York Times,* p. 1.
Garbarino, J. (1997). The role of economic deprivation in the social context of child maltreatment. In M. E. Helfer, R. S. Kempe, & R. D. Krugman (Eds.), *The battered child* (5th ed., pp. 49–60). Chicago: University of Chicago Press.
Garcia, J. (1992). Taste aversion and preference learning in animals. In L. R. Squire, J. H. Byrne, L. Nadel, H. L. Roediger, D. L. Schacter, & R. F. Thompson (Eds.), *Encyclopedia of learning and memory* (pp. 611–613). New York: Macmillan.
Garcia, J., & Koelling, R. A. (1966). Relation of cue to consequence in avoidance learning. *Psychonomic Science, 4,* 123–124.
Garcia, J., Ervin, F. R., & Koelling, R. A. (1966). Learning with prolonged delay of reinforcement. *Psychonomic Science, 5,* 121–122.
Gardiner, H. W., Mutter, J. D., & Kosmitzki, C. (1998). *Lives across cultures: Cross-cultural human development.* Needham Heights, MA: Allyn & Bacon.
Gardner, H. (1983). *Frames of mind.* New York: Basic Books.
Gardner, H. (1999). *Intelligence reframed: Multiple intelligences for the 21st century.* New York: Basic Books.
Gardner, H. (2004). *Changing minds: The art and science of changing our own and other people's minds.* Boston: Harvard Business School Press.
Garfield, S. L. (1992). Eclectic psychotherapy: A common factors approach. In J. C. Norcross (Ed.), *Handbook of psychotherapy integration* (pp. 169–201). New York: Basic Books.
Garfield, S. L. (1994). Research on client variables in psychotherapy. In A. E. Bergin & S. L. Garfield (Eds.), *Handbook of psychotherapy and behavior change* (4th ed., pp. 190–228). New York: Wiley.
Garlick, D. (2002). Understanding the nature of the general factor of intelligence: The role of individual differences in neural plasticity as an explanatory mechanism. *Psychological Review, 109,* 116–136.
Garlick, D. (2003). Integrating brain science research with intelligence research. *Current Directions in Psychological Science, 12,* 185–189.
Garpenstrand, H., Norton, N., Damberg, M., Rylander, G., Forslund, K., Mattila-Evenden, M., et al. (2002). A regulatory monoamine oxidase a promoter polymorphism and personality traits. *Neuropsychobiology, 46,* 190–193.
Garrett, M., & Carroll, J. (2000). Mending the broken circle: Treatment of substance dependence among Native Americans. *Journal of Counseling and Development, 78,* 379–388.
Gartlehner, G., Hansen, R. A., Carey, T. S., Lohr, K. N., Gaynes, B. N., & Randolph, L. C. (2005). Discontinuation rates for selective serotonin reuptake inhibitors and other second-generation antidepressants in outpatients with major depressive disorder: A systematic review and meta-analysis. *International Clinical Psychopharmacology, 20,* 59–69.
Gaunt, R. (2006). Couple similarity and marital satisfaction: Are similar spouses happier? *Journal of Personality, 74,* 1401–1420.
Gavin, L., MacKay, A. P., Brown, K., Harrier, S., Ventura, S. J., Kann, L., et al. (2009). Sexual and reproductive health of persons aged 10–24 years—United States, 2002–2007. *Morbidity and Mortality Weekly Report, 58,* 1–58.
Gawin, F. H. (1991). Cocaine addiction: Psychology and neurophysiology. *Science, 251,* 1580–1586.
Gazzaniga, M. S. (1967). The split brain in man. *Scientific American, 217,* 24–29.
Ge, X., Conger, R. D., & Elder, G. H. (1996). Coming of age too early: Pubertal influences on girls' vulnerability to psychological distress. *Child Development, 67,* 3386–3400.
Ge, X., Jin, R., Natsuaki, M. N., Frederick, X., Brody, G. H., Cutrona, C. E., et al. (2006). Pubertal maturation and early substance use risks among African American children. *Psychology of Addictive Behaviors, 20,* 404–414.
Gedo, J. E. (2002). The enduring scientific contributions of Sigmund Freud. *Perspectives in Biology and Medicine, 45,* 200–212.
Geer, J. H., & Robertson, G. G. (2005). Implicit attitudes in sexuality: Gender differences. *Archives of Sexual Behavior, 34,* 671–677.
Gehring, W. J., Himle, J., & Nisenson, L. G. (2000). Action-monitoring dysfunction in obsessive-compulsive disorder. *Psychological Science, 11,* 1–6.
Gelade, G. (2002). Creative style, personality, and artistic endeavor. *Genetic, Social and General Psychology Monographs, 128,* 213–234.
Gelfand, S. A. (1981). *Hearing.* New York: Marcel Dekker.
Geller, E. S., Russ, N. W., & Altomari, M. G. (1986). Naturalistic observations of beer drinking among college students. *Journal of Applied Behavior Analysis, 19,* 391–396.
Gendell, M., & Siegel, J. S. (1996). Trends in retirement age in the United States, 1955–1993, by sex and race. *Journal of Gerontology: Social Sciences, 51,* S132–S139.
Gentile, K., Raghavan, C., Rajah, V., & Gates, K. (2007). It doesn't happen here: Eating disorders in an ethnically diverse sample of economically disadvantaged, urban college students. *Eating Disorders, 15,* 405–425.
Georgiadis, J. R., Kortekaas, R., Kuipers, R., Nieuwenburg, A., Pruim, J., Reinders, A. A., et al. (2006). Regional cerebral blood flow changes associated with clitorally induced orgasm in healthy women. *European Journal of Neuroscience, 11,* 3305–3316.
Georgiou-Karistianis, N., Tang, J., Mehmedbegovic, F., Farrow, M., Bradshaw, J., & Sheppard, D. (2006). Age-related differences in cognitive function using a global local hierarchical paradigm. *Brain Research, 1124,* 86–95.
Gergen, K. J., & Gergen, M. M. (1988). Narrative and self as relationship. In L. Berkowitz (Ed.), *Advances in experimental social psychology* (Vol. 21, pp. 17–56). New York: Academic Press.
Gernsbacher, M. A. (1985). Surface information and loss in comprehension. *Cognitive Psychology, 17,* 324–363.
Gerressu, M., Mercer, C. H., Graham, C. A., Wellings, K., & Johnson, A. M. (2008). Prevalence of masturbation and associated factors in a British national probability survey. *Archives of Sexual Behavior, 37,* 266–278.
Gerrish, C. J., & Mennella, J. A. (2001). Flavor variety enhances food acceptance in formula-fed infants. *American Journal of Clinical Nutrition, 73,* 1080–1085.
Gershoff, E. T. (2002). Corporal punishment by parents and associated child behaviors and experiences: A meta-analytic and theoretical review. *Psychological Bulletin, 128,* 539–579.
Geschwind, N. (1975). The apraxias: Neural mechanisms of disorders of learned movements. *American Scientist, 63,* 188–195.
Geschwind, N., & Levitsky, W. (1968). Human brain: Left-right asymmetries in temporal speech region. *Science, 161,* 186–187.
Gheysen, F., Van Opstal, F., Roggeman, C., Van Waelvelde, H., & Fias, W. (2010). Hippocampal contribution to early and later stages of implicit motor sequence learning. *Experimental Brain Research,* doi:10.1007/s00221-010-2186-6.
Gibb, B. E., Alloy, L. B., Abramson, L. Y., Beevers, C. G., & Miller, I. W. (2004). Cognitive vulnerability to

depression: A taxometric analysis. *Journal of Abnormal Psychology, 113,* 81–89.

Gibbons, C. J., Fournier, J. C., Stirman, S. W., Derubeis, R. J., Crits-Christoph, P., & Beck, A. T. (2010). The clinical effectiveness of cognitive therapy for depression in an outpatient clinic. *Journal of Affective Disorders, 125,* 169–176.

Gibbs, W. W. (1996). Gaining on fat. *Scientific American, 275,* 88–94.

Gibson, H. B. (1995, April). Recovered memories. *The Psychologist,* pp. 153–154.

Giedd, J. N. (2004). Structural magnetic resonance imaging of the adolescent brain. *Annals of the New York Academy of Sciences, 1021,* 77–85.

Giedd, J. N., Blumentahl, J., Jeffries, N. O., Castellanos, F. X., Liu, H., Zijdenbos, A., et al. (1999). Brain development during childhood and adolescence: A longitudinal MRI study. *Nature Neuroscience, 2,* 861–863.

Gilbert, D. G., Stunkard, M. E., Jensen, R. A., & Detwiler, F. R. J. (1996). Effects of exam stress on mood, cortisol, and immune functioning. *Personality and Individual Differences, 21*(2), 235–246.

Gilbert, S. (1998, June 30). Optimism's bright side: A healthy, longer life. *New York Times,* p. F7.

Gilbertson, M. W., Shenton, M. E., Ciszewski, A., Kasai, K., Lasko, N. B., Orr, S. P., et al. (2002). Smaller hippocampal volume predicts pathologic vulnerability to psychological trauma. *Nature Neuroscience, 5,* 1242–1247.

Gildea, K. M., Schneider, T. R., & Shebilske, W. I. (2007). Appraisals and training performance on a complex laboratory task. *Human Factors, 49,* 745–758.

Gill, M. G. (2008). *How Starbucks saved my life: A son of privilege learns to live like everyone else.* New York: Gotham Books.

Gillam, B. (1980). Geometrical illusions. *Scientific American, 242,* 102–111.

Gillespie, C. F., & Nemeroff, C. B. (2007). Corticotropin-releasing factor and the psychobiology of early-life stress. *Current Directions in Psychological Science, 16,* 85–89.

Gilligan, C. F. (1982). *In a different voice.* Cambridge, MA: Harvard University Press.

Gillund, G., & Shiffrin, R. M. (1984). A retrieval model for both recognition and recall. *Psychological Review, 91,* 1–67.

Ginzberg, E. (1972). Toward a theory of occupational choice: A restatement. *Vocational Guidance Quarterly, 20,* 169–176.

Ginzberg, E. (1984). Career development. In D. Brown, L. Brooks, & Associates (Eds.), *Career choice and development.* San Francisco: Jossey-Bass.

Girandola, F. (2002). Sequential requests and organ donation. *Journal of Social Psychology, 142,* 171–178.

Gitelson, I. B., & McDermott, D. (2006). Parents and their young adult children: Transitions to adulthood. *Child Welfare League of America, 85,* 853–866.

Givens, B. (1995). Low doses of ethanol impair spatial working memory and reduce hippocampal theta activity. *Alcoholism: Clinical and Experimental Research, 19*(3), 763–767.

Gladwell, M. (2004, September 20). Annals of psychology: Personality plus. *New Yorker,* pp. 42–48.

Glanzer, M., & Cunitz, A. R. (1966). Two storage mechanisms in free recall. *Journal of Verbal Learning and Verbal Behavior, 5,* 351–360.

Glenberg, A. M., Smith, S. M., & Green, C. (1977). Type I rehearsal: Maintenance and more. *Journal of Verbal Learning and Verbal Behavior, 16,* 339–352.

Gliga, T., Volein, A., & Csibra, G. (2010). Verbal labels modulate perceptual object processing in 1-year-old infants. *Journal of Cognitive Neuroscience,* doi:10.1162/jocn.2010.21427.

Gluck, M. E., & Geliebter, A. (2002). Racial/ethnic differences in body image and eating behaviors. *Eating Behaviors, 3,* 143–151.

Glynn, M., & Rhodes, P. (2005). *Estimated HIV prevalence in the United States at the end of 2003.* National HIV Prevention Conference, Atlanta, GA. Abstract T1-Bll01.

Goddard, A. W., Ball, S. G., Martinez, J., Robinson, M. J., Yang, C. R., Russell, J. M., et al. (2010). Current perspectives of the roles of the central norepinephrine system in anxiety and depression. *Depression and Anxiety, 27,* 339–350.

Godden, D. R., & Baddeley, A. D. (1975). Context dependent memory in two natural environments: On land and underwater. *British Journal of Psychology, 66,* 325–332.

Goeders, N. E. (2004). Stress, motivation, and drug addiction. *Current Directions in Psychological Science, 13,* 33–35.

Goff, D. C., & Coyle, J. T. (2001). The emerging role of glutamate in the pathophysiology and treatment of schizophrenia. *American Journal of Psychiatry, 158,* 1367–1377.

Goh, J. O., & Park, D. C. (2009). Culture sculpts the perceptual brain. *Progress in Brain Research, 178,* 95–111.

Gold, M. S. (1994). The epidemiology, attitudes, and pharmacology of LSD use in the 1990's. *Psychiatric Annals, 24*(3), 124–126.

Goldberg, J. F. (2007). What psychotherapists should know about pharmacotherapies for bipolar disorder. *Journal of Clinical Psychology, 63,* 475–490.

Goldberg, P. D., Peterson, B. D., Rosen, K. H., & Sara, M. L. (2008). Cybersex: The impact of a contemporary problem on the practices of marriage and family therapists. *Journal of Marital and Family Therapy, 34,* 469–480.

Goldstein, D. G., Johnson, E. J., & Sharpe, W. F. (2008). Choosing outcomes versus choosing products: Consumer-focused retirement investment advice. *Journal of Consumer Research, 35,* 440–456.

Goldstein, I. (1998). Cited in Kolata, G. (1998, April 4). Impotence pill: Would it also help women? *New York Times,* pp. A1, A6.

Goldstein, I., Lue, T. E., Padmap, H. H., Rosen, C. Steers, W. D., & Wicker, P. A. (1998). Oral sildenafil in the treatment of erectile dysfunction: Sildenafil study group. *New England Journal of Medicine, 338,* 1394–1404.

Goldstein, J. M., & Lewine, R. R. J. (2000). Overview of sex differences in schizophrenia: Where have we been and where do we go from here? In D. J. Castle, J. McGrath, & J. Kulkarni (Eds.), *Women and schizophrenia* (pp. 111–141). Cambridge, UK: Cambridge University Press.

Goldstein, J. M., Seidman, L. J., Buka, S. L., Horton, N. J., Donatelli, J. L., Rieder, R. O., et al. (2000). Impact of genetic vulnerability and hypoxia on overall intelligence by age 7 in offspring at high risk for schizophrenia compared with affective psychoses. *Schizophrenia Bulletin, 26,* 323–334.

Goleman, D. (1982, March). Staying up: The rebellion against sleep's gentle tyranny. *Psychology Today,* pp. 24–35.

Goleman, D. (1995). *Emotional intelligence.* New York: Bantam.

Goleman, D. (1998). *Working with emotional intelligence.* New York: Bantam Books.

Goleman, D., Boyatzis, R. E., & McKee, A. (2002). *Primal leadership: Realizing the power of emotional intelligence.* Boston: Harvard Business School Press.

Gonzalez, H. M., Vega, W. A., Williams, D. R., Tarraf, W., West, B. T., & Neighbors, H. W. (2010). Depression care in the United States: Too little for too few. *Archives of General Psychiatry, 67,* 37–46.

Good, J. J., Woodzicka, J. A., & Wingfield, L. C. (2010). The effects of gender stereotypic and counter-stereotypic textbook images on science performance. *Journal of Social Psychology, 150,* 132–147.

Goodnick, P. J. (2000). The use of nimodipine in the treatment of mood disorders. *Bipolar Disorders, 2,* 165–173.

Goodwin, F. K., & Goldstein, M. A. (2003). Optimizing lithium treatment in bipolar disorder: A review of the literature and clinical recommendations. *Journal of Psychiatric Practice, 9,* 333–343.

Gorchoff, S. M., John, O. P., & Helson, R. (2008). Contextualizing change in marital satisfaction during middle age. *Psychological Science, 19,* 1194–1200.

Gordon, E. F. (2000). *Mockingbird years: A life in and out of therapy.* New York: Basic Books.

Gordon, S. (2008, June 15). Beware the "Blackberry thumb." *U.S. News & World Report.* Retrieved May 3, 2010, from http://health.usnews.com

Gorman, J. M. (2006). Gender differences in depression and response to psychotropic medication. *Gender Medicine, 3,* 93–109.

Gorsky, R. D., Schwartz, E., & Dennis, D. (1988). The mortality, morbidity, and economic costs of alcohol abuse: New Hampshire. *Preventative Medicine, 17,* 736–745.

Gosling, S. D., & Johnson, A. J. (2010). *Advanced Methods for Conducting Online Behavioral Research. Advanced methods for conducting online behavioral research.* Washington, D.C.: APA Books.

Gotlib, I. H., & Hamilton, J. P. (2008). Neuroimaging and depression: Current status and unresolved issues. *Current Directions in Psychological Science, 17,* 159–163.

Gottfredson, L. S. (1996). Gottfredson's theory of circumscription and compromise. In D. Brown, L. Brooks, & Associates (Eds.), *Career choice and development* (3rd ed., pp. 179–232). San Francisco: Jossey-Bass.

Gottlieb, G., Wahlsten, D., & Lickliter, R. (1998). The significance of biology for human development: A developmental psychobiological systems view. In W. Damon & R. M. Lerner (Eds.), *Handbook of child psychology* (Vol. 1, pp. 233–273). New York: Wiley.

Gottman, J. (1999a). *The marriage clinic.* New York: Norton.

Gottman, J. (1999b). *The seven principles of making marriage work.* New York: Crown.

Gould, R. A., Otto, M. W., Pollack, M. H., & Yap, L. (1997). Cognitive behavioral and pharmacological treatment of generalized anxiety disorder: A preliminary meta-analysis. *Behavior Therapy, 28,* 285–305.

Gouras, P. (1991). Precortical physiology of colour vision. In P. Gouras (Ed.), *The perception of colour* (pp. 163–178). Boca Raton, FL: CRC Press.

Government Printing Office. (2006). *USA Patriot Improvement and Reauthorization Act of 2005* (Public Law 109–177).

Graber, B. (1993). Medical aspects of sexual arousal disorders. In W. O'Donohue & J. H. Greer (Eds.), *Handbook of sexual dysfunctions: Assessment and treatment* (pp. 103–156). Boston: Allyn & Bacon.

Graber, J. A., Brooks-Gunn, J., & Warren, M. P. (2006). Pubertal effects on adjustment in girls: Moving from demonstrating effects to identifying pathways. *Journal of Youth and Adolescence, 35,* 413–423.

Graber, J. A., Seeley, J. R., Brooks-Gunn, J., & Lewinsohn, P. M. (2004). Is pubertal timing associated with psychopathology in young adulthood? *Journal of the American Academy of Child and Adolescent Psychiatry, 43,* 718–726.

Gracia, C. R., Freeman, E. W., Sammel, M. D., Lin, H., & Mogul, M. (2007). Hormones and sexuality during transition to menopause. *Obstetrics and Gynecology, 109,* 831–840.

Grados, M. A., Walkup, J., & Walford, S. (2003). Genetics of obsessive-compulsive disorders: New findings and challenges. *Brain Development, 25,* S55–S61.

Grady, C. L. (2000). Functional brain imaging and age-related changes in cognition. *Biological Psychology, 54,* 259–281.

Graf, P., & Schacter, D. L. (1985). Implicit and explicit memory for new associations in normal and amnesiac subjects. *Journal of Experimental Psychology: Learning, Memory, and Cognition, 11,* 501–518.

Graffin, N. F., Ray, W. J., & Lundy, R. (1995). EEG concomitants of hypnosis and hypnotic susceptibility. *Journal of Abnormal Psychology, 104*(1), 123–131.

Graham, K. S., Simons, J. S., Pratt, K. H., Patterson, K., & Hodges, J. R. (2000). Insights from semantic dementia on the relationship between episodic and semantic memory. *Neuropsychologia, 38,* 313–324.

Graham, R., Devinsky, O., & LaBar, K. S. (2007). Quantifying deficits in the perception of fear and anger in morphed facial expressions after bilateral amygdale damage. *Neuropsychologia, 45,* 42–54.

Graham, T. (2010). 10 teens found guilty of rioting in Feb. 16 "flash mob." *Philadelphia Inquirer.* Retrieved May 15, 2010, from http://www.philly.com/inquirer/local/pa/20100323_10_teens_found_guilty_of_rioting_in_Feb__16__flash_mob_.html#axzz0o2S8Rj00.

Grant, B. F., Hasin, D. S., Stinson, F. S., Dawson, D. A., Chou, S. P., Ruan, W. J., et al. (2004). Prevalence, correlates, and disability of personality disorders in the United States: Results from the National Epidemiological Survey on alcohol and related conditions. *Journal of Clinical Psychiatry, 65,* 948–958.

Grant, J. E., & Phillips, K. A. (2004). Is anorexia nervosa a subtype of body dysmorphic disorder? Probably not, but read on. . . . *Harvard Review of Psychiatry, 12,* 123–126.

Green, C. S., & Bavelier, D. (2007). Action-video-game experience alters the spatial resolution of vision. *Psychological Science, 18,* 88–94.

Green, J. G., McLaughlin, K. A., Berglund, P. A., Gruber, M. J., Sampson, N. A., Zaslavsky, A. M. et al. (2010). Childhood adversities and adult psychiatric disorders in the National Comorbidity Survey Replication I: Associations with first onset of DSM-IV disorders. *Archives of General Psychiatry, 67,* 113–123.

Green, J. P., & Lynn, S. J. (2000). Hypnosis and suggestion-based approaches to smoking cessation: An examination of the evidence. *International Journal of Clinical and Experimental Hypnosis, 48,* 195–224.

Green, S. K., Buchanan, D. R., & Heuer, S. K. (1984). Winners, losers, and choosers: A field investigation of dating initiation. *Personality and Social Psychology Bulletin, 10,* 502–511.

Greenberg, B. D., Li, Q., Lucas, F. R., Hu, S., Sirota, L. A., Benjamin, J., et al. (2000). Association between the serotonin transporter promoter polymorphism and personality traits in a primarily female population sample. *American Journal of Medical Genetics, 96,* 202–216.

Greenberg, L. S., & Rice, L. N. (1997). Humanistic approaches to psychotherapy. In P. L. Wachtel & S. B. Messer (Eds.), *Theories of psychotherapy: Origins and evolution* (pp. 97–129). Washington DC: American Psychological Association.

Greenberg, L. S., Elliot, R., & Lietaer, G. (1994). Research on humanistic and experiential psychotherapies. In A. Bergin & S. Garfield (Eds.), *Handbook of psychotherapy and behavior change* (4th ed., pp. 509–542). New York: Wiley.

Greenblatt, D., Harmatz, J., & Shader, R. I. (1993). Plasma alprazolam concentrations: Relation to efficacy and side effects in the treatment of panic disorder. *Archives of General Psychiatry, 50,* 715–732.

Greenfield, P. (1997). You can't take it with you: Why ability assessments don't cross cultures. *American Psychologist, 52,* 1115–1124.

Greenhaus, J. H. (2003). Career dynamics. In W. C. Borman, D. R. Ilgen, & R. J. Klimoski (Eds.), *Handbook of psychology: Industrial and organizational psychology, 12,* 519–540, New York: Wiley

Greenough, W. T., Wallace, C. S., Alcantara, A. A., Anderson, B. J., Hawrylak, N., Sirevaag, A. M., et al. (1993). Experience affects the structure of neurons, glia, and blood vessels. In N. J. Anastasiow & S. Harel (Eds.), *At-risk infants: Interventions, family, and research* (pp. 175–185). Baltimore: Paul H. Brookes.

Greenvale, J. K., Jeen-Su, L., & Mukesh, B. (1998). The role of affect in attitude formation: A classical conditioning approach. *Academy of Marketing Science Journal, 26,* 143–152.

Greenwald, A. G., & Draine, S. C. (1997). Do subliminal stimuli enter the mind unnoticed? Tests with a new method. In J. D. Cohen & J. W. Schooler (Eds.), *Scientific approaches to consciousness: Carnegie Mellon symposia on cognition* (pp. 83–108). Mahwah, NJ: Erlbaum.

Greitemeyer, T., & Osswald, S. (2010). Effects of proso-cial video games on prosocial behavior. *Journal of Personality and Social Psychology, 98,* 211–221.

Grekin, E. R., & Sher, K. J. (2006). Alcohol dependence symptoms among college freshmen: Prevalence, stability, and person–environment interactions. *Experimental and Clinical Psychopharmacology, 14,* 329–338.

Grieger, T. A., Fullerton, C. S., & Ursano, R. J. (2004). Posttraumatic stress disorder, depression, and perceived safety 13 months after September 11th. *Psychiatric Services, 55,* 1061–1063.

Griest, S. E., Folmer, R. L., & Hal Martin, W. (2007). Effectiveness of "Dangerous decibels," a school-based hearing loss prevention program. *American Journal of Audiology, 16,* S165–S181.

Griffiths, K. M., Calear, A. L., & Banfield, M. (2009). Systematic review on Internet Support Groups (ISGs) and depression: Do ISGs reduce depressive symptoms? *Journal of Medical Internet Research, 11,* e40.

Griffiths, M. D., Davies, M. N. O., & Chappell, D. (2003). Breaking the stereotype: The case of the online gaming. *Cyberpsychology and Behavior, 6,* 81–91.

Griffiths, M. D., Davies, M. N. O., & Chappell, D. (2004). Demographic factors and playing variables in online computer gaming. *Cyberpsychology and Behavior, 7,* 479–487.

Grinspoon, L., & Bakalar, J. B. (1995). Marijuana as medicine: A plea for reconsideration. *Journal of the American Medical Association, 273*(23), 1875–1876.

Grinspoon, L., Bakalar, J. B., Zimmer, L., & Morgan, J. P. (1997). Marijuana addiction. *Science, 277,* 751–752.

Grivetti, L. E. (2000). VI.13/ Food prejudices and taboos. In K. E. Kipple & K. C. Ornelas (Series Eds.), *The Cambridge world history of food* (Vol. 1, pp. 1495–1513). Cambridge, UK: Cambridge University Press.

Grossman, M. I., & Stein, L. F. (1948). Vagotomy and the hunger-producing action of insulin in man. *Journal of Applied Physiology, 1,* 263–269.

Grossman, P., Niemann, L., Schmidt, S., & Walach, H.(2004). Mindfulness-based stress reduction and health benefits. A meta-analysis. *Journal of Psychosomatic Research, 57,* 35–43.

Grossman, R. P., & Till, B. D. (1998). The persistence of classically conditioned brand attitudes. *Journal of Advertising, 27,* 23–31.

Grover, S. (2005). Reification of psychiatric diagnoses as defamatory: Implications for ethical clinical practice. *Ethical Human Psychology and Psychiatry, 7,* 77–86.

Gruen, R. J. (1993). Stress and depression: Toward the development of integrative models. In L. Goldberger & S. Breznitz (Eds.), *Handbook of stress: Theoretical and clinical aspects* (pp. 550–569). New York: Free Press.

Gugger, J. J., & Wagner, M. L. (2007). Rapid eye movement sleep behavior disorder. *Annals of Pharmacotherapy, 41,* 1833–1841.

Guilford, J. P. (1967). *The nature of human intelligence.* New York: McGraw-Hill.

Guilleminault, C., Palombini, L., Pelayo, R., & Chervin, R.D. (2003). Sleepwalking and sleep terrors in prepubertal children: What triggers them? *Pediatrics, 111,* e17–25.

Guisinger, S. (2003). Adapted to flee famine: Adding an evolutionary perspective on anorexia nervosa. *Psychological Review, 110,* 745–761.

Gurman, A. S., & Jacobson, N. S. (Eds.). (2002). *Clinical handbook of couple therapy* (3rd ed.). New York: Guilford Press.

Gustavson, C. R., & Garcia, J. (1974, August). Pulling a gag on the wily coyote. *Psychology Today,* pp. 68–72.

Gutchess, A. H., Kensinger, E. A., Yoon, C., & Schacter, D. L. (2007). Ageing and the self-reference effect in memory. *Memory, 15,* 822–837.

Guthrie, J. P., Ash, R. A., & Bendapudi, V. (1995). Additional validity evidence for a measure of morningness. *Journal of Applied Psychology, 80,* 186–190.

Guze, B. H., & Gitlin, M. (1994). New antidepressants and the treatment of depression. *Journal of Family Practice, 38,* 49–57.

Ha, T., Overbeek, G., & Engels, R. C. (2010). Effects of attractiveness and social status on dating desire in heterosexual adolescents: An experimental study. *Archives of Sexual Behavior, 39,* 1063–1071.

Haack, L. J., Dykman, B. M., Metalsky, G. I., & Abramson, L. Y. (1996). Use of current situational information and causal inference: Do dysphoric individuals make "unwarranted" causal inferences? *Cognitive Therapy and Research, 20,* 309–332.

Haas, L. (1999). Families and work. In M. B. Sussman, S. K. Steinmetz & G. W. Peterson (Eds.), *Handbook of marriage and the family* (pp. 571–612). New York: Plenum Press.

Haber, D. (1994). *Health promotion and aging.* New York: Springer.

Hackett, R. D. (1989). Work attitudes and employee absenteeism: a synthesis of the literature. *Journal of Occupational Psychology, 62*(3), 235–248.

Hackman, J. R., & Oldham, G. R. (1976). Motivation through the design of work: A test of a theory. *Organizational Behavior and Human Performance, 16*(2), 250–279.

Haefner, R. (2009). More employers screening candidates via social networking sites. Careerbuilder.com, June.

Haidt, J. (2008). Morality. *Perspectives on Psychological Science, 1,* 65–72.

Haie, L., & Do, D. P. (2007). Racial differences in self-reports of sleep duration in a population-based study. *Sleep, 30,* 1096–1103.

Haith, M. M., & Benson, J. B. (1998). Infant cognition. In W. Damon & R. M. Lerner (Eds.), *Handbook of child psychology* (Vol. 1, pp. 235–246). New York: Wiley.

Hakuta, K. (1999). The debate on bilingual education. *Developmental and Behavioral Pediatrics, 20,* 36–37.

Hakuta, K., Bailystok, E., & Wiley, E. (2003). Critical evidence: A test of the critical-period hypothesis for second-language acquisitions. *Psychological Science, 14,* 31–38.

Hall, D. R., & Zhao, J. Z. (1995). Cohabitation and divorce in Canada: Testing the selectivity hypothesis. *Journal of Marriage and the Family, 57,* 421–427.

Hall, D. T., & Nougaim, K. E. (1968). An examination of Maslow's need hierarchy in an organizational setting. *Organizational Behavior and Human Performance, 3,* 12–35.

Halpern, D. (1996). Public policy implications of sex differences in cognitive abilities. *Psychology, Public Policy and Law, 2*(3/4), 564.

Halpern, D. (2004). A cognitive-process taxonomy for sex differences in cognitive abilities. *Current Directions in Psychological Science, 13,* 135–139.

Halpern, D., & LeMay, M. L. (2000). The smarter sex: A critical review of sex-differences in intelligence. *Educational Psychology Review, 12,* 229–246.

Halpern, D. F., Benbow, C. P., Geary, D. C., Gur, R. C., Hyde, J. S., & Gernsbacher, M. A. (2007). The science of sex differences in science and mathematics. *Psychological Science in the Public Interest, 8,* 1–51.

Halpern, J. H., & Pope, H. G., Jr. (2003). Hallucinogen persisting perception disorder: What do we know after 50 years? *Drug and Alcohol Dependence, 69,* 109–119.

Hamani, C., Mayberg, H., Snyder, B., Giacobbe, P., Kennedy, S., & Lozano, A. M. (2009). Deep brain stimulation of the subcallosal cingulated gyrus for depression: Anatomical location of active contacts in clinical responders and a suggested guideline for targeting. *Journal of Neurosurgery, 111,* 1209–1215.

Hamann, S. (2005). Sex differences in the responses of the human amygdala. *Neuroscientist, 11,* 288–293.

Hamel, R., & Elshout, J. (2000). On the development of knowledge during problem solving. *Journal of Cognitive Psychology, 12,* 289–322.

Hamer, D. (2002). Genetics. Rethinking behavior genetics. *Science, 298,* 71–72.

Hamilton, C. E. (2000). Continuity and discontinuity of attachment from infancy through adolescence. *Child Development, 71,* 690–694.

Hammen, C. (2005). Stress and depression. *Annual Review of Clinical Psychology, 1,* 293–319.

Hammen, C. (2009). Adolescent depression: Stressful interpersonal contexts and risk for recurrence. *Current Directions in Psychological Science, 18,* 200–204.

Hampson, S. E., & Goldberg, L. R. (2006). A first large cohort study of personality trait stability over the 40 years between elementary school and midlife. *Journal of Personality and Social Psychology, 91,* 763–779.

Hanisch, K. A. (1992). The Job Descriptive Index revisited: Questions about the question mark. *Journal of Applied Psychology, 77*(3), 377–382.

Hanisch, K. A. (1995). Behavioral families and multiple causes: Matching the complexity of responses to the complexity of antecedents. *Current Directions in Psychological Science, 4*(5), 156–162.

Hanisch, K. A., & Hulin, C. L. (1990). Job attitudes and organizational withdrawal: An examination of retirement and other voluntary withdrawal behaviors. *Journal of Vocational Behavior, 37*(1), 60–78.

Hanisch, K. A., & Hulin, C. L. (1991). General attitudes and organizational withdrawal: An evaluation of a causal model. *Journal of Vocational Behavior, 39,* 110–128

Hanisch, K. A., Hulin, C. L., & Roznowski, M. A. (1998). The importance of individuals' repertoires of behaviors: The scientific appropriateness of studying multiple behaviors and general attitudes. *Journal of Organizational Behavior, 19,* 463–480.

Hanna, G. H. (2000). Clinical and family-genetic studies of childhood obsessive-compulsive disorder. In W. K. Goodman, M. V. Rudofer, & J. D. Maser (Eds.),

Obsessive-compulsive disorder: Contemporary issues in treatment (pp. 87–103). Mahwah, NJ: Lawrence Erlbaum Associates.
Hansen, T., Olkkonen, M., Walter, S., & Gegenfurtner, K. R. (2006). Memory modulates color appearance. *Nature Neuroscience, 9,* 1367–1368.
Hanson, G., & Venturelli, P. J. (1998). *Drugs and society* (5th ed.). Boston: Jones and Bartlett.
Hansson, R. O., DeKoekkoek, P. D., Neece, W. M., & Patterson, D. W. (1997). Successful aging at work: Annual review, 1992–1996: The older worker and transitions to retirement. *Journal of Vocational Behavior, 51,* 202–233.
Hardell, L., & Carlberg, M. (2009). Mobile phones, cordless phones and the risk for brain tumours. *International Journal of Oncology, 35,* 5–17.
Hardell, L., Carlberg, M., Söderqvist, F., Mild, K. H., & Morgan, L. L. (2007). Long-term use of cellular phones and brain tumours: increased Increased risk associated with use for > or = 10 years. *Occupational Environmental Medicine, 64,* 626–632.
Hargis, M. (2008). Social networking sites dos and don'ts. CNN.com. November 5. http://www.cnn.com/2008/LIVING/worklife/11/05/cb.social.networking/index.html
Harkins, S. G. (1987). Social loafing and social facilitation. *Journal of Experimental Social Psychology, 23,* 1–18.
Harlow, H. F., & Zimmerman, R. (1959). Affectional responses in the infant monkey. *Science, 130,* 421–432.
Harold, G. T., Fincham, F. D., Osborne, L. N., & Conger, R. D. (1997). Mom and Dad are at it again: Adolescent perceptions of marital conflict and adolescent psychological distress. *Developmental Psychology, 33,* 335–350.
Harris, C. R. (2003). A review of sex differences in sexual jealousy, including self-report data, psychophysiological responses, interpersonal violence, and morbid jealousy. *Personality and Social Psychology Review, 7,* 102–128.
Harris, C. R., & Christenfeld, N. (1996). Gender, jealousy, and reason. *Psychological Science, 7,* 364–366.
Harris, J. D. (1943). Habituatory response decrement in the intact organism. *Psychological Bulletin, 40,* 385–422.
Harris, J. R. (2000). Context-specific learning, personality, and birth order. *Current Directions in Psychological Science, 9,* 174–177.
Harris, S. R., Kemmerling, R. L., & North, M. M. (2002). Brief virtual reality therapy for public speaking. *Cyberpsychology and Behavior, 5,* 543–550.
Harrow, M., Sands, J. R., Silverstein, M. L., & Goldberg, J. F. (1997). Course and outcome for schizophrenia versus other psychotic patients: A longitudinal study. *Schizophrenia Bulletin, 23,* 287–303.
Hartmann, E. (1981, April). The strangest sleep disorder. *Psychology Today,* pp. 14, 16, 18.
Hartmann, U. (2009). Sigmund Freud and his impact on our understanding of male sexual dysfunction. *Journal of Sexual Medicine, 6,* 2332–2339.
Hartung, C. M., & Widiger, T. A. (1998). Gender differences in the diagnosis of mental disorders: Conclusions and controversies of the DSM-IV. *Psychological Bulletin, 123,* 260–278.
Haruki, Y. (2000). Human reinforcement: Conception of alien reinforcement. *Japanese Psychological Review, 43,* 501–518.
Haruki, Y., Shigehisa, T., Nedate, K., Wajima, M., & Ogawa, R. (1984). Effects of alien-reinforcement and its combined type on learning behavior and efficacy in relation to personality. *International Journal of Psychology, 19,* 527–545.
Harwood, H. (2000). *Updating estimates of the economic costs of alcohol abuse in the United States: Estimates, update methods, and data.* Report prepared by The Lewin Group for the National Institute on Alcohol Abuse and Alcoholism.
Hasin, D., Hatzenbuehler, M. L., Keyes, K., & Ogburn, E. (2006). Substance use disorders: Diagnostic and Statistical Manual of Mental Disorders, 4th edition (DSM-IV) and International Classification of Diseases, 10th edition (ICD-10). *Addiction, 101*(Suppl. 1), 59–75.
Hasin, D. S., & Grant, B. F. (2004). The co-occurrence of DSM-IV alcohol abuse in DSM-IV alcohol dependence: Results of the national epidemiological survey on alcohol and related conditions on heterogeneity that differ by population subgroup. *Archives of General Psychiatry, 61,* 891–896.
Hassett, J. M., Siebert, E. R., & Wallen, K. (2008). Sex differences in rhesus monkey toy preferences parallel those of children. *Hormones and Behavior, 54,* 359–364.
Hastings, E. C., Karas, T. L., Winsler, A., Way, E., Madigan, A., & Tyler, S. (2009). Young children's video/computer game use: relations with school performance and behavior. *Issues in Mental Health Nursing, 30,* 638–649.
Hatcher, R., Trussell, J., Stewart, F., Stewart, G., Kowal, D., Guest, E., et al. (1994). *Contraceptive technology* (16th ed.). New York: Irvington.
Haus, E., & Smolensky, M. (2006). Biological clocks and shift work: Circadian dysregulation and potential long-term effects. *Cancer Causes and Control, 17,* 489–500.
Havermans, R. C., & Jansen, A. (2007). Increasing children's liking of vegetables through flavour–flavour learning. *Appetite, 48,* 259–262.
Hawkley, L. C., & Cacioppo, J. T. (2007). Aging and loneliness: Downhill quickly? *Current Directions in Psychological Science, 16,* 187–191.
Hawks, S. R., Hull, M. L., Thalman, R. L., & Richins, P. M. (1995). Review of spiritual health: Definition, role, and intervention strategies in health promotion. *American Journal of Health Promotion, 9,* 371–378.
Hayden, E. P., Dougherty, L. R., Maloney, B., Emily Durbin, C., Olino, T. M., Nurnberger, J. I., et al. (2007). Temperamental fearfulness in childhood and the serotonin transporter promoter region polymorphism: A multimethod association study. *Psychiatric Genetics, 17,* 135–142.
Hayden, E. P., & Nurnberger, J. I., Jr. (2006). Molecular genetics of bipolar disorder. *Genes, Brain and Behavior, 5,* 85–95.
Hayes, E. R., & Plowfield, L. A. (2007). Smoking too young: Students' decisions about tobacco use. *American Journal of Maternal Child Nursing, 32,* 112–116.
Hayes, J. R. (1989). *The complete problem solver* (2nd ed.). Hillsdale, NJ: Erlbaum.
Hayes, R. D., Bennett, C. M., Fairley, C. K., & Dennerstein, L. (2006). What can prevalence studies tell us about female sexual difficulty and dysfunction? *Journal of Sexual Medicine, 3,* 589–595.
Hayne, H., & Rovee-Collier, C. (1995). The organization of reactivated memory in infancy. *Child Development, 66*(3), 893–906.
Heatherton, T. F., & Sargent, J. D. (2009). Does watching smoking in movies promote teenage smoking? *Current Directions in Psychological Science, 18,* 63–67.
Hebb, D. O. (1948). *Organization of behavior.* New York: Wiley.
Hebb, D. O. (1955). Drives and the C.N.S. (conceptual nervous system). *Psychological Review, 62,* 243–255.
Hebert, M., Tourigny, M., Cyr, M., McDuff, P., & Joly, J. (2009). Prevalence of childhood sexual abuse and timing of disclosure in a representative sample of adults from Quebec. *Canadian Journal of Psychiatry, 54,* 631–636.
Hedden, T., & Park, D. C. (2003). Contributions of source and inhibitory mechanisms to age-related retroactive interference in verbal working memory. *Journal of Experimental Psychology: General, 132,* 93–122.
Hedden, T., & Yoon, C. (2006). Individual differences in executive processing predict susceptibility to interference in verbal working memory. *Neuropsychology, 20,* 511–528.
Hedge, L. V., & Nowell, A. (1995). Sex differences in central tendency variability and numbers of high scoring individuals. *Science, 269,* 41–45.
Heidelbaugh, J. J. (2010). Management of erectile dysfunction. *American Family Physician, 81,* 305–312.
Heider, F. (1946). Attitudes and cognitive organization. *Journal of Psychology, 21,* 107–112.
Heider, F. (1958). *The psychology of interpersonal relations.* New York: Wiley.
Heim, C., Plotsky, P. M., & Nemeroff, C. B. (2004). Importance of studying the contributions of early adverse experience to neurobiological findings in depression. *Neuropsychopharmacology, 29,* 641–648.
Heine, S. J. (2008). *Cultural Psychology.* New York: Norton.
Heine, S. J., Foster, J. B., & Spina, R. (2009). Do birds of a feather universally flock together? Cultural variation in the similarity-attraction effect. *Asian Journal of Social Psychology, 12,* 247–258.
Heiser, P., Dickhaus, B. Schreiber, W., Clement, H. W., Hasse, C., Hennig, J., et al. (2000). White blood cells and cortisol after sleep deprivation and recovery sleep in humans. *European Archives of Psychiatry and Clinical Neuroscience, 250,* 16–23.
Hejmadi, A., Davidson, R. J., & Rozin, P. (2000). Exploring Hindu Indian emotion expressions. *Psychological Science, 11,* 183–187.
Helmers, K. H., Krantz, D. S., Merz, C. N. B., Klein, J., Kop, W. J., Gottdiener, J. S., et al. (1995). Defensive hostility: Relationship to multiple markers of cardiac ischemia in patients with coronary disease. *Health Psychology, 14,* 202–209.
Helmholtz, H. L. F. von. (1930). *The sensations of tone* (A. J. Ellis, Trans.). New York: Longmans, Green. (Original work published 1863)
Helms, J. E. (2006). Fairness is not validity or cultural bias in racial-group assessment: A quantitative perspective. *American Psychologist, 61,* 845–859.
Helmuth, L. (2001). From the mouths (and hands) of babes. *Science, 293,* 1758–1759.
Helwig, C. C. (1997). Making moral cognition respectable (again): A retrospective review of Lawrence Kohlberg. *Contemporary Psychology, 42,* 191–195.
Helzer, J. E., & Canino, G. J. (Eds.). (1992). *Alcoholism in North America, Europe, and Asia.* New York: Oxford University Press.
Hendrick, C., & Hendrick, S. S. (1983). *Liking, loving, and relating.* Pacific Grove, CA: Brooks/Cole.
Hennessy, M. B., Schiml-Webb, P. A., & Deak, T. (2009). Separation, sickness, and depression: A new perspective on an old animal model. *Current Directions in Psychological Science, 18,* 227–231.
Henry, B., & Moffitt, T. E. (1997). Neuropsychological and neuroimaging studies of juvenile delinquency and adult criminal behavior. In D. M. Stoff, J. Breiling, & J. D. Maser (Eds.), *Handbook of antisocial personality disorder* (pp. 280–288). New York: Wiley.
Henry, W. P., Strupp, H. H., Schacht, T. E., & Gaston, L. (1994). Psychodynamic approaches. In A. E. Bergin & S. L. Garfield (Eds.), *Handbook of psychotherapy and behavior change* (4th ed., pp. 143–189). New York: Wiley.
Hensley, L. G. (2002). Treatment of survivors of rape: Issues and interventions. *Journal of Mental Health Counseling, 24,* 331–348.
Herd, D. (1990). Subgroup differences in drinking patterns among Black and White men: Results from a national survey. *Journal of Studies on Alcohol, 51,* 221–232.
Herd, D. (1994). The effects of parental influences and respondents' norms and attitudes on Black and White adult drinking patterns. *Journal of Substance Abuse, 6,* 137–154.
Herman, L. M., & Uyeyama, R. J. (1999). The dolphin's grammatical competency: Comments on Kako (1999). *Animal Learning and Behavior, 27,* 18–23.
Herman, L. M., Kuczaj, S. A., II, & Holder, M. D. (1993). Responses to anomalous gestural sequences by a language-trained dolphin: Evidence for processing of semantic relations and syntactical information. *Journal of Experimental Psychology: General, 122,* 184–194.
Herrera, N. C., Zajonc, R. B., Wieczorkowska, G., & Cichomski, B. (2003). Beliefs about birth rank and their reflection in reality. *Journal of Personality and Social Psychology, 85,* 142–150.
Herrnstein, R., & Murray, C. (1994). *The bell curve.* New York: Free Press.
Hershman, E., Halberthal, M., Goldsher, D., Golz, A., & Bar-Joseph, G. (2009). Life threatening medullary injury following adenoidectomy and local anesthetic infiltration of the operative bed. *Paediatric Anaesthesiology, 19,* 164–167.
Hertlein, K. M. & Ricci, R. J. (2004). A systematic research synthesis of EMDR studies: Implementation of the platinum standard. *Trauma, Violence, and Abuse, 5,* 285–300.
Hertzog, C., Kramer, A. F., Wilson, R. S., & Lindenberger, U. (2008). Enrichment effects on adult cognitive development: Can the functional capacity of older adults be preserved and enhanced? *Psychological Science in the Public Interest, 9,* 1–65.
Herz, J., Zipp, F., & Siffrin, V. (2009). Neurodegeneration in autoimmune CNS inflammation. *Experimental*

Neurology. Retrieved December 17, 2009, from http://www.sciencedirect.com

Hesse, E., & Main, M. (2006). Frightened, threatening, and dissociative parental behavior in low-risk samples: Description, discussion, and interpretations. *Development and Psychopathology, 18,* 309–343.

Heston, L. L. (1966). Psychiatric disorders in foster home reared children of schizophrenic mothers. *British Journal of Psychiatry, 112,* 819–825.

Hettema, J. M., Neale, M. C., & Kendler, K. S. (2001). A review and meta-analysis of the genetic epidemiology of anxiety disorders. *American Journal of Psychiatry, 158,* 1568–1578.

Hewlett, W. A. (2000). Benzodiazepines in the treatment of obsessive-compulsive disorder. In W. K. Goodman (Ed.), *Obsessive-compulsive disorder: Contemporary issues in treatment* (pp. 405–429). Mahwah, NJ: Erlbaum.

Hewstone, M., Rubin, M., & Willis, H. (2002). Intergroup bias (social prejudice). *Annual Review of Psychology, 53,* 575–604.

Hicks, B. M., Krueger, R. F., Iacono, W. G., McGue, M., & Patrick, C. J. (2004). Family transmission and heritability of externalizing disorders: A twin-family study. *Archives of General Psychiatry, 61,* 922–928.

Hicks, T. V., & Leitenberg, H. (2001). Sexual fantasies about one's partner versus someone else: Gender differences in incidence and frequency. *Journal of Sex Research, 38,* 43–50.

Higbee, K. L., & Clay, S. L. (1998). College students' beliefs in the ten-percent myth. *Journal of Psychology, 132,* 469–476.

Hikosaka, O., Nakamura, K., Sakai, K., & Nakamura, H. (2002). Central mechanisms of motor skill learning. *Current Opinion in Neurobiology, 12,* 217–222.

Hilgard, E. R. (1977). *Divided consciousness: Multiple controls in human thought and action.* New York: Wiley.

Hilgard, E. R. (1992). Divided consciousness and dissociation. *Consciousness and Cognition, 1,* 16–31.

Hilgard, E. R., Morgan, A. H., & MacDonald, H. (1975). Pain and dissociation in the cold pressor test: A study of "hidden reports" through automatic key-pressing and automatic talking. *Journal of Abnormal Psychology, 84,* 280–289.

Hill, C. E., & Nakayama, E. Y. (2000). Client-centered therapy: Where has it been and where is it going? A comment on Hathaway (1948). *Journal of Clinical Psychology, 56,* 861–875.

Hill, P. C., & Pargament, K. I. (2003). Advances in the conceptualization and measurement of religion and spirituality. Implications for physical and mental health research. *American Psychologist, 58,* 64–74.

Hillix, W. A. & Rumbaugh, D. M. (2004). *Animal bodies, human minds: Ape, dolphin, and parrot language skills.* New York: Kluwer/Plenum.

Hill-Soderlund, A. L., & Braungart-Rieker, J. M. (2008). Early individual differences in temperamental reactivity and regulation: Implications for effortful control in early childhood. *Infant Behavior and Development, 31,* 386–397.

Hines, D. (2007). Predictors of sexual coercion against women and men: A multilevel, multinational study of university students. *Archives of Sexual Behavior, 36,* 403–422.

Hines, M. (2004). Psychosexual development in individuals who have female pseudohermaphroditism. *Child and Adolescent Psychiatric Clinics of North America, 13,* 641–656.

Hines, M., Ahmed, S., & Hughes, I. (2003). Psychological outcomes and gender-related development in complete androgen insensitivity syndrome. *Archives of Sexual Behavior, 32,* 93–101.

Hinton, G. E. (1979). Some demonstrations of the effects of structural descriptions in mental imagery. *Cognitive Science, 3,* 231–251.

Hirai, M., & Clum, G. A. (2005). An Internet-based self-change program for traumatic event related fear, distress, and maladaptive coping. *Journal of Traumatic Stress, 18,* 631–636.

Hiroto, D. S. (1974). Locus of control and learned helplessness. *Journal of Experimental Psychology, 102,* 187–193.

Hirshfeld, J. A. (1995). The "back-to-sleep" campaign against SIDS. *American Family Physician, 51*(3), 611–612.

Hirshkowitz, M., Moore, C. A., & Minhoto, G. (1997). The basics of sleep. In M. R. Pressman & W. C. Orr (Eds.), *Understanding sleep: The evaluation and treatment of sleep disorders* (pp. 11–34). Washington, DC: American Psychological Association.

Ho, B. C., Black, D. W., & Andreasen, N. C. (2003). Schizophrenia and other psychotic disorders. In R. E. Hales & S. C. Yudofsky (Eds.), *Textbook of clinical psychiatry* (4th ed., pp. 379–438). Washington DC: American Psychiatric Publishing.

Hobbs, F. B. (with Damon, B. L.). (1996). *65+ in the United States.* Washington DC: U.S. Bureau of the Census.

Hobson, J. A., & McCarley, R. W. (1977). The brain as a dream state generator: An activation-synthesis hypothesis of the dream process. *American Journal of Psychiatry, 134,* 1335–1348.

Hobson, J. A., Pace-Schott, E., & Stickgold, R. (2000). Dreaming and the brain: Toward a cognitive neuroscience of conscious states. *Behavioral and Brain Sciences, 23,* 783–842.

Hodges, F. M. (2005). The antimasturbation crusade in antebellum American medicine. *Journal of Sexual Medicine, 2,* 722–731.

Hodson, N. A., & Linden, R. W. A. (2006). The effect of monosodium glutamate on parotid salivary flow in comparison to the response to representatives of the other four basic tastes. *Physiology and Behavior, 89,* 711–717.

Hoff-Sommers, C. (2000). The war against boys. *Atlantic Monthly, 285,* 59–74.

Hofmann, S. G., & Smits, J. A. (2008). Cognitive-behavioral therapy for adult anxiety disorders: A meta-analysis of randomized placebo-controlled trials. *Journal of Clinical Psychiatry, 69,* 621–632.

Hogben, M. (1998). Factors moderating the effect of televised aggression on viewer behavior. *Communication Research, 25,* 220–247.

Hoge, C. W., Castro, C. A., Messer, S. C., McGurk, D., Cotting, D. I., & Koffman, R. L. (2004). Combat duty in Iraq and Afghanistan, mental health problems, and barriers to care. *New England Journal of Medicine, 351,* 13–22.

Holden, C. (1980, November). Twins reunited. *Science, 80,* 55–59.

Holland, A. J., Sicotte, N., & Treasure, J. (1988). Anorexia nervosa: Evidence of a genetic basis. *Journal of Psychosomatic Research, 32,* 561–571.

Hollon, S. D. (1996). The efficacy and effectiveness of psychotherapy relative to medications. *American Psychologist, 51,* 1025–1030.

Hollon, S. D., & Beck, A. T. (1994). Cognitive and cognitive-behavioral therapies. In A. E. Bergin & S. L. Garfield (Eds.), *Handbook of psychotherapy and behavior change* (4th ed., pp. 447–492). New York: Wiley.

Hollos, M., & Richards, F. A. (1993). Gender-associated development of formal operations in Nigerian adolescents. *Ethos, 21,* 24–52.

Holloway, S. R. (1998). Exploring the neighborhood contingency of race discrimination in mortgage lending in Columbus, Ohio. *Annals of the Association of American Geographers, 88,* 252–276.

Holmans, P., Weissman, M. M., Zubenko, G. S., Scheftner, W. A., Crowe, R. R., Depaulo, J. R., et al. (2007). Genetics of recurrent early-onset major depression (GenRED): Final genome scan report. *American Journal of Psychiatry, 164,* 248–258.

Holmes, T. H., & Rahe, R. H. (1967). The Social Readjustment Rating Scale. *Journal of Psychosomatic Research, 11,* 213–218.

Holroyd, J. (2003). The science of meditation and the state of hypnosis. *American Journal of Clinical Hypnosis, 46,* 109–128.

Holt, S., Brand, J. C., Soveny, C., & Hansky, J. (1992). Relationship of satiety to postprandial glycaemic, insulin and cholecystokinin responses. *Appetite, 18,* 129–141.

Holt-Lunstad, J., Birmingham, W., & Jones, B. Q. (2008). Is there something unique about marriage? The relative impact of marital status, relationship quality, and network social support on ambulatory blood pressure and mental health. *Annals of Behavioral Medicine, 35,* 239–244.

Holtzheimer, P. E., III, & Nemeroff, C. B. (2006). Advances in the treatment of depression. *NeuroRx, 3,* 42–56.

Hong, R. Y. (2007). Worry and rumination: Differential associations with anxious and depressive symptoms and coping behavior. *Behaviour Research and Therapy, 45,* 277–290.

Hood, D. C., & Finkelstein, M. A. (1986). Sensitivity to light. In K. R. Boff, L. Kaufman, & J. P. Thomas (Eds.), *Handbook of perception and human performance* (pp. 5.1–5.66). New York: Wiley.

Hooley, J. M., & Hiller, J. B. (1998). Expressed emotion and the pathogenesis of relapse in schizophrenia. In M. F. Lenzenweger & R. H. Dworkin (Eds.), *Origins of the development of schizophrenia* (pp. 447–468). Washington, DC: American Psychological Association.

Horgan, D. D. (1995). *Achieving gender equity: Strategies for the classroom.* Boston: Allyn & Bacon.

Horgan, J. (1996, December). Why Freud isn't dead. *Scientific American,* 106–111.

Horn, J. L. (1982). The aging of human abilities. In B. B. Wolman (Ed.), *Handbook of developmental psychology* (pp. 847–870). Englewood Cliffs, NJ: Prentice-Hall.

Horn, J. L., Donaldson, G., & Engstrom, R. (1981). Apprehension, memory, and fluid intelligence decline through the "vital years" of adulthood. *Research on Aging, 3,* 33–84.

Hornbacher, M. (1998). *Wasted: A memoir of anorexia and bulimia.* New York: Harper Perennial.

Horne, J. A., & Staff, L. H. E. (1983). Exercise and sleep: Body-heating effects. *Sleep, 6,* 36–46.

Horney, K. (1937). *The neurotic personality of our time.* New York: Norton.

Horney, K. (1939). *New ways in psychoanalysis.* New York: Norton.

Hoshi, Y., Huang, J., Kohri, S., Iguchi, Y., Naya, M., Okamoto, T., et al. (2009). Recognition of Human Emotions from Cerebral Blood Flow Changes in the Frontal Region: A Study with Event-Related Near-Infrared Spectroscopy. *Journal of Neuroimaging,* doi:10.1111/j.1552–6569.2009.00454.x.

Hosking, S. G., Young, K. L., & Regan, M. A. (2009). The effects of text messaging on young drivers. *Human Factors, 51,* 582–592.

Houry, D., Feldman, K. M., & Abbott, J. (2000). Mandatory reporting laws. *Annals of Emergency Medicine, 35,* 404.

Hovland, C. I., & Weiss, W. (1951). The influence of source credibility on communication effectiveness. *Public Opinion Quarterly, 15,* 635–650.

Howard, A., Riger, S., Campbell, R., & Wasco, S. (2003). Counseling services for battered women: A comparison of outcomes for physical and sexual assault survivors. *Journal of Interpersonal Violence, 18,* 717–734.

Howe, M. L. (2000). *The rate of early memories.* Washington, DC: American Psychological Association.

Howes, O. D., & Kapur, S. (2009). The dopamine hypothesis of schizophrenia: Version III—the final common pathway. *Schizophrenia Bulletin, 35,* 549–562.

Hoyert, D. L., Heron, M. P., Murphy, S., & Kung, H. (2006). Deaths: Final data for 2003. *National Vital Statistics Report, 54,* 1–120.

Hoyland, A., Dye, L., & Lawton, C. L. (2009). A systematic review of the effect of breakfast on the cognitive performance of children and adolescents. *Nutrition Research Reviews, 22,* 220–243.

Hsiung, R. C. (2001). Suggested principles of professional ethics for the online provision of mental health services. *Medinfo, 10,* 296–300.

Hu, J., Chiang, L. Y., Koch, M., & Lewin, G. R. (2010). Evidence for a protein tether involved in somatic touch. *EMBO Journal,* doi:10.1038/emboj.2009.398.

Huang, Y. H. & Bergles, D. E. (2004). Glutamate transporters bring competition to the synapse. *Current Opinions in Neurobiology, 14,* 346–352.

Hubel, D. H. (1990, February). Interview. *Omni,* pp. 74–110.

Hubel, D. H. (1995). *Eye, brain, and vision.* New York: Scientific American Library.

Hubel, D. H., & Weisel, T. N. (1965). Receptive fields of single neurons in two nonstriate visual areas (18 and 19) of the cat. *Journal of Neurophysiology, 28,* 229–289.

Hubel, D. H., & Weisel, T. N. (1979). Brain mechanisms and vision. *Scientific American, 214,* 150–162.

Huddleston, J., & Ge, X. (2003). Boys at puberty: Psychosocial implications. In C. Hayward (Ed.), *Gender differences at puberty* (pp. 113–134). New York: Cambridge University Press.

Hudson, A. J. (2009). Consciousness: physiological Physiological dependence on rapid memory access. *Frontiers in Bioscience, 14,* 2779–2800.

Huebner, D. M., & Davis, M. C. (2007). Perceived antigay discrimination and physical health outcomes. *Health Psychology, 26,* 627–634.

Huesmann, L. R. (Ed.). (1994). *Aggressive behavior: Current perspectives.* New York: Plenum Press.

Huff, N. C., Hernandez, J. A., Blanding, N. Q., & LaBar, K. S. (2009). Delayed extinction attenuates conditioned fear renewal and spontaneous recovery in humans. *Behavioral Neuroscience, 123,* 834–843.

Huff, W., Lenartz, D., Schormann, M., Lee, S. H., Kuhn, J., Koulousakis, A., et al. (2010). Unilateral deep brain stimulation of the nucleus accumbens in patients with treatment-resistant obsessive-compulsive disorder: Outcomes after one year. *Clinical Neurology and Neurosurgery, 112,* 137–143.

Huffcutt, A. I., & Arthur, W. Jr. (1994). Hunter and Hunter (1984) revisited: Interview validity for entry-level jobs. *Journal of Applied Psychology, 79,* 184–190.

Huffziger, S., Reinhard, I., & Kuehner, C. (2009). A longitudinal study of rumination and distraction in formerly depressed inpatients and community controls. *Journal of Abnormal Psychology, 118,* 746–756.

Hughes, J., Smith, T. W., Kosterlitz, H. W., Fothergill, L. A., Morgan, B. A., & Morris, H. R. (1975). Identification of two related pentapeptides from the brain with potent opiate agonist activity. *Nature, 258,* 577–579.

Hughes, M. E., & Waite, L. J. (2009). Marital biography and health at mid-life. *Journal of Health and Social Behavior, 50,* 344–358.

Hughes, Z. A., Liu, F., Marquis, K., Muniz, L., Pangalos, M. N., Ring, R. H., et al. (2009). Estrogen receptor neurobiology and its potential for translation into broad spectrum therapeutics for CNS disorders. *Current Molecular Pharmacology, 2,* 215–236.

Hulbert, A. (2003). Colour vision: Primary visual cortex shows its influence. *Current Biology, 13,* R270–R272.

Hull, C. L. (1943). *Principles of behavior.* New York: Appleton-Century-Crofts.

Hummel, M. & Unterwald, E. M. (2002). D1 dopamine receptor: A putative neurochemical and behavioral link to cocaine action. *Journal of Cell Physiology, 191,* 17–27.

Humphreys, K., Winzelberg, A., & Klaw, E. (2000). Psychologists' ethical responsibilities in Internet-based groups: Issues, strategies, and a call for dialogue. *Professional Psychology, Research, and Practice, 31,* 493–496.

Hunt, E. & Agnoli, F. (1991). The Whorfian hypothesis: A cognitive psychological perspective. *Psychological Review, 98,* 377–389.

Hunt, R. R. (2002). How effective are pharmacologic agents for alcoholism? *Journal of Family Practice, 51,* 577.

Hunter, E. C., Sierra, M., & David, A. S. (2004). The epidemiology of personalization and derealisation: A systematic review. *Social Psychiatry and Psychiatric Epidemiology, 39,* 9–18.

Hurt, H., Brodsky, N. L., Roth, H., Malmud, E., & Giannetta, J. M. (2005). School performance of children with gestational cocaine exposure. *Neurotoxicology and Teratology, 27,* 203–211.

Hurvich, L. M., & Jameson, D. (2000). An opponent-process theory of color vision. In S. Yantis (Ed.), *Visual perception: Essential readings* (pp. 129–144). New York: Psychology Press. (Originally published 1957)

Hussain, Z., & Griffiths, M. D. (2009). The attitudes, feelings, and experiences of online gamers: A qualitative analysis. *Cyberpsychology and Behavior, 12,* 747–753.

Huston, A. C., & Wright, J. C. (1998). Mass media and children's development. In W. Damon (Series Ed.), *Handbook of child psychology* (Vol. 4, pp. 999–1058). New York: Wiley.

Huttenlocher, P. R. (2002). *Neural plasticity: The effects of environment on the development of the cerebral cortex.* Cambridge, MA: Harvard University Press.

Hyde, J. S. (2007). New directions in the study of gender similarities and differences. *Current Directions in Psychological Science, 16,* 259–263.

Hyde, J. S., & McKinley, N. M. (1997). Gender differences in cognition: Results from meta-analyses. In P. J. Caplan, M. Crawford, J. S. Hyde, & J. T. E. Richardson (Eds.), *Gender differences in human cognition* (pp. 30–51). New York: Oxford University Press.

Hyde, J. S., & Oliver, M. B. (2000). Gender differences in sex-uality. Results from meta-analysis. In C. B. Travis & J. W. White (Eds.), *Sexuality, society, and feminism* (pp. 57–77). Washington, DC: American Psychological Association.

Hyde, J. S., Fenneman, E., & Lamon, S. (1990). Gender differences in mathematics performance: A meta-analysis. *Psychological Bulletin, 107,* 139–155.

Hyman, S. E., & Rudorfer, M. V. (2000). Anxiety dis-orders. In D. C. Dale & D. D. Federman (Eds.), *Scientific American Medicine* (Vol. 3, Sect 13, Subsect VIII). New York: Healtheon/WebMD Corp.

Iidaka, T., Anderson, N. D., Kapur, S., Cabeza, S., & Craik, F. I. M. (2000). The effect of divided attention on encoding and retrieval in episodic memory revealed by positron emission tomography. *Journal of Cognitive Neuroscience, 12,* 267.

Ikonomidou, C., Bittigau, P., Ishimaru, M. J., Wozniak, D. F., Koch, C., Genz, K., et al. (2000, February 11). Ethanol-induced apoptotic neurodegeneration and fetal alcohol syndrome. *Science, 287,* 1056–1060.

Ilgen, M. A., & Hutchison, K. E. (2005). A history of major depressive disorder and the response to stress. *Journal of Affective Disorders, 86,* 143–150.

Inciardi, J. A., Surratt, H. L., & Saum, C. A. (1997). *Cocaine-exposed infants: Social, legal, and public health issues.* Thousand Oaks, CA: Sage.

Ineichen, B. (1979). The social geography of marriage. In M. Cook & G. Wilson (Eds.), *Love and attraction* (pp. 145–149). New York: Pergamon Press.

Infante-Rivard, C., Fernandez, A., Gauthier, R., David, M., & Rivard, G. E. (1993). Fetal loss associated with caffeine intake before and during pregnancy. *Journal of the American Medical Association, 270*(24), 2940–2943.

Inglehart, R. Foa, R., Peterson, C., & Welzel, C. (2008). Development, freedom, and rising happiness: A global perspective (1981–2007) *Perspectives on Psychological Science, 3,* 264–285.

Ingram, R. E., Hayes, A., & Scott, W. (2000). Empirically supported treatments: A critical analysis. In C. R. Snyder & R. E. Ingram (Eds.), *Handbook of psychological change: Psychotherapy processes and practices for the 21st century* (pp. 40–60). New York: Wiley.

Innis, N. K. (1979). Stimulus control of behavior during postreinforcement pause of FI schedules. *Animal Learning and Behavior, 7,* 203–210.

Inzlicht, M., & Ben-Zeev, T. (2000). A threatening intellectual environment: Why females are susceptible to experiencing problem-solving deficits in the presence of males. *Psychological Science, 11,* 365–371.

Irwin, M., Clark, C., Kennedy, B., Christian Gillin, J., & Ziegler, M. (2003). Nocturnal catecholamines and immune function in insomniacs, depressed patients, and control subjects. *Brain, Behavior, and Immunity, 17,* 365–372.

Irwin, M., McClintick, J., Costlow, C., Fortner, M., White, J., & Gillin, J. C. (1996). Partial night sleep deprivation reduces natural killer and cellular immune responses in humans. *Journal of the Federation of American Societies for Experimental Biology, 10,* 643–653.

Isaac, M., & Chand, P. K. (2006). Dissociative and conversion disorders: Defining boundaries. *Current Opinion in Psychiatry, 19,* 61–66.

Isenberg, N., Silbersweig, D., Engelien, A., Emmerich, S., Malavade, K., Beattie, B., et al. (1999). Linguistic threat activates the human amygdala. *Proceedings of the National Academy of Sciences, USA, 96,* 10456–10459.

Iso, H., Simoda, S., & Matsuyama, T. (2006). Environmental change during postnatal development alters behavior, cognitions, and neurogenesis of mice. *Behavioural Brain Research, 179,* 90–98.

Ito, T., Takenaka, K., Tomita, T., & Agari, I. (2006). Comparison of ruminative responses with negative rumination as a vulnerability factor for depression. *Psychological Reports, 99,* 763–772.

Iverson, L. (2003). Cannabis and the brain. *Brain, 126,* 1252–1270.

Izac, S. M. (2006). Basic anatomy and physiology of sleep. *American Journal of Electroneurodiagnostic Technology, 46,* 18–38.

Jablensky, A. (2000). Epidemiology of schizophrenia: The global burden of disease and disability. *European Archives of Psychiatry and Clinical Neuroscience, 250,* 274–285.

Jablensky, A. (2002). The classification of personality disorders: Critical review and need for rethinking. *Psychopathology, 35,* 112–116.

Jablin, F. M. (1982). Organizational communication: An assimilation approach. In M. E. Rolff & C. R. Berger (Eds.), *Social cognition and communication* (pp. 255–286). Beverly Hills, CA: Sage.

Jackson, J. S., Williams, D. R., & Torres, M. (1997). *Perceptions of discrimination: The stress process and physical and psychological health.* Washington, DC: National Institute for Mental Health.

Jackson, S., & Blake, R. (2010). Neural integration of information specifying human structure from form, motion, and depth. *Journal of Neuroscience, 30,* 838–848.

Jackson-Triche, M. E., Greer Sullivan, J., Wells, K. B., Rogers, W., Camp, P., & Mazel, R. (2000). Depression and health-related quality of life in ethnic minorities seeking care in general medical settings. *Journal of Affective Disorders, 58,* 89–97.

Jacobs, B. L. (2004). Depression: The brain finally gets into the act. *Current Directions in Psychological Science, 13,* 103–106.

Jacobs, B. L., van Praag, H., & Gage, F. H. (2000). Adult brain neurogenesis and psychiatry: A novel theory of depression. *Molecular Psychiatry, 5,* 262–269.

Jacobsen, T., & Hofmann, V. (1997). Children's attachment representations: Longitudinal relations to school behavior and academic competency in middle childhood and adolescence. *Developmental Psychology, 33,* 701–710.

Jadack, R. A., Hyde, J. S., Moore, C. F., & Keller, M. L. (1995). Moral reasoning about sexually transmitted diseases. *Child Development, 66,* 167–177.

Jaffari-Bimmel, N., Juffer, F., van Ijzendoorn, M. H., Bakermans-Kranenburg, M. J., & Mooijaart, A. (2006). Social development from infancy to adolescence: Longitudinal and concurrent factors in an adoption sample. *Developmental Psychology, 42,* 1143–1153.

Jaffee, S., & Hyde, J. (2000). Gender differences in moral orientation: A meta-analysis. *Psychological Bulletin, 126,* 703–726.

James, W. (1884). What is an emotion? *Mind, 9,* 188–205.

James, W. (1899). *Talks to teachers on psychology and to students on some of life's ideals.* New York: Henry Holt.

James, W. (1950). *The principles of psychology.* New York: Dover. (Original work published 1890)

Jane, J. S., Oltmanns, T. F., South, S. C., & Turkheimer, E. (2007). Gender bias in diagnostic criteria for personality disorders: An item response theory analysis. *Journal of Abnormal Psychology, 116,* 166–175.

Jang, K. L., Hu, S., Livesley, W. J., Angleitner, A., Riemann, R., Ando, J., et al. (2001). Covariance structure of neuroticism and agreeableness: A twin and molecular genetic analysis of the role of the serotonin transporter gene. *Journal of Personality and Social Psychology, 81,* 295–304.

Janis, I. L. (1982). *Victims of groupthink* (2nd ed.). Boston: Houghton Mifflin.

Janis, I. L. (1985). Sources of error in strategic decision making. In J. M. Pennings (Ed.), *Organizational strategy and change* (pp. 157–197). San Francisco: Jossey-Bass.

Janoff-Bulman, R. (1992). *Shattered assumptions: Toward a new psychology of trauma.* New York: Maxwell Macmillan International.

Jarrett, R. B., Kraft, D., Doyle, J., Foster, B. M., Eaves, G. G., & Silver, P. C. (2001). Preventing recurrent depression using cognitive therapy with and without a continuation phase. *Archives of General Psychiatry, 58,* 381–388.

Jarvik, M. E. (1995). "The scientific case that nicotine is addictive": Comment. *Psychopharmacology, 117*(1), 18–20.

Javitt, D. C. (2007). Glutamate and schizophrenia: Phencyclidine, N-Methyl-d-aspartate receptors, and dopamine-glutamate interactions. *International Review of Neurobiology, 78,* 69–108.

Jemmott, J. B., III, Borysenko, M., McClelland, D. C., Chapman, R., & Benson, H. (1985). Academic stress, power motivation, and decrease in salivary secretory immunoglobulin: A secretion rate. *Lancet, 1,* 1400–1402.

Jenike, M. A., Baer, L., Ballantine, H. T., Martuza, R. L., Tynes, S., Giriunas, I., et al. (1991). Cingulotomy for refractory obsessive--compulsive disorder: A long-term

follow up of 33 patients. *Archives of General Psychiatry, 48*, 548–555.
Jenkins, J. G., & Dallenbach, K. M. (1924). Obliviscence during sleep and waking. *American Journal of Psychology, 35*, 605–612.
Jenkins, J. M., & Astington, J. W. (1996). Cognitive factors and family structure associated with theory of mind development in young children. *Developmental Psychology, 32*, 70–78.
Jenni, O. G., Achermann, P., & Carskadon, M. A. (2005). Homeostatic sleep regulation in adolescents. *Sleep, 28*, 1446–1454.
Jennings, J. R., Monk, T. H., & van der Molen, M. W. (2003). Sleep deprivation influences some but not all processes of supervisory attention. *Psychological Science, 14*, 473–479.
Jingde, Z., Xin, X., Entan, G., Junhui, L., Chunyu, X., & Xiaoyun, W. (2009). Surgical treatment of hermaphroditism: Experience with 25 cases. *Annals of Plastic Surgery, 63*, 543–551.
Johannes, C. B., Clayton, A. H., Odom, D. M., Rosen, R. C., Russo, P. A., Shifren, J. L., et al. (2009). Distressing sexual problems in United States women revisited: Prevalence after accounting for depression. *Journal of Clinical Psychiatry, 70*, 1698–1706.
Johnson, B. A. (2008). Update on neuropharmacological treatments for alcoholism: Scientific basis and clinical findings. *Biochemical Pharmacology, 75*, 34–56.
Johnson, J. A. (1997). Units of analysis for the description and explanation of personality. In R. Hogan, J. Johnson, & S. Briggs (Eds.), *Handbook of personality psychology* (pp. 3–93). New York: Academic Press.
Johnson, J. S., & Newport, E. L. (1991). Critical period effects on universal properties of language: The status of subjacency in the acquisition of a second language. *Cognition, 39*, 215–258.
Johnson, M. K., Hashtroudi, S., & Lindsay, D. S. (1993). Source monitoring. *Psychological Bulletin, 114*, 3–28.
Johnson, M. K., Mitchell, K. J., Raye, C. L., & Greene, E. J. (2004). An age-related deficit in prefrontal cortical function associated with refreshing information. *Psychological Science, 15*, 127–132.
Johnson, S. P., Amso, D., & Slemmer, J. A. (2003). Development of object concepts in infancy: Evidence for early learning in an eye-tracking paradigm. *Proceedings of the National Academy of Sciences, USA, 100*, 10568–10573.
Johnson, W., Turkheimer, E., Gottesman, I. I., & Bouchard, T. J., Jr. (2009). Beyond heritability: Twin studies in behavioral research. *Current Directions in Psychological Science, 18*, 217–220.
John-Steiner, V., & Mahn, H. (1996). Sociocultural approaches to learning and development: A Vygotskian framework. *Educational Psychologist, 31*, 191–206.
Johnston, L. D., O'Malley, P. M., Bachman, J. G., & Schulenberg, J. E. (2009). *Monitoring the future: National results on adolescent drug use; Overview of key findings, 2008* (NIH Publication No. 09–7401). Bethesda, MD: National Institute on Drug Abuse.
Johnston, L. D., O'Malley, P. M., Bachman, J. G., & Schulenberg, J. E. (2009, December 14). *Teen marijuana use tilts up, while some drugs decline in use.* University of Michigan News Service: Ann Arbor, MI. Retrieved April 26, 2010, from www.monitoringthefuture.org
Joliot, A. E. (2001). A comparative study of body image satisfaction and attitudes among American, Israeli, Spanish, & Brazilian college women (United States). *Dissertation Abstracts International: Section B: The Sciences and Engineering, 61*, 55–67.
Jonason, P. K. (2009). The value of physical attractiveness in romantic partners: Modeling biological and social variables. *The Journal of Social Psychology, 149*, 229–240.
Jones, E. E. (1979). The rocky road from acts to dispositions. *American Psychologist, 34*, 107–117.
Jones, E. E., & Nesbitt, R. E. (1971). *The actor and the observer: Divergent perceptions of the causes of behavior.* Morristown, NJ: General Learning Press.
Jones, J. (1962). Contiguity and reinforcement in relation to CS-UCS intervals in classical aversive conditioning. *Psychological Review, 69*, 176–186.
Jones, M. C. (1924). A laboratory study of fear: The case of Peter. *Pedagogical Seminary, 31*, 308–315.
Jones, M. C., Webb, R. J., Hsiao, C. Y., & Hannan, P. (1995). Relationships between socioeconomic status and drinking problems among Black and White men. *Alcoholism, Clinical and Experimental Research, 19*, 623–627.
Jones, N. P., Papadakis, A. A., Hogan, C. M., & Strauman, T. J. (2009). Over and over again: Rumination, reflection, and promotion goal failure and their interactive effects on depressive symptoms. *Behaviour Research and Therapy, 47*, 254–259.
Jones, R. T. (1971). Tetrahydrocannabinol and the marijuana- induced social "high" or the effects on the mind of marijuana. *Annals of the New York Academy of Sciences, 191*, 155–165.
Jones, S., Casswell, S., & Zhang, J. F. (1995). The economic costs of alcohol-related absenteeism and reduced productivity among the working population of New Zealand. *Addiction, 90*, 1455–1461.
Jones, S., & Dindia, K. (2004). A meta-analytic perspective on sex equity in the classroom. *Review of Educational Research, 74*, 443–471.
Jonsson, E. G., Burgert, E., Crocq, M. A., Gustavsson, J. P., Forslund, K., Mattila-Evenden, M., et al. (2003). Association study between dopamine D3 receptor gene variant and personality traits. *American Journal of Medical Genetics, 117B*, 61–65.
Jonsson, E. G., Ivo, R., Gustavsson, J. P., Geijer, T., Forslund, K., Mattila-Evenden, M., et al. (2002). No association between dopamine D4 receptor gene variants and novelty seeking. *Molecular Psychiatry, 7*, 18–20.
Jordan, A. S., & McEvoy, R. D. (2003). Gender differences in sleep apnea: Epidemiology, clinical presentation and pathogenic mechanisms. *Sleep Medical Review, 7*, 377–389.
Jorgensen, G. (2006). Kohlberg and Gilligan: Duet or duel? *Journal of Moral Education, 35*, 179–196.
Joule, R.-V., & Azdia, T. (2003). Cognitive dissonance, double forced compliance, and commitment. *European Journal of Social Psychology, 33*, 565–571.
Judge, T. A., & Livingston, B. A. (2008). Is the gap more than gender? A longitudinal analysis of gender, gender role orientation, and earnings. *Journal of Applied Psychology, 93*, 994–1012.
Julien, R. M. (1995). *A primer of drug action.* San Francisco: Freeman.
Jung, C. G. (1966). The psychology of the unconscious. In H. Read, M. Fordham, & G. Adler (Eds.), *Collected works of C. G. Jung* (Vol. 7). Princeton, NJ: Princeton University Press. (Originally published 1917)
Jung, C. G. (1967). *Collected works.* Princeton, NJ: Princeton University Press.
Jung, J. (2001). *Psychology of alcohol and other drugs: A research perspective.* Thousand Oaks, CA: Sage.
Juvonen, J., & Gross, E. F. (2008). Extending the school grounds? Bullying experiences in cyberspace. *Journal of School Health, 78*, 496–505.
Kaeser, F., DiSalvo, C., & Moglia, R. (2001). Sexual behaviors of young children that occur in schools. *Journal of Sex Education and Therapy, 25*, 277–285.
Kaestle, C. E., & Halpern, C. T. (2007). What's love got to do with it? Sexual behaviors of opposite-sex couples through emerging adulthood. *Perspectives on Sexual and Reproductive Health, 39*, 134–140.
Kahn, D. A. (1995). New strategies in bipolar disorder: Part II. Treatment. *Journal of Practical Psychiatry and Behavioral Health, 3*, 148–157.
Kahneman, D., & Tversky, A. (1973). On the psychology of prediction. *Psychological Review, 80*, 237–251.
Kahneman, D., & Tversky, A. (1984). Choices, values, and frames. *American Psychologist, 39*, 341–350.
Kahol, K., Leyba, M. J., Deka, M., Deka, V., Mayes, S., Smith, M., et al. Ferrara, J. J., & Panchanathan, S. (2008). Effect of fatigue on psychomotor and cognitive skills. *American Journal of Surgery, 195*, 195–204.
Kail, R., & Salthouse, T. A. (1994). Processing speed as a mental capacity. *Acta Psychologica, 86*, 199–225.
Kaiser Family Foundation (2006). *Media Violence and Children.* Retrieved June 12, 2010, from http://act-againstviolence.apa.org/mediaviolence/index.html.
Kako, E. (1999). Elements of syntax in the systems of three language-trained animals. *Animal Learning and Behavior, 27*, 1–14.
Kales, A., & Kales, J. (1973). Recent advances in the diagnosis and treatment of sleep disorders. In G. Usdin (Ed.), *Sleep research and clinical practice* (pp. 59–94). New York: Brunner/Mazel.
Kalish, R. A. (1985). The social context of death and dying. In R. H. Binstock & E. Shanas (Eds.), *Handbook of aging and the social sciences* (2nd ed., pp. 149–170). New York: Van Nostrand Reinhold.
Kan, P., Simonsen, S. E., Lyon, J. L., & Kestle, J. R. (2008). Cellular phone use and brain tumor: A meta-analysis. *Journal of Neurooncology, 86*, 71–78.
Kandel, D. B. (1978). Similarity in real-life adolescent friendship pairs. *Journal of Personality and Social Psychology, 36*, 306–312.
Kanoy, K., Ulku-Steiner, B., Cox, M., & Burchinal, M. (2003). Marital relationship and individual psychological characteristics that predict physical punishment of children. *Journal of Family Psychology, 17*, 20–28.
Kanwisher, N. (2003). The ventral visual pathway in humans: Evidence from fMRI. In L. M. Chalupa & J. S. Werner (Eds.), *The visual neuroscience* (pp. 1179–1190). Cambridge, MA: MIT Press.
Kaplan, C. A., & Simon, H. A. (1990). In search of insight. *Cognitive Psychology, 22*, 374–419.
Kaplan, D. A. (2010). SAS: A new no.1 best employer. *Fortune*, January 22, http://money.cnn.com/2010/01/21/technology/sas_best_companies.fortune/
Kaplan, H. S. (1974). *The new sex therapy: Active treatment of sexual dysfunctions.* New York: Brunner/Mazel.
Kaplan, R. E., Drath, W. H., & Kofodimos, J. R. (1991). *Beyond ambition: How driven managers can lead better and live better.* San Francisco: Jossey-Bass.
Kaplan, R. M. (2007). Should Medicare reimburse providers for weight loss interventions? *American Psychologist, 62*, 217–219.
Kaplan, R. M., & Saccuzzo, D. P. (1989). *Psychological testing: Principles, applications, and issues.* Pacific Grove, CA: Brooks/Cole.
Kaplan, S. J., Pelcovitz, D., Salzinger, S., Mandel, F., & Weiner, M. (1997). Adolescent physical abuse and suicide attempts. *Journal of the American Academy of Child and Adolescent Psychiatry, 36*, 799–808.
Kaplowitz, P. B., Oberfield, S. E., & the Drug and Therapeutics and Executive Committees of the Lawson Wilkins Pediatric Endocrine Society. (1999). Reexamination of the age limit for defining when puberty is precocious in girls in the United States: Implications for evaluation and treatment. *Pediatrics, 104*, 936–941.
Kapur, S., Craik, F. I. M., Tulving, E., Wilson, A. A., Houle, S., & Brown, G. M. (1994). Neuroatomical correlates of encoding in episodic memory. *Proceedings of the National Academy of Science, USA*, 91, 2008–2011.
Karch, D. L., Dahlberg, L. L., Patel, N., Davis, T. W., Logan, J. E., Hill, H. A., et al. (2009). Surveillance for violent deaths: National violent death reporting system, 16 states, 2006. *Morbidity and Mortality Weekly Reports: Surveillance Summaries, 58*, 1–44.
Karney, B. R., & Bradbury, T. N. (2005). Contextual influences on marriage: Implications for policy and intervention. *Current Directions in Psychological Science, 14*, 171–174.
Karni, A., Tanne, D., Rubenstein, B. S., Askenasy, J. J. M., & Sagi, D. (1994). Dependence on REM sleep of overnight improvement of a perceptual skill. *Science, 265*(5172), 679–682.
Karremans, J. C., Stroebe, W., & Claus, J. (2006). Beyond Vicary's fantasies: The impact of subliminal priming and brand choice. *Journal of Experimental Social Psychology, 42*, 792–798.
Kaskutas, L. A. (2009). Alcoholics Anonymous effectiveness: Fait meets science. *Journal of Addictive Diseases, 28*, 145–157.
Kaslow, F. W., Hansson, K., & Lundblad, A. (1994). Long-term marriages in Sweden: And some comparisons with similar couples in the United States. *Contemporary Family Therapy, 16*, 521–537.
Katigbak, M. S., Church, A. T., Guanzon-Lapeña, M. A., Carlota, A. J., & del Pilar, G. H. (2002). Are indigenous personality dimensions culture specific? Philippine inventories and the five-factor model. *Journal of Personality and Social Psychology, 82*, 89–101.

Katsuragi, S., Kiyota, A., Tsutsumi, T., Isogawa, K., Nagayama, H., Arinami, T., et al. (2001). Lack of association between a polymorphism in the promoter region of the dopamine D2 receptor and personality traits. *Psychiatry Research, 105,* 123–127.

Katz-Wise, S. L., Priess, H. A., & Hyde, J. S. (2010). Gender-role attitudes and behavior across the transition to parenthood. *Developmental Psychology, 46,* 18–28.

Kaufman, A. S., Kaufman, J. C., Liu, X., & Johnson, C. K. (2009). How do educational attainment and gender relate to fluid intelligence, crystallized intelligence, and academic skills at ages 22–90 years? *Archives of Clinical Neuropsychology, 24,* 153–163.

Kaufman, L., & Rock, L. (1989). The moon illusion thirty years later. In M. Hershenson (Ed.), *The moon illusion* (pp. 193–234). Hillsdale, NJ: Erlbaum.

Kawakami, N., Takeskima, T., Ono, Y., Uda, H., Hata, Y., Nakane, Y., et al. (2005). Twelve-month prevalence, severity, and treatment of common mental disorders in communities of Japan: Preliminary finding from the World Mental Health Survey 2002–2003. *Psychiatry and Clinical Neuroscience, 59,* 441–452.

Kaye, K. L., & Bower, T. G. R. (1994). Learning and intermodal transfer of information in newborns. *Psychological Science, 5,* 286–288.

Kazdin, A. E. (1977). *The token economy: A review and evaluation.* New York: Plenum Press.

Keck, P. E., Jr., & McElroy, S. L. (2002). Carbamazepine and valproate in the maintenance treatment of bipolar disorder. *Journal of Clinical Psychiatry, 63,* 13–17.

Keck, P. E., Jr., McElroy, S. L., & Arnold, L. M. (2001). Bipolar disorder. *Medical Clinics of North America, 85,* 645–661.

Keel, P. K., & Klump, K. L. (2003). Are eating disorders culture-bound syndromes? Implications for conceptualizing their etiology. *Psychological Bulletin, 129,* 747–769.

Keller, C. (2001). Effect of teachers' stereotyping on students' stereotyping of mathematics as a male domain. *Journal of Social Psychology, 141,* 165–173.

Keller, J., & Dauenheimer, D. (2003). Stereotype threat in the classroom: Dejection mediates the disrupting threat effect of women's math performance. *Personality and Social Psychology Bulletin, 29,* 371–381.

Kellner, C. H., Knapp, R., Husain, M. M., Rasmussen, K., Sampson, S., Cullum, M., et al., (2010). Bifrontal, bitemporal and right unilateral electrode placement in ECT: A randomised trial. *British Journal of Psychiatry, 196,* 226–234.

Kelly, D. J., Ge, L., Liu, S., Quinn, P. C., Slater, A. M., Lee, K., et al. (2007). Cross-race preferences for same-race faces extend beyond the African versus Caucasian contrast in 3-month-old infants. *Infancy, 11,* 87–95.

Kelly, M. M., & Forsyth, J. P. (2007). Observational fear conditioning in the acquisition and extinction of attentional bias for threat: An experimental evaluation. *Emotion, 7,* 324–335.

Kelman, C. A. (2001). Egocentric language in deaf children. *American Annals of the Deaf, 146,* 276–279.

Kemeny, M. E. (2003). The psychobiology of stress. *Current Directions in Psychological Science, 12,* 124–129.

Kemmelmeier, M., Jambor, E. E., & Joyce, L. (2006). The United States individualism and good works: Cultural variation in giving and volunteering. *Journal of Cross-Cultural Psychology, 37,* 327–344.

Kemp, M., Drummond, P., & McDermott, B. (2010). A wait-list controlled pilot study of eye movement desensitization and reprocessing (EMDR) for children with post-traumatic stress disorder (PTSD) symptoms from motor vehicle accidents. *Clinical Child Psychology and Psychiatry, 15,* 5–25.

Kenardy, J. A., Dow, M. G., Johnston, D. W., Newman, M. G., Thompson, A., & Taylor, C. B. (2003). A comparison of delivery methods of cognitive-behavioral therapy for panic disorder: An international multi-center trial. *Journal of Consulting and Clinical Psychology, 71,* 1068–1075.

Kendall, A. P., Kautz, M. A., Russo, M. B., & Killgore, W. D. (2006). Effects of sleep deprivation on lateral visual attention. *International Journal of Neuroscience, 116,* 1125–1138.

Kendler, K. S., McGuire, M., Gruenberg, A. M., & Walsh, D. (1994). Outcome and family study of the subtypes of schizophrenia in the west of Ireland. *American Journal of Psychiatry, 151,* 849–856.

Kennedy, S. H., Konarski, J. Z., Segal, Z. V., Lau, M. A., Bieling, P. J., McIntyre, R. S., et al. (2007). Differences in brain glucose metabolism between responders to CBT and venlafaxine in a 16-week randomized controlled trial. *American Journal of Psychiatry, 164,* 778–788.

Kenrick, D. T., & Sheets, V. (1993). Homicidal fantasies. *Ethology and Sociobiology, 14,* 231–246.

Kerns, K. A., Abraham, M. M., Schlegelmilch, A., & Morgan, T. A. (2007). Mother-child attachment in later middle childhood: Assessment approaches and associations with mood and emotion regulation. *Attachment and Human Development, 9,* 33–53.

Kessler, R. C., Berglund, P., Demler, O., Jin, R., & Walters, E. E. (2005). Lifetime prevalence and age-of-onset distributions of DSM-IV disorders in the National Comorbidity Survey Replication (NCS-R). *Archives of General Psychiatry, 62,* 593–602.

Kessler, R. C., Berglund, P., Demler, O., Jin, R., Koretz, D., Merikangas, K. R., et al. (2003). The epidemiology of major depressive disorder. Results from the National Comorbidity Survey Replication (NCS-R). *Journal of the American Medical Association, 289,* 3095–3105.

Kessler, R. C., Chiu, W. T., Demler, O., & Walters, E. E. (2005). Prevalence, severity, and comorbidity of twelve-month DSM-IV disorders in the National Comorbidity Survey Replication (NCS-R). *Archives of General Psychiatry, 62,* 617–627.

Kessler, R. C., McGonagle, K. A., Zhao, S., Nelson, C. B., Hughes, M., Eshelman, S., et al. (1994). Lifetime and 12-month prevalence of DSM-III-R psychiatric disorders in the United States: Results from the National Comorbidity Survey (NCS). *Archives of General Psychiatry, 51,* 8–19.

Kety, S. S., Wender, P. H., Jacobsen, B., Ingraham, L. J., Jansson, L., Faber, B., et al. (1994). Mental illness in the biological and adoptive relative of schizophrenic adoptees: Replication of the Copenhagen study in the rest of Denmark. *Archives of General Psychiatry, 51,* 442–455.

Khan, S. S., & Liu, J. H. (2008). Intergroup attributions and ethnocentrism in the Indian subcontinent: The ultimate attribution error revisited. *Journal of Cross-Cultural Psychology, 39,* 16–36.

Kiecolt-Glaser, J. K. (2009). Psychoneuroimmunology: Psychology's gateway to the biomedical future. *Perspectives on Psychological Science, 4,* 367–369.

Kiecolt-Glaser, J. K., Bane, C., Glaser, R., & Malarkey, W. B. (2003). Love, marriage, and divorce: Newlyweds' stress hormones foreshadow relationship changes. *Journal of Consulting and Clinical Psychology, 71,* 176–188.

Kiecolt-Glaser, J. K., Marucha, P. T., Malarkey, W. B., Mercado, A. M., & Glaser, R. (1995). Slowing of wound healing by psychological stress. *Lancet, 346,* 1194–1196.

Kiecolt-Glaser, J. K., McGuire, L., Robles, T. F., & Glaser, R. (2002). Emotions, morbidity, and mortality: New perspectives from psychoneuroimmunology. *Annual Review of Psychology, 53,* 83–107.

Kiehl, K. A., Bates, A. T., Laurens, K. R., Hare, R. D., & Liddle, P. F. (2006). Brain potentials implicate temporal lobe abnormalities in criminal psychopaths. *Journal of Abnormal Psychology, 115,* 443–453.

Kieseppa, T., Partonen, T., Haukka, J., Kaprio, J., & Lonnqvist, J. (2004). High concordance of bipolar I disorder in a nationwide sample of twins. *American Journal of Psychiatry, 161,* 1814–1821.

Kihlstrom, J. F. (1993). The continuum of consciousness. *Consciousness and Cognition, 2,* 334–354.

Kihlstrom, J. F. (2001). Dissociative disorders. In H. E. Adams & P. B. Sutker (Eds.), *Comprehensive handbook of psychopathology* (pp. 259–276). New York: Academic/Plenum Publishers.

Kihlstrom, J. F. (2005). Dissociative disorders. *Annual Review of Clinical Psychology, 1,* 227–253.

Kihlstrom, J. F., Glisky, M. L., & Angiulo, M. J. (1994). Dissociative tendencies and dissociative disorders. *Journal of Abnormal Psychology, 103,* 117–124.

Kilbride, H. W., Castor, C. A., & Fuger, K. L. (2006). School-age outcome of children with prenatal cocaine exposure following early case management. *Journal of Developmental and Behavioral Pediatrics, 27,* 181–187.

Kim, H., & Chung, R. H. (2003). Relationship of recalled parenting style to self-perception in Korean American college students. *Journal of Genetic Psychology, 164,* 481–492.

Kim, J. E., & Moen, P. (2001). Moving into retirement: Preparation and transitions in late midlife. In M. E. Lachman (Ed.), *Handbook of midlife development* (pp. 487–527). New York: Wiley.

Kim, J. E., & Moen, P. (2002). Retirement transitions, gender, and psychological well-being: A life-course, ecological model. *Journal of Gerontology: Psychological Sciences, 57B,* P212–P222.

Kim, S. J., Lee, H. S., & Kim, C. H. (2005). Obsessive-compulsive disorder, factor-analyzed symptom dimensions and serotonin transporter polymorphism. *Neuropsychobiology, 52,* 176–182.

Kim-Cohen, J., & Gold, A. L. (2009). Measured gene-environment interactions and mechanisms promoting resilient development. *Current Directions in Psychological Science, 18,* 138–142.

Kimura, D. (2000). *Sex and cognition.* Cambridge, MA: MIT Press.

Kinder, B. N., & Curtiss, G. (1988). Specific components in the etiology, assessment, and treatment of male sexual dysfunctions: Controlled outcome studies. *Journal of Sex and Marital Therapy, 14,* 40–48.

King, B. M. (2006). The rise, fall, and resurrection of the ventromedial hypothalamus in the regulation of feeding behavior and body weight. *Physiology and Behavior, 87,* 221–244.

King, K. R. (2005). Why is discrimination stressful? The mediating role of cognitive appraisal. *Cultural Diversity and Ethnic Minority Psychology, 11,* 202–212.

King, N. J., Gullone, E., Tonge, B. J., & Ollendick, T. H. (1993). Self-reports of panic attacks and manifest anxiety in adolescents. *Behaviour Research and Therapy, 31,* 111–116.

King, P. M., & Kitchener, K. S. (1994). *Developing reflective judgment: Understanding and promoting intellectual growth and critical thinking in adolescents and adults.* San Francisco: Jossey-Bass.

Kingsberg, S. (2007). Testosterone treatment for hypoactive sexual desire disorder in postmenopausal women. *Journal of Sexual Medicine, 4,* 227–234.

Kingsberg, S. A., & Janata, J. W. (2003). Sexual aversion disorder. In S. Levine (Ed.), *Handbook of clinical sexuality for mental health professionals* (pp. 153–166). New York: Brunner-Routledge.

Kinnish, K. K., Strassberg, D. S., & Turner, C. W. (2005). Sex differences in the flexibility of sexual orientation: A multidimensional retrospective assessment. *Archives of Sexual Behavior, 34,* 173–183.

Kinomura, S., Larsson, J., Gulyas, B., & Roland, P. E. (1996). Activation by attention of the human reticular formation and thalamic intralaminar nuclei. *Science, 271,* 512–515.

Kinsey, A. C., Pomeroy, W. B., & Martin, C. E. (1948). *Sexual behavior in the human male.* Philadelphia: Saunders.

Kinsey, A. C., Pomeroy, W. B., Martin, C. E., & Gebhard, P. H. (1953). *Sexual behavior in the human female.* Philadelphia: Saunders.

Kirkbride, J. B., Morgan, C., Fearon, P., Dazzan, P., Murray, R. M., & Jones, P. B. (2007). Neighborhood-level effects on psychoses: Re-examining the role of context. *Psychological Medicine, 37,* 1413–1425.

Kirkpatrick, S. A., & Locke, E. A. (1991). Leadership: Do traits matter? *Academy of Management Executive, 5,* 48–60.

Kirmayer, L. J., & Looper, K. J. (2007). Somatoform disorders. In M. Hersen, S. M. Turner, & D. C. Beidel (Eds.), *Adult psychopathology and diagnosis* (5th ed., pp. 410–472). Hoboken, NJ: Wiley.

Kirsch, I. (1994). Cognitive-behavioral hypnotherapy. In J. W. Rhue, S. J. Lynn, & I. Kirsch (Eds.), *Handbook of clinical hypnosis* (pp. 151–172). Washington, DC: American Psychological Association.

Kirsch, I. (2000). The response set theory of hypnosis. *American Journal of Clinical Hypnosis, 42,* 274–292.

Kirsch, I., & Lynn, S. J. (1995). The altered state of hypnosis. *American Psychologist, 50*(10), 846–858.

Kirsch, I., & Lynn, S. J. (1997). Hypnotic involuntariness and the automaticity of everyday life. *American Journal of Clinical Hypnosis, 40,* 329–348.

Kirsch, I., Montgomery, G., & Sapirstein, G. (1995). Hypnosis as an adjunct to cognitive behavioral psychotherapy: A meta-analysis. *Journal of Consulting and Clinical Psychology, 63,* 214–220.

Kisilevsky, B. S., Hains, S. M., Lee, K., Xie, X., Huang, H., Ye, H. H., et al. (2003). Effects of experience on fetal voice recognition. *Psychological Science, 14,* 220–224.

Kitayama, S., Mesquita, B., & Karasawa, M. (2006). Cultural affordance and emotional experience: Socially engaging and disengaging emotions in Japan and the United States. *Journal of Personality and Social Psychology, 91,* 890–903.

Kitterod, R. H., & Kjeldstad, R. (2002, October). *A new father's role? Employment patterns among Norwegian fathers in the 1990's.* Paper presented at the IATUR conference in Lisbon, Norway.

Klass, D. (1993). Solace and immortality: Bereaved parents' continuing bond with their children. *Death Studies, 17,* 343–368.

Klatzky, R. L. (1980). *Human memory: Structures and processes* (2nd ed.). New York: W. H. Freeman.

Klein, B., Mitchell, J., Abbott, J., Shandley, K., Austin, D., Gilson, K., et al. (2010). A therapist-assisted cognitive behavior therapy Internet intervention for posttraumatic stress disorder: Pre-, post- and 3-month follow-up results from an open trial. *Journal of Anxiety Disorders, 24,* 635–644.

Klein, D. N., Durbin, C. E., Shankman, S. A., & Santiago, N. J. (2002). Depression and personality. In J. H. Gotlib & C. L. Hammen (Eds.), *Handbook of depression* (pp. 115–140). New York: Guilford Press.

Klein, D. N., Lewinsohn, P. M., & Seeley, J. R. (2001). A family study of major depressive disorder in a community sample of adolescents. *Archives of General Psychiatry, 58,* 13–21.

Klein, M. J., & Simmers, C. S. (2009). Exergaming: Virtual inspiration, real perspiration. *Young Consumers, 10,* 35–45.

Klein, S. B. (1987). *Learning.* New York: McGraw-Hill.

Klein, T. W., & Newton, C. A. (2007). Therapeutic potential of cannabinoid-based drugs. *Advances in Experimental Medicine and Biology, 601,* 395–413.

Kleiner, K. (2004). What we gave up for color vision. *New Scientist, 181,* p. 12.

Kleinknecht, R. A. (1991). *Mastering anxiety: The nature and treatment of anxious conditions.* New York: Plenum Press.

Kling, K. C., Hyde, J. S., Showers, C. J., & Buswell, B. N. (1999). Gender differences in self-esteem: A meta-analysis. *Psychological Bulletin, 125,* 470–500.

Klinger, E., Bouchard, S., Legeron, P., Roy, S., Lauer, F., Chemin, I., et al. (2005). Virtual reality therapy versus cognitive behavior therapy for social phobia: A preliminary controlled study. *Cyberpsychology and Behavior, 8,* 76–88.

Klonoff, E. A., & Landrine, H. (1999). Cross-validation of the schedule of racist events. *Journal of Black Psychology, 25,* 231–254.

Klonoff, E. A., Landrine, H., & Campbell, R. (2000). Sexist discrimination may account for well-known gender differences in psychiatric symptoms. *Psychology of Women Quarterly, 24,* 93–99.

Kluft, R. P. (1999). Current issues in dissociative identity disorder. *Journal of Practical Psychology and Behavioral Health, 5,* 3–19.

Knox, D., Sturdivant, L., & Zusman, M. E. (2001). College student attitudes toward sexual intimacy. *College Student Journal, 35,* 241–243.

Knudsen, D. D. (1991). Child sexual coercion. In E. Grauerholz & M. A. Koralewski (Eds.), *Sexual coercion: A sourcebook on its nature, causes, and prevention* (pp. 17–28). Lexington, MA: Lexington Books.

Kobasa, S. C. (1982). Commitment and coping in stress resistance among lawyers. *Journal of Personality and Social Psychology, 42,* 707–717.

Kochanska, G. (1995). Children's temperament, mothers' discipline, and security of attachment: Multiple pathways to emerging internalization. *Child Development, 66,* 597–615.

Kochanska, G. (1997). Mutually responsive orientation between mothers and their young children: Implications for early socialization. *Child Development, 68,* 94–112.

Koehler, J. (2002). Vaginismus: Diagnosis, etiology, and intervention. *Contemporary Sexuality, 36,* i–viii.

Koh, K. B., Choe, E., Song, J. E., & Lee, E. H. (2006). Effect of coping on endocrinoimmune functions in different stress situations. *Psychiatry Research, 143,* 223–234.

Kohlberg, L. (1969). Stage and sequence: The cognitive-developmental approach to socialization. In D. A. Goslin (Ed.), *Handbook of socialization theory and research* (pp. 347–480). Chicago: Rand McNally.

Kohlberg, L., Levine, C., & Hewer, A. (1983). *Moral stages: A current formulation and a response to critics.* Basel, Switzerland: Karger.

Köhler, W. (1925). *The mentality of apes.* New York: Harcourt Brace.

Kolassa, I. T., & Elbert, T. (2007). Structural and functional neuroplasticity in relation to traumatic stress. *Current Directions in Psychological Science, 16,* 321–325.

Kolb, B. (1989). Brain development, plasticity, and behavior. *American Psychologist, 44*(9), 1203–1212.

Koles, Z. J., Lind, J. C., & Flor-Henry, P. (2009). Gender differences in brain functional organization during verbal and spatial cognitive challenges. *Brain Topography.* doi: 10.1007/s10548–009–0119–0.

Konkol, R. J., Murphey, L. J., Ferriero, D. M., Dempsey, D. A., & Olsen, G. D. (1994). Cocaine metabolites in the neonate: Potential for toxicity. *Journal of Child Neurology, 9*(3), 242–248.

Konttinen, H., Männistö, S., Sarlio-Lähteenkorva, S., Silventoinen, K., & Haukkala, A. (2010). Emotional eating, depressive symptoms and self-reported food consumption: A population-based study. *Appetite,* doi:10.1016/j.appet.2010.01.014.

Koob, G. F., & Bloom, F. E. (1988). Cellular and molecular mechanisms of drug dependence. *Science, 242,* 715–723.

Koob, G. F., & Le Moal, M. (2008). Review: Neurobiological mechanisms for opponent motivational processes in addiction. *Philosophical Transactions of the Royal Society of London. Series B, Biological Sciences, 363,* 3113–3123.

Kopelman, P. G. (2000). Obesity as a medical problem. *Nature, 404,* 635–643.

Kopta, S. M., Lueger, R. J., Saunders, S. M., & Howard, K. I. (1999). Individual psychotherapy outcome and process research: Challenges leading to greater turmoil or a positive transition? *Annual Review of Psychology, 50,* 441–469.

Koslowsky, M., & Babkoff, H. (1992). Meta-analysis of the relationship between total sleep deprivation and performance. *Chronobiology International, 9,* 132–136.

Koss, M. P., & Kilpatrick, D. G. (2001). Rape and sexual assault. In E. Gerrity (Ed.), *The mental health consequences of torture* (pp. 177–193). New York: Kluwer Academic/Plenum.

Kosslyn, S. M. (1994). *Image and brain: The resolution of the imagery debate.* Cambridge, MA: MIT Press.

Kosslyn, S. M., Ball, T. M., & Reiser, B. J. (2004). Visual images preserve metric spatial information: Evidence from studies of image scanning. In D. A. Balota & E. J. Marsh (Eds.), *Cognitive psychology: Key readings* (pp. 239–253). New York: Psychology Press. (Original work published 1978).

Koughan, M. (1975, February 23) Arthur Friedman's outrage: Employees decide their pay. *The Washington Post.*

Kowalski, K. (2003). The emergence of ethnic and racial attitudes in preschool-aged children. *Journal of Social Psychology, 143,* 677–690.

Kowalski, R. M. (1996). Complaints and complaining: Functions, antecedents, and consequences. *Psychological Bulletin, 119,* 179–196.

Kowalski, R. M., & Limber, S. P. (2007). Electronic bullying among middle school students. *Journal of Adolescent Health, 41,* S22–S30.

Kozart, M. F. (2002). Understanding efficacy in psychotherapy. *American Journal of Orthopsychiatry, 72,* 217–231.

Kozlowski, S. W., & Bell, B. S. (2003). Work groups and teams in organizations. In W. C. Borman, D. R. Ilgen, & R. J. Klimoski (Eds.), *Handbook of Psychology: Industrial and Organizational Psychology, 12,* 333–375.

Kraft, J. B., Peters, E. J., Slager, S. L., Jenkins, G. D., Reinalda, M. S., McGrath, P. J., et al. (2007). Analysis of association between the serotonin transporter and antidepressant response in a large clinical sample. *Biological Psychiatry, 61,* 734–742.

Kraft, J. M. (1996). Prenatal alcohol consumption and outcomes for children: A review of the literature. In R. L. Parrott & C. M. Condit (Eds.), *Evaluating women's health messages: A resource book* (pp. 175–189). Thousand Oaks, CA: Sage.

Krampe, H., & Ehrenreich, H. (2010). Supervised disulfiram as adjunct to psychotherapy in alcoholism treatment. *Current Pharmaceutical Design, 16,* 2076–2090.

Krantz, D. S., & McCeney, M. K. (2002). Effects of psychological and social factors on organic disease: A critical assessment of research on coronary heart disease. *Annual Review of Psychology, 53,* 341–369.

Krasnianski, A., Bartl, M., Sanchez Juan, P. J., Heinemann, U., Meissner, B., Varges, D., et al. (2008). Fatal familial insomnia: Clinical features and early identification. *Annals of Neurology, 63,* 658–661.

Kraut, R., Kiesler, S., Boneva, B., Cummings, J., Helgeson, V., & Crawford, A. (2002). Internet paradox revisited. *Journal of Social Issues, 58,* 49–74.

Kraut, R., Patterson, M., Lundmark, V., Kiesler, S., Mukopadhyay, T., & Scherlis, W. (1998). Internet paradox: A social technology that reduces social involvement and psychological well-being? *American Psychologist, 53,* 1017–1031.

Kraut, R. E. (1982). Social presence, facial feedback, and emotion. *Journal of Personality and Social Psychology, 42,* 853–863.

Kreibig, S. D. (2010). Autonomic nervous system activity in emotion: A review. *Biological Psychology,* doi:10.1016/j.biopsycho.2010.03.010.

Kreider, R. M. (2005). Number, timing, and duration of marriages and divorces: 2001. *Current Population Reports, P70–97.* Washington, DC: U.S. Census Bureau.

Kremer, I., Bachner-Melman, R., Reshef, A., Broude, L., Nemanov, L., Gritsenko, I., et al. (2005). Association of the serotonin transporter gene with smoking behavior. *American Journal of Psychiatry, 162,* 924–930.

Krijn, M., Emmelkamp, P. M., Olafsson, R. P., & Biemond, R. (2004). Virtual reality exposure therapy of anxiety disorders: A review. *Clinical Psychology Review, 24,* 259–281.

Kronenfeld, L. W., Reba-Harrelson, L., Von Holle, A., Reyes, M. L., & Bulik, C. M. (2010). Ethnic and racial differences in body size perception and satisfaction. *Body Image, 7,* 131–136.

Krstic, Z. D., Smoljanic, Z., Vukanic, D., Varinac, D., & Janiic, G. (2000). True hermaphroditism: 10 years' experience. *Pediatric Surgery International, 16,* 580–583.

Krug, D., Davis, T. B., & Glover, J. A. (1990). Massed versus distributed repeated reading: A case of forgetting helping recall. *Journal of Educational Psychology, 82,* 366–371.

Krystal, J. H., Staley, J., Mason, G., Petrakis, I. L., Kaufman, J., Harris, R. A., et al. (2006). Gamma-aminobutyric acid type A receptors and alcoholism: Intoxication, dependence, vulnerability, and treatment. *Archives of General Psychiatry, 63,* 957–968.

Kübler-Ross, E. (1969). *On death and dying.* New York: Macmillan.

Kübler-Ross, E. (1974). *Questions and answers on death and dying.* New York: Macmillan.

Kuepper, Y., Alexander, N., Osinsky, R., Mueller, E., Schmitz, A., Netter, P., et al. (2010). Aggression—Interactions of serotonin and testosterone in healthy men and women. *Behavioural Brain Research, 206,* 93–100.

Kumada, T., Jiang, Y., Cameron, D. B., & Komuro, H. (2007). How does alcohol impair neuronal migration? *Journal of Neuroscience Research, 85,* 465–470.

Kumari, V., ffytche, D. H., Williams, S. C., & Gray, J. A. (2004). Personality predicts brain responses to cognitive demands. *Journal of Neuroscience, 24,* 10636–10641.

Kung, H. S., Hoyert, D. L., Xu, J., & Murphy, S. L. (2008). Deaths: Final data for 2005. *National Vital Statistics Reports, 56* (10).

Kunstman, J. W., & Plant, E. A. (2008). Racing to help: Racial bias in high emergency helping situations. *Journal of Personality and Social Psychology, 95,* 1499–1510.

Kupelian, V., Link, C. L., Rosen, R. C., & McKinlay, J. B. (2008). Socioeconomic status, not race/ethnicity, con-

tributes to variation in the prevalence of erectile dysfunction. *Journal of Sexual Medicine, 5*, 1325–1333.
Kurdek, L. A. (1993). The allocation of household labor in gay, lesbian, and heterosexual married couples. *Journal of Social Issues, 49*, 127–139.
Kurdek, L. A. (1999). The nature and predictors of the trajectory of change in marital quality for husbands and wives over the first 10 years of marriage. *Developmental Psychology, 35*, 1283–1296.
Kuriyama, K., Stickgold, R., & Walker, M. P. (2004). Sleep-dependent learning and motor-skill complexity. *Learning and Memory, 11*, 705–713.
Kuypers, K. P., Wingen, M., & Ramaekers, J. G. (2008). Memory and mood during the night and in the morning after repeated evening doses of MDMA. *Journal of Psychopharmacology, 22*, 895–903.
Kuzelova, H., Ptacek, R., & Milan, M. (2010). The serotonin transporter gene (5-HTT) variant and psychiatric disorders: Review of current literature. *Neuroendocrinology Letters, 31*, 5.
Kwan, B. M., Dimidjian, S., & Rizvi, S.L. (2010). Treatment preference, engagement, and clinical improvement in pharmacotherapy versus psychotherapy for depression. *Behaviour Research and Therapy, 48*, 799–804.
LaBar, K. S. (2007). Beyond fear: Emotional memory mechanisms in the human brain. *Current Directions in Psychological Science, 16*, 173–177.
Lacayo, A. (1995). Neurologic and psychiatric complications of cocaine abuse. *Neuropsychiatry, Neuropsychology, and Behavioral Neurology, 8*(1), 53–60.
Laflamme, D., Pomerleau, A., & Malcuit, G. (2002). A comparison of fathers' and mothers' involvement in childcare and stimulation behaviors during free-play with their infants at 9 and 15 months. *Sex Roles, 47*, 507–518.
Lagana, L., McGarvey, E. L., Classen, C., & Koopman, C. (2001). Psychosexual dysfunction among gynecological cancer survivors. *Journal of Clinical Psychology in Medical Settings, 8*, 73–84.
Lahey, B. B., Pelham, W. E., Loney, J., Kipp, H., Ehrhardt, A., Lee, S. S., et al. (2004). Three-year predictive validity of DSM-IV attention deficit hyperactivity disorder in children diagnosed at 4–6 years of age. *American Journal of Psychiatry, 161*, 2014–2020.
Lakatos, K., Nemoda, Z., Birkas, E., Ronai, Z., Kovacs, E., Ney, K., et al. (2003). Association of D4 receptor gene and serotonin transporter promoter polymorphisms with infants' response to novelty. *Molecular Psychiatry, 8*, 90–97.
Lam, L. T., Peng, Z. W., Mai, J. C., & Jing, J. (2009). Factors associated with Internet addiction among adolescents. *Cyberpsychology and Behavior, 12*, 551–555.
Lambert, M. J., & Bergen, A. E. (1994). The effectiveness of psychotherapy. In A. E. Bergen & S. L. Garfield (Eds.), *Handbook of psychotherapy and behavior change* (4th ed., pp. 143–189). New York: Wiley.
Lambeth, G. S., & Hallett, M. (2002). Promoting healthy decision making in relationships: Developmental interventions with young adults on college and university campuses. In C. L. & D. R. Atkinson (Eds.), *Counseling across the lifespan: Prevention and treatment* (pp. 209–226). Thousand Oaks, CA: Sage.
Lancet, D. Ben-Arie, N., Cohen, S., Gat, U., Gross-Isseroff, R., Horn-Saban, S., et al. (1993). Olfactory receptors: Transduction diversity, human psychophysics and genome analysis. In D. Chadwick, J. Marsh, & J. Goode (Eds.), *The molecular basis of smell and taste transduction* (pp. 131–146). New York: Wiley.
Landabaso, M. A., Iraurgi, I., Sanz, J., Calle, R., Ruiz de Apodaka, J., Jimenez-Lerma, J. M., et al. (1999). Naltrexone in the treatment of alcoholism: Two year follow up results. *European Journal of Psychiatry, 13*, 97–105.
Landau, J., Garrett, J., & Webb, R. (2008). Assisting a concerned person to motivate someone experiencing cybersex into treatment: Application of invitational intervention; The arise model to cybersex. *Journal of Marital and Family Therapy, 34*, 498–511.
Landauer, T. K. (1986). How much do people remember? Some estimates of the quantity of learned information in long-term memory. *Cognitive Science, 10*, 477–493.
Landridge, D., & Butt, T. (2004). The fundamental attribution error: A phenomenological critique. *British Journal of Social Psychology, 43*, 357–369.
Landy, S. (2004). Migraine throughout the life cycle: Treatment through the ages. *Neurology, 62*, S2–S8.
Lang, A. J., & Stein, M. B. (2001). Social phobia: Prevalence and diagnostic threshold. *Journal of Clinical Psychiatry, 62* (Suppl. 1), 5–10.
Lange, T., Dimitrov, S., Fehm, H. L., Westermann, J., & Born, J. (2006). Shift of monocyte function toward cellular immunity during sleep. *Archives of Internal Medicine, 166*, 1695–1700.
Langlois, J. H., Roggman, L. A., Casey, R. J., Ritter, J. M., Rieser-Danner, L. A., & Jenkins, V. Y. (1987). Infant preferences for attractive faces: Rudiments of a stereotype? *Developmental Psychology, 23*, 363–369.
Langreth, R. (2000, May 1). Every little bit helps: How even moderate exercise can have a big impact on your health. *Wall Street Journal*, p. R5.
Lansford, J. E. (2009). Parental divorce and children's adjustment. *Perspectives on Psychological Science, 4*, 140–152.
Largo-Wight, E., Peterson, P. M., & Chen, W. W. (2005). Perceived problem solving, stress, and health among college students. *American Journal of Health Behavior, 29*, 360–370.
Larkin, M. (1998). On the trail of human pheromones. *Lancet, 351*, 809.
Lassman, D. J., McKie, S., Gregory, L. J., Lal, S., D'Amato, M., Steele, I., et al. (2010). Defining the role of cholecystokinin in the lipid-induced human brain activation matrix. *Gastroenterology, 138*, 1514–1524.
Lastella, D. D. (2005). Sexual harassment as an interpersonal dynamic: The effect of race, attractiveness, position power and gender on perceptions of sexual harassment. *Dissertation Abstracts International: Section B*, #0419–4217.
Latané, B., & Darley, J. (1969). Bystander "apathy." *American Scientist, 57*, 244–268.
Latané, B., & L'Herrou, T. (1996). Spatial clustering in the conformity game: Dynamic social impact in electronic groups. *Journal of Personality and Social Psychology, 70*, 1218–1230.
Lating, J. M., Sherman, M. F., Everly, G. S., Jr., Lowry, J. L., & Peragine, T. F. (2004). PTSD reactions and functioning of American Airlines flight attendants in the wake of September 11. *Journal of Nervous and Mental Disorders, 192*, 435–441.
Laubmeier, K. K., Zakowski, S. G., & Bair, J. P. (2004). The role of spirituality in the psychological adjustment to cancer. A test of the transactional model of stress and coping. *International Journal of Behavioral Medicine, 11*, 48–55.
Laugharne, J., Janca, A., & Widiger, T. (2007). Posttraumatic stress disorder and terrorism: Five years after 9/11. *Current Opinion in Psychiatry, 20*, 36–41.
Laumann, E. O., Gagnon, J. H., Michael, R. T., & Michaels, S. (1994). *The social organization of sexuality: Sexual practices in the United States.* Chicago: University of Chicago Press.
Laumann, E. O., Nicolosi, A., Glaser, D. B., Paik, A., Gingell, C., Moreira, E., et al. (2005). Sexual problems among women and men aged 40–80 years: Prevalence and correlates identified in the Global Study of Sexual Attitudes and Behaviors. *International Journal of Impotence Research, 17*, 39–57.
Laumann, E. O., Paik, A., & Rosen, R. C. (1999). Sexual dysfunction in the United States. *Journal of the American Medical Association, 281*, 537–544.
Laurent, S. M., & Simons, A. D. (2009). Sexual dysfunction in depression and anxiety: Conceptualizing sexual dysfunction as part of an internalizing dimension. *Clinical Psychology Review, 29*, 573–585.
Lavin, M. (2008). Voyeurism: Psychopathology and theory. In D. Laws & W. O'Donohue (Eds.), *Sexual deviance: Theory, assessment and treatment* (2nd ed., pp. 305–319). New York: Guilford Press.
Lavoie, C., & Desrochers, S. (2002). Visual habituation at five months: Short-term reliability of measures obtained with a new polynomial regression criterion. *Journal of Genetic Psychology*, 163, 261–271.
Laws, D. R. (2001). Olfactory aversion: Notes on procedure, with speculations on its mechanism of effect. *Sex Abuse, 13*, 275–287.
Lawyer, S., Resnick, H., Bakanic, V., Burkett, T., & Kilpatrick, D. (2010). Forcible, drug-facilitated, and incapacitated rape and sexual assault among undergraduate women. *Journal of American College Health, 58*, 453–460.
Lazarus, R. S. (1990). Theory-based stress measurement. *Psychological Inquiry, 1*, 3–13.
Lazarus, R. S. (1991). Cognition and motivation in emotion. *American Psychologist, 46*, 352–367.
Lazarus, R. S. (1993). From psychological stress to the emotions: A history of changing outlooks. *Annual Review of Psychology, 44*, 1–21.
Lazarus, R. S. (1995). Vexing research problems inherent in cognitive-mediational theories of emotion—and some solutions. *Psychological Inquiry, 6*, 183–197.
Lazarus, R. S. (2006). Emotions and interpersonal relationships: Toward a person-centered conceptualization of emotions and coping. *Journal of Personality, 74*, 9–46.
Lazarus, R. S., & Folkman, S. (1984). *Stress, appraisal, and coping.* New York: Springer.
Leaper, C., & Friedman, C. K. (2007). The socialization of gender. In J. E. Grusec & P. D. Hastings (Eds.), *Handbook of socialization: Theory and Research* (pp. 561–587). New York: Guilford Press.
LeBlanc, J., Ducharme, M. B., & Thompson, M. (2004). Study on the correlation of the autonomic nervous system response to a stressor of high discomfort with personality traits. *Physiology of Behavior, 82*, 647–652.
Lebovits, A. (2007). Cognitive-behavioral approaches to chronic pain. *Primary Psychiatry, 14*, 48–54.
Lebow, J. L., & Gurman, A. S. (1995). Research assessing couple and family therapy. *Annual Review of Psychology, 46*, 27–57.
Lecanuet, J. P., Manera, S., & Jacquet, A. Y. (2002, April). *Fetal cardiac responses to maternal sentences, to playback of these sentences, and to their recordings by another woman's voice.* Paper presented at the XIII International Conference on Infant Studies, Toronto, Ontario, Canada.
LeDoux, J. (1998). Fear and the brain: Where have we been, and where are we going? *Biological Psychiatry, 44*, 1229–1238.
Lee, A. Y. (2001). The mere exposure effect: An uncertainty reduction explanation revisited. *Personality and Social Psychology Bulletin, 27*, 1255–1266.
Lee, D. C., Sui, X., Ortega, F. B., Kim, Y. S., Church, T. S., Winett, R. A., et al. (in press). Comparisons of leisure-time physical activity and cardiorespiratory fitness as predictors of all-cause mortality in men and women. *British Journal of Sports Medicine.*
Lee, H. (1996). *Still life with rice.* New York: Simon and Schuster.
Lee, J., Pomeroy, E. C., Yoo, S. K., & Rheinboldt, K. T. (2005). Attitudes toward rape: A comparison between Asian and Caucasian college students. *Violence Against Women, 11*, 177–196.
Lefcourt, H. M. (2001). The humor solution. In C. R. Snyder (Ed.), *Coping with stress: Effective people and processes* (pp. 68–92). New York: Oxford University Press.
Lefcourt, H. M., & Davidson-Katz, K. (1991). The role of humor and the self. In C. R. Synder & D. R. Forsyth (Eds.), *Handbook of social and clinical psychology: The health perspective* (pp. 41–56). New York: Pergamon Press.
Lehrer, P. M., Feldman, J., Giardino, N., Song, H. S., & Schmaling, K. (2002). Psychological aspects of asthma. *Journal of Consulting and Clinical Psychology, 70*, 691–711.
Lehto, U. S., Ojanen, M., Dyba, T., Aromaa, A., & Kellokumpu-Lehtinen, P. (2006). Baseline psychosocial predictors of survival in localized breast cancer. *British Journal of Cancer, 94*, 1245–1252.
Leibowitz, S. F. (1991). Brain neuropeptide Y: An integrator of endocrine, metabolic, and behavioral processes. *Brain Research Bulletin, 27*, 333–337.
Leichliter, J. S., Chandra, A., Lidden, N., Fenton, K. A., & Aral, S. O. (2007). Prevalence and correlates of heterosexual anal and oral sex in adolescents and adults in the United States. *Journal of Infectious Diseases, 196*, 1852–1859.
Leichsenring, F., & Leibing, E. (2007). Psychodynamic psychotherapy: A systematic review of techniques, indications and empirical evidence. *Psychology and Psychotherapy, 80* (Pt. 2), 217–228.
Leigh, B. C. (1989). In search of the seven dwarves: Issues of measurement and meaning in alcohol expectancy research. *Psychological Bulletin, 105*, 361–373.

Leitenberg, H., & Henning, K. (1995). Sexual fantasy. *Psychological Bulletin, 117,* 469–496.

Leitenberg, H., Greenwald, E., & Tarran, M. J. (1989). The relation between sexual activity among children during preadolescence and/or early adolescence and sexual behavior and sexual adjustment in young adulthood. *Archives of Sexual Behavior, 18,* 299–313.

Leland, J. (1997, November 17). A pill for impotence? *Newsweek,* pp. 62–68.

Lemay, E. P., Clark, M. S., & Greenberg, A. (2010). What is beautiful is good because what is beautiful is desired: Physical attractiveness stereotyping as projection of interpersonal goals. *Personality and Social Psychology Bulletin, 36,* 339–353.

Lengagne, T., Jouventin, P., & Aubin, T. (1999). Findings one's mate in a king penguin colony: Efficiency of acoustic communication. *Behavior, 136,* 833–846.

Lenox, R. H., & Manji, H. K. (1995). Lithium. In A. F. Schatzberg & C. B. Nemeroff (Eds.), *The American Psychiatric Press textbook of psychopharmacology* (pp. 303–349). Washington, DC: American Psychiatric Press.

Lenze, E. J., Rollman, B. L., Shear, M. K., Dew, M. A., Pollock, B. G., Ciliberti, C., et al., (2009). Escitalopram for older adults with generalized anxiety disorder: A randomized controlled trial. *Journal of the American Medical Association, 301,* 295–303.

Leon, S. C., Kopta, S. M., Howard, K. I., & Lutz, W. (1999). Predicting patients' responses to psychotherapy: Are some more predictable than others? *Journal of Consulting and Clinical Psychology, 67,* 698–704.

Leonard, C. M. (1997). Corpus callosum: Sex or size? *Cerebral Cortex, 7,* 2.

LePine, J. A., Erez, A., & Johnson, D. E. (2002). The nature and dimensionality of organizational citizenship behavior: A critical review and a meta-analysis. *Journal of Applied Psychology, 87(1),* 52–65.

Lepore, S. J., Ragan, J. D., & Jones, S. (2000). Talking facilitates cognitive-emotional processes of adaptation to an acute stressor. *Journal of Personality and Social Psychology, 78,* 499–508.

Lepper, M. R., Corpus, J. H., & Iyengar, S. S. (2005). Intrinsic and extrinsic motivational orientations in the classroom: Age differences and academic correlates. *Journal of Educational Psychology, 97,* 184–196.

Lesch, K. P., & Merschdorf, U. (2000). Impulsivity, aggression, and serotonin: A molecular psychobiological perspective. *Behavioral Sciences and the Law, 18,* 581–604.

Lester, B. M., Andreozzi, L., & Appiah, L. (2004). Substance use during pregnancy: Time for policy to catch up with research. *Harm Reduction Journal, 1,* 5–49.

Lester, B. M., Corwin, M. J., Sepkoski, C., Seifer, R., Peucker, M., McLaughlin, S., et al. (1991). Neurobehavioral syndromes in cocaine-exposed newborn infants. *Child Development, 62(4),* 694–705.

Leuchter, A. F., Lesser, I. M., Trivedi, M. H., Rush, A. J., Morris, D. W., Warden, D., et al. (2008). An open pilot study of the combination of escitalopram and bupropion-SR for outpatients with major depressive disorder. *Journal of Psychiatric Practice, 14,* 271–280.

LeVay, S. (1996). *Queer science: The use and abuse of research into homosexuality.* Cambridge, MA: MIT Press.

Levenson, R. W., Carstensen, L. L., & Gottman, J. M. (1993). Long-term marriage: Age, gender, and satisfaction. *Psychology and Aging, 8,* 301–313.

Levenson, R. W., Ekman, P., & Friesen, W. V. (1990). Voluntary facial action generates emotion-specific nervous system activity. *Psychophysiology, 27,* 363–384.

Levin, R., & Nielsen, T. (2009). Nightmares, bad dreams, and emotion dysregulation: A review and new neurocognitive model of dreaming. *Current Directions in Psychological Science, 18,* 84–88.

Levine, B., Turner, G. R., Tisserand, D., Hevenor, S. J., Graham, S. J., & McIntosh, A. R. (2004). The functional neuroanatomy of episodic and semantic autobiographical remembering: A prospective functional MRI study. *Journal of Cognitive Neuroscience, 16,* 1633–1646.

Levine, J. A., & Pittinsky, T. L. (1997). *Working fathers: New strategies for balancing work and family.* Orlando, FL: Harcourt Brace.

Levine, M., & Thompson, K. (2004). Identity, place, and bystander intervention: Social categories and helping after natural disasters. *Journal of Social Psychology, 144,* 229–245.

Levine, R. A., & Campbell, D. T. (1972). *Ethnocentrism: Theories of conflict, ethnic attitudes, and group behavior.* New York: Wiley.

Levine, S. C., Vasilyeva, M., Lourenco, S. F., Newcombe, N. S., & Huttenlocher, J. (2005). Socioeconomic status modifies the sex difference in spatial skill. *Psychological Science, 16,* 841–845.

Levinson, D. F., Evgrafov, O. V., Knowles, J. A., Potash, J. B., Weissman, M. M., Scheftner, W. A., et al. (2007). Genetics of recurrent early-onset major depression (GenRED): Significant linkage on chromosome 15q25-q26 after fine mapping with single nucleotide polymorphism markers. *American Journal of Psychiatry, 164,* 259–264.

Levitt, A. G., & Utmann, J. G. A. (1992). From babbling towards the sound systems of English and French: A longitudinal two-case study. *Journal of Child Language, 19,* 19–40.

Levy, B. R., & Myers, L. M. (2004). Preventive health behaviors influenced by self-perceptions of aging. *Preventative Medicine, 39,* 625–629.

Levy, B. R., Slade, M. D., Kunkel, S. R., & Kasl, S. V. (2002). Longevity increased by positive self-perceptions of aging. *Journal of Personality and Social Psychology, 83,* 261–270.

Levy, D. L., Coleman, M. J., Sung, H., Ji, F., Matthysse, S., Mendell, N. R., et al. (2010). The genetic basis of thought disorder and language and communication disturbances in schizophrenia. *Journal of Neurolinguistics, 23,* 176.

Levy, G. D., Taylor, M. G., & Gelman, S. A. (1995). Traditional and evaluative aspects of flexibility in gender roles, social conventions, moral rules, and physical laws. *Child Development, 66,* 515–531.

Levy, K. N., & Kelly, K. M. (2010). Sex differences in jealousy: A contribution from attachment theory. *Psychological Science, 21,* 168–173.

Levy, N. A., & Janicak, P. G. (2000). Calcium channel antagonists for the treatment of bipolar disorder. *Bipolar Disorders, 2,* 108–119.

Levy-Shiff, R. (1994). Individual and contextual correlates of marital change across the transition to parenthood. *Developmental Psychology, 30,* 591–601.

Lewinsohn, P. M. (1974). A behavioral approach to depression. In R. J. Friedman & M. M. Katz (Eds.), *The psychology of depression: Contemporary theory and research* (pp. 157–185). Washington, DC: Winston-Wiley.

Lewinsohn, P. M., Clark, G. N., Hops, H., & Andrews, J. (1990). Cognitive-behavioral treatment for depressed adolescents. *Behavior Therapy, 21,* 385–401.

Lewinsohn, P. M., Rohde, P., & Seeley, J. R. (1994). Psychosocial risk factors for future adolescent suicide attempts. *Journal of Consulting and Clinical Psychology, 62,* 297–305.

Lewis, C. (2000). *A man's place in the home: Fathers and families in the UK.* York: Joseph Roundtree Foundation/YPS.

Lewis, D. O. (1992). From abuse to violence: Psychophysiological consequences of maltreatment. *Journal of the American Academy of Child and Adolescent Psychiatry, 31,* 383–391.

Lewis, D. O., Picus, J. H., Feldman, M., Jackson, L., & Bard, B. (1986). Psychiatric, neurological, and psychoeducational characteristics of 15 death row inmates in the United States. *American Journal of Psychiatry, 143,* 838–845.

Lewis, D. O., Yeager, C. A., Blake, P., Bard, B., & Strenziok, M. (2004). Ethics questions raised by the neuropsychiatric, neuropsychological, educational, developmental, and family characteristics of 18 juveniles awaiting execution in Texas. *Journal of the American Academy of Psychiatry and the Law, 32,* 408–429.

Lewis, M. (2009). *The Blind Side: Evolution of a Game.* New York: W.W. Norton.

Li, C. E., DiGiuseppe, R., & Froh, J. (2006). The roles of sex, gender, and coping in adolescent depression. *Adolescence, 41,* 409–415.

Li, D. K., Liu, L., & Odouli, R. (2003). Exposure to nonsteroidal anti-inflammatory drugs during pregnancy and risk of miscarriage: Population based cohort study. *BMJ, 327,* 368–372.

Li, S., Lindenberger, U., Hommel, B., Aschersleben, G., Prinz, W., & Baltes, P. B. (2004). Transformations in the couplings among intellectual abilities and constituent cognitive processes across the life span. *Psychological Science, 15,* 155–163.

Liberman, L. C., Lipp, O. V., Spence, S. H., & March, S. (2006). Evidence for retarded extinction of aversive learning in anxious children. *Behaviour Research and Therapy, 44,* 1491–1502.

Libersat, F., & Pflueger, H. J. (2004). Monoamines and the orchestration of behavior. *BioScience, 54,* 17–25.

Liberzon, I., Taylor, S. F., Amdur, R., Jung, T. D., Chamberlain, K. R., Minoshima, S., et al. (1999). Brain activation in PTSD in response to trauma-related stimuli. *Biological Psychiatry, 45,* 817–826.

Lichter, D. T., Qian, Z., & Mellott, L. M. (2006). Marriage or dissolution? Union transitions among poor cohabiting women. *Demography, 43,* 223–240.

Lieb, S., Thompson, D. R., Misra, S., Gates, G. J., Duffus, W. A., Fallon, S. J., et al. (2009). Estimating populations of men who have sex with men in the southern United States. *Journal of Urban Health, 86,* 887–901.

Lieberman, J., Chakos, M., Wu, H., Alvir, J., Hoffman, E., Robinson, D., et al. (2001). Longitudinal study of brain morphology in first episode schizophrenia. *Biological Psychiatry, 49,* 487–499.

Lieberman, J., Tollefson, G., Tohen, M., Green, A. I., Gur, R. E., Kahn, R., et al. (2003). Comparative efficacy and safety of atypical and conventional antipsychotic drugs in first-episode psychosis: A randomized, double-blind trial of olanzapine versus haloperidol. *American Journal of Psychiatry, 160,* 1396–1404.

Liebert, R. M., & Spiegler, M. D. (1998). *Personality: Strategies and issues* (8th ed.), Pacific Grove, CA: Brooks/Cole.

Liefbroer, A. C., & Dourleijn, E. (2006). Unmarried cohabitation and union stability: Testing the role of diffusion using data from 16 European countries. *Demography, 43,* 203–221.

Lilienfeld, S. O., Wood, J. M., & Garb, H. N. (2000). The scientific status of projective techniques. *Psychological Science in the Public Interest, 1,* 27–66.

Lillard, L. A., & Panis, C. W. A. (1996). Marital status and mortality: The role of health. *Demography, 33,* 313–327.

Lindau, S. T., & Gavrilova, N. (2010). Sex, health, and years of sexually active life gained due to good health: Evidence from two U.S. populations based cross sectional surveys of ageing. *BMJ, 340.*

Lindau, S. T., Schumm, L. P., Laumann, E. O., Levinson, W., O'Muircheartaigh, C. A., & Waite, L. J. (2007). A study of sexuality and health among older adults in the United States. *New England Journal of Medicine, 357,* 762–774.

Lindberg, L. D., Jones, R., & Santelli, J. S. (2008). Noncoital sexual activities among adolescents. *Journal of Adolescent Health, 43,* 231–238.

Lindenmayer, J. P., Khan, A., Iskander, A., Abad, M. T., & Parker, B. (2007). A randomized controlled trial of olanzapine versus haloperidol in the treatment of primary negative symptoms and neurocognitive deficits in schizophrenia. *Journal of Clinical Psychiatry, 68,* 368–379.

Lindroth, T., & Bergquist, M. (2010). Laptopers in an educational practice: Promoting the personal learning situation. *Computers and Education, 54,* 311–320.

Ling, D., Niu, T., Feng, Y., Xing, H., & Xu, X. (2004). Association between polymorphism of the dopamine transporter gene and early smoking onset: An interaction risk on nicotine dependence. *Journal of Human Genetics, 49,* 35–39.

Linhares, J. M., Pinto, P. D., & Nascimento, S. M. (2008). The number of discernable colors in natural scenes. *Journal of the Optical Society of America, 25,* 2918–2924.

Linville, P. W., Fischer, G. W., & Salovey, P. (1989). Perceived distributions of characteristics on in-group and out-group members: Empirical evidence and a computer simulation. *Journal of Personality and Social Psychology, 57,* 165–188.

Liossi, C., White, P., & Hatira, P. (2006). Randomized clinical trial of local anesthetic versus a combination of local anesthetic with self-hypnosis in the management of pediatric procedure-related pain. *Health Psychology, 25,* 307–315.

Lippa, R. (2003). Handedness, sexual orientation, and gender-related personality traits in men and women. *Archives of Sexual Behavior, 32,* 103–114.

Lipsitt, L.P. (2003). Crib death: A biobehavioral phenomenon? *Current Directions in Psychological Science, 12,* 164–170.

Lissek, S., Rabin, S., Heller, R. E., Lukenbaugh, D., Geraci, M., Pine, D. S., et al. (2010). Overgeneralization of conditioned fear as a pathogenic marker of panic disorder. *American Journal of Psychiatry, 167,* 47–55.

Littleton, H., Horsley, S., John, S., & Nelson, D. V. (2007). Trauma coping strategies and psychological distress: A meta-analysis. *Journal of Trauma and Stress, 20,* 977–988.

Liu, C. Y., & Kuo, F. Y. (2007). A study of Internet addiction through the lens of the interpersonal theory. *Cyberpsychology and Behavior, 10,* 799–804.

Livesley, W. J., Jang, K. L., & Vernon, P. A. (1998). Phenotypic and genotypic structure of traits delineating personality disorder. *Archives of General Psychiatry, 55,* 941–948.

Lloyd, G., Alexander, A. A., Rice, D. G., & Greenfield, N. S. (1980). Life events as predictors of academic performance. *Journal of Human Stress, 6,* 15–26.

Lockhart, R. S., & Craik, F. I. M. (1990). Levels of processing: A retrospective commentary on a framework for memory research. *Canadian Journal of Psychology, 44,* 87–112.

Lodewijkx, H. F., & Syroit, J. E. M. M. (2001). Affiliation during naturalistic severe and mild initiations: Some further evidence against the severity-attraction hypothesis [Special Issue]. *Current Research in Social Psychology, 6,* 90–107.

Lodewijkx, H. F. M., van Zomeren, M., & Syroit, J. E. M. M. (2005). The anticipation of severe initiation: Gender differences in effects on affiliation tendency and group attraction. *Small Group Research, 36,* 237–262.

Loewenstein, R. J., & Putnam, F. W. (2004). The dissociative disorders. In B. J. Sadock & V. A. Sadock (Eds.), *Posttraumatic stress disorder: DSM-IV and beyond* (8th ed., pp. 1844–1901). Baltimore, MD: Williams & Wilkins.

Loewenstein, W. R. (1960). Biological transducers. *Scientific American, 203,* 98–108.

Loftus, E. F. (1979). *Eyewitness testimony.* Cambridge, MA: Harvard University Press.

Loftus, E. F. (2000). Remembering what never happened. In E. Tulving (Ed.), *Memory, consciousness, and the brain* (pp. 106–118). Philadelphia: Psychology Press.

Loftus, E. F., & Palmer, J. C. (1974). Reconstruction of automobile destruction: An example of the interaction between language and memory. *Journal of Verbal Learning and Verbal Behavior, 13,* 585–589.

Loftus, E. F., & Zanni, G. (1975). Eyewitness testimony: The influence of the wording of a question. *Bulletin of the Psychonomic Society, 5,* 86–88.

Logie, R. H. (1996). The seven ages of working memory. In J. T. E. Richardson, R. W. Engle, L. Hasher, R. H. Logie, E. R. Stoltzfus, & R. T. Zacks (Eds.), *Working memory and human cognition* (pp. 31–65). Oxford, UK: Oxford University Press.

Logie, R. H. (1999). State of the art: Working memory. *The Psychologist, 12,* 174–178.

Logie, R. H., Della Sala, S., Wynn, V., & Baddeley, A. D. (2000, November). *Division of attention in Alzheimer's disease.* Paper presented at the Psychonomics Society meeting, Los Angeles, CA.

Logue, A. W. (1979). Taste aversion and the generality of the laws of learning. *Psychological Bulletin, 86,* 276–296.

Lohman, D. F., & Lakin, J. M. (2009). Consistencies in sex differences on the Cognitive Abilities Tests across countries, grades, test forms, and cohorts. *British Journal of Educational Psychology, 79,* 389–407.

Lomenick, J. P., Melguizo, M. S., Mitchell, S. L., Summar, M. L., & Anderson, J. W. (2009). Effects of meals high in carbohydrate, protein, and fat on ghrelin and peptide YY secretion in prepubertal children. *Journal of Clinical Endocrinology and Metabolism, 94,* 4463–4471.

Loney, B. R., Taylor, J., Butler, M. A., & Iacono, W. G. (2007). Adolescent psychopathy features: 6-year temporal stability and the prediction of externalizing symptoms during the transition to adulthood. *Aggressive Behavior, 33,* 242–252.

Long, B. C., & van Stavel, R. (1995). Effects of exercise training on anxiety: A meta-analysis. *Journal of Applied Sport Psychology, 7,* 167–189.

Lonsdorf, T. B., Weike, A. I., Nikamo, P., Schalling, M., Hamm, A. O., & Ohman, A. (2009). Genetic gating of human fear learning and extinction: Possible implications for gene-environment interaction in anxiety disorder. *Psychological Science, 20,* 198–206.

Lopez, C. M., Driscoll, K. A., & Kistner, J. A. (2009). Sex differences and response styles: Subtypes of rumination and associations with depressive symptoms. *Journal of Clinical Child and Adolescent Psychology, 38,* 27–35.

Lorenz, F. O., Simons, R. L., Conger, R. D., Elder, G. H., Jr., Johnson, C., & Chao, W. (1997). Married and recently divorced mothers' stressful events and distress: Tracing change across time. *Journal of Marriage and the Family, 59,* 219–232.

Lorenz, F. O., Wickrama, K. A., Conger, R. D., & Elder, G. H. Jr. (2006). The short-term and decade-long effects of divorce on women's midlife health. *Journal of Health and Social Behavior, 47,* 111–125.

Lourenco, O., & Machado, A. (1996). In defense of Piaget's theory: A reply to 10 common criticisms. *Psychological Review, 103,* 143–164.

Lowis, M. J., Edwards, A. C., & Burton, M. (2009). Coping with retirement: Well-being, health, and religion. *Journal of Psychology, 143,* 427–448.

Lu, N. Z., Eshleman, A. J., Janowsky, A. & Bethea, C. L. (2003). Ovarian steroid regulation of serotonin reuptake transporter (SERT) binding, distribution, and function in female macaques. *Molecular Psychiatry, 8,* 353–360.

Lucas, R. E. (2005). Time does not heal all wounds: A longitudinal study of reaction and adaptation to divorce. *Psychological Science, 16,* 945–950.

Ludtke, O., Trautwein, U., & Husemann, N. (2009). Goal and personality trait development in a transitional period: Assessing change and stability in personality development. *Personality and Social Psychology Bulletin, 35,* 428–441.

Luecken, L. J., & Compas, B. E. (2002). Stress, coping, and immune function in breast cancer. *Annals of Behavioral Medicine, 24,* 336–344.

Lumer, E. D., Friston, K. J., & Rees, G. (1998, June 19). Neural correlates of perceptual rivalry in the human brain. *Science, 280,* 1930–1934.

Luo, S. (2009). What leads to romantic attraction: Similarity, reciprocity, security, or beauty? Evidence from a speed-dating study. *Journal of Personality, 77,* 933–964.

Luszcz, M. A., Bryan, J., & Kent, P. (1997). Predicting episodic memory performance of very old men and women: Contributions from age, depression, activity, cognitive ability, and speed. *Psychology and Aging, 12,* 340–351.

Luxenberg, E. L., Goldenberg, F. D., Frank, J. I., Loch Macdonald, & R., & Rosengart, A. J. (2009). Locked-in syndrome from rostro-caudal herniation. *Journal of Clinical Neuroscience, 16,* 333–335.

Lykken, D. T., McGue, M., Tellegen, A., & Bouchard, T. J. (1992). Emergenesis. *American Psychologist, 47,* 1565–1567.

Lynch, W. J., Roth, M. E., & Carroll, M. E. (2002). Biological basis of sex differences in drug abuse: Preclinical and clinical studies. *Psychopharmacology, 164,* 121–137.

Lynn, S. J. (1997). Automaticity and hypnosis: A sociocognitive account. *International Journal of Clinical and Experimental Hypnosis, 45,* 239–250.

Lynne-Landsman, S. D., Graber, J. A., Nichols, T. R., & Botvin, G. J. (2010). Is sensation seeking a stable trait or does it change over time? *Journal of Youth and Adolescence,* doi:10.1007/s10964-010-9529-2.

Lytton, H., & Romney, D. M. (1991). Parents' differential socialization of boys and girls: A meta-analysis. *Psychological Bulletin, 109,* 267–296.

Maas, J. B. (1998). *The sleep advantage: Preparing your mind for peak performance.* New York: Villard.

Macfadden, W., Bossie, C. A., Turkoz, I., & Haskins, J. T. (2010). Risperidone long-acting therapy in stable patients with recently diagnosed schizophrenia. *International Clinical Psychopharmacology, 25,* 75–82.

Machado-Silva, A., Perrier, S., & Bourdon, J. C. (2010). p53 family members in cancer diagnosis and treatment. *Seminars in Cancer Biology.* doi: 10.1016/j.semcancer.2010.02.005.

MacIntyre, G. F. (1998). And what's keeping you from finishing your book? *Writer's Digest, 78,* 6.

Mackay, J. (2000). *The Penguin atlas of human sexual behavior: Sexuality and sexual practices around the world.* New York: Penguin Putnam.

MacKinnon, D., Jamison, K. R., & DePaulo, J. R. (1997). Genetics of manic depressive illness. *Annual Review of Neuroscience, 20,* 355–373.

Macmillian, N. A., & Creelman, C. D. (1991). *Detection theory: A user's guide.* Cambridge, UK: Cambridge University Press.

Macramalla, S., & Bridgeman, B. (2009). Anticipated effort in imagined self-rotation. *Perception, 38,* 79–91.

Maddi, S. R. (2005). On hardiness and other pathways to resilience. *American Psychologist, 60,* 261–262.

Maddi, S. R., Harvey, R. H., Khoshaba, D. M., Lu, J. L., Persico, M., & Brow, M. (2006). The personality construct of hardiness, III: Relationships with repression, innovativeness, authoritarianism, and performance. *Journal of Personality, 74,* 575–597.

Maddi, S. R., & Kobasa, S. C. (1984). *The hardy executive: Health under stress.* Homewood, IL: Dorsey Press.

Magley, V. J. (2002). Coping with sexual harassment: Reconceptualizing women's resistance. *Journal of Personality and Social Psychology, 83,* 930–946.

Magley, V. J., Hulin, C. L., Fitzgerald, L. F., & DeNardo, M. (1999). Outcomes of self-labeling sexual harassment. *Journal of Applied Psychology, 84,* 390–402.

Maguire, E. A., Woollett, K., & Spiers, H. J. (2006). London taxi drivers and bus drivers: A structural MRI and neuropsychological analysis. *Hippocampus, 16,* 1091–1101.

Magura, S., Laudet, A. B., Mahmood, D., Rosenblum, A., & Knight, E. (2002). Adherence to medication regimes and participation in dual-focus self-help groups. *Psychiatric Services, 53,* 310–316.

Mah, K., & Binik, Y. M. (2002). Do all orgasms feel alike? Evaluating a two-dimensional model of the orgasm experience across gender and sexual context. *Journal of Sex Research, 39,* 104–113.

Mahoney, R. (2007). *Down the Nile: Alone in a fisherman's skiff.* New York: Back Bay Books.

Main, M., & Solomon, J. (1990). Procedures for identifying infants as disorganized/disoriented during the Ainsworth Strange Situation. In M. Greenberg, D. Cicchetti, & M. Cummings (Eds.), *Attachment in the preschool years: Theory, research, and intervention* (pp. 121–160). Chicago: University of Chicago Press.

Maisonneuve, J., Palmade, G., & Fourment, C. (1952). Selective choices and propinquity. *Sociometry, 15,* 135–140.

Maj, M., Pirozzi, R., Magliano, L., & Bartoli, L. (1997). Long-term outcome of lithium prophylaxis in bipolar disorder: A 5-year prospective study of 402 patients at a lithium clinic. *American Journal of Psychiatry, 155,* 30–55.

Majdandzic, M., & van den Boom, D. C. (2007). Multimethod longitudinal assessment of temperament in early childhood. *Journal of Personality, 75,* 121–168.

Maki, M. T., & Kitano, H. H. (2002). Counseling Asian Americans. In P. B. Pedersen, J. G. Draguns, W. J. Lonner, & J. E. Trimble (Eds.), *Counseling across cultures* (5th ed., pp. 109–132). Thousand Oaks, CA: Sage.

Malaspina, D., Harlap, S., Fennig, S., Heiman, D., Nahon, D., Feldman, D., et al. (2001). Advancing paternal age and the risk of schizophrenia. *Archives of General Psychiatry, 58,* 361–367.

Maletzky, B. (1998). The paraphilias: Research and treatment. In P. E. Nathan (Ed.), *A guide to treatments that work* (pp. 472–500). New York: Oxford University Press.

Malina, R. M. (1990). Physical growth and performance during the transitional years (9–16). In R. Montemayor, G. R. Adams, & T. P. Gullotta (Eds.), *From childhood to adolescence: A transitional period?* (pp. 41–62). Newbury Park, CA: Sage.

Maltz, W. (2002). Treating the sexual intimacy concerns of sexual abuse survivors. *Sexual and Relationship Therapy, 17,* 321–327.

Maltz, W., & Boss, S. (2001). *Private thoughts: Exploring the power of women's sexual fantasies.* Novato, CA: New World Library.

Mann, R. D. (1959). A review of the relationships between personality and performance in small groups. *Psychological Bulletin, 56,* 241–270.

Manning, J. R., & Brainard, D. H. (2009). Optimal design of photoreceptor mosaics: Why we do not see color at night. *Visual Neuroscience, 26,* 5–19.

Manning, W. D. (2001). Childbearing in cohabiting unions: Racial and ethnic differences. *Family Planning Perspectives, 33,* 217–223.

Manoussaki, D., Chadwick, R. S., Ketten, D. R., Arruda, J., Dimitriadis, E. K., & O'Malley, J. T. (2008). The influence of cochlear shape on low-frequency hearing. *Proceedings of the National Academy of Sciences of the United States of America, 105,* 6162–6166.

Manuck, S. B., Flory, J. D., Ferrell, R. E., Mann, J. J., & Muldoon, M. F. (2000). A regulatory polymorphism of the monoamine oxidase-A gene may be associated with the variability in aggression, impulsivity, and central nervous system serotonergic responsivity. *Psychiatry Research, 95,* 9–23.

Marañon, I., Echeburúa, E., & Grijalvo, J. (2004). Prevalence of personality disorders in patients with eating disorders: A pilot study using the IPDE. *European Eating Disorders Review, 12,* 217–222.

Marazzitti, D., Rotondo, A., Presta, S., Pancioloi-Guasagnucci, M. L., Palego, L., & Conti, L. (1993). Role of serotonin in human aggressive behavior. *Aggressive Behavior, 19,* 347–353.

Marcia, J. E. (1966). Development and validation of ego identity status. *Journal of Personality and Social Psychology, 21,* 551–559.

Marcia, J. E. (1968). The case history of a construct: Ego identity status. In E. Vinache (Ed.), *Readings in general psychology* (pp. 325–332). New York: American Book.

Marcia, J. E. (1980). Identity in adolescence. In J. Adelson (Ed.), *Handbook of adolescent psychology* (pp. 159–187). New York: Wiley.

Marcia, J. E. (1993). The relational roots of identity. In J. Kroger (Ed.), *Discussions on ego identity* (pp. 101–120). Hillsdale, NJ: Erlbaum.

Marcia, J. E. (2002). Identity and psychosocial development in adulthood. *Identity, 2,* 7–28.

Mareschal, D. (2000). Object knowledge in infancy: Current controversies and approaches. *Trends in Cognitive Science, 4,* 408–416.

Marijuana as medicine: How strong is the science? (1997, May). *Consumer Reports,* pp. 62–63.

Mariscal, M., Palma, S., Liorca, J., Perez-Iglesias, R., Pardo-Crespo, R., & Delgado-Rodriguez, M. (2006). Pattern of alcohol consumption during pregnancy and risk for low birth weight. *Annals of Epidemiology, 16,* 432–438.

Markman, A. B., & Ross, B. H. (2003). Category use and category learning. *Psychological Bulletin, 129,* 592–613.

Marler, P. R., Duffy, A., & Pickert, R. (1986). Vocal communication in the domestic chicken: II. Is a sender sensitive to the presence and nature of a receiver? *Animal Behavior, 34,* 194–198.

Marques, J. F. (2010). The effect of visual deprivation on the organization of conceptual knowledge: Testing the grounded cognition hypothesis. *Experimental Psychology, 57,* 83–88.

Martin, C. L., & Halverson, C. F. (1981). A schematic processing model of sex typing and stereotyping in children. *Child Development, 52,* 1119–1134.

Martin, C. L., & Halverson, C. F. (1987). The role of cognition in sex role acquisition. In D. B. Carter (Ed.), *Current conceptions of sex roles and sex typing: Theory and research* (pp. 123–137). New York: Praeger.

Martin, C. L., & Ruble, D. N. (2010). Patterns of gender development. *Annual Review of Psychology, 61,* 353–381.

Martin, D. J., Garske, J. P., & Davis, M. K. (2000). Relation of the therapeutic alliance with outcome and other variables: A meta-analytic review. *Journal of Consulting and Clinical Psychology, 68,* 438–450.

Martin, G., & Pear, J. (1983). *Behavior modification: What it is and how to do it* (2nd ed.). Englewood Cliffs, NJ: Prentice Hall.

Martin, G., England, G., Kaprowy, E., Kilgour, K., & Pilek, V. (1968). Operant conditioning of kindergarten-class behavior in autistic children. *Behavior Research and Therapy, 6,* 281–294.

Martin, L. (1986). Eskimo words for snow: A case study on the genesis and decay of an anthropological example. *American Anthropologist, 88,* 418–423.

Martin, P. D., Specter, G., Martin, D., & Martin, M. (2003). Expressed attitudes of adolescents toward marriage and family life. *Adolescence, 38,* 359–367.

Martinko, M. J., Breaux, D. M., Martinez, A. D., Summers, J., & Harvey, P. (2009). Hurricane Katrina and attributions of responsibility. *Organizational Dynamics, 38,* 52–63.

Martorana, A., Mori, F., Esposito, Z., Kusayanagi, H., Monteleone, F., Codecà, C., et al. Sancesario, G., Bernardi, G., & Koch, G. (2009). Dopamine modulates cholinergic cortical excitability in Alzheimer's disease patients. *Neuropsychopharmacology, 34,* 2323–2328.

Mashal, N., & Faust, M. (2008). Right hemisphere sensitivity to novel metaphoric relations: application Application of the signal detection theory. *Brain and Language, 104,* 103–112.

Maslow, A. (1968). *Toward a psychology of being* (2nd ed.). New York: Van Nostrand.

Maslow, A. (1970). *Motivation and personality* (2nd ed.). New York: Harper & Row.

Maslow, A. (1971). *The farther reaches of human nature.* New York: Viking.

Masters, W. H., & Johnson, V. E. (1966). *Human sexual response.* Boston: Little, Brown.

Masters, W. H., Johnson, V. E., & Kolodny, R. C. (1993). *Biological foundations of human sexuality.* New York: HarperCollins.

Maston, C. T. (2010, March). *Criminal victimization in the United States, 2007—Statistical tables.* Bureau of Justice Statistics. Retrieved April 17, 2010, from http://bjs.ojp.usdoj.gov/index.cfm?ty=pbdetail&iid=1743

Mathew, R., Wilson, W., Blazer, D., & George, L. (1993). Psychiatric disorders in adult children of alcoholics: Data from the epidemiologic catchment area project. *American Journal of Psychiatry, 150*(5), 793–796.

Matlin, M. W., & Foley, H. J. (1997). *Sensation and perception.* Boston: Allyn & Bacon.

Matson, J. L., & Boisjoli, J. A. (2009). The token economy for children with intellectual disability and/or autism: A review. *Research in Developmental Disabilities, 30,* 240–248.

Matsuda, L. A., Lolait, S. J., Brownstein, M. J., Young, A. C., & Bonner, T. I. (1990). Structure of a cannabinoid receptor and functional expression of the cloned cDNA. *Nature, 346,* 561–564.

Matsumoto, D. (1994). *People: Psychology from a cross-cultural perspective.* Pacific Grove, CA: Brooks/Cole.

Maurer, T., & Robinson, D. (2008). Effects of attire, alcohol, and gender on perceptions of date rape. *Sex Roles, 58,* 423–435.

Maurice, W. L. (2005). Male hypoactive sexual desire disorder. In R. Balon & R. T. Segraves (Eds.), *Handbook of sexual dysfunction* (pp. 76–109). Boca Raton, FL: Taylor & Francis.

Mauss, I. B., Cook, C. L., Cheng, J. Y., & Gross, J. J. (2007). Individual differences in cognitive reappraisal: Experiential and physiological responses to an anger provocation. *International Journal of Psychophysiology, 66,* 116–124.

Maville, J., & Huerta, C. G. (1997). Stress and social support among Hispanic student nurses: Implications for academic achievement. *Journal of Cultural Diversity, 4,* 18–25.

Maxmen, J. S., & Ward, N. G. (1995). *Essential psychopathology and its treatment* (2nd ed.). New York: Norton.

Maxwell, J. C., & Spence, R. T. (2003). Profiles of club drug users in treatment. *Substance Use and Misuse, 40,* 1409–1426.

Mayberg, H. S. (1997). Limbic-cortical dysregulation: A proposed model of depression. *Journal of Neuropsychiatry and Clinical Neuroscience, 9,* 471–481.

Mayberg, H. S., Liotti, M., Brannan, S. K., McGinnis, S., Mahurin, R. K., Jerabek, P. A., et al. (1999). Reciprocal limbic–cortical function and negative mood: Converging PET findings in depression and normal sadness. *American Journal of Psychiatry, 156,* 675–682.

Mayberg, H. S., Lozano, A. M., Voon, V., McNeely, H. E., Seminowicz, D., Hamani, C., et al. (2005). Deep brain stimulation for treatment-resistant depression. *Neuron, 45,* 651–660.

Mayer, J. D., Salovey, P., Caruso, D. R., & Sitarenios, G. (2003). Measuring emotional intelligence with the MSCEIT V2.0. *Emotion, 3,* 97–105.

Mayer, R. E. (1983). *Thinking, problem solving, cognition.* San Francisco: Freeman.

Mayes, L. C., Bornstein, M. H., Chawarska, K., & Haynes, O. M. (1996). Impaired regulation of arousal in 3-month-old infants exposed prenatally to cocaine and other drugs. *Development and Psychopathology, 8*(1), 29–42.

Mays, V. M., & Cochran, S. D. (2001). Mental health correlates of perceived discrimination among lesbian, gay, and bisexual adults in the United States. *American Journal of Public Health, 91,* 1869–1876.

Maziade, M., Caron, C., Cote, R., Merette, C., Bernier, H., Laplante, B., et al. (1990). Psychiatric status of adolescents who had extreme temperaments at age 7. *American Journal of Psychiatry, 147,* 1531–1536.

Mazure, C. M., Keita, G. P., & Blehar, M. C. (2002). *Summit on women and depression: Proceedings and recommendations.* Washington, DC: American Psychological Association.

McAdams, D. P., & Olson, B. D. (2010). Personality development: Continuity and change over the life course. *Annual Review of Psychology, 61,* 517–542.

McAlpine, D. D., & Mechanic, D. (2000). Utilization of specialty mental health care among persons with severe mental illness: The roles of demographics, need, insurance, and risk. *Health Services Research, 35,* 277–292.

McAndrew, F. (1986). A cross-cultural study of recognition thresholds for facial expressions of emotions. *Journal of Cross-Cultural Psychology, 17,* 211–224.

McCallie, M. S., Blum, C. M., & Hood, C. J. (2006). Progressive muscle relaxation. *Journal of Human Behavior in the Social Environment, 13,* 51, 66.

McCann, U. D., Wilson, M. J., Sgambati, F. P., & Ricaurte, G. A. (2009). Sleep deprivation differentially impairs cognitive performance in abstinent methylenedioxy-methamphetamine ("Ecstasy") users. *Journal of Neuroscience, 29,* 14050–14056.

McCarley, R. W. (1998). Dreams: Disguise of forbidden wishes or transparent reflections of a distinct brain state? *Annals of the New York Academy of Sciences, 843,* 116–133.

McCarthy, B. W. (2001). Relapse prevention strategies and techniques with erectile dysfunction. *Journal of Sex and Marital Therapy, 27,* 1–8.

McClelland, D. C. (1987). *Human motivation.* Cambridge, UK: Cambridge University Press.

McClung, C. A. (2007). Circadian genes, rhythms and the biology of mood disorders. *Pharmacology and Therapeutics, 114,* 222–232.

McClure, H. H., Snodgrass, J. J., Martinez, C. R., Jr., Eddy, J. M., Jimenez, R. A., & Isiordia, L. E. (2010). Discrimination, psychosocial stress, and health among Latin American immigrants in Oregon. *American Journal of Human Biology, 22,* 421–423.

McConkey, K. M. (1995). Hypnosis, memory, and the ethics of uncertainty. *Australian Psychologist, 30,* 1–10.

McCrae, R. R., & Costa, P. T., Jr. (1998). Personality trait structure as a human universal. *American Psychologist, 52,* 509–516.

McCrae, R. R., Costa, P. T., Ostendorf, F., Angleitner, A., Hrebickova, M., Avia, M. D., et al. (2000). Nature over nurture: Temperament, personality, and life span development. *Journal of Personality and Social Psychology, 78,* 173–186.

McCrae, R. R., Costa, P. T., Jr., Pedroso de Lima, M., Simoes, A., Ostendorf, F., Angleitner, A., et al. (1999). Age differences in personality across the adult life span: Parallels in five cultures. *Developmental Psychology, 35,* 466–477.

McCrae, R. R., Costa, P. T., Terracciano, A., Parker, W. D., Mills, C. J., De Fruyt, F., et al. (2002). Personality trait development from age 12 to age 18: Longitudinal, cross-sectional, and cross-cultural analyses. *Journal of Personality and Social Psychology, 83,* 1456–1468.

McCullough, M. E., Hoyt, W. T., Larson, D. S., Koenig, H. G., & Thoresen, C. (2000). Religious involvement and mortality: A meta-analytic review. *Health Psychology, 19,* 211–222.

McElroy, S. L., Kotwal, R., Malhotra, S., Nelson, E. B., Keck, P. E., & Nemeroff, C. B. (2004). Are mood disorders and obesity related? A review for the mental health professional. *Journal of Clinical Psychiatry, 65,* 634–651.

McEvoy, P. M., & Nathan, P. (2007). Effectiveness of cognitive behavior therapy for diagnostically heterogeneous groups: A benchmarking study. *Journal of Consulting and Clinical Psychology, 75,* 344–350.

McFalls, J. A., Jr. (1990). The risks of reproductive impairment in the later years of childbearing. *Annual Review of Sociology, 16,* 491–519.
McGarvey, C., McDonnell, M., Hamilton, K., O'Regan, M., & Matthews, T. (2006). An 8 year study of risk factors for SIDS: Bed-sharing versus non-bed-sharing. *Archives of Disease in Childhood, 91,* 318–323.
McGehee, D. S., Heath, M. J. S., Gelber, S., Devay, P., & Role, L. W. (1995). Nicotine enhancement of fast excitation synaptic transmissions in CNS by pre-synaptic receptors. *Science, 269,* 1692–1696.
McGlashan, T. H., & Hoffman, R. E. (2000). Schizophrenia as a disorder of developmentally reduced synaptic connectivity. *Archives of General Psychiatry, 57,* 637–648.
McGrady, A. V., Bush, E. G., & Grubb, B. P. (1997). Outcome of biofeedback-assisted relaxation for neurocardiogenic syncope and headache: A clinical replication series. *Applied Psychophysiology and Biofeedback, 22,* 63–72.
McGregor, G., Desaga, J. F., Ehlenz, K., Fischer, A., Heese, F., Hegele, A., et al. (1996). Radioimmunological measurement of leptin in plasma of obese and diabetic human subjects. *Endocrinology, 137,* 1501–1504.
McGuffin, P., Rijsdijk, F., Andrew, M., Sham, P., Katz, R., & Cardno, A. (2003). The heritability of bipolar affective disorder and the genetic relationship to unipolar depression. *Archives of General Psychiatry, 60,* 497–502.
McHolm, A. E., MacMillan, H. L., & Jamieson, E. (2003). The relationship between childhood physical abuse and suicidality among depressed women: Results from a community sample. *American Journal of Psychiatry, 160,* 933–938.
McIntosh, D. N. (1996). Facial feedback hypotheses: Evidence, implications, and directions. *Motivation and Emotion, 20,* 121–147.
McIntosh, E., Gillanders, D., & Rodgers, S. (2010). Rumination, goal linking, daily hassles and life events in major depression. *Clinical Psychology and Psychotherapy, 17,* 33–43.
McKean, K. J. (1994). Using multiple risk factors to assess the behavioral, cognitive, and affective effects of learned helplessness. *Journal of Psychology, 128*(2), 177–183.
McKenna, M. C., Zevon, M. A., Corn, B., & Rounds, J. (1999). Psychosocial factors and the development of breast cancer: A meta-analysis. *Health Psychology, 18,* 520–531.
McKillip, J., & Reidel, S. L. (1983). External validity of matching on physical attractiveness for same and opposite sex couples. *Journal of Applied Social Psychology, 13,* 328–337.
McKim, W. A. (1997). *Drugs and behavior.* Upper Saddle River, NJ: Prentice Hall.
McKnight Investigators. (2003). Risk factors for the onset of eating disorders in adolescent girls: The results of the McKnight longitudinal risk factor study. *American Journal of Psychiatry, 160,* 248–254.
McKnight-Eily, L. R., Liu, Y., Perry, G. S., Presley-Cantrell, L. R., Strine, T. W., Lu, H., et al. (2009). Perceived insufficient rest or sleep among adults—United States, 2008. *Morbidity and Mortality Weekly Report, 58,* 1175–1179.
McLaughlin, K. A., Borkovec, T. D., & Sibrava, N. J. (2007). The effects of worry and rumination on affect states and cognitive activity. *Behavior Therapy, 38,* 23–38.
McLaughlin, K. A., Green, J. G., Gruber, M. J., Sampson, N. A., Zaslavsky, A. M., & Kessler, R. C. (2010). Childhood adversities and adult psychiatric disorders in the National Comorbidity Survey Replication II: Associations with persistence of DSM-IV disorders. *Archives of General Psychiatry, 67,* 124–132.
McLay, R. N., McBrien, C., Wiederhold, M. D., & Wiederhold, B. K. (2010). Exposure therapy with and without virtual reality to treat PTSD while in the combat theater: A parallel case series. *Cyberpsychology, Behavior, and Social Networking, 13,* 37–42.
McManus, M. A., & Baratta, J. E. (1992). *The relationship of recruiting source to performance and survival.* Paper presented at the annual meeting of the Society for Industrial and Organizational Psychology, Montreal, Canada.
McMillen, D. L., Smith, S. M., & Wells-Parker, E. (1989). The effects of alcohol, expectancy, and sensation seeking on driving risk taking. *Addictive Behaviors, 14,* 477–483.
McNeill, B., Prieto, L., Niemann, Y., Pizarro, M., Vera, E., & Gomez, S. (2001). Current directions in Chicana/o psychology. *Counseling Psychologist, 29,* 5–17.
McSweeney, F. K., & Swindell, S. (2002). Common processes may contribute to extinction and habituation. *Journal of General Psychology, 129,* 364–400.
McWilliam, L., Schepman, A., & Rodway, P. (2009). The linguistic status of text message abbreviations: An exploration using a Stroop task. *Computers in Human Behavior, 25,* 970–974.
Medicare to fund obesity treatment. (2004). CBS News. Available online at http://www.cbsnews.com/stories/2004/07/16/health/printable630141.shtml
Medina-Mora, M. E., Borges, G., Lara, C., Benjet, C., Blanco, J., Fleiz, C., et al. (2005). Prevalence, service use, and demographic correlates of 12-month DSM-IV psychiatric disorders in Mexico: Results from the Mexican National Comorbidity Survey. *Psychological Medicine, 35,* 1773–1783.
Mednick, S. A., Watson, J. B., Huttunen, M., Cannon, T. D., Katila, H., Machon, R., et al. (1998). A two-hit working model of the etiology of schizophrenia. In M. F. Lenzenweger & R. H. Dworkin (Eds.), *Origins of the development of schizophrenia* (pp. 27–66). Washington, DC: American Psychological Association.
Mehl, M. R., Vazire, S., Holleran, S. E., & Clark, C. S. (2010). Eavesdropping on happiness: Well-being is related to having less small talk and more substantive conversations. *Psychological Science, 21,* 539–541.
Mehroof, M., & Griffiths, M. D. (2010). Online gaming addiction: The role of sensation seeking, self-control, neuroticism, aggression, state anxiety, and trait anxiety. *Cyberpsychology, Behavior, and Social Networking, 13,* 313–316.
Meissner, J. S., Blanchard, E. B., & Malamood, H. S. (1997). Comparison of treatment outcome measures for irritable bowel syndrome. *Applied Psychophysiology and Biofeedback, 22,* 55–62.
Melke, J., Landen, M., Baghei, F., Rosmond, R., Holm, G., Bjorntorp, P., et al. (2001). Serotonin transporter gene polymorphisms are associated with anxiety-related personality traits in women. *American Journal of Medical Genetics, 105,* 458–463.
Mellet, E., Bricogne, S., Crivello, F., Mazoyer, B., Denis, M., & Tzourio-Mazoyer, N. (2002). Neural basis of mental scanning of a topographic representation built from a text. *Cerebral Cortex, 12,* 1322–1330.
Mellman, T. A., Alim, T., Brown, D. D., Gorodetsky, E., Buzas, B., Lawson, W. B., et al. (2009). Serotonin polymorphisms and posttraumatic stress disorder in a trauma exposed African American population. *Depression and Anxiety, 26,* 993–997.
Meltzer, L. J., & Mindell, J. A. (2006). Sleep and sleep disorders in children and adolescents. *Psychiatric Clinics of North America, 29,* 1059–1076.
Melzack, R., & Wall, P. D. (1988). *The challenge of pain* (2nd ed.). London: Penguin.
Memmler, R. L., Cohen, B. J., & Wood, D. (1992). *Structure and function of the human body* (5th ed.). Philadelphia: J. B. Lippincott.
Menard, K. S., Nagayama Hall, G., Phung, A., Erian Ghebrial, M., & Martin, L. (2003). Gender differences in sexual harassment and coercion in college students. *Journal of Interpersonal Violence, 18,* 1222–1239.
Mennella, J. A., & Beauchamp, G. K. (1991). Maternal diet alters the sensory qualities of human milk and nursling's behavior. *Pediatrics, 88,* 737–744.
Menzies, R. G., & Clark, J. C. (1993). A comparison of *in vivo* and vicarious exposure in the treatment of childhood water phobia. *Behaviour Research and Therapy, 31,* 9–15.
Merkl, A., Heuser, I., & Bajbouj, M. (2009). Antidepressant electroconvulsive therapy: Mechanism of action, recent advances and limitations. *Experimental Neurology, 219,* 20–26.
Merritt, J. M., Stickgold, R., Pace-Schott, E., Williams, J., & Hobson, J. A. (1994). Emotion profiles in the dreams of men and women. *Consciousness and Cognition, 3*(1), 46–60.
Mesch, G. S. (2001). Social relationships and Internet use among adolescents in Israel. *Social Science Quarterly, 82,* 329–340.
Mesch, G. S. (2009). Parental mediation, online activities, and cyberbullying. *Cyberpsychology and Behavior, 12,* 387–393.
Messner, M., Reinhard, M., & Sporer, S. L. (2008). Compliance through direct persuasive appeals: The moderating role of communicator's attractiveness in interpersonal persuasion. *Social Influence, 3,* 67–83.
Meston, C. M., Trapnell, P. D., & Gorzalka, B. B. (1996). Ethnic and gender differences in sexuality: Variations in sexual behavior between Asian and non-Asian university students. *Archives of Sex Behavior, 25,* 33–71.
Meyer, J. P., & Allen, N. J. (1991). A three-component conceptualization of organizational commitment. *Human Resource Management Review, 1,* 61–89.
Meyer, J. P., & Herscovitch, L. (2001). Commitment in the workplace: Toward a general model. *Human Resource Management Review, 11,* 299–326.
Meyer, L. (1999). Hostile classrooms. *The Advocate, 32*(1), 33–35.
Mezulis, A. H., Abramson, L. Y., Hyde, J. S., & Hankin, B. L. (2004). Is there a universal positivity bias in attributions? A meta-analytic review of individual, developmental, and cultural differences in the self-serving attributional bias. *Psychological Bulletin, 130,* 711–747.
Micco, J. A., Henin, A., Mick, E., Kim, S., Hopkins, C. A., Biederman, J., et al. (2009). Anxiety and depressive disorders in offspring at high risk for anxiety: A meta-analysis. *Journal of Anxiety Disorders, 23,* 1158–1164.
Michael, G. A., Boucart, M., Degreef, J. F., & Goefroy, O. (2001). The thalamus interrupts top-down attentional control for permitting exploratory shiftings to sensory signals. *Neuroreport, 12,* 2041–2048.
Michael, R. T., Gagnon, J. H., Laumann, E. O., & Kolata, G. (1994). *Sex in America: A definitive survey.* Boston: Little, Brown.
Michelson, D., Bancroft, J., Targum, S., Kim, Y., & Tepner, R. (2000). Female sexual dysfunction associated with antidepressant administration: A randomized, placebo-controlled study of pharmacological intervention. *American Journal of Psychiatry, 157,* 239–243.
Migliore, M., Novara, G., & Tegolo, D. (2008). Single neuron binding properties and the magical number 7. *Hippocampus, 18,* 1122–1130.
Milgram, S. (1963). Behavioral study of obedience. *Journal of Abnormal and Social Psychology, 67,* 371–378.
Milgram, S. (1965). Some conditions of obedience and disobedience to authority. *Human Relations, 18,* 57–76.
Milgram, S. (1974). *Obedience to authority: An experimental view.* New York: Harper & Row.
Millar, M. (2002). The effectiveness of the door-in-the-face compliance strategy on friends and strangers. *Journal of Social Psychology, 142,* 295–305.
Miller, B. C., & Benson, B. (1999). Romantic and sexual relationship development during adolescence. In W. Furman, B. B. Brown, & C. Feiring (Eds.), *The Development of Romantic Relationships in Adolescence* (pp. 99–121). New York: Cambridge University Press.
Miller, D. T., & Ross, M. (1975). Self-serving biases in the attribution of causality: Fact or fiction? *Psychological Bulletin, 82,* 213–225.
Miller, E. (1999). The pheromone androsterol: Evolutionary considerations. *Mankind Quarterly, 39,* 455–466.
Miller, G. A. (1956). The magical number seven, plus or minus two: Some limits on our capacity for processing information. *Psychological Review,* 63, 81–97.
Miller, G. E., & Blackwell, E. (2006). Turning up the heat: Inflammation as a mechanism linking chronic stress, depression, and heart disease. *Current Directions in Psychological Science, 15,* 269–272.
Miller, I. J., Jr., & Bartoshuk, L. M. (1991). Taste perception, taste bud distribution, and spatial relationships. In T. V. Gethell, R. L. Doty, L. M. Bartoshuk, & J. B. Snow, Jr. (Eds.), *Smell and taste in health and disease* (pp. 205–233). New York: Raven.
Miller, L. C., & Fishkin, S. A. (1997). On the dynamics of human bonding and reproductive success: Seeking windows on the adapted-for human-environmental interface. In J. A. Simpson & D. T. Kenrick (Eds.), *Evolutionary social psychology* (pp. 197–236). Hillsdale, NJ: Erlbaum.
Miller, N. S., & Gold, M. S. (1994). LSD and Ecstasy: Pharmacology, phenomenology, and treatment. *Psychiatric Annals, 24,* 131–133.
Miller, S. L., & Maner, J. K. (2010). Scent of a woman: Men's testosterone responses to olfactory ovulation cues. *Psychological Science, 21,* 276–283.

Miller, T. Q., Smith, T. W., Turner, C. W., Guijarro, M. L., & Hallet, A. J. (1996). A meta-analytic review of research on hostility and physical health. *Psychological Bulletin, 119,* 322–348.

Miller, T. Q., Turner, C. W., Tindale, R. S., Posavac, E. J., & Dugoni, B. L. (1991). Reasons for the trend toward null findings in research on Type A behavior. *Psychological Bulletin, 110,* 469–485.

Miller, W. R., & Seligman, M. E. P. (1975). Depression and learned helplessness in man. *Journal of Abnormal Psychology, 84,* 228–238.

Miller, W. R., & Thoresen, C. E. (2003). Spirituality, religion, and health. An emerging research field. *American Psychologist, 58,* 24–35.

Milliken, C. S., Auchterlonie, J. L., & Hoge, C. W. (2007). Longitudinal assessment of mental health problems among active and reserve component soldiers returning from the Iraq war. *Journal of the American Medical Association, 298,* 2141–2148.

Milling, L. S., Reardon, J. M., & Carosella, G. M. (2006). Mediation and moderation of psychological pain treatments: Response expectancies and hypnotic suggestibility. *Journal of Consulting and Clinical Psychology, 74,* 253–262.

Milner, B. (1962). Les troubles de la memoire accompagnant des lesions hippocampiques bilaterales. In P. Passonant (Ed.), *Physiologie de l'hippocampe* (pp. 257–272). Paris: Centre National de la Recherche Scientifique.

Milner, C. E., & Cote, K. A. (2009). Benefits of napping in healthy adults: Impact of nap length, time of day, age, and experience with napping. *Journal of Sleep Research, 18,* 272–281.

Minda, J. P., & Smith, J. D. (2002). Comparing prototype-based and exemplar-based accounts of category learning and attentional allocation. *Journal of Experimental Psychology: Learning, Memory, and Cognition, 28,* 275–292.

Mischel, W., & Shoda, Y. (1995). A cognitive-affective system theory of personality: Reconceptualizing situations, dispositions, dynamics, and invariance of personality structure. *Psychological Review, 102,* 246–268.

Miselis, R. R., & Epstein, A. N. (1970). Feeding induced by 2-deoxy-D-glucose injections into the lateral ventrical of the rat. *Physiologist, 13,* 262.

Mitelman, S. A., Buchsbaum, M. S., Brickman, A. M., & Shihabuddin, L. (2005). Cortical intercorrelations of frontal area volumes in schizophrenia. *Neuroimage, 27,* 753–770.

Miyaoka, Y., Sawada, M., Sakaguchi, T., & Shingai, T. (1987). Sensation of thirst in normal and laryngectomized man. *Perceptual and Motor Skills, 64,* 239–242.

Miyauchi, S., Misaki, M., Kan, S., Fukunaga, T., & Koike, T. (2009). Human brain activity time-locked to rapid eye movements during REM sleep. *Experimental Brain Research, 192,* 657–667.

Mobini, S., Chambers, L. C., & Yeomans, M. R. (2007). Effects of hunger state on flavour pleasantness conditioning at home: Flavour–nutrient learning vs. flavour–flavour learning. *Appetite, 48,* 20–28.

Moffitt, T. E. (2005). The new look of behavioral genetics in developmental psychopathology: Gene-environment interplay in antisocial behaviors. *Psychological Bulletin, 131,* 533–554.

Moffitt, T. E., Brammer, G. L., Caspi, A., Fawcet, J. P., Raleigh, M., Yuwiler, A., et al. (1998). Whole blood serotonin relates to violence in an epidemiological study. *Biological Psychiatry, 43,* 446–457.

Moffitt, T. E., Caspi, A., Taylor, A., Kokaua, J., Milne, B. J., Polanczyk, G., et al. (2009). How common are common mental disorders? Evidence that lifetime prevalence rates are doubled by prospective versus retrospective ascertainment. *Psychological Medicine,* doi:10.1017/S0033291709991036.

Mohr, C. (1964, March 28). Apathy is puzzle in Queens killing. *New York Times,* pp. 21, 40.

Mokhber, N., Azarpazhooh, M. R., Khajehdaluee, M., Velayati, A., & Hopwood, M. (2010). Randomized, single-blind trial of sertraline and buspirone for treatment of elderly patients with generalized anxiety disorder. *Psychiatry and Clinical Neurosciences, 64,* 128–133.

Molero, F., Navas, M. S., Gonzalez, J. L., Aleman, P., & Cuadrado, I. (2003). Paupers or riches: The perception of immigrants, tourists and ingroup members in a sample of Spanish children. *Journal of Ethnic and Migration Studies, 29,* 501–517.

Money, J., & Ehrhardt, A. (1972). *Man and woman, boy and girl.* Baltimore: Johns Hopkins University Press.

Mongrain, V., Lavoie, S., Selmaoui, B., Paquet, J., & Dumont, M. (2004). Phase relationships between sleep–wake cycle and underlying circadian rhythms in Morningness–Eveningness. *Journal of Biological Rhythms, 19,* 248–257.

Monroe, S. M., & Reid, M. W. (2009). Life stress and major depression. *Current Directions in Psychological Science, 18,* 68–72.

Montagu, A. (1986). *Touching: The human significance of skin.* New York: Harper & Row.

Monteith, M., & Winters, J. (2002, May–June). Why we hate; we may not admit it, but we are plagued with xenophobic tendencies. Our hidden prejudices run so deep, we are quick to judge, fear and even hate the unknown. *Psychology Today, 35,* 44–51.

Montgomery, J., Mitty, E., & Flores, S. (2008). Resident condition change: Should I call 911? *Geriatric Nursing, 29,* 15–26.

Monti-Bloch, L., Diaz-Sanchez, V., Jennings-White, C., & Berliner, D. L. (1998). Modulation of serum testosterone and autonomic function through stimuluation of the male human vomeronasal organ (VNO) with pregna-4, 20-diene-3, 6-dione. *Journal of Steroid Biochemistry and Molecular Biology, 65,* 237–242.

Montoya, M. R. (2008). I'm hot, so I'd say you're not: The influence of objective physical attractiveness on mate selection. *Personality and Social Psychology Bulletin, 34,* 1315–1331.

Mooney, D. K., Fromme, K., Kivlahan, D. R., & Marlatt, G. A. (1987). Correlates of alcohol consumption: Sex, age, and expectancies relate differentially to quantity and frequency. *Addictive Behaviors, 12,* 235–240.

Moore, D. S., & Johnson, S. P. (2008). Mental rotation in human infants: A sex difference. *Psychological Science, 19,* 1063–1066.

Moore, E. G. J. (1986). Family socialization and the IQ test performance of traditionally and transracially adopted black children. *Developmental Psychology, 22,* 317–326.

Moore, M. T., & Fresco, D. M. (2007). Depressive realism and attributional style: Implications for individuals at risk for depression. *Behavior Therapy, 38,* 144–154.

Moore, S. M. (1995). Girls' understanding and social constructions of menarche. *Journal of Adolescence, 18,* 87–104.

Morales, A. (2003). Erectile dysfunction: An overview. *Clinical Geriatric Medicine, 19,* 529–538.

Moreno, M. A., Parks, M., & Richardson, L. P. (2007). What are adolescents showing the world about their health risk behaviors on MySpace? *Medscape General Medicine, 11,* 9.

Moravec, C. S. (2008). Biofeedback therapy in cardiovascular disease: Rationale and research overview. *Cleveland Clinic Journal of Medicine, 75,* S35–S38.

Morgan, W. P. (1987). Reduction of state anxiety following acute physical activity. In W. P. Morgan & S. E. Golston (Eds.), *Exercise and mental health* (pp. 105–109). Washington, DC: Hemisphere.

Morgenstern, H., & Glazer, W. M. (1993). Identifying risk factors for tardive dyskinesia among long-term outpatients maintained with neuroleptic medications: Results of the Yale Tardive Dyskinesia Study. *Archives of General Psychiatry, 50,* 723–733.

Moreira, F. A., & Lutz, B. (2008). The endocannabinoid system: Emotion, learning and addiction. *Addiction Biology, 13,* 196–212.

Morin, C. M., Vallieres, A., Guay, B., Ivers, H., Savard, J., Merette, C., et al. (2009). Cognitive behavioral therapy, singly and combined with medication, for persistent insomnia: A randomized controlled trial. *Journal of the American Medical Association, 301,* 2005–2015.

Morisse, D., Batra, L., Hess, L., & Silverman, R. (1996). A demonstration of a token economy for the real world. *Applied and Preventive Psychology, 5,* 41–46.

Morlock, R. J., Tan, M., & Mitchell, D. Y. (2006). Patient characteristics and patterns of drug use for sleep complaints in the United States: Analysis of National Ambulatory Medical Survey data, 1997–2002. *Clinical Therapeutics, 28,* 1044–1053.

Morokoff, P. J. (1993). Female sexual arousal disorder. In W. O'Donohue & J. H. Greer (Eds.), *Handbook of sexual dysfunctions: Assessment and treatment* (pp. 157–199). Boston: Allyn & Bacon.

Morrison, P. D., Zois, V., McKeown, D. A., Lee, T. D., Holt, D. W., Powell, J. F., et al. (2009). The acute effects of synthetic intravenous Delta9-tetrahydrocannabinol on psychosis, mood and cognitive functioning. *Psychological Medicine, 39,* 1607–1616.

Morrow, E. M., Roffman, J. L., Wolf, D. H., & Coyle, J. T. (2008). Psychiatric neuroscience: Incorporating pathophysiology into clinical case formulation. In Theodore A. Stern, Jerrold F. Rosenbaum, Maurizio Fava, Joseph Biederman, & Scott L. Rauch (Eds.). *Massachusetts General Hospital Comprehensive Clinical Psychiatry.* Philadelphia: Mosby-Elsevier.

Mortensen, M. E., Sever, L. E., & Oakley, G. P. (1991). Teratology and the epidemiology of birth defects. In S. G. Gabbe, J. R. Niebyl, & J. L. Simpson (Eds.), *Obstetrics: Normal and problem pregnancies* (pp. 233–268). New York: Churchill Livingstone.

Morzorati, S. L., Ramchandani, V. A. Flury, L., Li, T.-K. & O'Connor, S. (2002). Self-reported subjective perception of intoxication reflects family history of alcoholism when breath alcohol levels are constant. *Alcoholism: Clinical Experimental Research, 26,* 1299–1306.

Mosedeghrad, A., Ferlie, E., and Rosenberg, D. (2008). A study of the relationship between job satisfaction, organizational commitment and turnover intention among hospital employees. *Health Services Management Research, 21,* 211–227.

Mosing, M. A., Gordon, S. D., Medland, S. E., Statham, D. J., Nelson, E. C., Heath, A. C., et al. (2009). Genetic and environmental influences on the comorbidity between depression, panic disorder, agoraphobia, and social phobia: A twin study. *Depression and Anxiety, 26,* 1004–1011.

Motivala, S. J., & Irwin, M. R. (2007). Sleep and immunity: Cytokine pathways linking sleep and health outcomes. *Current Directions in Psychological Science, 16,* 21–25.

Motomura, N., & Tomota, Y. (2006). Olfactory dysfunction in dementia of Alzheimer's type and vascular dementia. *Psychogeriatrics, 6,* 19–20.

Mottram, L., & Berger-Gross, P. (2004). An intervention to reduce disruptive behaviors in children with brain injury. *Pediatric Rehabilitation, 7,* 133–143.

Mousa, T. Y., Al-Domi, H. A., Mashal, R. H., & Jibril, M. A. (2010). Eating disturbances among adolescent schoolgirls in Jordan. *Appetite, 54,* 196–201.

Mowen, J. C., & Cialdini, R. B. (1980). On implementing the door-in-the-face compliance technique in a business context. *Journal of Marketing Research, 17,* 253–258.

Mroczek, D. K., & Spiro, A., III (2003). Modeling intra-individual change in personality traits: Findings from the Normative Aging Study. *Journal of Gerontology: Psychological Sciences, 58B,* P153–P165.

Mrug, S., Elliott, M., Gilliland, M. J., Grunbaum, J. A., Tortolero, S. R., Cuccaro, P., et al. (2008). Positive parenting and early puberty in girls: Protective effects against aggressive behavior. *Archives of Pediatrics and Adolescent Medicine, 162,* 781–786.

Mueller, C. W., Boyer, E. M., Price, J. L., & Iverson, R. D. (1994). Employee attachment and noncoercive conditions of work: The case of dental hygienists. *Work and Occupations, 21,* 179–212.

Mulrow, C. D., Williams, J. W., Jr., Chiquette, E., Aguilar, C., Hitchcock-Noel, P., Lee, S., et al. (2000). Efficacy of newer medications for treating depression in primary care patients. *American Journal of Medicine, 108,* 54–64.

Mumford, M. D. (2003). Where have we been, where are we going? Taking stock in creativity research. *Creativity Research Journal, 15,* 107–120.

Mumme, D. L., & Fernald, A. (2003). The infant as onlooker: Learning from emotional reactions observed in a television scenario. *Child Development, 74,* 221–237.

Munafo, M. R., Yalcin, B., Willis-Owen, S. A., & Flint, J. (2008). Association of the dopamine D4 receptor (DRD4) gene and approach-related personality traits: Meta-analysis and new data. *Biological Psychiatry, 63,* 197–206.

Munch, M., Knoblauch, V., Blatter, K., Schroder, C., Schnitzler, C., Krauchi, K., et al. (2005). Age-related attenuation of the evening circadian arousal signal in humans. *Neurobiology of Aging, 26,* 1307–1319.

Munson, C. (2006). *The effects of Leap Pad's text-to-speech support on kindergarten students' independent reading*. Unpublished master's thesis, University of Valdosta, Valdosta, Georgia. Retrieved February 22, 2010, from http://hdl.handle.net/10428/105

Murdoch, B. B., Jr. (1962). The serial position effect of free recall. *Journal of Experimental Psychology, 64*, 482–488.

Murillo-Rodríguez, E., Arias-Carrión, O., Sanguino-Rodríguez, K., González-Arias, M., & Haro, R. (2009). Mechanisms of sleep-wake cycle modulation. *CNS Neurological Disorder Drug Targets, 8*, 245–253.

Muris, P., Meesters, C., Morren, M., & Moorman, L. (2004). Anger and hostility in adolescents: Relationships with self-reported style and perceived rearing styles. *Journal of Psychosomatic Research, 57*, 257–264.

Murphy, K., & Delanty, N. (2007). Sleep deprivation: A clinical perspective. *Sleep and Biological Rhythms, 5*, 2–14.

Murphy, K. J., West, R., Armilio, M. L., Craik, F. I., & Stuss, D. T. (2007). Word-list-learning performance in younger and older adults: Intra-individual performance variability and false memory. *Neuropsychology, Development, and Cognition: Section B. Aging, Neuropsychology, and Cognition, 14*, 70–94.

Murphy, W., & Page, J. (2008). Exhibitionism: Psychopathology and theory. In D. Laws & W. O'Donohue (Eds.), *Sexual deviance: Theory, assessment and treatment* (2nd ed., pp. 61–75). New York: Guilford Press.

Murray, C. J., & Lopez, A. D. (Eds.). (1996). *Summary: The global burden of disease: A comprehensive assessment of mortality and disability from diseases, injuries, and risk factors in 1990 and projected to 2020*. Cambridge, MA: Harvard University Press.

Murray, H. A. (1938). *Explorations in personality*. New York: Oxford University Press.

Murray, J. (2000). Psychological profile of pedophiles and child molesters. *Journal of Psychology, 134*, 211–224.

Murray, S. O., Olshausen, B. A., & Woods, D. L. (2003). Processing shape, motion, and three-dimensional shape-from-motion in the human cortex. *Cerebral Cortex, 13*, 508–516.

Murray-Close, D., Ostrov, J. M., & Crick, N. R. (2007). A short-term longitudinal study of relational aggression during middle childhood: Associations with gender, friendship intimacy, and internalizing problems. *Development and Psychopathology, 19*, 187–203.

Muscari, M. (2002). Media violence: Advice for parents. *Pediatric Nursing, 28*, 585–591.

Muurahainen, N. E., Kisileff, H. R., Lachaussee, J., & Pi-Sunyer, F. X. (1991). Effect of a soup preload on reduction of food intake by cholecystokinin in humans. *American Journal of Physiology, 260*, R672–R680.

Myers, D. G. (2000). The funds, friends, and faith of happy people. *American Psychologist, 55*, 56–67.

Nacke, L. E., Nacke, A., & Lindley, C. A. (2009). Brain training for silver gamers: Effects of age and game form on effectiveness, efficiency, self-assessment, and gameplay experience. *Cyberpsychology and Behavior, 12*, 493–499.

Naegele, B., Thouvard, V., Pepin, J. L., Levy, P., Bonnet, C., Perret, J. E., et al. (1995). Deficits of cognitive functions in patients with sleep apnea syndrome. *Sleep, 18*(1), 43–52.

Nagel, B., Matsuo, H., McIntyre, K. P., & Morrison, N. (2005). Attitudes toward victims of rape: Effects of gender, race, religion, and social class. *Journal of Interpersonal Violence, 20*, 725–737.

Nairne, J. S. (2002). Remembering over the short term: The case against the standard model. *Annual Review of Psychology, 53*, 53–81.

Naish, P. L. (2010). Hypnosis and hemispheric asymmetry. *Consciousness and Cognition, 19*, 230–234.

Nakano, K. (1996). Application of self-control procedures to modifying Type A behavior. *Psychological Record, 46*(4), 595–606.

Nardi, A. E., Freire, R. C., Valenca, A. M., Amrein, R., de Cerqueira, A. C., Lopes, F. L., et al. (2010). Tapering clonazepam in patients with panic disorder after at least 3 years of treatment. *Journal of Clinical Psychopharmacology, 30*, 290–293.

Narvaez, D. (2010). Moral complexity: The fatal attraction of truthiness and the importance of mature moral functioning. *Perspectives on Psychological Science, 5*, 163–181.

Nash, J. M., & Thebarge, R. W. (2006). Understanding psychological stress, its biological processes, and impact on primary headache. *Headache, 46*, 1377–1386.

Nash, M. (1987). What, if anything, is regressed about hypnotic age regression? A review of the empirical literature. *Psychological Bulletin, 102*, 42–52.

Nash, M. (2005). Salient findings: A potentially ground-breaking study on the neuroscience of hypnotizability, a critical review of hypnosis' efficacy, and the neurophysiology of conversion disorder. *International Journal of Clinical and Experimental Hypnosis, 53*, 87–93.

Nassif, A., & Gunter, B. (2008). Gender representation in television advertisements in Britain and Saudi Arabia. *Sex Roles, 58*, 752–760.

Nathan, P. E., Stuart, S. P., & Dolan, S. L. (2000). Research on psychotherapy efficacy and effectiveness: Between Scylla and Charybdis? *Psychological Bulletin, 126*, 964–981.

Nathans, J., Merbs, S. L., Sung, C. H., Weitz, C. J., & Wang, Y. (1992). Molecular genetics of human visual pigments. *Annual Review of Genetics, 26*, 403–424.

National Association for Gifted Children (NAGC). (2010). *What is giftedness?* Retrieved April 23, 2010, from http://www.nagc.org

National Comorbidity Survey Replication data. Table 2. (2007). http://www.hcp.med.harvard.edu/ncs

National Highway Traffic Safety Administration (NHTSA). (2008). *Traffic safety facts, 2008*. Washington, DC: U.S. Department of Transportation.

National Highway Traffic Safety Administration (NHTSA). (2009). *Traffic safety facts: An examination of driver distraction as recorded in NHTSA databases*. Washington, DC: NHTSA's Center for Statistics and Analysis.

National Institute for Occupational Safety and Health (2010). *NIOSH power tools database (Milwaukee 6378 circular saw)*. Retrieved January 20, 2010, from wwwn.cdc.gov/niosh-sound-vibration/Default.aspx

National Institute of Mental Health (NIMH). (2002). *Suicide facts*. Retrieved May 9, 2004, from http://www.nimh.nih.gov/research/suifact.htm

National Institute of Mental Health (NIMH). (2007). *Suicide in the U.S.: Statistics and prevention* (NIH Publication No. 06–4594). National Institutes of Health, U.S. Department of Health and Human Services.

National Institute of Mental Health (NIMH). Genetics Workgroup. (1998). *Genetics and mental disorders*. NIH Publication No. 98-4268. Rockville, MD: National Institute of Mental Health.

National Institute on Drug Abuse (NIDA). (2001). *Research report series: Hallucinogens and dissociative drugs*. NIH Publication Number 01-4209.

National Institute on Drug Abuse (NIDA). (2006a). *Research report series: MDMA (Ecstasy) abuse*. NIH Publication Number 06-4728.

National Institute on Drug Abuse (NIDA). (2006b). *Research report series: Methamphetamine abuse and addiction*. NIH Publication Number 06-4210.

National Institute on Drug Abuse (NIDA) & University of Michigan. (2006). *Monitoring the Future National Survey Results on Drug Use, 1975–2005: Volume 11. College Students and Adults Ages 19–45.*

National Science Foundation (NSF). (2006). *U.S. doctorates in the 20th century*. NSF 06–319. Arlington, VA: Author.

National Sleep Foundation. (2004). *Summary Findings: 2004 Sleep in America Poll*. Washington, DC: Author.

National Sleep Foundation. (2005). *Summary Findings: 2005 Sleep in America Poll*. Washington, DC: Author.

National Sleep Foundation. (2006). *Summary Findings: 2006 Sleep in America Poll*. Washington, DC: Author.

National Sleep Foundation. (2009). *Summary Findings: 2009 Sleep in America Poll*. Washington, DC: Author.

National Sleep Foundation. (2010). *Summary Findings: 2010 Sleep in America Poll*. Washington, DC: Author.

Navarro, M. (1995, Dec. 9). Drugs sold abroad by prescription becomes widely abused in U.S. *New York Times*, pp. 1, 9.

Naylor, J. C., Pritchard, R. D., & Ilgen, D. R. (1980). *A theory of behavior in organizations*. New York: Academic Press.

Neher, A. (1991). Maslow's theory of motivation: A critique. *Journal of Humanistic Psychology, 31*, 89–112.

Neitz, J., Neitz, M., & Jacobs, G. H. (1993). More than three different cone pigments among people with normal color vision. *Vision Research, 33*, 117–122.

Neitz, J., Neitz, M., & Kainz, P. M. (1996, November 1). Visual pigment gene structure and severity of color vision defects. *Science, 274*, 801–804.

Nelson, R. (1988). Nonoperative management of impotence. *Journal of Urology, 139*, 2–5.

Nelson, R. A., & Strachan, I. (2009). Action and puzzle video games prime different speed/accuracy tradeoffs. *Perception, 38*, 1678–1687.

Nemeroff, C. B. (2007). The burden of severe depression: A review of diagnostic challenges and treatment alternatives. *Journal of Psychiatric Research, 41*, 189–206.

Neria, Y., Nandi, A., & Galea, S. (2008). Post-traumatic stress disorder following disasters: A systematic review. *Psychological Medicine, 38*, 467–480.

Nestler, E. J. (2006). The addicted brain: Cocaine use alters genes. *Paradigm, 11*, 12–22.

Nestler, E. J., & Carlezon, W. A., Jr. (2006). The mesolimbic dopamine reward circuit in depression. *Biological Psychiatry, 59*, 1151–1159.

Nestor, L., Roberts, G., Garavan, H., & Hester, R. (2008). Deficits in learning and memory: Parahippocampal hyperactivity and frontocortical hypoactivity in cannabis users. *NeuroImage, 40*, 1328–1339.

Neumark-Sztainer, D., Croll, J., Story, M., Hannan, P. J., French, S. A., & Perry, C. (2002). Ethnic/racial differences in weight-related concerns and behaviors among adolescent girls and boys: Findings from Project-EAT. *Journal of Psychosomatic Research, 53*, 963–974.

Nevin, J. A., & Grace, R. C. (2005). Resistance to extinction in the steady state and in the transition. *Journal of Experimental Psychology: Animal Behavior Processes, 31*, 199–212.

Nevonen, L., & Broberg, A. G. (2006). A comparison of sequenced individual and group psychotherapy for patients with bulimia nervosa. *International Journal of Eating Disorders, 39*, 117–127.

Newcomb, M. D., Munoz, D. T., & Carmona, J. V. (2009). Child sexual abuse consequences in community samples of Latino and European American adolescents. *Child Abuse and Neglect, 33*, 533–544.

Newcomb, T. M. (1961). *The acquaintance process*. New York: Holt, Rinehart & Winston.

Newland, M. C., & Rasmussen, E. B. (2003). Behavior in adulthood and during aging is affected by contaminant exposure in utero. *Current Directions in Psychological Science, 12*, 212–217.

Newman, D. L. (2005). Ego-development and ethnic identity formation in rural American Indian adolescents. *Child Development, 76*, 734–746.

Ni, X., Sicard, T., Bulgin, N., Bismil, R., Chan, K., McMain, S., et al. (2007). Monoamine oxidase A gene is associated with borderline personality disorder. *Psychiatric Genetics, 17*, 153–157.

Niccols, G. A. (1994). Fetal alcohol syndrome: Implications for psychologists. *Clinical Psychology Review, 14*, 91–111.

NICHD (National Institute of Child Health and Human Development) Early Child Care Research Network. (2002). The interaction of child care and family risk in relation to child development at 24 and 36 months. *Applied Developmental Science, 6*, 144–156.

NICHD (National Institute of Child Health and Human Development) Early Child Care Research Network. (2006). Child-care effect sizes for the NICHD Study of Early Child Care and Youth Development. *American Psychologist, 61*, 99–116.

Nicodemus, K. K., Callicott, J. H., Higier, R. G., Luna, A., Nixon, D. C., Lipska, B. K., et al. (in press). Evidence of statistical epistasis between DISC1, CIT and NDEL1 impacting risk for schizophrenia: Biological validation with functional neuroimaging. *Human Genetics*.

Nicolini, H., Arnold, P., Nestadt, G., Lanzagorta, N., & Kennedy, J. L. (2009). Overview of genetics and obsessive-compulsive disorder. *Psychiatry Research, 170*, 7–14.

Nie, N. H. (2001). Sociability, interpersonal relations and the Internet: Reconciling conflicting findings. *American Behavioral Scientist, 45*, 420–435.

Niedzwienska, A. (2003). Gender differences in vivid memories. *Sex Roles: A Journal of Research, 49*, 321–331.

Nielsen Co. (2009, June). *How teens use media: A Nielsen report on the myths and realities of teen media trends.* New York: The Nielsen Co.

Nielsen, M., Simcock, G., & Jenkins, L. (2008). The effect of social engagement on 24-month-olds' imitation from live and televised models. *Developmental Science, 11,* 722–731.

Nielsen, M. M., and Day, R. H. (1999). William James and the evolution of consciousness. Journal of *Theoretical and Philosophical Psychology, 19,* 90–113.

Nieuwenhuijsen, K., Verbeek, J. H., de Boer, A. G., Blonk, R. W., & van Dijk, F. J. (2010). Irrational beliefs in employees with an adjustment, a depressive, or an anxiety disorder: A prospective cohort study. *Journal of Rational-Emotive and Cognitive-Behavior Therapy, 28,* 57–72.

Nisbett, R. (1995). Race, IQ, and scientism. In Steven Fraser (Ed.), *The bell curve wars: Race, intelligence, and the future of America* (pp. 36–57). New York: Basic Books.

Nishino, S. (2007). Narcolepsy: Pathophysiology and pharmacology. *Journal of Clinical Psychiatry, 68,* 9–15.

Nivoli, A. M., Murru, A., & Vieta, E. (2010). Lithium: Still a cornerstone in the long-term treatment in bipolar disorder? *Neuropsychobiology, 62,* 27–35.

Noah, T. & Robinson, L. (1997, March 31). OK, OK, cigarettes do kill. *U.S. News & World Report,* pp. 29, 32.

Noble, M., & Harding, G. E. (1963). Conditioning of rhesus monkeys as a function of the interval between CS and US. *Journal of Comparative and Physiological Psychology, 56,* 220–224.

Nock, M. K., Hwang, I., Sampson, N., Kessler, R. C., Angermeyer, M., Beautrais, A., et al. (2009). Cross-national analysis of the associations among mental disorders and suicidal behavior: Findings from the WHO World Mental Health Surveys. *PLoS Medicine,* 6, e1000123.

Nolan, R. P., Spanos, N. P., Hayward, A. A., & Scott, H. A. (1995). The efficacy of hypnotic and nonhypnotic response-based imagery for self-managing recurrent headache. *Imagination, Cognition, and Personality, 14*(3), 183–201.

Nolen-Hoeksema, S. (2001). Gender differences in depression. *Current Directions in Psychological Science, 10,* 173–176.

Nolen-Hoeksema, S. (2002). Gender differences in depression. In I. H. Gotlib & C. L. Hammen (Eds.), *Handbook of depression* (pp. 492–509). New York: Guilford Press.

Nolen-Hoeksema, S., Larson, J., & Grayson, C. (1999). Explaining the gender difference in depressive symptoms. *Journal of Personality and Social Psychology, 77,* 1061–1072.

Nolen-Hoeksema, S., Stice, E., Wade, E., & Bohon, C. (2007). Reciprocal relations between rumination and bulimic, substance abuse, and depressive symptoms in female adolescents. *Journal of Abnormal Psychology, 116,* 198–207.

Nolen-Hoeksema, S., Wisco, B. E., & Lyubomirsky, S. (2008). Rethinking rumination. *Perspectives on Psychological Science, 3,* 400–424.

Nordin, S., Razani, J. L., Markison, S., & Murphy, C. (2003). Age-associated increases in intensity discrimination for taste. *Experimental Aging Research, 29,* 371–381.

Nordling, N., Sandnabba, N., Santtila, P., & Alison, L. (2006). Differences and similarities between gay and straight individuals involved in the SM subculture. *Journal of Homosexuality, 50,* 41–67.

Norman, R. M., & Malla, A. K. (1993). Stressful life events and schizophrenia: II. Conceptual and methodological issues. *British Journal of Psychiatry, 162,* 166–174.

Norton, N., Williams, H. J., & Owen, M. J. (2006). An update on the genetics of schizophrenia. *Current Opinion in Psychiatry, 19,* 158–164.

Norton, P. J., & Price, E. C. (2007). A meta-analytic review of adult cognitive-behavioral treatment outcome across the anxiety disorders. *Journal of Nervous and Mental Disease, 195,* 521–531.

Nosofsky, R. M., & Zaki, S. R. (2002). Exemplar and prototype models revisited: Response strategies, selective attention, and stimulus generalization. *Journal of Experimental Psychology: Learning, Memory, and Cognition, 28,* 924–940.

Nottelmann, E. D., Inoff-Germain, G., Susman, E. J., & Chrousos, G. P. (1990). Hormones and behavior at puberty. In J. Bancroft & J. M. Reinisch (Eds.), *Adolescence and puberty* (pp. 88–123). New York: Oxford University Press.

Nowell, P. D., Buysse, D. J., Morin, C. M., Reynolds, C. F., III, & Kuper, D. J. (1998). Effective treatments for selected sleep disorder. In P. E. Nathan (Ed.), *A guide to treatments that work* (pp. 531–543). New York: Oxford University Press.

Nunes, J., Jean-Louis, G., Zizi, F., Vasimir, G. J., von Gizycki, H., Brown, C. D., et al. (2008). Sleep duration among black and white Americans: Results of the National Health Interview Survey. *Journal of the National Medical Association, 100,* 317–322.

Nyberg, L., Marklund, P., Persson, J., Cabeza, R., Forkstam, C., Petersson, K. M., et al. (2003). Common prefrontal activations during working memory, episodic memory, and semantic memory. *Neuropsychologia, 41,* 371–377.

Nyer, P. U., & Dellande, S. (2010). Public commitment as a motivator for weight loss. *Psychology and Marketing, 27,* 1–12.

O'Brien, A., Terry, D. J., & Jimmieson, N. L. (2008). Negative affectivity and responses to work stressors: An experimental study. *Anxiety, Stress, and Coping, 21,* 55–83.

O'Brien, L. M. (2009). The neurocognitive effects of sleep disruption in children and adolescents. *Child and Adolescent Psychiatric Clinics of North America, 18,* 813–823.

O'Brien, M. (1996). Child-rearing difficulties reported by parents of infants and toddlers. *Journal of Pediatric Psychology, 21,* 433–446.

O'Bryan, M., Fishbein, H. D., & Ritchey, P. N. (2004). Intergenerational transmission of prejudice, sex role stereotyping, and intolerance. *Adolescence, 39,* 407–426.

O'Connor, D. B., Jones, F., Conner, M., McMillan, B., & Ferguson, E. (2008). Effects of daily hassles and eating style on eating behavior. *Health Psychology, 27,* S20–S31.

O'Connor, M. K. (1993). Hypotheses regarding the mechanism of action of electroconvulsive therapy, past and present. *Psychiatric Annals, 23,* 15–18.

Odgers, C. L., Caspi, A., Nagin, D. S., Piquero, A. R., Slutske, W. S., Milne, B. J., et al. (2008). Is it important to prevent early exposure to drugs and alcohol among adolescents? *Psychological Science, 19,* 1037–1044.

Okazaki, S. (2009). Impact of racism on ethnic minority mental health. *Perspectives on Psychological Science, 4,* 103–107.

O'Keefe, D. J., & Figge, M. (1997). A guilt-based explanation of the door-in-the-face influence strategy. *Human Communication Research, 24,* 64–81.

O'Leary Tevyaw, T., Borsari, B., Colby, S. M., & Monti, P. M. (2007). Peer enhancement of a brief motivational intervention with mandated college students. *Psychology of Addictive Behaviors, 21,* 114–119.

O'Leary, M. (2003). Early ejaculation. *British Journal of Urology International, 91,* 309.

Ogawa, R., & Haruki, Y. (2002). Modes of reinforcement and gender and culture of experimenter and subject: Effects of "alien" and external reinforcement for Japanese and American men and women. *Japanese Journal of Psychology, 73,* 305–313.

Oginska, H., & Pokorski, J. (2006). Fatigue and mood correlates of sleep length in three age-social groups: School children, students, and employees. *Chronobiology International, 23,* 1317–1328.

Ohsu, T., Amino, Y., Nagasaki, H., Yamanaka, T., Takeshita, S., Hatanaka, T., et al. (2010). Involvement of the calcium-sensing receptor in human taste perception. *Journal of Biological Chemistry, 285,* 1016–1022.

Olff, M., Langeland, W., Draijer, N., & Gersons, B. P. (2007). Gender differences in posttraumatic stress disorder. *Psychological Bulletin, 133,* 183–204.

Olfson, M., & Pincus, H. A. (1996). Outpatient mental health care in nonhospital settings: Distribution of patients across provider groups. *American Journal of Psychiatry, 153,* 1353–1356.

Oliver, M. B., & Hyde, J. S. (1993). Gender differences in sexuality: A meta-analysis. *Psychological Bulletin, 114,* 29–51.

Omar, H., McElderry, D., & Zakharia, R. (2003). Educating adolescents about puberty: What are we missing? *International Journal of Adolescent Medicine and Health, 15,* 79–83.

Ondersma, S. J., & Walker, C. E. (1998). Elimination disorders. In T. H. Ollendick & M. Hersen (Eds.), *Handbook of child psychopathology* (pp. 355–380). New York: Plenum Press.

Oquendo, M. A., Hastings, R. S., Huang, Y. Y., Simpson, N., Ogden, R. T., Hu, X. Z., et al. (2007). Brain serotonin transporter binding in depressed patients with bipolar disorder using positron emission tomography. *Archives of General Psychiatry, 64,* 201–208.

Ornstein, S., & Isabella, L. (1990). Age versus stage models of career attitudes of women: A partial replication and extension. *Journal of Vocational Behavior, 36,* 1–19.

Orr, E. S., Sisic, M., Ross, C., Simmering, M. G., Arsenault, J. M., & Orr, R. R. (2009). The influence of shyness on the use of Facebook in an undergraduate sample. *Cyberpsychology and Behavior, 12,* 337–340.

Ortega, L. A., & Karch, D. (2010). Precipitating circumstances of suicide among women of reproductive age in 16 U.S. states, 2003–2007. *Journal of Women's Health, 19,* 5–7.

Ortony, A., & Turner, T. J. (1990). What's basic about basic emotions? *Psychological Review, 97,* 315–331.

Osborne, R. H., Sali, A., Aaronson, N. K., Elsworth, G. R., Mdzewski, B., & Sinclair, A. J. (2004). Immune function and adjustment style: Do they predict survival in breast cancer? *Psychooncology, 13,* 199–210.

Osher, Y., Hamer, D., & Benjamin, J. (2000). Association and linkage of anxiety-related traits with a functional polymorphism of the serotonin transporter gene regulatory region in Israeli sibling pairs. *Molecular Psychiatry, 5,* 216–219.

Ostelo, R. W. J. G., van Tulder, M. W., Vlaeyen, J. W. S., Linton, S. J., Morley, S. J., & Assendelft, W. J. J. (2007). Behavioural treatment for chronic low-back pain. *Cochrane Database of Systematic Reviews,* Cochrane AN: CD002014.

Osterman, K., Bjorkqvist, K., Lagerspertz, K. M. J., Kaukianainen, A., Huesman, L. W., & Fraczek, A. (1994). Peer and self-estimated aggression and victimization in 8-year-old children from five ethnic groups. *Aggressive Behavior, 20,* 411–428.

Ostfeld, B. M., Perl, H., Esposito, L., Hempstead, K., Hinnen, R., Sandler, A., et al. (2006). Sleep environment, positional, lifestyle, and demographic characteristics associated with bed-sharing in sudden infant death syndrome cases: A population-based study. *Pediatrics, 118,* 2051–2059.

Ostroff, C., Kinicki, A. J., & Tamkins, M. M. (2003). Organizational culture and climate. In W. C. Borman, D. R. Ilgen, & R. J. Klimoski (Eds.), *Handbook of psychology: Vol. 12. Industrial and organizational psychology,* (pp. 565–593). Hoboken, NJ: John Wiley & Sons.

Osvold, L. L., & Sodowsky, G. R. (1993). Eating disorders of White American, racial and ethnic minority American, and international women [Special issue: Multicultural health issues]. *Journal of Multicultural Counseling and Development, 21,* 143–154.

Ou, L. C., Yeh, S. H., & Gean, P. W. (2009). Late expression of brain-derived neurotrophic factor in the amygdala is required for persistence of fear memory. *Neurobiology of Learning and Memory.* Retrieved December 17, 2009, from http://www.sciencedirect.com

Outland, L. (2010). Intuitive eating: A holistic approach to weight control. *Holistic Nursing Practice, 24,* 35–43.

Overman, W. H., Bachevalier, J., Schuhmann, E., & Ryan, P. (1996).Cognitive gender differences in very young children parallel biologically based cognitive gender differences in monkeys. *Behavioral Neuroscience, 110,* 673–684.

Overmier, J. B. (2002). On learned helplessness. *Integrative Physiological and Behavioral Science, 37,* 4–8.

Overmier, J. B., & Seligman, M. E. (1967). Effects of inescapable shock upon subsequent escape and avoidance responding. *Journal of Comparative and Physiological Psychology, 63,* 28–33.

Overstreet, L. S. (2005). Quantal transmission: Not just for neurons. *Trends in Neurosciences, 28,* 59–62.

Özgen, E., & Davies, I. R. L. (2002). Acquisition of categorical color perception: A perceptual learning approach to the linguistic relativity hypothesis. *Journal of Experimental Psychology: General, 131,* 477–493.

Ozturk, L., Pelin, Z., Karadeniz, D., Kaynak, H., Cakar, L., & Gozukirmizi, E. (1999). Effects of 48 hours sleep deprivation on human immune profile. *Sleep Research Online* [electronic resource], *2,* 107–111.

Ozturk, R., Niazi, S., Stessman, M., & Rao, S. S. (2004). Long-term outcome and objective changes of anorectal function after biofeedback therapy for faecal incontinence. *Aliment Pharmacology Therapy, 20,* 667–674.

Packer, D. J. (2009). Avoiding groupthink: Whereas weakly identified members remain silent, strongly identified members dissent about collective problems. *Psychological Science, 20,* 546–548.

Padela, A. I., & Heisler, M. (2010). The association of perceived abuse and discrimination after September 11, 2001, with psychological distress, level of happiness, and health status among Arab Americans. *American Journal of Public Health, 100,* 284–291.

Page, R. A., & Green, J. P. (2007). An update on age, hypnotic suggestibility, and gender: A brief report. *American Journal of Clinical Hypnosis, 49,* 283–287.

Paivio, A. (1971). *Imagery and verbal processes.* New York: Holt, Rinehart & Winston.

Paivio, A. (1982). The empirical case for dual coding. In J. Yuille (Ed.), *Imagery, cognition, and memory* (pp. 307–332). Hillsdale, NJ: Erlbaum.

Paivio, A. (1986). *Mental representations: A dual coding approach.* New York: Oxford University Press.

Pakkenberg, B., Pelvig, D., Marner, L., Bundgaard, M. J., Gundersen, H. J., Nyengaard, J. R., et al. (2003). Aging and the human neocortex. *Experimental Gerontology, 38,* 95–99.

Pallier, G. (2003, March). Gender differences in the self-assessment of accuracy on cognitive tasks. *Sex Roles: A Journal of Research,* 265–276.

Palmore, E. B., Burchett, B. M., Fillenbaum, G. G., George, L. K., & Wallman, L. M. (1985). *Retirement: Causes and consequences.* New York: Springer.

Papadakis, A. A., Prince, R. P., Jones, N. P., & Strauman, T. J. (2006). Self-regulation, rumination, and vulnerability to depression in adolescent girls. *Development and Psychopathology, 18,* 815–829.

Papelbaum, M., Moreira, R. O., Gaya, C. W., Preissler, C., & Coutinho, W. F. (2010). Impact of body mass index on the psychopathological profile of obese women. *Revista Brasileira de Psiquiatria, 32,* 42–46.

Paradis, S., & Cabanac, M. (2008). Dieting and food choice in grocery shopping. *Physiology and Behavior, 93,* 1030–1032.

Parasuraman, R., Masalonis, A. J., & Hancock, P. A. (2000). Fuzzy signal detection theory: Basic postulates and formulas for analyzing human and machine performance. *Human Factors, 42,* 636–672.

Parent, A. S., Teilmann, G., Juul, A., Skakkebaek, N. E., Toppari, J., & Bourguignon, J. P. (2003). The timing of normal puberty and the age limits of sexual precocity: Variations around the world, secular trends, and changes after migration. *Endocrine Reviews, 24,* 668–693.

Park, E. S., & Hinsz, V. B. (2006). Strength and safety in numbers: A theoretical perspective on group influences on approach and avoidance motivation. *Motivation and Emotion, 30,* 135–142.

Park, I. S., Lee, K. J., Han, J. W., Lee, N. J., Lee, W. T., Park, K. A., et al. (2009). Experience-dependent plasticity of cerebellar vermis in basketball players. *Cerebellum, 8,* 334–339.

Parker, E. S., Birnbaum, I. M., & Noble, E. P. (1976). Alcohol and memory: Storage and state dependency. *Journal of Verbal Learning and Verbal Behavior, 15,* 691–702.

Parker, G., & Brotchie, H. (2004). From diathesis to dimorphism: The biology of gender differences in depression. *Journal of Nervous and Mental Disorders, 192,* 210–216.

Parker, G., Roy, K., Wilhelm, K., & Mitchell, P. (2001). Assessing the comparative effectiveness of antidepressant therapies: A prospective clinical practice study. *Journal of Clinical Psychiatry, 62,* 117–125.

Parker-Pope, T. (2002, August 27). A new reason for teens to avoid sex: It could be harmful to their health. *Wall Street Journal,* D1.

Parkes, C. M. (1986). *Bereavement: Studies of grief in adult life* (2nd ed.). London: Tavistock.

Parkes, C. M. (1991). Attachment, bonding, and psychiatric problems after bereavement in adult life. In C. M. Parkes, J. Stevenson-Hinde, & P. Marris (Eds.), *Attachment across the life cycle* (pp. 268–292). London: Tavistock/Routledge.

Parkin, A. J., & Leng, N. R. C. (1993). *Neruopsychology of the amnesic syndrome.* Hove, UK: Psychology Press.

Parnas, J., Cannon, T., Jacobsen, B., Schulsinger, H., Schulsinger, F., & Mednick, S. (1993). Lifetime DSM-III-R diagnostic outcomes in the offspring of schizophrenic mothers. *Archives of General Psychiatry, 50,* 707–714.

Pascalis, O., & Kelly, D. J. (2009). The origins of face processing in humans: Phylogeny and ontogeny. *Perspectives on Psychological Science, 4,* 200–209.

Pasquet, P., Obeerti, B., Ati, J. El, & Hladik, C. M. (2002). Relationships between threshold-based PROP sensitivity and food preferences of Tunisians. *Appetite, 39,* 167–173.

Pate, J. E., Pumariega, A. J., Hester, C., & Garner, D. M. (1992). Cross-cultural patterns in eating disorders: A review. *Journal of the American Academy of Child and Adolescent Psychiatry, 31,* 802–809.

Patel, V. L., & Ramoni, M. F. (1997). Cognitive models of directional inference in expert medical reasoning. In P. J. Feltovich, K. M. Ford, et al. (Eds.), *Expertise in context: Human and machine* (pp. 67–99). Cambridge, MA: MIT Press.

Patrick, M. E., & Maggs, J. L. (2009). Does drinking lead to sex? Daily alcohol-sex behaviors and expectancies among college students. *Psychology of Addictive Behaviors, 23,* 472–481.

Patterson, C. J. (2006). Children of lesbian and gay parents. *Current Directions in Psychological Science, 15,* 241–244.

Patterson, D. R., Hoffman, H. G., Palacios, A. G., & Jensen, M. J. (2006). Analgesic effects of posthypnotic suggestions and virtual reality distraction on thermal pain. *Journal of Abnormal Psychology, 115,* 834–841.

Paul, G., Elam, B., & Verhulst, S. J. (2007). A longitudinal study of students' perceptions of using deep breathing meditation to reduce testing stresses. *Teaching and Learning in Medicine, 19,* 287–292.

Paul, P. (2008, March 28). Million-dollar babies. *Time.* Retrieved March 6, 2010, from time.com

Paulson, S. E., & Sputa, C. L. (1996). Patterns of parenting during adolescence: Perceptions of adolescents and parents. *Adolescence, 31,* 369–381.

Paulus, P. B. (Ed.). (1989). *Psychology of group influence* (2nd ed.). Hillsdale, NJ: Erlbaum.

Pavlov, I. P. (1960). *Conditioned reflexes: An investigation of the physiological activity of the cerebral cortex.* (G. V. Anrep, Trans.). New York: Dover. (Original work published 1927)

Paxton, J. L., Barch, D. M., Storandt, M., & Braver, T. S. (2006). Effects of environmental support and strategy training on older adults' use of context. *Psychology and Aging, 21,* 499–509.

Payne, J. D., Stickgold, R., Swanberg, K., & Kensinger, E. A. (2008). Sleep preferentially enhances memory for emotional components of scenes. *Psychological Science, 8,* 781–788.

Payte, J. T. (1997). Methadone maintenance treatment: The first thirty years. *Journal of Psychoactive Drugs, 29,* 149–153.

Pearlin, L. I. (1993). The social contexts of stress. In L. Goldberger & S. Breznitz (Eds.), *Handbook of stress: Theoretical and clinical aspects* (2nd ed., pp. 303–315). New York: Free Press.

Pearsall, M. J., Christian, M. S., & Ellis, A. P. (2010). Motivating interdependent teams: Individual rewards, shared rewards, or something in between? *Journal of Applied Psychology, 95,* 183–191.

Pedersen, D. M., & Wheeler, J. (1983). The Müller-Lyer illusion among Navajos. *Journal of Social Psychology, 121,* 3–6.

Pedersen, P. B. (2002). Ethics, competence, and other professional issues in culture-centered counseling. In P. B. Pedersen, J. G. Draguns, W. J. Lonner, & J. E. Trimble (Eds.), *Counseling across cultures* (5th ed., pp. 3–28). Thousand Oaks, CA: Sage.

Peelen, M. V., Glaser, B., Vuilleumier, P., & Eliez, S. (2009). Differential development of selectivity for faces and bodies in the fusiform gyrus. *Developmental Science, 12,* F16–F25.

Pelleymounter, M. A., Cullen, M. J., Baker, M. B., Hecht, R., Winters, D., Boone, T., et al. (1995). Effects of the obese gene product on body weight regulation in ob/ob mice. *Science, 269,* 540–543.

Pembrey, M. E., Bygren, L. O., Kaati, G., Edvinsson, S., Northstone, K., Sjöström, M. et al. (2006). Sex-specific, male-line transgenerational responses in humans. *European Journal of Human Genetics, 14,* 159–166.

Penley, J. A., Tomaka, J., & Wiebe, J. S. (2002). The association of coping to physical and psychological health outcomes: A meta-analytic review. *Journal of Behavioral Medicine, 25,* 551–603.

Peplau, L. A. (2003). Human sexuality: How do men and women differ? *Current Directions in Psychological Science, 12,* 37–40.

Pepperberg, I. M. (1991). A communicative approach to animal cognition: A study of conceptual abilities of an African gray parrot. In C. A. Ristau (Ed.), *Cognitive ethology* (pp. 153–186). Hillsdale, NJ: Erlbaum.

Pepperberg, I. M. (1993). Cognition and communication in an African gray parrot (*Psittacus erithacus*): Studies on a nonhuman, nonprimate, nonmammilian, subject. In H. L. Roitblat, L. M. Herman, & P. E. Nachtigall (Eds.), *Language and communication: Comparative perspectives* (pp. 221–248). Hillsdale, NJ: Erlbaum.

Pepperberg, I. M. (1999). Rethinking syntax: A commentary on E. Kako's "Elements of syntax in the systems of three language-trained animals." *Animal Learning and Behavior, 27,* 15–17.

Pereda, N., Guilera, G., Forns, M., & Gomez-Benito, J. (2009). The international epidemiology of child sexual abuse: A continuation of Finkelhor (1994). *Child Abuse and Neglect, 33,* 331–342.

Perez, M., Joiner, T. E., Jr., & Lewisohn, P. M. (2004). Is major depressive disorder or dysthymia more strongly associated with bulimia nervosa? *International Journal of Eating Disorders, 36,* 55–61.

Perina, K. (2002). Hot on the trail of flashbulb memory. *Psychology Today, 35,* 15–16.

Perlini, A. H., Bertolissi, S., & Lind, D. L. (1999). The effects of women's age and physical appearance on evaluations of attractiveness and social desirability. *Journal of Social Psychology, 139,* 343–344.

Perlis, R. H., Brown, E., Baker, R. W., & Nierenberg, A. A. (2006). Clinical features of bipolar depression versus major depressive disorder in large multi-center trials. *American Journal of Psychiatry, 163,* 225–231.

Perry, C. (1997). Admissibility and per se exclusion of hypnotically elicited recall in American courts of law. *International Journal of Clinical and Experimental Hypnosis, 45,* 266–279.

Perry, E., Walker, M., Grace, J., & Perry, R. (1999). Acetylcholine in mind: A neurotransmitter correlate of consciousness? *Trends in Neurosciences, 22,* 273–280.

Perry, W. G., Jr. (1981). Cognitive and ethical growth. In A. Chickering (Ed.), *The modern American college* (pp. 76–116). San Francisco: Jossey-Bass.

Person, E. S. (1990). The influence of values in psychoanalysis: The case of female psychology. In C. Zanardi (Ed.), *Essential papers in psychoanalysis* (pp. 305–325). New York: University Press.

Person, E. S. (2005). As the wheel turns: A centennial reflection on Freud's Three Essays on the Theory of Sexuality. *Journal of the American Psychoanalytic Association, 53,* 1257–1282.

Pesant, N., & Zadra, A. (2004). Working with dreams in therapy: What do we know and what should we do? *Clinical Psychology Review, 24,* 489–512.

Pesant, N., & Zadra, A. (2006). Dream content and psychological well-being: A longitudinal study of the continuity hypothesis. *Journal of Clinical Psychology, 62,* 111–121.

Petersen, J. L., & Hyde, J. S. (2010). A meta-analytic review of research on gender differences in sexuality, 1993–2007. *Psychological Bulletin, 136,* 21–38.

Peterson, B. E., & Duncan, L. E. (2007). Midlife women's generativity and authoritarianism: Marriage, motherhood, and 10 years of aging. *Psychology and Aging, 22,* 411–419.

Peterson, C. (2000). The future of optimism. *American Psychologist, 55,* 44–55.

Peterson, C., & Bossio, L. M. (2001). Optimism and physical well-being. In E. C. Chang (Ed.), *Optimism and pessimism: Implications for theory, research, and practice* (pp. 127–146). Washington, DC: American Psychological Association.

Peterson, C., & Seligman, M. E. (1984). Causal explanations as a risk factor for depression: Theory and evidence. *Psychological Review, 91,* 347–374.

Peterson, C., Maier, S. F., & Seligman, M. E. P. (1993). *Learned helplessness: A theory for the age of personal control.* New York: Oxford University Press.

Peterson, L. R., & Peterson, M. J. (1959). Short-term retention of individual verbal items. *Journal of Experimental Psychology, 58,* 193–198.

Petitto, L. (2009). New discoveries from the bilingual brain and mind across the lifespan: Implications for education. *Mind, Brain, and Education, 3,* 185–197.

Petrides, K. V., Furnham, A., & Martin, G. N. (2004). Estimates of emotional and psychometric intelligence: Evidence for gender-based stereotypes. *Journal of Social Psychology, 144,* 149–162.

Petry, N. M., Tedford, J., Austin, M., Nich, C., Carroll, K. M., & Rounsaville, B. J. (2004). Prize reinforcement contingency management for treating cocaine users: How low can we go, and with whom? *Addiction, 99,* 349–360.

Pettigrew, T. F. (2001). The ultimate attribution error: Extending Allport's cognitive analysis of prejudice. In M. A. Hogg & D. Abrams (Eds.), *Intergroup relations: Key readings in social psychology* (pp. 162–173). New York: Psychology Press.

Pettigrew, T. F., & Tropp, L. R. (2006). A meta-analytic test of intergroup contact theory. *Journal of Personality and Social Psychology, 90,* 751–783.

Petty, R. E., & Briñol, P. (2008). Persuasion: From single to multiple to metacognitive processes. *Perspectives on Psychological Science, 3,* 137–147.

Petty, R. E., & Cacioppo, J. T. (1986). *Communication and persuasion: Central and peripheral routes to attitude change.* New York: Springer-Verlag.

Petty, R. E., Cacioppo, J. T., & Goldman, R. (1981). Personal involvement as a determinant of argument-based persuasion. *Journal of Personality and Social Psychology, 41,* 847–855.

Petty, R. E., Fabrigar, L. R., & Wegener, D. T. (2003). Emotional factors in attitudes and persuasion. In R.J. Davidson, K.R. Scherer, & H.H. Goldsmith (Eds.), *Handbook of affective sciences* (pp. 752–772). Oxford, England: Oxford University Press.

Pfann, K. D., Penn, R. D., Shannon, K. M., & Corocs, D. M. (1998). Pallidotomy and bradykinesia: Implications for basal ganglia function. *Neurology, 51,* 796–803.

Pfaus, J. G. (2009). Pathways of sexual desire. *Journal of Sexual Medicine, 6,* 1506–1533.

Pfizer. (2002). *Pfizer global study of sexual attitudes and behaviors.* Retrieved September 4, 2004, from http://pfizerglobalstudy.com

Phares, E. J. (1991). *Introduction to personality* (3rd ed.). New York: HarperCollins.

Phelan, S., Nallari, M., Daroch, F. E., & Wing, R. R. (2009). What do physicians recommend to their overweight and obese patients? *Journal of the American Board of Family Medicine, 22,* 115–122.

Phelps, E. A., O'Connor, K. J., Cunningham, W. A., Funayama, E. S., Gatenby, J. C., Gore, J. C., et al. (2000). Performance on indirect measures of race evaluation predicts amygdala activation. *Journal of Cognitive Neuroscience, 12,* 729–738.

Phillips, M. R., Li, X., & Zhang, Y. (2002). Suicide rates in China, 1995–99. *Lancet, 359,* 835–840.

Piaget, J. (1929). *The child's conception of the world.* New York: Harcourt Brace.

Piaget, J. (1952). *The origins of intelligence in children.* New York: International Universities Press. (Original work published 1936)

Picht, T., Mularski, S., Kuehn, B., Vajkoczy, P., Kombos, T., & Suess, O. (2009). Navigated transcranial magnetic stimulation for preoperative functional diagnostics in brain tumor surgery. *Neurosurgery, 65,* 93–98.

Pickerell, J. (2003, July 8). Urine vision? How rodents communicate with UV light. *National Geographic News.* Retrieved on January, 19, 2004, from http://news.nationalgeographic.com/news/2003/07/0708_030708_ultravioletmammals.html

Pidoplichko, V. I., DeBiasi, M., Williams, J. T., & Dani, J. A. (1997). Nicotine activates and desensitizes midbrain dopamine neurons. *Nature, 390,* 401–404.

Pierce, J. P. (2005). Influence of movie stars on the initiation of adolescent smoking. *Pediatric Dentistry, 27,* 149.

Pieterse, A. L., & Carter, R. T. (2007). An examination of the relationship between general life stress, racism-related stress, and psychological health among Black men. *Journal of Counseling Psychology, 54,* 101–109.

Pike, K. M., Devlin, M. J., & Loeb, C. (2004). Cognitive-behavioral therapy in the treatment of anorexia nervosa, and binge eating disorder. In J. K. Thompson (Ed.), *Handbook of eating disorders and obesity* (pp.130–162). New York: Wiley.

Pillemer, D. B., Wink, P., DiDonato, T. E., & Sanborn, R. L. (2003). Gender differences in autobiographical memory styles of older adults. *Memory, 11,* 525–532.

Pinel, J. P. J. (1997). *Biopsychology* (3rd ed.). Boston: Allyn & Bacon.

Pinker, S. (1994). *The language instinct: How the mind creates language.* New York: Morrow.

Pinnell, C. M., & Covino, N. A. (2000). Empirical findings on the use of hypnosis in medicine: A critical review. *International Journal of Clinical and Experimental Hypnosis, 48,* 170–194.

Piper, A., & Merskey, H. (2004). The persistence of folly: A critical examination of dissociative identity disorder: Part I. The excesses of an improbable concept. *Canadian Journal of Psychiatry, 49,* 592–600.

Plazzi, B., Corsini, R., Provini, R., Pierangeli, G., Martinelli, P., Montagna, P., et al. (1997). REM sleep behavior disorders in multiple system atrophy. *Neurology, 48,* 1094–1097.

Pleis, J. R., & Lethbridge-Ceiku, M. (2007). Summary health statistics for U.S. adults: National health interview survey, 2006. *Vital Health Statistics, 10,* No. 235.

Plester, B., Wood, C., & Joshi, P. (2009). Exploring the relationship between children's knowledge of text message abbreviations and school literacy outcomes. *British Journal of Developmental Psychology, 27,* 145–161.

Pleyers, G., Corneille, O., Luminet, O., & Yzerbyt, V. (2007). Aware and (dis)liking: Item-based analyses reveal that valence acquisition via evaluative conditioning emerges only when there is contingency awareness. *Journal of Experimental Psychology: Learning, Memory, and Cognition, 33,* 130–144.

Plomin, R., DeFries, J. C., McClearn, G. E., & McGuffin, P. (2001). *Behavioral genetics* (4th ed.). New York: Worth.

Plutchik, R. (1984). Emotions: A general psychoevolutionary theory. In K. R. Scherer & P. Ekman (Eds.), *Approaches to emotion* (pp. 197–219). Hillsdale, NJ: Erlbaum.

Podd, J. (1990). The effects of memory load and delay on facial recognition. *Applied Cognitive Psychology, 4,* 47–59.

Pohl, R. F., Bender, M., & Lachmann, G. (2005). Autobiographical memory and social skills in men and women. *Applied Cognitive Psychology, 19,* 745–759.

Poldrack, R. A., Desmond, J. E., Glover, G. H., & Gabrieli, J. D. E. (1996). The neural bases of visual skill: An fMRI study of mirror reading. *Society of Neuroscience, 22,* 719.

Politi, P., Minoretti, P., Falcone, C., Martinelli, V., & Emanuele, E. (2006). Association analysis of the functional Ala111Glu polymorphism of the glyoxalase I gene in panic disorder. *Neuroscience Letter, 396,* 163–166.

Pollack, W. (1998). Mourning, melancholia, and masculinity: Recognizing and treating depresssion in men. In W. Pollack & R. Levant (Eds.), *New psychotherapy for men* (pp. 147–166). New York: Wiley.

Polmin, R. (1994). The Emanuel Miller Memorial Lecture 1993: Genetic research and identification of environmental influences. *Journal of Child Psychology and Psychiatry, 35,* 817–834.

Polotsky, V. Y., & O'Donnell, C. P. (2007). Genomics of sleep-disordered breathing. *Proceedings of the American Thoracic Society, 4,* 121–126.

Pomeroy, A. (2005). 50 best small and medium places to work: Money talks. *HR Magazine, 50(7),* 44–65.

Pomeroy, W. (1965, May). Why we tolerate lesbians. *Sexology,* 652–654.

Ponniah, K., & Hollon, S. D. (2009). Empirically supported psychological treatments for adult acute stress disorder and posttraumatic stress disorder: A review. *Depression and Anxiety, 26,* 1086–1109.

Pope, H. D., Jr., Oliva, P. S., Hudson, J. I., Bodkin, J. A., & Gruber, A. J. (1999). Attitudes toward DSM-IV dissociative disorders diagnoses among board-certified

American psychiatrists. *American Journal of Psychiatry, 156,* 321–323.

Pope, H. G., & Yurgelun-Todd, D. (1996). The residual cognitive effects of heavy marijuana use in college students. *Journal of the American Medical Association, 275(7),* 521–527.

Porkka-Heiskanen, T., Strecker, R. E., Thakkar, M., Bjorkum, A. A., Greene, R. W., & McCarley, R. W. (1997) Adenosine: A mediator of the sleep-inducing effects of prolonged wakefulness. *Science, 276,* 1265–1268.

Porte, H. S., & Hobson, J. A. (1996). Physical motion in dreams: One measure of three theories. *Journal of Abnormal Psychology, 105,* 329–335.

Porter, R. H. (1999). Olfaction and human kin recognition. *Genetica, 104,* 259–263.

Post, R., Frye, M., Denicoff, K. Leverich, G., Kimbrell, T., & Dunn, R. (1998). Beyond lithium in the treatment of bipolar illness. *Neuropsychopharmacology, 19,* 206–219.

Potter, W. J., Warren, R., Vaughan, M., Howley, K., Land, A., & Hagemeyer, J. (1997). Antisocial acts in reality programming on television. *Journal of Broadcasting and Electronic Media, 41,* 69–89.

Powell, L. H., Calvin, J. E., III, & Calvin, J. E. , Jr. (2007). Effective obesity treatments. *American Psychologist, 62,* 234–246.

Powell, L. H., Shahabi, L., & Thoresen, C. E. (2003). Religion and spirituality. Linkages to physical health. *American Psychologist, 58,* 36–52.

Powell, T. J., Silk, K. R., & Albeck, J. H. (2000). Psychiatrists' referrals to self-help groups for people with mood disorders. *Psychiatric Services, 51,* 809–811.

Pratkanis, A. R. (1992). The cargo-cult science of subliminal persuasion. *Skeptical Inquirer, 16,* 260–272.

Pratkanis, A. R., Epley, N., Savitsky, K., & Kachelski, R. A. (2007). Issue 12: Is subliminal persuasion a myth? In J. A. Nier (Ed.), *Taking sides: Clashing views in social psychology* (2nd ed., pp. 230–255). New York: McGraw-Hill.

Prentice, A. M. (2009). Obesity in emerging nations: evolutionary origins and the impact of a rapid nutrition transition. Nestle Nutrition Workshop Series. *Paediatric Programme, 63,* 47–54.

Prescott, C. A., Hewitt, J. K., Truett, K. R., Heath, A. C., Neale, M. C., & Eaves, L. J. (1994). Genetic and environmental influences on alcohol-related problems in a volunteer sample of older twins. *Journal of Studies on Alcohol, 55,* 184–202.

Pressman, S. D., Cohen, S., Miller, G. E., Barkin, A., Rabin, B. S., & Treanor, J. J. (2005). Loneliness, social network size, and immune response to influenza vaccination in college freshman. *Health Psychology, 24,* 297–306.

Preston, J. A. (2005, June). *Delaying a life: The consequences of career development for the Radcliffe class of 1950.* Paper presented at the IWPR's Eighth International Women's Policy Research Conference.

Price, C. A., & Balaswamy, S. (2009). Beyond health and wealth: Predictors of women's retirement satisfaction. *International Journal of Aging and Human Development, 68,* 195–214.

Price, W. F., & Crapo, R. H. (2002). *Cross-cultural perspectives in introductory psychology.* Belmont, CA: Wadsworth.

Pritchard, M. E., Wilson, G. S., & Yamnitz, B. (2007). What predicts adjustment among college students? A longitudinal panel study. *Journal of American College Health, 56,* 15–21.

Prosser, I. B. (1933). *Non-academic development of Negro children in mixed and segregated schools.* Unpublished doctoral dissertation, University of Cincinnati.

Proudfoot, J. G. (2004). Computer-based treatment for anxiety and depression: Is it feasible? Is it effective? *Neuroscience Biobehavior Review, 28,* 353–363.

Pruett, K. D. (2000). *Fatherneed.* New York: Broadway Books.

Prutkin, J., Duffy, V. B., Etter, L., Fast, K., Gardner, E., Lucchina, L. A., et al. (2000). Genetic variation and inferences about perceived taste intensity in mice and men. *Physiology and Behavior, 69,* 161–173.

Pullman, G. K. (1989). The great Eskimo vocabulary hoax. *National Language and Linguistic Theory, 7,* 275–281.

Purves, D., Augustine, G. J., Fitzpatrick, D., Katz, L., LaMantia, A. S., & McNamara, J. O. (1997). *Neuroscience.* Sunderland, MA: Sinauer.

Putnam, F. W. (2000). Dissociative disorders. In A. Sameroff, M. Lewis, & S. Miller (Eds.), *Handbook of developmental psychopathology* (2nd ed., pp. 739–754). New York: Kluwer Academic/Plenum.

Putnam, F. W., Guroff, J. J., Silberman, E. K., & Barban, L. (1986). The clinical phenomenology of multiple personality disorder: Review of 100 recent cases. *Journal of Clinical Psychiatry, 47,* 285–293.

Pyke, K., & Johnson, D. (2003). Asian American women and racialized femininities: "Doing" gender across cultural worlds. *Gender and Society, 17,* 33–53.

Qiu, J., Li, H., Jou, J., Liu, J., Luo, Y., Feng, T., et al. (2010). Neural correlates of the "aha" experiences: Evidence from an fMRI study of insight problem solving. *Cortex, 46,* 397–403.

Quattrone, G. A., & Jones, E. E. (1980). The perception of variability within ingroups and outgroups: Implications for the law of small number. *Journal of Personality and Social Psychology, 38,* 141–152.

Querido, J. G., Warner, T. D., & Eyberg, S. M. (2002). Parenting styles and child behavior in African American families of preschool children. *Journal of Clinical Child and Adolescent Psychology, 31,* 272–277.

Quickfall, J., & Crockford, D. (2006). Brain neuroimaging in cannabis use: A review. *Journal of Neuropsychiatry and Clinical Neurosciences, 18,* 318–332.

Quinn, P. C., & Liben, L. S. (2008). A sex difference in mental rotation in young infants. *Psychological Science, 19,* 1067–1070.

Quinn, P. C., & Tanaka, J. W. (2007). Early development of perceptual expertise: Within-basic-level categorization experience facilitates the formation of subordinate-level category representations in 6- to 7-month-old infants. *Memory and Cognition, 35,* 1422–1431.

Rabkin, S. W., Boyko, E., Shane, F., & Kaufert, J. (1984). A randomized trial comparing smoking cessation programs utilizing behavior modification, health education, or hypnosis. *Addictive Behaviors, 9,* 157–173.

Racsmany, M., Conway, M. A., & Demeter, G. (2010). Consolidation of episodic memories during sleep: Long-term effects of retrieval practice. *Psychological Science, 21,* 80–85.

Radiological Society of North America (2006, November 29). Violent video games leave teenagers emotionally aroused. *ScienceDaily*. Retrieved December 29, 2009, from http://www.sciencedaily.com/releases/2006/11/061128140804.htm

Rahman, Q. (2005). The neurodevelopment of human sexual orientation. *Neuroscience and Biobehavioral Reviews, 29,* 1057–1066.

Raichle, M. E. (1994). Visualizing the mind. *Scientific American, 270,* 58–64.

Raine, A. (1997). Antisocial behavior and psychophysiology: A biological perspective. In D. M. Stoff, J. Breiling, & J. D. Maser (Eds.), *Handbook of anti-social personality disorder* (pp. 289–304). New York: Wiley.

Raine, A. (2008). From genes to brain to antisocial behavior. *Current Directions in Psychological Science, 17,* 323–328.

Raine, A., Lencz, T., Bihrle, S., LaCasse, L., & Colletti, P. (2000). Reduced prefrontal gray matter volume and reduced autonomic activity in antisocial personality disorder. *Archives of General Psychiatry, 57,* 119–127.

Rainville, P., & Price, D. D. (2003). Hypnosis phenomenology and the neurobiology of consciousness. *International Journal of Clinical and Experimental Hypnosis, 51,* 105–129.

Rainville, P., Duncan, G. H., Price, D. D., Carrier, B., & Bushnell, M. C. (1997). Pain affect encoded in human anterior cingulate but not somatosensory cortex. *Science, 277,* 968–971.

Rakic, P. (1991). Plasticity of cortical development. In S. E. Brauth, W. S. Hall, & R. J. Dooling (Eds.), *Plasticity of Development*. Cambridge, MA: Bradford/MIT Press.

Rakofsky, J. F., Holtzheimer, P. E., & Nemeroff, C. B. (2009). Emerging targets for antidepressants. *Current Opinion in Chemical Biology, 13,* 291–302.

Ramnani, N., Toni, I., Josephs, O., Ashburner, J., & Passingham, R. E. (2000). Learning- and expectation-related changes in the human brain during motor learning. *Journal of Neurophysiology, 84,* 3026–3035.

Ramsey-Rennels, J. L., & Langlois, J. H. (2006). Infants' differential processing of female and male faces. *Current Directions in Psychological Science, 15,* 59–62.

Randall, S., Johanson, C. E., Tancer, M., & Roehrs, T. (2009). Effects of acute 3, 4 methylenedioxymethamphetamine on sleep and daytime sleepiness in MDMA users: A preliminary study. *Sleep, 32,* 1513–1519.

Rando, T. A. (1995). Grief and mourning: Accommodating to loss. In H. Wass & R. A. Neimeyer (Eds.), *Dying: Facing the facts* (3rd ed., pp. 211–241). Washington, DC: Taylor & Francis.

Ranganathan, M., & D'Souza, D. C. (2006). The acute effects of cannabinoids on memory in humans: A review. *Psychopharmacology* (Berlin), *188,* 425–444.

Rank, M. R. (2000). Poverty and economic hardship in families. In D. H. Demo, K. R. Allen, & M. A. Fine (Eds.), *Handbook of family diversity* (pp. 293–315). New York: Oxford University Press.

Rao, H., Hillihan, S. J., Wang, J., Korczykowski, M., Sankoorikal, G. M., Kaercher, K. A., et al. (2007). Genetic variation in serotonin transporter alters resting brain function in healthy individuals. *Biological Psychiatry, 62,* 600–606.

Rapiejko, P., Zielnik-Jurkiewicz, B., Wojdas, A., Ratajczak, J., & Jurkiewicz, D. (2008). The existence [of the] vomeronasal organ in adult humans. *Otolaryngologia Polska, 61,* 581–584.

Rapoport, J. L., Addington, A. M., Frangou, S., & Psych, M. R. (2005). The neurodevelopmental model of schizophrenia: Update 2005. *Molecular Psychiatry, 10,* 434–449.

Rappaport, V. J. (2008). Prenatal diagnosis and genetic screening: Integration into prenatal care. *Obstetrics and Gynecology Clinics of North America, 35,* 435–458.

Rasch, B., & Born, J. (2008). Reactivation and consolidation of memory during sleep. *Current Directions in Psychological Science, 17,* 188–192.

Rauch, S. L., Savage, C. R., Alpert, N. M., Dougherty, D., Kendrick, A., Curran, T., et al. (1997). Probing striatal function in obsessive-compulsive disorder: A PET study of implicit sequence learning. *Journal of Neuropsychiatry and Clinical Neuroscience, 9,* 568–573.

Rauch, S. L., Shin, L. M., & Phelps, E. A. (2006). Neurocircuitry models of posttraumatic stress disorder and extinction: Human neuroimaging research—past, present, and future. *Biological Psychiatry, 60,* 376–382.

Rauchs, G., Bertran, F., Guillery-Girard, B., Desgranges, B., Kerrouche, N., Denise, P., et al. (2004). Consolidation of strictly episodic memories mainly requires rapid eye movement sleep. *Sleep, 27,* 395–401.

Ravenna, H., Jones, C., & Kwan, V. S. (2002). Personality change over 40 years of adulthood: Hierarchial linear modeling analyses of two longitudinal samples. *Journal of Personality and Social Psychology, 83,* 752–766.

Ray, R. D., Wilhelm, F. H., & Gross, J. J. (2008). All in the mind's eye? Anger rumination and reappraisal. *Journal of Personality and Social Psychology, 94,* 133–145.

Raz, A. (2005). Attention and hypnosis: Neural substrates and genetic associations of two converging processes. *International Journal of Clinical and Experimental Hypnosis, 53,* 237–258.

Raz, A., Fan, J., & Posner, M. I. (2006). Neuroimaging and genetic associations of attentional and hypnotic processes. *Journal of Physiology* (Paris), *99,* 483–491.

Read, C. N., & Greenberg, B. D. (2009). Psychiatric neurosurgery 2009: Review and perspective. *Seminars in Neurology, 29,* 256–265.

Read, S., & Grundy, E. (in press). Mental health among older married couples: The role of gender and family life. *Social Psychiatry and Psychiatric Epidemiology.*

Ready, R. E., Marquez, D. X., & Akerstedt, A. (2009). Emotion in younger and older adults: Retrospective and prospective associations with sleep and physical activity. *Experimental Aging Research, 35,* 348–368.

Reba-Harrelson, L., Von Holle, A., Hamer, R. M., Swann, R., Reyes, M. L., & Bulik, C. M. (2009). Patterns and prevalence of disordered eating and weight control behaviors in women ages 25–45. *Eating and Weight Disorders, 14,* 190–198.

Reder, L. M., Park, H., & Kieffaber, P. D. (2009). Memory systems do not divide on consciousness: Reinterpreting memory in terms of activation and binding. *Psychological Bulletin, 135,* 23–49.

Regier, D. A., Narrow, W. E., Rae, D. S., Manderscheid, R. W., Locke, B. Z., & Goodwin, F. K. (1993). The de facto U.S. mental and addictive disorders service system: Epidemiologic Catchment Area prospective 1-year prevalence rates of disorders and services. *Archives of General Psychiatry, 50,* 85–94.

Rehder, B., & Hoffman, A. B. (2005). Thirty-something categorization results explained: Selective attention, eyetracking, and models of category learning. *Journal of Experimental Psychology: Learning, Memory, and Cognition, 31,* 811–829.

Reid, P., & Bing, V. (2000). Sexual roles of girls and women: An ethnocultural lifespan perspective. In C. Travis & J. White (Eds.), *Sexuality, society, and feminism* (pp. 141–166). Washington, DC: American Psychological Association.

Reinisch, J. M. (1991). *The Kinsey Institute new report on sex: What you must know to be sexually literate.* New York: St. Martin's Press.

Reisenzein, R. (1983). The Schachter theory of emotion: Two decades later. *Psychological Bulletin, 94,* 239–264.

Reiss, D. (2005). The interplay between genotypes and family relationships: Reframing concepts of development and prevention. *Current Directions in Psychological Science, 14,* 139–143.

Reissig, C. J., Strain, E. C., & Griffiths, R. R. (2009). Caffeinated energy drinks: A growing problem. *Drug and Alcohol Dependence, 99,* 1–10.

Reissing, E. D., Binik, Y. M., & Khalife, S. (1999). Does vaginismus exist? *Journal of Nervous and Mental Disease, 187,* 261–274.

Reite, M., Sheeder, J., Teale, P., Richardson, D., Adams, M., & Simon, J. (1995). MEG based brain laterality: Sex differences in normal adults. *Neuropsychologia, 33,* 1607–1616.

Reitzes, D. C., & Mutran, E. J. (2004). The transition to retirement: Stages and factors that influence retirement adjustment. *International Journal of Aging and Human Development, 59,* 63–84.

Rempel, D. M., Keir, P. J., & Bach, J. M. (2008). Effect of wrist posture on carpal tunnel pressure while typing. *Journal of Orthopaedic Research, 26,* 1269–1273.

Repetti, R., Wang, S., & Saxbe, D. (2009). Bringing it all back home: How outside stressors shape families' everyday lives. *Current Directions in Psychological Science, 18,* 106–111.

Repovs, G., & Baddeley, A. (2006). The multi-component model of working memory: Explorations in experimental cognitive psychology. *Neuroscience, 139,* 5–21.

Rescorla, R. A. (1967). Pavlovian conditioning and its proper control procedures. *Psychological Review, 74,* 71–80.

Resick, P. A., Nishith, P., Weaver, T. L., Astin, M. C., & Feuer, C. A. (2002). A comparison of cognitive-processing therapy with prolonged exposure and a waiting condition for the treatment of chronic posttraumatic stress disorder in female rape victims. *Journal of Consulting and Clinical Psychology, 70,* 867–879.

Resta, O., Foschino-Barbaro, M. P., Legari, G., Talamo, S., Bonfitto, P., Palumbo, A., et al. (2001). Sleep-related breathing disorders, loud snoring and excessive daytime sleepiness in obese subjects. *International Journal of Obesity and Related Metabolic Disorders, 25,* 669–675.

Reyna, V. F., & Farley, F. (2006). Risk and rationality in adolescent decision making. *Psychological Science in the Public Interest, 7,* 1–44.

Reynolds, C. R., & Brown, R. T. (Eds.). (1984). *Perspectives on bias in mental testing.* New York: Plenum Press.

Reynolds, J. R., & Burge, S. W. (2008). Educational expectations and the rise in women's post-secondary attainments. *Social Science Research, 37,* 485–499.

Reynolds, P., Hurley, S., Torres, M., Jackson, J., Boyd, P., & Chen, V. W. (2000). Use of coping strategies and breast cancer survival: Results from the Black/White Cancer Survival Study. *American Journal of Epidemiology, 152,* 940–949.

Reynolds, S., Stiles, W. B., Barkham, M., & Shapiro, D. A. (1996). Acceleration of changes in session impact during contrasting time-limited psychotherapies. *Journal of Consulting and Clinical Psychology, 64,* 577–586.

Rhoades, G. K., Stanley, S. M., & Markman, H. J. (2009). The pre-engagement cohabitation effect: A replication and extension of previous findings. *Journal of Family Psychology, 23,* 107–111.

Rhodes, N., & Wood, W. (1992). Self-esteem and intelligence affect influencability: The mediating role of message reception. *Psychological Bulletin, 111,* 156–171.

Rice, F. P. (1992). *Intimate relationships, marriages, and families.* Mountain View, CA: Mayfield.

Rice, V. H. (Ed.). (2000). *Handbook of stress, coping and health.* Thousand Oaks, CA: Sage.

Richards, J., Klein, B., & Carlbring, P. (2003). Internet-based treatment for panic disorder. *Cognitive Behaviour Therapy, 32,* 125–135.

Richardson-Klavehn, A., & Bjork, R. A. (1988). Measures of memory. *Annual Review of Psychology, 39,* 475–543.

Rich-Edwards, J., Krieger, N., Majzoub, J., Zierler, S., Lieberman, E., & Gillman, M. (2001). Maternal experiences of racism and violence as predictors of preterm birth: Rationale and study design. *Pediatric and Perinatal Epidemiology, 15,* 124–135.

Rickels, K., DeMartinis, N., Garcia-Espana, F., Greenblatt, D. J., Mandos, L. A., & Rynn, M. (2000). Imipramine and buspirone in treatment of patients with generalized anxiety disorder who are discontinuing long-term benzodiazepine therapy. *American Journal of Psychiatry, 157,* 1973–1979.

Ridley, M. (2003). What makes you who you are: Which is stronger, nature or nurture? *Time, 161*(22), 54–62.

Rieger, G., Gygax, L., & Bailey, J. M. (2008). Sexual orientation and childhood gender nonconformity: Evidence from home videos. *Developmental Psychology, 44,* 46–58.

Rieke, F., & Rudd, M. E. (2009). The challenges natural images pose for visual adaptation. *Neuron, 64,* 605–616.

Riemann, D., & Perlis, M. L. (2009). The treatments of chronic insomnia: A review of benzodiazepine receptor agonists and psychological and behavioral therapies. *Sleep Medicine Reviews, 13,* 205–214.

Rishi, M. A., Shetty, M., Wolff, A., Amoateng-Adjepong, Y., & Manthous, C. A. (2010). Atypical antipsychotic medications are independently associated with severe obstructive sleep apnea. *Clinical Neuropharmacology, 33,* 109–113.

Riskind, J. H., Williams, N. L., Gessner, T. L., Chrosniak, L. D., & Cortina, J. M., (2000). The looming maladaptive style: Anxiety, danger, and schematic processing. *Journal of Personality and Social Psychology, 79,* 837–852.

Rivers, P. C. (1994). *Alcohol and human behavior.* Englewood Cliffs, NJ: Prentice Hall.

Roberts, A., Cash, T. F., Feingold, A., & Johnson, B. T. (2006). Are Black–White differences in females' body dissatisfaction decreasing? A meta-analytic review. *Journal of Consulting and Clinical Psychology, 74,* 1121–1131.

Roberts, B. W., Caspi, A., & Moffitt, T. E. (2001). The kids are alright: Growth and stability in personality development from adolescence to adulthood. *Journal of Personality and Social Psychology, 81,* 670–683.

Roberts, B. W., & DelVecchio, W. F. (2000). The rank-order consistency of personality traits from childhood to old age: A quantitative review of longitudinal studies. *Psychological Bulletin, 126,* 3–25.

Roberts, B. W., Kuncel, N. R., Shiner, R., Caspi, A., & Goldberg, L. R. (2007). The power of personality: The comparative validity of personality traits, socioeconomic status, and cognitive ability for predicting important life outcomes. *Perspectives on Psychological Science, 2,* 313–345.

Roberts, B. W., & Mroczek, D. (2008). Personality trait change in adulthood. *Current Directions in Psychological Science, 17,* 31–35.

Roberts, B. W., Walton, K. E., & Viechtbauer, W. (2006). Patterns of mean-level change in personality traits across the life course: A meta-analysis of longitudinal studies. *Psychological Bulletin, 132,* 1–25.

Roberts, R. D., Schulze, R., O'Brien, K., MacCann, C., Reid, J., & Maul, A. (2006). Exploring the validity of the Mayer-Salovey-Caruso emotional intelligence test (MSCEIT) with established emotions measures. *Emotion, 6,* 663–669.

Roberts, R. E., Roberts, C. R., & Chan, W. (2006). Ethnic differences in symptoms of insomnia among adolescents. *Sleep, 29,* 359–365.

Roberts, S. M. (1995). Applicability of the goodness-of-fit hypothesis to coping with daily hassles. *Psychological Reports, 77*(3, Pt. 1), 943–954.

Robins, L. N., & Regier, D. A. (Eds.). (1991). *Psychiatric disorders in America: The Epidemiologic Catchment Area Study.* New York: Free Press.

Robins, R. W., Fraley, R. C., Roberts, B. W., & Trzesniewski, K. H. (2001). A longitudinal study of personality change in young adulthood. *Journal of Personality, 69,* 617–640.

Robinson, J. A., & Swanson, K. L. (1990). Autobiographical memory: The next phase [Special Issue: Applying cognitive psychology in the 1990s]. *Applied Cognitive Psychology, 4,* 321–335.

Robinson, L. A., Berman, J. S., & Neimeyer, R. A. (1990). Psychotherapy for the treatment of depression: A comprehensive review of controlled outcome research. *Psychological Bulletin, 109,* 30–49.

Robinson, N. M., Abbott, R. D., Berninger, V. W., & Busse, J. (1996). The structure of abilities in math-precocious young children: Gender similarities and differences. *Journal of Educational Psychology, 88,* 341–352.

Robles, T. F., & Kiecolt-Glaser, J. K. (2003). The physiology of marriage: Pathways to health. *Physiology and Behavior, 79,* 409–416.

Robles, T. F., Glaser, R., Kiecolt-Glaser, J. K. (2005). Out of balance: A new look at chronic stress, depression, and immunity. *Current Directions in Psychological Science, 14,* 111–115.

Rockafellow, B. D., & Saules, K. K. (2006). Substance use by college students: The role of intrinsic versus extrinsic motivation for athletic involvement. *Psychology of Addictive Behavior, 20,* 279–287.

Rodenburg, R., Benjamin, A., de Roos, C., Meijer, A. M., & Stams, G. J. (2009). Efficacy of EMDR in children: A meta-analysis. *Clinical Psychology Review, 29,* 599–606.

Rogers, C. R. (1942). *Counseling and psychotherapy.* Boston: Houghton Mifflin.

Rogers, C. R. (1951). *Client-centered therapy: Its current practice, implications, and theory.* Boston: Houghton Mifflin.

Rogers, C. R. (1959). A theory of therapy, personality, and interpersonal relationships, as developed in the client-centered framework. In S. Koch (Ed.), *Psychology: A study of science* (Vol. 3, pp. 184–256). New York: McGraw-Hill.

Rogers, C. R. (1961). *On becoming a person.* Boston: Houghton Mifflin.

Rogers, C. R. (1970). *Carl Rogers on encounter groups.* New York: Harper & Row.

Rogers, C. R. (1980). *A way of being.* Boston: Houghton Mifflin.

Rogers, C. R. (1986). Client-centered therapy. In I. L. Kutash & A. Wolf (Eds.), *Psychotherapists' casebook* (pp. 197–208). San Francisco: Jossey-Bass.

Rogers, M. A., Yamasue, H., Abe, O., Yamada, H., Ohtani, T., Iwanami, A., et al. (2009). Smaller amygdala volume and reduced anterior cingulated gray matter density associated with history of post-traumatic stress disorder. *Psychiatry Research, 174,* 210–216.

Rogers, N. L., Szuba, M. P., Staab, J. P., Evans, D. L., & Dinges, D. F. (2001). Neuroimmunologic aspects of sleep and sleep loss. *Seminars in Clinical Neuropsychiatry, 6,* 295–307.

Rogers, T. B. (1995). *The psychological testing enterprise: An introduction.* Pacific Grove, CA: Brooks/Cole.

Rogoff, B., & Chavajay, P. (1995). What's become of research on the cultural basis of cognitive development? *American Psychologist, 50,* 859–873.

Rohan, M. J., & Zanna, M. P. (1996). Value transmission in families. In C. Seligman & J. M. Olson (Eds.), *The psychology of values: The Ontario symposium* (Vol. 8, pp. 253–276). Mahwah, NJ: Erlbaum.

Rohrbach, L. A., Grana, R., Vernberg, E., Sussman, S., & Sun, P. (2009). Impact of Hurricane Rita on adolescent substance abuse. *Psychiatry, 72,* 222–237.

Roisman, G. I., Clausell, E., Holland, A., Fortuna, K., & Elieff, C. (2008). Adult romantic relationships as contexts of human development: A multimethod comparison of same-sex couples with opposite-sex dating, engaged, and married dyads. *Developmental Psychology, 44,* 91–101.

Roisman, G. I., & Fraley, R. C. (2006). The limits of genetic influence: A behavior-genetic analysis of infant-caregiver relationship quality and temperament. *Child Development, 77,* 1656–1667.

Rokicki, L. A., Holroyd, K. A., France, C. R., Lipchik, G. L., France, J. L., & Kvaal, S. A. (1997). Change mechanisms associated with combined relaxation/EMG bio-feedback training for chronic tension headache. *Applied Psychophysiology and Biofeedback, 22,* 21–41.

Rollins, B. C. & Feldman, H. (1975, February). Marital satisfaction over the family life cycle. *Journal of Marriage and the Family, 32,* 25.

Rolls, E. T. (2000). The representation of umami tastes in the taste cortex. *Journal of Nutrition, 130,* 960–965.

Rooney, N. J., Bradshaw, J. W. S., & Robinson, I. H. (2001). Do dogs respond to play signals given by humans? *Animal Behavior, 61,* 715–722.

Rosch, E. (1973a). Natural categories. *Cognitive Psychology, 4,* 328–350.

Rosch, E. (1973b). On the internal structure of perceptual and semantic categories. In T. E. Moore (Ed.), *Cognitive development and the acquisition of language* (pp. 111–144). New York: Academic Press.

Rosch, E., Mervis, C. B., Gray, W. D., Johnson, D. M., & Boyes-Braem, P. (2004). Basic objects in natural categories. In D. A. Balota & E. J. Marsh (Eds.), *Cognitive Psychology: Key Readings* (pp. 448–471). New York: Psychology Press. (Original work published 1976)

Rose, A. J., Carlson, W., & Waller, E. M. (2007). Prospective associations of co-rumination with friendship and emotional adjustment: Considering the socioemotional trade-offs of co-rumination. *Developmental Psychology, 43,* 1019–1031.

Rose, A. J., & Smith, R. L. (2009). Sex differences in peer relationships. In K. H. Rubin, W. M. Bukowski, & B. Laursen (Eds.), *Handbook of peer interactions, relationships, and groups* (pp. 379–393). New York: Guilford Press.

Rose, J. E., Behm, F. M., Salley, A. N., Bates, J. E., Coleman, R. E., Hawk, T. C., et al. (2007). Regional brain activity correlates of nicotine dependence. *Neuropsychopharmacology, 32,* 2441–2452.

Rose, R. J. (1995). Genes and human behavior. *Annual Review of Psychology, 46,* 625–654.

Rose, S. A. (1980). Enhancing visual recognition memory in preterm infants. *Developmental Psychology, 16,* 85–92.

Rosen, J. B. (2004). The neurobiology of conditioned and unconditioned fear: A neurobehavioral system analysis of the amygdale. *Behavior and Cognitive Neuroscience Reviews, 3,* 23–41.

Rosen, J. B., & Donley, M. P. (2006). Animal studies of amygdala function in fear and uncertainty: Relevance to human research. *Biological Psychology, 73,* 49–60.

Rosenbaum, J. E. (2009). Patient teenagers? A comparison of the sexual behavior of virginity pledgers and matched nonpledgers. *Pediatrics, 123,* e110-e120.

Rosenblith, J. F. (1992). *In the beginning.* Newbury Park, CA: Sage.

Rosenhan, D. L. (1969). Some origins of the concerns for others. In P. Mussen & M. Covington (Eds.), *Trends and issues in developmental psychology* (pp. 134–153). New York: Holt, Rinehart & Winston.

Rosenhan, D. L. (1973). On being sane in insane places. *Science, 179,* 250–258.

Ross, C. A. (1997). *Dissociative identity disorder: Diagnosis, clinical features, and treatment of multiple personality.* Toronto: Wiley.

Ross, S., & Peselow, E. (2009). Pharmacotherapy of addictive disorders. *Clinical Neuropharmacology, 32,* 277–289.

Roth, S., & Cohen, J. L. (1986). Approach, avoidance, and coping with stress. *American Psychologist, 41,* 813–819.

Roth, T., Krystal, A. D., & Lieberman, J. A. III (2007). Long-term issues in the treatment of sleep disorders. *CNS Spectrum, 12,* 1–13.

Roth, T., Schwartz, J. R., Hirshkowitz, M., Erman, M. K., Dayno, J. M., & Arora, S. (2007). Evaluation of the safety of modafinil for treatment of excessive sleepiness. *Journal of Clinical Sleep Medicine, 3,* 595–602.

Rothbart, M. K., Ahadi, S. A., & Evans, D. E. (2000). Temperament and personality: Origins and outcomes. *Journal of Personality and Social Psychology, 78,* 122–135.

Rothbaum, B. O., Hodges, L. F., Kooper, R., Opdyke, D., & Williford, J. (1995). Effectiveness of computer-generated (virtual reality) graded exposure in the treatment of acrophobia. *American Journal of Psychiatry, 152,* 626–628.

Rothbaum, B. O., Hodges, L., Watson, B. A., Kessler, G. D., & Opdyke, D. (1996). Virtual reality exposure therapy in the treatment of fear of flying: A case report. *Behavior Research and Therapy, 34,* 477–481.

Rothbaum, F., Schneider-Rosen, K. S., Pott, M., & Beatty, M. (1995). Early parent–child relationships and later problem behavior: A longitudinal study. *Merrill-Palmer Quarterly, 41,* 133–151.

Rotter, J. (1982). *The development and application of social learning theory.* New York: Praeger.

Rouch, I., Wild, P., Ansiau, D., & Marquie, J. C. (2005). Shiftwork experience, age, and cognitive performance. *Ergonomics, 48,* 1282–1293.

Rowe, T. (2006). Fertility and a woman's age. *Journal of Reproductive Medicine, 51,* 157–163.

Rowlett, J. K., Cook, J. M., Duke, A. N., & Platt, D. M. (2005). Selective antagonism of GABAA receptor subtypes: An in vivo approach to exploring the therapeutic and side effects of benzodiazepine-type drugs. *CNS Spectrums, 10,* 40–48.

Roy-Byrne, P. P., Joesch, J. M., Wang, P. S., & Kessler, R. C. (2009). Low socioeconomic status and mental health care use among respondents with anxiety and depression in the NCS-R. *Psychiatric Services, 60,* 1190–1197.

Ruark, J. (2009, August 3). An intellectual movement for the masses: 10 years after its founding, positive psychology struggles with its own success. *Chronicle of Higher Education.*

Rubin, K. H., Lynch, D., Coplan, R., Rose-Krasnor, L., & Booth, C. L. (1994). "Birds of a feather . . .": Behavioral concordances and preferential personal attraction in children. *Child Development, 65,* 1778–1785.

Rubin, S. S. (1993). The death of a child is forever: The life course impact of child loss. In M. Stroebe, W. Stroebe, & R. O. Hansson (Eds.), *Handbook of bereavement: Theory, research, and intervention* (pp. 285–299). Cambridge, UK: Cambridge University Press.

Ruderman, A. J. (1985). Dysphoric mood and overeating: A test of restraint theory's disinhibition hypothesis. *Journal of Abnormal Psychology, 94,* 78–85.

Rudgley, R. (1998). *The encyclopedia of psychoactive substances.* New York: Little, Brown.

Ruffin, C. L. (1993). Stress and health: Little hassles vs. major life events. *Australian Psychologist, 28*(3), 201–208.

Ruffman, T., Slade, L., & Redman, J. (2005). Young infants' expectations about hidden objects. *Cognition, 97,* B35–B43.

Rumelhart, D. E. (1980). Schemata: The basic building blocks of cognition. In R. Spiro, B. Bruce, & W. Brewer (Eds.), *Theoretical issues in reading comprehension* (pp. 33–58). Hillsdale, NJ: Erlbaum.

Ruscio, A. M., Brown, T. A., Chiu, W. T., Sareen, J., Stein, M. B., & Kessler, R. C. (2008). Social fears and social phobia in the USA: Results from the National Comorbidity Survey Replication. *Psychological Medicine, 38,* 15–28.

Rush, M. C., Schoel, W. A., & Barnard, S. M. (1995). Psychological resiliency in the public sector: "Hardiness" and pressure for change. *Journal of Vocational Behavior, 46*(1), 17–39.

Rushton, J. P., & Jensen, A. R. (2005). Thirty years of research on race differences in cognitive ability. *Psychology, Public Policy, and Law, 11,* 235–294.

Rushton, W. A. H. (1958). Kinetics of cone pigments measured objectively in the living fovea. *Annals of the New York Academy of Sciences, 74,* 291–304.

Rushton, W.A.H. (1975). Visual pigments and color blindness. *Scientific American, 232,* 64–74.

Russell, R. J. H., & Wells, P. A. (1994). Predictors of happiness in married couples. *Personality and Individual Differences, 17,* 313–321.

Rutherford, W. (1886). A new theory of hearing. *Journal of Anatomy and Physiology, 21, 166–168.*

Ruytjens, L., Willemsen, A. T. M., Van Dijk, P., Wit, H. P., & Albers, F. W. J. (2006). Functional imaging of the central auditory system using PET. *Acta Oto-Laryngologica, 126,* 1236–1244.

Rypma, B., Berger, J. S., Genova, H. M., Rebbechi, D., & D'Esposito, M. (2005). Dissociating age-related changes in cognitive strategy and neural efficiency using event-related fMRI. *Cortex, 41,* 582–594.

Saadat, H., Drummond-Lewis, J., Maranets, I., Kaplan, D., Saadat, A., Wang, S. M., et al. (2006). Hypnosis reduces preoperative anxiety in adult patients. *Anesthesia and Analgesia, 102,* 1394–1396.

Sable, M., Danis, F., Mauzy, D., & Gallagher, S. (2006). Barriers to reporting sexual assault for women and men: Perspectives of college students. *Journal of American College Health, 55,* 157–162.

Sachs, G. S., & Rush, A. J. (2003). Response, remission, and recovery in bipolar disorders: What are the realistic treatment goals? *Journal of Clinical Psychiatry, 64*(Suppl. 6), 18–22.

Sackett, P. R., & DeVore, C. J. (2001). Counterproductive behaviors at work. In N. Anderson, D. S. Ones, H. K. Sinangil, & C. Viswesvaran (Eds.), *Handbook of industrial, work and organizational psychology: Vol. 1. Personnel Psychology* (pp. 145–165). Thousand Oaks, CA: Sage Publications.

Sacktor, T. C. (2010). PINing for things past. *Science Signaling,* doi:10.1126/scisignal.3112pe9.

Sadker, D. (2000). Gender equity: Still knocking at the classroom door. *Equity and Excellence in Education, 33,* 80–83.

Sadler, W. A. (2000). *The third age: Six principles for growth and renewal after forty.* New York: Perseus.

Safarinejad, M. R. (2008). Evaluation of the safety and efficacy of bremelanotide, a melanocortin receptor agonist, in female subjects with arousal disorder: A double-blind placebo-controlled, fixed dose, randomized study. *Journal of Sexual Medicine, 5,* 887–897.

Sah, P., Faber, E. S. L., Lopez De Armentia, M., & Power, J. (2003). The aymgdaloid complex: Anatomy and physiology. *Physiological Reviews, 83,* 803–834.

Saito, A., Mikami, A., Kawamura, S., Ueno, Y., Hiramatsu, C., Widayati, K. A., et al. (2005). Advantage of dichromats over trichromats in discrimination of color-camouflaged stimuli in nonhuman primates. *American Journal of Primatology, 67,* 425–436.

Sajatovic, M., Valenstein, M., Blow, F., Ganoczy, D., & Ignacio, R. (2007). Treatment adherence with lithium and anticonvulsant medications among patients with bipolar disorder. *Psychiatric Services, 58,* 855–863.

Sakari, M. M. (1975). Small group cohesiveness and detrimental conformity. *Sociometry, 38,* 340–357.

Salend, S. J. (2001). *Creating inclusive classrooms: Effective and reflective practices* (4th ed.). Upper Saddle River, NJ: Prentice Hall.

Salgado, J. F., Viswesvaran, C., & Ones, D. (2003). Predictors used for personnel selection: An overview of constructs, methods and techniques. In N. Anderson, D. S. Ones, H. K. Sinangil, & C. Viswesvaran (Eds.), *Handbook of industrial, work and organizational psychology: Vol. 1: Personnel Psychology* (pp. 166–199). Thousand Oaks, CA: Sage Publications.

Salkovskis, P. M., Westbrook, D., Davis, J., Jeavons, A., & Gledhill, A. (1997). Effects of neutralizing on intrusive thoughts: An experiment investigating the etiology of obsessive-compulsive disorder. *Behaviour Research and Therapy, 35,* 211–219.

Salthouse, T. A. (1994). The aging of working memory. *Neuropsychology, 8,* 535–543.

Salthouse, T. A. (2004). What and when of cognitive aging. *Current Directions in Psychological Science, 13,* 140–144.

Salthouse, T. A., & Siedlecki, K. L. (2007). Efficiency of route selection as a function of adult age. *Brain and Cognition, 63,* 279–286.

Samarel, N. (1995). The dying process. In H. Wass & R. A. Neimeyer (Eds.), *Dying: Facing the facts* (3rd ed., pp. 89–116). Washington, DC: Taylor & Francis.

Sanaktekin, O. H., & Sunar, D. (2008). Persuasion and relational versus personal self-esteem: Does the message need to be one- or two-sided? *Social Behavior and Personality, 36,* 1315–1332.

Sanchez-Hucles, J. V., & Davis, D. D. (2010). Women and women of color in leadership. *American Psychologist, 65,* 171–181.

Sanders, J. D., Happe, H. K., Bylund, D. B., & Murrin, L. C. (2005). Development of the norepinephrine transporter in the rat CNS. *Neuroscience, 130,* 107–117.

Sanderson, C. A., & Cantor, N. (1995). Social dating goals in late adolescence: Implications for safer sexual activity. *Journal of Personality and Social Psychology, 68,* 1121–1134.

Sanes, J. N., Dimitrov, B., & Hallett, M. (1990). Motor learning in patients with cerebellar dysfunction. *Brain, 113,* 103–120.

Sangrigoli, S., & de Schonen, S. (2004). Recognition of own-race and other-race faces by three-month-old infants. *Journal of Child Psychology and Psychiatry, 45,* 1219–1227.

Santelli, J. S., Lindberg, L. D., Abma, J., McNeeley, C. S., & Resnick, M. (2000). Adolescent sexual behavior: Estimates and trends from four nationally representative surveys. *Family Planning Perspectives, 32,* 156–165 & 194.

Sanyal, S., & vanTol, H. M. (1997). Review the role of dopamine D4 receptors in schizophrenia and antipsychotic action. *Journal of Psychiatric Research, 31,* 219–232.

Sapolsky, R. M. (2000a). Glucocorticoids and hippocampal atrophy in neuropsychiatric disorders. *Archives of General Psychiatry, 57,* 925–935.

Sapolsky, R. M. (2000b). The possibility of neurotoxicity in the hippocampus in major depression: A primer on neuron death. *Biological Psychiatry, 48,* 755–765.

Sapolsky, R. M. (2002). Chickens, eggs and hippocampal atrophy. *Nature Neuroscience, 5,* 1111–1113.

Saskin, P. (1997). Obstructive sleep apnea: Treatment options, efficacy, and effects. In M. R. Pressman & W. C. Orr (Eds.), *Understanding sleep: The evaluation and treatment of sleep disorders.* Washington DC: American Psychological Association.

Saudino, K. J., McQuire, S., Reiss, D. Heatherington, E. M., & Plomin, R. (1995). Parent ratings of EAS temperaments in twins, full siblings, half siblings, and step siblings. *Journal of Personality and Social Psychology, 68,* 723–733.

Saunders, E. H., Scott, L. J., McInnis, M. G., & Burmeister, M. (2008). Familiality and diagnostic patterns of subphenotypes in the National Institutes of Mental Health bipolar sample. *American Journal of Medical Genetics Part B: Neuropsychiatric Genetics, 147b,* 18–26.

Sauter, D. A., Eisner, F., Ekman, P., & Scott, S. K. (2010). Cross-cultural recognition of basic emotions through nonverbal emotional vocalizations. *Proceedings of the National Academy of Sciences USA, 107,* 2408–2412.

Sava, F. A., Yates, B. T., Lupu, V., Szentagotai, A., & David, D. (2009). Cost-effectiveness and cost-utility of cognitive therapy, rational emotive behavioral therapy, and fluoxetine (Prozac) in treating depression: A randomized clinical trial. *Journal of Clinical Psychology, 65,* 36–52.

Savage-Rumbaugh, E. S. (1987). Communication, symbolic communication and language: Reply to Seidenberg and Petitto. *Journal of Experimental Psychology: General, 116,* 288–292.

Savage-Rumbaugh, E..S., McDonald, K., Sevcik, R., Hopkins, W., & Rupert, E. (1986). Spontaneous symbol acquisition and communicative use by pygmy chimpanzees (*Pan paniscus*). *Journal of Experimental Psychology: General, 115,* 211–235.

Savage-Rumbaugh, E. S., Rumbaugh, D. M., & Fields, W. M. (2006). Language as a window on rationality. In S. Hurley & M. Nudds (Eds.), *Rational Animals?* New York: Oxford University Press.

Savin-Williams, R. C. (2006). Who's gay? Does it matter? *Current Directions in Psychological Science, 15,* 40–44.

Saxena, S., Brody, A. L., Schwartz, J. M., & Baxter, L. R. (1998). Neuroimaging and frontal-subcortical circuitry in obsessive-compulsive disorder. *British Journal of Psychiatry, 173*(Suppl. 35), 26–37.

Sayette, M. A., Reichle, E. D., & Schooler, J. W. (2009). Lost in the sauce: The effects of alcohol on mind wandering. *Psychological Science, 20,* 747–752.

Schachter, S. (1951). Deviation, rejection, and communication. *Journal of Abnormal and Social Psychology, 46,* 190–207.

Schachter, S., & Singer, J. E. (1962). Cognitive, social, and physiological determinants of emotional state. *Psychological Review, 69,* 379–399.

Schacter, D. L., Alpert, N. M., Savage, C. R., Rauch, S. L., & Alpert, M. S. (1996). Conscious recollection and the hippocampal formation: Evidence from positron emission tomography. *Proceedings of the National Academy of Science, USA, 93,* 321–325.

Schaie, K. W. (1983). The Seattle longitudinal study: A 21-year exploration of psychometric intelligence in adulthood. In K. W. Schaie (Ed.), *Longitudinal studies of adult psychological development* (pp. 64–135). New York: Guilford Press.

Schaie, K. W. (1994). The course of adult intellectual development. *American Psychologist, 49,* 304–313.

Schaie, K. W. (1996). *Intellectual development in adulthood. The Seattle longitudinal study.* New York: Cambridge University Press.

Schaie, K. W., & Willis, S. L. (2000). A stage theory model of adult cognitive development revisited. In B. Rubinstein, M. Moss, & M. Kleban (Eds.), *The many dimensions of aging: Essays in honor of M. Powell Lawton* (pp. 173–191). New York: Springer.

Schaller, S. (1995). *A man without words.* Berkeley: University of California Press.

Schein, E. H. (1985). *Organizational Leadership and Culture: A Dynamic View.* San Francisco: Jossey-Bass.

Scheier, M. F., & Bridges, M. W. (1995). Person variables and health: Personality predispositions and acute psychological states as shared determinants for disease. *Psychosomatic Medicine, 57,* 255–268.

Scheier, M. F., & Carver, C. S. (1992). Effects of optimism on psychological and physical well-being: Theoretical overview and empirical update. *Cognitive Therapy and Research, 16,* 201–228.

Scherrer, J. F., True, W. R., Xian, H., Lyons., M. J., Eisen, S. A., Goldberg, J., et al. (2000). Evidence for genetic influences common and specific to symptoms of generalized anxiety and panic. *Journal of Affective Disorders, 57,* 25–35.

Schlesier-Stropp, B. (1984). Bulimia: A review of the literature. *Psychological Review, 95,* 247–257.

Schiffrin, H., Edelman, A., Falkenstern, M., & Stewart, C. (2010). The associations among computer-mediated communication, relationships, and well-being. *Cyberpsychology, Behavior, and Social Networking, 13,* 299-306.

Schinka, J. A., Letsch, E. A., & Crawford, F. C. (2002). DRD4 and novelty seeking: Results of meta-analyses. *American Journal of Medical Genetics, 114,* 643–648.

Schleifer, S. J., Keller, S. E., Camerino, M., Thornton, J. C., & Stein, M. (1983). Suppression of lymphocyte stimulation following bereavement. *Journal of the American Medical Association, 250,* 374–377.

Schmidt, H. D., & Pierce, R. C. (2006). Systematic administration of a dopamine, but not a serotonin or norepinephrine, transporter inhibitor reinstates cocaine seeking in the rat. *Behavioural Brain Research, 175,* 189–194.

Schmidt, L. A., Fox, N. A., Perez-Edgar, K., & Hamer, D. H. (2009). Linking gene, brain, and behavior: DRD4, frontal asymmetry, and temperament. *Psychological Science, 20,* 831–837.

Schmidt, U., Lee, S., Beecham, J., Perkins, S., Treasure, J., Yi, I., et al. (2007). A randomized controlled trial of family therapy and cognitive behavior therapy guided self-care for adolescent with bulimia nervosa and related disorders. *American Journal of Psychiatry, 164,* 591–598.

Schmidt-Hieber, C., Jonas, P., & Bischofberger, J. (2004). Enhanced synaptic plasticity in newly generated granule cells of the adult hippocampus. *Nature, 429,* 184–187.

Schmitt, D. P., Realo, A., Voracek, M., & Allik, J. (2008). Why can't a man be more like a woman? Sex differences in Big Five personality traits across 55 cultures. *Journal of Personality and Social Psychology, 94,* 168–182.

Schmitt, N., Cortina, J. M., Ingerick, M. J., & Wiechmann, D. (2003). Personnel selection and employee performance. In W. C. Borman, D. R. Ilgen, & R. J. Klimoski (Eds.), *Handbook of psychology: Vol. 12. Industrial and organizational psychology,* (pp.77–105). Hoboken, NJ: John Wiley & Sons.

Schoenborn, C. A. (1986). Health habits of U.S. adults, 1985: The "Alameda 7" revisited. *Public Health Reports, 101,* 571–580.

Schoppe-Sullivan, S. J., Mangelsdorf, S. C., Brown, G. L., & Sokolowski, M. S. (2007). Goodness-of-fit in family context: Infant temperament, marital quality, and early coparenting behavior. *Infant Behavior and Development, 30,* 82–96.

Schott, R. L. (1995). The childhood and family dynamics of transvestites. *Archives of Sexual Behavior, 24,* 309–327.

Schottenbauer, M. A., Glass, C. R., Arnkoff, D. B., & Gray, S. H. (2008). Contributions of psychodynamic approaches to treatment of PTSD and trauma: A review of the empirical treatment and psychopathology literature. *Psychiatry, 71,* 13–34.

Schouten, A. P., Valkenburg, P. M., & Peter, J. (2007). Precursors and underlying processes of adolescents' online self-disclosure: Developing and testing an "Internet-attribute-perception" model. *Media Psychology, 10,* 292–314.

Schredl, M. (2009). Dreams in patients with sleep disorders. *Sleep Medicine Reviews, 13,* 215–221.

Schredl, M., & Erlacher, D. (2008). Relation between waking sport activities, reading, and dream content in sport students and psychology students. *Journal of Psychology, 142,* 267–275.

Schuckit, M. A. (1998). Biological, psychological, and environmental predictors of the alcoholism risk: A longitudinal study. *Journal of Studies on Alcohol, 59,* 485–494.

Schuckit, M. A., & Smith, T. L. (1997). Assessing the risk for alcoholism among sons of alcoholics. *Journal of Studies on Alcohol, 58,* 141–145.

Schuh, K. J., & Griffiths, R. R. (1997). Caffeine reinforcement: The role of withdrawal. *Psychopharmacology, 130,* 320–326.

Schultz, D. P., & Schultz, S. E. (2000). *A history of modern psychology* (7th ed.). Fort Worth, TX: Harcourt Brace.

Schultz, D. P., & Schultz, S. E. (2005). *Theories of personality* (8th ed.). Belmont, CA: Wadsworth.

Schumm, W. R., Webb, F. J., & Bollman, S. R. (1998). Gender and marital satisfaction: Data from the National Survey of Families and Households. *Psychological Reports, 83,* 319–327.

Schwartz, P. D., Maynard, A. M., & Uzelac, S. M. (2008). Adolescent egocentrism: A contemporary view. *Adolescence, 43,* 441–448.

Schwartz, G., Kim, R. M., Kolundzija, A. B., Rieger, G., & Sanders, A. R. (2010). Biodemographic and physical correlates of sexual orientation in men. *Archives of Sexual Behavior, 39,* 93–109.

Schwartz, I. M. (1999). Sexual activity prior to coitus initiation: A comparison between males and females. *Archives of Sexual Behavior, 28,* 63–69.

Schwartz, M., O'Neal Chambliss, H., Brownell, K., Blair, S., & Billington, C. (2003). Weight bias among health professionals specializing in obesity. *Obesity Research, 11,* 1033–1039.

Schwarzwald, J., Bizman, A., & Raz, M. (1983). The foot-in-the-door paradigm: Effects of second request size on donation probability and donor generosity. *Personality and Social Psychology Bulletin, 9,* 443–450.

Scoboria, A., Mazzoni, G., & Kirsch, I. (2006). Effects of misleading questions and hypnotic memory suggestion on memory reports: A signal-detection analysis. *International Journal of Clinical and Experimental Hypnosis, 54,* 340–359.

Scoboria, A., Mazzoni, G., Kirsch, I., & Milling, L. S. (2002). Immediate and persisting effects of misleading questions and hypnosis on memory reports. *Journal of Experimental Psychology, Applied, 8,* 26–32.

Scollon, C. N., & Diener, E. (2006). Love, work, and changes in extraversion and neuroticism over time. *Journal of Personality and Social Psychology, 91,* 1152–1165.

Scott, S. K., Young, A. W., Calder, A. J., & Hellawell, D. J. (1997). Impaired auditory recognition of fear and anger following bilateral amygdala lesions. *Nature, 385,* 254–257.

Scott, T. R., & Plata-Salaman, C. R. (1991). Coding of taste quality. In T. V. Gethell, R. L. Doty, L. M. Bartoshuk, & J. B. Snow, Jr. (Eds.), *Smell and taste in health and disease* (pp. 345–368). New York: Raven.

Scoville, W. B., & Milner, B. (1957). Loss of recent memory after bilateral hippocampal lesions. *Journal of Neurology, Neurosurgery, and Psychiatry, 20,* 11–19.

Scully, J. A., Tosi, H., & Banning, K. (2000). Life events checklist: Revisiting the social readjustment rating scale after 30 years. *Educational and Psychological Measurement, 60,* 864–876.

Seaton, E. K., Scottham, K. M., & Sellers, R. M. (2006). The status model of racial identity development in African American adolescents: Evidence of structure, trajectories, and well-being. *Child Development, 77,* 1416–1426.

Seeman, P. (1999). Brain development, X: Pruning during development. *American Journal of Psychiatry, 156,* 168.

Segal, M. W. (1974). Alphabet and attraction: An unobtrusive measure of the effect of propinquity in a field setting. *Journal of Personality and Social Psychology, 30,* 654–657.

Segerstrom, S. C. (2000). Personality and the immune system: Models, methods, and mechanisms. *Annals of Behavioral Medicine, 22,* 180–190.

Segerstrom, S. C. (2007). Stress, energy, and immunity: An ecological view. *Current Directions in Psychological Science, 16,* 326–330.

Segerstrom, S. C., & Sephton, S. E. (2010). Optimistic expectancies and cell-mediated immunity: The role of positive affect. *Psychological Science, 21,* 448–455.

Segraves, R., & Woodard, T. (2006). Female hypoactive sexual desire disorder: History and current status. *Journal of Sex Medicine, 3,* 408–418.

Segrin, C., & Nabi, R. L. (2002). Does television viewing cultivate unrealistic expectations about marriage? *Journal of Communication, 52,* 247–263.

Seidler, G. H., & Wagner, F. E. (2006). Comparing the efficacy of EMDR and trauma-focused cognitive-behavioral therapy in the treatment of PTSD: A meta-analytic study. *Psychological Medicine, 36,* 1515–1522.

Seidler, R. D., Purushotham, A., Kim, S.-G., Ugurbil, K., Willingham, D., & Ashe, J. (2002). Cerebellum activation associated with performance change but not after motor learning. *Science* (Washington), *296,* 2043–2046.

Seiffert, A. E., Somers, D. C., Dale, A. M., & Tootell, R. B. H. (2003). Functional MRI studies of human visual motion perception: Texture, luminance, attention, and after-effects. *Cerebral Cortex, 13,* 340–349.

Sekuler, R., McLaughlin, C., Kahana, M. J., Wingfield, A., & Yotsumoto, Y. (2006). Short-term visual recognition and temporal order memory are both well-preserved in aging. *Psychology and Aging, 21,* 632–637.

Seligman, M. E. P. (1970). On the generality of laws of learning. *Psychological Review, 77,* 406–418.

Seligman, M. E. P. (1989). *Helplessness.* New York: Freeman.

Seligman, M. E. P. (1995). The effectiveness of psychotherapy: The *Consumer Reports* Study. *American Psychologist, 50,* 965–974.

Seligman, M. E. P., & Csikszentmihalyi, M. (2000). Positive psychology: An introduction. *American Psychologist, 55,* 5–14.

Seligman, M. E. P., & Maier, S. F. (1967). Failure to escape traumatic shock. *Journal of Experimental Psychology, 74,* 1–9.

Selling, L. H. (1940). *Men against madness.* New York: Greenberg.

Selmi, P. M., Klein, M. H., Greist, J. H., Sorrell, S. P., & Erdman, H. P. (1990). Computer-administered cognitive-behavioral therapy for depression. *American Journal of Psychiatry, 147,* 51–56.

Seltzer, J. A. (2001). Families formed outside of marriage. In R. M. Milardo (Ed.), *Understanding families into the new millennium: A decade in review* (pp. 466–487). Minneapolis: National Council on Family Relations.

Selye, H. (1976). *The stress of life.* New York: McGraw-Hill.

Sen, S., Burmeister, M., & Ghosh, D. (2004). Meta-analysis of the association between a serotonin transporter promoter polymorphism (5-HTTLPR) and anxiety-related personality traits. *American Journal of Medical Genetics, 127,* 85–89.

Sen, S., Villafuerte, S., Nesse, R., Stoltenberg, S. F., Hopcian, J., Gleiberman, L., et al. (2004). Serotonin transporter and GABA(A) alpha 6 receptor variants are associated with neuroticism. *Biological Psychiatry, 55,* 244–249.

Seto, M. C., & Barbaree, H. E. (1995). The role of alcohol in sexual aggression. *Clinical Psychology Review, 15,* 545–566.

Sexton, J. (1995, July 25). Reviving Kitty Genovese case, and its passions. *New York Times,* pp. B1, B5.

Seyam, R. M., Albakry, A., Ghobish, A., Arif, H., Dandash, K., & Rashwan, H. (2003). Prevalence of erectile dysfunction and its correlates in Egypt: A community-based study. *International Journal of Impotence Research, 15,* 237–245.

Shadish, W. R., Cook, T. D., & Campbell, D. T. (2002). *Experimental and quasi-experimental designs for generalized causal inference.* Boston: Houghton Mifflin.

Shafer, M., & Crichlow, S. (1996). Antecedents of groupthink: A quantitative study. *Journal of Conflict Resolution, 40,* 415–435.

Shaffer, A., Huston, L., & Egeland, B. (2008). Identification of child maltreatment using prospective and self-report methodologies: A comparison of maltreatment incidence and relation to later psychopathology. *Child Abuse and Neglect, 32,* 682–692.

Shah, D. B., Pesiridou, A., Baltuch, G. H., Malone, D. A., & O'Reardon, J. P. (2008). Functional neurosurgery in the treatment of severe obsessive compulsive disorder and major depression: Overview of disease circuits and therapeutic targeting for the clinician. *Psychiatry, 5,* 24–33.

Shallenberger, R. S. (1993). *Taste chemistry.* London: Blackie.

Shallice, T., & Warrington, E. K. (1970). Independent functioning of verbal memory stores: A neuropsychological study. *Quarterly Journal of Experimental Psychology, 22,* 261–273.

Shallice, T., & Warrington, E. K. (1974). The dissociation between long-term retention of meaningful sounds and verbal material. *Nueropsychologica, 12,* 553, 555.

Shamloo, Z. S., & Cox, W. M. (2010). The relationship between motivational structure, sense of control, intrinsic motivation and university students' alcohol consumption. *Addictive Behavior, 35,* 140–146.

Shanker, S. G., Savage-Rumbaugh, E. S., & Taylor, T. J. (1999). Kanzi: A new beginning. *Animal Learning and Behavior, 27,* 24–25.

Shapiro, F. (1991). Eye movement desensitization and reprocessing procedure: From EMD to EMD/R—a new treatment model for anxiety and related traumata. *Behavior Therapist, 14,* 133–135.

Shapiro, F. (2001). *Eye movement desensitization and reprocessing: Basic principles, protocols, and procedures* (2nd ed.). New York: Guilford Press.

Share, D. L., & Silva, P. A. (2003). Gender bias in IQ-discrepancy and post-discrepancy definitions of reading disability. *Journal of Learning Disabilities, 36,* 4–14.

Shaw, H., Ramirez, L., Trost, A., Randall, P., & Stice, E. (2004). Body image and eating disturbances across ethnic groups: More similarities than differences. *Psychology of Addictive Behaviors, 18,* 12–18.

Shaw, L. H., & Gant, L. M. (2002). In defense of the Internet: The relationship between Internet communication and depression, loneliness, self-esteem, and perceived social support. *Cyberpsychology and Behavior, 5,* 157–171.

Shaw, M., & Black, D. W. (2008). Internet addiction: Definition, assessment, epidemiology and clinical management. *CNS Drugs, 22,* 353–365.

Sheeks, M. S., & Birchmeier, Z. P. (2007). Shyness, sociability, and the use of computer-mediated communication in relationship development. *Cyberpsychology and Behavior, 10,* 64–70.

Sheldon, K. M., Arndt, J., & Houser-Marko, L. (2003). In search of the organismic valuing process: The human tendency to move towards beneficial goal choices. *Journal of Personality, 71,* 835–869.

Sheline, Y. I. (2000). 3D MRI studies of neuroanatomic changes in unipolar major depression: The role of stress and medical comorbidity. *Biological Psychiatry, 48,* 791–800.

Shen, B. J., McCreary, C. P., & Myers, H. F. (2004). Independent and mediated contributions of personality, coping, social support, and depressive symptoms to physical functioning outcome among patients in cardiac rehabilitation. *Journal of Behavioral Medicine, 27,* 39–62.

Shepard, G. M. (2006). Smell images and the flavour system in the brain. *Nature, 444,* 316–321.

Shepard, R. N. (1978). The mental image. *American Psychologist, 33,* 125–137.

Sherif, M. (1966). *In common predicament: Social psychology of intergroup conflict and cooperation.* Boston: Houghton Mifflin.

Sherif, M., Harvey, O. J., White, J., Hood, W., & Sherif, C. (1961). *Intergroup conflict and cooperation: The Robber's Cave experiment.* Norman: University of Oklahoma Press.

Shi, J., Levinson, D. F., Duan, J., Sanders, A. R., Zheng, Y., Pe'er, I., et al. (2009). Common variants on chromosome 6p22.1 are associated with schizophrenia. *Nature, 460,* 753–757.

Shields, M. (2004). Stress, health and the benefit of social support. *Health Reports, 15,* 9–38.

Shimoff, E., Catania, A. C., & Matthews, B. A. (1981). Unstructured human responding: Sensitivity of low-rate performance to schedule contingencies. *Journal of Experimental Analysis of Behavior, 36,* 207–220.

Shin, L. M., Rauch, S. L., & Pitman, R. K. (2006). Amygdala, medial prefrontal cortex, and hippocampal function in PTSD. *Annals of the New York Academy of Sciences, 1071,* 67–79.

Shiner, R. L., Masten, A. S., & Roberts, J. M. (2003). Childhood personality foreshadows adult personality and life outcomes two decades later. *Journal of Personality, 71,* 1145–1170.

Shinskey, J. L., & Munakata, Y. (2005). Familiarity breeds searching: Infants reverse their novelty preferences when reaching for hidden objects. *Psychological Science, 16,* 596–600.

Shintani, T., Hughes, C., Beckham, S., & O'Connor, H. (1991). Obesity and cardiovascular risk intervention through the ad libitum feeding of traditional Hawaiian diet. *American Journal of Clinical Nutrition, 53,* 1647S–1651S.

Shiraev, E., & Levy, D. (2010). *Cross-cultural psychology* (4th ed.). Boston: Allyn & Bacon.

Shneidman, E. S. (1987, March). At the point of no return. *Psychology Today,* pp. 54–58.

Shulman, S., Scharf, M., Lumer, D., & Maurer, O. (2001). Parental divorce and young adult children's romantic relationships: Resolution of the divorce experience. *American Journal of Orthopsychiatry, 71,* 473–478.

Siegel, J. M. (2001). The REM sleep-memory consolidation hypothesis. *Science, 294,* 1058–1063.

Siegel, J. M., & Boehmer, L. N. (2006). Narcolepsy and the hypocretin system: Where motion meets emotion. *Nature Clinical Practice Neurology, 2,* 548–556.

Siegel, L. S., & Hodkin, B. (1982). The garden path to the understanding of cognitive development: Has Piaget led us into the poison ivy? In S. Modgil & C. Modgil (Eds.), *Jean Piaget: Consensus and controversy* (pp. 57–82). New York: Praeger.

Siegel, S. (2005). Drug tolerance, drug addiction, and drug anticipation. *Current Directions in Psychological Science, 14,* 296–300.

Siever, L. J., & Koenigsberg, H. W. (2000). The frustrating no-man's-land of borderline personality disorder. *Cerebrum, The Dana Forum on Brain Science, 2*(4).

Signorielli, N., & Bacue, A. (1999). Recognition and respect: A content analysis of prime-time television characters. *Sex Roles, 40,* 527–544.

Silber, B. Y., & Schmitt, J. A. (2010). Effects of tryptophan loading on human cognition, mood, and sleep. *Neuroscience and Biobehavioral Reviews, 34,* 387–407.

Silva, C. E., & Kirsch, I. (1992). Interpretive sets, expectancy, fantasy proneness, and dissociation as predictors of hypnotic response. *Journal of Personality and Social Psychology, 63,* 847–856.

Sim, H. (2000). Relationship of daily hassles and social support to depression and antisocial behavior among early adolescents. *Journal of Youth and Adolescence, 29,* 647–659.

Simon, H. A. (1974). How big is a chunk? *Science, 183,* 482–488.

Simonson, K., & Subich, L. M. (1999). Rape perceptions as a function of gender-role traditionality and victim-perpetrator association. *Sex Roles, 40,* 617–634.

Simpson, G., & Yinger, J. M. (1985). *Racial and cultural minorities.* New York: Plenum Press.

Simpson, J. A., Collins, W. A., Tran, S., & Haydon, K. C. (2007). Attachment and the experience and expression of emotions in romantic relationships: A developmental perspective. *Journal of Personality and Social Psychology, 92,* 355–367.

Sinnott, J. D. (1998). *The development of logic in adulthood: Postformal thought and its applications.* New York: Plenum Press.

Sio, U. N., & Ormerod, T. C. (2009). Does incubation enhance problem solving? A meta-analytic review. *Psychological Bulletin, 135,* 94–120.

Skager, R., Frifth, S. L., & Maddahian, E. (1989). *Biennial survey of drug and alcohol use among California students in Grades 7, 9, and 11: Winter 1987–1988.* Sacramento, CA: Office of the Attorney General, Crime Prevention Center.

Skelton, C. (2006). Boys and girls in the elementary school. In C. Skelton, B. Francis, & L. Smulyan (Eds.), *The SAGE handbook of gender and education* (pp. 139–151). London: SAGE Publications.

Skinner, B. F. (1938). *The behavior of organisms.* New York: Appleton-Century-Crofts.

Skinner, B. F. (1953). *Science and human behavior.* New York: Macmillan.

Skinner, B. F. (1958). Teaching machines. *Science, 128,* 969–977.

Skodol, A. E., & Bender, D. S. (2003). Why are women diagnosed borderline more than men? *Psychiatry Quarterly, 74,* 349–360.

Slameka, N. J. (1966). Differentiation versus unlearning of verbal associations. *Journal of Experimental Psychology, 71,* 822–828.

Slattery, M. L., Curtin, K., Wolff, R. K., Herrick, J. S., Caan, B. J., & Samowitz, W. (2010). Diet, physical activity, and body size associations with rectal tumor mutations and epigenetic changes. *Cancer Causes and Control, 21,* 1237–1245.

Slijper, F. M., Drop, S. L., Molenaar, J. C., & de Muinck Keizer-Schrama, S. M. (1998). Long-term psychological evaluation of intersex children. *Archives of Sexual Behavior, 27,* 125–144.

Sloan, R. P., & Bagiella, E. (2002). Claims about religious involvement and health outcomes. *Annals of Behavioral Medicine, 24,* 14–21.

Small, B. J., Hertzog, C., Hultsch, D. F., & Dixon, R. A. (2003). Stability and change in adult personality over 6 years: Findings from the Victoria Longitudinal Study. *Journal of Gerontology: Psychological Sciences, 58B,* P166–P176.

Smetana, J. G., Campione-Barr, N., & Metzger, A. (2006). Adolescent development in interpersonal and societal contexts. *Annual Review of Psychology, 57,* 255–284.

Smith, A. D. (1996). Memory. In J. E. Birrent & K. W. Schaie (Eds.), *Handbook of the psychology of aging* (4th ed., pp. 236–250). San Diego, CA: Academic Press.

Smith, A. D., & Earles, J. L. K. (1996). Memory changes in normal aging. In F. Blanchard-Fields & T. M. Hess (Eds.), *Perspectives on cognitive change in adulthood and aging* (pp. 192–220). New York: McGraw-Hill.

Smith, A. M., Rosenthal, D. A., & Reichler, H. (1996). High schoolers' masturbatory practices: Their relationship to sexual intercourse and personal characteristics. *Psychological Reports, 79,* 499–509.

Smith, C. (1995). Sleep states and memory processes. *Behavioural Brain Research, 69*(1–2), 137–145.

Smith, C. A., Organ, D. W., & Near, J. P. (1983). Organizational citizenship behavior: Its nature and antecedents. *Journal of Applied Psychology, 68,* 653–663.

Smith, D. C. (1993). The terminally ill patient's right to be in denial. *Omega, 27,* 115–121.

Smith, D. E., & Cogswell, C. (1994). A cross-cultural perspective on adolescent girls' body perception. *Perceptual and Motor Skills, 78,* 744–746.

Smith, J. W., Frawley, P. J., & Polissar, N. L. (1997). Six- and twelve-month abstinence rates in inpatient alcoholics treated with either faradic aversion or chemical aversion compared with matched inpatients from a treatment registry. *Journal of Addictive Diseases, 16,* 5–24.

Smith, M. C., & Dust, M. C. (2006). An exploration of the influence of dispositional traits and appraisal on coping strategies in African American college students. *Journal of Personality, 74,* 145–174.

Smith, M. L., & Glass, G. V. (1977). Meta-analysis of psychotherapy outcome studies. *American Psychologist, 32,* 752–760.

Smith, M. L., Glass, G. V., & Miller, T. I. (1980). *The benefits of psychotherapy.* Baltimore: Johns Hopkins University Press.

Smith, P. C., Kendall, L. M., & Hulin, C. L. (1969). *The measurement of satisfaction in work and retirement.* Chicago, IL: Rand McNally.

Smith, T. W. (2006). Personality as risk and resilience in physical health. *Current Directions in Psychological Science, 15,* 227–231.

Smith, T. W., Glazer, K., Ruiz, J. M., & Gallo, L. C. (2004). Hostility, anger, aggressiveness and coronary heart disease: An interpersonal perspective on personality, emotion, and health. *Journal of Personality, 72,* 1217–1270.

Smock, P. J. (2000). Cohabitation in the United States: An appraisal of research themes, findings, and implications. *Annual Review of Sociology, 26,* 1–20.

Smyth, J., Litcher, L., Hurewitz, A., & Stone, A. (2001). Relaxation training and cortisol secretion in adult asthmatics. *Journal of Health Psychology, 6,* 217–227.

Snarey, J. (1995). In a communitarian voice: The sociological expansion of Kohlbergian theory, research, and practice. In W. M. Kurtines & J. L. Gewirtz (Eds.), *Moral development: An introduction* (pp.109–134). Boston: Allyn & Bacon.

Snyder, C. R., Ilardi, S., Michael, S. T., & Cheavens, J. (2000). Hope theory: Updating a common process for psychological change. In C. R. Snyder & R. E. Ingram (Eds.), *Handbook of psychological change: Psychotherapy processes and practices for the 21st century* (pp. 128–153). New York: Wiley.

Soares, J. C., & Mann, J. J. (1997). The functional neuroanatomy of mood disorders. *Journal of Psychiatric Research, 31,* 393–432.

Sohn, M., & Bosinski, H. A. (2007). Gender identity disorders: Diagnostic and surgical aspects. *Journal of Sexual Medicine, 4,* 1193–1207.

Solberg, E. E., Halvorsen, R., & Holen, A. (2000). Effect of meditation on immune cells. *Stress Medicine, 16,* 185–190.

Soloff, P. H., Lis, J. A., Kelly, T., Cornelius, J., & Ulrich, R. F. (1994). Self-mutilation and suicidal behavior in borderline personality disorder. *Journal of Personality Disorders, 8,* 257–267.

Solomon, A., Arnow, B. A., Gotlib, I. H., & Wind, B. (2003). Individualized measurement of irrational beliefs in remitted depressives. *Journal of Clinical Psychology, 59,* 439–455.

Solomon, R. L. (1980). The opponent process theory of acquired motivation: The costs of pleasure and the benefits of pain. *American Psychologist, 35,* 691–712.

Somers, V. K., Phil, D., Dyken, M. E., Mark, A. L., & Abboud, F. M. (1993). Sympathetic-nerve activity during sleep in normal subjects. *New England Journal of Medicine, 328,* 303–307.

Sonuga-Barke, E. J. S., Dalen, L., & Remington, B. (2003). Do executive deficits and delay aversion make independent contributions to preschool attention-deficit/ hyperactivity disorder symptoms? *Journal of the American Academy of Child and Adolescent Psychiatry, 42,* 1335–1342.

Soper, B., Milford, G. E., & Rosenthal, G. T. (1995). Belief when evidence does not support theory. *Psychology & Marketing, 12,* 415–422.

Soussignan, R. (2002). Duchenne smile, emotional experience, and autonomic reactivity: A test of the facial feedback hypothesis. *Emotion, 2,* 52–74.

Sowell, E. R., Thompson, P. M., Tessner, K. D., & Toga, A. W. (2001). Mapping continued brain growth and gray matter density reduction in dorsal frontal cortex: Inverse relationships during postadolescent brain maturation. *Journal of Neuroscience, 21,* 8819–8829.

Soyka, M., Preuss, U. W., Hesselbrock, V., Zill, P., Koller, G., & Bondy, B. (2008). GABA-A2 receptor subunit gene (GABRA2) polymorphisms and risk for alcohol dependence. *Journal of Psychiatric Research, 42,* 184–191.

Spanos, N. P. (1996). *Multiple identities and false memories: A sociocognitive perspective.* Washington, DC: American Psychological Association.

Spanos, N. P., Burnley, M. C. E., & Cross, P. A. (1993). Response expectancies and interpretations as determinants of hypnotic responding. *Journal of Personality and Social Psychology, 65*(6), 1237–1242.

Spark, R. F. (2000). *Sexual health for men: The complete guide.* Cambridge, MA: Perseus.

Spearman, C. (1904). The proof and measurement of association between two things. *American Journal of Psychology, 15,* 72–101.

Spector, I., & Carey, M. (1990). Incidence and prevalence of the sexual dysfunctions: A "critical" review of the empirical literature. *Archives of Sexual Behavior, 19,* 389–408.

Spencer, J. A., & Fremouw, W. J. (1979). Binge eating as a function of restraint and weight classification. *Journal of Abnormal Psychology, 88,* 262–267.

Spera, C., Wentzel, K. R., & Matto, H. C. (2009). Parental aspirations for their children's educational attainment: Relations to ethnicity, parental education, children's academic performance, and parental perceptions of school climate. *Journal of Youth and Adolescence, 38,* 1140–1152.

Sperling, G. (1960). The information that is available in brief visual presentations. *Psychological Monographs, 74*(Whole No. 498), 1–29.

Spiegel, D. (1997). Trauma, dissociation, and memory. *Annals of the New York Academy of Sciences, 821,* 225–237.

Spiegel, D. A. (1998). Efficacy studies of alprazolam in panic disorder. *Psychopharmacology Bulletin, 43,* 191–195.

Spriggs, M. (2009). Consent in cyberspace: Internet-based research involving young people. *Monash Bioethics Review, 28,* 1–15.

Squire, L. R. (1992). Memory and the hippocampus: A synthesis from findings with rats, monkeys, and humans. *Psychological Review, 99,* 195–232.

Squire, L. R., Knowlton, B., & Musen, G. (1993). The structure and organization of memory. *Annual Review of Psychology, 44,* 453–495.

Squire, L. R., Ojemann, J. G., Miezin, F. M., Petersen, S. E., Videen, T. O., & Raichle, M. E. (1992). Activation of the hippocampus in normal humans: A functional anatomical study of memory. *Proceedings of the National Academy of Science, USA, 89,* 1837–1841.

Srivastava, S., John, O. P., Gosling, S. D., & Potter, J. (2003). Development of personality in early and middle adulthood: Set in plaster or persistent change? *Journal of Personality and Social Psychology, 84,* 1041–1053.

Stacey, D., Clarke, T. K., & Schumann, G. (2009). The genetics of alcoholism. *Current Psychiatry Reports, 11,* 364–369.

Stahl, S. M. (1996). *Essential psychopharmacology.* New York: Cambridge University Press.

Stahl, S. M. (1998). Basic psychopharmacology of antidepressants: Part I. Antidepressants have seven distinct mechanisms of action. *Journal of Clinical Psychiatry, 59*(Suppl. 4), 5–14.

Stahl, S. M. (2001a). Dopamine system stabilizers, aripiprazole, and the next generation of antipsychotics: Part I. "Goldilocks" actions at dopamine receptors. *Journal of Clinical Psychiatry, 62,* 841–842.

Stahl, S. M. (2001b). Dopamine system stabilizers, aripiprazole, and the next generation of antipsychotics: Part II. Illustrating their mechanism of action. *Journal of Clinical Psychiatry, 62,* 923–924.

Stahl, S. M. (2007). Beyond the dopamine hypothesis to the NMDA glutamate receptor hypofunction hypothesis of schizophrenia. *CNS Spectrums, 12,* 265–268.

Stanley, S. M., Whitton, S. W., Sadberry, S. L., Clements, M. L., & Markman, H. J. (2006). Sacrifice as a predictor of marital outcomes. *Family Process, 45,* 289–303.

Stanovich, K. E., & West, R. F. (1998). Individual differences in rational thought. *Journal of Experimental Psychology: General, 127,* 161–188.

Stanton, J. L. (2004). The end of TV advertising: Technologies allow consumers to miss what once were the bedrock of consumer product advertising. *Food Processing, 65,* 26.

Starrels, M. E. (1994). Husbands' involvement in female gender-typed household chores. *Sex Roles, 31,* 473–491.

Statham, D. J., Heath, A. C., Madden, P., Bucholz, K. Bierut, L., Dinwiddie, S. H., et al. (1998). Suicidal behavior: An epidemiological study. *Psychological Medicine, 28,* 839–855.

Steadman, H. J., Mulvey, E. P., Monahan, J., Robbins, P. C., Applebaum, P. S., Grisso, T., et al. (1998). Violence by people discharged from acute psychiatric inpatient facilities and by others in the same neighborhoods. *Archives of General Psychiatry, 55,* 393–401.

Stear, S. (2003). Health and fitness series: 1. The importance of physical activity on health. *Journal of Family Health Care, 13,* 10–13.

Stebbins, G. T., & Murphy, C. M. (2009). Diffusion tensor imaging in Alzheimer's disease and mild cognitive impairment. *Behavioral Neurology, 21,* 39–49.

Steele, C. M. (1997). A threat in the air: How stereotypes shape intellectual identity and performance. *American Psychologist, 52,* 613–629.

Steele, C. M., & Aronson, J. (1995). Stereotype threat and the intellectual test performance of African Americans. *Journal of Personality and Social Psycholoty, 69,* 97–811.

Stefflre, V., Castillo-Vales, V., & Morley, L. (1966). Language and cognition in Yucatan: A cross-cultural replication. *Journal of Personality and Social Psychology, 4,* 112–115.

Stein, D. J., Ruscio, A. M., Lee, S., Petukhova, M., Alonso, J., Andrade, L. H., et al. (2010). Subtyping social anxiety disorder in developed and developing countries. *Depression and Anxiety, 27,* 390–403.

Stein, D. J., Westenberg, H. G. M., Yang, H., Li, D., & Barbato, L. M. (2003). Fluvoxamine CR in the long-term treatment of social anxiety disorder: The 12- to 24-week extension phase of a multicentre, randomized, placebo-controlled trial. *International Journal of Psychopharmacology, 6,* 317–325.

Steinberg, L., & Morris, A. S. (2001). Adolescent development. *Annual Review of Psychology, 52,* 83–110.

Steinberg, L., Lamborn, S. D., Dornbusch, S. M., & Darling, N. (1992). Impact of parenting practices on adolescent achievement: Authoritative parenting, school involvement, and encouragement to succeed. *Child Development, 63,* 1266–1281.

Steiner, M., & Born, L. (2000). Diagnosis and treatment of premenstrual dysphoric disorder: An update. *International Clinical Psychopharmacology, 15*(Suppl. 3) s5–s17.

Steiner, M., Dunn, E., & Born, L. (2003). Hormones and mood: From menarche to menopause and beyond. *Journal of Affective Disorders, 74,* 67–83.

Steinhausen, H. C., & Vollrath, M. (1993). The self-image of adolescent patients with eating disorders. *International Journal of Eating Disorders, 13,* 221–229.

Stephan, K. E., Marshall, J. C., Friston, K. J., Rowe, J. B., Ritzl, A., Zilles, K., et al. (2003). Lateralized cognitive processes and lateralized task control in the human brain. *Science, 301,* 384–386.

Stephens, C. E., Pear, J. J., Wray, L. D., & Jackson, G. C. (1975). Some effects of reinforcement schedules in teaching picture names to retarded children. *Journal of Applied Behavior Analysis, 8,* 435–447.

Stephens, E. A. (2000). H. G. 3/ Camels. In K. E. Kipple & K. C. Ornelas (Series Eds.), *The Cambridge world history of food* (Vol. 1, pp. 467–480). Cambridge, UK: Cambridge University Press.

Stephens, R. S., Roffman, R. A., & Simpson, E. E. (1994). Treating adult marijuana dependence: A test of the relapse prevention model. *Journal of Consulting and Clinical Psychology, 62*(1), 92–99.

Stephens, S. (2008, May 27). Will texting pupils make Shakespeare roll over? *Cleveland Plain Dealer.* Retrieved June 2, 2010, from http://www.jacquieream .com/pdfs/KISS%20in%20the%20News.pdf

Steriade, M., & McCarley, R. W. (1990). *Brainstem control of wakefulness and sleep.* New York: Plenum Press.

Stern, G. S., McCants, T. R., & Pettine, P. W. (1982). Stress and illness: Controllable and uncontrollable life events' relative contributions. *Personality and Social Psychology Bulletin, 8,* 140–143.

Stern, K. N., & McClintock, M. K. (1998). Regulation of ovulation by human pheromones. *Nature, 392,* 177–179.

Stern, S. L., Dhanda, R., & Hazuda, H. P. (2009). Helplessness predicts the development of hypertension in older Mexican and European Americans. *Journal of Psychosomatic Research, 67,* 333–337.

Sternbach, R. A. (1963). Congenital insensitivity to pain: A review. *Psychological Bulletin, 60,* 252–264.

Sternberg, R. J. (1985). *Beyond IQ: A triarchic theory of human intelligence.* New York: Cambridge University Press.

Sternberg, R. J. (1997a). The concept of intelligence and its role in lifelong learning and success. *American Psychologist, 52,* 1030–1037.

Sternberg, R. J. (1997b). *Successful intelligence.* New York: Plume.

Sternberg, R. J., Grigorenko, E. L., & Kidd, K. K. (2005). Intelligence, race, and genetics. *American Psychologist, 60,* 46–59.

Stevens, A., & Coupe, P. (1978). Distortions in judged spatial relations. *Cognitive Psychology, 10,* 422–437.

Stevens, S. B., & Morris, T. L. (2007). College dating and social anxiety: Using the Internet as a means of connecting to others. *Cyberpsychology and Behavior, 10,* 680–688.

Stewart, G. L., & Manz, C. C. (1995). Leadership for self-managing work teams: A typology and integrative model. *Human Relations, 48,* 347–370.

Stewart, R., Ellenburg, G., Hicks, L., Kremen, M., & Daniel, M. (1990). Employee references as a recruitment source. *Applied H.R.M. Research, 1*(1), 1–3.

Stice, E., Telch, C. F., & Rizvi, S. L. (2000). Development and validation of the eating disorder diagnostic scale: A brief self-report measure of anorexia, bulimia, and binge-eating disorder. *Psychological Assessment, 12,* 123–131.

Stickgold, R., & Walker, M. P. (2007). Sleep-dependent memory consolidation and reconsolidation. *Sleep Medicine, 8,* 331–343.

Stiles, W. B., Barkham, M., Mellor-Clark, J., & Connell, J. (2008). Effectiveness of cognitive-behavioural, person-centered, and psychodynamic therapies in UK primary-care routine practice: Replication in a larger sample. *Psychological Medicine, 38,* 677–688.

Stiles, W. B., Barkham, M., Twigg, E., Mellor-Clark, J., & Cooper, M. (2006). Effectiveness of cognitive-behavioural, person-centered, and psychodynamic therapies as practiced in UK National Health Service settings. *Psychological Medicine, 36,* 555–566.

Stine-Morrow, E. A., Parisi, J. M., Morrow, D. G., Greene, J., & Park, D. C. (2007). An engagement model of cognitive optimization through adulthood. *Journals of Gerontology. Series B, Psychological Sciences and Social Sciences, 62,* 62–69.

Stine-Morrow, E. A. L., & Soederberg Miller, L. M. (1999). Basic cognitive processes. In J. C. Cavanaugh & S. K. Whitbourne (Eds.), *Gerontology: An inter-disciplinary perspective* (pp. 186–211). New York: Oxford University Press.

Stock, W. E. (1991). Feminist explanations: Male power, hostility, and sexual coercion. In E. Grauerholz & M. A. Koralewski (Eds.), *Sexual coercion: A sourcebook on its nature, causes, and prevention* (pp. 61–73). Lexington, MA: Lexington Books.

Stoel-Gammon, C., & Otomo, K. (1986). Babbling development of hearing impaired and normal subjects. *Journal of Speech and Hearing Disorders, 51,* 33–41.

Stone, J. M., Morrison, P., & Pilowsky, L. S. (2007). Glutamate and dopamine dysregulation in schizophrenia: A synthesis and selective review. *Journal of Psychopharmacology, 21,* 440–452.

Storms, G., DeBoeck, P., & Ruts, W. (2001). Categorization of novel stimuli in well-known natural concepts. *Psychonomic Bulletin and Review, 8,* 377–384.

Storms, M. D. (1973). Videotape and the attribution process: Reversing actors' and observers' points of view. *Journal of Personality and Social Psychology, 27,* 165–175.

Stout, M. (2005). *The sociopath next door.* New York: Broadway Books.

Stoyva, J. M., & Budzynski, T. H. (1974). Cultivated low arousal—an anti-stress response? In L. V. DiCara (Ed.), *Recent advances in limbic and autonomic nervous systems research* (pp. 369–394). New York: Plenum Press.

Strassberg, D. S., & Lockerd, L. K. (1998). Force in women's sexual fantasies. *Archives of Sexual Behavior, 27,* 403–415.

Strassberg, D. S., Mahoney, J. M., Schaugaard, M., & Hale, V. E. (1990). The role of anxiety in premature ejaculation: A psychophysiological model. *Archives of Sexual Behavior, 19,* 251–257.

Strayer, D. L., Drews, F. A., & Crouch, D. J. (2006). A comparison of the cell phone driver and the drunk driver. *Human Factors, 48,* 381–391.

Strickland, B. R. (1989). Internal-external control expectancies: From contingency to creativity. *American Psychologist, 44,* 1–12.

Stright, A. D., Gallagher, K. C., & Kelley, K. (2008). Infant temperament moderates relations between maternal parenting in early childhood and children's adjustment in first grade. *Child Development, 79,* 186–200.

Stroebe, M. S. (1998). New directions in bereavement research: Exploration of gender differences. *Palliative Medicine, 12,* 5–12.

Stroebe, W., & Stroebe, M. (1987). *Bereavement and health.* New York: Cambridge University Press.

Stroebe, W., & Stroebe, M. (1993). Determinants of adjustment to bereavement in younger widows and widowers. In M. S. Stroebe, W. Stroebe, & R. O. Hansson (Eds.), *Handbook of bereavement* (pp. 208–226). New York: Cambridge University Press.

Stromquist, N. P. (2007). The gender socialization process in schools: A cross-national comparison. *Paper commissioned for the EFA Global Monitoring Report, 2008, Education for all by 2015: Will we make it?* 2008/ED/EFA/MRT/PI/71.

Strong, M., & Prinz, P. (2000). Is American Sign Language related to English literacy? In C. Chamberlain, J. P. Morford, & R. I. Mayberry (Eds.), *Language acquisition by eye* (pp. 131–141). Mahwah, NJ: Erlbaum.

Study reinforces that kids watch a lot of TV. (2009). Retrieved October 27, 2009, from http://news.yahoo.com/s/ap/20091026/ap_en_tv/us_preschool_tv/print

Stunkard, A. (1997). Eating disorders: The last 25 years. *Appetite, 29,* 181–190.

Substance Abuse and Mental Health Services Administration (SAMHSA). (2006). *Results from the 2005 National Survey on Drug Use and Health: National Findings.* Rockville, MD: Office of Applied Studies, NSDUH Series H-30, DHHS Publication No. SMA 06-4194.

Substance Abuse and Mental Health Services Administration (SAMHSA). (2007). *Results from the 2006 National Survey on Drug Use and Health: National findings.* Rockville, MD: Office of Applied Studies, NSDUH Series H-32, DHHS Publication No. SMA 07-4293.

Substance Abuse and Mental Health Services Administration (SAMHSA). (2009a). *Results from the 2008 National Survey on Drug Use and Health: National Findings.* Rockville, MD: Office of Applied Studies, NSDUH Series H-36, DHHS Publication No. SMA 09-4434.

Substance Abuse and Mental Health Services Administration (SAMHSA). (2009b). *The NSDUH report: Suicidal thoughts and behaviors among adults.* Rockville, MD: Office of Applied Studies.

Suh, J. J., Pettinati, H. M., Kampman, K. M., & O'Brien, C. P. (2006). The status of disulfiram: A half of a century later. *Journal of Clinical Psychopharmacology, 26,* 290–302.

Sullivan, J. W., & Horowitz, F. D. (1983). The effects of intonation on infant attention: The role of the rising intonation contour. *Journal of Child Language, 10,* 521–534.

Sullivan, M. A., & O'Leary, S. G. (1990). Maintenance following reward and cost token programs. *Behavior Therapy, 21,* 139–149.

Sullivan, P. F., Neale, M. C., & Kendler, S. K. (2000). Genetic epidemiology of major depression: Review and meta-analysis. *American Journal of Psychiatry, 157,* 1552–1562.

Super, D. E. (1957). *The psychology of careers.* New York: Harper & Row.

Super, D. E. (1976). *Career education and the meanings of work.* Washington, DC: U.S. Offices of Education.

Super, D. E. (1980). A life-span, life-space approach to career development. *Journal of Vocational Behavior, 16,* 282–298.

Super, D. E. (1991). A life-span, life-space approach to career development. In D. Brown, L. Brooks, & Associates (Eds.), *Career choice and development: Applying contemporary theories to practice* (2nd ed., pp. 197–261). San Francisco: Jossey-Bass.

Suzuki, H., Han, S., & & Lucas, L. R. (2010). Chronic passive exposure to aggression decreases D_2 and 5-HT_{1B} receptor densities. *Physiology and Behavior, 99,* 562–570.

Suzuki, K., Simpson, K. A., Minnion, J. S., Shillito, J. C., & Bloom, S. R. (2010). The role of gut hormones and the hypothalamus in appetite regulation. *Endocrine Journal,* doi:10.1507/endocrinj.K10E-077.

Swaby, A. N., & Morgan, K. A. (2009). The relationship between childhood sexual abuse and sexual dysfunction in Jamaican adults. *Journal of Child Sexual Abuse, 18,* 247–266.

Swain, I. U., Zelazo, P. R., & Clifton, R. K. (1993). Newborn infants' memory for speech sounds retained over 24 hours. *Developmental Psychology, 29*(2), 312–323.

Swan, G. E., & Carmelli, D. (2002). Impaired olfaction predicts cognitive decline in nondemented older adults. *Neuroepidemiology, 21,* 58–67.

Swartz, C. (1995). Setting the ECT stimulus. *Psychiatric Times, 12*(6), 33–34.

Swartz, M., Blazer, D., George, L., & Winfield, I. (1990). Estimating the prevalence of borderline personality disorder in the community. *Journal of Personality Disorders, 4,* 257–272.

Swayze, V. W. (1995). Frontal leucotomy and related psychosurgical procedures in the era before antipsychotics (1935–1954): A historical overview. *American Journal of Psychiatry, 152,* 505–515.

Swinson, J., & Harrop, A. (2009). Teacher talk directed to boys and girls and its relationship to their behaviour. *Educational Studies, 35,* 515–524.

Sysoeva, O. V., Kulikova, M. A., Malyuchenko, N. V., Tonevitskii, A. G., & Ivanitskii, A. M. (2010). Genetic and social factors in the development of aggression. *Human Physiology, 36,* 40–46.

Sytsma, M., & Taylor, D. (2001, May 2–6). *A model for addressing low sexual desire in married couples.* Paper presented at the 33rd Annual Conference of the American Association of Sex Educators, Counselors, and Therapists, San Francisco.

Szasz, T. S. (1987). *Insanity: The idea and its consequences.* New York: Wiley.

Szentirmai, E., Yasuda, T., Taishi, P., Wang, M., Churchill, L., Bohnet, S., et al. (2007). Growth hormone-releasing hormone: Cerebral cortical sleep-related EEG actions and expressions. *American Journal of Physiology. Regulatory, Integrative and Comparative Physiology, 293,* R922-R930.

Szkrybalo, J., & Ruble, D. N. (1999). "God made me a girl": Sex-category constancy judgments and explanations revisited. *Developmental Psychology, 35,* 392–402.

Tager-Flusberg, H. (2005). Putting words together: Morphology and syntax in the preschool years. In J. B. Gleason (Ed.), *The development of language* (5th ed., pp. 148–190). Boston: Allyn & Bacon.

Taghavi, M. R., Goodarzi, M. A., Kazemi, H., & Ghorbani, M. (2006). Irrational beliefs in major depression and generalized anxiety disorder in an Iranian sample: A preliminary study. *Perceptual and Motor Skills, 102,* 187–196.

Tajfel, H. (1982). *Social identity and intergroup relations.* Cambridge, UK: Cambridge University Press.

Takano, Y., & Sogon, S. (2008). Are Japanese more collectivistic than Americans? Examining conformity in in-groups and the reference-group effect. *Journal of Cross-Cultural Psychology, 39,* 237–250.

Tal-Or, N., & Papirman, Y. (2007). The fundamental attribution error in attributing fictional figures' characteristics to the actors. *Media Psychology, 9,* 331–345.

Tang, Y. Y., Ma, Y., Fan, Y., Feng, H., Wang, J., Feng, S., et al. (2009). Central and autonomic nervous system interaction is altered by short-term meditation. *Proceedings of the National Academy of Sciences of the United States of America, 106,* 8865–8870.

Tanguy, S., Quarck, G., Etard, O., Gauthier, A., & Denise, P. (2008). Vestibulo-ocular reflex and motion sickness in figure skaters. *European Journal of Applied Physiology, 104,* 1031–1037.

Tankova, I., Adan, A., & Buela-Casal, G. (1994). Circadian typology and individual differences. A review. *Personality and Individual Differences, 16,* 671–684.

Tanner-Smith, E. E. (in press). Negotiating the early developing body: Pubertal timing, body weight, and adolescent girls' substance use. *Journal of Youth and Adolescence.*

Tapert, S. F., Brown, G. G., Kindermann, S. S., Cheung, E. H., Frank, L. R., & Brown, S. A. (2001). fMRI measurement of brain dysfunction in alcohol-dependent young women. *Alcoholism: Clinical and Experimental Research, 25,* 236–245.

Tashkin, D. P. (2005). Smoked marijuana as a cause of lung injury. *Monaldi Archives for Chest Disease, 63,* 92–100.

Tata, D. A., & Anderson, B. J. (2009). The effects of chronic glucocorticoid exposure on dendritic length, synapse numbers and glial volume in animal models: Implications for hippocampal volume reductions in depression. *Physiology and Behavior.* Retrieved December 17, 2009, from http://www.sciencedirect.com

Taylor, C. B., & Luce, K. H. (2003). Computer- and Internet-based psychotherapy interventions. *Current Directions in Psychological Science, 12,* 18–22.

Taylor, D. J., Jenni, O. G., Acebo, C., & Carskadon, M. A. (2005). Sleep tendency during extended wakefulness: Insights into adolescent sleep regulation and behavior. *Journal of Sleep Research, 14,* 239–244.

Taylor, E. J., & Outlaw, F. H. (2002). Use of prayer among persons with cancer. *Holistic Nursing Practices, 16,* 46–60.

Taylor, H. (2002). Poor people and African Americans suffer the most stress from the hassles of daily living. *Harris Poll No. 66.*

Taylor, S. E. (2003). *Health psychology* (5th ed.). New York: McGraw-Hill.

Taylor, S. E. (2006). Tend and befriend: Biobehavioral bases of affiliation under stress. *Current Directions in Psychological Science, 15,* 273–277.

Taylor, S. E., Way, B. M., Welch, W. T., Hilmert, C. J., Lehman, B. J., & Eisenberger, N. I. (2006). Early family environment, current adversity, the serotonin transporter promoter polymorphism, and depressive symptomatology. *Biological Psychiatry, 60,* 671–676.

Teachman, J. D. (2003). Premarital sex, premarital cohabitation and the risk of subsequent marital dissolution among women. *Journal of Marriage and Family, 65,* 444–455.

Teachman, J. D., Tedrow, L. M., & Crowder, K. D. (2000). The changing demography of America's families. *Journal of Marriage and Family, 62,* 1234–1246.

Teasdale, J. D., & Russell, M. L. (1983). Differential effects of induced mood on the recall of positive, negative, and neutral words. *British Journal of Clinical Psychology, 22,* 163–171.

Teasdale, J. D., Scott, J., Moore, R. G., Hayhurst, H., Pope, M., & Paykel, E. S. (2001). How does cognitive therapy prevent relapse in residual depression? Evidence from a controlled trial. *Journal of Consulting and Clinical Psychology, 69,* 347–357.

Teicher, M. H. (2002). Scars that won't heal: The neurobiology of child abuse. *Scientific American, 286,* 68–75.

Teitelbaum, P., & Epstein, A. N. (1962). The lateral hypothalamic syndrome: Recovery of feeding and drinking after lateral hypothalamic lesions. *Psychological Review, 69,* 74–90.

Teitelbaum, P., & Stellar, E. (1954). Recovery from failure to eat produced by hypothalamic lesions. *Science, 120,* 894–895.

Teixeira, P. J., Silva, M. N., Coutinho, S. R., Palmeira, A. L., Mata, J., Vieira, P. N., et al. (2010) Mediators of weight loss and weight loss maintenance in middle-aged women. *Obesity, 18,* 725–735.

Temoshok, L. (1992). *The Type C connection: The behavioral links to cancer and your health.* New York: Random House.

Tenenbaum, H. R., & Leaper, C. (2003). Parent-child conversations about science: The socialization of gender inequities? *Developmental Psychology, 39,* 34–47.

Teng, C. I. (2008). Personality differences between online game players and nonplayers in a student sample. *Cyberpsychology and Behavior, 11,* 232–234.

Terman, L. M. (1916). *The measurement of intelligence.* Boston: Houghton Mifflin.

Terr, L. C. (1983). Chowchilla revisited: The effects of psychic trauma four years after a school-bus kidnapping. *American Journal of Psychiatry, 140,* 1543–1550.

Terracciano, A., Costa, P. T., & McCrae, R. R. (2006). Personality plasticity after age 30. *Personality and Social Psychology Bulletin, 32,* 999–1009.

Teyber, E., & McClure, F. (2000). Therapist variables. In C. R. Snyder & R. E. Ingram (Eds.), *Handbook of psychological change: Psychotherapy processes and practices for the 21st century* (pp. 62–87). New York: Wiley.

Thase, M. E. (2003). Effectiveness of antidepressants: Comparative remission rates. *Journal of Clinical Psychiatry, 64*(Suppl. 2), 3–7.

Thase, M. E., Jindal, R., & Howland, R. H. (2002). Biological aspects of depression. In H. Gotlib & C. L. Hammen (Eds.), *Handbook of depression* (pp. 192–218). New York: Guilford Press.

Thelen, E. (1995). Motor development: A new synthesis. *American Psychologist, 50,* 79–95.

Thies-Flechtner, K., Muller-Oerlinghausen, B., Seibert, W., Walther, A., & Greil, W. (1996). Effect of prophylactic treatment on suicide risk in patients with major affective disorders: Data from a randomized prospective trial. *Pharmacopsychiatry, 29,* 103–107.

Thomas, A., & Chess, S. (1977). *Temperament and development.* New York: Brunner/Mazel.

Thomas, A., & Chess, S. (1986). The New York longitudinal study: From infancy to early adult life. In R. Plomin & J. Dunn (Eds.), *The study of temperament: Changes, continuities, and challenges* (pp. 39–52). Hillsdale, NJ: Erlbaum.

Thomas, J., Kahn, S., & Abdulrahman, A. A. (2010). Eating attitudes and body image concerns among female university students in the United Arab Emirates. *Appetite, 54,* 595–598.

Thompson, L. A., Dawson, K., Ferdig, T. R., Black, E. W., Boyer, J., Coutts, J., et al. (2008). The intersection of online social networking with medical professionalism. *Journal of General Internal Medicine, 23,* 954–957.

Thompson, P. M., Giedd, J. N., Woods, R. P., MacDonald, D., Evans, A. C., & Togo, A. W. (2000, March 9). Growth patterns in the developing human brain detected by using continuum-mechanical tensor maps. *Nature, 404,* 190–193.

Thompson, V. L. (1996). Perceived experiences of racism as stressful life events. *Community Mental Health Journal, 32,* 223–233.

Thomson, E., & Colella, U. (1992). Cohabitation and marital stability: Quality or commitment. *Journal of Marriage and the Family, 54,* 259–267.

Thorndike, E. L. (1898). Animal intelligence: An experimental study of associative process in animals. *Psychological Review Monograph,* No. 8.

Thorndike, E. L. (1905). *The elements of psychology.* New York: Seiler.

Thorpe, G. L., & Olson, S. L. (1997). *Behavior therapy: Concepts, procedures, and applications* (2nd ed.). Boston: Allyn & Bacon.

Thorpy, M. (2007). Therapeutic advances in narcolepsy. *Sleep Medicine, 8,* 427–440.

Thurber, C. A. (1995). The experience and expression of homesickness in preadolescent and adolescent boys. *Child Development, 66,* 1162–1178.

Thurstone, L. L. (1931). The measurement of social attitudes. *Journal of Abnormal and Social Psychology, 26,* 249–269.

Thurstone, L. L. (1938). *Primary mental abilities.* Chicago: University of Chicago Press.

Tidwell, L. C., & Walther, J. B. (2002). Computer-mediated communication effects on disclosure, impressions, and interpersonal evaluations. *Human Communication Research, 28,* 317–348.

Tiedemann, J. (2002). Teachers' gender stereotypes as determinants of teacher perceptions in elementary school mathematics. *Educational Studies in Mathematics, 50,* 49–62.

Tienari, P., Wynne, L. C., Laksy, K., Moring, J., Nieminen, P., Sorri, A., et al. (2003). Genetic boundaries of the schizophrenia spectrum: Evidence from the Finnish Adoptive Family Study of Schizophrenia. *American Journal of Psychiatry, 160,* 1567–1594.

Tiggeman, M., Hargreaves, D., Polivy, J., & McFarlane, T. (2004). A word-stem completion task to assess implicit processing of appearance-related information. *Journal of Psychosomatic Research, 57,* 73–78.

Timonen, V., & O'Dwyer, C. (2009). Living in institutional care: Residents' experiences and coping strategies. *Social Work in Health Care, 48,* 597–613.

Tirindelli, R., Dibattista, M., Pifferi, S., & Menini, A. (2009). From pheromones to behavior. *Physiological Reviews, 89,* 921–956.

Tjaden, P., & Thoennes, N. (2006). *Extent, nature, and consequences of rape victimization: Findings from the National Violence Against Women Survey. Special Report.* Washington, DC: National Institute of Justice and the Centers for Disease Control and Prevention.

Tohidian, I. (2009). Examining linguistic relativity hypothesis as one of the main views on the relationship between language and thought. *Journal of Psycholinguist Research, 38,* 65–74.

Toledo, M. (2009, January 30). First comes marriage, then comes love. *ABC News/20/20.* Retrieved March 13, 2010, from http://abcnews.go.com/2020/story?id=6762309

Tolin, D. F., & Foa, E. B. (2006). Sex differences in trauma and posttraumatic stress disorder: A quantitative review of 25 years of research. *Psychological Bulletin, 132,* 959–992.

Tolman, E. C., & Honzik, C. H. (1930). "Insight" in rats. *University of California Publications in Psychology, 4,* 215–232.

Tomasello, M. (2000). Culture and cognitive development. *Current Directions in Psychological Science, 9,* 37–40.

Tomasello, M., Call, J., Nagell, K., Olguin, R., & Carpenter, M. (1994). The learning and use of gestural signals by young chimpanzees: A trans-generational study. *Primates, 35,* 137–154.

Tondo, L., & Baldessarini, R. J. (2009). Long-term lithium treatment in the prevention of suicidal behavior in bipolar disorder patients. *Epidemiologia e Psichiatria Sociale, 18,* 179–183.

Tormala, Z. L., Briñol, P., & Petty, R. E. (2007). Multiple roles for sources credibility under high elaboration: It's all in the timing. *Social Cognition, 25,* 536–552.

Torrey, E. F., Buka, S., Cannon, T. D., Goldstein, J. M., Seidman, L. J., Liu, T., et al. (2009). Paternal age as a risk factor for schizophrenia: How important is it? *Schizophrenia Research, 114,* 1–5.

Trafimow, D., Armendariz, M. L., & Madsen, L. (2004). A test of whether attributions provide for self-enhancement or self-defense. *Journal of Social Psychology, 144,* 453–463.

Treas, J., & Lawton, L. (1999). Family relations in adulthood. In M. B. Sussman, S. K. Steinmetz, & G. W. Peterson (Eds.), *Handbook of marriage and the family* (pp. 425–438). New York: Plenum Press.

Triandis, H. C. (1994). *Culture and Social Behavior.* New York: McGraw-Hill.

Triesman, A. M. (1964). Verbal cues, language, and meaning in selective attention. *American Journal of Psychology, 77,* 206–219.

Triller, A., Boulden, E. A., Churchill, A., Hatt, H., Englund, J., Spehr, M., et al. (2008). Odorant-receptor interactions and odor percept: A chemical perspective. *Chemistry and Biodiversity, 5,* 862–886.

Trimble, J. E., & Thurman, P. J. (2002). Ethnocultural considerations and strategies for providing counseling services to Native American Indians. In P. B. Pedersen, J. G. Draguns, W. J. Lonner, & J. E. Trimble (Eds.), *Counseling across cultures* (5th ed., pp. 53–92). Thousand Oaks, CA: Sage.

Triplett, N. (1898). The dynamogenic factors in pacemaking and competition. *American Journal of Psychology, 9,* 507–533.

Troisi, J. R., II. (2003). Spontaneous recovery during, but not following, extinction of the discriminative stimulus effects of nicotine in rats: Reinstatement of stimulus control. *Psychological Record, 53,* 579–592.

Tsao, J. C. I., & Zeltzer, L. K. (2005). Complementary and alternative medicine approaches for pediatric pain: A review of the state-of-the-science. *Evidence-Based Complementary and Alternative Medicine, 2,* 149–159.

Tsai, F., & Coyle, W. J. (2009). The microbiome and obesity: Is obesity linked to our gut flora? *Current Gastroenterology Reports, 11,* 307–313.

Tsai, G., Gastfriend, D. R., & Coyle, J. T. (1995). The glutamatergic basis of human alcoholism. *American Journal of Psychiatry, 152,* 332–340.

Tsapelas, I., Aron, A., & Orbuch, T. (2009). Marital boredom now predicts less satisfaction 9 years later. *Psychological Science, 20,* 543–545.

Tsuang, M. T., Fleming, J. A., & Simpson, J. C. (1999). Suicide and schizophrenia. In D. G. Jacobs (Ed.), *The Harvard Medical School guide to suicide assessment and intervention* (pp. 287–299). San Francisco: Jossey-Bass.

Tucker, M. A., & Fishbein, W. (2009). The impact of sleep duration and subject intelligence on declarative and motor memory performance: How much is enough? *Journal of Sleep Research, 18,* 304–312.

Tugrul, C., & Kabakci, E. (1997). Vaginismus and its correlates. *Sexual and Marital Therapy, 12,* 23–34.

Tulving, E. (1972). Episodic and semantic memory. In E. Tulving & W. Donaldson (Eds.), *Organisation of memory* (pp. 381–403). London: Academic Press.

Tulving, E. (1974). Cue-dependent forgetting. *American Scientist, 62,* 74–82.

Tulving, E. (1983). *Elements of episodic memory.* Oxford, UK: Oxford University Press.

Turati, C. (2004). Why faces are not special to newborns: An alternative account of the face preference. *Current Directions in Psychological Science, 13,* 5–8.

Turati, C., & Simion, F. (2002). Newborns' recognition of changing and unchanging aspects of schematic faces. *Journal of Experimental Child Psychology, 83,* 239–261.

Turk, C. L., Heimberg, R. G., & Hope, D. A. (2001). Social anxiety disorder. *Clinical handbook of psychological disorders: A step-by-step treatment manual* (3rd ed., pp. 114–153). New York: Guilford Press.

Turner, A. J., & Ortony, A. (1992). Basic emotions: Can conflicting criteria converge? *Psychological Review, 99,* 566–571.

Turner, P. J., & Gervai, J. (1995). A multidimensional study of gender typing in preschool children and their parents: Personality, attitudes, preferences, behavior, and cultural differences. *Developmental Psychology, 31,* 759–772.

Tversky, A., & Kahneman, D. (1974). Judgment under uncertainty: Heuristics and biases, *Science, 185,* 1124–1131.

Tversky, A., & Kahneman, D. (1980). Causal schemas in judgments under uncertainty. In M. Fishbein (Ed.), *Progress in social psychology* (pp. 49–72). Hillsdale, NJ: Erlbaum.

Tversky, B. (1981). Distortions in memory for maps. *Cognitive Psychology, 13,* 407–433.

Twitchell, G. R., Hanna, G. L., Cook, E. H., Fitzgerald, H. E., Little, K. Y., & Zucker, R. (1998). Overt be-havior problems and serotonergic function in middle childhood among male and female offspring of alcoholic fathers. *Alcoholism, Clinical and Experimental Research, 22,* 1340–1348.

Twyman, K., Saylor, C., Taylor, L. A., & Comeaux, C. (2010). Comparing children and adolescents engaged in cyberbullying to matched peers. *Cyberpsychology, Behavior, and Social Networking, 13,* 195–199.

Tylka, T. L. (2006). Development and psychometric evaluation of a measure of intuitive eating. *Journal of Counseling Psychology, 53,* 226–240.

UNICEF (United Nations Children's Fund). (2009). *State of the world's children.* New York: Author.

U.S. Census Bureau. (2006b). Nation's population one-third minority. U.S. Census Bureau News. Retrieved March 24, 2008, from http://www.census.gov/Press-Release/www/releases/archives/population/006808.html

U.S. Census Bureau. (2007). *Current population survey.* Washington, DC: U.S. Department of Commerce.

U.S. Census Bureau. (2008). *Current Population Survey, 2008 Annual Social & Economic Supplement. Current population survey, 2008 annual social and economic supplement.* Washington, D.C.: U.S. Department of Commerce.

U.S. Census Bureau. (2009). *2006–2008 American Community Survey.* Washington, DC: U.S. Department of Commerce.

U.S. Census Bureau. (2010). *Current Population Survey, 2009. Annual Social and Economic Supplement.* Washington, DC: U.S. Department of Commerce.

U.S. Department of Commerce. (2009). *Current Population Survey, 1996 through 2009.* Washington, DC: Author.

U.S. Department of Education. (2005). *1999 and 2004 National study of postsecondary faculty.* Washington, DC: National Center for Education Statistics.

U.S. Department of Education. (2009). *Condition of Education 2009, Indicator 24* (NCES 2009–081). Washington, DC: National Center for Education Statistics.

U.S. Department of Energy. (2007). *The human genome project information.* Available online at http://www.ornl.gov/ hgmis

U.S. Department of Justice. (2005). *Summary findings: Victim characteristics.* Bureau of Justice Statistics. Retrieved May 3, 2007.

Uchino, B. N. (2009). Understanding the links between social support and physical health: A life-span perspective with emphasis on the separability of perceived and received support. *Perspectives on Psychological Science, 4,* 236–255.

Uchino, B. N., Cacioppo, J. T., & Kiecolt-Glaser, J. K. (1996). The relationship between social support and physiological processes: A review with emphasis on underlying mechanisms and implications for health. *Psychological Bulletin, 119,* 488–531.

Ulibarri, M. D., Ulloa, E. C., & Camacho, L. (2009). Prevalence of sexually abusive experiences in childhood and adolescence among a community sample of Latinas: A descriptive study. *Journal of Child Sexual Abuse, 18,* 405–421.

Ullman, S. E., & Filipas, H. H. (2005a). Ethnicity and child sexual abuse experiences of female college students. *Journal of Child Sexual Abuse, 14,* 67–89.

Ullman, S. E., & Filipas, H. H. (2005b). Gender differences in social reactions to abuse disclosures, post-abuse coping, and PTSD of child sexual abuse survivors. *Child Abuse and Neglect, 29,* 767–782.

Ullman, S. E., Najdowski, C. J., & Filipas, H. H. (2009). Child sexual abuse, post-traumatic stress disorder, and substance use: Predictors of revictimization in adult sexual assault survivors. *Journal of Child Sexual Abuse, 18,* 367–385.

Ultan, R. (1969). Some general characteristics of interrogative systems. *Working Papers in Language Universals (Stanford University), 1,* 41–63.

Umberson, D., Williams, K., Powers, D. A., Meichu, D. C., & Campbell, A. M. (2005). As good as it gets? A lifecourse perspective on marital quality. *Social Forces, 84,* 493–511.

University of Michigan. (2008, April 8). Exactly how much housework does a husband create? *ScienceDaily.* Retrieved March 12, 2010, from http://www.sciencedaily.com/releases/2008/04/080403191009.htm

Ursu, S., Stenger, A., Shear, M. K., Jones, M. R., & Carter, C. S. (2003). Overactive action-monitoring in obsessive-compulsive disorder: Evidence from functional magnetic resonance imaging. *Psychological Science, 14,* 347–353.

Vainionpaa, L. K., Rattya, J., Knip, M., Tapanainen, J. S., Pakarinen, A. J., Lanning, P., et al. (1999). Valproate-induced hyperandrogenism during pubertal maturation in girls with epilepsy. *Annals of Neurology, 45,* 444–450.

Valensi, P., Doaré, L., Perret, G., Germack, R., Pariès, J., & Mesangeau, D. (2003). Cardiovascular vagosympathetic activity in rats with ventromedial hypothalamic obesity. *Obesity Research, 11,* 54–64.

Valente, S. M. (2005). Sexual abuse of boys. *Journal of Child and Adolescent Psychiatric Nursing, 18,* 10–16.

Valenza, E., Simion, F., Cassia, V. M., & Umilta, C. (1996). Face preference at birth. *Journal of Experimental Psychology, 33,* 711–723.

Valenzuela, M., & Sachdev, P. (2009). Can cognitive exercise prevent the onset of dementia? Systematic review of randomized clinical trials with longitudinal follow-up. *American Journal of Geriatric Psychiatry, 17,* 179–187.

Valkenburg, P. M., & Peter, J. (2007). Preadolescents and adolescents' online communication and their closeness to friends. *Developmental Psychology, 43,* 267–277.

Valkenburg, P. M., & Peter, J. (2009a). The effects of instant messaging on the quality of adolescents' existing friendships: A longitudinal study. *Journal of Communication, 59,* 79–97.

Valkenburg, P. M., & Peter, J. (2009b). Social consequences of the Internet for adolescents. *Current Directions in Psychological Science, 18,* 1–5.

Valkenburg, P. M., Peter, J., & Schouten, A. P. (2006). Friend networking sites and their relationship to adolescents' well-being and social self-esteem. *Cyberpsychology and Behavior, 9,* 584–590.

Valli, K., & Revonsuo, A. (2009). The threat simulation theory in light of recent empirical evidence: A review. *American Journal of Psychology, 122,* 17–38.

Valli, K., Revonsuo, A., Palkas, O., Ismail, K. H., Ali, K. J., & Punamaki, R. L. (2005). The threat simulation theory of the evolutionary function of dreaming: Evidence from dreams of traumatized children. *Consciousness and Cognition, 14,* 188–218.

van Apeldoorn, F. J., Timmerman, M. E., Mersch, P. P., van Hout, W. J., Visser, S., van Dyck, R., et al. (2010). A randomized trial of cognitive-behavioral therapy or selective serotonin reuptake inhibitor or both combined for panic disorder with or without agoraphobia: Treatment results through 1-year follow-up. *Journal of Clinical Psychiatry, 71,* 574–586.

Van de Castle, R. L. (1994). *Our dreaming mind.* New York: Ballantine.

Van den Bulck, J. (2003). Text messaging as a cause of sleep interruption in adolescents: Evidence from a cross-sectional study. *Journal of Sleep Research, 12,* 263.

Van den Bulck, J. (2007). Adolescent use of mobile phones for calling and for sending text messages after lights out: Results from a prospective cohort study with a one-year follow-up. *Sleep, 30,* 1220–1223.

Vandello, J. A., & Cohen, D. (1999). Patterns of individualism and collectivism across the United States. *Journal of Personality and Social Psychology, 77,* 279–292.

van der Kolk, B. A., Spinazzola, J., Blaustein, M. E., Hopper, J. W., Hopper, E. K., Korn, D. L., et al. (2007). A randomized clinical trial of eye movement desensitization and reprocessing (EMDR), fluoxetine, and pill placebo in the treatment of posttraumatic stress disorder: Treatment effects and long-term maintenance. *Journal of Clinical Psychiatry, 68,* 37–46.

VandeVusse, L., Irland, J., Healthcare, W. F., Berner, M. A., Fuller, S., & Adams, D. (2007). Hypnosis for childbirth: A retrospective comparative analysis of outcomes in one obstetrician's practice. *American Journal of Clinical Hypnosis, 50,* 109–119.

Van Goozen, S. H., Wiegant, V. M., Endert, E., Helmond, F. A., & Van de Poll, N. E. (1997). Psychoendocrinological assessment of the menstrual cycle: The relationship between hormones, sexuality, and mood. *Archives of Sexual Behavior, 26,* 359–382.

van Goozen, S. H. M., Fairchild, G., & Harold, G. T. (2008). The role of neurobiological deficits in childhood antisocial behavior. *Current Directions in Psychological Science, 17,* 224–228.

Van Heteren, C. F., Boekkooi, P. F., Jongsma, H. W., & Nijhuis, J. G. (2000). Fetal learning and memory. *Lancet, 356,* 9236–9237.

van Honk, J., & Schutter, D. J. L. G. (2007). Testosterone reduces conscious detection of signals serving social correction: Implications for antisocial behavior. *Psychological Science, 18,* 663–667.

van Hooren, S. A., Valentijn, A. M., Bosma, H., Ponds, R. W., van Boxtel, M. P., & Jolles, J. (2007). Cognitive functioning in healthy older adults aged 64–81: A cohort study into the effects of age, sex, and education. *Neuropsychology, Development, and Cognition, Section B: Aging, Neuropsychology, and Cognition, 14,* 40–54.

van Ijzendoorn, M. H., & Kroonenberg, P. (1988). Cross-cultural patterns of attachment: A meta-analysis of the Strange Situation. *Child Development, 59,* 147–156.

van Laar, M., Volkerts, E., & Verbaten, M. (2001). Subcronic effects of the GABA-agonist lorazepam and the 5-HT2A/2C antagonist ritanserin on driving performance, slow wave sleep and daytime sleepiness in healthy volunteers. *Psychopharmacology, 154,* 189–197.

van Solinge, H., & Henkens, K. (2005). Couples' adjustment to retirement: A multi-actor panel study. *Journals of Gerontology, Series B: Psychological Sciences and Social Sciences, 60,* S11–S20.

Vance, E. B., & Wagner, N. N. (1976). Written descriptions of orgasms: A study of sex differences. *Archives of Sexual Behavior, 5,* 87–98.

Vandeusen, K., & Carr, J. (2003). Recovery from sexual assault: An innovative two-stage group therapy model. *International Journal of Group Psychotherapy, 53,* 201–223.

Vandrey, R. G., Budney, A. J., Hughes, J. R., & Liguori, A. (2008). A within-subject comparison of withdrawal symptoms during abstinence from cannabis, tobacco, and both substances. *Drug and Alcohol Dependence, 92,* 48–54.

vanReekum, C., Johnstone, T., Etter, A., Wehrle, T., & Scherer, K. (2004). Psychophysiological response to appraisal dimensions in a computer game. *Cognition and Emotion, 18,* 663–688.

Varley, C. K., & Smith, C. J. (2003). Anxiety disorders in the child and teen. *Pediatric Clinics of North America, 50,* 1107–1138.

Vartanian, L. R. (2000). Revisiting the imaginary audience and personal fable constructs of adolescent egocentrism: A conceptual review. *Adolescence, 35,* 639–661.

Vartanian, L. R. (2001). Adolescents' reactions to hypothetical peer group conversations: Evidence for an imaginary audience? *Adolescence, 36,* 347–380.

Vassallo, S., Cooper, S. L., & Douglas, J. M. (2009). Visual scanning in the recognition of facial affect: Is there an observer sex difference? *Journal of Vision, 9,* 1–10.

Vaughn, B. E., Stevenson-Hinde, J., Waters, E., Kotsaftis, A., Lefever, G., Shouldice, A., et al. (1992). Attachment security and temperament in infancy and early childhood: Some conceptual clarifications. *Developmental Psychology, 28,* 463–473.

Vega, W. A., Karno, M., Alegria, M., Alvidrez, J., Bernal, G., Escamilla, M., et al. (2007). Research issues for improving treatment of U.S. Hispanics with persistent mental disorders. *Psychiatric Services, 58,* 385–394.

Venkatesh, K., Biswas, J., & Kumarasamy, N. (2008). Impact of highly active antiretroviral therapy on ophthalmic manifestations in human immune deficiency syndrome. *Indian Journal of Ophthalmology, 56,* 391–393.

Ventura, J., Nuechterlein, K. H., Subotnik, K. L., Hardesty, J. P., & Mintz, J. (2000). Life events can trigger depressive exacerbation in the early course of schizophrenia. *Journal of Abnormal Psychology, 109,* 139–144.

Vergne, D. E., & Nemeroff, C. B. (2006). The interaction of serotonin transporter gene polymorphisms and early adverse life events on vulnerability for major depression. *Current Psychiatry Reports, 8,* 452–457.

Verhaeghen, P., Marcoen, A., & Goosens, L. (1993). Facts and fiction about memory aging: A quantitative integration of research findings. *Journal of Gerontology: Psychological Sciences, 48,* P157–P171.

Vetterlein, T., Mandl, H., & Adlassnig, K. P. (2010). Fuzzy Arden Syntax: A fuzzy programming language for medicine. *Artificial Intelligence in Medicine,* doi:10.1016/j.artmed.2010.01.003.

Vieta, E., & Goikolea, J. M. (2005). Atypical antipsychotics: Newer options for mania and maintenance therapy. *Bipolar Disorders, 7*(Suppl. 4), 21–33.

Vigezzi, P., Guglielmino, L., Marzorati, P., Silenzio, R., De Chiara, M., Corrado, F., et al. (2006). Multimodal drug addiction treatment: A field comparison of methadone and buprenorphine among heroin- and cocaine-dependent patients. *Journal of Substance Abuse and Treatment, 31,* 3–7.

Villaneuva, A. T., Buchanan, P. R., Yee, B. J., & Grunstein, R. R. (2005). Ethnicity and obstructive sleep apnea. *Sleep Medical Review, 9,* 419–436.

Virgile, R. S. (1984). Locked-in syndrome: Case and literature review. *Clinical Neurology and Neurosurgery, 86,* 275–279.

Vitaliano, P. P., Scanlon, J. M., Ochs, H. D., Syrjala, K., Siegler, I. C., & Snyder, E. A. (1998). Psychosocial stress moderates the relationship of cancer history with natural killer cell activity. *Annals of Behavioral Medicine, 20,* 199–208.

Vitaliano, P. P., Young, H. M., & Zhang, J. (2004). Is caregiving a risk factor for illness? *Current Directions in Psychological Science, 13,* 13–16.

Voderholzer, U., Al-Shajlawi, A., Weske, G., Feige, B., & Riemann, D. (2003). Are there gender differences in objective and subjective sleep measures? A study of insomniacs and healthy controls. *Depression and Anxiety, 17,* 162–172.

Volkmann, C., & Volkmann, T. (2006). *From binge to blackout: A mother and son struggle with teen drinking.* New York: New American Library.

Volkow, N. D., Gillespie, H., Mullani, N., & Tancredi, L. (1996). Brain glucose metabolism in chronic marijuana users at baseline and during marijuana intoxication. *Psychiatry Research: Neuroimaging, 67*(1), 29–38.

Volkow, N. D., Wang, G. J., Fowler, J. S., Leonido-Yee, M., Franceschi, D., Sedler, M. J., et al. (2001). Association of dopamine transporter reduction with psychomotor impairment in methamphetamine abusers. *American Journal of Psychiatry, 158,* 377–382.

Volterra, A., & Steinhauser, C. (2004). Glial modulation of synaptic transmission in the hippocampus. *Glia, 47,* 249–257.

Voorspoels, W., Vanpaemel, W., & Storms, G. (2008). Exemplars and prototypes in natural language concepts: A typicality-based evaluation. *Psychonomic Bulletin and Review, 15,* 630–637.

Voyer, D., Voyer, S., & Bryden, M. P. (1995). Magnitude of sex differences in spatial abilities: A meta-analysis and consideration of critical variables. *Psychological Bulletin, 117,* 250–270.

Vygotsky, L. S. (1978). *Mind in society: The development of higher mental process.* Cambridge, MA: Harvard University Press.

Vygotsky, L. S. (1986). *Thought and language.* Cambridge, MA: MIT Press.

Vygotsky, L. S. (1987). Thinking and speech. In R. W. Reiber & A. S. Carton (Eds.), *The collected works of L. S. Vygotsky: Vol. 1. Problems of general psychology* (pp. 37–285). New York: Plenum Press. (Original work published 1934)

Vytal, K., & Hamann, S. (2009). Neuroimaging support for discrete neural correlates of basic emotions: A voxel-based meta-analysis. *Journal of Cognitive Neuroscience,* doi:10.1162/jocn.2009.21366.

Wack, E., & Tantleff-Dunn, S. (2009). Relationships between electronic game play, obesity, and psychosocial functioning in young men. *Cyberpsychology and Behavior, 12,* 241–244.

Wade, T. D. (2007). Epidemiology of eating disorders: Creating opportunities to move the current classification paradigm forward. *International Journal of Eating Disorders, 40,* s27–s30.

Wagner, B., Knaevelsrud, C., & Maercker, A. (2006). Internet-based cognitive-behavioral therapy for complicated grief: A randomized controlled trial. *Death Studies, 30,* 429–453.

Wagner, G. C., Beuving, L. J., & Hutchinson, R. R. (1980). The effects of gonadal hormone manipulations on aggressive target-biting in mice. *Aggressive Behavior, 6,* 1–7.

Waite, L. J., Laumann, E. O., Das, A., & Schumm, L. P. (2009). Sexuality: Measures of partnerships, practices, attitudes, and problems in the National Social Life, Health, and Aging Study. *Journals of Gerontology, Series B, Psychological Sciences and Social Sciences, 64,* i56-i66.

Wakefield, J. C. (1992). The concept of mental disorder: On the boundary between biological facts and social values. *American Psychologist, 47,* 373–388.

Wald, G. (1964). The receptors of human color vision. *Science, 145,* 1007–1017.

Wald, J., & Taylor, S. (2003). Preliminary research on the efficacy of virtual reality exposure therapy to treat driving phobia. *Cyberpsychology and Behavior, 6,* 459–465.

Waldron-Hennessey, R., & Sabatelli, R. M. (1997). The parental comparison level index: A measure for assessing parental rewards and costs relative to expectations. *Journal of Marriage and the Family, 59,* 824–833.

Walker, B. R., Diefenbach, K. S., & Parikh, T. N. (2007). Inhibition within the nucleus tractus solitarius (NTS) ameliorates environmental exploration deficits due to cerebellum lesions in an animal model for autism. *Behavioural Brain Research, 176,* 109–120.

Walker, E., & Tessner, K. (2008). Schizophrenia. *Perspectives on Psychological Science, 3,* 30–37.

Walker, L. J. (1989). A longitudinal study of moral reasoning. *Child Development, 60,* 157–166.

Walker, L. J. (1995). Sexism in Kohlberg's moral psychology? In W. M. Kurtines & J. L. Gewirtz (Eds.), *Moral development: An introduction* (pp. 83–107). Boston: Allyn & Bacon.

Walker, L. J., & Taylor, J. H. (1991). Stage transitions in moral reasoning: A longitudinal study of developmental processes. *Developmental Psychology, 27,* 330–337.

Walker, M. P. (2009). The role of sleep in cognition and emotion. *Annals of the New York Academy of Sciences, 1156,* 168–197.

Walker, M. P., & Stickgold, R. (2004). Sleep-dependent learning and memory consolidation. *Neuron, 44,* 121–133.

Walker, M. P., & van der Helm, E. (2009). Overnight therapy? The role of sleep in emotional brain processing. *Psychological Bulletin, 135,* 731–748.

Wallace, J., Schneider, T., & McGuffin, P. (2002). Genetics of depression. In I. H. Gotlib & C. L. Hammen (Eds.), *Handbook of depression* (pp. 169–191). New York: Guilford Press.

Wallentin, M. (2009). Putative sex differences in verbal abilities and language cortex: A critical review. *Brain and Language, 108,* 175–183.

Wallis, C. (2005, January 9). The new science of happiness. *Time.*

Walster, E., Aronson, E., Abrahams, D., & Rottman, L. (1966). Importance of physical attractiveness in dating behavior. *Journal of Personality and Social Psychology, 4,* 508–516.

Walters, S. T., Foy, B. D., & Castro, R. J. (2003). The agony of Ecstasy: Responding to growing MDMA use among college students. *Journal of American College Health, 51,* 139–141.

Wampold, B. E., Minami, T., Baskin, T. W., & Callen Tierney, S. (2002). A meta-(re)analysis of the effects of cognitive therapy versus other therapies for depression. *Journal of Affective Disorders, 68,* 159–165.

Wampold, B. E., Mondin, G. W., Moody, M., Stich, F., Benson, K., & Ahn, H. (1997). A meta-analysis of outcome studies comparing bona fide psychotherapies: Empirically, "All must have prizes." *Psychological Bulletin, 122,* 203–215.

Wang, S. H., Baillargeon, R., & Brueckner, L. (2004). Young infants' reasoning about hidden objects: Evidence from violation-of-expectation tasks with test trials only. *Cognition, 93,* 167–198.

Wang, Z., Nudelman, A., & Storm, D. R. (2007). Are pheromones detected through the main olfactory epithelium? *Molecular Neurobiology, 35,* 317–323.

Wanner, H. E. (1968). *On remembering, forgetting, and understanding sentences. A study of the deep structure hypothesis.* Unpublished doctoral dissertation, Harvard University.

Warburton, D. M. (1995). Effects of caffeine on cognition and mood without caffeine abstinence. *Psychopharmacology, 119,* 66–70.

Ward, C. (1994). Culture and altered states of consciousness. In W. J. Lonner & R. S. Malpass (Eds.), *Psychology and culture* (pp. 59–64). Boston: Allyn & Bacon.

Ward, J. (2003). State of the art synaesthesia. *Psychologist, 16,* 196–199.

Ward, R., Logan, J., & Spitze, G. (1992). The influence of parent and child needs on coresidence in middle and later life. *Journal of Marriage and the Family, 54,* 209–221.

Warner, R., & Steel, B. (1999). Child rearing as a mechanism for social change: The relationship of child gender to parents' commitment to gender equity. *Gender and Society, 13,* 503–517.

Warr, P. B. (1994). Age and employment. In M. D. Dunnette, L. Hough, & H. Triandis (Eds.), *Handbook of industrial and organizational psychology* (pp. 485–550). Palo Alto, CA: Consulting Psychologists Press.

Warrington, E. K., & Shallice, A. (1972). Neuropsychological evidence of visual storage in short-term memory tasks. *Quarterly Journal of Experimental Psychology, 24,* 30–40.

Waschbusch, D. A., Sellers, D. P., LeBlanc, M., & Kelley, M. L. (2003). Helpless attributions and depression in adolescents: The roles of anxiety, event valence, and demographics. *Journal of Adolescence, 26,* 169–183.

Wasserman, E. A., & Miller, R. R. (1997). What's elementary about associative learning? *Annual Review of Psychology, 48,* 573–607.

Wasserman, G. S. (1978). *Color vision: An historical introduction.* New York: Wiley.

Waterman, J., & Lusk, R. (1986). Scope of the problem. In K. MacFarlane et al. (Eds.), *Sexual abuse of young children: Evaluation and treatment* (pp. 3–14). New York: Guilford Press.

Watkins, D. C., Green, B. L., Goodson, P., Guidry, J. J., & Stanley, C. A. (2007). Using focus groups to explore the stressful life events for Black college men. *Journal of College Student Development, 48,* 105–118.

Watson, J. B., & Rayner, R. (1920). Conditioned emotional reactions. *Journal of Experimental Psychology, 3,* 1–14.

Watson, J. C., Schein, J., & McMullen, E. (2010). An examination of clients' in-session changes and their relationship to the working alliance and outcome. *Psychotherapy Research, 20,* 224–233.

Waylen, A., & Wolke, D. (2004). Sex 'n' drugs 'n' rock 'n' roll: The meaning and social consequences of pubertal timing. *European Journal of Endocrinology, 151,* U151–U159.

Webb, W. B. (1983). Theories in modern sleep research. In A. Mayes (Ed.), *Sleep mechanisms and functions* (pp. 1–17). Wokingham, UK: Van Nostrand Reinhold.

Webb, W. B., & Campbell, S. S. (1983). Relationships in sleep characteristics of identical and fraternal twins. *Archives of General Psychiatry, 40,* 1093–1095.

Webster Marketon, J. I., & Glaser, R. (2008). Stress hormones and immune function. *Cellular Immunology, 252,* 16–26.

Wechsler, D. (1939). *The measurement of adult intelligence.* Baltimore: Williams & Wilkins.

Weems, C. F., Watts, S. E., Marsee, M. A., Taylor, L. K., Costa, N. M., Cannon, M. F., et al. (2007). The psychological impact of Hurricane Katrina: Contextual differences in psychological symptoms, social support, and discrimination. *Behavior Research and Therapy, 45,* 2295–2306.

Wegener, D. T. & Carlston, D. E. (2005). Cognitive processes in attitude formation and change. In D. Albarracin, B. T. Johnson, & M. P. Zanna (Eds.), *The handbook of attitudes* (pp. 493–542). Hillsdale, NJ: Erlbaum.

Weibel, D., Wissmath, B., & Mast, F. W. (2010). Immersion in mediated environments: The role of personality traits. *Cyberpsychology, Behavior, and Social Networking, 13,* 251–256.

Weidner, R., & Fink, G. R. (2007). The neural mechanisms underlying the Müller-Lyer illusion and its interaction with visuospatial judgments. *Cerebral Cortex, 17,* 878–884.

Weijmar Schultz, W. C. M., & Van de Wiel, H. B. M. (2005). Vaginismus. In R. Balon & R. T. Segraves (Eds.), *Handbook of sexual dysfunction* (pp. 43–65). Boca Raton, FL: Taylor & Francis.

Weinrich, J. D. (1994). Homosexuality. In V. L. Bullough & B. Bullough (Eds.), *Human sexuality: An encyclopedia* (pp. 277–283). New York: Garland.

Weinstein, S., Woodward, T. S., & Ngan, E. T. (2007). Brain activation mediates the association between structural abnormality and symptom severity in schizophrenia. *Neuroimage, 36,* 188–193.

Weinstock, H., Berman, S., & Cates, W., Jr. (2004). Sexually transmitted diseases among American youth: Incidence and prevalence estimates, 2000. *Perspectives on Sexual and Reproductive Health, 36,* 6–10.

Weiss, A., Bates, T. C., & Luciano, M. (2008). Happiness is a personal(ity) thing: The genetics of personality and well-being in a representative sample. *Psychological Science, 19,* 205–210.

Weiss, R. D., & Mirin, S. M. (1987). *Cocaine.* Washington, DC: American Psychiatric Press.

Weissman, M. M. (1993). The epidemiology of personality disorders: A 1990 update. *Journal of Personality Disorders, 7*(Spring Suppl. 1), 44–62.

Weissman, M. M., & Olfson, M. (1995). Depression in women: Implications for health care research. *Science, 269,* 799–801.

Weissman, M. M., Bland, R. C., Canino, G. J., Greenwald, S., Hwu, H. G., Joyce, P. R., et al. (1999). Prevalence of suicide ideation and suicide attempts in nine countries. *Psychological Medicine, 29,* 9–17.

Weissman, M. M., Markowitz, J. C., & Klerman, G. I. (2000). *Comprehensive guide to interpersonal psychotherapy.* New York: Basic Books.

Welch, S. S. (2001). A review of the literature on the epidemiology of parasuicide in the general population. *Psychiatric Services, 52,* 368–375.

Welford, A. T. (1987). Ageing. In R. L. Gregory (Ed.), *The Oxford companion to the mind* (pp. 13–14). Oxford, UK: Oxford University Press.

Wellman, H. M., Cross, D., & Watson, J. (2001). Metaanalysis of theory of mind development: The truth about false-belief. *Child Development, 72,* 655–684.

Welsh, D. P., Grello, C. M., & Harper, M. S. (2006). No strings attached: The nature of casual sex in college students. *Journal of Sex Research, 43,* 255–267.

Welte, J. W., & Barnes, G. M. (1987). Alcohol use among adolescent minority groups. *Journal of Studies on Alcohol, 48,* 329–336.

Wertheimer, M. (1923). Principles of perceptual organization (Abridged trans. by M. Wertheimer). In D. S. Beardslee & M. Wertheimer (Eds.), *Readings in perception* (pp. 115–137). Princeton, NJ: Van Nostrand Reinhold. (Original work published 1923, *Psychologishe Forschung, 41,* 301–350)

West, S. G. (2009). Alternatives to randomized experiments. *Current Directions in Psychological Science, 18,* 299–304.

Westen, D. (1999). The scientific status of unconscious processes: Is Freud really dead? *Journal of the American Psychoanalytic Association, 47,* 1061–1106.

Westen, D., & Bradley, R. (2005). Empirically supported complexity: Rethinking evidence-based practice in psychotherapy. *Current Directions in Psychological Science, 14,* 266–271.

Westermeyer, J. F. (2004). Predictors and characteristics of Erikson's life cycle model among men: A 32-year longitudinal study. *International Journal of Aging and Human Development, 58,* 29–48.

Wetter, D. W., Cofta-Gunn, L., Fouladi, R. T., Irvin, J. E., Daza, P., Mazas, C., et al. (2005). Understanding the association among education, employment characteristics, and smoking. *Addictive Behaviors, 30,* 905–914.

Wever, E. G. (1970). *Theory of hearing.* New York: Wiley. (Original work published 1949)

Weyant, J. M. (1996). Application of compliance techniques to direct-mail requests for charitable donations. *Psychology and Marketing, 13,* 157–170.

Wheeler, D. S., & Miller, R. R. (2008). Determinants of cue interactions. *Behavioral Processes, 78,* 191–203.

Wheeler, J., Newring, K., & Draper, C. (2008). Transvestic fetishism: Psychopathology and theory. In D. Laws & W. O'Donohue (Eds.), *Sexual deviance: Theory, assessment and treatment* (2nd ed., pp. 272–285). New York: Guilford Press.

Wheeler, M. A., Stuss, D. T., & Tulving, E. (1997). Toward a theory of episodic memory: The frontal lobes and autonoetic consciousness. *Psychological Bulletin, 121,* 331–354.

Wheeler, M. D. (1991). Physical changes of puberty. *Endocrinology and Metabolism Clinics of North America, 20,* 1–14.

Whitbourne, S. K. (1996). *The aging individual.* New York: Springer.

Whitbourne, S. K. (2001). The physical aging process in midlife: Interactions with psychological and sociocultural factors. In M.E. Lachman (Ed.), *Handbook of midlife development* (pp. 109–155). New York: Wiley.

White, L. K., & Edwards, J. N. (1990). Emptying the nest and parental well-being: An analysis of national panel data. *American Sociological Review, 55,* 235–242.

White, L. K., & Rogers, S. J. (1997). Strong support but uneasy relationships: Coresidence and adult children's relationships with their parents. *Journal of Marriage and the Family, 59,* 62–76.

Whitehead, N. E. (2007). An antiboy antibody? Reexamination of the maternal immune hypothesis. *Journal of Biosocial Science, 39,* 905–921.

Whiting, B., & Edwards, C. P. (1988). *Children in different worlds.* Cambridge, MA: Harvard University Press.

Whorf, B. L. (1956). *Language, thought, and reality: Selected writings of Benjamin Lee Whorf.* New York: Wiley.

Wickelgren, I. (1997). Marijuana: Harder than thought? *Science, 276,* 1967–1968.

Widiger, T. A. (1998). Invited essay: Sex differences in the diagnosis of personality disorders. *Journal of Personality Disorders, 12,* 95–118.

Widiger, T. A. (2003). Personality disorder and Axis I psychopathology: The problematic boundary of Axis I and Axis II. *Journal of Personality Disorders, 17,* 90–108.

Widiger, T. A., & Chaynes, K. (2003). Current issues in the assessment of personality disorders. *Current Psychiatry Reports, 5,* 28–35.

Widom, C. S. (1999). Posttraumatic stress disorder in abused and neglected children grown up. *American Journal of Psychiatry, 156,* 1223–1229.

Wiechman Askay, S., & Patterson, D. R. (2007). Hypnotic analgesia. *Expert Review of Neurotherapeutics, 7,* 1675–1683.

Wiederhold, B. K., Jang, D. P., Kim, S. I., & Wiederhold, M. D. (2002). Physiological monitoring as an objective tool in virtual reality therapy. *Cyberpsychology and Behavior, 5,* 77–82.

Wiederman, M. W. (1997). Extramarital sex: Prevalence and correlates in a national survey. *Journal of Sex Research, 34,* 167–174.

Wiggins, J. S. (1997). In defense of traits. In R. Hogan, J. Johnson, & S. Briggs (Eds.), *Handbook of personality psychology* (pp. 97–115). New York: Academic Press.

Wilhelm, K., Mitchell, P. B., Niven, H., Finch, A., Wedgwood, L., Scimone, A., et al. (2006). Life events, first depression onset and the serotonin transporter gene. *British Journal of Psychiatry, 188,* 210–215.

Williams, D., Yee, N., & Caplan, S. E. (2008). Who plays, how much, and why? Debunking the stereotypical gamer profile. *Journal of Computer-Mediated Communication, 13,* 993–1018.

Williams, D. R., Gonzalez, H. M., Neighbors, H., Neese, R., Abelson, J. M., Sweetman, J., et al. (2007). Prevalence and distribution of major depressive disorder in African Americans, Caribbean Blacks, and non-Hispanic Whites. *Archives of General Psychiatry, 64,* 305–315.

Williams, D. R., Yu, Y., Jackson, J. S., & Anderson, N. B. (1997). Racial differences in physical and mental health: Socioeconomic status, stress and discrimination. *Journal of Health Psychology, 2,* 335–351.

Williams, J. E., Paton, C. C., Siegler, I. C., Eigenbrodt, M. L., Nieto, F. J., & Tyroler, H. A. (2000). Anger proneness predicts coronary heart disease risk: Prospective analysis from the Atherosclerosis Risk in Communities (ARIC) study. *Circulation, 101,* 2034–2039.

Williams, J. M., & Galli, A. (2006). The dopamine transporter: A vigilant border control for psychostimulant action. *Handbook of Experimental Pharmacology, 175,* 215–232.

Williams, K. N., & Kemper, S. (2010). Interventions to reduce cognitive decline in aging. *Journal of Psychosocial Nursing and Mental Health Services, 48,* 1–10.

Williams, L. M., Sidis, A., Gordon, E., & Meares, R. A. (2006). "Missing links" in borderline personality disorder: Loss of neural synchrony relates to lack of emotion regulation and impulse control. *Journal of Psychiatry and Neuroscience, 31,* 181–188.

Williams, R. (1993). *Anger kills.* New York: Times Books.

Willis, S. L., & Schaie, K. W. (1999). Intellectual functioning in midlife. In S. L. Willis & J. D. Reid (Eds.), *Life in the middle: Psychological and social development in middle age* (pp. 233–247). San Diego, CA: Academic Press.

Wills, T. A., & Fegan, M. (2001). Social networks and social support. In A. Baum, T. A. Revenson, & J. E. Singer (Eds.), *Handbook of health psychology* (pp. 209–234). Mahwah, NJ: Erlbaum.

Wilson, G. T., Grilo, C. M., & Vitousek, K. M. (2007). Psychological treatment of eating disorders. *American Psychologist, 62,* 199–216.

Wilson, K. G., Hayes, S. C., & Gifford, E. V. (1997). Cognition in behavior therapy: Agreements and differences. *Journal of Behavior Therapy and Experimental Psychiatry, 28,* 53–63.

Wilson, R. S., & Bennett, D. A. (2003). Cognitive activity and risk of Alzheimer's disease. *Current Directions in Psychological Science, 12,* 87–91.

Wingfield, A., & Kahana, M. J. (2002). The dynamics of memory retrieval in older adulthood. *Canadian Journal of Psychology, 56,* 187–199.

Winokur, G., Coryell, W., Keller, M., Endicott, J., & Leon, A. (1995). A family study of manic-depressive (Bipolar I) disease. *Archives of General Psychiatry, 52,* 367–373.

Wirtz, D., Chiu, C. Y., Diener, E., & Oishi, S. (2009). What constitutes a good life? Cultural differences in the role of positive and negative affect in subjective well-being. *Journal of Personality, 77,* 1167–1196.

Wise, S. M. (2000). *Rattling the cage: Toward legal rights for animals.* Cambridge, MA: Perseus Books.

Wiseman, C. V., Gray, J. J., Mosimann, J. E., & Ahrens, A. H. (1992). Cultural expectations of thinness in women: An update. *International Journal of Eating Disorders, 11,* 85–89.

Wiseman, S., & Tulving, E. (1976). Encoding specificity: Relations between recall superiority and recognition failure. *Journal of Experimental Psychology: Human Learning and Memory, 2,* 349–361.

Wisner, K. L., Peindl, K. S., Perel, J. M., Hanusa, B. H., Piontek, C. M., & Baab, S. (2002). Verapamil treatment for women with bipolar disorder. *Biological Psychiatry, 51,* 745–752.

Witt, L. A., Kacmar, M., Carlson, D. S., & Zivnuska, S. (2002). Interactive effects of personality and organizational politics on contextual performance. *Journal of Organizational Behavior, 23,* 911–926.

Witt, S. D. (1997). Parental influence on children's socialization to gender roles. *Adolescence, 32,* 253–259.

Wolf, D. H., Gur, R. C., Valdez, J. N., Loughead, J., Elliott, M. A., Gur, R. E., et al. (2007). Alterations of frontotemporal connectivity during word encoding in schizophrenia. *Psychiatry Research, 154,* 221–232.

Wolitzky, D. L. (1995). The theory and practice of traditional psychoanalytic psychotherapy. In A. S. Gurman (Ed.), *Essential psychotherapies: Theory and practice* (pp. 12–54). New York: Guilford Press.

Wolpe, J. (1958). *Psychotherapy by reciprocal inhibition.* Stanford, CA: Stanford University Press.

Woodward, S. (2003, September 7). Him, her—and the Internet. *Oregonian,* pp. L1, L8.

Woody, J. D., Russel, R., D'Souza, H. J., & Woody, J. K. (2000). Non-coital sex among adolescent virgins and nonvirgins. *Journal of Sex Education and Therapy*, 25(4), 261–268.

Woodzicka, J. A., & LaFrance, M. (2001). Real versus imagined gender harassment. *Journal of Social Issues*, 57, 15–30.

Woollett, K., Glensman, J., & Maguire, E. A. (2008). Non-spatial expertise and hippocampal gray matter volume in humans. *Hippocampus*, 18, 981–984.

World Health Organization. (2004). *The World Health Report 2004: Changing history*. Annex Table 3: Burden of disease in DALYs by cause, sex, and mortality stratum in WHO regions, estimates for 2002. Geneva: Author.

Wright, I. C., Rabe-Hesketh,, S., Woodruff, P. W., David, A. S., Murray, R. M., & Bullmore, E. T. (2000). Meta-analysis of regional brain volumes in schizophrenia. *American Journal of Psychiatry*, 157, 16–25.

Wrightsman, L. S. (1988). *Personality development in adulthood*. Newbury Park, CA: Sage.

Wrightsman, L. S. (1994). *Adult personality development: Vol 1. Theories and concepts*. Thousand Oaks, CA: Sage.

Wu, H. R., & Zhu, K. J. (2004). Path analysis on related factors causing Internet addiction disorder in college students. *Chinese Journal of Public Health*, 20, 1363–1364.

Wulsin, L. R., Vaillat, G. E., & Wells, V. E. (1999). A systematic review of the mortality of depression. *Psychosomatic Medicine*, 61, 6–17.

Wyatt, G. (1997). *Stolen women: Reclaiming your sexuality, taking back your lives*. New York: Wiley.

Xiao, Y., Wang, Y., & Felleman, D. J. (2003). A spatially organized representation of colour in macaque cortical area V2. *Nature*, 421, 535–539.

Xie, T., Tong, L., McLane, M. W., Hatzidimitriou, G., Yuan, J., McCann, U., et al. (2006). Loss of serotonin transporter protein after MDMA and other ring-substituted amphetamines. *Neuropsychopharmacology*, 31, 2639–2651.

Xiong, G. L., & Doraiswamy, P. M. (2009). Does meditation enhance cognition and brain plasticity? *Annals of the New York Academy of Sciences*, 1172, 63–69.

Xu, J., Kochanek, K. D., & Tejada-Vera, B. (2009). Deaths: Preliminary data for 2007. *National Vital Statistics Report*, 58, 1–51.

Xu, J., & Roberts, R. E. (2010). The power of positive emotions: It's a matter of life or death: Subjective well-being and longevity over 28 years in a general population. *Healthy Psychology*, 29, 9–19.

Xu, L., Sun, X., Lu, J., Tang, M., & Chen, J. D. (2008). Effects of gastric electric stimulation on gastric distention responsive neurons and expressions of CCK in rodent hippocampus. *Obesity*, 16, 951–957.

Yackinous, C. A., & Guinard, J. (2002). Relation between PROP (6-n-propylthiouracil) taster status, taste anatomy and dietary intake measures for young men and women. *Appetite*, 38, 201–209.

Yalom, I. D. (1989). *Love's executioner and other tales of psychotherapy*. New York: HarperCollins.

Yalom, I. D., & Leszcz, M. (2005). *The theory and practice of group therapy* (5th ed.). New York: Basic Books.

Yamagata, S., Suzuki, A., Ando, J., Ono, Y., Kijima, N., Yoshimura, K., et al. (2006). Is the genetic structure of human personality universal? A cross-cultural twin study from North America, Europe, and Asia. *Journal of Personality and Social Psychology*, 90, 987–998.

Yamamoto, T. (2008). Central mechanisms of roles of taste in reward and eating. *Acta Physiologica Hungarica*, 95, 165–186.

Yao, M. Z., Mahood, C., & Linz, D. (2010). Sexual priming, gender stereotyping, and likelihood to sexually harass: Examining the cognitive effects of playing a sexually-explicit video game. *Sex Roles*, 62, 77–88.

Yardley, L., & Kirby, S. (2006). Evaluation of booklet self-management of symptoms in Meniere disease: A randomized controlled trial. *Psychosomatic Medicine*, 68, 762–769.

Yatham, L. N., Liddle, P. F., Lam, R. W., Zis, A. P., Stoessl, A. J., Sossi, V., et al. (2010). Effect of electroconvulsive therapy on brain 5-HT(2) receptors in major depression. *British Journal of Psychiatry*, 196, 474–479.

Yau, K. W., & Hardie, R. C. (2009). Phototransduction motifs and variations. *Cell*, 139, 246–264.

Yeung, W. J., Sandberg, J. F., Davis-Kean, P. E., & Hofferth, S. L. (2001). Children's time with fathers in intact families. *Journal of Marriage and Family*, 63, 136–154.

Yingling, D. R., Utter, G., Vengalil, S., & Mason, B. (2002). Calcium channel blocker, nimodipine, for the treatment of bipolar disorder during pregnancy. *American Journal of Obstetrics and Gynecology*, 187, 1711–1712.

Yip, T., Seaton, E. K., & Sellers, R. M. (2006). African American racial identity across the lifespan: Identity status, identity content, and depressive symptoms. *Child Development*, 77, 1504–1517.

York, J. L., & Welte, J. W. (1994). Gender comparisons of alcohol consumption in alcoholic and nonalcoholic populations. *Journal of Studies on Alcohol*, 55(6), 743–750.

Youn, S., Lee, M., & Doyle, K. O. (2003) Lifestyles of online gamers: A psychographic approach. *Journal of Interactive Advertising*, 3, 1–13.

Young, A. H., McElroy, S. L., Bauer, M., Philips, N., Chang, W., Olausson, B., et al. (2010). A double-blind, placebo-controlled study of quetiapine and lithium monotherapy in adults in the acute phase of bipolar depression (EMBOLDEN I). *Journal of Clinical Psychiatry*, 71, 150–162.

Young, N. K. (1997). Effects of alcohol and other drugs on children. *Journal of Psychoactive Drugs*, 29, 23–42.

Yunker, G. W., & Yunker, B. D. (2002). Primal leadership: Realizing the power of emotional intelligence (book). *Personnel Psychology*, 55, 1030–1033.

Yutrzenka, B. A. (1995). Making a case for training in ethnic and cultural diversity in increasing treatment efficacy. *Journal of Consulting and Clinical Psychology*, 63, 197–206.

Zaalberg, R., Manstead, A. S. R., & Fischer, A. H. (2004). Relations between emotions, display rules, social motives, and facial behaviors. *Cognition and Emotion*, 18, 183–207.

Zaccaro, S. J., Mumford, M. D., Connelly, M., Marks, M., & Gilbert, J. A. (2000). Assessment of leader abilities. *Leadership Quarterly*, 11, 37–64.

Zadina, J. E., Hackler, L., Ge, L. J., & Kastin, A. J. (1997). A potent and selective endogenous agonist for the u-opiate receptor. *Nature*, 386, 499–502.

Zadra, A., Desjardins, S., & Marcotte, E. (2006). Evolutionary function of dreams: A test of the threat simulation theory in recurrent dreams. *Consciousness and Cognition*, 15, 450–463.

Zahn-Waxler, C., & Robinson, J. (1995). Empathy and guilt: Early origins of feelings of responsibility. In J. P. Tangney & K. W. Fischer (Eds.), *Self-conscious emotions* (pp. 143–173). New York: Guilford Press.

Zajonc, R. B. (1968). Attitudinal effects of mere exposure. *Journal of Personality and Social Psychology*, 9, 1–27.

Zajonc, R. B. (1965). Social facilitation. *Science*, 149, 269–274.

Zajonc, R. B. (1980). Feeling and thinking: Preferences need no inferences. *American Psychologist*, 35, 151–175.

Zajonc, R. B., Adelmann, P. K., Murphy, S. T., & Neidenthal, P. M. (1987). Convergence in the physical appearance of spouse. *Motivation and Emotion*, 11, 335–346.

Zajonc, R. B., Murphy, S. T., & Inglehart, M. (1989). Feeling and facial efference: Implications of the vascular theory of emotions. *Psychological Review*, 96, 395–416.

Zalenski, R. J., & Raspa, R. (2006). Maslow's hierarchy of needs: A framework for achieving human potential in hospice. *Journal of Palliative Medicine*, 9, 1120–1127.

Zanarini, M. C. (2000). Childhood experiences associated with the development of borderline personality disorder. *Psychiatric Clinics of North America*, 23, 89–101.

Zanarini, M. C., & Frankenburg, F. R. (1997). Pathways to the development of borderline person-ality disorder. *Journal of Personality Disorders*, 11, 93–104.

Zanarini, M. C., Skodol, A. E., Bender, D., Dolan, R., Sanislow, C., Schaefer, E., et al. (2000). The Collaborative Longitudinal Personality Disorders Study: Reliability of Axis I and II diagnoses. *Journal of Personality Disorder*, 14, 291–299.

Zee, P. C., & Manthena, P. (2007). The brain's master circadian clock: Implications and opportunities for therapy of sleep disorders. *Sleep Medicine Reviews*, 11, 59–70.

Zeitzer, J. M., Nishino, S., & Mignot, E. (2006). The neurobiology of hypocretins (orexins), narcolepsy and related therapeutic interventions. *Trends in Pharmacological Sciences*, 27, 368–374.

Zeman, A., Britton, T., Douglas, N., Hansen, A., Hicks, J., Howard, R., et al. (2004). Narcolepsy and excessive daytime sleepiness. *British Medical Journal*, 329, 724–728.

Zhang, A. Y., & Snowden, L. R. (1999). Ethnic characteristics of mental disorders in five U.S. communities. *Cultural Diversity and Ethnic Minority Psychology*, 5, 134–146.

Zhang, B., & Wing, Y. K. (2006). Sex differences in insomnia: A meta-analysis. *Sleep*, 29, 85–93.

Ziegler, D. J., & Leslie, Y. M. (2003). A test of the ABC model underlying rational-emotive behavior therapy. *Psychological Reports*, 92, 235–240.

Ziegler, D. J., & Smith, P. N. (2004). Anger and the ABC model underlying rational-emotive behavior therapy. *Psychological Reports*, 93, 1009–1014.

Zimbardo, P. G. (1972, April). Psychology of imprisonment. *Transition/Society*, pp. 4–8.

Zimmer, L., & Morgan, J. P. (1997). *Marijuana myths, marijuana fact: A review of scientific evidence*. New York: Lindesmith Center.

Zimmerman, M. E., Brickman, A. M., Paul, R. H., Grieve, S. M., Tate, D. F., Gunstad, J., et al. (2006). The relationship between frontal gray matter volume and cognition varies across the healthy adult lifespan. *American Journal of Geriatric Psychiatry*, 14, 823–833.

Zisook, S., Rush, A. J., Haight, B. R., Clines, D. C., & Rockett, C. B. (2006). Use of bupropion in combination with serotonin reuptake inhibitors. *Biological Psychiatry*, 59, 203–210.

Zorrilla, L. T., Cannon, T. D., Kronenberg, S., Mednick, S. A., Schulsinger, F., Parnas, J., et al. (1997). Structural brain abnormalities in schizophrenia: A family study. *Biological Psychiatry*, 42, 1080–1086.

Zottoli, M. A., & Wanous, J. P. (2000). Recruitment source research: Current status and future directions. *Human Resource Management Review*, 10, 435–451.

Zucker, K., Bradley, S., Oliver, J., Fleming, S., & Head, A. (1996). Psychosexual development of women with congenital adrenal hyperplasia. *Hormones and Behavior*, 30, 300–318.

Zuckerman, M. (1978). The search for high sensation. *Psychology Today*, 11, 38–99.

Zuckerman, M. (1994). *Behavioral expressions and biosocial bases of sensation seeking*. Cambridge, UK: Cambridge University Press.

Zuckerman, M., & Kuhlman, D. M. (2000). Personality and risk-taking: Common biosocial factors. *Journal of Personality*, 68, 999–1029.

Zurbriggen, E. L., & Yost, M. R. (2004). Power, desire, and pleasure in sexual fantasies. *Journal of Sex Research*, 41, 288–300.

NAME INDEX

SUBJECT INDEX

Module A
Industrial/Organizational Psychology

For Weiten's

Psychology:
Themes and Variations
Briefer Version, Seventh Edition

By Frank Landy, Kecia M. Thomas, and Matthew S. Harrison

THOMSON
WADSWORTH

Printed in the United States of America
1 2 3 4 5 6 7 11 10 09 08 07

ISBN-13: 978-0-495-40466-8
ISBN-10: 0-495-40466-7

Throughout this book we have seen many examples of how psychology has been applied to practical problems in a wide variety of settings. But we have yet to discuss in earnest one setting that has received a great deal of attention from the earliest beginnings of psychology—the work setting. *Industrial and organizational (I/O) psychology* is the branch of psychology concerned with the application of psychological principles in the workplace. The Society for Industrial and Organizational Psychology (SIOP), the primary professional organization for I/O psychologists, encompasses approximately 6,000 members, which includes representation from all 50 states and 42 countries. The membership of the society has more than doubled in recent years, and this growth trend is expected to continue. As the economy in Western nations changes to emphasize service and information, the influence and importance of I/O psychology is likely to increase. As an area of specialization in psychology, I/O psychology is second only to clinical psychology in the number of practitioners. I/O psychologists are mostly found in four sectors of the economy: industry, universities, government, and consulting firms (see Figure M.1). In this appendix, we will briefly describe the history of I/O psychology and then delve into its three main areas. But first we need a clearer picture of what I/O psychology encompasses.

Overview of I/O Psychology

Industrial and organizational psychology differs from other psychology subfields in the settings where it is practiced, in its content, and in its approach. It does *not* differ, however, in its reliance on the scientific method for its theories and research.

Settings

In one sense, I/O psychology is defined more clearly by *where* it happens than by *what* I/O psychologists actually do. I/O psychology is practiced in work settings, just as school psychology is practiced in educational settings. But even though the context in which research and application are carried out may be unique, I/O psychology makes use of the findings of many other branches of psychology. For instance, principles of human motivation are relevant to the study of productivity and safety behavior, theories of attitude formation help in understanding the job satisfaction of workers and organizational culture, the social psychology of groups helps us understand team performance and leadership dynamics, aspects of psychophysiology are relevant to a consideration of job stress, clinical theories of adjustment are applicable to the emotional consequences of job loss, and theories of intelligence are used to develop tests that might assist in hiring decisions. In fact, a good deal of the work of the I/O psychologist involves adapting or extending the basic principles of other specialty areas of psychology to the work setting.

With respect to *how* I/O psychologists practice their profession, they use most of the same techniques as their colleagues in other areas, such as developmental or social psychology. Like other psychologists, the I/O psychologist may do research in a laboratory or in a field setting (at the work site, for instance). I/O psychologists use the same basic experimental designs and statistical tests as other behavioral researchers, depend just as heavily on prior research for theoretical guidance, and publish the results of their research in scholarly journals. In other words, like their colleagues in other areas of psychology, I/O psychologists are scientists who depend on the scientific method to guide their work.

Content

More than anything else, the *content* of I/O psychology helps define it as a branch of psychology. As Figure M.2 shows, the I/O psychologist has three primary areas of interest: (1) personnel psychology, (2) organizational psychology, and (3) human factors (or human engineering) psychology. Although we will consider each of these areas in detail shortly, it might be helpful to briefly describe them here.

Personnel psychology deals with determining whether people have the knowledge, skills, abilities, and personality necessary to perform various types of work effectively. This subarea of I/O psychology is concerned with the broad topic of employment testing and with such related topics as job training, test validation, interviewing, and employment discrimination. Personnel psychologists see the job or work environment as the "given" and the population of individuals who might be workers as the vari-

Figure M.1
Employment of industrial/organizational psychologists. I/O psychologists are employed mainly in the settings identified here. As the pie chart shows, about three-quarters of I/O psychologists work in either universities or consulting firms. (Based on Society for Industrial and Organizational Psychology member database)

Source: Muchinsky, P. M. (2003). Psychology applied to work. Belmont, CA: Wadsworth. Reprinted by permission.

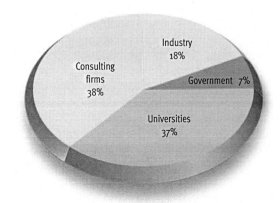

Industry 18%
Consulting firms 38%
Government 7%
Universities 37%

able factor. Their goal is to find the workers who have the right attributes to fit the demands of the job.

Organizational psychology is concerned with how people adapt emotionally and socially to working in complex human organizations. It focuses on work motivation, job satisfaction, leadership, organizational culture, teamwork, and related topics. From this perspective, the concern of the I/O psychologist is to understand the factors that contribute to the right emotional "fit" between people and their work. Eighty years ago, managers believed that money was the only work motivator. The modern I/O psychologist concentrates on making the job itself more interesting (in the jargon of the field, "enriching" the job), rather than getting workers to forget how boring the work actually is by paying them more. Other topics pursued by organizational psychologists are the relationships between work and nonwork (such as family life), the creation of cohesive workgroups within increasingly ethnically diverse workplaces, and the complexities of leadership in a dynamic workplace.

Human factors (human engineering) psychology examines the way in which work environments can be designed or modified to match the capabilities and limitations of human beings. From this perspective, the human being is the constant and the job or work environment is the variable in the behavior equation. The concept of the work environment is used broadly and includes the actual physical setting in which the work takes place, the tools and resources used in conducting the work (such as printing presses, cash registers, laptop computers, and other equipment), and the arrangement or design of the work tasks (including such things as the scheduling of work hours). Thus, the challenge to the human factors psychologist is to design or redesign a work environment so that it best fits the capabilities and allows for the limitations of the humans who will inhabit it. Unlike personnel psychology, in which the individual is being tested or selected to fit the job, human factors psychologists fit the work technology or environment to human capabilities in order to promote efficiency, effectiveness, and safety.

A Systems Approach

The division of I/O psychology into three facets is somewhat misleading because it implies that these areas operate independently. In practice, that is seldom the case. In fact, the actual work, the people who do the work, and the work environment define a larger entity that might be labeled the "sociotechnical system." Changes made in one part of the system usually affect other parts of the system.

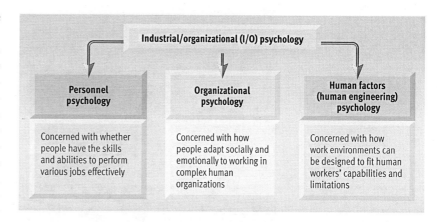

Industrial/organizational (I/O) psychology

Personnel psychology
Concerned with whether people have the skills and abilities to perform various jobs effectively

Organizational psychology
Concerned with how people adapt socially and emotionally to working in complex human organizations

Human factors (human engineering) psychology
Concerned with how work environments can be designed to fit human workers' capabilities and limitations

Figure M.2
Subfields of industrial/organizational psychology. The domain of I/O psychology can be divided into three specialized areas of interest: personnel psychology, organizational psychology, and human factors psychology.

Changing the design of a task so that it is more complex (a human factors activity) may have a substantial impact on the satisfaction that a worker derives from that task (an organizational topic) and who might do best at that task (a personnel psychology topic). As an example, consider the simple act of computerizing what had previously been a manual task. On the surface, this might be seen as a "human factor" change, since it is a modification of the tools of the job. But the new technology also changes other aspects of the work. A clerk may no longer need to go to the filing cabinet to insert or retrieve documents, as files can now be accessed electronically without moving from a desk. As a result, the clerk may become more isolated and lose opportunities for social interaction with other workers. In addition, the introduction of the computer changes the skill and ability mix necessary for success on the job. Unless the worker is capable of interacting effectively with the hardware and software of the computer system, he or she is likely to experience performance problems (and accompanying feelings of frustration). In addition to these changes, the performance of the worker might be more closely monitored. Keystrokes can be counted and an average per minute calculated, errors can be detected, and other measures of performance can be collected and used to reward or punish the worker. Finally, supervisors might interact with employees by sending messages via e-mail rather than by talking directly with them, losing a personal element. In short, computerizing a function is much more complex and dynamic than it seems on the surface.

The fact that the three areas of I/O psychology are not mutually exclusive is both a burden and an opportunity for I/O psychologists. The burden lies in being sensitive to the impact that making a change in one part of this sociotechnical system has on other parts of the system. The opportunity lies in having several options for dealing with real-world problems. For example, if an organization is having a problem

Web Link **M.1**

Society for Industrial and Organizational Psychology (SIOP) The Society for Industrial and Organizational Psychology (SIOP) is the leading professional organization for I/O psychologists. Although primarily intended for society members, its website provides a variety of resources for students and teachers interested in this growing specialty area. Included among the resources are excellent discussions of employment testing, the effects of coaching on employment testing, and ways I/O psychologists can contribute to organizational excellence.

The simple act of replacing a typewriter with a personal computer can have ramifications in many aspects of an employee's work besides interaction with the physical equipment. A systems approach helps explain the various repercussions of such changes.

with accidents or productivity, an I/O psychologist might suggest redesigning the work environment to be safer or more efficient. Alternatively, the psychologist might design a motivational program to encourage workers to engage in safer or more productive work. Finally, the psychologist might suggest changing the methods used to select or train workers. Any or all of these methods might be effective in reducing accidents or improving productivity. In all likelihood, the most effective intervention would combine elements of all three approaches. In a personal sense, the practice of I/O psychology is exciting because there are so many *different ways* to approach the same work-related issue.

A Brief History

Although psychology as a science was born in the late 19th century, various specialty areas, including I/O psychology, came along somewhat later. Hugo Munsterberg, one of the earliest practitioners of I/O psychology, was an original founder of the American Psychological Association in 1892. By 1910, Munster-

berg had written the first text in I/O psychology. The first Ph.D. granted in I/O psychology was in 1915. It was presented to Lilian Gilbreth by Brown University. In this section, we will examine the development of I/O psychology from a historical perspective.

Personnel Psychology

Personnel psychology was the first of the three I/O subfields to appear. The emergence of this subfield was the result of several forces, the foremost being psychology's increased interest in measuring and recording individual differences. As we saw in Chapter 9, Sir Francis Galton attempted to provide support for his cousin Charles Darwin's theory of evolution by showing that traits are inherited. Part of this demonstration involved the first efforts at psychological testing, including measurements of psychological abilities, such as memory and reaction time.

Mental tests were subsequently adopted by educational institutions to identify those children and young adults most likely to benefit from various forms of education. Alfred Binet developed his intelligence test to separate educable from uneducable children in the French primary school system. And Hugo Munsterberg developed tests for the selection of ships' captains, telephone operators, and trolley drivers. All of these instances of testing occurred before 1909, the year that Freud first visited America.

When the United States entered World War I, intelligence testing was introduced as a method of identifying those recruits with the greatest likelihood of becoming successful officers as well as steering nonofficers into specialties for which they were best suited (Yerkes, 1921). The respectability acquired by psychological testing from this wartime application carried over into industry following the war, and modern personnel psychology emerged. By 1932 there were dozens of texts describing the goals and methods of personnel psychology (such as Burtt, 1929; Viteles, 1932). Similar pressures for mass testing exerted by World War II further enhanced the importance of personnel testing, which retains a prominent role in I/O psychology today. Following World War II, there was a growing interest in personality and interest testing, and these new types of tests were added to the typical test battery given to job applicants.

Organizational Psychology

The prevailing belief in the early part of the 20th century was that money was the *only* motivator in business and industry. This belief was formalized by the theory of Frederick W. Taylor (1911), variously known as "scientific management" or "Taylorism."

Taylor believed that one need only identify the most efficient way to physically carry out a piece of work (lay a brick, shovel coal), pick a worker capable of the work and willing to follow orders without question, and pay that worker in proportion to production rate. At that time, the term "job satisfaction" was of little interest to employers. And "intelligence" among workers was to be avoided at all costs. Taylor preferred to apply his principles to workers "slightly dumber than an ox" (Taylor, 1911).

The Taylorists' views were eventually undermined by some influential experiments conducted at a Western Electric facility near Chicago in 1930. This work was described by Elton Mayo, an Australian psychologist working in the management school of Harvard University (Roethlisberger & Dickson, 1939). The research team discovered that employees' *attitudes* toward their supervisors and their company had substantial effects on productivity—effects that seemed to be independent of pay level or other working conditions, such as lighting or rest breaks. This was a revolutionary discovery because it implied that attitudes have direct effects on behavior. Previously, managers had believed that only physical or "real" stimuli, such as heat, light, and pay, affect behavior. The accuracy of Mayo's conclusions have been called into question over the years (Landsberger, 1958; Landy, 1988). Nevertheless, at the time the results appeared, they caused an earthquake in the world of business management. A new paradigm was introduced to replace scientific management, and the human relations movement was launched. This movement proposed that many factors beyond pay level contribute to the satisfaction and productivity of workers and that these factors can be identified in the attitudes that workers hold toward various aspects of their work. The implication was that supervisors should be more sensitive to the feelings of workers as a way of improving productivity. The human relations movement gave birth to 60 years of interest in job satisfaction, work motivation, and leadership, areas of study that remain important today.

Human Factors Psychology

Research and application of modern human factors psychology began with World War II. Airplanes, ships, submarines, and weapons had undergone a radical transformation since World War I, resulting in greater attention to developing technical systems that could be used effectively by humans. Of particular concern was the fact that far more accidents involving aircraft occurred than had ever been experienced in World War I. This situation was due, in

large part, to the fact that the military aircraft had become much more complex. In World War I, plane cockpits had a few primitive instruments indicating speed, altitude, and engine characteristics. Bombs were dropped by leaning out of the open cockpit and dropping a missile onto the target. In the two decades separating the wars, technology had advanced rapidly. The cockpit had become a dazzling array of gauges, controls, lights, and arrows. Worse yet, each type of airplane had a *different* configuration of controls and gauges. Bomber pilots were reaching for flap controls where they had been on the last plane they flew but accidentally activating landing gear and vice versa, resulting in fatal crashes. Human error, rather than equipment failure, seemed to play the major role in most such accidents. The simple standardization of the cockpits of the various airplanes drastically reduced these accidents. Gauges and controls were placed in the same spot in every aircraft, and unique knobs were assigned to various controls. Modern

Taylor's scientific management approach was popular with early 20th-century industrialists, who applied it to the factory system.

Human factors psychology plays an important role in the design of complex high-tech equipment, such as airplane control panels, to help reduce the risk of accidents.

human factors psychology was born out of this sort of need to design the best and safest combination of human and machine. Much of the complex equipment used today, particularly in high-technology arenas such as aviation, nuclear power, and computers, shows the influence of the human factors specialist.

In the next three sections of this appendix, we will consider each of the facets of I/O psychology in greater detail. Because of the breadth and complexity of I/O psychology, we will consider a representative sample of I/O issues rather than a comprehensive listing of those issues. In the final section, we will reconsider how the three facets of I/O psychology are bound tightly together in a sociotechnical system.

Personnel Psychology

Every three or four years, the New York City Police Department (NYPD) announces that it would like to hire new police officers. Over 50,000 people usually apply for the positions. About 2000 applicants will eventually be appointed to the Police Academy. How does the city decide *which* 2000 to appoint? By administering a series of tests that determine the mental and physical ability and emotional stability of the applicants. This is an example of personnel selection on its broadest scale.

Consider another example. A new mountain bike manufacturer decides to hire someone to design and maintain a website. The company has never had a website before. The company asks applicants to create a sample website, with the intent of hiring the person who develops the most attractive and effective site. This is an example of personnel selection on its narrowest scale.

An I/O psychologist working for either the NYPD or the mountain bike company would go about the development of the selection processes in the same general way. The first step is determining the most important duties of the job in question. The second step is to list the human attributes (skills, abilities, knowledge, experience, and personality characteristics) that will be necessary for successful completion of those important duties. The third step is to develop a way of assessing or measuring those attributes in applicants. The final task is to decide who will get job offers based on the results of those assessments. Let's look at this process in closer detail.

Job Analysis

The first step of determining the most important duties of the job is accomplished through what is known as a job analysis. *Job analysis* is a method for breaking a job into its constituent parts. It is a way to identify the most important parts of the job description—the requirements that are of primary interest to the employer. To use the job of police officer as an example, it is true that police officers give directions to lost motorists and pedestrians, fill in their log books on a regular basis, and put fuel in their patrol cars during their work shifts. But these are not the *central* or defining responsibilities of the police officer. The central responsibilities include enforcing traffic safety regulations, responding to calls for help from citizens and fellow officers, and apprehending individuals suspected of breaking laws.

A job analysis is a way of separating the less important aspects of a job (such as telling tourists how to find the Statue of Liberty) from the central aspects (such as intervening in a mugging). Once the task of identifying the truly important aspects of the job has been accomplished, the next step is to determine the knowledge, skills, abilities, or other personal characteristics necessary for successful completion of those tasks. When these key attributes have been identified, an appropriate test can be selected or developed. For the police officer, these attributes include memory and reasoning, communication skills, conflict resolutions skills, empathy, and physical abilities such as coordination and strength, to mention just a few.

Test Administration and Interviewing

The next step in personnel selection is assessing whether job candidates have the attributes required for the job. Standardized tests are used extensively in this phase. Employers can purchase tests from commercial test publishers or can develop special tests to meet their own needs. For example, the NYPD has its own 100-item multiple-choice test of mental abilities and uses a commercially published test of personality in its selection of new police officers.

Once a suitable test has been found or developed, the next step is to administer it to candidates and decide which of them has the greatest probability of being successful on the job. To continue with the police example, on a particular Saturday, NYPD will use several hundred public high schools and several thousand test administrators and monitors to assess tens of thousands of candidates. In most instances of employee selection, the prediction is that the higher the test score, the greater the likelihood of job success. Of course, this approach is based on the assumption that the employment test has acceptable reliability and validity. That is, the test must be a reasonably consistent measuring device, and there must be evidence that it really measures what it was designed to measure. As you might guess, employers are always looking for ways to improve their employee selection procedures. In recent years, personality testing has attracted increased interest as a means to enhance the hiring process. In part, this trend is the result of the popularity of the five-factor model of personality (see Chapter 12) as well as the appearance of standardized tests to measure the Big Five personality traits, such as the NEO Personality Inventory (Costa & McCrae, 1992).

Many organizations are beginning to consider the use of credit checks and integrity tests as part of the selection process. *Integrity tests* are standardized measures intended to predict respondents' honesty. From the perspective of employers, these sources of data may help them understand who among their applicants is most reliable and trustworthy. However, as with any assessment used for personnel decisions, the data from these tests must be evaluated in regard to the extent to which they provide valid job-related performance information. Unfortunately, studies have raised many doubts about how well integrity tests predict employee theft, rule breaking, and other forms of dishonest behavior (Brown & Cothern, 2002; Horn, Nelson, & Brannick, 2004). Moreover, many prospective employees perceive credit checks and integrity tests to be intrusive, since they can reveal private information about the applicant. The role of an I/O psychologist in such situations is to weigh the needs of the organization against those of the applicant. Every effort must be made to collect data that are directly relevant to the job for which applicants are applying (Turner et al., 2001).

At some point, it is important for the personnel psychologist to verify that the tests developed to identify the best job candidates are successful in doing so. Using a psychological test to hire people is analogous to testing a hypothesis in research (see Chapter 2). In this case, the hypothesis is that people who score better on the test will perform better on the job than those who score poorly on the test (see Figure M.3). If reliable performance measures are available, a statistical analysis can be used to test this hypothesis precisely. Such an analysis involves computing the correlation between test scores and performance scores (such as supervisory ratings). If the result is *a strong positive correlation* (see Appendix B), this finding supports the "hypothesis" that underlies using the test. This process of demonstrating that a test is a reasonably accurate predictor of job perfor-

mance is known as *validation*. Many other approaches can be used to demonstrate the validity of a test besides this correlational method, but all have the same goal—demonstrating that those who score better on the test will perform better on the job. To return to our police officer example, a validity study might consist of correlating test scores on the entrance examination with subsequent measures of police officer performance, including evaluations of supervisors as well as more objective indicators of

Many jobs, such as those of police officers, involve a diverse array of activities and responsibilities. Personnel psychologists engage in job analysis to determine which responsibilities are crucial to a specific job. These job analyses then influence the employee selection procedures that are developed.

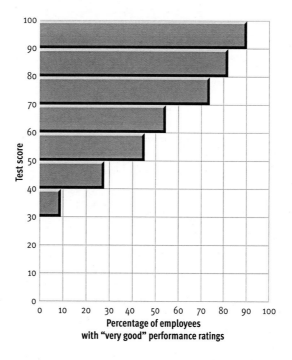

Figure M.3
A hypothetical example of the relationship between tests and job performance. When a standardized test is used to select the most promising job candidates, the implicit hypothesis is that higher scores on the test will be associated with better performance on the job. The relationship won't be perfect, but when employers collect data on the link between test scores and job performance, the findings should resemble the hypothetical data shown here. These data would yield a strong positive correlation between test performance and job performance, which is what employers always hope for. (Based on Jewell, 1998)

success, such as arrest-to-conviction ratios and response times to calls for assistance.

Although standardized mental ability and personality tests are commonly used in personnel selection, the most widely used device remains the interview. There are two types of interviews: unstructured and structured. *Unstructured interviews* consist of nonstandardized questions with no clear right or wrong answers and no method for assigning a score to an applicant. Although many employers rely heavily on this type of interview, research suggests that it is highly subjective and far from optimal. *Structured interviews* are more like standardized tests. The same questions or question types are asked of all candidates and are based on attributes or experiences necessary for success on the job in question; there are clear guidelines for judging the adequacy of answers, and the scores assigned to an applicant have known relationships to the attribute being measured. Structured interviews can be constructed to be reliable and valid (McDaniel et al., 1994). In addition, they hold the promise of supplying useful information *not* supplied by other forms of testing (about characteristics such as oral comprehension, listening skills, and motivation).

Equal Employment Opportunity and Testing

The final step in personnel selection is to decide which candidates will get job offers. It will come as no surprise to you that employment tests and hiring procedures are often the subject of debate and controversy. Mental ability tests have been variously portrayed as instruments of discrimination or as fair and objective ways to reduce discriminatory practices. The arguments often center on the differential test performance of white and minority applicants, whether the applications are for college, graduate school, police departments, or mountain bike companies. It is not uncommon for minority applicants, on average, to score more poorly on standardized tests than white applicants, on average. The same type of controversy has appeared with respect to differential test performance of men and women on physical ability tests, of older and younger individuals on mental ability and physical ability tests, and of applicants with and without disabilities on both mental and physical ability tests.

In the United States, the Equal Employment Opportunity Commission and the Department of Justice are responsible for assuring that tests are fair to all applicants, regardless of race, religion, gender,

age, or disability. This rather simple goal has led to a complex tangle of legal, administrative, and philosophical disputes—a tangle that has resulted not just from the need to demonstrate that a test is "fair" to all applicants but also from an attempt to correct inequities in past hiring practices. In the past, this correction often involved a requirement that hiring decisions conform to a certain numerical goal until an imbalance (such as too few women in a workforce) has been eliminated. Thus, the notion of "hiring quotas" was introduced. Although strict hiring quotas were made illegal by the Civil Rights Act of 1991, many companies still strive to increase the diversity of their workforce.

This situation has created a good deal of debate among representatives of the federal government, employers, and personnel psychologists. Much of this debate has centered on the validity of the tests used in hiring decisions. The debate often occurs in the context of legal suits brought against employers by unsuccessful applicants, who typically claim that the tests disproportionately favor majority applicants and work to the disadvantage of minority or female applicants (often referred to in legal jargon as "adverse impact"). As a result, the federal courts have become heavily involved in the evaluation of the technical merits of tests and have issued rulings regarding what can and cannot be done in making hiring decisions. It is unlikely that the basic debate will change in the next decade. Many unsuccessful job applicants will continue to believe that the tests used are unfair. Many employers and personnel psychologists will continue to believe that the tests are valid and that their use is warranted. In addition, many politicians will continue to use the issue to their advantage. The modern personnel psychologist needs to cut through the ideological and political smoke and continue to develop and administer good tests. By applying what they know, they can help applicants, employers, and society as a whole.

As an example, consider the way police entry testing used to be done and how it is practiced today. In the 1980s, applicants were selected *solely* on the basis of general intelligence. Although intelligence is valuable in police work, other attributes are also highly desirable, including physical abilities, communication skills, and personality characteristics. Today, applicants are given a battery of tests in which high scores on one attribute (such as communication skills) can compensate for less than stellar scores on another attribute (such as physical abilities). When hiring decisions are based on *several* important attributes, it is likely that ethnic minority applicants will fare considerably better. I/O psychologists have been at the forefront of attempts to create selection systems that are fair to all applicants.

New Trends and Challenges

Other areas often addressed by the personnel psychologist include *training and education* and *performance assessment* of current employees. In recent years, the emphasis has shifted from the act of "training" someone to the development of a "learning" environment in which the employee seeks out job and career information and the employer provides user-friendly resources and environments to ensure effective learning. The challenge in performance assessment is to construct a system (usually a series of rating scales) that is easy to use, fair and unbiased, and capable of providing information to the employee for skill development.

Under normal conditions the process of conducting a job analysis and developing valid and fair selection instruments is a complicated and lengthy endeavor. However, at times demanding circumstances can create increased pressure to engage in this work in a rapid, expeditious manner. In fact, at times it is even a matter of national security. After the terrorist attacks on the United States on September 11, 2001, the importance of personnel psychology took on new meaning. In response to these attacks, the Department of Homeland Security (DHS) was created and I/O psychologists who had previously worked in many separate agencies became part of a new team. A recent interview of I/O psychologists working in the DHS provided many details about their urgent, challenging, and crucial work (McFarland, 2005). Like other I/O psychologists, these individuals engage in personnel psychology research that is applied to the selection, development, and assessment of workers who need to be effective in their jobs. The federalization of airport screeners in 429 airports in the U.S. gave I/O psychologists working in the DHS only a few months to assess, select, and hire over 55,000 federal airport screeners. These psychologists accomplished this monumental task while executing their other responsibilities, which include engaging in ongoing evaluation and quality assurance, training development and deployment, organizational assessment surveys, and leadership development. An emerging responsibility for these psychologists is studying the DHS workforce's response to the increasingly advanced technology that is used within the agency and ensuring that their selection systems, training programs, and work environments are revised to keep

© 2005 AP Images/Misha Japaridze

pace with these advances (McFarland, 2005). The mission-critical work of DHS psychologists provides another example of how each of the three branches of I/O psychology are intimately interrelated.

Organizational Psychology

Most people do not work alone. They work with colleagues, subordinates, and supervisors, often on project teams. As we saw earlier, *organizational psychology* is concerned with the human relations aspects of work. Organizational psychologists are interested in how organizational factors influence workers' social and emotional functioning. In this section, we'll discuss several topics that have been of special interest to organizational psychologists: work motivation, job satisfaction, teams, leadership, and organizational culture.

Work Motivation

Why do some people spend their free time in athletic activities while others choose to read books or go to concerts? Why do some people approach tasks enthusiastically while others are more passive or uninterested? Over the years, many theories have been proposed to account for these differences in motivation.

As you might expect, employers and I/O psychologists have a particular interest in motivational principles as they apply in the work setting. Why do some

The task of improving airport screening of passengers and their baggage illustrates how problems in the workplace are often multifaceted. The federalization of airport screeners was a massive, complicated personnel psychology project that had to be accomplished with remarkable swiftness.

employees accept the goals of the organization and their supervisor while others reject those goals? Why do some employees work hard while others appear lazy and uncooperative? The answers to these questions might make the difference between survival and failure for a business. There is no one "correct" theory of motivation. Instead, several valuable theories contribute to our understanding. Let's look at some theories that have been used by I/O psychologists over the last few decades to understand work behavior.

The two most popular theories of work motivation in the 1960s were Frederick Herzberg's (1966) *job enrichment theory* and the application of B. F. Skinner's (1969) *reinforcement theory* to work settings. Herzberg proposed that the nature of the work is motivating in and of itself, aside from any rewards. His prescription for increasing the motivation of a worker is to enrich the job by increasing the worker's responsibilities and the job's challenges. He conceded that external rewards such as money and praise are also necessary to attract and keep a worker, but ultimately, he proposed that motivation depends on whether the job is interesting. The implications of Skinner's reinforcement theory are just the opposite. Reinforcement theory postulates that jobs acquire interest *only* through their association with extrinsic or external rewards. Attempts to motivate workers are based on ensuring that desired work behavior is followed by meaningful rewards.

Both of these theories have value. Consider reinforcement theory. There can be no doubt that associating certain rewards with work behavior can result in an increased probability that this behavior will occur again. If you get $20 each time you take a phone order for a telemarketing firm, you will probably stay on the phone for many hours a day. The problem is that not all work behaviors are as simple and discrete as taking a phone order. How would one apply contingent rewards to a police officer, a teacher, or a nuclear power plant control operator? Would everyone be equally motivated by money? Problems arise with Herzberg's job enrichment theory as well. It seems that some people don't *want* enriched jobs and that some jobs *can't be* enriched without massive, expensive, and time-consuming work redesign. Each theory has its strengths, but neither approach works in all situations.

Two additional theories of work motivation that have attracted interest are *expectancy theory* and *self-efficacy theory.* Expectancy theory (Porter & Lawler, 1968; Vroom, 1964) has a cognitive slant. It is based on the premise that people operate based on a prediction of what rewards they will receive for certain

work behaviors. Unlike reinforcement theory, which assumes that associations are stamped in automatically, expectancy theory asserts that individuals make mental calculations about what is being asked of them and the probability of their receiving something they desire for specified performance, then take action based on these estimates. Albert Bandura's (1995) self-efficacy theory proposes that individuals gradually develop confidence (or lack of confidence) about their ability to overcome obstacles and successfully complete difficult tasks. This confidence can be diminished or enhanced by their actual work experiences.

Today, the concept of self-efficacy is often considered within broader models of *self-regulation,* which refers to people's capacity to direct, control, and alter their behavior. Self-regulation includes making and executing plans, initiating and inhibiting behaviors, taking responsibility, and exhibiting self-discipline. Self-regulation is important to many aspects of employee behavior, including "fitting in" with co-workers. Winning acceptance from colleagues requires good social skills, as one must have the ability to form relationships, build a positive reputation, and behave in ways that are deemed acceptable. To succeed in these tasks, individuals must often be able to modify their behavior to conform to the ideals regarded as acceptable in their groups (Baumeister et al., 2005).

Expectancy, self-efficacy, and self-regulation theory are all highly regarded models that have been applied with some success in work settings. Expectancy theory is implemented by making sure that workers have a clear understanding of the likelihood that successful performance will be followed by a desired reward. Self-efficacy theory has been applied in the workplace by selecting workers with high self-efficacy and then creating conditions that maintain and enhance workers' feelings of competence. Self-regulation theory is important as it suggests why some individuals are self-starters or why some are better able than others to work in the teams that modern companies often rely on today.

Another motivational theory that has received considerable attention is *goal-setting theory* (Locke, 1968, 1970). This theory is potent in its simplicity. It proposes that the best way to increase effort is to set specific, challenging goals for a worker. You will recognize the same principle at work in athletic training. For example, if you want to run a sub-40 minute 10K, you need to set challenging training goals (such as running at least one 6-minute mile in every 5-mile run, and so forth). According to goal-setting theory, even if you do not reach your goal, you will perform better and work harder than if you had not set specific goals.

Job Satisfaction

Closely associated with work motivation is *job satisfaction*. Recently, the term "quality of working life" has been used as a synonym for job satisfaction. Presumably, people want to gain satisfaction from their work and to avoid dissatisfaction. What factors lead to job satisfaction and what are its consequences?

More research has been done on these topics than almost any subject in I/O psychology. Thousands of studies have led to the basic finding that the primary sources of job satisfaction are interesting and challenging work, pleasant co-workers, adequate pay and other financial benefits, opportunities for advancement, effective and supportive supervisors, and acceptable company policies. In contrast, job dissatisfaction results from the absence of these characteristics. Many of us have had what we called "boring" jobs. This is the other side of the satisfaction coin. For a fascinating glimpse at the most unsatisfying jobs that one might have, read the entertaining and illuminating books of Barbara Garson (1988, 1994), which describe boring jobs and how people cope with them.

Most organizations take the emotional temperature of their employees by periodically administering questionnaires. These questionnaires typically ask workers to rate their levels of satisfaction on the basic factors we've listed. Organizations go to the trouble of gathering this information because they believe that job satisfaction is related to employee absenteeism, turnover, and productivity. For instance, most managers believe that dissatisfied employees are likely to take excessive sick leave or to seek employment elsewhere. Because absenteeism and turnover are costly, employers try to reduce them by increasing job satisfaction. Most managers also believe that job satisfaction leads to increased productivity. That assumption is more questionable. Several decades of research have failed to demonstrate that satisfaction causes productivity. Some research, however, does indicate that *productivity causes satisfaction* (Locke, 1976). In other words, it appears that workers who are able to accomplish work goals and overcome work-related challenges are happier than those who do not have such experiences.

What are the implications of the research findings on job satisfaction? First, if a company wants a stable workforce, it should try to minimize employee dissatisfaction with key job factors (pay, opportunities for advancement, and so on). The concerned employer can make necessary adjustments based on the analysis of work-related attitude questionnaires distributed on a regular basis. In addition, an employer that wants high productivity and happy employees should ensure that they have the necessary resources (equipment and technical support) and should solve any problems that arise on the job. In short, the employer's job is to remove obstacles to success.

There are, of course, other reasons for fostering job satisfaction beyond boosting productivity and reducing absenteeism. There is no reason that people should not derive happiness from their work, just as there is no reason that they should not derive happiness from other activities. Conversely, evidence suggests that dissatisfying and stressful work environments can lead to physical and psychological damage (Karasek & Theorell, 1990; Landy, Quick, & Kasl, 1994). Any environment in which people spend half or more of their waking hours is bound to have the potential for affecting psychological well-being. Organizational psychologists look for ways to make these effects more positive.

Up to this point, we have been considering the individual as a social-emotional island in the larger organization in which he or she works. Let's expand that picture a bit. Workers go about their business in a number of social contexts. For example, in most jobs the individual works most closely with a group of others, often called a *team*. Furthermore, the team works within a psychological environment created by the person supervising it, commonly referred to as the *leader*. Finally we have the "personality" of the organization itself, which is often referred to as the *culture* of the organization. Each of these variables—the team, the leader, and the organizational culture—can influence workers' motivation and satisfaction. Let's briefly consider each of these variables.

Work Teams

Until 20 years ago, the concept of a work team was an unusual one for companies in the United States. Although work teams were used extensively by European companies (such as Volvo in Sweden), they were the exception in North America. The downsizing epidemic of the 1980s changed that. American companies decided to radically reduce their workforces. This move usually meant eliminating many mid-level management positions. Fewer people were expected to do more work with less supervision. As a result, teams began to emerge as the new paradigm for effective organizations. Other forces were at work as well. Using loosely managed teams had the effect

© Yellow Dog Productions/The Image Bank/Getty Images

of increasing accountability and ownership at increasingly lower levels of the organization. This change improved both work motivation and job satisfaction (through participative goal setting and job enrichment). Since the shift toward team work, I/O psychologists have devoted a good deal of effort to understanding team formation processes, the advantages of teams, and the optimal conditions for team functioning (Guzzo & Dickson, 1996).

Additionally, with the emergence of the Internet, I/O psychologists are asked more and more frequently to help facilitate the effective operation of *virtual teams.* Virtual teams are very much like traditional work teams in that all members work on the same project. The main difference is that these members are working from various locations. In some cases they may be separated by thousands of miles and many time zones. Because of the globalization of commerce, the use of virtual teams is increasing. While technological advances have made virtual teams a valuable and convenient option, several possible disadvantages must also be considered. Virtual teams can experience problems resulting from time differences, local/cultural differences, and inadequate face-to-face interactions. Moreover, they may lead to excessive reliance on technology, which can be a risk factor in striving to complete a project (Gibson & Cohen, 2003). Thus, I/O psychologists who work this arena must study the most effective ways virtual teams can be implemented and managed.

Leadership

A more traditional area of interest for organizational psychologists has been the study of *leadership.* Are leaders born or made? Based on decades of research, the answer appears to be a little of both. In recent years, I/O psychologists have been particularly interested in *transformational* and *charismatic* leadership. The term "transformational" is used because *change and adaptation to change* are emerging as the hallmarks of the successful modern company. The transformational leader is one who has a compelling vision of what he or she wants to accomplish and transforms followers' beliefs, values, and needs (Bass, 1990, 1995). Transformational leaders seek to realize their goals by making workers or followers more aware of the importance of what they are doing, persuading them to put the good of the organization or team ahead of their own self-interest, and appealing to their achievement and mastery needs (Hughes, Ginnett, & Curphy, 1996). Charismatic leadership depends more on the sheer force of a leader's personality, as opposed to the appeal of the leader's vision. Charismatic leaders elicit trust in others, are willing to take personal risks, and are sensitive to others' needs (Conger & Kanungo, 1994). Charismatic leaders are able to get followers to suspend disbelief and to accept challenges that they would ordinarily reject.

A more recent topic in this area is the concept of *emancipatory leadership* described by Corson (2000). Emancipatory leadership's guiding principle is that leadership should reflect the constituency it serves. Emancipatory leaders make sure that those affected by leadership's decision making play a role in those decisions and are responsible for their implementation. The power and presence of leaders are minimized while democracy and inclusion are maximized. Emancipatory leaders understand their own boundaries and biases. They strive to empower their employees rather than to rule them. Moreover, they resist stereotypes and limits that impede the progress of members of minority groups. This leadership model has been proposed to be ideal in situations where an organization is undergoing change related to increasing diversity.

Another emerging line of research suggests that leaders' *emotional intelligence* has a considerable impact on their leadership effectiveness. According to Jennifer George (2000), emotional intelligence—the ability to understand and manage moods in oneself and others—contributes to effective leadership in organizations. For example, Zhou and George (2003) review research suggesting that the emotional intelligence of leaders plays a critical role in fostering creativity in workers. Emotionally intelligent leaders may help team members who have recently experienced a work-related disappointment to productively use their emotions to analyze the situation and make necessary changes. George believes that emotional intelligence is a talent that anyone can develop through self-reflection, reading, mentoring, and coaching. In any event, as organizations continue to evolve and change, leadership will remain a critical area of interest for organizational psychologists as well as for society overall (Hogan & Kaiser, 2005).

Organizational Culture and Climate

Every organization, no matter how small or large, has a "personality." In simple terms, it is this personality and the value system of the organization that is referred to as *culture* in organizational psychology jargon (Denison, 1996). The culture of the organization is manifested in its rituals, language, traditions, symbols, and unwritten rules. I/O psychologists are primarily interested in how *employees* (as opposed to clients or customers) experience organizational culture. Employees' perceptions of their organizational culture can create variations in workplace climate. *Climate* consists of shared perceptions among workers about specific aspects of the workplace environment that can affect workers' behavior and social interactions. For example, I/O psychologists might be interested in an organization's "climate for diversity," its "climate for service," its "climate for innovation and creativity," or its "climate for safety." An organization's culture and climate can have a dramatic impact on its effectiveness and productivity.

Different companies cultivate different organizational cultures. For example, the culture of a Silicon Valley Internet company might hinge on innovation. The culture of a fast food delivery service like Domino's Pizza tends to be dominated by—what else—time urgency. In regard to organizational culture, the chief issue for I/O psychologists is to understand how this culture is developed, maintained, and changed and the resulting climate for employees. For example, in the late 1970s and early 1980s, a number of nuclear power plant mishaps occurred, including those at Three Mile Island and Chernobyl. Controversies swirled regarding the safety of the entire global nuclear power industry. From those debates, a new culture emerged that placed a much greater emphasis on safety. Virtually every organization that produces goods and services that could affect public safety at the broadest level (such as power plants, aircraft manufacturers, and companies that produce toxic waste byproducts) now attempts to impress on workers the need to commit to a culture that values safety. The challenge for the I/O psychologist is how to facilitate the development of this culture through the implementation of human resource systems (such as selection, performance appraisal, and promotion programs). The frequent monitoring of employees' attitudes regarding safety through annual surveys helps employers learn the extent to which

The organizational culture of a company can have an enormous impact on employee productivity and satisfaction. The importance of organizational culture often surfaces when corporate mergers occur (such as the merger between US Airways and America West Airlines, which generated the protest pictured here).

the importance of safety has been assimilated by employees. Zohar and Luria's (2005) research on almost 4,000 production workers in 401 different work groups in manufacturing plants suggests that safety climates should be assessed regularly at various levels within organizations.

Balancing Work and Other Spheres of Life

Another emerging trend in organizational psychology is increased interest in how employees balance work obligations and their personal lives. Research in this area often focuses on the design and evaluation of programs intended to reduce stress at work. Ultimately, the goal is to develop programs that enhance employees' work life and their family life.

A recent review of the work-family literature (Eby et al., 2005) revealed that this research has focused on nine topics: (1) work-family conflict, (2) work role stress, (3) work-family assistance, (4) work schedules, (5) job-related relocation, (6) career and job-related outcomes, (7) gender and the relationship between work and family domains, (8) the challenges of dual-earner couples, and (9) relationships among life domains. Although the work-family interface has traditionally fallen within the realm of organizational psychology, it is also relevant to other branches of I/O psychology. For example, personnel psychologists may be interested in how family obligations tend to affect workers' performance, while human factors psychologists may be interested in how different work schedules correlate with workers' productivity and their quality of life outside work. For instance, Fritz and Sonnentag (2005) examined the impact of weekend downtime on health and job performance. They found that time off from work, the extent of work-related hassles, and the level of nonwork stress are significant correlates of subsequent work-week performance, as well as of employee health.

Human Factors Psychology

Whenever you get into an unfamiliar rental car and begin to search for the controls for the lights and the windshield wipers, you are dealing with a human factors issue. When you turn the right handle on a faucet in a hotel room and get a glass of hot water instead of a glass of cold water, you are dealing with a human factors issue. In fact, human factors psychology has been referred to facetiously as "knobs and dials" psychology (Carter, 1978) because early in its development the field concentrated on devising the most effective ways of displaying information (the best designs for dials and gauges) and of taking actions (the best designs for knobs and faucet handles). This research dealt with the best placement of knobs and dials, the arrangement associated with the fewest performance errors, and so forth. Human factors specialists were also referred to as *human engineering psychologists,* because they designed environments and equipment to match the capabilities and limitations of human operators. They took both human attributes and engineering principles into account.

Human factors specialists seek to understand the human-machine relationship in various environments. Although such psychologists might be involved in designing home environments, health care environments, educational environments, and consumer products, we will concentrate on the application of human factors principles to the work environment. The basic challenge in human engineering efforts is depicted in Figure M.4.

As you can see, the human-machine system has several components. An important component is *in-formation* in the environment. That information is *displayed* to the human being through devices such as dials, meters, computer screens, and printouts. In your car, the gas gauge is a display that provides important information, as are the speedometer, the odometer, and the oil and temperature lights. The fact that you must interpret and possibly use this information creates a design challenge. How can this information be *best* displayed? Systems specialists refer to this "confrontation" of the individual and the information as an "interface" problem and strive to make the interface as effective as possible. As Figure M.4 illustrates, the individual must *interpret the information in the display* and choose a course of action (or inaction) based on that information. Doing so creates a second interface, between the individual and the device that modifies or has an influence on the system.

Let's take the simple example of a machine operator adjusting the speed of a machine. The actual speed of the machine is presented in a digital readout on the face of the machine. This is the *display* part of the system. If the speed is too fast or too slow, it can be adjusted with a series of keyboard buttons on the machine console. This is the *control* part of the system. Thus, the operator looks at the digital display for information, keys in a series of commands that speed up or slow down the machine, and then reexamines the display to make sure that the target speed has been achieved. If the speed is still too fast or too slow, or if the adjustment has been too extreme, the operator keys in new and more refined information and keeps checking the digital display until the desired speed has been achieved. This is a description of a simple combination of human, display, and control. A less elegant but equally relevant example is the system that includes the driver of an automobile, the speedometer, the cruise control system, and the gas pedal. The driver wants to maintain a constant speed compatible with the speed limit posted for that highway. The driver activates the cruise, presses the gas pedal down until the desired speed registers on the speedometer, presses the "set" button on the cruise control, and watches to see whether the speedometer settles in at the desired speed. The speed of the car may be slightly faster or slower than the driver desired, so another round of actions may be needed to achieve the final desired speed. This is an excellent example of the interface between a machine and an operator, complete with a feedback loop.

Most of the early human factors research was geared toward achieving satisfactory interfaces between human and display and human and control. For example, it was discovered that many of the air-

Interpretation

Information indicator (output)

Operator

Information reception (input)

Control action (output)

Control mechanism (input)

Machine

plane accidents that occurred in World War II were caused by either faulty displays or faulty controls. Faulty displays included dials that were placed outside of the pilot's line of vision or that presented information in a way that was difficult to interpret. Many of the control problems came from confusion of one control with another. For example, the knobs that activated the flaps were identical in shape to those that activated the landing gear. As a result, many pilots who meant to retract the landing gear shortly after takeoff actually engaged the flaps, causing a crash. The solution to this problem turned out to be relatively simple. Each knob was given a distinctive shape that conveyed its particular function. Thus, the knob that controlled the landing gear was shaped like a wheel, whereas the knob that controlled flaps was actually shaped like a flap. Meanwhile, dials were arranged more centrally so that they were easier to see and were given a standard location in all planes.

Similar principles of human engineering are applied today in many areas of technology. As an example, the design of control rooms for nuclear power plants has been influenced greatly by human factors psychology. Consider the control panel shown in the photos on the right. Just drawing lines and borders and providing labels for clusters of controls and displays helps make the information-processing task easier. The simple act of grouping similar information sources can reduce the probability of errors.

Consider the consequences of a situation in which information was *not* presented efficiently. At the Dallas–Fort Worth Airport, American Airlines flies out of several terminals. This means that you cannot simply pick the correct terminal for your departing flight by knowing you will fly American. The Airport Authority decided to display individual flight information on a large electronic billboard at the ramp for each terminal. So if you planned to take an American Airlines flight to Denver, you needed to scan that billboard while steering your car through dense traffic, at speeds often exceeding 40 miles per hour. To make matters worse, there could be *several* flights on American to Denver, each leaving at a different time from a different terminal. So you would need to look not only for the Denver flight but for the *correct* Denver flight. As you might expect, a serious accident was caused by a motorist looking for the correct American Airlines flight while trying to navigate through a maze of similarly confused drivers. As a result of a successful lawsuit filed by the injured driver, the information about flights has now been moved to the entrance to the airport where drivers must stop at a toll booth to obtain a parking ticket. To learn more about the importance of human factors

to the design of both simple and complex equipment that people use daily, look for Don Norman's *The Psychology of Everyday Things* (1988) and *The Design of Everyday Things* (2002) and visit www. baddesigns.com.

Human factors specialists follow a number of principles in designing equipment and environments. One central principle is *response stereotype*, which is people's tendency to expect that a control will work in a particular way. Most people believe that when they want to open a door, they should turn the knob clockwise or push the handle down. When they have to turn the doorknob counterclockwise or pull the handle up, they become confused and act less efficiently. Therefore, one of the basic design principles is to see how people will carry out

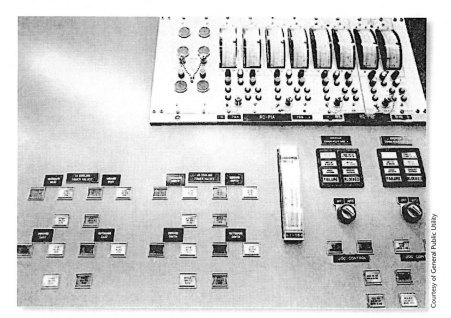

Courtesy of General Public Utility

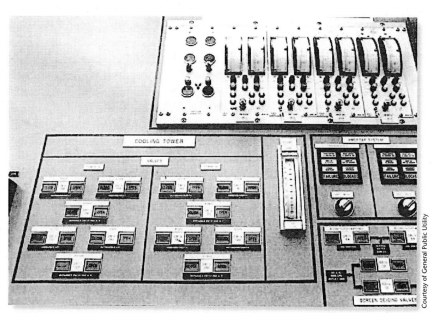

Courtesy of General Public Utility

Visual displays can often be enhanced to help workers find information more quickly. The top photo shows a section of a display panel from a nuclear power plant control room before it was redesigned. The bottom picture shows how this display panel was modified to make it easier for operators to locate needed information quickly.

Figure M.5
Guidelines for reducing stress in the workplace. Work stress is an important matter that has been the subject of a great deal of research. The guidelines shown here are based on a review article by Sauter, Murphy, and Hurrell (1990), as summarized by Jewell (1998). The guidelines draw on research from all three domains of I/O psychology (personnel, organizational, and human factors psychology), showing once again that the three areas are highly interdependent.

an action when left to themselves. If they show a clear preference (or response stereotype), the operator actions should be designed to take advantage of that preference. If people show no clear preference, other principles of design can be used.

Human factors specialists face many other challenges in today's work environment. One such challenge is robotics at the work site. Specialists must design controls for robots to be compatible with the response tendencies of those who will command or operate them. Similarly, engineers need to determine the best interface for remote computer-controlled devices used by operators in nuclear power plants, chemical plants, and similar facilities who cannot "see" what they are doing.

Another challenge for human factors specialists is finding ways to reduce work-related stress. Some work designs can lead to greater stress than others. Research suggests that workers' stress level depends on three key factors: how demanding the job is, how much decision control one has, and how much social support one has in the work setting (Karasek & Theorell, 1990). To illustrate how changes in the workplace may or may not be stressful, consider how the introduction of a computer can turn out to be a blessing or a curse. If the computer is fast and failure-free, it can be a real enhancement. But if it is slow in responding or difficult to control through software, it can create frustrations. Similarly, a system in which either too much or too little information is presented to the operator can create stress, leading to both health-related problems and performance errors. No

one wants to be a passenger in a plane flown by a pilot under stress or to live in the vicinity of a nuclear power plant where the control room operators feel overwhelmed. The guiding principle in work design is to prevent the demands of a job from exceeding the resources or capacities of the person who holds that job. Figure M.5 summarizes some guidelines derived from research in all three domains of I/O psychology that can help reduce stress in the workplace (Sauter, Murphy, & Hurrell, 1990).

Advancing technology will continue to make human factors research important in many sectors of the economy. For example, human factors issues are at the forefront of the growing use of distance education in colleges and universities. How do distance learning programs compare to traditional classrooms in terms of learning outcomes? Are some distance learning formats, such as those that allow for interaction between the teacher and audience, more effective than others in promoting learning? The biomedical fields also are presenting all sorts of new challenges for human factors experts. Have you seen the commercial in which a doctor in one part of the world is guiding the surgery that another doctor is performing elsewhere? Human factors psychologists may ask, are there ways to enhance the technology used by the medical profession to convey information more accurately and efficiently, with minimal mistakes?

A Systems Approach to Work Safety: Putting It All Together

Workplace safety can serve as an example of the interrelation among personnel psychology, organizational psychology, and human factors psychology. Consider the problem of pizza delivery drivers who have excessive accidents when trying to deliver pizzas in under 30 minutes. How could accidents be reduced? Working from a personnel psychology perspective, one approach would be to determine whether particular individuals seem to have more accidents than others. If that is the case, experts could examine the basic abilities of these people and institute either a training or a selection program to reduce the accident rate. We know, for example, that younger drivers and older drivers tend to have more accidents than middle-aged drivers. We also know that pizza delivery drivers tend to be young (and newly licensed) drivers. Thus, it would be important to provide a careful training and monitoring program to make sure that the drivers know and obey the rules of the road.

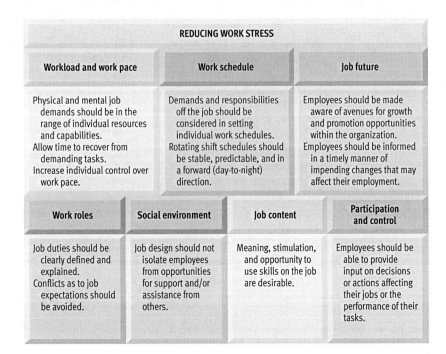

REDUCING WORK STRESS		
Workload and work pace	**Work schedule**	**Job future**
Physical and mental job demands should be in the range of individual resources and capabilities. Allow time to recover from demanding tasks. Increase individual control over work pace.	Demands and responsibilities off the job should be considered in setting individual work schedules. Rotating shift schedules should be stable, predictable, and in a forward (day-to-night) direction.	Employees should be made aware of avenues for growth and promotion opportunities within the organization. Employees should be informed in a timely manner of impending changes that may affect their employment.
Work roles	**Social environment**	**Job content**	**Participation and control**
Job duties should be clearly defined and explained. Conflicts as to job expectations should be avoided.	Job design should not isolate employees from opportunities for support and/or assistance from others.	Meaning, stimulation, and opportunity to use skills on the job are desirable.	Employees should be able to provide input on decisions or actions affecting their jobs or the performance of their tasks.

An organizational psychologist might approach the problem by assuming that the drivers are being strongly influenced by a speed culture. As an example, the founder of Domino's Pizza, Tom Monaghan, wrote a book and gave motivational speeches preaching that on-time delivery was a matter of life and death for the Domino's manager (Monaghan & Anderson, 1986). Similarly, drivers were expected to call out times when they left the store and returned to the store so that fellow workers would know whether they had made an on-time delivery. This approach could be seen as the antithesis of the safety culture described earlier.

Alternatively, it might be just as effective to work from a human factors perspective and prevent a driver from delivering more than one pizza every 30 minutes. Thus, speeding to and from the store would be largely useless. Changing the nature of the task would enhance safe deliveries. A "new" and safer job would have been designed. The safest system would probably be achieved by using all three approaches rather than just one. In the pizza delivery example, this approach would include a careful selection and training program, a work environment that did not glorify speed and time urgency, and a set of tasks optimally arranged for safe and efficient deliveries.

Bandura, A. (1995). Exercise of personal and collective efficacy in changing societies. In A. Bandura (Ed.), *Self-efficacy in changing societies.* New York: Cambridge University Press.

Bass, B. M. (1990). *Bass and Stogdill's handbook of leadership: Theory research, and managerial applications.* New York: Free Press.

Bass, B. M. (1995). Theory of transformational leadership redux. *Leadership Quarterly, 6.*

Baumeister, R. F., DeWall, N. C., Ciarocco, N. J., & Twenge, J. M. (2005). Social exclusion impairs self-regulation. *Journal of Personality and Social Psychology, 88,* 589–604.

Burtt, H. E. (1929). *Psychology and industrial efficiency.* New York: Appleton.

Carter, D. (1978). Knobology underwater. *Human Factors, 20,* 641–647.

Conger, J., & Kanungo, R. N. (1994). Charismatic leadership in organizations: Perceived behavioral attributes and their measurement. *Journal of Organizational Behavior, 15,* 439–452.

Corson, D. (2000). Emancipatory leadership. *International Journal of Leadership in Education, 3*(2), 93–120.

Costa, P. T., Jr., & McCrae, R. R. (1992). *Revised NEO Personality Inventory: NEO PI and NEO Five-Factor Inventory* (Professional Manual). Odessa, FL: Psychological Assessment Resources.

Eby, L. T., Casper, W. J., Lockwood, A., Bordeaux, C., & Brinley, A. (2005). Work and family research in IO/OBL: Content analysis and review of the literature (1980–2002). *Journal of Vocational Behavior, 66*(1), 124–197.

Fritz, C., & Sonnentag, S. (2005). Recovery, health, and job performance: Effects of weekend experiences. *Journal of Occupational Health Psychology, 10*(3), 187–199.

Garson, B. (1988). *The electronic sweatshop.* New York: Simon & Schuster.

Garson, B. (1994). *All the livelong day.* New York: Penguin.

George, J. M. (2000). Emotions and leadership: The role of emotional intelligence. *Human Relations, 53,* 1027–1055.

Gibson, C. B., & Cohen, S. G. (2003). *Virtual teams that work: Creating conditions for virtual team effectiveness.* San Francisco: Jossey-Bass.

Guzzo, R. A., & Dickson, M. W. (1996). Teams in organizations: Recent research on performance and effectiveness. *Annual Review of Psychology, 47,* 307–338.

Herzberg, F. (1966). *Work and the nature of man.* Cleveland: World Publishing.

Hogan, R., & Kaiser, R. B. (2005). What we know about leadership. *Review of General Psychology, 9*(2), 169–180.

Horn, J., Nelson, C. E., & Brannick, M. T. (2004). Integrity, conscientiousness, and honesty. *Psychological Reports, 95*(1), 27–38.

Hughes, R. L., Ginnett, R. C., & Curphy, C. G. (1996). *Leadership: Enhancing the lessons of experience.* Chicago: Irwin.

Jewell, L. N. (1998). *Contemporary industrial/organizational psychology.* Belmont, CA: Wadsworth.

Karasek, R., & Theorell, T. (1990). *Healthy work.* New York: Basic Books.

Landsberger, H. A. (1958). *Hawthorne revisited: Management and the worker, its critics and developments in human relations in industry.* Ithaca: New York State School of Industrial and Labor Relations.

Landy, F. J. (1988). The early years of I/O: "Dr. Mayo." *The Industrial and Organizational Psychologist, 25,* 53–55.

Landy, F. J., Quick, J. C., & Kasl, S. (1994). Work, stress, and well-being. *International Journal of Stress and Management, 1,* 33–73.

Locke, E. A. (1968). Toward a theory of task motivation and incentives. *Organizational Behavior and Human Performance, 3,* 157–189.

Locke, E. A. (1970). Job satisfaction and job performance. *Organizational Behavior and Human Performance, 5,* 484–500.

Locke, E. A. (1976). The nature and causes of job satisfaction. In M. D. Dunnette (Ed.), *The handbook of industrial and organizational psychology.* Chicago: Rand McNally.

McDaniel, M. A., Whetzel, D. L., Schmidt, F. L., & Maurer, S. D. (1994). The validity of employment interviews: A comprehensive review and meta-analysis. *Journal of Applied Psychology, 79,* 599–616.

McFarland, L. A. (2005). The career column: I-O psychologists in the Department of Homeland Security. *The Industrial-Organizational Psychologist, 42*(3), 49–54.

Monaghan, T., & Anderson, R. (1986). *Pizza tiger.* New York: Random House.

Norman, D. A. (1988). *The psychology of everyday things.* New York: Basic Books.

Norman, D. A. (2002). *The design of everyday things.* New York: Basic Books.

Porter, L. W., & Lawler, E. E. (1968). *Managerial attitudes and performance.* Homewood, IL: Dorsey Press.

Roethlisberger, F. J., & Dickson, W. J. (1939). *Management and the worker.* Cambridge, MA: Harvard University Press.

Sauter, S. L., Murphy, L. R., & Hurrell, J. J. (1990). Prevention of work-related psychological disorders: A national strategy proposed by the National Institute for Occupational Safety and Health. *American Psychologist, 45,* 1146–1158.

Skinner, B. F. (1969). *Contingencies of reinforcement.* New York: Appleton-Century-Crofts.

Taylor, F. W. (1911). *The principles of scientific management.* New York: Harper & Row.

Turner, S. M., DeMers, S. T., Fox, H. R., & Reed, G. M. (2001). APA's guidelines for test user qualifications: An executive summary. *American Psychologist, 56,* 1099–1113.

Viteles, M. (1932). *Industrial psychology.* New York: Norton.

Vroom, V. H. (1964). *Work and motivation.* New York: Wiley.

Yerkes, R. M. (1921). *Memories of the National Academy of Sciences: Psychological examining in the United States Army* (Vol. 15). Washington, DC: U.S. Government Printing Office.

Zhou, J., & George, J. M. (2003). Awakening employee creativity: The role of leader emotional intelligence. *Leadership Quarterly, 14,* 545–568.

Zohar, D., & Luria, G. (2005). A multilevel model of safety climate: Cross-level relationships between organization and group level climates. *Journal of Applied Psychology, 90,* 616–628.

Notes